Twentieth-Century Literary Criticism

Guide to Gale Literary Criticism Series

When you need to review criticism of literary works, these are the Gale series to use:

If the author's death date is:

You should turn to:

After Dec. 31, 1959
(or author is still living)

CONTEMPORARY LITERARY CRITICISM

for example: Jorge Luis Borges, Anthony Burgess,
William Faulkner, Mary Gordon,
Ernest Hemingway, Iris Murdoch

1900 through 1959

TWENTIETH-CENTURY LITERARY CRITICISM

for example: Willa Cather, F. Scott Fitzgerald,
Henry James, Mark Twain, Virginia Woolf

1800 through 1899

NINETEENTH-CENTURY LITERATURE CRITICISM

for example: Fedor Dostoevski, Nathaniel Hawthorne,
George Sand, William Wordsworth

1400 through 1799

LITERATURE CRITICISM FROM 1400 TO 1800
(excluding Shakespeare)

for example: Anne Bradstreet, Daniel Defoe,
Alexander Pope, François Rabelais,
Jonathan Swift, Phillis Wheatley

SHAKESPEAREAN CRITICISM

Shakespeare's plays and poetry

Antiquity through 1399

CLASSICAL AND MEDIEVAL LITERATURE CRITICISM

for example: Dante, Homer, Plato, Sophocles, Vergil,
the Beowulf Poet

Gale also publishes related criticism series:

CHILDREN'S LITERATURE REVIEW

This series covers authors of all eras who have written for
the preschool through high school audience.

SHORT STORY CRITICISM

This series covers the major short fiction writers of all nationalities
and periods of literary history.

ISSN 0276-8178

R

Volume 36

Twentieth-Century Literary Criticism

**Excerpts from Criticism of the
Works of Novelists, Poets, Playwrights,
Short Story Writers, and Other Creative Writers
Who Died between 1900 and 1960,
from the First Published Critical Appraisals
to Current Evaluations**

Paula Kepos
Editor

Marie Lazzari
Thomas Ligotti
Joann Prosyniuk
Laurie Sherman
Associate Editors

080/599

Gale Research Inc. · *DETROIT* · *NEW YORK* · *LONDON*

Toll-free Telephone Number: 1-800-347-GALE

STAFF

Paula Kepos, *Editor*

Marie Lazzari, Thomas Ligotti, Joann Prosyniuk, Laurie Sherman, *Associate Editors*

Susan Windisch Brown, Tina N. Grant, Grace N. Jeromski, Michael W. Jones, David Kmenta,
Michelle L. McClellan, Ronald S. Nixon, Debra A. Wells, *Assistant Editors*

Jeanne A. Gough, *Permissions & Production Manager*
Linda M. Pugliese, *Production Supervisor*
Jennifer E. Gale, David G. Oblender, Suzanne Powers,
Maureen A. Puhl, Linda M. Ross, *Editorial Associates*
Donna Craft, *Editorial Assistant*

Victoria B. Cariappa, *Research Supervisor*
H. Nelson Fields, Judy Gale, Maureen Richards, *Editorial Associates*
Jill M. Ohorodnik, *Editorial Assistant*

Sandra C. Davis, *Permissions Supervisor (Text)*
Josephine M. Keene, Kimberly F. Smilay, *Permissions Associates*
Maria L. Franklin, Michele Lonoconus, Camille P. Robinson, Shalice Shah,
Denise M. Singleton, Rebecca A. Stanko, *Permissions Assistants*

Patricia A. Seefelt, *Permissions Supervisor (Pictures)*
Margaret A. Chamberlain, *Permissions Associate*
Pamela A. Hayes, Lillian Quickley, *Permissions Assistants*

Mary Beth Trimper, *Production Manager*
Shanna G. Philpott, *External Production Assistant*

Arthur Chartow, *Art Director*
C. J. Jonik, *Keyliner*

Laura Bryant, *Production Supervisor*
Louise Gagné, *Internal Production Associate*

Library of Congress Catalog Card Number 76-46132
ISBN 0-8103-2418-0
ISSN 0276-8178

Printed in the United States of America

Published simultaneously in the United Kingdom
by Gale Research International Limited
(An affiliated company of Gale Research Inc.)

Contents

Preface

Since its inception more than ten years ago, *Twentieth-Century Literary Criticism* has been purchased and used by nearly 10,000 school, public, and college or university libraries. With this edition—volume 36 in the series—*TCLC* has covered over 500 authors, representing 58 nationalities, and more than 25,000 titles. No other reference source has surveyed the critical response to twentieth-century authors and literature as thoroughly as *TCLC*. In the words of one reviewer, "there is nothing comparable available." *TCLC* "is a goldmine of information—dates, pseudonyms, biographical information, and criticism from books and periodicals—which many libraries would have difficulty assembling on their own."

Scope of the Series

TCLC is designed to serve as an introduction for students and advanced readers to authors who died between 1900 and 1960, and to the most significant interpretations of these authors' works. The great poets, novelists, short story writers, playwrights, and philosophers of this period are frequently studied in high school and college literature courses. In organizing and excerpting the vast amount of critical material written on these authors, *TCLC* helps students develop valuable insight into literary history, promotes a better understanding of the texts, and sparks ideas for papers and assignments. Each entry in *TCLC* presents a comprehensive survey of an author's career or an individual work of literature and provides the user a multiplicity of interpretations and assessments. Such variety allows students to pursue their own interests; furthermore, it fosters an awareness that literature is dynamic and responsive to many different opinions.

TCLC is designed as a companion series to Gale's *Contemporary Literary Criticism*, which reprints commentary on current writing. Because of the different periods under consideration (*CLC* considers authors who were still living after 1959), there is no duplication of material between *CLC* and *TCLC*. For additional information about *CLC* and Gale's other criticism titles, users should consult the Guide to Gale Literary Criticism Series preceding the title page in this volume.

Coverage

Each volume of *TCLC* is carefully compiled to present:

- criticism of authors who represent a variety of genres and nationalities

- both major and lesser-known writers of the period (such as non-Western authors increasingly read by today's students)

- 14-16 authors per volume

- individual entries that survey the critical response to each author's works, including early criticism to reflect initial reactions; later criticism to represent any rise or decline in the author's reputation; and current retrospective analyses. The entries also indicate an author's importance to the period (for example, the length of each author entry reflects the amount of critical attention he or she has received from critics writing in English, and from foreign criticism in translation)

An author may appear more than once in the series because of continuing critical and academic interest, or because of a resurgence of criticism generated by such events as a centennial or anniversary, the republication or posthumous publication of a work, or the publication of a new translation. Several entries in each volume of *TCLC* are devoted to criticism of individual works that are considered among the most important in twentieth-century literature and are thus frequently read and studied in high school and college literature classes. For example, this volume includes entries devoted to André Gide's *The Counterfeiters* and Mark Twain's *A Connecticut Yankee in King Arthur's Court*.

Organization of the Book

An author entry consists of the following elements: author heading, biographical and critical introduction, list of principal works, excerpts of criticism (each preceded by explanatory notes and followed by a bibliographic citation), and a bibliography of further reading.

- The *author heading* consists of the author's full name, followed by birth and death dates. The unbracketed portion of the name denotes the form under which the author most commonly wrote. If an author wrote consistently under a pseudonym, the pseudonym will be listed in the author heading and the real name given in parentheses on the first line of the biographical and critical introduction. Also located at the beginning of the introduction to the author entry are any name variations under which an author wrote, including transliterated forms for authors whose languages use nonroman alphabets.

- The *biographical and critical introduction* outlines the author's life and career, as well as the critical debate surrounding his or her work. References are provided to past volumes of *TCLC* and to other biographical and critical reference series published by Gale, including *Short Story Criticism, Children's Literature Review, Contemporary Authors, Dictionary of Literary Biography,* and *Something about the Author.*

- Most *TCLC* entries include *portraits* of the author. Many entries also contain reproductions of materials pertinent to an author's career, including manuscript pages, title pages, dust jackets, letters, and drawings, as well as photographs of important people, places, and events in an author's life.

- The *list of principal works* is chronological by date of first book publication and identifies the genre of each work. In the case of foreign authors with both foreign-language publications and English translations, the title and date of the first English-language edition are given in brackets. Unless otherwise indicated, dramas are dated by first performance, not first publication.

- *Criticism* is arranged chronologically in each author entry to provide a perspective on changes in critical evaluation over the years. All titles of works by the author featured in the entry are printed in boldface type to enable the user to easily locate discussion of particular works. Also for purposes of easier identification, the critic's name and the publication date of the essay are given at the beginning of each piece of criticism. Unsigned criticism is preceded by the title of the journal in which it appeared. Many of the excerpts in *TCLC* also contain translated material. Unless otherwise noted, translations in brackets are by the editors; translations in parentheses or continuous with the text are by the critic. Publication information (such as publisher names and book prices) and parenthetical numerical references (such as footnotes or page and line references to specific editions of works) have been deleted at the editors' discretion to provide smoother reading of the text.

- Critical excerpts are prefaced by *annotations* providing the reader with information about both the critic and the criticism that follows. Included are the critic's reputation, individual approach to literary criticism, and particular expertise in an author's works. Also noted are the relative importance of a work of criticism, the scope of the excerpt, and the growth of critical controversy or changes in critical trends regarding an author. In some cases, these annotations cross-reference excerpts by critics who discuss each other's commentary.

- A complete *bibliographic citation* designed to facilitate location of the original essay or book follows each piece of criticism.

- An annotated *list of further reading* appearing at the end of each author entry suggests further reading on the author. In some cases it includes essays for which the editors could not obtain reprint rights.

Cumulative Indexes

Each volume of *TCLC* includes a cumulative index listing all the authors who have appeared in *Contemporary Literary Criticism, Twentieth-Century Literary Criticism, Nineteenth-Century Litera-*

ture Criticism, Literature Criticism from 1400 to 1800, Classical and Medieval Literature Criticism, and *Short Story Criticism,* along with cross-references to the Gale series *Children's Literature Review, Authors in the News, Contemporary Authors, Contemporary Authors Autobiography Series, Dictionary of Literary Biography, Concise Dictionary of American Literary Biography, Something about the Author, Something about the Author Autobiography Series,* and *Yesterday's Authors of Books for Children.* Useful for locating an author within the various series, this index is particularly valuable for those authors who are identified with a certain period but who, because of their death dates, are placed in another, or for those authors whose careers span two periods. For example, F. Scott Fitzgerald is found in *TCLC,* yet a writer often associated with him, Ernest Hemingway, is found in *CLC.*

Each volume of *TCLC* also includes a cumulative nationality index, in which authors' names are arranged alphabetically under their respective nationalities.

Title Index

This volume of *TCLC* also includes an index listing the titles of all literary works discussed in the volume. The first volume of *TCLC* published each year contains an index listing all titles discussed in the series since its inception.

Suggestions Are Welcome

In response to suggestions, several features have been added to *TCLC* since the series began, including annotations to excerpted criticism, a cumulative index to authors in all Gale literary criticism series, entries devoted to a single work by a major author, more extensive illustrations, and a title index listing all literary works discussed in the series since its inception.

Readers who wish to suggest authors to appear in future volumes, or who have other suggestions, are cordially invited to write the editors or call our toll-free number: 1-800-347-GALE.

Acknowledgments

The editors with to thank the copyright holders of the excerpted criticism included in this volume, the permissions managers of many book and magazine publishing companies for assisting us in securing reprint rights, and Anthony Bogucki for assistance with copyright research. We are also grateful to the staffs of the Detroit Public Library, the Library of Congress, the University of Detroit Library, Wayne State University Library Complex, and University of Michigan Libraries for making their resources available to us. Following is a list of the copyright holders who have granted us permission to reprint material in this volume of *TCLC*. Every effort has been made to trace copyright, but if omissions have been made, please let us know.

COPYRIGHTED EXCERPTS IN *TCLC*, VOLUME 36, WERE REPRINTED FROM THE FOLLOWING PERIODICALS:

American Literature, v. XXXVI, November, 1964; v. XLIV, May, 1972; v. 50, November, 1978. Copyright (c) 1964, 1972, 1978 Duke University Press, Durham, NC. All reprinted with permission of the publisher.—*The American Scholar,* v. 39, Winter, 1969-70 for "Swinburne" by A. E. Housman. Copyright © 1969 by The Society of Authors. Reprinted by permission of The Society of Authors on behalf of the Estate of A. E. Housman.—*Criticism,* v. ll, Spring, 1969 for "Gide and the Fantasts: The Nature of Reality and Freedom" by David Haberstich. Copyright, 1969, Wayne State University Press. Reprinted by permission of the publisher and the author.—*The Dalhousie Review,* v. 48, Autumn, 1968 for "Swinburne's Poetry and Twentieth-Century Criticism" by Robert E. Lougy. Reprinted by permission of the publisher and the author.—*The Emerson Society Quarterly,* v. 37, 1964 for "Higginson, Emerson, and a National Literature" by Edgar L. McCormick. Copyright © 1968 by Kenneth Walter Cameron. Reprinted by permission of the author.—*The French Review,* v. XLV, February, 1972. Copyright 1972 by the American Association of Teachers of French. Reprinted by permission of the publisher.—*International Philosophical Quarterly,* v. XVI, March, 1976 for "The Modern State and the Search for Community: The Anarchist Critique of Peter Kropotkin" by Vincent C. Punzo. Reprinted by permission of the author.—*Mark Twain Journal,* v. XI, Summer, 1960; v. XV, Summer, 1970. Both reprinted by permission of the publisher.—*Modern Fiction Studies,* v. 32, Spring, 1986. Copyright © 1986 by Purdue Research Foundation. West Lafayette, IN 47907. All rights reserved. Reprinted with permission.—*The Nation,* New York, v. 187, November 29, 1958. Copyright 1958, renewed 1986 by *The Nation* magazine/The Nation Company, Inc. Reprinted by permission of the publisher.—*The New England Quarterly,* v. XXXIX, December, 1966 for "Mark Twain's Yankee" by Gerald Allen; v. XLVIII, March, 1975 for "Merlin's Grin: From 'Tom' to 'Huck' in 'A Connecticut Yankee'" by Clark Griffith. Copyright 1966, 1975 by *The New England Quarterly.* Both reprinted by permission of the publisher and the respective authors.—*The New York Review of Books,* v. XXIII, October 28, 1976. Copyright © 1976 Nyrev, Inc. Reprinted with permission from *The New York Review of Books.*—*The New York Times Book Review,* October 2, 1927. Copyright 1927 by The New York Times Company. Reprinted by permission of the publisher.—*Partisan Review,* v. XLIV, 1977 for "Myth of the Primitive" by Vincent Crapanzano. Copyright © 1977 by *Partisan Review.* Reprinted by permission of the publisher and the author.—*The Polish Review,* v. XI, Summer, 1966; v. XIV, Spring, 1969. © copyright 1966, 1969 by the Polish Institute of Arts and Sciences of America, Inc. Both reprinted by permission of the publisher.—*Science and Society,* v. XXXI, Winter, 1962. Copyright 1962 by S & S Quarterly, Inc. Reprinted by permission of the publisher.—*South Atlantic Quarterly,* v. 61, Autumn, 1962. Copyright © 1962 by Duke University Press, Durham, NC. Reprinted by permission of the publisher.—*Studies in the Novel,* v. XIX, Winter, 1987. Copyright 1987 by North Texas State University. Reprinted by permission of the publisher.—*Studies in Romanticism,* v. 18, Spring, 1979 for "Swinburne: The Sublime Recovered" by Pauline Fletcher. Copyright 1979 by the Trustees of Boston University. All rights reserved. Reprinted by permission of the publisher.—*Texas Studies in Literature and Language,* v. XIV, Winter, 1973 for "Yankee Showman and Reformer: The Character of Mark Twain's Hank Morgan" by Judith Fetterley. Copyright © 1973 by the University of Texas Press. Reprinted by permission of the publisher and the author.—*Theatre Journal,* v. 31, October, 1979. © 1979, University and College Theatre Association of the American Theatre Association. Reprinted by permission of the publisher.—*The Times Literary Supplement,* n. 4236, June 8, 1984. © Times Newspapers Ltd. (London) 1984. Reproduced from *The Times Literary Supplement* by permission.—*The Tulane Drama Review,* v. 8, Winter, 1963 for "Re-Read Artaud" by Romain Weingarten, translated by Ruby Cohn; v. 8, Winter, 1963 for "The Artaud Experiment" by Paul Arnold, translated by Ruby Cohn. Copyright © 1963, *The Tulane Drama Review.* Both reprinted by permission of MIT Press and the translator.—*The Victorian Newsletter,* n. 51, Spring, 1977 for "Swinburne's Craft of Pure Expression" by Antony H. Harrison. Reprinted by permission of *The Victorian Newsletter* and the author.—*Victorian Poetry,* v. 26, Winter, 1988. Reprinted by permission of the publisher.

COPYRIGHTED EXCERPTS IN *TCLC,* VOLUME 36, WERE REPRINTED FROM THE FOLLOWING BOOKS:

Adler, Joseph. From *The Herzl Paradox: Political, Social and Economic Theories of a Realist.* Hadrian Press, 1962. © 1962 Hadrian Press, Inc., and the Herzl Press, New York, N.Y. All rights reserved. Reprinted by permission of the

Authors to Be Featured in Forthcoming Volumes

Karel Čapek (Czechoslovakian novelist and dramatist)—Čapek is celebrated for his science fiction novels and dramas in which he warned against the dehumanizing aspects of modern civilization and satirized a wide range of social, economic, and political systems.

Charles Waddel Chesnutt (American short story writer and novelist)—Chesnutt was one of the first black American writers to receive widespread critical and popular attention. He is best known for short stories about the antebellum South that incorporate subtle and ironic condemnations of slavery.

Benedetto Croce (Italian philosopher and critic)—Considered the most influential literary critic of the twentieth century, Croce developed aesthetic theories that became central tenets of modern arts criticism while establishing important critical approaches to the works of such authors as William Shakespeare, Johann Wolfgang von Goethe, and Pierre Corneille.

Countee Cullen (American poet)—One of the foremost poets of the Harlem Renaissance, Cullen is best remembered for his numerous poems treating contemporary racial issues.

Ford Madox Ford (English novelist)—Ford was a major English novelist and a strong influence on modern trends in both poetry and prose. *TCLC* will devote an entry to *The Good Soldier,* a novel that is often considered Ford's most important.

Charlotte Perkins Gilman (American fiction writer and essayist)—Gilman was a prominent social activist and leading theorist of the women's movement at the turn of the century. She examined the role of women in society and propounded her social theories in *Women and Economics* and other nonfiction works, while she depicted the realization of her feminist ideals in her novels and short stories.

Henrik Ibsen (Norwegian dramatist)—Ibsen is regarded as the father of modern drama for his introduction of realism and social concerns to the European theater of the nineteenth century. *TCLC* will devote an entry to one of his most important and best-known dramas, *A Doll's House.*

Sinclair Lewis (American novelist)—One of the foremost American novelists of the 1920s and 1930s, Lewis wrote some of the most effective satires in American literature. *TCLC* will devote an entry to his novel *Babbitt,* a scathing portrait of vulgar materialism and spiritual bankruptcy in American business.

Jack London (American fiction writer and essayist)—London was a popular writer of Naturalist fiction in which he combined high adventure with elements of socialism, mysticism, Darwinian determinism, and Nietzschean theories of race. *TCLC* will devote an entry to his most widely read work, *The Call of the Wild.*

Katherine Mansfield (New Zealand short story writer)—Mansfield was an innovator of the short story form who contributed to the development of the stream-of-consciousness narrative.

Claude McKay (American poet)—A prominent figure of the Harlem Renaissance, McKay was the author of powerful poems of social protest that are considered among the most significant of the early American civil rights movement.

Edmond Rostand (French novelist)—Significant for his revival of romantic verse drama at a time when Naturalism and Symbolism dominated the French stage, Rostand combined an excellent sense of theatrical effect with a keen wit. His optimistic idealism found its best expression in the comedy *Cyrano de Bergerac,* which achieved a lasting international reputation.

John Millington Synge (Irish dramatist)—Synge is considered the greatest dramatist of the Irish Literary Renaissance of the late nineteenth and early twentieth centuries. *TCLC* will devote an entry to his drama *The Playboy of the Western World,* which is regarded as his masterpiece.

Yevgeny Zamyatin (Russian novelist)—Censored in the Soviet Union for his best-known work, the dystopian novel *We,* Zamyatin wrote satiric fiction characterized by experimentation with language and imagery that made him one of the most influential Russian writers in the decade following the Russian Revolution.

Emile Zola (French novelist)—Zola was the founder and principal theorist of Naturalism, one of the most influential literary movements in modern literature. His twenty-volume series *Les Rougon-Macquart* is a monument of Naturalist fiction and served as a model for late nineteenth-century novelists seeking a more candid and accurate representation of human life.

Antonin Artaud

1896-1948

(Also wrote under the pseudonym Le Révélé) French essayist, dramatist, poet, novelist, screenwriter, translator, and actor.

For further discussion of Artaud's career, see *TCLC*, Volume 3.

Artaud is considered one of the most influential drama theorists in the development of modern theater. His concept of Theater of Cruelty—which he outlined in *Le théâtre et son double (The Theater and Its Double)* and other works—extended the possibilities of theatrical presentation by repudiating Western theatrical traditions of realistic social drama in favor of an antirationalist spectacle intended to provoke in his audience an awareness of a higher order of truth and reality.

Artaud was born in Marseilles, the son of a prosperous ship-fitter and his wife. Throughout his childhood and adolescence Artaud suffered ill health, chiefly headaches that were believed the result of an acute case of meningitis in 1901. He attended the Marist school in Marseilles, where he founded a student journal in which he published his own poetry. In 1915, suffering from depression, headaches, and other ailments, he sought treatment at a local sanatarium. The following year he was drafted into the army but given a medical discharge a few months later. He spent two years in a Swiss hospital, where his artistic tendencies were encouraged as part of his therapy. After Artaud's condition had improved, he moved to Paris under the care of Dr. Edouard Toulouse, a psychoanalyst and editor of the literary magazine *Demain.* Toulouse published Artaud's poetry in *Demain* and employed him to help with editorial duties. In 1923 Artaud submitted several poems to Jacques Rivière, the editor of the *Nouvelle revue française.* Although Rivière rejected these works as incomprehensible, he did publish Artaud's correspondence which comprised a defense of his works and a statement of his poetic theory, as well as a disclosure of the mental problems that afflicted him.

In Paris, Artaud became fascinated by the theater, and he joined a series of experimental theater groups, including that of Charles Dullin at the Théâtre de l'Atelier. His associates in Paris included many of the artists and writers of the Surrealist group, and for a time Artaud was identified with that movement. However, Artaud, with Roger Vitrac and Robert Aron, was repudiated by the Surrealists when he refused to embrace Marxism. Together, the three founded the Théâtre Alfred Jarry in 1926, stating that their intention was "to contribute by strictly theatrical means to the ruin of the theater as it exists today in France." Throughout the late 1920s and early 1930s, Artaud worked in theater and film and grew increasingly dependent on narcotics, which he found relieved the symptoms of his mental disorders. In 1931 he attended a performance by a Balinese theater troupe and was fascinated by the predominance of movement over speech in their art, something he later sought to emulate in his own theatrical works. In 1936 he traveled to Mexico to study the Tarahumaras, a tribe of native Americans living in the Sierra Madre

whose religious rituals include the use of peyote. Artaud's experiences among the Tarahumaras had a profound influence on his perception of the value of mystical religious experience, and he later incorporated this understanding into his work in the theater. He subsequently became interested in Irish mythology as well, and traveled to Ireland in 1937 in possession of a walking stick he believed to have once belonged to St. Patrick. Although details of the event are unclear, Artaud was deported after causing a disturbance in a Dublin monastery. Upon his arrival in France he was judged mentally ill and institutionalized in Rouen. Artaud spent nine of his last eleven years confined in mental asylums and died of cancer in 1948.

Artaud is considered most important as a drama theorist, and his concept of Theater of Cruelty has greatly influenced the development of theater in the second half of the twentieth century. By cruelty, Artaud meant subjection to a theatrical experience in which both audience and actors would confront the fundamental realities of human existence. In his collection of theoretical writings, *The Theater and Its Double,* Artaud asserted that Western theater was in need of radical transformation because its well-ordered plots, realistic presentation of characters, and preoccupation with language no longer had any connection to life. To counteract these conventions of traditional drama, Artaud proposed devaluation of the written text and increased use of movement and sound. He maintained that emphasizing symbolic gestures, nonverbal chanting, and sound effects in a stage production would have the power of a primitive rite in releasing the repressed emotions of the audience. Artaud described what he envisioned in his "First Manifesto of the Theater of Cruelty": "Every spectacle will contain a physical and objective element, perceptible to all; cries, laments, arguments, surprises, all kinds of theatrical shocks, magic beauty, and costumes taken from certain ritual models. Resplendent lighting, incantatory beauty of voices, charm of harmony, rare notes of music, colors of objects, physical rhythms of movements whose crescendo will blend with the pulsation of movements familiar to everyone, the concrete appearance of new and surprising objects, masks, puppets several yards high, sudden changes of light, the physical play of light which causes feelings of warmth and cold."

In addition to his theoretical works, Artaud produced a wide variety of writings, including screenplays, dramas, poetry, and extensive correspondence. His best-known cinematic work is the controversial surrealist screenplay *La coquille et le clergyman,* which in 1927 was made into a film directed by Germaine Dulac. Upon its release Artaud angrily claimed that he had been shut out of Dulac's production and that her realization of his script had radically transformed his work. For some time thereafter, critics largely disregarded *La coquille et le clergyman,* but Artaud's criticisms of the production are now used as a basis for discussion of his film aesthetics. Of his dramas, *Le jet de sang* (*The Jet of Blood*), has received the most critical attention. A violent work considered difficult to produce, *The Jet of Blood* concludes with a prostitute biting the giant wrist of God and causing a stream of blood to splash onto the stage. Artaud's nontheatrical writings include nonfiction works detailing his experiences in Mexico as well as letters and essays on suicide, alienation, madness, and drug use.

Artaud's illness, drug addiction, and alienation have caused him to be linked with such figures as Arthur Rimbaud and Gérard de Nerval as a cult hero of the avant-garde whose work presents an often moving portrait of a tortured mind. Because of his mental illness some critics have dismissed his work as illogical and valueless, but others submit that he purposefully rejected formal logic, intent instead on developing the emotive powers of his work. Artaud's various theories have never been realized in a single production, but aspects of his work have been incorporated into the works of prominent dramatists of the late 1950s and early 1960s, including Jean Genet, Eugene Ionesco, and Peter Weiss.

(See also *Contemporary Authors,* Vol. 104.)

PRINCIPAL WORKS

Tric-trac du ciel (poetry) 1923
*L'ombilic des limbes (poetry, essays, and dramatic dialogues) 1925
Le pèse-nerfs (poetry) 1925
La coquille et le clergyman (screenplay) 1927
Correspondance avec Jacques Rivière (letters) 1927
        [*Artaud-Rivière Correspondence* published in journal *Exodus,* 1960]
L'art et la mort (essays) 1929
Le manifeste du théâtre de la cruauté (manifesto) 1932

Héliogabale; ou, L'anarchiste couronné (novel) 1934
Les Cenci (drama) 1935
        [*The Cenci,* 1969]
Les nouvelles révélations de l'etre [as Le Révélé] (essays) 1937
Le théâtre et son double (essays) 1938
        [*The Theater and Its Double,* 1958]
D'un voyage au pays des Tarahumaras (essays) 1945
        [*Concerning a Journey to the Land of the Tarahumaras* published in *City Lights Journal,* 1964]
Artaud le Momo (poetry) 1947
        [*Artaud the Momo,* 1976]
Ci-git, précédé de la culture indienne (poetry) 1947
Van Gogh: Le suicidé de la société (essay) 1947
        [*Van Gogh: The Man Suicided by Society* published in *The Tiger's Eye,* 1949]
Lettres de Rodez (letters) 1948
Pour en finir avec le jugement de Dieu (radioscript) 1948
        [*To Have Done with the Judgment of God* published in journal *Northwest Review,* 1963; also published as *To End God's Judgment* in *Tulane Drama Review,* 1965]
Supplément aux lettres de Rodez, suivi de Coleridge, le traitre (letters and essay) 1949
Œuvres complêtes. 20 vols. (essays, poetry, drama, novel, letters, sketches, dramatic dialogues, dramatic sketches, interviews, screenplays, and diaries) 1956-84
Antonin Artaud Anthology (essays, poetry, and drama) 1965
Collected Works. 4 vols. (essays, poetry, drama, dramatic sketches, dramatic dialogues, letters, and interviews) 1968-75
Love Is a Tree That Always Is High: An Artaud Anthology (poetry, drama, and essays) 1972
Antonin Artaud: Selected Writings (essays, poetry, drama, letters, dramatic dialogues, screenplay, interview, and diaries) 1976
The Peyote Dance (essays) 1976

*Includes the first publication of *Le jet de sang;* English translation *The Jet of Blood* published in *Modern French Theatre,* edited by Michael Benedikt and George E. Wellwarth, 1964.

PAUL GOODMAN (essay date 1958)

[*Goodman was an American poet, novelist, short story writer, dramatist, critic, and social commentator. Considered a prophet of the radicalism that flourished on college campuses during the 1960s, he challenged the bureaucratic organization of society and advocated a philosophy uniting principles of anarchism, nonviolence, and political decentralization. In the following excerpt, Goodman praises Artaud's insight into theater while challenging several arguments presented in* The Theater and Its Double.]

Artaud's [***The Theater and Its Double***] is by a man in love and banking everything on his love. He wills this love to give a meaning to life and he wills by this love to counterattack in the society where he is desperate. What he says is often wrong-headed and he often contradicts himself, but he also sees and says important truths with bright simplicity. "I will do what I have dreamed or I will do nothing"—naturally this comes to doing very little; yet since his death the passion of his dream has moved and conquered theatre people. "He was the only one of our time who understood the nature and greatness of theatre," they say of this confused little book (I am quoting Julian Beck). Now if here for a few paragraphs I try to distinguish the true and false voices of this explosion, it is not to diminish the idol of the theatre people; his passion is more important than sound sense; but it is to help simplify their discussions, in order that that passion can be more effectual.

Everywhere Artaud betrays the attitudes and prejudices of a puritan, self-depriving and with a nausea for ordinary food. I should guess that he clung precariously to his sanity by warding off fantasies of cannibalism and other things he thought depraved. When the theatre broke through this shell and provided him a real excitement, he inevitably thought of it as totally destructive and hellish; it had raped him. The theatre, he says, is "the exteriorization of a depth of latent cruelty by means of which all the perverse possibilities of the mind are localized."

He is wearing blinders. He does not seem to conceive of the more ordinary neurotic or simply unhappy man to whom the magic of the work of art is its impossible perfection, its promise of paradise. And for the happy there is no art: "Where simplicity and order reign, there can be no theatre."

So he famously derives the theatre from the last stages of the Plague, when "the dregs of the population, immunized by their frenzied greed, pillage the riches they know will serve no purpose or profit. At that moment the theatre is born, i.e., an immediate gratuitousness provoking acts without use of profit." He goes on to quote St. Augustine's horror of the theatre's poison. And he ends with a rhapsody on [John] Ford's *Whore,* whose content seems to him to be the plague itself. All this is brilliantly told, with good oral savagery; it may be only a partial view of theatre, but it is a hot one that could give birth to fine works.

Alas! as he thinks it, he becomes frightened of his love, and he begins to reiterate a tediously moralistic theory of illusion and catharsis, false in itself and in direct contradiction to the best things he has to say elsewhere. The action, he reiterates, is only on the stage, it is "virtual" not actual, it develops an illusory world like alchemy; its aim is to "drain abscesses collectively." He seems to think that this symbolic action is the primitive theatre magic, but the very point of the primitive magic is that it is not virtual, it makes the grass grow and the sun come back; the primitive is not afraid of the forces he unleashes.

Artaud's theory of draining the abscesses seems to look like the Greek view of catharsis, but there is a crucial difference: for when it had purged the passions, the Greek play restored its audience to a pretty good community, further strengthened by the religious rite that the play also was, that sowed the corn with the dismembered limbs. But Artaud's play would purge the audience of such vital vices as they have and let them down into the very world from which there is no escape but the asylum. Just so, Artaud is beguiled by the wonderful combination in the Balinese theatre of objective and accurate complexity with trance and indeed witchcraft; but he astonishingly does not see that this is possible because it rises in and still rests in the village, its everyday way of life, and its gamelan. Artaud makes the fantastic remark that the Balinese dances "victoriously demonstrate the absolute preponderance of the *metteur en scène*"—there is a delusion of grandeur indeed!

Artaud betrays little humor, but his view of comedy brings him to the same dilemma, the fear of total destruction. Comedy, he says, is "the essential liberation, the destruction of all reality in the mind." No, *not* all. Comedy deflates the sense precisely so that the underlying lubricity and malice may bubble to the surface. Artaud always thinks the bottom will drop out and that through the theatre one is "confronted with the absolute." But it is not the absolute but always a risky next moment that is very real.

But let us start again on a positive tack, and see where Artaud is strong. Artaud is great when he insists that theatre, like any art, is an action in the sense of a physical cause; it is not a mirroring or portrayal that can be absorbed by the spectator and interpreted according to his own predilections. It is not a fantasy. He rightly compares it to psychoanalysis: "I propose to bring back into theatre the elementary magical idea, taken up by psychoanalysis, which consists in effecting the patient's cure by *making* him assume the apparent and exterior attitudes." Let me say this my own way: the moment of communication we are after is not that in which a structure of symbols passes from the system in one head to the system in another, when people "understand one another" and "learn something." The semanticists, the language-reformers, the mathematicians of feedback do not give us what we are after; the interesting moment is when one is physiologically touched and one's system is deranged and must reform to cope with the surprise. This Artaud wants to say and does say.

It is in the context of theatre as effectual action that Artaud comes to his celebrated assault on literary plays, his refusal to use text to direct from. It is not that he means to attack speech as such, for he understands perfectly that speech is a physical action, it has intonation, it is continuous with outcries and natural signals. He wants, he says beautifully, "to manipulate speech like a solid object, one which overturns and disturbs things, in the air first of all." And his remarks on breathing in the essay on Affective Athleticism are solid gold; for the breathing of anger or some other affect has far more theatrical value than the verbalizing or confabulation about it, which can certainly profitably be diminished.

But there is an aspect of the action of speech that he quite neglects and that makes his attack far too sweeping. Words have inter-personal effect, they get under the skin, and not only by their tone but especially by their syntax and style: the mood, voice and person of sentences, the coordination and subordination of clauses. The personalities of men are largely their speech habits, and in the drama of personalities the thing-language that Artaud is after is not sufficient; we need text, but a text not of ideas and thoughts, but of syntactical relations. Artaud polemically condemns Racine as literary, but he surely knew that Racine's theatre did not depend on the content of those speeches, but on the clash of personalities in them, and especially on the *coup de théâtre* of the sudden entrances and the carefully prepared big scenes. *Coup de théâtre* is theatre as action. If the old slow preparation makes us impatient, the fault may be ours.

Artaud neglects these obvious things because he has, I am afraid, one basically wrong idea: he says that the art of theatre aims at utilizing a space and the things in the space; and therefore he makes quite absolute claims for the *mise en scène*. But this is too general; for the theatre-relation is that some one looks at and is effected by, not a space with things and sounds, but persons behaving in their places. Theatre is actors acting on us. So the chief thing is neither interpreting the text nor the *mise en scène,* but the blocking-and-timing (conceived as one space-time solid): it is the directedness of the points of view, the confrontation of personalities, the on-going process of the plot. Artaud was misled, perhaps, by his experience of cinema, where the one who makes the montage, the so-called "editor," is paramount, for what we experience is the flow of pictures. But for the blocking-and-timing of theatre we need, as is traditional, the collaboration of three: the actor, the director and the dramatic poet. (pp. 412-14)

Paul Goodman, "Obsessed by Theatre," in The Nation, *New York, Vol. 187, No. 18, November 29, 1958, pp. 412-14.*

CLAUDE MAURIAC (essay date 1958)

[*The son of Nobel–prize-winning author François Mauriac, Mauriac is a French novelist, dramatist, and critic who is best known for his association with the New Novel movement in France during the late 1950s. In the following excerpt from his study* The New Literature, *Mauriac examines the motivations for Artaud's experimental literature.*]

As in the case of Kafka, it is difficult if not impossible to evaluate the works of Artaud without reference to the man who created them. His poetry is almost intransmissible. It is not inexpressive, but rather it is expressive in the way that human cries can be. **"Cry,"** moreover, is the title of one of his very first poems. It was printed in the *Nouvelle revue française* of September 1, 1924, not for its poetic value, but because it happened to be quoted by Artaud himself in the course of one of his letters about his work of that time. Jacques Rivière had inserted these letters in his review in place of the works themselves, which he considered unpublishable.

When Artaud evokes the *men tortured by language* and names them (François Villon, Charles Baudelaire, Edgar Poe, Gérard de Nerval), he knows that he belongs to the same breed: the poets who *suffer their works.* Reproved, accursed, they *transude* rather than write. As far back as 1923, in the letters to Jacques Rivière, Antonin Artaud makes a diagnosis of the metaphysical illness with which he was afflicted. "I am suffering from a frightful malady of the mind. My thoughts evade me in every way possible. (It is a question of) a total absence, an actual loss." The few fragments which he submitted to the editor of the *N.R.F.* constitute "those remnants which he was able to win away from complete oblivion." Rivière's condemnation was for Artaud equivalent to denying him any sense of reality. If these passages do not succeed in *existing as literature,* their author will be deprived of his only claim to existence: "The whole problem of my thinking is at stake. For me it is a question of nothing less than knowing whether or not I have the right to continue to think, in verse or in prose."

Jacques Rivière replied that "the awkwardness and disconcerting strangeness" of his poetry did not preclude the possibility "that with a little patience he will reach the point of writing perfectly coherent and harmonious poems." Artaud describes his real problem, which will be the real problem throughout his life: *as a central crumbling of the soul, a kind of erosion of thought, essential and at the same time fugitive.* He is "a man who has had great mental suffering and who, by this token, has the right to speak." His weaknesses "have living roots, roots of anxiety."

There is something that is destroying my thinking, something that does not prevent me from being whatever I shall be able to be, but that leaves me, so to speak, in suspense. Something furtive which takes away the words *that I have found,* which diminishes the intensity of my mind, which, step by step, destroys in its substance the bulk of my thinking, which goes so far as to take away from me the memory of the figures of speech and devices by which one expresses oneself. . . .

His whole generation is suffering, Artaud indicates, from a "weakness that touches the very substance of what has been conventionally called the soul, and which is the emanation of our nerve forces coagulated around objects." In 1924 he wrote that Tristan Tzara, André Breton, and Pierre Reverdy showed symptoms of this sickness: "But in their case, their soul is not affected in a physiological way, nor is it deeply affected. It is only affected at all points where it touches upon something else, so that it is not affected anywhere *except in their thinking.*" They do not suffer, while the pain that afflicts him tortures him "not only in the mind, but in the everyday flesh": "This non-application to the object which is characteristic of all literature is in my case a non-application to life. I can truly say that I am not of this world and this is not simply an attitude of mind."

Jacques Rivière understood. Therefore, in the *N.R.F.,* in place of Artaud's poems he published the letters in which the poet comments on them, as well as his own replies. These are fine, intelligent and such as one could hope for from this man who was himself in a state of continual uneasiness and self-doubt. Two lines from Jacques Rivière show how far he entered into the drama of Artaud, a drama which is not so much of a period as of Man (but which, in this accursed poet, as in Kafka, is carried to a point of exemplary incandescence): "Proust described the *intermittences of the heart;* now one must describe the intermittences of human beings."

Antonin Artaud loses contact with his ego; it is continually in retreat and as though cut off from him. As he points out again to Rivière: "He is not completely himself, not as tall, thick or wide as he really is." His entire life will be spent chasing after his real self, trying to catch his double, in order to fuse with it and at last become only one being. Yes, Jacques Rivière understood Antonin Artaud as much as one could understand him at that time. But we, who know the sequel and the end of his life, give these letters of 1923–24 a significance which escaped not only Rivière but even Artaud. Fortunately for him, Artaud never believed himself to be incurable and regardless of how much his disorder became aggravated he never gave up all hope. If he submitted manuscripts to Rivière, it was in order to prove to himself "that he could still be something," and, above all, a writer: "This is my particular weakness and my *absurdity,* to want to write at any price and express myself."

Some of Artaud's work finally appeared in the December 1, 1925, issue of the *N.R.F.* (Jacques Rivière died at the beginning of the year and probably it was not he but Jean Paulhan who decided to publish it). These are no longer letters in which he explains that he wants to write and that it is his only hope of salvation, but actual literary works. These three fragments: **"Positions de la chair," "Manifeste en langage clair"** and **"Héloïse et Abélard,"** bring us new proof of Artaud's permanent place in letters which was, once and for all, established from this time on. When he writes that "the Sense and Science of every thought is hidden in the nervous vitality of the bones," we recognize one of his fundamental convictions, and also that word *bones,* used in the Kafkaian sense. The same is true of **"Correspondance de la momie,"** which appeared in the *N.R.F.* in March, 1927:

> . . . All this which makes of me a mummy of live flesh gives God an idea of the void in which I have been placed by the necessity of being. . . . But from the top to the bottom of this pitted flesh, through this non-compact flesh, the undeveloped fire always circulates. The lucidity which hour after hour glows in its braziers is joined by life and its flowers.

Or, commenting on Jean de Boschère's *Marthe et l'enragé,* in a note in the September 1st issue of the same year: "A marvelous flowering of mica trembles in the midst of the submarine beams of the subconscious come to light." But 1927 is the year of **Pèse-nerfs** (**Nervometer**), followed by **Fragments d'un journal d'enfer** (**Fragments of a Diary in Hell**), titles that are in themselves significant: "There is nothing in me, nothing in what makes up my personality, which was not produced by the existence of an evil *antedating* me, *antedating* my will." He is in *despair from solitude.* Drugs? Certainly. But they are the consequence, not the cause. To a woman whom he reproves for judging him sexually and not intellectually, he writes (still in **Pèse-nerfs**):

> I have only one more thing to tell you: that is, that I have always had this disorder of the mind, this crushed feeling in body and soul, this kind of contraction of all my nerves, at more or less closely spaced periods; and if you had seen me a few years ago, before I could even have been suspected of the practice for which you reproach me, you would no longer be surprised now at the reappearance of these phenomena. . . . Whatever the outcome, I can no longer count on you in my distress, since you refuse to take an interest in the most affected part of me: my soul. Besides, you have never judged me except on my exterior appearance, as all women do, as all idiots do, while it is my inner soul that is most destroyed, most ruined: and for that I cannot forgive you, for the two, unfortunately for me, do not always coincide.

I have spent a little time on these early writings to indicate that the deterioration of his mental state, which became more and more clear-cut, would subsequently overwhelm Antonin Artaud without producing any essential modification in the spiritual ordeal that he had experienced and known for a long time. Even in his worst moments of aberration he would never lose sight of it. Insanity, if it was insanity, is, therefore, no explanation, even if it was the cause of the intellectual perdition which the patient continually describes. Artaud's dementia reveals the dementia of all living men who think. It is the deflagration that leads to the discovery of the explosive charge cautiously carried by all of us. Thanks to this amplification what has escaped detection by being in a latent state becomes apparent. It is not so much insanity as the impossibility of being, the horror of essential solitude. "I live and was born with the unlimited temptation of the human being: what shall I be, where am I from, where shall I go and how?" [**Supplément au voyage au pays des Tarahumaras** (**Supplement to the Voyage to the Land of the Tarahumaras**)]. As he wrote in October, 1945, from the asylum at Rodez, to Henri Parisot: "With me it is the absolute or nothing, and that is what I have to say to this world which has neither soul nor agaragar." The absolute or nothing. Such is the greatness of this

man. For most of us, the alternative is the same, but we turn our attention, at no matter what price, from this fundamental dilemma.

As far back as 1917 Antonin Artaud was mentally ill. At that time he underwent a mystical crisis and experienced violent nervous suffering. At the end of 1918 he entered a Swiss rest home, where he remained for two years. Sent to Paris by his parents, he stayed, to begin with, at Villejuif, under the care of Dr. Toulouse. By 1921 he was considered cured. But we have seen what he could write to Jacques Rivière two years later. He was to be confined again in 1939 at Ville-Evrard, which he left in 1943 to be confined at Rodez under somewhat less unpleasant conditions until 1946 (two years before his death). A frightful calvary, because Antonin Artaud, though he thought and acted at times like an insane person, did not feel more at odds with himself then than when he was at liberty. He never ceased to be conscious of his difference, if not of his illness, and he lived as well—or rather as badly (but without danger to others)—free as incarcerated. On the one hand, he knew more about his sickness than the psychiatrists who treated him. On the other hand, he was not unaware that in its essence this illness was not exclusively his. This was something that the doctors, distracted by their specialty from the true drama of humanity, forgot.

> And human beings can stammer in vain that things are as they are, and that there is nothing further to seek. I see, indeed, that they have lost their bearings and that for a long time *they have no longer known what they were saying,* for they no longer know where they used to go in search of the states of mind with which they can stretch out upon the flow of ideas and from which they get words with which to speak.

If he often speaks of madness—his madness—it is as a rational person. Comparing the European to the Tarahumara, he notes that the European, in contrast to the latter, would never accept the possibility "that what he has felt and perceived in his body, that the emotion which has shaken him, that the strange idea which has just stirred him with its beauty, was not his own but that of another person who has felt and experienced all this through his body; otherwise he would believe himself to be mad and people would be tempted to say that he had become a lunatic." [**"Le rite du peyotl"** (**"The Peyote Rite"**)]

He insists that peyote does not *make one take dreams for reality,* nor does it "confuse true images and emotions with perceptions borrowed from depths that are fleeting, unnurtured, not yet ripe, not yet raised from the hallucinations of the subconscious." If he defends himself in this way it is because he is aware that his mind may be accused of wandering. By convincing his contradictors that peyote does not affect the essence of thinking, he is also trying to justify those of his hallucinations that are due to no drug other than that borne by his sick blood. "I also," he points out, "had false sensations and perceptions and I believed in them. But since then I have felt my energy and clarity return. [**"Le rite du peyotl"**] In the **Lettres de Rodez,** we see him constantly trying to get back his bearings, even when he seems to be most astray. In the letter of October 6, 1945, for example, he begins in a rational way, only to fall back into delirium. But by the third page he emerges from the shadows. "I need poetry in order to live, and I want to have it around me. And I do not concede that the poet in me was locked up in an insane asylum because he wanted to achieve poetry in its natural state." After this, he immediately sinks again: "I concede even less that groups of bewitchers, made up of the entire population of Paris, taking turns endlessly night and day, place themselves in the streets and boulevards at certain hours that they have agreed and decided upon in advance in order to cast upon me floods of hatred. . . ."

In almost all of his last works Antonin Artaud tries desperately to *prove* the existence and reality of these spells. To Henri Parisot he points out: "I want the last friends that I may have on this earth and who are my last readers, to be enlightened, and to understand that I was never mad, or ill, and that my incarceration is the result of a frightful occult plot in which all sects of the *initiated,* Christians, Catholics, Mohammedans, Jews, Buddhists, Brahmans, plus the lamas of the Tibetan monasteries, have participated." Warnings, reproofs, supplications, of the same order are numerous. One could cite several dozen. In his lecture at the Vieux Colombier on January 13, 1947, he elaborates: "At Rodez, it was never possible for me to mention the word 'spell' in front of Dr. Ferdière without immediately being accused of being delirious." Artaud himself reports this pathetic dialogue in which he calls upon the most subtle resources of dialectics to defend his hallucinations:

> —Come, come, Monsieur Artaud, I think your delirium is taking hold of you again.
> —What do you mean, my delirium? I am citing facts and I'll show you proof.
> —But that's it, that's it exactly, delirium with stubbornness. Well, I am going to recommend a series of electric shocks for you and write to your friend Jean Paulhan that I am going to give you shock treatments again.
> —But, in short, I am not the only writer to have spoken about witchcraft, and Huysmans in *Là-bas*—
> —Huysmans was crazy, like you, and all those who believed in the afterlife were crazy; look at Nietzsche and Gérard de Nerval. As for the spells, never has there been scientific proof of a spell, and since you are obstinate about it you will never leave this house and will remain confined throughout your life.

One might say that Artaud is exhibiting the logic of paranoia. It is so forceful, however, that the psychiatrist speaks to him as to a sane man, trying in turn to convince Artaud and threatening him with sanctions as though he were a responsible person. In this type of illness the patient is healthy in everything that does not touch on his particular mania. Hence the alternating lucidity and delirium. After his lecture at the Vieux Colombier, Antonin Artaud wrote to Maurice Saillet: "I noticed particularly (in your review in *Combat*) the sentence concerning enchantments where you say that my revelations about them elicited no interest. I noticed it all the more since, like you, I was aware that they had indeed fallen upon empty air. However, the facts that I cited should have been enough to arouse a whole hallful of spectators. . . ."

That Artaud's mind was damaged, no one can doubt. His last writings are for the most part devoid of significance or even reduced to onomatopeia. He even goes so far as to think he is Jesus Christ. Certainly there must have been physical causes for his aberration, but Artaud always realized that his illness was above all (like Kafka's) metaphysical in nature. He never stopped evoking God: sometimes to adore him, more often to blaspheme him, but, with or without the capital letter, God was always there. Artaud felt excluded from a reality which he happened to believe was supernatural. As far back as 1927 he exclaimed: "The most diseased part of me: my soul."

At one period, Antonin Artaud was converted to Catholicism. Later, he could not find enough insults, sarcasm, and obscenity with which to dissociate himself from what he considered thereafter to be a new, particularly subtle and noxious, form of enchantment. He points out in a postscript: "I wrote the **"Rite du peyotl"** in a state of conversion, with a hundred and fifty or two hundred hosts already in my body; these were the cause of my occasional delirium about Christ and the cross of Jesus Christ. Nothing now seems to me more ominous and ill-fated than the stratifying and limiting sign of the cross, etc." It was for this reason that, in September, 1945, Antonin Artaud asked Henri Parisot to exclude from the **Pays des Tarahumaras** the **Supplément au voyage** "in which I was imbecile enough to say that I had been converted to Jesus Christ, whereas the Christ is what I have always abominated most. This conversion was only the result of a frightful enchantment. At Rodez it made me swallow a fearful number of hosts disguised as communion; these were supposed to keep me for as long as possible, and, if possible, eternally, inside a being which is not my own." This **Supplément au voyage au pays des Tarahumaras** was, therefore, sacrificed in the original edition published by *Fontaine* in 1945. Its disavowal does not, however, make it not worth quoting from.

Antonin Artaud begins by evoking the demons who are attacking him, "this being that I constantly see faltering before my eyes as long as God has not placed his key in my heart. One sees God when one wants to, and to see God is not to be satisfied with the little enclave of terrestrial sensations. . . . One day I was far from God but never had I also felt so far away from my own self, and I saw that without God there is neither identity nor being, and that the man who still believes he is living will never again be able to understand himself." In the Ciguri of the Tarahumaras, *he could not but recognize Jesus Christ.* A letter to Henri Parisot of December 10, 1942, states: "I shall pray especially to Jesus Christ about this, for my whole Voyage to Mexico concerns Him, and it is He, the Word of God, whom the Tarahumaras adore, as I was able to observe in the rite of the *Tutuguri* which takes place at sunrise." As for the **Supplément,** it concludes: "And it is this God of Eternal Charity whom I went and found the following year among the Icelanders." This refers to another trip, his last, about which he makes these comments in a letter to Jean-Louis Barrault dated October, 1943:

> The thought which permitted me to support my ordeals without flinching: God. I came back to Him in Dublin in September, 1937, and it was there that I took confession and communion after twenty years of estrangement from the Church and several years of atheism and blasphemy with which all my works are studded. This means that, except for my correspondence with Rivière, the **Théâtre et son double** and **Nouvelles révélations de l'etre,** I disavow all my written works and I shall have them all destroyed.

According to this passage, he apparently kept his faith until 1917 (the period of his first mental disturbance), then reverted to it again from 1937 to 1944. By what right, then, should we accept his denunciation of his Christian rather than his blasphemous works?

Whether he refers to a metaphysical system or to a system

of magic, it is obvious that Antonin Artaud is interpreting them according to his own concepts. No doubt this is what all believers do. As objective observers, however, we cannot give preference to one or other of these spiritual positions. Artaud's interpretative approach is noticeable, for example, in his ideas concerning mescaline. He assures us in the **"Rite du peyotl"** that "Mystics must pass through similar states before attaining supreme illumination." And in the *Supplément au voyage:* "It is then that the peyote given by Jesus Christ intervenes. It takes the soul from behind and sets it in the eternal light, such as comes from the Spirit on high. . . ." A note written after the **"Rite"** pokes fun at this interpretation: "As for peyote, it does not lend itself to these offensive spiritual assimilations, for MYSTICISM has never been anything but a copulation of a very learned and very refined *tartufferie* against which peyote thoroughly protests, for with it MAN is alone, desperately rattling the music of his skeleton, without father, mother, family, love of god or society." But in the *Supplément* he wrote what seems incontestable, whether or not it is considered from the Christian point of view: "*I had certainly never experienced anything of God* (thanks to peyote), *for it is not by means of an experimental physical test that one reaches the Godhead. . . .*"

Here the madman Artaud seems more rational than the wise Aldous Huxley, according to whom mescaline enables one *to experience the heights of contemplation.*

Whether Artaud recognizes himself as a Christian or not, whether he reveres Christ or blasphemes him, seems less important to me than to the pseudo-rebels of the *nth* surrealist generation who go into a trance at the very name of Jesus while they feel respect for the bloodiest beliefs of the Aztecs or the Tarahumara rites. Such sensitivity surprises observers who consider themselves unconnected with any form of supernaturalism. It is the credulity of these pseudo-atheists that is impressive. A subconscious nostalgia for the faith causes them to disown Christianity the better to abandon themselves to a metaphysical appeal whose heterodox, exotic, and indeterminate form reassures them. As for me, it makes no difference whether this poet, who is visibly *inspired,* claims this or that religion. Artaud went to Christ just as he went to Ciguri. It was not by chance that he happened to confuse them. It would be unfair to use this as an argument in favor of the conception of Artaud as a Christian. But it is also just as unacceptable to overlook the date of his conversion, as has been done too often, and only remember his blasphemies and *other* beliefs. What really matters is not Artaud the Christian, nor Artaud the magician, nor Artaud planning to go "the way of the Himalayas" to be initiated into new mysteries. No, what is important is Artaud at constant and direct grips with metaphysics.

In one of his letters from Rodez, Antonin Artaud admits that, above all, he went to seek in Mexico a race that would follow his ideas. This indicates that he, too, was only looking for what he had already found. Very much along the same lines is this declaration from a letter of April 2, 1926: "I plan to leave Mexico City shortly for the interior of Mexico. I am leaving in search of the impossible. We shall see whether I shall find it." In the **"Rite du peyotl"** he carried this search for the impossible toward an objective that was scarcely more modest: "I told him (the Priest) also that I had not come to the Tarahumaras out of simple curiosity but to rediscover a Truth, conserved by his Race, which has eluded the European world." His commentary, in the *Supplément au voyage,*

changes nothing essential in this: "Thus it was that, driving on toward God, I rediscovered the Tarahumaras."

Antonin Artaud spoke a great deal also about good and evil. He never ceased to know what was good and what was evil. Here again citations abound. He writes that "Evil is in the order of things and man can no longer feel pure." He adds that "the struggle between Good and Evil is not yet finished. In order for the reign of God to arrive on earth, we must be chaste." These notes are from Rodez, but the same theme is found again after his renunciation of Christianity in the poems written during the last months of his life, published by the review *84.* In them, Artaud denounces "the hideous world of lubricity and the obscene proposition of a world without judgment or ethics. . . . This true story of mine is shocking. It is the story of a man who wanted to be good and pure but nobody wanted him, because men can can never get along with anything but impurity, impiety, injustice and assassination. It is very difficult to be pure, but when one must be pure in the face of general ill will that does everything it can to keep one in a state of evil, as if by force, it becomes a desperately difficult chore." On this point the judgment of Arthur Adamov appears definitive and cannot be questioned even by our pious fanatics of impiety. We find it in the same issue of the review *84:* "He believed in enchantments, and in a literal way. But I have reason to think that in large measure Antonin Artaud's belief in enchantments was born from an impossibility, from a refusal to admit the existence of evil in the world, and I would say almost from too great a love."

There is nothing to add, except perhaps to quote the Dominican, Father Laval: "In short, here is the true language of a man who is suffering." (pp. 35-49)

Claude Mauriac, "Antonin Artaud," in his The New Literature, *translated by Samuel I. Stone, George Braziller, Inc., 1959, pp. 35-49.*

PAUL ARNOLD   (essay date 1963)

[*In the following essay, Arnold discusses the cultural context out of which Artaud's experimental theater emerged, the development of his dramatic theories, and the influence of his work.*]

With the intransigence of an innovator who feels himself inspired, Antonin Artaud, by an imperious gesture of the pen, by an imperious gesture of the mind, wrote off about two thousand three hundred years of theatre.

Of Western theatre.

We are in the early thirties. This was the period when Louis Jouvet successfully produced the masterpieces of Jean Giraudoux: the period of *Electra* and her half-god, half-prophet Beggar, just before the Trojan War would not take place, and a little longer before Ondine would glisten in the first rays of another world. This was the period when Charles Dullin created the terrifying protagonist of *Richard III,* the saraband of *'Tis a Pity She's a Whore,* tragedies as frenzied as tragedies can be, in which howling, cursing, death-bed laments alternate with love songs and sweet tenderness. This was the period when George Pitoëff preserved from mere fashionable success Chekhov's *Sea Gull, Three Sisters, Uncle Vanya,* Ostrovsky's *Storm,* and an extraordinary Hamlet-like Romeo. This was a miraculous period for the theatre in France.

But it was not enough for Artaud. Nor was he the only one

to think that all this was too discreet, too ordinary, too "true to life," and that there was no effort being made to know "up to what point one could push further," as Jean Cocteau so nicely phrased it. This was the period when Autant-Lara scandalized Paris with his "Companions of Art and Action," with spectacles in which they "walked on their hands." Artaud was not afraid to accept it literally. One day, while rehearsing the role of Charlemagne under Dullin's direction, Artaud, in order to portray his character better, crawled toward the throne on all fours. Barrault, who reports the incident and the stupefaction of Dullin, describes Artaud's indignation when, repudiated by the master, he got up waving his arms and with a regal air cried out: "Oh, if only you would work with the simple truth!"

It was the period when Jean-Louis Barrault, lying all night in the stage-bed of Volpone, "knocked the theatre over" with the haunting pantomime *As I Lay Dying,* and what Artaud would call the "marvelous horse-centaur" by means of which "Jean-Louis Barrault gave us magic." For Artaud this show of June, 1935 was "an event worthy of the highest acclaim."

In the very depths of the art theatre, the new generation did not really try to "continue the Cartel," as Gaston Baty would have wished. Not only revolutionary, but actively rebelling, this young, giddy, rude generation was seized by a hope as high as it was vague, a hope that glistened with the last sparks of the explosion of surrealism. Opposed to those who created with the masterliness of Goethe, there were others who preferred the eruptive genius of Büchner or Gérard de Nerval. Opposed to Renoir, they preferred van Gogh. More was at stake than a cabal of artists, a quarrel of schools. A whole culture, a new civilization hung in the balance. It was no longer merely a matter of reform, whether prudent or brutal: it was a question of ending any utilitarian orientation in art and in life; of ending all aesthetic pragmatism; even better, of ending the logical mentality in order to bring about the triumph, or rather the resurgence, of the "primitive" prelogical mentality. It was a question of profiting at last from the message of Arthur Rimbaud. Of such hopes Artaud became the standard-bearer.

The idea is not completely new. In opposition to the Théâtre Libre, Maeterlinck, Rémy de Gourmont, Paul Fort, and then Alfred Jarry had founded theatres of liberty, theatres of the supernatural and the mysterious, such as Mallarmé demanded. Just after the first World War, in opposition to the Henry Batailles, the Bernsteins, the François de Curels, the Caillevets, a group of "madmen" sprang up: the Marcel Achard of *Do You Want to Play with Me? (Voulez-vous jouer avec moi?),* the Salacrou of *The Blusterer (Casseur d'assiettes)* and *Bridge of Europe (Pont de l'Europe),* the Neveux of *Juliette (Juliette ou la clef des songes),* the Jean-Victor Pellerin of *Replaceable Head (Tete de rêchange).* And these seemed like classics when compared to Apollinaire's *Breasts of Tiresias (Mamelles de Tirésias).*

But all of this was the fruit of intelligence, the intellect, a superior kind of trickery to which Crommelynck contributed some linguistic distinction. Artaud did not want this kind of theatre. It was a beginning, to be sure, and in it one could welcome "the spirit of profound anarchy that is at the base of all poetry," and which Artaud felt the contemporary theatre had "broken with." And if, since the time of his protest, Anouilh, Sartre, Achard, Aymé and many others have consolidated the position of the "theatre of human passions," of that Western theatre against which Artaud revolted, their re-

action does not change the fact that there is a new orientation in the history of the theatre—an orientation that strives to realize the malediction uttered by Artaud [in *The Theatre and Its Double*]:

> When we pronounce the word life, we must understand that it is not the life of external facts, but of that fragile, secret interior which outer forms do not touch. And if there is still something infernal and truly accursed in our day, it is to linger artistically upon these outer forms, instead of being like martyrs at the stake, who make signs through the flames.

Is the Artaud experiment over? Rather has it even begun? Has not Artaud conceived a lofty mission that the future may fulfill?

> On the moral and psychological level, the Orphic mysteries which captivated Plato must have had something of this transcendental and final aspect of the alchemical theatre. Along with its elements of extraordinary psychological density, the mysteries, conversely, must have evoked alchemical symbols which provided the spiritual means to decant and transfuse matter, and they must have evoked the burning and decisive transfusion of matter by spirit.

In these phrases, which may at first seem obscure, Artaud has perhaps best stated the essence of his quest. Roughly, humanity may be divided into "primitive" or "pre-logical" and civilized or logical beings. All true exaltation breaks the bounds of intellect, but our insufficient human reason will not permit us wholly to accept this fact. This is what Artaud suddenly understood when he saw performances of the Balinese Theatre at the Colonial Exposition of 1931; this theatre of living tradition was as different from ours as a religious ceremony is from a Molière comedy. Without knowing the Indonesian language, Artaud was struck by the hieroglyphics of performance, conventional movements and positions that were completely different from the corporeal expression we are accustomed to, "spiritual signs which have a precise meaning that strikes us only intuitively but with enough violence to render superfluous any translation into discursive, logical language."

This is the touchstone of the Artaud mystery.

We know little about the Orphic mysteries or the Eleusinian mysteries. With the help of stimulants, strange dances, terrifying or spell-binding scenes suddenly revealed in dark depths, the hierophants "transported" the veils, exalted or horrified the initiated in the way that certain Negro or Tibetan rites do today (the rite of Choeud, for example). In every case it is a matter of shocking man until he momentarily loses control of his reasoning mind and a destructive "second state" springs forth from the discursive intelligence.

In this anarchy of thought, which is not stupidity but a new comprehension, mystics assure us that the human being sees and seizes new superhuman truths. Transported outside and beyond himself (or what he believes to be himself, but is only an apparent and superficial aspect of his being), he is reintegrated into the universal, into that which is sensible beyond the senses. Artaud wanted this experience for the theatre in order to give rise to the "metaphysical identity of the concrete and the abstract," the unity of all the revealed world, of all the created universe. It was therefore a kind of savage mystique.

From the moment of "transport," immediate reality, everyday experience, became insufficient, inoperable; it was no longer a complete reality, it was no longer truly "realistic." It was necessary to introduce a super-reality (not to be confused with surrealism) which would not be limited to expressing tangible reality, but which would embrace tangible daily appearances, *plus* spiritual leverage, *plus* an immanent metaphysical and metapsychological power for which daily appearances would be a most incomplete medium. To speak in images, it was a matter of lifting the veil, of uncovering an interior reality, a "divine" mechanism. By these means reality would appear "to the nth degree," as called for by Artaud.

And because this super-reality would be stripped of the contingent, of the "case in point" (as the jurists have it), it would transcend the petty, incomplete news item (it is because any given apple differs in some way from every other apple that *it* cannot represent all apples). Thus, the process of unveiling would reveal reality to the nth degree in a stylized form: a pure shape, which is also, and not accidentally, pure theatre.

It goes without saying that this super-reality is not simply made up of words; nor is it a question of mental attitude, for we know that everyday consciousness does not attain transcendence. One has to reach a different level, the "second state" of metaphysics and parapsychology. How can one get there? By what practical means is this attainment possible? Once he knew his goal, all of Artaud's research went to answer these questions. And after giving him the key, the Balinese theatre gave him the method. What struck Artaud in the Balinese theatre was that the characters no longer obeyed what we believe to be our psychological center, our deliberate will, our liberty of action. Artaud rightly thought that Balinese characters are dehumanized, "mechanized"; what they feel does not seem to belong to them, or come through their own resolution; rather it is inspired in them, "dictated" by superior forces. For this reason their gestures, their actions, everything that happens before our eyes, spills over and goes beyond the *apparent* will of the individuals and takes possession of the actors so that they become the involuntary (automatic) participants in a divine ritual. Their theatre has all the solemnity of a sacred rite whose goal, like that of any religious service, is to reveal the superhuman, the miraculous.

And Artaud claims to have experienced this transport through "the kind of terror" evoked in him, which should be evoked in us, by the sight of these mechanized, dehumanized beings moved by superhuman powers. I have already mentioned that terror is always the principal ingredient in initiation rites, both among the magicians of so-called primitive peoples and the heirophants of Eleusis. Terror arouses in us, certain people claim, that particular sensation which leads to the mystic state (we need not discuss this point, but there is no doubt that this is an oversimplification of the mystic phenomenon, and I shall have more to say about this). This second state found in certain collective rites (in the South Sea Islands, for example) is contagious. For example, among the Kriss dancers in Bali (who are so well described by Beryl de Zoete in *Dance and Drama in Bali*) once a single dancer attains a certain level of delirium, the others succumb much more quickly. And it is this contagious quality of delirium that interested Artaud; he compared it to the plague. It is this communicable, contagious delirium that he intended to put on the stage, where it would submerge everyone and everything.

This is the essential difference between what Artaud called the false theatre, which is practiced generally, and what he felt to be the true theatre. Rather than being limited by what the psychologically oriented Aristotle saw in the theatre, the theatre should become the mouthpiece for the supernatural. This enables us to put our finger on the weak point of Artaud's reasoning.

Artaud constantly defended himself against the charge of religiosity. He expressed himself vehemently on that point, saying that the special mysticism of what he called the Theatre of Cruelty must not be confused with the ignorance of a church-warden or what he called a Buddhist priest outside the temple; and this drove him to the most frightful blasphemy. However, when he tried to analyze the essence of this delirium that he claimed to create, he found nothing more than "the latent depth of cruelty" in an individual or in a people, which focuses "all the perverse possibilities of the spirit" and which he also called "dark forces." These shadowy forces have to be brought to the surface, made to triumph in and through the theatre, and to constitute "the time of evil." Further, Artaud assures us that these infernal forces are fed by still deeper forces, about which he says nothing more except that these deeper forces will eliminate the dark forces through stimulating them (purity through purgation).

In other words, by giving free rein to all of man's evil in this delirium, man will be cleansed of all evil. Artaud does not add that this delirium will bring about the time of the good; he prefers to limit himself to the first phase, which he sees in certain ancient tragedies, and whose secret he feels is indispensable. It is thus clear that his whole theory is based philosophically on the axiom that the complete liberation of evil forces (even beyond the libido) would bring about the good. This is an obvious philosophical, psychological, and historical error. If certain exceptional people were able to somersault from a delirium of perversity to beneficent mysticism, recent history has shown that the psychology of modern mobs tends in exactly the opposite direction. Another of Artaud's misconceptions was to believe that an actor in the throes of a tragic "fury" needed more virtue *not* to commit a crime than an assassin needed courage to commit his crime. This is taking the meaning out of words. The problem of the actor's identification with the character he portrays has just about been solved: we know that, hot or cold, he never completely splits his personality, he never completely loses control of himself while playing a role. He would never go as far as a real crime, and therefore needs no special virtue to stop himself. And similarly, any true mystic, any authentic yogi will teach us that the release of evil is different from the release of good and that the latter cannot be nourished by the former even if evil disappears in the process. Quite the contrary; certain paths of evil must be sealed off in order to approach a true state of mysticism. Actually, Artaud's illusions about Balinese theatre were based on a misunderstanding; the goal of this theatre was never to reveal the latent cruelty in man, but to reveal nonhuman forces which attack man from without, and which he fears with all the terror of primitive man face to face with the mysteries of external nature. On the other hand, the Tibetan priests teach (and this is the goal of certain of their initiations) that this kind of terror is ignorance of the true nature of phenomena, and that these so-called demons are evoked by our imagination alone.

Thus the entire philosophical basis of **The Theatre and Its Double** is erroneous. But that is not our problem; the problem is one of theatrical effectiveness. It is a question of seeing how

Artaud intended to reach his goal, how he intended "to bring our demons to the surface." What practical way, what method, what theatrical technique can accomplish this metamorphosis? How can the metaphysical theatre, the alchemical theatre be made a reality?

By creating "poetry in space."

And for that one needs all the sources of expression that the theatre has always had. Of course, "the language of gesture, attitude, dance, music is less able than verbal language to depict a character, to reveal a clear, specific state of consciousness." But verbal language itself should assume another function than it has now. It should be torn from its reasoning and degrading function, and it should be made to create a metaphysics of language.

> It is not a matter of abolishing spoken language, but of giving words the approximate importance they have in dreams. To make metaphysics out of spoken language is to make language express what it usually does not express: it is to use it in a new, uncommon, unusual way; to restore its possibility of physical shock, to divide it and distribute it actively in space; to use intonation in a concrete and absolute way in order to restore its power of shattering and of really manifesting something; to turn against language and its merely utilitarian, one might say alimentary, worries, turn against its origins of hunted beast; finally, to make a metaphysics of language is to consider language as a form of Incantation.

Incantation is the magic function of language. In these lines there is both the foreknowledge of genius and an excusable error. Did Artaud know that in restoring to language its incantatory function he was only restoring its primitive magic value? For—as studies of the language and mentality of oceanic peoples have proven—originally language did not have a "basely utilitarian," "alimentary" function; it was not a tool of a "hunted beast," but a holy, magic, and fearful thing, inspiring not articulated sounds, but supernatural actions that were incantatory in the powerful sense of casting spells. In Kanaka *no* means word, act, and action. And when the war-song sounds, the Kanakan warrior says, "I have begun a word"; the chief, seeking the help of magic in waging war, says, "I shall seek for my service the man who begins the words and who flings the enemy house into the air."

Artaud wanted to restore a comparable magic power to language, the same power that Rimbaud and Mallarmé sought for poetry. Not the surrealist frenzy which had merely made noise, and which Artaud criticized:

> I propose to renounce this dominance of images supplied haphazardly by the unconscious, and dropped haphazardly also, images called poetic and therefore hermetic, as though the kind of trance that poetry evokes did not have its effect on all the feelings, in every nerve, and as though poetry were a vague force that does not vary its movements.

Refusing cerebration, Artaud wanted an interior and subtle music that would hypnotize us as the flute-player charms the cobra:

> If music acts upon snakes, it is not through the spiritual idea it supplies to them, but because snakes are long and they wind their length across the earth so that their body touches the earth at almost every point; and the musical vibrations which are com-

municated to the earth reach the snake in the form of a very subtle, very long massage; I propose acting upon spectators as music upon snakes, causing them to return to the subtlest ideas through their entire being.

There must be no caesura between this incantatory, vibratory function of the word and the musicality of all other elements in the spectacle: "sounds, noises, cries are sought first for their vibratory quality, then for what they represent." For vibration itself has a quality that acts magically upon us.

Finally, theatrical action. Despite what others have claimed for him, action is and remains the focal point of Artaud's productions (I do not say their goal). "Action and the dynamism of action" are decisive. Not the futile reflection of a more or less sensational news item. The action itself should tend to make one aware of the presence of extra-sensory powers. How does one go about making these intentions evident? As in the Balinese theatre, it must be understood that the joys and sorrows of the characters do not belong exclusively to them, but that these beings follow the ritual and the will "dictated by superior intelligences." This can be attained by a hubris that transcends human will, through "*a theatre in which violent physical images* destroy and hypnotize the sensitivity of the spectator." It is the orchestration of such elements that will restore the magic power of the Balinese theatre to the spectacle. For here,

> there is something which takes part magically in this intense liberation of signs that are at first withheld, then suddenly flung into the air. Sputtering through this effervescence of painted rhythms is a chaotic seething that is full of guidemarks, and occasionally it is curiously well-ordered; in this effervescence pauses play endlessly, interrupting with well-planned silence.

We are very far from the ravelling and unravelling of a plot. All these surface phenomena are only brute matter out of which the man of the theatre, like the alchemist, precipitates through sublimation a secret and sacred essence.

> The director . . . becomes a kind of magic creator of order, a master of sacred ceremonies. And the matter upon which he works, the subjects to which he gives life, are not his own, but of the gods.

We shall pass by the element of intellectual drunkenness expressed here. Artaud summarizes what such a spectacle might be like visually and psychologically:

> Certain paintings of Grünewald or Hieronymus Bosch give sufficient indication of the quality of a spectacle where natural objects appear as temptations, as in the mind of a saint. In this spectacle of a temptation in which life has everything to lose and the spirit everything to gain, the theatre must recover its true meaning.

Difficulties began when Artaud tried to translate these lofty ideas into technical, practical terms. The Balinese theatre whose spirit inspired him depends upon a magic or pre-logical mentality that is buried too deeply in Western man under layers of customs, reactions, and habits of logical thinking. Because it was necessary to relinquish the spell-binding power of myth, whose mere recitation to the oceanic primitive was enough to give reality to legend, restoring its activating and inspiring force, as faith liberated the ecstasy of the saint, because actor and spectator were reduced to artificial inspiration, there remained only paltry means for arousing poetic or mystic exaltation.

Artaud is not very original in enumerating these means in the **"First Manifesto of the Theatre of Cruelty"**:

> Every spectacle will contain a physical and objective element, perceptible to all; cries, laments, arguments, surprises, all kinds of theatrical shocks, magic beauty, and costumes taken from certain ritual models. Resplendent lighting, incantatory beauty of voices, charm of harmony, rare notes of music, colors of objects, physical rhythms of movements whose crescendo will blend with the pulsation of movements familiar to everyone, the concrete appearance of new and surprising objects, masks, puppets several yards high, sudden changes of light, the physical play of light which causes feelings of warmth and cold, *etc.*

It must be said that most of these scenic effects, as far as they can be identified through this brief description, have been used for a long time. Even their orchestration is not very far from the theatre demanded by Gordon Craig long before Artaud.

Perhaps the novelty lies more in the intensity, the degree of incandescence of all these means, which are feeble in themselves. One can feel a desire to guide the theatre toward occultist experiments; such a tendency is clearly reflected in Artaud's requirement that "belief in a fluid materiality of the soul is indispensable to the profession of acting." That remark alone permits one to foresee the revolution announced by the **"First Manifesto of the Theatre of Cruelty."**

Artaud's repertory itself was unreliable and was not enough to insure the revelatory aspect of the material. At the top of the list was an "Elizabethan work"—which finally turned out to be *The Cenci,* adapted by Artaud from Shelley and Stendhal: the sole production of the Theatre of Cruelty and Horror. Then came a play "of extreme poetic liberty, by Léon-Paul Fargue," who was a magician of language (delighting in rare words and unexpected images) but was as far as he could be from the dynamism of action that Artaud demanded. Fargue never wrote the promised play. Next on the program was "an extract from the Zohar," the principal book of the Jewish Cabal, and one may doubt whether the nonoccultist spectator would be at all moved by the recitation. As for Büchner's *Wozzeck,* which was also on the list, one can imagine that its frenzied rhythm, the intensity and compression of its scenes, might have permitted an experiment using this text whose stripped quality and language are almost untranslatable. The productions of this play by different French companies since 1945 have sometimes striven for a hallucinatory, convulsive action, which is quite far from that imagined or desired by Artaud, who inspired them all; these post-war productions were unconvincing, and they lead us back to the worst scenic techniques, using as a pretext a work that is after all rotten with romanticism.

Artaud's conception of the "place" where the Spectacle of Horror would be presented is probably more original:

> We abolish the stage and the auditorium, which will be replaced by a single site, without partition or boundary of any kind, and this will become the theatre for the action. Direct communication between spectator and spectacle will be restored. . . . We will take some hangar or barn which will be rebuilt by methods which have result-
> ed in the architecture of certain churches or holy places, and of certain Tibetan temples.

One may doubt whether Artaud had a clear idea of these "holy places" and "temples." I visited several in the East without seeing the desired instrument for Artaud's theatre. Artaud continues:

> Special positions will be reserved for the actors and for the action at the four corners of the room.

But the conclusion is less daring:

> However, there will be a central area set aside, which, although not strictly speaking a stage, will permit most of the action to be concentrated and to be brought to a climax whenever that is necessary.

Thus we come back finally to a most classical idea, or at least to the theatre-in-the-round used since classical times with varying results; and in this theatre the playing is scattered in the manner of the Mystery plays, where the action moved from station to station with the audience following.

Thus when Artaud passed from the abstract to the concrete, from theory to practice, the visionary flight was halted.

Nor could it be otherwise. For even the most frenzied external methods can never create a spectacle capable of transporting us into the second state, or even into a state of basic receptivity. At best such methods can excite our curiosity or our appetite. Food for the "magic process" can come only from the dramatic poet inventing a myth in new language. Outside of that, a spectacle can offer no more than certain dazzling moments, as Artaud said Barrault did with his "marvelous horse-centaur." Artaud wanted to see in *As I Lay Dying* a "magic spectacle, as the incantations of Negro sorcerers are magic." But it is a lesser Artaud, disappointed by the recent failure of his *Cenci,* who wrote that appreciation, hoping that he had met a disciple who would save the Theatre of Cruelty from disaster. The years which followed have not shown us that Artaud was right in proclaiming that Barrault's pantomime "transformed the atmosphere so that an antagonistic public is suddenly and blindly immersed, and invincibly won over."

What Artaud truly saw and foresaw was something quite different. Those who have seen Japanese Nô plays (and let us not speak of the poor Western translations) know that this kind of density spreads and lasts all through the spectacle, not only because of the vocal tones and dance postures, but also because of the suggestive, enchanting power of the subject, because of the philosophy and the human sorrow underlying the plays, which is truly that of "martyrs at the stake, who make signs through the flames."

Only once did Artaud have the opportunity to express himself fully—in his *Cenci.* I attended that production. Subjective observations are out of place here, and if one attempts to form an opinion from the reviews, one is confused. Rehearsals and manifestoes had aroused the curiosity and the skepticism of the critics. Many were receptive to the heightened presentation, but none could see the psychological power desired by Artaud. Was his goal nevertheless attained in this between-war Paris, eager for strong sensations? Was it understood that the problem was, as Artaud declared in an interview, "to give to theatrical production the appearance of a blazing hearth, and at least once during the production to drive action, situation, images to that degree of relentless incandescence which, in the domain of the psychological or comic, may be identified with cruelty?" It is doubtful, and the failure of **The Cenci** was financially decisive: it brought about Artaud's ruin, leading to his abandonment of the theatre, and his escape into the virgin Mexican forest, where he went to study the habits of the Tarahumaras.

But this kind of throwing of the dice pays off many years later. And it may be said that the entire presently fashionable generation sprang from Artaud—which does not mean it has carried out his message. Where he is not entirely original, Barrault derives in large part from Artaud; and Jean Vilar, perhaps with more cause, does not deny that Artaud is his inspiration. But both these actor-directors have compromised with the habitual theatre so that Artaud's quest is less betrayed in them than forgotten. It might be taken as axiomatic that Artaud's kind of visionary theatre cannot surrender an inch of its intransigence without completely betraying itself. A mixture of Ingres and Picasso is unthinkable; Picasso turned away from Ingres, the master of his early Blue Period, when he became himself. The development of a theatre—and particularly of a national theatre—cannot be reconciled with a path as absolutely experimental as Artaud's. At a time when no one claims his authority any longer, something else is being done whose value need not be discussed now. A few of the "young" have worked in the same spirit, above all Nicolas Bataille with his haunting production of Dostoyevsky's *The Possessed* and his violent rendering of Ionesco's *The Bald Soprano.*

If we look at those playwrights who claim a relationship with Artaud (Adamov, Beckett, Schéhadé, Ionesco, Vauthier, etc.), we find human anguish resulting in intellectual games, paradox, the mystery of nothingness (for example, the vain wait for Godot) and a doubletalk which seeks to dismantle language, to explode it, to dynamite through it in order to offer us, or claim to offer us, a super-reality. Was this what Artaud wanted? Was it this vituperative or sarcastic vehemence, or did he want rather a deep and serious exaltation? Was it Ionesco's way of squaring the circle, or a tearing at the heart, as in **The Cenci?**

What we have to see is whether Artaud's philosophical error, which I have discussed, can be rectified by present or future generations, so that Artaud's goals can be won. But first let us see how those goals are interpreted. I have already said that the release of evil in order to extinguish it can not bring about a mystic purge. The confusion of the contemporary world has produced the mental anarchy that is at the root of Artaud's reasoning. In a spirit comparable to Arthur Miller's, our avant-garde has learned from Artaud only his vehemence, his scandalous aspect—flinging bile and excrement at all institutions, beliefs, ideas, feelings, without having any substitute idea or feeling to offer us. This negativity can take the virulent form of apostrophe or parody which claims that it is philosophical or social criticism, or it can take the less harmful form of illogicality (which is confused with prelogic), the somewhat clumsy fantasy of a steady-stream syringe in which the blunted sensibility of our generation allows itself free rein and reveals its utter triviality. All this is in large part arbitrary because it lacks all philosophical basis, even one that is tainted with error like Artaud's. He claimed to know the sources of the occult; our "youth" has forgotten his rather solid basis, and they are working in a void, unbalanced, doing their best (and sometimes fooling themselves)

to hide beneath a scandalous exterior a position of social or political criticism, some on the Left, others on the Right. The essence of this attitude was already in Artaud's thought, which certain political groups used without his having the slightest idea of it.

So that his message, already shaky when it left him, has been completely betrayed. Can it still serve to build and improve what Artaud perceived vaguely? For he did define a kind of incandescence and through it a renaissance of ancient tragedy.

We would need an exceptional social climate of peace, stability, and confidence—a climate in which the spiritual life of the people would be the main and almost sole concern. Along with these basic conditions, we would need exceptionally pure beings for whom "the time of evil" would be a means and not an end, for whom scandal would be abandoned in order to go beyond the half-hidden man and undertake the quest for the superhuman. These "pure beings" would not stop the trilogy with *The Libation Bearers* but would push on to *The Eumenides;* they would not stop with *Prometheus Bound* but with *Prometheus Freed.* But time passes swiftly, and the messages of precursors are forgotten. We must look for a new Artaud who will rethink the message of **The Theatre and Its Double** and who will transcend it. (pp. 15-29)

Paul Arnold, "The Artaud Experiment," translated by Ruby Cohn, in The Tulane Drama Review, *Vol. 8, No. 2, Winter, 1963, pp. 15-29.*

Artaud as Gringalet in the film Le juif errant, *1926.*

ROMAIN WEINGARTEN (essay date 1963)

[*In the following excerpt, Weingarten examines aspects of Artaud's dramatic theory.*]

> On viscous, foul-smelling, bloody streams (the
> color of anguish and opium) which spurt out of
> corpses, pass strange characters dressed in wax,
> with noses as long as sausages, and with glass eyes;
> they are mounted on a kind of Japanese sandal
> made of double wooden slats, one vertical and the
> other horizontal, serving as the sole, and these pro-
> tect them from the polluted fluids; they chant ab-
> surd litanies which do not stop them from sinking
> into the blaze in their turn.
> ### The Theatre and Its Double

This is the outline of a spiritual landscape which has continued to deteriorate from the 1720 outbreak of the plague in
Marseilles to 1938 (publication date of **The Theatre and Its
Double**) and on to our own day. The "strange characters"
have been in the process of engulfing the world. But after the
war, in St. Germain-des-Pres, the last inhabitant of an increasingly unexplored continent appeared and offered the minority a choice: to live or not to live. For several, the word
"theatre" represented the possibility of completely changing
our way of life. This is more than a paradox; it is the very purpose of **The Theatre and Its Double.**

Since his death, Artaud's name has been linked with almost
every theatrical undertaking. And one may wonder—without
passing any judgments—to what degree Artaud has influenced our theatre.

ACTION. The central problem of the theatre is that of the
actor. There is no escape from the need to define a notion of
"act" which applies both to the actor and to theatrical action.

> Our idea of a civilized man is someone conversant
> with systems, thinking in systems, forms, signs,
> representations. He is a monster who has developed
> to an absurd degree the ability to derive thoughts
> from acts instead of identifying thoughts and acts.
> If our life lacks brimstone and magic it is because
> we look at our acts and lose ourselves in fantasies
> about them, instead of being propelled by them.

I will add this: for us the actor is someone who is acted upon,
not someone who acts. And here I must insist that metaphysics underlies Artaud's notion, despite his statement that "I
very much regret pronouncing that word." It is metaphysical
in the traditional sense that consciousness is equivalent to the
act and every act is therefore a relationship between con-
sciousnesses. Each movement in the "outer world" (where all
acts take place) implies a level of consciousness which underlies all reality: a metaphysical, life-source, level.

> The actor who never repeats the same gesture, but
> who gestures and moves, does violence to accepted
> forms; but behind these forms, and precisely
> through their destruction, he comes upon what out-
> lives them and insures their continuation.

The fundamental difference between thought and things
(which has evoked so much violent idolatry) no longer exists.
Instead there is only a difference in degree, and all levels of
reality are reflected in and modified by all others at every moment. One can readily see the infinite register of relationships
and correspondences that such an idea uncovers for the artist.
If action consists not in changing the *position* of things but
the *level* on which they are understood, then all levels of reality can be revealed on the physical space of the stage. Theatrical action takes on a wider meaning. The spectator can be
given a complete representation of life which will liberate and
exalt him.

> Briefly, the highest idea of theatre seems to be one
> which will reconcile us philosophically with Be-
> coming. Rather than concerning itself with changes
> and conflicts represented by words, this theatre will
> suggest, through all kinds of objective situations,
> the stealthy notion of the transmutation of ideas
> into things. Furthermore (and the theatre arose
> from this), the theatre should present man and his
> appetites only when man is pitted against destiny.
> Not to suffer that destiny, but to measure himself
> against it.

If we accept this point of view it becomes clear that there is
nothing at any time that we can consider simply as a means.
Every means is at the same time an end—that is a *being,* and
a being is a certain possibility of action, a certain liberty.

It is in this spirit that we must view all the elements of theatre. We must treat them with reverence if we want to project
the feeling of *presence*—which is more necessary than ever in
a world overflowing with an extraordinary number of means
whose hypothetical ends are racing away from us at the speed
of light; presence is leaving us. And we turn towards yesterday's worlds, but for us the "old totemism of animals, stones,
thunderous objects, bestial costumes—in short, everything
that can influence, direct, and arouse forces—is a dead thing,
which we can use only statically and aesthetically, use, that
is, as spectators, not as actors."

POETRY. Poetry may be viewed as anything opposed to the
world of pure utility in which we grind out our lives. As far
as the language of the theatre is concerned, it would be confusing to discuss poetry, because with few exceptions it
doesn't exist yet.

> This very difficult and complex poetry takes on
> many aspects. First of all it includes every method
> of expression available to the stage, such as music,
> dance, plastic arts, pantomime, mimicry, gestures,
> intonations, architecture, lighting, and décor.

Put all that together and the spectator, crushed under so
many tedious components rolled into one, pleads for mercy
and asks that as soon as possible he be given a little of that
theatre in which he suffers a boredom which is at least peaceful and discreet. In Artaud there are so many noises, cries,
gestures, and actions lumped crudely together that if we add
to these a general free-for-all between actors and spectators
the result will be widespread carnage and fire in the auditori-
um. Usually only the picturesque part of Artaud's description is retained and no effort is made to understand him. Accustomed as we are to the classical development of thought
(in "our profound ignorance of the spirit of synthesis and
analysis") we cannot accept ideas that do not flow and follow
one after another, but which, instead, catch fire and spring
forth almost simultaneously from a living, flaming center. In
this profusion and hammering of explosive images, and even
in this literary sumptuousness, there is the danger that we
will be diverted from the care for absolute *stripping down* that
evoked it all.

> In this poetic and active way of envisaging stage ex-
> pression, everything urges us to turn away from a
> human, contemporary, and psychological meaning
> for the theatre in order to rediscover the religious

and mystical meaning that our theatre has completely lost.

PSYCHOLOGY. "Something is taking place" ["Il se passe quelque chose"]. This common sense way of expressing the mysterious concretization of the theatre leads me to the idea of action as the passing of a living force from one level to another. This passing is theoretically impossible according to most of our present notions, which see the impossibility of communication as the only tangible reality. The "impossibility of communication" has become the very object of a theatre whose art lies in nothing taking place.

> Stories about money, worry over money, social climbing, pangs of love without altruism, sex stories sprinkled with eroticism without mystery—all this may be the province of psychology, but not of the theatre. These torments, seductions, and lusts in the face of which we are mere voyeurs turn sour and incite revolt. We must realize that.

The stage is there, and the troupe of actors, and moveable objects; but all these placed outside of life are no more than "a tale of sound and fury, signifying nothing." Signs without thickness dissolving into the night; why should one need a space for all that?

SPACE. Every thought or feeling has a concrete existence in some point of space, just as everything in space at some time is expressed in thought or feeling. But even before it fills space, the theatre *is* space. In the theatre things are as they are in consciousness: scenic space is the very interior of life. And as soon as one grants to the actor a *personal* interior quality that differs from this universal common place, the stage is empty, theatre vanishes, and exhibitionism begins. It is for this reason that the portrayal of a state of the soul, no matter how moving, does not belong to the theatre. Language, a useless transcription of what might be seen, has no force for us.

> To change the goal of theatrical language is to use it in a concrete and spatial sense; that is, to blend it with everything in the theatre that is spatial and concretely meaningful. To change the goal of language is to manipulate it like a solid object which turns things topsy-turvy, first in the air, then in an infintely more mysterious and secret domain that itself may be extended, and it will not be very difficult to identify this secret but extended domain with formal anarchy on the one hand, and with continuous formal creation on the other.

It is one thing to say "I am angry" and to make a face, and another to suggest anger by lighting, music, or an unusual way of placing an object. Above all, it is important for the actor to be angry in space—that is, to inject space into anger. But again, what is this space? And where does the action take place? The action is not onstage. One does not actually kill there, or build dams, or have children. The action is represented on the stage. But the action takes place in the consciousness of the audience, which climbs onstage to meet the consciousness of the actor. And this is the stuff he plays upon and which he shapes in his own way; which he can illuminate if he is gifted with the necessary purity.

PASSIONS. There is room here for a whole science of the theatre. In order to believe in this anger which is as mysterious as space itself, one has to believe in the real existence of certain relationships verified by common sense. In addition to the grimace there are other active physical outlets (in other

words, creative outlets) for feeling. Hysterical actors push this face-twisting to an extreme and the cry is heard, "Ah, Artaud!"—when it is just the contrary. In the one case I feign a passion of which I am soon no longer the master, and this leads to the destruction of the theatre. In the other case I free myself completely from this passion, but I arouse its presence in my body and *outside* of me. The more overwhelming and exciting it is, the more I act with coldness and precision. I play with this inflamed being which is given life by the audience; I play with it as with an object distinct from myself. The exercise is dangerous, but it is less harmful than the art of the actor.

> To know that a passion is material, that it is subject to the plastic fluctuations of matter, gives us an authority over the passions which extends our sovereignty. . . . To know that the soul has a bodily outlet permits the actor to get at this soul from the other direction, and to discover its very being through mathematical analogies. To be acquainted with the secret of the rhythm of the passions, of that kind of musical tempo which regulates the harmonic beat—this is an aspect of the theatre that our modern psychological theatre has not thought of in a long time.

THEATRE. A theatre of man comprising what will be, what is no longer, and what is not of man. Within the limited area of the stage, the unlimited area of life's exchanges makes of each element in turn the basis of "that frail and shifting center that forms do not touch." Many people familiar with contemporary theatre keep discussing what must be done. Décor or no décor, abstract or figurative, ancient or modern—and above all, what subject to treat. But what can all this accomplish in the theatre? One can perform good theatre with all of that; one can do everything—there is no rule, no law, no interdiction. But there is one source, there is one center. The very conception of acting and the indefinable idea of the presence of the actor are the only elements which deserve discussion.

Let the spectator look at the empty stage, without décor, before the appearance of the first actor, and perhaps he will be nostalgic for the living theatre. Perhaps he will be nostalgic for "that frail and shifting center" that can not be exhausted by all the social, psychological, psychoanalytic and other forms in which it has been rigged up. Let no one say that it is a matter of a theatre of dreams (by which they mean escape). The dream of the sleeping man is not the dream of the man who is awake. When the dreamer takes up his dream in life, there where sleep left it, perhaps he is waking up already, no longer dreaming. Or isn't life itself the dream of those who are dying? It is true that nothing resembles the theatre so much as dreams. One doesn't commit the crime of one's dreams. One avoids the catastrophe of one's dreams. Moreover, we can learn a good deal from the logic of dreams (which is not a different logic but a shorthand of reality), and, adding effort, give theatrical language the profound effectiveness of dreams.

This theatre does not exist. It is futile to want to throw it back upon the compost-heap of the past, or to confuse it with experiments that are contrary to its spirit. And it would be dangerous to use all these means merely to stir up the monsters of the extreme compartmentalization of our civilization, for that would constitute a turning back to shadowed, demonic communication instead of forward to a communication that is luminous in its proper time and place. What we need is a powerful contribution beyond the efforts of any individual, for without such immense power, all bodies would stop moving (we might as well lie down and die). If we do not derive *our* force from the flowing sources of life, nothing is of any use. It is not a question of principle but of true participation and "preparation." Only then will we be able to see the trajectory of thought in forms, and forms in thought; then we will be able to draw upon this force and recreate ourselves in it, as in a new body, freed of fantasies; and we will see that if life "draws back from us" on one side, it climbs back into us on the other.

> That is why I propose a theatre of cruelty. With this mania we all have today for depreciating everything, people will at once take the word "cruelty" to mean "blood." But "theatre of cruelty" means a theatre that is difficult and cruel first of all for myself. And on the level of performance, it is not a question of the cruelty we can practice on one another by hacking at each other's bodies, carving up our anatomies, or, like Assyrian emperors, sending through the mail parcels of human ears, noses, or neatly detached nostrils, but the much more terrible and necessary cruelty that things exercise against us. We are not free. And the heavens can still fall down on our heads. The theatre was created to teach us that first of all.

Discussions of the merits of the Marquis de Sade are unbearable, and we may be glad, for once, that not everybody carries out his thoughts and deeds. Unfortunately, thought is also a deed. Here at least there is no ambiguity:

> I use the word cruelty in the sense of appetite for life, of cosmic rigor and implacable necessity, in the gnostic sense of a whirlwind of life devouring the shadows, in the sense of that pain outside of whose ineluctable necessity life could not be lived. . . . A play would be futile and unsuccessful without this will, this blind appetite for life, capable of overriding everything, visible in gesture, act, and transcendental aspect of the action.

For Artaud, cruelty is an idea that is both cosmic and moral. But we mustn't get lost on this point, or the result will be strained and still far short of its goal. If a violent effort, a real torture is needed to finish with "psychology," if this effort is inevitable for anyone who wants to leave the circle of closed worlds, for anyone who simply wants to continue to live, if this effort constitutes the prime goal of the theatre, I am not forgetting the *other side,* that evocation of tenderness that is the loftiest and most difficult creation of the theatre. Nor am I thinking, for example, of Romeo and Juliet. These two people in conflict with an evil God in the person of the author had no opportunity to measure themselves against their destiny; the curtain falls before the play begins, and Artaud was right to trace the downfall of Western theatre to Shakespeare.

MORALITY.

> It is a question of knowing what we want. If we are all ready for war, plague, famine, and slaughter, we do not even have to say so; we merely have to continue as we are. Continue behaving like snobs, going in droves to this singer, to that admirable show that never passes beyond the limits of art (and even the Russian ballet at its most splendid never passed beyond the limits of art), to this exhibition of painting in which impressive forms may explode, but at random, without any real consciousness of the forces they could arouse.

The theatre always arouses forces. The spectator lends his soul for the actor to enjoy, flattering its lowest and laziest qualities; then, abandoning it, the actor leaves it even more debased. I have already said that the theatre would be still more dangerous if we drove the monsters from their lairs, and I apologize for returning to this point. But I would like to convey some sense of this medicine. Crime discovered finishes its trajectory upon the stage, accomplishes its task and purges the spectator, not through the spectacle of the punishment of the "wicked," but on the contrary, because the spectator followed all the steps of the crime with passionate attention, having himself become the criminal in the prey of his passion, and having lived that passion. Thus the real crime becomes pointless, and the spectator, like the actor, will be better disposed to make that incessant effort that every life demands. Beyond the dark developments on stage, both actor and spectator will enter a universal level of life; they will turn their own cruelty against themselves. I can only touch upon this question, whose ramifications are infinite.

> The action of the theatre, like that of the plague, is beneficial, for, impelling men to see themselves as they are, it causes the masks to fall; it uncovers lying, dullness, baseness, hypocrisy; it shakes up the stifling inertia of matter which touches even the clearest information of the senses; and by revealing men's dark power and hidden force to them, it invites them to take a heroic and superior attitude to their destiny, which they could never have done otherwise.

RITES. As far as ways and means are concerned, we in the West certainly do not have a tradition of "metaphysical" theatre, as it exists in the East. Artaud's whole book is based on this opposition between Eastern and Western theatre.

> In the Oriental theatre of metaphysical tendencies, as opposed to the Occidental theatre of psychological tendencies, this whole complex of gestures, signs, positions, sounds, of which the language of theatre and performance consists (this language which develops all the physical and poetic consequences on every level of consciousness and in every direction) must lead to profound attitudes which might be called *metaphysics in action.*

It must be admitted that these millennial rites of proven but limited effectiveness have wearied the patience of gods and men in certain parts of the globe. For that matter, Artaud's own position varied, and in **The Theatre and Its Double** we already see him torn between his attraction towards rites and the call of the dark force of a total revolution going further and deeper than the most astonishing productions of Balinese theatre. Life, always ahead of rites, proposes a much loftier rite, which would upset all the temporary medicines of "man-carrion."

But it cannot be denied that in Eastern as in Western traditions (but the Eastern follows the smallest details of life more closely) there lies precise information about the transportation of the soul and the world into the physics of the human body, and this information is most interesting, most "urgent," if I may phrase it in this way. It would be desirable for men of the theatre to obtain at least some idea of them. Now that science will soon become fiction, the field of action of Oriental rites lies open to the investigation and the *responsibility* of the West. But here one would have to speak of religion, and that is not my subject. In art, what we find in rites is the same precision we find in science. The more terrible the transports, the more rigorous the precision; results are obtained through danger; precision is beauty that gives birth to the sublime. All true art bears witness to it. We have kept the transports but not the precision. We want an art that puts us to sleep and diverts us, not an art that is dangerous, difficult, and thus precise, an art that would awaken us. This precision, which controls the ritual gestures and makes them effective, is basically the idea of the theatre. How much more indispensable it is to us in the West, who have no lifeline, and who have to rediscover a whole life! We have the choice between destruction on the one hand and danger on the other.

There are certainly lessons to be learned from the Japanese cinema, from actors in the Peking Opera (however they may restrict great myths such as *War in Heaven*) and from all forms of Oriental theatre. It is not a question of recreating the same theatre, but neither is it something entirely different. We must hope that among us and among our actors are people who want to do something different, and who agree to learn something new, or at least to unlearn in order to invent, for everything has to be invented and reinvented, beginning with our attitude towards life.

> There is a risk, but I think that in these circumstances it is worth running that risk. I do not believe that we can succeed in reviving the status quo, and I do not believe that it is worth clinging to. I propose something to rescue us from stagnation, instead of continuing to bemoan the stagnation, boredom, inertia, and stupidity of it all.

Even if we could find the actors, funds, and audiences for a new kind of theatre, the difficulty is that it would take years before one could speak of a *profession*. But it would be easier if we understood that, in spite of the bottomless past, we are at the very beginning, at the first faltering, even in the case of the most venerable masterpieces; and if we understood, too, that the possibilities are infinitely greater than our theories and oppressive habits allow us to imagine.

RE-READ ARTAUD?

> And perhaps I will no longer need a table, but will be able to plant forests to free so much matter buried eternally in the earth. Forests of bodies that are souls, and of souls that have finally become beings because they will be flame-bodies.
>
> Letter from Rodez, 1946.

Can we still hear this voice of a great poet who did more than dream of an impossible theatre, who, since he was reduced to words in spite of himself, carried words to a degree of incandescence that they had never attained? Did Artaud's theatre die with him, who alone proclaimed it?

There are contradictions in Artaud's thought. But also a unique effort, always faithful to itself, *against all baseness*. I think that no one who reads or rereads *The Theatre and Its Double* will challenge my statement that it has remained a dead letter in spite of its great importance and literary merit. As far as I am concerned, Artaud's highly personal production plans are the least important part of the book. Besides, these plans demand an abundance of means lacking to avant-garde theatres. But these means are not necessary for the reform of the acting profession, nor for the very meaning of that profession. Any stage at all, no matter how bare, will do. The rest, worthy though it may be, comes second. Since my intention is not to write criticism, I am reluctant merely to add to whatever is being written, and I would prefer the silence of

the forests. But what is at stake is a book that is impossible to find, and I only hope that I have given some people the desire to read it, or, more presumptuously, to reread it.

> And what is infernal and truly accursed in our time, is that we dally aesthetically over forms, instead of being like martyrs at the stake, who make signs through the flames.

(pp. 74-84)

Romain Weingarten, "Re-read Artaud," translated by Ruby Cohn, in The Tulane Drama Review, *Vol. 8, No. 2, Winter, 1963, pp. 74-84.*

JACQUES GARELLI (essay date 1974)

[*In the following excerpt, Garelli examines significant characteristics of Artaud's poetry as manifested in "Invocation of the Mummy."*]

What strikes one first in the work of Artaud is the identity felt, thought, repeated, but perhaps also established, between the text as it is read and the mind as it is seen. In this sense, the title of Eluard's "Donner à voir" could be thought of as exactly applying to this work as the common place finally "realized" of the spiritual will to knowledge and self-knowledge in, by, and through the act of linking words one to the other. From the first letters to Jacques Rivière onwards, the identification is felt as a suffering, as a scandal, and even in its imperfections as an irrefutable evidence that the objective faults of the written page do nothing to controvert. In this perspective, the text is presented as "the palpable radiation of a soul." And it is significant that the poem accompanying the postscript of a letter wherein certain literary theses were discussed is entitled: **"Cry,"** a term whose existential weight is manifest. Moreover, in this postscript, Artaud affirms his right to speak by reason of his spiritual suffering, the poem itself manifesting a provisional moment of that suffering which although fugitive has existed nonetheless, and which the reader must re-experience or relive, in and by means of the text, if he means to judge it.

Furthermore, we know that the relationship strongly established, not only between the text and the spirit but between the book and life is posed in an abrupt and peremptory fashion at the outset of **L'ombilic des limbes.** It is in the understanding of this strange affirmation that we must take up our place in order to question this text in its smallest details. Now the spirit in act is identified with existence to such an extent that Artaud uses the terms "existence" and "life" without distinguishing between them. If "life is burning the questions," the text-writing itself is none other than the temporal process of this consuming. Thus Artaud can never conceive of the work as detached from life. Each singular work he presents as if it were carved out of the stuff and the living tissue of existence. In that way can the following proposition be understood:

> Each of my works, each of my levels within myself, each of the glacial flowerings of my interior soul drivels on me.

It is clear in this proposition that the text is treated as one of the levels of existence and that the image of the "glacial flowering of the soul" shows the impossibility of treating the work as a pure essence, the necessity of incorporating it within an existential problematics which poses in its very center the question of the subject, and which implies, on the critical level, an "egology." Now the three following paragraphs insist on the absolute necessity of incorporating the work within the future of a life put in question as it gropes its way along, and of treating the book as a manifestation of existence. First, by stressing the discovery of the existential dimension of the self as it is manifested in the course of its epistolary questionings; second, by refusing all the objectifying conceptions of the mind's activity which are blind to the specificity of its "dimension" of life; and third, by the clearly defined meaning of his inaugural gesture which, according to his expression, "places the book suspended in life," so it will be directly connected with the attacks of the exterior world as well as with the incoherent hesitations of the self as it seeks its own being. From then on, the identification of the text with the spirit declares itself in a new movement; first by affirming the immersion and in some sense the fusion of the book's pages to take place in the "bain" of the spirit. Against that effort for identity is outlined the categorical refusal to distinguish heterogeneous levels in the life of the spirit and to separate the daily existence from the existence lived by the writer in his relation to words.

It is in that perspective that Artaud attacks the verbal dualism which places the mind and literature in two heterogeneous areas. From now on, the book is conceived as the opening of the Self on life, as a communication between thinking existence and reality inventing itself, an attitude so novel, thinks Artaud, that it cannot fail to upset the traditional thought processes. Thus the idea of a topology as an art of the description of the place opened by, spread out by, the book in the movement leading to its juncture with reality: "A few of us at the present time have tried to assault things themselves, creating in ourselves spaces open to life, spaces which never existed before and seemed to have no room in space." To inspect these new spaces, created afresh by the unfolding of the text—precisely the task of a topology—a double danger must be avoided. First, the refusal to consider the originality, the specificity, the irreducibility of this space and by a sort of reductive fatality, to conceive of it only with the mental instruments and the criteria adapted to the space of daily life. This danger is that of realism. The second, just as dangerous, is the one we might call essentialist, that of linguistic positivism, which consists of refusing any system of exchange between language and the world. Artaud makes very clear the importance he accords to what one might call the existential dimension or thickness of language and to its opening on and communication with the world, the refusal to cut off language as it is spoken from existence as it is lived, to enclose its problematic in a linguistic ghetto, thus betraying language, spirit, existence, and life. A rigorous topology must therefore steer its way between the shoals of reductive realism and reductive essentialism.

For this third path, the notion of "chair" is indispensable; in the text entitled **"Position of the Flesh,"** Artaud stresses the extreme difficulty of this new knowledge which leads to the working out of a new method:

> But the path of dead stones must be trodden with a slow step, especially by the man who has lost the *knowledge of words*. It is an indestructible science which explodes in slow stages. And he who possesses it knows it not. But the Angels also know it not, for all true knowledge is *obscure*. The clear Spirit belongs to the realm of matter.

It is this third path of knowledge, this obscure knowing of the "flesh," this new space to be surveyed that the present essay inscribes under the name of topology.

Now the flesh is for Artaud an immediate mode of knowing incarnate, at once substance and knowledge whose ambiguity the intellectual dichotomies of subject and object, the for-itself (*pour-soi*) and in-itself (*en-soi*), of spirit and matter cannot grasp. In fact, it is not within the framework of an "ontic" thought that the notion of flesh can be understood but in what Artaud defines as the **"Metaphysics of Being."** To speak of knowledge is to speak of evidence. So Artaud affirms an order of the evidence of the body which cannot be reduced to that of logical reason. And it is to that order that the poetic image belongs, as it reveals its lucidity in the flesh of its substance.

In this convergence of vocabulary between the poet and the philosopher is a profound relationship of thought according to which the flesh is that element of Being which does not belong to the reign of objectified things. It is exclusively on the level of the ontology of language that the muffled and hidden life of a text can be perceived, in that space where the opening of sense and the exchange of meanings are covered over by the apparent game of disguise and dispersion. This ontological character of the poetic text as it opens, this dividing line of critical discourse between the reign of the ontic and the ontological, is convincingly described by Eluard:

> For the artist as for the least cultivated man, there are neither concrete forms nor abstract forms. There is only communication between what sees and what is seen, an effort of understanding, of relationship, occasionally of determination, of creation. To see is to understand, to judge, to transform, to imagine, to forget or to forget oneself, to be or to disappear.

So the interrogation of the poem should be carried out neither as a study of objectified signs nor as meanings fossilized into a series of objective themes, nor as an intellectual structure to be built abstractly from a global reading of the signifieds of the work and of its signifiers considered as material things to be observed, but rather in the temporal unveiling of the text conceived as an operation which renders visible ("donne à voir") one which, according to its success or its failure, leads the way to *being* or to disappearing.

"Invocation de la momie"

Ces narines d'os et de peau
par où commencent les ténèbres
de l'absolu, et la peinture de ces lèvres
que tu fermes comme un rideau

Et cet or que te glisse en rêve
la vie qui te dépouille d'os
et les fleurs de ce regard faux
par où tu rejoins la lumière

Momie, et ces mains de fuseaux
pour te retourner les entrailles,
ces mains où l'ombre épouvantable
prend la figure d'un oiseau

Tout cela dont s'orne la mort
comme d'un rite aléatoire,
ce papotage d'ombres, et l'or
où nagent tes entrailles noires

C'est par là que je te rejoins,
par la route calcinée des veines,
et ton or est comme ma peine

le pire et le plus sûr témoin.

"Invocation of the Mummy"

These nostrils of bone and skin
where the shadows of the absolute
begin, and the painting of those lips
which you close like a curtain

And that gold slipped to you in dream
by life which strips you of bones
and the flowers of that false gaze
by which you join the light again

Mummy, and those spindle hands
to turn your entrails inside out
those hands where the frightening shadow
takes the shape of a bird

All that with which death bedecks itself
like a ritual of happenstance,
that banter of shadows, and the gold
where your black entrails swim

By the way of all those things I join you,
by the calcified road of veins,
and your gold is like my sorrow
the worst and surest witness

"A solitary dialog," this poem takes on, by its aridity, the form of an "absolute monolog." But then, who is speaking, of whom or of what, and to whom? Invocation: to invoke, to supplicate by means of the voice. A being of language, the invocation opens a way, a correspondence with the other, originating in the self—even if it were to be a one-way path, it would remain a correspondence. But the mummy is not in this case the receiver of the message, rather the subject of discourse. The strange dialog initiated between "the mummy" of fresh substance that we are and the dead mummy progressively awaking to the consciousness of its being by the work of the word is heard in the long and breathless first sentence of a text we must join to the first, **"Correspondance de la momie"**:

> Cette chair qui ne se touche plus dans la vie,
> cette langue qui n'arrive plus à dépasser son écorce,
> cette voix qui ne passe plus par les routes du son,
> cette main qui a oublié plus que le geste de prendre,
> qui n'arrive plus à déterminer l'espace où elle réalisera sa préhension,
> cette cervelle enfin où la conception ne se détermine plus dans ses lignes,
> tout cela qui fait ma momie de chair fraîche donne à dieu une idée du vide où la nécessité d'être né m'a placé.

> (This flesh which is no longer touched in life,
> this tongue which no longer extends beyond its outer surface,
> this voice which no longer passes by the roads of sound,
> this hand which has forgotten more than the gesture of taking,
> which will no longer determine where its grasp is realised,
> this brain where conceiving no longer decides within its lines,
> all that which makes up my mummy of living flesh gives god an idea of the emptiness where the necessity of being born has placed me.)

A parallel analysis of the two texts shows a similar construction: nothing is known of the beginning series of statements in its grammatical and logical functioning, either in its meaning or its cause, until the neuter demonstrative: "all that" picks up the totality of what has been said in order to make

of it, in the **"Correspondance de la momie"** the subject of what constitutes "ma momie de chair fraîche," and in **"Invocation de la momie"** the circumstantial complement of manner, means, instrument, or place, or perhaps all these complements at once, by means of which a subject saying "I" declares the possibility of meeting another subject whose singularity has been guessed at in a way as gradual as it is insistent—that is, by the second person pronoun "tu," invoked in the last line of the first quatrain, confirmed as the poem develops, and then revealed by the title and the initial vocative of the third quatrain as the mummy to whom the "I" of the last stanza is speaking even while he claims to be meeting it: ("que je te rejoins"). In other words, the invocation accomplishes by the temporal use of the poetic voice a union, or, in the words of Artaud, a "junction" which modifies the subject of the poem in his being, because from the being who speaks at the poem's outset he progressively reveals himself as the mummy to whom he is speaking. Now since the formal process of constituting and of "junction" is the same in the two texts, the notion of the "momie" in each must be clarified. In the **"Correspondance,"** the proposition immediately following the initial statements declares:

> Ni ma vie n'est complète, ni ma mort n'est absolument avortée.

> (Neither is my life complete, nor my death absolutely aborted.)

Which reveals the mummy as a mixture of life and death, a sort of composite midway between the fullness of being and the dissolution of nothingness. The mummy of fresh substance tends toward being at the same time as it accomplishes the movement which undoes it. Less evocative of Hegel than preparatory for Beckett, this figure describes the course of a life which only keeps itself going by self-destruction and of a death which only manifests itself by an indefinite suspension of the act which would permit it to attain its final limit.

But on the other hand it is clear that by the term of "flesh" Artaud means all the ambiguity of the living, which Merleau-Ponty designated by the same term at the end of his life. He means at once the origin of opening and of resistance, source of light and of opacity, wherein the meshing of meanings embodied or incarnate forms an intersection with the world, so that, by a gesture, the world suddenly takes on a soul and a body.

> Ce sens qui court dans les veines de cette viande mystique dont chaque soubresaut est une manière de monde. . . .

> (This sense coursing through the veins of the mystic flesh [literally: meat] whose every motion is a manner of the world. . . .)

The being invoked is thus living and dead, the being of the mummy, of the invocation, and of the text constructing in its verbal unfolding the fragile figure of the mummy speaking to itself.

A field of verbal and conceptual presence is spread out in the act of poetic speech extending from the speaker to the object addressed. Now this crisscrossing of notions developed in the dynamic of reading is sufficiently resistant to constitute a being to which, according to the poet, he is joined. The study of this space itself, by the analysis of its surfaces and the display of its paths as they are laid out implies the working method of a *topological approach*. In this instance, the particularity of this space is constituted by the enunciation as it forms the being of the person speaking. Here language belongs not to the order of representation but to that of constitution, since the "I" constructs itself in its saying. It does not reveal itself; it originates itself. Before being said, nothing existed. Only by the act supposing the thing does it come into being.

The difficulty of this text, then, is in its particular portraiture, alone able to create, transform, accomplish its subject, of which no model existed; nondescriptive, therefore, and opening the way to paradox. In this poem, death intrudes its visage in the open field of life, but only reveals itself as death for the one who names it. Perhaps one could conceive of the constitution of the mummy according to the progressive *prise de conscience* by the For-Others (*Pour-Autrui*) of an existent which would objectify itself in language. Then the poetic text constituting the route of this coming to consciousness would be at the same time consciousness of self and one of its modes of being.

The poem does not try to bring into presence a represented object, but to make real the movement constituting it. It is the intentional aim—that is to say the mind as it acts, operative intentionality—which has become poetic matter. The "work" of poetic constitution, to which this type of verbal creation corresponds, consists precisely of this realizing and making palpable, audible, and sensible this intentional consciousness, and not just in representing an object or a series of objects and facts of which one becomes conscious. The difficulty of the text, the resistance it offers to an unwary reader, the impossibility of treating it according to the traditional systems of ontic explanation, have to do with this uprooting from the ordinary world of the intentional object as it is carried out simultaneously with the work of its transformation.

In this perspective Artaud's untiring declarations that each of his texts manifests the movement of his mind at work should be understood: the self constructing its being in the text by the work of the word. The whole difficulty of the critical enterprise has to do with the nature of this aim. The object of our analysis of Artaud's text is to show the divisions and the junctions of these two components of intentional consciousness.

The intentional objects composing this poem, upon which the work of constitution relies are five:

> 1) line 1, these nostrils
> 2) line 3, these lips
> 3) line 7, this gaze
> 4) line 9, these hands
> 5) line 10, the entrails

We are omitting in line 5 "this gold," since as we shall show, it is not a matter of a specified object which exists or has an equivalent in the world.

Starting with these five points of reference, whose realistic component is undeniable and without which the poem would be incomprehensible, the work of constituting the unreal field of transformation and unrealization begins, incommensurable with daily perception. Although the poetic starting point has its place in the perceptive reality from which the poem progressively and forcibly removes itself, this particular type of poetic activity must be understood within the process of transformation into unreal or surreal intentional objects. The poem refers to reality without representing it, designates it

without imitating it; constitutes an autonomous world while never ceasing to speak of the real world; creates without relying for its creation on a mute thing pre-existing before the act of verbal utterance.

Scarcely has the first intentional object been named than "these nostrils" are presented not just as a physiological organ perceived and strongly underlined on the realistic level ("these nostrils of bone and skin") but also as a path, a canal, a way which, while it belongs to the world of the flesh, opens on a beyond which seems to be the reign of absence, of night, of the absolute and of death. The prophetic, rhythmically marked tone of the lines conveys the sense of the irremediable absolute of the universe to which this path leads:

> Ces narines d'os et de peau
> par où commencent les ténèbres
> de l'absolu . . .

If these nostrils in their bodily being open onto the beyond of death, they act as a boundary separating the real world from the "realm of shadows." By his flesh man meets the opening of the absolute. His "metaphysical" dimension is thus constituted by the vision interpreting the intentional object of the nostrils as a magic canal opening directly on to death, introduced and introducing into the reign of the beyond. It is this ambiguous situation which defines the status of "chair" in Artaud's usage. The object originally seen has become "unrealized": the poetic act of Artaud consists very clearly in rendering present and sensible the intentional current envisaging the nostrils as a path toward the shadows of the absolute, not as an organ to be sniffed through, wiped, and so on.

In the following perspective:

> . . . et la peinture de ces lèvres
> que tu fermes comme un rideau

the part of intentionality is still greater than in the first instance, because the reader is uncertain whether the object in question is "these lips" or "the *painting* of these lips." In fact, the chain of the objects visualized in this poem is constituted by the parts of the body, so that it would seem to be the former. But the precise determination, "the *painting* of these lips" seems to belong to the field of the knower since the proposition: "that you close like a curtain" suggests the idea of spectacle that the lips might reveal or close off imperiously. This suggestion creates an oscillation of meaning wherein poetic reverie causes the mind to hesitate between the unreal color of the lips and the spectacle (painting) that they offer in the act of utterance. But if it is the intentional undertaking that makes visible in its hesitation a wavering between color and spectacle, this is because the poem constitutes the unreality of this undertaking verbally, makes the hesitation present in its soul and body. The surreal does not concern the noematic object here: the lips are lips, nothing more. But the poem becomes surreal insofar as it renders visible intentionality at its noetic level. Contemporary esthetics has never thought of asking what is surreal in the poem: the object or the gaze leveled on it, transforming it by its particular outlook? Plainly the latter, in this case. It is not the thing, which is poetic in itself, but the current of consciousness enveloping it, transforming it and nevertheless leading to it.

However, in the third intentional perspective:

> Et cet or que te glisse en rêve
> la vie qui te dépouille d'os

unreality monopolizes the totality of the intentional field to such a degree that "this gold" which is formally treated as a term of the poetic undertaking cannot be spoken of as an object. It is in itself an element of intentionalizing, not the object on which that aim is trained. We can neither understand this proposition, nor know what it concerns and what its purpose is. But this element is integrated in the general intentional movement of the poem. Here, swept along by its own movement of unrealizing or, if one prefers, transfiguring, the apprehending frees itself from any real object as a resting place; and between the perspective taken on the "lèvres" and on the "regard" accomplishes, as if in emptiness, its route of reverie. In the vain efforts of decoding, in these turnings over of the line in its emptiness, the sentence takes on a density and a weight, imposes itself as an object to be known. The absence of realistic support becomes surreality, the surreal defining itself here as the unreal of the intentional outlook which takes itself as being, intentionality becoming its own object. Whence the opening of the two following lines on a vocative which lends its reality to this movement of invocation:

> et les fleurs de ce regard faux
> par où tu rejoins la lumière
>
> Momie . . .

A perfect symmetry is established between the structure of these two lines and lines 3 and 4 of the first quatrain. In both cases, the hesitation occurs over the precise choice of the intentional perspective: The false gaze or the flowers of that gaze? The flowers seem rather to belong to the gaze as a means, an instrument, a place and path by which the mummy rejoins the light. Strange association between the essential (work or light) and the realm of the lie, which appears frequently in Artaud, understandable only by a problematics of *constitution.* For what is constituted by language is exactly that which is not "real," what is falsified by language. Thus in **"L'enclume des forces"**: "A block, an immense false block separates me from my lie. And this block is of any color one wishes."

That the flesh is in its ambiguity both nature and intellection is the result of poetic language. The same movement interprets the intentional object as "spindles": an actor-agent suggested by the disturbing figure of the bird as the celebrant of mysterious and cruel funeral rites:

> . . . et ces mains de fuseaux
> pour te retourner les entrailles,
> ces mains où l'ombre épouvantable
> prend la figure d'un oiseau.

These hands at once spindles and bird figure rise up from the intentionality posing them, supposing them.

The constitutive movement of the mummy having been elaborated before the reader by the verbal chain of the poem, Artaud can henceforth declare thetically the junction he operates between this notional being and the self speaking: thus can the last two stanzas be understood:

> Tout cela dont s'orne la mort
> • • • • •
> C'est par là que je te rejoins

In this intentional movement logically thematized, and in the series of intentional perspectives presumably of the same order as those discussed above ("ce papotage d'ombres, l'or où nagent tes entrailles, la route calcinée des veines, l'or qui est le plus sûr témoin"), the difference from the preceding perspectives is noticeable. These have only a referential and complementary value, secondary to what was initially postulated, constituted: a reference which folds the poem back on itself, develops and prolongs what was accomplished before. In this sense, the creative moment of the poem is found in the three first quatrains, the last two unfolding, explicating the initially abrupt creation. At first—in the first moment—the verb constitutes. In the second moment, it logically develops what was postulated, savagely and irrefutably. (pp. 172-84)

Jacques Garelli, "The Search for the Place of Poetry: Artaud's 'Invocation de la momie'," translated by *Mary Ann Caws, in* About French Poetry from Dada to "Tel Quel": Text and Theory, *edited by Mary Ann Caws, Wayne State University Press, 1974, pp. 172-85.*

J. H. MATTHEWS   (essay date 1974)

[*Matthews is a Welsh critic and educator who has written extensively on Surrealist art and literature. In the following excerpt he discusses the influence of the Surrealist movement on Artaud's work in the theater.*]

Of all those whose names have been linked with surrealism, for whatever length of time, Antonin Artaud is without doubt the one generally associated most readily with the stage. The immense influence his theories have come to exert over the theatre in the second half of the twentieth century is self-evident. Less clear is the extent to which the ideas embodied in his conception of the Theatre of Cruelty may be traced to surrealism. Specifically, the relationship between the principles underlying the Théâtre Alfred Jarry, of which Artaud was co-founder, and those advocated in surrealism has been subject to contradictory evaluation. At one extreme, Henri Béhar assures us [in *Etude sur le théâtre dada et Surrealiste,* 1967] that, after 1930, Artaud's theatrical ambitions developed directly from the propositions underlying the Théâtre Alfred Jarry—and that means, ultimately, from surrealism. At the other, Eric Sellin, . . . [in his *Dramatic Concepts of Antonin Artaud,* 1968], declares that "for all intents and purposes his surrealist period ended in 1927." Meanwhile the surrealist origins of Artaud's first play, **Le jet de sang (The Spurt of Blood**), have never been established with any degree of clarity.

As early as 1923 Artaud became interested in what André Breton was doing. In 1924 he became a member of the newly formed surrealist group, although his name does not figure . . . among those mentioned in the first manifesto as having "given proof of ABSOLUTE SURREALISM." Among the early surrealists he distinguished himself as the author of some of the most violently aggressive open letters signed by participants in the movement, earning this praise from Breton in *Entretiens:* "no one had more spontaneously put his means, which were great, at the service of the surrealist cause." It was Artaud, commended by Breton for his uncompromising fury "which spared so to speak no human institution," who in 1925 drew up a statement on the activities of the Bureau of Surrealist Research, opened on the Rue de Grenelle in Paris in 1924. When, having closed its doors to the public in 1925, the bureau continued to operate in private, he became its director. To Artaud fell also responsibility for preparing the April 1925 number of *La révolution surréaliste,* the last issue to appear before Breton took over the magazine and edited it himself from the fourth number onward.

All that Artaud wrote, during his period of enthusiastic support of the ideas set forth in Breton's *Manifeste du surréalisme,* shows him to have been unreservedly committed to the cause he had espoused. To insist, as Sellin does, that Artaud "made no changes in himself, no adjustment, to become 'surrealistic' " and so to imply that Artaud's outlook was in no way modified through contact with surrealism proves nothing, one way or the other. This makes Artaud's case by no means as exceptional as Sellin and Virmaux [in his *Antonin Artaud et le théâtre,* 1970] apparently believe. What really counts is that, for a while, surrealism offered Artaud encouragement to demand complete satisfaction of needs that he, Breton, and their friends all had in common.

If we examine, for example, Artaud's statement on the activities of the Bureau of Surrealist Research, we find nothing suggesting either that he had significant reservations about the action to be taken in furthering surrealism's aims, or that he brought any remarkably distinctive proposals to the pursuit of surrealist ambitions. We do not even come across proof that he was possessed of exceptional gifts for achieving these aims, however talented he proved to be at giving them vehement expression. Antonin Artaud's definition of the problems facing surrealists and his recommendations for handling these were entirely orthodox, substantively distinguishable in no way from what others in the movement were saying during the mid-twenties. Speaking of the surrealist revolution, for instance, he asserted:

> This revolution aims at a general devaluation of values, at the depreciation of the mind, at the demineralization of evidence, at the absolute and renewed confusion of tongues, at changing the level of thought.
> It aims at breaking and disqualifying logic, which it pursues unto the eradication of its original entrenchments.

While still a willing participant in surrealism, Artaud published his first play, *Le jet de sang,* in his *L'ombilic des limbes* of 1925. Confined to this one text, tangible evidence of his ideas on theatre during the period when he was directly involved in surrealist activities is limited. But it is no less so, proportionately speaking, than the evidence Artaud was able to bring forward in support of his conception of the Theatre of Cruelty, when he decided to found his Théâtre de la Cruauté in order to stage his only full-length play, *Les Cenci*—an adaptation from Stendhal and Shelley—in May 1935. If, then, there is a major difference between his contribution to the theatre during his time as a surrealist and later on, it is this: while militating for surrealism, Artaud, who within a decade was to distinguish himself as one of the most original theoreticians of the theatre, advanced not a single observation upon the principles according to which *Le jet de sang* had been written, either in explanation or in defense of what he had tried to do.

Of course, we must bear in mind that Artaud felt drawn to the theatre before he made Breton's acquaintance. Coming to Paris from his home town of Marseilles in 1920, he attracted the attention of A.-F. Lugné-Poë, director of the Théâtre de l'Œuvre, who gave him a small role in Henri de Régnier's *Les scrupules de Sganarelle.* In 1921, Artaud made contact with Charles Dullin, for whom he played a variety of roles at the Théâtre de l'Atelier. He also acted with the Georges and Ludmilla Pitoëff troupe at the end of its 1922-23 season and during the 1923-24 season. At about the same time he began to find roles in films. All the same, in the absence of proof that, by the time he joined surrealism, Artaud had already begun to view the theatre in a way that would set him apart from those with whom he was about to consort voluntarily, there is no reason to treat *Le jet de sang* as anything other than an attempt to bring surrealism to the stage. Indeed, where-as a consequence of Artaud's direct experience of stage productions—one might expect to see signs that the author of *Le jet de sang* was not only far more aware of the needs of the theatre than his fellow surrealists but also much more responsive to them, we encounter instead indisputable evidence of unwillingness to compromise surrealist iconoclasm through any concession at all to the practicalities of staging. We are reminded in this play, therefore, of an affirmation made by Artaud in his statement on the activities of the Bureau of Surrealist Research, an affirmation that noticeably stressed the negative rather than the positive aspects of the surrealist program: "Surrealism, rather than beliefs, registers a certain order of repulsions."

Le jet de sang has not fared well with the critics. So we find ourselves seeking an explanation for the general reluctance displayed by commentators to discuss this play. One may be found, it seems, if we consider Sellin's criticism of the stage directions Artaud places just after the action has begun with an avowal of love between a young man and a young woman:

> A silence. We hear something like the sound of an immense wheel turning and setting off a wind. A hurricane breaks them apart.
> At this moment, we see two astral bodies come into collision and a series of legs of living flesh falling with feet, hands, hair, masks, colonnades, doorways, temples, alembics, falling, but more and more slowly, as if they were falling in a vacuum, then three scorpions one after the other, and lastly a frog, and a beetle that comes to rest with heart-rending slowness, sickening slowness.

The young man cries, "The sky has become mad." But this, apparently, is not enough to placate Sellin who, despite the fact that *Le jet de sang* was staged in London by Peter Brook in 1964, complains, "This is as unstageable as it is unscientific. Furthermore, it is strangely static in essence and—like so many scenery descriptions by surrealist playwrights—reminds us more of a Max Ernst collage than a blueprint for dramatic action" [in "Surrealist Aesthetics and the Theatrical Event," *Books Abroad* 43, No. 2 (Spring 1969)].

It would be helpful to know which playwrights Sellin has in mind, since at least one of those he mentions in his article—Jean Cocteau—certainly had nothing to do with surrealism. All the same, the drift of his argument does not escape detection. Nor do its consequences elude us. To anyone looking to *Le jet de sang* to provide "a blueprint for dramatic action"—looking, in other words, for ideas that can be expected to contribute materially to giving the theatrical event new direction—Artaud's first play must necessarily offer little excitement. Far from helping supply the theatre with the kind of impetus most drama critics are equipped to measure, *Le jet de sang* exemplifies surrealist anti-theatre. To the very extent that such critics find it worth no more than a brief mention, it is valuable to those concerned with the role of theatre in surrealism.

Surrealism places in our hands the only instrument sensitive enough to register accurately the effects obtained in *Le jet de sang.* Speaking of surrealism in the course of his comments on the Bureau of Surrealist Research, Artaud pointed out most pertinently, "But, in the final analysis, it is in the mind, it is from within that it is judged, and, faced with its thought, the world does not carry much weight." The stage directions Sellin has condemned rest neither upon science, which he invokes to dispose of them, nor upon admission of the primacy of practical considerations in theatrical production. Instead, they take their meaning from an attitude reflected in what Artaud has to say about surrealism:

> In the name of an inner liberty, of the exigencies of its peace, its perfection, its purity, it spits on you, world given over to dessicated reason, to the bemired mimetism of the centuries, and who have built your houses of words and established your lists of precepts where the surrealist spirit, the only one to which we owe being uprooted, can no longer explode.

It is surely in relation to this affirmation of faith in the power of surrealism to release man from inherited and inculcated thought processes that we must consider the instructions given in *Le jet de sang* at a time when a violent storm is raging on the darkened stage: "At a given moment an enormous hand seizes the bawd's hair which catches fire and grows visibly." The bawd, we notice, recognizes the "gigantic voice" that orders, "Bitch, look at your body!" as her clothing becomes transparent, showing her in hideous nudity. She exclaims, "Leave me, God." All the same, instead of accepting divine retribution as just, "She bites God on the wrist," causing an immense spurt of blood to strike the stage. Such unexpected behavior indicates that Artaud's play was not written to reaffirm familiar moral precepts. So does the fact that, when the footlights come up again, everyone else—including a priest—lies dead, while the bawd, still very much alive, is talking to the young man "as though at the extreme point of a love spasm."

It is not in staging alone, therefore, that Artaud calls for rejection of convention in *Le jet de sang.* He demands no less radical a change in our predispositions with respect to dramatic action. As the play opens, the banal exchange of stock phrases between lovers is given new vitality, taking an inhabitual direction. As each of the two characters varies pitch, when delivering lines stripped of all vestiges of novelty, words we know only too well assume a strange aspect, thanks mainly to arbitrary emphasis. This is not attributable to psychology so much as to the degree of intensity granted the sounds we hear.

Sellin speaks accurately of "new tonalities" being "sprung from the traditional rhythms of speech by the artificial registers employed." Where we cannot follow him is in treating this effect as "perhaps more silly than dramatic." In fact, his first adjective betrays Sellin's prejudice toward a mode of drama that concerned Artaud little, if at all, during the writing of *Le jet de sang.* Meanwhile something that to a critic of Sellin's persuasion seems silly is revelatory of a characteristic feature of surrealist dialogue, as described in the first manifesto. Examination of the examples furnished in Breton's text reveals that the *exchange* authorizing us to speak of "dialogue" is not necessarily of the kind that takes meaning from the logical advancement of a plot. Indeed, by standards usually considered applicable in drama, dialogue of the sort in question is stationary, not progressive. Halting rational intercourse, it replaces this with a confrontation that merits classi-

fication as poetic, surrealists agree, by virtue of its nonconsecutive nature.

After the hurricane has separated the lovers at the beginning of *Le jet de sang,* a medieval knight and a swollen-breasted wet nurse, who may or may not be the young woman's parents, trade insults. Now the young man returns, declaring, "I have seen, I have known, I have understood," but without making any attempt to share his insights with the audience. In his continuing quest for the young woman he has lost, he receives no assistance or encouragement from figures of authority like a beadle and a priest, who remarks significantly, "We don't see it that way" (literally: "We don't hear it with that ear").

Although capable of retaliating against God with impunity, the bawd cannot distract the young man with her amorous conduct. He hides his head in his hands, while the wet nurse returns, flat-chested now and with the corpse of the young woman under her arm, like a package. A momentary diversion occurs. The knight demands the Gruyère cheese we saw him eating earlier. "There you are," says the wet nurse, lifting her skirt. Unaccountably reduced to marionettelike stiffness in his movements, the young man pleads in a ventriloquist's voice, "Don't hurt Mummy." The knight displays horror as a large number of scorpions "come out from under the wet nurse's dress and begin to swarm into her sex which swells and splits, becomes vitreous, and flashes like a sun." The young man and the bawd run off together "like trepaned people," while the young woman, miraculously returned to life, has the closing line of the play: "The virgin! ah that's what he was looking for."

Just as significant as the shock administered to conventional religious feeling through the element of blasphemy introduced quite casually in *Le jet de sang* is the shock it offers well-established assumptions about the structure and function of drama. On the technical plane no less than on the moral plane, this play faithfully reflects the surrealist attitude. Thus the discontinuous character of *Le jet de sang* is entirely in accord with the belief common to surrealists that sustained plot development is not mandatory in the theatre. On the contrary, it seems to them that plot consistency may be sacrificed without hesitation or regret to more pressing concerns. If, for instance, we look at that part of the play where Artaud appears content to mingle horror with the scabrous, when the scorpions swarm under the wet nurse's skirt, there is reason to believe that this spectacle is by no means as gratuitous as it appears at first. True, no explanatory statement is to be found in the stage directions, and none is made in the dialogue. In fact we should have no guidance from the author when interpreting this part of *Le jet de sang,* had not Artaud later drawn up a scenario for a play called *La conquête du Mexique* (*The Conquest of Mexico*), which was to have been the first of his Theatre of Cruelty productions. In the outline for the third act of *La conquête du Mexique* occurs the sentence, "Montezuma cuts through true space, splits it open like a woman's sex to make the invisible spurt from it." In the last verb we hear a distinct echo of the title *The Spurt of Blood.* Even without this, however, the recurrence of the arresting image of splitting a woman's sex would suffice to bring to our notice an allusion that illuminates the whole of *Le jet de sang.*

It could well be that only the passage of time made it possible for Artaud to recognize, in the bold image from *Le jet de sang* to which he returned after 1930, the projection of a need to bring the invisible forth from the visible. In the circumstances, it might not be wise to credit him with full awareness of what he was doing, while working on his first play. But if we may suppose he was less than clear in his mind about the implications of what he was saying, this still does not detract from the validity of *Le jet de sang* as an expression of surrealism. On the contrary, under these conditions that play might be regarded profitably as testimony to Artaud's refusal to set reasonable bounds upon a drama he was writing at a time when, as he noted in his open letter to the Schools of Buddha, "We are suffering from a rot, from the rot of Reason."

Be that as it may, we have no difficulty tracing the orientation of Artaud's thinking during the period to which *Le jet de sang* belongs. We can do this most conveniently through the open letters he drafted for the surrealist group to issue as collective challenging statements. Thus the one addressed to the directors of insane asylums—particularly noteworthy, when we recall how many years its author was to spend as a patient in mental institutions—begins accusingly, "Laws and customs grant you the right to measure the mind. This dangerous sovereign jurisdiction you exercise with your intelligence. Forgive us if we laugh." Soon Artaud is asserting, "We do not admit that the free development of a delirium should be hindered. It is as legitimate, as logical as any other succession of human ideas or acts." And a moment later he affirms "the absolute legitimacy" of insane people's conception of reality and of "all the acts stemming from it."

Being attentive to Artaud's approach to life as a surrealist means something quite different from getting ready to write off his first play as proof of mental imbalance. The value of the open letter just cited lies elsewhere. It establishes the relative unimportance, from where he stands beside the surrealists, of rational criteria, both in the creative act itself and in interpretation of its fruits. Without risk of ascribing undue importance to *Le jet de sang,* therefore, we can safely claim that its significance lies in the following areas. This is a text in which premeditation is sufficiently questionable—here and there, at all events—for spontaneity of an irrational nature to be a feature of the creative process we cannot discount, when asking how the play came to be written. When we ask, next, why it was written, we have to recognize that *Le jet de sang* poses a question regarding the nature of reality that is fundamental to surrealism, and does this whether or not we estimate that conscious intent is largely absent here. "Existence is elsewhere," declares Breton at the very end of his *Manifeste du surréalisme.* "We are not in the world," observes Artaud, after Rimbaud, as he condemns the Pope in an open letter for being "confined to the world." When, finally, we ask how Artaud's drama was put together, with what degree of concern for character and plot, we cannot help noticing the effects of an underlying spirit of rejection likely to promote consternation and epitomizing the surrealist approach to dramatic form.

Le jet de sang conforms to the anti-aesthetic of surrealism so faithfully that someone thoroughly familiar with the latter's demands upon the theatre is likely to find this play offers him no real surprises. Indeed, such a viewer might reasonably expect that Antonin Artaud could have gone on producing texts just as representative of the surrealist outlook as his first play, in which there are no signs that he was finding the surrealist mode irksome or inadequate to his needs. However, while internal evidence in his drama does foster the belief that Artaud could have remained faithful to surrealism, certain events taking place soon after *Le jet de sang* was published made continued fidelity impossible for its author.

In 1927, after much soul-searching, five members of the surrealist group, Aragon, Breton, Eluard, Benjamin Péret, and Pierre Unik, joined the Communist Party, determined to give political expression to the surrealist revolution. Explaining their reasons in a public statement printed under the title *Au grand jour* (*In Broad Daylight*), they took the opportunity to attack two former members of their circle "in the name of a certain principle of honesty which, in our opinion, must come before everything else." These two were Philippe Soupault and Antonin Artaud.

The accusations against two formerly valued members remained generally vague. Only one of their shortcomings was specified: "their *isolated* pursuit of the stupid literary adventure." Years later, Breton was to comment less abruptly upon his reservations vis-à-vis Artaud. Referring to the celebrated open letters for which Artaud was responsible, Breton remarks in *Entretiens:*

> However . . . it did not take me long to become disturbed by the atmosphere they created . . . I had the impression that, without quite knowing it, we had caught a fever and that the air was becoming rarefied about us. . . . This new direction, half-liberative, half-mystical, was not quite mine and I came to regard it rather as a dead-end than as a new direction (I was not the only one, by the way).

Only when he criticizes the "verbal" nature of these documents in *Entretiens* does Breton come close to justifying the attack made in *Au grand jour.* What he says does go a little further, though, toward helping us understand how ridiculous political involvement must have seemed to Artaud, who confided in one of his letters, "*I* can say, truly, that I am not in the world, and this is not a mere attitude of mind."

Artaud's response to *Au grand jour* was not long delayed. It took the form of a privately printed counterattack, *A la grande nuit; ou, le bluff surréaliste* (*In the Darkest Night; or, The Surrealist Bluff*), dated June 1927. As one might anticipate, where the authors of the former talk of him as having been expelled, Artaud speaks of having withdrawn voluntarily because surrealist action has become sterile, whatever the framework selected for it. Hence he is led to define surrealism from the standpoint of his own demands upon it. "The revolutionary forces of any movement," he comments, "are those capable of throwing the present basis of things off axis, of changing the angle of reality." While certain surrealists now feel constrained to consider the social implications of their attitude of revolt, Artaud avers, "I am speaking of a metamorphosis of the inner conditions of the soul." This is how he comes to refer to surrealism in terms that set *Le jet de sang* in perspective, as "that conflagration of the basis of all reality," insisting that for him, "It is a matter of that shift in the spiritual centre of the world, of changing the levels of appearances, of that transfiguration of the possible which surrealism was to contribute to provoking. All matter begins in spiritual derangement."

The longer he talks of surrealism, the more clearly Artaud indicates the nature of the motivation from which his first play originated. Surrealism, he declares, was never to his mind anything but "a new sort of magic." Imagination and dreams are "that intense liberation of the unconscious which has as its aim to bring flowing to the surface of the soul that which the soul is accustomed to keep hidden," with consequent "profound transformations in the scale of appearances, in the value of signification and the symbolism of the object created." Thus the beyond, the invisible "push back reality." Taking issue with those he feels no longer have anything in common with him, Artaud announces, "They can howl as much as they like in their corner and say it is not this, I will reply that for me surrealism has always been an insidious extension of the invisible, the unconscious within reach. The treasures of the invisible unconscious, become palpable, lead the tongue directly in one spurt."

What is interesting above all is that Artaud's definition of surrealism is still quite orthodox. It presents no noteworthy divergence from the one that continued to be defended by the surrealists after his departure and regardless of the need felt by some of them to extend their protest against the reality principle to the plane of social reality. In other words, had Artaud not quarrelled with the surrealists over politics, it would not be difficult at all to imagine him capable of writing a play after *Le jet de sang,* no less expressive of the surrealist point of view while yet communicating his own preoccupation with "the equivocal, fathomless domain of the unconscious" with its "signals, perspectives, glimpses, a whole life growing when one stares at it and showing itself capable of still disturbing the mind."

Something else noticeable is that, when attacking his former friends, Artaud speaks of their having sacrificed spiritual revolt to social revolution. He is content to allude regretfully and with no sign of insincerity to "that magnificent power of evasion" to which, it seems to him, surrealists held the secret. Nowhere in *A la grande nuit,* though, does he face and attempt to meet the accusation that he has already betrayed an interest in creating literature, a commodity most suspect in surrealist eyes. Meanwhile, the authors of *Au grand jour* ignore, just as he does, a factor that contributed measurably to bringing about a deterioration in Artaud's relationship with the surrealist group. Neither *A la grande nuit* nor *Au grand jour* mentions the Théâtre Alfred Jarry, founded by Artaud, Vitrac, and Robert Aron in September 1926, fully eight months before *Au grand jour* appeared in May 1927. (pp. 133-45)

The Théâtre Alfred Jarry was to have staged its first production in early 1927. Already in October 1926 the following unsigned text had been given to the newspapers:

> A group of young writers brought together to revive the idea of an absolute theatre is going to found a new theatrical company, under the name Théâtre Alfred Jarry. Their efforts are directed toward creating a theatre which will develop in the direction of complete liberty and which will have no other aim than satisfying the most extreme demands of the imagination and of the spirit. For them, the theatrical event can no longer rest upon an illusion but corresponds to a reality of the same order as the other tangible realities.

To promote interest in the Théâtre Alfred Jarry it was decided that a public lecture should be given. This was delivered by Aron at the Ecole des Hautes Etudes on November 25, under the title "Genèse d'un Théâtre." In the absence of Aron's text, which was not preserved, we have to rely for a report of the content of his talk upon a review published by Guy Crouzet in *La grande revue*'s December 1926 issue. Aron spoke of "a free exchange between the stage and the au-

ditorium," stressing removal of the barriers traditionally marked by the footlights. "From each play must result the creation of a world," imitation of everyday acts and gestures being replaced by "the limitless freedom of dream and the spirit."

A circular letter signed by Yvonne Allendy on December 12, 1926, records that, when Artaud and his friends came to visit her and her husband on September 26, 1926, asking for assistance in raising funds, they wanted to found a theatre dedicated to putting on "a programme including plays by Jarry, Strindberg, Roger Vitrac, etc." As it happened, Artaud never produced a play by Jarry, whom the surrealists revered. After a first spectacle in which all three co-founders were represented, a second, given on January 14, 1928, consisted of Pudovkin's film *Mother,* banned in French movie houses, and unauthorized presentation of an act taken from a play not identified in advance but in which Breton recognized *Partage de midi* by Paul Claudel, French Ambassador to the United States or, as Artaud called him from the stage, when keeping his promise to name the author of the play, "an infamous traitor." Then came Strindberg's *A Dream Play* (June 2 and 9, 1928). Finally Artaud produced Vitrac's *Victor* on December 24 and 29, 1928, and January 5, 1929.

The Théâtre Alfred Jarry's was a mixed program, one that could hardly be expected to appeal to the surrealists in its entirety. Artaud, of course, had ceased to care about pleasing Breton and his associates. Had this not been the case, it would be less interesting to observe how closely the principles underlying the ideas upon which the Théâtre Alfred Jarry

Artaud as Frère Massieu in Carl Dreyer's film La passion de Jeanne d'Arc, *1927.*

rested parallel those we have found to be characteristic of surrealist practice in the theatre. Much remains vague in what we know of Aron's lecture. The same is true of the statement given to the press. Yet in the original plans for a new theatre outlined by Artaud, what we notice above all is that the most concrete proposals relate quite closely to those exemplified in plays of surrealist inspiration.

The aim of the Théâtre Alfred Jarry, Artaud informs us, is that "everything obscure in the mind, buried deep, unrevealed should be manifested in a sort of material projection, real." Still true to surrealist principles, he asserts, "In the theatre that we want to produce, chance will be our god." He expresses contempt, meanwhile, for "all theatrical means properly so called," for "all that constitutes what people generally agree to call the *mise en scène,* like lighting, sets, costumes, etc.," insisting that the Alfred Jarry Theatre is intended for "all those who do not see in the theatre an end but a means, all those disturbed by concern for a reality of which the theatre is only a sign." In short, the Théâtre Alfred Jarry was created, he declares, "in reaction against the theatre."

Not surprisingly, Jarry's example appealed to Artaud as much as to the surrealists. Like them, he saw in the author of *Ubu Roi* a man who "was able to contemplate the abolition of the theatre." For this reason, *Ubu Roi* meant very much the same to Artaud as to those from whom, in helping found the Théâtre Alfred Jarry, he was asserting his independence. Thus it was respect for Jarry and for what he had made possible in the theatre that maintained continuity in Artaud's theatrical principles, when he left the surrealist group.

Persuasive evidence of continuity in Artaud's ideas at the time when, moving away from surrealism, he was planning a new theatre is the first spectacle presented by the Théâtre Alfred Jarry on the stage of the Théâtre de Grenelle, June 1 and 2, 1927. It consisted of three plays—Aron's *Gigogne,* Artaud's ***Ventre brûlé; ou, la mère folle*** (***Burnt Belly; or, The Mad Mother***) and Vitrac's *Les mystères de l'amour*—of which the last was by far the most substantial. In the brochure *Le Théâtre Alfred Jarry et l'hostilité publique* Aron's play is described as "written and presented with the systematic purpose of provocation." It was never published. Artaud's musical sketch, "a lyrical work that humorously denounced the conflict between cinema and theatre," was not preserved either, and was a modest effort. Vitrac's is the only play of the three to have been published. It came out, we recall, in November 1924, within a month of Breton's *Manifeste du surréalisme,* two and a half years before its production under Artaud's direction.

Artaud and Vitrac met in 1924, within the surrealist group and a year after *Les mystères de l'amour* was completed. They became close enough to spend their summer vacation together in 1925. Upon their return to Paris, each submitted an article to *La nouvelle revue française.* Publication of Vitrac's, a note on ***L'ombilic des limbes,*** was delayed until December, but Artaud's laudatory review of his friend's play appeared in the September 1925 issue. Artaud's admiration for *Les mystères de l'amour* led him, in the hope of seeing it staged, to approach Lugné-Poë. However, arrangements to present it under the latter's direction in December 1925 fell through. In November 1926 Robert Aron's lecture on the Théâtre Alfred Jarry was followed by readings from Jarry, Raymond Roussel, and *Les mystères de l'amour.* Meanwhile the previous month Vitrac's play had been mentioned as figuring in the first Théâtre spectacle announced in the press for produc-

tion at the Vieux Colombier on January 15, 1927. When lack of funds halted plans for January, Yvonne Allendy and her husband set about raising money that permitted Artaud to begin rehearsal of Vitrac's drama in May 1927, at the Théâtre de l'Atelier, where Dullin made space available.

The dates speak for themselves and really should leave no room for confusion. Nevertheless commentators have tended to ignore them when interpreting the relationship of Vitrac's "surrealist drama" to Artaud's ideas on the theatre.

Indisputably, Artaud was preoccupied with *Les mystères de l'amour* for quite a time before he produced it in 1927. However, to some observers his interest appears directly influenced by his own exclusion from surrealism in November 1926. Specifically, their comments reveal their judgment to have been affected by the postscript, dated January 8, 1927, to Artaud's **"Manifeste pour un théâtre avorté(("Manifesto for an Aborted Theatre"),** published in the *Cahiers du sud* (February 1927) after its author had reached the conclusion that financing the Théâtre Alfred Jarry would be impossible. This postscript takes up the surrealists' contention that Artaud and Vitrac were engaged in literature and, by their efforts to establish a theatre, had proved themselves to be counter-revolutionaries. Implying that, being no longer associated with surrealism, he and Vitrac had ceased to be indebted to it, Artaud appears to be inviting reactions that are, at best, ambiguous.

The truth is that, to explain the steadfastness of Artaud's faith in Roger Vitrac's play *Les mystéres de l'amour,* we have to look beyond their friendship. We have to recognize the compelling influence of ideas about the nature and function of theatre that derived from surrealist thinking, in Artaud's case as much as in Vitrac's, far more than from anywhere else. Personal differences aside, it seems at first conceivable that Artaud might have been capable, if not of placing the Théâtre Alfred Jarry at the service of surrealism, then at least of welcoming those surrealists who wished to take advantage of a stage where their plays would have been guaranteed sympathetic presentation by a director sensitive to their aspirations in drama. To see why speculation of this kind is inadmissible, we must look at the facts more closely.

In advance of his disagreement with the group over politics, Artaud took a step in 1926 that carried him outside the surrealist circle. Not only did he show willingness to risk censure for collaborating with Vitrac, expelled more than a year before, but he also demonstrated his readiness to devote himself to a project tempting to no other surrealist: he was preparing to involve himself in a theatrical venture that inevitably entailed commercial considerations. Moreover, he freely admitted in **"Théâtre Alfred Jarry, 1re année,"** "the works we shall put on belong to literature." Confessing a tendency toward literature of which he stood accused by the surrealists, Artaud went on to employ the unfortunate phrase "pure theatre," far too evocative for surrealist taste of the abbé Brémond's *"poésie pure."* In the circumstances he could not hope to escape suspicion from former friends who had not ceased to fear the concessions they felt must attend any effort to meet the public on terms other than their own. Indeed one has the distinct impression that Artaud's conduct was calculated to provoke the surrealists to caution and to keep at a distance those with whom he was no longer associated.

While, to begin with, it may seem pure coincidence that Artaud and Vitrac waited until they had severed contact with surrealism before attempting to found a theatre, this is hardly likely. The reaction they would have stirred up by taking such a step earlier is easy to imagine, so fearful was Breton of compromising the demands of surrealism in ways he soon had cause to believe that Artaud and Vitrac were quite willing to accept: not only did they stage a Strindberg play with the backing of the Swedish Embassy, but they even called in the police to prevent the surrealists from disrupting the performance. Anger at Artaud and Vitrac had the effect of blinding Breton and his followers to the simple fact that, in some significant ways, the Théâtre Alfred Jarry stood for the same things as they. Thus not one of them would have raised any objection to adding his signature to the following statement, had it not been written by Artaud in his **"Manifeste pour un théâtre avorté"** of 1927: "Everything belonging to the illegibility and magnetic fascination of dreams, all this, those dark layers of consciousness which are all that preoccupies us in the mind, we want to see it radiate and triumph on stage, content to lose ourselves and to expose ourselves to a colossal failure."

On the face of it, then, the surrealists had only themselves to blame for not appreciating the possible benefit to their movement of active cooperation with Artaud. From one important point of view, however, they had good reasons for withholding their support. From the surrealist standpoint Artaud and Vitrac appeared altogether too inclined to pursue in the theatre alone their effort to attain those ambitions that they had in common with surrealism. In this sense, they fully deserved categorization as "men of the theatre." Their dedication to a medium they hoped to serve while making it conform to their special requirements had a consequence that no surrealist could envisage for long without alarm. "Before thinking of his ideas," remarked Artaud, when announcing *Victor* in the program of the Théâtre Alfred Jarry's 1928 season, "Roger Vitrac, like any good dramatic author, thinks of the theatre but remains at the same time close to his thought." Essentially, it was the question of precedence that separated the surrealists' values from those Artaud was defending by reference to Vitrac's theatre.

Weighing this question, the surrealists did not take long to find both Artaud and Vitrac guilty of *"arrivisme ignoble"* ["vulgar ambition"]. The offhand manner in which this judgment is delivered in the course of a 1929 article not aimed primarily at taking Artaud and Vitrac to task, tends to conceal its central importance with regard to the special problems the theatre raises for surrealists. To the extent that Artaud credited Vitrac with placing concern for his medium above dedication to the material that medium was to communicate, he removed Vitrac's plays from the context of surrealist endeavor, situating them instead in relation to the demands drama imposes upon writers. If it were true that, as Béhar wants us to believe, the original purpose of the Théâtre Alfred Jarry was simply to "contribute to ruining the theatre as it exists by specifically theatrical means," then the surrealists could only have applauded Artaud's undertaking. But Artaud necessarily fell into disfavor with them when attempting to make a contribution to the medium of theatre, rather than requiring the theatre to comply with standards given precedence in surrealism.

Criticizing Vitrac in an undated letter, Antonin Artaud wrote, "If you want to make a theatre to defend certain ideas, political or otherwise, I will not follow you in that direction. In the theatre only that which is theatrical interests me, to use the theatre to launch any revolutionary idea (except in the domain of the spirit) seems to me the basest and most repugnant opportunism." Less important to us as a sign of the growing disagreement that finally came between Vitrac and Artaud, this letter is valuable as an expression of its author's point of view, which is, he concedes, "the point of view of a stage director if you like, but basically theatre is everything that has to do with staging. . . ."

Henri Béhar talks of a "tragic misunderstanding" between the promoters of the Théâtre Alfred Jarry and the surrealists. But for this, he contends, Artaud might have furthered the cause of surrealism in the theatre, much as Antoine had served that of naturalism, and Paul Fort and Lugné-Poë had served Symbolism. But we can follow this line of reasoning only if we gloss over the serious differences that, above and beyond personal disagreements, set Artaud the man of the theatre apart from his former associates. These differences make clear why, from the early days of group action, the surrealists shunned contact with professionals who might have brought their form of theatre to public notice. (pp. 146-52)

"The Théâtre Alfred Jarry was created to use the theatre and not to serve it," declared a manifesto announcing its 1928 season. If only Artaud had kept to this plan of campaign, he might still have gained the surrealists' confidence. However, the scope of the program he was able to see through to production was altogether too limited to command the surrealists' trust. From within the surrealist camp it seemed that he was doing more to confirm deep-rooted fears about the sad consequences of a public theatrical venture than to allay misgivings. (p. 154)

> *J. H. Matthews, "Antonin Artaud and the Théâtre Alfred Jarry," in his* Theatre in Dada and Surrealism, *Syracuse University Press, 1974, pp. 133-54.*

CHARLES I. GLICKSBERG   (essay date 1976)

[*Glicksberg is an American educator and critic best known for his studies of American literature. In the following excerpt from his* Literature of Commitment, *he focuses on Artaud's rejection of political commitment and his formulation of an alternative aesthetics.*]

[Antonin Artaud] was not interested in radical politics as a means of attaining a secular type of salvation. In Artaud, the categorical imperative of Marxist doctrine and its urgent call for commitment was countered by the metaphysical vision that his recurrent states of madness accentuated. He recognized that there are limits beyond which no revolution, regardless of its degree of "success," can go. No matter what sweeping reforms are instituted in the form of government and in the equitable distribution of wealth, man's fate still remains ineluctably tragic. No political or economic panaceas can save him from the ultimate effects of the human condition. This perception of the inexorable limits that the revolutionary must perforce acknowledge and abide by, despite all his brave efforts to change the world closer to the heart's desire, serves in some cases to weaken his will and to shake his faith.

Other writers had caught intimations of this metaphysical vision. In *Danton's Death,* Büchner, who was active in the revolutionary movement of his time (he died in 1837 at the age of twenty-three), includes in his play a glimpse of the nullity of man's struggle to build the Kingdom of Heaven on earth.

Dostoevski, after his release from five years of exile in Siberia, attacked the revolutionary mystique that affirms the myth of the political apocalypse. Hermann Hesse used the novel as a vehicle for communicating the meaning and intrinsic purpose of his spiritual quest. He had started this search for integral selfhood with *Demian,* which reveals his reaction to the First World War. He became convinced at this period of his life of the basic irrationality of human behavior. Society could be saved and its destructive conflicts eliminated not by political means but only through the mediation of personal insight. He questioned the value of reforms externally imposed.

> In the last resort the crises of politics were for Hesse (and always remained) only pointers to the ultimate issues in the inner world of man. He feels that he cannot really be engaged in a political cause, at most in a moral one; poets and artists were always, in his view, essentially *Aussenwelter* (outsiders). *Littérature engagée* distorts their nature. . . . His was the revolt of a religious, not a political conscience; he knew very well that intellectuals and artists could have little hope of influencing men of power. [Mark Boulby, *Hermann Hesse*]

A confident believer in the myth of Prometheus, the Communist asserts that such reactionary views as Hesse propounds are typical of the encapsulated self of the bourgeois writer, who retreats into a mysticism that shields him from the disturbing challenge of social reality. Promethean man can conquer his environment and become the architect of his destiny. The thought of death does not frighten him. He can shape the laws of heredity and determine the process of sexual selection. No longer the slave of instinct, he will learn how to defeat those forces which seal his doom as a mortal creature. Leon Trotsky, in *Literature and Revolution,* said: "Emancipated man will want to attain a greater equilibrium in the work of his organs and a more proportional developing and wearing out of his tissue, in order to reduce the fear of death to a rational reaction of the organism toward death." The morbid fear of death, Trotsky prophesies, will be gradually reduced so that mankind will no longer be tempted to nourish "stupid and humiliating fantasies about life after death."

Marxism has never been able to give a satisfying answer to the haunting question of death. I. Kataev, in speaking of the man of the future, knows that he will be happy since he will inherit the benefits of Socialism. Kataev then asks:

> How will he sense the space of the universe, time, the cosmos, his own existence, the approach of death? Will he retain the will to change himself and the world around him, to aim at distant, faintly flickering ends? ["Art on the Threshold of Socialism," *International Literature* (April 1934)]

Soviet literature has never tackled this problem. Solzhenitsyn, in *Cancer Ward,* does not deal with this archetypal theme, and yet it cannot be passed over in silence. Daniel Bell believes that as faith in the religious absolute collapsed, the "fear of death as total annihilation, unconsciously expressed, has probably increased." Even the dedicated Communist cannot free himself at times from this metaphysical obsession. For Paul Nizan the thought that one day his consciousness would be extinguished for all eternity was unbearable. When he was in the grip of such a mood he drank steadily to drown the pain of this realization.

He had asked himself whether the Socialist creed

might not somehow help him to exorcise it [the thought of annihilation that would last forever] and felt quite optimistic as to prospects; but his lengthy interrogation of young Russian Communists concerning this topic had elicited a unanimous reply—in the face of death, comradeship and solidarity were no help at all, and they were all scared of death themselves. . . . It had been a great blow to him to discover that, in Russia as in France, the individual was alone when he died, and knew it. [Simone de Beauvoir, *The Prime of Life*]

Those writers who were not drawn to the Marxist evangel and saw no reason for submitting to a code of commitment that demanded their abdication of individual freedom of judgment and their willingness to accept the dictates of the Communist Party—such writers had to depend on their own inner resources to survive. They knew full well the impurity and impotence of the medium they worked in. Language was an imprecise and treacherous instrument. Hence in their quest for authenticity they decided to create "aliterature": writing that would seek to rid itself of the artifices and stifling conventions of the past. The apostles of "aliterature" took no pride in their new venture; they were secretly ashamed of their continued dependence on words, words, words, but in their worst moments of despair they kept on writing.

The high priest of "aliterature" was Antonin Artaud, who describes with anguish the loss of his sense of identity; he does not know what he is thinking; he cannot put his house of thought in order. He has no control over the tumultuous flow of thought—thoughts that cause him to fall into the dementia of incoherence, but he stubbornly persists in his search for the undiscovered Absolute. He tries to picture for us the civil war that rages on the confused battlefield of his mind, the progressive disintegration of his ego. "There is something that is destroying my thinking, something that does not prevent me from being whatever I shall be able to be, but that leaves me, so to speak, in suspense." Artaud suffered from recurrent attacks of an acute anxiety neurosis.

But the onset of madness led him to create what was virtually a new literary genre. Mental illness made it possible for him to gain deeper insights into the meaning of life and the strange mutations of the self than the method of rational inquiry affords. In his painful attempts to set down the truth about his condition, he writes about the feverish inner conflicts that made him feel that he was not himself. He struggled hard to become a writer, to establish communion with the world of men, even though he frankly acknowledged the preposterous folly of harboring such an ambition. "This is my particular weakness and my absurdity, to want to write at any price and express myself." That is why he was so desperately preoccupied with the disorder of his mind; he was driven by the need to find out, if he could, the cause of his accursed mental affliction. Claude Mauriac remarks [see excerpt dated 1958]: "Artaud's dementia reveals the dementia of all living men who think. . . . It is not so much insanity as the impossibility of being, the horror of essential solitude." Artaud experimented with peyote, a drug that induces dreams and projects images dredged from the primordial depths of the unconscious. He is fascinated by the esoteric art of weaving spells and reciting magic incantations; he is trying to master the difficult, unprecedented technique of using these fits of insanity for a creative purpose. He is aware of the fact that he is striving to create the literature of madness. There are times, in fact, when he enjoys the euphoria brought on by madness. He seeks to reach God through the medium of peyote, but he learns that drugs cannot call forth this ineffable vision of God.

Artaud gives expression to the supreme craving of alienated twentieth-century man to discover a truth that is commensurate with the whole truth of life. That "truth," Artaud realizes, resists conceptual formulation. Life comes first; it must be lived; only later does there arise the compelling need to understand and, above all, to believe in the "force" that makes us want to live. For life, as Artaud apprehends it, is more than the biological organization of matter; it is an abiding mystery, a perpetual source of magic. The old, dying forms must be interred so that modern man can reestablish contact with the fountainhead of being: partake of the elixir that will bestow on him the gift of timeless spontaneity, restore his faith in the reality of magic, and enable him to recover the pristine purity of perception that is the mark of the true poet. To experience all this and give it adequate expression, a new language must be forged. The revitalized theater Artaud envisaged must break through the barriers of language and liberate the power of dreams. Modern man must root himself once again in the primordial matrix of the great myths of the race and build the new theatre on a foundation of archetypal conflicts. Concretely, what Artaud wishes the theater to recapture is the language of action and gesture, the ritual of the dance, the organic function of music in the drama. He does not want the theater to concern itself with the essentially sterile task of psychological analysis. He sounds a call for a theater that will release the untapped potentialities of the metaphysical vision.

Unlike Brecht, Artaud took no interest in the propagandist type of "proletarian" drama that Piscator was experimenting with in Berlin. According to Artaud, the object of the new theater he hoped to found was not to mirror reality but to come to grips with a reality that transcends the restricted sphere of the human. Artaud rejected the shallow technique of realism in order to concentrate his energy on depicting spiritual states in an expressive language of gesture. Words, he pointed out, are ambiguous and even treacherous conveyors of meaning. The effort to capture the life of feeling in words and communicate it on the stage often fails because feeling is essentially untranslatable. To express true feeling "is to betray it. But to translate it is *to dissimulate it.*"

In his **"First Manifesto on The Theater of Cruelty,"** Artaud formulates the general aesthetic principles that would guide him; he calls for the creation of a unique language of gesture that would supplant the printed text used in the past. By "cruelty" Artaud means the lucid recognition of necessity. Unlike the Marxists with their conception of the omnipotent factor of economic necessity, Artaud provides this singular definition of cruelty:

> death is cruelty, resurrection is cruelty, transfiguration is cruelty, since nowhere in a circular and closed world is there room for true death, since ascension is a rending, since closed space is fed with lives.

The Theater of Cruelty affirms that life is conflict, contradiction, strife, irrational suffering, and gratuitous cruelty. In these dramatically presented affirmations, the importance of the Word steadily diminishes. "Renouncing psychological man, with his well-dissected character and feelings, and social man, submissive to laws and misshapen by religions and

precepts, the Theater of Cruelty will address itself only to total man."

Before total man could come to life on the stage, the fragmentary man, torn by internecine psychological conflicts, would have to acquire a sense of identity and learn how to master the language he must use in the interminable debates conducted by the inner self. This language was shadowy, unreal, phantasmal. Who, after all, is involved in the process of thinking? What is consciousness? How determine the identity of the various contentious voices that speak in its name? Words are elusive, protean creatures to work with; they seem to have a will of their own and willfully distort the meaning of what the writer is trying to say. Suffering from the disintegration of his sense of reality and the loss of self, Artaud observed how his language deteriorated into frozen ciphers.

> I suffer from a fearful mental disease. My ideas abandon me at every stage, from the mere fact of thought itself to the exterior phenomenon of its materialization in words. Words, the forms of sentences, inner directions of thought, the mind's simplest reactions:—I am in constant pursuit of my intellectual being.

Artaud, at this point no longer concerned with that which can be expressed, leaves behind him the realm of literature and plunges into the unknown world of myth and the oceanic depths of the ineffable. In this ultima Thule, words utterly fail him; language exists only for what has already been said, not for that which he is now experiencing for the first time. He is, as it were, cut off from himself; a lost monad floating in the space-time continuum, he is nevertheless passionately in search of unity of being; he breaks down all barriers in his determined quest for the Absolute.

Artaud explores the negative pole of mysticism; he is cut off from the mundane plane of existence but he has no assurance that he has gained admittance to a higher or lower world of the spirit. All he knows and can declare with the utmost conviction is that the language of literature is pretentious nonsense. "All writing," he says, "is rubbish." That which can be caught in the net of words is not worth putting down on paper. The damning charge he hurls against the writers of his time is that they repeat the obvious. He dismisses the entire literary tribe as "a pack of rubbish-mongers, especially today." Artaud bids farewell to the fossilized fund of language preserved in a literary tradition.

Artaud rebelled against this effete, anachronistic tradition. The modern writer, he insisted, must have the courage to face his naked self and reveal the civil war raging within him. Artaud sought to orient himself in a reality that is spectral, unknown, undefined, and indefinable. He realizes that he is creating a literature born of mental illness. He is tensely aware that the road he has taken leads to suicide or madness. He refuses to yield to the insidious power of madness just as he had resisted the siren song of death. Day after day he fights this battle inside the locked cage of his mind. He feels the throbbing pain of consciousness, the unrelenting pressure of his phobias and obsessions, the fear born of his nameless anxieties and his solipsist fixation. yet he does not look upon his abnormality as a threat. In order not to become the slave of conventional social reality, he turned to the experimental theater and endeavored to bring forth drama that is elemental in content and cosmic in scope, drama that faithfully reflects the implacable cruelty of existence. Artaud singled out Heliogabulus as the hero of the absurd. In his **"Letter on Lautréa-**

mont" he voiced his admiration of this remarkable poet and his work. Isidore Ducasse, he declares, is neither a madman nor a visionary but a daring explorer of the unconscious. He pays an even more lavish tribute to the genius of Van Gogh, who belongs to the race of genuine lunatics, as Artaud calls them. A genuine lunatic he defines as one "who prefers to go mad in the social sense of the word, rather than forfeit a certain higher idea of honor." Society persecutes and shuts up in asylums those who refuse to play the game of adjustment according to the prescribed rules, those who persist in their effort to proclaim a number of intolerable truths.

Artaud collaborated with the Surrealists, but with them, too, he felt misunderstood. They loved life while he despised it. There was also the troublesome matter of political commitment that divided them. He could not endorse their eager acceptance of Marxism nor their decision to join the Communist Party. Communism, he felt, was not a panacea for the spiritual suffering of mankind. Politics was a distraction, a snare. Those among the Surrealists who did not believe in the cause of Communism were drummed out of the movement. Artaud was one of those who did not fit into this doctrinaire scheme of political salvation. He was accused of pursuing literature as an isolated activity, instead of devoting his talent to the supreme task of changing the world. He was *persona non grata* because he continued to dwell in the hermetic fastness of the mind, lost in a world of dreams. Artaud replied to these charges by rejecting the simplistic view that political revolution in and of itself could transform the nature of man. (pp. 132-40)

> *Charles I. Glicksberg, "Artaud and Metaphysical Madness," in his* The Literature of Commitment, *Bucknell University Press, 1976, pp. 131-40.*

VINCENT CRAPANZANO (essay date 1977)

[*In the following excerpt, Crapanzano reviews* The Peyote Dance.]

"There where others propose works, I claim nothing more than to reveal my mind." With these words Antonin Artaud began his second book, *L'ombilic des limbes,* published in 1925. He was beginning, too, a scriptorial trajectory that was to challenge not only the assumptions of Western theater, *le théâtre digestif* as he called it, but the problematic of language itself—a language through which, inevitably condemned, he had yet to seek liberation. Artaud was doomed, despite his foray into surrealism, his theatrical iconoclasm (now, perversely, mainstream avant garde), his experimentation with the hallucinogenic rituals of the Tarahumara Indians of Mexico, the ostensible subject of *The Peyote Dance,* his *protestations verbales contre le verbe,* his pleas for a material, corporeal language, his pun-beleaguered poetry, despite even his madness. The unconscious, Lacan reminds us aphoristically, is the discourse of the Other.

Artaud did not then, at the age of twenty-nine, conceive of his oeuvres as detached from life.

> Each of my works, each of the sketches of myself, each of the icy blossomings of my inner soul drools over me.

Artaud, in fact, could never permit himself the luxury of the genitive. The "of," better still the *"de"* with its ablative connotations, remained always a copulative which he had either

to accept totally, accepting thereby his martyrdom, or to reject totally, rejecting thereby his mind, his spirit, his *esprit.* "Nor do I conceive of the mind as detached from myself," he wrote in *L'ombilic.* A year earlier, in a letter to Rivière, he complained:

> I suffer from a frightening disease of the mind. My thought abandons me at all levels. From the simple fact of the thought to the external fact of its materialization in words. Words, sentence forms, interior thought directions, simple reactions of the mind, I am in constant pursuit of my intellectual being. When then I can grasp a form, however imperfect, I fix it, in the fear of losing the entire thought. It is beneath me, I know, I suffer from it, but I agree to it in the fear of not dying altogether.

It was this constant pursuit of his intellectual being, this attempt to undo the primordial self-alienating experience of language that motivated Artaud's work and provoked its harrowing images. Just as the mind, through the word, is detached from itself (whatever the authorial protest) so, too, life as the subject of representation, theatrical or other, is detached from itself—an illusion, a creation even, of such (verbal) representation. One can say that in Artaud's vision what is represented has never been presented. Artaud, who was a passionate man, sought escape in the surrealist dream of that other reality, in the "metaphysical" theater of the Orient, in his own theater of cruelty, and in the supposedly self-transcending rituals of the primitive.

Artaud left for Mexico in the winter of 1936, disappointed and bitter. His second theatrical venture, *Les Cenci,* had been a failure. "Because I kept seeing around me men lying, lying about the source of ideas, idiotically refusing to advance as far as ideas, I felt the need to leave mankind and go away to a place where I could at least freely advance my heart. . . ." In Mexico, Artaud hoped to find a civilization where the metaphysical values he tried to put on stage were still alive. "I have come to Mexico to make contact with the Red Earth." The primitive afforded him, as so many others, the possibility of a Romantic quest which he might otherwise have found embarrassing. He had, of course, been fascinated by Mexico for years. He lectured at the University and lived with the Tarahumara from the end of August to the beginning of October. He returned to France, flirted briefly with normal bourgeois life, and then suffered progressive estrangement, delusional thinking, and paranoia that resulted in his arrest and hospitalization in LeHavre in 1937. (He was on his way back from Ireland where he had hoped to meet the Druids and to return a cane he thought had belonged to St. Patrick.) A year later his most influential book, *Le théâtre et son double,* was published.

The Peyote Dance is a collection of essays, postscripts, supplements, letters, a poem, and notes that Artaud wrote about his Mexican trip and his experience with peyote. They were written over a period of ten years, most of which Artaud spent in insane asylums. They blend, if not always explicitly, the two encounters. In **"The Peyote Rite,"** for example, Artaud moves from a description of his experience with peyote to his belief (confirmed in the works of ancient Chinese) that the liver is "the organic filter of the Unconscious," to the effect of incarceration, hunger, and electroshock therapy on him. "And I could not face each new treatment without despair, for I knew that once again I would lose consciousness and that for one whole day I would be gasping for air inside myself, unable to find myself, knowing perfectly well that I

was somewhere but the devil knew where, as if I were dead."
He writes four years later in a postscript to this essay that it

> represents my first effort to return to myself after
> seven years of estrangement and total castration. In
> it a recent victim of poisoning, sequestered and
> traumatized, recalls what happened before his
> death. This explains why the text can do no more
> than stammer.

He adds—in what must be taken as more than sensationalist
rhetoric—that it was written "in the dulled mental state of
a convert whom the magical spells of the priestly rabble, taking advantage of his momentary weakness, were keeping in
a state of enslavement." Thirteen days later, in a continuation
of the postscript, he claims to have between 150 and 200 hosts
in him. Nothing appears "more erotically pornographic than
Christ, ignoble sexual materialization of all false psychic
enigmas. . . ." It was this state of conversion, Artaud maintains, that accounted for his "delirium" on the subject of
Christ and the cross in the essay. There is continual movement—shifts in perspective, in lucidity, in mental disposition—in the essays.

The Peyote Dance, in its contorted and involuted totality,
comes (unwittingly I suspect) as close to Artaud's ideal discourse as anything he wrote. It is, despite its ostensible subject, its own subject. It is an encounter, created and recreated,
distorted and corrected, symbolized and resymbolized, discussed and digested, though never fully. It cannot be read as
an ethnographic text (though some pedestrian anthropologists have tried to do so), as a psychiatric history, an adventure story, or a spiritual quest. This is its fascination. Artaud
came as close to achieving *here,* in his text, what he sought
there, among the Tarahumara.

Though planned in his life time, *The Peyote Dance* was not
published until 1955—eight years after his death. Now comes
the Farrar, Straus and Giroux translation which, with the exception of a few banalities on the dust jacket, abandons the
work to its readers without an introduction, an epilogue, a
chronology, or a justification for the order of the selections—
all essential to appreciate the development of Artaud's response to his encounter with the Tarahumara. My French
edition, which reflects Artaud's wishes concerning this order,
is significantly different. Artaud would probably have been
pleased with his American achievement, were it not that it
hangs on the commercial force of "peyote" and "Artaud."

Artaud is, nevertheless, subject to language—to the myth of
the primitive, of his thought and words, through which the
Westerner defines himself. Were Artaud not cognizant of
this—and at times he appears not to be—it would be simple
enough to dismiss *The Peyote Dance* as the work of yet another armchair philosopher of the primitive who insists that
his myth is *their* reality. Artaud's stance is considerably more
complicated. In one essay he declares that had he not met the
Tarahumara, whom, he claims, believe themselves to be a
Primeval Race, he would have thought "a primeval race" to
be nothing more than a myth. More often, the source of his
perception is left open. In **"The Mountain of the Signs,"** one
of the most impressive essays, Artaud describes the signs,
forms, and natural effigies he sees on the Tarahumara mountains: a naked man, tortured, nailed to a rock, and worked
on by forms which the sun made volatile; an enormous statue
of Death with an infant in its hands; a woman's bosom with
perfectly delineated breasts; an animal carrying in its own
jaws its effigy which it devoured. He seems "to read every-

where a story of childbirth in war, a story of genesis and
chaos. . . . " He remarks: "Between the mountain and myself, I cannot say which was haunted. . . . " He writes in another essay:

> For anyone who pursues the mental side of things
> with his heart, there is a point, as in the Peyote rite
> of the Tarahumara, when the fabric of perception
> opens in a cross, and cracks in such a way that one
> no longer knows whether it is from one's own heart
> that this cross has emerged, or from the head of the
> Other, who then is no longer the Other, any Other,
> but THAT ONE, the Only Source of Flames, whose
> tongue pierces and gathers the taste for the Word,
> when the heart which was beating like a Double,
> recognizes its GENERATOR.

Subject and object are blended in the image, which has for
Artaud the power of bringing one closer to a hidden reality.
"Whatever belongs to the realm of the image," Artaud wrote
in his Surrealist days, "cannot be subjected to reason; it must
remain within this realm, or be annihilated." Of course, Artaud attempts in *The Peyote Dance* (as in some of his writings on the Theater of Cruelty) just such an annihilation.
Some of the most painfully tedious pages of *The Peyote
Dance* are his translations of images into (verbally meaningful) signs.

Artaud could not escape his own personal mythology either;
it is carried in his images. Images of castration, mutilation,
sexual antagonism, purity, pollution, and bewitchment, of
Christ and the cross, as well as grander philosophic, linguistic, and esthetic themes, that characterize Artaud's writings,
are attributed to the Tarahumara. Despite some extraordinary descriptions of the peyote rites and his own experience
of peyote, the book is impersonal, aloof, and distant. The Indians do not come alive; they remain always icons within Artaud's personal mythology. *The Peyote Dance* is very much
the work of a lonely man—a man tormented by an inability
either to detach himself from experience or to accept it
wholly. It is, in its way, a record of Artaud's martyrdom.

When Artaud writes, for example, at the beginning of the first
essay (in the American edition) "incredible as it may seem,
the Tarahumara Indians live as though they were already
dead," we are at first tempted to read this as an extravagant
image that is somehow descriptive of the Indians. By the end
of the essay—it is only six pages long—we know it is Artaud
speaking of himself, of the mummy (Artaud le Momo) dead
and yet paradoxically preserved as alive. Death for Artaud,
we must remember, is a means "to regain the emptiness of
a crystalline liberty." It is a liberation from life—life which,
in a meditation on suicide, he describes as "a consenting to
the apparent readability of things and their relationship to the
mind." The image of man, neither alive nor dead, the
mummy, god even (Artaud had such delusions) mutilated,
castrated, martyred, Christ, Osiris, Adonis, appears in ritual
splendour at the end of **"Tutuguri."** The poem was written
two weeks before Artaud's death of rectal cancer on March
4, 1948.

> there, the advancing horse bears the torso of a man,
> a naked man who holds aloft
> not a cross,
> but a staff of ironwood
> attached to a giant horseshoe
> that encircles his whole body,
> his body cut with a slash of blood,
> and the horseshoe is there

like the jaws of an iron collar
which the man has caught
in the slash of blood.

Artaud explains in a letter to his publisher Marc Barbizat
that "The new Tutuguri that I am writing for you is heavy
with a blood experience which I did not have in 1936. This
blood experience is that I had here three attacks in which I
was found bathing in my blood, in an entire sea of blood, and
Tutuguri comes out of this." (pp. 458-62)

Vincent Crapanzano "Myth of the Primitive," in
Partisan Review, *Vol. XLIV, No. 3, 1977, pp. 458-
62.*

RUBY COHN   (essay date 1979)

[*An American critic and educator, Cohn has published numerous critical works on modern drama, including several studies
of Samuel Beckett. In the following excerpt, she compares* The
Jet of Blood *with Armand Salacrou's one-act play* Le boule de
verre *(1924), discussing Artaud's use of parody and the ways
in which* The Jet of Blood *foreshadows his Theater of Cruelty.*]

Densely packed as it is, Artaud's *Jet de sang* can be read
aloud in about five minutes, but duration of a performance
would depend upon scenic effects, and it may have been these
that prompted choice of the play in the 1964 Royal Shakespeare Company Season of Cruelty, "played through first in
sounds; then as Artaud wrote it." Other than reviews of that
production, only two critics have accorded *Le jet de sang* sustained attention—both writing in English, although with
good knowledge of French, as is not always true of Artaud
enthusiasts.

Bettina Knapp believes that Artaud is mocking many contemporary attitudes, even while he objectifies his inner life.
She summarizes the play's meaning [in her *Antonin Artaud:
Man of Vision*]: "*The Jet of Blood* reveals youth's optimism
and idealism, the desire for independence and the need to belong, the nostalgic world of the past and the pain to come."
Albert Bermel finds the brief play largely inclusive; he reads
it as "a nightmarish, comic story in miniature of the creation
of the world and its desecration by people, especially by
women" [see excerpt in TCLC, Vol. 3, p. 61]. Bermel also fits
Artaud's cast into his own *Contradictory Characters:* "The
Boy seeks virginity and traffics with a whore. The Girl loves
the Boy and leaves him. The Priest is not interested in God.
The Wetnurse is a mother who frightens her son. The Knight
is neither chivalrous nor valiant but selfish and impotent.
Even the omnipotent, unseen God bleeds from a chewed
wrist." Neither critic is apparently aware of the fact that Artaud entitled his manuscript: "Le jet de sang ou la boule de
verre." *La boule de verre* is a one-act play by Armand
Salacrou. Like Artaud, young Salacrou frequented the Surrealists, and he took a lively interest in poetry and painting as
well as theatre. Unlike Artaud, Salacrou was later able to
produce his plays with money earned in publicity. His favorite director was Charles Dullin, who had earlier won Artaud's admiration. Salacrou's sympathies remained on the
political and artistic Left, but his voluminous drama balances
between cautious experiment and mainstream taste. He later
called his one-act *Boule de verre* "une pièce à lire" ["a play
for reading"], and I know of no productions.

La boule de verre is preceded by an epigraph ascribed to
Thomas Edison: "For a man to be completely alone, he must

contemplate the stars." Salacrou sets his play in a traveling
fair, replete with clown, fortune-teller, organ-grinder, bal-
loons, lottery tickets, and shooting gallery. Salacrou's titular
glass ball hangs above the shooting gallery, and the Gallery-
Owner circles the ball with a large flaming candle. The speaking characters number fifteen, of whom four lead directly to
Artaud's *Jet de sang:* Young Man, Young Girl (named
Marie-Ann), Knight, and Wetnurse.

Salacrou's Young Girl, dressed in a bygone fashion, tells the
Young Man of her unknown mother before they exchange
declarations of love, amidst disapproving comments of people at the fair. Quite suddenly, the Young Man bursts into
tears at the evanescence of all experience. The young couple
disappear into the crowd, whereupon they are replaced by a
Knight who keeps picking up candy-wrappers and a Wetnurse who calls out for Marie-Ann. The Knight, who is Marie-
Ann's father, has allowed the Wetnurse to serve her on condition that the older woman not reveal herself as Marie-Ann's
mother. The Young Man returns, contemplates the glass ball,
and falls into a wild depression. After dialogues with a Fortune-teller and a Clown, the Young Man tries his skill in the
shooting gallery. He wins an alarm clock. As Marie-Ann returns, followed by the Knight and the Wetnurse, the alarm
rings. A passerby reveals that the Wetnurse is Marie-Ann's
mother, seduced from him by the Knight, who thereupon explains that he was married to the most noble and beautiful
of women, who was stricken with "le mal du ciel" ["sky sickness"]. Marie-Ann was therefore born of a substitute mother,
the Wetnurse. The Young Man reacts violently against "le
mal du ciel," threatening to destroy all mysteries, extinguish
the stars, perforate the moon. Then he collapses, dead. Marie-
Ann wishes to follow him to heaven, but the Knight, tearing
candy-wrappers over the Young Man's body, declares that he
will cure her of "le mal du ciel." The play's final line is spoken
by the Gallery-Owner: "Dans sa monotonie, le soleil . . . Au
moins, éteignez-moi ce bec de gaz. (*criant:*) Mettez-le en
berne." (Monotonously, the sun . . . At least extinguish that
gas-lamp. [*shouting:*] Lower it to half-mast.)

Salacrou's play is about five times as long as Artaud's, but a
plot summary can embrace both (with a little forcing): the
Young Girl is the product of a momentary union between a
half-crazed nobleman and a crass commoner. The Young
Man's love for her cannot slake his thirst for the absolute.
However, both plays reach for a meaning beyond the plot (as
Knapp and Bermel rightly sensed in the case of Artaud);
Salacrou's glass ball is a metaphor for the earth, and the
blood spurting from God's wrist is prophetic of what Artaud
would later call cosmic cruelty.

A sustained comparison of the two plays has been made by
Paule Thévenin, editor of Artaud's *Oeuvres complètes:*

> In writing this short play, Antonin Artaud dis-
> played a rather ferocious humor. It is a parody of
> a one-act play by Armand Salacrou, *The Glass Ball,*
> which had just been published in the periodical
> *Intentions.* . . . From Armand Salacrou's work he
> kept only the main characters, and he took apart
> the mechanism of their dialogue to show the stereo-
> typical aspect. One detail reveals the way he
> amused himself in parody; in *The Glass Ball,* which
> is set in a traveling fair, the Knight collects tinfoil
> candy wrappers; in ***The Spurt of Blood*** he calls for
> his papers, each one of which wraps an enormous
> slice of Swiss cheese, which he eats; paper and

cheese were stuffed at the bottom of the Wetnurse's pockets, as swollen as her large breasts.

Considered in inverse order, Thévenin's points present increasing difficulty: parodic tic, characters' parodic dialogue, total parody. The Knight's wrapper compulsion is a parodic detail, and what is wrapped may also be related in the two plays. What I have translated as "candy" is French *nougat,* a white pulpy sweet studded with nuts or candied fruit, so that Swiss cheese resembles an enlarged version. Salacrou's Knight admires the beauty of tinfoil wrappers, but Artaud's Knight devours the contents of wrappers—Swiss cheese, which, as Bermel mentions, may relate him to the Swiss accent of the Priest, or more probably, as Knapp suggests, ties him to the swollen, milk-filled breasts of the Wetnurse; the holes of the cheese suggest female sexuality. Salacrou's esthetic candy-wrappers become Artaud's food-wrappers associated with women. This may be parody, but the image has a broader significance.

Moving from the Knight's obsession, we examine Thévenin's claim that Artaud was indebted to Salacrou for his main characters, taking apart the mechanism of their lines to show their stereotypicality. Artaud's two couples clearly do derive from Salacrou, replete with essential characteristics—anachronism of the Knight, dependence of the Wetnurse, fidelity of the Young Girl, idealism of the Young Man. It is the dialogue of the young lovers whose mechanism is taken apart, as noted by Thévenin, perhaps to show its stereotypical aspect, but also its egocentricity and exaltation. The dialogue of the Knight and the Wetnurse, in contrast, is vulgar and atypical of stage convention. If the repetitions and tonal variations of the lovers' lines mock stereotypical stage lovers (and only directorial pointing could convince me that they do), such typicality disappears from the abrasive dialogue of the rest of the brief play.

Does Artaud's "rather ferocious humor" in *Le jet de sang* constitute parody? Other grotesquely comic details do not depend upon Salacrou. With the same flat word "Voilà," the Young Girl faces her beloved, and the Wetnurse lifts her dress for the Knight. The Young Man hides his face from the Bawd in orgasm, and the Knight hides his face from the Wetnurse spawning scorpions. The colloquial "ça" links key lines toward the end of the play.

> La Maquerrelle. Racontez-moi comment ça
> vous est arrivé.
> La Jeune Fille. La vierge! ah c'était ça qu'il cherchait.
>
> The Bawd. Tell me how that happened to you.
> The Young Girl. The virgin! ah that's what he
> was looking for.

The first "ça" is a sexual climax, the second a quest climax. "Ça," "voilà," and shamefaced gesture can be pointed in direction toward humor, but it would be the Black Humor of the Surrealists, rather than parody.

Completed and perhaps wholly written on 17 January 1925, *Le jet de sang* was included with *Paul les oiseaux* and *Le vitre d'amour* in a folder labeled *Trois contes*. *Le jet de sang* is not mentioned in Artaud's published letters, and it is not discussed by his acquaintances or biographers. Artaud evidently liked the brief play enough to place it in his second book *L'ombilic des limbes,* his first to be published by the prestigious press of the *Nouvelle revue française,* and his zest for that publication sprinkles his letters. The 1926-27 publici-

ty blurb for his Alfred Jarry Theater announces the première of *Le jet de sang,* but no steps toward performance were apparently taken. In 1946, when Artaud withdrew his first book *Tric-trac du ciel* from the projected publication of his complete works, he left the *Ombilic* volume intact.

Despite Artaud's sporadic homage to humor, comic forms were not his forte, and he imposed an idiosyncratic meaning on "parody" as on "cruelty." The OED defines parody: "An imitation of a work more or less closely modelled on the original, but so turned as to produce a ridiculous effect." Artaud cites a curious example of parody in his letter of 27 November 1932 to Jean Paulhan, editor of *La nouvelle revue française:* "On y [in the anonymous *Arden of Feversham*] perçoit un désir de parodier Shakespeare. . . . Quoique cette volonté parodique soit par moments assez peu accusée." (A desire to parody Shakespeare is evident. . . . Although that parodic wish is at times not very pronounced.) One might say the same of Artaud's desire to parody Salacrou, if indeed that was his desire—assez peu accusé (not very pronounced). Although Knapp finds that *Le jet de sang* mocks contemporary attitudes, and Bermel calls it "a *comic* story" (my emphasis), neither critic shows how humor operates in the play. The Royal Shakespeare Company production—the only professional production known to me—sought cruelty rather than humor, although Ronald Hayman notes [in his *Artaud and After*] that the performance "drew laughter of the wrong kind from the audience." The question remains whether Artaud desired laughter of *any* kind, and whether, if *Arden of Feversham* is parody, his conception of parody intended laughter at all.

The purpose of parody is to ridicule another work, and that demands recognition of the mocked work. Two competent critics analyze *Le jet de sang* without even referring to Salacrou's insemination, and it is improbable that any reader—certainly not I—would notice Salacrou's unfamiliar *Boule de verre* without Thévenin's editorial note, which is in turn based on Artaud's manuscript. A parodic intent may have been the springboard for Artaud's play, which, however, contains more on heaven and earth than is dreamed of in Salacrou's play.

Despite the Knight's farcical tic, *Le jet de sang* evidences Artaud's serious interest in "le mal du ciel," which is analogous to his own malady described in his 1923-24 correspondence with *Nouvelle revue française* editor Jacques Rivière, and which predicts his Gnosticism as analyzed by Susan Sontag in the Introduction to her *Antonin Artaud: Selected Writings* [excerpted in *TCLC,* Vol. 3, pp. 56-8]. More provocative in this play is a hovering cruelty. Artaud's young lovers are star-crossed, and on his stage stars literally collide, wreaking widespread and flamboyant havoc. Salacrou's Young Man has heaven-sickness, but Artaud's hero declares that the heavens have gone mad. Like his author, he recognizes cosmic cruelty. Having seen, known, and understood that, this Young Man finds mundane life intolerable. He is not merely the "contradictory character" claimed by Bermel; he reflects his author's desire for unity of flesh and spirit. When the Priest asks the Young Man what part of the Young Girl's body he refers to most often, her brother-lover answers: "To God." This is not simple blasphemy but an excarnation, not spirit made flesh, but a flesh-spirit union, a constant through Artaud's writing. Because the Young Man desires the pure virgin, he exits with the foul Bawd, as the resurrected Young Girl implies. The "ça" of Bawd and Young Girl, the "Voilà" of Wetnurse and Young Girl, may suggest synonymity—at this stage of Artaud's thinking (before the last years when he viewed any sexual activity as an unmitigated evil).

After the publication in 1924 of Artaud's correspondence with *Nouvelle revue française* editor Jacques Rivière, the young writer may have expected a sympathetic reception to a record of his suffering, his consciousness of void, his devaluation of literature in favor of intensely lived life—all suggested by his title **Umbilicus of Limbo.** Since that slim volume was published by the *Nouvelle revue française* press, we may assume director Jacques Rivière's acquiescence to Artaud's rejection of traditional literary forms. The thirteen texts of *L'Ombilic des limbes,* like the far better known *Théâtre et son double,* is a mixture of genres: three poems (two previously published); three letters (one to a cinema official, one to a doctor, and one to the legislator of the law on narcotics); three vivid evocations of suffering, a description of an André Masson painting, *Paul les oiseaux* about three Italian Renaissance artists, and *Le jet de sang*—these introduced by a preface passionately declaring Artaud's commitment to "Esprit" (mind or spirit). Only in a long footnote does Artaud mention his title: "Si j'avais, moi, ce que je sais qui est ma pensée, j'eusse peute-être écrit *l'Ombilic des limbes,* mais je l'eusse écrit d'une tout autre façon." (If I possessed what I know is my thought, I might perhaps have written *The Umbilicus of Limbo,* but I would have written it in a wholly different way.) In the way that he did write, however, the pieces are paradoxically nourished by Artaud's sense of Limbo. Penetrated by a void, the dissimilar pieces are energized in words.

Paul les oiseaux may be usefully compared with *Le jet de sang,* written about a year later. The latter is a play, the former a scenario. Both are rooted in the work of another author—*Le jet de sang* in Armand Salacrou's *Boule de verre,* and *Paul les oiseaux* in Marcel Schwob's *Vies imaginaires.* Originally published in 1898, Schwob's anecdotal biographies were reprinted by Gallimard in 1923, and Artaud was apparently drawn to only one of these twenty-two figures.

Again Artaud appropriates four characters from his source—the painter Paolo Uccello, his wife Selvaggia, and the sculptors Donatello and Brunelleschi. Schwob tells a short simple story of a painter so obsessed with the geometry of his canvases that he does not notice either the beauty or the death of his wife, as he continues to paint her. At the end of his life Uccello shows his masterwork to Donatello, who exclaims: "O Paolo, recouvre ton tableau." Uccello takes this as a tribute to his achievement, but Donatello has seen only a hodgepodge of geometric figures.

Artaud not only destroys the linearity of this tale of monomania, he also introduces himself into his composition, and he converts a story into what he calls "théâtre mental"—"Car nous sommes *uniquement* dans l'Esprit" (For we are *solely* in the mind)—with setting, description, dialogue. Artaud explicates Paolo Uccello as detached mind, Donatello as elevated mind, whereas Brunelleschi, bound to the earth, in love with Selvaggia, thinks only of sex, and the scenario ends with his ejaculation in the form of a great white bird. The piece is remarkable in imagery, intensity, and fragmented quality. Editor Thévenin does not label this piece parody, but remarks that Artaud took his subject from Schwob. I find *Paul les oiseaux* more vivid than *Le jet de sang,* but the two pieces depart similarly from their sources, each expressing Artaud's own preoccupations rather than being distorted into parody.

Both pieces predict Artaud's view of theatre as space to be filled rather than problem to be solved. Both pieces treat sex shockingly, and both enlarge characters far beyond realism. However, *Paul les oiseaux* is a scenario whereas *Le jet de sang* is a play exhibiting several features that Artaud would incorporate into his vision of theatre. Repetition and tonal variation (as well as a Swiss accent) stress the purely sonic qualities of language and may have no parodic intention whatsoever. Nonverbal sounds, zigzags of lightening, a gigantic hand, a suddenly transparent dress are today part of theatre idiom, but they must have been striking in 1925.

More telling than these innovations, however, is the density of Artaud's early effort to stage cosmic cruelty with such obsessive images as circle, fire, blood, incest, giantism—the last three absent from Salacrou's *Boule de verre.* The circle is faintest since the hurricane sounds as though created by a giant wheel, and I cannot imagine how an audience would know that. Fire attacks the Bawd's hair. Blood spurts from God's wrist. The Young Man and the Young Girl are brother and sister as well as husband and wife. Giantism is manifest in God's hand and spurt of blood. Unlike Christ's blood that Marlowe's Faustus sees as a redemptive agent, this God's blood litters the stage with corpses and awakens lust in those who are left alive—the Bawd and the Young Man. This giantism is a sign of that cruelty which will become the fulcrum of Artaud's vision of theatre. Although Artaud would intend actor and spectator, not character, to undergo purgation by cruelty, perhaps the resurrective recognition by the Young Girl is an early Artaud sketch of an apocalyptic vision that was to have such wide and varied impact after his death—decades afterward. (pp. 312-18)

> *Ruby Cohn, "Artaud's 'Jet de Sang': Parody or Cruelty?," in* Theatre Journal, *Vol. 31, No. 3, October, 1979, pp. 312-18.*

STEVEN KOVÁCS   (essay date 1980)

[*In the following excerpt, Kovács provides descriptive analyses of Artaud's film scenarios and writings on film.*]

During the premiere of *The Seashell and the Clergyman* on the night of February 9, 1928, the hushed silence of the audience at the Studio des Ursulines was broken by the following loud exchange:

> —Who made this film?
> —Madame Germaine Dulac.
> —What is Mme. Dulac?
> —She is a cow.

Armand Tallier, director of the theater, had the house lights turned on and pinpointed the disrupters, Antonin Artaud, Robert Desnos and a couple of Surrealist buddies. He asked them to apologize, but instead of excuses he received a stream of obscenities. Friends of the establishment quickly joined forces to evict the troublemakers, but they succeeded only after an exchange of kicks and blows. The undesirables broke some of the mirrors of the lobby and shouted more obscenities before they abandoned the premises.

The fury of this outburst was indicative of the great concern with which Artaud approached film. He had certain ideas about the demands of Surrealism on the screen which he was determined to put into practice. During the period of his most serious involvement with the cinema, between the years 1926 and 1930, he attacked the medium with the uncompromising fervor that characterized all of his artistic ventures. He wrote film reviews, articles on the theory of film, answered questionnaires and interviews, but above all he devoted himself to writing film scenarios which he hoped to see made into movies. (p. 155)

Artaud bases his first . . . scenario for a film on a concept which readily lends itself to cinematic adaptation.

Eighteen Seconds is the unfolding of a man's thoughts during that short period of time as he is standing on a street corner. As Artaud himself comments, "The whole interest of the scenario lies in the fact that the time during which the described events take place is really eighteen seconds while these events will require an hour or two to be projected on the screen." Artaud emphasizes this duality of interior and exterior time by showing the close-up of a watch on which the seconds pass with infinite slowness. True to his precepts about the role of films, he chooses a subject of direct psychological import, namely, the individual's optical thought process. Sharing the Surrealists' attitude that the cinema is the medium which best approximates dreams, he assigns the screen the role of transmitting the daydreams of a man. His reflections are shown on the screen precisely because Artaud believes the psychological process to be of paramount importance. Not only is interior time longer than exterior but it is also infinitely more powerful: the man's daydreaming finally leads him to commit suicide.

Because Artaud saw the cinema as being especially apt for showing the internal state of man, he chose an appropriately psychological topic for his first film plan. Because of his belief in the potential of the cinema, he projected his own inner turmoils into that scenario more directly than into any other piece of fiction he produced. The story is of an actor. He is close to winning glory and just as close to winning the woman he has loved. He is struck by a strange malady, however, which disrupts all his plans. He becomes unable to reach his own thoughts. Although he is completely lucid, he cannot give his thoughts an exterior form, to translate them into the appropriate words. He is reduced to seeing a parade of images unfold in his mind. As a result he becomes incapable of sharing the lives of others and of giving himself to any activity.

The situation thus described in the opening scenes of the scenario fits Artaud's own situation exactly. He was a young actor in love with the actress Génica Athanasiou. He surely felt that his theatrical career never blossomed because his nervous disorders compelled him to act with an intensity which was unacceptable on the stage. His inability to win her total love stemmed from this same malady. In his famous correspondence with Jacques Rivière in 1923 Artaud talked about the problem he had in expressing his thoughts: "I suffer from a frightful disease of the mind. My thought abandons me at all stages. From the simple act of thinking to the external act of its materialization into words. Words, forms of phrases, interior directions of thought, simple reactions of the spirit, I am in constant pursuit of my intellectual being. When, therefore, *I can seize a form,* imperfect that it may be, I fix it, for fear of losing all my thoughts." According to his own testimony, therefore, simply writing about his affliction, both in his letters and in the scenario, was an achievement, the seizing of a form for the expression of his thoughts, a cure for his illness through a literary form.

Confronted with his mental infirmity, the actor curses his fate. In his desperation he swears that he is ready to change

places with anyone, even the hunchback selling newspapers on the street, in order to exercise control over his faculties. The mental disorder is much more serious than any physical defect could be. The hunchback is shown thinking while images of power and success flash by. At some point the actor becomes the hunchback as he hopes that his hump will also be removed when he finds the central problem. He begins his quest for sanity. We see him at meetings, on the road, in front of books trying to find the answer. He is arrested and placed in an insane asylum, where he becomes truly mad but remains intent on finding the cause of his problem. A revolution frees him, the crowds acclaim him as their king. Now it seems that he has everything, yet he is still not in possession of his mind. He finds himself in a theater watching an act when he realizes that the hunchback on the stage with his mistress is only an effigy of himself, a traitor who stole his love and his mind. Once this moment of recognition comes, the two characters merge into one on the screen. The suicide of the actor that follows is an indication that the problem cannot be resolved. The hunchback who stole his mind is indeed only an effigy of himself, yet it was he who thought of himself as the hunchback, so that the problem is circular and resides within his own head. As in this scenario, so in real life Artaud was forever in quest of a seminal truth without ever being able to resolve the mental problems that were tormenting him. (pp. 159-60)

Artaud's best-known film scenario is, of course, the one which was realized by Germaine Dulac, **The Seashell and the Clergyman,** and which provoked the ruckus at the Studio des Ursulines. The story is as complicated as that of **Eighteen Seconds.** It opens with a clergyman in a laboratory pouring liquid from a huge shell into various beakers, each of which he proceeds to smash on the floor. A military man appears and breaks the shell with his sword. The clergyman appears following a carriage on all fours. Inside the carriage is the officer and a beautiful woman, who eventually enter the confessional of a church. The clergyman attacks the officer, but as he does so the officer turns into a priest. He throws this double away on top of a mountain. We then see the clergyman and the woman in the confessional. He hurls himself at her and rips off the bodice of her dress. Underneath is a shell protecting her breasts which he tears away and waves in the air. We then see him in a crowded ballroom where the officer and woman appear on a dais. He continues to chase the woman in various places as we see images of her float by. He goes down a corridor opening doors with a large key, until he finds the officer and the woman in the last room. A chase begins. We see his fingers searching for a neck as various landscapes appear between his hands. The clergyman is asleep. He dreams that servants enter a room with a glass bowl in it and start to do some cleaning. A governess dressed in black enters who turns out to be the same beautiful woman. Two young people enter from the garden: they are the woman and the clergyman and they are to be married by a priest. Visions from the clergyman's dream interrupt the process. Now the headless clergyman appears carrying a package. It is a glass bowl, which he breaks in order to take his own head out of it. The head melts into a blackish liquid as it rests on an oyster shell: the clergyman drinks it with closed eyes. The British Board of Censors banned the film with an illogic of a different sort: "The film is so cryptic as to be almost meaningless. If there is a meaning, it is doubtless objectionable."

Although this scenario is not so clearly autobiographical as **Eighteen Seconds,** it still presents as the main problem themes which haunted Artaud throughout his life. In this scenario as in the previous one he presents a quest for a woman as well as a quest for self-knowledge. As Bettina Knapp has rightly pointed out, "Such a quest begins in a scientific manner, usually in a laboratory of some sort, as it had with the alchemists of old." In fact Artaud's quest, as it was projected into his theories of theater, at least parallels the processes of alchemy if it does not directly issue from them. At least in one other of Artaud's works the scientific laboratory plays an important symbolic role in the discovery of Self. In a play written in 1931 called *The Philosopher's Stone* a Dr. Pale carries out experiments to find the philosopher's stone, the object of all alchemical processes. His experiments consist mostly of chopping away at the body of his double, Harlequin, who incorporates in himself the sexual appetites noticeably absent from the doctor. Mrs. Knapp observes that "mythologically speaking, it is through the *cleansing, burning,* or *dismemberment process,* that transformation and rebirth can occur." Comparable to this destructive act in the laboratory is the clergyman's titration of liquids which ends with his breaking of beakers as well as the officer's smashing of the shell with his sword.

Just as in *Eighteen Seconds* the actor's quest for the woman was related to his attempt to gain control of his own mind, so in *The Seashell* . . . the beautiful woman is but a focal point of the clergyman's attempt to break through the divisive forces of his character. The officer represents the other side of the clergyman's nature. He is the obstacle to the clergyman attaining wholeness through union with the woman. He appears in the laboratory as a disruptive force. He seems to usurp the clergyman's role even in the church when he seats himself in the confessional. The clergyman attains the power to destroy his double only once they are in the church, in his own domain. It is while the officer is being choked by the clergyman that his true identity emerges: his face changes to that of a priest. Once he is destroyed, the clergyman thinks he has removed the chief obstacle to his union with the woman, yet she keeps on eluding him. His triumph over his officer double was only temporary. The officer keeps reappearing by the side of the woman in the involved chase scenes. The clergyman even dreams of being united with his love, but that is only a dream. Since it is his psyche which is split in two, he cannot reach a state of inner unity by the external act of union with a woman. He must alter the very chemistry of his being by drinking the mysterious liquid. Is the liquid totally life-restoring or is it deadly? Whichever it may be, the act of drinking is as final a step as the suicide of the actor in *Eighteen Seconds.*

After reading Artaud's scenario, a viewing of the film will confirm that Germaine Dulac closely followed the script in shooting the movie. Yet when Artaud first saw the film he was so greatly dissatisfied with it that he caused the great uproar at its premiere. As a result of his immediate disclaimer, observers have tended to side with Artaud in judging the film to be a distortion of Surrealism on the screen. Lately, Alain Virmaux has come along to clarify the nature of the relationship between Artaud and Mme. Dulac in their participation on the film. Virmaux has documented the change from Artaud's respectful attitude toward Mme. Dulac in the first few months of the venture to his total disillusionment by the time of the opening. Briefly, Artaud emphatically denied newspaper rumors that he wanted to interfere in the making of the film, writing to Mme. Dulac, "I do not have the slightest pretention to collaborate with you. It would be a stupid preten-

tion." Yet as time went on he started giving suggestions to her on the "conception" if not the "realization" of the film. What her reaction was we do not know, but there is a gap of two and a half months between Artaud's first batch of letters and his last of September 25 in which he complains to Mme. Dulac of not knowing anything about the progress of the film. In a letter of August 29 to Jean Paulhan he says that he would like to write an article for *La nouvelle revue française* "to defend my film without attacking anyone, but to determine my position with respect to this film." Thus, Artaud was already suspect of the way the film would turn out long before he actually saw it.

Why was Artaud so totally dissatisfied with the finished film? He had certainly decided in advance to make his own attitude on it public. That decision was made after he had had time to think about how he wanted his film to be made. Although at first he wanted no part of the production, he gradually began to envision certain scenes shot in certain ways. As he realized in his own mind the possibilities of the cinema, he was more and more eager to have a hand in the actual production. Of course, there were a few specific misinterpretations in the movie, but by and large the movie was faithful to the script. What made Artaud disclaim the movie was not so much that his intentions were distorted, but rather that he could not participate in their cinematization. Having entrusted his scenario to Mme. Dulac, Artaud then wanted to assist in the execution of the film. "[T]here are a series of nuances, of detail, of subtleties, even of sleight-of-hand turns which I see exactly how to do, but which can only be indicated when shooting. I also had a rather precise conception of the way in which the actors should play, of a certain rhythm to ask of them, to communicate to them." For Artaud the smallest details of the movie became significant. He began to imagine a certain tempo which he wanted to create in the film through the performance of the actors. His ideas, in fact, combine certain theatrical suggestions with purely cinematic considerations.

> In the scene of the ball I see after one or two very distant shots taken from high up, exactly as you had in mind, other shots where the camera would be placed on the ground and aimed vertically towards the sky, so as to show the bottom of the chin and the cavity of the actors' eyebrows. And I believe that this would be possible. About these same dancers, I see them now dancing in regular fashion and without expression like ordinary dancers, now dancing in a paroxysm of anger with their faces in convulsions and their bodies swinging normally, now an expression of voluptuousness, of amorous delirium but completely stereotyped. [Letter from Artaud to Dulac, June 17, 1927]

Certain other suggestions in the letters further clarify for us the way in which Artaud imagined his film. He sought to create a powerful psychological undercurrent through a number of devices. He proposed, for example, an actor for the role of the officer whom he had picked in order to emphasize "a great contrast in expression between the head of the officer and that of the clergyman." In order to create a particular mood, he suggested a total simplicity of decor and went so far as to envision the ballroom filmed without any walls.

What emerges from these scanty letters is the germ of a particular kind of vision that Artaud had for the cinema. That vision was rooted in his experience with the theater and was to be more precisely articulated in his essays of the 1930s, *The*

Theater and Its Double. He is already demanding highly exaggerated performances from his actors which border on a nervous fit. He wishes to accentuate these extreme states of mind through the assistance of the camera, which can show a somber close-up of human faces taken from an unusual angle. He wants to make the decor absolutely simple precisely in order to emphasize the actors. Yet their performances are to be ruled by a certain rhythm which he will try to recreate again in imitating the rhythmic patterns of Oriental theater.

His opposition to the film prompted Artaud to elaborate his attitude to the cinema in more general terms in the years 1927 and 1928. In an article entitled **"Witchcraft and the Cinema"** of the summer of 1927 he stressed the sense of mystery unique to movies. "I have always noticed in films a special quality in the hidden movement and in the very substance of the images. There is in the cinema something unforeseen and mysterious which is not to be found in the other arts." Artaud then compared movies to dreams: "If the cinema is not made for translating dreams or all that which in the waking life is connected to the domain of dreams, then the cinema does not exist. Then nothing differentiates it from the theater." Movies were not just related to dreams, but to all imaginary experience. "The cinema is essentially a revealer of the occult life with which it puts us directly in contact. . . . Raw film, taken as it is, in the abstract emits a little of this atmosphere of a trance eminently favorable to certain revelations." Artaud explained why the film was so closely related to these forms of the imagination: "The smallest detail, the most insignificant object take on a meaning and a life which belongs to them exclusively. This, over and above the value of the meaning of the pictures themselves, beyond the thoughts they translate or the symbols they form. By the fact that it isolates the objects, the cinema endows them with a separate life which tends to become more and more independent and detached from the ordinary meaning of the objects." He would have surely emphasized this independent life of the object as image in his film, as is indicated by his suggestion to focus on the eyebrows of the dancers, for example. Because of its extraordinary powers over the mind, motion picture was for Artaud the medium which could best express the contemporary liberation of the spirit. "There will not be on the one hand the cinema which represents life, and on the other that which represents the functioning of thought. Because more and more life, that which we call life, will become inseparable from the spirit. A certain hidden realm tends to surface. The cinema, better than any other art, is capable of translating the representation of this realm since stupid order and habitual clarity are its enemies."

Artaud became especially concerned about the way his movie would be received when he was convinced that Mme. Dulac would greatly distort his scenario. In having his scenario published in *La nouvelle revue française,* he added an explanatory preface about his artistic intent. In it he returned to a discussion of the role of dreams in response to Mme. Dulac's advertising the film as a "dream by Antonin Artaud."

> This scenario is not the reproduction of a dream and must not be considered as such. I will not try to excuse its apparent incoherence by the simple loophole of calling it a dream. Dreams have more than their logic. They have their life, where only a dark and intelligent truth appears. This scenario searches for the somber truth of the mind, in images issuing only from themselves, and which do not draw their meaning from the situation where they develop but from a sort of powerful and interior necessity which illuminates them with merciless clarity.

Contrary to what most critics have deduced, this passage is not an attempt by Artaud to dismiss dreams. He is merely saying that he did not write his scenario on the basis of a dream he had, but wrote it to expose certain deeply felt inner psychic images. A careful reading of the passage will confirm that Artaud thinks of dreams as powerful manifestations of the spirit ("Dreams have more than their logic. They have their life."). If anything, he is attempting to recreate the impact of a dream as it is being dreamed rather than to jot down a waking man's memories of a dream. His aim is to capture its power rather than its irrationality. Thus, there is nothing inconsistent about Artaud's previous attitude toward the cinema as a medium which best explores the realm of dreams.

In the preface to his scenario Artaud situated his cinematic efforts within the context of contemporary movie production. He saw two main types of film being produced: "pure cinema," which attempted to present visual abstractions, and commercial cinema, which was based on "psychological situations which would be perfectly in place on a stage or in the pages of a book, but not on the screen." The problem with the former was that "one can only remain insensible to purely geometric lines, without a value of signification by themselves." For Artaud abstraction meant nothing. As far as he was concerned, "As one delves deep into the mind, one finds at the source of all emotion, even the intellect, a physical sensation which comes from the nervous system. This sensation is nothing but the recognition . . . of something substantial, of a certain vibration which recalls states either known or imagined. . . . " Abstract cinema simply could not reach this nervous base of all emotions. Commercial movies, on the other hand, by attempting to translate a text exactly into pictures, did not exploit the potential of the image, and hence failed to attain the possibilities of motion pictures. Artaud, therefore, sought to create a solution which would correct the faults of both types of films. He wanted to make movies which worked directly through the unfolding of images (as did abstract movies) and which would engage the audience psychologically (as commercial movies tried to do). In regard to *The Seashell* . . . he wrote, "In the following scenario I sought to realize this idea of visual cinema where even psychology is devoured by acts. . . . Not that the cinema must dispense with all human psychology: this is not its principle, quite the contrary, to give to this psychology a much more alive and active form." *The Seashell and the Clergyman* does not tell a story but develops a series of states of mind which are deduced from each other as thought issues from thought, without this thought having reproduced a rational chain of events. True psychic situations are produced from the clash of objects and gestures."

Now we know what kind of film Artaud sought to create, but in what kinds of films did he see his ideas best realized? In the favorite genre of the silent era, the comic film. It is instructive to see exactly what the appeal of comic film was for him.

> [The cinema] does not separate itself from life but rather it rediscovers the primitive state of things. The most successful films in this sense are those where a certain humor reigns, as in the early Buster Keatons, and in the least human Charlie Chaplins. Motion pictures studded with dreams, which give

you the physical sensation of pure life, attain perfection in the most excessive humor. A certain movement of objects, of forms, of expressions can only be appropriately expressed through the convulsions and somersaults of a reality which seems to destroy itself with an irony in which one hears the extremes of the spirit crying out.

In fact, Artaud considered the comic film to be the first example of a successful use of subjective images. He saw *The Seashell* . . . as a further step in an evolution which began with the comic film.

> *The Seashell and the Clergyman* is the first film ever written which makes use of subjective images untainted by humor. There were other films before it which introduced a similar break in logical thought patterns, but humor always provided the clearest explanation for breaking the *links* between patterns.
> The mechanics of this type of film, even when applied to serious subjects, is modeled on something rather similar to the mechanics of laughter. Humor is the common factor, known to all, by which the mind communicates its secrets to us.
> *The Seashell and the Clergyman* is the first film of a subjective type where an attempt was made to deal with something other than laughter, and which even in its comic segments, does not rely exclusively on humor.
>
> (pp. 163-69)

The film scenarios that followed were generally inferior to the first he had written, lacking their power and originality. Their weakness may be due in large part to Artaud's recognition of the fact that movies were above all a commercial venture. If he wanted his scenarios to be produced, he had to cater to commercial tastes. As he wrote in a letter to Yvonne Allendy in connection with his scenario *Flights,* "Evidently this is for me *only* a matter of money." He was aware of the lower quality of these scenarios, agreeing in a letter with the judgment of a man named Kruger who put *The Seashell* . . . much above *The 32.* The scenarios are inferior in a number of respects. They include fewer scenes of truly cinematic potential. Images do not arise from previous images as he had planned before and as they did in his earlier scenarios. A rather straight narrative style dominates. Only the subject matter continues Artaud's preoccupation with the magic created by the screen. (pp. 169-70)

Flights is a simple detective story of a young lawyer who pursues his pretty client's father-in-law for stealing a document which names her as the beneficiary of a great fortune. The interest of the scenario lies in its rich visual exploration of the theme of flights. When the young lawyer first daydreams of his attractive client, we see a flight of seagulls, then a view of the ocean taken from an airplane. Later, among the girl's daydreams appear the flight of a sparrow and again the flight of seagulls. When we see the thief running, he is shown from high up, as from an airplane. The father-in-law's escape to Constantinople takes place on the Orient Express, but the progress of the train is again shown from a flying plane. Once the young lawyer retrieves the precious document from the thief, he rushes with it to the nearest post office, where he posts it airmail. The story closes with a shot of a mail plane flying in a clear sky.

We have remaining a two-page fragment of an eight-page scenario entitled *The Solar Airplane.* The scene is set in the Far

East and in the extant pages we are given a detailed description of the experiences of a pilot flying in unusual weather. He attempts to clear clouds, a whirlwind shakes the fuselage, the plane is surrounded by flames and sparks. The propeller of the plane seems to make even the ground tremble. We have also remaining the first and last lines of the scenario: "For a few days a strange terror weighs . . . and it is the wait for news about him which created this nightmare." The whole scenario is therefore concerned with a kind of nightmarish terror which is somehow connected to the flight of an airplane. The flight itself is a total sensory experience, approaching certain hallucinatory states.

Artaud's interest in flight is related exclusively to his cinematic works. While the theme frequently occurs in his film scenarios, it is absent from all of his other writings. Artaud seems to have evoked this subject repeatedly in his scenarios because of a certain relationship he felt between airplane flight and the cinema. The airplane was a time machine ("how the plane swims over time"); it was a vehicle which could enter the realm of the occult ("mist of occultism for aviation"); it was also the vehicle for entering extraordinary sensory states in *The Solar Airplane.* In many ways it symbolized the effects of the cinema as Artaud perceived them. Of course, the airplane symbolized for him the flight of thought as it did for many other poets, but it also created a sensation equivalent to that of a deeply stirring poem ("the vibrating propeller imitates the radiation of poetry"), and at one point he even described it in terms that apply directly to the cinema ("being transported in an uncontrollable, vibrationless machine, representing a direct line of action"). For Artaud the airplane proved to be the most appropriate cinematic symbol: in his scenarios he invested it with the transcendental qualities he found in the movies, perhaps because only the exhilaration of flying could approach the enchantment of the movies.

Although Artaud dealt with flight only in film scenarios, not all of his scenarios are concerned with air travel. All those that do not, share another theme, that of a split or dual personality. While obviously the airplane was specifically linked to Artaud's conception of the cinema, his concern with a dual identity was such a fundamental, lifelong preoccupation that it surfaced in all of his writings That a number of his film scenarios revolve around this latter theme testifies not only to the existence of this psychological state in him but also to his inclination to use the media first and foremost as so many vehicles for self-purification through the outward projection of his own emotional instability.

The early film scenarios give ample evidence of Artaud's interest in the problem of dual identity. *Eighteen Seconds* presents a double duality, as it were. First, we have the man on the street corner and his vision of himself as the actor who goes through the adventures of his daydreams. Second, the actor is both the king and the hunchback, the former having a mental deficiency, while the latter is marked by physical deformity. The hunchback is the darker aspect of Artaud's personality who stole the king's mistress and mind. The conflict is resolved with the merging of the two characters into one. In *The Seashell* . . . the officer acts as a psychological double of the clergyman. The officer stands as an embodiment of the clergyman's desires. Yet he also stands in the way of the realization of those desires. There is actual conflict between the two. The officer symbolically intrudes into the clergyman's laboratory and smashes his shell. The clergyman in turn attacks the officer inside the church and temporarily succeeds in casting him off. Obviously the two characters represent the two opposite sides of a single personality. This is why the officer is not eliminated permanently: his presence is a symbol of the divisive forces which prevent the clergyman from exercising his will. It was with the difference of these two characters in mind that Artaud wrote to Mme. Dulac, "I had wanted a great opposition of expression between the head of the officer and that of the clergyman."

Artaud's interest in a dual personality kept surfacing in his scenarios. *The 32* is the story of a handsome young professor whose aid is requested by one of his pretty students who was abandoned when she became pregnant. She asks the young man for occult intervention. In the course of her visit to him he is suddenly overtaken by a fit. He is placed under medical care. The girl keeps visiting him. During one visit the young man conjures up a ghost that looks a lot like him. Another time the girl begins to dream once a glass bowl is put into motion. She dreams of an aquatic world, of bestial faces, of masks, of animals' paws. Suddenly the vision disappears and in its place in the mirror we see the head of the young man, but completely transformed into something hideous. He takes out a black noose, at which the girl cries out and turns around. The young man is suddenly calmed down, but we do not know if all this was a dream or not. A war comes and the young man leaves. The house stays abandoned for a long time. The mayor and the commissioner of the town decide to search the premises. In the cellar they find the bodies of thirty-two women with a black noose around their necks. Investigation of the murders leads to a vampire in Turkey. The girl enters a hospital with the mayor and the commissioner. When they ask to see the young professor, they are led to the bed of a man with a terribly distorted, pockmarked face who looks nothing like the young man.

In this work once again a character is presented with dual personality. He is a handsome professor ready to help a young girl in trouble, but he is also a hideous vampire who had murdered thirty-two women. It is significant that these two aspects do not exist peacefully side by side, but are the source of continuous conflict. The split is like a disease which erupts in strange fits when the character passes from one identity to another. Artaud created this scenario partly out of *Bluebeard* and partly from *Dr. Jekyll and Mr. Hyde,* because he found in them a way to express his ambivalent attitude toward women and his preoccupation with split personality. (pp. 170-72)

[In *The Revolt of the Butcher,* Artaud] created a work comparable in strength and originality to *Eighteen Seconds* and *The Seashell*. . . . In fact, Artaud saw the scenario as picking up where *The Seashell* . . . had left off. In a prefatory note he wrote, "*The Revolt of the Butcher* originates in a similar intellectual impulse, but the elements which were latent in *The Seashell* . . .—eroticism, cruelty, blood-lust, thirst for violence, obsession with horror, dissolution of moral values, social hypocrisy, lies, perjury, sadism, perversity, etc.— have been made as explicit as possible." The scenario is even less coherent than the early ones. It presents symbolic images and acts which have actually very little to do with each other. Each situation, however, creates a certain sensation, evokes certain associations of a violent nature. Much of the power of the scenario lies in its presenting certain highly charged emotional states from which there is no adequate psychological release, thus building anxiety in the audience.

The scenario opens with a man in anguish pacing around a deserted square, having the compulsion to bite. A butcher's van drives by, swerves to avoid the man, and drops a beef carcass. The man walks into a bar, arousing the curiosity of the clientele. A prostitute enters with a gigolo and smiles at him. We see the madman inspecting the customers who are lined up at the bar standing absolutely still. Then we see a mad race, each customer rolling down a steep slope on a particular object. The madman is on the running board of a taxi with the whore and the gigolo inside and a heavy butcher sitting on top. Meanwhile, a little woman enters the bar and is taken to the police as soon as she admits that she is waiting for the madman. She escapes and the whole police force races after her. They scatter, and when we see them again, they are marching together entranced, playing bagpipes. We see seminarists and soldiers running in slow motion. The madman sees the butcher unload the stiff body of the woman. When he approaches he sees only a side of beef. He finds the woman under wood shavings. Butcher and madman sit down amidst the cutting of carcasses, with the woman laughing between them. We have a view of the woman in a basket, with her arms spread out and bloody. The butcher gets ready to cut her up but cannot do it. There is a big festivity for the butcher and the little woman, who are getting married. In front of the slaughterhouse the whore and the gigolo are consoling the madman. He closes the gates and goes off driving a herd of cattle in front of him. In his final plan for a film Artaud produced a work of unprecedented violence and great cinematic potential. (pp. 174-75)

Artaud at the clinic of Dr. Delmas in Ivry-sur-Seine.

[Artaud's break with the cinema came in] an essay written in 1933, entitled **"The Premature Senility of Film,"** [in which] he launched into a full-scale attack of movies. Writing as an outsider, he divides films into two types, dramatic movies and documentaries. He makes no mention of himself and of his efforts since they are a thing of the past. He condemns the dramatic film for suppressing poetry in principle. The documentary, on the other hand, presents a fragmentary vision of the external world. It attempts to discover the real nature of things by its arbitrary manner of recording. Through the very process of filming the camera imposes its own order on the spectacle, an order which the eye recognizes as being valid insofar as it corresponds to certain memories of external events. Yet such a film is unable to discover a deeper reality. For Artaud, "The world of the cinema is a dead world, illusory and truncated." It is largely talking pictures which brought about such state of affairs, for, in being too explicit, they arrested "the unconscious and spontaneous poetry of images." They excluded chance from playing a part in films. For Artaud chance had been a crucial factor in movies before he actually started writing scenarios. In 1925 he had written, "The cinema is the actualization of chance." Now, once again a spectator, he complained about the elimination of chance from movies. "We knew that the most characteristic and most striking virtues of the cinema were always, or almost, the effect of chance, that is to say, a sort of mystery whose fatality we could not explain." (pp. 177-78)

By 1933 it was in the theater that Artaud expected to find the myths of the present revealed. He was in the midst of writing the essays which were to form the core of his ideas on the theater, *The Theater and Its Double.* It was in this year that he wrote his play *The Conquest of Mexico,* which best exemplified the theater of cruelty. He was to stage his sensational *Cenci* only two years later. He became the apostle of the theater of cruelty, for which he is best remembered today. Yet for a long time he sought his personal answer in the cinema. Perhaps it was only because of his inability to realize his scenarios as films that he totally abandoned the medium.

The line between Artaud's cinematic and theatrical work is not at all clear. He worked in both media at the same time. What he attempted to achieve on the stage was often remarkably similar to the effects he sought to attain on the screen. He wrote of the theater in terms which he applied to the cinema as well: "We conceive of the theater as a veritable magic operation. We do not address ourselves to the eyes, nor to the direct emotion of the soul; that which we seek to create is a certain *psychological* emotion where the most secret energies of the heart are laid bare." He often presented the same motifs in both plays and film scenarios, such as the idea of dual personality, which haunted him throughout his life. Ultimately both the theater and the cinema served as artistic projections of Artaud's search for his own identity. (p. 178)

> Steven Kovács, *"What the Surrealist Film Might Have Been: Artaud and the Cinema,"* in his From Enchantment to Rage: The Story of Surrealist Cinema, *Fairleigh Dickinson University Press, 1980, pp. 155-82.*

JEAN-PIERRE LALANDE   (essay date 1986)

[*In the following excerpt, Lalande examines the affinity between the fantastic tradition in literature and the literary and philosophical theories of Artaud as manifested in his work in film and the theater.*]

Antonin Artaud's use of the fantastic in cinema and theatre must be viewed in conjunction with Surrealism, that is to say, as an attempt to discover a new definition of reality and a new approach to it. For the Surrealists, rationalism cannot provide an accurate knowledge of the real because it limits reality to the confines of logic. As a result, the Surrealist movement will search for a new set of criteria whereby to define reality which, in the Second Manifesto, Breton expresses in these terms: "Everything leads us to believe that there exists a certain point in the mind from which life and death, the real and the imaginary, the past and the future, the communicable and the uncommunicable, . . . cease to be perceived as contradictory. And it is in vain that one would seek in Surrealism another motive but the hope to determine this point." With Breton (and in Artaud's case without him), the Surrealists will undertake a similar exploratory task which will lead them beyond reason to the investigation of such little-known domains as the imaginary, the unconscious, the irrational, and the uncanny.

Given their goal, it is no wonder that the fantastic plays an important role in their works, both as a source of inspiration and as a means of expression. Indeed, the Surrealist and the fantastic approaches to the world share a common nature. Both are expressions of a mind determined to revolt against rules and institutions in an attempt to follow its own imaginative and unconscious inclinations. This explains why Breton writes: "The marvelous [which he does not here differentiate from the fantastic] is always beautiful, any kind of marvelous is beautiful, nothing but the marvelous is beautiful."

After a brief initial period devoted to the writing of poetry, Artaud chose the theatre and cinema (in its very infancy then) as a means of expression. He felt that their reliance on visual rather than on verbal images (the latter being for him the vehicle of rational thought) might have greater appeal for the imagination and the unconscious. The cinema (at least as Artaud knew it) simply showed or suggested things instead of naming them; it also had the magical ability to conjure up illusions, thereby giving the imagination an opportunity to be creative. The same applies, of course, to theatrical productions as long as they do not merely strive to illustrate a text. Being an actor, Artaud never lost his interest in the theatre, but in a theatre which would break away from realism, for he sees realism on the stage as producing nothing but a superficial, dull, and distorted image of reality. Superficial because it takes no account of the subconscious imagination and deals only with banalities, dull because it discourages curiosity, and distorted because, for clarity's sake, it represents reality according to an order that does not correspond to its true nature: "Clear thinking is no longer sufficient. . . . What is clear is what is immediately accessible, but the immediately accessible is only the very surface of life."

Initially Artaud considers both cinema and theatre as means of escape for the imagination. He wants to harness their power of suggestion in order to cause "a liberation . . . of all the dark forces of our thinking process" which have been stifled by reason and logic. By aiming toward the representation of some of the "secrets which lie buried in our consciousness," cinema helps us achieve a better knowledge of ourselves and of our environment. We should go to the cinema or the theatre to "escape from ourselves, or, if you prefer, to find ourselves again in . . . our innermost unicity."

These few remarks make it clear that Artaud assigns to the cinema the same definitions and purpose as Marcel Schneider and Eric Rabkin attribute to the fantastic. [In his *La littérature fantastique en France*] Schneider describes the fantastic as "a literature of escape in the sense that we escape in order to find ourselves again, in the most hidden retreat of our mind," and [in his *The Fantastic in Literature*] Rabkin comments: "In the literature of the fantastic, escape is the means of exploration of an unknown land, a land which is the underside of the mind of man. The fantastic is used to reveal the truth of the human heart." Artaud himself is aware of such a resemblance when he writes: "The cinema will take after the fantastic, a fantastic which, as we realize it more and more, is actually nothing but the real in its totality."

Two of Artaud's film scripts illustrate how and to what purpose he intends to make use of the fantastic.

His first scenario, **The Eighteen Seconds,** was primarily an attempt to demonstrate the artificiality of rational thinking. Here Artaud imagines a succession of images in the same order as they come to the mind of a man who has no control over his thinking process during a time period of eighteen seconds. The author's first intention is obviously to oppose two ways of perceiving the world: the rational way with which everybody ordinarily complies and the spontaneous way which the character in the scenario follows. In order to communicate with others, the first one is mandatory because it is the only code universally recognized as legitimate and acceptable. Whoever fails to abide by it is rejected as an outsider or even a lunatic (like the character in the scenario who, as a result of ostracism, commits suicide).

Based upon this opposition, Artaud contends that what is commonly called reality is in fact only a very partial aspect of it. It is partial because it amounts to nothing more than the outcome of a rational perception of the world, that is to say, the logically ordered world where everything is assigned a significance and a function. Furthermore, he considers such an approach to reality as highly arbitrary and artificial because, as he attempts to demonstrate, it does not even coincide with the way the mind, once left to its own spontaneity, naturally operates. Logic is the result of an effort and therefore is contrived.

The author's second intention with the scenario is obviously the representation of what he considers the authentic aspect of reality. As irrational as they might be, the images that generate spontaneously in the mind of the character are illustrations of that other aspect of reality. For Artaud believes that behind the logical order lies a hidden life which the mind can detect and recognize, but which reason instantly represses.

Finally, the last and most important purpose of the scenario consists of convincing the audience of the existence of that hidden life. To this effect, Artaud turns to the fantastic and makes use of two elements that characterize the genre, the dream and the occult. Because it expresses the way in which the psyche spontaneously apprehends the world, Artaud uses the structure of a dream, which Penzoldt calls "the language of the subconscious" [Peter Penzoldt, *The Supernatural in Fiction*]. It is also convenient in that it is a familiar and intriguing phenomenon which appeals to the imagination and arouses curiosity as well as interest by revealing unusual and unexpected facets of ordinary things. The occult, on the other hand, is equally convenient because, by suggesting the existence of phenomena that cannot be explained logically, it offers an unusual conception of the world which, therefore, appeals to the imagination.

For Artaud, the occult, like the dream, possesses a reality of its own which the cinema must express: "The cinema is essentially the revelation of an occult world with which it puts us directly into contact." A later scenario, **The 32,** is even more fantastic than **The Eighteen Seconds.**

Here the author imagines a banal setting where strange events will make a sudden eruption into everyday life. His main character, who must initially appear as a very social chemistry teacher, turns into a mad killer whenever he has hallucinations; and, in the end, it becomes known that he has killed thirty-two women and that he may indeed be a vampire. Until this moment the spectators are kept in a state of suspense and fright.

After an initial scene presenting the professor in his classroom, Artaud immediately wants to arouse the curiosity and the apprehension of his audience. He does so in the following segment, where the professor makes an appointment with a young girl for midnight on the next day. From that moment until the arrival of the young girl at the professor's house, the camera must focus on the surrounding environment. First, the dark and quiet town, then the professor's house, its dark and empty rooms, his lab where nothing can be seen besides bottles and strange instruments, the professor himself whose nervous state is evident, and finally the door of his house.

The nature of the scenario coincides exactly with Schneider's description of the fantastic: "The fantastic is not confined to the thrill of terror or to the diabolical. It must also be seen as a step toward things which are beyond appearances and discursive logic." After making use of the dream and the occult, Artaud now employs fear in the same way as in a fantastic story, that is, as a means to manipulate the spectator, to make him vulnerable and receptive to what he sees, while keeping his attention. Fear stimulates the imagination as well as the unconscious and permits the audience to suspend its disbelief without realizing it. Artaud hopes that once fear sets in, the spectator will stop rationalizing what he sees and will perceive the objects presented to him by the camera, not according to their practical or logical functions, but rather according to what their appearance on the screen triggers in his imagination or subconscious: "I can visualize very well all the things of real life reorganized and crystallized according to a revolutionary order which would derive its meaning from nothing but the solicitations of the unconscious."

In other words, Artaud is convinced that if the camera can present the objects with enough force of persuasion, it will be able to create a certain atmosphere conducive to manipulating the spectator's mind or unconscious. The very same ordinary objects will then be looked upon differently, and, as a result, they will take on new and different meanings which, even if they are not logical, will nevertheless make sense for the observer in a process similar to the dream-work. One thing may become something else, familiar objects may become disturbing, threatening, mysterious and yet remain quite real. The professor, for example, may be seen as a solitary alchemist of sorts and his lab a setting for some black magic performance. These various potential aspects that things may take constitute what Artaud calls the "hidden life behind the logical order" or "the occult life of things."

It is now clear that Artaud uses these fantastic devices because he is in the same situation as the writer of a fantastic story. He wants to present an illogical aspect of something that he considers to be reality, and he wants his spectator to accept it as real. Therefore, he must choose a theme which will appeal to the imagination and the unconscious of his audience and which can create an atmosphere of mystery or fear so that the spectator will be sensitive to it, and finally he must present it in the most concrete way possible.

Unfortunately, nothing came out of either of the two film scripts, and, disappointed, Artaud turned again to the theatre with the same purpose in mind: to illustrate the occult nature of reality. The themes remain the same—they all pertain to the fantastic—but Artaud's use of them becomes more sophisticated and more indicative of his conception of reality.

In 1928 Artaud chose to stage Strindberg's *A Dream Play.* In this drama Strindberg creates a world in which people are driven to misery and despair because their hopes and expectations—though reasonable—are repeatedly destroyed. These misfortunes stem from the fact that man does not see his world as it is and therefore cannot fully relate to it. Strindberg shows that too often people organize their environment logically and act accordingly, a phenomenon that invariably leads to disaster because the laws of nature are not always rational. Because things never follow their expectations, the characters are so bewildered that they can no longer differentiate between true and false, real and unreal.

Artaud is attracted to the play because it presents a situation which is both concrete and mysterious, and he attempts to emphasize these two contrasting aspects. He wants the staging to be as concrete as possible so that the reality of the action can never be challenged (in other words, he does not want the play to be looked upon as the representation of a dream or of a fantasy world). He also wants the staging to magnify the mysterious nature of things and, for that reason, he focuses on the objects themselves. But his interpretation is different from Strindberg's.

Strindberg suggests that things are deceptive because their existence is just an empty appearance without meaning or substance. Artaud, on the contrary, wants to convey that they are deceptive because we are unable to capture their full meaning and that consequently they do not answer our expectations. Here again, his staging borrows heavily from the repertoire of the fantastic but for different purposes. He now decides to intrigue the spectator by giving mysterious appearances to the props themselves. He elaborates on Strindberg's idea of using the same objects in different scenes for different purposes, to show that there is no limit to their potential. This effect, along with the atmosphere of mystery that prevails, must give the impression that things possess an occult life. But Artaud goes even further: he hopes to show the alienating effect of this occult life on the characters. He feels that because the environment is constituted of objects, man is compelled to react to them, to give them a meaning in order to organize and thereby dominate his world. However, these objects escape from his grasp as they inevitably take on other meanings. Artaud's intentional manipulation of the play consists in showing that, as a result, man can never dominate his environment and, for this reason, is eventually overwhelmed by it.

Because of financial problems, Artaud was given only one opportunity to stage the play, but very soon afterward he had several projects for new productions. At that time he was working on a translation and an adaptation of Matthew

Lewis's novel *The Monk.* This growing interest in the fantastic and the occult is perhaps best reflected in a proposal he wrote in 1930 for the staging of yet another play by Strindberg, *The Ghost Sonata.* It is also in this proposal that Artaud gives full significance to elements pertaining to the fantastic.

Strindberg's play, *The Ghost Sonata,* is already rich in fantastic elements. After a seemingly realistic opening scene, the atmosphere becomes eerie. Most characters are skeletal figures, moving about in what seems to be a peaceful environment. Their behavior also seems normal until a feeling of fear and death begins to prevail without any obvious reason. For Artaud it is another perfect play to appeal to the imagination because it invites any number of interpretations. It resembles a dream in that it juxtaposes the familiar and the mysterious while not appearing to follow a rational development; and it also conveys "the feeling of something which, without being supernatural, non-human, belongs to some sort of inner reality." Through his interpretation of the play, we can understand that this "inner reality" is in fact the expression of what Artaud views as the true nature of reality, stemming from the relationship between the fantastic and the real, which theatre must manage to communicate.

Whereas Strindberg intrigues his spectator by opposing appearance and reality, Artaud wants to disorient him from the very beginning by focusing on the material objects themselves. He immediately eliminates Strindberg's seemingly realistic opening by suggesting a transparent house where some of the objects inside appear much larger than their normal size. He also wants to make it obvious that the mystery comes from the very presence of these objects and their respective situations vis-à-vis one another. In other words, before the play even begins, the objects must attract the spectator's curiosity and become the agent of the mystery. As the play unfolds, Artaud intends to continue focusing on them to maintain their power over the spectator's interest.

His staging directions revolve around the idea of an overwhelming magical attraction which would emanate from things. In order to make the audience sensitive to this magnetic power, the actors are directed, throughout the play, to appear spellbound. This is where Artaud's interpretation of the play becomes truly fantastic. The actors must give the impression that they are drawn to the house by some superior force: "This feeling of invincible attraction, of bewitchment, or magic, is oppressing, overwhelming." To create such an effect, Artaud suggests that they appear as depersonalized and lifeless near-corpses doomed to revolve mechanically and endlessly around their tiny world. He goes so far as to portray them at times in the form of mannequins.

Clearly, Artaud presents this attraction as all-powerful and universal: there is no escape; and, as in *A Dream Play,* he sees it as a destructive force which deprives each individual of his will power, turns him into a mechanical puppet, and eventually consumes him. No one will escape from destruction and death, and Artaud goes on to illustrate that this destruction is caused by the concrete world which brings about alienation. In his staging, the character of the cook (who provokes the slow death of almost everybody in the house) is represented at all times by a mannequin. Here matter literally takes life in order to destroy, and this is not an isolated instance: the old lady who brings about the death of the man who appeared to be the main character is represented by the form of a mummy coming out of a closet. At crucial moments, Artaud envisions the action as being dictated by the presence of particular objects.

As mentioned earlier, Artaud's work involves discovering a new approach to reality and a new definition of it. His interpretation of *The Ghost Sonata* reveals the main evolution of this effort. To a rational world where everything is labeled and classified, Artaud opposes a world where things are in perpetual motion and therefore impossible to apprehend, let alone explain. When he says that the theatre (and also the cinema) must help us detect the occult life of things, he means precisely that it must teach us how to perceive and acknowledge this constant transformation of things in spite of its irrationality and unpredictability.

Artaud explains the ever-changing nature of things by the existence of cosmic forces running the universe. These forces, which are active and destructive at all times, constitute for Artaud the "point" mentioned by Breton from which "life and death, the real and the imaginary, the past and the future . . . cease to be perceived as contradictory." The most fundamental element of reality becomes, then, the recognition of the existence of such a cosmic fatality which accounts for all phenomena. Artaud is of the opinion that man can achieve an awareness of this destructive fatality through careful observation of his relationship with the physical world, and it is the purpose of his theatre to provoke such an awareness. This is why Artaud calls it a Theatre of Cruelty.

It is cruel because it shows man that his method of apprehending the world—namely reason—has brought about nothing but false assumptions and frustrations, as evidenced by Strindberg's two plays. It is also cruel because it compels man to realize his inability to explain and control his environment due to its constantly changing nature. He must accept the fact that the least he can do is to be aware of these changes. Finally, it is most cruel because it places man, forever alone and defenseless, before this uncontrollable and mysterious fatality which will inevitably destroy him as it has destroyed the characters in *The Ghost Sonata*. Artaud expresses this theatrical ambition in one sentence: The ultimate goal of the theatre is "to reintroduce into each theatrical gesture the idea of a cosmic cruelty without which there would be neither life nor reality."

In conclusion, we can say that Artaud's theatre is metaphysical in purpose and fantastic in nature. Moreover, aside from the author's use of such motifs as dreams, ghosts, vampires, and magic, it would be helpful to point out briefly some general characteristics which relate this theatre to the fantastic genre as defined by such critics as Todorov, Caillois, Rabkin, and Schneider.

All four agree that the fantastic is based on the existence of mysterious and sometimes frightening phenomena which disturb the familiar order of the world and which cannot be explained logically. Schneider and Rabkin emphasize the fact that the fantastic is a means of escape that allows the individual to explore the other side of himself, his imagination and unconscious. Schneider also points out that the fantastic author's originality consists in the fact that he does not change the nature of the outside world and of the objects he uses, but instead multiplies their significance and power. Artaud's theatre shares all these characteristics.

However, it does not seem to follow Rabkin's theory of a reversal of perspective. Artaud's theatre is not "reality turned 180° around." According to Rabkin, the fantastic presup-

poses the presence of two contradictory orders: the natural order with its well-known laws and the supernatural order with its unknown laws. Artaud (who dislikes the term "supernatural" because of its misleading religious connotations) does not see the fantastic as the opposition of the natural and the supernatural, but as the coexistence of these two complementary aspects of the same reality. The fantastic for Artaud is not the reversal of reality but one aspect of it, its hidden and therefore unknown facet, because, as Todorov says, "If a fantastic event is part of reality, it means that reality operates according to laws unknown to us." [Tzvetan Todorov, *Introduction à la littérature fantastique*].

As a matter of fact, Artaud's theatre appears most fantastic when compared with Todorov's definition of the genre. Todorov sees the fantastic as a hesitation on the part of the individual whose familiar world has been disturbed by illogical phenomena. Artaud's theatre can be seen then as provoking the ultimate hesitation. It not only reveals the presence of these phenomena which baffle all rational explanation, but it also shows the individual that his life is dramatically altered by them in a way that will always escape his understanding and consequently will leave him forever in a state of powerless hesitation in front of his own destiny. (pp. 113-20)

Jean-Pierre Lalande, "Artaud's Theatre of Cruelty and the Fantastic," in Aspects of Fantasy: Selected Essays from the Second International Conference on the Fantastic in Literature and Film, *edited by William Coyle, Greenwood Press, 1986, pp. 113-20.*

FURTHER READING

Balakian, Anna. "To Transform the World." In her *Surrealism: The Road to the Absolute*, rev. ed., pp. 231-44. New York: Dutton, 1970.
    Includes a brief, negative appraisal of Artaud, whom Balakian calls the "dark angel of Surrealism, representing the initial pessimism and revolt of the group, rather than its later manifestation of constructive poetic vision."

Cadden, Michael. "Artaud at the Crossroads." *Theater* 9, No. 3 (Summer 1978): 60-6.
    Discusses Artaud's affinity to the doctrines of Gnosticism.

Campbell, R. J. "On Saying the Unsayable." *Critical Quarterly* 22, No. 3 (Autumn 1980): 69-77.
    Relates Artaud's notion of the expression of " 'metaphysical' ideas which elude verbal language" to similar ideas found in the works of dramatist Samuel Beckett and philosopher Ludwig Wittgenstein.

Caws, Mary Ann. "Artaud's Myth of Motion." In her *The Inner Theatre of Recent French Poetry*, pp. 125-40. Princeton: Princeton University Press, 1972.
    Discusses the importance of myth and movement in Artaud's dramatic theory.

Chafer, A. D. "Antonin Artaud and the Critique of Language." *Nottingham French Studies* 19, No. 1 (May 1980): 1-21.
    Reassesses Artaud's contributions to drama, suggesting that critics who study his work in terms of Western theater are missing the significance of his work, which lies in his rejection "of the type of language, with the arbitrary nature of its representation of reality, that is the primary means of expression of this form of theatre."

Corti, Victor. Introduction to *To End God's Judgment,* by Antonin Artaud. *Tulane Drama Review* 9, No. 3 (Spring 1965): 56-60.

Traces the biographical circumstances surrounding Artaud's writing of the radio drama *To End God's Judgment,* its censorship and private presentation in 1948, and its publication history.

Croyden, Margaret. "Artaud's Plague." In her *Lunatics, Lovers and Poets: The Contemporary Experimental Theatre,* pp. 55-71. New York: McGraw-Hill, 1974.

Introductory sketch tracing Artaud's involvement in Parisian experimental theater, his interest in Balinese drama, his formulation of the principles of the Theater of Cruelty, and his influence on dramatists of the 1950s and 1960s.

Demaitre, Ann. "Artaud and the Occult Tradition." In *Literature and the Occult: Essays in Comparative Literature,* edited by Luanne Frank, pp. 111-24. Arlington: University of Texas, 1977.

Discusses the relationship between various occult and mystical traditions, including Gnosticism and the Cabbala, and Artaud's writings and worldview.

Derrida, Jacques. "La Parole Soufflée" and "The Theater of Cruelty and the Closure of Representation." In his *Writing and Difference,* translated by Alan Bass, pp. 169-95 and pp. 232-50. Chicago: University of Chicago Press, 1978.

Examines Artaud's poetic language and drama theories.

Dufresne, Nicole. "Toward a Dramatic Theory of Play: Artaud, Arrabal, and the Ludic Mode of Being," pp. 181-91. In *Myths and Realities of Contemporary French Theater: Comparative Views,* edited by Patricia M. Hopkins and Wendell M. Aycock. Lubbock: Texas Tech Press, 1985.

Discusses Artaud's theater in terms of modern concepts of ritual, play, and drama.

Flitterman-Lewis, Sandy. "The Image and the Spark: Dulac and Artaud Reviewed." In *Dada and Surrealist Film,* edited by Rudolf E. Kuenzli, pp. 110-27. New York: Willis Locker & Owens, 1987.

Traces the conflict between Artaud and director Germaine Dulac over the realization of Artaud's scenario *The Seashell and the Clergyman.* Flitterman-Lewis attributes their clash to a fundamental opposition of aesthetics, with Artaud representing Surrealism and Dulac exemplifying the Symbolist tradition.

Greene, Naomi. "Artaud and Film: A Reconsideration." *Cinema Journal* 23, No. 4 (Summer 1984): 28-40.

Examines several aspects of Artaud's film aesthetics, including the relation of his ideas to Surrealism, his insistence that film art not be representational, his debate with Germaine Dulac over *The Seashell and the Clergyman,* and his preoccupation with the theme of the double.

Hayman, Ronald. *Artaud and After.* Oxford and New York: Oxford University Press, 1977, 189 p.

Biography written in conjunction with the National Book League exhibition "Artaud and After" (19 October–12 November 1977) in London. Hayman provides biographical discussion of Artaud's theater and literary careers, a catalog of exhibits, bibliography, and chronology of Artaud's work in theater and film.

Hellman, Helen. "Hallucination and Cruelty in Artaud and Ghelderode." *The French Review* 41, No. 1 (October 1967): 1-10.

Uses the "hallucinatory tradition" in literature and art—represented by the works of Hieronymus Bosch, Pieter Brueghel, and Charles Baudelaire, among others—as a context in which to compare the dramaturgy of Artaud and Michel de Ghelderode (1898-1962).

Hivnor, Mary Otis. "Barrault and Artaud." *Partisan Review* 15, No. 3 (March 1948): 332-38.

Discusses the mutual influence between Artaud and French stage director Jean-Louis Barrault.

Kenny, Neil. "Changing the Languages of Theatre: A Comparison of Brecht and Artaud." *Journal of European Studies* 13, No. 51, part 3 (September 1983): 169-86.

Compares the careers of Artaud and German dramatist Bertolt Brecht, admitting fundamental opposition of the aim of each in transforming the structure of modern theater, but finding similarities in the way each sought to effect change. According to Kenny, "Both men restructure the theatre around a framework of interplay; speech comes to constitute only one of many dramatic languages, the others being produced by the dialogue, or dissonance, between components such as other verbal forms, music, costume, the audience, the actor and his body."

Lyons, John D. "Artaud: Intoxication and Its Double." *Yale French Studies* 50 (1974): 120-29.

Discusses Artaud's attempt to formulate a new artistic language for the Theater of Cruelty in order to re-create on a cultural level the fragmentation and reintegration of the self induced by opium.

Marowitz, Charles. "Notes on the Theatre of Cruelty." *Tulane Drama Review* 11, No. 2 (Winter 1966): 152-72.

Recounts the explorations of Artaudian theater staged by the experimental theater group formed by Marowitz and Peter Brook in 1963 in affiliation with the Royal Shakespeare Company.

———. "Artaud at Rodez." *Evergreen Review* 12, No. 53 (April 1968): 65-7, 81-4, 86.

Sympathetic account of the events surrounding Artaud's institutionalization at Rodez which extensively quotes the doctor who treated him there.

Martin, Mick. "Theatre of Cruelty: Artaud's Impossible Double." *Nottingham French Studies* 22, No. 1 (May 1983): 52-64.

Discusses the failure in practice of Artaud's Theater of Cruelty, the fault of which, Martin suggests, lies in "the nature of the proposals themselves" not in the misinterpretation or misapplication of those principles by playwrights. According to Martin, Artaud's genius is "flawed by a logical inconsistency which lies at the very core of his theories."

Robinson, Ione. "The Death of a Poet: Antonin Artaud." *Renaissance and Modern Studies* 22 (1978): 63-86.

Personal reminiscence of Artaud's final month, including the controversial broadcast of his radio play *To End God's Judgment,* his home at Ivry, and his death and funeral.

Saillet, Maurice. "Close to Antonin Artaud." *Evergreen Review* 4, No. 13 (May-June 1960): 79-83.

Appreciative sketch recounting Artaud's poetry reading and lecture at the Vieux-Colombier Theatre in January 1947.

Savacool, John K. "More about the Metaphore of Cruelty: An Essay Composed to Please Antonin Artaud." In *From Dante to García Marquez: Studies in Romance Literatures and Linguistics,* edited by Gene H. Bell-Villada, Antonio Giménez, and George Pistorius, pp. 286-96. Williamstown, Mass.: Williams College, 1987.

Overview of important concepts of Artaud's Theater of Cruelty.

Thompson, Peter S. "The Temptation of Antonin Artaud." *Romance Notes* 21, No. 1 (Fall 1980): 42-7.

Defines key terms used in Artaud's definition of theater of cruelty, including his use of "tentation" ("temptation") and "le vide" ("the void"), and how the use of these terms reflects his artistic values.

Tonelli, Franco. "From Cruelty to Theatre: Antonin Artaud and the Marquis de Sade." *Comparative Drama* 3, No. 1 (Spring 1969): 79-86.

Discusses Artaud's Theater of Cruelty in relation to aesthetic and philosophical concepts utilized in the works of Marquis de Sade (1740-1814), particularly associating Artaud's theater with Sade's novels.

Virmaux, Alain. "Artaud and Film." *Tulane Drama Review* 11, No. 1 (Fall 1966): 154-65.

Recounts Artaud's role in creating the film *The Seashell and the Clergyman,* the controversy surrounding its production, and the relation of the film to other Surrealist films of the era.

Weightman, John. "Saint Artaud." In his *Concept of the Avant-Garde: Explorations in Modernism,* pp. 145-52. London: Alcove Press, 1973.

Reprint of 9 January 1965 *Times Literary Supplement* article tracing Artaud's life and theories, occasioned by performances of Peter Weiss's *Marat/Sade* produced at the London's Aldwych Theater by Peter Brook and greatly inspired by Artaud's principles.

Gamaliel Bradford

1863-1932

American biographer, diarist, essayist, dramatist, novelist, and poet.

Bradford is best known for his development of the "psychograph," a type of biography that focuses on analyzing personality rather than providing a chronological account of a subject's life. He wrote numerous studies of political, literary, and intellectual figures, including Robert E. Lee, Charles Darwin, Benedict Arnold, and Emily Dickinson. Bradford's innovation in this field led John Macy to call him "the supreme biographer of our time."

Born into a wealthy New England family, Bradford grew up in Boston. He was a sickly child and remained a semi-invalid all his life, suffering from various health problems including severe vertigo, sciatica, rheumatism, and a number of intestinal disorders. He enrolled at Harvard in 1882 but withdrew after only six weeks because of illness and was privately tutored in Greek, Latin, and mathematics. Married in 1886, Bradford enjoyed a comfortable standard of living as a result of financial support provided by his father, a prosperous businessman. Initially Bradford wanted to be a creative writer but was unsuccessful in attempts to publish his numerous plays, novels, and poems. In 1888, the *New Princeton Review* accepted his essay on Ralph Waldo Emerson, and he began to concentrate on biographical writing. His first book, *Types of American Character,* was published in 1895 and has been viewed as an early example of his interest in character analysis for its consideration of such personality types as "The American Pessimist" and "The American Man of Letters." Following the publication of this work, Bradford published the novels *The Private Tutor, Between Two Masters,* and *Matthew Porter* and the poetry collection *A Pageant of Life,* and contributed essays to the *Atlantic Monthly* and other periodicals. His first important biographical work, a collection of essays about Robert E. Lee which appeared in 1912, exhibited Bradford's psychographic method of biography. During the next two decades he employed this technique in such works as *Damaged Souls*—whose subjects, including Benedict Arnold and P. T. Barnum, were men whom Bradford found to have tragic character flaws—and *Daughters of Eve,* a collection of essays on illustrious women from the seventeenth to the twentieth centuries, including Catherine the Great, George Sand, and Sarah Bernhardt. Bradford died in 1932.

Bradford coined the term "psychograph" early in his career, then discovered it had been used by George Saintsbury to describe the works of the French critic Charles Augustin Sainte-Beuve (1804-1869). Most critics suggest that while Bradford was influenced by the biographical writings of Sainte-Beuve, the method he developed was ultimately his own. Believing that certain fundamental aspects of a person's character remain constant throughout life, Bradford sought to uncover those traits through an examination of his subject's thoughts, feelings, and actions, and then to compose an integrated analysis of the person's character. Psychography thus differs from biography in that it is organized topically, according to aspects of a subject's personality, instead of

chronologically. Bradford has been praised for anticipating elements of psychoanalytic theory and other psychological concepts in his works, but he believed there was an important difference between the two approaches: all of his psychographs focused on an individual, while psychology emphasized generalizations about human nature.

Bradford based his psychographs on primary source materials, examining the autobiographies, correspondence, and diaries of his subjects, and critics have praised his apt selection of detail, skillful integration of fact and analysis, and insights into his subjects' personalities. Most commentators, including Bradford himself, prefer his shorter studies, which are collected in various volumes, to his longer works, such as *Darwin* and *D. L. Moody: A Worker in Souls,* maintaining that the additional length and the chapter divisions in his book-length studies result in less integrated interpretations of his subjects. His portraits of literary figures, such as William Cowper and Emily Dickinson, are generally considered stronger than his portrayals of military leaders and statesmen, such as Theodore Roosevelt and Woodrow Wilson. Critics agree that Bradford's later works, including *Bare Souls, Wives,* and *Daughters of Eve,* are superior to his earlier ones, such as *Confederate Portraits* and *Union Portraits,* as he continued to refine his technique throughout his career. With psychography, Bradford developed an innovative method of examining personality and broadened the scope of biographical writing.

(See also *Dictionary of Literary Biography,* Vol. 17.)

PRINCIPAL WORKS

Types of American Character (essays) 1895
A Pageant of Life (poetry) 1904
The Private Tutor (novel) 1904
Between Two Masters (novel) 1906
Matthew Porter (novel) 1908
Lee the American (biography) 1912
Confederate Portraits (biography) 1914
Portraits of Women (biography) 1916
Union Portraits (biography) 1916
A Naturalist of Souls: Studies in Psychography (biography) 1917; revised edition, 1926
Unmade in Heaven (drama) 1917 [first publication]
Portraits of American Women (biography) 1919
A Prophet of Joy (poetry) 1920
Shadow Verses (poetry) 1920
American Portraits, 1875-1900 (biography) 1922
Damaged Souls (biography) 1923
Bare Souls (biography) 1924
Her Only Way (novel) 1924; published in journal *The Stratford Monthly*
The Soul of Samuel Pepys (biography) 1924
Wives (biography) 1925
Darwin (biography) 1926
D. L. Moody: A Worker in Souls (biography) 1927
Life and I: An Autobiography of Humanity (essays) 1928
As God Made Them: Portraits of Some Nineteenth-Century Americans (biography) 1929
Daughters of Eve (biography) 1930
The Quick and the Dead (biography) 1931
Biography and the Human Heart (essays) 1932
Saints and Sinners (biography) 1932
The Journal of Gamaliel Bradford, 1883-1932 (journal) 1933
The Letters of Gamaliel Bradford (letters) 1934

GARLAND GREEVER (essay date 1912)

[*In the following excerpt from a review of* Lee the American, *Greever praises Bradford's portrayal of the Confederate general.*]

Mr. Bradford . . . has the sense of Lee's character as a part of our national inheritance. He regards it not as a sectional but as our common possession. His dedication reads:

> To the young men both of the North and of the South who can make or unmake the future of the America of Washington, of Lincoln, and of Lee.

Three other passages that I cannot forbear quoting at length show the depth of his insight and the rightness of his attitude:

> *Abandon all these local animosities, and make your sons Americans.* What finer sentence could be inscribed on the pedestal of Lee's statue than that? Americans! All the local animosities forgiven and forgotten, can we not say that he too, though dying

only five years after the terrible struggle, died a loyal, a confident, a hopeful American, and one of the very greatest?

· · · · ·

One was a man of the eighteenth century, the other of the nineteenth; one of the old America, the other of the new. Grant stands for our modern world, with its rough business habits, its practical energy, its desire to do things no matter how, its indifference to the sweet grace of ceremony and dignity and courtesy. Lee had the traditions of an older day, not only its high beliefs, but its grave stateliness, its feeling that the way of doing things was almost as much as the thing done. In short, Grant's America was the America of Lincoln, Lee's the America of Washington. It is in part because of this difference, and because I would fain believe that without loss of the one we may some day regain something of the other, that I have given so much thought to the portrayal of Lee's character and life.

· · · · ·

America in the twentieth century worships success, is too ready to test character by it, to be blind to those faults success hides, to those qualities that can do without it. Here was a man who failed grandly, a man who said that "human virtue should be equal to human calamity," and showed that it could be equal to it, and so, without pretense, without display, without self-consciousness, left an example that future Americans may study with profit as long as there is an America.

A young sophomore was once summoned and gently admonished that only patience and industry would prevent the failure that would inevitably come to him through college and through life.

"But, General, you failed," remarked the sophomore, with the inconceivable ineptitude of sophomores.

"I hope that you may be more fortunate than I," was the tranquil answer.

Literature can add nothing to that.

In reaching an understanding of Lee's character, Mr. Bradford has discarded legend and engaged in exhaustive research. "A complete bibliography of sources," he declares, "would be practically a bibliography of the war literature both Northern and Southern." Yet he does not present . . . in epic narrative a multitude of facts about Lee's career. Nor does his familiarity with the background of general conditions upon which Lee's actions were projected—his knowledge of the social and moral issues, and of the larger phases of the technical and administrative problems—lure him from his peculiar theme. Happily, we are promised the fruitage of these by-studies in a subsequent volume, ***Portraits of the Confederacy.*** Wise readers will not expect the forthcoming studies to reveal any such ideal as Lee. The other leaders had merits and weaknesses: we may be sure Mr. Bradford will be blind to neither. He will show the men as they were,—and that is all we can ask.

Here, as I have suggested, Mr. Bradford has made it his purpose to portray Lee's soul. He has shown this in the various relations suggested by the titles of all the chapters save one: "The Great Decision," "Lee and Davis," "Lee and the Confederate Government," "Lee and his Army," "Lee and Jackson," "Lee in Battle," "Lee as a General," "Lee's Social and Domestic Life," "Lee's Spiritual Life," and "Lee after the War." It will be seen that Mr. Bradford falls in with the new school of writers who in their treatment of historical figures lay stress upon character rather than upon deeds. So vital and so valuable is this aim, and so successful is Mr. Bradford in carrying it out, that readers will be especially interested in his own comments on his method of approach. These comprise an attractive and illuminating appendix, "Lee and Psychography." He says:

> What I have aimed at in this book is the portrayal of a soul. We live in an age of names, and a new name has recently been invented—psychography. This means, I suppose, an art which is not psychology, because it deals with individuals, not general principles, and is not biography, because it swings clear of the formal sequence of chronological detail, and uses only those deeds and words and happenings that are spiritually significant.

After explaining the dangers, both subjective and objective, that threaten the psychographer's poise, he maintains that the chief advantage in studying great men is in finding their resemblance to ordinary mortals. He parts company with the believers in Lee's absolute perfection when he shows us that Lee was the barest trifle aloof, and that the invasion proclamations were prompted by sound common-sense as well as by lofty principles. But the purpose is not to belittle his subject. It is rather to inspire us. The process need not be, as might seem, disillusioning. Mr. Bradford's method is that of thorough sanity; yet he finds Lee "a human being as lovable as any that ever lived." "I have loved him," he declares, "and I may say that his influence upon my own life, though I came to him late, has been as deep and as inspiring as any I have ever known."

Mr. Bradford's chapter on "The Great Decision" shows us that Lee's actions were guided "strictly and loftily by conscience." The severest test came at the outbreak of hostilities. Then, as always, Lee excluded personal considerations; but he was not satisfied with either party. "While I wish to do what is right," he wrote, "I am unwilling to do what is wrong at the bidding of the South or of the North." He felt that the destruction of the old balance between local and central authority would "be an end to Republican government in this country"; on the other hand, he considered slavery "a moral and political evil"—an evil which a decision for the South would force him to uphold. "It is precisely this network of moral conditions," affirms Mr. Bradford, "that makes his heroic struggle so pathetic, so appealing, so irresistibly human. . . . Lee is one of the most striking, one of the noblest tragic figures the world ever produced." The most perfect comment on his life is his own statement that to do our duty is "all the pleasure, all the comfort, all the glory we can enjoy in this world."

The chapters on Lee's relations with Davis, with the Confederate government, with his army, and with Jackson, are absorbing. Of these, the first two show his fine modesty and courtesy; they also show his patience under trying difficulties that lead Mr. Bradford to write, "He was never free." The third explains his extraordinary hold upon his men through the confidence he inspired, his personal magnetism, his own love for his soldiers, and his recognition of the fact that he was leading an army of American freemen. The fourth shows his wisdom in dealing with the most inflexible personalities.

Nothing is more characteristic of him than the suggestion through which he reconciled differences between Jackson and A. P. Hill: "He who has been the most aggrieved can be the most magnanimous and make the first overture of peace."

The chapter on "Lee in Battle" reveals to us again that nice balance of Lee's gifts which accounts for Alexander's dictum "Probably no man ever commanded an army and at the same time so entirely commanded himself." The treatment of "Lee as a General" shows the enormous difficulties with which he had to contend, and finds four outstanding military qualities: organizing power, boldness, rapidity and perhaps energy of action, and a knowledge of human nature. The last quality enabled him to deal effectively with subordinate and foeman. Mr. Bradford thinks it the chief of his military merits, and hence believes Colonel Henderson's words are the most satisfying eulogy: "He was the clearest-sighted soldier in America."

In "Lee's Social and Domestic Life" we see his dignity, not stiff and pompous, but natural, and softened by the inborn deference of the true democrat. He had charm and thoroughgoing kindliness; his inherent moderation bordered a little on reserve. In "Lee's Spiritual Life" we learn that the bent of his character was "absolutely moral and practical." He had passions and sensibilities, but he kept them under control. Perhaps he was a little too precise, a little too scrupulous; yet we like to think of him as worrying a little after Gettysburg because he could not lay his hands upon officials to whom he might pay his taxes. He had no desire for rank or honors, no jealousy, no impatience under criticism, no wish to justify himself at the expense of others even when those others were at fault. His religion was "a pure and vivifying light"; it was compact of love. God was the cardinal fact of his life.

"Lee before the War" is the only chapter which is largely narrative. It further traces early influences and the growth of high motives which were to govern him so thoroughly when his role became conspicuous. "Lee after the War" presents a period as instructive and inspiring as any in his life. Whatever he did was sure, as Grant asserted, to have tremendous influence in the South. What, then, shall we say of his restraint, of his hopefulness, of the fact that, "so far as his limited opportunities will allow us to judge, he was a thinker in education as he was a thinker in war"? His programme was one of constructive labor: "Tell them they must all set to work, and if they cannot do what they prefer, do what they can." (pp. 160-62)

[Mr. Bradford's *Lee the American*] must be considered an altogether indispensable book. Its discriminating analysis is supported by a wealth of humanized evidence and vital illustration, and it gives a superb and convincing portrayal of the actual soul of Lee. One wonders as he reads it whether the resurrection of human character is not almost the equal of great creative writing—especially when the character resurrected is one so noble as is here portrayed. (p. 162)

Garland Greever, "A Heritage of American Personality," in The Dial, *Chicago, Vol. LII, No. 617, March 1, 1912, pp. 159-62.*

GAMALIEL BRADFORD   (essay date 1915)

[*In the following excerpt from an essay originally written in 1915, Bradford outlines the purpose and methodology of psychography.*]

Some one asked Zola why he used the term, "Naturalism," when there was nothing about his work that was essentially different from realism or from other literary forms that had been employed for thousands of years before his time. "I know all that," he said. "You are perfectly right. But I needed a name to attract the attention of the public. When I repeat the word over and over, it is bound at last to make people think there is something in it. It is like driving a nail. The first blow does not amount to much; but as you add another, and another, and another, in the end you make progress."

I confess that my use of the word, "Psychography," was at first something like Zola's use of "Naturalism." It was not even my own original invention, though I had coined it for myself before I discovered that it had been used by Professor Saintsbury a few years earlier in discussing the work of Sainte-Beuve. I did not suppose that it meant anything particularly new, but it seemed to sum up processes that have been rather vaguely employed before and to give them a name which might be useful in attracting the attention of the jaded, overloaded American reader.

I should not now claim that the word meant anything new in substance. All literary and historical methods have been employed over and over again and the most we can hope to do is to improve and modify them. But the more I practise psychography, the more it seems to me to represent definite phases of literary or historical production, phases worthy not only of a distinct name, but of careful study and consideration.

I can best introduce what I have in mind by making clear one or two things that psychography is not. In the first place, it is not at all properly conveyed or suggested by the word, portrait. I have hitherto used this term, because it has the excellent authority of Sainte-Beuve and many others, and because I have not yet found courage to talk about "psychographs," and even if I had, publishers and editors have not. But "portraits" is very unsatisfactory. To carry the terms of one art into another is always misleading, and I have experienced this in the complaint of many critics that as a portrait painter I could present a man at only one moment of his career, that I depicted his character in only one phase, one situation, one set of conditions and circumstances.

Now the aim of psychography is precisely opposite to this. Out of the perpetual flux of actions and circumstances that constitutes a man's whole life, it seeks to extract what is essential, what is permanent and so vitally characteristic. The painter can depict a face and figure only as he sees them at one particular moment, though, in proportion to the depth and power of his art, he can suggest, more or less subtly, the vast complex of influences that have gone to building up that face and figure. The psychographer endeavours to grasp as many particular moments as he can and to give his reader not one but the enduring sum total of them all.

But, it is urged, if the object is thus chronological completeness, in what respect does psychography differ from biography? Simply that biography is bound to present an elaborate sequence of dates, events, and circumstances, of which some are vital to the analysis of the individual subject, but many are merely required to make the narrative complete. From this vast and necessary material of biography, psychography selects only that which is indispensable for its particular purpose, and as the accumulation of books becomes yearly great-

er and greater, it seems as if this principle of condensation must become more and more pressing in its appeal.

Finally, psychography differs from psychology in that the latter does not deal primarily with individuals, but with general principles, and uses individuals only for the discovery, development, and illustration of those principles.

Psychography, then, is the attempt to portray character, and in discussing psychography we must evidently begin with a clear understanding of what character means. The reader will perhaps pardon my rehearsing the no doubt crude metaphysical analysis which I have found satisfactory for my own purposes. Character is quite distinct from individuality. Individuality, so far as we appear to others in this world, is a vast complex, based primarily upon the body, the material, physical organisation, and consisting of all the past history of that organisation, its name and all its actions and utterances in their sequence and concatenation with other circumstances and events.

It is, of course, perfectly evident that no words, no possible abstract instruments of thinking, will ever suffice to render this individuality in its completeness. The brush of the painter can at once attain a result that is impossible to language, and although the artist in colour never conveys anything like the fulness of individuality, yet the physical portrayal he achieves is to all intents and purposes distinct from the portrayal of any other human being, and so far individual.

But we poor workers in words have to toil vaguely after a result which is far less conclusive and satisfying. Even the concrete method, employed by the novelist and dramatist, of letting a personage do his own deeds and speak his own words, rarely makes any approach to complete individuality. No single human action, as verbally recorded, can be confined to one human being more than to another, and scarcely any complication of actions. In the same way no word or combination of words is distinctively yours or mine, or Cæsar's or Napoleon's. A thousand women might have murdered Duncan as Lady Macbeth did, and a million men might have said with Hamlet, "To be or not to be, that is the question."

Fortunately, in the weltering chaos which is totaled by the word, individuality, there is one clue that we can seize, though it is frail and insecure. As we observe the actions of different men, we find that they follow certain comparatively definite lines, which we call habits, that is, the same man will perform over and over again actions, and speak words, which have a basis of resemblance to each other, though the basis is often obscure and elusive. And back of the words and actions we assume from our own experience motives of sensation and emotion, which serve to strengthen and confirm such resemblance. On this vague basis of fact is built the whole fabric of our study and knowledge of our fellow men. The generalisation of these habits of action, sometimes expressing itself very obscurely and imperfectly for the acute observer in features and manifestations of the body, constitutes what we call qualities. And the complex of these qualities in turn forms the fleeting and uncertain total which we sum up in the word, character. An honest man is one who does honest actions. A simple man is one who does simple actions. An ambitious man does ambitious actions. A cruel man, cruel actions. And so on, almost without limit. The importance of these quality terms is so enormous in our practical daily lives that we are apt, as with many other abstractions, to look upon them as mysterious entities, functions, elements, in some way existing by themselves and entering into the very fibre and substance of the man's inmost soul. And so far as his habits of action are ingrained, vital, rooted deep down in the solid foundations of education and inheritance, these words which express habit are permanent and significant, but their significance comes only from the acts they generalise and the inferred feelings and emotions that prompt those acts, nothing more.

Character, then, is the sum of qualities or generalised habits of action. Psychography is the condensed, essential, artistic presentation of character. And it is now perfectly obvious how frail, how infirm, how utterly unreliable is the material basis upon which psychography rests. First, before we can analyse and generalise a man's habits of speech and action, we must deal with the historical record of that speech and action. And here, of course, we meet the ordinary difficulties in regard to accuracy, which have become so many and so glaring in the light of modern historical research. Most of our knowledge of men's actions in the past depends upon the testimony of others. That testimony, when limited in amount, is extremely uncertain, as shown by the fact that, when abundant, it is usually conflicting. In the small number of cases in which we have the testimony of the man himself, we are apt to be more puzzled and perplexed than when we are without it. As with actions, so with words. It is rare indeed that we can be sure of having even the substance of a man's speech correctly reported to us. Yet for the interpretation of his character it is often of the utmost importance that we should have his exact language, and, if possible, the tone and gesture and emphasis that double or halve its significance.

But these concrete, historical difficulties are but the smallest part of the problem we have to deal with in psychography. Supposing that we have the most reliable record of a man's deeds and utterances, we have advanced but a very little way in establishing the qualities of his character. What actions are just, what actions are generous, what actions are cruel, what actions are foolish? To determine these points requires wide reflection on the bearing of actions in reference to all sorts of conditions and circumstances, and on a man's own judgment and others' judgment of that bearing. The result of such reflection will be different in different minds, and the colour than an action assumes to you will be very different from what it assumes to me or to the next critic who considers it.

Further, the generalisation of actions is always imperfect. A man may do one or several kindly actions, yet not have the essential habit of kindliness. A man whose ordinary life runs in the conventional groove of honesty may meet some sudden crisis with an entire reversal of his honest habit. The most minute study, the widest experience in the investigation of human actions and their motives, only makes us feel more and more the shifting, terrible uncertainty of the ground under our feet.

The natural question then arises, of what use is psychography? Why perplex and torment one's self with the study of character, when the difficulty is so great and the result so uncertain, when we seem to begin with nothing and to end with nothing, to be weaving a skein of shadows into a fabric of clouds?

The answer is first, that there is no possible study more fascinating. The problems of character, in others and in ourselves, are teasing us for solution every moment of our lives. The naturalist spends years in studying the life and habits of a bird,

or a frog, or a beetle. But every beetle is a beetle, and when you have studied the class, the individual is practically nothing. With the human class every individual is infinitely varied from every other and the field of study is as inexhaustible as it is absorbing.

Moreover, if psychography is an impossible science, it is a necessary one. The psychographer is not a curious dilettante, investigating odd facts to pass an idle hour. The one form of knowledge that is practical above all others is the knowledge of ourselves and of other men. We are all psychographers from the cradle. The child, almost before it can speak, learns just what will affect its father or its mother, and what will not. In our business and in our pleasure, in our hope and in our fear, in our toil and in our repose, we are always considering, examining, calculating upon the action of others. We miscalculate and mistake and blunder disastrously again and again, but we still pursue our instinctive psychography, because it is more important than anything else to the successful conduct and even to the mere living of our lives.

Of course, in the vast chaos of individual action and speech, certain elements are far more significant than others, and it is largely in the discovery and interpretation of these elements that the claim of psychography consists. A man may deliver a formal oration, carefully framed after conventional models and tell us practically nothing about himself. I long since learned that such material as the fifteen volumes of Sumner's collected works was of little or no value for my purposes. Again, a careless word, spoken with no intention whatever, a mere gesture, the lifting of the hand or the turning of the head, may fling open a wide window into a man's inmost heart.

When one gets to watching for these subtle indications of character, the delight of them is inexpressible. All history and biography are strewn with them, but in astonishingly varying abundance. *The Diary of Pepys* contains new light on the writer's soul in every page and paragraph. The equally extensive *Diary of Madame D'Arblay* is artificial, literary, external, and tells comparatively little about Madame D'Arblay herself. General Sherman wears his heart upon his sleeve. Material for depicting him is so plenty that there is only the difficulty of selecting. General Lee conceals himself instinctively behind a barrier of formal reserve, and it is only by long study that one comes across such vivid revelations as his remark at Fredericksburg, "It is well that war is so terrible, or else we should grow too fond of it."

Of course these revelations of soul are not confined to books or to historical personages. The men and women we meet in casual daily intercourse are always telling—or concealing— the same story of what they are and what they are not. One or two apparently trifling instances have stuck in my memory from their singular significance. A man's wife was caught unexpectedly, in travelling, with little or no money, and obliged to explain her difficulties to the hotel keeper and telegraph to her husband for assistance. The husband sent it at once, but his comment was, "To think that *my* wife should be stranded in a hotel without money." Just reflect upon all that little sentence tells of the person who wrote it. Again, I was explaining to a friend a terrible disaster that had happened to another friend and I was myself so agitated and overcome that I could not make anything approaching a lucid story. My hearer was dumfounded by my condition and after a moment's effort to gather what I was driving at, his first word was, "Tell me, at least, does this trouble concern me?" Think of the depths of human nature revealed in that! Take still another instance. A most worthy, affectionate, devoted husband, who was trying to do all that could be done for an invalid wife, used often to remark, "When I stand by her grave, I do not wish to have anything to reproach myself with." Simple, natural words, perhaps, yet they seem to me distinctly significant of a certain type of man.

So, every day, every hour, every minute, we are all of us writing our own psychographs, at any rate piling up ample material for some one else to do it for us.

It is sometimes urged that attention to such minute details in the conduct of historical personages, not to speak of our neighbours, savours of mere gossip. We degrade history and biography, it is said, when we make them depend on careless words and unregarded actions. But if it be true, as I have suggested, that the knowledge of others' characters is absolutely vital to living our own lives and that just such careless words and unregarded actions give us this knowledge of character, then assuredly it is right we should observe them, no matter how trivial and apparently insignificant.

It must be admitted that psychography is always in danger of degenerating into gossip. The difference between the two is simply that gossip springs from the desire to saturate our own emptiness with the lives of others, from a mere idle curiosity about things and persons, bred by an utter lack of interest in ourselves. Gossip makes no distinction of significance between different facts, but gapes wide for all, only more eagerly for those that offer more violent and abnormal distraction. Psychography picks, chooses, and rejects; in a bushel of chaff finds only a grain or two of wheat, but treasures that wheat as precious and invaluable.

Thus far I have spoken of psychography as a science, that is, of the material with which the psychographer deals. Before I touch upon psychography as an art, let me turn for a few moments to the writer from whom I think the psychographer has most to learn, Sainte-Beuve.

It is curious that Sainte-Beuve should have been all his life the most exquisite practitioner of psychography and never have known it. I do not mean that he did not use the word. That is a small matter. But he always thought and spoke of himself as a literary critic, all the while that he was doing work far different from literary criticism.

Indeed, as a mere critic, I do not think that Sainte-Beuve quite deserves the rank usually assigned him. He had little knowledge of any literature beside the classics and his own. Even in speaking of things French, he is a very unsatisfactory guide, outside of the sixteenth, seventeenth, and eighteenth centuries. If he writes of his contemporaries, his judgments, when just, are apt to be intertangled with a personal element of jealousy, which is very unpleasant. Such pure criticism as his study of Theocritus has great and peculiar charm, but it is much less common in his work than is generally supposed.

Where he is really distinguished and original and unrivalled, is as what he himself called, in a rare moment of analysis, "a naturalist of souls." In insight into the deep and hidden motives and passions of the soul, in power of distinguishing and defining them, best of all, in cunning and subtle gift of winnowing material so as to select just those significant and telling illustrative words and actions I have spoken of,—in all these admirable qualities he had no predecessor and has had no follower who can at all approach him. His vast collection

of studies of great and striking figures in French history is something quite unmatched in any other literature, and it is coming to stand out more and more and be better appreciated, as it is more widely known. Best of all are his many portraits of women. Madame de Sévigné, Madame de Maintenon, Madame Du Deffand, Madame d'Epinay, and a score of others, representing entirely different aspects of character, are depicted with a fidelity, a sympathy, a delicacy, a just appreciation of mental and moral strength and weakness, which make you feel as if you had known every one of them all your life.

Now it seems evident enough that it is a mere misuse of terms to call such work as this literary criticism. Is it not strange, then, that Sainte-Beuve should never have got really clear with himself about what he was doing, but should have insisted that because these various women wrote letters, therefore, in discussing them, he was discussing literature? The explanation is closely connected with an essential element of his greatness. For he was not an abstract thinker, not a man of theories or formulæ. His attempts to analyse the general character of his work are rare, and those that do occur are not lucid or satisfactory. What he did have was an immense, insatiable desire for observation, investigation. Few men have personified more completely than he the spirit of pure scientific curiosity, the love and reverence for the fact in itself, independent of argument, or of any effort to use facts as foundations for theories. One of the ablest of his followers, Scherer, points out that in all Sainte-Beuve's vast work there is little or no repetition. This is true, but Scherer fails to note the significant reason. It is because Sainte-Beuve adores and imitates the immense individuality of nature. Scherer himself, Brunetière, France, Lemaître, Faguet, Matthew Arnold, all admirers and imitators of Sainte-Beuve, miss his excellence in this point entirely. Not one of them left a quarter part as much work as Sainte-Beuve did. Yet not one of them but in those narrower limits repeats himself over and over in some philosophical discussion or some abstract theory, as all readers will immediately realise in regard to Matthew Arnold. To Sainte-Beuve theories were misleading and unprofitable. Human beings were unlimited in fascination and charm.

Thus, no one was more widely conversant with the material of psychography than he. Moreover, so far as the art of psychography consists in the cunning and exquisite selection of illustrative details, no one has ever surpassed or ever will surpass him.

But there is another phase of psychographic art, which becomes daily of greater interest to me, and which Sainte-Beuve practised comparatively little. This is the phase of composition. His method of procedure was usually that of simple biography. After a brief introduction, he followed the chronology of his subject, developing different points of character in connection with different circumstances or periods. No doubt great variety can be obtained in this way, as every skilled biographer knows. At the same time, it seems to me that there is a gain in swinging clear from this chronological sequence altogether, and in attaching oneself solely to the presentation of a man's qualities of character, arranged and treated in such logical sequence as shall give a total impression that will be most effective and most enduring. I confess that I had grave doubts about this procedure at first. I feared that the discussion of qualities in the abstract would be academic, pedagogic, monotonous. Even yet I am not prepared to affirm that this will not prove true and that in the end I shall not have to fall back on simple biographical structure. But my doubt in the matter diminishes daily. Indeed, it is in this regard that the originality and significance of psychography impresses me most, and I am astonished to find how rich and varied are the possibilities of artistic presentation with every individual character. Instead of a monotonous renewal of the same qualities in the same order, every individual seems to suggest and to require a different arrangement, a different emphasis. So that I come to feel that Nature herself is the artist and that all one has to do is to lend a patient, earnest ear to her dictation. It is true that not one but a dozen possibilities of composition are indicated in every case and this seems largely to accentuate the uncertainty and unreliability of psychographic art. But, as I have already shown, such wide variety in methods of treatment corresponds to a far wider variety in the material employed, and the search for the best form of developing the material is as delightful as the discovery of the material itself. (pp. 3-20)

> Gamaliel Bradford, "Psychography," in his A Naturalist of Souls: Studies in Psychography, *Dodd, Mead and Company, 1917, pp. 3-24.*

ARTHUR HOBSON QUINN   (essay date 1924)

[*In the following excerpt, Quinn evaluates the psychographies collected in* Damaged Souls.]

Perhaps it is the paucity of great novels that is turning readers more and more to biography and memoirs. It is a healthy reaction to reality, yet such work as Mr. Bradford's is animated to a certain extent by the spirit of fiction. Fielding's opinion that everything in history is false except the names and dates while everything in a novel is true except those necessary evils, is perhaps a sufficient authority for the modern biographers who insist upon letting their imagination play upon their gathered facts. There is, of course, nothing new in this attitude. The scientific historian, who insisted upon facts first and interest afterwards, had his reward. But some years ago, there was a reaction against mere accuracy, and it brought forth a number of *True Benjamin Franklins* and *True Thomas Jeffersons,* some of which were original and some of which were good. The aim of these books . . . is to present a portrait and not a photograph, and in the case of the author of **Damaged Souls,** he has been careful to hold the camera a bit askew.

The method has its obvious advantages. For years the present writer assigned as a subject to a college class in composition the treatment of historical characters from a point of view different from that usually taken, and he recalls with pleasure consequent gems, among them a portrait of "Lot's Wife" which would have astounded biblical criticism had it ever been published. The dangers inherent in this method are also apparent. To be effective the subjects must be sufficiently well known to make popular appreciation of the new point of view immediate, and the reconstructor of history is tempted to emphasize unduly these undiscovered phases of his subjects' natures or to set up straw men to knock down.

Mr. Bradford has undoubtedly felt himself upon the defensive in this last respect, for in his introduction he has explained his choice of the **Damaged Souls** he is endeavoring to rehabilitate. It is truly at first glance a strange collection: Benedict Arnold, Thomas Paine, Aaron Burr, John Randolph of Roanoke, John Brown, P. T. Barnum, Benjamin F.

Butler. How different in historic importance, in immediate appeal, in permanent interest are those "palely damaged, but not completely damned souls." Barnum and Butler seem negligible, Randolph is remote in present interest. Paine seems hardly in need of defense, for the country he helped to found has lasted, the religion he tried to destroy can afford to forget his attacks. But after all the sketches in this well-written and stimulating book have been completed, a likeness evolves out of the confused events of their lives, a likeness Mr. Bradford doubtless felt although he does not express it concretely. They are examples of men in whom personality was developed at the expense of character. That is why, in moments of temptation, Arnold, Burr, and Butler disgraced themselves, in large and in little things, while Paine, Randolph, and Brown, brooding too intensively, struck at the foundations of religion and government.

In a book like this, the treatment is of course uneven. Arnold, Burr, and Brown are the best portraits, probably because they really were damaged souls. The quotation from Burr's farewell to the Senate, "If the Constitution be destined ever to perish by the sacrilegious hands of the demagogue or the usurper, which God avert, its expiring agonies will be witnessed on this floor," almost justifies the article alone. And the concluding paragraph on John Brown is masterly in its depiction of the influence of Brown on the Civil War and on posterity. The portrait of Paine is well drawn, and Mr. Bradford rightly shows the lofty aims of that sometimes misguided man. He points out, also quite truly, that Paine writes in phrases rather than in words. But to one who has read Paine's own works, the essay is a bit disappointing. Perhaps Mr. Bradford had to keep his greatest figure down to the level of the others to prevent him from escaping altogether from the common category.

Randolph's portrait is disappointing for another reason. Mr. Bradford does not understand the southern landholder. He speaks of Randolph as though he contained a "multiplicity of conflicts" within him, because "he was a slaveholder and a lover of liberty" "an aristocrat and a lover of democracy," because he denounced the slave trade and yet hated abolitionists. Such apparent inconsistencies did not bother Randolph. In his conception of society, a few leaders ruled by right of superior intelligence the rest of mankind, who were equal to each other and who were relieved of all responsibility, who were to be protected as well as governed, and whose rights their leaders would allow no one to infringe but themselves. It is the clan theory of society and it differs radically from that which Mr. Bradford understands as democracy. Yet it is democracy of a certain kind, and we may be sure that its workings caused Randolph no spiritual disturbance. (pp. 401-03)

[In] this day when we are suffering from an excess of personality and a lack of character, in public and private life, perhaps the representation of damaged personalities may not be without its significance. (p. 404)

> Arthur Hobson Quinn, "Chronicles of Personality," in The Yale Review, *Vol. XIII, No. 2, January, 1924, pp. 401-04.*

JOSEPH WARREN BEACH   (essay date 1926)

[*Beach was an American critic and educator who specialized in American literature and English literature of the Romantic and Victorian eras. In the following excerpt, he examines aspects of Bradford's prose style.*]

We are rightly grateful to Mr. Bradford for his many and interesting studies of the souls of notable men and women. Mr. Bradford has many qualifications for his task. He has patience, industry, sympathy, fairness, subtlety, a sense of form. He has had one real inspiration in the title of his *Damaged Souls.* He writes well, and very well; and it is perhaps ungracious to note that he does not often write supremely well. He writes well when he will let himself go. There is, for example, the inimitable opening paragraph of his chapter on General Butler:

> And still I am looking for a real, live rascal, one who knows and confesses himself to be such, and boasts of it, who does not dodge and shift and palter and whip the devil around the stump, to whom principle is nothing, conscience is nothing, God is nothing, and self and pleasure and success are all. If I could find him, he should have first place among these palely damaged, but not completely damned souls. I have not found him yet and he is certainly not General Benjamin Franklin Butler.

The trouble is that Mr. Bradford, with his New England nerves all taut, will seldom let himself go. He takes his task so seriously, and he always lets us know how seriously he takes it. In 1916 he tells us of his *Portraits of Women:*

> The nine portraits contained in this volume are preliminary studies or sketches for the series of portraits of American women which will follow my Union portraits. Such a collection of portraits of women *will certainly fill a most important section* in the gallery of historical likenesses selected from the whole of American history, which it is my wish to complete, if possible.

In 1922 he tells us, of his *American Portraits,* "This group of portraits is the first of a series *in which I hope to cover American history,* proceeding backwards with four volumes on the nineteenth century, two on the eighteenth, and one on the seventeenth," and he goes on to set forth at length the difficulties he must encounter in performing this task fully and fairly. In 1924 he explains that "*The Soul of Samuel Pepys* and *Bare Souls* represent a digression from the extensive series of American portraits to which *I mean in future to devote all my time and energy.*" It is all very well for the student to propose to cover American history and to assure himself that a given collection of portraits will fill a most important section in a gallery which he wishes to complete. But the reader cares for the product and not the labor, and the well-advised author will do away with all traces of the reading-lamp and the green shade of the student.

One of the difficulties of the follower of this "psychographic method"—God save the mark!—is to present every aspect of the soul under investigation and yet to spare us the intolerable burden of scholarly detail. And Mr. Bradford has shown, indeed, great courage in his eliminations, great skill in reducing his enormous material to the compass of an essay. There are often left, however, traces of this labor of condensation. We have too much the sense of the student passing constantly from one topic to another in a carefully outlined progression. One is bothered by the clocklike recurrence of formal transitional phrases, as in the essay on Madame de Sévigné:

> Let us trace further the charming many-sidedness. . . . Yet though she could make. . . .

Yet though she had many friends. . . . it must not be supposed. . . . Nevertheless, it would be wholly unjust. . . . The fact is. . . . Yet she makes the best. . . . It will naturally be asked. . . . She has her moments, also. . . . So we have seen Madame de Sévigné to be. . . . For the most part, however, . . . But it makes no difference. In spite of. . . . Thus you see, this sweet and noble lady. . . .

Such rhetorical devices, though an evidence of rhetorical expertness, are at the same time a betrayal of the fact that the author has not achieved that final synthesis and crystallization of his subject matter which is demanded of a good portraitist, and which we recognize with joy in the English gallery of *Eminent Victorians.* They are an evidence of care and pains, but not of that final joyous simplification which is the fruit of leisure and saturation.

Mr. Bradford makes for himself another difficulty which Mr. Strachey has shed with a shrug of the shoulders—that of judging his characters as well as presenting them. Mr. Strachey is content to be a portraitist pure and simple. He does not even let us know that he is interpreting, as Mr. Bradford does on every page; and if we feel that he is fair to his characters, it is not because he tells us so. Mr. Bradford, in presenting Mark Twain, feels called upon gravely to consider the question whether that writer for the man in the street did more harm than good, and whether the world was made wholly better by his presence. Even where he is most liberal and indulgent in his interpretation, he seems to have an eye on an audience of censorious puritans. Thus Roosevelt's abhorrence of Thomas Paine, whom he called a "filthy little atheist," stirs Mr. Bradford to a defense which is a credit to his open-mindedness, but which would be superfluous and a little quaint in Mr. Lytton Strachey writing for Mr. Strachey's audience:

> No doubt it is good to be clean and sober and conservative and do what your fathers did and shun ideals. But some of us occasionally like to think new thoughts and step out of the beaten track, and we like one who makes us do these things, even if he is a trifle untidy in his person. Here is a man who upset the world and you say that he did not brush his clothes. Here is a man who beat and shook conventions, who stirred up dusty and old titles, till he showed their rotten vanity, and you complain because some of the dust got on himself. This is childishness.

This is very good writing indeed, and the best thing in his essay on Paine. But there is in it a note of nervousness and the consciousness of a daring greater than the subject calls for. And in all of Mr. Bradford's writing we have a sense of labor and responsibility that rather weighs upon us. (pp. 54-9)

Joseph Warren Beach, "Unripe Fruits," in his The Outlook for American Prose, *The University of Chicago Press, 1926, pp. 21-60.*

JOHN MACY　(essay date 1932)

[*Macy was an American literary critic and an editor of the* Boston Herald *and the* Nation. *His best-known critical work is* The Spirit of American Literature *(1913), which denounced the genteel tradition and called for realism and the use of American subjects. In the following excerpt, Macy offers an*

Bradford did not invent but developed in his own way a method or kind of biography which he calls psychography, literally "soul-writing"—though this does not translate it at all. About the time that his first published work appeared, *The Century Dictionary* (1889, 1895) defined "psychography" as "the natural history of mind; the description of the phenomena of mind; a branch of psychology." In the Appendix to *Lee the American* (1912) Bradford calls it a "new name recently invented." What is new is Bradford's personal application of it. In the first chapter of *A Naturalist of Souls* (1917) he discusses the word and his general theory of biography. The gist of it is in a single sentence: "Psychography is the condensed, essential, artistic presentation of character." It is free from the chronological pattern of narrative biography. A psychograph is not quite a "portrait," because it is not static but fluid. And Bradford would deny that psychography is a "branch of psychology," because psychology deals with principles and uses individuals to illustrate the principles, whereas psychography deals with individuals and uses the principles of psychology, and of any other "ology," to throw light on the character of this and that person. It is interesting that Bradford, having coined the word for himself, as he says, found that Saintsbury had used it a few years earlier in relation to Sainte-Beuve. But Bradford, though excellently precise in his use of words, is no stickler for terms, and he smilingly admits that "psychograph" will not do, for publisher or public, in the title of a book.

Terms and labels aside, what has Bradford done? He has written a hundred short studies, portraits of men and women, including some literary-critical essays; four volumes, each devoted to an individual, Lee, Darwin, Pepys, D. L. Moody; and the quintessence of his experience, reading, and reflection, *Life and I: An Autobiography of Humanity.* He has examined and rejoiced in a wide diversity of creatures, a gallery in which are all sorts and conditions of men and women of many races, nations, periods of history: Jesus and Saint Francis of Assisi; Talleyrand and Benjamin Butler; Madame de Maintenon and Emily Dickinson; Ovid and Henry Adams. And which of them is not treated with sagacity and skill? Almost no one reader is intimate with all the persons of whom Bradford has chosen to write. So that his work as a whole offers a double experience: he gives you his view of a man whom you think you know, or thought you did; he introduces you to a man whom in a life of miscellaneous reading you have missed, but whom you forthwith determine to know if life lasts long enough. More than half his subjects are American, obviously because he knows more about America than about the rest of the world, and also because he takes patriotic pride in celebrating his countrymen—it is a kind of patriotism which admits no scoundrel.

Why did Bradford undertake to exemplify in his work the truth that the proper study of mankind is man? Partly because he was ambitious to be a writer; he made excursions, not very startling, into verse and fiction. But his greater impulse was to find out for himself how men have lived, with what motives, with what results, in order to become a better and wiser man himself. He says, quite understandably, that he "lived for ten years with the soul of Robert E. Lee and it really made a little better man of me". Then he says: "Six months of Mark Twain made me a worse. I even caught his haunting exaggeration of profanity. And I am fifty-six years old and not over-susceptible to infection. What can he not do to children of sixteen?" One answer might be that Mark Twain would do the children much good and no harm, that they would not get his bitterness any more than they would be poisoned by the satiric venom of Gulliver. Bradford's attitude seems to me a bit too anxiously moralistic even for a New England moralist, which in a high, fine sense he is. But his concern for self-improvement and for the welfare of the race is not incompatible with an adventurous enthusiasm, an inquisitive gusto in observing, appraising, enjoying, sometimes not too violently damning, that variously engaging creature, the human being.

With man as subject you can play a selfish game, a continuous theft which much enriches you and makes none poor indeed; you see what you can get out of your fellow man for your amusement and instruction; and then you can free yourself from all selfishness (and at the same time fatten your ego) by passing on to others what has amused and instructed you. Such is the main motive of makers of song and story, of historians, biographers, dramatists, writers of fiction, essayists, and (a few) philosophers. Idle people as well as scholars and thinkers find the study of humanity not only necessary but fascinating. "It is," says Bradford, "perhaps the most justifiable of pursuits, since in studying others we are studying ourselves and fitting ourselves for larger and more perfect adjustment to life." Bradford writes of Henry Ford, who said that history is bunk and then collected Wayside Inns and antiques: "The explanation seems to be that he is immensely interested in the past, provided it concerns himself. Perhaps a little wider study would have taught him that the history of the whole world exists only to throw light upon you and me and Henry Ford." More generally, he says that after all there is not one of the essential elements of character "that is not present to some extent in you and me, and it is endlessly delightful to consider why they have not put you and me where they put Roosevelt and Mussolini." So Mark Twain found in himself all the qualities of human nature, good and bad, in sufficient quantities to enable him to understand them in others. The gift of understanding human nature is itself a possession common to human nature, and we all have it to some degree. Without it we could not run a peanut stand or manage a government or write a biography. The man of action driving to a practical end needs special kinds of understanding according to his goal. The philosophic biographer has no end in view except understanding for its own sake. Or at least that is his chief end.

We may all have the motives and ambitions of Napoleon or of Bradford. Motive and ambition amount to nothing without equipment. Bradford's equipment, inborn and acquired, is almost perfect for his purpose. Regarded in its totality, his work makes him the supreme biographer of our time, though no doubt any one of a score of biographies written in this century can be advanced as superior even to his best. It has become tiresomely usual to group him, in resemblance and contrast, with Lytton Strachey. The two men are not much alike, except in the generally inclusive sense that they are alert modern minds with biography as their subject. There seems little point in saying that Bradford preceded Strachey, as if they were contestants for priority in a patent right. One admires rather the intended praise than the critical justice of Mencken's saying that "this Bradford is the man who invented the formula of Lytton Strachey's *Queen Victoria.*" I doubt if a formula can be found in Strachey's book or if one can be deduced from all his books, and I think he never analyzed and codified his method, as Bradford did. Certainly the excellent qualities of the two men are not the same. Bradford is the better informed and more careful historian, and the scope of his subjects is much broader. Strachey's brilliant mind was unscholarly, if not lazy; he did not delve assiduously into sources, but seemed content with secondary information. You cannot always trust him round the corner with a fact, though you applaud the grace with which he turns the corner. Strachey shapes his material to dramatic effects and to some effects that are not dramatic but are a clever, whimsical indulgence of the spirit of caricature. His most splendid passages are beyond the reach of Bradford's more prosaic talent. But this is not to say that Bradford is incapable of dramatic effect and poetic phrasing. His concluding paragraphs, if not dramatic, are marvellously well-turned, luminous finalities that leave you satisfied as if a curtain had dropped. The end of *Lee the American* brings tears; the lovely littleness of the episode is tremendous, not a smashing climax nor even the repose of death, but the more than tragic completion of a life perfect in failure. "Literature can add nothing to that."

Neither Bradford nor Strachey is guilty of adding to the mongrel breed of "fictionized biography," which is a deliberate mixture of genres and is quite different from the confusion of fact and fiction due to the source material or to the biographer's honest failure to discriminate. Bradford's discrimination and the keenness of his interpretations are extraordinary. He handles evidence like a super-detective. He would have been a great lawyer and judge; fortunately he was not so wasted but was directed to the higher wisdom of literature. In his examination of character he sets down some recorded fact; then he considers whether the fact as reported is credible; then he reflects on what it means. It may mean two or three things, and he ponders each possible meaning. Finally he takes you adroitly into his argument, as if you were deciding for yourself, and so he tells you what a fact means, without a touch of dogmatism, and you find that you have accepted his interpretation. A person has been drawn for you, and unless you are an expert student of this particular historic figure or unless your inexpert opinions are too stubbornly fixed, you have no disposition to change Bradford's delineation. He makes you respect, if not love, people whose actions and beliefs you oppose or even detest. I found myself almost not disliking Frances Willard of the Woman's Christian Temperance Union, whom Bradford says he could not bear but whom because of his aversion he made all the more effort to appreciate. Bradford's persuasion is not the too cunning, insinuating kind that takes you unawares and tricks your confidence. He can be downright, point-blank and assertive when he chooses to be. But he is always flexible. He establishes the lines of a character; yet it is as if the clay had not quite set and stiffened into unyielding permanence. That is why he objects to the word "portrait" and is wary of ultimates. "If the psychographer had not become hardened to the feeling that no conclusion about human character is ever final, he would have given up a hundred times in despair."

This feeling for the human being as an unsettled problem is due to a fundamental tolerance of human nature, which is itself one of the good qualities of human nature. Bradford's avowed master, Sainte-Beuve, is tolerant, but in a cool intellectual way. So that Bradford is not wholly in sympathy and agreement with the French "naturalist of souls." Bradford says that the wisest observers of humanity, even when they have teased and mocked and ridiculed, have always loved. "It is in this point of love that Sainte-Beuve is weakest. He prided himself on understanding everything—and I think a little on loving nothing. Therefore his very subtlest work is sometimes

bitter, and bitterness is no help to psychography or to anything else." It may be questioned whether bitterness is such a useless quality; to some of us it is exhilarating rather than depressing when we meet it in literature—in Swift and in Mark Twain. But the passage is a declaration of Bradford's faith and character. He loves human beings. He hates mean qualities but he can have affection for people who are damaged by them; for him a defect is a damage rather than a reprehensible sin.

One mode of tolerance, or ingredient of it, is humour. The Yankee Bradford has the kind of humour which is sometimes miscalled "dry," and is really a fluent under current of quiet comment, never a crackling joke, and seldom detachable for quotation. At the risk of disturbing the easy and dignified motion of his thought, I quote this from *Life and I:* "There are the more physiological abnormalities, such as perversion, Sadism, Masochism, words become so pleasantly familiar to the astonishing youth of the present day that one has no hesitation in using them anywhere. In fact, they appear to be taught in the kindergarten, with, or without, the alphabet."

In analyzing a personality into its component elements Bradford discerns certain qualities, love of power, ambition, cruelty, generosity, kindness, the hundred abstractions the common names of which we use every day. But a collection of qualities does not make a person. We must go deeper and find out, if we can, what those qualities are in themselves and in association. Bradford loves to play with the quality of qualities, with the meaning of this virtue and that vice, with the meaning of the inclusive abstractions, vice and virtue. For example, a reformer is devoted to a Cause, a general is devoted to the welfare of his army and to the national loyalties he serves. How far does the reformer enjoy having an evil to fight, how deeply is he thrilled at the thought of himself as leader? How far does the most patriotic and self-sacrificing general, disclaiming all thought of personal glory, find, in the very act of renunciation and sacrifice, delicious satisfaction of the ego? How far is identification with the will of God, self-annihilating humility, a form of self-aggrandizement, consoling and flattering to the proud I? Bradford's discussions of these fine questions are wise contributions to psychology and to ethics, the more so because they are specifically applied, because they illuminate and are illuminated by a single separate person. At least for the moment a single person is under consideration, though other persons are called in as parallel cases, contrary witnesses, counter-advocates.

The culmination of Bradford's work and play is *Life and I: An Autobiography of Humanity,* written four or five years before he died; it is a beautiful book, philosophic in the derivative meaning of the word. The "I" is any individual I, for which Bradford is the spokesman, and there is just enough of a private nature to make the book his intellectual autobiography. The most striking chapter is a psychographical examination of Jesus and the New Testament, which would have been a daring thing to try in America forty years ago and in itself shows how far we have come from the age of Moody—and of Ingersoll. The dominant interests of life—Love, Power, Beauty, Thought, and Faith—which compose and embrace the individual, are related to each other in *Life and I* and summarized into a unit as coherently and solidly constructed as a great bridge. But the image is not rigid, for over the bridge moves humanity.

To be impartial and yet not to straddle and trim and compromise; to be both reverent and sceptical; to be moderate in tone and yet firm, even passionate, in conviction; to understand both sides and yet place unequivocally a preponderance of emphasis on one side—all this is to be endowed with a truly balanced mind and a rich, generous nature. Bradford, a modest, timid man, as he says of himself, full of misgivings, afraid of making decisions, lacking confidence and assurance, fearful each day that in spite of encouraging success he can write no more, has erected from the lives of stronger and weaker men a glorious egotism, has effected an *entente cordiale* between the individual and the universe. The character that emerges from his many studies of character is Bradford's.

Perhaps there is no need for someone else to write a psychograph of him; he has written it. (pp. 144-49)

> *John Macy, "Gamaliel Bradford: Portrayer of Souls," in* The Bookman, *New York, Vol. LXXV, May, 1932, pp. 144-49.*

GRANVILLE HICKS   (essay date 1933)

[*Hicks was an American literary critic whose study* The Genteel Tradition: An Interpretation of American Literature *since the Civil War (1933) established him as the foremost advocate of Marxist critical thought in Depression-era America. Throughout the 1930s, he argued for a more socially engaged brand of literature and severely criticized such writers as Henry James, Mark Twain, and Edith Wharton, who he believed failed to confront the realities of their society and, instead, took refuge in their own work. In the following excerpt, Hicks identifies Bradford's limitations as a writer.*]

Gamaliel Bradford began his journal in 1883, when he was nineteen years old, and his first entry implied a hope that it would some day be published. Now Van Wyck Brooks has selected for publication approximately one-tenth of that journal, which grew to over a million words. Though the first entry is dated 1883, five-sixths of the book is devoted to the last decade and a half of Bradford's life. [*The Journal of Gamaliel Bradford, 1883-1932*] has no value as an account of the outside world; it is all Bradford. Three topics recur to the exclusion of almost everything else: the author's health, his reading, and his work. Mr. Brooks, in a rather extraordinary preface, praises the journal as the revelation of the mind of an American author. It is certainly that—the revelation, though Brooks implies quite the contrary, of one more case of Brooksian frustration. (p. 358)

To the spiritual isolation characteristic of all the literary New Englanders of Bradford's generation his illness added a very real physical isolation. He both needed and desired solitude, and he was happy only in his own home and in the Athenaeum. He lived almost entirely with his books, which he read and reread according to a marvelous schedule. For contemporary literature, except detective stories and French comedies, he had little regard, reading only what he felt obliged to, and that with abhorrence. There is no evidence in the journal of any acute interest in current events, and his reading, except in so far as it was dictated by the exigencies of his work, was wholly belletristic.

Yet Bradford wanted, above everything else, to be a poet and novelist, and it was to poetry and fiction that he devoted his early years. Even in 1921, after his success as a biographer was established, he fervently threw himself into the composition of a novel. But soon he was back at his biographies, and thereafter he made the best, though not without moments of rebellion, of the field in which he had triumphed. It was, obvi-

ously, the only field in which he could hope for success, the only field in which his isolation, his almost fantastic remoteness from the life of his age, was not a fatal handicap.

And even as a biographer Bradford could not escape the effects of his isolation. It is not fanciful, perhaps, to suppose that his whole method was the product of his singular mode of life. What he wanted to do—what he thought he did do—was to select the essential characteristic of the man he was studying. He disregarded chronology and thus the whole process of character development; he disregarded, in most of his studies, the social and economic conditions of the time; he dealt in only the most superficial fashion with intellectual currents. His whole conception of character was abstract and academic. Look, for example, at the neat formula for *The Soul of Samuel Pepys*: Pepys and his diary, his office, his money, his humanity, his intellect, his wife, God. Even the more substantial *Darwin* is static and lifeless. Of the shorter studies, some of the early American portraits are unpretentious and within limits shrewd; but the later work is almost uniformly shallow and mechanical, and its defects are emphasized by the expression, as in the preface to *Bare Souls,* of the grandiose theories of psychography that Bradford developed, perhaps as compensation for his failure as a creative writer.

On all his weaknesses as a writer the journal sheds a cruel light. It is a pathetic book, with its record of constant ill health, of literary disappointments, of uneasy skepticism. It is at times, when the smug tory is revealed behind the mask of urbanity and tolerance, an irritating book. But it is never, despite Bradford's fine courage in the face of obstacles, a stirring book. Nor is it even a tragic book, for one does not feel, as one so often does in reading American journals and autobiographies, the waste of a great talent. What one really feels, harsh as it may seem to say it, is that Gamaliel Bradford, with his hours of reading and his brief moment of fame, got all he deserved. "Of what account are one's personal miseries," he asked on January 1, 1918, "especially when they are so trifling and balanced by so many comforts as mine, in comparison with the horrible state of the world at large?" And he answered his question, "I find that, for me at any rate, the only relief is to keep my thoughts so far as possible on the larger, higher, more permanent interests of life." It may be difficult to find the larger, higher, more permanent interests of life in the journal, but Gamaliel Bradford had his relief. (pp. 358-59)

> *Granville Hicks, "An Insulated Litterateur," in* The Nation, *New York, Vol. CXXXVII, No. 3560, September 27, 1933, pp. 358-59.*

FRANCES WENTWORTH KNICKERBOCKER   (essay date 1934)

[*In the following excerpt, Knickerbocker examines Bradford's assessment of his own works as presented in his* Journal.]

Bradford's attitude towards his work is two-fold, a paradox that runs through all his life: on the one hand, ardent enthusiasm; on the other, keen self-criticism. On almost every page of the [*Journal of Gamaliel Bradford*] eager absorption in his work alternates with moods of exhaustion, even desperation, when that work is perforce put aside.

> I do not believe that the mystic's rapture can carry
> away a man and wrap him out of himself more

thoroughly than the work I am doing now for an hour and a quarter each day. And then, as always, for the remainder of the day I am dead, and simply wait in passionate self-collection for the arrival of the next morning.

So, and so only, did Bradford escape for a time from the terror and suffering of his recurrent vertigo into the inexhaustible adventure of others' lives. Yet in this absorption he never lost the power to objectify his work. And thus in the *Journal* we discover him anticipating most of the defects that critics have found in his art. For instance, he picks up at the Athenaeum a journalist's book, the record of one who has knocked against all sorts of life, who has seen everybody and been everywhere, and he cries out despairingly: "And I, poor I, who try to know and understand the heart solely from my own poor and limited specimen . . . shut up with my own soul and books." For the biographer needs so much of the surface, "and of the surface I have nothing—except what my weak imagination gives me."

Bradford's portraits do lack surface, the play of movement, the variety of setting and costume, the color and glitter which he sought so eagerly in the theatre. Naturally, surface plays a larger part in some lives than in others; it is almost absent with Darwin, it is of the essence of Pepys. The saints transcend it, the sinners are immersed in it. We feel the lack of it most in some of Bradford's studies of men of action, and daughters of Eve. Casanova, P. T. Barnum, Ninon de Lenclos, Sarah Bernhardt—such vivid creatures need the word-painter's art.

This lack of surface is but one aspect of another defect. It is due not so much to "weak imagination," or even to limited experience, but to imagination concentrated on character analysis. Bradford put his finger on the real weakness when in describing his creative process he adds: "There is the horrible danger of formulas, so especially threatening for a born and bred generalizer like myself." It is "the born and bred generalizer," the "naturalist of souls," dissecting and classifying human character in terms of motive, that sometimes overwhelms the artist. The tendency grew upon him to reiterate a few dominant motives: ambition, love of money, love of women, need of God—those common human elements that he analyzes in *Biography and the Human Heart* (1932). So intent is Bradford upon laying bare those hidden desires that link you and me with Mussolini and Thomas à Kempis, that he forgets his own principle that "every individual seems to suggest and to require a different arrangement, a different emphasis." And yet, here again he was aware of the danger of "monotonous iteration"; and in the Preface to *The Quick and the Dead* (1931) he explains that the very fascination of these men of action is the variations wrought by character and circumstance in the recurring pattern of motive.

This tendency to formula inevitably led Bradford to understress the development of his characters. Here, too, he is aware of this criticism and argues it in several passages of the *Journal.* He states his theory, a theory too near dogma for a scientific thinker, though he warns himself against letting it become fixed:

> With Sainte-Beuve, I feel that the larger traits of character are fixed and remain so from the cradle to the grave. . . . Doubtless there are cases of striking development. . . . Doubtless there are modifications in every case. . . . But the character

of the individual is given him at birth and hardly changes.

Yet in spite of this conviction, he is concerned, when working on George Sand "whether the psychographical method allows enough for development in character." In truth, he must have realized that it does not. Probably, in his dislike of all psychology he had avoided the behaviorists on this issue. For although he tended to choose subjects that fitted his theory, with dominant traits that are early and strongly marked, his method fails to do justice to amazing personalities like D. L. Moody or Mussolini, whose end no man could forsee from their beginnings. He seems never to have realized that he was thus neglecting a chief source of our interest and delight in biography. For what makes us linger over the early years of our hero or villain is the fascination of discovering how or why he became what he was—and what we might have become.

"I do feel," writes Bradford, "that structure, architectonic, is my secret." So it is, but it is a secret both of strength and of weakness. That this very insistence on structure often led to fixity of conception Bradford recognizes . . .:

> In these successive portraits there is a sort of grouping at first. I cannot seem to find my way, all is hazy, confused, obscure. Then suddenly somehow I get hold of a thread, a clue, and gradually all reduces itself to order and symmetry. Of course, what I have to guard against is the illusion that the order is really in the subject instead of being merely a creation of my own fertile fancy, a mould into which I am trying to force nature.

This search for the one clue or motive sometimes sacrifices reality to clarity. Bradford's pictures of FitzGerald as a complete idler, of Gray as the futile recluse, make it almost incredible that the one could have created the matchless *Rubaiyat,* the other, the best-loved poem in the English language! The very habits of work enforced by his ill-health, the method of outlining in advance every chapter, section, and paragraph, of rehearsing the outline and even composing the sentences as soon as he woke in the morning so that when he sat down to the typewriter, it was scarcely more than "letting my fingers follow a process of dictation," although splendid training in concentration and clarity, must have been fatal to spontaneity. And when he repeatedly rearranges his men and women into climactic categories: physical, social, intellectual, spiritual, we feel that the pattern has displaced the person.

But artifice is not the last word to be said of Bradford's portraits. The best of them are memorable interpretations, in which motive and detail are blended in one clear image. Some of these are among the short early studies collected in *A Naturalist of Souls* (1926). **"A Gentleman of Athens," "Ovid Among the Goths,"** and **"The Portrait of a Saint,"** are compact of economy and variety. Bradford's three longer studies, the *Pepys* (1924), *Moody* (1927), and *Darwin* (1926) are not the most successful, although he poured into them, as he tells us, "the thought and experience and longing and desire of a lifetime." But the psychographic method with its analysis into aspects: as Darwin the Observer, the Thinker, the Loser, the Lover, the Destroyer, inevitably weakens not only the unity, but the reality of the portrait. Deeply moved as Bradford was by the dramatic human values of his material, he lost the living man amidst discussions of the destructive effects of Darwinism on faith. Indeed all three books are haunted by the refrain of Bradford's own search after God. The climax of his life-work seemed to him to be his *Life and I: An Autobiography of Humanity* (1928), into which he distilled the essence of his dearest books and thoughts. Yet here again his purpose is thwarted by the form and habit of his thought; instead of the "incessant play of my own with that of others" which he intended, we have a discussion, subtle and stimulating, but too abstract and impersonal, of the I in its relations to Love and Power and Beauty and Thought and Christ, its struggles to escape from the Not-I of denial into the More-than-I of idealism. Bradford himself realized that these longer books had led him into "riots of generalizations," and that "it is far better for me to concentrate my attention on the brief, intense, compact portrayal."

Among these brief, intense portrayals, *Damaged Souls* (1923) is deeply characteristic of Bradford's range of sympathy ("Give me these children of Hell every time!" he cried) and of his refusal of the cheap and easy debunking. It was like Bradford to seek the real humanity beneath the legends of Benedict Arnold and Aaron Burr. The most difficult subjects he treated were the contemporary statesmen and leaders of *The Quick and the Dead.* Bradford was both too close in time and too remote in temper from their social and political issues. Yet all the more did he labor to unravel that tragic tangle of ambitions and ideals that was the career of Woodrow Wilson, or to probe "the dry and unprofitable soul" of that "genius of the average, Calvin Coolidge." Wherever "the damnable effort to be just and fair" is hardest, wherever his prejudice or antipathy is the strongest, there the play of his irony is most marked. Of Frances Willard's *Autobiography* he notes, "the impression of a naturally modest lady undressing in public"; of Henry Ford's activities, "but nothing is impossible with Henry Ford; has he not made the automobile?"; of Mussolini's glorification of "beautiful violence," "to the victims of Fascist brutality, these distinctions may seem somewhat fine spun." (The pity that he did not live to do Hitler!) His is an irony that plays like heat lightning, but never sears, like Strachey's. Sometimes it turns to sheer wit, like his epigram on the elder Pliny: "After perpetrating forty books of lies, he died of the desire to discover the truth"; or to the dry, delicious humor of his "if Moody's God had been half as clever as Moody"; and his allusion to "perversion, Sadism, Masochism, words so pleasantly familiar to the astonishing youth of the present day that . . . they appear to be taught in the kindergarten, either with, or without, the alphabet."

There are instances of prejudices not overcome, to which the *Journal* supplies a revealing clue. Speaking of Frances Willard, he traces his dislike of reformers to his secret sympathy with them and his secret self-reproach that he has not sided with them. And he adds characteristically, "At any rate, I do not love reformers, and there is all the more charm in trying to distil the good from them and to represent their motives, their labors, and their hopes as fairly and as sympathetically as possible". The portrait of Henry Adams (*American Portraits, 1875-1900,* 1922), with all its searching criticism of the man, fails to grasp his contribution to modern thought. In the *Journal,* we follow Bradford's first absorbed delight in *The Education of Henry Adams,* then his growing impatience with its aloof egotism. "The whole book is a demand on the universe that it should educate Henry Adams." Bradford was indeed incapacitated, by his aversion to philosophic thought and his distaste for the medieval mind, for appreciating the deeper syntheses of *The Education* and *Mont-Saint-Michel.* But the real cause of his antipathy comes out in this searching

self-criticism, apropos of his unsuccessful portrait of Henry James:

> And it is odd that, when I have so much sympathy with him [Henry James] and Adams, I should condemn them so completely; but it is precisely because I condemn in them what is so odious and damnable in myself. *I,* too, think only of *my* art, I, too, cannot approach human beings or dwell with them. My poor artistic efforts also fail from utter absence of real, instinctive contact with life. But I hate the limitation in myself and I hate it in them.

Over against Bradford's under-estimate of Henry Adams one should place his fine appreciation of the contemporary with whom he was most often and most inaptly compared. There is no subtler temptation than to depreciate a rival; but Bradford's comparison of Lytton Strachey's work with his own is a model of justice and discernment. Of course he perceives the utter inaccuracy of Mencken's unfortunately still-quoted dictum: "This Bradford is the man who invented the formula of Lytton Strachey's *Queen Victoria.*" He realizes the total difference between Strachey's "epic continuity and digression" and his own psychography with its "elaborate arrangement of contrast and climax." Moreover, he recognizes, first with poignant distress, then with a fine objectivity, the genius that surpassed him: "his [Strachey's] extraordinary, penetrating, illuminating, vivid clarity, which seems to dart right down into men's souls, where I can only stumble and grope." He sees, too, defects of Strachey's style and structure which confirm his faith in his own method, but he says little of those deeper defects of judgment which have made Strachey so brilliant but so dangerous a guide of modern biography. That Bradford was not tempted to follow another brilliant contemporary is suggested by his note on his difficulty in finding material for one of his portraits. "Of course, I can fall back upon the imagination, *à la Maurois,* which is precisely what I never mean or want to do."

And so we come back, at the last, to Bradford's finest portraits, in which imagination interprets without replacing fact. There is, for instance, the **"Cowper"** in *Bare Souls* (1924), which he himself placed among his best, with its memorable final image: "Women petted him, cats purred about him, he held endless skeins of worsted, cracked his pleasant little jokes, drank oceans of tea. And all the time, within an inch of his unsteady foot, opened that black, unfathomable gulf of hell." There is Emily Dickinson, that white ethereal vision with "her contagion of eternity." It was to women that Bradford, like Sainte-Beuve, gave his finest discernment, his deepest sympathy. And so it is in the last two of his four volumes on women: *Wives* (1925) and *Daughters of Eve* (1930) that much of his best work is found. There is Sarah Butler, pouring out her heart to the husband unworthy of her; Mrs. Lincoln, overshadowed by the mighty tragic figure beside her; Madame Guyon, difficult saint; Ninon de Lanclos, fearless daughter of joy.

Whether the method of Gamaliel Bradford proves to be, as he once anticipated, "a mere biographical will-o'-the-wisp," or whether it has made a real contribution to the biography of tomorrow it may be too soon to say. Meantime, it seems unjust to dismiss him, as certain of our younger critics have done, to the limbo of the decayed and discarded, merely because his world is not theirs. To be sure, as he once protested, life to him did not mean "the collective, sociological unity" that it does to them. "Life to me," he went on, "is the human individual and that only, but—and here is the profound point—through the human individual I penetrate to inexhaustible depths of human passion and suffering and joy and hope." To reread the Bradford portraits in the light of the *Journal* is to feel that here was an artist who gave his life not in vain to understanding and interpreting his fellowmen. In words that recall the creed of a greater artist, Joseph Conrad, he once set down the aim to which he was faithful:

> Not to be true, not to be final, not to be exhaustive, simply to make one's readers think, to make them feel, and so for a few moments live, that is all I can expect and all I aim at.

(pp. 93-9)

Frances Wentworth Knickerbocker, "Gamaliel Bradford Looks at His Art," in The Sewanee Review, *Vol. XLII, No. 1, Winter, 1934, pp. 91-9.*

MARK LONGAKER (essay date 1934)

[*In the following excerpt, Longaker analyzes Bradford's point of view, method, and style in his writings.*]

In Bradford's point of view toward his subjects there is nothing especially distinctive. Although he is too positive to be called equivocal, he is always conservative in his deductions. The few passages of self-conscious boldness stand out conspicuously from the mass of cautious, tentative judgments and condensations of the implications of the sources. He rarely escapes from the wise but disconcerting thought that the records from which he works are often undependable and inadequate. Too often he is willing to seek refuge in that which he never tires of calling "delightful inconclusiveness." While attempting to determine whether or not Benedict Arnold was tormented by conscience in his exiled years, Bradford observes cautiously: "We cannot prove it or disprove it: we can only deduce possibilities from external facts. . . . The facts certainly indicate that Arnold's life was not a comfortable one." An innate modesty, or perhaps an acute realization of human limitations in interpreting the lives and characters of others, robs his convictions of force and curbs his flashes of insight before they can illuminate the lineaments of character.

Bradford's conservatism is interestingly revealed in the remark with which he closes his study of Thomas Paine. "I sometimes wish," he concludes wistfully, "I had the courage and character to be a rebel myself." In his own mind there undoubtedly lurked the consciousness of a troublesome kind of restraint. With surmise, which to more robust literary personalities often extends to conviction and dogma, he will have nothing to do. He is chary of those interpretations of character which cannot be deduced plainly from the records; and when he finds himself on the border line between clear deductions from well-established evidence and intuitive surmise, he scurries back to the safety of his sources in a fashion that often leaves both his courage and acumen in doubt.

Good taste—the kind of which New England, I hope, will continue to be proud—keeps Bradford's eye from lingering minutely on all aspects of human nature. When the question of Whitman's masculinity inadvertently slips into the study of Walt Whitman (*Biography and the Human Heart*), Bradford makes a wry face as he announces that this topic affords "an ample field for analysts of Freudian propensities." Prudishness does not characterize his attitude; it is rather sensitivity to any detail which might convey a highly colored revela-

Bradford in his later years.

tion. He refuses to allow his curiosity to become tinged with the morbid and vulgar; and when his kindly eye detects features that are distasteful to his sensibilities, he moves his glance elsewhere.

Impartiality, it is agreed, is a biographical virtue, but the impartiality which results in aloofness cannot be named unreservedly as a commendable quality. One feels Bradford's detachment too keenly; without waiting for verification from the *Journal,* one suspects that Bradford knew men largely through books and not through a profound richness of personal experience. The warmth and intimacy which come from poignant sympathy with life itself are rarely felt; there is only that sympathy with which we regard the race at large. To select a figure from the one hundred and more characters which stand in Bradford's galleries and say, "Here is supreme adaptability between subject and biographer" is impossible, for there is no instance in which one feels that the author was keenly attuned to the inner nature of his subject. Individual character comes to Bradford not through an acute feeling of dual sensibility, but rather from his ability to see objectively those distinguishing traits of personality as they are implied in the rich storehouses of autobiographies, diaries, and personal letters. Although he is more than an impartial agent between sources of information and the reader, his point of view lacks that subjective depth which underlies the penetrating re-creation of character.

Perhaps, too, a native benevolence is in some measure responsible for Bradford's inability to be rugged in his convictions concerning the true nature of man. His kindliness is refreshing in an age in which biography has become a fertile province for iconoclasts and lampooners; but it is this kindliness and generosity in viewing human frailty which have often caused him to seek refuge in an inscrutable smile. He is cognizant of the fact that the reader of biography is seeking some kind of identification between his own life and that of the figure portrayed, but in his attempt to offer the reader this identification he is never inclined to drag great men down to the reader's level, but rather he seeks to raise the reader's level to theirs. Disarming as such a procedure undoubtedly is to criticism, the fact remains that benevolence is not necessarily the path to truth. Even when Bradford is portraying figures around whom gossip and irrefutable evidence have woven the soiled garment of stigma, he is more largely concerned with detecting the noble features of character than he is with exposing and ridiculing the bad. His Yankee shrewdness rescues him from outright Pollyannaism, and one feels that were it not for this quality of shrewdness—which is a by-product of true conservatism—Bradford's portrayals of character would be in large measure a tribute to the nobility of human character.

In spite of the fact that he does not set out deliberately to exonerate and justify, his smile is kindly and forgiving. His shrewdness in observing man does not become the source from which an ironic attitude springs. Rather it serves as a check on that which could readily become eulogy. Irony, which appears only at rare intervals, is unbecoming to Bradford; and invective is beyond—and perhaps below—his aim. When the editor of *Harper's Magazine* suggested that he write a series of iconoclastic portraits, and informed the author that "in dealing with such a gallery we should expect you to proceed ruthlessly and with scant deference to tradition," Bradford replied that such a proposal made "a fascinating appeal to the worst elements in [his] nature."

The remainder of his reply is illuminating.

> I objected that such a work of destruction was not really worth doing, and that in the end it was likely to do more injury to the critic than to the character criticized. I urged that I did not want "to undermine, to overthrow, to destroy, even the things which deserve it," and I pointed out that "in every character I have portrayed so far it has been my endeavor to find the good rather than the evil, to set the figure firmly on its common human basis, but at the same time to insist that if the human heart were not worth loving, my work should not be worth doing." After reflecting on the matter, I made the counter-proposition to do "a group of somewhat discredited figures, and not endeavor in any way to rehabilitate or whitewash, but to bring out their real humanity and show that, after all, they have something of the same strength and weakness as all of us."

In his treatment of those who form the gallery of *Damaged Souls,* and the other "somewhat discredited figures" who occasionally force their way into his range of observation, Bradford's kindliness is pronounced. At times he reminds one of gentle Izaak Walton who saw all men in the rosy light of his own goodness, and again his attitude is tinged with a near approach to Pollyannaism. There is no instance in Bradford's varied galleries in which he is inclined to present a devasting exposé. In spite of the fact that he deals with no out-and-out rascals, one is led to believe that he would have made Iago less villainous and Goneril less despicable. He is, no doubt, aware of the frailty of human nature, but his innate goodness

and his conservatism help him to curb his flickering inclination to expose. His detachedness and sweet charity are pleasing to those who have a surfeit of the highly subjective, ironic kind of portraiture; but it is necessary, unhappily, to reflect on the superficiality into which his aloofness and goodness often led him. It is also fitting to reflect that such benevolence is its own reward.

The method which Bradford adopted is in large measure a product of his conservative point of view. The responsibility of re-creating he left for the lesser responsibility of selecting, condensing, and unifying. Working almost entirely from autobiographies, memoirs, diaries, and letters, he made it his chief task to disentangle those details which declare character most vividly from the mass of the inconsequential, and to fuse the characteristic qualities into a unified, complete impression. "The art of the psychographer," he writes, "consists in distinguishing these qualities, in developing and emphasizing them according to their relative importance in the particular subject. It is just here that the absorbing interest of psychography—as a business—lies, and I may say that it is a perpetual revelation to find how nature herself, as it were, takes a hand, and seems to dictate the structure and composition of the psychograph, suggesting a new order, a new treatment, a new richness and splendor of development with every new subject that presents itself."

Although nature herself may take a hand in dictating the structure and composition of the psychograph, the author who exploits the form to the extent to which Bradford goes in treating a hundred and more figures, becomes naturally inclined to follow a fairly consistent formula. In his essay **"Biography and the Human Heart,"** which gives its title to a posthumous collection of psychographs, he describes the formula by which he has often proceeded. Man's character, he believes, can be most satisfactorily studied by noting his characteristic reactions to dominant desires. Love, ambition, money, and religion, with their ramified attendant desires, and their antonyms, are the principal channels through which men reveal themselves most vividly and completely. The psychographical process, as Bradford applies it in his later studies, is to select from the biographical materials which he has collected or found readily available, those details which will characterize the individual's reactions to these four dominant desires. As an organizing principle, this formula has considerable usefulness.

This method of procedure, Bradford realized, could not always be applied. When an author swings clear of chronological sequence, he has a wide variety of arrangements from which to choose. "Instead of a monotonous renewal of the same qualities in the same order," writes the author, "every individual seems to suggest and require a different arrangement, a different emphasis." While attempting to trace the characters of scores of widely different figures, he probably allowed nature herself to take a hand and "dictate the structure and composition of the psychograph." For instance, in the gallery entitled *Wives,* he seeks to reveal character through a different set of dominants from those which he employs in *Biography and the Human Heart.* Although considerable variety exists in the arrangement, the sketches of Wives are developed by answering with more or less consistency and insight such questions as: Was she a woman who submerged herself largely in her home and husband? Did she really love her husband? Did religion play an important part in her life? Was she skilful in managing her domestic affairs?

Was she happy? A great deal of penetrating characterization is bound to result when such questions are answered discerningly.

At times the Bradford method consists chiefly in playing one authority against another, as in the study of Mrs. Abraham Lincoln, in which Herndon and Rankin are made to tell what they know, while Bradford sits in judgment of their acumen and authority. In a few of the psychographs there is a kind of genus-differentia process: the figure is identified with a type, and then individualized. It is scarcely profitable or inspiring to extend the list of Bradford's methods: it is enough to observe that there is little monotony which comes from a "renewal of the same qualities in the same order."

But no matter how nature takes a hand in dictating the organizing principles of the psychograph, selection, compression, and unification play the major rôles in the application of the various formulae. It is in the use of these three fundamental psychographical principles that the true essence of the Bradford method lies. Unless a judicious selection of detail is made from the mass of biographical materials, the psychograph cannot offer the essential character; and unless the carefully selected materials are compressed and unified with consummate skill, the study becomes little more than an accumulation.

Bradford's selection of details is generally discriminating. His ability to distinguish the essential qualities of character is especially remarkable in those instances in which the sources from which he worked are heavy with characteristic, revealing detail. He knows, with Sainte-Beuve, that "it is detail which makes things live." But he also knows that "there is nothing like detail to kill things. It is all a question of choice. The biographer must not overwhelm us with formless, inconsequent gossip. He must know how to go straight to the poignant touch which reveals, to pick that out, to stress it, without overstressing it, and to leave entirely aside the mass of the insignificant which merely confuses and obscures." The problem of separating the significant from the trifling is rarely difficult, but within the province of the highly characteristic alone, choices must be made which call for the most acute kind of discrimination. Will, for instance, the revealing detail of Alexandre Dumas' child-like temper be of as much value in portraying the essential Dumas as a notice of his vanity? In both details there lurks a richly suggestive lineament of character, but, hypothetically, limitation of space will not permit the author to stress them both. It is with such problems that the psychographer must deal, and Bradford's discernment of the highly significant rarely fails him.

Although his ability to distinguish the essential qualities of character is sufficiently remarkable to be called a talent, he is generally more successful in his selection of details in his studies of literary figures than he is in his accounts of military and political figures. His portraits of Pepys, Walpole, Keats, and Lamb are richer characterizations than those of Robert E. Lee, Theodore Roosevelt, and Woodrow Wilson. This can be accounted for, at least in part, by considering the fact that he was able, by reason of his own life, to see in searching perspective the features which declare most significantly the characters of men of letters; and by recalling that with literary figures he usually had excellent sources from which to draw his materials. In no instance, however, in his studies of military and political figures does his selection become random. If his study of Woodrow Wilson fails to indicate a discerning choice of details, it is owing to the fact that Bradford had an inadequate comprehension of what dominates such a life.

In the compression and unification of his carefully selected materials, Bradford encounters obstacles which he is not always able to surmount. His talent for condensation lies not in the concise presentation of details, but in the essential quality of the details themselves: his ability to compress reverts to his talent to select. For concise development of materials, his leisurely nature left him unendowed. And in his unification of details, he is too often prone to forget that the space devoted to brief transitional passages is of considerable value to the reader. Such passages give coherence to that which is otherwise little more than an arbitrary accumulation. Then, too, it is at times difficult to justify the order in which the author presents the essential aspects of character; but when personality is to be revealed in thirty pages, one cannot be too insistent on knowing why Lady Mary Wortley Montagu's letter-writing propensities are considered on the same page as her experiments with vaccination. At times it would seem that "nature herself" failed to come to Bradford's assistance in the arrangement of his materials. The urge for epitome is responsible for many an inconsecutive discussion.

Psychography, we are told, is not only the condensed, essential presentation of character; it is the artistic presentation as well. In the essay which appeared in the *Saturday Review of Literature* on May 23, 1925, under the title **"The Art of Biography,"** Bradford, while rehashing his earlier convictions about the uses of psychography, happily digresses for a brief paragraph in order to consider style. ". . . As with history," he writes, "a man is tempted to think that he can write a good life simply because he has a wide acquaintance with the facts. This is only the beginning. It is style that makes all books live that do live, style that makes poetry, that makes fiction, that makes drama. It is style and style alone, the form and quality of the words they utter, that makes the characters of Shakespeare the profoundest and loftiest creations of dramatic art. And the biographies which live are those in which the material is fused, transfigured, glorified by the imaginative intellect of the artist, working with the instrument which we call style. This it is that has made the instant success and enduring appeal of the biographical studies of Mr. Strachey."

The observation that "it is style that makes all books live that do live," and the reference to Strachey's "enduring appeal," leave the critic quite disconsolate when he undertakes to evaluate this side of Bradford's work. One might even wish for the sweet charity which Bradford himself used in his consideration of all mankind. Bradford's enduring appeal—if it is enduring—cannot rest on the same qualities as Lytton Strachey's. There is no more eloquent illustration of the well-worn maxim that the style is the man than in Gamaliel Bradford. The style of his biographical studies is the constrained manner of the mental and literary conservative.

One cannot read many of his works before he feels that Bradford is afraid of words. He is never completely their master; he fears the subtleties of their implications, and he is usually willing to compromise with adjectives which carry suggestion to only a moderate pitch. As a result, richness of phrase gives way to that which approaches frugality. With boldness, he will have little to do; and when, apparently tiring of his own moderation, he flings restraint to the winds and reaches verbal abandon with such phrases as "ravishing fascination," the reader is no more startled than the author, who, after committing this outrage of immoderateness, tiptoes hastily back to the use of the more timid adjectives.

There are times while reading Bradford that one wishes that the author would commit some verbal indecency in order to free the atmosphere of oppressive constraint. Restraint is a commendable literary virtue, but Bradford's manner suggests tightness and repression. His diction is fastidious only in so far as it is cautious. When a surge of impulsiveness manages to take hold of his pen, the passage which results is so different from his usual manner that the reader senses a perceptible interruption. Bradford enjoys his occasional verbal abandon, especially if it yields a passage heavy with sententiousness; but one feels that he is not completely comfortable while he is indulging in this form of pleasure.

Of brevity, Gamaliel Bradford spoke almost unceasingly in his consideration of the form of biography which he adopted. But of the "becoming brevity" of Lytton Strachey he had little. His ability to compress, as I have observed, lies in his remarkable talent for selecting highly characteristic details, not in his ability to be concise in their presentation and development. He lacked the talent for saying little and suggesting much; and although he was acutely conscious of the connotations of words, he was not always able to make one word say everything that the one word can say. His inability to be brilliantly concise—a virtue for which he constantly longed—can be traced again to his conservatism. The use of a strong adjective unqualified left Bradford uneasy. Two mild words are less dangerous than one strong word, and an adjective such as "uncomfortable" is safer than "anguished" or "tormented." True conciseness, however, is dependent not only on a feeling for words, but on the courage to use them.

In spite of the fact that his style lacks the boldness which often makes for brilliance, Bradford's manner illustrates in goodly measure the beauties of restraint, clarity, and refinement. With smartness he has no traffic; he escapes completely from any charge of cleverness. For *le mot rare* and epigram he does not strive, for his talent is unresponsive to their use. In rhetoric for its own sake he does not indulge, nor does he attempt to heighten lights and shadows merely for artistic effect. The same conservatism which robs him of boldness of phrase guards him against any inclination toward mere stylistic prettiness. Of the beauty of clarity, he is a supreme master. His most lucid effects are dependent not on sharpness of outline, but on the illumination which comes from simplicity and relative thoroughness. Bradford is never impatient with the reader who cannot grasp a lineament of character in a single phrase. He is willing to view the subject from many angles and—as is the case in the study of Dwight L. Moody—even to repeat. And his patience with the reader is quite consonant with his stylistic refinement. Bradford's refinement is not that of urbanity and studied grace—of pretentiousness there is nothing; it is the deeper refinement of modesty and simplicity. We have became so accustomed to look for refinement in urbanity that we are often prone to confuse fastidious dilettantism with literary aristocracy. Although Bradford's style lacks the glitter of brilliance, one must feel that the author is a literary thoroughbred.

His patience with the reader is the result of his quiet friendliness, a quality native to Bradford, and one which saves his style from coldness. At times an entire passage is given warmth by a kindly smile. Of the aloofness which comes from the demonstration or affectation of erudition, there is nothing. One is never told of the prodigious reading of the author

in the preparation of a portrait, nor is he made to feel Bradford's unapproachable authority. There is something peculiarly American in his warmth of manner, for there lurks in his attitude toward his subjects and his readers the conservative democracy which eschews the dictatorial, refuses to sit in austere judgment, but which insistently cherishes the right to think.

In addition to the qualities of restraint, clarity, and refinement of which he is master, Bradford has an ear for structural beauty. His style, generally free of arresting phrase, is marked by an evenness which is not without grace. In his evenness there is little monotony: it can be compared to the slow, well-modulated grace of a minuet. There are no sharp parentheses, no stirring crescendos; nor are there dissonances. The euphony of his manner is not dependent on facile variety, but rather on subtle quickenings and modulations of tone and tempo. Listen, for instance, to a representative passage which stands near the beginning of *The Soul of Pepys:*

> He had the average practical instincts of life, could do a day's work, groan over it and rebel against it, but do it. He could drive a hard bargain, and then, when his sympathy or vanity was touched, give away a round sum, or throw it away. He had an average intelligence, could apply a keen analysis to a problem that affected his own interest, made mistakes, imbibed prejudices, misjudged men and life and God and paid for it. Take him all in all, and allowing for his surroundings, he was average in morals, indulged his passions and regretted the indulgence, made good resolutions and broke them and made them again, judged others severely and himself leniently and severely also, fought the old battle with the flesh and the devil, sometimes shamefully, sometimes triumphantly, but always humanly. In short, he was a man amazingly like you and me, and the chief among the many interests of his wonderful Diary is that it reveals him and you and me with a candor, an unparalleled, direct, sincere clarity, which has never been equalled, except perhaps in the Essays of Montaigne. If he was average in the essentials of his character, his power of displaying that character and his frankness in doing so were not average at all.

Such a passage, and his style at large, indicate that Bradford was more than a journeyman of letters. He succeeded in giving his readers not only the condensed, essential presentation of character, but the artistic presentation as well. He was no "rugged individualist" in either thought or manner, and he must be content without the insignia of intellectual and literary brilliance. But his talent for selection, and the beauties of restraint, clarity, refinement, and euphony which mark his style are completely reconcilable with true literary distinction. His conservatism of thought and manner is not always a positive virtue; but in an age in which all manner of hypotheses are advanced in a desperate effort to yield a doubtful truth, and in which style is often confused with cleverness, Bradford's moderateness is not without value to the race of biographers at large. Despite his unwillingness to offer highly subjective interpretations of character, there is probably more biographical truth in Gamaliel Bradford's careful deductions than in the works of the whole school of fiction writers who feel that they have intuitively found the answer to the riddle of human character. Then, too, it is pleasant to reflect that Bradford's benevolence to mankind may have revealed a share of the larger truth of human nature. (pp. 76-87)

Mark Longaker, "A Naturalist of Souls: Gamaliel
Bradford," in his Contemporary Biography, University of Pennsylvania Press, 1934, pp. 67-90.

EDWARD WAGENKNECHT (essay date 1982)

[*Wagenknecht is an American biographer and critic who knew
Bradford personally and used his psychographic technique in
his own studies of Charles Dickens and Mark Twain. In the
following excerpt from his biographical and critical study of
Bradford, Wagenknecht surveys Bradford's career, examining
his poetry, drama, and fiction as well as his psychographies.*]

Poetry was Gamaliel Bradford's first and dearest love. He
was only nineteen when he wrote that if he could not be a
great poet, he expected either to commit suicide or die mad.
He did none of these things, but before the year was out, he
had produced nearly two volumes of short poems, was working on the narrative **Bertha** and the poetic drama **Bacchus
and Ariadne,** and was planning another narrative, **Angelica,**
a comedy in the style of Aristophanes, and the novel **Girard.**
Even as late as 1920 he wrote a correspondent that he
thought of his prose as merely a means of making people read
his poetry.

His verses divide themselves into two classes—lyrics and narratives. He got two collections of the former into print—*A
Pageant of Life* (1904) and *Shadow Verses* (1920)—and one
long narrative, *A Prophet of Joy* (1920). Most, not all, of the
narratives are early. Lyrics he continued to write, with certain hiatuses, throughout his life (by 1928 he counted well
over 2,000), the only important change being that, as he grew
older, he ceased to write about the historical and cultural
themes he had treated in his early sonnets and concentrated
on personal interests, reflections, and emotions. (p. 33)

Bradford considered [*A Prophet of Joy*] his major poetic enterprise, perhaps his supreme work. . . . Though it was not
published until 1920, there were three earlier versions, two
in prose and one in verse. It is a kind of novel in verse, on the
model of the long narrative poems of Byron and his contemporaries, written in iambic pentameter eight-line stanzas,
rhymed *abababcc,* of which there are 567, divided into six
books. Lo, here, as Chaucer would say, "the forme":

> Miss Theodora Perkins was unwed
>   At thirty-five, yet delicately charming,
> An idle and bewitching life she led,
>   And thought love's snares perhaps somewhat alarming,
> In earlier days she had been city-bred,
>   Then bought a country place, and played at farming,
> Had hens and cows but did not milk herself,
> Nor touch the polished pans upon the shelf.

Bradford feared he would be accused of imitating Byron, but
he told William Lyon Phelps that John Fletcher had been
more important to him, and it is clear that Cervantes also
contributed. Perhaps his own best description of the poem
was made in a letter to Ellery Sedgwick:

> Meanwhile, I amuse my leisure in what you will no
> doubt consider the singularly futile diversion of
> composing a vast narrative, semi-epic, semi-
> humorous poem. It is something I have had in mind
> and worked over at odd times for thirty years, a
> long story of an enthusiastic youth who preaches
> an inspired gospel of joy to a cold world and in
> doing it meets with many strange characters and
> singular adventures and is loved by many women

> and finally gives his life for his cause and in the long
> process of his history touches all phases of our com-
> plicated modern life, Bolshevism and Christian Sci-
> ence and Christian sacrifice and capital and com-
> promise and politics, all in a broad and light and
> laughing way, but with love and sunshine and with-
> out satire or bitterness. At least I would have it so,
> and I am weaving it all in octave stanzas after the
> fashion of Byron and the great Italian epics, and it
> is an endless amusement and distraction to me and
> would probably be an endless weariness to every-
> body else.

Percival Smith, a millionaire's son, starts out, Don Quixote-
like, to teach men how to enjoy life. He stays for a time with
Miss Theodora, a distant cousin, who half falls in love with
him and from whom he takes french leave with her purse,
after which he falls in with one Jarvis, whom he encounters,
with two girls, in an amusement park. He meets Morgan, a
reporter, addresses a meeting of radicals, and embarks upon
a high-flown romance with a film actress, Aurelia McGoggin.
Aurelia's aunt and her brother, Slippery Bill, burn Jarvis's
books in imitation of Cervantes. Percival is taken to a Christian Science meeting, where he addresses the worshippers.
After having been introduced to Ezekiel Waters, an apostle
of violence, he is caught in a police raid on an anarchist meeting, but Aurelia pleads for him and he is discharged. Theodora tries to interest him in a fair but rich and fickle cousin,
Cecilia. He falls in with Peter Scrimp, a multi-millionaire,
speculates in Zona Oil, and becomes a director. Stocks crash;
he is persuaded to go into politics and is elected. There is a
strike at Scrimp's factory. Percival pleads with the men to
avoid violence and is warned off by Waters. He refuses to
leave, faces the mob, and is killed. Aurelia vows to carry on
his work.

From this incomplete summary it may be seen that *A Prophet of Joy* has a very wide range and touches a variety of
American aspects and concerns. Charles Wharton Stork
called it the most important book of verse since *The Congo*
and *Spoon River Anthology,* and William Lyon Phelps found
it an original contribution to literature, resembling nothing
else that had been written in America. But Barrett Wendell,
who read it with care and admired it in many aspects,
thought the treatment too genteel, and Bradford at least half
agreed with him.

> I appreciate fully what you mean about the lack of
> boldness and freedom. The thing should have more
> of a large vigor and sweep of movement, should ap-
> pear to pour and really should pour out a fullness
> and abundance of life which should suggest much
> wider possibilities behind it than could be crowded
> and compressed into any such compass. And the
> Bohemian world should be rougher, more eminent-
> ly and intimately alive. I felt the need of this and
> hoped I had got it by suggestion at least, but I can
> well understand that I haven't.

Perhaps. Or perhaps Wendell was asking for a different kind
of poem. One cannot but wonder whether an admixture of
the kind of realism he desired might not have vitiated the fundamental idea of a lighthearted crusade in the interest of joy.

As usual, Bradford's own attitude wavered. He was enrap-
tured when he reread the second canto, and he said of the oc-
taves that they "writhe like serpents, and glitter like stars,
and rattle and clatter like mad castanets." Perhaps he was
only half satirical in looking forward to the day when his

poem should be established "as one of the humorous classics of the world" and editors would study the earlier versions "as they gathered up the early drafts and paralipomena of Faust." On the other hand, though he was sure the *Prophet* ought to sell as well as *Spoon River* and *North of Boston,* in his heart he thought a sale of 300 to 1,000 copies more likely. The fundamental weakness of the poem is that it is not sufficiently of a piece, and the tragic ending comes as a shock. The light, almost flip tone of the earlier portion is simply junked, and the work is not sufficiently focused so that one can be quite sure just what the author was trying to say. (pp. 42-4)

There are so many contradictions and so much self-mockery in Bradford's comments on his poetry that it is hard to believe he ever arrived at a settled evaluation of it. Intellectually he was sure that the practically universal view that he had talent as a biographer but not as a creative writer was probably correct. Yet hope refused to die. "But when my prose has made my reputation," he wrote in 1922, "I have an intimate confidence that my verse will in the end come to stand as high, or higher". . . . (pp. 46-7)

There can be no question as to Bradford's immense cleverness and fecundity in poetry, and perhaps his characteristic note is strongest in those poems in which he achieves a surprising, sometimes illuminating, slightly cynical twist in the closing verses. Rhymes chased themselves without let or hindrance through his head; he wrote verse as easily as prose, and everything was poured out *mit einem Gusse* ["with a gush"].

This gift was not an unmixed blessing, however; like the gifts of the fairies, it imposed conditions. Bradford certainly wrote far too many lyrics, playing infinite variations upon the same theme and expressing the same idea hundreds of times. He himself once wrote:

> A multitude of songs will come
>   Upon me in the night.
> If out of all the number some
>   Were good enough to write!
>
> And some have speed and some have flow
>   And some perchance have wit
> But not a single one, I know,
>   Is really exquisite.

However this may be, he was simply not the kind of writer who can spend hours or days over a lyric, polishing it to an impossible perfection. (p. 48)

Bradford attempted dramatic composition in both prose and verse. *Unmade in Heaven* was the only play ever to see print, and none was ever acted. (p. 49)

"I see more and more," wrote Bradford in 1927, "that my plays are all skeletons. They need the flesh of richer observation and more varied color, and above all again, just that same quality of style that makes Sophocles and Shakespeare, and without which the gates of Parnassus will never be opened to us." But the stage door, if not Parnassus, has certainly opened to many who were neither Shakespeare nor Sophocles, and all in all, Bradford's plays are probably about as good as we could expect to have written by an intelligent man and a gifted writer with no practical theatrical experience. He understood his characters, and he knew how to develop a theme, but his action is often stiff and a little awkward (even in *Unmade in Heaven* he does not always manage his "curtains" well), and the analytical note is often overplayed. Except when he was president of the Playgoers Club, he

never even had any contacts with theater people; then he got an evening behind the scenes, "on the strict promise on my part that I should not 'monkey with the ballet girls.' Fancy me monkeying with the ballet girls! I should have been more afraid of them than of a collection of wild tigers." Yet the dream "of having one of my comedies acted to a crowded house, of being called before the curtain and making the speech that I have made to myself so many times that I know it better than the Apostles' Creed" never died, and when he participated in a reading of *Unmade in Heaven* in his house, almost at the end of his life, "I had all I could do to restrain my sobs." That same year, he was greatly excited when a woman in Seattle expressed interest in achieving a production and "immediately began to imagine a great triumph for *Unmade in Heaven* on Broadway and all over the country. Incredible child!" (pp. 57-8)

Bradford wrote nine novels, of which four—*The Private Tutor, Between Two Masters, Matthew Porter,* and *Her Only Way*—were published. There are also a novelette, *Bags of Gold,* and a few short stories—"The Photograph," conjecturally assigned to the 1890s, and **"Death's Dainty Ways"** and **"The Meteor,"** both written in 1920. (p. 59)

Since the novel is a far more flexible form than the drama, Bradford had less difficulty here in getting his characters on and off, but still with a tendency to stiffness and overreliance for development on one arranged confrontation after another. The author's weakness for subplots led him to use a larger number of characters than he needed or had time and space to develop, and if his people sometimes seem to understand themselves and each other more completely than we do in life, the reason probably is that his mind was essentially that of a critic or essayist rather than, in the narrower sense of the term, a creative writer. His dialogue is often excellent, and if his subject matter sometimes seems trifling, we must remember his rooted conviction that humor and lightness of tone were the qualities in which contemporary fiction was most deficient.

In 1920 he thought he liked *Autumn Love* and *Woodbine Lodge* best among his novels; two years later, he rated *Matthew Porter* a great book. He could sell himself short, as when he wrote Lyman Beecher Stowe, then associated with Doubleday, that his novels were

> quaint, old-fashioned things, depending on ease and naturalness of dialogue and character-study, and with altogether too little story interest. Especially are they entirely out of the current style: no adultery in them, no sordidness, no Main Street or Babbitt detail whatever, just pleasant people doing and saying pleasant things, after the much-despised Victorian way, with the author trying to lift a little bit of the veil that always shrouds our souls.

Sometimes, too, he thought his novels failures because he had not had sufficiently wide contacts with life. But probably his most considered comment was the one he addressed to himself and ended with a question:

> I have such a wonderful gift of words, and I have such power of constructing, of putting things together with symmetry and adaptation and emphasis and climax, and I have such knowledge of human nature, and above all I have, what counts more for intelligent readers in a novel than anything else, the gift of brilliant and telling and natu-

ral dialogue. Why cannot I write novels? Why?
Why? Why, My God, why?

(pp. 70-1)

The general reader knows Gamaliel Bradford almost exclusively as the inventor and leading exponent of psychography. A psychograph is a picture of the soul or the psyche, a study of the character and personality of a human being. Bradford coined the word for himself and then discovered that George Saintsbury had already used it to describe the work of Charles Augustin Sainte-Beuve (1804-1869). Though it indicates accurately what the character writers try to do, the uninitiated are always in danger of supposing that it must have an affinity with psychoanalysis or some kind of psychological vagary. This troubled Bradford sufficiently that by 1924 he had stopped pushing the word. Unfortunately there is no really satisfactory substitute. (p. 72)

What . . . is the difference between psychography and biography as commonly conceived? A biography tells the story of a man's life; a psychograph probes his character and personality. A biographer arranges his materials chronologically, a psychographer topically.

As for formal psychology, Bradford saw it as the antithesis of all biography. "Biography is the study of the individual, pursued with all the aids of psychology, but always centered on the individual at last. Psychology is constantly and properly occupied with the general and uses the individual only to illustrate its general laws and conclusions." In Freud he found only "a distortion and exaggeration and fantastic elaboration and misunderstanding of perfectly plain and long known facts." But he got nothing from Roback or MacDougall either, or, in a different area, from such a writer as Spengler. "I was brought up in a storm of general principles. My father lived with them, delighted in them, and talked about them perpetually. He was quick and keen to note facts, but every fact instantly became the text for some large, sweeping deduction and assertion." Since the son had tied himself to reality by concentrating on the individual, he could hardly have been expected to be pleased when the psychologists threatened to take biography over. (p. 73)

Bradford's ideal was to build his psychographs into a tight structure in which one topic led to another in order of climax so that the character emerged at last in terms of an almost organic unity. Structure and the use of quotations were the two aspects of his work to which he gave the most careful attention, using quotations both as evidence, to support his own observations, deductions, and generalizations, and for atmosphere, to bring the reader, as it were, into the subject's presence and allow him to hear his voice. Unlike Sainte-Beuve's, his quotations are characteristically short and woven into his text.

In an early letter, he went so far as to describe his portraits as consisting "largely of carefully selected brief quotations from the person's own words, woven together so as to give as complete and rounded a portrayal of him as possible." But this was an exaggeration even then, and it became more an exaggeration as time marched on. When he wrote of the politicos treated in [*As God Made Them: Portraits of Some Nineteenth-Century Americans*] and *The Quick and the Dead,* he found himself quoting much less than of old. "I come more and more to sum up and condense the results of my own thought and study and depend less and less upon the actual words of the subject for illustration." This was partly because

his subjects were now somewhat less eloquent or quotable than the more imaginative figures with whom he had concerned himself in, say, *Bare Souls,* but he also thought that his work on the religious trilogy [*Darwin, D.L. Moody: A Worker in Souls,* and *Life and I: An Autobiography of Humanity*] had encouraged his tendency toward generalization. (pp. 77-8)

Bradford used exclamations, rhetorical questions, and addresses to the reader freely, especially in his earlier work. "Oh, the truth of history!" "Oh, to have been present at that dinner!" "How I should like to have heard him!" "Something to love here, is there not?" "Could you imitate her, madam?" "Remember this, when you read some of the following extracts and you will wonder as I do." "God knows, a husband's love is a pitiful thing." Even, "Whew!" He was also capable of directly expressing his attitude toward a subject and of open reference to his own experience. Thus he speaks of Madame de Sévigné as "this beautifully rounded character," parts from Seward with the greatest reluctance, thanks heaven that General Sherman did not talk more, is glad that Stanton did not write his contemplated book on the Bible (since in this case Bradford would have had to read it), and is so moved by an utterance of General Thomas that he feels the tears in his eyes. We know that he was thinking of his father when he wrote of Theodore Roosevelt's perpetual vehemence, "I speak with feeling, having passed a considerable portion of my life with just such a character," and he was obviously thinking of himself when he wrote of the health of Alexander H. Stephens, "How far this fiery energy of the soul was responsible for the failure of the body, who shall say?"

He could build up to a quotation when he thought it necessary or interpret its implications after he had presented it. Thus when Mrs. James G. Blaine calls her husband "the best man I have ever known," and then adds, "Do not misunderstand me. I do not say that he is the best man that ever lived, but that of the men I have thoroughly known, he is the best," Bradford adds, "Could the interplay of qualifying analysis and passionate affection be better illustrated than in that? The more one ponders on the sentence, the more one is impressed by the rich significance of it." (pp. 82-3)

[Bradford's] outstanding characteristic as a psychographer was a wide-ranging sympathy and pity; . . . he saw the absence of this element as Sainte-Beuve's greatest limitation. When Dr. W. W. Keen thought he had handled Catherine the Great too gently, he replied, "But it [is] always my principle not indeed to slight the frailties but to make them comparatively unimportant where there are great human qualities beside them." It was characteristic that he should admit the addiction of both Toombs and Hooker to alcohol but treat it only incidentally, yet he is generally pretty scrupulous about noting exceptions to his generalizations about character, even when he plays them down.

Though he could not help liking some of his subjects better than others, Bradford opposed Maurois's view that the biographer should select only persons with whom he felt sympathy.

The truth is he should be in sympathy with all his subjects. For the time he should become the soldier, the saint, the scholar, the artist, the lover, the toiler, even the sinner, not in the fact of his sin, but in the possibility of it. It is by this universal sympathy that he makes his biography real and alive, and he can thus awaken in his readers the sympathy that he feels himself.

In 1930 he expressed the view that "just because I have no character of my own, it sometimes seems to me that I have a lot of other peoples' " and that "though I have no life of my own, I live passionately in the lives of others," and that same year, characteristically adapting himself to his correspondent, he played down the moral element in his work in a letter to Mencken:

> More and more, I am afraid, I get to study all kinds of human beings for the pure interest of them, without the slightest desire to commend or the opposite. I see so much to admire as well as so much to disapprove of in myself, that I am singularly tolerant of the weaknesses and even of the virtues—which sometimes require more tolerance—of other people.

But he was truer to his own temperament and practice when he confided to his journal concerning Moody:

> I must try above all to enter into Moody's own state of mind and inner life, to see the world as he sees it and interpret it as he interprets it. But all that time, as always, there is and must be the play of my own spirit above and beyond all this.

In the vast majority of his psychographs, Bradford achieved both these ends. The first achievement made him one of the most perceptive of biographers, and the second explains why, though they read most biographers because they are interested in their subjects, people read Bradford, regardless of this consideration, because they are interested in him. (pp. 84-5)

[*A Naturalist of Souls*] is the key document for the study of Bradford's psychography, for it is the only volume in which we see his method in the making. The first studies were planned as straight literary criticism, but as one turns the successive pages, psychography emerges, develops, and at last takes over altogether, the pivotal chapter being the one on Clarendon, analyzing "the work and the character of one to whom psychography is deeply indebted for models and inspiration." Finally, as Bradford himself points out, "the last four portraits [in the 1926 edition] are elaborate specimens of psychography working consciously, and the last two are as finished psychographs as it is in my power to produce." (p. 87)

Psychography first appears at the beginning of the Leopardi [psychograph], whose Section I might well be the first, orientational, biographical section of a full-fledged psychograph. Section II deals with Leopardi's scholarship, and Section III considers him as a man of letters, but the interest in character delineation persists throughout. The succeeding papers from the Trollope through the Lemaître weave back and forth between description and evaluation of the work and commentary on the personality; in the Burton, the emphasis is on the work, as the title shows. Contrasts and comparisons involving many writers, in many times and countries, abound. Of Trollope Bradford remarks that "he accomplishes with Titanic effort what Shakespeare, Fielding, Miss Austen, Thackeray, and Dickens do with divine ease and unerring instinct," which must be very nearly the only kind thing he ever said about Dickens. If his enthusiasm over Trollope's hunting scenes seems surprising, it is only one more example of his ability to respond to the interests of subjects wholly unlike himself. The study of Dumas is generous toward both man

and writer and remarkable for the author's ability to understand the fine qualities which coexisted with both extraordinarily naive egotism and a flagrant disregard of what a New England writer might be expected to regard as imperative moral principles. Because of its preoccupation with an art his commentator shares with the subject, the study of Clarendon is the most professional in the volume; it shows knowledge of Burnet and Lauderdale as well as Clarendon and includes many references to Tacitus and Saint-Simon.

It seems curious that of the four climactic papers in *A Naturalist of Souls,* the first three should, alone among Bradford's portraits, deal with classical subjects. The title "Ovid among the Goths" comes from *As You Like It,* and Bradford himself called attention to its inaccuracy, since it was to "Tomi, a little colony, half Greek, half barbarian, on the Black Sea, near the mouth of the Danube" that Ovid was exiled. To the extent that the study is focused upon this period in the subject's life, it is more specialized than the others, but the concentration is not complete. Xenophon is called "one of the most sweetly, most wholesomely religious natures that ever lived," and the modern reader of "Letters of a Roman Gentleman" is likely to be pulled up sharply and enviously by the opening sentence, which begins, "To us who dwell in settled peace." With all three of the classical subjects, however, the reader must feel strongly the absence of the memorabilia which the writer would have had available in studying more modern figures.

The portrait of Saint Francis of Sales may seem specialized, too, in its concentration upon the subject as a shepherd of souls, but after all this was his life, and certainly Bradford brings in many more general "human" qualities. There is one priceless quotation which has lost nothing since either Francis wrote it or Bradford quoted it. One of the saint's penitents, worried about whether it was right for her to follow the current fashion of powdering her hair, sent him a message imploring his counsel. "Tell her to powder her hair, if she likes," he replied, "so long as her heart is right; for the thing is not worth so much bothering about. Don't get your thoughts entangled among these spider-webs. The hairs of this girl's spirit are more snarled up than those of her head."

Bradford claimed to have spent fifteen years on his Civil War books, ten of them on Lee, and *Lee the American* was his first published volume of psychography. Its individual chapters attracted considerable attention when published serially in the *Atlantic Monthly,* the *South Atlantic Quarterly,* and the *Sewanee Review* between 1910 and 1912, and the book was one of his most successful, being welcomed with special enthusiasm in the South, where considerable pleasure and surprise was felt that a New Englander could respond with such warmth to the great hero of the Confederacy.

The body of the book comprises eleven chapters: "Lee Before the War," "The Great Decision," "Lee and Davis," "Lee and the Confederate Government," "Lee and His Army," "Lee and Jackson," "Lee in Battle," "Lee as a General," "Lee's Social and Domestic Life," "Lee's Spiritual Life," and "Lee after the War."

It will be clear at once that what we have here is a much less highly integrated psychograph than the author was later to achieve; indeed he himself once spoke of the book as "a series of studies on Lee." Remnants of the chronological method of conventional biography survive at both the beginning and the end, and in the chapters on "Lee and Davis" and "Lee and Jackson" the focus is almost as much on the others as on Lee. Transitions are sometimes awkward, and the introduction of quotations less gracefully managed than in later years; neither is their application always entirely clear and obvious. (pp. 88-91)

There are four generals in *Confederate Portraits*—Joseph E. Johnston, J. E. B. Stuart, James Longstreet, and P. G. T. Beauregard—and one "Rear Admiral" or privateer, Raphael Semmes. Alexander H. Stephens was Vice President of the Confederacy, and Judah P. Benjamin held several Cabinet posts. Robert Toombs served in both military and civil capacities, but his service in the second field was the more important.

In the Preface the author apologizes for what some readers may consider his harshness, and it is true that only the Stuart and Stephens portraits are wholly admiring in tone. The studies of all the generals except Stuart are essentially studies in failure, the whole first part of the Johnston being devoted to a discussion of what was wrong with him and why he did not accomplish more. Aside from his faults as a commander, the answer is sought in his "schoolboy petulance" and "constant attitude of disapproval, of fault-finding, of resentment even approaching sullenness," and the problem becomes that of reconciling these things with his charm and amiability in personal relationships. Though both aspects are adequately described, Bradford does little to reconcile them, and the net result is an impression of incompleteness.

Longstreet and Beauregard are both given credit for honest patriotism, but both were handicapped by vanity, jealousy, and an overdeveloped tendency to criticize. Beauregard had too a weakness for devising elaborate plans to meet contingencies which never developed; Davis called it "driveling on possibilities," and the phrase haunted Bradford. Stuart, on the other hand, was a kind of D'Artagnan. Bradford was always remarkable for his ability to understand and sympathize with persons wholly unlike himself (in this case, exceptional purity in personal conduct would seem to be the only outstanding trait they shared), and the author is quite carried away by his subject's exuberance, his laughter and song, and his genuine joy in life. He cannot deny that Stuart's reports were flowery, yet he declares he loves them. He does not, however, deny the man's limitations, especially on the intellectual side ("Again and again he reminds me of a boy playing soldiers"), and he felt that he was fortunate in being killed at thirty-one.

The portrait of Semmes has the most self-indulgent beginning of any Bradford wrote. He opens with a playful speculation about names, suggested by but not limited to his subject's, and proceeds to develop his own delighted boyhood conception of Semmes as a pirate. Psychography properly speaking does not begin until the ninth page of a twenty-eight-page study, after which we learn that, though capable of coarseness, Semmes had elements of the Christian gentleman about him. The odor of piracy is not wholly blown away, however, and one gets the impression that the author rather relished it. (pp. 92-3)

At the suggestion of Ellery Sedgwick, and rather against his own preference, Bradford used for the first time in *Union Portraits* the numbered divisions within each paper which appeared in nearly all his subsequent work, and this apparently both accented his structure and made for easier reading. Here are five generals—George B. McClellan, Joseph Hooker, George Gordon Meade, George Henry Thomas, and Wil-

liam T. Sherman; two Cabinet officers—Edwin M. Stanton and William H. Seward; one senator—Charles Sumner; and one journalist—Samuel Bowles. (p. 94)

Since Bradford's skill as psychographer never ceased to develop, it should go without saying that many of his later portraits are more consummately done than those in the Civil War trilogy. Moreover, the writers and artists to whom he so often later devoted himself had considerably more substance than the men of action with whom he dealt here. The greatest shortcoming of the Civil War books, however, is that Bradford never faces, or even shows himself aware of, the war problem. Having observed in the Thomas that "a man's conscience is, of course, higher than his military duty," he adds weakly that "the instances where the two should be separated are very rare indeed." Interestingly enough, this matter is most troublesome in connection with Lee himself. Here was one of the most high-minded and winning of human beings, yet he owes his fame to having set thousands of his fellow countrymen to slaughtering each other. Bradford quotes two of Lee's own immensely suggestive utterances on this point but discusses neither of them: "The great mistake of my life was taking a military education" and "For my own part, I much enjoy the charms of civil life, and find too late that I have wasted the best part of my existence."

On the other hand, Bradford was never to achieve a more impressive ending than that of *Lee the American,* where he tells his reader that he wished to do the book partly because, in a country which worships success, Lee was a man who remains great although he failed, who believed that "human virtue should be equal to human calamity" and proved that it could be. The final words are devoted to this incomparable and beautifully told anecdote about Lee's postwar days as president of a small southern college:

> A young sophomore was once summoned to the president's office and gently admonished that only patience and industry would prevent the failure that would inevitably come to him through college and through life.
>
> "But, General, you failed," remarked the sophomore, with the inconceivable ineptitude of sophomores.
>
> "I hope that you may be more fortunate than I," was the tranquil answer.
>
> Literature can add nothing to that.

Portraits of Women was conceived as "preliminary studies or sketches" for several volumes of psychographs of American women which Bradford planned to have follow his Civil War books. . . . Bradford himself thought it superior to its immediate successor and was always inclined to resent its modest sale, though he admitted that it was not planned "deliberately as a whole" but had "grown in a rather haphazard way." He wrote it in odds and ends of time while mainly occupied with the Civil War trilogy, "merely gathering what I could from such correspondence and gossip as came in my way. To be sure, they were all subjects that I had long been more or less familiar with." It is the only one of his books which contains nine portraits, and it lacks bibliography, annotations, index, and formal divisions within each paper. Not surprisingly, its organization of materials, while not rambling, is considerably less schematic than in most of the later portraits. An interesting passage in the Preface explains the necessity when portraying women of dealing with exceptions rather than with average personages. The psychographer must have abundant material, and usually it is women who have lived exceptional lives that leave such material behind them. The psychography of queens and artists and authors and saints is little, if any, more interesting than that of your mother or mine, or of the first shopgirl we meet. I would paint the shopgirl's portrait with the greatest pleasure, but the material is lacking.

The subjects are Lady Mary Wortley Montagu, Lady Holland, Jane Austen, Fanny Burney, Mrs. Samuel Pepys, Madame de Sévigné, Madame du Deffand, Madame de Choiseul, and Eugénie de Guérin. (pp. 96-8)

Jane Austen is the only one of his subjects in this book that Bradford could have expected his readers to know much about in advance. After having established her provenance, he gives much attention to her mockery, citing his evidence first from her books, then from her letters. Thence he proceeds to his second theme, finding warm humanity under the "demure demeanor" and "an infinite fund of tenderness, a warm, loving, hoping, earnest heart," especially in familial relationships. Yet, in the final analysis, it remains true that though Jane Austen loved mankind in general, or at least took great interest in it, she found "most individual specimens unattractive and even contemptible." (p. 99)

Portraits of American Women might almost, as the author was aware, have been called "Portraits of New England Women," since of its eight subjects only Frances Willard did not hail from that region. There are four writers—Harriet Beecher Stowe, Margaret Fuller, Louisa May Alcott, and Emily Dickinson; one educator—Mary Lyon; one reformer—Frances Willard; and one First Lady—Abigail Adams. In a class by herself is the author's great-aunt, Sarah Alden Bradford Ripley (1793-1867), one of the learned ladies of her time, who was studied largely from private papers.

The Harriet Beecher Stowe has one of Bradford's characteristic quick beginnings:

> She was a little woman, rather plain than beautiful, but with energy, sparkle and vivacity written all over her. I always think of her curls, but they were not curls of coquetry or curls of sentiment, they were just alive, as she was, and danced and quivered when she nodded and glowed.

We proceed to background and achievement, basic equipment, fundamental interests, and the impulse toward expression and reform, in life and in writing. There is some literary criticism in Section IV, and the discussion of Mrs. Stowe's sunny temperament leads to an amusing excursus in which Bradford, taking his key from the unexpected interest in Rubens which he shared with his subject, indulges himself by wondering whether, had she been "a pagan suckled in a creed outworn," she might have followed it with the same proselytizing ardor that she gave to Christianity," and conjures up an image of her, "thyrsus in her hand, undraped in a dainty, if limited, garment of fawnskin, careering over the pastures by the sea, at the head of a Bacchic squadron of middle-aged New England matrons." But after this "piquant, if indecorous," passage, he pays his closing tribute to *Uncle Tom's Cabin* as "one of the greatest moral agencies the world has seen." (pp. 101-02)

Bradford's first impression of [Frances Willard, the founder of the Women's Christian Temperance Union] was favorable, but he soon found that she repelled him and even worried about whether he might bring the wrath of the WCTU down upon both the *Atlantic Monthly* and himself, and in the introductory essay to *Wives,* he would write, "She was a splendid woman, only I could not bear her, would have walked miles to avoid meeting her, and that got into my portrait too."

Yet the study is eminently fair and dispassionate and structurally perhaps the most interesting in the book. It has a good opening sentence: "She had the great West behind her; its sky and its distances, its fresh vigor and unexampled joy," and this is followed by an effective summary of Miss Willard's life experience and personality traits, which leads in turn to the quotation which strikes Bradford's keynote: "The chief wonder of my life is that I dare to have so good a time, both physically, mentally, and religiously." Next he describes her work, first in its effect upon others and then upon herself. What a wonderful story is that of the hostess who thoughtlessly offered her a glass of wine. "The blood flashed in cheek and brow as I said to her, 'Madam, two hundred thousand women would lose something of their faith in humanity if I should drink a drop of wine.' " And Bradford comments: "Think what it must be to feel the eyes of two hundred thousand women fixed upon you from the time you wake till the time you sleep again. That is the way Miss Willard lived."

Bradford's third book about women, *Wives* (1925), differed from its predecessors in being devoted to women who would never have been heard of save that they happened to marry famous or infamous men. (pp. 105-06)

The publication of *Wives* followed hard upon that of *Bare Souls* (1924), and there could not be a sharper contrast than that between the two. *Bare Souls* presented the writer the challenge of superb material, the matchless self-revelation of a group of writers, several of whom touched genius. Except for Mrs. Butler, the material for *Wives* was scattered and scanty and the problem often that of determining the woman's traits from what had been written about her husband. (p. 106)

[The] two most remarkable portraits in *Wives* are those of Sarah Butler and Harriet Blaine. The latter is very interesting structurally, for the author surrounds Mrs. Blaine with concentric circles, seeing her in the world, in her home, in her relations with her husband and, finally, with her own soul. The peculiarity of Sarah Butler's portrait is that virtually all the material is derived from the letters she wrote between 1860 and 1865, which have been printed only in connection with Butler's own much more extensive correspondence. These letters are superb in quality, though limited in extent; if she had less "ease and natural expression" than Harriet Blaine, Mrs. Butler had more "imaginative depth and power" and was a much more charming person. Naturally we see her mainly, though not exclusively, in her relations with her husband, and Bradford passes over the question of how such a woman could have loved such a man on the ground that "we see the love of higher, finer natures just so erring every day," yet, for all his admiration for Sarah Butler, he does not hesitate to point out her shortcomings—"a touch of . . . acerbity" and "just the slightest trace . . . of that lack of higher, finer delicacy" which is so much more prominent in her husband. (pp. 108-09)

The Soul of Samuel Pepys was the first book Bradford had devoted to a single figure since *Lee the American.* It was divided into seven chapters: "The Man and the Diary," "Pepys and His Office," "Pepys and His Money," "Pepys and Humanity," "Pepys and His Intellect," "Pepys and His Wife," and "Pepys and God." If this is compared with the chapter headings in *Lee the American,* the advance in integration and consequent mastery of psychographic structure will be evident. (p. 131)

[Bradford] sees Pepys as a very able man and a worthy public servant, honest at least by the standards of his time, an average man in character but much more than that in his ability to reveal it, and far above the average in his passion for books and music. Since Bradford had already written of Mrs. Pepys in *Portraits of Women,* he had to be careful to avoid repetition when he came to the chapter on domestic life. He presents the lady sympathetically, making a valiant effort to recover her own point of view wherever it can be ascertained. All in all, this is a delightfully human chapter, with just enough spice supplied by the husband's occasional brutality, oddly and inconsistently intermingled with his consideration, and by the incurable infidelities in which he engaged. The subject being what he was, the closing chapter on religion is surprisingly rich and varied and develops many unexpected angles, and the masterly and characteristic closing paragraph shows that the author himself was fully aware of this:

> Perhaps it will be thought that, in discussing a busy, active, external, material life, I am giving too much weight to God altogether. It is because the vast, brooding consciousness of God alone gives such a life all its significance—and all its emptiness, and because I believe the busy, active, external, material life of America to-day, so much the life personified by the great Diarist, needs God more than anything else to save it. How the need is to be satisfied is another question and one that can never be answered from the Diary of Pepys.

The subjects in *Bare Souls* are Voltaire, Thomas Gray, Horace Walpole, William Cowper, Charles Lamb, John Keats, Gustave Flaubert, and Edward Fitzgerald, and the materials are almost wholly drawn from their correspondence. The title comes from Sainte-Beuve: "All at once the surface of life is torn apart, and we read bare soul."

These men were all writers, and one may well say all were bachelors, for only Fitzgerald ever led a woman to the altar and he hardly kept her long enough to count. For all that, there is no lack of variety in these pages. Voltaire was preeminently a creature of superb spiritual vitality ("I have never been able to understand how anybody could be cold; that is too much for me"), Walpole essentially a dilettante. The "whole purpose" of Flaubert's existence was "to interpret life in beautiful words." "Though Keats burned out his life at twenty-five, consumed by the passion for creating great poetry, he was no visionary, no crack-brained dreamer, but a sane, sound, normal human being, as Shakespeare was." Gray's life was set in solitude; he "supported himself with decency and dignity, lived long in his remote, sequestered corner and melted out of the world, apparently, as a man, a perfect bit of alms for the vast erasure of oblivion." Charles Lamb was "a creature of whim and frolic fancy, turned life upside down and inside out, sported with it, trifled with it, tossed it in the air like soap bubbles or thistledown, regardless of where it fell or whom it might light upon," a fact which gave Bradford an excellent opportunity to compare him to the Elizabethan or Shakespearean Fools he loved so much. But he does not suppress the tragedy of madness in the Lamb

family, which, though it reached its height in Charles's sister Mary, did not leave him totally unscathed.

The study of Keats is notable for both its passionate response to Keats as a poet and for the complete sympathy with which it portrays his love for Fanny Brawne. (pp. 132-33)

But the masterpiece in *Bare Souls* is the portrait of Cowper. Bradford never did a finer piece of work, and it may well be doubted that any other writer ever surpassed it in kind. The basis for the study of Cowper is hell, for the man lived all his later life under the shadow of the conviction that, since he had committed the unpardonable sin, hell must be his eternal home. That fact the reader must never be permitted to forget, for Cowper never forgot it. Once when he was crossing a cemetery at night, a gravedigger accidentally struck him with a skull. "The incident impressed him deeply, and skulls were hitting him from somewhere all his life." When he was dying, a friend tried to convince him that God's mercy could embrace even him, but "up to the very end he preferred being damned to being convinced." (p. 134)

It is interesting to note that *The Soul of Samuel Pepys* and *Bare Souls* were both written between April and December 1923.

Saints and Sinners appeared when Bradford was on his death-bed. . . . On the assumption that three saints ought to be able to balance four sinners, it covers "The Riot of Youth: Caesar Borgia," "God's Vagabond: Saint Francis of Assisi," "The Devil's Vagabond: Casanova," "Alone with God: Thomas à Kempis," "The Prince of Darkness: Talleyrand," "God and the World: Fénelon," and "The Glory of Sin: Byron." (p. 136)

[*Saints and Sinners*] is one of Bradford's very best and shows him, at sixty-nine, at the height of his powers, capable of making the saints quite as vivid as the sinners.

Caesar Borgia represents the Renaissance physical man, bent on "glory through conquest and cruelty," while Talleyrand, the indifferent skeptic who "accumulated money by crooked means," was so different from him that about the only thing Bradford can give him credit for, aside from his social charm, is the love of peace, or at least hatred of war, which made him a brake upon Napoleon.

The two predominantly sexual sinners, Casanova and Byron, could not well have been more unlike each other either. Casanova, the wanderer, adventurer, idler, and charlatan, who got his money by gambling and "projects" and was always as ready to give as to grasp, "kept up a sexual revel for the endless varied delight of it, without a moment of compunction or remorse." To the Puritan Byron, who used sin as an avenue to glory, or at least a means of attracting attention, "the remorse was the stamp of sin, without which the whole exhibition would have been worthless." He was not in the least like Pepys, "who sinned against his will and suffered the pricks of conscience afterwards, real pricks. To Byron the pricks were theoretical, like the sin, and both made gorgeous material to flaunt before a gasping world." The study of Casanova is, on the whole, denigrating; Bradford finds that Casanova had little to say and has difficulty crediting the man's veracity. He finds vulgarity in Byron, too, "the wayward, mischievous, malignant child," and quotes with approval Goethe's judgment: *"Sobald er reflectiert, ist er ein Kind"* ["As soon as he reflects, he is a child"]. Yet the portrait of Byron is drenched in the same glamour that informs his poetry, and its creator's failure to perceive this is one of his most glaring misjudgments of his own work. (pp. 137-38)

Though Bradford once said that Saint Francis was too close to insanity easily to come to terms with, nobody could have made "God's Vagabond" more winning than he made him. It is true that, even here, he is characteristically impressed by the inability of even the saints to achieve complete unselfishness ("the day will come," Francis is quoted as having said, "when I shall be adored by the whole world"). Yet the great thing about this saint is that, despite all his excesses, he never lost sight of the fact that though "he wanted to make over the world, . . . he wanted to make it over by love, and love does not destroy." And, for all the antipathy between modern freedom and medieval asceticism, it is this portrait which contains the most directly autobiographical passage in all Bradford's psychographs, the account of how, when he was engaged to be married, he and his love were tempted to set up their lives on the basis of something like a Franciscan poverty, and how, though they yielded at last to pressure from their elders, "there are times when I wish I had behaved as Francis did."

Naturally we do not see Thomas à Kempis with anything like the clarity that obtains with Saint Francis. Much of the first section is devoted to a description of the monastic life and consideration of whether Thomas really was the author of [*The Imitation of Christ*]. Nevertheless the analysis of the praise of solitude, negation of self, and complete subjection to the will of God is masterly, as is the closing section on "the extraordinary qualities of literary beauty, which make the *Imitation* one of the masterpieces of the world." Who but Bradford could have dreamed of writing, "The Daphnis and Chloë of Longus is a monument of Pagan naturalism, but the delicate rippling cadences of the Greek and the simple human touch all through the book often remind one of the *Imitation*"?

The complicated and sophisticated François de Salignac de la Mothe Fénelon, an aristocrat, a gentleman, an aspiring statesman, almost an exquisite, a lover of literature and art, and himself the author of a French educational classic, seems far removed from the heavenly simplicities of Thomas and Francis, yet his saintly character is clearly established, and Bradford might well have extended his admiration for the last page of his psychograph to the whole closing section, for it is a masterly analysis of religious feeling, as manifested by Fénelon in his final phase. Incidentally, one of Bradford's most astonishing personal statements is that Fénelon and Talleyrand were the two subjects in **Saints and Sinners** that he found most congenial because they were most like himself! (pp. 138-40)

In his preface to Bradford's **Journal** [see Further Reading], Van Wyck Brooks spoke of "a literary life impressive in its devotion and continuity, a life which, in its steady integrity, its adaptation of means to valuable ends, its coherence and well-directed intensity, recalls the classical age of American letters." Taking into consideration the handicaps under which Bradford labored, one might add that it was also an heroic life. His idiosyncrasies harmed only himself; if in his journals and his **Autobiography** he made a habit of selling himself short by emphasizing and often exaggerating all the limitations which most of us do our best to excuse and to conceal, he not only stands clear of having inflicted them upon others, but so conducted himself that his fellows never even

suspected their existence. One might well apply to him what he said of Mark Twain, that his faults were incidental to humanity and that as an individual he stood with the best. He left a shelf of sensitive, penetrating, humane, and aspiring books behind him, and his memory has been cherished by all who had the good fortune to know him. (p. 192)

Edward Wagenknecht, in his Gamaliel Bradford, *Twayne Publishers, 1982, 220 p.*

FURTHER READING

Britt, Albert. "The Moderns." In his *The Great Biographers*, pp. 183-218. New York: Whittlesey House, 1936.
    Discusses characteristic features of works by Bradford and other contemporary biographers, including Lytton Strachey and André Maurois.

Brooks, Van Wyck. Preface to *The Journal of Gamaliel Bradford, 1883-1932*, by Gamaliel Bradford, edited by Van Wyck Brooks, pp. vii-xiii. Boston: Houghton Mifflin Co., 1933.
    Overview of Bradford's career, noting the value of the *Journal* for "the light it throws on the writer in his study, engaged in the work the public knows so well."

Carver, George. "Bradford." In his *Alms for Oblivion: Books, Men, and Biography*, pp. 278-86. Milwaukee: Bruce Publishing Co., 1946.
    Biographical and critical sketch.

Grant, Robert. "Gamaliel Bradford." In *Commemorative Tributes to Hastings, French, Hill, Bradford, Melchers, John Van Dyke, Henry van Dyke, Babbitt, Platt, Shorey, Gilbbert, Whitlock, Thomas, Baker, and Loeffler*, pp. 35-48. New York: American Academy of Arts and Letters, 1936.
    Appreciative overview of Bradford's life and career.

Hough, Lynn Harold. "A Magnificent and Meticulous Dilettante." In his *Vital Control: Forest Essays, First Series*, pp. 39-68. 1934. Reprint. Freeport, N.Y.: Books for Libraries Press.
    Surveys Bradford's major works, praising his insight into the personalities of his subjects.

Hutch, Richard A. "Explorations in Character: Gamaliel Bradford and Henry Murray as Psychobiographers." *Biography: An Interdisciplinary Quarterly* 4, No. 4 (Fall 1981): 312-25.
    Compares the lives and works of Bradford and the psychologist Henry A. Murray, suggesting that "Murray's psychological notions are pre-figured in Bradford's biographical sketches."

McCormick, Virginia Taylor. "Bradford, Naturalist of Souls." *Personalist* 9, No. 1 (January 1928): 27-37.
    Analyzes the development of Bradford's method of psychography.

Pattee, Fred Lewis. "The New Biographers." In his *The New American Literature, 1890-1930*, pp. 447-59. New York: D. Appleton-Century Co., 1935.
    Examines Bradford's role in the development of modern biographical writing.

Warren, Dale. "Gamaliel Bradford: A Personal Sketch." *The South Atlantic Quarterly* 32, No. 1 (January 1933): 9-18.
    Outlines Bradford's life and career.

Federico Gamboa

1864-1939

Mexican novelist, memoirist, and dramatist.

Referred to as "the patriarch of Mexican letters," Gamboa is best known for naturalistic novels in which he explored the problems of his country's middle and lower classes. Gamboa's subject matter and approach were influenced by Emile Zola, the principal theorist of literary Naturalism, who viewed the novel as an illustration of how human behavior is determined by various social, psychological, and hereditary forces. In his later works, Gamboa attempted to transcend the deterministic aspect of Naturalism with a more idealistic philosophy. In addition to his novels, Gamboa's extensive memoirs are also highly valued, their clear rationality and balanced assessments providing unique insight into Mexican political and literary life of the late nineteenth and early twentieth centuries.

Gamboa was born in 1864 in Mexico City. Beginning his career as a court clerk and journalist, he was appointed in 1888 to a diplomatic post, serving as undersecretary in Mexican legations in Guatemala, Argentina, Brazil, and the United States, and later as Minister Plenipotentiary in several European nations. He published his first book, the short story collection *Del natural,* in 1889 and continued to write works of fiction and drama throughout his career in the diplomatic service. In 1901 a gambling problem resulted in what Gamboa referred to in his diary as "a psychological crisis." He credited his recovery to his return to the Catholic church, and critics attribute the idealism of his later works to this renewed faith. In 1913, Gamboa was forced into exile after running as the vice presidential candidate for the Catholic party, which lost the election to the dictator Victoriano Huerta. When Gamboa returned to Mexico, he resumed his career in journalism, began teaching Mexican literature at the National University, and worked on his memoirs until his death in 1939.

In his novels, Gamboa described the plight of individuals manipulated by psychological and social forces beyond their control. He used this naturalistic approach to portray such subjects as corrupt courts, adultery, and prostitution, connecting these to the more fundamental problems of poverty and class oppression. For example, in his depiction of the Mexican prison system in *Suprema ley,* Gamboa criticized society for concerning itself with the poverty-stricken only when they have committed a crime. His best known novel, *Santa,* explores the life of a young country girl who turns to prostitution to support herself after she is deserted by her lover and disowned by her family. Arthur Wallace Woolsey praises Gamboa's forceful use of naturalistic techniques to present her life: "At times he is almost photographic in his description of some of the more sordid scenes. He presents his 'slices of life' in a powerful and effective manner, and the reader does not soon forget the poverty, the squalor, and the oppression found in the lives and places which are presented to him." Some critics contend that while Gamboa treated themes common to Naturalism in his novels, he cannot be classified as a Naturalist writer. Instead, they see him as simply observing details rather than organizing these materials

to reveal a pattern of scientific laws, concluding that his moral judgments and explicit didacticism do not conform to the Naturalist goal of objectivity. Others, however, see his moralizing as the result of his return to Catholicism and contend that his earlier works, such as *Santa,* do represent a Naturalist philosophy.

Although not as widely known as his novels, Gamboa's extensive memoirs are considered important documentation of Mexican politics in the late nineteenth and early twentieth centuries, providing not only a first-hand report on the dictatorships of the period, but also information on Mexican and U. S. activities in Central America. Gamboa's recollections of the major literary figures in Mexico, Spain, and Central and South America are also considered valuable documents of literary history. Ernest R. Moore summarizes Gamboa's achievements by stating: "Outstanding as an incorruptible career diplomatist and as the first important Mexican writer of memoirs, Federico Gamboa will nevertheless best be remembered as the foremost and most prolific novelist of his age."

PRINCIPAL WORKS

Del natural (short stories) 1889

Apariencias (novel) 1892
Impresiones y recuerdos (memoirs) 1893
Suprema ley (novel) 1896
Metamórfosis (novel) 1899
Santa (novel) 1903
La venganza de la gleba (drama) [first publication] 1907
Mi diario. 5 vols. (memoirs) 1907-38
Reconquista (novel) 1908
La llaga (novel) 1910

ERNEST R. MOORE (essay date 1940)

[*In the following excerpt, Moore summarizes Gamboa's major works.*]

In *Impresiones y recuerdos* and *Mi diario* [Gamboa] leaves an exciting record of his career which will be much consulted by literary and political historians in the future. The historical value of these works lies in his intimate and accurate observations on Mexican and American activities in Central America, on the Díaz and Huerta dictatorships, and on American intervention in Mexico during the early days of the Revolution. His story vies with José Vasconcelos' in scope and surpasses it in unimpassioned, balanced judgments. His literary associations with Rubén Darío, Rafael Obligado, Martín Coronado, and a host of other *modernistas* in Buenos Aires, with Agustín Gómez Carillo, Salvador Falla, and Antonio Batres Jáuregui in Guatemala, and with numerous contemporary writers in Spain and Mexico, will contribute much to an understanding of the tide of literary ideas in his time. Because of his close friendship with all Mexican writers of importance during his long directorship of the Academia Mexicana, maintained despite his years of travels abroad, his comments on the intellectual and artistic life in Mexico represents the best single literary history of the last five decades which has yet been published in Mexico. (p. 365)

[Gamboa's] writings and his conversation revealed a heartening rationality. From it he drew his beliefs; and that these were good, humane, his writings and his conduct have long since proved. He was a man of convention, yes, but never to the point of abandoning for it a commiseration for his fellowmen; he was a man of common sense, "common" implying that he always thought of himself as a member of a group for whose good, which included his own, he wrote and taught; he was a man of moral firmness, of order, and of intellectual integrity. . . .

Outstanding as an incorruptible career diplomatist and as the first important Mexican writer of memoirs, Federico Gamboa will nevertheless best be remembered as the foremost and most prolific novelist of his age. He introduced into Mexican literature the benefits, but not the absurdities of the French naturalists, Zola and the Goncourt brothers, whom he personally knew and openly admired; and with his novels of social import bridged the wide gap between the realist triumvirate, Emilio Rabasa, Rafael Delgado, José López-Portillo y Rojas, and the post-Revolution novelists, best represented by Mariano Azuela and Martín Luis Guzmán. His novels, of which *La llaga, Suprema ley,* and *Santa* are the best, all present an objectively described and psychologically interpreted vivisection of Mexican bourgeois society. Each novel, documented by personal experience and observation, deals with

a limited social problem: *La llaga* records the tribulations of a former inmate of the notorious San Juan de Ulúa prison as he attempts to make a comeback in "decent" society; *Suprema ley* analyzes a theme important in his writings (as indeed in Mexican society), the psychological and sociological consequences of carnal love; *Santa* is an originally conceived Mexican *Nana*. Better known than any other of his literary productions, *Santa* has gone into more editions than any other Mexican novel and has become one of the most widely read Hispanic American novels. It typifies his best work; an artistic, sympathetic, exact, and stereoscopic study of a closely related group of people who, in their dark little corner of society, grope about for an opening into a better world where nature is less unfavorable and man more humane. (p. 366)

Ernest R. Moore, "Federico Gamboa, Diplomat and Novelist," in Books Abroad, *Vol. 14, No. 4, Autumn, 1940, pp. 364-67.*

ROBERT J. NIESS (essay date 1946)

[*An American educator and critic, Niess specializes in French literature, particularly the works of Emile Zola. In the following excerpt, he demonstrates the influence of Zola's novel* L'oeuvre *on the themes and plot of Gamboa's* Reconquista.]

Although Federico Gamboa is often called the leading exponent of literary naturalism in Mexico and as such was inevitably a follower of Zola, it is difficult to demonstrate that he borrowed heavily or continuously from the French master. His work provides only scattered examples of direct appropriation from Zola and the latter's influence on him was rather general than specific, bearing mainly on his choice of subject-matter, method of treatment and overall social outlook. But in at least one novel it is possible to see more than this general influence, to find evidence of an attempt on Gamboa's part not only to imitate Zola but to take a form already developed by his predecessor and to turn it to his own philosophic and artistic ends. That novel is *Reconquista.* Lacking specific declarations from Gamboa himself, we cannot reach definite conclusions, but certain evidence indicates that the work may have been based on Zola's *L'oeuvre,* based on it not as an imitation but as an answer to the basic idea that Zola had expressed in that long and turgid novel.

Gamboa's interest in such a work as *L'oeuvre,* that is, in a semi-autobiographical work dealing with life in artistic circles, seems to date from fairly early in his career. In 1893, for example, when he visited Zola in Paris, he questioned him rather closely about *L'oeuvre* and indeed that novel is the only one he mentions when describing the interview in his *Diario.*

Now, even if he did have the intention of rivaling with Zola on the latter's own ground, it could not be demonstrated that *Reconquista* is a close or direct copy of *L'oeuvre. Reconquista* is a story of the artist Salvador Arteaga, who, after the death of his wife and under the influence of the pessimistic and materialistic ideas of the German philosophers, steadily slips into a life of dissipation and idleness and thus ruins his promising career as painter and teacher. Things go from bad to worse for him until at last he finds hope of salvation in the love of Carolina, a young girl of simple and honest faith. He determines to marry her but—almost in spite of himself—seduces and abandons her. After a long period of idleness and self-doubt and after a fearsome psychological crisis, followed by a desperate illness, he seeks Carolina out and eventually they are married. Under her guidance Salvador recovers his lost faith in the Church and sets out toward the rebuilding of his life. He has completed his reconquest; his principle will be "Creer, crear" [to believe, to create].

It is obvious that, in plot and idea at least, the work owes little to *L'oeuvre*. But certain aspects of the novel lead to a different conclusion. First and most important is the fact that both novels are autobiographical to a degree. In both, the author appears in a strange, double capacity: in each he is the artist, the protagonist of the work, and in each also he appears as the friend of the artist, the novelist *porte-parole*. This double rôle of the author in his own work is the strongest argument for the hypothesis that Gamboa composed *Reconquista* with *L'oeuvre* as his conscious or unconscious guide. Let us look first at the autobiographical element in *Reconquista.* There are indications that the novelist Covarrubias, the only constant friend of Salvador, represents Gamboa himself. Like the latter, Covarrubias is a municipal employe and has produced four novels with some success—the same number that Gamboa himself had written to this time. Moreover, he sounds surprisingly like Gamboa: his ethical and sociological doctrines are no more than a repetition of what his creator had said and was to say over and over in such autobiographical expansions as the *Diario* and *Impresiones y recuerdos.* His reasonable, often didactic tone is an exact echo of Gamboa's own in these personal works.

As for Zola's relationship to the novelist Sandoz in *L'oeuvre* it is abundantly clear. His son-in-law and editor, Maurice Le-Blond, declares that ". . . nul n'ignore que Zola s'est mis lui-même en scène sous les traits de Pierre Sandoz" ["no one is unaware that Zola put himself in the scene under the lineaments of Pierre Sandoz"], and in the notes to the work Zola declares this in fact to be the case. In the previously mentioned interview Zola had revealed to Gamboa that he himself had been the model for the character of Sandoz.

But both Zola and Gamboa seem to have depicted themselves with more psychological exactness and intimate detail in the figures of their artists. Claude Lantier of *L'oeuvre* is of course Paul Cézanne in many of the exterior details of his life, but he is also Emile Zola himself, as M. LeBlond specifically declares. There is likewise good reason for thinking that Salvador Arteaga represents his creator in *Reconquista.* It is no secret that for some time Gamboa's career as diplomat was in jeopardy because of certain weaknesses which he indulged too freely. He too had his period of decline, of pessimism, of near-failure. And, as in the case of his creature Salvador, this period was terminated by a psychological crisis of such intensity that it threatened to ruin his entire life: ". . . ¡la noche de hoy, la noche de hoy! yo me la he pasado con Ana Radcliffe, Hoffmann y Poe, en una pesadilla imborrable, que quién sabe si no me dejará lacrado para siempre" ["Last night, last night! I passed it with Ann Radcliffe, Hoffmann and Poe, in an unforgettable nightmare, which, who knows, might have left me permanently injured"]. Again, this psychological crisis brought in its wake a reconversion to religious faith, a "reconquest" of the beliefs of his youth that he had so long forgotten. . . . (pp. 577-79)

It is clear that *Reconquista,* like *L'oeuvre,* was a novel written *ad hoc,* to give expression to the torments its creator had suffered, to reveal his inmost thoughts and fears and hopes, in short, to give a portrait of the artist as a man.

A number of less important similarities support the hypothesis that *Reconquista* and *L'oeuvre* have a resemblance that is more than coincidental. It is true that many of these similarities are no more than details, but their number is so considerable that they can scarcely be dismissed as the product of mere chance. It may be pointed out for instance that both painters, Lantier and Arteaga, are men of rural origin, that both are sent to the capital (Paris in the one case, in the other Mexico City) to study art at the expense of protectors, that both arrived in the metropolis full of fire and faith, eager to put into concrete form the ideal of art—naturalistic art—which they carry within themselves. But in the capital each undergoes the same experience: the prevailing skeptical ideas so corrupt each that he eventually finds himself incapable of attaining his artistic ideal. The ideas of Schopenhauer, of Nietzsche, of the other pessimists and materialists are so corrosive that the artists soon find themselves defenseless before the attacks of the self-doubt that was so much a part of the spirit of the times. (pp. 579-80)

This philosophical influence of the metropolis is indeed one of the distinguishing characteristics of both novels; its rôle in *L'oeuvre* is great, in *Reconquista* it is decisive, all-important.

Both young artists, moreover, soon find themselves surrounded by groups of other young intellectuals, painters, writers, musicians. In both cases a café is the gathering-place for these groups, in *L'oeuvre* the café Baudequin, an unnamed "cervecería alemana" ["German beer hall"] in *Reconquista.* And in both cases the protagonist is abandoned by this group of intellectuals as he slips toward failure and as his early promise gives little sign of fruition. In each case only one of the group remains true and faithful, the novelists Covarrubias of *Reconquista* and Sandoz of *L'oeuvre.* In each work the novelist represents the only link that remains between the artist and the intellectual world he once knew, the only counselor left to give him hope and courage.

It is a curious and notable fact that in both these novels the young artists set out to paint their wives in the nude, hoping thus to give some measure of permanence to the fleshly love that brightened their early years of hope and effort. Most curious of all, though, is the fact that in both novels the painting modeled by the wife remains unfinished and one can scarcely escape the conclusion that both Zola and Gamboa wished thus to symbolize the artistic impotence of their creatures. In the case of *Reconquista* it is probable that the incomplete portrait of Salvador's first wife, Emilia, is the symbol of the marriage that death cut short, just as it demonstrates the inability of Salvador to attain full creative power in the years that preceded his "reconquest." In *L'oeuvre* it is patent that Zola intended the unfinished portrait of Christine to symbolize the flaw in Claude's artistic makeup; the incomplete painting is indeed the crux of the whole novel, the essential fact of its economy.

Again, both young artists are gripped by the fever to glorify on canvas the city that enfolds them, to translate its soul into the reality of line and color. . . . Neither of them succeeds in creating this physico-moral portrait of the metropolis, Salvador because the novel ends before he is able to busy himself with the task, Claude because he cannot, because his incomplete genius bars him from finishing the great and complex scene which drives him to final despair and suicide.

When their great projects do not turn out, both artists are seized by the fury of the thwarted; both are moved to violence, to a holocaust of canvas that will leave them fresh and purified, to start anew. And, as they both sink further and further toward failure, both are forced to prostitute their talents in order to live, to paint shades and snuffboxes and the walls of taverns for the few francs or the few pesos that will enable them to follow their hopeless dream. And, driven at last to heartbreak, both find their only surcease in long night-wanderings through the great city; here, in the glimpses given us of the silent cities, the two works are strikingly similar.

But Salvador and Claude are most evidently alike in their artistic doctrines. Both are artists of rebellion who would revolutionize their epoch with their attacks on the conventional and the academic. The Academia of the Mexican capital is for Salvador exactly what the Salon is for Claude—the refuge of the stuffy conservatism of outmoded schools. Both cry for realism, for naturalism, for the direct copy of real life. Salvador's task, as he sees it, is to "defender y rescatar la Belleza" ["to defend and redeem Beauty"]; he knows that he will be condemned by the bourgeoisie, by "los de Panurgo" ["the Panurgoans"], that he will be ignored or attacked, yet he will persist until his goal is reached. That goal is the creation of a new art in Mexico, an honest art, based on observation of the real and living, freed of the shackles of conventional copying, a fit instrument for the works of tomorrow. His ideal is in no essential different from that of Claude. . . . (pp. 580-82)

In spite of these similarities, there is an essential cleavage between *Reconquista* and *L'oeuvre,* a cleavage which becomes evident when we consider the explanations which the authors advance, explicitly or implicitly, for their characters' evolution. Both Claude and the early Salvador are fundamentally unable to create the works they envisage. In Claude's case the obstruction is material: he cannot paint what he wishes because of "sa physiologie, sa race, la lésion de son œil" ["his physiology, his race, the injury of his eye"], as Zola himself says. He is radically impotent. Gamboa goes one step further with Arteaga. Where Zola had been content merely to state the fact of Claude's impotence, laying it to factors beyond human control, Gamboa attempts a philosophic explanation of the artist's weakness. In his early years Arteaga cannot reach full artistic stature because he has no faith, no "soul." . . . And, when Arteaga acquires a soul through his own "reconquest," he finds that clarity of vision, that skill of hand which will guarantee the attainment of his ideal. Here is justification for the hypothesis that Gamboa composed *Reconquista* as an answer to *L'oeuvre,* as a document which should go beyond the hopeless materialism of that work to a higher sphere of logic. Thus seen, this "naturalistic" novel stands full in the current of "idealistic" literature which set so strongly at the turn of the century.

The evidence adduced here does not of course indicate that Gamboa was in any sense the literary slave of the man he called master. He was artist enough constantly to remain himself and to find within himself the force to accomplish what he wished. But *L'oeuvre* and *Reconquista* present such similarities of broad outline and of detail that it is difficult to believe that the one did not provide a source for the other. However, if Gamboa did in fact imitate Zola here, he very probably did so not to duplicate his work but to answer it; employing the same basic idea, he turned the novel to an opposite end. Like most of the followers of Zola, he went beyond the master, but the original debt remains. *Reconquista* appears today as a solid artistic structure, but its foundations must surely be sought in *L'oeuvre.* (pp. 582-83)

Robert J. Niess, "Zola's 'L'oeuvre' and 'Reconquista' of Gamboa," in PMLA, Vol. LXI, No. 2, June, 1946, pp. 577-83.

A. W. WOOLSEY (essay date 1950)

[*Woolsey is an American educator, translator, and critic who specializes in Spanish-American society and literature. In the following excerpt, he discusses several of the social problems considered by Gamboa in his novels.*]

Federico Gamboa, Mexican novelist of the late nineteenth and early twentieth centuries, has given a great deal of attention to social problems and conditions in his country. Although the whole subject is too broad to be considered in a short article, one aspect of it can be reviewed briefly. In *Reconquista, Suprema ley,* and particularly in *La llaga* class oppression is given extensive treatment by Gamboa. *Reconquista* has for its dominant theme the groping of a wandering soul after its Maker, but there are in it recurring references to the oppressed classes. Salvador, the protagonist, cannot reconcile himself to the indifference of the upper classes towards those of lower rank and those who are more unfortunate than they, and he is satirical in his consideration of the attitude of self-complacency and the pride with which those more fortunately situated point to the few hospitals, orphanages and similar institutions when they are reproached for their heartless disregard for suffering.

Gregorio, the main character of *La llaga,* is the vehicle for some of Gamboa's thoughts regarding class oppression and the possibility for improvement of conditions. In the prison camp, with ample opportunity for studying the soldiers as well as the convicts over whom they have power, he suddenly awakens to a realization of the fact that essentially there is no difference between soldiers and convicts. Both are of the lower class, both are "under dogs," both are victims, practically slaves of society—that is to say, of the powerful classes. He stands amazed before this discovery so new to his thinking.

In *La llaga* the author presents the conclusion that the prison inmate is in fact society's victim because the social organism evinces no interest in him until such time as he has committed some overt act which causes him to be regarded as something dangerous to the established order. There are realistic pictures of prisons and prison life in different parts of Mexico, but especially in the prison of Ulúa at Vera Cruz.

The novel opens with a view of the convicts at the close of the day when they have had their evening meal, and there is little left for them to do but to tumble into their bunks for the night. Some of them talk, but the majority of them have nothing to say. In addition to Gregorio, there is a certain Martiniano whom Gamboa uses as spokesman for much of his philosophy and for many of his ideas. The prisoners are non-communicative concerning the causes of their incarceration, and they do not care to talk of these things even to those in similar circumstances.

The prison is an unutterably filthy place, and when Gregorio laments the fact that it has fallen to his lot to go out to work, he is told by one of the older prisoners that he should be glad of the opportunity to get out into the sun and fresh air away from the rotten hole where he has been. The eternal longing of man for affection is shown in a description of the convicts and a pack of stray dogs. The dogs belong to no one in particular and remain at a distance while the convicts are at work, but when the men are at ease, the animals approach and race madly about, yelping and barking to express their affection.

In a contemplative mood Gregorio considers the place of prisons in human existence. Why should man in all his wisdom build a snare to which he himself falls victim? His imagination and intellect produce cathedrals, halls of justice and other beautiful edifices, but alas!—this same fertile inventiveness also builds prisons which serve for the undoing of the planner. Even the beasts of the forest do not set traps with which to ensnare themselves.

Suprema ley furnishes further scenes of prisons and corrupt courts which illustrate the evils of class oppression. Cartera, the court official, and his method of obtaining confessions remind one of modern day gangster methods in the United States. What is wanted is the confession, and the method does not matter. The prisoner is made to feel that although he is not guilty, the easiest thing for him is to confess to the crime of which he is accused.

In the conviction and execution of a certain Apolonio there is presented the question of society's bringing a man back to health in order that it may take his life in its own way. There is a discussion of the general subject of capital punishment, a pondering of the right of the group to take the life of one of its members, and a consideration of society's obligation to the accused person; again the question: Why does society not concern itself with a man *before* he commits a crime?

In an indirect manner a vividly horrible picture of the actual execution is painted. The memory of the event weighs upon the mind of Julio Ortegal, a court clerk, causing him to fall ill; during his illness he constantly speaks of the execution, the curious crowds that attended, the café nearby that did not even close its doors, and the fact that the judge who had passed sentence did not attend the execution. Through hearing the ravings of Julio his entire family came to know the story almost as well as he.

In all the court scenes of *Suprema ley* there are portrayed inefficiency and justice at a price; that price may be money, influence, or a pretty face. The terrible fact of taking human life, even by society, is powerfully impressed upon the reader in the example of Apolonio. Gamboa prefers to lay the blame for the crime upon society and to consider the man to be executed as the victim. His picture of criminal procedure as presented in *Suprema ley* shows what great reforms are necessary before anything like justice will be achieved.

The poverty of the masses is another problem with which Gamboa deals at length and is one that is related to the preceding discussion of class oppression. Poverty is seen on every hand, especially in the great metropolis, and the novelist brings it forcibly to the reader's attention in all of his important novels. In *Apariencias* the thoughts of a poor clerk portray most vividly the wretched state of affairs that exists in his own home which is typical of many. He sees the stark poverty, days without food and nights without shelter, insufficient furniture; his wife is reduced to selling her wedding ring, the very sheets from the bed, and finally the image of the Virgin which their child has worn as a protective amulet since birth.

In *Metamórfosis* we find a picture of the poverty and the oppressed condition of the people of the country. (pp. 294-96)

Widespread immorality with its attendant evils of disease, adultery, and desertion is an important problem of Mexico and is often related to the poverty of the masses. Gamboa recognizes this problem and considers it repeatedly in his works. The theme of both *Apariencias* and *Suprema ley* is that of adultery, which in the former causes Pedro to forget his gratitude to his foster father, and in the latter causes Julio to desert his wife. More than this the author has set himself in *Santa* the task of writing the life story of a prostitute. He has done this fearlessly, omitting none of the details, and has presented a realistic though sordid picture of the workings of vice in Mexico half a century ago.

Gamboa tells us that he had often considered as a subject for one of his books the life of a woman of the streets. He sees this question of vice as one of the greatest problems that confront his country, and he feels that the people as a whole is to blame. Again he feels that the fault is primarily that of society and not altogether that of the woman—the breaker of the precepts. He reaches the conclusion that usually the woman is driven to such a life by the attitude which the family and society take when she makes the first misstep. Rather than to try to help her, they hasten her on her downward way. The title page of the novel bears the words of Hosea 4:14 that bespeak forgiveness for the woman because the fault is man's. . . . (pp. 296-97)

Santa, the chief character of the book, is deceived by a soldier whom she loves. When he deserts her, and her sin is discovered by her family, she is turned out into the street. She sees no remedy but starvation or the course that she ultimately takes. Remembering that once at a fair a woman had told her that if ever she were in need of money, she knew of a place for her in the city, Santa goes to this place and becomes one of its inmates. Immediately upon her arrival she sees the living image of what she will become through such a life. There is a sort of prophecy, of foreshadowing, in this bringing together of one who has led a life of vice and one who stands upon the threshold of such a life.

There is no doubt as to the influence of the French naturalists upon Gamboa, and he was personally acquainted with Emile Zola and Edmond de Goncourt. The subjects discussed above are the type of material treated by these authors, and his methods of treatment are very similar to theirs. At times he is almost photographic in his descriptions of some of the more sordid scenes. He presents his "slices of life" in a powerful and effective manner, and the reader does not soon forget the poverty, the squalor, and the oppression found in the lives and places which are presented to him. Federico Gamboa remains the outstanding exponent of the nineteenth century novel in Mexico, the novel as it was before the earth shaking events of 1911 and subsequent years, but he is a novelist in the European and especially the French tradition. He belongs to the regime of Porfirio Díaz and not to the era of the Mexican Revolution, yet one may find in his novels a portrayal of conditions that provided fertile ground for the seeds of the whirlwind. (p. 297)

A. W. Woolsey, "Some of the Social Problems Considered by Federico Gamboa," in The Modern Language Journal, *Vol. XXXIV, No. 4, April, 1950, pp. 294-97.*

JOHN S. BRUSHWOOD (essay date 1966)

[*An American educator, translator, and critic, Brushwood has written extensively on the Spanish-American novel. In the following excerpt, he surveys Gamboa's novels.*]

Gamboa's *Del natural* (1889) is a collection of short stories which represents his entry into fiction. His later work gives a much more complete view of the author's reality, but the Naturalist basis of the first work is important to an understanding of how . . . [he saw his] world. "Vendía cerillos" is perhaps the most typical of the stories. Its protagonist is kept from becoming the person he wants to be, by a series of circumstances quite beyond his control. His suicide at the age of fifteen seems improbable to some readers. I can think of few acts more likely than the suicide of a boy who is effectively dead already, since he is separated from all apparent means of self-realization.

"Vendía cerillos" is typical of Gamboa's later work also in its portrayal of a sentimental hero. These heroes are romantically sensitive and, in the opinion of some readers, keep Gamboa from being a Naturalist. Such an attitude is all right if one wishes to toy with words. What is important is not whether you call Gamboa a Naturalist or don't call him a Naturalist, but the fact that he saw, as a part of reality, a number of people who could not be what their wills would have made them. It matters little whether they were sentimental or not. The pessimism of this view limits the possibility of individual improvement and even casts doubt on the efficacy of fundamental social change. (pp. 133-34)

The whole question of style is something of a barrier to consideration of Gamboa's novels. This man, who was the best novelist Mexico had produced up to his time, has often been underrated because of repeated criticism of his style, described as academic, dull, pretentious. The criticism is not entirely without justification, because Gamboa's careful writing occasionally creates the impression that he was trying too hard, and the popular elements that he injects from time to time are surprising rather than unobtrusive. But for reasons that are hidden from me, adverse criticism of his style has acquired prominence in commentaries on his fiction that is entirely out of proportion to its real importance. Really there are far more good things than bad to be said about it. It is clear, accurately descriptive, and appropriate to his theme. There is nothing about it that inhibits participation in the novels, nothing that removes the reader from the world in which the author wishes to place him.

Following the stories of *Del natural,* Gamboa published his first novel, *Apariencias,* in 1892. His only advance over the stories was to write a longer work. *Apariencias,* which combines a story of the French Intervention with an almost separate story of adultery, is a failure because the author simply did not have enough to say. Gamboa was just learning how to surround his protagonists with society and to give them backgrounds that justify their actions. He shows his interest in creating an identifiable Mexican setting; and he reveals the mixture of Christian hope and Naturalism that has made many people say he could not possibly be a Naturalist. The fact is that neither his Naturalism nor his Christianity is strictly orthodox, and his novels are the more probable for that very reason. His characters are controlled by circumstances which frequently could be altered by Christian concern; but that concern, like the hope that is its corollary, is not always present.

Gamboa's first mature novel, *Suprema ley* (1896), is one of his best, though it is overshadowed by the tremendous fame of *Santa* (1903). Since its characters are more "average" than those that frequent Santa's world of prostitution, it gives us a somewhat better idea of how Gamboa viewed life. The story is the fall of Julio Ortegal, an unimportant court clerk. Ortegal married less for love than because it was the thing to do. His conjugal bliss gradually gives way to the boring exigence of family responsibility. At court he meets a woman who is accused of murdering her lover. Although she is acquitted, she is friendless and is taken into the home of the Ortegal family. At first, she saves this family that was already on the brink of disaster. But later Julio seduces her, and the ensuing adulterous affair destroys Ortegal's family, and eventually Ortegal himself.

Suprema ley deserves several amplifying comments concerning Gamboa's approach to fiction. The surrounding circumstances for the plot are provided by his detailed description of the court and its employees, and by a similarly detailed description of theater life, when Ortegal takes a backstage job in order to supplement his income. The two sets of circumstances offer a remarkable contrast to each other. The court employees represent a struggling middle class shrouded in dullness; the theater offers glitter, but no more genuine happiness than the contrasting drabness. Both groups are dishonest. Ortegal bribes the jury; success in the theater has no direct relationship to talent. Ortegal's home life is based on common sense, but it is ruined primarily by the fact that there is no common sense in his financial situation. The home, the court, and the theater form a triangle which Gamboa uses as a means of taking the reader through the life of the city. He makes it a good experience because his accurate view catches the reader up in the contrasts that are typically urban.

Both the reader and the characters are involved in life. Neither withdraws to consider the circumstances. For example, even before the coming of Clotilde, Julio and his wife, Carmen, are struggling to keep their marriage in good working order. Without knowing what is happening, they sense that an extra effort is necessary. Gamboa's description of their reaction to the problem is pathetically human. Before and after Clotilde's coming, Julio is only partly aware of what is happening to him. In the first stages of his relationship with Clotilde, he is apparently moved only by human compassion. His later obsession does not kill his paternal concern. It is as if he were suffering from an illness. Clotilde is never in love with him, although she accepts him as a lover. When finally she is forgiven by her family and leaves the city, death is the only course available for Ortegal, although he dreams of rehabilitating himself and his family.

Obviously, *Suprema ley* is Naturalism rampant. Gamboa took a middle-class situation similar to many other novels, and based the action on the common sense and conformist attitude that were so dear to the time. He supplemented the situation with commendable human concern, and then let circumstances destroy the whole thing. In a way, *Suprema ley* was even more shocking than Nervo's novels, because the fundamental setting was so familiar.

Metamórfosis (1899) is like *Suprema ley* in most matters of technique, but the theme of the novel is even farther removed than *Santa* from commonplace living. It deals with the transformation of a woman from religious commitment to the male protagonist's lover. Gamboa's careful development, of course, makes the metamorphosis reasonable, and the nature of the change reveals the author's understanding of what love means. Unfortunately, the change takes place at an irregular pace; that is, the change in Sor Noeline appears to move too slowly at one point and too fast at another. The effect is to remove the reader and make him critical of the process while it is going on. The nature of the theme also makes it hard for Gamboa to maintain the general movement of the novel. The hero abducts Sor Noeline and hides her in the house of a friend. Once this mission is accomplished, there is no way to involve her in action going on outside the house. So we are taken from her presence to more or less extraneous happenings, and then brought back.

One rather long section of **Metamórfosis** takes place on a hacienda, where Gamboa's detail is interesting enough, but the episode doesn't have much to do with the rest of the novel. Among the characterizations, Gamboa makes very interesting use of the hero's young daughter, who is Sor Noeline's pupil, and an unwitting catalyst to the transformation of the woman.

Gamboa's best novel, **Santa,** has had an odd critical fate. It has had an exceptionally wide reading, which it deserves because it is an excellent novel, but which it has gotten largely because of its reputation for being risqué. The critics, as a result of a kind of reflex negativism, have tended to concentrate on its faults—a difficult task, because its faults are few.

Santa, a dishonored country girl, suffers rejection by her family and comes to Mexico City where she becomes a prostitute. She starts at the top and goes to the bottom, with interludes as the mistress first of a *torero* and later of an unhappy husband. In spite of some inclination to reform, she is never quite able to do so; indeed, she even deceives the *torero* who is the provider of at least a semirespectable life. Finally, she is rescued from the gutter by Hipólito, who has loved her from the beginning, but she is near death when this happens. She is, in fact, redeemed by Hipólito's love—an outcome that displeases many of Gamboa's readers. Incidentally, this may well be the only case in Mexican fiction where a woman has been redeemed by a man—usually it is the other way.

The honest care with which Gamboa wrote **Santa** is the novel's greatest asset. Perhaps some of the scenes may be regarded as risqué, certainly many are repulsive; but Gamboa must be respected for his wisdom in writing details that contribute to the impact of the novel and omitting those that are unnecessary. He might have been able to omit some of the uglier details if he had used narrative techniques more complicated than objective statement. But given his technique, he was compelled to use the details. Still he chooses his words carefully, and avoids pornography—except for those who can make pornography of any mention of sex—by adopting a clinical attitude toward sexual matters.

Hipólito has always been a highly controversial character because many regard him as being too "sentimental." He is an ugly, blind pianist who worked in the brothel where Santa lived. At the very beginning he fell in love with her, partly because she was kind to him, partly because he recognized her fundamental decency. The picture is completed by a description given Hipo by his guide. This is a fine, poetic piece—perhaps a little too elegant for its source—but an appropriate way for Santa to be seen through the "eyes" of Hipo. His love endures even after Santa's fundamental decency has changed to fundamental immorality, because Hipo's picture of her does not change. I suspect Hipo is an example

of what Delgado and some others meant when they spoke of the reality of sentiment, a better example than Delgado was able to create.

The changes of mood throughout the novel are interesting and extremely convincing. The intransigent family honor of Santa's brothers is felt as keenly as a raucous celebration at the brothel. One particularly good episode is the coming of the brothers to inform Santa of her mother's death, when Santa is the toast of the town. Into the glitter and gaiety stride the brothers, somber, deliberate, hermetic. Gamboa does not push his reader in either direction, but lets him feel the reality of the contrast. He was capable also of catching the simple goodness beneath the flamboyance of "El Jarameño," the *torero*. The jealousies and intrigues of the women are equally real, as are Santa's moments of happiness and her gradual decline. We may well argue about the matter of Santa's will power and whether or not she could have changed the course of her life. I think Gamboa's purpose was not to present an air-tight case for the dark powers of destiny, but to show a situation in which Santa's possibilities for choice were limited. A Mexican student of mine has noted, regarding the change in Santa's character, that she, like Mexico, followed a particular course until, having reached a point-of-no-return, she found it easier—almost necessary—to go the wrong way rather than to turn back.

The comparison of Santa and the nation suggests that Gamboa was one of the few writers, if not the only one, of his time who wrote beyond himself. That is, he actually said more than his original design intended. López Portillo may have done so in *Nieves,* but Gamboa did so more generally. His novels suggest a revision of values because the basis of common sense doesn't work. It is a risky thing to compare specific characters to general conditions; but there is no doubt at all that these novels, written during the years of the "establishment," are novels of questioning unrest. This general mood is communicated to the reader who, at the end of each novel, has a feeling of vague uneasiness that the world is not turning as it should. (pp. 150-55)

[The years between 1907 and 1912, when] Mexico moved into the Revolution, were agonizing times of searching for solutions that were hidden behind the wall built by the establishment. (p. 159)

The agony of uncertainty is amply apparent in the novel. Some of the writers—López Portillo, Ceniceros y Villarreal, Cayetano Rodríguez Beltrán—held fast to the hope of man's individual improvement. While this improvement was associated with Christianity, it was really morality that concerned them; and the morality they advocated is more sensibly associated with traditionalism than with Christian faith. The *costumbrista* element of their novels serves as more than an interesting picture of customs. It is the basis of morality. They show how people acted, differentiating good from evil, and they propose that these traditional customs be a standard of conduct. The example of good conduct may also be an exponent of Christian faith; but the implication that Christianity and morality are equal to each other is just another example of the manufactured reality of the period. (p. 160)

Federico Gamboa's last two novels, both published during this period, are somewhat different from the traditionalist position and also from his own earlier works. They have many of the characteristics of Naturalism, and the style is still much the same; but they are inferior to the earlier novels because Gamboa wrote under the compulsion of solving his protagonists' problems. He fell into the trap of direct moralization, and he bent his characters almost to the breaking point to make them turn out the way he wanted them. It is interesting that he now felt the need of solving the problem, something that didn't bother him in his earlier novels. It is interesting also that the problem of the protagonist is related, in both novels, to a national problem. This fact, by the way, supports the idea that Santa's life can be associated with the circumstances of the Mexican nation. In the two late novels, there is a great deal of social protest. The national problems are not resolved, in spite of the author's vague discourses on the meaning of patriotism and the soul of Mexico, and in spite of the resolution of the problems of individual characters.

Reconquista (1908) deals with the spiritual rehabilitation of a gifted Mexican painter. Because he is a freethinker, his personal problems nearly destroy him. He loses both his professional job and his inspiration. He talks a lot about the soul of Mexico, which he proposes to discover among the poor and miserable. When he is asked by a magazine in the United States to paint a series of pictures of Mexico, he decides to paint the real Mexico, which is, in his opinion, the misery of the underprivileged. He believes only in the committed artist, saying that art for its own sake is of no importance. However, he is never really successful in capturing the soul of Mexico until he formally accepts the Church.

There is never any question of the artist's concern for social justice, though he is no moralist in his personal life. Gamboa apparently did not base his hope for a better society on personal morality. Indeed his closest approach to the traditionalist position is his assumption that the painter cannot discover the soul of Mexico until he has professed his Christian faith. And in this regard, no half measures would do. The act of conversion is not a dramatic, single moment in his life, but a gradual change. He is impressed by the persistent faith of another person, and moves toward Christianity. But his artistic inspiration does not come until after his definitive confession of faith. However, the meaning of Christianity in *Reconquista* is quite different from its meaning in . . . traditionalist novels. Gamboa is less concerned with its moral values than with the quality that feeds the artist's inspiration. The mystic quality of this inspiration is not entirely clear. From one standpoint it seems that Gamboa considers Christian faith to be the source of the painter's creative power. From a slightly different point of view, he seems to say that commitment to Christianity is necessary before the artist could really comprehend the soul of Mexico. The second assumption makes more sense in view of the author's obvious interest in social justice. It also means that Gamboa was probing into Mexican reality, trying to discover what was meaningful to the Mexican people and to relate that meaning to the social circumstance. His choice of Christianity as a means of understanding was somewhat different from the traditionalist approach, because it was an act of looking beyond visible reality rather than settling for superficial morality.

La llaga (1910) is the story of another kind of rehabilitation, this time of an ex-convict. Gamboa is likely to please and to annoy his reader alternately in this novel. It is full of preaching that makes one want to tell him to stay out of the way; on the other hand there are many fine novelistic touches that are typical of Gamboa at his best—for example, when Eulalio leaves prison, one of the first things he does is buy some flowers, without having any idea of why he wants to buy them.

The act is a symbol of his re-entry into the world. And that re-entry is far from simple. He finally makes a place for himself in an entirely different social situation from the one he had known before. Gamboa finds the opportunity to praise manual labor and to study the living conditions of the working class.

Gamboa speaks of the absence of patriotism in Mexico; and what he seems to mean is that genuine patriotism demands less personalism in the national life. He complains of economic and moral injustices on the part of the *hacendado,* and says that the Mexican peon is prepared for insurrection rather than for civic responsibility. He is not educated as a child. Later, the insurgents tell him the government is always bad, and the government tells him all insurgents are bandits. In the end, he discovers that insurrection does nothing to help him, whether he participates or not. For the national dilemma, Gamboa's only solution is gradual enlightenment, and he expresses his hope in Eulalio's becoming a father.

The *llaga* (sore) is apparent in several different forms. Eulalio bears it psychologically as a result of his imprisonment. He bears it physically as the result of mistreatment in prison, and of a later accident. It also exists nationally in the social rejection of Eulalio and in the nation's inability to cure its ills. There is no suggestion of revolution in Gamboa's novels, unless we presuppose the rejection of gradualism. In both *La llaga* and *Reconquista,* he struggles to find a ray of hope within the existing situation, but the result of his efforts could hardly be satisfactory to him or to anyone else. There is not the slightest doubt that by the time Gamboa wrote these novels, he was acutely aware of the dichotomy in Mexican society, and convinced that different circumstances should prevail. In a way, his hope was also based on the past, but it seems to require a deeper change in individuals than would be required by the *costumbrista* morality of the traditionalists. (pp. 163-65)

> *John S. Brushwood, in his* Mexico in Its Novel: A Nation's Search for Identity, *University of Texas Press, 1966, 292 p.*

JOHN S. BRUSHWOOD   (essay date 1981)

[*In the following excerpt, Brushwood uses Roman Jakobson's model of communication to discuss message and meaning in Gamboa's* Suprema ley.]

Federico Gamboa is generally and properly thought of as the leading naturalist among Mexican novelists. His most productive years in prose fiction extend from 1892 to 1913, coinciding roughly with the glory and decline of the Porfirio Díaz dictatorship. Undoubtedly his best known novel is *Santa,* a work that owes much of its fame to a sensationalist (for that period) story line—the fallen woman becomes a prostitute and continues her descent through several levels of her profession. This novel's reputation as a scandalous book (more recently shaded toward "camp") has tended to distract attention from its carefully developed story line and rich symbolic code. *Suprema ley* has also been obscured by its younger sister's flamboyant shadow. Its publication clearly antedates the author's supposed affirmation of a new religious faith in 1902—an act pointed out by Alexander C. Hooker, Jr., in his study of Gamboa [*La novela de Federico Gamboa*], as a turning point in the novelist's use of naturalism. The important difference seems to be that Gamboa was less pessimistic—possibly more idealistic—in the resolution of his later fictions. Whether or not a naturalist novelist must be committed to a pessimistic ending is a question that might be discussed at considerable length. The only relevance to the present study is that criticism of Gamboa's works often turns on the proposition that he was not really a naturalist. The choice of *Suprema ley,* rather than one of the later novels, makes consideration of a religious change unnecessary. There is no doubt that Gamboa was a practicing Roman Catholic, and he apparently did not take his interest in naturalism to be in conflict with his religious beliefs. With or without pessimism, religion is a factor in all his novels.

Studies of Gamboa have tended to deal with his life, the themes of his books, his view of society, and his understanding of naturalism. Analytical criticism has been less frequent. A recent note by Emmanuel Carballo is a good example of contemporary ideas on Gamboa and his novels. Basing his definition of naturalism on his reading of Joaquín Casalduero and Edmond de Goncourt, Carballo finds Gamboa deviating from the naturalist norm in several different ways: he considers him an observer of detail rather than an experimenter; he regards his religious concerns, moral judgments, and explicit preaching as inappropriate to naturalism; he believes Gamboa to have been naturalistic in themes but not in technique. Nevertheless, he thinks Gamboa was a good novelist, with a well-intentioned, bourgeois sensibility, who saw many of the sordid aspects of Mexican reality. The common people, for him, held a certain "exotic" attraction. Carballo says nothing about the naturalist novelist being less objective than the realist. He does note Casalduero's statement that naturalism proposes neither the study of characters nor of types, but of temperaments.

To a very considerable extent, *Suprema ley* accomplishes a study of temperaments. It would be difficult to eliminate the concept of "characters" from an analysis of the novel, because the temperaments, after all, are appreciated in terms of individuals. It is also worth noting that individualization (the discrete, human entity as against a social generalization) is evident in Gamboa as it is in Zola. The tendency toward the study of temperaments (an application of a "scientific" theory) involves the choice of cases that illustrate the point. A delicate balance between the study of characters and the study of temperaments is maintained in *Suprema ley* by the special characteristics of the narrative voice(s). This function can be illustrated by using Roman Jakobson's model of the communication act. There are variations in the sender that appear to be modifications or subdivisions of the omniscient narrator who is outside the story writing about someone other than himself. Such modifications alter the narrative situation and one may wonder, early in the novel, whether or not they contribute to a difference between the treatment of Julio and the treatment of Clotilde. It turns out that Julio is treated as the typical naturalist case but that Clotilde is not, and this difference is related to the balance maintained in the novel between study of character and study of temperament. Jakobson's model can be used to show how the variations function; however, it is necessary, first, to point out the differences between the basic anecdote and the developed plot of *Suprema ley.*

The plot emphasizes the emotional crisis of Julio Ortegal, an insignificant bureaucrat, and his subsequent moral and physical deterioration. Born late into a family identified by the long line of males who have held minor positions in the judicial system, Julio is pampered into ineffectiveness as an individual. He does all the things expected of him and, at the proper time, becomes a minor court official. Following the deaths of his parents, it occurs to him that maybe he should marry. The consequent choice is Carmen, an honest and unspectacular young woman; Julio marries her and they establish a household. Too little income and too many children keep them on the brink of economic desperation. Then Clotilde Granada is brought into court, accused of having murdered her lover. She is exonerated, but has been cut off from her family. Julio befriends her. His kindness and her gratitude lead them into an affair that destroys Julio's marriage and worsens his already weak physical condition. Clotilde becomes reconciled with her family; Julio dies of tuberculosis and of his inability to extricate himself from the trap of alienation.

The major *time* difference between basic anecdote and plot is that the latter begins when Clotilde is imprisoned. Information about the protagonists' earlier lives is supplied by the narrator, in different ways, after this fact. In addition to the time difference, two other factors in the plot development deserve special attention. First, Gamboa's use of detail creates the general ambience of the period and also underlines the meanness of Julio's life, by association with squalid surroundings. Second, the attitudes of Julio and Clotilde develop in such a way that they seem to fall into their love affair rather than seek it. The result is that this passion—the only extraordinary thing that ever happened to Julio—does nothing to enhance his self-esteem, since it is produced by accident rather than by design.

The Jakobson model of the communication act involves six factors, as follows:

$$\text{sender} \underset{\substack{\text{contact} \\ \text{code}}}{\overset{\substack{\text{context} \\ \text{message}}}{\rule{6em}{0.4pt}}} \text{receiver}$$

A fiction text, of course, contains a very large number of communication acts. It seems reasonable, however, to deal with the total text in terms of the Jakobson model, and later to use the same model as a means of illustrating some of the important variations within the narrative process. First we will consider *Suprema ley* to be one huge communication act.

The sender-receiver line obviously deserves first attention, and particularly in view of the importance of the narrative voice(s) in maintaining the balance between character study and temperament study in the novel to be analyzed. The sender should be understood as three different but related entities, suggested by Wayne Booth: (1) author, (2) implied author, and (3) narrator. The author of *Suprema ley* is rather clearly defined in the observations of Emmanuel Carballo, already referred to. Gamboa belonged to a conservative, traditionalist family. His father had fought against the Juárez government at the time of the French Intervention. The novelist himself supported the Díaz dictatorship, though he was able to see many social problems of the time. He was a diplomat, and served as foreign minister in the Huerta government— the reactionary backlash against the government of Francisco Madero. As a diplomat, he learned to get along well with people, and became highly cosmopolitan in his awareness of literature. Carlos González Peña points out Gamboa's interest in new people and new things, in spite of his basically traditionalist attitude. It is not difficult to imagine a receiver—a reader completely exterior to the text—with similar characteristics. This correspondence, however, is more relevant to an author named Federico Gamboa than it is to a novel entitled *Suprema ley.*

There are obvious points of contact between the author and the implied author, but it is important to note that the implied author may vary greatly in two or more novels by the same author. The implied author of *Suprema ley* believes that the established social institutions of his culture are good and that they exercise a potentially redemptive function. This function operates for Clotilde, but not for Julio—a difference that is perfectly credible as explained by the narrative study of the two temperaments. (Clotilde's separation from her family is basically accidental, and her orientation is always toward reunion. Julio, the mediocrity, is pulled into the affair by his need for some kind of distinction; separation from his family causes him to feel more guilt than regret.) The point is that *Suprema ley*'s implied author assumes there are forces in society that are capable of destroying established institutions. He is also aware of widely practiced vices like gambling and excessive drinking, and tends to regard them as foolish and futile. He obviously is well acquainted with the bureaucracy and is sensitive to its inadequacies.

The implied author is close to the narrator in *Suprema ley,* since the basic narrative position is outside the story. Narrator is different from implied author, however, because the narrator determines how the action is rendered (to borrow a term from Brooks and Warren); that is, the narrator controls the techniques of narration, though he may share the implied author's view of the reality portrayed. In dealing with the court officials, he is inclined to use a put-down that has a judgmental effect—for example, "El juez llegó a su hora, es decir, tarde" ("The judge arrived at the usual time, that is to say, late"). He achieves a similar tone on certain occasions when he is narrating in third person, but actually in lieu of the person whose case he is revealing. In such cases, his language takes on a colloquial coloring through the use of cliché, as when he is describing Julio's selection of Carmen: "Carmen Terno se llamaba la vencedora, quien se acercaba a los veinte años, sana y limpia que era una gloria verla" ("The name of the winner was Carmen Terno, almost twenty, so healthy and pure that she was a joy to behold").

The narrator chooses to emphasize unpleasant details of the setting as a means of intensifying the ugliness of a situation. Julio's reaction after the seduction (near rape) of Clotilde is underlined by a description of the carriage in which it happened: "la agravante del coche sucio y mojado por la lluvia; un cristal roto, grasientos los cojines" ("the exacerbation of the dirty carriage, wet because of the rain; a broken window, grimy cushions"). Although, in many instances, the third-person narrator seems very close to a character, there are times when he withdraws to a clinical position, examines the situation carefully, and even forecasts what a character will do later on: "Muchas ocasiones, cuando ya su drama carecía de remedio, achacó a esta condescendencia el origen de la catástrofe" ("On many occasions, when the course of his drama could not be altered, he imputed to this condescension the beginnings of the whole catastrophe"). [Later] the narrator actually detaches himself to explain, with a "No digo . . . ," but this narrative position evolves within the same paragraph into a third-person exposition of Julio's attitude, stating the case as if the protagonist's thoughts were being transposed into the narrator's language. It is interesting to note that the narrator virtually concedes his role to the implied author and then reclaims it. Equally interesting, in the

same passage, is another variation, one in which the narrator is obviously speaking *for* Julio, but it is doubtful that Julio would be *thinking* these thoughts. Rather, they seem to have turned into the thoughts of the implied author, stated as a proposition intended for examination in the naturalist manner. A similar investigative approach takes the form of a psychological exposition, later in the novel, with reference to Julio's and Clotilde's attitudes toward their love affair. In this case, the narrator uses the first-person impersonal ("se") to create greater distance between himself and the characters.

We may think of an implied reader who fits into the "receiver" position in Jakobson's model. This reader stays close to the narrator as he approaches or draws away from the characters, and is assumed to be ready to adapt to dialogue, pure narration, or exposition of a case. The reader presumably will join the narrator in judgmental attitudes. The characteristic of adaptability on the part of the reader is demanded by the nature of the contact. It is not enough to say that the contact is a bound series of printed pages called a "novel." These printed pages themselves include different forms of contact that anticipate different kinds of reaction. The *code,* on the other hand, tends to consolidate rather than diversify the reader's role. It is orthodox, literary Spanish of the period. The most important modification that may be called a sub-code is the occasional shading that has a judgmental or hyperbolic effect.

The most complicated problem is the *message.* Hooker says that the "fundamental concept" of *Suprema ley* is contained in a passage that incorporates the title.

> El amor está lleno de sorpresas; preséntase cuando menos se le espera y bajo todas las formas; arrolla y domina; no conoce resistencias ni parentescos ni obligaciones; vence a todas las leyes, las divinas y las humanas, porque es él la suprema ley!
>
> (Love is full of surprises; it presents itself when one least expects it, and it comes in all forms; it overwhelms and dominates; it does not recognize resistance or relationships or obligations; it conquers all laws, divine and human, because it is itself the highest law.)

These opinions are attributed to Berón, one of Julio's professional associates, who is given to delivering disquisitions of this kind. Indeed, it may be taken as a superficial description of what happens to Julio, but certainly not of what happens to Clotilde. Its function in the story is very interesting because it appears, not as a quotation, but as a report by the narrator of what Berón says. Immediately after this passage, the narrative manner changes back to dialogue, with Berón addressing Julio. The passage quoted is, in effect, a kind of summary of what Berón presumably said during part of an extended dialogue. It would be reasonable to think of Berón as the sender, Julio as the receiver, and the narrator's summary as the contact. This formulation changes the implied reader into a text act reader removed from the context of this subordinate communication act. The narrative process focuses first on characterization, then on temperament, and after that, on characterization again.

The passage quoted is clearly a subordinate communication act and should not be taken as a substitute for, or summary of, the overall communication act that is *Suprema ley.* The message of the novel may be thought of as a series of propositions concerning the nature and power of love. Message is very different from meaning, which takes into account all aspects of the communication act. The message is sent in many different ways—all within the possibilities, of course, of the contact. Thinking in terms of the power of love as a theme, the message appears in thirteen principal propositions:

1. The narrator reveals Julio's thoughts regarding the innocent love of childhood, followed by the disturbing presence of Clotilde in his reverie.
2. A prisoner realizes the redemptive power of love. The narrator summarizes part of the prisoner's story of his life.
3. The narrator analyzes Julio's attitude, pointing out his fear of the passion he senses, his ignorance of love, and his natural desire to experience it.
4. In a conversation with Clotilde's father, Julio reveals—through the narrator's description—a morbid curiosity in Clotilde's past and a corollary desire to possess her.
5. The "suprema ley" passage quoted above.
6. A reprise of a Biblical quotation by Berón, remembered by Julio, that gives scriptural authority to the notion of *femme fatale*.
7. Clotilde's wishful thinking (her thoughts reproduced in third person by narrator) finds a refuge in her religious training and concludes that Julio will leave her alone and return to his family.
8. In a discourse on the disappearance of love, the narrator indicates the effective end of the Julio-Carmen marriage.
9. In a reverie (reported in the intimate third person by the narrator), Julio recalls the Garden of Eden story and contemplates his guilt.
10. The narrator sets forth Clotilde's attitude after she is deeply involved in the affair with Julio (again the intimate third person approaches interior monologue). She knows she loves him, recognizes her guilt, but still cannot believe that a person will be condemned to hell for having loved, even though the love be illicit.
11. Julio breaks ties with his family completely in order to save his love affair.
12. In conversation with Berón, Julio, fearing separation from Clotilde, changes the "suprema ley" statement: "—Es una equivocación, Licenciado; la única suprema ley es el dolor!" ("It is a mistaken idea, Licenciado; suffering is the highest law").
13. Julio, now alone, explains to a poor watchman how Clotilde's confession to a priest put an end to their love affair, and says he cannot understand how a priest can prohibit love.

The meaning of the communication act depends on the message conveyed in these thirteen propositions and on all the other aspects of the model, including the context. There is a context within the communication act itself and a context outside the act. The latter takes into account the complex society of the middle years of the Díaz dictatorship, during which the author was a member of the establishment. The interior context takes into account the attitudes of the implied author as expressed by the narrator and of the reader who corresponds to him. The relatively new interest in psychology is an important factor in this context, as is the skeptical view of bureaucracy combined with acceptance of an orderly, if repressive, political organization. This context also incorporates the ambience of the city at a particular time in its history, including its entertainment media as well as its home life.

If the series of passages on the theme of love may be taken as the message, this message has meaning only in terms of the context and the way the message is sent. The meaning seems to depend to a great extent on variations in the narrative procedure that affect the characterization and the study of temperament. This phenomenon can be illustrated by describing a series of subordinate communication acts.

The basic presentation of Julio Ortegal takes place in the first chapter, beginning in an office setting and using the narrator's knowledge of his past to furnish all the information needed. Substituting particularities of the case in the Jakobson model, we have this scheme:

> *context:* characterizations
> of Julio's co-workers
> *message:* Julio's biography

sender: narrator   *receiver:* implied
close to implied ——————————————— reader interested in
author   bureaucratic types

> *contact:* summary
> *code:* standard Spanish
> for period and author's
> social milieu, with some
> derogatory expressions

This passage is a normal procedure used by realist and naturalist novelists as a basis for characterization. The ambience is established before the biographical section begins. The "code" indicates the narrator's (and the implied author's) lack of respect for the protagonist. The message contains information that suggests Julio's temperament—a mediocrity frustrated without even being aware of his frustrations. Although the language occasionally suggests a closing of the gap between narrator and protagonist, the scornful tone maintains an emotional separation.

The essential information regarding Clotilde Granada's past is presented in a very different way. It is revealed in the course of examination by Julio, following her arrest.

> *context:* questioning in
> court by Ortegal
> *message:* Clotilde's
> illicit love

sender: Clotilde;   *receiver:* Ortegal; im-
narrator's para- ——————————————— plied reader interpret-
phrase of Clotilde   ing paraphrase

> *contact:* summary and
> scene
> *code:* standard Spanish

Whereas the presentation of Julio is objective, with great distance between the narrator and Julio, the presentation of Clotilde places her in a give-and-take situation with another character. Scene and summary alternate, in contrast to the predominance of summary when Julio is first presented. The passage analyzed here is more a study of character than of temperament, as far as the woman is concerned. On the other hand, Julio Ortegal's response as receiver reveals an interest that is overtly sympathetic but that suggests he is aware of dealing with an unfamiliar kind of person. This reaction not only serves to set forth his own temperament but also, because of this sense of unfamiliarity, focuses attention on the temperament of Clotilde. When the narrator paraphrases in third person, condensing Clotilde's words, he seems closer to her than he is to Julio, in the latter's introductory scene, specifically because the code does not include derogatory expressions.

The presence of the implied author is felt more intensely in the interpolated story of Apolonio, a convicted murderer. He is a member of the lower class, a victim of the social framework that defines his position, his values, and his fate. In addition to the experience of this story in its own right, we appreciate its influence on Julio's reaction to Clotilde's plight, since he is close enough to see all the horror of Apolonio's execution and the time immediately preceding it. Apolonio has no interest in religion, but a priest leads him into confession by asking him to tell the story of his life.

context: situation
preliminary to
Apolonio's execution
message: Apolonio's
biography

sender: Apolonio   —————————   *receiver:* priest and
and narrator   implied reader

contact: summary
and scene
code: standard Spanish

Major interest in this passage focuses on the sender. When the narrator's third-person voice substitutes for Apolonio's part of the dialogue, it is not in the nature of a paraphrase of his presumed words, but more like an exposition and commentary on his life. In the presentation of Julio, the narrator was separated from the protagonist by his feeling of disrespect. In the case of Apolonio, the narrator is separated by an objective position that is almost clinical. He seems to explain to an implied reader what life is like for poor people like Apolonio, bringing out points that Apolonio would not make if he were simply talking about himself. Apolonio's speech is hardly differentiated from the narrator's explanation—nothing more than a diminutive, like "cervecita" ["short beer"], for example. The language of the narrator himself changes as much or more in a few instances when he moves toward paraphrasing. However, this tendency never really takes hold, so Apolonio's story becomes a case history—not an unexpected phenomenon in a naturalist novel. In the present case, the Apolonio episode, taken as a whole, contributes to the characterization of Julio by supporting his inclination to help Clotilde.

Julio is pushed closer to the brink of disaster when Clotilde's father asks him to receive and deliver to Clotilde a monthly allowance to be sent by her father. Again Julio's temperament comes into prominence as he experiences a sense of power cloaked in the rhetoric of helping someone

context: Julio ill from Apolonio episode and association
of it with Clotilde's fate
message: Agustín Granada's
version of Clotilde's story

sender: Granada ————————— *receiver:* Ortegal
and narrator   and implied reader

contact: dialogued interviews
—scene with intercalated
summary
code: standard Spanish;
Granada's is flowery

The sender role is dominated by Granada. Naturally, Julio speaks. What he says does not constitute part of the message unless we turn the model around every time the dialogue

changes, so making Julio an alternating sender. Preserving the sense of the interview taken as a whole, the narrator's intervention serves only to abbreviate the dialogue. Granada's "sub-code" (his courtly speech) is a very important part of the meaning of the passage because it enhances Julio's appreciation of the circumstance as extraordinary. That is, Granada's manner is impressive to Ortegal. The context shows him in an extremely vulnerable position.

Once exonerated, Clotilde lives with the Ortegal family until she realizes the nature and extent of Julio's interest in her. Then she establishes a residence of her own. After going to her new quarters, she takes account of the situation, recognizing Julio's passion, her own love for him, and the related problems.

context: Clotilde, separated from
others, evaluates her situation
message: Clotilde's reaction
to new environment

sender: narrator ————————— *receiver:* im-
close to implied   plied reader
reader

contact: narrator's analysis, plus
questions that could reflect
Clotilde's thoughts
code: standard Spanish

This passage is remarkably different from the early presentation of Clotilde. Here she is not in contact with another character, and the narrator's analysis tends toward the clinical. Some occasional questions may be taken to reflect or paraphrase Clotilde's verbal formulation of the problems before her. If this sender identification were developed in the narrative process, Clotilde might well become the receiver, in a kind of conversation with herself. However, this possibility remains only a suggestion, and the questions are equally plausible as formulations set forth by the narrator and then answered or discussed by him, with the direction clearly toward the implied reader rather than toward a character in the story. The effect is that attention is focused on the aspects of the problem rather than on the plight of an individual. This passage is the most intensely clinical point in the treatment of Clotilde. Subsequently, the narration emphasizes her character rather than her temperament, and builds toward her reconciliation (or redemption).

When Julio's affair with Clotilde becomes flagrantly apparent, the situation of the deserted wife and children takes on added importance in the story. The adherence of both author and implied author to established institutions makes the survival of the Ortegal family (without Julio, of course) almost a foregone conclusion. The instrument of salvation is the devotion of the first-born, Julito, to his mother. There are many details and several useful passages that might be pointed out in this connection, but a very short and significant one is the first description of the relationship.

context: Julio gives money to family, but otherwise ignores them
message: Julio reads to his
mother

sender: narrator ————————— *receiver:* im-
                                          plied reader

contact: summary
code: standard Spanish,
imperfect tense

The particular value of this passage is in a detail of the message. The narrator uses the imperfect tense to describe what habitually went on in the Ortegal family at this time, and pictures Carmen sewing while Julito studies or reads her a serial novel, "de esas que conmueven a las mujeres y a los niños por lo enmarañado de la trama y lo bien parada que a todos tiros queda la virtud") ("one of those that move women and children because of the entanglements of their plots and how well virtue bears up under all attacks"). There is, therefore, another (subsubordinate) communication act described by the narrator, one in which Julito is the sender, Carmen is the receiver, the contact is a melodramatic novel, the code is unknown, the context is an abandoned mother and son, and the message is whatever the contents of the novel may be as Julito reads it. We know only what the narrator says about it, but that is enough to identify a familiar kind of text. It is interesting that what happens to Carmen and her children in the rest of *Suprema ley* is remarkably similar to the kind of novel the narrator describes in this passage. The effect is that Julio is separated from his family in more than one way—that is, the story of Julio follows a naturalist line while the story of his family relates an idealized, virtue-rewarded situation. It makes the Julio-Clotilde study look even more like a case history.

The disruption of the family and the virtue of the mother-son relationship are emphasized in a brief passage in which Julito describes the ceramics school to which he has been admitted.

context: Julito seeking gainful
employment
message: description of school

sender: Julito ——————————————— *receiver:* Carmen

contact: scene
code: standard Spanish

Julito's enthusiasm is reassuring to Carmen and indicates his maturity. An aspect of secondary interest is the usefulness of the passage as an indication of the implied author's ideas about education. Julito's enthusiasm is founded on the practical, job-oriented nature of the school. There is no derogatory shading by the narrator, so it seems safe to assume that a point is being made about education. However, it is worth noting that the narrator, in this case, allows a character to state the case. It is not easy to find him so relaxed in explaining the Julio-Clotilde relationship. More frequently he seems anxious to control the differentiating lines between his two characters. The present scene, of course, emphasizes the alienation of Julio by focusing on the growing maturity of his son. In combination with the much earlier comments derogating Julio's profession, it suggests that the latter might have fared better as a tradesman. However, his temperament would never have permitted it.

The plot crisis (not necessarily the major point in the study of characters or temperaments) comes when Clotilde's Aunt Carlota arrives in Mexico City to act as intermediary between Clotilde and her family. Her arrival immediately separates the lovers, since Julio cannot spend nights with Clotilde, and threatens an eventual break. The basic communication of this change is a letter from Agustín Granada to his daughter.

context: Carlota and Clotilde
alone in latter's home
message: Clotilde's father's
proposed reconciliation

sender: Carlota ——————————————— *receiver:* Clotilde
reading letter

contact: letter
code: histrionic Spanish

The code is more important here than in any of the other passages analyzed. The exaggerated emotions expressed in the letter place the Clotilde-family relationship in a class with the saga of Julio's wife and children. Julio is left unredeemed and, apparently, unredeemable.

After Clotilde makes the final break with Julio, he goes to the neighborhood of her house. A sleepy watchman is the only person available for company, so Julio tells him his story.

context: Julio separated from
Clotilde and from family
message: Julio's view of
affair (reprise)

sender: Julio ——————————————— *receiver:* watchman
and narrator   and implied reader

contact: scene and summary
code: standard Spanish

The words actually spoken by Julio are little more than introductions to the narrator's summary of what Julio talks about. The predominant theme is Julio's need to justify his actions and to blame someone for his most recent loss. If the communication act were stated with the dialogue reversed, that is, with the watchman in the sender position, the message is the only other component of the diagram that would be changed. The watchman's role in this passage is to emphasize the absurdity of Julio's position. The watchman has a common-law wife and some children. He is attached to them and does not see anything complicated about the conjugal relationship. Julio's discourse simply bores him.

The extraordinary factor that entered Julio's life has vanished. He is out of contact with the institutions of the world he lives in. Spiritually, he is destroyed. There is a suggestion of possible reconciliation with his family, but his physical demise comes before that can take place.

Consideration of the series of propositions concerning love as the overall message of *Suprema ley* seems accurate and, at the same time, very inadequate. It is not sufficient, for example, to explain Julio's dilemma by saying that he is the victim of the power of love. In fact, the experience of the novel emphasizes his insignificance more than the power of love. The dynamic factor in the novel (the principal factor in the transformation of basic anecdote into developed plot) is not the definition of the role of love but the changing idiosyncrasies of the sender. The passages examined in terms of the Jakobson model indicate that the sender varies in such a way that the distance between narrator and character at times may indicate a clinical evaluation or at other times may reflect a more personal involvement. A few differences in the code (far fewer than might have been advantageously used) contribute to the effect; basically, the sender variation sets Julio apart from the others. He alone is not saved by some form of reconciliation. Gradually, the experience of the novel involves awareness of Julio as a mediocrity whose emotional inclinations are unknown even to himself. The force that leads to his destruction is not the power of love—or certainly not as it is explained in any of the propositions made in the novel—but his deep need to stand out from the mediocrity that identifies him. To the extent that this need expresses itself in a bizarre love affair, the message of the novel is indeed the series of propositions concerning love. On the other hand, it might be better to say that the message is an alternating personal and clinical view of Julio, in which the clinical aspect becomes dominant.

There are moments in the novel when the view of Clotilde is also clinical, and the experience of the work admits briefly the possibility of alternating views of two characters, balanced against each other. However, Clotilde achieves reconciliation, and reasonably so within the context of the novel as a whole. It might be possible to think of her as a case study, but it is much easier to think of Julio in this way because, gradually, his plight becomes more important than his person—the study of a temperament is more impressive than the character study of a man named Julio. This development is the meaning of the communication act, because it synthesizes the experience of the novel. (pp. 158-74)

John S. Brushwood, "Message and Meaning: Federico Gamboa's 'Suprema Ley'," in his Genteel Barbarism: Experiments in Analysis of Nineteenth-Century Spanish-American Novels, *University of Nebraska Press, 1981, pp. 158-74.*

FURTHER READING

Niess, Robert J. "Federico Gamboa: The Novelist as Autobiographer." *Hispanic Review* 13, No. 4 (October 1945): 346-51.
    Explores the autobiographical basis of Gamboa's novel *Reconquista.*

André (Paul Guillaume) Gide

1869-1951

French novelist, diarist, dramatist, critic, autobiographer, essayist, and poet.

The following entry presents criticism of Gide's novel *Les faux-monnayeurs* (1925; *The Counterfeiters*, 1927). For discussion of Gide's complete career including criticism of *The Counterfeiters,* see *TCLC,* Volumes 5 and 12.

The Counterfeiters is Gide's most ambitious work, integrating discussions of literary theory and reflections on ethics and psychology into a fictional narrative. Compared for its technical innovations and its concern with the process of literary creation to James Joyce's *Ulysses* (1922) and Marcel Proust's *A la recherche du temps perdu* (1913-27; *Remembrance of Things Past*), *The Counterfeiters* uses a variety of experimental techniques in an attempt to create a more authentic picture of reality than could be achieved by traditional novelistic methods. A complex network of characters and events enabled Gide to treat such widely varying themes as hypocrisy, the relationship between evil and progress, and the conflict between self-fulfillment and responsibility to society. The structural and thematic intricacy of the novel, along with Gide's commentary in *Le journal des faux-monnayeurs* (*Journal of the Counterfeiters*), have resulted in conflicting critical assessments of the work.

Although Gide had considered writing a novel concerned with "the *relations* between a dozen characters" as early as 1902, he did not begin writing *The Counterfeiters* until 1919. He had saved newspaper articles from two events in 1906 and 1909 in order to incorporate them into his novel: one incident involved a group of adolescents from respected families who had been caught passing counterfeit coins, and the other, a high school student who had killed himself to fulfill a suicide pact with his friends. During the six years he took to complete the novel, he worked on several other projects, including a series of lectures on Fyodor Dostoevsky. Dostoevsky's theories, such as the importance of evil to intellectuality, and his literary techniques, such as interruptions in action at moments of great intensity, influenced Gide's composition of *The Counterfeiters*. Some critics believe an even greater influence on *The Counterfeiters* can be found in Gide's separation from his wife in 1918 and his growing intimacy with Marc Allégret. An entry about Allégret in Gide's diary supports this theory: "It was for him, to win his attention, his esteem, that I wrote *Les faux-monnayeurs,* just as all my preceding books were written under the influence of Em. [Gide's wife], or in the vain hope of convincing her." A dedicated diarist, Gide kept a separate journal for his thoughts about *The Counterfeiters,* which he published in 1926 as *Journal of the Counterfeiters*. Although some critics consider the journal an essential companion to the novel, Germaine Brée spoke for others when she observed: "The *Journal of the Counterfeiters* is neither a guide to Gide's novel nor an explanation of it. At most, it can raise certain questions in the reader's mind concerning Gide's intentions, the merits of the techniques he used, and the scope of the book itself."

The Counterfeiters is structured to relate a number of simul-

taneous events, often connecting them only through distant relationships among the characters. The action is divided among several groups and individuals, including the Profitendieu and Molinier families; the pastor Vedel, his wife, and the students and faculty at their school; the novelists Edouard and Passavant; and the counterfeiter Strouvilhou. Edouard provides a tenuous focus for the novel through his connections to other characters and his attempts to incorporate many of the events of the novel into a novel of his own, also called *The Counterfeiters*. He, like Gide, maintains a *Journal of the Counterfeiters,* comprising almost half of Gide's book, in which he records his impressions of people and events and his theories about the novel as a genre. As the half-brother of Mme. Molinier, Edouard has at least a peripheral view of the events that surround her three sons, Vincent, Olivier, and Georges. Vincent has impregnated Laure Douviers, daughter of Vedel and a close friend of Edouard, and subsequently abandons her for Lady Griffith, whom he eventually murders. Edouard has romantic feelings for Olivier, who, though reciprocating the writer's interest, becomes involved with Edouard's literary rival, Passavant. Olivier's friend Bernard Profitendieu, having learned of his illegitimacy, leaves home and becomes Edouard's secretary for a period. Georges, who is involved in a gang of high school students passing counterfeit coins, becomes part of a hoax that leads Boris, the grandson of Edouard's old piano teacher La Perouse, to commit suicide. The intricacy of the plot, only briefly outlined here, has both been praised as an accurate reflection of the complexity of reality itself and criticized as overly complicated and melodramatic.

In the *Journal of the Counterfeiters,* Gide said he wanted to write a "pure novel," a novel that would be aesthetically perfect and would include no elements that served merely to create a realistic representation of life without contributing to the artistic and philosophic scheme of the narrative. Gide considered *The Counterfeiters* to be his first novel, classifying his earlier works as *récits,* or psychological narratives, such as *La porte étroite* (*Strait Is the Gate*) and *La symphonie pastorale* (*The Pastoral Symphony*), or as farcical *soties,* such as *Paludes* (*Marshlands*) and *Les caves du Vatican* (*Lafcadio's Adventures*). Viewing these works as too narrowly focused, Gide wished to incorporate into *The Counterfeiters* all of his experiences and observations. Unlike the traditional linear storyline, his decentralized plot attempts to reproduce the actual simultaneity and multiplicity of events in reality. Gide began each chapter on a fresh subject, having vowed "never to take advantage of momentum already gained." Gide also rejected using an omniscient narrator and consistent characterization as too divorced from reality. At the same time he used many techniques that emphasized the artificiality of his novel, including direct comments from the author in the chapter titled "The Author Judges His Characters" and the many implausible coincidences that advance the plot.

Critics have often been led to a biographical reading of *The Counterfeiters* by Edouard's similarity to Gide in personality, life-style, and profession. Both Edouard and Gide theorize about the "pure novel," and Edouard's desire to write a novel "which would be at once as true and as far removed from reality, as particular and as general, as human and as fictive as *Athalie, Tartuffe,* or *Cinna,*" resembles the plan for *The Counterfeiters* Gide originally discussed in his journal. Assuming Edouard to be Gide's mouthpiece, some critics have judged *The Counterfeiters* a failure because it does not fulfill the intentions Gide ascribed to Edouard for his own novel. The sample of Edouard's novel provided in *The Counterfeiters* is considered more analytical, abstract, and self-conscious than Gide's, and of inferior quality. Other critics conclude from this discrepancy that Gide's aims differed from Edouard's.

One of Gide's primary artistic and philosophical concerns was authenticity. He discussed his life in a way that has been called self-consciously candid and exhibitionistic by some critics, while others see religious overtones in his "unremitting search for self-correction and self-purification." The much-discussed Gidean notions of "sincerity," which Germaine Brée has summarized as signifying the "struggle of human beings with truths compulsively followed" and *"disponibilité,"* which Gide explained as "following one's inclinations, so long as they lead upward," were products of his lifelong passion for self-awareness. In *The Counterfeiters,* Gide's concerns are implied not only by the title of the novel and by the main activity of the teenage gang, but also by the emotions and ideas of most of the characters. J. C. Davies finds that "the story of *real* counterfeiters, designated in the title of the book, takes on a symbolic significance as serving to illustrate the essential theme of psychological 'counterfeiters,' those who fabricate false ideas and sentiments and who spend their whole lives in an atmosphere of hypocrisy, without ever knowing their true selves." For example, Pastor Vedel assumes the role of devout Christian, which he continues to play long after he has ceased to believe the tenets of Christianity. Even Edouard, who prides himself on his sincerity, plays the role of benefactor when the primary reason for his interference in others' lives is his curiosity. The struggle against hypocrisy is best embodied in Bernard, who strives for self-knowledge and to act honestly on that knowledge. Gide counterbalances this approval of self-determination with an imperative of moral responsibility to others, an issue that most conspicuously arises in the relationship between Boris and the many characters who thoughtlessly influenced his suicide. Never indicating a definitive opinion on any issue he raises, Gide proliferates questions and themes that expand beyond the scope of the novel.

Critics vary widely in their interpretation of *The Counterfeiters,* claiming variously that it is a novel of ethics, a novel about the novel, or a novel about perceptions of reality. Attempts to place it in a school or determine Gide's intentions have never produced a consensus, and most critics, for varied reasons, have judged *The Counterfeiters* to be a partial failure. Some critics contend that Gide did not achieve his goals of creating a "pure novel," or of accurately reflecting a wide range of human experience, while others criticize the book for lack of unity and consistent characterization. Nevertheless, the structural and thematic complexity of *The Counterfeiters* has led to its status as an exemplary modern novel and as Gide's major fictional work.

(See also *Contemporary Authors,* Vols. 104 and 124, and *Dictionary of Literary Biography,* Vol. 65.)

LOUIS KRONENBERGER (essay date 1927)

> [*A drama critic for* Time *from 1938 to 1961, Kronenberger was a distinguished historian, playwright, novelist, and literary critic highly regarded for his expertise in eighteenth-century English history and literature. In an assessment of Kronenberger's critical ability, Jacob Korg states: "He interprets, compares, and analyzes vigorously in a pleasingly epigrammatic style, often going to the essence of a matter in a phrase." In the following excerpt, Kronenberger praises* The Counterfeiters *as an advance in the great tradition of the novel.*]

Unlike Anatole France, Gourmont and Proust, André Gide has not been given by intelligent Americans the recognition which his great talents deserve. It is to be hoped that with this magnificent book, **The Counterfeiters,** he will come more into his own, as Thomas Mann has come into his own over here with the publication of *The Magic Mountain.* For out of a fair familiarity with recent French literature, I can think of no fiction since Proust which offers as much, which means as much, as this present novel of Gide's.

In an age of experimentation Gide has produced a novel which is original without being experimental, which is large without being unwieldy, and which is intellectual without being dialectic. It was his ambition in **The Counterfeiters,** an ambition in which he has succeeded, "to purge the novel of all those elements which do not belong specifically to the novel." His book has no secondary aims whatsoever; it tells the story of a dozen interplaying lives. But besides purging it of all excesses, he has written it as, in a significant sense, no other novel has altogether been written. He has rejected the kind of reality achieved by established schools of writing—by realists, by naturalists, by students of manners. What all novelists do unconsciously to a certain degree, Gide has done deliberately to the ultimate degree; he has discarded "the real world" for "the representation of it which we make to ourselves." With Gide it has not been merely the inevitable question of a writer's "interpretation." Gide's characters are alive in a living world, never for an instant abstractions in an abstract world, yet Gide has virtually dispensed with the materialistic. He has found neither need nor place in *The Counterfeiters* for backgrounds of any kind, for surfaces, for sensory impressions, for telling trivialities which give life an "air of naturalness." The people of *The Counterfeiters* lead neither the customary inner nor the customary outer lives. We are shown them growing through their experiences with and influence upon one another; the rest, unimportant by comparison, is left to our imagination. For *The Counterfeiters,* in a word, is a novel of the development of related lives. Some of these lives grow, others decline, while two or three of the characters in the book act as catalysts.

It is not possible to summarize *The Counterfeiters* with any accuracy. Its chief characters are young fellows who react upon one another and who, each one, come into contact with some one older. . . .

And these people live vividly, significantly, as people. Bernard, Olivier, Vincent, George, fed by life and passing under the influences of Edouard, Passavant, Lillian, Gheridanisol, grow through mental and moral upheavals and move on toward their destinies. Gide is not the old-fashioned novelist who ties up their lives in permanent knots at the end of his story; but he is no mere spectator; he is a creator and an artist, and if they do not reach their final destinies, he lets us see, at least, something of what they may be. For *The Counterfeiters* is a superbly rounded novel with a beginning and a conclusion. From a masterly introduction of its characters one after another in a beautifully patterned sequence, through a long series of scenes which never confuse us, no matter how many lives must be kept in sight, it proceeds to a point where its own interests are exhausted and where its characters stand on new thresholds of activity—the exact point at which it should end.

The Counterfeiters restores the novel to us in all its creative freshness. It is an advance, but a logical advance, in the great tradition. It throws out the photographic and observational method extending from Flaubert to Joyce, to resume the creative and panoramic method of Balzac and Tolstoy. What fascination there is to most of these characters, and what a world they form! One can hardly forget the meeting of Edouard and Olivier at the railway station, the return of Passavant, Lillian and Vincent from Rambouillet, the Argonaut's dinner, the suicide of Boris. Yet *The Counterfeiters* belongs to the great tradition in a new way, and one distinction must be made. It has not universal qualities; it is, after all, a kind of intellectualist's novel. For it presupposes that the reader will bring to it an imaginative and mental equipment that will do very much work of their own, rather than directly inciting us as, say, *Père Goriot,* incites us; and its characters are too complexly alive to have the immediate memorableness of a Goriot. Like *Hamlet, The Counterfeiters* was made for rereading, and nobody can get all the rich compensations of its art and the vivid excitement of its reality by reading it once. For never in all his career has Gide had so much to give.

Louis Kronenberger, "André Gide's New Novel Is in the Great Tradition," in The New York Times Book Review, *October 2, 1927, p. 2.*

JOSEPH WARREN BEACH (essay date 1932)

[*Beach was an American critic and educator who specialized in American literature and English literature of the Romantic and Victorian eras. Of his work, Beach noted: "I do not aim so much to render final judgements and deliver certificates of greatness, which is something manifestly impossible and a trifle ridiculous, as to analyze and interpret stories and poems as expressions of our humanity and as effective works of art." In the following excerpt, Beach examines the great diversity of subject matter and points of view in* The Counterfeiters.]

Exactly contemporary with *Manhattan Transfer* and *Mrs. Dalloway* was *The Counterfeiters* (*Les faux-monnayeurs,* 1925), from which novel we have taken our phrase "the breadthwise cutting." In this case we do not have to guess what the author was undertaking to do. Gide is one of the most self-conscious of writers. During the years while he was planning and writing *The Counterfeiters,* he kept a notebook, like those kept by James in his later years, in which he made a record of his artistic ideals, his gropings for an idea, and to some extent of his progress in the composition of the book. This note-book he has published as *Le journal des faux-monnayeurs.* In many respects it corresponds very closely to the note-book of Edouard in the novel itself.

To begin with, there is his wish to be comprehensive, to get everything in. In the *Journal* he speaks more than once of his wish to make his work *touffu,* that is, dense or crowded with matter.

> As dense as I hope to make this book, I can't dream of getting everything in. And yet it is just the wish for that which still embarrasses me. I am like a composer who seeks to juxtapose and overlap, in the manner of César Franck, an andante motif with an allegro.

A question that arose in this connection was whether to have the story told by one of the characters. Gide, who was an admirer and translator of Conrad, had inclined in earlier books to Conrad's way of having the story told by some one who was involved in it. He had also Conrad's fondness for documents. *L'immoraliste* (1902) is a frame story like *Heart of Darkness,* which saw the light in the same year. It was recited by the leading character, Michel, to a group of friends gathered one night on the terrace of his house in Algeria. Thus it has the restricted point of view of a first-person narrative. But it is introduced and concluded by the friend who explains the circumstances under which the story was told; and the whole has the form of a letter written by the friend to his brother, a person in high office, who may be able to help Michel. So that it has the character of one of those documents beloved of romancers. *La porte etroite* (1909), again, is told in the first person by some one mainly involved in the story; and then, to give it higher documentary value, there is included a large part of the diary of another leading character.

Thus, in each of these books, Gide manages to reconcile his concern for point of view with his interest in having light fall from several different directions on the same subject.

Point of view is important to any one who conceives fiction in terms of picture. "First of all study the direction from which the light falls; all the shadows depend on that." In *The*

Counterfeiters Gide's first thought was to have the story told entirely by Lafcadio. Lafcadio is the name of a principal character in his *sotie, Les caves du Vatican,* (1922); I assume that his first intention was to revive him in the new book and give him some rôle like that of Bernard. But eventually he dropped him. "For several days I have been in doubt whether to make Lafcadio tell the story. It would be a recital of events which he discovered little by little and in which he interested himself through curiosity, idleness, and perversity." Later he considers having the story pass through the hands of several narrators. "I should like to provide a succession of interpreters: for example, these notes of Lafcadio would occupy the first book; the second book would be Edouard's note-book; the third a lawyer's brief, etc. . . . "

The reason why he is not satisfied with a single interpreter is that it is too difficult to bring in through him all that he wishes in the way of events and of psychological interpretation. In writing another of his books, he says—but the whole passage is highly worth quoting:

> In the course of writing, I was brought to consider that intimacy, penetration, psychological investigation, may, in some ways, be pushed farther in the novel proper than even in "confessions." In these latter, one is somewhat handicapped by the "I"; there are certain complexities which one can't expect to unravel, to develop, without seeming to force things. All that I see, all that I learn, everything that happens to me in the course of several months, I'd like to work into this novel, and make use of to give it a richer texture. I should like to manage it so that the events are never recounted directly by the author, but rather set forth (and several times, from various angles) by those among the actors on whom these events have had a certain influence. I should like, in the account which they give, for these events to appear slightly deformed; there is a sort of interest for the reader in the simple fact of making his corrections. The narrative demands his collaboration if the drawing is to be right.

There are in this passage half a dozen matters of extreme interest. But I wish to lay my stress for the moment on Gide's desire to work in a great diversity of matter, to have his story spread out over a wide range of human experience. He realizes that this means departing from the usual type of novel (*le type convenu du roman*), and he finds that it involves him in many difficulties, but the difficulties tend to fall away "the moment that he deliberately takes advantage of the queerness" of his undertaking.

> From the moment that I reconcile myself to the impossibility of making this like anything else (and it suits me that it should be so) why try so hard to find motivation, consistency, a way of grouping everything around a central plot? Can't I find a way, with the form which I adopt, of indirectly criticizing all that sort of thing? Lafcadio for example would try in vain to tie the threads together; there would be useless characters, gestures without significance, talk that leads nowhere, and an action that never gets started.

Gide never quite says in so many words *why* it is he wants to make his work so different from the usual type of novel: why he wants to neglect such excellent principles as motivation, consistency (or consequentiality), and a systematic arrangement of matter around a central plot. But here it is easy to guess what he is after. He is after a nearer approach to the truth of human experience. He wants his work to be *more like life.* And life he has found to be more surprising, more elusive, less formally consistent, than it has been portrayed in "the usual type of novel." He has come under the influence of that tendency to *deformalization.* . . . And he wants to get away from the logical neatness of the Jameses, the Flauberts, the Bourgets, the Prévosts. He wants to take life by surprise, after the manner of the Conrads, the Joyces.

This is not a new notion with him. In *Les caves du Vatican* he has already introduced a character who was disposed to "criticize all that sort of thing." Lafcadio has been reading a novel by his distinguished brother, Julius de Baraglioul, and he finds that it is spoiled by excessive logic. The trouble with your hero, he tells Julius, is consistency. "You take such pains to keep him, always, everywhere consistent, towards us and towards himself, faithful to his obligations, to his principles,—that is to say, to your theories." And in the end Julius comes to agree with him.

> The logic, the consequentiality, which I demand of my characters,—in order to insure this, I demanded it first of all from myself; and that was not natural. We live disguised, rather than not resemble the picture which we made of ourselves to begin with; it is absurd; in doing so, we run the risk of distorting whatever is best in us. . . .

Pursuing this line of reasoning, he arrives at a brilliant idea for his next novel: a crime committed without a motive. And curiously enough, before the book is over, he breaks his shins against an actual case of murder without motive, or at least without any motive which is clear to the murderer himself. And the murderer is his brother Lafcadio! It goes without saying that he is greatly taken aback at finding so prompt a confirmation of his artistic theory.

In *The Counterfeiters* still more is made of this quaint parallelism and contrast between reality and the logic of fiction. One of the central characters is the novelist, Edouard; and he shares the ambition of Gide to work into his book as much as possible of what he actually experiences. But the culminating event of the book is the suicide of a young boy in a boarding-school; and this event Edouard is unable to get into his story, for the simple reason that he cannot understand it. André Gide understands it fairly well, in its motivation and circumstances, and makes it the climax of his book. But his imaginary author says:

> While I don't pretend to give a precise explanation of anything, I shouldn't like to present any fact without sufficient motivation. That is why I don't intend to make use in my *Counterfeiters* of little Boris's suicide; I find too much difficulty in understanding it. . . . I grant that reality may come to the support of my thought, as a confirmation; but not that it should anticipate it. It distresses me to be surprised. The suicide of Boris seems to me like an impropriety [*une indécence*], for I was not expecting it.

In many respects the artistic intentions of Edouard are identical with those of André Gide. But in the present instance he is clearly in a class with Julius, who goes by logic and consistency. He is dominated by the standard of the "usual type of novel." And that is why, as Gide says in the *Journal,* "he is unable to write his book. He understands many things; but he is constantly in pursuit of himself, through all the characters, through everything. A true devotion [to his subject] is practically impossible for him. He is an amateur, a missfire." And that, he tells us, is the underlying subject of the book and what makes it so difficult to write.

> There is properly speaking no single center to this book, round which my efforts converge; it is about two focal points, in the manner of ellipses, that these efforts are polarized. On the one side the event, the fact, the exterior circumstances; on the other side, the very effort of the novelist to make a book out of all that. And just there is the principal subject, the new center which throws the narrative off its axis and draws it towards the fanciful and visionary.

Gide does not tell us much about the precise nature of the book which Edouard is writing, and just how the pedantic following of his own logic prevents him from making the best use of his material. But he does show us Edouard theorizing about the proper way of writing fiction, and setting down in a note-book what he observes and what he thinks. And then, all about him, he shows us Life spinning its intricate webs so much faster and farther than Edouard can follow. And while Edouard is losing himself in a cloud of abstract ideas like Carlyle in "Sartor Resartus" (it is Gide's own comparison), Life is piling up concrete facts so startling that Edouard's ideas fade into insignificance.

Edouard does not even appreciate the full import of the title of his novel. On one occasion he is discussing his work with his young secretary Bernard. Bernard has shown himself a little impatient with Edouard's notion of a novel of ideas. And who are these counterfeiters? he asks. What Edouard meant by counterfeiters was certain of his confrères who were offering the public literary products without value, and especially his rival, the novelist, the Comte de Passavant. And his mind was filled with ideas of exchange, devalorization, inflation, etc., which really were supplanting the very characters in his book.

> "Did you ever hold in your hand a piece of counterfeit money?" he asked. . . . "Well, imagine a gold piece of ten francs which is counterfeit. In reality it is only worth two sous. It is worth ten francs so long as it is not recognized as false. So then, if I start with this idea that . . . "

> "But why start with an idea?" Bernard interrupted impatiently. "If you would start with a fact well set forth, the idea would come of its own accord and take up its abode there. If I were writing *The Counterfeiters,* I should begin by exhibiting the counterfeit money, this little coin of which you were just speaking . . . and here it is!"

And he throws upon the table a ten-franc piece, explaining that it is counterfeit money which he has received in change from a grocer.

Now, what Bernard and Edouard do not realize is that this false coin has been put in circulation by one of a band of young boys several of whom are well known to them both, one of them being Edouard's nephew, Georges Molinier. And what even the reader does not know as yet is that the person responsible for this and other vicious ways into which these boys have fallen is none other than Edouard's rival, the Comte de Passavant. So that while Edouard has been concerning himself with the comparatively mild crime of feeding the public adulterated wares in the form of novels, Reality be-

hind his back is offering the highly significant fact of a generation of school-boys corrupted and turned into criminals. It is this same group of boys in the end who are responsible for the death of little Boris. But Edouard, as we have seen, is shut up so tight in his ivory tower of consistency that he cannot take advantage of this prime exhibit offered him by Reality.

There is still another matter of the very highest importance which Edouard would never be able to get into his book; and that is his own character, his motivation. The Comte de Passavant is his rival not merely for the interest of the reading public, but also for the affections of certain school-boys, and in particular for those of Edouard's nephew, Olivier. The Comte de Passavant is in every respect the evil genius of these boys. Edouard is the soul of benevolence. His aim is to help every one with whom he has to do. But does he understand how far the simple passion of jealousy is the moving power in his behavior? And there is more to it than that. Both Edouard and his rival are by all indications of that race of men who find their emotional satisfaction in men instead of women. Has it ever occurred to Edouard that it might be rather difficult for one of his race to play the good angel to adolescent boys? The question even arises whether this difficulty has been met by Edouard's creator.

It will be impossible for me to recount the plot of *The Counterfeiters,* or even to list the many strands woven into it. The important matter is to note the deliberate and systematic way in which the author alternates the many related subjects and methods of approach. Of the forty-four chapters, some dozen only are devoted to Edouard's note-book, which is more or less regularly followed by passages of ordinary narrative. The other leading character, Bernard, makes his appearance in about half the chapters, sometimes in company with Edouard. And all along are interspersed chapters dealing with Passavant, with Bernard's father, with Olivier, with Olivier's brothers Vincent and Georges, and with several other characters, each one of whom has his independent story.

Gide makes no attempt, like Dos Passos and Wassermann, to give a cross-section of society as a whole. And yet this torch seems to light up the darkness in every direction with its fitful illuminations. One has an extraordinary sense of the infinite ramifications of human life, its unpredictableness, its inconclusiveness. As one of the characters says, "In life, nothing is settled; everything keeps going on. [*Dans la vie, rien ne se résout; tout continue.*]" The author has dropped a stone into these still waters, and the circles keep widening out, to infinity. (pp. 449-57)

> *Joseph Warren Beach, "Logic and Life: Gide," in his The Twentieth Century Novel: Studies in Technique, Appleton-Century-Crofts, Inc., 1932, pp. 449-57.*

KLAUS MANN   (essay date 1943)

[*Mann was a German novelist, essayist, and playwright. The son of novelist Thomas Mann, he left Germany in 1933 and settled soon afterward in the United States, where he served as editor of the literary magazine* Decision. *Mann's works reflect his active interest in cultural issues and his advocacy of greater political awareness. In the following excerpt, Mann compares the structure of* The Counterfeiters *to that of a fugue and explores the idea of evil as the unifying element of the novel.*]

[The structure of *Les faux-monnayeurs*] is organized around a center of moral, intellectual energies. The drama developed in this ample and diffuse composition is primarily ideological. Gide's novel is a novel of ideas.

That is why it appears comprehensive and yet exclusive—almost anarchic in its bountiful variety, and at the same time lucid, architectonic, pure. An amplitude of elements is fused in the microcosm of this extraordinary book; but all elements it contains are essential, *pure*—no accessories and arabesques are admitted.

"To purge the novel of all elements which do not belong specifically to its character!" demands the author of *Les faux-monnayeurs,* and continues:

> One does not bring about anything worthwhile by mixing incoherent patterns. I have always abominated what they call "the synthesis of arts," and which, according to Richard Wagner, should be effected in the theater. Hence my horror of the theater—and of Wagner. . . .
>
> Tragedy and comedy have attained, in the seventeenth century, a high degree of purity; the same is true, by the way, for all other genres, whatever their scope and their significance—fables, character sketches, maxims, sermons, memoirs, letters, and so forth. Lyric poetry can be purely lyric—and the novel could not be purely a novel? (Purity, in art, as everywhere, is the only thing that matters.)
>
> Nobody has succeeded, neither then nor later, in creating the *pure novel*—not even the admirable Stendhal, who came closer to this ideal than any other novelist. As for Balzac, however, he may be our most potent narrator, but he certainly is the one who surpassed all others in fusing and amalgamating the most heterogeneous elements. His novels are crammed with ingredients essentially strange and inadmissible to the novelistic form. That is why each of his massive books overwhelms us with its power and its imperfection, its flaws and its dynamics. It is remarkable that the English, whose drama has never become perfectly *pure* (in the sense in which the tragedies of Racine are perfect and are pure) have attained so early a much higher degree of purity in the novels of Defoe, Fielding, and even Richardson.

This statement, paraphrased from Gide's *Journal des faux-monnayeurs,* may be apt to clarify the innermost intentions and aspirations that induced him to write his "first novel." The composition he dreamt of, would have to be informed with the whole confusion and disquietude of this critical moment in human history—not just echoing the anxieties, but elucidating, dramatizing, purifying their impact. To render the chaos transparent, to organize the disorder, to rationalize the crisis—what a bold, wonderful task! The result might turn out to be something at once intricate and lucid, a labyrinth constructed with mathematical precision, akin—to what? To the fugues of Johann Sebastian Bach, perhaps.

"What I would like to produce," Gide admitted, "is something in the line of the *Kunst der Fuge.* I don't see why it should be impossible to accomplish in literature what has been possible in the sphere of music."

Gide acknowledges that a novel can be "impure" and yet great. (The case of Honoré Balzac.) The reader might be inclined to ask whether a "pure" novel is necessarily a great novel; or, more bluntly, whether *The Counterfeiters* may be called a great book.

An outstanding connoisseur of novels, and an outstanding novelist, E. M. Forster, answers this question in the negative. Gide's book is, according to Mr. Forster, "among the more interesting of recent works: not among the vital: and greatly as we shall have to admire it as a fabric, we cannot praise it unrestrictedly now." Whereupon he chooses to "glance again at *War and Peace:* here the result is vital."

The book from which I just quoted, *Aspects of the Novel,* is one of the acutest, most delightful achievements in the field of literary criticism. Forster has an admirable manner of discussing Proust and Meredith, Tolstoi and Joyce, Anatole France and Dickens. It is from Dickens that he jumps directly to André Gide. He senses an affinity between *Bleak House* and *The Counterfeiters*—"a novel which for all its modernity has one aspect in common with *Bleak House:* it is all to pieces logically. Sometimes the author is omniscient: he explains everything, he stands back, *il juge ses personnages;* at other times his omniscience is partial; yet again he is dramatic, and causes the story to be told through the diary of one of his characters. There is the same absence of viewpoint, but whereas in Dickens it was instinctive, in Gide it is sophisticated; he expatiates too much about the jolts. The novelist who betrays too much interest in his own method can never be more than interesting."

The last sentence is strikingly, scathingly true. Besides, Gide is fully aware of the dangers inherent in his constant self-observation and auto-analysis. His double and mouthpiece in *Les faux-monnayeurs*—the novelist Edouard, who is occupied with writing a novel about counterfeiters himself—muses over his diary: "A good novel should be conceived and composed much more naïvely and instinctively. . . . "

But what is a "good" novel? Or an "interesting" or a "vital" novel? Both Edouard and E. M. Forster employ their evaluating epithets in a somewhat arbitrary fashion. Why should an interesting novel not be good, or vital, or even great? That is to say, great and vital in its historic function, and according to the demands and standards of its period.

Why compare a novel of ideas with an epic saga of Homeric dimensions? It's like comparing a tennis champion with a heavy-weight pugilist. They are of different statures; they respond to different requirements; in short, they do not compete with each other. The same is true of the two novels, *War and Peace* and *The Counterfeiters.*

Of course, Gide may look slim in comparison with the Russian giant. But then, who wouldn't? Who does live up, nowadays, to the impressive dimensions of the nineteenth-century masters?

The stature of an individual is something relative—not an absolute. Each epoch has its specific pattern of greatness—an inherent maximal norm which an individual may attain, if he can. In the Renaissance this "maximal norm" was of tremendous caliber: Ibsen or Degas would appear ridiculously puny with Michelangelo or Shakespeare around, as would our contemporaries contrasted with the creative plethora of the preceding period. True, André Gide is not quite Tolstoi or Dostoevski, just as Stravinski falls short of Bach; Claudel, of Dante; Picasso, of Rembrandt and Leonardo.

But the only relevant question is whether Gide can compete with the maximal stature of this century, and also whether *The Counterfeiters* represents the highest and finest attainable to this artist. Both questions must be answered in the affirmative. No doubt, Gide's rank matches the most exacting standards set by our epoch; and, undoubtedly again, he gives in *Les faux-monnayeurs* the best he has to offer, the crown and climax of his genius.

And now let us have a look at the novel proper.

We must keep in mind, first of all, that the opus we are dealing with is a fugue, not a symphony. That is to say, the novel is not built in several major episodes, each with an individual theme of its own; but the whole polyphonic score develops one central theme, varying and transforming it most ingeniously, according to strict contrapuntal rules. As for this central theme. . . . But perhaps we ought first to outline the scheme of the variations.

The texture of the novel consists of a multitude of dramas, all of which are interwoven with the utmost skill and a great deal of musical tact. The reader is allowed, or required, to visualize every character as belonging to several groups simultaneously and as playing a rôle in several actions at one time. That is the way life works. A schoolboy, say, is not exclusively a schoolboy: he is also a son and a brother, and perhaps he is a lover or a criminal or a genius or what not. So every actor in the ample cast of *The Counterfeiters* has his function on several stages and in various capacities. The central character, if there is such a thing in this book, is involved in all dramas at once.

This central character, if anybody, is Edouard, the novelist who is engaged in writing a novel called *Les faux-monnayeurs*. Edouard is André Gide, almost undisguised. Through Edouard's diary Gide expresses his own views and reflections with regard to *The Counterfeiters* and the world in general. While Gide attempts to bring about a novel of ideas, a pure novel, his character, Edouard, dwells theoretically on all problems involved in such a delicate task.

But Edouard is by no means just a commentator; he actively takes part in the various plots. There are links between him and all other groups. His position is mainly, but not solely, that of a go-between, mediator, confessor, and confidant. Somehow ageless of type, he belongs half to the camp of the youngsters, half to the side of the grown-ups. Both parties trust him and tell him about their troubles. And they have plenty of troubles, all of them.

It may be more correct to speak of three main camps, not just two. For the youth sector is split in itself: the children and the young people live on different planes. The young men, between seventeen and twenty-five, are as remote from their little brothers of ten to fifteen as they are from their aging parents and professors.

The most prominent characters of the intermediate group—in fact, the two leading figures, after Edouard, of the whole composition—are Bernard and Olivier, intimate friends but very different from each other. (pp. 179-85)

Bernard is more virile, more adventurous, more resilient than his friend Olivier. Olivier needs a mentor and wavers between two; Bernard is in search of himself, of his star and his demon. He runs away from home when he finds out that he is not really the son of the dignified old gentleman whom he has thought to be his father. He is a bastard, like Lafcadio [in *Les caves du Vatican*], with whom he has also other features in common. The *Journal des faux-monnayeurs*—Gide's commentary on his book when it was in process of construc-

tion—tells us that Lafcadio was supposed to be the leading character, according to the original plan. Is Bernard, then, Lafcadio in disguise?

No, he resembles too much the Prodigal Son to be Lafcadio's double. He is less irresponsible, less impish and primitive than the radiant vagabond of *Les caves du Vatican.* Bernard is reflective, not without a certain youthful gravity, for all his dashing élan.

"For what cause should I use the forces that I sense in me?" Lafcadio is not likely to ask this question which occupies Bernard.

"How to make the best out of myself?" Bernard muses. "By concentrating on one particular goal? But as for this goal, how could I select it? How can I know what it is like, as long as I have not yet attained it?"

And as Edouard says something to the effect that "to live without a goal means to live without direction," Bernard replies, "I'm afraid you don't quite understand what I am trying to say. When Columbus discovered America, did he realize what he was up to? His sole goal was to move, just to go ahead. His goal—he carried it in himself. . . . "

Is this, then, the clue, the leading thought in virtue of which the incongruous elements of this book cohere and can become a living entity? Is Bernard's angel the secret center of the composition, rather than Edouard's diary with all its incisive reflections?

Yes, the heart and hero of the book is the demon—not just Bernard's, but the demon in general and as such.

The demon is not sheer, rampant energy such as impels Lafcadio to commit his inspired larks. Nor is this demon of a purely spiritual nature like the one haunting Alissa and the Immoralist. The demon of *Les faux-monnayeurs*—Bernard's demon: André Gide's demon—is double-faced, complex, dialectic, as is the demon of the Prodigal Son.

Reason and Energy, Love and Hate, destructive and constructive impulses are combined in the truly demoniac disposition. We can trace the authority of the demon in all characters of the novel, with the one exception of Lady Griffith. She belongs completely to the realm of nature. Her cynicism is natural. Nature is not demoniac; spirit is.

The demon manifests itself, diabolically, in the cynical elegance of Robert de Passavant, in Vedel's hypocrisy, in La Pérouse's rigid and arrogant gloom. No doubt, Georges and his fellow-pupils, or fellow-felons, are possessed by the demon; their grisly and dangerous plays are obviously inspired by his genius. Who stands behind Laura when she abandons her husband? As for Vincent, the *Journal des faux-monnayeurs* makes it very plain what force it is that guides and confuses him:

> Vincent complies with the diabolic spirit, who penetrates him little by little. He feels himself becoming diabolic; just when everything he touches prospers and succeeds, he realizes his doom more than ever. He would like to warn his brother Olivier, but everything he tries in order to save him turns out damaging to the other, profitable to himself. . . . He senses the grip of Satan, but at the same time continues to wonder if the Evil One exists in reality. His mind is haunted by the Devil's terrible whisper: "Why are you afraid of me? You know perfectly

well that I do not exist. . . . " In the end Vincent comes to the point of believing in the reality of Satan *as he believes in his own reality;* that is to say, he identifies himself with the Devil.

The demon harasses and mystifies the smug, canting citizens: the pastors and housewives, teachers and officials, who lie to each other and commit by stealth their dreary little crimes, unaware of the demoniac lights and voices alluring and leading them. Bernard is stronger and more lovable than his demure father (who is neither really his father nor really so demure), as he, Bernard, attempts at least—and how passionately! how bravely!—to scrutinize his own being and to disentangle the staggering pellmell of devastating and constructive impulses.

For the demon has always a twofold tendency and a double appeal; the important thing is to recognize the ambivalent impact of his spell and persuasion. That is what Socrates was driving at when he advised the youth of Athens to listen to the demoniac whisper of their inner voices. If the unconscious is the Devil's retreat, we have to lift the darkness from this hiding place. Sigmund Freud agrees with Socrates: what matters is to shed light upon the shadowy realm of the unconscious.

Gide agrees with both. Those characters in his novel who openly admit the presence and the power of the demon are in a better position, and are better characters, than the others who deny or conceal their own devilish tendencies. Even the murderous youngsters in Vedel's boarding school are preferable to the mendacious pastor. They follow their demon into mortal adventures, blindly and naïvely; whereas the old liar protects himself and breeds pestilence as do those who desire but act not.

Edouard recognizes his demon and follows him, unafraid. "Every being acts according to his inherent law," says Gide, "and that of Edouard compels him to experiment incessantly. He has a good heart, to be sure; but at times I would prefer to see him act out of interest, rather than out of a generosity which is often only the companion of his indomitable curiosity. And this curiosity might become very cruel."

And yet Edouard's greatest adventure does not spring from his demoniac curiosity; or, if it does, it changes its character, almost miraculously. There is nothing playful or cruel about Edouard's "experiment" with Olivier. Ennobled and transfigured by love, the demon reveals, for once, the sacred flame of his divine descent.

But only for transient moments, never in the long run, is the demon altogether good or altogether evil. "There are in every man, in every moment, two simultaneous tendencies," Baudelaire remarks in his *Journal intime,* "one toward God; the other toward Satan." Gide, who quotes this sentence in his admirable preface to *Les fleurs du mal,* underlines, in parentheses, the cardinal importance of the word "simultaneous" in this particular context, and then dwells on the double proclivity of human nature. The will of every individual to maintain his own identity coherent and consistent, is constantly counterbalanced and at times counteracted by the reverse instinct which is centrifugal and disintegrating, tending towards division, dissociation, and dissolution. Prodded by this uncanny, this truly demoniac impulse, the individual is always inclined to jeopardize his own logic, to run risks, to gamble, to split, to go to pieces, to lose his poise or to transcend his limitations. And André Gide—although fully aware, of course, of all dangers inherent in this "centrifugal," schizophrenic trend—suggests nevertheless: "Are here not the first signs of a new radioactive energy of incalculable value, the power of which may be such that the ancient theories, laws, conventions, and pretensions, all of them, may fade away before long?"

Do we recognize him, this revolutionary, dynamic demon, whose contradictory magic can compel us to fall into dire depths or to soar to glorious heights? William Blake, for one, was on appallingly intimate terms with that divinely devilish Being. "This Angel," we read in the *Marriage of Heaven and Hell,* "who is now become a Devil, is my particular friend; we often read the Bible together in its infernal or diabolical sense, which the world shall have if they behave well."

Gide invokes the "Proverbs of Hell" in his fascinating essay on Dostoevski. . . . The work in question, a cycle of lectures delivered in 1922, at the *Théâtre du Vieux-Colombier,* is what remains of one of Gide's favorite projects: a "Life of Dostoevski" for which he compiled material as far back as 1910. (pp. 188-93)

The rousing shock of the First World War was necessary, perhaps, to reveal to Gide the whole impact of Dostoevski's mysticism—"so much closer to Asia than to Rome"—and of his psychological profundity. It may be that this perspicacious critic, André Gide, had to pass through many a calamity and many a transformation himself, to grasp fully the inherent logic of what appears as morbid inconsistency in Dostoevski's figures. Far from concealing this uncanny desultoriness of his heroes, the great Russian displays and emphasizes it deliberately. That is to say, what fascinates him most in a human character is the profusion of incoherent, contradictory trends and energies coexisting in his shadowy, unfathomable depth. That coexistence appears often all the more paradoxical and disconcerting as Dostoevski pushes the emotions of his characters to the extreme or even exaggerates them to the point of absurdity.

And what of André Gide? Are not the emotional reactions of his figures often pitched to almost unbearable heights? Olivier's attempted suicide is as illogical, as "inconsistent" as any mystic vagary of any Dostoevski character. The demon who corrupts Georges and destroys Boris is hardly more rational than Raskolnikov's murderous whim or the reveries of Prince Myshkin in *The Idiot.* If Dostoevski's martyrs and visionaries are split personalities, divided within themselves, what should be said of the Prodigal Son or the Immoralist?— or of Lafcadio? *"Je suis une être d'inconséquence!"* ["I am an inconsequential being!"] he rants in his childlike fashion. The double optics of ***Les faux-monnayeurs,*** with Edouard's fictitious novel reflecting and criticizing the methods of André Gide's fiction, suggest a mild case of schizophrenia. Or is it just that genius has a penchant for complicated devices and by instinct prefers the indirect approach? William Blake is right, then, when he says: "Improvement makes strait roads; but the crooked roads without Improvement are roads of Genius."

To Blake's "Proverbs of Hell," quoted by Gide with so much amused approval, he adds these two tenets of his own credo: "It is with fine feelings that one produces poor literature"; and: "There is no work of art without the collaboration of the demon." Then he tells us that every work of art is a token of the marriage of Heaven and Hell, which serves him as a pretext to cite Blake once more: "The reason Milton wrote in fetters when he wrote of Angels and God, and at liberty when of Devils and Hell, is because he was a true poet and of the Devil's party without knowing it."

But after having dwelt on the demoniac aspects of Blake's and Dostoevski's genius, Gide reminds his listeners of the essential fact that both are so utterly overwhelmed by the truths of the Gospel that their "ferocity" cannot but be of transitory nature, the momentary consequence of a kind of holy blindness. Gide would like to quote some of Blake's "Songs of Innocence" to counterbalance and rectify the impression he conveyed by citing the "Proverbs of Hell." As for Dostoevski, his Christian ethos has by no means always a somber or savage tinge. He is also a great lover; he adores this life and this world—this "vast world of delights," to use another of Blake's phrases. To illustrate this streak of exuberant optimism in Dostoevski, Gide reads to his listeners this suggestive fragment of a dialogue from *The Possessed:*

"Are you fond of children?"

"I am," said Kirilov, in a rather indifferent way.

"Are you fond of life too, then?"

"Yes, I do like life too. Does that astonish you?"

André Gide is interested in children because he is interested in life—in its growth and development, in its unending potentialities, in the unending promise it enfolds. That which *is* fascinates him more than what *has been.* But even more exciting than the present is the future—that which could be and, therefore, *will* come into being. "What is now proved was once only imagin'd," William Blake says. And his spirited disciple, André Gide, adds, "What we imagine now will be proved in the future."

One might object, at this point, that Gide's imagination is dismaying as far as the coming generation is concerned. Are his callow counterfeiters and suicides, his little runaways and neurotics, the future we have to look forward to?

Yes and no. They bear the germs of the future, those erratic youngsters who perform their drama in *Les faux-monnayeurs.* True, their drama is lurid and disorderly. But is it their fault? Or rather is it not the fault of a society which abides by untruthfulness, oppresses the instincts, postpones and pollutes the evolution of man? The disorderly demon of youth, iridescent, uncertain, dynamic, might become the demiurgos of a truly new order.

Boris and Georges go astray—poisoned by the blight of hypocrisy that palls M. Vedel's institute. But perhaps Olivier will find his way, guided by Edouard? And Bernard—did he not come out victorious from his fight with the angel? And what do we know about Bernard's younger brother, Caloub? Edouard is curious to find out what this little stranger may be like. The voluminous, involved composition of *Les faux-monnayeurs* ends with a casual but suggestive reference to this imminent meeting. The last entry in Edouard's diary, the last sentence of the novel reads: *"Je suis bien curieux de connaître Caloub"* ["I'm very curious to know Caloub"].

Thus the fugue resumes and reaffirms its intrinsic theme, which connotes and guarantees new themes and new fugues to come. The infinite melody of which romantic musicians dreamt—there it is, full of prospects and promises, severe and serene, playful and faithful and proud.

Gide shows us, with relentless realism, a generation bewil-

dered and confused in the midst of the rampant turmoil that is our present life and our present society. He shows the struggle, the efforts, the vices secret or open, the triumphs, the aberrations. He wants future generations to receive this dialectic confession, the fugue of our contradictory drama, *le roman pure* ["the pure novel"], the undisguised account of our crisis. He supposes that it may be profitable for the generations to come to be familiar with our adventures and our sufferings. He is an optimist, the author of *Les faux-monnayeurs.* To write for future generations indicates optimism.

Gide never cared much for the immediate success of his writings. In the beginning, however, when he composed *Les cahiers d'André Walter,* this detachment had a rather melancholy flavor. In that time, he was not interested enough in the present to aspire to present success. But thirty-five years later, at the time of *Les faux-monnayeurs,* he was too keenly interested in the future to be primarily concerned with his prestige among contemporary critics. The indifference as such remained the same. But the feelings from which it springs had altered.

André Walter said, somewhat drearily, "I don't care whether or not I am understood and liked by my generation."

André Gide—the André Gide of *The Counterfeiters*—says, "My fervent hope is that I may be understood and liked by generations to come."

"Why," he says, "why should we not be able to attain a sympathetic perspicacity, in virtue of which we could anticipate what is in the offing and in the making? What problems will perturb the coming generation? It is for these coming ones that I write. To answer yet unspoken questions! To respond to yet indistinct longings! Those who are children now will be surprised, one day, to find me on their path." (pp. 193-98)

> *Klaus Mann, in his* André Gide and the Crisis of Modern Thought, *Creative Age Press, Inc., 1943, 331 p.*

JUSTIN O'BRIEN   (essay date 1953)

[*O'Brien was an American critic who wrote extensively on modern French literature and translated important works by André Gide, Albert Camus, and Paul Valéry. In the following excerpt, he examines the theme of personal autonomy and fulfillment in* The Counterfeiters.]

[The] problem of how to live dominates *Les faux-monnayeurs* (*The Counterfeiters* in America, *The Coiners* in England). That massive novel, which first appeared in 1925, had been in the author's mind since at least 1914, and consequently embodies his mature thought on the subject. Here the question, alluded to early in *L'Immoraliste* and implicit throughout *Les caves du Vatican,* rises to the fore to be treated in sharper and more positive form. More than any other of Gide's works, this is a true *Bildungsroman,* a novel of growing up and finding oneself.

From among the many characters of this complex, Dostoevskian fiction, against the drab background of their conservative middle-class families, two adolescents emerge in the very first pages; and the novel tells the story of their self-integration. Bernard, bold and apparently assured, is close to Lafcadio. The discovery of his illegitimacy offers just the excuse he needs to revolt and break with his family. When he indulges in further daring by stealing Edouard's suitcase and seeking out Laura, he wins our esteem by his show of energy. Olivier, despite Edouard's and the author's evident preference for him, loses some of our regard by missing his chance to hold his uncle and by falling, through spite, to the artificial Passavant, who serves as a sort of caricature of Edouard. But later, the night of the banquet, Olivier sacrifices his pride and achieves himself through self-renunciation. By the end of the novel, consequently, he is happy and integrated whereas his friend Bernard is still striving.

As the preceding paragraph shows, it is impossible to summarize the story of the two adolescents without constant reference to Edouard, for it is in relation to him that they both define and assert themselves. Yet Edouard, the novelist who is so much like Gide that even the most damning comments the author makes about him have been used against Gide, is not the hero of the novel. Despite the extent to which he holds the center of the stage, despite the large part of the book formed by his journal, he remains a marginal observer of others' actions. He is the commentator, and as such he is occasionally obliged to intervene in order to keep the action alive or to give it a sudden turn in another direction. Like the author himself, he serves as the point of intersection of the various plots. He is, above all, an original and effective literary device, the culmination of Gide's life-long experiment with *composition en abyme,* or the story within a story.

Commenting on Laura's almost tragic adultery, Edouard says: "It can happen to anyone to make a bad start. The important thing is not to persist. . . . " The remark is more comprehensive than anyone but the author could recognize at the time it is made, for everyone in the novel makes a false step at the outset. Most of the characters remain permanently warped as a result, but a few, such as Laura, Olivier, and Bernard, make up for their bad start by correcting that false step later. They all do so by an act of will, without which there can be no genuine self-assertion.

As far back as one can go in André Gide's career, that element of will is present and consciously recognized. Under the date of 1887, in one of his earliest journal-entries, which he incorporated into *Les cahiers d'André Walter,* he wrote: "May will dominate in everything: make oneself as one wants oneself." Gide was not yet eighteen when he voiced such a resolve. Five years later, on 3 January 1892, he noted that instead of recounting his life as he has lived it, the artist must live his life as he will recount it; "In other words, the portrait of him formed by his life must identify itself with the ideal portrait he desires. And, in still simpler terms, he must be as he wishes to be." Again, in 1904, while prefacing an exhibit of Maurice Denis's paintings, he reduced the formula to "Will to be who one is."

This does not imply a mere fatalistic self-acceptance, but rather—as in the Pindaric motto "Become who you are," which Nietzsche used—a realization of one's best potentialities. In the capital conversation toward the end of *Les faux-monnayeurs* when Bernard asks Edouard's advice, the youth wonders whether or not it is necessary to fix one's eyes on an objective in life. "When Columbus discovered America," he asks, "did he know toward what he was setting sail? His objective was to go ahead, straight ahead. His objective was himself, and he who projected it in front of him. . . . " Edouard tells Bernard to find his rule in himself, "to have as an objective the development of oneself." And when Bernard fears that in learning how to live he may meanwhile make mistakes, his mentor replies: "That itself will teach you. It is good to follow one's inclination, provided one go upward." How often that wise injunction was to be misunderstood by readers who, consciously or unconsciously, omitted or forgot its essential proviso! In the same spirit Gide speaks of Edouard's love for Olivier and the care with which he would have matured the boy: "With what loving respect would he not have guided, supported, carried him to his self-fulfillment?"

Such integration of one's possibilities and realization of the self is the theme of the novel. At one point Edouard voices the author's thought when he deplores the fact that literature, concerned with the hardships of fate, social relationships, and conflicts of passions and characters, has largely neglected another form of tragedy which is "the very essence of the individual." We know that he is here speaking for Gide because the latter stated the same idea more precisely in his lectures on Dostoevsky, delivered while he was writing his own novel. There he notices that in the Occident "the novel, except for very few exceptions, is concerned solely with relationships among men, relationships of passion or intellect, family or society relationships or those of social classes—but never, almost never, of the individual's relationships with himself or with God—which here take precedence over all others." (pp. 194-97)

Gide had done just this in his own writings—not all novels, to be sure, yet at least *L'immoraliste* (1902) and *La porte étroite* (1909) were novels. But in those works he had abstracted Candaules, Philoctetes, Michel, and Alissa, for instance, from society in general, showing how each one struggled with himself and progressed to his salvation or damnation in unreal isolation. At most, each one stands in contrast or in conflict with a single other person, at the expense of whose happiness, often, he finally achieves full expression. On the other hand, Dostoevsky showed Gide how the conquest of the individual can be attained even amidst numerous external relationships by a man deeply rooted in surrounding society. For this reason Gide had already praised Dostoevsky, in 1908 while writing about the Russian novelist's correspondence, for having reconciled individualism and collectivism: "And, opposite Nietzsche, he becomes an admirable example to show us how little conceit and complacency often accompany that belief in the value of the ego. He writes: 'The hardest thing in the world is remaining oneself'; and 'one must not waste one's life for any objective'; for, according to him, without individualism, as without patriotism, there is no way of serving humanity."

Les caves du Vatican, with its numerous characters and multiple plots all interlocking, had already marked a step in this direction. Yet Lafcadio committed his experimental act of self-assertion without reference to anyone else or to the rest of the novel. Only when it was beyond recall did he become aware that he had murdered his half-brother's brother-in-law, confirmed Julius's theory of the gratuitous act, and played into the hands of Protos. In his initial disregard for consequences, he had not stopped to think what a "crossroads" a mothy, provincial traveler can turn out to be. But Bernard of *Les faux-monnayeurs,* who begins with some of the same fine, careless abandon, progresses far beyond his predecessor. Gide tells us: "His struggle with the angel had matured him. Already he had ceased to resemble the carefree luggage-thief who thought that in this world it is enough to dare. He was beginning to realize that the happiness of others is often the price of one's daring." The Bernard who goes out into the world at the end of this novel is far more mature and integrated a personality than the Lafcadio whom we left waking up in Geneviève's arms at the end of the *Caves.*

Before his discovery of Dostoevsky, however, André Gide was aware of the interdependence of all—even in relation to the problem of self-assertion. In the *Nourritures terrestres* of 1897, just before the Envoi, he had inserted an allegorical, Dantesque "Hymn to serve as Conclusion" that seems completely out of harmony with the Dionysiac tone of the book to which it belongs. It was doubtless its abstract quality that permitted him to dedicate discreetly to his wife, under the initials "M. A. G." for Madeleine André Gide, this uncharacteristic fragment of a book of which she disapproved in general. The "Hymn" describes the stars in their ardent and fixed course through the heavens: "They are all linked to one another by bonds that are virtues and powers, so that each depends on another and the other depends on all. The course of each is marked out and each finds its own course. It could not change course without making all the others deviate, each being involved with every other one. And each chooses the course it *was* to follow; what it is to do it must do willingly, and that course, which to us seems decreed in advance, is the preferred course for each, for each has an independent will. A dazzled love guides them; their choice determines laws and we are dependent on them; we cannot escape." Obviously the stars, enjoying freedom of choice and yet obeying predetermined laws, parallel the human lot. In effect Gide is here expressing the same thought that Goethe voiced in his *Dichtung und Wahrheit:* "A man may turn whither he pleases, and undertake anything whatsoever, but he will always return to the path that nature has once prescribed for him."

The individual must *will* to become the man he is ordained to be, must, in Edouard's words, follow his inclination *upward.* The true self is not achieved without a struggle; hence Bernard's wrestling with the angel. Furthermore, such self-realization must take into account the human community and our inevitable interdependence. In the struggle many succumb, whereas others elude the problem by compromise or falsification of their true personalities. The latter are the counterfeiters who pass off upon the world an artificial, social self with nothing but the appearance of the genuine. Terms like "counterfeit" or "fabricated personality" occur throughout the novel, into which—as a further reflection of the theme—Gide has mischievously introduced the minor plot of the boys who circulate false coins. The anarchistic Strouvilhou talks of demonetizing sentiments, and Bernard, on the other hand, longs to "ring true" in every circumstance of life. Edouard, fascinated by what *might be* rather than by what has been, says: "I lean vertiginously over the possibilities of each individual and weep over all that the lid of conventions atrophies."

That lid presses most heavily on the older people in the novel, the representatives of conservatism and members of bourgeois families. Indeed, one of the most obvious themes in *Les faux-monnayeurs* is that of the decay of the middle-class family, living as it does on false and empty principles and unable to stand the inevitable conflict between the generations. Bernard's family and Olivier's, both belonging to what was once known as the *noblesse de robe* or magistrature, are disintegrating rapidly, until Pauline Molinier can finally confess: "I wish I had never had any children!" Behind its facade of hypocrisy, the numerous Vedel clan is even more decayed at the heart, its adulterous Laura, pathological Armand, and facile

Sarah all rebelling against the grandfather's blind benignity and the father's sanctimonious agitation. Even the limited group formed by the old music-teacher, La Pérouse (the most Dostoevskian of Gide's characters), his wife, and his grandson crumbles before our eyes. Finally, Robert de Passavant belongs to a wealthy, noble family whose instability we sense during the vivid scene when little Gontran keeps vigil over his father's body. To be sure, the only reason for introducing the father and Gontran is simply to provide one more example for the demonstration.

The family is indeed the social cell, as Paul Bourget, the defender of tradition, claimed; but it is also, Edouard insists, a prison cell. Edouard has no family, save for his half-sister Pauline and her sons, to whom he hardly behaves in the usual avuncular manner. He belongs to the parents' generation by age and to that of the children by temperament; not involved in the struggle, he can observe and comment from the sidelines. He is not quite dispassionate, however, for he shares the attitude of the original Ménalque who cried: "Families, I hate you!" and of Gide, who longed to see children raised by anyone but their own parents. Edouard reflects that "The future belongs to the bastards. What significance in the expression: *a natural child!* Only the bastard has a right to the natural." Bernard owes his initial liberation, as Lafcadio owed his exceptional liberty to his illegitimacy; but, as we now know, this is but a beginning of a solution to their problem. Inasmuch as the real difficulty lies in *being free,* there is no easy, a priori solution; everyone must pass through a struggle and attain the conquest of himself. (pp. 197-200)

Justin O'Brien, in his Portrait of André Gide: A Critical Biography, *Alfred A. Knopf, 1953, 390 p.*

MARTIN TURNELL   (essay date 1959)

[*Turnell was an English critic, translator, and author who wrote widely on French literature and made significant translations of the works of Jean-Paul Sartre, Guy de Maupassant, Blaise Pascal, and Paul Valéry. In the following excerpt, he examines the themes of authenticity and counterfeiting in* The Counterfeiters.]

In an extract from the diary of Edouard, the middle-aged novelist who is [Gide's protagonist in *Les faux-monnayeurs*], we read:

> Les livres que j'ai écrits jusqu'à présent me paraissent comparables à ces bassins des jardins publics, d'un contour précis, parfait peut-être, mais où l'eau captive est sans vie. A présent, je la veux laisser couler selon sa pente, tantôt rapide et tantôt lente, en des lacis que je me refuse à prévoir.
>
> (The books that I have written up to now seem to me to resemble the ponds in public parks. Their contour is precise, perhaps even perfect, but the water in them is captive and lifeless. At present, I want to let it flow in accordance with its inclination, sometimes rapidly and sometimes slowly, forming patterns which I refuse to predict.)

The passage, with the familiar image of still or stagnant water, is an interesting comment on Gide's earlier works of fiction and on his intentions in this one. He had consistently refused to describe them as novels, and in his dedication he speaks of the *Faux-monnayeurs* as "my first novel." The *récits* are, in the best sense, small-scale works. Gide was plainly attempting something on a much larger scale. He was also attempting something which would be different not only from his own earlier work, but from anything which had previously been written. The emphasis shifts in this book from the conflicts in the material world or in the minds of the characters, which normally provide the novelist with his subject, to the conflict between reality and the form in which he presents it:

> Je commence à entrevoir ce que j'appellerais le "sujet profond" de mon livre. C'est, ce sera sans doute la rivalité du monde réel et de la représentation que nous nous en faisons.
>
> (I am beginning to perceive what I might call the "essential theme" of my book. It is, it will be no doubt the rivalry between the real world and our representation of it.)

He is working out a theory of the "pure novel." It must be purged of all the elements which do not belong specifically to the novel. "Nothing good," he remarks, "can be obtained from a mixture."

The actual method is well described in another passage:

> Ce que je veux, c'est présenter d'une part la réalité, présenter d'autre part cet effort pour la styliser, dont je vous parlais tout à l'heure.
>
> (What I am anxious to do is on the one hand to present reality, and on the other to reveal the effort to stylize it of which I was speaking a few minutes ago.)

Gide takes as his starting-point a coining scandal in which schoolboys had been concerned in 1906-7 and a suicide which had occurred at a French school in 1909. He then proceeds to write a novel about a novelist who is also writing a novel called the *Faux-monnayeurs,* only to find that the imaginary incident is actually happening in the world in which he is living. Bernard's production of the counterfeit coin prompts the famous exchange with Edouard:

> "Alas! I see that reality doesn't interest you."
>
> "Yes, it does," said Edouard; "but it embarrasses me."
>
> "That's a pity," retorted Bernard.

Edouard's diary is a method of playing off "reality" and "our representation of it," of describing what happens to him and how he intends to work it into his book. This may be called the inner as opposed to the outer diary. For in addition to making his central character keep a diary, Gide himself kept and published as a separate work the *Journal des "Faux-monnayeurs"* in which he recorded the progress of the novel, and many of his own theories of novel-writing which he later transferred to Edouard's diary in the novel itself.

"He is a character," Gide said of Edouard, "who is all the more difficult to make convincing because I have put a lot of myself into him. I must step back and place him at a distance so that I can get a better view of him."

He may perhaps have put more of himself into Edouard than he realized. It is necessary for the reader, too, to step back in order to obtain a good view of the highly personal element which helps towards an understanding of the book.

"At that innocent age," said Gide on the first page of his autobiography, "when our minds are supposed to be nothing but transparency, tenderness and purity, I find in my own mind nothing but darkness, ugliness and slyness."

In spite of an obvious element of bravado, it is a fact that throughout his life Gide exhibited a marked taste for anything that was clandestine, furtive or *louche.* He was particularly interested in the clandestine activities of children, in the disreputable things that they did at an age when they were supposed to be models of innocence and purity. Juvenile delinquents play a large part in his fiction, and there was something of the juvenile delinquent in his own make-up. He was in certain respects a case of arrested development and his taste for the clandestine was undoubtedly connected with his peculiarly infantile form of sexuality. When he was a grown man he went on indulging in practices which were a continuation of the forbidden "games" of childhood. They had, however, acquired an added attraction: they had become criminal.

The incidents at the two French schools in the early years of the century made a deep impression on Gide. He preserved the newspaper reports and allowed them to ferment slowly in his mind. Ten years later they were used as the foundation of the novel. For the *Faux-monnayeurs* is among other things a story of juvenile delinquency—the story of a school "prank" which was lifted out of the world of the classroom and developed into a public scandal. Gide naturally invests it with an elaborate symbolical significance. The schoolboys involved in the circulation of the counterfeit coins are all children of good family, and two of them are the sons of magistrates. Their activities are transformed into a plot against law and order which is going on secretly beneath the surface of an outwardly respectable society.

The action of the novel takes place in a Protestant or nominally Protestant milieu. This explains the special importance of the Pension Azaïs. For the Pension, with its dubious clergyman and his chequered family, is a picture of the disintegration of the Protestant cell from a fresh angle. Its disintegration is not caused by the impact of an outsider on it or the flight of one of its members; it is caused by the spiritual failure of its head. Instead of providing a standard of integrity it has become a "coining" establishment—an establishment for the circulation of counterfeit religious values, a source of infection which poisons first the inmates, then the whole environment.

Gide's protagonist is placed in the position of an "old boy" who looks in on the activities of the younger generation. This enables Gide to combine the functions of novelist and *voyeur,* and to obtain a vicarious satisfaction from the spectacle of childish corruption and crime. His personal hostility to religion during the years that followed the first world war and an intensification of his taste for "the underside of things," which was not unexpected in a man of fifty, account for the sensational nature of much of his material. It includes not only coining and suicide, but murder, a clergyman who is a slave of Gide's main vice, a clergyman's son who pushes his sister into bed with a friend, and an uncle who seduces his nephew with the connivance of the mother.

Although Gide occasionally makes a personal appearance in the novel, takes the reader by the arm and comments on the behaviour of some of the characters, he was a strong critic of the novelist's traditional assumption of omniscience. One of his aims in the *Faux-monnayeurs* was to introduce what might be called a multiple point of view. The themes are "orchestrated" in the manner of the nineteenth-century novelists, but the novel also creates the impression of being a collection of mirrors in which the characters are continually seen, and are continually seeing themselves, from different angles and in different guises. Edouard is Gide's own reflection in one mirror, the clergyman his reflection in another. Boris is a glimpse of him as a child, reminding us of a reflection in a cracked and spotted mirror or a faded snapshot from a family album. Edouard, Olivier and Laura all hold up a different mirror to Bernard. Olivier sees his reflection in the different mirrors represented by Edouard and Passavant, as they see themselves reflected in him. All the characters have one thing in common: they are trying to discover which of the reflections is a true likeness. This brings us to the heart of the book.

"The novel," remarks Edouard, "has dealt with the setbacks of destiny, good and ill fortune, the conflicts of passion and character, but not with *l'essence même de l'être*" ["the very essence of being"]. In spite of Edouard's reservation, the central theme of the *Faux-monnayeurs* is a theme with which Gide had already dealt in a string of earlier books. It is the difference between the "counterfeit" and the "authentic being," which is symbolized here by the difference between the counterfeit and the genuine currency.

Clandestine activities always breed groups, parties and secret societies. Their overt intentions are usually different from their real activities and they are inevitably hostile to the life of the community. There are four main groups in the *Faux-monnayeurs* which are engaged, whether they realize it or not, in the manufacture and circulation of counterfeit coins: the parents, the schoolboys, the Pension, and the literary coteries. The schoolboys are in rebellion against the false values instilled into them by the older generation, but their rebellion against one set of false values leads them to propagate another set of false values of their own. The Pension, as we have seen, is the source of "counterfeit" religious values, and the literary coteries are engaged in the dissemination of "counterfeit" literary values.

It is tempting to assume that Edouard is the "authentic" and Passavant the "counterfeit" novelist, but this explanation is too simple. He may be "authentic" compared with Passavant, but a good deal of irony and not a little mystification went into his creation. It is significant that the only sample of his novel that we are shown is obviously "counterfeit," is the worst piece of writing in the book and a caricature of Gide's own work. This is really the crux of the matter. Although there are some black and some white sheep in the fold, Gide's aim was to avoid the sharp contrasts, the simple division into black and white of his earlier works. The larger canvas was designed to enable him to introduce finer shades and gradations, to deal with the greys as well as the blacks and whites. Bernard, who is one of Gide's few sympathetic characters, states the positive ideal and reveals the drama which is going on beneath the surface in a passage that contains a direct allusion to the counterfeit coins:

> Oh! Laura! Je voudrais, tout le long de ma vie, au moindre choc, rendre un son pur, probe, authentique. Presque tous les gens que j'ai connus sonnent faux.

> (Oh, Laura! All my life I should like to give, at the slightest touch, a pure, true and genuine ring. Almost all the people I've known ring false.)

The characters find themselves in a world of counterfeit values. They cannot avoid contamination completely. For there is something of the "counterfeit" in the "authentic being," as there is an element of the authentic being in the counterfeit. The sympathetic characters try to discriminate between the counterfeit and the authentic, to purge themselves of the counterfeit elements. That is why they scrutinize themselves, or rather their reflections, so eagerly, and interrogate their friends so anxiously. That is why Edouard feels so uneasy about his novel and why, in addition to keeping a diary, he persists in discussing his theories with the other characters for as long as they will listen to him.

In the course of the novel Gide examines the degree of contamination of the various characters and its causes. The schoolboys are divided broadly into bad, weak and mixed. Bernard is an incarnation of the Prodigal, but he ends by returning to his father. Olivier is not exactly a prodigal, but he is almost carried away, almost distracted from his "authentic" self by the counterfeit novelist, and rescued at the last moment by Edouard. There are similar contrasts in the four children of the clergyman, which repeat the conflict of parents and children in a specifically religious setting. Armand is the prodigal son who rebels violently against the religion of his father. Sarah is the prodigal daughter who goes completely to the bad. Rachel, the pious daughter with a heart of gold, is going blind. Religious blindness is a recurrent theme in Gide. Blindness stands for innocence, but also for an inability to face reality. This is the cause of Gertrude's suicide after the recovery of her sight in the *Symphonie pastorale.* Rachel's blindness appears to be psychological, to be the result of her inability to go on facing the reality represented by her father. In this way it reinforces her brother's criticism of the baleful effects of their father's religion, or lack of "authentic" religion. The splendid Laura is another of Gide's sympathetic characters, but though there is a good deal of the "authentic being" in her, she has made the mistake of marrying a "counterfeit" being on the rebound from Edouard.

The book is filled with Gide's usual dicta which in one way or another reflect the main theme. In view of what I shall have to say later about the characters of Edouard and Laura, Edouard's comment on the man whom she preferred to him, then abandoned, is of particular interest:

> "Je le plains beaucoup," dit Bernard. "Mais pourquoi n'admettez-vous pas que lui aussi, dans ce prosternement, se grandisse?"

> "Parce qu'il manque de lyrisme," dit Edouard irréfutablement.

> "Que voulez-vous dire?"

> "Qu'il ne s'oublie jamais dans ce qu'il éprouve, de sorte qu'il n'éprouve jamais rien de grand."

> ("I'm very sorry for him," said Bernard. "But why won't you admit that in his present state of prostration, he too gains in stature?"

> "Because he's lacking in poetry," said Edouard unanswerably.

> "What d'you mean by that?"

> "That he never manages to forget himself in what's he's feeling, with the result that he never feels anything great.")

"Lyrisme" recalls the "ferveur" of the *Nourritures terrestres.* It is evidently one of the qualities of the "authentic being." It is also the opposite of "contrainte," which either prevents people from becoming wholly authentic or makes them into counterfeits. It is associated in Gide's mind with religion and the comments on the "counterfeit" clergyman take us back to the world of the *récits.* The clergyman's son is speaking:

> Tu ne sais pas ce que peut faire de nous une première éducation puritaine. Elle vous laisse au coeur un ressentiment dont on ne peut plus jamais se guérir . . .
>
> Oui, c'est un convaincu professionnel. Un professeur de conviction. . . . Mais quant à savoir ce qui se passe dans ce qu'il appelle "son for intérieur"? . . . Ce serait indiscret, tu comprends, d'aller le lui demander. Et je crois qu'il ne se le demande jamais lui-même. Il s'y prend de manière à n'avoir jamais le temps de se le demander.
>
> (You don't know what an early puritan education can do to us. It leaves you with a feeling of resentment in your heart which can never be cured. . . .
>
> Yes, he's a professional believer. A professor of belief. . . . But as for finding out what goes on in what he calls "his heart of hearts"? . . . It would be indiscreet, you know, to ask him. And I don't think he ever asks himself. He arranges things so that he never has time to ask himself the question.)

Although the emphasis appears to fall mainly on the distinction between "authentic" and "counterfeit" beings, it is not by any means confined to people. Gide clearly intended it to be a universal standard which could be applied equally to people, institutions and beliefs. Religion, politics and literature all come under scrutiny in the novel, and by the time we reach the end we find that the distinction has been erected into something very like a method or a system. It is well illustrated by the activities of Edouard. Although he is used as a foil for Passavant, he is not entirely the "authentic" novelist; he is trying, as Gide himself was, to become the authentic novelist. That is why he spends so much of his time theorizing about the nature of the novel. For you cannot become an authentic novelist without first discovering what constitutes an "authentic" novel. I think we are entitled to assume that the "authentic" novel means the "pure" novel. The "pure" novel, we remember, is the novel which has been purged of all elements which do not belong specifically to the novel, which means the "counterfeit" elements. The book ends like most of Gide's other works on a mark of interrogation. The problem is not to decide whether Gide has written an authentic novel; it is to discover whether it is possible to write a novel which corresponds to Gide's definition, whether we can in fact represent "reality" without some "counterfeit" elements entering into "our representation of it."

In spite of the praise that it has received, it does not seem to me that the *Faux-monnayeurs* is an artistic success, or that the larger canvas was suited to Gide's particular talents. It remains a fascinating experiment which in the nature of things was bound to fail. The prose is an admirable example of Gide's plain style—the style which offers "aucun intérêt de surface, aucune saillie" ["no surface interest, no ornamentation"]—and unlike his other fiction it is immensely readable. But we cannot fail to perceive that there is no real advance on the earlier works, that compared with them it re-veals not development but embroidery. Gide was obliged by the nature of the undertaking to sacrifice the shapeliness and finish of the shorter books, but he does not seem to have replaced them by anything of genuine artistic worth. The fact that he elected to present all the familiar themes in a more elaborate setting draws attention to the nature of the failure. The variety is essentially a surface variety; his best qualities appear in dilution and are spread out over a wider area. His speculations about the nature of fiction are interesting and entertaining, are indeed the best pages in the book, but they do not offer the sort of experience we expect to find in the "authentic" or any other kind of novel. We can hardly escape the conclusion that by deliberately taking us into the workshop and by directing attention from *experience* to its *presentation,* he was making a virtue of what for a writer like Flaubert was plainly a necessity. For this preoccupation with technique is the clearest sign of the absence of any new or vital experience. (pp. 263-69)

> *Martin Turnell, "The Protestant Cell," in his* The Art of French Fiction: Prévost, Stendhal, Zola, Maupassant, Gide, Mauriac, Proust, *Hamish Hamilton, 1959, pp. 245-71.*

PHILIP THODY   (essay date 1960)

[*Thody is an English educator and critic who specializes in twentieth-century French literature. In the following excerpt, he explores the theme of responsibility in* The Counterfeiters.]

One of the main attractions of *Les faux-monnayeurs,* for both critic and reader, lies in its extreme complexity. It can be read for aesthetic motives as a meditation on the art of the novel and an attempt to realize Gide's ideal of "purity" in fiction. The historian of manners and censorship can find in it the first open defence of homosexuality, while for the moralist it seems to give Gide's final version of his ethic of individualism—"Il est bon de suivre sa pente, pourvu que ce soit en montant" ["It is good to follow one's inclination, as long as one is going upward"]. By the side of a criticism of bourgeois society and ready-made moral systems, it contains what is probably Gide's most convincing demonstration of the abuses of Protestant morality. As a satire, it attacks both psychoanalysts and littérateurs, as a novel of manners it presents a fascinating picture of [Alfred] Jarry, as an expression of despair it contains the suicide of Boris, the character of Armand, and the ideas of La Pérouse on the cruelty of God. It has been said, however, that this complexity is achieved only at the expense of an almost complete sacrifice of unity: that the novel has no central plot and that the story of the schoolboys distributing false coins, which provides the symbolic title of the work, never progresses beyond the stage of a minor intrigue. Indeed, one of the many problems which the book presents to the critic is that of deciding whether it has any unity other than that provided by the presence of Edouard, and, more important, of discovering whether the various plots are anything more than a series of fascinating embroideries on a very tenuous central theme.

The critic's task is not made easier by the apparent contradictions in Gide's own statements about the novel. In the *Journal des faux-monnayeurs* he tells us that it was written backwards in order to explain the *fait divers* ["news item"] of the suicide of the *lycéen* ["high school student"] at Rouen. In his *Journal* for 1 December 1921, however, he says of the composition of "ce livre"—presumably *Les faux-monnayeurs*—that "tout ce que j'écris c'est au courant de la plume . . . je ne sais pas où je vais et crains de me trouver bientôt arrêté" ["all that I write is off the top of my head . . . I do not know where I am going and fear to find myself stopped too soon"]. It is difficult to see how Gide could at one and the same time have been writing "without knowing where he was going" and following a plan of composition which was to explain a definite event. There is another difficulty in reconciling the perfectly balanced construction of the novel—eighteen chapters in the first part, seven in the second, eighteen in the third—with Gide's stated intention to present the reader with something which is not complete in itself and "could be continued." This formal unity is also accompanied by an internal structure on a fugal pattern, with Bernard's discovery of his illegitimacy balancing, in the first part, Laura's pregnancy, and, towards the end, Jarry's foolery with a revolver and Olivier's false suicide announcing the real death of Boris. This again contrasts very strongly with the idea which Gide put into Edouard's mouth that the novel attracts him because it is the most "lawless" of genres, for *Les faux-monnayeurs* is anything but a work from which formal planning, art and artifice are missing. It is possible, however, that these contradictions were present in Gide's own mind, and that they were in fact intended to form part of his openly stated intention of disturbing the reader, forcing him to return to the book again and again in order to solve the problems which it set and discover the meaning implicit in it. The *hypothèse de lecture* which this essay presents is based on the following invitation in the *Journal des faux-monnayeurs:* "D'abord procéder à l'inventaire. On fera les comptes plus tard. Il n'est pas bon de mêler. Puis, mon livre achevé, je tire la barre, et laisse aux autres le soin de l'opération: addition, soustraction, peu m'importe: j'estime que ce n'est pas à moi de la faire. Tant pis pour le lecteur paresseux: j'en veux d'autres." ["At first proceed to the inventory. One will make the calculations later. It is never good to mix them. Then, my book finished, I close the list, and leave to others the trouble of the operation: addition, subtraction, it doesn't much matter to me: I consider that it's not for me to do. Too bad for the lazy reader: I want others."]

Its aim is to show that *Les faux-monnayeurs* has, in its plot, a much greater unity than has often been suggested.

A unifying theme in *Les faux-monnayeurs,* implicit in the plot but never openly stated, is the idea of responsibility. This theme is primarily expressed through the suicide of Boris, but it also recurs as a factor in the other relationships between the different characters. The suicide of Boris, directly caused by the machinations of Strouvilhou and Ghéridanisol, is closely linked with the plot of the circulation of false coins which gives the novel its title. It is also indirectly caused by the inefficiency of the people around him—Edouard, Mme Sophroniska, Azais, Vedel—and is thus also linked with the criticism in the novel of social attitudes. The link with the "bande de faux-monnayeurs" is precise and definite. It is Ghéridanisol, Strouvilhou's cousin, who alone knows that the pistol is loaded. It is because Boris has been excluded from the activity of passing false coins that he is anxious to prove himself and become a member of the *Confrérie des hommes forts* ["Brotherhood of Strong Men"]. It is Strouvilhou, the chief of the "real" counterfeiters, who has made Boris's desire to join this fraternity even greater by communicating to Ghéridanisol the piece of paper bearing the magic formula "Gaz . . . téléphone,. . . . Cent mille roubles . . . " ["Gas . . . telephone . . . one hundred thousand rubles,"]

which the latter places on Boris's desk. The sight of this talisman plunges Boris even further into the despair caused by the death of Bronja and by his loneliness, and makes him prepared to do anything in order to be accepted by his companions. Strouvilhou, however—and here the link between the real and the symbolic counterfeiters becomes apparent—has been given this piece of paper by Mme Sophroniska during the visit which he made to Saas-Fée. The responsibility for Boris's death thus begins to be shared.

It is fairly clear, from the comments which Gide puts into Edouard's mouth, that he does not entirely approve of the Freudian technique of analysis which Mme Sophroniska is attempting to apply to Boris, and the majority of readers would agree with Edouard's judgement. Yet even the most convinced Freudian could not for a moment approve the action of a doctor who confides an immensely important document concerning one of her patients to a complete stranger. However, she is not the only person in a position of responsibility who makes a mistake which forms a link in the chain leading to Boris's death. It is Edouard who decides that Boris shall go to live in the Pension Azais-Vedel, in spite of the fact, as Gide points out, that he knows the peculiar atmosphere which reigns there, and the effect which it is likely to have upon so delicate a person as Boris. It is true that in making this decision Edouard is thinking first of all of the pleasure which La Pérouse will have in living with his grandson near him, and the profit which Boris himself may receive. Nevertheless, Gide specifically intervenes as narrator in order to criticize Edouard's motives: "Ce qui ne me plaît pas chez Edouard, ce sont les raisons qu'il se donne. Pourquoi cherche-t-il à se persuader, à présent, qu'il conspire au bien de Boris? Mentir aux autres, passe encore; mais à soi-même. *Le torrent qui noie un enjani pretend-il lui porter à boire? . . .* " (my italics) ["What displeases me about Edouard is the reasons he gives. Why does he try to persuade himself, at present, that he conspires for Boris's good? To lie to others, that's one thing; but to oneself. Does the torrent that drowns an infant maintain that it brings him to drink? . . . "] Both Edouard and Sophroniska add something to the torrent which drowns Boris, and their responsibility for his death does not involve themselves alone. They are both representative figures, Sophroniska of medical science, Edouard of art and literature. If, as D. L. Thomas has suggested, *Les faux-monnayeurs* marks the stage in Gide's thought where he begins to doubt the sufficiency of "the ethic of the artist" and turns to social and political problems, then the idea of Edouard's responsibility for Boris's death fits into a wider pattern.

The responsibility of the symbolic coiners does not, however, stop at Edouard and Sophroniska. False religious values also play their part in killing Boris. It was in revolt against the Puritanism of the Pension Vedel that Strouvilhou accepted the facile pseudo-Nietzscheanism which justifies, in his and Ghéridanisol's eyes, the killing of the weak by the strong. An indication of this is provided by Gide's comments on Puritanism in the *Journal des faux-monnayeurs:* "C'est par haine contre cette religion, cette morale qui opprima toute sa jeunesse, par haine contre ce rigorisme dont lui-même n'a jamais pu s'affranchir, que Z travaille à débaucher et pervertir les enfants du pasteur. Il y a là de la rancune. Sentiments forcés, contrefaits." ["It is by hatred of this religion, this morality which oppressed all his youth, by hatred of this rigorism from which he could never free himself that Z works to debauch and pervert the pastor's children. There is malice there.

Forced, counterfeit sentiments."] It is also the blind and stupid acceptance by Azaïs of ready-made religious ideas, his refusal to recognize that the children committed to his charge are anything but angels of purity—witness his reaction to Georges's buttonhole—which creates exactly the right atmosphere in which the passing of false coins and the *Confrérie des Hommes Forts* can flourish. Vedel, constantly fleeing reality in a whirl of occupations, is indubitably guilty, by the most obvious of sins of omission, for what goes on under his own roof. Even La Pérouse, who suffers most from the death of Boris, is responsible in that it was the pistol with which he had tried to take his own life, and which he had left loaded to remind himself of his failure, which was used for the crime. It is surely to this multiplicity of causes which led to Boris's death that Gide refers in the only passage in the *Journal des faux-monnayeurs* which specifically mentions the idea of responsibility: "Il n'est pas d'acte, si absurde ou si préjudiciable, qui ne soit le résultat d'un concours de causes, conjonctions et concomitances; et sans doute est-il bien peu de crimes dont la responsabilité ne puisse être partagée et pour la réussite desquels on ne se soit mis à plusieurs—fût-ce sans le vouloir ou le savoir. Les sources de nos moindres gestes sont aussi multiples et retirées que celles du Nil." ["There is not an action, however absurd or however injurious, which is not the result of a concurrence of causes, conjunctions, and concomitances; and without doubt it is very few crimes for which the responsibility cannot be shared and the success of which one cannot attribute to many—even if it was without their desire or knowledge. The sources of our least deeds are as multiple and as secluded as those of the Nile."] If the suicide of Boris is the last of the *actes gratuits* in Gide's work, it is for the very good reason that it is not at all *gratuit* when the circumstances which led up to it are analysed. It is an act which was planned by some people, but for which the carelessness, blindness and stupidity of others were almost equally responsible.

It is when we come to study the motives which inspired those immediately responsible for Boris's death that *Les faux-monnayeurs* takes on a metaphysical rather than a social significance. Strouvilhou's motives are not difficult to understand, and a very slight analysis is sufficient to reveal the superficiality of his character. It is Ghéridanisol who presents the greatest problem. Here, surely, is an absolute in unexplained wickedness and perverse cruelty. Iago can be at least partly understood or explained in terms of professional and sexual jealousy, Smerdyakov by resentment at his illegitimacy, and even Stravrogin by an intense metaphysical despair, but Ghéridanisol remains wholly and inexplicably evil. His only possible motive for killing Boris is pure malignity. It may be that he is one of the incarnations of the Devil who weaves his way in and out of the plots of *Les faux-monnayeurs,* but if this is the case he is very different from the amiable one who inspires works of art or drives Vincent to gamble. Rather than a representative of the pleasant Gidean Devil, whose only power is to tempt, Ghéridanisol is the representative of a more vicious and active type of evil which, in the novel, can be understood only by reference to the ideas of La Pérouse.

Gide invites us to see in the character of La Pérouse a genuine rarity in the novel, for it is true, as he says, that fiction is but little preoccupied with the aged. It is important to note that before Edouard goes off again at the end in pursuit of Caloub—thus beginning a completely new novel—the last word on the events of *Les faux-monnayeurs* is left to La Pé-

rouse. It is his verdict upon God which remains ringing in the reader's ears while Edouard, the artist with no moral conscience, is preoccupied with new loves. "Et savez-vous ce qu'il a fait de plus horrible. . . . C'est de sacrifier son propre fils pour nous sauver. Son fils, son fils. La cruauté, voilà le premier des attributs de Dieu." ["And do you know what he did that is more horrible. . . . He sacrificed his only son to save us. His son, his son. Cruelty—that is the foremost attribute of God."] A hint at a partial identification of Boris with Christ has been made by Jacques Lévy in his study of *Les faux-monnayeurs,* when he talks of his death as being "l'offrande de l'innocent" ["the offering of the innocents"], but it is difficult to accept it as having been willed by a benign Providence. If Boris is a child martyr, killed by a combination of natural perversity (Ghéridanisol) and false ideas (Strouvilhou, Azaïs, Sophroniska), he is one whose death can bring no salvation. It is merely a pointless tragedy which could have been avoided. It is, moreover—and the words which Gide puts into the mouth of La Pérouse invite us to this conclusion—an overwhelming proof of the cruelty and indifference of God, as well as a testimony to the perverseness and carelessness of man. After *Les faux-monnayeurs* (1925), Gide's next important metaphysical work is *Oedipe* (1931), one of the most convincing expressions of his anti-religious thought. Implicit in the character of La Pérouse—the plaything of God—and in the tragedy of Boris's death is the condemnation of God as the greatest coiner of them all. As far as his religious opinions are concerned, the Gide who wrote *Les faux-monnayeurs* in the 1920's is very little different from the Gide who, in 1947, refused to believe in God because of the existence of suffering. Replying to his interrogator in the second of the *Interviews imaginaires* in 1947, he said that he preferred the attitude implicit in the *Credo quia absurdum* to any attempt to base religion on reasoning.

> Car, pour moi, croire à ce Dieu qu'il [= 'l'effort ratiocinant'] me propose m'amènerait vite à dire, avec Oreste:
>
> De quelque part sur moi que je tourne les yeux
> Je ne vois que malheurs qui condamnent ce Dieu.
>
> [Because, for me, to believe in this God which it (= 'ratiocinative effort') proposes to me would quickly lead me to say, with Orestes:
>
> Whichever way I turn
> I see nothing but the miseries which condemn this God.]

Both on a metaphysical and a religious plane, *Les faux-monnayeurs* announces the agnostic Gide of the 1940's and the "socially conscious" Gide of the 1930's. The demonstration that religion, science and literature can all, by their aberrations and insufficiencies, bring about the death of an innocent child causes the novel to open out into a broad condemnation of society and to demand that new remedies be found for its ills. (pp. 351-55)

The principal objection to this *hypothèse de lecture*—which by no means claims to be exclusive—lies in the fact that it depends almost completely upon a personal interpretation of the plot. It is true that Gide himself invited the reader to make any interpretation he wanted, within reason, and even went so far as to hint that there was a hidden meaning in *Les faux-monnayeurs* which he would allow the reader to discover for himself, and thereby acquire a flattering impression of his superior intelligence. Yet the one quotation from the *Journal des faux monnayeurs* made above, although it does mention the idea of responsibility, does so only in an extremely indirect and ambiguous way. It is also curious that Gide, who was seldom reluctant to suggest interpretations of his work, never once mentioned, either in respect of *Les faux-monnayeurs* or of his other works of fiction, the idea of responsibility. As one looks closer, this becomes even more curious, because each one of the three best known of his serious fictions—*L'immoraliste, La porte etroite, La symphonie pastorale*—can be studied from this point of view. In *L'immoraliste,* Michel, to all intents and purposes, kills Marceline. Whether this is merely through the indifference of absolute selfishness or through a deliberate attempt to get rid of this obstacle to a full life of the senses is not made clear, but Michel's guilt is in any case complete. It is in Marceline's death that the true results of his "immorality" can be seen, and it is in the results of his immorality that the best support can be found for the view which interprets *L'immoraliste* as a satirical novel. Similarly, it is the results of Alissa's virtue which most clearly illustrate the idea that *La porte etroite* is correctly read as an attack on certain religious tendencies. The denial of all natural affection and happiness which Alissa's virtue involves leads not only to her own unhappiness and final disillusion, but also to the melancholy bachelordom of Jérôme and the unsuitable marriage of her sister. Alissa's rejection of the links which tie her to other people—as absolute in its way as that of Lady Griffiths or Michel—has exactly the same result: the growth of unhappiness. Through the abdication of the most fundamental human value, that each person is responsible for those about him, the characters of Gide's serious fiction leave behind them a trail of ruined lives. This ruin may be brought about by a failure to recognize one's motives for what they are—the example here is that of the pastor in *La symphonie pastorale,* who drives Gertrude to death, and his son to a despairing abdication of his personality in Catholicism—or by the adoption of deliberately antisocial ethical systems. In spite of the great differences in technique and subject-matter, the same themes which inform *La porte etroite, L'immoraliste* and *La symphonie pastorale* recur in *Les faux-monnayeurs* when this is read in the light of the problem of responsibility. Those responsible for the death which ends each of these works—the death of Marceline, of Gertrude, of Alissa, of Boris—can be divided into those who follow definitely wrong principles and those whose principles are insufficient. Definitely wrong are the principles of Alissa, Michel, Strouvilhou and Ghéridanisol, insufficient those of the pastor, of Edouard, of Madame Sophroniska, of Vedel and of Azais. Throughout the fiction of Gide this same pattern can be perceived. If it is genuinely a "pattern in the carpet" and not a purely subjective impression, then the following questions must be considered: was Gide himself conscious of this pattern, or was it the result of largely subconscious forces in his mind? In either case, how does it affect our estimate of the ethical value of his work?

It is easier to discuss the second question first because it shows the relative unimportance of the first. The most generally held and correct view of Gide's ethical system is that it is first and foremost an invitation to individuality. In his own epitaph, in the closing pages of *Thésée,* he wrote "Il m'est doux de penser qu'après moi, grâce à moi, les hommes se reconnaîtront plus heureux, meilleurs, et plus libres" ["It is sweet to think that after me, thanks to me, men will find themselves happier, better, and more free"]. Sartre wrote of him [in "Gide vivant," *Les temps modernes* (March 1951)] that he was the writer who had delivered twentieth-century man from God. In attacking the stultifying effect of conventional thought, in casting off the heritage of Puritanism, in ac-

cepting himself as a homosexual and claiming for the individual the right to follow his sexual nature wherever it did not actively harm others, in pleading for greater understanding of the criminal, in rejecting the whole tradition of both Christian and lay morality which sees in fixed laws the only safeguard to morality, Gide made an essential contribution to the progress of liberal thought. Yet, as his adversaries never wearied of pointing out, such liberation cannot be wholly and exclusively good. It is possible, without falling into the exaggerations of a Massis or a Du Bos, to recognize that certain aspects of Gide's thought are potentially dangerous. If his work revealed no awareness of the fact that the development of individualism can hurt others, then these criticisms would be justified and well founded. As it is, however, the pattern of responsibility which his work reveals is proof that a genuine concern for the individual carries within it its own corrective against excess, and can dispense with fixed ethical systems based on dogmatic creeds. Seen in this light, the problem of whether or not Gide was aware of this pattern takes on a new appearance. No one was more alive than he to the danger of preaching morality through works of art. To have deliberately insisted upon this theme of responsibility, either in the works of fiction themselves or in his commentaries upon them, would have appeared to Gide himself as preaching. To allow the theme to be perceived is much more subtle and much more in keeping with Gide's aesthetic ideals. If it did happen that this theme were something of which he was unconscious, it would be, paradoxically enough, an even greater triumph for Gide the individualist, though less flattering to Gide the artist. It would be evidence that the genuine moralist who composes works of art cannot help but express all aspects of the problems with which he deals. Yet when one considers the complexity of the plot of *Les faux-monnayeurs,* and the inevitability with which so many of the apparently irrelevant incidents contribute towards Boris's death, it is difficult to accept the idea of Gide's unawareness of this theme. His failure to mention it must be attributed to his realization that what matters in a novel is its plot and construction, and not the author's comments upon them. (pp. 356-58)

Philip Thody, "'Les Faux-Monnayeurs': The Theme of Responsibility," in The Modern Language Review, *Vol. LV, No. 3, July, 1960, pp. 351-58.*

GERMAINE BRÉE (essay date 1963)

[*Brée is a French-born American critic and translator. Her critical works are devoted to modern French literature and include* André Gide, l'insaisissable Protée: Etude critique de l'oeuvre d'André Gide *(1953; Gide). Concerning her work as a critic, Brée has written: "I do not consider myself a writer and should probably be classed among the 'academic' critics. . . . I have no particular critical method and am, in fact, an eclectic. Each writer seems himself to suggest to me the method of approach I should use as I attempt to elucidate the kind of book he has written. . . . I attempt, with a good deal of difficulty, to communicate what seems to me essential about each, rather than to prove, attack or praise." In the following excerpt, Brée relates the characters and narrative structure of* The Counterfeiters *to its themes.*]

Gide had always wanted to rid the novel as a genre of the "parasitic elements" that superficial realism had burdened it with. When he discussed the "pure novel" and the necessity for working toward the "erosion of contours" in fiction he was working out the formula best suited to his own intellectual bent. This was to discover, beneath the complicated network of appearances, the deeper outline of a story in the making. When Gide spoke of "purging the novel of all the elements that do not specifically belong to the novel," this rather vague statement referred quite exactly to what he was attempting to achieve in *The Counterfeiters.* He wanted to subordinate characters and plot to their often episodic role in the formation of one underlying pattern. "I am trying to wind the various threads of the plot and the complexities of my thoughts around the little living bobbins that are my characters."

If the little living bobbins were to become characters, unwinding on their own the threads of a plot indistinguishable from themselves, Gide had to make a great effort at stylization. He had in fact to create characters both "new" and "invented" who could live and breathe only in terms of the novel he had abstracted from reality. It was not a new psychology he was experimenting with but rather a new architecture, a new way of projecting his characters into space: "First study the source of light; all the shadows will depend on that. Every form rests on and finds support in its shadow." The bulk of the novel does indeed remain in the shadow, while Gide brings the greater part of his effort to bear on certain brilliantly lighted surfaces, so much so that these are the ones critics have tended to see to the exclusion of all others. This new architecture accounted for Gide's heroic efforts to avoid a sustained narrative. "With each chapter I must start anew. *Never take advantage of the momentum gained*—such is the rule of my game." He wants each facet of the whole to appear to the reader independently, no single one revealing the pattern of which it is a part. It is not astonishing, therefore, that Gide often worked out his novel, as he said, in reverse, perpetually strengthening the hidden lines whose ultimate convergence would reveal a hidden, guiding intent. But what events? What grouping? The novel is there to elucidate this point and it does not always correspond to what Gide says about it in *The Journal of the Counterfeiters.* For example, he starts the second notebook of the *Journal* with the following statement:

> Properly speaking, there is no single center to this book, around which my various efforts converge; it is in relation to two foci, as in an ellipse, that they become polarized. On the one hand, the event, the fact, the external datum; on the other, the very effort of the novelist to make a book out of it all. That effort is the main subject, the new center that throws the plot off its axis, drawing it away toward the imaginative.

But Edouard never really tries to "make a book" out of what he observes, or, at least, Gide shows us two brief and very mediocre passages of a book that, he warns us, Edouard will never write. It is Gide who writes the book, and if he does not really let us into his secrets, it is perhaps because he himself was not clearly conscious of what they were. *The Journal of the Counterfeiters* is quite enlightening on this point. Up to almost the last instant, until May, 1925, Gide thought he was writing a novel in two parts. At the last moment it inevitably became a novel in three parts; the first and last, each with eighteen chapters, are situated in Paris, while the seven central chapters take place in Saas-Fée, in Switzerland. As usual, the novel had taken shape as an ascending curve, a plateau, a descending curve, ending with the disintegration of the main themes rather than a conclusion. Instinctively Gide had worked out the structure which was fundamentally his

"own" and which seen from without might appear contrived and artificial:

"I hold that the composition of a book is of the first importance and I hold that it is through a lack of composition that most works of art sin today. . . . It is best to let the work compose its own order, and above all it is best not to *force* it." Apparently this is how all Gide's works took shape. They are fashioned from the inside out. Gide's form, or *design,* for each, perfect as it may seem, even to the point of artificiality when completed, is the end result of a long fumbling and groping. That is why his novels are not merely "thesis-novel" demonstrations. From the fictional debate instigated in the novel about the novel, certain principles do emerge most subtly. This is true too of his ethics. Abstracted from his novels, however, Gide's thought often seems vague, closer to common sense than to wisdom. He sometimes even pontificates, and in rather facile fashion. Fiction alone provided him the means of transmitting in its entirety the inner climate of sensitivity from which his ideas drew their singular and persuasive force.

There is something truly admirable in the discipline Gide imposed upon himself in the writing of *The Counterfeiters.* The creation of a novel was for him adventure par excellence, a veritable Odyssey. He succeeds in projecting something of the excitement and poetry of his creative experience into the very prosaic and mediocre world which the novel sets in motion. It took all Gide's intelligence and vast experience as a writer to make of this strange novel a work of great scope. He succeeded, because he imposed upon his material a form as restrained and controlled as the fugue. (pp. 226-29)

On the whole, [*Journal of the Counterfeiters*] stresses those characteristics of fiction which Gide wanted to do away with: descriptions in the realistic manner, a plot around which to drape his story, motivational analysis explaining the characters' behavior, the kind of narration so smoothly organized that it carries the reader along on a kind of conveyer belt, and the traditional sort of conclusion.

Yet all these customary habitual ingredients have a place in *The Counterfeiters.* Gide provides a geographic and social setting, a main plot, and several subordinate plots. The succession of events is carefully timed and the novel is brought to a conclusion by means of two, perhaps even three, successive denouements, the first two partially happy endings, the third tragic. All the energies set in motion in the first part of the novel come to a temporary rest at the end, an equilibrium on which the book closes.

Gide situates his story carefully: in the Luxembourg section of Paris and in Saas-Fée, Switzerland—a narrow geographic area but with ramifications in France, England, Corsica, Poland, America and Africa. The effect is of a small brilliantly lighted stage beyond which the entire world extends. Lady Griffith's America, the Africa of Vincent, the Poland of La Pérouse's son are the faraway frontiers of a region in which even Pau, in southern France, is considered a place of exile. The setting of *The Counterfeiters* resembles the universe of the ancients: a small flat space surrounded by the vague masses of mythical continents. Gide had wanted the setting of his novel to be "saturated with myth," his Luxembourg Gardens to be as imaginary as Shakespeare's Forest of Arden in *As You Like It.* Actually one may feel rather constrained by the naïveté and narrowness of the Gidian perspective. The borders of the known world in *The Counterfeiters* are rather quickly reached.

The small coherent group of characters belong to a part of the respectable Parisian bourgeoisie, shut in upon itself and limited in its contacts. The foreigners who happen to intrude are promptly thrown out: little Boris, from Poland, commits suicide and Lady Griffith is assassinated by Vincent.

The Protestant milieu, as always, furnishes the main contingent of characters, the family of the Vedel-Azaïs, the Moliniers and the novelist Edouard; but a variety of so-called Protestant righteousness even hangs over the Catholic Profitendieus. Gide did not wish to raise the denominational issue as he had done in *Strait Is the Gate.* What the four families most actively involved in his story have in common is their connection with liberal professions: they are magistrates, professors, pastors, writers. On the fringes, the aristocratic Passavants and the politically inclined Adamantis suggest further upper-middle class connections. Quite late in the story there appears a character who seems out of place in such a respectable group, the counterfeiter Strouvilhou. The social setting, like the geographic, stretches farther than is at first apparent. What shuts the characters in is their own limited point of view, whereas in truth they are "imbricated," as Gide would say, in an apparently unlimited social world.

Gide may have had trouble initially in attaching his heroes to definite families and "relating" them to each other. Nevertheless, he did so with the greatest care, although he leaves it to his reader to spell out the relations that operate implicitly through the story. M. Profitendieu and M. Molinier are magistrates. The wealthier Profitendieus have four children of whom only one, the illegitimate son Bernard, plays a part in the novel. Gide winds the main threads of his plot around the three sons of the Moliniers: Vincent, Olivier, and Georges. The Vedel-Azaïs family, educators and pastors, people the novel with their five children: Rachel, Laure, Sarah, Alexandre and Armand. Boris, the grandson of the music teacher, La Pérouse, attends the Azaïs school as does the nephew of Strouvilhou, Ghéridanisol. All the characters are thus interconnected in a thousand ways and from generation to generation. Gide stresses the continuity within which the opposition of the generations will operate. The friendship of Olivier and Bernard is echoed in the mutual esteem of their fathers. Ghéridanisol goes to the Azaïs school because his uncle went there before him. The web of connections stretches backward in time, giving the story temporal dimensions rather than the more traditional spatial ones.

At the center of the web is Edouard, Mme. Molinier's half brother. He is connected to the Vedel-Azaïs family through his halfhearted love affair with Laure and by having boarded in their school, where he met Strouvilhou and had La Pérouse as his music teacher. He knows Count Passavant, who is one of his literary colleagues, and he will greatly influence Bernard and Olivier. All the events of the novel, in some way, direct or indirect, move within Edouard's orbit. Incidental characters cross his path, wending their way in and out of the main stream of the story, suggesting further perspectives that Edouard's limited attention cannot encompass.

The fabric of the novel is not pieced together to fit the dimensions of the story; the story, Gide implies, stretches beyond his novel in space, time, and human connections. The characters fall into two main groups: the parents and grandparents; the younger generation, all under forty. Edouard, who is just thirty-six when the story begins, moves between the two groups. The conflict between the generations and yet the continuity of the heritage that binds them together is an integral theme.

The young group initiates the action, their parents being immobilized in a sort of social and mental status quo. Some of the lively characters under forty are young adults, already "committed," engaged in life—Edouard, Count Passavant, Vincent, Rachel, and Laure. Others—Bernard, Olivier, Armand, and their friends, all around eighteen—are uncertainly poised between their dependence as schoolboys and their passage into adult life. The baccalaureate, the terminal high-school examination in France, symbolizes this transition, which is one of the major themes in the novel. The younger teen-agers—Georges, Boris, Ghéridanisol, and Phiphi—are at the difficult stage between childhood and adolescence. As the novel progresses, the spotlight moves from group to group, concentrating sometimes on one and sometimes on the other. But whether they are at the center of the stage or in the wings, all the characters are present and active in the novel from the very beginning.

When the story begins one intrigue, involving Edouard, Vincent, Laure, and her husband Douviers, is coming to its end; a second involving Bernard, Olivier, Edouard and Passavant is shaping up; a third is vaguely suggested: the illegal, clandestine activity of the high-school boys which preoccupies the two magistrates. It will emerge fully only in the third part of the book.

The characters are tied to their milieu and few break away. When Bernard Profitendieu decides to be adventurous and break with his family, he does nothing more hazardous than to become secretary to Edouard, the uncle of his closest friend, Olivier, and then subsequently to find a job at the Azaïs boarding school. Laure Vedel, in love with Edouard, ventures as far as Pau, only to be seduced there by Edouard's oldest nephew, Vincent.

The professional ambitions of the characters are equally limited. The most arduous profession these young men envisage is literary journalism; the most violent political commitment, joining a right-wing party. Aside from usual and less usual love affairs, the main cause of excitement is the launching of an avant-garde review; the most fascinating adventure of the year is a literary dinner; and the greatest trial is the baccalaureate. Even the reprehensible activities of the boys, which so gravely concern the two magistrates, are cut to scale. They are merely those of a group of schoolboys, cynically indulging with prostitutes in their first sexual experiences.

The rare "explorers" like Vincent Molinier and Alexandre Vedel, who take off for darkest Africa, are deliberately relegated to the periphery of the novel. They come to a bad end or disappear in those obscure regions that extend beyond the boundaries of Gide's stage. The small world Gide chose to depict has nothing very glorious to recommend it. It is ethically and socially refined almost to the point of effeteness. Yet it has the characteristic traits of the well-to-do and well-meaning upper-middle class in Western Europe, as it was before the series of brutal wars which disrupted its righteous tranquillity.

Gide's approach to this world may seem surprising, but the people with whom he deals are quite recognizably related to those also depicted in novels as different from Gide's as Proust's and Martin du Gard's. Galsworthy and Meredith treat their English counterparts and Mann describes their German equivalents in those "people of the plain" whom Hans Castorp rejects in *The Magic Mountain.* Gide merely eliminated from his story all economic or social considerations. His characters interest him only in so far as they are connected with the self-appointed guardians of the ethical values in their society, those values embodied in the law, the church and the educational system.

Nothing in *The Counterfeiters* suggests that the earth is not peopled entirely by persons of this type, and this is perhaps a weakness. Rare are the novels with characters so far removed from the concerns of average human beings. Toward the end of the novel, as Bernard hesitates at a sort of crossroads in his life, Gide imagines that an angel takes him by the hand and leads him "into the poor sections of the town, whose wretchedness Bernard had never suspected. Evening was falling. They wandered for a long time among tall, sordid houses, inhabited by disease, prostitution, shame, crime and hunger." Bernard's angel turns aside to weep, but the reader is tempted rather to shrug his shoulders. It is all too obvious that for Gide the "sordid crimes" perpetrated by the poor are not of the same kind as the more elegantly reprehensible activities of his young heroes.

Gide's human world, in spite of his good will, was limited. The only dramas that flourish in this milieu are the casual, carefully concealed complications of adultery. At worst, the pious pastor Vedel is inwardly tormented because of his addiction to masturbation, to which he alludes in secret code in his journal. The taboo concerning sex is total and on the whole Freud is still almost unknown in the fictional universe described. Yet Gide's characters are all involved in a web of trite clandestine love affairs which keep them on the go: Laure's adultery; Vincent's liaisons; the brief encounter of the two adolescents, Bernard and Sarah; Edouard's and Passavant's seduction of Olivier. Edouard, attracted by Olivier, forgets his love for Laure. Laure, disappointed with Edouard, marries Douviers and has a liaison with Vincent. Vincent abandons Laure for Lady Griffith. Bernard leaves home when he discovers he is illegitimate. Armand contracts syphilis in some sordid adventure.

The love affairs are handled casually. Sex plays a role in all these lives, but it is a role neither glamorous nor mysterious. Fortunately Gide does not intend to make it a source of romance; otherwise his novel might have foundered in the embarrassing honeyed sweetness of Edouard's love for Olivier. Sex in *The Counterfeiters* merely opens the way for more disruptive, dangerous and perturbing forces. It sets the characters in motion and its omnipresence suggests that all, in some vital fashion, are governed by its exigencies.

This undercover sexual activity, general though it is, is carefully concealed by everyone. The children would never guess that their parents had ever yielded to erotic impulses were there not to inform them of what goes on behind the scenes the secret letters and locked drawers dear to eighteenth-century fiction which quite naturally find their place in Gide's novel. The parents, in turn, pretend not to notice the love affairs of their children: Oscar Molinier, for example, dwells at some length on the edifying aspects of his two sons' most questionable friendships. Only at the end does Olivier's mother admit the truth concerning her son's homosexual affair, an indirect and reluctant admission.

The clandestine activities of Georges Molinier and his teen-age gang are more brutal. They involve not only current concepts of morality but also the law, and they culminate in what is in fact a murder. Gide used to advantage the insights he had gained into adolescent crime when he was a member of the jury in the Assize Court of Rouen. The gang psychology and brutality of his teen-agers are depicted clearly and forcefully. At the beginning of the novel M. Molinier and M. Profitendieu, we learn, are concerned about a vice ring which M. Profitendieu is investigating, which he now knows implicates schoolboys with respectable backgrounds. These are no longer the "scissor thieves" of *The Immoralist,* the picturesque little Arabs whose exoticism accounts for their untoward actions. But the investigators whose job it is to detect crime and make it inoperative cannot tolerate the thought that it has infected their own social class. Silence is preferable to truth. Like the illicit sexual relationships of their elders, the teen-ager antisocial activities are hushed up.

While the love intrigues in *The Counterfeiters* give the novel its picaresque atmosphere, the hidden criminal activity is a source of mystery. The reader, rather like Profitendieu, the investigating magistrate, comes upon certain clues and coincidences and begins to glimpse a rather alarming reality beneath the quiet surface of the story, as Strouvilhou and a counterfeit coin make their simultaneous entrance toward the middle of the book. The mystery attached to both, at first intriguing to the reader, soon becomes sinister. A menace hangs over Gide's pleasant and insignificant set of characters, so full of good will and so self-absorbed. Georges Molinier's trail leads to the mysterious Strouvilhou, but so do many others. As soon as he puts in an appearance it becomes clear that Strouvilhou's influence is all pervasive, that Gide's whole cast of characters is connected with him. They are all prevaricators and, to varying degrees, counterfeiters. All proffer their false coins in the hope that they will be accepted as real, or at least that no detective will appear to investigate their origin.

This is the heart of the novel. Gide's characters and their concerns may seem insignificant. The narrative tone, rapid, detached and slightly mocking, emphasizes the picaresque quality of the story. But the real subject Gide is handling is neither commonplace nor slight. It brings to light a deep-seated equivocation governing the relationships in the group, exemplified in the acts of all the characters.

"The combats of truth and error," wrote Blake, "is eating of the Tree of Life." Eating of the Tree of Life is what Gide's adolescents do, as their parents have done before them. But nothing prepares them for the flavor of the fruits they taste. Of their educators one could say with Blake:

> They take the two contraries which are called qualities, with which
> Every substance is clothed. They name them good and evil.
> From them they make an abstract which is a negation
> Not only of the substance from which it is derived
> A murderer of its own body, but also a murderer
> Of every Divine Member.

Wherever they turn the youngsters find good and evil inextricably mixed, yet their elders righteously proclaim that good alone reigns around them.

In contrast, Gide's novel is conceived to bring out a deeper pattern and truth as Gide sees it. The intrigues of the counterfeiters notwithstanding, the "combats of truth and error" are fought in the novel on all levels by each character. They give the story the hidden epic value with which Gide strove to suffuse his tale.

Each character follows his own path, journeying through temptations and dangers. Bernard is a winner in this contest, but the novel is strewn with those who are defeated, temporarily or permanently; those who wander around aimlessly; and those who, somewhere along the way, were taken captive or joined the wrong faction. There is a kind of "pilgrim's progress" involved, particularly for the adolescents. Their struggles at this level take place in solitude. Social institutions, family, justice, schools, religion all league together to maintain the righteous fiction of social and moral order. The love affairs secretly weld individuals to one another in a conspiracy of silence. The teen-age delinquents band together to challenge the restraints imposed upon them. The counterfeiters are linked together by their defiance of the law. But nothing binds the Gidian pilgrims to anyone else. Entangled as they are, they can either accept the struggle between truth and error or join the ranks of the counterfeiters, thus alienating themselves from the "substance" of life.

At different levels, therefore, Gide's characters go through solitary trials and adventures through which they are led to an active organic participation in the fight with or against the counterfeiters. In these encounters their spiritual solitude gives them a freedom untrammeled by the tight social bonds which link them to each other. This freedom, the empty space that surrounds each one, is a device whereby Gide emphasizes the inner quality that determines their respective orientations.

At one point Bernard says that he would like his life "to ring true, with a pure, authentic sound." Gide has endowed each character with his own sound. The most serious source of counterfeit is the attempt, whether individual or social, to reduce all dissonance in favor of that universal and wholly theoretical perfect and continuous chord which haunts the imagination of the old piano teacher, La Pérouse. For the sake of some form of harmony all the characters in the novel, at times and more or less deliberately, indulge in counterfeit. The theme is taken up in turn by each instrument in Gide's human orchestra.

Certain characters are centers of emission of the false coin; in varying degrees what they put forth can be deceptive and dangerous. Passavant is a counterfeiter from vanity, from the need to cut a figure in the world: through counterfeit literary pursuits, counterfeit sentiments, and a counterfeit wit. He deals in small coin and deceives no one except, temporarily, young Olivier. The Englishwoman, Lady Griffith, more dangerous, perverts Vincent, a promising young doctor, to the extent that Gide eventually throws him out of the novel, literally "to the devil." At the very end of the story we learn that Vincent, by this time having killed Lady Griffith, has gone mad and thinks he is the devil in person—a very moral ending. The sense of his adventure is pointed up in the well-known anecdote told by Lady Griffith at the beginning of the novel. Once shipwrecked, Lady Griffith, herself safely hauled into one of the lifeboats, saw the sailors cut off the hands of those unlucky survivors who tried to clamber on after the boat had been filled to capacity. Since then luck and an unscrupulous ferocity had appeared to her perversely romantic eyes to be the only safe guiding principles in life. In a few quick stages she teaches Vincent to gamble on his luck and to cut off all restraining hands, Laure's the first among them.

Vincent's unbridled commitment to his appetite is self-destructive, but destroys him alone, not others. Vincent is not, as he thinks, the devil but merely one of the devil's victims.

The master "counterfeiter" and his mint are a good deal more dangerous: pious old Azaïs and his establishment. Strouvilhou, the real-life counterfeiter, is only one of its by-products. All the major characters in the book wander through the precincts of the school. It is the Vatican of the novel. Just as Profitendieu, on the trail of crime, is gradually led back to Strouvilhou, so the story inevitably leads to the school where the major plot is hatched that brings about the one irreparable event, the death of young Boris. There in his study old Azaïs reigns as though he were God. Azaïs, himself, has a certain pleasing innocence that "rings true." But everyone around him must echo back to him his own sound. Systematically he acknowledges only the purest good around him, every day casting the serpent out of Paradise. He is an unbearable burden upon his family and students, who are forced to conceal or overlook all that does not jibe with Pastor Azaïs's "perfect chord." Their only resort is lying, and prevarication teems around the old gentleman. The insigne that young George wears in his buttonhole, the insigne of his teen-age gang, becomes in Azaïs's eyes the emblem of an association for moral improvement. All his children live under the shadow of guilt, unable to grapple with the ambivalence in their own motivations and impulses. In the Azaïs boarding school, the combats of truth and error are impossible. Evil thrives unchallenged, and Strouvilhou has no trouble recruiting his accomplices there.

Strouvilhou is the natural complement of the old headmaster. He is bitterly aware of the illusory nature of Azaïs's idyllic view of things. A nihilist, he sees only the lie beneath the façade and, revolted, openly declares war on the lie. He has become a perverter out of a disappointed idealism akin to Azaïs's own. Detecting everywhere only the counterfeit, he cynically decides to live on it. Morally speaking, the other characters fall somewhere between Azaïs and Strouvilhou. On the headmaster's side there is society, the myth of harmonious family life, the myth of childish innocence, the myth of punishment and reward, and the myth of parental infallibility—every counterfeit that can help put up a decorous screen between people and the plain truth they all know. On Strouvilhou's side there are the young people, apparently cynical but actually counterfeiters only because of ignorance, bafflement or distress.

Bernard becomes a counterfeiter when he discovers the large crack behind the family façade of perfect respectability. Georges and Phiphi at fourteen become counterfeiters because no other outlet is offered for their violent and unrecognized physical energies. Armand becomes a counterfeiter out of despair, unable to live up to his pious family's exigencies. Boris becomes a counterfeiter out of his great desire for purity and the intimate distress caused by the sense of his own unworthiness. Edouard is a counterfeiter because he cannot face such brutal realities as Boris's death, preferring to bypass them in his novel as in his life. Wherever fiction takes the place of truth, counterfeit coin starts to circulate. Like Edouard, the counterfeiters are bad novelists, peddling their ersatz substitutes for truth.

Azaïs and Strouvilhou both judge on appearances, hence the confusion they generate. "Go," said Blake, "put off holiness and put on intellect." That is just what Gide, humorously, proposes we do. Intelligence regulates the play of light and shadow in the novel, suffusing it with a slightly ironic, non-dogmatic form of intelligence. The perceptive moralist in Gide lent a hand to the artist. There may have been in Gide himself a Strouvilhou and, even more, an Azaïs, an Edouard, and a Passavant, but in *The Counterfeiters* he succeeded in keeping them at a distance. The humor which pervades the book gives his characters an autonomous yet recognizably human flavor. Semiallegorical, semireal, they disconcert the dogmatic moralist in Gide's readers, far more prone than he was to reduce novels to reassuring parables. To distinguish truth from error requires a perspicacity incessantly alert to the thousand snares laid by gullibility.

There are no general conclusions to be drawn from any individual situation in *The Counterfeiters,* no ready-made roles to be assumed. At the beginning of the novel Vincent tells Lady Griffith about the surprising discoveries concerning the organism of deep-sea fish. They had been thought to be blind, but it was found that almost all had eyes. "Why eyes with no means of seeing? . . . And at last it was discovered that each of these creatures which people first insisted were creatures of darkness, gives forth and projects before and around it its *own* light." Bernard is a character who learns to trust his own light. But no conclusion can be drawn as to what Olivier should do, for to his fish story Vincent adds another. Each species of ocean fish subsists only in waters containing certain solutions of salt, varying with the species. They move in layers. When an individual fish moves too far up or too far down, it weakens and becomes easy prey for alien fish. To each, therefore, his own dosage of good and evil. Gide's symbol thus accommodates an inexhaustible number of connected images and themes with many variations.

The reading of the novel itself is something of an adventure, so finely meshed are the wheels which regulate its movement. Wherever possible, Gide used the present tense for his narrative, as he had in *Lafcadio's Adventures,* to emphasize his departure from the traditional "story told in retrospect" that relies on various combinations of past tenses. The narrator's comments along the way are calculated to give the impression that things are actually developing as the novel advances. And yet, somewhat as in a movie, they take place in a different world, submitting to different necessities and rhythms. No single point of view directs the narrative. The narrator, whom one naturally first identifies with the author, starts to tell the story. Almost immediately he turns it over to Bernard and thenceforward the point of view travels back and forth as characters move in and out of the scene. Gide handles these shifts in perspective with great smoothness, relying mainly on a rapid, conversational tone to give the story an easy, uninterrupted flow. But the narration projects light only on the narrow segment of the action that each character perceives. No one, not even the unidentified first narrator himself, sees the complete sweep of circumstance relating to each event.

Bernard runs away from home, steals a suitcase, and by chance gets a job as Edouard's secretary; Vincent wins heavily at roulette, abandons Laure and becomes Lady Griffith's lover; Edouard comes back from London, collects Laure and also Bernard, and promises old La Pérouse to bring his grandson, Boris, back to Paris. Olivier meets Passavant and becomes editor of an avant-garde review. Old La Pérouse resolves to commit suicide on a given day: all this occurs within thirty hours or so between a certain Wednesday afternoon in late June and the following Thursday night. But Bernard uncovers a set of old letters, and reads and so does the reader with him—Edouard's *Journal*—so that along the way the reader acquires a sense of continuity and pattern that the characters lack.

Within the novel paths crisscross unexpectedly. The characters, like balls on a narrow billiard table, bump against each other, deflecting each other, continually diverting each other from their original paths. Bernard's intrusion into Edouard's life is just such an unforeseeable diversion. The successive diversions caused by such impacts seem to scatter the balls at random. But from diversion to diversion they finally bring about the culminating event in the novel, Boris's death.

All the events noted in Edouard's *Journal,* which Bernard discovers, touch upon Laure's wedding nine months previously, and mesh in with the random set of events which take place in June. Laure, pregnant and abandoned by Vincent, calls Edouard back to Paris. He is attracted by Olivier but lets himself be persuaded rather to take Bernard as his secretary. Not knowing what to do with himself, he decides, on the spur of the moment, to go and get Boris in Saas-Fée. On his return his real inner concern reasserts itself, he becomes engrossed in Olivier's concerns.

But, as a rebound of all these movements, young Boris meanwhile has been transferred to the Azaïs school. As he arrives there and the third part of the story begins, all the apparently unrelated threads of the action come together, and all the characters, including Azaïs and Strouvilhou. No single character sees what is taking place, though all have their part in it. Gide's deconcentrated plot has a significance and an invisible line of progression reflects his intent. In the third part of the story all the "diversions" are rapidly dealt with. The only love story that really interested Gide, Edouard and Olivier's, ends happily after the latter's attempted suicide. Bernard, like the prodigal son, is on his way back home, and Laure on her way to her husband, Douviers. Armand has joined the counterfeiters. The Azaïs school is quite prosperous. Frightened by the message Edouard relays from Profitendieu, the schoolboy gang seems to have stopped its profitable dealings in counterfeit coins. La Pérouse and his grandson are reunited. All is for the best in the best of all possible worlds.

The schoolboys' secret society of "strong men" now takes the center of the stage. The first suicide victim, Boris, is picked in a fake drawing of lots. The fast-moving tempo suddenly halts as the whole novel plunges into a nightmarish reality. While all the main characters have been absorbed in their own lives, the novel itself, operating in a large framework comprising these individual lives, has been leading up to this single shocking event. Boris's fate develops in the shadow cast by the errors and blindness of the others. When he steps forward in front of his grandfather's desk into the chalk circle prepared by the gang and raises the pistol to his forehead, suddenly, in retrospect, all the characters and actions in the novel appear trivial and singularly irresponsible. Like Lafcadio's tossing Fleurissoire off the train, Boris's death changes the perspectives on the whole story.

Boris is the victim of the counterfeiters. Edouard, when he learns of Boris's death, waves it aside as too brutal for his novel, with a few righteous remarks on how inopportune it was for the poor Vedel-Azaïs family, just as he had waved aside the false coin Bernard had brought to his attention. But so far as Gide is concerned, the counterfeit coin and the schoolboy suicide are the very substance of his novel, its central inner core. A glance backward over the story reveals all the responsibilities at work in Boris's death. Edouard is easily the most responsible. But had Bernard, to whom Boris is entrusted, been less concerned with himself; had La Pérouse not loaded the pistol; had Profitendieu really done his job; had Azaïs, enamoured with his image of innocent childhood, not emboldened the gang; had the psychiatrist to whom Boris had been entrusted not put Boris's secret into Strouvilhou's hands; had his little friend Bronja not died. . . .

Gide planned his novel so that it might approximate his view of how a great many events come about, *not* through a straight, relatively simple interplay of chance, situation and motivation. An event such as the death of Boris combines innumerable chance factors and, in each, a share of human weakness. Boris's fate is not the consequence of any one set of circumstances. It is made possible by the conjunction of several disparate and random series of activities. All the events in the first part of the novel create a pattern of relationships among the characters. But these are not fixed constellations, each character proceeds along his own path. Edouard's *Journal* is not a Proustian plunge into the past. It is a fictional device which allows Gide to enlarge the temporal dimensions of the novel, so that he can plot trajectories in time, orientations which determine new patterns, and future dispersions. Certainly this is the most original part of *The Counterfeiters* and by far the most arresting.

The novel, which begins at an almost frenzied pace, seems to bog down during Edouard's stay at Saas-Fée, and then to break up at random into a series of secondary plots, connected only by one moral theme—the theme of counterfeit. Only at the very end does Gide's scheme become clear. He wanted his novel to be an "imitation" of an action in the manner of a classical play, revealing all the forces, whether visible or not, which determine an act like Boris's: chance, circumstance, motivation, atmosphere, error working through human contacts, intentions, failures. All the events and characters are seen in relation to that act, so that the whole may realize the "erosion of contours" Gide wanted to obtain.

The Counterfeiters has the free lines, the abstract planes, the multiplication of perspectives, the interplay of form and idea as well as the humor characteristic of the soties. But unlike the soties, Gide's novel treats characters who are not mere pawns, and it has a serious, human significance. *The Counterfeiters* seems to convey something life had disclosed to Gide, who is not Edouard.

The second part of the novel, which takes place in the Alpine Saas-Fée, introduces an interval of repose in the story. But Gide's "infernal machine" is in the background all wound up and set for the dénouements. Meanwhile Edouard, Laure, and Bernard discuss Edouard's novel and Boris's cure with Sophroniska, the psychoanalyst. Strouvilhou passes through leaving behind the counterfeit gold piece Bernard finds in a shop and takes to Edouard. At this point the theme of counterfeit coin brings up a more basic problem, the paradox of its resemblance to real coin. When the action again moves forward, in line with Gidian dialectics, truth has become the main concern, not counterfeit. As always during the interval of repose, Gide clarifies and intellectualizes his theme. Sophroniska deals with the same problems as Profitendieu in his criminal investigation, but in the realm of individual psychology. Boris, with his "Yes-No" answers and his nervous furies, shows clear evidences of deep disorder. Observing the

symptoms, Sophroniska patiently attempts to track down the hidden ill, to dislodge it, and to free Boris from its grip. Edouard suggests, and subsequent events tend to corroborate his opinion, that Boris's trouble, if mercilessly tracked down, will only change its aspect and take root more deeply in less accessible parts of his psyche. In the same way, when Profitendieu shuts up the house where the schoolboy orgies are held, the boys turn to peddling counterfeit money. Warned by Profitendieu that their activities are known to the police, they turn to sadism and organize a kind of "superman club." Unhappily, Sophroniska has prepared a ready victim for them.

Boris suffers terrible feelings of guilt for indulging in what he calls the "magic" which relieves him of his solitude, and which he somehow connects with a certain talisman. Believing that good always triumphs, Sophroniska attempts to circumvent evil by eliminating it. She takes away Boris's talisman, but makes the error of handing it over to Strouvilhou, who in turn gives it to the schoolboys. Newly enrolled at the Azaïs school, Boris joins their gang, wistfully wanting to be accepted as one of the boys, wistfully anxious to harbor no suspicion of evil intent in their advances. And yet he is well aware that all is not as they describe it to him. Boris's enemy lurks in recesses well out of Sophroniska's reach, in the person of Ghéridanisol, who does evil for the sake of evil. Boris, unprepared for battle, is totally defenseless.

Meanwhile, cozy in his own comfortable realm, the literary Edouard toys with the word "pure." He plagiarizes Gide, imagining a novel whose hero, a novelist, writes the story of the genesis of a novel. Its theme is to be the struggle between reality as observed and the novelist's idea of the nature of that reality. Edouard reads two pages of his book—a kind of parody of *Fruits of the Earth*—to Georges, in the hope of influencing him. He fails completely. Edouard is not Gide's spokesman but, like other of the characters, he introduces those variations on Gide's main themes that apply to his particular profession as novelist. Edouard moves to the periphery of the action as events converge toward the central catastrophe. He ends up as a sort of supernumerary. The range of his vision falls short of the requirements of his art. He wants reality to "ring" exclusively according to a "chord" of his own choosing.

Gide's *Counterfeiters* is a novel of adolescence, a novel of orientation which depicts young people emerging from various forms of myth into the reality of life. For the first time Gide's work has really deep social implications. He portrays the struggle of the young to discover through trial and error the genuine forces and limits of their personalities, in the face of obsolete social forms and ethics which tend to impose stereotyped feelings and attitudes upon them. Experience teaches Edouard nothing, since he ignores it, whereas Georges, shaken by Boris's death, alters his disastrous course. For Gide, to live, as to write a novel, is to undergo the test of reality.

By the time he wrote *The Counterfeiters* Gide had left behind him the ironic, critical novel. For his young people the "trial by life" ends with a return to their own social orbit. From error to authenticity, the way is difficult but open. Each separate adventure in the novel, as well as the novel as a whole, converges toward the discovery of the real and the true as opposed to the false. Bernard gets rid of his silly ideas, while Georges discovers what real monsters lurked behind his revolt. Neither devils nor angels, the characters simply become more human: "As for these antinomies," wrote Gide of devils and angels, "I believe them to be all imaginary . . . but the mere fact of living calls them up, creates them." Gide's novel is oriented away from finding antinomies in life. According to him, life does not long put up with counterfeit. It neither deceives nor disappoints. It is we who disappoint and deceive ourselves:

> In this world: real sufferings; imaginary sufferings. The first can be attenuated; the second almost suppressed. They most often result from a belief in *idols*—or in *bogeymen*. The former are constructions that are venerated and do not deserve to be. The latter are phantoms that are feared and do not deserve to be feared.

Gide felt, as did Proust, that the artist is "prompted" by life but that one of the elements given him is an inner orientation and sensitivity to which he must remain faithful; "it is the secret of the depths of his flesh that prompts, inspires and decides," he said of the artist. There is really no possible counterfeit in art; there are only individual limitations, success and failure.

The "given elements" of life on which Gide worked are slight, perhaps, but at least they are authentic. The point of view that molded them into a novel, however, is quite broad in scope and original. Gide succeeded in setting up for his story a form which is complex without being arbitrary. It is highly intellectual, yet permeated with a special poetry, made up of humor, lucidity, and that very mystery which springs from "the depths of the flesh." *The Counterfeiters* has neither the power nor the density of Proust's novel or of Joyce's *Ulysses,* its two great contemporaries. The reader can accept it straightforwardly without ever filling in the empty spaces, re-establishing the perspectives, or being moved to laughter by its implicit humor. It will seem outmoded, slight and artifi-

cial, and its curious transparency irritating, when the boldness of its structural movement goes unnoticed.

In *The Counterfeiters* Gide overcame his difficulties and facilities as a writer. The antiromantic yet poetic stylization of all the elements of the novel, the orchestration of the diverse voices, the lively pace of the story, the concern with permanent human values, the stringency of the language—all contribute to make *The Counterfeiters* an unusual book. To the ordinary pleasures of novel reading it adds, for the sensitive amateur, the "pure" pleasure of aesthetic understanding. No novel ever written was more "literary" and yet more free of literary influences. What Gide really investigated in his novel is what happens to all forms of "literature," in contact with life. It was perhaps the only real adventure that he himself had fully lived, and as a result, *The Counterfeiters* is the only one of his novels which fully expresses him. (pp. 230-50)

> *Germaine Brée, in her* Gide, *Rutgers University Press, 1963, 302 p.*

W. WOLFGANG HOLDHEIM   (essay date 1968)

[*Holdheim is a German-born American critic who specializes in French and comparative literature. In the following excerpt, he assesses Gide's theoretical aims for the structure and themes of* The Counterfeiters *and his success in achieving them.*]

Ever since Gide's "first novel" (as he provocatively calls it in the dedication to Roger Martin du Gard) was published in 1926, the general tendency has been to consider it a failure, albeit a brilliant one. Several *Journal* entries show how the author was bothered by this judgment. His difficulties in writing the book had been extreme. Both the diary and the *Journal des faux-monnayeurs* present a vivid picture of his long and painful effort. It is understandable that Gide attributed the relatively negative reception of his work to its novelty. Above all he saw the cause in his desire for conciseness and economy, which demands the active collaboration of the reader. He bitterly reflects, for example, that he could much more easily have flattered the public's laziness by following accepted patterns. Sometimes he almost regrets that he did not do so, but then he persuades himself that he has written for the future: "Avant vingt ans l'on reconnaîtra que ce que l'on reproche à mon livre, ce sont précisément ses qualités" ["In twenty years, it will be recognized that what is criticized in my book now are precisely its merits"]. Thus writes Gide in 1927, yet forty years later the general judgment has not significantly changed. What is the cause of the persistent uneasiness of readers and critics in front of Gide's ambitious enterprise? Has he correctly diagnosed the nature of this reaction? An answer to this question would go far toward illuminating the problems of the work.

Perhaps we can gain a clue by describing the novel's atmosphere, by clarifying the general impression which it makes upon the reader. One is immediately struck by the complexity of the texture. This novel seems truly a *summa* of Gidean themes, ideas and experiences. Characters like the old piano teacher La Pérouse, the minister Vedel and the cynical Armand are familiar to readers of *Si le grain ne meurt . . .*, and the cruelty of the schoolboy Ghéridanisol to Boris is reminiscent of little Gide's persecution by the bully Gomez in the lycée in Montpellier. A host of such autobiographical facts could be enumerated. However, transposed as they are into the context of the novel, they are often transformed to the point of unrecognizability. The same holds true for the ideas,

Gide about the time he wrote The Counterfeiters.

which Gide, emulating Dostoevsky, has deliberately relativized in function of his characters. Thus the notion that ideas live at the expense of men, in the **Prométhée** a universal statement of human self-transcendence, here becomes a mere expression of Edouard's intellectualism. Gide's critique of symbolist aesthetics is almost literally repeated by the literary opportunist Passavant in a conversation with young Olivier, but in his mouth it becomes a somewhat obscene attempt at seduction. Other well-known notions, such as the condemnation of fake psychological consistency and the Nietzschean morality of the strong, are taken over but subverted by the diabolical Strouvilhou in a conspiratorial meeting with Passavant (an echo, incidentally, of Pyotr's dialogue with Karmazinov in *The Possessed,* for literary reminiscences as well are legion in Gide's novel). We also have a complete integration of old-established "conceptional" themes into the narrative texture of the work. One example is the "gratuitous act." In the *soties* it had already developed from a philosophical problem (**Paludes**) via a narratively presented metaphysical hypothesis (**Prométhée**) into a narratively enacted human deed (**Caves**). **Les faux-monnayeurs** completes this progressive "novelization": only upon reflection can the suicide of little Boris, tragic but after all quite credible, be identified as a successor of Zeus' divine spontaneity. Here again examples could be multiplied. All in all, Gide vies with Dostoevsky in living "dispersed in his heroes." He has followed the tenets of novelistic self-expression, his experiences have grown into a world.

Let us note, however, that this world remains basically quite traditional. Most of the procedures which Gide uses to loosen up the structure were not unknown to previous novelists, who merely applied them more discreetly. In the last analysis we still have a coherent story, easy enough to follow, built around the conventional nuclei of character and plot. Though experimental, the **Faux-monnayeurs** is much less so (and makes far less strenuous demands on the reader) than other novels which appeared at the same time and since. This is undoubtedly one reason why those contemporary critics who gravitate around the "new novel" are downright anxious to minimize Gide's importance as a precursor—an unjust treatment which they accord neither Joyce nor Proust.

We can no longer say, then, that it is chiefly the difficulty of Gide's work which has kept it from being properly appreciated. Indeed in a way we can almost turn the statement upside down: instead of unduly straining the reader, the book does not strain him enough. Does he not often feel as if he were drifting along with a story that flows on without encountering resistance? Events, themes and ideas pop up and vanish in a confusing merry-go-round of change. The trouble is that they leave no traces: this kaleidoscopic flux has something irremediably inconsequential. The reader has nothing to hold on to, he is faced with an elusive substance that slips through his fingers like sand. The result is a sense of irritating disorientation, the kind we would experience in empty space. In a sense the critic finds no solid point of departure for his interpretation, no major problem into which he could set his teeth.

This, however, is only half the story. The autocritical elements in the book, which we have hitherto ignored, do offer substantial food for interpretation. Yet their very existence is an additional cause for the widespread doubts concerning the value of the novel, especially in the eyes of those critics who are committed to the ideal of realistic persuasiveness. Claude-Edmonde Magny, for example, views the intervening

author as a "non-novelistic" carry-over from the *soties*. Let us note that Gide's novel actually goes further than his *soties*. We have much more than an intervening author, the critical component grows into full-fledged technical and theoretical considerations, especially in Edouard's diary and in his discussions in Saas-Fée. This is all the more astonishing in view of Gide's pointed efforts to integrate ideas into the course of the narrative. On this one point he does not appear to have succeeded, and the lengthy disquisitions on theory seem to stand within the novel in weighty self-sufficiency, unassimilable and superimposed. This creates an additional feeling of disorientation which has been well expressed by Albert J. Guerard. He argues that we really have two manners that appeal to two different types of reader. Basically and to the general reader, **Les faux-monnayeurs** is a good and swiftly moving novel of adventure. As for the technical component, centering on Edouard, it is largely supererogatory and of importance only for critics who want to write essays on André Gide. Naturally this view is far too radical. It reflects the inveterate conviction of many Anglo-Saxon critics that the story is the *alpha* and *omega* of a novel, and that intellectuality is either German or otherwise suspicious. We should admit that a simple adventure story would have been anticlimactic after Gide's *soties!* Yet Guerard's clear distinction does seem to have a basis in Gide's book. The relative orthodoxy of the story imposes a more or less traditional perspective which is then irritatingly upset by the theoretical substance.

The reader's uneasiness thus appears to have a dual cause: disorientation in the midst of an unseizably Protean atmosphere, and further disorientation through the unexpected juxtaposition of the novel and its critique. These are guidelines to be kept in mind for closer examination. (pp. 235-37)

As we know, it was the advice of Martin du Gard which made Gide adopt the traditional solution of running various plots into one, after a long struggle with the problem. Let us see how he nevertheless tries to maintain deconcentration in the midst of centrality, in order to accord the demands of art and life.

There are various nuclei of plot structure (individuals or groups, often family units) that are progressively welded into one huge ensemble of social interaction. There is the Azaïs-Vedel group, which consists of the old Protestant minister Azaïs, his daughter and her husband Vedel and their children Laura Douviers (née Vedel), Rachel, Sarah and Armand. There are the families of the two magistrates: Molinier with his wife and three sons Vincent, Olivier and Georges; Profitendieu and his wife and sons, the most important of whom is the illegitimate Bernard. The chief individuals are the novelist Edouard, the fashionable author Passavant (inspirer of an avant-garde literary circle), Strouvilhou (the leader of a gang of counterfeiters) and old La Pérouse. The developing story creates an increasingly intricate system of ramifications, too complex to be reported here in detail but important enough to be sketched in some of its outlines. Vincent, the oldest Molinier son, becomes the lover of Laura Douviers but forsakes her when she expects a child. Anxious at first to find money for an abortion, Vincent falls into the hands of Passavant who takes him to a gambling house and finally delivers him to the amoral Lady Griffith. Passavant is merely interested in Vincent's younger brother Olivier, with whom Edouard as well has fallen in love, so that the two are rivals *in eroticis* as well as in literature. There is of course a professional relation between the two magistrates. In fact it goes further than

Molinier suspects, for Profitendieu, who is on the track of Strouvilhou's gang that uses children to float counterfeit coins, discovers that his colleague's youngest son Georges is involved. As for Bernard Profitendieu, he flees from home and turns to his schoolmate Olivier for lodging. Having heard about Edouard, who happens to be Olivier's uncle, Bernard seeks the author's acquaintance and becomes his secretary. All that remains is to weave in Edouard's old piano teacher La Pérouse. He has a grandson who lives in Poland with his widowed mother by whom he is neglected. The lonely old man longs to see little Boris. Upon his request Edouard goes to Saas-Fée, where Boris is staying with a woman psychoanalyst (Dr. Sophroniska). He takes along Bernard and also his old friend Laura, who is still smarting from her abandonment by Vincent. Later in Paris, events continue to evolve and intertwine. Olivier leaves Passavant (with whom he had spent the vacation) and finally finds his way to Edouard. Many of the others are united at the Azaïs-Vedel school for boys: Bernard as a tutor (and as Sarah Vedel's lover); La Pérouse as a supervisor; little Boris (whom Edouard had brought from Switzerland) as a pupil. Even Passavant's younger brother Gontran is an intern there. So is Georges Molinier, who is friendly with a certain Ghéridanisol, Strouvilhou's cousin and tool. These two, evil and sadistic, prevail upon Boris to show his mettle by shooting himself in class before his grandfather's eyes.

This brief account suffices to show the melodramatically strained character of systematic assimilation. If there is confusion, it is caused (as in Dostoevsky's *Raw Youth*) by overcomplexity rather than lifelike openness, by an exaggerated integration of events, intrigues and coincidences. Nowhere is it clearer that coincidence is necessity posing as contingency. The waiter, that universal creator of ramifications, has really been working full-time here. And yet this novel has special pretensions to openness which one major difference from the *Prométhée* can illustrate. The story of the *sotie* is more obviously closed because it has a definite (indeed an absolute) beginning. Zeus' act initiates the relations which the waiter then develops. *Les faux-monnayeurs* as well starts out from anterior relations, but these are not created all at once, not given from the transcendent (extratemporal) perspective that sees absolute beginnings: they are presented from the immanent point of view of the unfolding story and go back to various periods. In other words, the story appears as an evolving present that is *open to the past*. I have already alluded to some of the anterior ramifications, many of which are centered on Edouard. La Pérouse is his former music teacher. The writer is also Mme. Molinier's half-brother and therefore the uncle of Georges, whom he nevertheless does not know and meets by chance. Moreover, Edouard used to be intimate with Laura, the mistress of his other nephew Vincent (who has, however, met her by chance, in a sanatorium). In fact Laura had only married Douviers because her real love Edouard had proved averse to marriage. This had happened when the author lived with the Azaïs-Vedel family, who also used to run a boarding house. That house is truly a universal meeting place! Thus the mysterious Strouvilhou had boarded there as well, albeit at yet another period, and Mme. Molinier had sent all her boys to the Azaïs school. We see the paradoxical result, and hence the questionable character, of this "openness to the past": effectively it still enhances the global domination of the plot. Pretending to loosen up the system, the flashbacks add to its disorienting complication. The web of multiple ramifications becomes so inescapably all-embracing that it reminds one of the parodistic practices of the *Caves*.

An even more essential requirement of the vitalistic novel is its *openness to the future*. Gide goes to great lengths to ensure that his work should "s'éparpiller, se défaire" ["disperse, become loose"]. The universal gathering chez Vedel disperses after the catastrophe. Bernard returns to his stepfather and becomes a journalist. The destinies of the characters are like threads which, having been temporarily intertwined, separate again and remain hanging in the air—to be continued. Armand Vedel is perhaps seriously ill, but we do not find out for certain. Strouvilhou may be caught, but here again we can only speculate. "Je suis bien curieux de connaître Caloub" ["I am very curious to know Caloub"] says Edouard at the very end, referring to a minor character who had played virtually no role before and thus pointing toward an unknown future. More such examples could be given. They all have one thing in common: they are conscientiously and ingeniously contrived.

Contrived: here lies the key to the impression of artificiality which clings to the whole process of "becoming" as it is reproduced in the novel of André Gide. Time is a flowing present, inherently deconcentrated; it has no beginning and no end. Man, the temporal being, is engaged in a creative structurization of chaos that is perpetually incomplete. Gide pretends to give us such a "slice of time" cut out (no: briefly lit up) in the confused welter of becoming, organizing it partly in the process. But what he actually does is the reverse. His point of departure is form, not chaos—spatial concentration and not temporal dispersion. His "evolving present" is really nothing else than the systematically unfolding plot. It does not truly move from infinity to infinity, from an open past to an unknown future: it just tries to suggest such movement by cleverly loosening up at both ends. Instead of an active structurization of chaos we have a mimetic "chaotization" of structure; instead of an irremediably incomplete formalization there is a finished system that strives to create the impression of temporal non-completeness. This would-be decentralization is itself purely formal. The flux of time has as it were been reduced to its external structure. Assiduously the formalizing consciousness goes through all the motions of change, reproducing its mechanism but failing to grasp its creative quality. What Gide's novel presents is the abstract pattern, the architecture of duration.

The *soties* showed a growing prevalence of movement accompanied by a softening of the system. *Les faux-monnayeurs* clearly represents the final step. From the implied immobility of movement (in *Paludes*) we have progressed to a full-fledged mobilization of structure. Even in *Les caves du Vatican*, dynamism remains structurally external to the systems (which are all tributaries of the overall aesthetic configuration). As a movement *between* systems that reveals their hollowness, it remains a gauge applied from the outside: the "cellars" remain circularly closed and formally autonomous. In the *Faux-monnayeurs*, the circle itself paradoxically tries to break its formal intactness. Dynamism becomes inherent in the structure qua structure, the system as such begins to move. The weakening of form has become a specifically *formal* enterprise, a systematic "ironization" which poses as an image of time.

Protos' imitation of becoming is still without structural sophistication. It concentrates exclusively on the obvious element of changeability, which it parodistically presents as interchangeability and disguise. The detailed mimesis of temporal architecture in *Les faux-monnayeurs*, on the other hand, seems designed to be taken seriously and is in principle much more credible—and yet one is not entirely convinced. We are no longer subjected to the deliberately antirealistic levitation of the *saugrenu* ["absurd"], which finds only a remote successor in the somewhat picaresque tone of the narration in part I. Nevertheless, there remains an overall sense of levity—more subtle than in the *Caves,* less palpable but fully as pervasive. Its prime cause is precisely the ironic mobilization of structure, the intellectual travesty of time. This, more than anything, is what creates the impression of disorienting insubstantiality which I described. Everything moves, but somehow its movement is thinly theoretical. Has the author sought realistic credibility without succeeding? Determined as he was to dissolve the fake solidity of the literary universe, it seems that he has treated it with the wrong solvent, so that the result has been intellectual dilution. Something about the novel's atmosphere, about the whole aura in which it bathes, strikes us as fundamentally *false.* (pp. 237-41)

To begin with, I must emphasize a striking parallel that has not been sufficiently noticed: *"Falschmünzer,"* the exact German equivalent of *"faux-monnayeurs,"* was Friedrich Nietzsche's chief polemical term in his exposure of moral and psychological mendacity, a favored weapon in the arsenal of his struggle against "idealism." It appears throughout his work in many contexts. Thus Carlyle, "jener grosse Falschmünzer wider Wissen und Willen" ["one of the great counterfeiters against his knowledge and will"], is held responsible for our infatuation with emptily grand gestures and heroic attitudes. The priests are pious forgers and notably Paul (who perverted Jesus' teaching) was a "Falschmünzer aus Hass" ["counterfeiter out of hatred"]. The philosophers are " 'unbewusste' Falschmünzer" [" 'involuntary' counterfeiters"] and Nietzsche, the first truthful thinker, sits in judgment over four millennia of forgery. As for the poets and artists, who should interest us particularly, they have deformed our view of reality—but "die Zeit der harmlosen Falschmünzerei ist zu Ende" ["the time of innocent counterfeiting is at an end"]. The unmasking of beautiful feelings and grand ideas is also a typically Gidean activity, although Gide's version has of course neither Nietzsche's scope nor Nietzsche's violence. The correspondence in terminology is highly significant, whether it indicates a downright influence or "only" a profound affinity. Most important, the Gidean theme refers to the same series of closely interconnected phenomena as Nietzsche's *mot de guerre:* make-believe, the refusal to face reality, and a subversion of true values.

In the universe of Gide's novel, falsification is so all-pervasive that there is virtually no particle of the book which is not somehow a variation on the theme. No character is immune from the virus of inauthenticity, which lurks even in the extreme situations of misery or death. Thus old La Pérouse desecrates and perverts his unhappiness by casting himself in theatrical attitudes (reminiscent of those of the old Saint-Auréol couple in *Isabelle*). His projected suicide is a pose, and his revolver becomes a veritable symbol of falsity. Doubly so, in fact: not only does it stand for La Pérouse's abortive act, it also serves for Boris' suicide which (conversely) is real but engineered under false pretenses—Ghéridanisol had led his associates to believe that it was unloaded. Boris himself is counterfeit to the core. His nervous disorders, connected with onanism (the substitution of imaginary satisfactions for real ones), result in a tendency toward mystification and mythomania. Gide makes even psychoanalysis serve his purposes: neurosis is a refusal to face reality, free association a

way to bring out the "truth"—a possibility in which Dr. Sophroniska believes just as naïvely as the minister Azaïs. True, Boris kills himself willingly since he apparently never doubts the gun is loaded—but is this desperate act his moment of truth or a final escape? As for Armand Vedel, his cynicism does not make him any less a counterfeiter, in fact it is a pose adopted in revolt against his moralistic environment. And he deliberately turns his back on reality when he declines to consult a doctor about a disquieting tumor in his mouth.

The falsity of individuals, like Armand's cynicism, is usually in some way related to their surroundings. Indeed we are particularly struck by the counterfeiting activities of social groups. There is first of all Gide's old *bête noire,* the bourgeois family. The Profitendieus, "pillars of society" in the sense of Ibsen, think that the skeleton in their closet (Bernard's illegitimacy) has ceased to exist because it is hidden. The Moliniers live in an even more complicated maze of mendacity: the husband has a mistress whom he hides from his wife, and the latter knows it but conceals her knowledge from her husband. Social corruption already affects the children and adolescents. When they gather in a group, the lycéens cease to be natural, and Bernard and Olivier dare not show their friendship. The children have fabricated personalities, they lie, brag and cheat—and Georges and his little friends literally turn the truth upside down when they found a "society of strong men." But the atmosphere is downright suffocating in the Azaïs-Vedel milieu, that geographical center of falsification through which all characters seem (symbolically) to have passed. Social perversion is here intensified by an oppressive Huguenot piety. Vedel, perpetually busy so he need not face himself, leaves all financial burdens to his daughter Rachel and merely supports her with his prayers. As for the tyrannical yet gullible Azaïs, he insists on complete "sincerity" in human relations but demands at the same time that the "truth" should conform to his austere moralistic preconceptions. (This makes him a counterpart of Michel in *L'immoraliste,* who believes with equal cecity that truthfulness is equivalent to evil). What wonder that Azaïs' school is one of hypocrisy where already the children learn to dissemble!

Though the symbol and the method are Nietzschean, the overall perspective has a distinctly Rousseauistic slant. Azaïs believes in a direct and unhampered communication between men, in a "transparency" without "obstacles" (to use Starobinski's terms). But man is alienated from his true being and lives in a world of appearances that is a function of social togetherness. Some of the modalities of social perversion are clearly exposed in *Les faux-monnayeurs.* Why, for example, have Georges and his friends set up their group? For the sole purpose of excluding Boris. The children have here discovered one of the basic principles of social association—Proust's analyses lead to the same result. The dynamics of social existence are negative, the members of a group derive their value from the sole fact that they are *not* outsiders. This essential negativity and indirection is well understood by the master coiner Strouvilhou. "La société des faux-monnayeurs . . . n'admet que des gens *compromis*" ["The society of counterfeiters . . . only admits compromised people"] we read in the *Journal des faux-monnayeurs* of 25 July 1919. "Il faut que chacun des membres apporte en otage de quoi pouvoir le faire chanter." ["It is necessary that each of the members supplies as a hostage something with which he can be blackmailed."] And the children in Strouvilhou's gang bring him letters and other documents that could be used against their families. The system which they thus enable him to establish reflects the fundamental structure of social cohesion. (Already Protos had insisted on the social usefulness of blackmail). In the horizontal realm of interrelations, vital commitment is corrupted into universal "compromise." Instead of transparent communication we have a web of negative interdependence founded on concealment, a complete reversal of all true values. Such a "transvaluation" appears, in yet another context, from Profitendieu's and Molinier's attitude toward their sons. Surely their conviction that their children must be free from evil instincts is the acme of social falsification, a fact that is underlined when Molinier sees in Bernard's escapades a natural result of his illegitimate birth. In a ludicrous bourgeois emulation of extinct aristocratic beliefs, social status is confused with innate value, convention with nature—another instance of the anti-epic (and anti-lyrical) assimilation of nature by sociality which has been demonstrated à propos of the landscape of Saas-Fée.

Social forgery also affects and perverts literary life. Passavant is the very type of the mundane literary coiner who floats second-hand witticisms in drawing rooms. In his works and in his literary magazine he is always anxious to reflect the latest fads. He is in every respect an exponent of *fashion*. The fact has more importance than a hasty look might reveal. For what is fashion? An image of change—which it translates, however, into an empty succession of prejudices. Social counterfeiting here takes a particularly insidious form, it becomes a corrupt imitation of temporal movement: fashion is a "socialization" of time itself. In a nutshell, it expresses the role of counterfeiting in the entire *Faux-monnayeurs*. Falsification is this world's principle of movement, the mainspring of a universal dynamism based on appearance and make-believe. Appropriately it is Strouvilhou who finds the perfect definition of this theme in Gresham's law: "la mauvaise monnaie chasse la bonne" ["the bad coins drive away the good"]. There rises the image of inflation, which is nothing else than false (devaluative) growth—a perpetually active substitution of the false for the genuine, a qualitatively degraded version of "becoming."

The novelistic enterprise seems a failure. Its ideal task was to "conquer" sociality, to render it meaningful in terms of development in time. Instead we are faced with a social corruption of the novel's entire substance and with a deterioration of temporality itself. This is why already the *Caves,* as a contrast, revived the image of lyrical authenticity. However, there is a counterweight in the *Faux-monnayeurs* as well: the story of Bernard's growth toward the maturity of voluntary commitment. Is not this after all the triumph of an authenticity that is temporal, social, novelistic? So it seems, and this is probably what Gide meant it to be. But we cannot help remaining unconvinced by Bernard's somewhat schematic maturing, which is very much a deliberate demonstration employing the consecrated formulae of the *Erziehungsroman*. Besides, Georg Lukács has brilliantly shown the problematical nature of the post-Goethean *Erziehungsroman*. Often it merges with the romantic novel of disillusionment. But when it does not, when the reconciliation between self and world is not a defeat but a freely accepted resignation, the experience remains purely private and has no validity for anyone but the hero. Bernard is not more than such a radically relativized hero, at his very best.

Strouvilhou is among others a veritable philosopher of literary fashion. But there is also a specifically aesthetic type of forgery which goes beyond his competence. This is the "harmless counterfeiting," the whole complex of novelistic elaboration and artistic consciousness which the preceding section has analyzed in detail. The line of forgery runs from Bernard's false coin via the contortions of social behavior to the novelist's "creative" enterprise. The opposition between Passavant the socially unauthentic author and Edouard the aesthetically authentic one is relative: in a deeper sense, it is precisely the genuine artist's procedure that is profoundly unauthentic. The ensemble of social and criminal falsification points to its genius and inspirer, Strouvilhou. The aesthetic prejudgments of Edouard and the make-believe of *je* ["I"] point to the Author, who is also the supreme Coiner. But the two are essentially homogeneous. The implied condemnation of social falsity goes hand in hand with the self-exposure of the work of art. As in the *soties,* the critique of existential attitudes is connected with (and as it were sifted through) the autocritique of the novel. What we have, in effect, is a negativization of the pre-established harmony between the social and the aesthetic which we found in the traditional realistic novel. There, the eidetic horizontality of the social system was completed and harmonized by the spatial balance of artistic form. Here this *positive* correspondence in terms of structure is supplemented and superseded by a *negative* one in terms of creation and movement. In *Les faux-monnayeurs,* the process of artistic forgery corresponds to, refines upon and intensifies the fake dynamics of social life, thus exposing the tainted nature of reality. Gresham's law applies to the literary nature of the work as much as to its specific content. The novel itself is an inflationary triumph of mere paper which displaces the true values by the false, reality by illusion—propelled by an ironic travesty of time.

Does Gide's work have any universal significance or is it a mere personal whim? And—a related question—is it "novelistic" at all or is it still a belated *sotie,* as "realistic" critics tend to think? Even a brief look at literary history suggests that it is both universal and novelistic. The *mise en question* of the novel's world by a self-conscious author is surely more than the coquettish pose of a 20th-century raffiné. Beyond 19th-century trends connected with German romanticism, beyond 18th-century writers like Fielding and Sterne, it points back to the *Don Quixote,* that first and most exemplary of modern novels. Nor is it new that the autocritique of the novel parallels and implies a critique of reality. "A l'affirmation une et arbitraire de l'*être* de ses personnages" ["For the single and arbitrary affirmation of the *existence* of his characters"], wrote Benjamin Crémieux shortly after the publication of Gide's novel, "André Gide préfère une profusion de *'paraîtres'*. C'est là sans doute la nouveauté essentielle de son roman, celle qui ouvre le plus de routes et de possibilités." ["André Gide prefers a profusion of 'seemings.' That is without a doubt where the essential newness of his novel lies, that which opens the most routes and possibilities."] Undoubtedly, but this "novelty" also reactivates the past, for the problem of being and appearing is at the very core of the original inspiration of the genre. Let us again think of Cervantes' work! Viewed in this wider perspective, *Les faux-monnayeurs* appears as nothing less than a reconquest, laboriously prepared by the *soties,* of the sources of the Western novel—after the realistic interlude. One must wear realistic blinkers to doubt its novelistic character! The notion that the novel reflects a reality that is somehow tainted runs through many modern theories of the novel. This corruption is defined in various ways on which we cannot expatiate here, but there are recurrent themes which often strikingly apply to *Les faux-monnayeurs* and already to the *Caves:* the question of truth in an equivocal reality, the prevalence of appearance and illusion, the impossibility of genuine communication between men. As for Georg Lukács' still exemplary considerations in *Die Theorie des Romans,* they sometimes read as if they had been written with Gide's work in mind, long before its appearance. The novel deals with a problematical hero in quest of (or in any case vitally concerned with) authenticity in a problematical world. Here we have Gide's central theme and his chief hero! Counterfeiting is not just any subject, it is *the* Subject of the novel: Gide has in a sense written the Novel *par excellence.* As for the problematical hero, menaced in his authenticity and unsure of his being, more even than in Bernard we recognize him in the Gidean Novelist—so strangely absent in his very omnipresence, so ubiquitously active in his very absence. And here lies the specifically contemporary element of *Les faux-monnayeurs.* It is traditional that a crisis of life should be reflected by the ironic self-examination of art, especially of the novel, that "epic" or "anti-epic" of modernity. It remained for our era to pose the question of art and life with a sharpness and a radicalism which had never been attained before. Gide's novel has pushed this tradition to its conclusion: the absorption of the existential critique by the literary auto-critique in the person of the hero. The trend could be traced in its historical development—for example, in the growing scope and importance of the *Künstlerroman,* down to *Felix Krull* and *Les caves du Vatican.* In the *Faux-monnayeurs* at last, the self-conscious novelist in his different incarnations or disincarnations (is not this in itself an image of fragmentation?) coincides with the problematical individual in quest of being, the Author as such becomes the prototype of modern Man.

In this schema of the novel's tradition, what is the place of those works (usually 19th-century) which are not pseudo-mimetic but "truly" mimetic, which do not strive for irony but for narrative persuasiveness? The question has been touched upon before: the realistic interlude reflects an attempt to take both the novel and reality for granted. If the author dogmatically affirms the being of his characters, it is in the hope of escaping from their equivocality. The desired unambiguity of the world is projected into the univocality of form and vision. Let us be precise: the depicted reality can be (and usually is) still problematical in content; however, this remains a surface phenomenon, since reality is tamed by form, knowable and describable "as it is." This *anti-problematical* enterprise is one way of dealing with the existential data of the genre.

This account, historically satisfactory, seems to create problems when considered from a theoretical point of view. For does not the source of the novelistic inspiration, and the concomitant importance of the ironic novel, suggest that irony is essentially connected with the genre? Realistic critics tend to dismiss it as "non-novelistic"; are we forced into the opposite extreme of denying novelistic status to narrative seriousness, thus removing the realistic interlude from the mainstream of the novel's development? We need not do so, for there is no such thing as non-ironic imitation. However "serious," it is never the thing itself but is built upon a split between a hidden and a manifest content, thus exemplifying the very structure of irony. We said that irony is essentially mimetic. Conversely, all mimesis is essentially ironic, every actor is to some degree the actor of Diderot. Realistic credibility is simply a state of affairs where the hiatus between the

imitator and the imitated is almost unnoticeable, where illusion and reality pretend and seem to coincide. What then is the nature of "narrative seriousness"? It may reflect a mimetic activity that is naïvely unconscious of its ironic structure. On the other hand, it may represent the subtlest form of ironic self-awareness: does not the subtlety of irony grow with its decrease in obviousness? Not-yet-consciousness can here no longer be distinguished from overconsciousness, extreme naïveté merges with extreme finesse.

Two important principles, then, emerge from these considerations: the ironic structure of imitation and the coincidence of awareness and naïveté. They permit us to give the finishing touch to this entire analysis, for they furnish the theoretical key to the two crucial questions on which it ultimately hinges: that of the transition from simple narration to critical consciousness in the *Faux-monnayeurs* and that of the homogeneity of novel and *sotie.* To his interlocutors Protos may be indistinguishable from an Italian peasant or abbé, but the reader is never even supposed to be fooled by his (or anyone's) performance. The manifest content in the *Caves* never strives to obscure the hidden one, the stylization always shines through the "true little fact." *Les faux-monnayeurs* has moved considerably closer to realistic persuasiveness. All in all, stylization (be it of names, be it of situations) is not more evident than in the work of Dickens or Balzac. True, there is the overall aura of falsity, but it is often almost unseizably subtle—just strong enough to make us suspicious (and if that suspicion turns against Gide's mimetic capacities and not against imitation as such, this is in itself a victory of the naïve perspective to which the parodistic obviousness of the *Caves* cannot give rise). In its most simply narrative passages, Gide's work invites credibility like any 19th-century novel. Compared to the *Caves,* the *Faux-monnayeurs* is here no longer a parody of the novel but a pastiche. And therefore very much the thing itself, since there is no essential difference between a "true novel" (even conceived in narrowly realistic terms) and a pastiche. A speaking imitation of an imitation, a "pastiche" is ontologically homogeneous with its model. What the term stresses is merely the element of consciousness, the ironic self-awareness of naïveté. The parody is nothing but a pastiche that is more evident, the pastiche a parody that is less so, to the point where it is "genuine" (which means: not any falser than what it imitates). The road from the obvious to the hidden, from pseudo-mimesis to mimesis is gradual. The transition from the *Caves* to the *Faux-monnayeurs,* from the *sotie* to the novel is merely one of degree.

Yet falsity cannot be ignored. One cannot isolate the simple narrative parts except provisionally, for purposes of logical definition and analysis. Their very juxtaposition with the critical and theoretical components suffices to undermine their realistic credibility. But is it really a juxtaposition of contrasting elements? Only if we take credible narration at face value. Then, of course, we will have to agree with those critics who can conceive of no osmosis of elements that are different in kind. The principle of the intellectual structure of mimesis, however, reveals that there is no such heterogeneity, thus enabling us to confirm the results of the preceding section from another angle. It explains how from serious narration to the autocritique and theory of the novel there can be one truly homogeneous chain of gradation, a line of increasing abstraction which marks a continual growth of self-awareness. And here the supplementary principle comes in, that of the coincidence of awareness and naïveté. It is a final commentary on the "pantheistic" assimilation of the novelistic world by the Author's consciousness. What is "serious narration" in the *Faux-monnayeurs*—is it true simplicity or intellectuality at its most intense, the ignorance or the hyperconsciousness of ironic structure, the base of the system or its top? The answer can hardly be doubtful. The chain from "naïvely" conventional practice to theory is continued and retraced by that other one which ranges from theory via hypothesis to ironic practice, and the end is identical with the beginning. Gide's novel is truly his great synthesis. It bears within itself, after all, and accords the two "contrary" movements of gradation, one of which had been previously identified with the *Journal des faux-monnayeurs* alone. Again we have a line that curls into a circle. It is a circle of irony, a circus of intellectuality, the very quintessence of a literary universe. The system of gradation is a huge "song of degrees" where everything emanates from and flows back to an Author diluted into creative transcendentality. It is a universal chain of Non-Being. (pp. 254-62)

The interpretation of *Les faux-monnayeurs* brings us to the conclusion of this analysis. Gide's ambitious work stands at the end of a line that runs through the *soties,* at the point of scission between art and life and at the intersection of novelistic theory and practice, and somehow it unites the author's various aesthetic doctrines. It is truly "un carrefour—un rendez-vous de problèmes" ["a crossroads—a rendezvous of problems"], a huge synthesis of Gidean concerns and endeavors under the aegis of irony. This could be demonstrated at great length. One might examine in detail, for example, just how this novel deals with each and every one of the specific theoretical and technical problems which arouse during the investigation of part I. But we would be led *ad infinitum* if we were to tie up all loose ends. Suffice it to reiterate that *Les faux-monnayeurs* really does effect a kind of paradoxical fusion between the vitalistic ideal and the artistic one. Does it not succeed in combining theistic with pantheistic patterns, Zeus with Protos? The Author is a "central hero" who is both universal and multifariously particularized, at the same time diffused through his whole world and almost absent through his lack of "being" Similarly, falsification is in a sense both "all subjects" and "no subject": all subjects because of its unlimited pervasiveness, and because it is the novelistic Subject *par excellence;* no subject because it is by definition that which pretends to be but is not, negativity in its visible form. Ironic negativity, in fact, is the key to this fusion of contraries. Vitalistically, it is a characteristic that betokens imperfection, but in idealistic terms it can be considered the acme of perfection, the purity of Non-Being which is also that of the Idea. Seen in this light, Gide's work actually satisfies the contrary demands of totality and purity, of vitalization and ascesis. Does not its "everything" come down to nothing? In a self-negating movement that is an ironic radicalization of "critical art," the "total novel" turns on its own essence, as it were canceling itself and thus tending toward the inexorable purity of the white page.

Much has been made of the shifting relationship (through the *soties* and the novel) between the system and movement, the circle and the line, enclosure and the dynamic *saugrenu* ["absurd"]. The importance of these dialectics can indeed hardly be exaggerated. We know that the poles which here seem to struggle to get together stand for spatiality and temporality, form and life, the artistic and the vitalistic ideal. But we can go beyond the immediate Gidean context and relate them to the basic movements of 19th-century philosophy: on the one hand the gigantic effort to fix the whole of reality in an idealistic system, on the other the existential revolt against the systematic spirit. In its own way, the Gidean enterprise reflects and enacts the crucial problem of modern thought, the archetypal opposition between Hegel and Kierkegaard. This association is capable of lengthy and fruitful developments. Let us here only repeat that the dynamic pole, in Gide, is always "falsified." It is clearly a successor to the ironic procedures of the German romanticists. But the romantic artist was a God. He could believe that his imaginative license equals the workings of nature and is an essential expression of the flux of things. Not so Gide, for whom the chasm between *Geist* and life has become unbridgeable, for whom "artist" has become a more restrictive term. *Geist,* contracted into intellectuality, can no longer offer more than a counterfeit resemblance of "becoming." The ironist is but a negative image of the vitalist; Protos is not really Proteus, he is Proteus aped by the actor of Diderot. And the Gidean interaction between structure and movement is nothing but an interplay between the systematizing and the mimetic forms of mind. Propelled by a demand for anti-intellectualistic authenticity, Gide's works nevertheless remain irremediably caught in the closed sphere of intellection. (pp. 263-64)

> *W. Wolfgang Holdheim, in his* Theory and Practice of the Novel: A Study on André Gide, *Librairie Droz, 1968, 269 p.*

DAVID HABERSTICH   (essay date 1969)

[*In the following excerpt, Haberstich shows how* The Counterfeiters *illustrates Gide's relationship to the movements of Cubism, Surrealism, and Dadaism.*]

André Gide was not a symbolist, nor a dadaist, nor a surrealist. He was a relativist and an eclectic moralist who borrowed freely from philosophies, artistic and literary styles, the external world of factual-historical events (whether personally experienced or culled from published documentation), and from imagination—as any novelist must—in order to construct his *Weltanschauung* and the themes and plots of his novels. The climax of Gide's creative evolution may be the complex and controversial *Les faux-monnayeurs,* which appeared in 1925 and is considered his masterpiece by many critics. Gide pronounced the work his "first novel" and published his self-conscious *Journal of "The Counterfeiters"* in order to illuminate his creative struggles over the book. He had recorded in this special journal his shifting attitudes and the aesthetic problems which he encountered during the writing of the novel from 1919 to 1925, and he offered the account to the public as freely and deliberately as the source material from which significant themes and incidents were drawn for the novel.

The themes of the novel are: (1) that we face a dichotomy of the counterfeit versus the genuine, in terms of both tangibles (e.g., currency) and intangibles (e.g., emotion, personality, values, subjective reality); (2) that the attainment of the good and full life is dependent upon vigorous intellectual and moral exercise; and (3) that one must be true to himself and follow his own peculiar star, no matter what the consequences may be. The *subject* of the novel is "the rivalry between the real world and the representation of it which we make to ourselves." This is the subject of the novel entitled *The Counterfeiters* being written by Gide's character Edouard, and we may safely assume that he is speaking for his creator. Edouard struggles with the problem of writing the "pure" novel, as Gide himself was struggling to make *Les faux-monnayeurs* a pure novel (but had to be content to "stylize life" in the literary genre of the epic). The metaphysical problem of the nature of reality—an obsession of the cubists and the surrealists—is Gide's preoccupation.

Gide has been called a cubist because of the collage-like narrative structures of *Les faux-monnayeurs* and an earlier novel, *Les caves du Vatican.* The spare, stylized treatment of these works also contributes to this cubist classification. Before 1914 the cubist painters Braque, Gris, and Picasso were constructing their first collages or paste-pictures, while Gide was assembling *Les caves du Vatican,* wherein the novelistic structure is interrupted by references to the author himself at work. Gide further developed his technique of intentional disintegration of the narrative in *Les faux-monnayeurs:* in this work the complex plot gradually is revealed from divergent viewpoints—those of the characters in conversations, letters and journals, and the viewpoints of both an omniscient narrator and a personally involved artist-creator-observer named André Gide. In its adherence to multiple viewpoints and its refusal to integrate disparate ingredients, the novel resembles cubist paintings and *papiers collés* which utilized the juxtaposition of various images of the same object as seen from several angles. The impact of this device and of Gide's insistence upon beginning anew with virtually every chapter—breaking the rhythm he had already established—is startling. "Gide's art has the excitement of interruption, of fracture" [Wylie Sypher, *Rococo to Cubism in Art and Literature*].

If *Les faux-monnayeurs* is cubist, it is also mildly dadaist. Indeed, Gide has been called the *first* dadaist by some, chiefly for *Les caves du Vatican.* The ambiguous introduction of the real-life proto-dadaist Alfred Jarry, who wreaks havoc in the banquet scene of the later novel, immediately springs to mind, but there are also "anti-artistic" devices, such as the deliberately inconclusive *dénouement* of the novel, in which certain aspects of the dadaist spirit appear. The refusal of the author to resolve the majority of his sub-plots derives partly from a certain contempt for his public. Gide said that his role was to disconcert, to disturb, and it is not always easy to distinguish this intellectual, cubist penchant from the genuine hostility of Dada's programs. Following Gide's early influence by Mallarmé and the symbolists, he was naturally interested in the ideas of the dadaists and surrealists of the early 1920s, but he was never an official member of their circles. . . . The vestiges of Dada are apparent in *Les faux-monnayeurs,* but by the publication date of the novel, Dada had spent itself, and Gide's influence fell upon Surrealism.

[In his *Age of Surrealism*] Wallace Fowlie has called Gide, Henri Bergson, and Sigmund Freud the originators of the "myth of Surrealism." Bergson provided the theory of intuition or the irrational and its superiority to intellect or the rational, while Freud—without question a chief god of the surrealist pantheon—taught the lessons on the subconscious, without which Surrealism as an organized, coherent artistic movement would be unthinkable. From Gide and the others, according to Fowlie, the surrealists derived a "subterranean impetus and confirmation," and specifically from Gide they obtained the notion of "the sincerity of individual morality" and the Nietzschean "lessons on self-affirmation." Ultimately the surrealists rejected Gide for the most part (as he later rejected them and their theories) and accepted whole-heartedly only one of his works, *Les caves du Vatican. Inquiétude,* the modern frame of mind, may lead to a denial of reality when conventional "realistic" life becomes meaningless or seems to fetter the human spirit. Lafcadio, whose raison d'être is to commit a "gratuitous" act, epitomizes the radical literature which sought to administer an antidote for the inadequacies of realism. The new hero of the literature is typically introspective, irrational, and schizoid.

Lafcadio's *geste gratuit* is the unmotivated murder of a stranger. In *Les faux-monnayeurs* the exploration of the gratuitous act receives new emphasis in the suicide of the schoolboy Boris, which is a more rational event than Lafcadio's murder, but it has the same bizarre inevitability, lending it a kind of convulsive, surrealist beauty.

The element of chance, so vital to dadaist and surrealist art (the popular surrealist parlor game of "Exquisite Corpse" is only one manifestation), was a fundamental strand in Lafcadio's adventures; it is also woven into the fabric of *Les faux-monnayeurs.* Gide tried to destroy the usual logical organization of plot by cubist techniques, but in a manner which should have been congenial to surrealist aesthetics. As in a Ionesco fantasy, the characters of the novel meet, part, and may or may not form relationships, making the plot, like life, surprising, incongruous, and irresolute. By accident Edouard encounters his nephew George, whom he does not recognize, attempting to steal a book. Again, by chance, Edouard's frustrating interview with his other nephew, Olivier Molinier, leads him to discard his luggage ticket absent-mindedly, and the newly ordained vagabond, Bernard, retrieves it. After coming to know Edouard through his "borrowed" journal, Bernard forms a relationship with him which temporarily alienates Olivier from Edouard, but which ultimately misfires.

In the novel which Edouard seeks to create, he attempts to mold a book from the raw stuff of life which he is living and observing, and calls for an anarchy of novelistic technique. He wishes to transcend the bounds of predetermined subject matter because his interest lies more in the "gestation" of the literary work than in the completed book—which indeed, he admits, may never transpire. Here Gide's interest in the avant-garde is patent, and the dadaists and surrealists endorsed such artistic freedom. A cubist stylistic device retained by Surrealism is the motif of recession to infinity in the novel-within-a-novel format—Gide's *Counterfeiters* and Edouard's *Counterfeiters*—Gide the novelist and his novelist Edouard, who is also writing about a novelist—and so on. This receding "Quaker Oats" motif is a mild but provocative device popular with several surrealist artists. It is symptomatic of a concern with the relationship between—indeed, the distance between—art or artifice, and reality. This problem is at least as old as the play with which Hamlet caught the conscience of the king, and it was fundamental to the theories of both Cubism and Surrealism.

Many of the characters of Gide's *roman* were calculated to appeal, at first glance, to the surrealists. The literary efforts of the young men who contribute to the avant-garde reviews in the novel reflect the same iconoclastic surgings which propelled the dadaists and surrealists into the literary spotlight; Gide's contemporaries could readily identify with his characters. Like Lafcadio, they are preoccupied with questions of free will and morality, revolting against conventional art and conventional mores. A masochistic wish for alienation leads them into crime—from Bernard's impulsive theft of Edouard's suitcase to the organized activities of the counterfeiting ring—and compels them to sever ties with their families. The *sincere* man, like Lafcadio or Bernard, escapes the counterfeit values and sentiments of conventional society (represented in the institution of the family), denounces them, and become natural—*à la* Rousseau—and sincere, because he has nothing to gain and nothing to lose by being so. In Bernard's masochism, he welcomes the lacerating discovery of his illegitimacy, which he believes will free him.

[In his study *The Contemporary French Novel*] Henri Peyre wrote that "Gide *had* to compose novels in order to escape from the pitfall of solipsism, to which not only his physical temperament and his education but the example of many self-centered symbolists in Paris cénacles exposed him. Only through *half-imaginary* creatures could he, at first, prolong and liberate some of the obsessions that tormented him." Gide's "half-imaginary" characters (the italics were mine) are keys to his conception of reality in *Les faux-monnayeurs*. He explicitly demonstrates that certain episodes and characters are drawn from life. Old La Pérouse, the music master, is based upon Gide's own piano teacher. Olivier's attempted suicide was inspired by a letter describing the suicide of a man who, after being "happier than he had ever been" reacted to a remark by the writer of the letter that he would kill himself "only after a joy so great that I could be certain that I was never going to feel another like it." The bizarre but inexorable suicide of Boris, who shoots himself in a crowded classroom as part of a ritual contrived by his cruel and cynical schoolmates, has its counterpart in the actual suicide of Nény at the Lycée Blaise-Pascal in Clermont-Ferrand, 1909. The title of the novel itself ostensibly refers to a band of counterfeiters who exploit a group of schoolboys for the purpose of passing illicit money, and this situation is based upon the historically factual *modus operandi* of the criminal trio of Djl, Monnet, and Tournet in 1906. Finally, Gide boldly introduced the name and fantastic, pistol-brandishing personality of a real French literary figure, Alfred Jarry.

A biography of Gide reveals real-life antecedents for other characters and events of the book. Both Bernard, the "natural" and sincere youth, and the novelist Edouard, through whose journal much of the action is narrated, are idealized portraits of Gide himself. In the case of Edouard, the fact that he is a novelist trying to write a book entitled *The Counterfeiters*, and who, like Gide, maintains a *Journal of "The Counterfeiters,"* drawing upon the external world for characters and incidents, leaves little doubt about his relationship to Gide. In a less obvious manner, Boris is the reincarnation of Gide as a child, who in an oppressive puritanical milieu led a guilt-ridden life due to his problem of masturbation.

The "stranger-than-fiction" realities which Gide has incorporated into the novel are convincing because his scrupulous documentation makes their plausibility irrefutable. It is profoundly disconcerting, therefore, when this ring of truth is abruptly silenced by the appearance of Bernard's encounter with the angel. The episode has several important functions in the story, but it is also of interest for its jarring surrealist tonality. It is chiefly the philosophical aspects of the novel which inclined toward Surrealism, for the structure and technique are more cubist than surrealist, even if the emphasis upon chance corroborates the official surrealist theories of chance and automatism. The external events—the plot—of the novel generally seem to display fidelity to life, especially when factual sources of inspiration are adduced to establish plausibility. Why are we suddenly faced by a non-terrestrial being, a spirit, an angel?

On the mythical level, it is clear that the demon-angel duality is present in Gide, although it might be a mistake to search too assiduously for these symbolisms in *Les faux-monnayeurs*. Robert de Passavant and Lady Griffith have demonic characters and Vincent Molinier eventually comes to believe that he is the devil. There is also the devilishness of Strouvilhou, Armand, and George and his associates. At the opposite extreme, it must be admitted that Bronja and Rachel are angelic. Gide claimed an artistic abhorrence for sharply delineated opposites of good and evil, but the duality is present for those who seek it in *Les faux-monnayeurs*. But now in this novel, an angel materializes: it is one of the disquieting features of the work which, like the author's deliberate, self-conscious pause in the middle of the book to parade and review his creations before us, functions in part to surprise, if not to exasperate, the reader (as Gide surely intended). We are not certain how we are expected to react to the angel, who is so reminiscent of Dickens' Christmas ghosts in *A Christmas Carol*. Is he an angel in the biblical sense? an hallucination? a symbolic or allegorical figure? or a dream? Whatever may be the nature of his existence, it acts as a surrealist juxtaposition amid the sequence of cubist juxtapositions. In Cubism the juxtapositions of elements offer variegated views of conventional reality, but in Surrealism they are contrived to evoke impressions of a universe which transcends conventional reality. The angel device is surrealistic if he represents a dream or hallucination—and is therefore psychologically realistic—for the occasional blurring of the demarcation between the waking and dreaming states is a fact of life. The author does not define the nature of the angel's existence, and the reader is left with an unresolved chord, one of the many in the symphony of dissonances and *inquiétude* which constitutes *Les faux-monnayeurs*. Paradoxically, it is precisely this element which is simultaneously realistic and surrealistic. It is realistic because life truly is "like that"—filled with loose ends and unconcluded problems, endless dilemmas. Humans are unpredictable, and in an anti-classical manner constantly are stepping "out of character," as do some of the protagonists of Gide's novel.

The onus of convention bears heavily upon the popular notion of reality, so the unconventional and the uncommon have to be regarded as "unreal" in an individual, relative sense, whereas, cosmically, all events—including apparent miracles and everything "fantastic" must finally be considered *real*. The surrealists did not theorize about the *un*real: rather, they proclaimed the existence of a greater, higher, more profound reality than the pedestrian, pre-Freudian idea of reality. When the events and characters of Gide's book develop unpredictably and disconcertingly, they are more lifelike. They embody some of the seeds which erupted into the Surrealism of the 1920s, and occasionally attained an imperfect surrealist bloom such as the self-destruction of Boris.

Not only did Surrealism adopt the Gidian concept of relative morality—as Dada had adopted as its central feature the *geste gratuit* whose literary prototype was the pointless murder by Gide's Lafcadio, a few years earlier—but his theory of reality adumbrated theirs. In a similar manner, the photographer Eugène Atget photographed Paris so lyrically, discovering strange and fantastic juxtapositions in the nostalgia of the streets and in the superimposed reflections and objects in store windows, that the surrealists published his pictures in

La révolution surréaliste in 1926. Atget's vision confirmed photographically—hence, irrefutably—the *sur*reality of visual reality. The great difference between an Atget and a Gide may be that Atget was a primitive while the writer was a sophisticate. Gide was acutely aware of his incipient Surrealism in his exploration and experimentation with the nature of reality, but Atget may have been ingenuous. Sometime seaman, actor, painter, and finally from 1898 until his death in 1927, a photographer whose ambition was to record the artistic and picturesque face of Paris, Atget's life has been recorded almost too perfunctorily to permit a detailed analysis of his artistic aims. Indeed, it is perhaps too much to say whether he considered himself an artist in the sense that Gide manipulated and synthesized factual events into what he considered an artistic production, or as simply an honest and humble documentarian with no pretense to artistry.

If an evaluation of Atget's intent is either impossible or at least unfair, it is certainly possible to assess the impact of his photography within the framework of surrealist theory. In the same way that Gide contributed a "subterranean impetus" to literary Surrealism, Atget lent a "subterranean impetus" to visual Surrealism. They each transcended the artificial and superficial limits of *a priori* conventional reality and achieved a significant position within the surrealists' heritage. But while docile Atget made his quiet contribution and departed, Gide remained to undermine the very movement he had helped to create.

While Gide was incorporating dadaist and surrealist elements into *Les faux-monnayeurs,* he had already become disenchanted with Dada and with those addicted to the newly fermented elixir of Surrealism (sensing perhaps its potential for enslavement). The avant-gardists in the novel form a coterie of counterfeiters. Passavant nurtures avant-garde poets from counterfeit, selfish motives, for at heart he is little more than a prevaricator and a dilettante. Scarcely any of the diners at the argonauts' banquet—including Alfred Jarry, true life iconoclast and author of the fantastic play *Ubu Roi* at the age of fourteen—are represented in a complimentary fashion. The contributors to Passavant's review parallel in fiction the actual dadaist and surrealist writers and artists contemporary with Gide's book, but his reaffirmation of certain aspects of Surrealism was mitigated by his derision of avant-garde personalities; it is for this reason that Lafcadio's adventures formed an acceptable surrealist novel, while the story of the counterfeiters did not. Indeed, Gide's *Journal of "The Counterfeiters"* implies the revision of his attitude toward the French avant-garde, for his original plan was to use Lafcadio as the narrator of the novel. In his decision to tell the story from multiple viewpoints instead, he reverts to Cubism, finally dispensing with Lafcadio altogether by transforming him into the less iconoclastic Bernard Profitendieu. This modification demonstrates Gide's repudiation of the destructive side of relativist morality.

Little Boris speaks to Bronja in a childishly meaningless language of his own and constantly contradicts himself. The recitation of poetry devoid of recognizable meaning was a regular feature of dadaist *soirées,* and in the context of the times, Boris's speech is reminiscent of such poetry readings by Kurt Schwitters and others. Boris, however, had a deep psychological affliction; was Gide suggesting that the dadaists were mentally aberrant? It is interesting that Gide chooses to annihilate Boris (thereby also disposing of certain painful memories of his own childhood). Armand Vedel, impulsive and

cynical, masquerading behind a façade of nonchalance, is at heart one of the most desperate of characters. It is he who finally edits Passavant's review. Heartsick in the knowledge that he has contracted syphilis, he exhibits sado-masochistic tendencies in his mutually lacerating relationships with others, and is probably the most psychologically unhealthy character of the book: is this the stuff from which editors of surrealist and dadaist publications are made? Cob-Lafleur, another contributor to Passavant's review, is also mentally unsteady, but he does have the ability to see through Passavant's system of counterfeit values. The literary counterfeit ring embodies both moral decadence and intellectual deceit. It is both deceit and *con*ceit in the avant-garde to which Gide objects.

Bernard's encounter with the angel is one of two hinges of the novel, another being the Argonauts' dinner. After wrestling the angel, Bernard matures. He receives from Edouard the new motto that one must follow his own inclinations, but only if they are constructive. Bernard, with Gide, abjures the destructive aspects of the avant-garde, as Lafcadio could not have done, and the prodigal son Bernard returns to the foster father whose saving virtue is his love for him. Bernard's refusal to ally himself with constricting philosophies recapitulates Gide's denial of the dictatorship of Dada and Surrealism.

Although himself a creator of the surrealist myth, Gide incurred the wrath of the surrealists by ridiculing their heroes, and by softening the "hard line" he had taken in *Les caves du Vatican.* It is almost a truism that the dadaists and surrealists were anti-cubist, but to imagine that the cubist construction of *Les faux-monnayeurs* antagonized them is virtually to presuppose their acquaintance with Wylie Sypher's much later exposition of Gide's cubism [see excerpt dated 1949]. The multitude of styles which obtained in dadaist and surrealist art indicates, moreover, that formal considerations were less important than the philosophical. One of many examples of dadaist antipathy for Cubism is Francis Picabia's portrait of the proto-cubist Paul Cézanne as a monkey, but it is more likely that Picabia was deriding Cézanne's cool intellectualism than his style *per se.* Similarly, even if Gide's style in *Les faux-monnayeurs* is more recognizably cubist than dadaist or surrealist, it could scarcely be such a paramount factor in his fall from grace in the eyes of the fantasts. He alienated himself from them not in terms of style but in terms of an implicitly cubist intellectualizing philosophy: intuitive Dada and Surrealism revolted against the cubist's rational, unemotional detachment. If the dadaist spirit is at all present in Gide's determination to "disconcert" his readers, as has been suggested, it is admittedly far from the bombastic, uninhibited hostility toward the artist's audience which is found in full-blown, authentic Dada, and perhaps Sypher is correct in saying that Gide is not at all contemptuous of his readers. Gide's contempt for the organized French avant-garde is much more evident than any hostility toward the reader, and the fantasts readily understood this. They resented his apparent reversion to a certain social conservatism, or at least a qualified liberalism, with its emphasis upon living the "constructive" life.

Gide was a relativist in that he constantly reaffirmed his emotional independence after absorbing new philosophical systems, deriving what benefit he could from them, and rejecting the undigestible portions. In a similar manner, a decade later, he would again assert his independence after his flirtation with Communism. Communism, like most dictatorial philosophies, he would discover, promised more than it could give.

Fowlie rightly stated that Gide helped to create the surrealist myth in *Les faux-monnayeurs,* but in the same work he emphatically rejected Surrealism's blinding excesses and its restrictions upon the artist's spiritual and emotional freedom. (pp. 140-50)

David Haberstich, "Gide and the Fantasts: The Nature of Reality and Freedom," in Criticism, *Vol. 11, Spring, 1969, pp. 140-50.*

ALBERT J. GUERARD (essay date 1969)

[*An American novelist, educator, and critic, Guerard is esteemed for his studies of the twentieth-century novel, particularly his works on Joseph Conrad and André Gide. While occasionally criticized for some of his psychoanalytical interpretations, Guerard is generally praised for his ordered, lucid explications and critical rigor. In the following excerpt, he analyzes three types of narrators in* The Counterfeiters *to determine their effect on the realism of the novel.*]

The historic importance of *Les faux-monnayeurs* in the general drift away from realism is greater than that of many more daring experiments—and not merely because its author paused to explain what he was doing. Lautréamont or Raymond Roussel could be of major profit only to surrealists as extreme as themselves, but Gide proposed ways of making the ordinary novel more entertaining. His most obvious assaults on realism are in fact his least successful ones. He intended to give his opening chapter a "certain element of the fantastic and supernatural" in order to authorize later "unrealities." But little remains of this effort to make the Luxembourg gardens as "mythical" as the Forest of Arden. The ambulatory Devil virtually disappears; Strouvilhou is more sinister than Protos, but distinctly less occult. Only Bernard's excursion with the Angel promises a frankly supernatural chapter, but his all-night wrestling match returns it to frayed symbolism. The attempt to shatter realistic illusion is too obvious and too willful, yet too modest. The same thing may be said of the famous chapter "The Author Reviews His Characters," which so baldly announces its eighteenth-century freedom.

Gide's anti-realism is far more successful where it rests on the actual movement of the story: on the "roving conductor's" witty and intruding presence, on startling abruptness of transition and economy of narrative, on an unabashed use of coincidence. The series of events that leads Bernard to Laura's bedroom and to his meeting with Edouard (Chapters X—XIV) depends on a lost cloakroom ticket, and on Bernard's own alert impudence. What would life be if, in order to penetrate others' lives, we had only to make a wish or rub a magic lamp? These chapters distort life only to render life more amusing. Here for once Edouard's diary serves a dramatic purpose, though the vivacity of Bernard's two chapters makes the realism of the intervening diary seem all the more cumbersome. Coincidence, impudence, surprise, humor, speed—these are the novel's immediate properties, when either Bernard or the roving conductor is on the scene. Then *Les faux-monnayeurs* becomes, but with more plausible human beings, another *Caves du Vatican.* Its author recovers, after how many years of effort, the theory of fiction of the young Thomas Hardy. He even achieves some of Hardy's freedom from inhibition.

At the farthest extreme from Hardy, however, Gide controls every impulse to describe at length. . . . "Precision in the reader's imagination should be obtained not by accumulating

details but by two or three touches put in exactly the right places." However perfect the description, Edouard realized, the reader will substitute his own picture. Gide found pure realism, with its absence of shadow, banal as well as uneconomical. "Study *first of all* the place from which the light comes; all the shadows will depend on it. Each figure rests in and leans upon its shadow." The one thing to avoid was the clear, constant, explanatory light of traditional realism, which destroys all perspective. The contrary danger is that the use of shadow may become an excuse for defective understanding. The obscurity of Strouvilhou, who remains in the deep shadow of frankly incomplete knowledge, is perhaps more justifiable than the final ambiguity of Armand, whose surrounding shadow is much less dark. But the changing source of light and the changing intensity of that light give to the portrait of Boris a pathos, depth, and uncertainty.

Claude-Edmonde Magny's brilliant essay on *Les faux-monnayeurs* finds in it many of the techniques of the modern motion picture, including calculated variations in the distance of the camera. But this matter of distance returns us—as does very nearly everything else that is successful in the novel's technique—to "point of view," to the central problem of narrating consciousness. The lasting novelty and antirealism of the novel, and the reasons for its vivacity, lie here. But these matters have been described inaccurately so often that it is necessary to look at them very closely. How many narrators in fact are there? Which of them is the most successful? And how much is gained or lost by the intervention of Edouard and his diary?

1. *The alleged author of "Les faux-monnayeurs."* This is the personage who speaks in Chapter VII of the second part, "The Author Reviews His Characters"—the hypothetical author who wonders where the story will take him, who is mildly annoyed by Edouard, and has been disappointed by Bernard, Lady Griffith, and Vincent. Some critics have identified Gide with Edouard, many of them with the "roving conductor," and nearly all of them with this "alleged author." Even Claude-Edmonde Magny takes his judgments to be Gide's—and she is of course right when she says that Gide here attempted an extreme degree of stylization.

But is Gide really as ignorant of his characters' destinies as he claims to be in this chapter? The "alleged author" must be separated from Gide, from the actual author of *Les faux-monnayeurs* as we have it. It is Gide who conceives of the ambulatory Devil, who carefully conceals the motivation of Strouvilhou, who drops clues and supplies letters, and who (through Vincent and Lady Griffith) slyly offers the book's most direct thematic image:

> Vincent says there are certain kinds of fish which die according as the water becomes more salt or less, and that there are others, on the contrary, which can live in any degree of salt water; and that they swim about on the edge of the currents, where the water becomes less salt, so as to prey on the others when their strength fails them.

The "alleged author" is less subtle than Gide, has a more primitive curiosity concerning his characters. (The complete identification of Edouard and Gide is still less justified. Edouard is a milder person than Gide, even the relatively tranquil Gide of 1925, and a more rational novelist than he. His refusal to use Boris' suicide in his "Faux-monnayeurs" is not a merely whimsical dissociation. He would indeed want to find a motive for every act he dramatized. It goes without saying that Gide did see much of himself in Edouard, and often spoke through him.)

2. *The omniscient narrator or "roving conductor."* This is the amusing personage who takes us through the first seven chapters and who appears fitfully thereafter. The problem of fictional identification (half-conscious identification by the author as he writes) is here most interesting for anyone willing to read closely. We know that Lafcadio [the protagonist of *Les caves du Vatican*], who was to have been the narrator, became Bernard at some point in the novel's germination, and in the change lost his "conducting" functions. It would therefore be reasonable to assume a tripartite identification, or to suppose that some of Gide's feeling for this new Lafcadio would carry over into his characterizations of both Bernard and the roving conductor. And this is what we actually find. The roving conductor still betrays a kinship with Bernard. Thus he loses much of his sprightliness after the first three chapters, when the plot turns from Bernard to Vincent. Heretofore Gide's sense of Bernard's energy has carried over to the narrator. But now the roving conductor has lost some of his own flesh and blood. In other words, he could profit from Gide's feelings about Bernard as long as Bernard remained on the scene. This is a rather fine point, which no doubt escaped Gide's attention at the time of writing; it is one of the commonest yet least conscious aspects of novel-writing. One can hazard, more generally and more safely, that the roving conductor inherited much of his impertinence and laconic wit from *Les caves du Vatican* and from the Lafcadio of that book.

On one occasion this personage foresees the future, and once he makes the serious mistake of referring to "the body of the book" (thus temporarily fusing with the "alleged author"). In the early chapters, however, his position and personality are distinct. He is truly omnipotent, since he can comment on Bernard's dreams and enter into his waking reveries. But on more than one occasion he disclaims omniscience. "I am not very sure how he and Vincent became acquainted." God both knows and watches, yet protests that man is free. The roving conductor is a camera with a personality and a man reading stage-directions aloud: conducting, observing, and listening to a life that unrolls in an eternal present. He is telling the story, as the events occur before him, not writing a book. Until late in the novel—and it would be hard to overemphasize the importance of this—he speaks in the present tense.

Although he gets about Paris with supernatural ease, the roving conductor has a distinct and very human personality. *Nil admirari?* This ambulatory observer is shocked when the characters are shocked and pleased when they are pleased, yet he can be shocked or pleased by them. He is the unseen guest at every banquet, the shadow walking at one's elbow. One moment he is watching Bernard, and at the next moment is inside him. But usually he remains outside, an amused ghost who can follow any whim. He walks down the Boulevard St. Michel with Bernard and Olivier, listening to their conversation; then sees Georges Molinier and his friends a few steps away, and follows them instead. He may, as the occasion demands, watch, listen, remember, analyze. The saving grace of his omnipotence is that he knows when not to abuse it: "I should be curious to know what Antoine can have told his friend the cook. But it is impossible to listen to everything. This is the hour appointed for Bernard to go to Olivier. I am not sure where he dined that evening—or even whether he dined at all. He has passed the porter's room without hindrance; he gropes his way stealthily up the stairs. . . ." The plausible speaking voice here masks much complexity. For in these few sentences the narrator has defined himself as a person who can be in only one place at one time, as a fatalist who foreknows Bernard's destiny, as a man ignorant of the immediate past, and as the living observer of action only now occurring. The opening chapters of *Les faux-monnayeurs* (which may seem the least self-conscious and most traditional of any) are by far the most complex in artistry.

The roving conductor—and it should be clear by now that he conducts the reader not the characters—addresses us directly. Yet he achieves a fuller illusion by convincing us of his physical presence. "Her parents were right when they said to her: 'You never know your own mind.' Let us leave her . . ." "No, it was not to see his mistress that Vincent Molinier went out every evening. Quickly as he walks, let us follow him." Occasionally he permits himself a few lines of conventional psychological analysis. But the brevity and laconic tone always give, as they do in Stendhal, an overtone of irony. Life may be an ironic adventure, but it is still adventure—and an incomplete adventure if known only from the outside. The distance of the roving conductor from the action varies constantly: from cold omniscience to a sympathetic rephrasing of the characters' thoughts and feelings to a full submersion in them.

This impertinent narrator, a personage both sympathetic and *sympathique,* was an ideal vehicle for Gide's attack on conventional realism. He can maintain a pace as swift as that of *Les caves du Vatican* and can manage a difficult transition in a few lines: "How hot it is going to be in Paris! It is time to return to Bernard. Here he is, just awaking in Olivier's bed." As a rule we look over his shoulder, at the free present. But now and then he glances back at us. He can interrupt the dialogue of his characters to identify someone who has been mentioned, or to supply us with essential background information—not with a feigned casualness but frankly, at the moment we need it. He even permits himself the economical eighteenth-century convention of summarizing dialogue while seeming to report it (by using the third not the first person). He thus interrupts that "deluge of dialogue" to which James and Edith Wharton had already objected. Even interior monologue is sometimes reduced to the economy of shorthand notation, a reduction which very few novelists have been able to manage successfully. The monologues of Bernard sometimes read like Elizabethan soliloquies. At other times the glib summations serve as parodies of this traditional device for psychological revelation.

The roving conductor, violating all the rules of realism, yet achieves a particular kind of realism. The characters seem (and this is a much rarer occurrence than is commonly supposed) to have an existence independent of the reader, the author, the book. This is not a simple matter, and cannot be explained simply. The conductor rarely conceals his intruding presence and rarely loses his ironic detachment. He never stays long in one place or with one character; he offers us little of the surface texture of life and none of its connective ligaments. He leaves few important psychological facts in shadow, but leaves everything else to the reader's imagination: faces, voices, atmospheres. Perhaps Gide's intention was, once again, to involve the reader by making him fill in the details. But the effect is exactly the opposite. Carried at such a swift pace, the reader ceases to care about these details. The result is to repel reader-identification and involvement almost completely, and to conceal the identification and involvement of the author. Thus the classic achievement of the realistic novel, to insert the reader in the action and make him one of the characters, is almost wholly lost. But the characters of the novel—so freed from both reader and author, seen as it were by chance, so integrally keeping their distance—lead lives which are all the more independent. We look at them over the narrator's shoulder, yes. But they go on living after we have looked away. Bernard exists apart from us as palpably and unpredictably as Candide or Trabb's boy. No reader would be satisfied by a steady diet of such "unrealistic" realism. We want, after all, to be involved more intimately in lives which are not our own. But we can rejoice in its occasional appearance—whether in the *Arabian Nights* or Stendhal or Voltaire, or here fitfully in Gide—as perhaps the purest form of fictional *creation*.

3. *Edouard and his diary*. The diary represents, to a degree that has not been sufficiently emphasized, a concession to subjectivity and old-fashioned realism. Admittedly the *Kunstlerroman* asks for some equivalent of Philip Quarles's notebook or of Mark Rampion's didactic harangues. Admittedly too Edouard's diary has a real value for anyone interested in the art of fiction. But the first seven chapters of *Les faux-monnayeurs* promised something much more interesting than an intelligent *Kunstlerroman*. Edouard's diary is deplorable precisely because it interrupts the "roman d'aventure" and even threatens to destroy it. How much is gained in compensation? Perhaps the roving conductor could not have achieved some of Edouard's deeper tones: the pathos of Pauline, La Pérouse, and Armand, or the story of his own love for Olivier. We could further defend the diary by saying that Edouard's abstract discussion of "depersonalization" (Chapter VIII) offers a necessary respite, after so much swiftly dramatized action, or that the dark realism of his visits to La Pérouse is a necessary preparation for the tragedies of Armand and Boris. Finally, we could argue that the didactic Edouard saved the roving conductor from all obligation to moralize and explain. Edouard's digressive impurity as a narrator left the roving conductor's purity intact.

This is a dangerous hypothesis, however—improper because it exists outside the book as we have it. What we do have, in Edouard's diary, is a distinct recession to an older manner and to the devices Gide found easiest: narrative in the first person or through letters and diaries, slow realism, an intelligent brooding on the action. The paradox of Gide's most obvious innovation is that it readmits and even invites the techniques he was trying to avoid. The retrospective diary permitted anything. It invited the conventional realism of minutely described appearance. It permitted the realism and pathos of Edouard's interview with Pauline (Part III, Chapter VI), a chapter almost wholly written in dialogue. It encouraged the filling in of background and motivation. It permitted incessant recapitulation and the old "flashback" in a novel whose chief charm was its presentness. (Even the roving conductor, reappearing after so many pages of the diary and corrupted as it were by it, talks to us in the past tense.) Finally, it allowed Gide to indulge in prolonged psychological analysis. Edouard was a vehicle through whom he could indulge all his most familiar temptations—the temptations to realism, to careful ordering and elaboration, to the intelligent "roman-à-thèse" ["thesis novel"]. The plausible drama of everyday suffering observed by Edouard is interesting and moving; we would have, without him, a less complete impression of life.

But is a more ample "impression of life" the achievement that, in this particular book, matters? Many other novelists in our time have attained the sympathy which Edouard conveys, and at least a few have offered refractions of experience as subtle and as intelligent as his. But the first seven chapters of *Les faux-monnayeurs* are unique in their swiftness and vivacity. There is nothing quite like them in our century of gloomy fiction. They fulfill at last and though briefly Gide's old wish—to rival the energy and pure creativity of Stendhal. (pp. 165-74)

Albert J. Guerard, in his André Gide, *second edition, Cambridge, Mass.: Harvard University Press, 1969, 287 p.*

CATHERINE A. BARRY   (essay date 1972)

[*In the following excerpt, Barry examines the influence of Fyodor Dostoevsky on Gide as revealed in* The Counterfeiters.]

As early as 1908 Gide had launched his discovery of Dostoevsky upon the French literary scene through his **Dostoïevsky d'après sa correspondance,** partly in protest at de Vogüé's surprising neglect and distortion of the giant of the Russian novel, but in larger part, to hold up to the French literary public a mirror of Gide's own convictions as a man and writer. In 1911 a program note to Copeau's dramatic adaptation of *Les Frères Karamazov* emphasized the bond which Gide professed to discover between Dostoevsky and himself, though it added little bulk to Gide's previous critique of the Russian. The epigraph which preceded Gide's article on *Les Frères Karamazov* quotes Nietzsche's personal appreciation of Dostoevsky in echo of Gide's own praise: "Dostoïevsky—le seul qui m'ait appris quelque chose en psychologie" ["Dostoyevsky—the only one who taught me something about psychology"]. Although Gide would continue to mention Dostoevsky in his *Journal* beyond the twenties, his last stage of concerted criticism on Dostoevsky occurred in 1922 in connection with a series of lectures, six in all, which Gide presented at the Vieux-Colombier.

Several major interrelated themes are woven into the six Gide lectures later published under the simple title, **Dostoïevsky.** The first, previously stated in **Dostoïevsky d'après sa correspondance,** is that of *contradictions* and *inconséquences;* this is expressed in Gide, according to Guérard, as the "theory of the divided ego" and of an "absolute ambivalence"; the second, the affirmation of the individual by renunciation, is transposed in Gide into the *acte gratuit* ["gratuitous act"], Gidian *dénuement* ["denudement"], and sincerity. Since the third major theme, evangelism and Satanism, holds the key to all the others, it is the Dostoevskian evangelic-satanic diptych transposed in Gide which has caused most of the dissension among critics as to Gide's real message. Pfleger, for instance, states that the radical difference between Dostoevsky and Gide in respect to the Gospel is the crowning stress in Dostoevsky on the triumph of the Christian cosmos and in Gide, that of a Satanic conception "purement irrationnelle" and "éternellement problématique." Alibert, taking a completely opposite stand, accuses Gide of accentuating the "sur-evangelism" of Dostoevsky to the detriment of the demoniac element. But more recently, Holdheim in *Theory and Practice of the Novel* has moved the whole question onto another plane out of range of possible semantic contradiction. Holdheim sees little basic difference in Gide's admiration for Dostoevsky from that which Gide had expressed earlier for

Nietzsche. The chief theoretical distinction between the early Nietzsche writings and the lectures of 1922 are, in Holdheim's words, "the addition of evangelical religiousness." Holdheim continues: "Gide's criterion (of Dostoevsky and Nietzsche), then, is not mystical, but vitalistic, and this applies equally to the ideal of evangelical bliss."

Of special interest here, too, is the critic's insight as to Gide's admiration of Dostoevsky: ". . . we touch upon the most secret cause of Gide's admiration: it is precisely that Dostoevsky is a 'questioner' whose production can yet be interpreted (imagined!) as 'vitalistic.' But Gide's consciously expressed theoretical opinions do not acknowledge such subtleties. Dostoevsky is primarily the daemonic artist, the Creator who expresses his being 'comme le lion sa force, ou comme le tonnerre sa vertu' ['like the lion his strength, or like the thunder its force'], and whose literary creativity is identical with action. And in the Dostoevskian novel, Gide finds a chaotic vitality which seems to prove that the disjunction between life and art has been overcome."

Nowhere, of course, did Gide himself attempt to overcome this disjunction more than in *Les faux-monnayeurs.* To look for structural traces of Dostoevsky in Gide's novel within a novel would be most interesting, but this study limits itself to the more purely conceptual traces of Dostoevsky in *Les faux-monnayeurs* and centers upon the evangelic-satanic element and its above-mentioned related themes.

One might consider first, arbitrarily, the twin Dostoevskian phenomena of *contradictions* and *inconséquences.* The strongly "Western" or "French" character of Gide's transposition of *contradictions* and *inconséquences* in *Les faux-monnayeurs* is immediately apparent, however anxious Gide may have been to break through the barriers of over-self-consciousness. With Dostoevsky *contradictions* and *inconséquences* seem linked to mysterious, vital, subconscious forces under neither the at least partly conscious control of the characters involved nor under the control of the analyzing commentary of the author as they are in *Les faux-monnayeurs.* If there is absurdity in Gide, it is linked rather to the despair of philosophical, existential absurdity rather than to a life surge, however disordered or horrific that surge may be. The suicide of Kirilov in *The Possessed,* for example, though its driving force is extreme, insane self-assertion, is motivated, also, in its reverse aspect, by the hallucination of a warped Christ-figure who wishes to sacrifice himself for humanity. There are two suicides in *Les faux-monnayeurs,* one successful and the other abortive, that of Boris and Olivier, respectively. The first seems allied with Gidian absurdity, while the second, to be treated later in a discussion of the *acte gratuit,* bears a greater resemblance to that of Kirilov. The positive assertiveness of Kirilov's suicide is entirely missing in the suicide of Boris. Boris' suicide is horrific in its complete meaninglessness. It is not supported by the positive interior motivation of Kirilov's *acte gratuit.* Boris destroys himself to prove that he exists (not as Kirilov, that God does not exist)—a cul-de-sac contradiction. If there is a positive motive force behind the act, it is the diabolic Strouvilhou who stands behind the group of "possessed" accomplices whose slogan is intrinsically contradictory: "L'homme fort ne tient pas à la vie" ["The strong man does not value life"]. Boris is fully aware that he will prove nothing and gain nothing by his suicide. The fact that none of the group acknowledges his person in the least seals the horror of the act: Boris destroys not self, but a shadow.

The inescapable intellectuality of Gide's treatment of *contradictions* reveals itself again in his own gift of *globalisme* (René Lalou's expression) to Edouard. Gide and Gide's extension, Edouard, accept, as a point of departure, the human soul in all its antinomies. But understanding everything too well makes it difficult to choose anything. Gide speaks of himself in the *Journal des faux-monnayeurs* as essentially contradictory under this peculiarly "global" aspect: "De même dans la vie, c'est la pensée, l'émotion d'autrui qui m'habite, mon coeur ne bat que par sympathie. C'est ce qui me rend toute discussion si difficile. J'abandonne aussitôt *mon* point de vue. Je me quitte et ainsi soit-il. Ceci est la clef de mon charactère et de mon oeuvre" ["Likewise in life, it is the thought, the emotion of others which lives in me, my heart does not beat but by sympathy. That is what makes all discussion for me so difficult. I soon abandon *my* point of view. I separate from myself and that's the way it is. That is the key to my character and my work"]. In Lalou's words: " . . . choisir, pour lui, c'est accueillir délibérément tout l'univers, accepter d'avance de ne rien nier" [" . . . to choose, for him, is to welcome deliberately all the universe, to accept in advance to deny nothing"].

Edouard in his refusal of ultimate responsibility is totally aware how responsible the choice not to choose is: "Cette force antiégoiste de décentralisation est telle qu'elle volatilise en moi le sens de propriété—et, partout, de la responsabilité. Un tel être n'est pas de ceux qu'on épouse. Comment faire comprendre cela à Laure?" ["This anti-egotistical force of decentralization is such that it volatilizes in me all sense of propriety—and, moreover, of responsibility. Such a being is not the sort that one marries. How can I make Laura understand that?"]

The danger is immediately apparent: can one in an eternal hesitation ultimately choose both life (God?) and self-consciousness (Satan?)? In introducing in his second lecture at the Vieux-Colombier Dostoevsky's famous theory of the layers of the soul, Gide stressed how the region of hell, for Dostoevsky, is found in the least profound layer, the pride-filled intellect. Dostoevsky has, in Gide's estimation, a "dépréciation évangélique de l'intelligence" ["evangelical depreciation of intelligence"]. The evangelical poverty of renunciation of intellectualism in Dostoevsky which will lead to "God" or life will become in Gide *dénuement.* How to gain life ("God," "purity") without losing self-awareness and artistic fulfillment and before one is killed by over-consciousness is what Gide is really after. Gide's "satanism" is by no means as clear-cut as Gide himself would have us believe Dostoevsky's "satanism" is. Of course, on the most obvious level, both Dostoevsky and Gide accept implicitly the efficacy of the satanic quality in art: "C'est avec les beaux sentiments que l'on fait la mauvaise littérature et qu'il n'est point de véritable oeuvre d'art où n'entre la collaboration du démon" ["It is with beautiful sentiments that one makes bad literature and there is not one true work of art where the collaboration of the devil is not employed"]. One can, therefore, move quickly to the next level: Dostoevsky's and Gide's exposition of the necessity of evil in life as well as in art. Gide's conscious presentation of Dostoevsky in this regard revolves upon the now classic notion that the Russian soul finds its God only at the end of a tortuous path of suffering, degradation, and sin. In the classic conception of Dostoevsky passed on to us by Gide, the death of sin is swallowed up in the victory of God's redemptive mercy and love. Whatever Gide might justifiably attack in de Vogüe's critique of Dostoevsky, this is little more than de Vogüé's "religion de la souffrance" ["religion of suffering"] in Gidian dress. As for Gide's own transposition of Dostoevskian evil in *Les faux-monnayeurs,* evil does not appear to be swallowed up there; it is not essentially a negative force. In his effort to create for the French the equivalent of *The Possessed,* Gide presents in *Les faux-monnayeurs* two express Satan-figures, Strouvilhou and Vincent. Strouvilhou, the overt Satan of the novel, is the concentrated incarnation of the spirit which Gide had already stated prowls diffusely throughout the book. But Strouvilhou's ironic impact is strong and his diabolism so obvious that Hytier considers him a Gidian caricature: "Gide nous a même donné la caricature de son enterprise de démonétisation: c'est la théorie outrancière de Strouvilhou qui se propose, oui, de ruiner les vrais valeurs" ["Gide has even given us a caricature of his demonization enterprise: it is the extremist theory of Strouvilhou which proposes itself, yes, to ruin the true values"]. In his "éternellement problématique" fashion Gide is playing at deliberately mystifying us. Vincent, who in his progressive *dévalorisation* imagines himself to be Satan, is much more to the point. Vincent is destroyed not really by his loves, but rather by his own over-conscious self-torture: "Vincent se laisse lentement pénétrer par l'esprit diabolique. Il se croit devenir le diable; et c'est quand tout lui réussit le plus qu'il se sent le plus perdu" ["Vincent let himself be slowly penetrated by the diabolic spirit. He believes that he has become the devil; and it is when all succeeds for him the most that he feels himself the most lost"]. The process of *décristallisation* of which Laura and Lady Griffith are only the agents demoralizes him completely. Yet it would seem that Bernard Profitendieu is the real key of vitalistic force in evil, rather than Vincent, for it is in Bernard that we see that if evil does not work positively for some, it does for others, and that without benefit of grace. The cruel, adolescent rejection of M. Profitendieu by Bernard, his devil-may-care daring with Edouard and Laura, his lusty adventure with Sarah, all serve a creative purpose. In Bernard an ascetism of evil comes closest to a glorious justification. Thus, absurdity and slow destruction do not constitute the essence of Gidian "evil"; if the Borises, the Vincents, and the Lady Griffiths fall by the wayside, they deserve it.

Certainly, as one sees it in Bernard, the *dénuement* which is most typically Gidian is that which produces fervor. In *Les faux-monnayeurs,* even as Edouard represents Gide's globalism, Bernard figures as another of Gide's ideals, that of youth whose sights are always set on the future, youth which acts. Time, so hard on all the other characters in the novel, with its accompanying *dévalorisations* and its gradual unmasking of failures and disappointments, is conquered by Bernard alone. Bernard alone is created, not destroyed, through his successive loves and *engagements.* His successive sheddings and recapitulations (his *dénuement*) win for him not the childhood of Gospel joy, but a natural élan whose robust vigor is questioned only implicitly by Gide in his "Pourrait être continué ["Could be continued"]. Neither Gide nor Bernard know what may become of a purely natural freedom, nor do they wish to shoulder the responsibility for its possible issue. Linking this state of enthusiasm with that of artistic inspiration, Gide suggests that it is the full development of the individual which is really first and not God, or that the individual's full development *is* "God." Gide-Bernard will go on; Gide-Edouard, in their creation of a great novel (the marriage of awareness and action), too, will go on. The setting in *Les faux-monnayeurs* is a conversation between Edouard and Bernard immediately after Olivier has been saved from death by Edouard's intervention: "Tenez: je crois que j'appelle lyrisme l'état de l'homme qui consent à se laisser vaincre par Dieu.—N'est-ce pas là précisément ce que signifie le mot: enthousiasme?—Et peut-être le mot: inspiration" ["Listen: I believe that I would call lyricism the state of the man who consents to let himself be conquered by God.—Isn't that precisely what is meant by the word enthusiasm?—And maybe the word: inspiration"]. Gide assigns individual fulfillment as the most important consequence of renunciation and seems to impute the same hierarchy to Dostoevsky: " . . . la première et la plus importante conséquence de cette soumission [of Dostoevsky before Christ] fut . . . de préserver la complexité de sa nature" [" . . . the first and most important consequence of this submission (of Dostoevsky before Christ) was . . . to preserve the complexity of his nature"]. Be this more *gidisme* of Dostoevsky or not, it finely illustrates Gide's use of the master. Holdheim expresses it thus: "Gide seems to believe that the vitalistic work of art is possible. Its model has become the Dostoevskian novel. But Dostoevsky is more for Gide than a novelist, although therein lies his ultimate significance. He sums up and personifies the full range of Gide's irrationalist experiment, in all its complexity and with all its contradiction."

Of course, no treatment of Gide's *dénuement* as essential to fervor can ignore the Gidian *acte gratuit.* For Dostoevsky the *acte gratuit* had represented the supreme illusory joy of the false moment. Kirilov's suicide in *The Possessed* is allied with epileptic seizure, as Gide notes. It is epilepsy which brings Kirilov five seconds of pure, creative joy. A friend warns him of the illusions of such a joy, but Kirilov smiles mysteriously: he will kill himself so that in any case the epilepsy "won't have time." The Russian nihilist roots of such abandon had already been introduced to the French by de Vogüé in his explanation of *otchanié,* "la séduction et l'épouvante du pays de folie froide" ["the seduction and fright of the country out of cold madness"]. In Gide's early transposition of the *acte gratuit* he had radically diminished motivation, but by 1922 he had already posited the limits of the famous act: it is an act without *exterior* motivation. Emile Gouiran has clearly presented the psychological and philosophical bases of the *acte gratuit* by defining it as an act fully consented to and integrally lived, the consciousness of the being realizing itself entirely, since the supreme sin for Gide is to abandon his being. All things being integrally good at each instant of the act's duration by virtue of its interior dynamism, the act is its own reward. Kirilov's suicide is an obvious springboard to Olivier's *acte gratuit* in *Les faux-monnayeurs.* The terrible meaninglessness of Boris' suicide is complemented by the immense joy inherent in Olivier's act. Yet, again, dark, satanic shadows linger in the background because even as the ecstatic moment of Kirilov's false epileptic joy precedes his suicide, so the unbearable joy of Olivier's fulfillment in Edouard's questionable love is the prelude to Olivier's attempted suicide. Olivier does not want to give *his* "epilepsy" time to destroy him, either. It is Bernard who explains Olivier's act to Edouard in the following passage from *Les faux-monnayeurs:* "C'est moi qui lui parlais de suicide, dit-il à Edouard. Je lui demandais s'il comprenait qu'on puisse se tuer par simple excès de vie, 'par enthousiasme,' comme disait Dimitri Karamazov. J'étais tout abandonné dans ma pensée et je n'ai fait attention alors qu'à mes propres paroles: mais je me rappelle à présent ce qu'il m'a répondu . . . Qu'il comprenait qu'on se tuât, mais seulement après avoir atteint un tel moment de joie, que l'on ne puisse, après, que redescendre" ["It is me who talked to him about suicide, he said to Edouard. I asked him if he understood that one could kill himself by simple excess of life, 'by enthusiasm,' as Dimitri Karamazov said. I was entirely caught up in my thought and therefore did not pay attention to my own words: but I remember now what he answered . . . That he understood that one could kill himself, but only after having attained such a moment of joy, that one could not, afterwards, but redescend"].

Rachel, daughter of the minister Vedel, appears to be the only example in the novel of Gospel renunciation and poverty in Gide's *expressed* Dostoevskian sense: "Rachel s'est effacée toute sa vie, et rien n'est plus discret, plus modeste que sa vertu. L'abnégation lui est si naturelle qu'aucun des siens ne lui sait gré de son perpétuel sacrifice" ["Rachel effaced herself all her life, and nothing is more discreet, more modest than her virtue. The abnegation is so natural to her that none of her relations is grateful to her for her perpetual sacrifice"]. The whole treatment of the Protestant Vedel family reflects Gide's horror of "religious" households: "Azaïs impose autour de lui l'hypocrisie" ["Azaïs imposes hypocrisy all around himself"]. Rachel seems to be the willing but frightfully self-deceived victim of this garden of "simple souls." Indeed, Armand Vedel, for example, speaks of the self-deception of the minister Vedel: "Tout ce qu'il demande c'est de ne pas y voir clair" ["All he asks is not to see clearly"]. Like Alissa in *La porte étroite* Rachel's utter renunciation ends not in joy, but in bitterness, bitterness, the reader feels, that she has desperately tried to hide from herself. The rebel Sarah, Rachel's sister, mirror of Gide's revolt against the Calvinistic gospel, ultimately crushes Rachel, and her "religion de la souffrance" drowns midway through the novel as a disconcerting myth. Not only the Vedels, but all in *Les faux-monnayeurs,* reveal themselves as counterfeiters of some sort or other; that is, all but Bernard: "Seul le bâtard a droit au naturel" ["Only the bastard has the right to naturalness"]. So, from another point of view, Dostoevsky's renunciation or "humility" has become in Gide "sincerity," the truth of one's being. Gide's creative transpositions again transcend his critical appraisal of Dostoevsky, the only one who had taught him anything in psychology. To repeat Holdheim: "Gide's consciously expressed theoretical opinions do not acknowledge such subtleties."

Gide on Dostoevsky in *Les faux-monnayeurs,* certainly; but then, a deeper and more problematic Dostoevsky on Gide than in the early Dostoevsky critique. "Pourrait être continué." (pp. 580-87)

> *Catherine A. Barry, "Some Transpositions of Dostoevsky in 'Les Faux-Monnayeurs'," in* The French Review, *Vol. XLV, No. 3, February, 1972, pp. 580-87.*

MICHAEL TILBY (essay date 1981)

[*In the following excerpt, Tilby considers the strengths and weaknesses of* The Counterfeiters *and its importance to the development of the modern novel.*]

Coming to a conclusion, however tentative, about *Les faux-monnayeurs* is far from easy. The impossibly ambitious nature of Gide's novel and his inevitable recourse to compromise make criticism easy. On the other hand, appropriate criteria for a judgment of individual features are notoriously hard to establish. As Francis Jammes once noted [in a letter to Gide] with reference to *Les nourritures terrestres:* "Chacune de tes pensées portait en elle, DIRECTEMENT,

sa propre réfutation" ["Each of your thoughts carries in itself, DIRECTLY, its own refutation"]. Yet it would be wrong to claim that the critic's hands are tied in every respect. When the novel is viewed as a whole, it is possible to form an opinion of its contribution to the development of the French novel and to enumerate some of the recurrent strengths and weaknesses of Gide's writing.

It would be absurd to deny that *Les faux-monnayeurs* has the capacity to make its readers think. But we should, I feel, ask ourselves whether it encourages us to discover truths that are in any way novel or profound. It may be thought that, as Germaine Brée has claimed, "la pensée, pour lui [i.e. Gide] reste toujours trop générale pour s'individualiser; elle tend vers le lieu commun" ["thought, for him (i.e. Gide), always remains too general to individualize itself; it tends toward common ground"]. We may feel that Gide shows an obsessive concern with his own self, or that, in comparison with Proust, he seeks above all to justify and gratify himself instead of embarking on a truly illuminating voyage of self-discovery. Thus *Les faux-monnayeurs* may present a densely populated world of clearly differentiated characters but it might be objected that we are given none of the rich diversity that we observe in everyday life. According to such a view, the novel is dominated by Gide's own personality, the characters being presented solely in terms of a limited number of distinctly Gidean preoccupations. Objection may also be made to a tendentiousness that is at odds with the author's much vaunted commitment to open-endedness. To mention a single example, Gide skilfully presents his fictional world in such a way that the reader may well find himself accepting the superiority of Edouard's homosexual leanings somewhat against his will. Not all Gide's readers will recognize as valid the uniformly pessimistic treatment given love and marriage. How can one avoid the conclusion that Gide is indulging in implausible wishful-filment when he makes Pauline sanction Edouard's "protection" of her son?

We need also to ask whether the impression of superficiality in this composition is totally dispelled by our awareness of its calculated subtlety. It is difficult to be sure that this subtlety is not sometimes an exercise in obfuscation or that Gide's practice does not allow him to shirk vital issues, presenting with sometimes questionable sleights of hand his weaknesses as virtues. For so many of the precepts illustrated by *Les faux-monnayeurs* hinge on the impossibility of a particular intellectual, moral or artistic ambition. The relationship between Gide and Edouard may give rise to particular misgivings. While there may be some who, like Edmond Jaloux, regret that Gide did not make his superiority over Edouard an undisputed fact, others may be tempted to assume that by leaving in some doubt the precise distinctions to be drawn between the two, Gide was spared the need to come to terms with himself and his ideas. More than one critic has been moved to complain that Gide is playing an elaborate game of hide and seek with his reader.

At every turn, Gide's strange practice can be justified by the particular needs of his composition but this does not mean that the reader is obliged to accept that the realization of the aims the author has set himself is as worthwhile as the latter would have us believe, however brilliant the stratagems to that end. Speaking more generally of Gide's work, Aldous Huxley (whose novel *Point Counter-Point* (1929) is, incidentally, all too often seen as an English *Faux-monnayeurs*) once observed that the author had "refined his work till that rather gross, almost physical quality, which is called life, has been distilled out of it along with other crudities." Some sympathy may also be found for the view of Henry Bidou, who defined Gide's novel as "ce cours d'eau faussement libre" ["that stream falsely free"].

When it comes to Gide's attempt to rescue the Novel from the impasse in which he felt it was trapped, it is perhaps significant that the post-war *nouveaux-romanciers* have been loath to enrol Gide among their precursors, preferring to derive their experiments from the work of Flaubert, Proust and Raymond Roussel. Seen in the light of the post-war experimentalists and *contestataires*, Gide's novel does little to undermine the conventions on which the "realist" or "naturalist" novel had rested. Initially, **Les faux-monnayeurs** may thwart the reader's expectations but any questioning of the novel as an adequate means of representation is, it may be thought, severely limited by Gide's over-riding concern with the quest for the *roman pur*.

On the other hand, it is undoubtedly true that **Les faux-monnayeurs** is "déjà un livre de l'impuissance du romancier dévoré par ses problèmes de romancier" ["already a book about the impotence of the novelist devoured by the problems of the novelist" (Claude Martin)], and that as such it has fostered further thinking about a genre which was often felt to be the product of Nature rather than a reflection of the epistemological assumptions of a particular age. It may be true that in the final analysis "son univers romanesque n'est pas la société humaine, c'est seulement le monde étroit de l'écrivain André Gide" ["his novelistic universe is not human society, it is only the narrow world of the writer André Gide" (Pierre de Boisdeffre)], but Gide's ability to embody his preoccupations and attitudes in different fictional characters and to allow them to be reflected in instinctive responses to precise physical settings prevents the novel from being as limited as such a statement suggests. The wider relevance of the fictional world he has created is indeed seen in the way the novel questions the moral assumptions of the age in which he lived. Anyway, we should, I think, ask ourselves whether the fact that this novel is to a large extent an expression of the character of André Gide is necessarily a reason for censure. Alongside a certain pessimism, there is present in this novel a humanity, sensitivity and critical intelligence that may well be found appealing. As the Belgian poet and critic Roger Bodart so rightly says [in *Cahiers André Gide*]: "Gide écrit non pas pour écrire, mais pour être" ["Gide writes not in order to write, but in order to live"], and while his novel obviously demands from the reader a high degree of intellectual participation, we are constantly made aware of Gide's lively personality. The shape of his composition may bring us still further pleasure. We may perhaps also agree with Crémieux's approval of "l'admirable économie de l'oeuvre" ["the admirable economy of the work"].

Much will depend on how we choose to approach **Les faux-monnayeurs.** Are we to consider it a completed novel or, in Naomi Lebowitz's words, "a diagnostic work which concerns itself inevitably with the competition of the possible attitudes and frameworks which could be used by more committed novelistic talents"? [see Further Reading.] The problem is that Gide wants it to be both of these at once. An ambiguous response may therefore be thought the only one appropriate to this ambiguous composition. Yet to call it a partial failure, as many have done, is perhaps too easy. For it might well be argued that Gide is aware that, in certain respects, it is bound to be a failure. (The criticisms he levels against Edouard suggest also that he is only too aware of his own possible shortcomings.) It seems highly plausible to suggest therefore that he was trying to find out how far he could go in the directions he had set himself, exploring in the process the nature of both the difficulties which faced him and the various achievements that prove possible. Perhaps, paradoxically, he was, though, too successful in creating certain illusions, thereby undermining the attempt to make us reflect on the inevitability of his failure. Yet, however we decide to approach this matter, there can, as we have seen, be no doubt that an assessment of Gide's novel must bear in mind its ability to make the reader explore the vast range of complex questions it poses, with a degree of critical rigour that obliges him constantly to reconsider the conclusions he has only just reached.

In the final analysis, much will depend on the temperament of the individual reader. Some will claim that Gide is trying to do too much within the bounds of a single work, thereby making unrealistic demands on his readers. Others will welcome the opportunity to become active and "self-conscious" readers, and they will reach a conclusion that reflects the perennial fascination this text holds for them. Those of us who belong to this second group would, however, perhaps do well to ponder a recent definition of the literary critic as "un lecteur perverti" ["a perverted reader"].(pp. 97-101)

> *Michael Tilby, in his* Gide: "Les Faux-Monnayeurs", *Grant and Cutler Ltd., 1981, 105 p.*

FURTHER READING

Bouraoui, H. A. "Gide's *Les faux-monnayeurs:* Hidden Metaphor and the Pure Novel." *Australian Journal of French Studies* 8, No. 1 (January-April 1971): 15-35.

   Asserts that Gide suggests the "existence of a unified vision or sensibility" in *The Counterfeiters* through the use of recurrent metaphors and opposing philosophical views that are presented throughout the novel.

Brosman, Catharine Savage. "The Relativization of Character in *Les faux-monnayeurs.*" *Modern Language Review* 69, No. 4 (October 1974): 770-78.

   Concludes that in *The Counterfeiters* Gide "helped to show that the individual, as an absolute, was dead, and that understanding man and his deeds depends upon the angle of vision."

————. "The Novelist as Natural Historian in *Les faux-monnayeurs.*" *Essays in French Literature* 14 (November 1977): 48-59.

   Investigates Gide's use in *The Counterfeiters* of metaphors from natural history to comment on social and ethical questions, concluding that Gide "seems to want to make the point that human conduct is first of all rooted in nature, where cruelty predominates and all life and growth are based on the sacrifice of some."

Chambers, Leland H. "Gide's Fictional Journals." *Criticism: A Quarterly for Literature and the Arts* 10 (Fall 1968): 300-12.

   Includes a discussion of the purposes of Edouard's journal in *The Counterfeiters,* such as the encouragement Bernard draws from reading it and its usefulness in creating reader sympathy for Edouard.

Ciholas, Karin Nordenhaug. *Gide's Art of The Fugue: A Thematic*

Study of "Les faux-monnayeurs." Chapel Hill, N.C.: North Carolina Studies in the Romance Languages and Literatures, 1974, 125 p.

Proposes to "demonstrate that *Les faux-monnayeurs* is a unified composition based on an interrelationship of themes. By considering the themes in their linear and causal sequence and in their reciprocal relatedness based on their affinity of similarity or contrast I hope to prove that the novel's most outstanding compositional and artistic feature is its intrinsic coherence, its 'satisfied and satisfying harmony'."

Cook, Albert. "Reflexive Attitudes: Sterne, Gogol, and Gide." In his *The Meaning of Fiction,* pp. 24-37. Detroit, Mich.: Wayne State University Press, 1960.

Includes a discussion of the reflexive structure of *Les faux-monnayeurs,* concluding that Gide's novel-within-a-novel composition is imperfectly achieved.

Cordle, Thomas. "Social Realism." In his *André Gide,* pp. 116-62. New York: Twayne Publishers, 1969.

Thematic study which emphasizes Gide's use of realism and understatement to express the hopelessness of the characters' struggles to escape the "middle class morass of mendacity, duplicity, and abdication of duty and ideals."

Davies, J. C. "Sincerity and Self-Delusion in *Les faux-monnayeurs.*" *Australian Journal of French Studies* 7, Nos. 1-2 (January-August 1970): 123-41.

Maintains that Gide's treatment of sincerity in *The Counterfeiters* is essentially pessimistic, portraying most characters as not understanding their motives for action.

————. "Gide's *Faux-monnayeurs:* Edouard, the Man and the Novelist." *Australian Journal of French Studies* 19, No. 3 (September-December 1982): 266-87.

Judges Edouard as lacking self-awareness and favorably assesses his potential as a novelist, despite Gide's stated opinion to the contrary.

Fadiman, Clifton P. "Pure Novel." *The Nation* 125, No. 3251 (26 October 1927): 454-55.

Discusses Gide's techniques for achieving the pure novel and praises the emotional impact of *The Counterfeiters.*

Fokkema, D. W. "A Semiotic Definition of Aesthetic Experience and the Period Code of Modernism." *Poetics Today* 3, No. 1 (Winter 1982): 61-79.

Uses a semiotic definition of aesthetic experience and of Modernism in order to "justify the weak plot, the lack of character description, the impression of incoherence and the open ending" of *The Counterfeiters.*

Fowlie, Wallace. "The Art of the Novel: *Les faux-monnayeurs* (1925)." In his *André Gide: His Life and Art,* pp. 85-97. New York: Macmillan Co., 1965.

Discusses *The Counterfeiters* as an "attempt to renovate and even upset the usual logical presentation of material, and to diminish the importance of traditional psychological analysis."

Freedman, Ralph. "The Inner Landscape." In his *The Lyrical Novel: Studies in Hermann Hesse, André Gide, and Virginia Woolf,* pp. 165-81. Princeton, N.J.: Princeton University Press, 1963.

Explores Gide's emphasis on perception in his themes, characterization, and social criticism in *The Counterfeiters.*

Garzilli, Enrico. "The Fictive Self and Identity." In his *Circles without Center: Paths to the Discovery and Creation of Self in Modern Literature,* pp. 118-27. Cambridge, Mass.: Harvard University Press, 1972.

Asserts that both the form and content of *The Counterfeiters* reflect Gide's concern with artistic and personal identity.

Hytier, Jean. "*Les faux-monnayeurs* and the Art of the Novel." In his *André Gide,* pp. 206-36. London: Constable and Company, 1963.

Analyzes the narrative structure and themes of *The Counterfeiters* in order to judge its success as a novel.

Jackson, Elizabeth R. "The Evanescent World of the *Faux-monnayeurs.*" *Symposium: A Quarterly Journal in Modern Literatures* 16, No. 2 (Summer 1962): 103-14.

Finds that *The Counterfeiters* resembles French literature of the Baroque period in its stylistic and thematic manifestations of instability, mobility, metamorphosis, and illusion.

Kadish, Doris Y. "Structures of Criminality in Gide's *Les faux-monnayeurs.*" *Kentucky Romance Quarterly* 25, No. 1 (1978): 95-107.

Analyzes three types of crimes in *The Counterfeiters:* theft and fraud, sexual crimes, and physical violence, concluding that Gide intended the reader to judge the characters relativistically, taking into consideration not only the crimes but also the perpetrators' feelings of guilt, covertness in performing the crimes, and their degree of self-deception.

Lebowitz, Naomi. "The Counterfeiters and the Epic Pretence." *University of Toronto Quarterly* 33, No. 3 (April 1964): 291-310.

Maintains that Gide experimented with epic and tragic forms in *The Counterfeiters* in order to explore what is possible in the modern novel.

Ljungquist, Gary. "*Les faux-monnayeurs* as a Radical Statement on Homosexuality." In *Selected Proceedings 32nd Mountain Interstate Foreign Language Conference,* edited by Gregorio C. Martin, pp. 199-205. Winston-Salem, N.C.: Wake Forest University, 1984.

Asserts that the "fundamental radicalism of Gide's representation of homosexuality stems from the textually problematic nature of the novel and from Gide's use of a subtly perceptible homosexual sub-text whose relationship to the reader is critically ambiguous and ultimately corrupting."

March, Harold. "Counterfeit." In his *Gide and the Hound of Heaven,* pp. 265-95. Philadelphia: University of Pennsylvania Press, 1952.

Presents biographical background to the writing of *The Counterfeiters* and ties together the various situations and characters of the novel with the theme of counterfeiting.

Moore, Ann M. "Women, Socialization, and Language in *Les faux-monnayeurs.*" *Stanford French Review* 11, No. 2 (Summer 1987): 211-28.

Asserts the fundamental importance of women's roles to the themes of self-fulfillment in *The Counterfeiters,* concluding that in the novel women's efforts at self-expression are thwarted by society and themselves.

"*The Counterfeiters.*" *The New Republic* 53, No. 682 (28 December 1927): 170-71.

Unfavorable review.

O'Brien, Justin. "*The Counterfeiters* and *Point Counter Point.*" In his *The French Literary Horizon,* pp. 103-08. New Brunswick, N.J.: Rutgers University Press, 1967.

Finds Aldous Huxley's *Point Counter Point* an ineffective imitation of Gide's *The Counterfeiters,* unsuccessfully using Gide's novel-within-a-novel structure and contrapuntal plots.

Painter, George D. "'My First Novel': *The Coiners,* Dostoevsky, *Journal of 'The Coiners'.*" In his *André Gide: A Critical Biography,* pp. 88-98. New York: Atheneum, 1968.

Discusses personal and literary influences on *The Counterfeiters.*

Peters, Arthur King. "Rivalry—the Root and the Flower." *Jean Cocteau and André Gide: An Abrasive Friendship,* pp. 279-308. New Brunswick, N.J.: Rutgers University Press, 1973.

Analyzes Gide's personal life, particularly his relationship to Marc Allégret and Jean Cocteau, for insight into the Bernard-Passavant-Edouard triangle in *The Counterfeiters.*

Purdy, Theodore Jr. "A Spreading Plant." *Saturday Review of Literature* 4, No. 16 (12 November 1927): 301-02.

Review of *The Counterfeiters* which claims that Gide's "tact and skill in construction, the classic quality of his style . . . , and the continued intelligence of his observation, combine to make *The Counterfeiters* rich beyond all but the best of twentieth-century fiction."

Rieder, Dolly S. "*Les faux-monnayeurs:* Gide's Essay on Bad Faith." *Romantic Review* 62, No. 2 (April 1971): 87-98.

Maintains that Gide was forced to abandon his original intention to make *The Counterfeiters* a "pure novel" because of the impossibility of achieving that goal, but asserts the importance of Gide's effort.

Romney, Jonathan. "Forgery and Economy in Gide's *Les faux-monnayeurs.*" *Neophilologous* 71, No. 2 (April 1987): 196-209.

Examines the theme of forgery in *The Counterfeiters,* particularly the idea of Gide's novel as a forgery itself. Romney concludes, "The very substance of *Les faux-monnayeurs* is its lack of substantial value, for by duplicating the process by which value is established, it reassesses the notion of literary value itself."

Shepard, Leslie A. "The Development of Gide's Concept of Personality." *Bucknell Review: A Journal of Letters, Arts and Sciences* 17, No. 2 (May 1969): 47-66.

Includes a discussion of the mutability and self-contradictory nature of personality in *The Counterfeiters* and identifies this theme as central to the novel.

Stock, Irvin. "A View of *Les faux-monnayeurs.*" *Yale French Studies* 7 (1951): 72-80.

Sees in *The Counterfeiters* a skepticism toward reality, but concludes, "Though every image of reality is counterfeit, we need not despair, there remains a basis for choice among them. That basis is the self's needs, honestly acknowledged."

Tashjian, Dickran L. "*The Counterfeiters* by André Gide: The Esthetic Ontology of Dada." *Minnesota Review* 6, No. 1 (1966): 50-7.

Examines the anti-art ideology behind *The Counterfeiters,* asserting the success of the book as a Dadaist anti-novel.

Thomas, Lawrence. "*Les faux-monnayeurs.*" In his *André Gide: The Ethic of the Artist,* pp. 190-209. London: Secker and Warburg, 1950.

Critical analysis which focuses on Gide's integration of individualism with social obligation.

Tilby, Michael. " 'Self-Conscious' Narration and 'Self-Reflexivity' in Gide's *Les faux-monnayeurs.*" *Essays in French Literature* 15 (November 1978): 56-81.

Places *The Counterfeiters* within the tradition of self-conscious narration and explores various techniques Gide used to achieve this effect, such as the numerous coincidences which point to the presence of the author.

Ullman, Stephen. "The Development of Gide's Imagery." In his *The Image in the Modern French Novel,* pp. 1-98. Oxford: Basil Blackwell, 1963.

Divides the imagery in *The Counterfeiters* into three categories—imagery in the narrative, in Edouard's diary, and in the direct speech of the characters—and concludes that *The Counterfeiters* marks the height of Gide's image-making power.

Walker, David H. "Continuity and Discontinuity in *Les faux-monnayeurs.*" *French Studies* 40, No. 4 (October 1986) 413-26.

Proposes to "examine the novel in the light of one particular cluster of contradictory postulates from which it appears to have grown: on the one hand, the need for continuity as a condition of the form and a response to reader expectations; and on the other, the various discontinuities with which the text is ultimately concerned."

Watson-Williams, Helen. "The Principle of Duality in Gide's *Les faux-monnayeurs.*" *Australian Journal of French Studies* 7, Nos. 1-2 (January-August 1970): 234-53.

Analyzes the characters, themes, and narrative techniques of *The Counterfeiters* in terms of polarities.

Theodor Herzl

1860-1904

Austro-Hungarian essayist, journalist, dramatist, novelist, and short story writer.

Herzl is best known as the founder of the Zionist movement, an international campaign to establish a Jewish homeland. He was also a prolific author whose works include plays, novels, essays, and short stories. While Herzl attained some literary success during his lifetime, particularly as an essayist and playwright, most of his writings have been overshadowed by the Zionist theory developed in his three most important works—the political tract *Der Judenstaat (The Jewish State),* the drama *Das neue Ghetto (The New Ghetto),* and the novel *Altneuland (Old-New Land).*

Born in Pesth, one of the two cities later merged to form Budapest, Herzl was the son of upper-middle-class assimilated Jews who provided him with little background in Jewish traditions. His father was a merchant and his mother was a strong-minded woman whose admiration for German culture had a lifelong influence on her son. Herzl attended specialized schools to prepare for a career in engineering, but he eventually found that his abilities were better suited to literature. He began writing short stories and essays, and in 1875 he transferred to a school with a broader curriculum. Following the sudden death of his sister from typhus in 1878, Herzl and his parents moved to Vienna, where he studied law at the University of Vienna and wrote feuilletons and plays. After receiving his law degree in 1884, Herzl began working as a judicial clerk. His first literary success, achieved in 1885 when his short story "Das Alltägliche" was published in the journal *Wiener Allgemeine Zeitung,* convinced him that he could succeed as a writer and he resigned his position as a clerk. He was further encouraged when his play *Tabarin,* a one-act melodrama set in Paris during the 1620s, was performed in New York that same year as a showpiece for a famous German actor. When his subsequent efforts did not meet with similar success, he began to travel, relying on his parents for financial support and submitting essays describing his journeys to various Viennese journals. After returning to Vienna, he published two collections of feuilletons—*Neues von der Venus* and *Das Buch der Narrheit*—and in 1891 he accepted a position as Paris correspondent for the *Neue freie Presse,* a Viennese newspaper.

During his years in Paris, Herzl became interested in the plight of the Jews in Europe, where anti-Semitism was becoming increasingly prevalent. In 1894 Alfred Dreyfus, a Jewish officer in the French army, was falsely accused of treason and imprisoned. Although Dreyfus was later exonerated, his case demonstrated that hatred of the Jewish people was deeply ingrained in European culture, and the furor aroused by what became known as the Dreyfus Affair lasted well into the twentieth century. Some commentators have argued that the Dreyfus Affair precipitated Herzl's interest in the problem of anti-Semitism, but others maintain that Herzl had already displayed a concern for the situation of European Jewry. He had, for example, proposed a series of duels to prove Jewish honor, with himself challenging the major anti-Semites of the day, or a dramatic mass Christian baptism of

Jews intended to alleviate anti-Semitism. He had also examined the situation of Viennese Jews in *The New Ghetto,* suggesting that Jews, no longer confined to a geographical ghetto, had to free themselves of the negative characteristics they had acquired as a result of ghetto life.

Although Herzl had initially advocated assimilation as the best way for Jews to achieve equality, during the mid-1890s he became increasingly convinced of the need for a separate Jewish state, and in 1896 he published *The Jewish State,* a political pamphlet outlining the process by which such a state would be organized. Believing that control of the new nation must be achieved through formal diplomatic means rather than by settlement, he met with various statesmen, including European leaders and the Sultan of the Ottoman Empire, in attempts to secure a charter. Unlike many other Zionists, Herzl was not committed to Palestine as the Jewish homeland and pursued the possibilities of Jewish settlement in Argentina, Cyprus, the Sinai Peninsula, and other parts of Africa. In 1897 he organized the First Zionist Congress, which was held in Basel, Switzerland, and was attended by approximately two hundred delegates who debated various questions and formulated a resolution defining the Zionist program. Although Herzl and others considered the Congress a success, sources of conflict were evident among Zionists and with the rest of the Jewish community. Herzl's willingness to consider alternatives to Palestine angered many Zionists, and he was also attacked by Orthodox Jews who, believing that only God could restore their homeland, considered him a false messiah. In addition, many criticized his belief that anti-Semitism could benefit the Jews by prompting them to leave Europe. Challenged from within the movement at subsequent Zionist Congresses, frequently frustrated in his diplomatic negotiations, and suffering from steadily worsening heart disease which biographers believe was aggravated by emotional stress, Herzl once again turned his attention to writing during the last years of his life, publishing the utopian novel *Old-New Land,* in which he envisioned a thriving Jewish state in Palestine. Herzl died after a series of heart attacks in 1904.

Although Herzl wrote in numerous genres, critics generally agree that his literary talents were best displayed in journalistic essays known as feuilletons. These essays are marked by controlled organization, an eloquent and forceful prose style, and the clear expression of acute observations and original insights. Herzl was a skilled descriptive writer, and his travel essays are considered among his best work. His reflections on French parliamentary proceedings, collected in the volume *Das Palais Bourbon,* though occasionally criticized for their stilted style, have been described as a "brilliant record of an epoch not usually remembered for its political life." These writing skills—keen observation and clear presentation—make his extensive diaries, totalling approximately 500,000 words for the period from 1895 to 1904, important documents valued by biographers, critics, and historians. Indeed, biographer Desmond Stewart considers the diaries Herzl's "literary masterpiece."

As a playwright, Herzl's only important work is *The New Ghetto,* in which he specifically addressed the position of Jews in European society. The work focuses on Jacob Samuel, a Jewish man modeled on Herzl, and his personal and business dealings with other Jewish and gentile characters, many of whom were based on people in Herzl's life. Challenged to a duel, Samuel feels that refusing would cast doubt on Jewish honor, and he is fatally wounded. According to critics, the theme of escape from the ghetto is central to the play; Herzl maintained in this work that Jews must liberate themselves from a psychological ghetto that resulted from centuries of gentile oppression and contempt. Ritchie Robertson suggests that *The New Ghetto* marks an important phase in the development of Herzl's Zionist philosophy, asserting that the superficial assimilation of some of the characters in the play indicates that Herzl no longer believed that assimilation was a viable solution to the problems faced by the Jews.

Herzl's answer to the "Jewish Question" is presented in *The Jewish State,* which Alex Bein has called "Herzl's life work." In this pamphlet, Herzl asserted the need for a separate Jewish homeland and proposed the manner in which this goal might be realized. Herzl stated that the Jews were a people, not simply a religious group; as a result, they could never be genuinely assimilated into European society. Anti-Semitism would never be eradicated, Herzl continued, and would in fact increase, especially in western Europe as more Jews immigrated from Russia and eastern Europe. Thus, he argued that the only solution was for the Jewish people to have their own independent nation where they would be free of the threat of anti-Semitism. While Herzl's initial concept of a Jewish state referred only to Jewish sovereignty over a specific, but unnamed region, other factions of the Zionist movement insisted on Palestine, and Herzl eventually agreed. He proposed two groups, both based in London until a territory could be obtained, to organize the formation of the Jewish state: the Society of Jews, which would handle political and administrative groundwork, and the Jewish Company, which would oversee the practical implementation of the plans for the state's development. The ideas presented in *The Jewish State* were not entirely original; many aspects of Herzl's program were similar to the ideas presented in J. L. Pinsker's *Auto-Emanzipation: Ein Mahnruf an seine Stammesgenossen* (1882; *Auto-Emancipation*), an earlier Zionist tract that Herzl claimed he had not read when he wrote his own manifesto. *The Jewish State* was met with diverse responses, including criticism from Jews who feared that Zionism would endanger their own success in European society and praise from anti-Semites who encouraged the Jews to leave Europe. Despite such a mixed reaction, *The Jewish State,* considered the "bible of modern Zionism," has had a tremendous impact on world politics.

Herzl presented a fictionalized version of his image of the Jewish state in *Old-New Land,* which has been characterized as a utopian novel. In this work, a young Jewish man and the Prussian aristocrat to whom he is a companion visit Palestine in 1903 and 1923 and are amazed on their second visit at the changes that have taken place as the result of Jewish control. The modernist society depicted in *Old-New Land* demonstrates Herzl's faith in the power of technology to solve human problems. Herzl's image of the culture of the new state also reflects the admiration for German culture that his mother had encouraged: the citizens of Old-New Land speak German, not Hebrew, and there is little that is uniquely Jewish about the new society. Some Zionists argued that Herzl's proposed nation, lacking any specifically Jewish cultural traditions, would lead to the obliteration of those traditions, but as Desmond Stewart explains, "To Herzl what seemed distinctly Jewish was simply the result of gentile persecution." Tolerance and universalism are dominant features of Herzl's Jewish state. Like his other major works, *Old-New Land* is considered important for the insight it provides into Herzl's thought and political activities, both of which contribute to an understanding of world politics and the origins of the modern state of Israel.

PRINCIPAL WORKS

Tabarin (drama) 1885
Neues von der Venus (essays and short stories) 1887
Das Buch der Narrheit (essays and short stories) 1888
Seine Hoheit (drama) 1888
Das neue Ghetto (drama) [first publication] 1894
    [*The New Ghetto,* 1895]
Das Palais Bourbon, Bilder aus dem franzosischen Parlamentsleben (essays) 1895
Der Judenstaat, Versuch einer modernen Losung der Judenfrage (manifesto) 1896
    [*The Jewish State: An Attempt at a Modern Solution of the Jewish Question,* 1896]
Philosophische Erzählungen (essays and short stories) 1900
Altneuland (novel) 1902
    [*Oldnewland* published in journal *The Maccabean,* 1902-03; also published as *Old-New Land,* 1941]
Feuilletons. 2 vols. (essays and short stories) 1904
Zionistische Schriften. 2 vols. (essays) 1905

Theodor Herzls Tagebücher, 1895-1904. 3 vols. (diaries)
    1922-23
Theodor Herzl: A Portrait for This Age (essays, addresses,
    diaries, drama, and short stories) 1955
The Complete Diaries of Theodor Herzl. 5 vols. (diaries)
    1960

LEWIS MUMFORD (essay date 1923)

[*Mumford is an American sociologist, historian, philosopher,
and author whose primary interest is the relation between the
modern individual and his or her environment. An expert in
city and regional planning, he is the author of several important studies of cities, including* The Culture of Cities (*1938*)
and The City in History (*1961*). Many of his works reflect his
conviction that firm moral values are necessary to the growth
of civilization. In the following excerpt, Mumford discusses the
Zionist state Herzl depicted in* Altneuland.]

It is customary, I believe, to regard the pamphlet entitled *The
Jewish State* as Herzl's capital contribution to Zionism, and
to look upon his Utopia, *Altneuland* (published in 1904), as
a fanciful and scarcely necessary popularization, in more
graphic form, of the ideas that were definitively put forward
in 1896. I confess that a cursory reading gave me the same
impression. When one compares the prospectus and the utopia proper a little more carefully, however, one discovers that
the second essay represents a real development in Herzl's
thought, and that in *Altneuland* he grapples with the difficulties of Zionism in a much bolder fashion than he did in the
original effort. The Zionist movement, it seems to me, has
been following broadly along the road paved by the pamphlet
without sufficiently grasping the fact that *Altneuland* implicitly suggests certain new departures; and that, in essential respects, *The Jewish State* and *Altneuland* are in conflict.

A word about the original pamphlet before I set out to examine the less systematic but more concrete presentation of the
utopia itself.

The title to the pamphlet of 1896, *The Jewish State,* is the
prime clue to its contents. The plan of colonization there set
forth is too familiar now to require any exposition; but the
interesting point is this: the plan specifically demands that
"the sovereignty be granted us over a portion of the globe
large enough to satisfy the reasonable requirements of a nation." Those of us who adopt the anomalous phrase, "a Jewish national homeland" are not quite as honest as Theodor
Herzl in defining the concept of nationality, as opposed to
simple "culturism," for Herzl left no doubt as to what a nation was. "A nation is," he said, "in my mind a historic group
of men of a recognizable cohesion, held together by a common enemy." His scheme for the settlement of a "national
homeland" therefore presupposed the existence of a common
enemy, and required the formation of a special instrument for
combating that enemy—a Jewish National State.

As Zionism was originally conceived by Herzl, then, it was
a weapon of defence rather than a positive effort to establish
the good life; and necessarily, since it was such a weapon, it
conceived of drawing under its national standard the whole
population of *Judentum.* So the idea stood before the Congress of Basle; before Herzl himself took further steps to realize this prospectus in some sort of working organization. The

original pattern in Herzl's mind was fixed by the myth of the
national state. The mechanism was to be improved, of course,
but the ends for which it existed were those which five centuries of aggression and warfare in national units had hallowed.
Israel was to become a nation among the nations, ever ready
to beat its ploughshares into swords.

By the time Herzl came to write *Altneuland,* the accent and
emphasis had changed; he was no longer treating of some hypothetical settlement in the Argentine or in Syria, but definitely dealing with the old homeland of Palestine. Although
his plans in *Altneuland* are developed with a greater wealth
of imaginative detail than in *The Jewish State,* they are at the
same time a little closer to the realities of the world as they
are known to science, and a little further away from contemporary myths, particularly the myth of the unitary, indivisible National State. One of the symptoms of this change is that
Herzl counts less upon pressure from the outside to effect the
change, and more, as Mr. Benjamin Kidd would have said,
upon the inherent emotional power of the ideal. In *The Jewish State* he emphasizes anti-Semitism and the miseries of a
persecuted race, as the propulsive force behind the movement; in *Altneuland* he was less conscious of the power of inimical Christian groups and more conscious, perhaps, of the
powers of Jewry; and so he writes on his title page: "What
people powerfully desire, they will indisputably achieve." He
was no longer thinking of a "nation held together by a common enemy"; he was thinking of a cultural community, held
together by a common literature and common idola. Zion
was to be established not because Europe was hateful but because the Promised Land itself was attractive.

Merely as a work of literature, in spite of a certain technical
naïveté, *Altneuland* is an interesting book. The dream of *Altneuland* passes through the mind of a young Jew, Dr. Friedrich Löwenberg, who has been overwhelmed in his struggles
with the world as it is, and is on his way to take refuge, as
companion to a genial old misanthropist, in an island in the
South Seas. That South Sea island characteristically represents one utopia of escape for the Jew—its success being conditioned by the completeness with which one can eliminate
other human beings and human contacts, with their opportunities for hope and disappointment. The other utopia of escape is the dream of Zion, which needs only an exertion of
will and the formation of a concrete "building-plan" to become a genuine utopia of reconstruction. This new Zion is to
be blessed by all the knowledge and invention and skill and
imagination that the world at large—and not merely Jewry—
can give.

For the purposes of the story, Dr. Löwenberg is supposed to
return to Palestine after a twenty year sojourn in idleness on
the South Sea island; and the country he finds is the outcome
of a generation of intense effort, led by a young Jew who had,
with all the innocent zealousness of youth, dreamed again the
dream of the Promised Land restored.

How does Herzl's utopia differ from [those presented in Edward Bellamy's *Looking Backward* and Theodor Hertzka's
Freeland]? Well, to begin with, it appeals not so much to a
vague, rational desire for the good society, as to the Jewish
myth, and to the passion for fulfillment in some concrete
form which has always been latent in the Jewish myth. Neither Hertzka nor Bellamy departed very widely from existing
institutions; and Herzl's utopia, in its economic framework,
scarcely can come any closer to concrete realities than those
of his excellent contemporaries. The great difference between

Herzl and his fellow-utopians was that he was keenly conscious of a fatal weakness in their proposals which vitiated their most level-headed pragmatism; that is—I am translating roughly—"they took for granted the very thing which was to be proved; namely, that people had already the maturity and the freedom to judge what things were necessary for the arrangement of a different society. Or perhaps they were clear about this, only they needed a fixed point, like that which Archimedes needed to move the world. They believed that machinery was the most important matter in the creation of a modern order. On the contrary, what is most important is power."

Herzl distinguishes himself, then, by the fact that he purposes to tap a brimming reservoir of power; on one hand, his utopia gets a part of its initial momentum from the misery of the Jews in Europe; on the other, and this is perhaps even more important, from the perpetuated glory of the Jewish myth.

Here is the situation as Herzl puts it in the mouth of his anomalous misanthropist: "With the ideas, knowledge, and means, that today, the 31 December, 1902, are in the possession of mankind, they could remedy their situation themselves. One doesn't need any philosopher's stone or any dirigible airship. All that is necessary to make a better world is already at hand. And do you realize, my friend, who could show the way? You! The Jews! Precisely because everything is going badly with you. You have nothing to lose. You could create an experimental society for mankind—over there in Palestine, on the old soil, you could create a new community—Altneuland."

So one might say that whereas each of the classical utopias was chiseled coldly out of the imagination of some particular thinker, Herzl's *Altneuland,* while perhaps germinating in the mind of a single man, was nevertheless attached, by a sort of placental cord, to the main body of Jewish utopian tradition. More than once, before the Diaspora, the Promised Land had been laid waste and the Temple destroyed; more than once the land had been recultivated and the temple rebuilt. It was another return to Zion that Herzl planned; but the return was not to be a mere reversion: it was to be enriched by all the treasures of thought, imagination, and systematic learning that Israel had encountered on her long wanderings through foreign lands. The Jew was not to come back to Palestine barehanded, facing an impoverished country with no better knowledge of industry, agriculture, and science than that with which his fathers had faced the rich, unexhausted soil at the end of their exodus. If the Zion of old was to be worth rebuilding, it must be such a Zion as had not yet been given body and form. Zion was not merely to reestablish an old habitation for the Jews, but create a new habitation for humanity.

If the first sketch of Herzl's utopia had suggested a Jewish state, on the conventional, more or less military pattern familiar to Western Europe, the completed drawing—as I have pointed out already—substituted for this conception the notion of a New Society working out by direct economic means all that a political state would attempt to accomplish by political methods. Let me emphasize the essential difference between these two points of view. The pat definition of the political state is that it is a territorial organization in which there is a distinction between the governors and the governed: the chief functions of the political state, if one takes a cool historical account of its activities, is to collect tribute, to wage war, and to extend the area from which tribute may be collected.

None of these functions have any necessary connection with the good life; neither do they represent essential economic or cultural activities. For other purposes than waging war, collecting tribute, and preserving privilege—three activities which are so closely related to each other that separation is almost impossible—the political state is an anachronism. It is only, as it were, by an accident that the political state may occasionally serve the legitimate interests of culture or industry.

In fine contrast to the political state, is Herzl's outline of the New Society. For the purpose of recolonizing Palestine, recultivating the land, and restoring Jewish culture, Herzl purposes to use a voluntary, economic corporation, of the type which had grown up in Western Europe during the second half of the nineteenth century. This colonization company was to perform the initial tasks of purchase, transportation, and settlement. As soon as colonies had been successfully planted, however, this corporation was transformed, we find in *Altneuland,* into a *Genossenschaft*—a Society or Association—which therewith took over the capital, the machinery, and the political responsibilities of the pioneer organization.

Where are we to find parallels for this *Genossenschaft?* Is it a state? Plainly not: it lacks a united parcel of territory and it cannot exercise coercive powers over every inhabitant that dwells therein. Is it merely a local administrative unit, like a modern municipality? No: because membership in the *Genossenschaft* does not come automatically by mere residence within a certain area, but implies active participation and an active use of the various instrumentalities possessed by the society. Indeed, the *Genossenschaft* stands for something which is neither a local society, *per se,* nor an industrial organization, *per se,* nor a cultural institution *per se*: it is rather a new form of organization which conforms to modern conditions of technology and culture. There is no exact parallel to this *Genossenschaft* in either the craft guilds of the Middle Age or the Free Cities: the only organization it suggests is that of the First Garden City Association which, by a curious but not irrelevant coincidence, was formed in England about the same time. Economically, the *Genossenschaft* performs functions which used to be in the hands of private corporations or co-operative organizations; politically, it exercises directly controls which used to be exercised in a roundabout way by the political state.

The existence of a *Genossenschaft* does not imply dependence upon an external political state: it only calls for freedom from intrusion and interference by the State. For such a congeries of societies to come into existence in any country, and to attract new members the only provisos that need be made are those calling for complete freedom in immigration and complete freedom in economic intercourse, including freedom to purchase land, make contracts, and transport goods without blockade by customs. The opposition to such a society does not exist anywhere except in the traditional dues, loyalties, and superstitions of the National State. Hence *Altneuland,* instead of being an embodiment of the National State, turns out to be a challenge to it.

To have arrived at such a clear and definite conception of a new organic polity was a singular achievement. Perhaps Herzl did not realize its importance; perhaps he did not see how thoroughly his plans for a scientifically designed polity in *Altneuland* were at odds with the notions outlined in *The Jewish State.* If Herzl himself did not see this great disparity, and did not follow out its implications—a fact partly accounted for, perhaps, by his early death—it is not altogether surprising that those who were immersed in the Zionist movement did not observe it either. At any rate, the piece of original thinking which makes **Altneuland** a distinctive contribution to politics, by suggesting the expedience of forms of political co-operation and government outside the framework of the national state, has remained unnoticed; with the result that the classic modern discussion of the *Genossenschaft* and *Genossenschaftsrecht* is currently supposed to be solely that of Gierke in his *Political Theories of the Middle Ages.*

One more point on behalf of Herzl's deep originality. While **Altneuland** did not posit a national state, neither did it advocate merely a more systematic policy of colonization on the lines that had already been followed in America and Palestine. On the contrary, Herzl added an indispensable program to these somewhat cut-and-dried efforts: he related the immediate, practical step to a comprehensive scheme for social, economic, and cultural development. In short, he provided the Zionist movement with a definite objective, a utopia, so that each particular, concrete step forward had the significance of the movement of a battalion in the execution of a plan of battle. The difference between colonization by itself and colonization towards utopia is the difference between merely grubbing for food or security and achieving a civilized life. Herzl's utopia used the Jewish myth as a propulsive force, as a reservoir of energy: it did not look upon the Jewish myth as an end in itself. Escape from oppression was one thing; reconstruction was quite another. Herzl's utopia pointed to the fact that if the Jews wanted a new material world, in which their spiritual aspirations might be better fulfilled, they would have to create for themselves an intellectual building plan, as complete and accurate as that an engineer constructs before he builds a bridge, or an architect before he starts to erect a house. So Herzl's contribution as a utopian is perhaps even more important to the Zionist movement than his work and example as a Jew: he visualized its implications. Zionism had been a phrase: Herzl made it a picture and a plan. (pp. 158-64)

Lewis Mumford, *"Herzl's Utopia,"* in The Menorah Journal, *Vol. IX, No. 3, August, 1923, pp. 155-69.*

S. BERNSTEIN (essay date 1929)

[*In the following excerpt from* Theodor Herzl: A Memorial, *essays commemorating the twenty-fifth anniversary of Herzl's death, Bernstein, a Zionist philosopher, discusses the purpose and ideology of* Der Judenstaat.]

There is a widespread but erroneous impression that Theodor Herzl's **Judenstaat** represents the program of Zionism. Erroneous because it was in Basle that this program received its clear formulation. Herzl's book is more: it is the spirit, the very essence, so to speak, of Zionism. He himself characterized his work most expressively: "I want this book to have wings."

In the **Judenstaat** there is an element that seems paradoxical, a touch of divine comedy; for fundamentally it is by no means a specifically Jewish book. It is universal in its basis. In its ideas and intellectual tendencies it seems to spring from considerations of general humanity as much as from the Jewish point of view. Throughout the volume the author is impelled equally by the idea of saving the wretched, helpless Jewish masses and by the ideal of the seven-hour working-day, whose realization in the Jewish State is to present a compel-

ling example to the entire world. Actually, however, no conflict exists here. In Herzl's mind Jewry and humanity are so closely bound together that it is difficult to distinguish the line of differentiation. As a matter of fact, the **Judenstaat** was not written for Jews alone, but was designated by its author as an appeal to all mankind. Indeed, Herzl stresses, with some sarcasm, that his plan concerns not the Jewish, but the Christian question. (p. 87)

Herzl's plan for the Jewish State is by no means conceived from a narrow nationalistic and exclusively Jewish point of view. In it he is concerned not so much with Palestine as with the entire Orient. It is characteristic of Herzl's entire attitude that the geographic concept of Palestine plays a relatively subordinate part. The element of Jewish patriotism is merely incidental with him. His primary interest is in the opening of the continent of Asia to Western civilization. "The problem of Asia," he writes, "is becoming more serious every day; and I fear it may lead to a bloody conflict. It is in the interests of the civilized nations to create, as soon as possible, a cultural center on the road to Asia, to serve the cause of Occidental civilization. This center is Palestine; and the civilized nation that is ready to sacrifice its possessions and its blood for this cause is the Jewish people. The political-minded must see this immediately. Such a procedure would help the Jews, and further the interests of all humanity." This is the essential ideology of the **Judenstaat.** But the Jews are not the only civilized people to feel drawn to the East. "England, the great country of freedom, whose possessions touch on every sea, will understand our aspirations. She will broaden the scope of the Zionist ideal—of that we may rest assured."

The **Judenstaat** has frequently been criticized for its mistaken conception of Jewish nationalism. Herzl bases his idea of the Jewish State chiefly upon the *Judennot* (wretched condition of the Jews), and, therefore, upon anti-Semitism. Many Zionists, indeed, regard this as the weakest point of his ideology. Actually, however, it is a very strong point. To Herzl the *Judennot* is the theoretic fundament of his plan; he confesses this quite frankly. As a matter of fact, he considers it the most powerful and, perhaps, the only motive that may impel the Jewish masses to attempt a "flight to the heights." "To achieve anything at all," he remarks, "is difficult for those who are not a little desperate." And he answers with a decided affirmative the question of whether the Jews are capable of taking up the colossal difficulties which such a plan must involve. "Their wretched condition is the miraculous motive power that urges the Jews forward into their new country, that will force them to the greatest sacrifices." Nor can any one deny that the course of Jewish life in the last ten years has proved the correctness of this view.

Although the **Judenstaat** is no longer the official program of the Zionist Organization—the First Congress having incorporated in its program the demand for an internationally recognized and secured Homeland in Palestine—its spirit and basic ideology nonetheless guided the entire Zionist policy of Herzl. The idea about which the **Judenstaat** centers is that of evolution. (pp. 87-8)

Herzl's flexibility in his negotiations and in his pursuit of his ultimate aim was a curious phenomenon. It is unusual to find a party leader so extremely willing and ready to compromise and reach an agreement on even the most important points. To him the slogan of the **Judenstaat** was the secret of his success, the cry that aroused the Jewish masses; yet the moment he realized that a change of tactics would further his cause, he yielded, and accepted the formula of the "Homeland." Seeing that the question of language and culture would cause some serious conflicts among the Zionists, he had the courage to set the entire problem aside, and to declare it of no great significance. "The Jews of the new country will discover for themselves which language is most useful and convenient for them." Indeed, in his readiness for compromise he even went so far as to give up, for a time, the entire idea of Palestine. In order to open the way for negotiations and to obtain the political co-operation of England he agreed to the Uganda plan.

It seems strange that a leader of this sort was able to maintain his position at all, not to mention the fact that he was regarded as the absolute ruler of the popular will. But this was because every one received and felt the clearly defined, invincible will power which Herzl brought into Jewish life. Every one knew that he was not actually deviating from the idea of Palestine by a hair's breadth, or for a single moment. Every one knew that his policy of compromise was directed toward Palestine. He was merely waiting for more favorable conditions; all this was but a device to ease the long, thorny road of the preparation of public opinion. Some day, however, it would develop that all these devious paths led to Jerusalem. Never did Herzl relinquish the idea of the *Judenstaat;* but he felt that it was immaterial how this goal was reached.

Herzl's willingness to compromise was due to the fact that fundamentally his was the nature of a fighter. To Herzl's mind struggle was necessary to the life of society; but it was not to be engaged in unless all other means had failed, unless there was no other way out, unless there was no more hope for friendly co-operation. For a long time he patiently carried on an intensive campaign of propaganda in order to win over the Jewish religious communities of Western Europe. But only after he saw that his peaceful efforts would never succeed, and after the leaders of these congregations, at a moment they considered favorable to their purposes, suddenly launched an attack against Zionism, did he come out with his battle-cry: "Conquer the communities!" He never relinquished his hopes of convincing and winning over his opponents. And when he failed, he was quick to blame himself. "I probably did not know how to handle him," he writes in his diary after his unsuccessful attempt to interest Baron de Hirsch in his idea for Palestine. On another occasion he says: "Some day they will all be our friends, the Rothschilds, the Montagus and the rest. The only question is how to manage them, how to present the cause to them." In order to facilitate the reaching of an agreement, and to prevent the possibility of opposition, he was willing to resort to the most extreme measures. Thus he strictly forbade any sort of connection between the "land policy" and the Zionist movement. Zionism, he believed, must be the bond that unites all the Jews, and must avoid any course that might lead to differences. The Jewish "oligarchy," again, felt offended when the Zionists designated its activities as "philanthropy"; whereupon Herzl came and explained the unreasonableness of such an attitude toward philanthropic work: "When philanthropy is extended to an entire people it becomes a policy."

He was ready to make any sacrifice that might bring him the co-operation of the great Jewish financiers, whose help he considered absolutely indispensable to the success of his enterprise; indeed, he even offered the leadership of the entire movement to the Rothschilds and Montagus. He knew that all these compromises would inevitably lead to the final victory of Zionism. There is no need to fear for the future of a movement based not upon a whim, but upon the solid ground of a scientific conception of reality, of actual life. "Its success must be as certain as the delivery of a letter through the mails." The only question remaining is that of when the time for action shall come; the Jewish policy must take this great moment into account, and must prepare for it. It is in this work of preparation that Herzl saw the secret of Jewish political development and statesmanship; like a scarlet thread this concept runs through his entire work. Herzl's *Judenstaat* describes the art of Jewish statesmanship for all time. (p. 88)

S. Bernstein, "Fundamentals of the Judenstaat: Herzl's Conception of the Jewish State," in Theodore Herzl: A Memorial, *edited by Meyer W. Weisgal, n.p., 1929, pp. 87-8.*

ALEX BEIN (essay date 1934)

[*A German-born historian, Bein served as Director of the Central Zionist Archives in Jerusalem and is the author of numerous studies of the Zionist movement and of Herzl's life and works. In the following excerpt from his* Theodore Herzl: A Biography, *he discusses the subjects and style of Herzl's early feuilletons and plays,* Altneuland, *and* Das Palais Bourbon.]

[In 1887 Herzl published] his first book, a collection of articles, sketches and stories under the rather unfortunate title of *News from Venus.* Some of the material had already appeared in print; some was new. The unifying theme was love as it comes to expression in a variety of circumstances and societies. It was all light, chatty, and distinguished in a minor way.

The introductory *causerie* was devoted to disillusionment, which always resulted, according to the author, when the object of longing was transferred from the dream-distant horizon into the proximity of reality; Venus, the bright star, examined too closely and realistically by the scientist, loses its charm, and so does love when it is similarly treated. It is only the earthy, the massively real, which can sustain such scrutiny, and the dreamer stands before it helpless and disillusioned.

This theme recurs not only in Herzl's first collection of theses; it is one of the basic psychic motifs of all his life.

The closing sketch, **"The Thought-Reader,"** tells of a man who has the peculiar gift of sensing in human beings the transition from the true to the false, from the fullness of feeling to the emptiness of the gesture. "The division into good and bad people is as old fashioned as blood and thunder melodrama," Herzl has this character say. "I believe that in the beginning everyone is good, or as I would put it, genuine. . . . Then something intervenes, it may be only the passage of time, and they become ungenuine. Of love nothing remains then but the tender glance, of friendship nothing but the warm handshake. But I observe the change at once, however deceptively alike the two phenomena may be. . . . I have a nose for the decay of the genuine. . . . I see the transformation into the ungenuine going on all about me. . . . Put yourself in the condition of that unhappy man who can with the naked eye see the infusoria swimming about in the water which he drinks. He perishes between revulsion and thirst. In such case am I. . . ."

This closing article supplied the basic motif of Herzl's second collection of journalistic pieces [*Das Buch der Narrheit*], which appeared a year later under the imprimatur of the same publishing house. He chose as his motto the following quotation from Swift's *Tale of a Tub*: "This is the sublime and refined point of felicity, calling the possession of being well deceived, the serene, peaceful state of being a fool among knaves." After long hesitation he chose for this collection the title of *The Book of Folly*. . . .

It differed from the first collection no less in value than in form. It was a definitely superior work. Instead of a loose succession of scenes, dialogues and monologues, we have a genuine orchestration of feuilletons—that art-form which Boerne and Heine had transferred from the French to the German and which reached its highest form in literary Vienna.

The most characteristic section of the book is the very first, and the theme unfolds most clearly in the story "**Second-Class Gods.**" Here Herzl tells us how he travelled with a fourth-rate theatre, working among the actors, putting up and taking down the tent, arranging the benches for the audience—and participating as an equal in the lives of his fellow artists. Each one of them considered himself a genius, and by means of this self-deception and of hearty mutual lying, they made life tolerable for themselves and for each other. "One disillusionment more, my friends! Not every unrecognized poet is a genius; not every one who fights against windmills is a Don Quixote; not every travelling comedian is the pure idealist which I thought him to be in my youthful passion for superlatives. . . ." And when one of the friendly actors happens to get a little more applause than usual, his nose is suddenly in the air and he looks down it contemptuously at the others. "Ah, you second-class gods, how well I know you now! A little success, a little luck and sunshine, and the weeds shoot up like a thicket: dishonesty, hypocrisy, arrogance, ingratitude! For all of us are like that."

This feuilleton reflects adequately the tone of his mind and the tenor of his thoughts. It is the disillusionment of a kindly spirit: "For all of us are like that." All of us live by the grace of lies. None of us is morally any better, and the height of happiness is, in Swift's phrase, "to be a fool among knaves."

A total of seven or eight lines is devoted to Jews—Herzl's impressions of the Ghetto in Rome. "What a steaming in the air, what a street! Countless open doors and windows thronged with innumerable pallid and worn-out faces. The ghetto! With what base and persistent hatred these unfortunates have been persecuted for the sole crime of faithfulness to their religion. We've travelled a long way since those times: nowadays the Jew is despised only for having a crooked nose, or for being a plutocrat even when he happens to be a pauper." Pity and bitterness inform these lines, but they are written by a detached spectator. He did not know how much of the Jew there was in him even in this detachment of his, in this feeling of remoteness from a world which offered him not living reality but folly.

These fragmentary productions of Herzl's pen are relatively unimportant when placed side by side with his later creations; they are not those masterpieces of craftsmanship which he was yet to produce in the realm of the feuilleton. But the best of them are already luminous with those characteristics which stamp the inspirations of his maturity: originality of perception, clarity of outline, gentleness of expression, perfect balance between content and phraseology. The slight affectation of the grand manner was already evident in his prose, giving it its individual and inimitable features. He has

not yet achieved for every sentence that exactitude and relevance which is the mark of perfection, but neither has he reached that super-refinement of style which later on was to emerge occasionally as the excess of a virtue. In very few instances does he content himself with straightforward, simple narrative; for the most part it is *causerie,* casual conversation. He seems to be addressing a listener, and his remarks flow from him effortlessly, carrying with them no part of his own emotions; or if there is an emotional attitude, it is restricted to a kind of self-irony. No cry of the heart of a poet breaks through; and if now and again there is a hint of the heart's participation, of sorrow or indignation, it is served up delicately, like a finely prepared dish at a gourmet's banquet, in such wise as to make no heavy calls on the digestion of the guest. (pp. 55-8)

[Between] the first and second books Herzl . . . scored his first dramatic success. In February 1888 his comedy *Seine Hoheit* was produced by an excellent cast in Prague, and was well received by public and critics alike. On March 18 the play was transferred to Berlin. "Its success there was considerably greater than in Prague, even though the production was immeasurably inferior," the triumphant author wrote his parents, who had travelled to Prague to attend the premiere. The Berlin critics were for the most part generous in their treatment of the beginner. There were a few sharply negative pieces, but in the big newspapers the comedy "was either mildly praised or gently criticized." There was, however, complete unanimity in the allusions to "the superb feuilletonist." (p. 59)

Unfortunately the first rush of luck soon died down. By the early part of September 1889, he had already completed a new comedy, *Was Wird Man Sagen?*, which dealt with the conventionality of fear of public opinion, and satirized the proneness of men and women to judge their deeds by the reactions of their class. The play was refused by the *Burgtheater* in October, but in March 1890 it was produced in Berlin and Prague, and was an ignominious failure with both critics and public.

Then followed a number of attempts with varying degrees of success and failure. There was the musical comedy *Das Teufels-Weib,* the libretto of which Herzl adapted from Henri Mailhac and A. Mortier's *Madame le Diable,* with music by Müller; it was well enough received, but did not make up for the failure of *Was Wird Man Sagen?* Then Herzl collaborated [with journalist Hugo] Wittmann in *Die Dame in Schwarz,* which was produced on February 6, 1890 by the *Burgtheater,* and was damned by the critics as hokum. Then followed the comedy *Prinzen aus Genieland,* which was excellently received at the *Carltheater* in Vienna on November 21, 1891, but achieved only a short run.

How was it that this successful and gifted feuilletonist could not achieve enduring success in the theatre, even when he put into his dramatic work something more than the play for popular acclaim? There are many reasons. The foremost—it would suffice of itself—was that he did not populate his plays with genuine, living figures. They were schematic, synthetic puppets, whose existence was justified by the witty things they said in behalf of the author. They were inventions, not the transcriptions of observation. "Let life itself be your source, and not your brain," Hartmann wrote to Herzl in 1887. "Take actual persons as your models, instead of clay figures in the museum of the theatre. You are obviously gifted, you have talent, inventiveness, everything that a playwright needs. But it seems to me that you ought to have a somewhat more respectful attitude toward humanity, you ought to look deeper into it."

But Herzl's attention was unfortunately riveted more on the public, and not on the reality of life. He frequented society and, as we have seen, tried to make of his dramatic productions a sort of criticism of society. But the flood of life beyond society, the thunder of that tide which Hauptmann clearly caught, came through to him as a faint murmur, for there intervened not only his own middle class attitude but the delicate musical attunement of his ear. He was frightened off by that realism in art which was, in those days, about to conquer the theatre. But it was impossible to fob off the great social problems of the time with superior and sceptical psychological ingenuities—which is what Herzl tried to do.

To this inadequacy must be added another: Herzl lacked the quality of genuine humor. He had wit, spirit, the sense of the comical in human situations, which accounts, indeed, for his success with the more concentrated form of the feuilleton. But genuine humor, which provokes hearty and liberating laughter, and which calls, in the author, for the power to lift himself clear of his own life and the life of those around him, was denied him; he took himself too seriously.

This subjectivity was an advantage in the semi-philosophic form of the feuilleton, within which he passed on steadily to higher and higher achievement. He poured into it the results of his daily experience, he was able to convert to its purpose his contact with the theatre, and to liven it with the observations gathered on his frequent travels. Other values were also created in him. He came in contact with the masses, for the first time, via his audiences, and obtained his first glimpses into the art of the manipulation of the masses. His failures were object lessons in the loss of such manipulative power, for which another name is—leadership. (pp. 64-7)

Between October 21 and November 8, 1894 . . . [Herzl] completed *The Ghetto,* or, as he later renamed it, ***The New Ghetto.***

The story of the play is easily told. Its hero is the young lawyer Dr. Jacob Samuel, the son of simple, decent people (modelled faithfully after Herzl's own parents). Samuel marries the good-hearted but spoiled and showy Hermine Hellman, daughter of a wealthy merchant. Until the time of his marriage a pure idealist, whose friends have been almost exclusively non-Jews, Samuel, who was introduced to the Hellman family by Dr. Bichler, a baptized Jew, becomes linked with the wealthy class of Jewry, till then an unknown world to him. His closest friend, the Christian Franz Wurzlechner, breaks with him because he dislikes the contact with stock exchange Jews, and also because the association would be harmful to his political career. Samuel's new brother-in-law, Rheinberger, a typical parvenu who toadies to the aristocracy, and his partner Wasserstein, a good natured, ignorant broker, are stock exchange speculators. They see life only under the money-making aspect, and in their eyes Samuel, who continues to stand by his ideals, is an impossibly highstrung individual.

The action of the play develops round the business relationship between Rheinberger and Wasserstein on the one hand, and a certain Rittmeister von Schramm, the owner of a mine, on the other, with Samuel between them. Samuel is called in to draw up the articles of incorporation of a company which is to take over the mine, and of which the chief shareholders

are to be Rheinberger, Wasserstein and von Schramm. It so happens that von Schramm, the distinguished descendant of a long line of aristocrats, was no stranger to Samuel. They had met years before, and had quarreled; Schramm had challenged Samuel to a duel, and Samuel had avoided the duel by tendering an apology—the unrevealed reason being that he dreaded the effect of a duel not on himself, but on his old, sick father.

Samuel has no illusions about von Schramm's opinion of him; the gallant aristocrat undoubtedly thinks of him contemptuously as a coward. Nevertheless he accepts the assignment offered him by Rheinberger and Wasserstein—and that chiefly because he wants to protect the Christian aristocrat against the possible machinations of his brother-in-law, who is infinitely more skilful in business than his new partner.

In the midst of the negotiations Samuel, who has already defended without charge a number of socialists, receives a visit from the delegate of Schramm's miners. The delegate complains that the mine is in bad condition, and a catastrophe may take place any day. Samuel, who has borrowed some money from his brother-in-law, returns the loan and withdraws from his assignment, to take up the cause of the workers. He proceeds at once to the town of Dubnitz, where the mine is situated, and calls the miners out on strike. The strike collapses. On the day when the miners return to work, the waters, which have been accumulating during the period of the strike, break through, and a frightful accident ensues. The result is—on the business side—that the shares of the mine take a sharp fall; the value of the shares held by Rittmeister von Schramm no longer covers the loan which he has made. He is ruined. Rheinberger, whom Schramm holds responsible for the situation, refuses to receive the ruined aristocrat. Samuel interviews him instead and denounces him in the sharpest terms for his treatment of his workers. Von Schramm retorts that Samuel is hand in glove with his thievish brother-in-law. Samuel: "That is a lie!" Schramm: "Jewish pack of thieves!" Samuel: "Take that back!" Schramm: "And if I don't? You'll apologize, just as you did last time. I know you! You'll apologize for yourself, and you'll apologize for your brother-in-law! Jewish pack of thieves!" Samuel flies into a rage and slaps von Schramm. There is a duel. Rittmeister von Schramm kills Dr. Jacob Samuel.

With this play—by far the best of his dramatic creations—Herzl completed his inner return to his people. Until then, with all his emotional involvement in the question, he had stood outside it as the observer, the student, the clarifier, or even the defender. He had provided the world-historic background for the problem, he had diagnosed it and given the prognosis for the future. Now he was immersed in it and identified with it.

He has become its spokesman and attorney, as he is spokesman and attorney for other victims of injustice. It is no accident that the hero of the play is a lawyer by vocation and avocation. For the hero is Herzl himself, and the transformation which unfolds in Dr. Jacob Samuel is the transformation which is unfolding in Theodore Herzl.

There are powerful scenes in the play which throw a blinding light on the working out of the transformation. When Franz Wurzlechner tells Jacob Samuel that, without feeling differently toward his old friend, he is compelled to give up the friendship because he would ruin himself politically if he associated with these stock exchange Jews, Samuel is deeply stirred, but quite clear as to what he is to do. He had learned much from Wurzlechner, he admitted: bearing, manner, gestures. "I have learned from you how to honor a man without crawling at his feet, how to be proud without being arrogant." With the help of Wurzlechner he had "taken a number of steps out of the Jewish street," so that now he was able to continue the exit by himself. At the same time he knows that no credit for this is due his friend. "To be frank with you, what I have admired in you is your family, just as you despise my family now. For some hundreds of years you have been citizens—while we . . ." he smiles painfully. "You became a lawyer because the Wurzlechners of Vienna have always been lawyers or doctors. And Wasserstein, too, is what his forefathers were, he is that which destiny made his ancestors. It's not his fault. Neither is it your achievement. The moral element comes in later, when conscious effort begins. It comes in when the deliberate effort is made to overcome that which has always been instinctive. As for us Jews, we have been made what we are not even by nature, but by history."

"It's all over between us, Wurzlechner! But if you were to offer me your friendship again, if you were to give me the choice, to go with you or with Wasserstein, I would know where I belong. I belong with Wasserstein, whether he is rich or poor. I can't reproach him with anything, any more than I can praise you. Each of you stands there where your history has placed you. But we must not be satisfied with that. We must go onward, upward. Do you hear me? That is what it means to be a man!"

He belongs utterly to the Jews; it is for them that he fights, and, dying, he still sees himself as the fighter for their future. "Jews, my brothers," are his last words, "there will come a time when they will let you live again—when you know how to die. Why do you hold me so fast? . . ." Murmurs: "I want to get out! . . ." With all his strength: "Out! Out—of—the—ghetto!"

What future Jacob Samuel foresaw for the Jews in his dying moments remains unclear. It would appear that Herzl himself still believed that a deepening of mutual understanding between Jews and non-Jews might bring the solution. It is only thus that we can interpret another passage in the dying speech of the hero of the play: "Do you know what else I want? I want reconciliation and forgiveness. . . ."

But Herzl had travelled so much further by this time that he could not have in mind the "reconciliation" which would come by the capitulation of baptism. Indeed, the play emphasizes as a first prerequisite in human relations the element of self-respect. "If you become untrue to yourself," says the clever mother to the son, in the play, "you mustn't complain if others become untrue to you." A man could only be true to himself if he continued to stand by the particular world in which he had grown up and in which nature and history had placed him. And it was the duty of every man to rise consciously, in vision and comprehension, above the limits of his particular little world. The ghetto, Herzl teaches in the play, brings frustration in bearing and being; it is the narrow, the oppressed, the unmanly, it is the distortion of character. The emancipation took away the physical ghetto; the internal ghetto, however, the invisible ghetto, has to be destroyed by ourselves. It is in this sense that Jacob Samuel stands forth as the symbol of a better future.

What Herzl sought, in the writing of this play, was to unburden himself of his crushing obsession. . . .[He] did not suc-

ceed in this. But *The New Ghetto* was a tremendous step forward in his development; it was the beginning of a new Jewish political method. Henceforth the Jewish question was to be lifted out of the trivial atmosphere of minor groups and obscure tea-party meetings, and put by the Jews on the stage of public action. It was like a fresh wind blowing suddenly through the choking atmosphere of a lightless room. It was a new attitude: decent pride! (pp. 102-07)

Between the end of June and the middle of July [1895, Herzl] wrote the last three articles of his series "Pictures of the Parliamentary Life of France," which were later to be published under the book title of *Das Palais Bourbon.* The collection represents the most polished, balanced work that Herzl did for the *Neue Freie Presse.* It is not, however, his best book. Many of the individual pieces are too forced, too polished and too deliberately reflective. "There are pages," wrote Max Nordau, the unbending critic, "which are masterpieces of temperamental, artistic prose. But for my taste others are not simple enough; they do not seem to have been written for inner satisfaction but with an eye on the reader, and in a confusion of native impulse and desire for effect. Such confusion does not produce the best work."

Whatever these objections may be worth, the *Palais Bourbon* is for the most part a composite of brilliant pictures and of penetrating thought. One may apply to Herzl the remark which he applied to Deschanel: he thinks, even though he chatters. He observes, and his first question is directed at the essence, meaning and value of what he sees. He uncovers, behind the facade of magniloquence and great gestures, the trivial humanity of the speakers. To use the phrase of a critic, he sees these parliamentarians not as they create laws but as they create themselves. But his study of personalities is only the psychological springboard for his observations on great questions of political and social import, questions of the structure and instrumentalities of the state, their use and their abuse.

In his studies of the elections of 1893, Herzl had already revealed his critical attitude toward parliamentary democracy as it functioned in France. He was critical of the indecisiveness, the rapidity of change, the general lowering of the level of thought and action, to which it led. It exaggerated the significance of the empty word, it dealt carelessly with great personalities, it gave the advantage to mediocrity. Everything is directed toward the applause of the people. The "free" representative of the people exists in theory only; actually this representative is under the thumb of the election committee; he cannot vote according to his conscience if he expects to be reelected. There are important questions of domestic, and, even more, of foreign policy, which cannot be treated with theatrical boldness, and which do not even permit of a simple yes or no decision. "The public character of the decisions, demanded by democracy, is false and fictitious. Behind that frontage of public discussion things continue to happen which ultimately break out in scandals, like the Panama affair and others of its kind."

On the other hand Herzl perceives clearly that only the normal man, and not the excessively big man such as democracies seek, is fit to direct a government. "These giants, these monster figures, are necessary for the creative eruption, but they are dangerous for the values that exist. . . . The existing values must be guarded and directed by average persons." A clear distinction must be made between government principle and the form of the state, is the opinion of this admirer of Machiavelli, Montesquieu and Rousseau. "There are only two principles of government: the aristocratic and the democratic. And I believe that the principle of government must stand in complementary contrast to the form of the state. The principle of government and the form of the state must mitigate each other. . . . For the aristocratic Republic and the democratic Monarchy are certainly the finest forms of the completed state." (pp. 146-47)

[Herzl completed *Old-New Land* on 30 April 1902] and another half year passed before it appeared in print. It is definitely a book with a purpose, a utopia novel. Its purpose is to body forth the Palestine of the future, to show "how much justice, goodness and beauty can be created on earth if only there is a decent will to it."

It has the weaknesses of every tendencious novel, the weaknesses of all of Herzl's plays: the figures are not full-grown and three-dimensional, they are types embodying a specific outlook or expressing a specific view. This does not, however, alter the fact that most of the fictitious persons are based on living personalities, whose characters or peculiarities have been incorporated in this or that protagonist. Indeed, it was Herzl's purpose to memorialize his friends, as well as some of his opponents; the truth remains, however, that most of the *dramatis personae* are figures in a play; the entire work has something of the stage about it, and proceeds in scenes rather than by way of narrative. We perceive in it, as in all of Herzl's literary productions, his special ability to arrest a moment in time and to outline swiftly and simply the elements of a situation or subject; we perceive also that he lacks the breath, endurance and patience to master a great literary form, as well as the creative power to round out and fill with life the figures which he presents. Regarding himself Herzl said, in his diary, that he was "a writer of great mold," who "had not put forth his full strength because he had been disgusted and discouraged." But the truth seems to be that he overestimated his literary gifts. His talent was of another kind: he had a flair for development and growth, he saw the full fruit in the seed, the future lying concealed in the present. He pictured forth the future, he showed the way to it, he called upon others to tread the path, and he himself courageously led the way—a road-builder and banner-bearer. (pp. 396-97)

> *Alex Bein, in his* Theodore Herzl: A Biography, *translated by Maurice Samuel, The Jewish Publication Society of America, 1940, 545 p.*

JOACHIM PRINZ   (essay date 1952)

[*A German-born American scholar and rabbi, Prinz has written numerous works on Jewish history, religion, and culture. In the following excerpt, he recounts the genesis of* Der Judenstaat *and delineates Herzl's ideology as presented in the work.*]

Most great Jewish books are anonymous in a profound sense. Not that the author is generally unknown, but the details of his biography have become unimportant. At times the author's name has been forgotten, and he is remembered only by the title of his work.

But the *Judenstaat* is Theodor Herzl's book. Neither its content nor its influence can be understood without an analysis of the author. It is the first Jewish book that stirred Jewry after the Western emancipation. Not that Herzl's topic or even his approach to the Jewish problem had been utterly novel. Moses Hess wrote his *Rome and Jerusalem* in 1862, and it is far superior to Herzl's *Judenstaat.* Leon Pinsker's

Auto-Emancipation, published twenty years later, is more concise and in parts more impressive than the *Judenstaat.* Neither of the two, however, was able to create the movement that was to implement their ideas. The *Judenstaat* did. Its consequences and its impact upon masses of people can only be compared with Karl Marx's *Das Kapital* and with the Communist *Manifesto.*

Three factors account for the success of the little book which Herzl called, "my pamphlet": the unusual spiritual-political circumstances of the times; the post-emancipatory disappointment of world Jewry, and the unique personality of Theodor Herzl.

Few decades in the world history can boast of so many accomplishments in almost every field of human endeavor: Bell invented the telephone; Edison the electric bulb; Henry George wrote *Progress and Poverty* and Tolstoy preached Socialism in novels; Brahms and Wagner were but two of the galaxy of great composers; Rodin and Renoir, Toulouse-Lautrec and Degas began to emerge from the great battle of the impressionists; the great French novel (Victor Hugo and Emile Zola); the dramatic play of social significance (Shaw and Wilde in England, Ibsen and Strindberg in Scandinavia, Tolstoy in Russia and Hauptmann in Germany); the organization of trade unions; the revolutionary discoveries in chemistry; the final emergence of the middle class and the bourgeois military caste; the widening conflict between a newly awakened nationalism and the beginnings of liberalism in political as well as social thinking. It is against this background of events that the *Judenstaat* must be viewed. Is it any wonder that a generation so wide awake, so profoundly alerted to the new miracles and so piously devoted to faith in progress should have listened attentively to a call for a "new order" in the affairs of the Jewish people? Herzl himself was part of the dreams and ideals of his time.

The Jewish world was sharply divided into East and West. Oriental Jewry was not even known. Elkan N. Adler's book on Oriental Jewry came as a shocking surprise. Western Jewry looked with disdain upon the unemancipated masses of the East. Of their Jewish life, their creativity and piety and their Jewish devotion, they knew nothing. Nobody would have dared to sing a Yiddish folk song in society or at a Jewish meeting anywhere in the Western Jewish world. Of Jewish literature, only the sweetish romanticism of Karl Emil Franzos and Israel Zangwill's ghetto stories seemed acceptable. Any real contact with East European Jewry was avoided.

The reason for this lay in fear and basic insecurity. Although the decrees of Jewish emancipation had been solemnly signed and although prosperity among the Western Jews of Herzl's generation was widespread, there was a general feeling of insecurity. To determine the real Jewish situation underneath the surface happiness and success, one needed a seismograph. The slightest disturbance spelled catastrophe: the tragic comedy of Alfred Dreyfus (Clemenceau, then a young lawyer, claimed that Dreyfus was the only one who did not comprehend the anti-Semitic nature of his own case) removed at once the veneer of French civilization and good French citizens crowded the streets of Paris and yelled, "*a bas les Juives*" ["down with Jews"]; an alleged shabby business deal of the Jewish ammunition manufacturer, Loewe, elevated a miserable school master, Ahlwart, to leadership of the anti-Semitic movement in Berlin; and the black Friday at the stock exchange in 1893 was the beginning of a mass movement against the "international Jew." Nor could the Jews be made to believe that these attacks upon their emancipation were caused by the base instincts of the masses. After all, Richard Wagner the composer, Heinrich Treitschke the historian, Houston Stewart Chamberlain the writer, and Adolf Stoecher the Protestant minister, were among the leaders. . . .

It was necessary for Western Jewry to comfort itself with a theory that would explain the strange "medieval movement of anti-Semitism." To the Western Jews, anti-Semitism was the manifestation of lack of enlightenment and thus they proceeded to enlighten the Christian world. This was done through the *Alliance Israelite Universelle* in Paris, the *Central Verein* in Berlin, the *Union* in Vienna, which were the leading Jewish organizations of these countries and fully represented the beliefs of the majority of the Jewish people. The magazines and books published at that time reassured the world of Jewish patriotism; recorded proudly every Jew who had died "on the field of honor" or had made an important scientific contribution; denied emphatically any tie with world Jewry; and sought to emphasize the ethical foundations of Judaism rather than the colorful customs which distinguished Judaism from Christianity. Anti-Semitism was a real force in the life of the majority of the Jews in Western countries. It was difficult to prevent Jews from intermarrying; more than one hundred twenty-five thousand had changed their religion since the emancipation was proclaimed.

Theodor Herzl, it must be remembered, was not far removed from this world. There was a time when to him, too, conversion was the only possible solution. "Two years ago," he wrote in the spring of 1895, "I meant to solve the Jewish problem with the help of the Catholic Church, at least in Austria. I meant to go to the Pope and ask him to help us in the fight against anti-Semitism. 'If you do as I say, I shall make myself the leader of a huge movement aiming at a voluntary and honest conversion to Christianity.' " His plan was to lead a solemn procession of Viennese Jews "on a Sunday morning at twelve o'clock noon to Stephan's Cathedral with church bells ringing. It should be done unashamedly and proudly." Ironically enough, it took Benedikt, his publisher, a confirmed anti-Zionist and assimilationist, to convince him how undignified and impractical the plan was. "For one hundred generations your family preserved its ties with the Jewish people. Yet now, you take it upon yourself to terminate it. You can't do it. You must not do it. Furthermore, the Pope won't see you anyway." It is not clear which of the two arguments convinced him; at any rate, Herzl gave up the idea.

A few days later in a conversation with a friend, Ludwig Speidel, music critic of the *Neue Freie Presse,* he began a new train of thoughts, the first beginnings of the *Judenstaat.* He recorded it thus:

> I begin to understand anti-Semitism. It is the consequence of our emancipation. . . . But anti-Semitism which lives in the masses as something strong and subconscious will not hurt the Jews. On the contrary, it will serve us well. . . . Hardships are good means of education. It will lead to Darwin's mimicry. The Jews will be integrated. They are sea lions which world accident threw into water. Thus they pretend to be fishes. They adopt the appearance and characteristics of fishes. Yet if they ever were to land again on dry land and were permitted to stay there for a few generations, their fins would change into feet. Only new pressure can remove the traces of pressure.

Speidel was impressed with what he called "a world historic concept" of the Jewish problem. A few experiences which followed this conversation are recorded in Herzl's diary: some anti-Semitic incidents; a service at the famous synagogue on *rue de la Victoire* in Paris; and a discussion with Fredrich Beer who did Herzl's bust. During the excited discussion with Beer, Herzl conceived the idea of a play which was to deal with the Jewish problem. It took him "three glorious weeks" to write *The New Ghetto.* As a play it was mediocre, and offered no real solution. The duel between the anti-Semitic nobleman and the Jew ends with the death of the Jew. The death of his hero in the play was in reality a suicide. Indeed the idea of suicide plagued Herzl throughout his lifetime. In terms of a real solution of the Jewish problem as a problem of the people, personal and individual solutions meant little.

It was at that time that his plan for a pamphlet began to be formulated. He meant to call it, "A Survey on the Jewish People" (*Zustaende der Juden*). It represented a reporter's approach to the problem. "I intended to visit those places into which world-accident had scattered them: Russia, Galicia, Hungary, Bohemia, later the Orient and the new Zionist colonies and then again, West Europe." The aim of this survey was to prove to the world that the Jews were innocent victims and that "they were being slandered without being known." This is still the ideology of the assimilationist. It is still apologetic. The plan, however, was dropped in favor of a novel.

A novel was closer to Herzl's heart. Alphonse Daudet, the French novelist and an anti-Semite, reminded him of the far-reaching influence of *Uncle Tom's Cabin* upon the emancipation of the American Negro. The plot for the novel was almost ready. Again suicide played a central role. This time it is not the hero but a symbolic Jew, Samuel Kohn, who commits suicide "because he was not able to discover his Promised Land." The plot is meager and Herzl's love for the melodrama would have made this an almost unbearable novel. Happily, he decided upon what he called "a practical idea." This meant a serious political pamphlet.

Although Herzl could not account for the sudden change to this new form, it seems abundantly clear that his letters to Baron Hirsch and the conversation that followed, were responsible for this. The first letter is vague. The second (May 4, 1895), however, has all the characteristics of style and approach of the *Judenstaat.* "So far" he writes to Hirsch, "you were merely a philanthropist. I shall show you how to grow." This is the almost impertinent style of most of Herzl's letters. There is an abruptness and directness of speech which is at once insulting and appealing. The conversation which followed was decisive. Herzl, who during the entire period watched himself as though he were looking at a historic drama and did things deliberately in the light of it, played his role well. Although he did not admit it immediately, he played the role of Moses before Pharaoh. The real Pharaohs were yet to come. In his conversation with Hirsch he speaks almost in Biblical terms: "I shall go to the German Kaiser. He will understand me for he was trained to understand big things. I shall tell him, 'Let us go. We are strangers. One does not permit us to assimilate and we can't do it. Let us go'." This role fits him well. He begins to like it. And perhaps with a trembling heart he pretends to be bold. His language is. "Do you have a full hour for me?" he says to Hirsch. "If you don't, let's not even start." Herzl's summary of the conversation is: "I was not disappointed. On the contrary, I was stimulated."

The *Judenstaat* was the result of this stimulation. "At home something pulled me to the desk. I wrote walking, standing, in the street, at the table and at night when I could not sleep." At times he was not quite sure of his sanity. "Were it not so logical, I should call it 'compulsion neurosis'." In older days such a state of mind was called "inspiration." In this state of exultation he wrote some seventy pages of the most fantastic plans which he wanted to incorporate into the *Judenstaat.* In the final version, however, many of these "thought splinters" were left out. They are part of what he called "Address to the Family Circle of the Rothschilds." The idea became an obsession with him that the fortune of the Rothschild family should finance his plans. As he began to think in terms of a catastrophe which sooner or later would overwhelm the Jewish people, he considered this plan the only means of saving the huge fortune of the family.

The manuscript was to be read to two friends, Rabbi Moritz Guedemann, the Chief Rabbi of Vienna, and Heinrich Mayer-Cohen, a philanthropist from Berlin. Herzl thought of a gigantic setting—the Alps in Glion, Switzerland. Only snow-covered mountains could form the proper background for an idea that tried to reach the stars and was as gigantic in his mind as the eternal snow on the mountain-tops. The plans, however, were changed and he had to choose the drab surroundings of a Jewish restaurant in Munich. The two men were impressed, even enthusiastic. Guedemann called him a Moses. It was then that he realized that his plan which he wanted subsidized by the Rothschilds, transcended the concern of one family and that it could only be carried out by the people for whom it was intended—a factor mightier than any bank or any family fortune. The Jewish people were included in the plans. And so, the frills and trimmings disappeared and the *Judenstaat* was conceived and written. It is not a uniform book, either in style or in content. Some of the "thought splinters" disturb the flow of the book. Yet it contains two important parts: the theory of the Jewish question and a sketch of the apparatus which was to lead to its solution. When the English translation appeared in London in 1896, its title was, *The Jewish State—An Attempt at a Modern Solution of the Jewish Question.*

The slightly more than seventy pages that constitute the *Judenstaat* made fantastic reading. They contained the theory of the new movement and a plan of action. Although the plan was widely discussed and formed the basis for practical work in Palestine, it was the theory that converted Jewry to the new movement. For a theory was badly needed, particularly in Europe where no movement could grow without accepting a clearly defined ideology. Herzl's *Judenstaat* became literally the Bible and the catechism of European Zionism. The decades following the publication of the *Judenstaat* were devoted to ideological discussion rather than merely practical work. The interpretation of this Bible of Zionism in hundreds of books and thousands of articles, not to speak of the endless discussions at Zionist meetings all over the world, formed the backbone of the movement at a time when colonization and immigration were virtually at a standstill. European Jewry in the West, by virtue of tendencies of assimilation, in the East as a result of Haskalah, the movement of enlightenment, was passing through a crisis of Jewish religion. Zionism was the secular substitute for it and the new ideology created by the *Judenstaat* almost replaced the religious dogma.

The starting point of the ideology presented in the *Judenstaat* was the "understanding" and new interpretation of anti-Semitism. Herzl was not satisfied with the definition of anti-Semitism in the literature of his contemporaries. Anti-Semitism could not be due to a lack of enlightenment. Anti-Semitism was much more deep-seated and therefore beyond the reach of rational enlightenment. "The old prejudices against us still lie deep in the hearts of the people. One only needs to listen to the people where they speak frankly and simply: both proverb and fairy tale are anti-Semitic." This anti-Semitism so profoundly imbedded in the character of the Christian world must therefore be considered a reaction to the *existence* of the Jewish people rather than to any *action* on their part. This anti-Semitism causes oppression and pogroms. Since the Jewish people are not better than other people, it does not improve their character. "Oppression naturally creates hostility against oppressors and our hostility aggravates the pressure. It is impossible to escape from this vicious circle." Nor can anti-Semitism be cured by assimilation. "We have honestly tried everywhere to merge ourselves into the social life of our environment and to preserve only the religion of our fathers. They will not permit us to do so."

What then is the *cause* of anti-Semitism? It is contained in one sentence which we consider the basic statement in the *Judenstaat.* It became the slogan of the new movement. With this simple, short sentence which sounds trite today, Herzl began the revolution in Jewish thinking. The sentence reads: "We are a people—one people." Here was the theory of anti-Semitism and the explanation for the abnormal existence of the Jewish people. Scattered all over the globe, the Jews remained a people within the nations among whom they lived. The proof was the existence of the Jewish question: "The Jewish question exists. Nobody can doubt it." The Jews remained not only *a* people among the various nations, but also *one* people across all the borders, transcending language, habit and national custom which they may have accepted in the countries of their adoption. Since the Jews constituted one people, the interpretation of anti-Semitic phenomena by contemporary writers was wrong. There must be an approach that would apply to the affair of Alfred Dreyfus in France as well as to the pogroms in Russia, to the anti-Semitic movements in Germany, to the anti-Jewish trials in Hungary and to the violent anti-Semitism in Vienna. These were not to be regarded as isolated national occurrences but as manifestations of a single phenomenon. This phenomenon was called "the Jewish question," and it was the entire problem which the *Judenstaat* proposed to solve.

A very important point of the *Judenstaat* is usually overlooked in the many interpretations of the book. It is what Herzl calls "the propelling force." This is, to our mind, the very crux of the movement which Herzl founded and without which the *Judenstaat* would have been forgotten and the Zionist movement would not have existed. It shows not only Herzl's daring but his understanding of the elements of a political movement. Against the background of Jewish prosperity in the Western countries, where Jews were successful in contemporary banking, manufacturing, sciences, literature and music, he dared to predict that anti-Semitism, instead of disappearing, would increase to such an extent as to make the life of the Jews in the West as well as in the East, utterly unbearable. He introduced into the discussion, a new term: *Judennot*—Jewish misery. It corresponds in his theory to the place which the idea of the "increasing misery of the working masses" has in the socialist theory of Karl Marx. Political movements are doomed to failure if they lack the daring to predict for their whole foreseeable future, the economic and political development of the group at which they are aimed. But daring alone is not enough. Daily reality must furnish sufficient proof that the political theory is more than a sermon. The labor movement based upon the theory of the "increasing misery of the working masses" grew because the theory proved to be true. Herzl's *Judenstaat* would have remained a pamphlet and a Utopian idea without the prediction of increasing Jewish misery and without the fulfillment of this prophecy. "In Russia the Tzar will kill us, in Germany the Kaiser will issue decrees and there will be expropriation from above." These were daring words at a time when everybody was speaking of progress.

For the complexities of the Jewish question, Herzl had a relatively simple solution. "The whole plan is in its essence simple, as it must be if everybody is to understand it. Let sovereignty be granted us over a portion of the globe large enough to satisfy the rightful requirements of a nation. The rest we shall manage for ourselves. The creation of a new state is neither ridiculous nor impossible . . . the governments of all countries, plagued by anti-Semitism, will be keenly interested in assisting us to obtain the sovereignty we want."

The idea of the state is clear, yet Herzl was in doubt as to the country where the Jewish State was to be established. "Shall we choose Palestine or Argentina? . . . Argentina is one of the most fertile countries in this world, extending over a vast area. It has a sparse population and a mild climate. . . . Palestine is our ever-memorable historic home." Thus the idea of the *Judenstaat* does not necessarily mean Palestine. It aims at a state. It means sovereignty. And it means, above all, an international guarantee in the form of a charter to be obtained from one of the existing governments. But the choice of the land is left to a commission which will decide between Argentina and Palestine, or even other countries in the world. Herzl was as undecided about the country as he was about many other matters, particularly in regard to the Hebrew language. Assimilated Jew that he was, he could not conceive of Hebrew as the language of the people and was quite surprised when Dr. M. Berkowicz asked for permission to translate the *Judenstaat* into Hebrew. He was certain that one of the European languages would be acceptable to most Jews. There are other parts of the "practical plan" which make strange reading today, yet its framework remains an ingenious part of the *Judenstaat.*

Herzl envisaged the creation of two organizations: "The Society of Jews" and "The Jewish Company." It is interesting that in the German original, the two terms are used in English. Headquarters of both organizations were to be in London. Herzl was convinced that whatever country would be selected, England would play a major part in the creation of the state. "The Society of Jews will do the preparatory work in the fields of science and politics," and The Jewish Company will be responsible for the practical implementation. The Society of Jews will represent the Jewish people in the Diaspora. It will be its national address. It will take the place of the state as long as the state does not exist.

What Herzl envisaged by his Society of Jews was fulfilled by the World Zionist Organization and later by the Jewish Agency for Palestine. And his Jewish Company found its counterpart in those organizations which did the practical work in the upbuilding of the land. A good many of the details in Herzl's plan for the Jewish State became obsolete: his

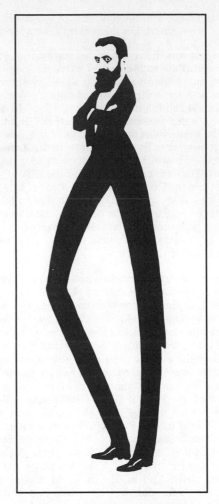

Viennese cartoon of Herzl with the caption "The Biggest Jew Alive."

concept of an "aristocratic republic," his general tendency toward some mild form of dictatorship; some of his proposals for practical implementation. But the strange details did not obscure the sublime message of the *Judenstaat,* nor detract from its influence. Had Herzl limited his book to his theory of the Jewish question and to the bare outline of his plan, the *Judenstaat* would still have been the most stirring and influential of modern Jewish books. It captured the imagination of the Jewish people. It invested Jewish life with new meaning. The *Judenstaat* became the credo of the modern Jew. (pp. 254-67)

> Joachim Prinz, "*Judenstaat (The Jewish State),*" in The Great Jewish Books and Their Influence on History, *edited by Samuel Caplan and Harold U. Ribalow, Horizon Press, 1952, pp. 254-67.*

MARVIN LOWENTHAL   (essay date 1956)

[*In the following excerpt from the introduction to his 1956 translation of Herzl's diaries, Lowenthal emphasizes the literary and historical importance of Herzl's autobiographical writings.*]

A diary of consequence, a great diary, owes its distinction to the window it opens on some vanished day—to its historical value—and to the floodlight it pours on the diarist himself as a man of his time or, in rare cases, of all time. . . .

The diaries of Theodor Herzl . . . have the singular quality of being written by an unpremeditated statesman who didn't wait until the returns were in, and his career fairly over, to compose his memoirs and thereby, even if in good faith, reshape his memories. Instead, he gives us statesmanship in the raw, undraped and undoctored—history on the spot and caught in the act. Then too, unlike most statesmen who have kept a journal, he was a trained dramatist who knew how to do literary and human justice to his remarkable experience. (pp. ix-x)

From the moment the idea of a Jewish state took form, still inchoate and vague, in his mind, he felt the writer's compulsion to put his thoughts and feelings on paper. Day by day the idea grew wilder in eruption and yet clearer and firmer as the flaming particles began to cohere and cool into a logical structure; and the diary entries display, in perhaps unparalleled detail, the creative process at work. When the writer turned to action, as he quickly did, the diaries recount how starting from scratch Herzl forged the tools for converting his idea into a reality: a world-wide organization to express the Jewish people's will, a Congress to serve as its national assembly, and the financial institutions to implement its decisions.

Simultaneously the diaries capture the story, unfolded step by step, of how with little or no backing he negotiated single-handed with the rulers, statesmen, and financiers who controlled the destinies of Europe and the Near East: Kaiser Wilhelm II and Foreign Minister von Bülow in Germany; the Sultan of Turkey, Abdul Hamid, and his favorite minions of the moment; Joseph Chamberlain and Lord Lansdowne in England; Ministers Plehve and Witte in Russia; Pope Pius X, Cardinal Merry del Val, and the King of Italy at Rome; Baron de Hirsch and the Rothschilds among the Jews; and scores of lesser figures, the most important sometimes having the least standing. Anyone today, professional historian or amateur of the human spectacle, who seeks to understand our civilization on the eve of its plunge, with the First World War, into a new era will gain fresh insights and vistas from the window opened by the diaries.

Every episode they report was a maneuver in a grand but endless strategy, and, because of Herzl's literary skill, presents a living breathing portrait of the participants. Each encounter runs like a scene from a play which transports the onlooker from London to Constantinople, from Jerusalem to St. Petersburg, from Potsdam to Rome, across the stage of world history at the turn of our century. Great names are transmuted into actors who know how to speak their parts but cannot cease to be plain human beings. The diaries, in a word, have a line—like that of a sweeping novel or drama. While none of the characters, including the diarist, can know what will happen next, while suspense rules and cross-currents and distractions abound, an underlying purpose—Theodor Herzl's purpose—imbues the whole with a unity to be found only in art or in a man whose life is so dedicated as to become a work of art. The diaries, then, are at once autobiography, history, and literature.

Perhaps their most unusual trait is the freedom with which Herzl, in the engaging candor of a man who is both the doer and the observer, retails the daily adventures, the ups and downs, the misjudgments and inconsequentialities, the hopes,

schemes, and disillusionments, the whole serio-comic aspect of statescraft. But to the extent to which politics are comic, the politician in the case of Herzl becomes poignantly tragic. A politician who never discerns the comedy of politics, who is never vouchsafed a detached glimpse of himself and his activities, who can never evaluate, with a cosmic sense of proportion, himself, his fellow actors, and their mutual behavior, and who never once cries out, like Alice, "You are nothing but a pack of cards!" is of course most comic of all. Herzl was far from this. On the other hand, a politician who would persist in seeing nothing but the comedy could not remain a politician. Herzl had again and again the flash of comic insight, yet a stronger power than himself held him to the contest. He was keen enough never to be surprised at failure, yet the idea of Zion which had seized him and manipulated him against the frequent dictates of reality, compelled him always to hope and strive for victory. Zion ruled him as fate governed a Greek hero or as the burden of the Lord weighed on a Hebrew prophet, and kept him fighting when he knew that the opposing odds were overwhelming and, worse, when he knew that the tactics and human figures in the battle were on occasion tawdry. He was tragic not because he was a Don Quixote winning our indulgent sympathies, but because he was a Don Quixote who recognized his own Quixotism and yet, in obedience to the ideal, never lowered his lance . . . and drove himself to an untimely grave.

Literature is not only richer for his diaries, written in the heat of each day's work and catching the pulse and color of their time and of the men who played imposing parts in it, but through their pages a new character is delineated in history. The Utopist is a familiar figure. The Utopist who strives to make his news from nowhere a reality to be chronicled in the morning papers is also not altogether unknown. But such constructive Utopists have never before, one may venture to say, left a minute and palpitating record, dated sometimes hourly, of themselves and their quest. And that Herzl's life, from the day he penned the first line of his journal, was devoted without condition or remittance to his people, that he achieved significance and even grandeur through this devotion should be an especial human treasure. (pp. x-xii)

Marvin Lowenthal, "Introduction: The Diaries and the Man," in The Diaries of Theodor Herzl, *edited and translated by Marvin Lowenthal, The Dial Press, 1956, pp. ix-xxvi.*

ALEX BEIN (essay date 1960)

[*In the following excerpt, Bein examines the development of themes and style in Herzl's short stories.*]

In the mind of the public, Herzl the statesman, the founder of the Jewish State, and Herzl the writer, are two separate and distinct figures. The former receives only the highest praise, but the latter is generally considered a second-rate journalist who wrote brief, entertaining articles for "the lower half of the page," articles which required little intellectual effort on the part of the reader and would quickly be forgotten. It is believed that before he became a Zionist, literature was Herzl's chief occupation (and indeed he did write many essays, sketches and plays), but that he was not very serious about his profession. On the other hand, when he took up the cause of Zionism, he devoted himself to it wholeheartedly, and continued to turn out minor literary pieces simply to fulfill his obligation to the *Neue Freie Presse,* of which he was literary editor. He was always afraid that he would lose this job because of his Zionist activities, and thus be left without either a livelihood or a respectable position in the world—a position which meant so much for the furthering of his Zionist ambitions.

Certain notes in Herzl's diaries and letters give evidence of this. When the great change occurred in his life, in the 1890's, he viewed his previous life and literary work with scorn. His new goal was so inspiring, the tasks he had taken upon himself so absorbing, that everything he had written before seemed frivolous by comparison. The necessity for retaining his position on the *Neue Freie Presse,* which never mentioned Zionism during his lifetime, was a constant source of irritation to Herzl, and friction between himself and the newspaper owners embittered his entire existence. Thus, depression and irritability frequently appear in his diary entries and letters. Such moods are, of course, quite irrelevant to a just estimate of his merit as a writer.

Herzl felt he had been destined to become a great writer, but that his talent had never reached full development because his attention had been diverted in other directions. But all his life, he longed to produce finished works of art, works that would express his deepest yearnings and convictions. And precisely during those years when he was most preoccupied with Zionism, his literary achievement reached its greatest depth and clarity. The characters and events he described were closer to reality then, and frequently he expressed through parable and allegory concepts he was forbidden, as a Zionist, to express openly in his newspaper. Thus, there is slight justification for making a distinction between Herzl the Zionist and Herzl the writer: these are different aspects of the same personality. Moreover, Herzl's whole orientation toward life, the evolution of his philosophy covering justice, free will, the relation between the sexes, and between parents and children, ethics, and the relation between society and the state were given expression in his literary work. Thus he sent such a book as his *Philosophical Tales* to the various men with whom he was negotiating on behalf of Zionism—the German Kaiser, Bulow, the Grand Duke of Baden, Walter Rathenau and others. He specially requested the Grand Duke of Baden to read the story entitled **"Solon in Lydia,"** and the Duke replied that he had read not only this story, but all of them. He found in them, he wrote, abundant food for thought that completely justified the title *Philosophical Tales.* "Each story stimulates a new train of thought that compels self-examination."

Walter Rathenau wrote to him on August 16, 1901, "I finished your book yesterday. You appealed to my discretion in asking that I not review it, but I am going even further, and shall not discuss it with you at all, except to make one comment. Please do not take this as simply politeness; the book gave me the feeling, which I had not had before, that the author really knew life." These remarks apply especially to the first half of *Philosophical Tales.*

The title *Philosophical Tales* was chosen by Herzl in 1900 when the stories were first published in a single volume, and he used it again in 1904, when he appended four "philosophical tales" to his two volumes of *feuilletons.* The four tales included in this publication had appeared in the *Neue Freie Presse* after publication of the previous book.

Another story, not included in the above-mentioned volumes, was published in 1887 with Herzl's first collection of *feuille-*

tons, entitled *News about Venus.* This brief story, **"The Mind Reader,"** seems typical of Herzl's way of seeing things, which is also expressed in his dispatches from Paris (a small selection of which he put together under the title *Palais Bourbon*), as well as in his plays. The hero of **"The Mind Reader,"** who is also the narrator, says of himself that he has the power to detect deception. "Or perhaps I should say," he replies to a question,

> that I am aware of transitions. It's a very special faculty. Have you ever watched the twilight fall? Have you ever noticed how the light of both dawn and evening brightens and pales in a split second? Well, I have a very sharp eye: I see each of these transitions as a separate event. And transitions of this sort also appear in the human personality. I can see these just as clearly. The division of men into good and evil is completely antiquated and melodramatic. . . . There are no such things as "good" and "bad" men. At the outset, I believe, every man is good, or, rather, I should say, genuine. The woman loves and she pours all her love into the tenderness of her glance. The friend is devoted, and he presses your hand with warmth. Then something happens—perhaps merely the flow of time itself—and they lose their genuineness. Of love, nothing remains except the tender glance; of friendship, only the warm handclasp. But I discover this immediately, however deceptively it looks like the genuine thing; so deceptively that one is inclined to take the holiest oath upon its genuineness. I can read the thoughts. I can smell the odor of the decay of sincerity. . . . I can feel it in the lyrics of a poet writing of feelings which left him long ago; in politics, I see it in the opportunistic orator whose voice still thunders as in the days when he was young and filled with passionate enthusiasm, although inwardly he has become utterly cold and indifferent. Wherever there is lack of genuineness, I am aware of it. With this power of seeing into men's souls, I could be a successful diplomat or businessman, but I have wasted the gift and am only an idler and a *boulevardier.* What power I could wield over men, I, who recognize the rot and corruption of their hearts!

Isn't this the same power of "seeing into things"—into the very souls of men—that Herzl displayed when he examined the Jewish question? Here, too, he tore away the veils of pretense and revealed the truth in all its ugliness, but with all its potentialities for beauty. These stories mark stages along Herzl's journey into the depths of his own psyche, which had to precede his understanding of the world in general and of the Jewish problem in particular.

In **"The Mind Reader,"** as well as in several of Herzl's other stories, the literary qualities are often weak. Herzl did not realize his characters sufficiently. Nor was he a born storyteller, as are the great novelists and short story writers. His talent was rather that of the brilliant conversationalist who can recount an amusing anecdote or make a witty comment. He was also a thorough-going romanticist: "the lyricist of the Viennese *feuilletonists*" one critic called him. But above all, Herzl was a philosopher, a man who looked into the heart of things, in order to determine the nature of reality, both in the present, and in the future. Thus, the plot in most of his tales is superficial elaboration with no organic relation to the ideas expressed. The point of departure for most of the stories and sketches is the surroundings in which the hero or narrator finds himself, and his seemingly insignificant impressions of

Vienna, his home town, or on his extensive travels. But these external events serve only as an entering wedge into the main subject matter.

The world of the theatre, of journalism and advertising, occupied him for many years. Thus in **"The Dressing Room,"** as in many other stories, Herzl tears the veil of illusion from a world which appears entirely glamourous, and reveals the life of frustration and disappointment behind the superficial glitter. We catch a glimpse of the wounded pride that subsequently led him to defend the honor and rights of the Jewish people, as well as the compassionate understanding of a man who had felt keenly the suffering and persecution of others. The link between personal suffering and great achievement in the fields of the arts, science and public service, was perceived and shown by him almost ten years later in his tragic story **"Sarah Holzmann."** Here Herzl combines, and compares philosophically, the story of dogs trained by cruel discipline, of a young woman pianist who perfects her art through silent personal suffering, and of a scientist who does research in the wilds of Africa. Of the scientist who flees from a nagging wife to far-off lands, Herzl says,

> Science should be grateful to this woman. The motivations for our achievements are sometimes strange, and often pathetic. You, members of the comfortable middle class, haven't the slightest notion of the source of the songs which enchant you or the deeds you so ardently admire. You enjoy a song which springs out of suffering, but you don't understand it. Of course, in order to be creative, a man must have the kind of soul which transforms affliction into exquisitely poignant expression.

With regard to the world of the theatre, Herzl was always interested in the "how" and "why." How were the matinee idols created? Why did the theatre exert so magnetic an attraction? Why did the circus draw such enormous audiences? Who was behind it? Who organized and directed it all? And behind this lay another, even more engrossing question: what was the relationship between an individual leader and the masses he sought to sway? The search for the solution to the latter problem was manifested in Herzl's many adventure stories, written over a period of years. Spangelberg was apparently a shallow man, whose entire ambition was to attract audiences to his performances, but he never ceased being amazed by the strange phenomenon called "mass response." Certain sketches in Herzl's files indicate that for years he wanted to write a full-length book about this adventurer who struggled to control people, to make them do his bidding. We may suppose that the stories **"Pygmalion," "The Riot at Amalfi,"** and perhaps even **"A Good Deed"** and **"Mumbo"** were to be part of this book which was never written.

In two stories, both written in 1890, we can feel the change beginning to assert itself in Herzl. **"The Son"** was written a short time after he became a father. "When my son was born, the world suddenly became full of meaning," says the hero. "You know that I come from a good family and that I received a well-rounded education. In my youth I was a playboy. I also entered into marriage lightheartedly. . . . Our children are our greatest teachers. My son taught me truly to savour life and love. For he was my life, my limitless continuation, the security that I shall always walk under the sun, in my son, my grandson, always young, always handsome and strong, always nobler and nobler. . . ." The conception and execution of the story **"Beautiful Rosalinda"** can be traced from the first sketch written after his visit to the

Wiertz Museum in Brussels, through various intermediate versions, to the final, completed work.

The failure of some of his plays after he had enjoyed years of success in the best theatres was proof in his eyes that he did not as yet know how to reach the masses in the way he was seeking so eagerly. At the same time, the crisis in his marriage compelled him to examine his own life critically and, through it, the life of others.

In 1891, he went to live in Paris. From 1891 to 1895, when he was Paris correspondent for the *Neue Freie Presse,* the largest paper in Vienna, and one of great influence on the political, cultural and financial life of all Europe, he turned his full attention to journalism. In addition to his prolific reportorial writings, done in the polished style of the *feuilletonist,* he wrote book reviews and critical articles on drama and art. One philosophical tale, **"Cure for Melancholy,"** appeared at the outset of this period. It was the story of a man who had nothing to live for and wanted to be cured of the boredom which poisoned his life, a life which to all outward appearances was one of extreme happiness. This story was followed by a four-year break. Only after Herzl became a Zionist, in 1896, did he again begin to write and publish philosophical tales.

A new man emerges from the new series. No longer is Herzl the witty conversationalist who is almost ashamed of making a serious remark and conceals his petty truths in shallow plots. From now on, most of his philosophical stories are real stories and the reflections in them truer, more tranquil, simpler and less affected in both mood and style. For example, consider two stories, **"The Dirigible Air-Ship"** and **"The Anilin Inn,"** both written shortly after publication of his book *The Jewish State.* To his contemporaries, these stories were the literary expression of his general views as a Zionist. His new faith in himself and in mankind is apparent, replacing the paradoxical, cynical quips of earlier days. Of the inventor of the dirigible airship, who burns his invention because he despises certain men who have embittered his life and whom he deems unworthy of enjoying revolutionary inventions of this type, Herzl has one of the characters say at the conclusion of the story, "He should not have thought of the men of his time, and least of all, of the miserable people of his immediate environment. Those who work for the future must learn to look beyond the present. The future will bring forth better men." Whereupon another character in the story, a woman, remarks, "The hero of your tale lacks only one thing for greatness: the ability to forgive." In a similar manner, he shows in **"The Anilin Inn,"** as he had tried to show in a different way in *The Jewish State,* how it is possible to turn misfortune and despair into strength and an unlimited capacity for altruistic action.

The problem of understanding the common people, and how to control them, occupied him now on another level. Once he had found his way to his own people, and was entirely engrossed in attempting to establish the Jewish State, the impresario was no longer the hero of his tales. Solon of Athens, the great lawgiver, was the hero of one of his most carefully constructed stories, which he later adapted for the theatre. The material for the story of **"Solon in Lydia"** was taken from ancient myth, as was the story of Sulla (**"Epaphroditos"**) which was drawn from Plutarch's *Lives.* This writer, historian and philosopher (46-125 C.E.) was the tutor of many statesmen, from the time he was rediscovered and translated into many modern languages at the beginning of the 16th century.

Herzl's feeling about the fate of the Jews is contained in his words about the gladiator, condemned to death by the crowd, in the story **"Epaphroditos"**: "They demanded the blood of the Thracian for one reason only, because he was the weaker. To the extent that they hated him, just so much would they have loved him, had he by chance been the stronger!"

Most of his stories end with a glance toward the future. This looking forward is especially evident in the story **"Däumerle und Bäumerle or The Future,"** and in **"The Treasures of Life."** The poverty stricken hero of the latter story dedicates his life to the poor in order to restore their faith in themselves and the future. He considers his "vision of the future" to be the treasure of his life. "Yes, this is springtime itself. Even the thought of my own passing away is no longer painful. Already I am a citizen of the future, because I labor in its behalf. Didn't even he himself, the great pessimist Schopenhauer, always turn to his future community? He too believed, beyond all negation, in futurity. It is the one and only thing which holds no disillusion for us."

Herzl often referred to Schopenhauer, whose philosophy apparently made the greatest impression on him. But he did not accept his outlook unreservedly as a closed system. Herzl's intellectual processes were not those of a systematic philosopher, who organizes his thoughts according to rigorous logic, but rather those of a highly sensitive individual, soaking up impressions, which he reacts to associatively and emotionally. This was typical too of Heinrich Heine's thinking, who in many respects was Herzl's literary ideal.

As one who has transcended the illusions of Maya—if we translate the words of his mind-reader into the terms of Hindu philosophy—he sees suffering, ugliness, and evil behind the world's external glitter. And he was constantly storing up impressions—impressions which become purer, that is, less related to the self, as time goes by, until they merge and become identical with the emotion of love.

Herzl's views and reactions came increasingly to reflect the teachings of Spinoza, particularly his way of regarding the earthy and transitory in the light of the eternal, and his concept that what is visible to the eye is the expression and symbol of invisible reality. This outlook implies that the future already exists in the present, as the essence of all manifestations, hidden from our eyes only by the human category of time. Our task, therefore, is to seize what is inherently "real" in the present (rather like the sparks of the *Shekhinah* in the teachings of the Kabbalah), and carry it by means of our present actions forward into the future.

This same ability to discern in current events the developing forms of the future distinguished Herzl's *feuilletons* on technological subjects and transportation. Even as a child, Herzl had been interested in technological developments. When the Suez Canal was opened to ships in 1869, the boy dreamed that he would one day accomplish what Lesseps had done, and build a great canal linking the Atlantic with the Pacific through the Isthmus of Panama. Early in his life, he saw in technology a means of freeing humanity from poverty and slavery, and when he became a Zionist, these dreams took on reality. What he wrote in the introduction to **The Jewish State,** "that electric light was not invented for the purpose of illuminating the drawing rooms of a few snobs, but rather for the purpose of throwing light on some of the dark problems of humanity" including the Jewish question, served always to epitomize his convictions. He always saw the world

around him as a man who was destined to implement the founding of the Jewish State, an ideal economy and society, which would embody the finest elements of the civilized world. In his novel **Altneuland,** Herzl described in detail and from many aspects, this new life, based on the existing institutions of his time. The *feuilletons* concerning methods of transportation and their development are a kind of groping attempt in this direction. In order to evaluate them, we must bear in mind that transportation was then only beginning to develop: the bicycle had only recently ceased to be a toy and begun to be used as a means of transportation; the automobile was seen only rarely in the streets, and an airship was still a dream. The airplane as we know it had not yet been invented. When a volume of Herzl's **Philosophical Tales** appeared in 1900, a serious critic of one of the large German newspapers commented, "The second story, **"The Dirigible Air-Ship,"** deals in the same delicate way with the latest problem of the modern idealist—the flight of Icarus, a problem that no man has ever solved or ever will."

At the beginning of this story, which appeared early in 1896, Herzl wrote a kind of philosophical preface which was to apply to his entire transportation series. A man just back from Paris—that is Herzl himself—begins the story with some observations on the bicycle, remarking that it is changing the appearance of the streets.

> Who would have thought a few years ago that this toy could bring about such drastic changes? And now horseless carriages are appearing! What innovations will these not bring about? Each new form of transportation brings in its wake profound and unexpected changes which have a marked effect on the masses of the people—on their welfare and morality. New diseases appear, or, conversely, the human race becomes healthier. The conditions of life are changing more rapidly than they ever have in any period of history.

He felt changes occurring everywhere, and heard the future echoing in each stirring of the present—stirrings which were either not heard by others of his generation, or else were regarded as irritating noise. For Herzl, everything was changing as the result of these developments—both conditions themselves and man's perception of them. Country landscapes and city vistas alike were taking on new shapes; narrow, filthy streets were giving way to broad, shining thoroughfares. Herzl also contemplated the machine, less vulnerable than the human being who must master it, and who would perhaps be mastered by it. Control of the explosive energy of engines and its conversion into powerful constructive force became symbolic for him. It was a symbol he had already described in the preface to **The Jewish State** as the force of Jewish agony which could be converted into a purifying and creative power, through proper organization and direction.

The potentialities of technology whether for the benefit of humanity or otherwise, is the subject, treated lightly and in verse, of **"The Legend of the Telegraph,"** one of Herzl's *feuilletons* on children. These *feuilletons* are brief sketches of a loving father watching the development of children—both his own and other people's. We have already mentioned the change that affected Herzl when he became a father. "I know," he wrote to a friend at this time, "that the experience of fatherhood will open the gates of philosophy to me."

His children frequently served as a point of departure for his reflections on life in general and especially on politics. Children, who held the seeds of the future, inspired Herzl's special affection. Here, too, his emotion often began as compassion stemming from his participation in the hardships of their development. He was ever sympathetic toward their struggles and despair over problems which appeared so trivial to the adults around them. Herzl's compassion sprang from the memory of his own early youth, and allowed him to achieve the complete identification with others which is love. But how do his reflections on the latent possibilities of technology and the rearing of children fit together? The connection can be found in a sketch called **"Toys of 1900,"** written after Herzl had perused the catalog of a large toy manufacturer.

Two tales published after Herzl's death, were intended as folk-stories and were thus written in the form of legend and parable. They concern man's struggle for honesty and justice. The one on **"Lieschen"** is especially interesting. Its theme is essentially the same as that of **"The Mind-Reader."** Here too, the characters—in this case a man and a woman—are able to penetrate into the hearts of men and read their secret thoughts. But how different are these characters from the earlier ones. The mind-reader of 1887 was an idler, an aimless drifter who had no use for his rare talent. When he discovers by means of his insight the faithlessness of his wife and friends, he wreaks a cruel, almost sadistic revenge on them. In contrast, the hero of 1904 is a judge by profession, whose daughter has been deliberately blinded. She is not embittered because of this, however; she does not plot revenge; her soul becomes more selfless as her power to penetrate into the mysteries of the human heart increases. Herzl the dandy, the socialite who played with his talent, had become the moralist who sought for truth, and wanted to turn the truth into living reality. Thus, the circle of Herzl's life, which always found expression in his stories, was closed.

Herzl's literary style is derived from conversation. It is simple and direct, polished, but precise. Each word is carefully weighed and balanced in the sentence to achieve maximum conciseness and clarity. His incisive thought, broad education, natural courtesy, and restraint in the expression of his feelings, as well as his self-doubt and suspicion of others were all expressed and crystallized in his style. His command of the German language, from the standpoint of both nuance and tradition, was superb. He was called the best of the young Viennese prose-writers even by his severe opponent, Karl Kraus. All of the traditions of the *feuilleton* and the philosophical tale—from Voltaire and the French literature of the 19th century through Boerne and Heine, and including the Viennese *feuilletonists* from Speidel to Wittman—influenced Herzl's style, and many of his works maintain the standards of the greatest. (pp. 153-64)

> *Alex Bein, "Herzl's Short Stories," translated by Chayym Zeldis, in* Herzl Year Book, Vol. III, *edited by Raphael Patai, Herzl Press, 1960, pp. 153-64.*

JOSEPH ADLER (essay date 1962)

[*Adler is the author of* The Herzl Paradox: Political, Social and Economic Theories of a Realist. *In the following excerpt from that work, he analyzes Herzl's political and socioeconomic theories as presented in* Der Judenstaat *and* Altneuland.]

Theodor Herzl's goal was the regeneration of the Jewish nation as a political entity. The task seemed an impossible one.

The Jews had settled throughout the world; they were a minority everywhere; they possessed no common territory; they spoke many languages; they followed different traditions; and their religious ideology had become splintered as a result of emancipation and reform. There was no Jewish nation in the political sense, only Jewish communities scattered throughout the world.

Herzl was only partially aware of the many barriers that would confront him in trying to achieve his goal of a Jewish state. But he realized the power inherent in the idea of a national territory for the Jews when he noted that:

> No human being is wealthy or powerful enough to transplant a people from one place of residence to another. Only an idea can achieve that. The state idea surely has that power. The Jews have dreamt this princely dream throughout the long night of their history. "Next year in Jerusalem:" is our ancient watchword. It is now a matter of showing that the vague dream can be transformed into a clear and glowing idea.

Der Judenstaat suggested a political solution to the Jewish Question at a time when both Eastern and Western European Jewry were divided and faced serious crises. In the West, there was a general feeling of insecurity among the Jews due mainly to the failure of the policy of assimilation and the rise of anti-Semitism. In the East, the Jewish Enlightenment had weakened orthodox Judaism, and the governments of that vast geographic area had intensified their nationalistic programs.

The starting point of Herzl's ideology, as presented in *Der Judenstaat,* was his analysis of the Jewish Question. For Herzl there were two aspects to the question: persecution and the Jew's feeling of homelessness; and at the root of both of these was anti-Semitism. The forms of persecution varied according to nation and circumstance, but one thing was clear to Herzl; anti-Semitism existed wherever Jews lived in large numbers. Moreover:

> The longer anti-Semitism lies dormant, the more violently will it erupt. The infiltration of immigrating Jews attracted to a land by apparent security, and the rising class status of native Jews, combine powerfully to bring about a revolution. Nothing could be plainer than this rational conclusion.

Coupled with persecution was the Jew's feeling of being unwanted, of being an alien even in the country of his birth. This sense of homelessness existed, Herzl declared, even though the Jews had:

> Sincerely tried everywhere to merge with the national communities in which we live, seeking only to preserve the faith of our fathers. It is not permitted us. In vain are we loyal patriots, sometimes super-loyal; in vain do we make the same sacrifices of life and property as our fellow citizens; in vain do we strive to enhance the fame of our native land in the arts and sciences, or her wealth by trade and commerce. In our native lands where we have lived for centuries we are still described as aliens, often by men whose ancestors had not yet come at a time when Jewish sighs had long been heard in the country. The majority decide who the alien is. . . .

But, Herzl asked, what were the causes of anti-Semitism? The most remote of these, he believed, was the factor of religious differences, and its time of origin could be traced back to the

Middle Ages. Modern anti-Semitism, however, was due largely to economic factors and had developed out of the emancipation of the Jews following the French Revolution. He states:

> When civilized nations awoke to the inhumanity of discriminatory legislation and enfranchised us, our enfranchisement came too late. Legislation alone no longer sufficed to emancipate us in our old homes. For in the Ghetto we had remarkably developed into a bourgeois people and we emerged from the Ghetto a prodigious rival to the middle class. Thus we found ourselves thrust upon emancipation into this bourgeois circle, where we have a double pressure to sustain from within and from without.

Moreover, following a common nineteenth century Western and Central European belief, Herzl asserted that " . . . the equal rights of the Jews before the law cannot be rescinded where they have once been granted." Hence, he reasoned, anti-Semitism would grow because " . . . the very impossibility of getting at the Jews nourishes and deepens hatred of them."

No matter what the cause of anti-Semitism—economic, political, or religious—the results were always the same. It led almost inevitably to bloodshed, poverty, destruction of property, and demoralization. It was a vicious cycle, Herzl believed, because " . . . oppression naturally creates hostility against oppressors, and our hostility in turn increases the pressure."

Herzl believed that the constant oppression of the Jews could produce one positive effect: it could weld the Jews into a single people. A feeling of fellowship among the Jews, which had begun to crumble after the era of emancipation, was strengthened anew by anti-Semitism. He concluded:

> Thus, we are now and shall remain, whether we would or not, a group of unmistakable cohesiveness.

> We are a people [*Wir sind ein Volk*]—our enemies have made us one whether we will it or not, as has repeatedly happened in history. Affliction binds us together, and thus united, we suddenly discover our strength.

It is difficult to capture the full significance of Herzl's statement, *"Wir sind ein Volk"*—in its English translation, "We are a people." It clearly implied that the Jews were *a people entitled to national self-determination* (*"Volk"*), and this claim must be understood in the context of German political theory.

The concept of *"Volk"* in German political thought came to denote, beginning with Hegel, and later in the writings of Friedrich Ernst Daniel Schleiermacher (1768-1834), Friedrich Karl von Savigny (1779-1861), and Johann Kasper Bluntschli (1808-1881), a collectivity and a rather arbitrarily defined cultural heritage. This development had taken place because of the attempts by these German theorists to distinguish between a people and a nation in their philosophies of the state. In general they tended, under the sway of German nationalism, to use the word *"Volk"* in the sense of "nation" when the idea of race was to be stressed, and in the sense of "people" when governmental institutions or functions were referred to. Among German thinkers the concepts "nation" and "people" were therefore often intimately blended. (pp. 61-5)

Herzl's nationalistic appeal to the Jewish people was heightened by its Messianic overtones. Among the Eastern European Jews, in particular, Herzl stimulated the old dream of a return to the Promised Land; the beginning of an era of universal knowledge of God; permanent peace and freedom. The Messianic appeal was not anticipated by Herzl but was inherent in the concepts of nationalism. For, modern European nationalism had drawn from the "old monotheistic religions not only their exclusiveness, but also their profound belief in a forthcoming end of days, an era of ultimate fulfillment."

Throughout his exposition in *Der Judenstaat* Herzl showed an awareness of the power of nationalism—its attractions and its dangers. He wrote:

> It might be said that we ought not to create new distinctions between people; we ought not to raise fresh barriers but make instead the old ones disappear. But men who think in this manner are amiable visionaries, and the idea of a native land will still flourish when the dust of their bones will have vanished tracelessly in the winds. . . .

Herzl knew there was considerable danger in bringing Jewish nationalism into the glaring light of international politics. His was an age of political unrest, where strong currents of national revolt and international rivalry could be discerned under the smooth surface of apparent peace. Had Herzl's theory contained the faintest suggestion of the use of force, his efforts to gain the support of both the international community of nations and the Jews themselves would have miscarried. It was as a peaceful emancipator, therefore, that Herzl appeared before the Jews of Europe. His plan contemplated no force of arms. It depended largely upon international discussion, diplomacy, and positive political action.

From time to time in his Zionist career Herzl, however, was confronted by groups or individuals who tried to persuade him to abandon his peaceful course of action. Thus, in 1896 he was approached by representatives of the Jewish student group *Kadimah* who proposed that he sanction the formation of a battalion of one or two thousand volunteers for an attempted landing at Jaffa in the Holy Land. On still another occasion an adventurous Swede who called himself Ali Nouri Bey Dilmec (1861-1937) came to Herzl with a request for aid in launching a military expedition against Constantinople. Herzl remained aloof to all such ill-conceived schemes.

The very nature of Herzl's approach to the Jewish Question produced, in his work *Der Judenstaat,* a rejection of those solutions that advocated the use of violence and those that ignored the question of nationalism. In the latter category Herzl placed two concepts that enjoyed some popularity among the Jews in the last quarter of the nineteenth century: the doctrine of assimilation and the ultra-religious, or Ghetto, doctrine.

The idea of assimilation can be traced back to the era of emancipation. It was based on the belief that the Jews were not a people at all but only an aggregation with vestigial religious doctrines and tenets that separated them from their neighbors. The supporters of assimilation were convinced that the Jews would eventually become an organic part of the peoples among whom they lived. Assimilation, they reasoned, would eliminate the causes of anti-Semitism.

Herzl had been reared in a family that believed in assimilation, and he had great difficulty trying to shed its effects. His struggle with the concept of assimilation is strongly evident in his diary notes and to some extent in *Der Judenstaat* itself. Prior to writing this book he even believed that anti-Semitism, if exerted steadily, could act as a stimulant to hasten the assimilation process. Thus, he once wrote:

> However, anti-Semitism which is a strong and unconscious force among the masses will not harm the Jews. I consider it to be a movement useful to the Jewish character. It represents the education of a group by the masses, and will perhaps lead to its being absorbed. Education is accomplished only through hard knocks. A Darwinian mimicry will set in. The Jews will adapt themselves. They are like the seals which an act of nature cast into the water. These animals assume the appearance and habits of fish, which they certainly are not. Once they return to dry land again and are allowed to remain there for a few generations, they will turn their fins into feet again. The traces of one kind of pressure can be effaced only by another kind.

Nevertheless, it can be seen in *Der Judenstaat* that Herzl's attitude was undergoing a fundamental change and that he had taken a new position on assimilation. He began to see that assimilation was disagreeable and even impossible for the Jewish people as a whole. He felt that assimilation was dependent on factors beyond the control of the Jews: a desire for widespread intermarriage on the part of the majority population and sufficient time—at least one or two generations—to allow for nearly complete assimilation to take place. Neither of these conditions seemed likely to obtain. The rapid rise of anti-Semitism made this clear. Furthermore, from a nationalistic point of view assimilation was undesirable.

> The distinctive nationality of the Jews neither can, will nor must perish. It cannot because external enemies consolidate it. It does not wish to; this it has proven through two millennia of appalling suffering. It need not; that, as a descendant of countless Jews who refused to despair I am trying once more to prove in this pamphlet. Whole branches of Jewry may wither and fall away. The tree lives on.

The second solution to the Jewish Question that Herzl rejected was the Ghetto, or ultra-religious, concept. The followers of this viewpoint argued that an unbridgeable chasm separated the Jews from other peoples, and it was therefore incumbent upon Jews to remain passive and be dependent on the good graces of the people among whom they dwelt until the advent of the Messiah. Herzl considered this point of view sterile.

The Jewish Question, he believed, was neither a social nor religious problem, even though it sometimes took these forms.

> It is a national question, and to solve it we must first of all establish it as an international political problem to be discussed and settled by the civilized nations of the world in council.

Since the Jewish Question was a national one with international ramifications, it could only be resolved, Herzl concluded, by the creation of a special instrument to encompass both these factors; a Jewish state, recognized and secured by international agreement, and to which Jews could migrate and freely colonize on a large scale.

Anti-Semitism, the source of the Jewish Question, Herzl was convinced would be stifled by the rise of the Jewish state. He reasoned that with the large scale migration of the great bulk of European Jewry to the new state, the economic foundations of anti-Semitism (the modern cause of this evil) would crumble and collapse. Those Jews who chose to remain behind in Europe after the creation of the Jewish state could then easily be absorbed, as all bars to assimilation would be let down in the absence of economic competition from the Jewish middle classes.

In *Der Judenstaat* Herzl attempted to elevate the Jewish Question into a challenging international issue. He tried to remove the discussion of the problem from the synagogues and temples, the salons of the wealthy Jewish philanthropists, and the debating halls of the assimilationists and to place it squarely before the European powers. He tried to make what had been considered a religious and racial problem into a political and diplomatic question. He had taken the first significant step forward in creating a Jewish nation. He envisioned a Jewish state, and this became his goal.

Herzl described *Der Judenstaat* in a sub-title as "an attempt at a modern solution of the Jewish Question," and the pamphlet consists of a close and dispassionate examination of the Jewish people among the nations as well as a detailed scheme for creating a state in which the Jews would reconstitute their national life in a territory of their own.

How was this national state to be achieved? The first step, Herzl believed, was to convince the Jewish people of the need for a Jewish state. He recognized that if one man were to attempt to create a state it would be folly, but he believed it practicable if the will of a whole people were behind it. It was not enough "to feel and know that we are a nation; national consciousness must lead to the awakening of the national will." And, he said, "Those Jews who want a state will have it."

Did the Jewish *"Volk"* have the right to assume such an undertaking? Herzl believed they did, for:

> Smaller nations have dared to claim a piece of the earth for themselves, and because they dared, they acquired it too. Shall our *"Volk,"* as famous as it is unhappy, not dare to make its claim? Does it not feel the very fact that it makes the claim assures it of the esteem of the whole world? We have at least the same rights as other people to ask for a country that would form the basis of our national existence. We have acquired this right through our sufferings that are unparalleled in the history of mankind. Streams of blood have accompanied us on our way through the centuries. Our sufferings would be incomprehensible senseless tortures if we have endured them without hoping for national rebirth.

The skills and knowledge the Jews had acquired since their emancipation would now serve them in laying the foundation of a modern state, Herzl felt. "We are strong enough to form a state, and indeed a model state, for we possess all the requisite human and material resources." Furthermore, other people in recent history had successfully achieved statehood.

> Were the founders of the states which now are great—mightier, cleverer, better educated, wealthier than we Jews of today? Poor shepherds and huntsmen have founded communities which later became states. In our own time, Greeks, Rumanians, Serbs, Bulgarians have established themselves—and should we be incapable of doing so?

The task of creating a state Herzl stressed, could be carried out effectively and in a relatively short span of time. In commenting on this Jacob de Haas wrote:

> He was timing the restoration of the Jewish state within his own lifetime. His reaction to speed was modern American in its acclaim of "hustle." This arose from contemplation of the change in the world's power of mobility. He admired modern methods of concentrated efficiency. Two similes ran repeatedly through his earlier addresses; the small cramped villages of Europe had taken centuries to develop, while great spacious modern cities were built comparatively in a few years. Before the 12th century kings crossed their domains in two wheeled chariots drawn by oxen. In 1895 the poorest traveller covered in an hour the distance kings had made in a day. A new state to be founded in the tempo of the cable.

It seemed to Herzl that anti-Semitism would provide the motive for creating the Jewish state. The sheer force of Jewish suffering and misery (*Judennot*) would act as a propelling force to set in motion a migration to the projected state. Elaborating on this theme, Herzl wrote:

> The present scheme [the creation of a Jewish state], on the other hand, involves the use of a motive force which exists in reality. In view of my own limitations, I shall do no more than suggest what cogs and wheels constitute the machinery. I propose, trusting that better mechanics than myself will be found to carry the work out. The decisive factor is our propelling force. And what is that force? The plight of the Jews. . . . Now everyone knows how steam is generated by boiling water in a kettle, only rattling the lid. The current Zionist projects and other associations to check anti-Semitism are tea kettle phenomena of this kind. But I say that this force if properly harnessed is powerful enough to propel a large engine and to move passengers and goods, let the engine have whatever form it may.

Herzl's plan for creating a state, as he outlined it in *Der Judenstaat,* called for the formation of two organizations: the "Society of Jews" was one and the "Jewish Company" was the other. To the Society of Jews would go the task of making the necessary preparations for the establishment of a state, and to the Jewish Company would go the job of looking after the economic interests of the Jews in the countries to and from which they were migrating. The Society of Jews was to be created first and would consist of upright men who could not derive any material advantage from their membership in the Society. The Society was to provide the Jews with an authoritative political organ, explore and educate public opinion, determine the political preconditions for mass migration and provide statistical data on the conditions of migration, search out a suitable territory for a state, and negotiate with the Great Powers for the acquisition of this territory and for the granting of a political charter which would guarantee Jewish sovereignty. If successful in these efforts, the Society of Jews would next give instructions to the Jewish Company concerning immigration, purchase of land, and colonization and would entrust the Company to implement them. In addition the Society would engage in preparing the legal and administrative groundwork for the future state. In brief, the Society would be the forerunner of the state; for, it " . . . will be recognized, to put it in the terminology of international law, as a state creating power, and this recognition will in effect mean the creation of the state."

Of course, the task of establishing a state could not be carried out without adequate financial support. The body that Herzl called the Jewish Company would have the task of supplying such aid. The Company would be responsible for the migration, colonization, and resettlement of the Jews. It would help those who chose to leave their old homes and would organize commerce, trade, and industry in the new country. In retrospect, the Jewish Company would provide an orderly and equitable method of liquidating the business interests of Jewish emigrants and would compensate the various countries for the loss of Jewish income and taxes. In the new country the Jewish Company would purchase land and equipment for settlement, erect temporary housing quarters for workmen, and provide financial help for incoming settlers. The Company, as Herzl conceived it, was transitional in nature, and he assumed that its functions in the new land would eventually be assumed by the state.

How and where would the Company be organized? Herzl stated:

> The Jewish Company will be set up as a joint-stock company, incorporated in England, under British laws and protection. Its principal center will be in London. I cannot tell yet how large the Company's capital should be; I shall leave that calculation to our numerous financiers. But in order to be specific, let us put it at a billion marks [two hundred million dollars]; it may be even more or less than that sum. . . .

Herzl offered three possible approaches to the task of creating the capital stock of the Jewish Company, leaving the selection of the best method to the Society of Jews, which would use its prestige to establish the credit of the Company among the Jewish people. It was Herzl's hope that wealthy Jewish financiers would subscribe the necessary funds. He favored this method because it seemed to be the most simple and swift means of obtaining the financial resources for the Company while providing investment opportunities with the possibility of a fair return. Herzl's second approach, to be used in the event of reluctance to help on the part of the financiers, called for an appeal to small banks. If this second method proved to be unsuccessful Herzl proposed to capitalize the Jewish Company through a direct subscription of funds from the Jewish masses. He wrote:

> The Company's capital might be raised without the aid of a banking syndicate, by means of a direct subscription on the part of the public. . . . A new and peculiar form of the plebiscite would thus be established, whereby each man voting for this solution of the Jewish Question would express his opinion by subscribing for a certain sum conditionally. This condition would constitute his security. The full funds subscribed would only be paid in if their sum total reached the required amount, otherwise the initial payments would be returned. But if the whole of the required sum is raised by popular subscription, then each little amount would be secured by the great numbers of other small amounts.

How would the Society of Jews, the forerunner of the state, come into being? Could it legally act on behalf of the Jewish communities of the world? To answer these questions Herzl drew upon his knowledge of Roman Law, and in particular upon the ancient juristic institution of the *negotiorum gestio.* Under this concept which fitted in neatly with Herzl's belief in an elite, any person or group could protect the property of an incapacitated or absent party without receiving a warrant from the owner to do so. A person acting in this manner derived his mandate from what the law deemed to be a "higher necessity" and was designated a *gestor*—the director of affairs not strictly his own. Herzl noted:

> A state is created by a nation's struggle for existence. In any such struggle it is impossible to obtain proper authority in due form beforehand. In fact, any preliminary attempt to obtain a regular decision from the majority would probably ruin the undertaking at the outset, for partisan divisions would render the people defenseless against external dangers. We cannot all be of one mind; the *gestor* therefore simply takes the leadership into his hands and marches in the van.
>
> Action by the *gestor* of a state is sufficiently authorized if the *dominus* [people] is prevented either by want of will or by some other reason, from helping itself. However, the *gestor* by his intervention becomes similar to the *dominus* and is bound by the agreement *quasi ex contractu*. This is the legal relationship existing before, or more correctly, created simultaneously with, the state.

Since the Jews were a people dispersed throughout the world they were not in a position to conduct their own political affairs, nor could they protect themselves against common dangers. They were, Herzl believed, unable to create a state without the help of a *gestor*. The Jewish *gestor*, however, would not be a single individual because such a person would appear ridiculous. Furthermore, since he might appear to be working for his own gain he might seem contemptible. The *gestor* of the Jews was to be a corporate person such as the Society of Jews. After 1897 the *gestor* became in fact the World Zionist Congress.

Herzl was intensely proud of the *negotiorum gestio* concept which he believed to be one of the theoretical highpoints of his work **Der Judenstaat.** In a letter to the sociologist Ludwig Gumplowicz (1838-1909) he noted:

> It is a source of considerable amusement to me that universities and other serious circles do not seem to have observed or understood this movement up to now. A pretty detail: in my first pamphlet about a Jewish state, with which publication the Zionist Movement, now world-wide in scope, began, I devoted a chapter to the legal foundation of government. In the place of the miserably opportunistic theory of "*Naturnotwendigkeit*"—not to talk anymore about the contract social—I put the theory of *negotiorum gestio* which, I believe, can stand up to your sociological interpretation. This theory which at the very least could be made the object of scholarly discussion, has not been deemed worthy of so much as a glance by anyone up to this moment. Obviously, I am not employing the proper scientific jargon. . . .

Inherent in Herzl's theory of the *negotiorum gestio* were the answers to the important political questions: who shall rule? and what group or class should enjoy a privileged position in the Jewish state? The Society of Jews, or *gestor*, he wrote in **Der Judenstaat,** would "arise out of the circle of energetic English Jews whom I apprised of my scheme in London." Herzl had in mind the Maccabean Club, an organization of prominent English Jews. The Maccabean Club, he felt, would either become the Society of Jews or the model for the Society. In terms of class structure, the Society, if it closely paralleled its model, would be composed of an elite of Jewish community leaders—religious, economic, and intellectual—drawn from the upper and middle classes.

It would be the middle class of Jewry, however, that would benefit most from a Jewish state. It would be this class that would do the most to spread the idea of a state and that would provide the necessary technical and professional manpower for the national movement.

> The middle classes will be drawn willy-nilly into the outward current, for their sons will be officials of the Society or Company employees "over there." Lawyers, doctors, technicians of every description, young business people—in fact, all Jews who are in search of opportunity, who are now fleeing oppression in their native lands to earn a living in foreign lands—will assemble on a soil so full of fair promises.

Once the state was established, Herzl contemplated very little change in the power structure no matter what form the government took. Both power and privilege would remain in the upper and middle classes, with the latter acting as the backbone of the state's bureaucracy. From the ranks of the middle class, Herzl predicted, would come a "surplus intelligentsia" who would provide the state with an aristocracy of talent.

Even before the publication of **Der Judenstaat** Herzl had been obsessed by the idea of using the Jewish "surplus intelligentsia" in his projected state. This theme emerges sharply in a letter he wrote to Baron de Hirsch June 3, 1895. It read:

> and this undertaking [the creation of a state] will even in its first stages provide employment for an aspiring multitude of our young people: all the engineers, architects, technologists, chemists, physicians, lawyers, who have emerged from the Ghetto during the last thirty years and who thought they would gain their livelihood and their bit of honor outside the higgling and haggling Jewish trades. They must now be getting desperate and are beginning to constitute a frightful proletariat of intellectuals. But all my love belongs to them, and I want to increase their numbers even as you wish to decrease them. In them I see the future, as yet dormant strength of the Jews. In a word, my kind of people. Out of this proletariat of intellectuals I shall form the general staff and the cadres of the army which is to seek, discover and take over the land.

Herzl was convinced that his plans for the intelligentsia would meet with their full approval. A unity of interest existed between the needs of the intelligentsia and the needs of the Jewish state. The differentiation that had marked the rise of this new middle class had created a strong class solidarity. Economic pressures brought about by older and more firmly established social groups were threatening to destroy this class feeling of union.

The "surplus intelligentsia" of the Jewish middle class, Herzl believed, would gradually sink and become a helpless revolutionary-minded proletariat unless their energies were diverted toward the goal of creating a Jewish state. These factors would be quickly grasped by the intelligentsia and compel them to support a state that would strengthen their claims as a class. It would secure their own ends and at the same time give to the state the power and authority it required.

Apart from this description of the forces and instruments that would make possible a Jewish national state, Herzl filled the pages of *Der Judenstaat* with many practical suggestions on statecraft. These ideas, which were in large measure derived from his personal observations and experiences as a foreign correspondent, made the book more readable and gave additional substance to his theory of the state. (pp. 66-79)

For more than six decades most Zionist thinkers have generally agreed that Herzl's conception of a Jewish state was his greatest theoretical contribution. Unfortunately, the adherents of this viewpoint have almost invariably ignored the ideas in Herzl's last work, *Altneuland,* believing them to be at best a highly fanciful popularization in more graphic form of the concepts set forth in *Der Judenstaat.* Upon closer examination, however, these assessments of the theoretical content of *Altneuland* are found to be wanting. For the book represented the maturation point in Herzl's political and socio-economic thought and contained many new ideas that were both at variance with and more profound than his earlier theory of the state.

Altneuland marked a transition in Herzl's political and socio-economic thinking. In *Der Judenstaat* he had blueprinted a Jewish political national state on the conventional pattern familiar to Europe, complete with army and flag, and with an economic base strongly suggestive of benevolent capitalism. In *Altneuland,* however, Herzl abandoned the traditional form of a political state as well as capitalism and depicted a Jewish "commonwealth" governed by a giant cooperative association called the New Society. (pp. 86-7)

Two principles regulated the economic growth of the commonwealth: the belief in modern technocracy and the practical application of the cooperative idea to all phases of economic life. Technocracy was central to almost all of Herzl's writings. He was convinced that "the word impossible had ceased to exist in the vocabulary of technical science . . ." and that properly used, science could become the great benefactor of mankind.

> Today: With the ideas, knowledge and facilities that humanity possesses . . . it could save itself. No philosopher's stone, no dirigible airship is needed. Everything needful for the making of a better world exists already.

The commonwealth that Herzl described in *Altneuland* was built upon the foundations of modern technology. What had once been a wasteland had been turned by the New Society into a veritable "land of milk and honey." How had this come to pass? "We merely had to transplant," a cooperative leader notes, "existing inventions to this country," for the commonwealth was evolved "out of experiments, books and dreams. . . ." The New Society had borne the burden of this gigantic experiment but the results "did not derive from the brains of its leaders nor from the pockets of its founders alone . . . ," for it had drawn upon "the ideas which were the common stock of the whole civilized world."

All that was most modern had been introduced into the country. (p. 92)

The second principle guiding the economic development of the commonwealth involved the application of cooperative methods to the production, consumption, and distribution of goods. It indicated a novel economic system—an intermediary form spanning both capitalism and socialism. The idea, however, had old roots and a history of struggle. One member of the commonwealth informs a visitor:

> The whole merit of our New Society is merely that it fostered the creation and development of cooperatives by providing credits, and—what was even more important—by educating the masses to make use of them. Economic science had long ago recognized the significance of the cooperatives. But in practical life they succeeded—when they did succeed—by accident and with much difficulty. Their members were usually too poor to hold out until the inevitable success could be achieved. . . . The combined power of habit, friction and the inhibitions imposed by old customs worked against the formation of the cooperatives. And yet their method provides the mean between individualism and collectivism.
>
> (pp. 94-5)

Herzl's use of the cooperative principle in *Altneuland* was extensive and included many variants and novel suggestions. Although his discussion centered chiefly on the New Society's cooperative efforts in the fields of industry and commerce he did not forget agriculture. This was not surprising; for, Herzl was keenly aware of the great agricultural revolution that had passed over Europe. He knew that the Great Powers had been as much upset by the transformation of their peasantry, which had accompanied the agrarian upheaval, as by the more spectacular and exciting revolution in industry. His philosophy had been shaped by these latter considerations and he looked forward eagerly to the day when a coeval development of industry and agriculture would be possible.

The balanced industrial-agricultural economy that Herzl described in *Altneuland* was in many respects contrary to the views held by many of his followers; notably those former Lovers of Zion and religious and socialist Zionists who believed that the Jews could only be redeemed by a return to the soil of Palestine and the creation of a traditional type of peasantry. He was quite certain that the creation of a traditional type of peasant out of the Jewish masses was neither practical nor feasible. A city-bred intellectual, Herzl was too much a modernist to admire the various cycles of toil and play associated with tilling the earth. He regarded such activity as a moribund phase of human history that had to be swept away by modern technology. In developing this point in *Der Judenstaat* he had written:

> Those who would attempt to convert Jews into peasants are committing a truly astonishing error. For the peasant is a creature of the past, as seen by his style of dress, which in most countries is centuries old, and by his tools, which are identical with those used by his earliest ancestors. His plow is unchanged; he sows his seed from the apron, mows with the time honored scythe, and threshes with the flail. But we know that all this can now be done with machinery. The agrarian question is only a question of machinery. America must conquer Europe, in the same way as large landed possessions absorb smaller ones. The peasant is consequently a type which is on the way to extinction. Wherever he is preserved by special measures, there are involved political interests who hope to gain his support. To create new peasants on the old pattern is absurd and an impossible undertaking. No one is wealthy or powerful enough to make civilization take a single step backward. The mere preservation

of obsolete institutions is a task vast enough to strain the capacities of even an autocratic state.

Will anyone, then, suggest to Jews, who know what they are about, that they become peasants of the old cast? That would be like saying to the Jew, 'Here is a crossbow; now go to war!' What? with a crossbow, while others have small arms and Krupp cannon? Under these circumstances the Jews would be perfectly right in remaining unmoved when people try to place them on the farm. The crossbow is a pretty piece of armament, which inspires a lyrical mood in me whenever I can spare the time. But its proper place is the museum. . . .

Although, Herzl in his political brochure did not spell out his agrarian plans in any great detail it is quite obvious that he had given some thought to the idea of cooperative farming. Some indication as to what he had in mind can be gathered from a letter which he wrote to Saul Rafael Landau (1870-1943) a Viennese journalist ten days after the publication of **Der Judenstaat.** It read in part:

> Naturally, we will have a population who will cultivate the land but not in the old manner. We will have productive agricultural societies to whom the Jewish Company will give land and credits for machinery. There will also be a small agricultural industry which will also receive credits for machinery. . . .

In **Altneuland** Herzl's general impressions on the need for a new type of Jewish farmer and for modern agricultural methods merged completely with his ideas on cooperation. Farmers banded together in agricultural cooperatives worked the land. Improved scientific methods of cultivation and afforestation had been introduced by the New Society, which had also planted many cooperative villages in the midst of the rejuvenated lands. (pp. 99-101)

Herzl's giant cooperative association, the New Society, was novel. Equally unique and diverse were the sources of Herzl's ideas on cooperation. He drew heavily upon English, Irish, French, German, Austrian, and American experiments in industrial and agricultural producer and consumer cooperation. He was familiar with the writings and theories of many prominent social reformers in many nations. In addition, his ideas on agricultural cooperatives received a new impetus when his activities as leader of the World Zionist Organization brought him into contact with many "land reformers" and with the Bible itself. From each source Herzl drew inspiration, but the theory of cooperation that he outlined in **Altneuland,** although enriched by many borrowings, was distinctively his own. (p. 102)

Joseph Adler, in his The Herzl Paradox: Political, Social and Economic Theories of a Realist, *Hadrian Press, 1962, 178 p.*

ANDREW HANDLER   (essay date 1983)

[*Handler is the author of* Dori: The Life and Times of Theodor Herzl in Budapest (1860-1878), *an examination of a phase of Herzl's life which Handler claims is often overlooked or misrepresented by other biographers. In the following excerpt from that work, he compares Herzl's early German and Hungarian essays and discusses the biculturalism Herzl experienced during his development as a writer. Throughout the excerpt, Handler refers to Herzl as Dori, which was his childhood nickname.*]

Dori's compositions were indisputably the products of his bicultural bilingualism, revealing no emotional conflict of loyalties. He managed to effect the transition from German to Magyar and back again, both linguistically and conceptually, without allowing the one to advance at the expense of the other. He expressed his thoughts clearly in either language. Though the subjects of Dori's compositions reveal a remarkably wide range of interests and a knowledge of respectable depth, they are similar in many respects.

Each composition, whether written in German or Magyar, whether on a topic taken from ancient times or contemporary events, whether from the sciences or the humanities, contains an invariably recurring set of ingredients that reflect Dori's reservoir of emotions and graceful elegance. There is no trace of the forced, clumsy style and mechanical, predictable patterns of thought so commonly associated with students of his age, laboring to fulfil the length requirement of their compulsory school assignments in composition. Dori's compositions, whether written in a serious mood or a lighthearted manner, retain a high standard of quality. Their verbal beauty, stylistic grace and contextual depth invariably succeed in capturing and sustaining the reader's interest. The fluid style creates a deceptive impression of effortless spontaneity. Though the youthful author threw himself into themes with firm resolve and unbridled enthusiasm, he rarely abandoned his meticulous care for form. He worked hard at his prose, often rewriting compositions many times until his increasingly finely honed literary taste and sense of stylistic propriety were satisfied.

An interesting feature of Dori's compositions is the absence of a strict thematic demarcation between his two vehicles of literary expression. The crossover, however, is largely unidirectional. Whereas the Magyar compositions generally contain no German topics, those in German, such as the descriptions of Budapest and the essay entitled "Im transilvanischen Parlament," often incorporate Magyar themes.

He clearly possessed the gift of narrative. The confident, facile choice of words and elaborate yet rarely faltering construction of sentences, molding his prose into a graceful and flexible form, testify to an unmistakable talent. (pp. 66-7)

Dori's compositions reveal no evidence of the spiritual inclination or preoccupation with matters of faith that are supposedly revealed by his celebrated childhood dream of being carried off in the arms of "King Messiah" to meet the great figures of the Bible. Indeed the most striking aspect of Dori's literary efforts at this time was the virtual absence of Jewish themes. In fact, having read the compositions, one may be hard put to identify their author as a Jew. (p. 67)

Drawing conclusions from Dori's essays, stories, sketches, and critiques is, of course, any reader's prerogative and should thus be left to his or her discretion. Many such interpretations and conclusions bear the undeniable imprint of having been influenced by Herzl's awe-inspiring prophetic vision and his political philosophy, neither of which is found in the compositions themselves. Dori's personality and manners, as evident in both verbal and written communication, leave little room for success in such a search for unspoken and unwritten clues. He was not a subtle, subdued, and dreamy-eyed child, inextricably caught up in a world of childhood fantasies. He was a spirited and adequately thorough researcher for his age, a freely expressive writer, a severe critic, often flamboyant, and at times blunt. Hints and allusions were simply not part of his style. (p. 68)

As Patai rightly noted [in his "Herzl's School Years"] Dori's compositions "written in German have already received sufficient attention and are well known." Indeed they outnumber the ones written in Magyar, and because of the attention received they alone seem to encompass Dori's literary interests and range of emotions. In this instance, however, numerical superiority is not the determinant. Content is. At first glance, to be sure, Dori's compositions in German offer the reader a generous measure of gratification. Sometimes Dori wrote in a light-hearted vein, reporting a spirited competition held in Venice in 1714 for the title of "the world's first violinist," describing the deceitful woman whose husband uses her to blackmail his wealthy friends, or relating the life and marriage of Professor Theophilos Misogyn. At other times he wrote in a more serious manner, reflecting on the way in which people changed as a result of the inventions of the modern age, or on the emancipation of women, or on Naples, a seaside resort, or some of the notable sights of Budapest. At all times he remained an engaging, entertaining essayist and witty anecdotalist whose graceful style and sophisticated thinking belied his tender age.

Perhaps too much so. For notwithstanding the favorable impression they create of the author's undeniable literary talent, Dori's compositions written in German reveal what they had tried to conceal so carefully: the fundamental predicament that every writer of the German language and reader of German literature must have felt in the midst of an increasingly constricting and intolerant Magyar environment. As a *deutscher Schriftsteller* he would have been limited to the periphery of the cultural mainstream, addressing a rapidly diminishing sector of the population. More importantly, the German writer in Dori was by circumstance removed from the inspiring and exciting realities of daily life and necessarily caught up in the memories of the past and a world of make-believe. There are, as Patai pointed out, sentences and paragraphs that give evidence of Dori's inquisitive mind and deep reservoir of emotions. His German compositions in toto, however, form only a glittering armor of *l'art pour l'art*. They provided him little more than protective isolation as he stood teetering on the brink of the intellectual limbo occupied by any German writer in Magyarized Budapest. The geographic distance of Austria and Germany and the cultural pressures of the Hungarian capital would surely have banished him to obscurity if he had chosen to defy the all too obvious warning signals and continue to pursue his literary activities in that direction. (pp. 69-70)

The compositions written in Magyar are not the mirror image of those in German; they may not be regarded as interchangeable ingredients of Dori's bicultural bilingualism. A comparative analysis of them reveals that the Magyar compositions, on the whole, provide a better account of Dori's personality and intellectual and emotional involvement than the German. While the German compositions depended for their substance on his skillful use of imagination and speculation, the ones written in Magyar were born of the reality of experience and the immediacy of impression. Stylistically they are similar, containing gracefully flowing sentences carried forward by the effortless succession of sophisticated, well-chosen words and expressions. Beyond form, however, the favorable comparison ends. The Magyar compositions were written by a Magyar boy whose formal education and social

contact were interwoven with his predominantly Magyar environment, whereas the German compositions were written by a Magyar boy who admired German culture from afar. (pp. 70-1)

Dori's Magyar compositions parallel the German ones in range of interests, construction of form, and fluidity of style. It is, however, the quality of content that gives the Magyar essays the winning edge.

Indeed, on that ground, none of Dori's writings in German compare favorably with the two Magyar compositions that form the emotional apex of the initial stages of his literary activity. In them a remarkable though not unexpected metamorphosis takes place: the impeccably elegant, supranational stylist gives way to an unabashedly fervent Magyar patriot, whose sole perspective is the love of the fatherland rather than any striving for literary excellence. His interest in the famous personalities of the past and the outstanding statesmen and men of letters of his time led Dori to two of the most popular nineteenth-century Hungarian poets: Mihály Vörösmarty (1800-55) and János Arany (1817-82).

Vörösmarty, whom Antal Szerb, the noted literary historian, called "the poet laureate of Magyardom," appealed to Dori's imagination and sensitivities to the past. The author of "Szózat" developed a panoramic, history-oriented perspective that became the cornerstone of his creative world. Through the epic tales and heroic events of ancient times—the favorite themes of his early poems—Vörösmarty eventually reached the exalted plateau where "the Magyar people, Magyar land, and Magyar stars converged in unity, transfused by a common circulation of blood, and where he whose heart beats in unison with the rhythm of the Magyar cosmos, may truly live his Magyardom."

Dori payed an enthusiastic homage to Vörösmarty in a composition entitled **"A magyar költo" ["The Magyar Poet"]**. He successfully recaptured Vörösmarty's fascination with decay and death, bittersweet flight from reality into the soothing depth of self, and unabating love of the fatherland.

> On trackless crags treads the Magyar poet, singing melancholy songs of the heroic age of the fatherland, when the patriot was still faithful to the last drop of his blood and with weapon in hand defended the rights of the fatherland. He sings songs of the heroes who, like the rare ideals of courage, glitter on the pages of history. He sings songs of a youth's love, of a maiden's charms. And while he sings, tears well up in his eyes and his face becomes clouded.
>
> All is in vain. Do not sing! The golden age of the fatherland has long passed, and with it died the heroes whom we wreathed with the laurels of poetry. The youth loves no more, the maiden feels no more, and your love is unrewarded. If you do sing, sing only for yourself, joylessly, by the nocturnal lair of beasts of prey.
>
> And the youth wanders on homeless, the fire of his heart extinguished and his song stilled.
>
> The falling leaves gently cover the body of the dead poet, who dreams sweet dreams in his quiet resting place.

Like the generations of schoolchildren who came under the spell of Miklós Toldi, the powerful hero of János Arany's monumental trilogy, Dori was fascinated by the inspiring ex-

Herzl's tomb, in Jerusalem.

ploits of the legendary Magyar warrior. A more nationalistic topic he could hardly have found. "The most Magyar of Magyar poets" gave his people the gift of love they needed most: the true peasant hero, the exemplary Magyar. In addition to its immense popularity, for Dori, *Toldi's* appeal must have been heightened by a circumstance in which elements of time, location, and personality converged. Arany moved to Budapest, shortly before Dori was born, to become a member and eventually secretary-general of the Hungarian Academy of Sciences, as well as director of the Kisfaludy Society. Thus Dori may have seen the great poet in the flesh. Moreover, Dori was drawn to *Toldi* because of two character traits which he shared with its hero: an inclination to become emotional and quick-tempered in responding to the manifold challenges of life, and the deep strain of devotion between mother and younger son, a central feature of the epic drama.

Entitled **"Toldi Miklós,"** Dori's carefully written Magyar composition is a skillful synopsis of Arany's monumental work. A number of additions and deletions in the text attest to the author's punctilious observance of the correct elements of style.

> Many years have passed and many generations have been born and descended into the tomb since Miklós Toldi died, yet the memory of his deeds persists. People still talk about the huge warrior whose powerful voice would terrify us and whose armor would pin even the strongest man to the ground.

> The field hands are sprawled out in a shady spot, leaving things the way they are, doing nothing though there would be plenty to do, but in the heat of the sun no one is in the mood for working. Across the steppe, as far as the eye can see, only one

young man is up on his feet. On his shoulder an awesome wooden pole quivers. Though the sun is shining brightly his eyes wander to faraway lands. He watches, not the dust that the whirlwind has stirred up, but the troops that march in the distance. They are going to war against the Turks and Tatars, and to win laurels, muses the valiant Miklós Toldi. You lucky ones, how I wish I could accompany your formations, you proud knights!

> Followed by his army, the palatine Endre Lacfi pushes on. Upon noticing him, Lacfi addresses Toldi haughtily, "You, peasant! Show me the way that leads toward Buda!" The words, however, offend Toldi very much, for his father, Lorinc Toldi, was a great warrior, and his deceitful brother, György, is a great noble and the king's good friend. "I, a peasant?" But he said no more about it. As he thought of György amid a torrent of curses, he lifted the monstrous pole with one hand, showing where the road turned toward Buda. Every one of the palatine Lacfi's soldiers wonders at his deed, and despite Lacfi's call none of them dares to wrestle with him or lift the pole.

> It has been a long time since the army marched off; still Miklós keeps his arm ramrod straight, holding the heavy pole. At last, when not even the dust shows any sign of the dashing young men, he goes home with a heavy heart.

> In Nagyfalu big preparations are under way as Miklós arrives home, for during his absence his brother, György, arrived with forty of his warriors and servants to spend half of his inheritance on feasting and pocket the other half. Entering the room, Miklós automatically stretches out his arms

to embrace his perfidious brother, but the latter firmly pushes him away and gives him a severe tongue-lashing. By then Miklós's anger is roused; he reproaches his brother for everything he has done and asks for his paternal inheritance. However, György, who had no intention of complying, slapped the face of his upright, good-hearted brother. With that the ties which bind even the prodigal to his closest relative are broken. If Miklós struck him even once he would no longer enjoy the light of the sun. But he changes his mind and does not do it. He walks out of the room quietly and sits down in a corner of the courtyard; giving vent to his sorrow, he weeps bitterly.

There he sat for a long time. At last the feast was over and in their exuberance György's warriors started throwing lances and wrestling in the courtyard. György Toldi watched the revelry from under the eaves. He notices his brother sitting at the end of the courtyard and urged his men . . .

Not all of Dori's Magyar compositions are confined to subjects taken from the history and literature of the Magyars. If they were, a case could be made out for the "German Boy in Budapest" theory. Although one would have to disregard the implications of their patriotic fervor and stylistic elegance, one could argue that the Magyar essays reflect a talented Germanophile student's ability to conceal his true feelings for the purpose of producing a perfunctory exercise in patriotism that met the requirements of a constraining and nationalist Hungarian educational system. That, however, is not the case. The conclusion that the observant reader is more apt to reach is that when the youthful author was free to select the language of his compositions, he chose impulsively rather than in conscious deference to a linguistic and cultural predisposition.

The compositions in Magyar that did not incorporate Magyar themes are in many ways the mirror image of the ones he wrote in German. The impressive literary characteristics that he had acquired in the course of the brief but productive association with Wir [a literary society founded by Herzl and his friends] are readily discernible in most of the Magyar compositions. These were written at a later date, to judge from the more assured and sophisticated handwriting. The wide range of interest, uncompromising outspokenness, fluid style, and skillful choice of words and expressions form an authoritative, albeit thin façade that a less scrupulous person might have used to conceal superficiality in approach and execution.

The carefree young man-about-town who virtually flaunted his pedantic concern with the proprieties of appearance and the formalities of etiquette, however, did not have the makings of a diletante littérateur. Neither did he search for shortcuts to achieve his objectives. Dori worked honestly and hard at becoming a writer. He set high standards for himself and strove indefatigably not to fall short of them. He remained his own severest critic and taskmaster, patiently and meticulously correcting words or sentences, often rewriting even entire compositions. He did not differentiate between light-hearted topics and those of a somber nature. His goal, to become a writer of impeccable taste and consummate skill, was to remain untarnished in the years to come.

Dori's Magyar compositions embrace widely disparate topics, both fictional and nonfictional, and follow one another in an unpredictable sequence. One of the most interesting is a rare, perhaps unique piece of writing on a scientific subject, yielding important clues to the author's unhappy frame of mind in the science-oriented *főreáltanoda*. Entitled **"Az Oxigén" ["The Oxygen"]**, it affords the reader more than a fleeting glimpse of the teenage author's laborious approach to creative writing. In technical execution **"Az Oxigén"** is reminiscent of the rest of his compositions. At least three drafts attest to the hard-to-please Dori's tenacious struggle to attain excellence in penmanship and depth of substance. But the elegant, gracefully fluid style and effortless choice of expressions, his usual hallmarks, give way to a clear, concise, and simply constructed narrative that traces the evolution of the theories explaining the chemical process that takes place in burning. He then examines the words for *oxygen* in English, French (*calorique*), German (*Sauerstoff*), Greek (*oxys* and *genes*), and Magyar (*éleny*), and lists its chemical characteristics. Next he identifies the scientists (Stahl, Lavoisier, Priestley, Sheele, and the Hungarian Irinyi) who had conducted important experiments with it. Observes Dori in the concluding sentence, "Substances like iron that do not burn easily disintegrate (rust) slowly when exposed to air; in pure oxygen they burn intensely." (pp. 72-6)

Of the compositions still extant, this is the only one devoted to science. His Muse soon nudged him toward other topics. He gave vent to his fine sense of humor in an untitled short story in which he relates the experiences of a two-week vacation at a nearby spa. Prompted by a whim, the excursion turns into a chain of minor mischances that could not have been more annoying if an evil demon had meticulously planned them. He arrives at the height of the season, following a short but tiring journey. When a long search for a suitable room ends satisfactorily, his success is quickly soured by the landlord's interminable tirade about the finer points of the room and the desirable location of the house. Dori falls asleep exhausted, only to be awakened at midnight by an insomniac pacing up and down in the adjacent room. Still, he does not allow the series of petty annoyances to get the better of him. "I felt sorry for that poor man who could not sleep, spending the long hours of the night alone in his thoughts, which perhaps were tormenting him with memories of the past." Well, things would be better the next day after meeting some friends. "I got up early the next morning and went to the promenade in front of the mineral spring, where, notwithstanding the early hours, the well-groomed guests of the spa had already gathered. I scrutinized the rows of strolling people. I had no success. I did not see a single acquaintance."

In another untitled composition Dori lets his imagination roam in a sensitive description of the early seventeenth-century German countryside. He observes, somewhat sadly, the passing of summer and the approaching signs of autumn: an inevitable cycle of decay and rebirth shared by man and nature. "It is the law of nature that after long years the tall-treed forest withers so that it may give way to young sprouts that will grow and become sturdy trunks, only to give way to new shoots again. That is also how a careful forester works, preserving the forest from century to century by handing it over to other, equally caring persons. And even if he is long dead, his remains turned to dust, and even if not one old dusty picture arouses in the offspring remembrance of the ancestor, the memory of his caring will still be crackling among the merry treetops."

Perhaps the most entertaining of Dori's Magyar compositions is the one entitled **"A bölcsek köve (humoristicus novel-**

la)" ["**The Philosophers' Stone (Humorous Short Story)**"]. Like the brief account of his vacation woes, "**A bölcsek köve**" is written in flawless, idiomatic Magyar, revealing no hidden dissatisfaction with that language, but only a thorough familiarity with its grammatical and stylistic rules and intricacies. There simply is no evidence in "**A bölcsek köve**" of a struggle to find the appropriate words and expressions. Nor is there any sign that the sentence structure is hampered by the cumbersome process of thinking in German and translating into Magyar. In fact, when read aloud, the informal style and use of words and expressions not usually found in literary compositions offer the reader a rare opportunity to hear what Dori sounded like when speaking in his native tongue.

The hero of "**A bölcsek köve**" is a tantalizingly named academic, Crysostomos Bombastus Elysaus Pfanhauerius, both rector-dean of Hundsheim University and chairman of its Department of Chemistry. The reader is hardly surprised to learn that the bearer of such a name should live in a time "when quackery was thought to be synonymous with science, and whoever merely dabbled in alchemy was regarded as a genius." The name of the university, which in English would be "dog's home," reinforces the point. We read that the door of the laboratory where this "greatly respected and long-titled gentleman" is conducting an experiment slowly opens to admit someone wearing an ominously nondescript cape, whose identity as a "representative of the *genus masculinus*" is not apparent until his long, gray beard becomes visible by the light of a burner. Frightened, the good rector-dean-chairman quickly concludes that the best way to defend himself is to grab a test tube, an act of such uncertain menace that it promptly draws a smile to the lips of the intruder. He, it turns out in the course of a polite introduction, is Robertus Caribatus Stockbeinius, dean and professor of chemistry at Pformesberg University. The test-tube-armed Pfanhauerius regains his composure and politely greets his eminent colleague. The two are soon absorbed in their highly specialized shoptalk, though it seems that the visitor is attempting to overwhelm the Hundsheim rector-dean with a torrent of names and technical terms.

Soon the rapidly changing topics of the conversation touch on the philosophers' stone, which, Stockbeinius contends could easily be produced by mixing a variety of strange-sounding liquids and solids in a pot on St. Bartholomew's night, accompanied by an appropriate blessing. Pfanhauerius promptly decides to perform the experiment with the help of his knowledgeable colleague. He throws, among other things, some of his less than popular or profitable books into the pot. On the fateful night when "people search after or use untested nostrums, recommended by gypsy women and soothsayers, which assure love, perpetual health, and long life," Pfanhauerius and Stockbeinius place the pot in the middle of a meadow. Stockbeinius even scrapes into it some greasy substance off his well-worn hat, creating a stench that would make both man and beast run for shelter. "Such a phenomenon is well known by every herdsman on the *Alfold,* who puts it into use when he wants to chase his cattle from another man's land or prevent them from grazing on unhealthy herbs."

Then as the dense, white, stinking vapors nearly engulf the two academics, the brave Stockbeinius invokes the exalted spirit of the philosophers' stone to lead them to the precious stone itself. Suddenly a stentorian voice, which only the awe-struck and befuddled Pfanhauerius could fail to recognize, rings out.

> You impudent, good-for-nothing ignoramus! You rascally lazybones! You flaunt your learning, but you really know nothing. Now you've met your master! I, whom you thought to be Stockbeinius, am Jeremiás Holzer, a student who has been expelled from Hundsheim University. You're trembling, aren't you? It was on account of you that I was expelled. But now I've taken my revenge. All that humbug, the books that have been burned and the money you've spent, was for naught. At this very moment my friends are scavenging your cellars, pantries, and cupboards. And if you dare think of prosecuting me, I'll tell everyone that you didn't know that there's no Pformesberg, thus it could have neither a university nor a dean, and that you let me make a fool of you and followed me here so that I might produce for you the philosophers' stone from the witches' brew. Go ahead, do it! They'll lock me up for a few years, but you'll lose your scholarly reputation. As of now only I and my friends know that you're an ass, but the whole world will know then. Here, you can have these for what you let yourself be made a fool of.

After he has his "colleague's" wig and beard thrown at him and his face slapped, the crestfallen Pfanhauerius is unceremoniously told to "get lost."

The respected rector-dean never exposes the student, but keeps his silence. "Only a few people learned that he was an ass. I was one of those who knew. Herzl Tivadar."

The ebullient signature—the family name is executed in exemplary penmanship, whereas the given name is slapdash, taking a floundering downward direction—is a fitting end to this exercise in nonsense.

Whenever he left the realm of fiction Dori's personality underwent a strange metamorphosis. The witty, chatty, and entertaining raconteur disappeared and was replaced by a somber, sharp-tongued, keen-eyed, and opinionated reviewer of the events of the past and a cautious admirer of its heroes. This serious side, however, was not employed as a convenient subterfuge. For even in his most impressive academic pose, Dori would take pride only in a painstakingly prepared and flawlessly finished piece of literary work.

The evolution of the essay on Girolamo Savonarola, the ill-fated fifteenth-century Dominican friar of Florence, is a good example. Dori made four drafts, each with a different title. The first, "**Egy olasz reformátor**" ["**An Italian Reformer**"], begins, "In our days that old feud between Church and State is rekindled, and again men are fighting with weapons of the mind so that they may put the affairs of the Church in order and end the dispute once and for all. Man needs something that will save him from despair when the hard blows of fate weigh heavily on him, when the foundations of his good fortune crumble, when he senses death approaching. That is religion." The hard-to-please Dori started anew. "Jeromos Savonarola was born on 21 September 1452. His childhood. . . ." The second draft grew somewhat longer before it too fell apart. Might a new title help? The third draft, "**Egy lázadó pap**" ["**A Rebellious Priest**"], had a new opening paragraph. "A few decades before the Reformation there lived in Florence a Dominican who was destined to play a great role for political as well as religious reasons. A man of moral purity, in contrast to his contemporaries, he threw down the gauntlet at the corrupt princes of the Church and stepped on the spiritual battleground where the inspired and noble-minded martyrs confront the haughty tyrants, and with the blood of their hearts set their seal on the warnings to the mighty."

Not even a fresh start placated the fickle Muse. Dori's fourth and mightiest effort, however, was crowned with at least partial success. He seemed determined to get to the bottom of things. He prepared an elaborate outline listing the prominent personalities in Italy in the last quarter of the fifteenth century—popes Pius II, Paul II, Sixtus IV, Eugene VIII, and Alexander VI, the talented but ruthless Medicis, and King Charles VIII of France—and described the chronological evolution of the conflict between Alexander VI and the French king. Unfortunately, the outline turned out better than the final version, which bore the simple title, **"Girolamo Savonarola."**

In the course of a spirited outburst of indignation, scathingly critical of the medieval Church, Dori declares, "The tiara had never rested on the head of a more evil, sanguine, and dissolute man than Alexander VI. Celibacy notwithstanding, Alexander VI lived in open adultery with the beautiful Julia Farnese and legitimized his children by her. His second son was the rapacious cardinal Caesar Borgia who had killed his brother and committed adultery with his sister Lucrezia. The debauchery of the papal court was bound to kindle the wrath of every noble-minded man." Thus speaks a Jewish boy living in the proud nineteenth-century Hungarian bastion of Christianity!

Dori took a different tone in the effortlessly written, lengthy essay, **"Catilina összeesküvése" ["Conspiracy of Catiline"]**. He seemed to have regained the intellectual balance that had almost deserted him among the unending intrigues of medieval Florence. The sole extant version of the essay (corrections throughout indicate that it was not a fair copy, although it may have been preceded by earlier drafts) attests to Dori's sure-footedness in the maze of ancient Rome's social strife. The author's perspective is worth noting. The young "Pest Jew," who since birth had been surrounded by the amenities of wealth, became an outspoken critic of the "dissolute and immoral" Roman patricians, whose extravagance, he believed, was responsible for the spread of waste from private life into the public realm. Government institutions absorbed enormous sums, as did the construction of public buildings like the theater that "accommodated 80 thousand people and into which 360 marble columns and 3,000 bronze statues had been placed." Such waste was bound to affect the wealth of the patricians adversely, and many of them went into debt.

One such impoverished patrician was Lucius Sergius Catiline. "He was one of those rare men on whom nature had bestowed pleasant and noble qualities and who feared nothing." Having won the support of a large number of people, young and old, he set out to challenge Cicero for the leadership of the Senate. His rumored interest in putting through relief measures for the poor was his undoing. Frustrated, he planned to wrest by force what he had failed to attain by election. Dori, like a learned guide, takes the reader on an informative and leisurely stroll through the streets and institutions of ancient Rome, describing Cicero's active political life as a backdrop to the unfolding drama of Catiline's ill-fated conspiracy. All in all, the essay is an impressive tour de force that Dori took an almost visible delight in writing—the same is true of his compositions on Cicero and Vergil—causing him

none of the moments of consternation that accompanied his labors over the cumbersome drafts of the Savonarola essay.

Similar success crowned Dori's attempt to pay homage to another great man in history. Entitled **"I Napoleon,"** the brief biographical composition accurately reflects the impression the Napoleonic legend had made on generations of nineteenth-century schoolboys in Hungary. The opening sentence sets the admiring tone that is the most easily discernible leitmotif of the essay. "From time to time in world history we meet outstanding men who accurately represent before us the virtues of our century, whose lives constitute a chain of earth-shaking feats, whose stars glitter with blinding light until they become covered with dark clouds. One such man was Napoleon I."

Except for its brevity—the sole feature that prevents favorable comparison with the other compositions—the Napoleon essay attests to Dori's firm grasp of the meaning of the revolutionary events that paved the way for Bonaparte's rise to military and political power, and to thorough research resulting in an accurate description of the emperor's achievements, victories and defeats, and exile. Dori had no misgivings about the enduring fame of the illustrious subject of his essay and concluded, "I will bravely state that like Julius Caesar, who will forever be mentioned in world history, N. will be praised for his virtues by our descendants for millennia to come." A noble thought. The thirteen-year-old author seemed to think so too. The decorative, oversized "No. 1" followed by "8/12 [1]873" below the last handwritten line stand out like a well-earned seal of approval.

The evidence Dori's Magyar compositions offer is clear. He felt at ease in both the culture of his Magyar environment and that of his Germanophile parents. He could put to creative use the tools of the writer in both Magyar and German. The event that would change this well-balanced bilingual biculturalism was his parents' unforeseen decision to leave Budapest for Vienna. In the better part of the 1870s, however, Dori still had the option to become either Theodor Herzl, *deutscher Schriftsteller,* or Herzl Tivadar, *magyar író.* Had it not been for his sister's sudden, tragic death, the consequences of which dramatically altered his life, realistic assessments of his budding literary career would undoubtedly have prompted the practical Dori to realize that his chances for success as a German writer in Budapest were no better than those of a Magyar writer in Vienna. Living in Budapest, Dori would have become the like of his cousin, Jenő Heltai (1871-1957), a prolific writer-playwright and a graceful, eloquent supplier of the light entertainment demanded by Budapest's middle class. (pp. 77-83)

> *Andrew Handler, in his* Dori: The Life and Times of Theodor Herzl in Budapest (1860-1878), *The University of Alabama Press, 1983, 161 p.*

JACQUES KORNBERG (essay date 1987)

[*In the following excerpt, Kornberg describes the utopia Herzl envisioned in* Old-New Land, *noting ideological differences between this work and the earlier* The Jewish State *and discussing Herzl's understanding of the European political climate of the late nineteenth century.*]

Herzl wrote the utopian novel ***Old-New Land*** for a variety of reasons. Utopian novels were a popular genre in the late nineteenth century, and Herzl hoped his work would be widely read. In addition, pouring his thoughts and feelings into a novel was a creative act for Herzl the writer and balked playwright, convinced he had given up a promising career in German letters by attaching himself to the Jewish cause. The novel was an affair between Herzl and his conscience, an interior monologue, a refuge from the compromises of day-to-day Zionist politics.

In the nineteenth century images of the ideal society conveyed through novels had spurred influential political movements. In 1840 Etienne Cabet's *Voyage en Icarie* had led to the birth of an active, well-organized political movement among French artisans. Later in the century the utopian novel enjoyed even wider popularity: Samuel Butler's *Erewhon* (1872) was followed by Edward Bellamy's *Looking Backward, 2000-1887* (1888), the Australian Theodor Hertzka's *Freeland: A Social Image of the Future (Freiland: Ein Sociales Zukunftbild, 1890)* and William Morris' *Notes from Nowhere; or An Epoch of Rest, Being Some Chapter from a Utopian Romance* (1891). *Freeland* went through ten editions in five years and led to the emergence of Freeland Associates in Germany and Austria that sought to purchase land in Africa to realize Hertzka's ideal society. Herzl wished to ride the tide of this success.

Still, Herzl's choice of the genre needs further explanation, for he had always considered the utopian novel an inappropriate literary mode for a statesman and man of action. When he first read Bellamy's *Looking Backward,* Herzl had scoffed at the novel as an "ideal fancy." The utopian genre functioned best as a critique of society's absurdities. The more it distanced itself from the real world, the "more amusing" it was. For Herzl, his plan was either realistic or an "ingenious fantasy," that is to say, "a novel." He concluded in 1895 that an inquiry into "The Condition of the Jews" would best evoke the mood of immediacy and realism that suited his political ends. Later, when writing *Old-New Land,* Herzl saw his novel no differently. In a draft of a letter of October 1902 to Lord Rothschild accompanying a copy of the novel, Herzl put his misgivings starkly: "I realize all the dangers it holds for me, namely that they'll once more revile me for being a 'dreamer of dreams' (in English in the original). But I had to choose this entertaining form because I want it to be read."

However, this exercise in ideal fantasies offered Herzl something more than the prospect of a wide readership. Behind the protective shield of the fictional form, less precise or binding than speeches and resolutions and easier to disclaim or qualify, Herzl expressed his own vision of Zionism in its purest, most uncompromising form. Herzl himself thought of *Old-New Land* as a work removed from the sphere of day-to-day political tactics, a creative personal catharsis in the midst of his political difficulties. On June 3, 1900 he wrote in his diary: "shall we hear a categorical no from Yilduz [The Sultan's palace]? If this came, I would resume work on my novel *Altneuland.* For then our plan will be only for the future and a novel." On March 4, 1901 he linked *Old-New Land* to his political reversals, to his miscarried time-table: "I am now industriously working on *Altneuland.* My hopes for practical success have now disintegrated. My life is no novel now. So the novel is my life."

Anticipated political failure was bitter, but also liberating. Reacting to the prospect, Herzl abandoned the constraints of day-to-day Zionist coalition politics and recklessly set out on an intransigent assertion of his own vision of Zionism. If his political hopes were in disarray, at least he would retain the

integrity of his convictions. In the end Herzl payed a price for his challenge, for the publication of *Old-New Land* unleashed a bitter debate in the Zionist press. The debate was launched by Ahad Ha-Am's critique of *Old-New Land* in *Ha-Shilo'ah* in December, 1902, and soon engaged prominent Zionists in bitter controversy. The vehement tone of the debate threatened to rupture the alliance between East European and Western Jewry and destroy the universality of the Zionist movement. All sides retreated from the brink, but the publication of *Old-New Land* ended up strengthening the hand of Herzl's Zionist opposition.

To understand why Herzl's novel provoked such opposition, its ideological tendency must be understood. In composing a utopian novel, Herzl was engaged in nationalist mobilization through myth-making. Nineteenth century utopias were based on the premise that for the first time in human history science, technology and industry would enable humanity to fully master its natural and social environment. These utopias were powerful political instruments, promising to end once and for all age-old oppression and injustice, and to gratify age-old longings for satisfying labor and self-fulfillment.

Old-New Land was not a blueprint for the settlement of Palestine. With its free farmers and agricultural co-operatives, *Old-New Land* bears a superficial resemblance to the schemes of Franz Oppenheimer, an influential German-Jewish economist whom Herzl brought into the Zionist movement in 1901. In his proposals for Jewish settlement, spelled out in a series of articles in *Die Welt,* Oppenheimer had stressed the need for the gradual creation of a broad agricultural base in Palestine consisting of farm cooperatives. These would bring economies of scale while sustaining a broad stratum of free, self-reliant Jewish farmers. Oppenheimer wished to forestall a danger endemic to colonial development: the creation of large plantations worked by a native agricultural proletariat that would as well become the basis for a low-paid industrial reserve army. In Oppenheimer's scheme a varied and versatile agricultural base would promote economic self-sufficiency and provide a market for eventual industrial development. But trade and industrial cooperatives would come gradually, only in so far as the agricultural market could support them. Oppenheimer offered a coherent plan for the gradual settlement of Palestine. Herzl's own description in *Old-New Land* actually diverged widely from Oppenheimer's scheme.

What Herzl depicted was not a practical scheme of settlement but a futuristic utopia created *de novo,* with no links to the past. The real advantage of settling in Palestine, Herzl insisted, was that it was so "primitive and neglected." As a result, Jews could start afresh, without being encumbered either by inherited institutions, pre-industrial social classes, or an obsolete technological infrastructure. It was on this basis that Herzl now sought to rally Jews to Palestine, not by evoking sacred memories and hallowed traditions. Palestine was a blank slate on which human will and ingenuity could write what it wished. Palestine answered to a futuristic vision; humanity's desire to shed the past and start absolutely afresh, on virgin territory. Herzl did not even link his utopian vision to Jewish continuities, to the ancient yearnings of Jewish messianism. Instead, he attributed the utopian spirit animating *Old-New Land* to the "gigantic social-economic labors of the nineteenth century." The foundations for *Old-New Land* were laid in modern Europe. Finally, the tone of *Old-New Land* is more anti-clerical than Herzl's earlier work, *The Jewish State.* In the novel no concessions are made to the "noble functions" of the clergy. Herzl was responding to those who feared that the Jewish rebirth "would be a stupid reaction, a kind of millenial terrorism," by asserting that religion had no role in "public affairs."

Herzl depicted a fully developed, advanced industrial society in Palestine just twenty years from the time the Ottoman authorities had granted a charter to the Jews. When Friedrich, the novel's protagonist, and his friend, the Prussian ex-cavalry officer, Kingscourt, enter Haifa after twenty years of misanthropic isolation on a South Sea island, they find themselves in a busy urban metropolis. Because of its geographical position linking Europe, Asia and Africa, Palestine has become a major entrepôt, a hub of international trade. Automobiles rush by on the wide streets. A network of elevated electric trains ring the city. Jerusalem has become a twentieth century metropolis. In a breathtaking imaginative leap, Herzl depicted Palestine as far more advanced than Europe. "You're a damned shrewd nation," the Prussian Kingscourt exclaims, "left us with the old scrap iron, while you travel about in the latest machines!" Starting with a blank slate, the settlers were able to introduce the most advanced technology immediately, and as a result Palestine boasts every advanced technology and industry known to the civilized world. Between Spring and Autumn during the first year of the Charter, a half million immigrants were settled in Palestine—an outlandish claim that was to be mocked by the Russian Zionist, Ahad Ha-Am. The Dead Sea Canal, stretching from the Mediterranean to the Dead Sea, feeds a series of electric power stations and pours limitless gallons of water into the desert, sustaining its rich agricultural yields.

Old-New Land must be read against a particular historical background. The novel is a relatively late product of Herzl's political career; first begun in July 1899 and written over a period of three years, it was completed in April 1902. By then long-simmering quarrels between Herzl and opposition forces within the Zionist movement were coming to a head. The novel was a challenging response to these quarrels, which had first broken out during the early years of the movement. To understand *Old-New Land*'s significance, a knowledge of the quarrels that beset Zionism from the very beginning is necessary.

Initially, members of Hovevei Zion, the Russian Zionist movement that predated Herzl, had serious reservations about even responding to Herzl's call for a Zionist Congress, for they feared that Herzl's program as enunciated in *The Jewish State* would override their own priorities. The main issues that divided them from Herzl were Hovevei Zion's absolute and unreserved concentration on Palestine as the locus for a Jewish state, its program of agricultural settlement there, and its desire to foster a Hebrew revival and a modern Hebraic culture, all of which were keyed to a gradualist, long-range time frame. Herzl, in *The Jewish State,* had considered other possible locations for a Jewish state, notably Argentina. Furthermore, he aimed first of all for the maximalist goal of Jewish sovereignty, which he expected to attain quickly, within months or at most years, and he considered all other goals—such as settlement activity or the Hebraic revival—as distracting from and undermining the maximalist aim.

Quarrels over priorities were rooted in deeper ideological differences. Influenced by Russian Populism, Hovevei Zion sought to create in Palestine a Jewish peasant stratum close to nature, rooted in the soil. Herzl considered peasants a reactionary class; his model of Jewish society was urban, and

technological. For Herzl, Zionism's first creation was to be a highly centralized state which would lever Jews into modernity. Hovevei Zion, influenced by the experience of Tsarist bureaucratic tyranny, was hostile to the modern state, preferring a minimalist state hedged in by a self-reliant Jewish society and a highly developed Hebraic national spirit. Herzl was antagonistic to the modern Hebrew revival which, he believed, would perpetuate Jewish isolation and cut Jews off from the European cultural mainstream. In addition, Herzl contemplated a state and society liberated from the yoke of the Jewish past. For Hovevei Zion the Hebraic revival was central and could only occur in Palestine, because Palestine alone evoked sacred Jewish traditions; a modern, even secular Hebrew culture would have to preserve links to past Jewish practices and beliefs.

Differences on these issues could have split the Zionist movement from the outset had not Herzl responded by a combination of substantial concessions as well as vague, deft compromises that would not tie his hands as he pursued his priorities. The Basle Program at the First Zionist Congress affirmed the centrality of Palestine and the importance of incremental settlement activity there. But Herzl continued to hedge on these issues. After ignoring the resolutions of the Second Congress, in order to avert a split he finally agreed at the Third Congress to alter the statutes of the Jewish Colonial Trust and restrict its tasks to Palestine. At the Fourth Congress he was still able to sidetrack a resolution to promote Hebrew culture, but by the Fifth Congress, he had to bow to the opposition and agree to set up a Cultural Commission to implement a resolution favoring the Hebraic revival. Whatever concessions Herzl made he always endeavored to ignore, or indeed to torpedo in practice. As an example, the Smaller Actions Committee, made up of Herzlean loyalists, hampered the work of the Cultural Commission set up by the Fifth Congress.

With each Congress opposition to Herzl had mounted. Simultaneously, Herzl's extravagant promises of imminent success were wearing thin; his failures on the diplomatic front were weakening his hand; Russian Zionists kept pressing for a return to land purchase and colonization efforts in Palestine.

By August 1902, Herzl was forced to acknowledge that his negotiations with the Ottoman régime had come to nothing and that no diplomatic break-throughs were imminent. The argument that Zionism would have to return to the gradualist program of Hovevei Zion in order to avoid stagnation now acquired great force. Open challenges to the Herzlean program increased. Herzl's response was to go on the offensive by launching a feverish campaign for a charter, first in the Sinai Peninsula, then in East Africa. Herzl's campaign culminated in the Uganda Affair, which in the face of massive opposition he insisted on turning into an issue of confidence in his leadership. No longer the deft strategist, he launched a frontal assault against the opposition, that threatened to split the movement apart. Only at the eleventh hour did both sides retreat from the brink.

It is against this background of the creeping erosion of Herzl's leadership and his reluctant concessions to an opposition, gradually gaining in strength, that *Old-New Land* must be viewed.

Indeed, *Old-New Land* represented a move away from some of Herzl's own nationalist reflections in the years 1895 to

1897, when he was first developing his ideas. He was now recoiling, after several years in the Zionist movement, from what he originally had acknowledged both in theory and practice. In particular, Herzl had now become far more suspicious, far less patient, with what he saw as the irrationalist side of nationalism, whereas at first he had appreciated, indeed affirmed, its central importance.

In a pathbreaking study of Herzl [see Further Reading], within the all-important context of fin-de-siècle Vienna, Carl Schorske has depicted the founder of political Zionism as a rebel against Austrian liberalism and as one of Vienna's pioneers in "post-rational politics." With the decline of Austrian liberalism resulting from the entrance of the masses into the political arena after the wide extension of the Austrian suffrage in the 1880s, Herzl had come to grasp "the irrational psychological dynamic of politics." Herzl was educated by the mass movements that were now divesting Austrian liberalism of its ascendancy—Czech nationalism, Social Democracy, Christian Socialism and Pan-Germanism, and he was to apply the lessons he had gained in mobilizing the Jewish masses on behalf of Zionism. This meant abandoning the rationalist tone of liberalism and adopting a politics that appealed to the heart, the feeling of the masses. As such, Herzl "affirmed dream, waking fantasy, the unconscious, and art" as instruments of political mobilization. Specifically, this meant evoking memories of an ancient national solidarity mystically tied to a sacred homeland, national myths and symbols, and messianic expectancy. Reading Herzl's first Zionist tract, *The Jewish State* and the early entries in his Zionist diary, to all indications Herzl had learned the lessons of mass politics well. He summoned Jews to rejoin their ancient nation, to revive an archaic communion, identified by him as "the faith of our fathers."

Herzl's early schemes for mobilizing nationalist fervor included the cult of festivals—a feature of German nationalism—which linked the modern striving for national unity to historic memories of an ancient tribalistic communion. Such festivals were to feature archaic dress, a flag. To parallel the ancient Germanic tribal brotherhood with its warrior austerity, Herzl evoked the memory of the Maccabees. For the oak and the sacred flame, archaic symbols from Germany's tribal past, Herzl substituted the seven-branched candelabrum used in the Temple, the menorah. The menorah's form, he believed, was based on that of the tree. Herzl also called for "Jewish National Passion Plays," a copy, we can assume, of the passion play performed every ten years at Oberammergau, considered to be genuine *völkisch* theater, rooted in popular nativist traditions.

Herzl's early entries in his Zionist diary constitute a virtual handbook in nationalist political mobilization. The problem, as he saw it, was how to bind a physically dispersed and culturally heterogeneous people into a common sentiment of nationhood. The most powerful common element among Jews, shared by the still traditionalist masses of Eastern Europe and the assimilated Jews of Western and Central Europe, was Judaism, what Herzl had termed "the faith of our fathers." Hence the rabbis would play a central role in Zionism, stirring mass enthusiasms. Zionism would even transport to Palestine the Hasidic wonder rabbi of Sadagora from the benighted Bukowina, creating a focus of religious pilgrimage equal to Mecca and Lourdes.

As he had insisted in *The Jewish State:* "we intend to keep sacred all emotional attachments to the past." Herzl had grasped that a great deal of the emotional power of nationalism derived from its ability to tap the realm of the sacred common historical myths, rituals, and dogmas, endowed with charismatic power. Nationalism's superior attractive power to creeds like liberalism and even socialism was that while the latter emphasized their break with the past with its over-abundant superstition and injustice, nationalism linked itself up to the past, to history, reviving the memory of ancient greatness, an ancient culture, ancient customs, all that had made the nation unique.

At the same time, Herzl's image of the Jewish State was modernistic and liberal, a state featuring progressive labor legislation, advanced technology and rational administrative planning and direction. The Jewish state was to be a model of modern liberty and economic justice. As such it was to be purged of historical anachronisms. Herzl criticized the efforts of Hovevei Zion to create a Jewish peasantry in Palestine. In an age of large-scale agricultural production, the peasant was economically obsolete. In addition, efforts to create a Jewish peasantry meant preserving "obsolete cultural conditions," "turn[ing] back the clock of civilization by force." Herzl was denying the value of simple piety and mystic attachment to the ancient soil. By the same token the role of the rabbis was to be restricted, subordinated to the state's policy of religious pluralism. Rabbis were to have "no privileged voice in the state." They were to stir national enthusiasm and teach patriotism, beyond that their influence would be restricted.

For Herzl, faith was meant to be an instrument of political mobilization, an expedient, a means, nothing more. "Faith unites us, knowledge makes us free." Faith was not to impinge upon the absolute primacy of science and reason. The appeal to ancient tribal memories, myths and customs, messianic longings, the attachment to the sacred Land of Promise, were all to be highly controlled means, expedients for the ends of political unification and heightened national morale and self-confidence. Herzl had taken the measure of the masses. "With nations one must speak in a childish language: a house, a flag, a song, are the symbols of communication." (The house was to be a specially designed building for Zionist congresses.) Through the controlled use of archaic motivations—"childish language"—he wished to lever the Jewish masses into a modernistic political community.

Qualifying reflections, reservations expressed by Herzl both in the early years and later, indicate a dawning realization that non-rational means and rational ends could not be kept separate in practice. Either the irrational means would override the rational ends, or, what Herzl opted for, irrational means would have to be abandoned. Accordingly, Herzl's attitude to the Hebraic cultural revival highlighted his opposition to any substantive links between Zionism and Jewish cultural continuities. There was nothing wrong with evoking memories of the Maccabees, for in Herzl's mind this awakened civic virtues, the value of heroic self-sacrifice on behalf of national independence. Beyond this he would not go, for he viewed the Hebrew cultural revival as a form of nativism. "If we found a neo-Hebrew state," he had commented in his diary, "it will be only a New Greece." Herzl's reference to Greece was to the course its nationalism had taken since Greek independence in 1829, when the country became locked in a struggle between Westernizers, oriented to the heritage of the Enlightenment and the French Revolution and anti-Westernizers, who wished to build on Greece's Eastern, Byzantine and Greek Orthodox past. If Herzl rejected the Greek model, all the more was he repelled by another nativist example, the Orange Free State and the Transvaal—the Afrikaner republics—engaged in the 1890's in a bitter war of independence against the British. "After all," Herzl commented in his diary, "we don't want a Boer state, but a Venice." Later, Zionists of a different persuasion saw in the hardy independent warrior-cattle-farmers who had carved out the Boer republics in a hostile and threatening environment the model for a "Jewish Peasant State." What stood out for Herzl was that the Boers rejected the liberal and humanitarian values of contemporary European civilization in its dominant British mode in South Africa, and developed a Biblically-based nationalism that asserted Afrikaner superiority over other races and cultures. Herzl seems to have feared any religious influences on Zionism, even those purportedly in harmony with Western values. At the Third Congress in August 1899, the Chief Rabbi of the Sephardic communities of England, Moses Gaster, delivered an address on the importance of the Hebraic revival. In his speech Gaster asserted that traditional Jewish messianism found its modern expression in the longing for a world in which justice and love ruled. Though he linked Judaism with progressive modern ideals, his insistence on the continuing relevance of Judaism seems to have irritated Herzl who, in his diary, called the speech "a theological beerhall rant."

In **The Jewish State** Herzl had sought to appeal, at least in part, to non-rational sentiments in his attempt to create a modern Jewish political movement. In **Old-New Land** Herzl was now engaged in a concerted effort to override these sentiments. In a letter to Lord Rothschild on August 22, 1902, which accompanied a copy of **Old-New Land,** he sought to allay Rothschild's opposition to Zionism: "I will not concede that the Jewish commonwealth I wish to found will be small, orthodox and illiberal. For three years I have labored on a coherent response to these and similar misgivings." Herzl's quarrels with his Zionist opposition had heightened his distrust of the non-rational side of nationalism. By the time he wrote **Old-New Land** he was determined to resist such trends by posing a counter-image of the Jewish State as an implacably futuristic utopia.

Herzl's efforts to counter what he considered archaic trends in Jewish nationalism through futuristic myth-making had a political dimension as well. **Old-New Land's** institutional framework was to promote hegemony by a technocratic elite and undercut the political power of the common people, considered by Herzl the carriers of nationalistic atavism.

Herzl's view of the common people comes to light several times in **Old-New Land.** In his only depiction of free farmers, shaped ostensibly by enlightened cooperative institutions, we actually encounter the first sour note in what Herzl called the New Society, for what we meet are Russian Jews depicted as Yiddish-speaking, nativist bigots. Once more Herzl seemed to repudiate his previous efforts at coalition politics within Zionism. After the First Zionist Congress in 1897, Herzl had gone so far as to criticize Western European Jews for their "arrogance" toward East European Jews. On the contrary, he insisted "they [East European Jews] have the inner unity which most European Jews have lost." Hence, they are on "the right track," and are able to resist assimilation. In **Old-New Land** Herzl cast such views aside; the only virtuous Russian Jews are fervent Westernizing assimilationists like Dr. Eichenstamm, the New Society's first President (modelled on

Max Mandelstamm, a Herzl loyalist who later, along with Israel Zangwill, founded the Jewish Territorial Organization) and David Littwak (modelled on David Wolffsohn, a Herzl associate and his successor as head of the World Zionist Organization). Indeed, Herzl's famous and often quoted claim that Zionism is the "return to Judaism" seemed now merely a passing thought, a concession to Russian Zionist sensitivities.

Spurred by the farmer Mendel, (Herzl's caricature of Menachem Mendel Ussishkin, perhaps his most determined and outspoken opponent among Russian Zionists) the men of Neudorf (New Village) a prosperous producer's cooperative, follow a political demagogue, Doctor Geyer, who is eager to flatter their base instincts. He does this by appealing to "immediate advantage" rather than "lasting good," strengthening the resolve of the men of Neudorf to exclude gentiles from the New Society. (Whether Dr. Geyer refers to an actual person remains a mystery. Desmond Stewart has concluded that Geyer stands for Richard Wagner. Ludwig Geyer was Wagner's stepfather, and there is some evidence he was Wagner's biological father too. Some have claimed Geyer was Jewish, though the evidence is inconclusive.) Dr. Steineck (modelled after the Viennese architect and Herzl loyalist, Oskar Marmorek) muttering sotto voce "I shall set their peasant skulls to rights," lectures the farmers of Neudorf on the need for "liberality, tolerance, love of mankind." "The applause was slight," we learn.

In another instance, Herzl expressed his concern about the democratic tendencies of cooperatives. When told that newspapers, too, had become cooperatives, owned by subscribers both sharing in the newspaper's profits and electing deputies who made policy, Friedrich objects that this must "debase the popular intelligence," since mass instinct unchecked by the leadership of "gifted individuals" tended to political extremes. David Littwak then explained that privately owned newspapers also existed, so that "a new tendency" or "a creative spirit," did stand a chance of prevailing.

The utopian novels of the 1880s and 1890s had dealt with the problem of the masses. Their common solution was shared by Herzl. In their magisterial study of utopian thought [*Utopian Thought in the Western World* (1979)], the Manuels have called this solution "Victorian socialism." Reacting to the emergence of the "social question," the mass misery produced by capitalism's cycles of speculative boom and subsequent collapse, crises of over-production and periodic waves of unemployment, these utopias provided mechanisms to tame and channel the power of capital and dispense its benefits to all. Such schemes were meant to offer an enlightened alternative to class conflict and revolutionary violence. Contrary to the Marxist image of a new society ushered in by apocalyptic revolutionary upheaval, Victorian socialism relied on reason and enlightened self-interest to effect a major transfer of wealth and power.

But it was not only the cycle of bloodshed brought about by revolutionary violence and state repression that the utopians wished to undercut. Universal suffrage in France and Germany, and the widening of suffrage in the United Kingdom and Hapsburg Austria in the 1880s had seen the rise of anti-liberal, anti-capitalist mass parties that now sought power through the ballot box. There was a danger that the new age would be shaped by the power of the masses, by a regimented state socialism and egalitarian levelling. Danger from the left was also matched by danger from the right. In Austria in the early 1890s, the Christian Social Party under Karl Lueger was a major electoral force, and by 1897 Lueger had become Mayor of Vienna. The Christian Social party included a large petty bourgeoisie clientele, artisans in particular, suffering from the consequences of capitalist modernization. The Christian Socialists combined opposition to large-scale capitalism with anti-liberalism, anti-Semitism and militant clericalism.

The utopians of the 1880s and 1890s aimed to short-circuit the rise of mass politics by offering the benefits of capitalism without its ills. Monopoly ownership of land and capital was to be eliminated and access to land and easy credit furnished to all. There was to be no wage labor. Utopia consisted of a network of producers' cooperatives and individual enterprises. Both made possible economies of large scale production; at the same time the eradication of poverty increased overall purchasing power. Competitiveness remained; earnings depended on initiative and talent. Utopia made possible the freedom of individual enterprise, competition and differential rewards for merit without gross inequality and endemic want.

The advantage of the free market and the free movement of labor and capital were to be supplemented by technocratic planning. In Hertzka's *Freeland,* the state was responsible for building the railroads and for massive public works projects. A state statistical bureau eliminated speculation from economic decision-making. Moreover, cooperatives appointed managers with wide powers (though they were removable by popular vote). Utopia amounted to combining the freedom of liberalism with technocratic planning in order to forestall the revolt of the masses. *Old-New Land* incorporated these same mechanisms.

In Herzl's account of the Zionist acquisition of the Old-New Land, the people play no role. In the new version, Herzl carried through his original plan—conceived in 1895—of appealing to wealthy Jews to acquire a charter from the Turks. There is, then, no need to create an alternative power base in the Jewish masses, or to rely on them for financial resources. The initial two million pounds sterling paid to the Turkish government comes from the philanthropic foundations for Jewish colonization financed by Jewish millionaires. Indeed, the charter agreement is signed behind the scenes and kept secret so as to prevent a rush of immigrants, so little are the masses actively involved.

The story of the acquisition of Palestine is told by Joe Levy "the man who carried through the new Jewish national project." A benevolent technocrat, Levy combines "sound observation and an iron will." (Levy was modelled after Joseph Cowen, an English businessman and associate of Herzl.) Levy is shrouded in charismatic mystery. Incessantly travelling to purchase the latest technology for Old-New Land, he is never seen; his "strong masculine voice" is heard on a phonograph recounting the story of Old-New Land's founding. Zionist politics were made from above, by exceptional personalities, platonic rulers in the shape of technocrats and financiers.

During the general elections for the President of the New Society the party of Jewish nativists, who wish to exclude gentiles from the New Society, launch an attack on Joe Levy for "his all-too-unlimited powers over the millions of the New Society." Professor Steineck cannot contain his indignation at the ungrateful author of this assault: "He knows how Joe

sweated to bring the New Society up to its present level." Centralized decision-making by technical experts—Levy and his appointed Department Heads—has created the infrastructure of Palestine, its cities, its industries, its land allocation, the settlement of its immigrants, its labor allocation. The New Society continues to be run largely by benevolent technocrats. Experts manage the public sector, provided for out of public funds, which includes schools, hospitals, orphanages, public kitchens and vacation camps—institutions ensuring lifelong security and universal access to opportunity. Though Old-New Land possesses an elected Congress and President, Congress sits only a few weeks each year, and the President's position is purely honorary.

Herzl had solved the problem of mass politics through the suspension of politics; benevolent technocrats replaced professional politicians at the centers of power. As a consequence the New Society has no mass parties, no outlet at all for the mobilization of the masses. "There is a healthy prejudice against [political] partisans of any kind whatsoever." The key decisions in the New Society are politically neutral technocratic decisions; the promotion of political ideology had been read out of the system. In this regard *Old-New Land* was not a harbinger of the new, since the urgent political challenge of turn of the century European politics was to incorporate mass parties into the policy in ways that softened—but hardly eliminated—class and ideological conflict, and stabilized the political order. Herzl's scheme was not up to this challenge. Instead, he posited a society in which collectivist, supra-individual ideologies lacked all function or appeal.

The basic social unit for Herzl remained the individual, in an economic system that had eliminated extreme poverty and wealth but that still allowed for income differentials. Indeed, there was a second society in Old-New Land outside the cooperatives of the New Society, one of private capitalism and wage labor. Though enlightened, typically including profit-sharing schemes for its employees, this sector made possible the private accumulation of substantial wealth. The great achievement of Old-New Land did not lay in subordinating the individual to larger aggregates but in transforming "raw egotism" in to enlightened egotism.

As David Littwak, who was to become the next President of the New Society, expressed it: "mutualism has not made us poorer in strong personalities; the richer, if anything. . . . We recognize and respect the importance of the individual." "Talent must have its due reward; effort as well. We need wealth so that we may tempt the ambitious and nurture unusual talent." Old-New Land was "a society of citizens seeking to enjoy life through work and culture." Sharing in an economy of abundance, the Jewish masses now found their satisfaction in work, the play of talents and capacities and inner cultural development. The pursuit of individual self-enhancement had deflected nativist and nationalist passions.

For Herzl the fortunes of Zionism and those of European liberalism were intertwined. Zionism was no flight from liberalism but was meant to sustain and reinforce liberalism. *Old-New Land* was a social-liberal utopia, a blueprint for a liberal New Society in Palestine, not only for Palestine, but for the restoration of liberal prospects in Europe as well.

In the early 1890s Herzl had pondered ways to reform Austrian liberalism in order to restore its universalistic appeal. Well before he became a Zionist, Herzl had become alarmed by the growing political paralysis of Austro-liberalism, its defensiveness on the "social question" and consequent inability to halt the rise of democratic mass parties. Only by demonstrating their relevance on issues of mass distress could liberals stem a political tide that could well sweep them away. Clinging stubbornly to their program of economic laissez-faire, liberals, he declared, "gradually bring freedom into disrepute." What they have failed to understand is that "The conditions that foster individualism change with the times." The task of liberalism, as he saw it, was to broaden its political appeal among the masses with a social reformist program.

Zionism, too, was to play a major role in rescuing the fortunes of liberalism. Herzl hopes that the mass transfer of Jews to Palestine would take the edge off European social discontent. In *The Jewish State,* Herzl described the gentile acquisition of Jewish property, the movement into the professions vacated by Jews, as a peaceful appropriation that would bring about an upward tide of gentile social mobility. Jewish immigration would produce a bloodless version of a property transfer, such as had occurred during the French Revolution, this time with Jews as the willing émigrés. Revolutionary forces would be stalled. With a breathing space of several decades, developing technology might succeed in easing the misery of the European masses. Liberalism would then have a chance to reassert itself. Indeed, the institutions of *Old-New Land* were a model for Europe, for there, too, the rise of producers' co-operatives was "inevitable." These co-operatives would evolve out of the industrial cartels, that had brought industry-wide stability through their control of the price and supply of commodities, and that had pioneered in enlightened paternalism towards workers. The transition from cartels to co-operatives would be gradual and peaceful. European states would further the New Society which, in turn, "serves, strengthens and supports" the state. Revolutionary pressures would be undercut, labor and capital would be reconciled, private property would be placed on solid foundations, the regime of talent would flourish.

Zionism would also further liberalism by hindering the radicalization of the Jews. Jews had produced a surplus of professionals now losing out in competition with gentiles and, in embittered response, had become "the petty officers of all revolutionary parties." Enticed by the prospect of "brilliant careers in Palestine," these Jews would "waste no more time on political tomfoolery" and would rejoin the liberal ranks. In addition, anti-Semitism threatened to alienate the Jewish masses from the social order and win them for the revolutionary parties, whereas Zionism would deflect them from this course.

One might think that the emergence of political anti-Semitism would have caused Herzl to lose faith in the promise of European liberalism. Austrian liberals had, after all, shown themselves to be politically timid and opportunistic in their response to Christian Social anti-Semitism. Zionism, on the face of it, represented the Jewish abdication from Europe. But Herzl did not believe that the rise of political anti-Semitism signalled the bankruptcy of European liberalism. Instead, he considered anti-Semitism "a dragged out piece of the Middle Ages," a historical remnant on its way to extinction.

Herzl maintained his faith in liberalism by viewing anti-Semitism as a comprehensible response to a specific social irritant, rather than as a symptom of Europe's continuing anti-Jewish pathology. Jewish emancipation had, to his mind, created a problem that taxed human good will to its limits. Jews had been a pariah people in the Middle Ages. Alien ethnically and by religion, they had been welcomed in Europe in order to fulfill a commercial role that was ethically and socially problematic for Christians. Subsequent emancipation coincided with rising industrialization, a socio-economic situation congenial to Jewish habits and capacities. Former aliens now acquired economic power and positions of status. For gentiles, the status order had become reversed, their world had been turned upside down. "In the long run", Herzl believed, "the people cannot possibly put up with such a conquest by the low class Jew." He also stressed the socio-economic dynamics of anti-Semitism, the economic rivalry with native artisans and shopkeepers. Anti-Semitism, in this view, was a result of the sudden onrush of a people just recently considered aliens, into the interstices of an economically and socially strained society. By relieving Europe of its surplus Jewish population, eliminating Jewish competition for scarce resources, Zionism would put a definitive end to anti-Semitism; the condition of Jews everywhere would improve.

For Jews like Herzl, European liberalism had promised a deeply longed-for, full integration of Jews into the mainstream of European humanity. The rise of anti-Semitism had frustrated this prospect, and Jews had remained pariah-like second-class citizens. Through Zionism Jews were to enforce the equality denied to them in Europe by transforming themselves into state-makers. With the acquisition of the modern symbol and substance of power, a state, Jews would gain by their own efforts the status their European compatriots had so far withheld from them and join—indeed be enthusiastically welcomed into—the ranks of European humanity as equal partners. Zionism for Herzl, was the fulfillment of his assimilationist aspirations, fuelled by the realization that only by developing a state of their own could Jews cease to be outsiders and become like everyone else.

The goal of Herzl's Zionism was Jewish integration into European civilization on a new, equal and autonomous basis. Indeed, by eliminating anti-Semitism, Zionism even enabled Jews in Europe to realize assimilation without suffering the stigma of second-class citizenship. The Jewish state in Palestine was to be no standing reproach to those Jews remaining in the Diaspora, but a spur to their integration in their native lands. For these reasons Zionism had to uphold the values of European cosmopolitanism.

In his critique of *Old-New Land,* Ahad Ha-Am complained that there were no signs of Jewish cultural creativity in the New Society. Its culture was European: the language of its educated classes was German, not Hebrew. Jews were not depicted as creators of culture, merely transmitters, carrying the culture of the West to the Middle East. All this, of course, was in keeping with Herzl's vision.

Old-New Land is inhabited by Jews of different nations and cultures, and different languages, united not on the basis of a restored Hebraic culture but only "on the basis of their common humanity." What binds them together in a common cultural enterprise is European cosmopolitanism, which also emphasizes the common humanity of Jews, Christians and Moslems. Jews, as recent outsiders, shared no common roots with Europeans. But cosmopolitanism transcended all differences of nationality and religion, rejecting the particularist identities that separated rather than united peoples. Assimilated European Jews had been dedicated upholders of the cosmopolitan European Enlightenment because its rejection of "historical traditions" and the "world of myth and symbol" undercut just those factors that divided Jews from their European compatriots. The Enlightenment stressed reason, uniting humanity, rather than feeling, which fragmented humanity by tapping the emotional subtratum of particularistic myths and rituals. Through reason Jews shared with Europeans a common present and even more, a common future.

As a modern nationalistic politician, Herzl understood that political power depended upon mass mobilization. At the same time mobilizing the Jewish masses threatened to bring to the fore just those archaic and particularist sentiments fostering the age-old sense of Jewish separateness, exactly the condition he wished to avoid. His solution, formulated in **Old-New Land,** was a futuristic myth. He set forth a bold vision of economic abundance, technological mastery and individual Jewish self-enhancement, coupled with a firm insistence that Zionism thrust forward toward unequivocal modernity, with full Jewish integration into the European vanguard. (pp. v-xxix)

> *Jacques Kornberg, in a preface to* Old-New Land *(Altneuland) by Theodor Herzl, translated by Lotta Levensohn, Herzl Press, 1987, pp. v-xxxi.*

FURTHER READING

Arendt, Hannah. "The Jewish State: Fifty Years After—Where Have Herzl's Politics Led?" *Commentary* 1, No. 7 (May 1946): 1-8.
Examines Herzl's Zionist political views and the socio-historical developments that influenced them. Arendt then evaluates Herzl's policies, discussing their relevance to and application in post-World War II society.

————. "Herzl and Lazare." In her *The Jew as Pariah: Jewish Identity and Politics in the Modern Age,* edited by Ron H. Feldman, pp. 125-30. New York: Grove Press, 1978.
Describes the relationship between Herzl and Bernard Lazare and compares their Zionist theories.

Busi, Frederick. "Anti-Semites on Zionism: The Case of Herzl and Drumont." *Midstream* 25, No. 2 (February 1979): 18-27.
Analyzes Herzl's *The Jewish State,* comparing the philosophies of Herzl and Edouard Drumont, the leading exponent of anti-Semitism in France. Busi also notes similarities and differences between Zionist and anti-Semitic tenets and suggests causes for the negative criticism Herzl received from fellow Jews.

Cohen, Israel. *Theodor Herzl: Founder of Political Zionism.* New York: Thomas Yoseloff, 1959, 399 p.
Biography focusing on Herzl's career as the leader of the Zionist movement.

Cohn, Henry J. "Theodor Herzl's Conversion to Zionism." *Jewish Social Studies* 32 (1970): 101-10.
Examines the factors that inspired Herzl to become a Zionist. Citing the evidence of Herzl's diaries and other documents, Cohn emphasizes the importance of Herzl's awareness of the anti-Semitism in Vienna rather than the Dreyfus Affair, which many commentators consider the precipitating event in Herzl's involvement with Zionism.

Elon, Amos. *Herzl.* New York: Holt, Rinehart and Winston, 1975, 448 p.
Describes Herzl's life and works.

Fraenkel, Josef. "Herzl in Paris: Dossier No. 92, 509 in the Paris Police Archives." *The Menorah Journal* 36, No. 1 (Winter 1948): 140-44.
Describes Herzl's experience in Paris in the early 1890s and presents excerpts from documents maintained by the Paris police concerning what they construed as Herzl's potentially subversive activities.

Lewisohn, Ludwig. "Theodor Herzl: A Portrait for This Age." In *Theodor Herzl: A Portrait for This Age,* edited by Ludwig Lewisohn, pp. 19-91. Cleveland: The World Publishing Company, 1955.
Introductory biographical essay that also provides historical and political background to Herzl's career. This volume also includes selected works by Herzl and a preface by David Ben-Gurion.

Liptzin, Solomon. "Theodor Herzl." In his *Germany's Stepchildren,* pp. 113-23. Philadelphia: Press of the Jewish Publication Society, 1944.
Summary and discussion of *The Jewish State* and Herzl's Zionist philosophy.

Loewenberg, Peter. "Theodor Herzl: A Psychoanalytic Study in Charismatic Political Leadership." In *The Psychoanalytic Interpretation of History,* edited by Benjamin B. Wolman, pp. 150-91. New York: Basic Books, 1971.
Psychoanalytic evaluation of Herzl's personality, behavior, and writings. Loewenberg explains, "By correlating his plays, stories, essays, and novels with his political fantasies, we may observe the interaction of the literary creativity with the psyche of the author."

Patai, Josef. *Star Over Jordan: The Life of Theodor Herzl,* translated by Francis Magyar. New York: The Philosophical Library, 1946, 356 p.
Sympathetic biography.

Patai, Raphael, ed. *Herzl Year Book,* vols. I-III. New York: Herzl Press, 1958-60.
Collection of essays on the development of political Zionism and on Herzl's philosophy, writings, political career, and relationships with other Zionist leaders. Contributors include Joseph Adler, Alex Bein, David Ben-Gurion, Josef Fraenkel, Ludwig Lewisohn, Joseph Patai, and Stefan Zweig.

Robertson, Ritchie. "The Problem of 'Jewish Self-Hatred' in Herzl, Kraus, and Kafka." *Oxford German Studies* 16 (1985): 81-108.
Examines the writings of Herzl, Karl Kraus, and Franz Kafka, exploring their attitudes toward their Jewishness.

Samuel, Maurice. "Dedicated to an Idea." *New York Times Book Review* (21 May 1961): 6.
Positive review of the first full edition of Herzl's diaries to appear in English. Samuel maintains that the diaries "are fascinating as history, as a picture of *fin de siècle* personalities, as a description of unreal yet creative political maneuvers, but above all as the record of a human spirit committed beyond rescue to a fantastic and 'impossible' ideal."

Schorske, Carl. "Politics in a New Key: An Austrian Trio." In his *Fin-de-Siècle Vienna: Politics and Culture,* pp. 116-80. New York: Alfred A. Knopf, 1961.
Compares the lives and careers of Herzl, Georg von Schönerer, a radical Pan-German nationalist, and Karl Lueger, a strongly anti-Semitic mayor of Vienna.

Stewart, Desmond. *Theodor Herzl.* Garden City, N.Y.: Doubleday and Co., 1974, 395 p.
Biography which the author describes as "an attempt, not to contribute to the polemics for or against the political movement with which [Herzl] is identified, but to discover the human being who lived from 1860 to 1904 and who combined the qualities of dreamer and man of action to a unique degree."

Waxman, Meyer. "Herzl's *Diaries*." In his *A History of Jewish Literature,* vol. IV, pp. 850-66. New York: Bloch Publishing Co., 1941.
    Outlines Herzl's Zionist career as presented in the *Diaries*. Waxman describes Herzl's diaries as documents "of exceptional importance and of deep human interest."

Whitman, Sidney. "Theodor Herzl." *The Contemporary Review* 86 (September 1904): 371-76.
    Obituary tribute that recounts Herzl's life and his commitment to Zionism.

Thomas Wentworth Higginson

1823-1911

American essayist, critic, historian, biographer, autobiographer, editor, poet, novelist, short story writer, and translator.

An American social reformer and man of letters, Higginson had a varied career that began with his association with the New England Transcendentalists during the 1830s and 1840s and lasted into the twentieth century. He was an active abolitionist and campaigner for women's rights as well as a prominent literary figure who wrote essays, criticism, history, biographies, and fiction.

The youngest of ten children, Higginson was born in Cambridge, Massachusetts, and grew up in an environment that encouraged intellectual pursuits. His father served as the bursar of Harvard College and director of Harvard Divinity School, and literary figures, including Henry Wadsworth Longfellow and Margaret Fuller, were often guests at the Higginson home. When Higginson was ten, his father died, and he was raised by his mother and aunt. After attending local schools, Higginson entered Harvard at the age of thirteen. There he studied languages, history, mathematics, and natural science, wrote verse, and became interested in Transcendentalism and in the reform movements, especially abolitionism, that were prominent in New England in the 1830s. Unsure of the vocation to which his talents were best suited, Higginson worked as a tutor and studied independently following graduation, then attended Harvard Divinity School. He married in 1847 and accepted a position at a church in a small town north of Boston. Some members of the congregation found his abolitionist views unacceptable, however, and he was soon forced to resign.

For the next several years, Higginson supported himself by lecturing. In 1852, he became pastor of the Free Church in Worcester, where his liberal interpretation of Christian doctrine and his emphasis on social reform were well received. During this period, he edited *Thalatta,* an anthology of poetry, and his essay "Saints and Their Bodies," in which he asserted the importance of physical exercise for a person's overall health, appeared in the *Atlantic Monthly.* Throughout the 1850s, he contributed essays to the *Atlantic,* often addressing social issues or describing nature. He was also an active reformer, advocating abolitionism, women's rights, temperance, and penal and labor legislation. His abolitionist activities included participation in an attempt to free an escaped slave being held in the Boston Court House, assisting Free Soil settlers in Kansas, and supporting John Brown's raid at Harper's Ferry. In 1862, Higginson was offered the command of the First South Carolina volunteers, the first regiment of former slaves organized by the Union Army. He served for two years before being wounded and discharged in 1864.

Following his military service, Higginson settled in Newport, Rhode Island, where he resumed his career of writing and reform. His essay "A Letter to a Young Contributor" in the *Atlantic Monthly,* in which he encouraged aspiring writers, inspired Emily Dickinson to send him four of her poems. Higginson corresponded with the poet until her death in 1886, and he visited her twice in Amherst. During the 1860s and

1870s, he contributed numerous essays to the *Atlantic,* recorded his experiences during the war in *Army Life in a Black Regiment,* and composed historical works, biographies, and fiction. He continued to promote such causes as women's suffrage and the desegregation of Newport's schools. Following his wife's death in 1877, he returned to Cambridge and eventually remarried. During the 1880s, he served in the state legislature, where he argued for civil service reform and encouraged religious and cultural pluralism and tolerance. In 1890, at the request of the Dickinson family, he and Mabel Loomis Todd, a Dickinson family friend, edited the first published volume of Dickinson's poems. Through the last decades of his life, he continued to write and engage in reform activities, publishing *Common Sense about Women, A Larger History of the United States, Such as They Are: Poems,* and the autobiography *Cheerful Yesterdays,* and helping to establish the Anti-Imperialist League with Mark Twain, William James, and Andrew Carnegie. Higginson died in 1911.

Higginson's reform interests inspired the writings that most critics consider his best. In *Army Life in a Black Regiment,* which is generally regarded as his most important work, Higginson hoped to correct what he viewed as Northern misconceptions about freed slaves by recounting their performance as soldiers. More than a simple diary of wartime experiences, however, the book has been praised for its evocative description of the American South and as an important source of folk history. Among Higginson's most influential writings were his essays on women's rights. In "Ought Women to Learn the Alphabet?" and other essays, Higginson argued that women were men's equals, and he demanded equality of opportunity for women in all aspects of life, particularly education and politics.

Some biographers speculate that Higginson's emphasis on women's intellectual equality encouraged Emily Dickinson to write to him. Since Higginson's letters to the poet have not survived, reconstructing their relationship is difficult. Some Dickinson biographers have attacked Higginson's role, maintaining that he discouraged her from publishing and tried to change the style of her poetry, but other scholars, in support of Higginson, point out that the continued correspondence between Higginson and the poet suggests that Dickinson found value in Higginson's comments and apparently did not ask for help with publication. When editing Dickinson's poetry after her death, Higginson and Todd added titles to her poems and "corrected" her unconventional grammar, punctuation, and capitalization. Higginson has been censured for this decision, but some scholars argue that other nineteenth-century editors would have made similar alterations and that Higginson deserves credit for presenting Dickinson's unorthodox poetry to the reading public of the time. In fact, James W. Tuttleton has called Higginson's "discovery" of Dickinson "perhaps his chief contribution to American literature."

As a literary critic, Higginson evaluated works by many of his contemporaries and expressed strong opinions on the state of American literature. Higginson believed, as he outlined in his essay "Americanism in Literature," that circumstances unique to the United States—a democratic government and large numbers of immigrants—would contribute to the formation of a national character which would, in turn, produce a genuinely American literature. He thought that American literature should address indigenous subjects and should be concerned with social issues, but because his view of American society was essentially positive, he criticized many naturalists and realists for their pessimistic perspectives. In poetry, Higginson advocated the use of American subjects and preferred conventional rhyme and meter. His own fiction and poetry were neither critically nor commercially successful. His most ambitious work as a creative writer was the novel *Malbone,* which is generally considered unconvincing and moralistic.

Higginson wrote a number of essays, biographies, and historical works. Usually regarded as examples of his finest writing, his nature essays have been praised for their presentation of scientific fact in a sophisticated literary style. Other essays discuss reform issues or describe historical events such as slave uprisings. His biographical sketches of New England intellectuals and reformers whom he knew are valued for providing unique perspectives on their subjects despite a lack of scholarly research. Higginson also wrote several full-length biographies, including one of his ancestor Francis Higginson, the first minister in the Massachusetts Bay Colony, and another of his grandfather Stephen Higginson, a Revolutionary War-era patriot. Critics suggest that his biographical writing was strongest when he described people he knew and events he had experienced. He had been acquainted with Margaret Fuller, and his biography of her is often considered his best for the insight provided by his personal knowledge and his

extensive use of unpublished manuscript sources. Higginson's *Young Folks' History of the United States* is considered a pioneering work in history for children, and *A Larger History of the United States,* which Higginson wrote with his brother-in-law Edward Channing, has been praised for its engaging narrative. In the latter work, Higginson sought to correct misconceptions about the American past, and he also emphasized the role of women in American history.

For several decades after his death, Higginson's works were largely ignored and he was remembered primarily as the editor of Emily Dickinson's poems. Beginning in the 1960s, perhaps partly as a result of the reform movements of that decade, his life and works have received renewed attention. A prolific author who wrote in several genres, Higginson explored in his works a wide range of subjects that defined American life and culture of his time. Writing in 1978, Tuttleton stated, "Higginson is a memorable example of what an American man of letters in the nineteenth century could be."

(See also *Dictionary of Literary Biography,* Vols. 1 and 64.)

PRINCIPAL WORKS

Thalatta: A Book for the Seaside [editor with Samuel Longfellow]   (poetry)   1853
Outdoor Papers   (essays)   1863
Harvard Memorial Biographies. 2 vols. [editor]   (biography)   1866
Malbone   (novel)   1869
Army Life in a Black Regiment   (nonfiction)   1870
Atlantic Essays   (essays)   1871
Oldport Days   (sketches)   1873
Young Folks' History of the United States   (history)   1875
Common Sense about Women   (essays)   1882
Margaret Fuller Ossoli   (biography)   1884
A Larger History of the United States to the Close of President Jackson's Administration [with Edward Channing]   (history)   1885
The Monarch of Dreams   (novella)   1887
Women and Men   (essays)   1888
Life of Francis Higginson   (biography)   1890
Poems of Emily Dickinson [editor with Mabel Loomis Todd]   (poems)   1890
Poems of Emily Dickinson: Second Series [editor with Mabel Loomis Todd]   (poems)   1891
Such as They Are: Poems [with Mary T. Higginson]   (poems)   1893
Book and Heart: Essays on Literature and Life   (essays)   1897
Cheerful Yesterdays   (autobiography)   1898
Contemporaries   (biography)   1899
The Writings of Thomas Wentworth Higginson. 7 vols. (essays, history, biography, autobiography, criticism, nonfiction, and poems)   1900
Henry Wadsworth Longfellow   (biography)   1902
John Greenleaf Whittier   (biography)   1902
A Reader's History of American Literature [with Henry W. Boynton]   (criticism)   1903
Part of a Man's Life   (autobiography)   1905
Life and Times of Stephen Higginson   (biography)   1907
Things Worth While   (essays)   1908
Carlyle's Laugh, and Other Surprises   (essays)   1909

WILLIAM DEAN HOWELLS (essay date 1869)

[*Howells was the chief progenitor of American Realism and the most influential American literary critic during the late nineteenth century. Through realism, a theory central to his fiction and criticism, Howells sought to disperse "the conventional acceptations by which men live on easy terms with themselves" that they might "examine the grounds of their social and moral opinions." To accomplish this, according to Howells, the writer must strive to record detailed impressions of everyday life, endowing characters with true-to-life motives and avoiding authorial comment in the narrative. In the following excerpt, Howells praises* Army Life in a Black Regiment.]

[Colonel Higginson's **Army Life in a Black Regiment**] is a series of carefully wrought studies of negro character as a phase of humanity, and of graphically recounted episodes of regimental or personal adventure, all full of the peculiar life and color of Southern scenery. A man who took command of the first negro regiment formed during the war, who led it throughout the struggle, and who, having fought the Rebels, turned and fought the more disgraceful government for the pay of its true and faithful soldiers, might be expected to write in a spirit of extravagance and even exaggeration; but there is nothing of this kind in Colonel Higginson's records, and nothing is more taking in him than his perfect temperance and reserve. As to the different parts of the book, it has its better and worse; and we suppose the "Camp-Diary" is the best; it came first and freshest, and is certainly easiest in manner. In some other chapters, as "A Night in the Water," the premeditation of effect and the literary purpose are plainer; and generally we should say that we like our author most when he does not remember that he is an essayist as well as an officer.

A very delightful quality in many of his reminiscences is their familiar and kindly, not to say domestic tone. He is not only proud of those picturesque, brave black soldiers, but he has an affection for his simple childlike warriors that is almost paternal; and in this feeling toward his regiment all its circumstances are given a home-like air. It would be hard to find anywhere a prettier bit of *genre* than that account of "The Baby of the Regiment": the various contrasts of the whole situation are most delicately and artfully suggested; the softness and sweetness of the Quartermaster's baby, and the accommodation of the camp-life's rudeness to its lovely helplessness and innocence, are shown with the happiest touches. "Out on Picket" pleases us almost as well, in a quite different way; and we have no need to recall to our readers the charm of its pictures, and its agreeable humor. It has attractions common to all the sketches, with not so much of the analytical tendency as some. A faculty to which we are indebted for such faithful and accurate work as this, however, is one that is scarcely to be blamed even when it wearies; we are not certain that it quite does this, and are not prepared to say more than that sometimes we could wish a little more pencil and a little less scalpel.

The beauty of Colonel Higginson's style is something that one is so apt to enjoy unconsciously, that we must make a point of speaking of it. The nature of his subject has relieved him in this book of the care which he sometimes, however seldom, feels, to write finely, and he has throughout written delightfully. The diction is always clear and bright, with just sufficient movement to have the graces that distinguish good prose from bad rhythm; and that excellent taste and moderation with which the papers are written is thoroughly imparted to it. As we remember, it never oversteps the modesty of the best English, and even in its negative qualities is full of comfort and enjoyment in these days of verbal attitudinizing. (p. 644)

> *William Dean Howells, in a review of "Army Life in a Black Regiment," in* The Atlantic Monthly, *Vol. XXIV, No. CXLV, November, 1869, pp. 643-44.*

THE NATION, NEW YORK (essay date 1875)

[*In the following excerpt, the critic commends Higginson's skill in presenting the American past in* Young Folks' History of the United States.]

Colonel Higginson's book [**Young Folks' History of the United States**] is quite a model of its kind—compact, clear, and accurate. Even in our short-lived annals there are myths which, having done duty as history for past generations, are now made over to confiding young people as facts. Colonel Higginson relates none of these, unless we except the apparition of Goffe the regicide when the Indians attacked Hadley. This story has recently been challenged, and apparently shown to be without any better foundation than tradition. It belongs probably to a very old class of myth. Castor and Pollux were seen at the battle of Lake Regillus; a pair of saints fought in the air for Constantine against Maxentius at the Milvian Bridge; and the army of Cortes was saved in Mexico by San Iago in person. It is only remarkable as having originated so recently and in New England. Many of our books for children are disfigured by Americanisms and colloquial vulgarisms, and some writers for the young adopt the sort of patronizing, jocular tone which visitors of ragged-schools are apt to assume when addressing the pupils of these institutions. It is kindly meant, no doubt, but instinctively irritating to any boy not descended from a long and unbroken line of paupers. This history is free from such blemishes. Its tone is always quiet and gentlemanlike, without exaggeration or conceits of language. There are no symptoms of rampant patriotism or spread-eagleism; even manifest destiny has been omitted. It is especially grateful not to be told that America is the home of the oppressed of all nations, and the only hope of liberty and civilization.

Unless we are mistaken, children of a larger growth will find this little book a most useful manual of American history. Nowhere can they get the facts so well stated in so small compass. The first three chapters treat of the "pleistocene" aborigines, the mound-builders, and the Indians; the next three relate the apocryphal story of the Norse colony, the voyages of Columbus and of his successors. These are followed by an account of the settlement of the thirteen colonies, which gives a clear and comprehensive view of the subject, and by capital sketches of colonial life and customs in New England, among the Dutch in New York, and the Friends in Pennsylvania. The narrative of the French and Indian wars, from 1689 to 1763, closes the history of the ante-revolutionary period . . . ; but Colonel Higginson has selected his incidents with so much judgment and arranged them so skilfully, that a careful perusal of this half of his book will give the ordinary reader all that he would probably take away, or care to remember, if he had the time and courage to master the eight volumes of Bancroft on the same subject. In the remainder of the volume the history of the country is brought down to the election of Grant. In our own times and in the war of secession, the author is as impartial as in his earlier chapters. There is no trace of party feeling or prejudice. (p. 100)

There are good monographs on particular periods of American history, but neither Graham, Hildreth, nor Bancroft is entirely satisfactory. This unpretending little book is the best general history of the United States we have seen. It contains all of it that the average citizen requires in order to go through life comfortably and creditably. With this well-drawn outline fixed in his mind he will always know where to place any additional facts that may be brought to his notice; and we hope that Colonel Higginson's readers, both young and old, will take pains to imitate his simple, straightforward style, which is not the least attractive feature in the work. (p. 101)

> *A review of "Young Folks' History of the United States," in* The Nation, *New York, Vol. XX, No. 502, February 11, 1875, pp. 100-01.*

FRANKLIN SANBORN   (essay date 1886)

[*An American biographer, editor, and educator, Sanborn belonged to the Transcendental community in Concord and participated in abolitionist efforts with Higginson and other activists. In the following excerpt, he lauds the literary qualities of* A Larger History of the United States.]

[In the United States] we have so far had no general history which can rest its hope of long life upon its artistic quality. Possibly it is not time yet to look for such a book, but it is pleasant to see promise of it in the fragmentary work which Colonel Higginson has put forth [*A Larger History of the United States*]. We say fragmentary, not only because the book stops just as the drums are beginning to beat for the great fray which gives reality to all American history, but because the plan of the work as so far carried out does not seem to show an attempt at true perspective. While, for example the early, half-legendary history is given in a charming manner, so important a phase as the relations between the French and the English is hardly more than allusively treated. If one accepts the book, however, as a graceful series of sketches of interesting passages in United States history, one will not be disappointed in his reading. Especially does Colonel Higginson give life to his story when he comes down to a period just beyond the memory of man, and we are confident that he could write a history of the Union from 1837 to 1861 which would contain so fine an infusion of personality as would give the book a long life in literature.

That he regards this history as an historical essay rather than a full, comprehensive survey is evident from several slight indications. There is almost an entire absence of reference to authorities, and there is also a curious fashion of appeal in the text to personal authorities. "Boat-building had there begun" (in New England, that is), he tells us, "according to Colonel C. D. Wright, in 1624;" but whether Colonel Wright mentioned this fact to him at the club, or set it down in some book, the reader is not told. Such pleasant little trivialities, also, as "The landing of Columbus has been commemorated by the fine design of Turner, engraved in Rogers's poems," help to give a discursive character to the history, and to relieve the reader from too severe a habit of mind.

It is not our purpose to give a detailed examination of this

book, but to welcome it as an indication that there is a view of history which is not scientific, but strictly literary. A writer of Colonel Higginson's strong aesthetic tendencies takes up the subject of United States history. His book is sure to be eagerly read and enjoyed. It may be hacked to pieces by a critic bred in the scientific school, but it has, what the scientific history is very apt to lack, a sense of form, a grace of style, those agreeable qualities which win readers who are indifferent to the subject, but are ready to be pleased. The conception of our history as a theme capable of artistic presentation has not commonly been held, but the reason for this has been largely in the failure to grasp the true meaning of American development. (pp. 558-59)

> *Franklin Sanborn, "Historical Methods," in* The Atlantic Monthly, *Vol. LVII, No. CCCXLII, April, 1886, pp. 553-59.*

THE NATION, NEW YORK   (essay date 1888)

[*In the following excerpt, the critic discusses the essays collected in* Women and Men.]

[In *Women and Men*] Mr. Higginson has reprinted in book form the series of articles, chiefly on women and incidentally on men, which have already appeared in *Harper's Bazaar*. They discuss, with great good sense and judgment, the changes in the condition of women produced by the extinction of her home-sheltered occupations of spinning and weaving, and by the coincident extinction of that profound ignorance which was once thought essential to modesty. The curious slowness with which many people—aged and conservative people of both sexes—recognize the changes in character and career which are necessarily produced by such great changes in circumstances, will cause articles of this sort to serve an important function, doubtless, for many years to come; but to one who has a keener vision for the signs of the times, they have already a somewhat antiquated air. It is only the slow-of-going and the hard-of-seeing who have still to be convinced that a good education is not wasted when spent upon a woman, and that she can tie her bonnet-strings with modesty and virtue as she passes down the elevator and out of the door of some mammoth manufacturing establishment. Of the various causes, however, which have hastened in this country the complete recognition of woman's right to an independent existence, not the least important, perhaps, is the steady stream of sound and careful argument which . . . has poured from Mr. Higginson's pen. No one is more deserving than he of the warm feeling which the victims of a resisted oppression must have for their tried and true knight-errant.

Of the articles which do not concern women, the best is that on the novelists of the Howells school. It is an admirable defence of the position that because commonplace characters are capable of being accurately painted, it does not follow that a writer of sufficient genius cannot make as fine a picture of characters that are not commonplace.

> *A review of "Women and Men," in* The Nation, *New York, Vol. XLVI, No. 1177, January 19, 1888, p. 59.*

THE NATION, NEW YORK   (essay date 1900)

[*In the following excerpt, the critic examines selected biographical and critical essays from the collection* Contemporaries.]

Many readers will be grateful for the resurrection of these papers [collected in *Contemporaries*], some of which have been a long time buried in the files of one or another periodical. It would have been most proper for Mr. Higginson to give with each the date and place of its original appearance. In a prefatory note he simply states that they are from the *Nation, Atlantic,* and so on, without indicating which was in this publication, which in that. The list does not include the *Outlook,* in which **"The Eccentricities of Reformers"** appeared not long ago. Some changes have been made where it might have been better, we think, to let the original form remain and make the necessary change or criticism in a note, after the manner of Ruskin in his *Seven Lamps* and elsewhere. Such a method would have better furnished us with genuinely contemporary appreciations. All the changes we have noted are in the direction of a severer taste and a more cautious blame.

That several of these papers were originally obituary notices takes nothing from their worth. Possibly here and there we have reserves prompted by kindly feeling at a moment shadowed by the death of a great man. In some of them there is more mere information than there would have been if the writer had been self-stirred to his work. The first number of the series, **"Ralph Waldo Emerson,"** is less adequate to its subject than the Phillips, which reaches the high-water mark, and some others. The amount of Emerson's preaching after his first return from England is unduly minimized. The word "sonorous" as applied to his oratory gives us a moment's pause. Dr. Hedge would, we think, have denied that Horace Greeley was "one of the first, if not the first, to claim for [Emerson] a rank at the very head of our American bards." Dr. Hedge took that honor to himself, and averred that he instigated Emerson to more frequent ventures in poetry. The remarks on Alcott have an unobtrusive flavor of depreciation. We read of him as "in a stately way penniless," and of his "high-souled attitudinizing." Of the **"Summer School of Philosophy"** it is neatly said that "there was plenty of summer, something of philosophy, and very little school." There is a mere allusion to Alcott's splendid behavior on the night of the attempted Burns rescue, but a note referring to the full account in *Cheerful Yesterdays.* In the passage dealing with Emerson's and Alcott's mutual appreciation we would gladly have been told that Alcott's account of Emerson's manner of lecturing is the best ever written.

The article on Theodore Parker is a testimony to Lowell's courage in his editing of the *Atlantic,* in which it appeared soon after Parker's death. We miss in it the expected emphasis on Parker's anti-slavery work, than which Mr. Higginson admired nothing of his more. The lack is stranger measured by the fact that the article was written in the heat of the first Lincoln electoral campaign. The sketch of Whittier is a delightful interpretation of both the man and the poet, with little reference to that canny politician under the singing robes, with whom Pickard's biography shows a fascinated engagement. The assonance is possibly responsible for the coming of Whitman next to Whittier. This chapter differs a good deal from the original form. The drastic criticism on Whitman's priapism (with the suggestion that Whitman's broken health was the penalty of an immoral life) "glares through its absence"—the fine phrase of Emerson which Mr. Higginson thinks an improvement on the *eo ipso præfulgebant* of Tacitus. In fact, Mr. Higginson does his sternest criticism of Whitman by proxy, in his sketch of Sidney Lanier, whose description of Whitman's poems as "huge raw callops cut from the rump of poetry" is more suggestive of Whitman's worst

than of Lanier's best manner. **"An Evening with Mrs. Hawthorne"** is very brief, but tells a charming story of Hawthorne's first reading of *The Scarlet Letter* to his wife. With this personal experience must be classed the remarkable chapter, **"A Visit to John Brown's Household in 1859."** The visit was after the trial of Brown, and shortly before his execution. The story of the visit is a human document of imperishable significance.

The two concluding chapters somewhat mar the unity of the collection. **"The Eccentricities of Reformers"** is almost too amusing for the company which it keeps, and **"The Road to England"** diverges sharply from the main highway. Mr. Higginson is no Anglomaniac. If, like the vase in the fable, he boasts that he has been with the rose, there is some disparagement of the rose. For Lowell's "Certain Condescension in Foreigners" we have a certain condescension *to* foreigners. The highest praise reserved for any English face or voice or manner is that there was something American about it.

> A review of "Contemporaries," in The Nation, New York, Vol. LXX, No. 1807, February 15, 1900, p. 135.

MARY THACHER HIGGINSON   (essay date 1914)

[*In the following excerpt from her biography of her husband, Mary Thacher Higginson presents selections from Higginson's diaries in which he describes the writing of* Malbone *and* Army Life in a Black Regiment.]

On New Year's Day, 1866, the thought first came to Colonel Higginson, while reading Hawthorne's *Marble Faun,* that he might write a romance, a project always before rejected. The thought rapidly took shape in his mind, too rapidly, he wrote in his diary, for his own comfort, being overworked as editor of the *Harvard Memorial Biographies.* In March, he reports himself as still crushed under letters and memoirs, having himself written thirteen of the biographies for these volumes. But on his long solitary walks, he dreamed happily about the projected story. He wrote in his diary:—

> A wild afternoon and I imagined a scene for my romance so vividly that it now seems real to me. . . . Walked to cliffs late in afternoon—it is astonishing how much dearer is one spot to me since I planned a scene there for my romance.

In 1866, he finished the *Memorial Biographies* and wrote, "Liberty at last." A few days later his diary chronicles, "Offer from Fields to write 10 articles for *Atlantic* for $1000—from Jan. 1." Of one of these papers, **"A Driftwood Fire,"** he wrote in his diary:—

> Jan. 24, 1867. When I print a thing like the **"Driftwood Fire"**—which seems to me to have a finer touch in it than anything I ever wrote—I feel as if it were thrown into the sea and as if nobody living cared for it. How can a man write who does not enjoy intensely the writing itself as I do? When I first read anything of mine in print, it is with perfect delight—then comes depression and the doubt whether anybody cares for such things and then I let it go, and get interested in something else.

His birthday meditations that year ran thus:—

> Looking back . . . I feel renewed gratitude for that wonderful cheerfulness and healthiness of nature I inherited from my mother. This season always

gives some feeling of loneliness to one of my temperament who is childless . . . and whose home is a hospital and who sees the only object of his care in tears of suffering daily. . . . And while literary sympathy or encouragement come slowly, I yet do surely feel an enriching of the mind this winter, more ideality, more constructive and creative faculty—such as I should think my **"Driftwood Fire"** would prove to all, if anybody cared for such things. For I am sometimes haunted with the feeling that it is too soon for any ideal treatment in America. Who reads *Twice-Told Tales?"*

In 1867, Colonel Higginson translated various sonnets from Petrarch, wrote essays and short stories for the *Atlantic,* continued his army papers, and compiled a little book by request of Ticknor and Fields, called **Child Pictures from Dickens,** which was issued at the time of Dickens's second visit to this country.

The summary of a single day's occupation, jotted down in the diary, illustrates the truth of Mr. A. Bronson Alcott's description of Colonel Higginson as "a man of tasks." In one day he had revised a memoir for one of the numerous literary aspirants who continually sought his sympathetic aid, written a book notice and several letters, made the first draughts of two *Independent* articles, aided in a written examination of the high school for one and a half hours in the afternoon, and spent two and a half hours examining school papers in the evening, besides his usual exercise.

In the summer of this year (1867), he embodied some of his translations of Petrarch's sonnets in a paper which he thus described in a letter to J. T. Fields, whom he called his poet-publisher:—

> I am writing a species of rhapsody called Sunshine and Petrarch, supposed to be written out-of-doors; a kind of plum pudding, Nature furnishing the pudding—Petrarch the plums, translated sonnets being inserted at proper intervals. It is charming *to the writer* which is dangerous, as the ratio of fascination is generally inverted ere reaching the public. As puddings should be thoroughly boiled, I shall keep this the rest of the week, probably.

His diary records:—

> For the first time took my Petrarch writing outdoors . . . sat at different points, chiefly at Myers House—yard full of spiræa, lilac, clover, grass in blossom, daisies—robin's nest oddly placed in birch tree far out on bough. A delicious time!

In 1903, a dainty volume of these sonnets was published and a copy sent through the American ambassador to Queen Marguerite of Italy who received it with gracious commendation. The book also received a flattering reception from an Italian society at Arezzo formed to honor Petrarch's memory.

The beginning of Colonel Higginson's work on **Malbone** is thus noted:—

> To-day I felt an intense longing to work on my imaginary novel. . . . The impulse was so strong I yielded to it and got a first chapter into shape that satisfied. This was enough and afterwards I could return to the essay.

January 1, 1868, he continued:—

> I know that this Romance (**Malbone**) is in me like the statue in the marble, for every little while I catch glimpses of parts of it here and there. I have rather held back from it, but a power within steadily forces me on; the characters are forming themselves more and more, . . . and it is so attractive to me that were it to be my ruin in fame and fortune I should still wish to keep on.

On March 11, he wrote four pages for the story, and says, "I enjoy this extremely and am much encouraged, but cannot afford to reject the offer to write Margaret Fuller's life." This was an article for a volume by different writers called *Eminent Women of the Age,* and for the same publication Mr. Higginson wrote a memoir of Lydia Maria Child. His biography of Margaret Fuller Ossoli was published sixteen years later in the *American Men of Letters Series.*

A few days later, he had accomplished—

> 5 pages **Malbone**—and letter to N.Y. Standard. I have now 50 pages of this novel. For the first time perhaps I have something to write which so interests me it is very hard to leave it even for necessary exercise. I hate to leave it a moment—and yet I have to write about Margaret Fuller.

A week later, he added:—

> 6 pages Ossoli. Like this very well, but grudge the time taken from **Malbone,** about which I was beginning to feel very happy.

> I do not think that anything except putting on uniform and going into camp has ever given me such a sense of new strange fascinating life, as the thought that I can actually construct a novel. It is as if I had learned to fly.

In April he decided not to interrupt **Malbone** again, but to postpone **Army Life** if necessary, and adds:—

> Told Fields about **Malbone**—and he was very sympathetic and asked many questions and said must have it in *Atlantic.*

Before the book appeared, the author reflected:—

> It is impossible for me to tell what will be thought of this book, whether it will be found too shallow or too grave, too tragic or too tame; I only know that I have enjoyed it more than anything I ever wrote (though writing under great disadvantages) and that the characters are like real men and women to me, though not one of them was, strictly speaking, imitated from life, as a whole.

Yet two of the characters in **Malbone** were suggested by real persons. Many of Aunt Jane's witty sayings had originated with Mrs. Higginson, and Philip Malbone was drawn from memories of Hurlbut, the author's early friend. On September 25, he had ended the story and sent it to Fields, and quoted in his diary a passage from Browning's "Paracelsus":—

> Are there not . . .
> Two points in the adventure of a diver,
> One—when, a beggar, he prepares to plunge,
> One—when, a prince, he rises with his pearl?
> Festus, I plunge!

In November he had finished working over the manuscript and says:—

> There is, with all my fussy revising and altering, al-

ways a point where a work seems to take itself into its own hands . . . and I can no more control it than an apple-tree its fallen apples.

The advent of *Malbone* was announced to the writer's sisters with this comment:—

> I expect dismay on your part, my dear sisters, before you see it and perhaps after—but I had to write it. I enjoyed it so much, so we must acquiesce.

After the book was actually published (1869), he wrote:—

> As for my new literary venture, it is received with quiet approbation apparently though not with eagerness. . . . It seemed strange to me to hold my own novel in my hand, after all the thought and feeling I had put into it—and after thinking for so many years that I never could or would write one.

The announcement of an English reprint of *Malbone* pleased the author, and when in after years he revisited the scene of the story, he wrote in his diary:—

> Walked along the bay, beside the empty houses, and the dismantled house where I wrote *Malbone.* The fog bell tolled and the whole scene was full of ghosts; how long it seemed since those dreamy summers! That was the ideal epoch of my life: I have written nothing like that since and may not again.

In January, 1869, he continued:—

> I begin this year with a feeling of publicity and perhaps assured position such as never before. This is due to the reception of *Malbone* and my paper on the Greek Goddesses and also to lecturing more and to my participation in Woman's Suffrage Movement, Grand Army affairs and (prospectively) Free Religious Convention . . . I like it—and especially in view of the diminished society around me in Newport.

In April he felt "rather tired of writing," and held back from his *Army Life,* adding, "Shall I compel myself to it?" However, he was soon hard at work on this collection of army papers, and on September 22, wrote:—

> *Army Life in a Black Regiment* published today. It is amazing how indifferent I feel as to the reception of this book, compared with *Malbone,* which was so near my heart. It scarcely awakens the slightest emotion.

But a little later this feeling changed:—

> After reading a graphic military novel turned to my *Army Life* and read it with surprise and interest; and with a sort of despair at the comparative emptiness of all other life after that.

Twenty years afterward, he wrote to Dr. Rogers:—

> Those times are ever fresh and were perhaps the flower of our lives.

(pp. 275-82)

Mary Thacher Higginson, in her Thomas Wentworth Higginson: The Story of His Life, *Houghton Mifflin Company, 1914, 435 p.*

CHARLES FRANKLIN THWING   (essay date 1933)

[*An American critic, educator, and historian, Thwing wrote numerous books on the development of American higher education and served as president of Western Reserve University. In the following excerpt, he assesses Higginson's career as a man of letters.*]

[While] one thinks of Higginson as a political and a social protestant and as a great friend, one is also to remember that he was primarily the writer. He was essayist, historian, biographer, poet.

In the citation which was used in conferring the degree of LL.D. upon Higginson at the Harvard commencement of 1898, a degree which could fittingly have been given much earlier, President Eliot said, "minister, teacher, early Abolitionist in theory, and in practice, Colonel of the First South Carolina Colored Volunteers in the Civil War, historian and man of letters." "Man of letters" is the formal and most comprehensive term. Early came the impulse to write, and the impulse continued for a longer period than with any one of his contemporaries. It manifested itself in subjects most diverse. In all this diversity of theme, two qualities are constructive. They are, as he himself confesses, fineness and fire. These two elements are characteristic. It is, however, rather fineness than fire that dominates. The common remark that the style is the man is also quite as true when reversed, the man is the style. Fineness of thinking, fineness of feeling, fineness of appreciation, ever seem to me to belong to him, and therefore to form, or to give at least atmosphere to, his writing. This fineness belongs to his interpretation of his contemporaries, to his interpretation of historic periods, and also to his appreciation of nature. Fire belongs more to his understanding of movements. When he confesses that he has "some want of copiousness and fertility which may give a tinge of thinness to what I write," I find myself not at all sympathetic. Yet I do feel a certain "thinness" which seems to spring from writing under mere "inspiration" at the "golden moment." In this inspiration I do not feel the concentrated laboriousness, conscious or unconscious, which belongs to the great and the enduring works.

The fact is that Higginson, though a hard worker, was a hard worker in many fields. If he had concentrated his interests and brought his many and diverse activities to a single point, literature would have been more deeply enriched, enriched indeed as it has been by his many and miscellaneous contributions. At the age of nineteen he said, "My great intellectual difficulty has been having too many irons in the fire." After his death his wife wrote, confirming the early self-judgment. Such a condition is not exceptional. In the very midst of his career Longfellow confessed, "I find no time to write. I find more and more the little things of life shut out the great. Innumerable interruptions—letters of application for this and for that; endless importunities of foreigners for help here and help there—fret the day and consume it."

It may also be said that one cause of Higginson's desultoriness may lie in his not having the sustaining and controlling power of a regular vocation. The demands of a professorship were to Lowell, for instance, the force which gave form and substance and a certain concentration to his essays and poems. It would have been well if Higginson had been thus confined. The brook needs the limitations of banks for getting power. The wandering stream becomes thin, and lacks directness and force.

Yet even despite this dissipation of interest and of activity, Higginson's contributions as a man of letters have, I believe, enduring qualities. His hymns and poems possess noble lyric and devotional elements. The best hymn writers of his generation were adherents of the Unitarian faith. The names of Oliver Wendell Holmes, of Hosmer, of Gannett, of Samuel Longfellow, are the most eminent. To this small number Higginson belongs. His hymn, **"Pantheism and Theism,"** deserves to be sung with Holmes' "Lord of All Being, Throned Afar":

> No human eyes Thy face may see,
> No human thought Thy form may know;
> But all creation dwells in Thee,
> And Thy great life through all doth flow!
>
> And yet, O strange and wondrous thought!
> Thou art a God who hearest prayer,
> And every heart with sorrow fraught
> To seek Thy present aid may dare.

The whole volume of poems, *The Afternoon Landscape,* dedicated to "James Russell Lowell, schoolmate and fellow townsman," is not unworthy of the personal and neighborly association. Of the verses of one **"Decoration Day"** I quote two and two only:

> Youth and beauty, dauntless will,
> Dreams that life could ne'er fulfil,
> Here lie buried; here in peace
> Wrongs and woes have found release.
>
> Turning from my comrades' eyes,
> Kneeling where a woman lies,
> I strew lilies on the grave
> Of the bravest of the brave.

But more characteristic than the poems and hymns, and more enduring than the essays and novels, is the appeal which his biographies make. They are, as a whole, his most important achievement in letters. For they embody those elements which that prince of biographers, William Roscoe Thayer, interprets as of essential worth. They incarnate the constructive element of human sympathy, they are real. They also possess the supreme gift or achievement, felicity of style. They describe, moreover, men and women who lived and wrought in his own atmosphere. Their times were his years; their feelings his experiences; their struggles his battles; their achievements his victories; and their purposes his ideals. In biography as in painting the one who makes the portrait is quite as important as the man of whom the portrait is made. Thayer intimates [in his *The Art of Biography*] that "four-fifths depends on the biographer." It is necessary for each to see and understand alike. Higginson writes of his *Contemporaries.* He interprets in the *Harvard Memorial Biographies,* which he in part wrote and in part edited, the men who gave their all in the struggle in which he rather hoped he might lose his own life. The *Cheerful Yesterdays* he had himself lived. His *Army Life in a Black Regiment* was his life and career. His biographies are essentially autobiographies. We see, hear, understand, feel him. As he writes of Whittier or of Wendell Phillips he is essentially writing of himself. One can hardly forbear believing that novel and essay, too, are personal interpretations. *Malbone* is a picture of Newport. *Old Cambridge* is his home, earliest and latest. His *Hints on Writing and Speech Making* grew out of his long continued and fruitful experiences. Chapters in the *Atlantic Essays,* as "A Plea for Culture," are a bugle call of hope and achievement; and other chapters, like **"Ought Women to Learn the Alpha-**bet?"** teem with wit as well as with wisdom of a very personal sort. The translations of Epictetus bear evidence that his interpretations grew out of the richest soil of his own disciplined thinking. The understanding which he gave to the great causes had for their standards of measurement the eternal principles of thought, of morals, which were the elements of his own manhood. In fact, as I read these twenty-five volumes, I am surprised, and yet not surprised, at their essentially autobiographic impression and impressiveness. (pp. 122-27)

> *Charles Franklin Thwing, "Thomas Wentworth Higginson: Soldier of Humanity," in his* Friends of Men, *1933. Reprint by Books for Libraries Press, 1968, pp. 111-32.*

VAN WYCK BROOKS   (essay date 1940)

[*An American scholar, Brooks is noted chiefly for his biographical and critical studies of Mark Twain, Henry James, and Ralph Waldo Emerson, and for his influential commentary on the history of American literature. Early in his career, Brooks asserted that America had no culture of its own and that American literature relied almost exclusively on its European heritage, but after studying Ralph Waldo Emerson he found much in America's past to be unique and artistically valuable. While Brooks initially attacked Higginson as an example of the decline of New England culture [see Further Reading], he later applauded Higginson's contribution to American literature. In the following excerpt, he comments on Higginson's life and works, praising* Army Life in a Black Regiment *and noting the importance of his role as mentor to women writers.*]

A generous, valorous, hopeful soul, [Higginson] was always ready to write or speak on subjects suggested by the *zeitgeist,*—the function of culture, the manners of tourists, the future of country towns, domestic service. He had produced one book of permanent interest, *Army Life in a Black Regiment,* a first-rate human document of the Civil War. This was the story of the "military picnic" of the First South Carolina Volunteers. Higginson had looked for the arming of the Negroes for six years before the war began, ever since the days of the Kansas troubles, and he had already raised a Massachusetts company when he was placed in command of the camp at Beaufort. His mind was filled with military matters, but the training of eight hundred slaves,—the first Southern regiment of Negroes, as Colonel Shaw's, in Boston, was the first in the North,—might well have taxed the skill of Grant or Sherman. They felt they were fighting with ropes about their necks, for the officers and soldiers of all the Negro regiments suffered a felon's death when they were captured. Higginson kept a diary in camp, as Dana had kept a diary on the *Pilgrim,* and the story of this "gospel army," fighting for its freedom, had much of the spirit and charm of Dana's book. It was filled with grotesque and dramatic adventures, like those of Marion's band in the Revolution, when the "old swamp fox" eluded his foes in these same forest-paths of Carolina, in the pine-barrens and muddy creeks, embosomed in blossoming shrubs, where the mocking-birds sang in the magnolias. There were foraging expeditions up the rivers,—up the Edisto, for one, to destroy the bridge on the railroad,—where the cotton-fields were white with fleecy buds and the air was full of hyacinthine odours. Never could one forget the fascination of these nocturnal ascents of unknown streams, leading far into the enemy's country, as one slipped in the moonlight through the meadows, passing the picket-fires on the silent banks,—the rippling water, the veiled lights, the anxious watch, the whispered orders, while the reed-birds wailed overhead and one heard the yelp of a dog on some distant plantation. Nor could one forget the nights on picket, under the live-oak branches with their trailing moss, among the wax-myrtles and the oleanders, the japonicas, oranges, lemons, the date-palms and fig-trees, in the endless bridle-paths of the flowery forests.

In retrospect, the colonel saw himself adrift on a horse's back in a sea of roses. He had spent scores of nights in the saddle, in the starlight, in a mist or densest blackness, while the chuck-will's-widow droned above and the great Southern fireflies rose to the treetops or hovered close to the ground, till the horse raised his hoofs to avoid them, riding through pine-woods and cypress-swamps, or past sullen brooks and clustered tents, or the dimly seen huts of sleeping Negroes. He had spent a whole night swimming in one of the rivers, alert for every sound on the glimmering shore; and often, returning from rides on the plover-haunted barrens, he had silently entered the camp in the midst of a "shout." The dusky figures about the fire moved to the rhythm of the dance,—the kind of scene that Winslow Homer loved,—chanting, sometimes harshly, but always in the most perfect time, a monotonous refrain, "Bound to Go" or "When the War is Over." Higginson loved the Border ballads that Child was collecting in Cambridge. He had always envied Scott the delight of tracing them out and writing them down; and here was a kindred world of unwritten songs, as indigenous and simple as those of the Scotsmen, usually more plaintive, almost always touching and often as essentially poetic. He listened to these spirituals, "Wrestling Jacob," "Hold Your Light," "My Army Cross Over," "One More River," and jotted down the words, as best he could, and carried them to his tent, like captured birds or insects, to study them and print them at his leisure. Had Europe or America seen an army so religious since Higginson's own forbears fought with Cromwell? The fatherly colonel thought of the Negroes as the world's perpetual children, docile, lovable and gay. The regular troops were mundane and rough beside them.

In later years, Higginson never rose again to the literary heights of some of these chapters, the superb "Up the Edisto" and "A Night on the Water." He had written one of those rare books that recall a passage of history as the works of the formal historians cannot recall them. Meanwhile, he had thrown himself into miscellaneous writing and was one of the chief supports of the *Atlantic.* A linguist and an excellent scholar, he had never known a moment of boredom, nor could he imagine such a thing while there was still a language or science to learn. He remembered a time when a prison-cell would have looked rather alluring to him if he had had a copy of Laplace to read. He wrote historical essays, papers describing Newport,—*Oldtown Days,*—a romance called *Malbone,* rather feeble, and pleas for literature and culture that were tonic in their effect on younger writers. In **"A Charge with Prince Rupert"** and **"Mademoiselle's Campaigns,"** he was almost as good as Carlyle in a similar vein; and he followed Thoreau in his essays on birds and flowers. But the interests of women were his special study, as befitted a friend of Margaret Fuller who had spent days on the Rhine visiting the scenes that recalled Bettina and the spot where Günderode died. **"Ought Women to Learn the Alphabet?"** was one of his essays; and in **"Saints and Their Bodies"** he preached the gospel of out-door life, quoting Catherine Beecher's remark that in all the vast acquaintance of the Beechers there were not a dozen healthy women. He formed a collection of books on the status of women, the Galatea collection, which he left to the Public Library in Boston.

[Julia Ward] Howe and Higginson were voices of a Boston epoch that might have been described as a "second growth." This feminizing Boston, this Boston that followed the war, wished to believe in itself rather than did so. But Mrs. Howe and Higginson still believed, with the faith of old and some of the force, in this resembling also Dr. Hale; and, if the faith had waned a little and lost its old effectiveness, it was full of generosity and goodness. For the rest, one of Higginson's hobbies was discovering talent. He had offered a prize at Newburyport, the bait that caught Harriet Prescott Spofford. He was one of the earliest friends of Celia Thaxter. It was he who sent Elizabeth Stuart Phelps her first letter of praise. He called upon Rose Terry Cooke at Hartford, when she was still unknown, living in a sort of moated grange, a mile out of town, an old brick house with an air of decay, where she dwelt with an old grey father. He discovered Emily Dickinson. He encouraged "H. H.," later known as Helen Hunt Jackson, Emily Dickinson's friend as a child at Amherst, who was Higginson's neighbour at Newport. If the new age of writers was largely an age of women writers, Higginson was the first to find them and read them. (pp. 129-33)

> *Van Wyck Brooks, "The Radical Club," in his* New England: Indian Summer, 1865-1915, *E. P. Dutton & Co., Inc., 1940, pp. 115-39.*

HOWARD MUMFORD JONES   (essay date 1960)

[*A distinguished twentieth-century American critic, Jones is noted for his illuminating commentary on American culture and literature. Awarded the Pulitzer Prize for his study of American culture in* O Strange New World (*1964*), *he is also acclaimed for his criticism in* The Theory of American Literature (*1948*) *and similar works in which he examines the relationship between America's literary and cultural development. In the following excerpt from his introduction to* Army Life in a Black Regiment, *Jones commends the work, especially Higginson's evocation of life in the South.*]

Army Life in a Black Regiment (1870) is a forgotten masterpiece from a neglected literary period by an author who is not supposed to have written masterpieces but who in fact produced two—*Army Life,* and *Cheerful Yesterdays* (1898). To some consideration of the first title I shall come in a moment. Regarding the second let it be said that such is the conventional-mindedness of literary historians, they do not recognize the autobiography as an art form. Nevertheless, American letters have produced a great number of these admirable memoirs, and the long golden afternoon of New England gave us a whole library of them, of which Higginson's is one of the most charming.

Thomas Wentworth Higginson wrote too much. He tells us that the index to the first twenty volumes of the *Atlantic Monthly* shows he contributed more largely to it than any other person except Lowell and Holmes. His books, moreover, range from a school history of the United States to a translation of Epictetus, and from the stately two-volume *Harvard Memorial Biographies* to an amateur but not unreadable novel, *Malbone,* draped over the shoulders of a divinity student who, says Higginson, could not in real life buy an apple of an old woman without making her feel that she alone had really touched his heart, and who came to a bad end—"the name of that youth is not mentioned among the poets of Greece." Yet Higginson's considerable talent condensed into memorability only once or twice. Why should this be so?

He was, in the first place, the victim of a liberal education. Entering Harvard as the youngest member of the class of 1841, he was to spend about ten years in that institution, and his undergraduate career was lived during an uneasy interim period in which the old prescriptive curriculum was watered down by unsteady experimentalism, especially in foreign languages and mathematics. Higginson read five languages other than English when he left college, and excelled in mathematics; nevertheless nothing in the curriculum encouraged a gifted youngster to develop his bent towards any specific calling. Irritating restrictions kept the undergraduates in a pupillary state. "When I entered Harvard College," Higginson wrote,

> an "Abstract of Laws and Regulations" of the University was given me. The one thing that now seems of peculiar interest in that circular is an item headed, "Dress. On Sabbaths and Exhibition days, and on all public occasions, each student in public shall wear a black or black-mixed coat, with buttons of the same color."

Debating his entrance into the Divinity School at the mature age of twenty, our author wrote his mother, "I want to be a boy as long as I can. . . . Could I figure in proctorial dignity, figure . . . in blouses and bobtailed frocks?"—the costume of the beatniks of the 1840's. Higginson read omnivorously as a student and gained something from the instruction of Edward Tyrrell Channing, Boylston professor of rhetoric and oratory, under whom, he says, "the classic portion of our literature came largely into existence," but he also observed that "young men in my time who would have graduated in these later days with highest honors in some department of physics or biology," because of the restricted curriculum, "were then at the very foot of the class, and lost for life the advantage of early training in the studies they loved." Once when the college assembled for compulsory chapel, he found that 200 panes of glass had been blown out of the windows, the hands had been wrenched from the clock, the panels removed from the pulpit, and some rebel had written on the wall, "A Bone for old Quin to pick." "Old Quin" was President Josiah Quincy, who had once been popular but who had lost his popularity because he threatened to turn over to the grand jury the name of any students suspected of destroying college property. If Channing taught Higginson anything about writing, the college never taught him what to write about.

Nor did his environment help him. Higginson was a child of Bostonian culture, though he was born in Cambridge. Cambridge, however, was merely a suburb of Boston, it was not Concord, which was several light years away, and living in Cambridge was, he tells us in a picturesque figure, "like dwelling just outside a remarkably large glass beehive" through which you could see "the little people inside" "without the slightest peril to the beholder." When he entered Harvard, he entered this glass beehive, from which it took him a good many years to escape. Chapter III of *Cheerful Yesterdays* has to do with the "Newness," by which we moderns understand the radicalism of Emerson, *Walden,* and Brook Farm. But Brook Farm was not really radical, it was a mild protest by children of the genteel, who, born into a decaying Federalist culture, not only did not know what to do with their lives (a phrenologist once told Higginson he had splen-

did talents and no application), but were also prevented by the value system of their generation from following any particular occupation. To adopt law or medicine or the ministry or a mercantile career was to warp one's soul, was to do violence to the "ideal." Higginson was, moreover, steeped in German romanticism. He read the memoirs of Jean Paul Richter and his *Siebenkäs,* he read Fouqué's *Undine* ("oh, how dreadful it is to be in a land where there are no supernatural beings visible"), he read other dreamy books which taught him to be "above following Ambition." When old gentlemen asked him about his plans, he formed the resolution of "not studying a profession," a decision that left him "perfectly settled and perfectly tranquil." His adoring mother acquiesced. He could not bear Blackstone and the law. He drifted into the Divinity School, but he did not know why. Cursed with versatility, he experienced "an eager desire to fill all the parts" and abandoned divinity because "I cannot obtain the equilibrium and peace of mind I need." But he came back after a year, discovering "a higher tone of spiritual life" than he had anticipated (one wonders whether his approaching marriage had anything to do with this change), took a degree, and was appointed to the First Religious Society of Newburyport in 1847 and afterwards (1852) to the Free Church of Worcester, that "seething centre of all the reforms."

Ethical commitment turned Higginson into an effective writer. When Cambridge students later on asked him how to train for political speech-making, he said: "Enlist in a reform." Anger at the fugitive slave law condensed Higginson's prose into forcefulness. Consider, for example, this paragraph from his first "book," a pamphlet entitled *A Ride Through Kansas* (1856):

> Our train included about one hundred and forty men and some twenty women and children. There were twenty-eight wagons—all but eight being horse-teams. Our nightly tents made quite a little colony, and presented a busy scene. While some watered and fed the stock, others brought wood for the fires; others prepared the tents and wagons for sleeping; others reloaded pistols or rifles, and the leaders arranged the nightly watch or planned the affairs of the morrow. Meanwhile, the cooks fried pork, made coffee, and baked bread, and a gaping crowd, wrapped in blankets, sat around the fire. Women brought their babes, and took the best places they could find, and one worthy saddler brought out his board and leather every night and made belts and holsters for the men. We slept soundly in spite of the cold and of the scarcity of wood, and each kept watch for an hour, striding in thick boots through the grass, heavy with frost.

German sentimentality has been replaced by narrative energy, and this narrative energy is in turn a function of moral zeal. Whatever aesthetes may say, effective writing is as often the product of a crusade as it is of metaphysics and sensibility. Witness Dante, Burke, Carlyle, and Bernard Shaw.

Higginson was temperamentally opposed to Negro slavery, but as in the case of Lincoln it took an actual case of slave-trading—the separation by one Mr. Lynch in St. Louis of a likely colored girl from her mother—to electrify his convictions. As he told the Massachusetts Anti-Slavery Society on its twenty-fifth birthday:

> All my life I had been a citizen of a Republic where I had seen my fellow-citizens retreating, and retreating, and retreating, before the Slave Power,

and I heard that away off, a thousand miles west, there was one town where men had made their stand, and said to Slavery, "Thus far, but no farther!" I went the thousand miles to see it, and I saw it. I saw there the American Revolution, and every great Revolution of bygone days in still living progress.

From bleeding Kansas to the command of the First South Carolina Volunteers was, despite Higginson's initial hesitation, an inevitable transition.

He never forgot that in the mismanaged attempt to free Anthony Burns in 1854 a black man had leaped ahead of him into the Boston courthouse, an experience "of inestimable value to me, for it removed once for all every doubt of the intrinsic courage of the blacks." *Army Life in a Black Regiment* therefore has modern meaning, among other reasons, because it is a document in desegregation.

On May 4, 1863, Major-General David Hunter, who authorized the raising of Higginson's regiment of blacks, wrote the Governor of Massachusetts:

> I am happy to be able to announce to you my complete and eminent satisfaction with the results of the organization of negro regiments in this department [Department of the South]. In the field, so far as tried, they have proved brave, active, enduring, and energetic, frequently outrunning, by their zeal, and familiarity with the Southern country, the restrictions deemed prudent by certain of their officers. They have never disgraced their uniform by pillage or cruelty, but have so conducted themselves upon the whole, that even our enemies, though more anxious to find fault with these than with any other portion of our troops, have not yet been able to allege against them a single violation of any of the rules of civilized warfare.

Higginson's book validates General Hunter's estimate. *Army Life in a Black Regiment* contains, to be sure, nothing like the bloody assault on Fort Wagner by Robert Shaw's soldiers, and may even be accused of gentility in omitting or softening certain unlovely features of army life, but a lively humor, a fine eye for the picturesque, indignation against injustice, and real affection for his men create one of the few classics of military life in the national letters.

Amateurs of the Civil War will be interested in a number of components making up Higginson's narrative. He pays unexpected tribute to the "methods and proprieties" of the regular army as creators of discipline—unexpected, because Higginson's previous martial experience was confined to a brief glimpse into border warfare, half a dozen drill clubs, and a few months as a Union officer. His subordinates came from a dozen different states and from all branches of the service, a distinct advantage to him, since they had no uniform and preconceived notions about the Negro. Their morale was sustained by a psychological blunder of the Confederates, who threatened any officers of Federal colored troops with death when captured, a measure that raised the self-esteem of Higginson's whole staff (the Confederates conveniently forgot they had some colored troops of their own). As the private soldiers knew that for them the issue was literally freedom or slavery, Col. Higginson had no trouble about *esprit de corps*. He entered sympathetically into the psychology of his ex-slaves, in whom he found "a certain tropical element" and "great individual resources when alone,—a sort of Indian wiliness and subtlety of resource." His chapter on the Negro

soldier quietly corrects the myth that the African is sub-human; and his New England righteousness was amazingly tolerant of sexual laxity, which, he says, was "modified by the general quality of their temperament, and indicated rather a softening and relaxation than a hardening and brutalizing of their moral natures," and he thought the general drift was towards matrimony. The soul of his regiment was religion; his graphic pages dramatize for us the crusading nature of the experiment. His own ethical idealism responded to this simple faith, an idealism evident in his stinging rebuke of the United States for not keeping its word in the matter of his soldiers' pay. He disapproved of the haphazard strategy of the War Department but he contents himself with saying that if the colored regiments had not held the islands, Sherman's march to the sea could never have been performed.

But to read *Army Life in a Black Regiment* as a mere military chronicle is like reading *Hamlet* as a contribution to ghost-lore. Higginson's book is a study in enchantment, a single volume in that vast library wherein the North records its longing for the South. One finds this yearning everywhere above . . . the Ohio. (pp. vii-xii)

Higginson's book is a volume in this library of the South, and it is astonishing. Under the moral guise of saving the Union and of doing right by our colored brother this Worcester clergyman transforms himself into a sea-island pagan more imperceptibly than if it were done by Circe. He lets himself go, he yawns, he laughs, he expands like Emerson's famous corn and melons, he accepts and delights in all that is warm, colorful, lazy, and exotic. Read his account in Chapter VII of swimming by night; in addition to being an escapade in which Huck Finn would have delighted, it conveys an intense sensuous pleasure uncommon in New England literature. Once or twice he remembers with regret the "pure, clean, *innocent* odors" of the spring in Massachusetts, but they are drowned in the "luscious, voluptuous, almost oppressively fragrant" scent of the magnolias, which belongs, he says, not to Hebe, but to Magdalen. One would not be surprised to hear him murmur with Baudelaire. "Bizarre déité, brune comme les nuits" ["bizarre god, dark as night"]. The world is sometimes a universe "of profuse and tangled vegetation," sometimes of "bare sand-plains, gray above," "always yellow when upturned," (and then there seemed to be "a tingle of Orientalism in all our life") sometimes all "blackberries and oysters, wild roses and magnolias, flowery lanes instead of sandy barrens," green alleys and miles of "triumphal arches of wild roses" through which he galloped endlessly. The sea, in which the sun set "like a great illuminated bubble," is as romantic as the land: "innumerable sea-fowl" at the entrance of an outer bar make a low, continuous noise, more "wild and desolate than anything in my memory can parallel. It came from within the vast girdle of mist, and seemed like the cry of a myriad of lost souls . . . Dante became audible." He describes Hilton Head, "always like some foreign military station in the tropics," as if it were an early water color by Winslow Homer, and at Jacksonville the mocking birds sang all night like literary nightingales, "their notes seeming to trickle down through the sweet air from amid the blossoming boughs."

Consider these vignettes. In the first he

> looks through the broken windows of this forlorn plantation-house, through avenues of great live oaks, with their hard, shining leaves, and their branches hung with a universal drapery of soft,

long moss, like fringe-trees struck with grayness. Below, the sandy soil, scanty, covered with coarse grass, bristles with sharp palmettoes and aloes; all the vegetation is stiff, shining, subtropical, with nothing soft or delicate in its texture.

Can this be America? Here is a second, a vivid picture of the camp on a dark, mild, drizzling evening while Higginson listens to the

> melodies and strange antics from this mysterious race of grown-up children. . . . All over the camp the lights glimmer in the tents, and as I sit at my desk in the open doorway, there come mingled sounds of stir and glee. Boys laugh and shout,—a feeble flute stirs somewhere in some tent, not an officer's,—a drum throbs far away in another,—wild kildeer plover flit and wail above us, like the haunting souls of dead slave-masters . . . from a neighboring cook-fire comes the monotonous sound of that strange festival, half pow-wow, half prayer-meeting, which they know only as a shout.

Here is a third picture, a soldier's burial at night, like something painted by Delacroix or Géricault:

> . . . only the light of pine-splinters, as the procession wound along beneath the mighty moss-hung branches of the ancient grove. The groups around the grave, the dark faces, the red garments, the scattered lights, the misty boughs, were weird and strange. The men sang one of their own wild chants. Two crickets sang also, one on either side, and did not cease their little monotone, even when the three volleys were fired above the grave.

Daylight was likely to bring "that peculiar Mediterranean translucency which Southern islands wear," and at night he might overhear an escaped slave telling his story to the soldiers, "the brilliant fire lighting up their red trousers and gleaming from their shining black faces," "the mighty limbs of a great live-oak with their weird moss swaying in the smoke and the high moon gleaming faintly through." The depth psychologist notes the images of sexuality and death in this prose as Higginson tries to remember and record, but the book is about neither death nor sex, it is about enchantment.

The sense of enchantment in this environment helps make credible Higginson's instinctual sympathy for his ex-slaves. The white race scarcely appears in these pages, and when it does, its representative may be treated with asperity, as in the case of the loan-shark in Jacksonville or the wonderful confrontation of Corporal Robert Sutton and his former mistress—" 'Ah,' quoth my lady, 'we called him Bob!' " The anecdote sums up a whole moral situation, on which Higginson, with superb reticence, makes no comment, just as he does no more than enumerate the contents of the slave jail that filled him with "unutterable loathing." It is true, he sees the Negro only from the outside as, being the commander of the regiment, he was bound to do, and a militant desegregationist might complain of paternalism when Higginson writes that "their griefs may be dispelled like those of children, merely by permission to utter them." But this is to read 1862 in terms of 1961, and Higginson has small belief in Uncle Toms. His book is a shrewd and sympathetic example of sociological analysis, and his collection of spirituals in Chapter IX an invaluable record of folk art. The militant modern is likely to be as humorless about oppressed racial groups as he charges his predecessors with being complacent, but surely it is possible to sense the colonel's profound sympathy beneath the graphic humors of what happened during his raid up the South Edisto River:

> With the wild faces, eager figures, strange garments, it seemed, as one of the poor things reverently suggested, "like notin' but de judgment day." Presently they began to come from the houses . . . with their little bundles on their heads; and then with larger bundles. Old women, trotting on the narrow paths, would kneel to pray a little prayer, still balancing the bundle; and then would suddenly spring up, urged by all the accumulating procession behind, and would move on till irresistibly compelled by thankfulness to dip down for another invocation. Reaching us, every human being must grasp our hands, amid exclamations of "Bress you, mas'r," and "bress de Lord," at the rate of four of the latter ascriptions to one of the former. Women brought children on their shoulders; small black boys carried on their backs little brothers equally inky, and gravely depositing them shook hands. Never had I seen human beings so clad, or rather so un-clad, in such amazing squalidness and destitution of garments. I recall one small urchin without a rag of clothing save the basque waist of a lady's dress, bristling with whalebones, and worn wrong side before, beneath which his smooth ebony legs emerged like those of an ostrich from its plumage. How weak is imagination, how cold is memory, that I ever cease for a day of my life, to see before me the picture of that astounding scene!

Army Life in a Black Regiment is, then, a document of considerable importance from several points of view. As a contribution to military history its account of a regiment, under fire and in camp, on garrison duty or as a raiding force, has, one supposes, value. But as a study of a race that was, for most Northerners, as unknown as the Koreans, it has even greater worth. Yet its supreme appeal is as an expression of yearning of the North for the South, for color, for warmth, for a simpler and healthier way of life than that of industrialized cities. For once the pen of its writer was touched with the incommunicable power that turns writing into literary art. (pp. xiii-xvii)

> *Howard Mumford Jones, in an introduction to* Army Life in a Black Regiment *by Thomas Wentworth Higginson, Michigan State University Press, 1960, pp. vii-xvii.*

ANNA MARY WELLS (essay date 1963)

[*Wells is an American educator and critic. In the following excerpt from her biography of Higginson, she discusses some of his essays that appeared in the* Atlantic Monthly.]

Higginson's first *Atlantic* essay appeared in March, 1858. It was called **"Saints and Their Bodies"** and proposed a very simple thesis, that physical and spiritual health are not mutually exclusive. The length at which he labored the point and the tremendous impression the article made on its readers implies a great deal about the society in which he lived. (pp. 110-11)

"Saints and Their Bodies" was followed by **"The Murder of the Innocents,"** in which he made his attack on the hothouse forcing of young intellects. The highly competitive school systems he knew required from eight to eleven hours a day of children's time. Some of these could, as a result, multiply

351,426 by 236,145 mentally for a public exhibition, and some of them died "raving of algebra." Sunday school contests in which children memorized five or six thousand Scripture texts he found equally objectionable.

> When some young girl incurs spinal disease for life from some slight fall which she ought not to have felt for an hour . . . the . . . observer sees the retribution for the folly of those misspent days which enfeebled the childish constitution instead of ripening it. . . . Though hard study at school is rarely the immediate cause of insanity, it is the most frequent of its ulterior causes.

"A Letter to a Dyspeptic" dealt in even livelier and much more entertaining fashion with the bad health habits of the ordinary American. Breakfasts of beefsteak, sausage, fried potatoes, baked beans, mince pies, pickles, saleratus biscuits, and coffee; dinners of fried pork, beefsteak, cucumbers, potatoes and gravy, mince pie, apple pie, lemon pie, and coffee; teas of pound cake and tea, and suppers of doughnuts and cheese he felt put an undue strain on the digestive apparatus. He also asserted the value of fresh air in bedrooms and of frequent bathing, amenities which many well-to-do Boston families denied themselves.

"It is as easy to be healthy as to be wealthy," he said in summation.

> After health, indeed, the other necessaries of life are very simple and easily obtained;—with moderate desires, regular employment, a loving home, correct theology, the right politics, and a year's subscription to the *Atlantic Monthly,* I have no doubt that life . . . may be . . . happy.

There is more than a hint of impatience with neurotic invalidism in this essay.

> You are undoubtedly, as you claim, a martyr to Dyspepsia; or if you prefer any other technical name for your disease or diseases, I will acquiesce in any except, perhaps, the word "Neurology". . . . You are haunting water-cures, experimenting on life-pills, holding private conferences with medical electricians, and thinking of a trip to the Bermudas. . . . These long consultations with the other patients in the dreary parlor of the infirmary, the morning devoted to debates on the nervous system, the afternoon to meditations on the stomach, and the evening to soliloquies on the spine will do you no good.

In **"A New Counterblast"** he objected with equal vigor to the use of tobacco. **"Barbarism and Civilization," "Gymnastics,"** and **"The Health of Our Girls"** all dealt with aspects of the same subject.

This is not to say, however, that his *Atlantic* articles were merely expressions of irritation at the discomfort of sharing his life with an invalid. Obviously the abuses of which he wrote must have been sufficiently widespread to be recognizable wherever the *Atlantic* went, and his attacks on them were admittedly effective in some areas at least. Health, however, physical or mental, was only one of the subjects on which he held forth in these pages. His second essay, in July, 1858, was a lively historical narrative, **"Mademoiselle's Campaigns."** It retold the story of the military adventures of Anne Marie Louise D'Orléans, princess of the age of Louis XIV, and did it so effectively that *Atlantic* readers demanded more. **"A Charge with Prince Rupert"** the next year used the same technique on a battle at Oxford between Puritan and Cavalier. Higginson's popularity as a historical writer was established, and endured throughout his life.

His third essay in the *Atlantic,* **"Water Lilies,"** in September, 1858, was again entirely different in subject matter and treatment. It was purely descriptive, a long and, for twentieth-century taste, overelaborate account of a day on Lake Quinsigamond, which began with an overnight camping trip so that the watchers might be on hand to see the lilies opening at dawn.

> On every floating log, as we approach it, there is a convention of turtles, sitting in calm debate, like mailed barons, till, as we draw near, they plump into the water and paddle away for some subaqueous Runnymede. . . . But we must return to our lilies. There is no sense of wealth like floating in this archipelago of white and green. The emotions of avarice become almost demoralizing. . . . Yonder steep bank slopes down to the lakeside, one solid mass of pale pink laurel, but, once upon the water, a purer tint prevails. The pink fades into a lingering flush, and the white creature floats peerless, set in green without and gold within.

Like **"Mademoiselle's Campaigns"** and **"Saints and Their Bodies," "Water Lilies"** set a pattern which Higginson was to follow for some years. His nature essays have survived the century since they were written with more vigor, perhaps, than anything else he wrote. **"April Days," "My Outdoor Study," "Snow," "The Life of Birds,"** and **"Procession of the Flowers"** were widely popular in their own day and are still eminently readable. Henry Thoreau and Emily Dickinson were among those who expressed their admiration, and of Thoreau's praise Higginson noted: "He is the only critic I should regard as really formidable on such a subject."

The fourth *Atlantic* essay in 1858 was **"Physical Courage"** in November. Higginson was established as a regular contributor to "the new magazine." Everywhere he went to lecture he found its readers his own admirers. In 1859 he contributed four essays again, in 1860 five, and in 1861 eight. None was signed, but the *Atlantic* frequently listed him in its announcements of coming attractions, and even after a hundred years a reader finds the regular contributors to the early numbers of the *Atlantic* as easy to recognize as a familiar face or voice. The Autocrat of the Breakfast Table, Mrs. Stowe, Whittier, Emerson, and Higginson all speak with unmistakable individuality.

In view of his commitment to the Abolitionist cause, it is rather remarkable that there was nothing about slavery during Higginson's first two years as contributor. Early in 1859 he got around to the subject of woman's rights with **"Ought Women to Learn the Alphabet?"** Lowell, who had succeeded Underwood as editor, hesitated over it because he thought it "too radical," but allowed himself to be persuaded. It is a plea not merely for the education of women but also for their admission to business and the professions. Higginson himself was so fond of it that he had it reprinted as a Woman's Suffrage tract and later used it as the core of a book, *Common Sense About Women.* (pp. 111-14)

Immediately after the affair at Harper's Ferry, Higginson visited John Brown's family at North Elba and wrote an account of the visit for Redpath's *The Public Life of Captain John Brown.* In the February and May numbers of the *Atlantic Monthly* for 1860 appeared two more of his historical essays,

"The Maroons of Jamaica" and **"The Maroons of Surinam,"** describing successful slave uprisings of the kind John Brown had planned. In October he published a biographical sketch of Theodore Parker, who had died that summer in Rome, and in November an article about his experiences four years earlier in Fayal.

His 1861 essays covered practically the full range of his interests. There were two more about slave rebellions, one directly concerned with the outbreak of hostilities between the North and South, three about health, and two about nature.

During the latter part of 1861 Higginson was hard at work recruiting a regiment and bitterly discouraged by the obstacles he was encountering. His two *Atlantic* articles early in 1862 reflected this discouragement in different ways, **"Snow"** by turning his back on it for another contemplation of the beauties of nature, and **"A Letter to a Young Contributor"** by various pessimistic side glances in his figures of speech. He had been invited to write the latter essay and considered it a potboiler. It was to be in some ways the most important publication of his life. Like everything he wrote it was sound and conscientious work.

He spoke of the necessity for painstaking effort in forming a style but pointed out that the result of such labor does not look laborious.

> There may be phrases which shall be palaces to

Higginson as a senior at Harvard Divinity School, 1846.

> dwell in, treasure houses to explore; a single word may be a window from which one may perceive all the kingdoms of the earth and the glory of them. Oftentimes a word shall speak what accumulated volumes have labored in vain to utter; there may be years of crowded passion in a word, and half a life in a sentence. Such being the majesty of the art you seek to practise, you can at least take time and deliberation before dishonoring it . . . When I think how slowly my poor thoughts come in, how tardily they connect themselves, what a delicious prolonged perplexity it is to cut and contrive a decent clothing of words for them, as a little girl does for her doll—nay, how many new outfits a single sentence sometimes costs before it is presentable, till it seems at last, like our army on the Potomac, as if it never could be thoroughly clothed,—I certainly should never dare to venture into print, but for the confirmed suspicion that the greatest writers have done even so.

From the question of difficulties he passed to that of rewards and of the writer's relation to his audience.

> If one were expecting to be judged by a few scholars only, one might hope somehow to cajole them; but it is this vast, unimpassioned, unconscious tribunal, this average judgment of intelligent minds, which is truly formidable—something more undying than senates and more omnipotent than courts, something which rapidly cancels all transitory reputations, and at last becomes the organ of eternal justice and infallibly awards posthumous fame.

The problem of posthumous fame, of the fluctuating scale of values which sends reputations skyrocketing up and down within a decade, was one that had always interested him. One of his college essays was concerned with it; in 1838 he noted in his journal that he had spent all day writing his essay for Saturday on the changes of public opinion with regard to distinguished men. And in the intervening years he had returned repeatedly to the topic.

> Charge your style with life, and the public will not ask for conundrums . . . If, therefore, in writing, you find it your mission to be abstruse, fight to render your statement clear and attractive, as if your life depended on it; your literary life does depend on it, and, if you fail, relapses into a dead language.

He continued with some excellent advice about vocabulary and the use of erudition and then paused to consider the situation of the author who felt himself to be unappreciated.

> Do not waste a minute, not a second, in trying to demonstrate to others the merit of your own performance. If your work does not vindicate itself, you cannot vindicate it . . . Yet do not be made conceited by obscurity any more than by notoriety. Many fine geniuses have been long neglected; but what would become of us if all the neglected were to turn out geniuses?

Toward the end of the essay he turned back to his own immediate preoccupations and discussed the advantages and disadvantages of a military life as compared to a contemplative one.

"Of all gifts eloquence is the most short-lived," he recorded sadly. "A book is the only immortality." (pp. 117-20)

Anna Mary Wells, in her Dear Preceptor: The Life

and Times of Thomas Wentworth Higginson, *Houghton Mifflin Company, 1963, 363 p.*

EDGAR L. McCORMICK   (essay date 1964)

[*In the following essay, McCormick examines Higginson's ideas on the development of a national literature in nineteenth-century America.*]

Those who pass off Thomas Wentworth Higginson as narrowly traditional and superficially romantic have overlooked his vigorous insistence that nineteenth-century America was establishing its own literature and that Ralph Waldo Emerson was its first great writer. The mastery of conventional modes of expression and the use of native subjects could not create a national literature. According to Higginson, the democratic ideal, especially as it was restated by the Transcendentalists, had to inspire writing that was truly American. In the *Independent* (Sept. 24, 1868) he declared that although European "resources and standards brought polish" to Longfellow's poetry, "there was something wanting." What he missed was the "American breath" that quickened the work of Emerson.

In the 1850's and 1860's, in Massachusetts, Kansas, and South Carolina, Higginson had defended the democratic belief in human freedom; in 1870, in the *Atlantic,* he identified this ideal as the basis of what he chose to call "Americanism in literature." He held that self-government is the very "oxygen" of American life, "the basis of all culture." In a land too immense to be dominated by prejudice or partiality (or even by economic problems, Higginson assumed), political freedom assured every individual of the opportunity for the maximum development of his talents. Such promise of human progress made the American into the "advancing figure" Higginson had described in his *Atlantic* **"Letter to a Young Contributor"** (1862), a figure whose very language is unique, expressing with suitable "dash" and "accuracy" the vigorous life of the Republic. All that is distinctively American, he believed, is inspired by this ideal. His own commitment to it lay behind his efforts to define an American literature and to know and encourage its makers.

Higginson was certain that an American literature exists by its own right with its unique place in world literature. It earned this place not so much by its treatment of indigenous subjects as by its concern for the importance of every man. He never agreed with Barrett Wendell, who maintained (*A Literary History of America*) that the literary historian should describe "what America has contributed to the literature of the English language." Higginson held, consistently, the view that he expressed in the *Independent* (Feb. 10, 1887): "American literature is not, and never again can be, merely an outlying portion of the literature of England." With Emerson had come a declaration of literary independence and we "ceased to be colonial" (*The New World and the New Book*).

Americans, however, were slow to recognize the merit of their authors, and the writers themselves were tardy in throwing off their deference to England. The old bondage persisted, even after the Civil War, and Higginson advocated thorough emancipation. He believed that Americans had earned the recognition they were hesitant to accept. When he traveled in England in 1872 he found no greater writers than those his own country had produced. "I never felt for an instant that I had really encountered in England men of greater calibre than I had met before, for was I not the fellow countryman of Emerson and Hawthorne, of Webster and Phillips?" (*Cheerful Yesterdays*).

It was evident to him, of course, that the first mark of an American literature was its concern with native subjects. "It must be indigenous, if it is to be anything at all." (*Nation,* May 31, 1883). As late as October 8, 1896, when he reviewed Emily Dickinson's *Poems, Third Series* (*Nation*), he believed it still necessary to stress the importance of American subjects in poetry where the tenacious hold of convention hindered assimilation of the native and local:

> Some consideration is also due to the peculiarly American quality of the landscape, the birds, the flowers, [Emily Dickinson] delineates. What does an Englishman know of the bobolink, the whippoorwill, the Baltimore oriole, even of the American robbin or blue-jay? These have hardly been recognized as legitimate stock-properties in poetry, either on the part of the London press or of that portion of the American which calls itself "cosmopolitan." To use them is still regarded, as when Emerson and Lowell were censured for their use, "a foolish affection of the familiar." Why not stick to the conventional skylark and nightingale? Yet, as a matter of fact, if we may again draw upon Don Quixote's discourse to the poet, it is better that a Spaniard should write as a Spaniard and a Dutchman as a Dutchman. If Emily Dickinson wishes to say in her description of a spirit, " 'Tis whiter than an Indianpipe" . . . let her say it, although no person born out of her own land may ever have seen that wondrous ghost of a flower. . . . Perhaps in the end, the poet who is truest to his own country may best reach all others. An eminent American librarian, lately visiting in England, made it a practice to inquire in the country bookstores what American poet was most in demand with their customers, and was amazed at the discovery that it was usually Whittier.

In *Cheerful Yesterdays* Higginson recalled the pleasure he experienced when, in the period of the Concord "Newness," familiar things became common subjects in American writing. "Probably no one who did not live in those days can fully realize what it was to us to have our own aspects of nature, our own historic scenes, our own types of character, our own social problems brought up and given prominent place." But infinitely more significant to the new literature was the vital meaning the Transcendentalists expressed. To the "Disciples of the Newness" all things were important. Their belief in "the essential and the inalienable value of the individual man" not only played the major role in freeing and nationalizing American literature, but also provided the touchstone by which it could be identified. (*The New World and the New Book*). Transcendentalism was the "one strongly original movement in American literature," he affirmed (*Nation,* Jan. 15, 1903) as he noted that the Rowland Club of Cleveland had reprinted "the old *Dial,* the land-mark of the ever interesting Transcendental period."

In a review of *Society and Solitude* (*Atlantic,* July, 1870), he declared that Emerson's essays constituted "the high-water-mark of American literature," being "unequalled in the literature of the age." Emerson "took his allusions and his poetic material from the woods and waters around him; his vital idealism had the "effect of revelation." (*Contemporaries*). In his tribute to Emerson in the *Nation* (May 4, 1882), he recognized the passing of an author who, with "full and conscious purpose," had been the founder of a school of thought:

> From the beginning to the end of his first volume ("Nature"), the fact is clear that it was consciously and deliberately a new departure. Those ninety brief pages were an undisguised challenge to the world. On the very first page the author complains that our age is retrospective—that others have "beheld God and nature face to face; we only through their eyes. Why should not we," he says, "also enjoy an original relation to the universe? Why should not we have a poetry and philosophy of insight and not of tradition?" Thus the book begins, and on the very last page it ends, "Build, therefore, your own world!" At any time, and under any conditions, the first reading of such words by any young person would be a great event in life, but in the comparative conventionalism of the literature of that period it was a new heaven and a new earth.

Emerson awakened "the first great need in a new literature—self-reliance." His was a stimulus "quite unequalled during the era when our original literature was taking form." Standing "among the poets, not among the philosophic doctors," he also brought greatness to American writing itself: ". . . it may be fearlessly said that, within the limits of a single sentence, no man who ever wrote the English tongue put more meaning into words than Emerson."

But few could approach this "high-water-mark," and Higginson did not expect any sudden maturation of a great national literature. He was hopeful that the democratic ideal was motivating the post-Civil War realists. They, too, he was certain, were interested in all men and their problems. William Dean Howells, particularly in such novels as *The Rise of Silas Lapham* and *A Hazard of New Fortunes,* expressed "the dignity and importance of the individual man." Fulfillment, however, belonged to the future. Neither the Puritan tradition (in its best ethical sense) nor materialism, nor science need be inimical to the realization of the democratic ideal and the attendant growth of an American literature. The vigor and devotion of Puritanism could contribute strength to life and art; practical pursuits could bring the leisure and security necessary for individual growth and creativity; science, concerned with the tangible, need not intrude upon the realm of intuition or inspiration where the ideal reveals itself. So Higginson reasoned, perhaps naively, (*A Reader's History of American Literature*) as the new century began. He was sure that one day a literature would appear that would be truly commensurate with the active faith he considered American.

He was aware, of course, of serious obstacles to the development of such a literature. Americans neglected culture and overlooked art. They were beguiled by material prosperity and drawn to scientific thought. But neither money nor science threatened to deter the growth of an American literature so much as did the genteel tradition. In 1903 (*A Reader's History of American Literature*), Higginson repeated what he had said in 1870 (**"Americanism in Literature"**), recognizing the real obstacle to "the new birth of literature and art in America" as "the timid and faithless spirit that lurks in the circles of culture, and still holds something of literary and academic leadership in the homes of the Puritans. . . . How can any noble literature germinate where young men are constantly told by some of their professors that there is no such thing as originality, and that nothing remains for us in this effete epoch of history but the mere re-combing of thoughts

which sprang from braver brains?" Despite the great economic changes, his optimism had not faltered, and he still was certain in the early years of the new century that "Out of our strong forward-bearing American life, with its apparent complications, and its essential simplicity, is to come, some day, a purer national expression than we have known." (pp. 71-3)

> Edgar L. McCormick, "Higginson, Emerson, and a National Literature," in The Emerson Society Quarterly, *Vol. 37, No. IV, 1964, pp. 71-3.*

HOWARD N. MEYER (essay date 1967)

[*Meyer is an American lawyer who has written and edited works on American race relations. In the following excerpt from his biography of Higginson, he discusses Higginson's influential essay "Ought Women to Learn the Alphabet?"*]

"Ought Women to Learn the Alphabet?" [Higginson] asked. That was the title and the recurrent theme of one of his most influential essays. His starting point was the proposal of a satirist of Napoleonic France of 1801 who suggested a law forbidding women to read. The earlier writer had given examples based on the prejudices of more primitive times when it was thought that knowledge rarely made men attractive, and females never. Higginson wrote:

> It would seem that the brilliant Frenchman touched the root of the matter. Ought women to learn the alphabet? There the whole question lies. . . . Resistance must be made here or nowhere. . . . Woman must be a subject or an equal: there is no middle ground.

He paid his respects to the great names of the bench and bar of the period, lawyers, jurists, and scholars whose opinions he ridiculed. He topped off the series of quotations with the solemn finding of a lord high justice who declared "The wife is only the *servant* of the husband" in the eyes of the law.

[Higginson] needed no argument to answer this. He simply quoted a barbaric four-thousand-year-old Oriental doctrine that had been recently excavated, "A man, both day and night, must keep his wife so much in subjection that she by no means be mistress of her own actions. If the wife have her own free will, notwithstanding she be of a superior caste, she will behave amiss."

He reviewed the consistently increasing amount of published work by women of the eighteenth and nineteenth centuries. There was special interest in the highlights of their forgotten tracts and appeals, in all languages, arguing the case for their freedom and proving their right to equality of opportunity. Male predecessors in the fight were not neglected. The implication of the continued debate was summed up, "Ancient or modern, nothing in any of these discussions is so valuable as the fact of the discussion itself. There is no discussion where there is no wrong."

A brief glance at the other side of the question brought the appraisal:

> The obstacle to woman's sharing the alphabet, or indeed any other privilege, has been thought by some to be the fear of impairing her delicacy, or of destroying her domesticity, or of confounding the distinction between the sexes. These may have plausible excuses. They may have even been genu-

ine, though minor, anxieties. But the whole thing, I take it, had always one simple, intelligible basis—sheer contempt for the supposed intellectual inferiority of woman.

This was the issue he wanted to meet. In the first place, he said, "it obviously does a good deal towards explaining the facts it assumes. If contempt does not originally cause failure, it perpetuates it." In the second place, he pointed out, "Women being denied, not merely the training which prepares for great deeds, but the praise and compensation which follow them, have been weakened in both directions. . . . Single, she works with half-preparation and half-pay; married, she puts name and wages into the keeping of her husband. . . ." When given equal opportunities and training, he proved with ancient and modern examples, woman will make her contribution, ". . . great achievements imply great preparations and favorable conditions." Who knows of what the world has been deprived by its prejudices, ". . . how many mute, inglorious Minervas may have perished unenlightened, while Margaret Fuller Ossoli and Elizabeth Barrett Browning were being educated 'like boys'. . . . Give an equal chance and let genius and industry do the rest."

The stock contentions of critics of the women's rights movement were answered with wit, ingenuity, and examples from history. He returned again and again to his theme, "woman must be a subject or an equal; there is no middle ground. . . . It is an alarming feature of this discussion, that it has reversed, very generally, the traditional positions of the sexes: the women have had all the logic; and the most intelligent men, when they have attempted the other side, have limited themselves to satire and gossip."

He closed on a note of good-humored optimism:

> In how many towns was the current of popular prejudice against female orators reversed by one winning speech from Lucy Stone! Where no logic can prevail, success silences. First give woman, if you dare, the alphabet, then summon her to her career; and though men, ignorant and prejudiced, may oppose its beginnings, they will at last fling around her conquering footsteps more lavish praises than ever greeted the opera's idol,—more perfumed flowers than ever wooed, with intoxicating fragrance, the fairest butterfly of the ball-room.

When he submitted **"Ought Women to Learn the Alphabet"** to Atlantic editor James Russell Lowell, there was much grumbling and shaking of the head. Abolitionist though he was, Lowell thought the ideas Wentworth put forward on freedom for half the population a little too radical. It did not take long to win him over, and when published, the article was given place of honor. Reprinted often, it probably had a wider circulation and greater effect than any other single article [Higginson] had written. Not only were bastions of prejudice toppled in many circles but there was a very practical effect: at least two women's colleges, one of them Smith, were founded as a direct answer to the question, "Ought women to learn the alphabet?" (pp. 170-73)

Howard N. Meyer, in his Colonel of the Black Regiment: The Life of Thomas Wentworth Higginson, *W. W. Norton & Company, Inc., 1967, 346 p.*

TILDEN G. EDELSTEIN   (essay date 1968)

[*In the following excerpt, Edelstein examines Higginson's poetry, his role as the editor of Emily Dickinson's poems, and his critical writings on American authors of his time.*]

Infrequently written poetry and very frequently published criticism of poetry helped establish Higginson's literary reputation. During his adolescence and early manhood he had published a few reform-oriented poems; after the war his poetry, while occasionally maintaining this concern, more often described domestic life. **"Sixty and Six: Or a Fountain of Youth"** and **"The Baby Sorceress,"** for example, described his reaction to his young daughter Margaret. The beginning of the latter poem is representative of their genre:

> Joy of the morning,
> Darling of the dawning,
> Blithe, lithe little daughter of mine!
> While with thee ranging
> Sure I'm exchanging
> Sixty of my years for six years like thine.

Occasionally more inspiring were Higginson's poems about nature. But in **"Sea-Gulls at Fresh Pond"** he frankly acknowledged the truth about his poetry.

> I am no nearer to those joyous birds
> Than when, long since, I watched them as a child;
> Nor am I nearer to that flock more wild,
> Most shy and vague of all elusive things,
> My unattainable thoughts, unreached by words.
> I see the flight, but never touch the wings.

Higginson's most popular poems were those commemorating the Civil War. Most publicly recited was **"Waiting for the Bugle,"** first read in 1888 before a group of Cambridge war veterans. The last lines read:

> Though the sound of cheering dies down to a moan
> We shall find our lost youth when the bugle is blown.

Dedicatory poems to Whittier, Helen Hunt Jackson, and Edward Bellamy express far less disappointment and pessimism than his other types of poetry. Whittier is credited with opening the nation's eyes to the need for abolition, and Mrs. Jackson for "Lifting with slender hand a race's wrong." **"Heirs of Time"** assures Bellamy that the "tread of marching men / The patient armies of the poor . . .

> Some day, by laws as fixed and fair
> As guide the planets in their sweep,
> The children of each outcast heir
> The harvest-fruits of time shall reap.

Higginson's poems are generally lyric in structure. Conventional meters and verse forms, four-line stanzas, alternating rhyme, and iambic pentameter are most often employed. While there is some lyric variety, he showed no interest in experimenting with unorthodox forms. In this traditionalism his poetry remained akin to antebellum poetry and to such postwar contemporaries as Edmund Clarence Stedman and Thomas Bailey Aldrich. It has been correctly suggested that Higginson was more adept as a translator than as an original poet. In [*Fifteen Sonnets of Petrarch*] for example, the weakness of his poetic fancy does not excessively mar the result.

Poetry, Higginson believed, was the "highest kind of literature . . . for it culls the very best phrase of the language, instead of throwing a dozen epithets to see if one may chance to stick." He knew, however, that his own poetic efforts achieved no such height. A volume of 1893 containing the best poems from Higginson and his wife was modestly titled [*Such as They Are: Poems*]. But humility did not character-ize his conception of himself as a critic of poetry. Recognized as a major literary critic by his contemporaries, Higginson believed that poetry could do what the novel or the essay could not: raise the mind and carry it "into sublimity by con-forming the show of things to the desires of soul, instead of subjecting the soul to external things." His responses to the poetry of Emily Dickinson, Walt Whitman, and Sidney La-nier provide a revealing test of his literary opinions. (pp. 340-42)

If Higginson, during the twenty-four years he corresponded with Emily Dickinson, bears the major responsibility for dis-couraging the publication of her poetry—though certainly she exerted some choice—he also deserves much of the credit, after her death, for bringing it to the world's attention. Mrs. Mabel Loomis Todd, the wife of the professor of astronomy at Amherst College and a friend of the Dickinson family, met with Higginson in early November 1889 to show him some two hundred Dickinson poems which Mrs. Todd had copied from the poet's manuscripts. Mrs. Todd, at the request of the Dickinson family, had come for his advice and help in editing and publishing them. After some hesitation because of his own ill-health, other literary projects, and the poet's "pecu-liarities of construction," Higginson consented to collaborate if Mrs. Todd would do the bulk of the editorial work. He would be responsible for the final editing, the preface, pub-lishing arrangements, and publicity. It seemed unlikely that the volume, its printing plates paid for by the Dickinson fami-ly, would succeed in doing more than provide a modest me-morial to Emily Dickinson. But Higginson, who previously had received more than a hundred poems during the poet's lifetime, examined those chosen for the volume by Mrs. Todd and suddenly discovered that Emily Dickinson was not just a private poet. With some incredulousness he wrote to Mrs. Todd: "I can't tell you how much I am enjoying these poems. There are many new to me which take my breath away & which also have *form* beyond most of those I have seen before. . . . My confidence in their *availability* is greatly in-creased."

To recall that Emily Dickinson already had sent him many of her best poems suggests that what most impressed Higgin-son with the new ones indeed was the presence of *form*. Form meant maximum revision by the poet to conform to accepted literary standards. Neither of the two poems which Higgin-son judged to be of the highest quality, it should be noted, was markedly unconventional in rhyme, meter, or imagery. And both poems had themes common to New England verse.

> Glee! the great storm is over!
> Four have recovered the land;
> Forty gone down together
> Into the boiling sand . . .

The other poem, which Higginson titled "The Lonely House,"—"I know some lonely houses off the road . . ."—paralleled his own poem, **"The Dying House,"** previously published in a collection of his verse. For those Dickinson poems with more obscure themes, Higginson sought to guide future readers by grafting on titles. Also titles like "Rouge et Noir," "Rouge Gagne," and "Astra Castra" were added to give the poems a learned weight.

How to edit the body of the poetry, recent scholars have

noted, was a complex matter, partly because it was difficult to know which poems had been considered final versions by Miss Dickinson. Although Higginson's own poetry employed standard rhyme, he conceded in his published criticism that the traditional roundel had been cloying. And while reading the Dickinson verse in December 1889, he wrote, unlike most critics of his day, that Thomas Bailey Aldrich's "most ad-mired gems are really the mere resetting of what came first from someone else." Still, Emily Dickinson's originality seemed to him very remarkable, though odd. So with an eye to public acceptance and standard grammar he sought to modify some of the oddity. Far too unorthodox for Higginson was "The grass so little has to do / I wish I were a hay." He asserted: "It cannot go in so, everybody would say that *hay* is a collective noun requiring the definite article. Nobody can call it *a* hay!" Therefore, he sent "the hay" to the printer along with the alteration of the line, "And what a Billow be," to "And what a wave must be." In other poems Higginson and Mrs. Todd eliminated unorthodox capitalization and added conventional punctuation.

Perhaps the most important alteration of a major poem oc-curred in "Because I could not stop for death." Higginson ti-tled it "The Chariot," changed some words, and omitted an entire stanza. His editing suggests that he interpreted the poem as only depicting the soul's ascension to heaven in a chariot. A birds-eye view of the ground, rather than the si-multaneous existence of mortal remains and immortal soul, was the resulting emphasis. Thus he changed the last line from "The Cornice—in the Ground" (meant to be a coffin's cornice) to "The cornice but a mound" (a house's cornice viewed from above). The original stanza and Higginson's re-visions are here illustrated:

We paused before a House that seemed	We paused before a house that seemed
A Swelling of the Ground—	A swelling of the ground;
The Roof was scarcely visible—	The roof was scarcely visible,
The Cornice—in the Ground—	The cornice but a mound.

Omission of the revealing fourth stanza further changed the poem's intent:

> Or rather—He passed Us—
> The Dews drew quivering and chill—
> For only Gossamer, my Gown—
> My Tippet—only Tulle—

Again, the coexistence of mortality and immortality is lost. Also the symbolic interchangeability of love with death is eliminated or obscured because the editor never displays the woman in her bridal dress traveling to her marriage with God. Here and elsewhere, Higginson missed the central fact of Emily Dickinson's symbolism. He, as has been said about Emerson, was "remote from the specific possibilities of the *literary* symbol." But in "The Chariot," as well as in other poems, alterations were probably less drastic than would have been made by any other editors of the era—if indeed anybody else would have consented to associate his name with such poetry. Higginson, for example, accepted the un-conventional rhyming of "pearl" with "alcohol," and "own" with "young." (Tennyson, however, provided precedent for such assonance.) As editor, Higginson was torn by a personal obligation to Emily Dickinson's memory and a historical ob-ligation to documentary truth as against his own conception of good poetry and the hostile reception expected from critics and public. Not only was this conflict reflected in the editorial results but also in his prefatory remarks which introduced Emily Dickinson to the world.

To publicize this forthcoming volume, Higginson wrote an article for the *Christian Union*. While similar to his subsequent preface to the poems, it was less guarded in discussing the poet's motives and the level of the poetry. Emily Dickinson, he suggested, was akin to those poets "who wrote for the relief of their own mind and without thought of publication." Granting that she had a standard of her own, he likened her verse to poetry plucked up by the roots, with earth, stones, and dew adhering—it was wayward and unconventional in the last degree; defiant of form, measure, rhyme, and even grammar. But he hoped that the faulty rhyme and defect of workmanship would be compensated by its power. He chose to publish, for the first time, fourteen of the poems she had sent to him during their many years of correspondence.

To explain why no volume of her poetry had been printed during her lifetime, he wholly blamed the poet by asserting that she had been asked again and again for verses to be published. It should be recognized, however, that neither Higginson nor any of his defenders have produced any documentary evidence showing that he ever had asked her. And if the primary blame for altering Emily Dickinson's verse is Mrs. Todd's, as a recent Higginson biographer has argued, it also must be acknowledged that he was a willing accomplice, with a long-held conviction that much revision and criticism were prerequisites to publication. His marked antipathy to the other poetic innovators of his day makes even a circumstantial defense tenuous. On the eve of the first volume's appearance, Higginson conceded some misgiving in allowing its publication at all.

In the preface to the first edition, Higginson neither admitted misgiving nor said that the verse was written for mental relief. Instead, he stressed that Emily Dickinson had absolutely no choice in the *way* she wrote and the way she received flashes of wholly original and profound insight into nature and life. Now praising this recluse woman for touching the "very crisis of physical or mental conflict," he confined his criticism to the uneven vigor and the lack of a sustained lyric strain. And he assured readers that the poems "are here published as they were written, with very few and superficial changes."

On publication day, November 12, 1890, Higginson wrote to Mrs. Todd: "Books just arrived—bound. I am *astounded* in looking through. How could we have doubted them." No less astounding was the success of the public sale; the first edition of five hundred copies was quickly sold and followed by second, third, and fourth editions. The prestige of the printed word and the extent of the sale caused him to reconsider, once again, the meaning of Emily Dickinson's life and poetry. To Mrs. Todd, who was planning another collection of Dickinson poetry, Higginson suggested: "Let us alter as little as possible now that the public ear is opened." The second series received less editing than its predecessor.

Just prior to its publication, Higginson promoted the collection by writing a revealing biographical essay for the *Atlantic* which outlined his meetings with Emily Dickinson and quoted extensively from her letters to him. He stressed the tension in her "abnormal life," but for the first time insisted that he had always known that she was a genius. And from then on, some thirty years after he first received her poems, the image of a raw genius characterized his comments about her work.

Reviewing the second series in his unsigned column in the *Nation,* Higginson urged that the poems be read as "sketches, not [as] works of conscious completeness." Her work made it appear "as if she had been in at the very birth of her birds and flowers." When a young man, Higginson had described in precisely these terms the romantic work of Jean Paul Richter. Now Emily Dickinson's work had incorrectly come to exemplify what Schiller had called the naïve and sentimental in poetry.

Mrs. Todd edited a third series of Dickinson poems without Higginson's assistance (he had been paid a very small sum by the Dickinson family for his past work), but he reviewed them in the *Nation.* He found that the poet had heeded Emerson's plea for a distinctive national literature in her representation of "the peculiarly American quality of the landscape, the birds, the flowers." Her poetry, he concluded, with all "its flagrant literary faults" could be appreciated only in terms of what "Ruskin describes as 'the perfection and precision of the instantaneous line'." Once having said that Emily Dickinson would "wait many days for a word that satisfied," he increasingly turned to the opinion that her poetry lacked the traditional care of revision and was primarily the spontaneous expression of a "pitifully childlike poetic genius," who was strange, solitary, and morbidly sensitive. For him the obscure, inscrutable quality of her poetry with its fractured grammar and "defiance of form" could best be comprehended by believing that it "rests content with a first stroke" and therefore lacks the "proper control and chastening of literary expression." Incredible as it may seem today, Emily Dickinson's poetry and her personality were being measured against Helen Hunt Jackson's.

It was "H. H." whom Higginson viewed as the best kind of "poet of passion," one who tempered her waywardness and controlled her poetic impulses by being always ready to revise and correct her verse at his suggestion. Aided by the openness and frankness Mrs. Jackson showed toward him, he had achieved the everyday comradeship lacking in his relationship with Emily Dickinson. Mrs. Jackson was also able to combine an ardent and impetuous nature with an ability to be pleasantly sociable and congenial. Her prejudices against Negroes and her lack of sympathy with the woman's rights cause were less important to him, he granted, than her personal generosity. At a time when he criticized Longfellow's poetry for being too easily and quickly comprehended, and Whittier's for having an obtrusive moral, Higginson found that Mrs. Jackson's best poetry contained just enough obscurity to compliment the intelligent reader.

While obviously impressed that 30,000 copies of Miss Dickinson's poetry had been sold by 1895, Higginson privately noted that her work was not valued by the finest minds. Publicly he acknowledged its quality by ranking her with those women poets he esteemed most: Helen Hunt Jackson and Elizabeth Barrett Browning. He began to use her poetry as a standard with which to criticize other poets who were seeking a new means of expression. Mrs. Annie Fields' poetry was inferior to Mrs. Jackson's and Miss Dickinson's in "passion and originality." And when the Dickinson poems sold poorly in England he defended her work against the poetry that he most disdained: "Apparently the English polite cannot stand the unconventional except with a good coarse flavor as in Whitman." With the appearance of Stephen Crane's *The Black Rider and Other Lines,* Higginson noted that Crane grasped "thought as nakedly and simply as Emily Dickinson," but was an amplified Emily Dickinson. Here too was "poetry torn up by the roots." Apparently reconsidering, however, his own previous praise for Emily Dickinson in this regard, Higginson suggested that such a style was "always interesting to the botanist, yet bad for the blossoms." Edward Arlington Robinson, one of the most promising of our younger poets, he said, was also given credit for displaying an "obscurity that is often like that of Emily Dickinson when she piques your curiosity through half a dozen readings and suddenly makes all clear." But while Higginson acknowledged the poet's right to be obscure, Robinson sometimes came near the unintelligible. The cause of such a flaw was working too much alone—exactly his criticism of Emily Dickinson.

Higginson's final estimate of American poets devoted a scant two pages to Emily Dickinson. He predicted that the poem most likely to bring her lasting fame was one he had titled "Vanished." It ended:

> Her little figure at the gate
> The angels must have spied,
> Since I could never find her
> Upon the mortal side.

The paternal compassion and fascination that attracted Higginson to Emily Dickinson and her enigmatic poetry and personality were wholly absent in his response to Whitman and his poetry. This was true despite Higginson's willingness to be critical of the renowned Aldrich, to label Bayard Taylor a "champion imitator," and to charge that Richard Henry Stoddard was "burnt out." He suggested that writing *Leaves of Grass* was no discredit to Whitman—"only that he did not burn it and reserve himself for something better." Claiming to have read the poem in 1855, during his rough sea voyage from the Azores, Higginson was uncertain about which had more upset his stomach. But when he reviewed the Boston edition of *Leaves of Grass* in 1881 he was sure that its "nauseating quality remains in full force." Republication of the poem only could provide satisfaction for those who feared the dominance of "Anthony Comstock and his laws respecting obscene publications." According to Higginson, Whitman displayed the animal impulse of the savage who knocks down the first woman he sees and drags her to the cave. The savage, however, wrote no resounding lines about it. Responding to an expurgated Boston edition of *Leaves of Grass* in 1892, Higginson said that it may be left openly about the house but its profuseness and wordiness remain.

"Drum-Taps" was tasteless in a different manner. It was hypocritically hollow because Whitman, who had been trumpeted by his admirers as having the finest physique in America, had avoided Civil War battlefields and instead served in the hospital with the noncombatants. Whitman's patriotism was the sheer bravado of thousands of Fourth of July orations. And similarly, the poet's celebration of the laborer rang false because he had never labored; Whitman tried to use folk language without having studied the localisms of the day.

The modicum of tolerance Higginson had exhibited toward Emily Dickinson's poetic style was absent. In Whitman's verse the reader was not pierced by the "rifle-bullet effect" of the instantaneous line, but instead was assaulted by the poet's "bird-shot," his endless enumerations, and the ostentatious effort at cosmopolitanism exhibited in the sudden use of French words. Reminded of the long rambling lines and excessive romantic effusiveness of Martin Tupper, the English

aphorist he had admired in his youth, Higginson concluded that Whitman lacked the stylistic control required of a poet.

This virulence was unmatched in Higginson's many pieces of criticism except for his comment that Rudyard Kipling's poems have "that garlic flavor which makes a very little of them go a great way, and makes the reader himself soon wish to go a great way off." Whitman, and Kipling to a lesser extent, represented a repugnant kind of manliness. Holding to a chivalric conception, he believed that Whitman epitomized an exclusively muscular manliness. Higginson's views ranged close at times to an Anglo-Saxonism that looked upon the best American man as a transplanted Englishman transformed into a "type more high bred, more finely organized, and also more comprehensive and cosmopolitan." Or in another way, Higginson conceived of himself in relation to the Greek ideal, relegating Whitman to the role of a Roman Bacchus. In his article **"The Greek Goddesses,"** for example, Higginson equated Greece with high-minded purity, and derided both Ovid and Aristophanes for writing irreverent indecencies about women and for failing to recognize Aphrodite's essential modesty. He also was critical of writers who "find some indecency in every ancient symbol."

With acuteness and venom, Higginson compared Whitman to Oscar Wilde by noting that they wrote about nudity in a way not comparable to the "sacred whiteness of an antique statue, but rather [to] the forcible unveiling of some insulted innocence." A real man would never read such literature aloud in the presence of ladies. True literature combined power with delicacy, and elevated mankind to a realization of its higher nature. What Whitman valued as "the sexual fibre of things," Higginson judged as animalism and a failure to understand love as an ideal emotion. Defending a tradition infused with transcendentalism and puritanism against a poet who believed that the absence of a significant American literary tradition made personal vision necessary, Higginson believed that Whitman was a sheer egoist. The poet's failure to distinguish between a goddess and a streetwalker showed only blindness to moral verities.

Whitman believed that Higginson was responsible for much of the hostility toward him in Boston. And only later in life did Higginson discover a spark of greatness in the poet's work. In reviewing a collection of Whitman's complete writings, he noted "occasional bursts of fine humility which are too rarely visible in the writings of this remarkable man," and which by their "manly modesty . . . atone for a multitude of sins." But Higginson never forgave Whitman's failure to fight in the Civil War, nor forgot that this self-styled democratic poet received not one popular vote for the Hall of Fame of Immortals. There were only two poems Higginson ever praised. One was "My Captain," which came nearest to regularity of rhythm and proved the importance of adhering to recognized poetic method. It ranked, in his estimation, with some of the best American poems of the nineteenth century. "Joy, Shipmate, Joy," he praised for the "fine outburst" and "sunny spirit" in Whitman's conception of death and immortality; these lines, Higginson said at age eighty-two, could be a fitting inscription on his own memorial stone. But in assessing all of Whitman's poetry he agreed with Sidney Lanier's criticism: " 'A republic depends on the self-control of each member; you cannot make a republic out of muscles and prairies and rocky mountains; republics are made of the spirit.' " For Higginson, restraint and spirit were the "austere virtues" that had been bequeathed to American literature by puritanism and transcendentalism.

Not until after Lanier's death in 1881 did Higginson appreciate this southern poet and rate him among the "master singers." In **"Recent Minor Poetry"** Higginson had previously reviewed the only volume of collected verse published in Lanier's lifetime; he found little of real poetic sentiment. Although "Corn" displayed a genuine feeling for nature, and "The Psalm of the West" had some moving passages, Higginson discovered "no symptom of relaxing that convulsive and startling mode of utterance" of the "Centennial Cantata." He concluded that the entire absence of simplicity spoiled everything.

Lanier's death, and the subsequent publication of the tragic details of his life that accompanied a collection of his poetry, enabled Higginson to write about him again in the *Nation*. Responding, as he had repeatedly done with other poets, to personal character, he now called Lanier a man of genius whose fame would grow. If his verse was not simple, this must be excused and attributed to youth and ill health and "an almost morbid conscientiousness in the direction of certain theories of sound and phrase." "Sunrise" was declared to be his best poem, and Higginson recommended it to the young followers of Whitman, because it seemed to be constructed on Whitman's methods; but instead of "bald and formless iteration, it is everywhere suffused with music as with light; every stanza chants itself, instead of presenting a prosaic huddle of long lines." He viewed Lanier as the first distinctly southern poet—comparable in his lyricism to Poe.

Now transformed from critic to advocate, Higginson noted in an article about Paul Hamilton Hayne that Lanier was "by far the most gifted of Southern bards." Comparing Lanier's manliness in life and poetry with Whitman's, he extolled this southerner's service in the Confederate Army in contrast to Whitman's hospital service for the North. There was "refined chivalry" in "The Symphony," but "fleshiness" in "Leaves of Grass." Lanier's poetry was always single-minded, noble, and pure. Higginson was as sympathetic to his portraits of southern scenes as he had been to Whittier's northern ones. (This appreciation for local color would cause him also to commend the Celtic scenes found in the early poetry of William Butler Yeats.) Higginson would never acknowledge that Lanier had praised Whitman, nor would he ever comment upon Lanier's attacks on radical Reconstruction, but he did sympathetically quote the southerner: " 'with us of the younger generation in the South since the war, pretty much the whole of life has been merely not dying'." Lanier, he concluded, was the "Sir Galahad among our American poets."

Higginson's biographies of Fuller, Longfellow, and Whittier and his innumerable essays about other antebellum writers reveal his reliance upon the New England writers of the forties and fifties as a guide for developing postwar American literature. Although he was sympathetic to Emerson's plea for a distinctly American literature of insight, not tradition, he also agreed with a postwar critic, Horace Scudder, that half a dozen great writers before the war had provided a viable tradition. Higginson understood that Emerson had loosened American writers from their dependence upon European literature by having mastered a national idiom with distinctly American images. Emerson's condensed style packed each word with thought.

Of lesser note, but important because its recognition in Europe gave American writers hope of ultimate acceptance, was Longfellow's work. Higginson suggested that though it lacked profundity it would survive for more homely qualities. Whittier, in contrast to Longfellow, he considered the poet of the people, the leading bard of the antislavery crusade, the Burns of the Merrimack Valley. If his poetry too often was marred by a superfluous moral, his skill in depicting American domestic life provided a tradition that united art and democracy.

In praising Henry Thoreau and Margaret Fuller, Higginson was rare among postwar literary critics. He appreciated Thoreau's protest against worldly materialism which simultaneously stayed close to the world of labor and literature. Before the war, Higginson had been exceptional in praising *A Week on the Concord and Merrimack Rivers;* after the war he published sympathetic reviews of both *The Maine Woods* and *Cape Cod,* finding in them a lyrical strain superior to Emerson's. He also advocated the publication of Thoreau's journals. Margaret Fuller, he believed, stressed the ideal but still succeeded far more than Emerson in recognizing that thought and action were inseparable, that the best part of intellect was action. Higginson was her first sympathetic biographer, denying, unlike others, that egomania characterized her life.

Higginson considered the work of Holmes and Lowell less admirable. He realized that recognition of Holmes' serious writing had been submerged by the popularity of his "delightful trifles," and yet Higginson failed to acknowledge the uniqueness of this writer's scientific orientation. Instead, he criticized the excessive stylistic self-consciousness and accepted the oversimplified view that Holmes should be remembered primarily because he epitomized the past ascendancy of Boston Brahminism. Higginson, to some degree, acknowledged his link to Holmes by recalling those antebellum *Atlantic* dinners at which Holmes' wit highlighted the proceedings, but he carefully noted little rapport with Holmes' conservatism regarding slavery. Higginson did not recognize the similarity of his own literary style to that of Holmes. To follow Emerson was Higginson's desire, but he seldom emerged from Holmes' shadow.

Higginson found little in Lowell to commend except his odes commemorating Lincoln and Grant. He judged him personally disagreeable and his poetry lacking in finish. Also Lowell had arrogantly denigrated Thoreau and Fuller.

Nathaniel Hawthorne was the greatest artist of the transcendental era, and indeed of American literature; Higginson judged him a writer who synthesized the two most important elements of the American experience: the "spiritual subtlety" of transcendentalism and the "moral earnestness" of puritanism. And Hawthorne was a truly American writer because he chose his country's past for literary themes. For Higginson, as for many other postwar writers, Hawthorne served as model and inspiration. Higginson refrained from criticizing either his denial of transcendental optimism or his view about the central place of sin in human character. And he uncritically accepted Hawthorne's assertion of having been an Abolitionist in feeling but not in fact.

Higginson, like most of his contemporaries, could find no value in Melville. He was never aware of that author's literary worth.

About Edgar Allan Poe's work, he was uncertain. While conceding that Poe's place in "imaginative prose-writing is as questionable as Hawthorne's," Higginson suggested that he lacked Hawthorne's philosophical profundity. Poe's failure to comprehend Hawthorne's originality and his ferocious attack on Longfellow for plagiarism convinced Higginson that no one had ever done more in America to lower the tone of literary criticism. The "weird" and lyric quality of Poe's verse—especially "Israfel"—attracted Higginson despite the poet's excessive absorption "in his own fantastic life of the mind." But he concluded that Poe's work was a dangerous model to emulate and that the austere virtues, the virtues of Emerson, Hawthorne, and Whittier, were more conducive to quality.

Higginson had confessed to Emerson that he was "lured by the joy of expression itself." It accurately explained more than Higginson's literary interests, for much of his reform activity had depended upon the desire to speak forcefully to people. Now he called for a vigorous literary style, one which would appeal to thirty million auditors who would reject stale pedantry. To attract a mass audience through literature, the cultivated writer must avoid mere ornamentation; he must make simplicity and freshness his instruments of expression and be willing to revise his manuscript thoroughly. He criticized Emerson for lacking freedom and "self-abandonment," but Higginson emphasized spontaneity far less than the need for culture. Unlike Emerson in the "American Scholar," he judged poise and proportion, not inspiration, to be the main ingredients of literary artistry. Learned and rational literary craftsmanship—with "one drop of nervous fluid" to distinguish it from the British product—was the formula bequeathed, in Higginson's view, by the antebellum New England writers.

Higginson encouraged a didacticism and an ideological commitment in fiction which he had come to condemn in good poetry. Central to this concept was the role he envisioned for the postwar intellectual. Upon withdrawing active support for Reconstruction in 1867 he had said that American politics no longer needed the artist's skilled hand to do the plain work of politics. The writer's responsibility, however, should not be limited to mere felicity of expression: writers of romance should provide imaginative insights into American society and draw plans for shaping the nation's future. Men participating in politics were not able to do this and could not be expected to state the problem confronting the future. By utilizing and transcending the facts of daily life, and by using literary skill to convince his readers, the imaginative writer would be serving a major social function by illuminating society's problems and suggesting their solution. Such social consciousness was not demanded from the poet, who must seek the joy of expression and "fill the desires of the soul instead of subjecting the soul to external things."

Higginson found in Hawthorne's fiction the best model of the writer as seer. Others like Charles Brockden Brown, Washington Irving, and James Fenimore Cooper, in their early portraits of America, lacked a larger insight, and too often they viewed America as merely a province of England. While Mrs. Stowe, in *Uncle Tom's Cabin,* had shown that Negroes, like Cooper's Indians, were a picturesque, heroic, and interesting race, her evangelical fervor and excessive melodrama hampered the credibility of the tale. An American writer with Hawthorne's plastic imagination was needed to portray the variety of American character and explore the depths of individuals.

Applying his criteria for good fiction to the work of Henry

James, Higginson highly praised two early short stories—"Madonna of the Future" and "Madame de Mauve"—but he claimed that *Daisy Miller* and *The American* were ruined by "the conventional limits of a stage ending." These two books, like *Portrait of a Lady,* were chiefly objectionable to him because they stressed America's failure to prepare its people—depicted as rich and innocent—to deal with the immoral European aristocracy.

James' attitude toward America was central to Higginson's criticism. Fleeing to Europe had a literary parallel in the author's indifference to accurate descriptions of American locales. James' care in describing European scenes and his failure to appreciate the cosmopolitan and cultured people living in America offended Higginson's national and personal pride. In response to James' assertion that a monarchical society is "more available for the novelist than any other," he argued that a republic develops "real individuality in proportion as it diminishes conventional distinctions." He concluded that James suffered from being out of touch with the mass of mankind. James, in turn, wished that "Higginsonian fangs" would stop "bespattering public periodicals with my gore."

As James' reputation grew, Higginson, whose most critical comments predate *The Ambassador* and *The Golden Bowl,* came to appreciate his skill in character delineation. But he also became disdainful of the author's involved and often puzzling style; Higginson believed that James had rejected the standard of stylistic simplicity set by Thoreau, Hawthorne, and Emerson. And he would not forgive him for abandoning America and favoring everything that condemned America, nor for being like those writers who "become oblivious of the outer world altogether, and entangle themselves more and more in intellectual subtleties of their own weaving."

For a time it appeared to Higginson that Edward Bellamy would would become the American novelist as seer. In *Dr. Heidenhoff's Process* and *Miss Ludington's Sister,* romances running counter to the realism of James and Howells, he found imaginative conceptions unmatched since Hawthorne's work. But after the publication of his two most important novels of social analysis, *Looking Backward* and *Equality,* Higginson's sense of literary craftsmanship tempered his praise. He was enthusiastic about the author's ideas but felt that Bellamy lacked Hawthorne's technical skill. By the turn of the century, when Higginson reviewed American literary accomplishments, Bellamy was eliminated from his list of important writers.

Higginson never accepted Mark Twain as more than a light humorist or *Huckleberry Finn* as more than regional literature. In his opinion, the best novelist of the postwar era was William Dean Howells. As early as 1862, in the same *Atlantic* article that attracted Emily Dickinson's attention, Higginson had become one of the first influential American critics to attack the dominant sentimental fiction of the day. Declaring that the familiar and commonplace should provide the material for fiction, he, like Howells, revered Jane Austen's treatment of everyday life with what Higginson called grace and Howells called an exquisite touch. In *Malbone,* Higginson had failed to follow his own advice about avoiding melodrama and an involved plot (in a later edition of the novel he complained that no one had believed that there actually had been a secret staircase in the home he had depicted), but he appreciated Howells' ability to do so. He recognized a skilled craftsman who sought to confront the "essential forces" of

American society. He also liked his repugnance for the extravagant emotionalism of sentimental fiction and his allegiance, in the early books, to the imaginative romance. Assuring Higginson that he was aware of the moral function of the novel, Howells wrote to him of feeling "ashamed and sorry if my work did not teach a lenient, generous, and liberal life." Higginson, in 1879, responded favorably to *A Chance Acquaintance, Out of the Question,* and *The Lady of the Aroostook. Chance Acquaintance,* depicting a clash between an independent western woman and a Bostonian of caste and etiquette, contributed insights into the future of our society. "How is it to be stratified? How much weight is to be given to intellect, to character, to wealth, to antecedents, to inheritance?" Such questions again were posed to Higginson's satisfaction in Howells' farcical play, *Out of the Question,* where the natural gentleman confronts education, social standing, and wealth in Back Bay Boston.

Higginson and Howells began to differ as early as the seventies. Higginson deplored Howells' declaration that *A Foregone Conclusion,* with its neurotic and hopeless characters, was his first genuine novel because neither lofty language nor idealized character was employed. Undersized characters dominated the book while full-sized humanity was absent, observed Higginson. Such devotion to the commonplace, if it meant omitting individuals with emotional or intellectual maturity, was not the new fiction he sought. Also *The Lady of the Aroostook,* which he largely approved, presented another objectionable part of Howells' early efforts at realism. "It was only necessary," Higginson suggested, "for a refined woman like the heroine to know the *fact* of the man's intoxication and not the facts."

But when Howells, in *The Undiscovered Country,* wrote a romance, Higginson applauded and discerningly compared it to *The Blithedale Romance.* He also approved of its sweetness and wholesomeness. The publication of *The Rise of Silas Lapham* further pleased him. Judging that the characters, especially Irene Lapham, were sketched in full dimension, he wrote Howells: "You are trusting yourself in these deeper motives of human emotion in which I always wanted to see you—your place is with Tourganef & not with Trollope or even with James." Only Turgenev, in Higginson's view, treated a variety of social classes. Despite Howells' allegiance to the "photographic school" of realism, Higginson praised him for treating American social problems in an optimistic way.

Higginson thought that Howells' best book, despite the devotion of the first six chapters to the hero's search for an apartment, was *A Hazard of New Fortunes.* It appealed to the cultivated reformer of principle who was interested in observing the variety of people living in postwar urban America: the self-made capitalist, the European-bred socialist, the aristocrat, the laborer. Confirmed here also was Higginson's belief in the essential goodness of man and in the eventual power of the ballot box to correct social evils. Soon after reading the book, he wrote Howells: "If I could write fiction as you do, I would leave criticisms to those who cannot create."

Higginson's response to *A Hazard of New Fortunes* marked the height of rapport between the two men. Howells' increasing commitment, by the late eighties, to realistic fiction and to criticism of American society began to trouble Higginson. Even their mutual devotion to Turgenev became a source of difference. Higginson, who had met Turgenev at a Paris meeting of the International Literary Congress in 1878 and described him as uniting the "fine benignant head of Longfel-

low with the figure of Thackeray," denied that the Russian was a truly realistic writer. Although at first praising *Virgin Soil* (a reformist novel that advocated gradual change, not revolution) as second only to *War and Peace,* he ultimately decided that Turgenev's greatness was best illustrated by *Poems in Prose,* where allegory and aphorism abound. To Howells, however, Turgenev was a model realist devoted to portraying the common life without romantic plot and melodrama. And in Howells' essays, *Criticism and Fiction,* the line that separated him from Higginson was visible when he criticized those "pastured on the literature of thirty or forty years ago . . . [who] preach their favorite authors as all the law and prophets." Higginson, in response, called Howells a narrow critic: "It is not necessary, because one prefers apples, to condemn oranges."

By comparing Howells to George Eliot, Higginson marked his position between the realists and their enemies. Eliot, unlike Howells, does not banish "the ideal side of life. . . . She only asserts the so-called little things of life to be equal in importance to the great, and does not claim for them a superior, much less an exclusive importance; . . . [she] does not deride the other half of art, and banish Raphael and Shakespeare to the domain of Jack the Giant-killer."

Higginson also disagreed with some of Howells' social views. He did not support the anarchists convicted after the Haymarket riot and criticized Howells for doing so. He rejected the indictment of American society in *Traveler from Altruria:* to characterize America as a plutocracy ignored, in Higginson's view, the high degree of social democracy prevailing in America in the nineties. Howells, he concluded, had become sad and morbid, and blinded to the noble and beautiful in life. Having lost sight of the basic theme of democratic literature—the dignity and inalienable value of the individual man—Howells had found in "altruism an entanglement as ineffectual as that met by Mr. James in introspection." Such social criticism further displayed by pessimistic determinists like Theodore Dreiser and Ellen Glasgow had brought American literature, Higginson complained, to a point where even Hawthorne's masterpieces were forgotten.

Far worse, however, were the cynical writers who embraced the *fin de siècle* spirit and autocratically emphasized the stupidities of democratic government. "Better a thousand times to train a boy on Scott's novels or the Border ballads," argued Higginson, "than educate him, on the one side, that chivalry was a cheat and the troubadours imbeciles, and on the other hand, that universal suffrage is an absurdity and the real need is to get rid of our voters."

Insisting that a writer should be interested in more than the development of his own petty talent, he endeavored to separate himself from the reigning genteel writers and critics who sought to avoid major postwar social problems. In the tradition of his generation of Transcendentalists he still looked to experience as the microcosm of truth. Neither his allegiance to the ideal side of life nor to Scott's novels kept him from giving the highest praise to the "war photography" found in both *War and Peace* and *The Red Badge of Courage.* He fully appreciated Stephen Crane's ability to present "the real tumult and tatters of the thing itself." And he understood a part of Tolstoy's greatness when he wrote that *War and Peace* "reveals both the brilliancy of war and its tediousness and dreariness—its waste, aimlessness, and disconnection."

But while he agreed with Howells by esteeming Crane and

Tolstoy, Higginson remained a critic of America's realist and naturalist writers. They failed, in his opinion, to touch the essence of the American spirit by forsaking the optimism and faith in the individual; they failed to utilize, therefore, the basic reality of American society. At first he was hopeful that the triumph of the abolitionist crusade had returned the alienated intellectual to the center of American life, as a respected spokesman for society's problems and their solutions. Higginson came to fear, however, the result of fleeing democracy like Henry Adams and Henry James, disdaining it like Thomas Bailey Aldrich, or harshly criticizing it like either Howells or the naturalists. Such behavor, he believed, once again deprived America of intellectual leadership and alienated the intellectual. Higginson always rejected the idea that intellectual alienation might be, to a large degree, a permanent and even necessary thing.

Higginson so often reflected prevailing literary and social views that posterity has relegated him to anonymity and failed to recognize the degree of uniqueness that was his. His literary criticism, despite severe limitations, deserves attention because of his role in publishing Emily Dickinson and in praising Sidney Lanier's poetry, Thoreau's essays, and the work of Crane and Howells. His acute criticism of the day's most popular writers—Aldrich, Taylor, Stoddard, and Kipling—reveals a man who eludes the category of literary Brahmin. (pp. 345-67)

> *Tilden G. Edelstein, in his* Strange Enthusiasm: A Life of Thomas Wentworth Higginson, *Yale University Press, 1968, 425 p.*

JAMES W. TUTTLETON   (essay date 1978)

[*Tuttleton is an American critic and educator. In the following excerpt, he assesses Higginson's writings and his place in American letters.*]

As a writer Higginson is perhaps most memorable for his brief sketches of important contemporaries like Emerson, Thoreau, Lowell, Margaret Fuller, Wendell Phillips, Garrison, Bronson Alcott, Holmes, and Whittier. Taken singly, these charming personal reminiscences may seem negligible. But taken together, they create a vivid picture of the Concord-Cambridge milieu in the great age of the Transcendental Newness and the revolutionary abolition movement. Shaped by the major literary and political currents of his time, Higginson made his portraits come to life for us as almost no other writer of the time was able to do. Though Higginson lacked a deep analytic mind, Howard W. Hintz has rightly remarked [in his 1937 dissertation "Thomas Wentworth Higginson: Disciple of the 'Newness' "] that "with his natural love of people, his wide capacity for rich and varied friendships, his propensity for anecdote, and his remarkably retentive memory, he was to the manner born in the realm of intimate biography, reminiscence, and autobiography." Something of a Boswellian figure reflected in the glory of his subjects, Higginson outlived them all, and achieved a lesser greatness thanks to the lucidity and charm of a richly varied style that made him extraordinarily popular throughout the country.

Higginson's moral fervor and adherence to the "rules" has inevitably led him to be grouped with Thomas Bailey Aldrich, E. C. Stedman, and Hamilton Wright Mabie as an exemplar of the Genteel Tradition in criticism. To a great extent this classification is accurate, for Higginson always affirmed good taste—the taste of ladies and gentlemen—in the writer's choice of subject and in his execution. He held high standards of style, based on the classics, and deplored wayward genius defiant of form. Yet his fiery abolitionism, his radical views on social democracy, and his labor in behalf of woman's suffrage—together with his sometimes perplexed appreciation of writers as diverse as Dickinson, Crane, Howells, and Wharton—suggest that it would be a serious mistake to identify him too closely with those genteel-era contemporaries.

As a poet, Higginson's talent was negligible, though his Romantic verses reveal a competent craftsman skilled enough in mere technique, but lacking a creative imagination. Nevertheless, he rendered a useful service to the poetic criticism of his time in exploring—intelligently, on the whole—the merits of Emerson and Thoreau, Holmes and Lowell, and Helen Hunt Jackson and Sidney Lanier. His moral and aesthetic biases blinded him to some of the unorthodox achievements of Poe, Whitman, and Dickinson. Yet he was candid enough to acknowledge, uneasily, the force of their poetry. As a novelist and sporadic short-story writer, Higginson was comparably limited—*Malbone, The Monarch of Dreams,* and other tales being clearly works of a minor order. His models—Hawthorne and Austen—were suitable, but they failed to unify in his imagination, so that he excelled neither as a novelist nor as a romancer. Of the fiction he produced, only *The Monarch of Dreams* still interests—largely, though, as a revelation of deep unconscious impulses fascinatingly deployed as dream symbols of inner conflict. Recognizing the thinness of his narrative achievement, he wisely abandoned fiction.

At his best, Higginson's essays on Nature approach Thoreau's in appreciation, though not in intellectual power, and lead directly to the work of John Muir and John Burroughs. While nature studies like his **"Water Lilies," "The Life of Birds," "Snow,"** and **"April Days"** do not yield much in the way of knowledge, they reveal an attentive witness to the ways of the winds and tides, the bluejays and butterflies, the thistles and wood-anemones. Celebrations of the natural order, these essays richly record Higginson's sense of the "lessons of faith and beauty" communicated by external nature, the veil of the noumenal Spirit, or what Goethe had called "the living garment of God." So winsome are his meditations on the flora and fauna of the Cambridge and Newport environs that Hintz has even called his nature studies "comparable with the best American writing that has been done in this form." And Fred L. Pattee, in *History of American Literature Since 1870,* has praised him for avoiding "the overliterary element on the one hand and the over-scientific on the other," with the effect that he became "the first of what may be called the modern school of nature writers."

As a biographer and historian, Higginson excelled only in occasional moments, chiefly when dealing with artists whom he had personally known or with events in which he had directly participated. None of the biographies is definitive—although the studies of Longfellow and Margaret Fuller stood up for a number of years. Superseded now in every way, they are still works of sustained (though superficial) narrative portraiture, enlivened by personal reminiscence and anecdote. The less than original scholarship they reveal also characterizes his historical prose, which was useful in its own time but has also been totally superseded. As Romantic history, done better by Bancroft and Parkman, Higginson's historical prose yet made up a tributary in the mighty stream of patriotic chronicle that shaped the nineteenth-century sense of America's "manifest destiny." Lucidly written, lively, and informative, they served especially well the young people of their day, but have not survived in that great tribunal to which he always appealed—the public mind. Similarly, his social criticism—diversified and finally superficial—remains interesting only for the student of American radical thought. Most effective when the issues were apparently black and white, when an Absolute Principle could be invoked, his argumentative prose has faded with the causes later won. Yet his account of the attempted rescue of the slave Anthony Burns, of his ride through Kansas during the border wars, of his command of black troops during the Civil War, and of his feminist and temperance campaigns are told in a stirring prose charged with high moral fervor. Later, after the Civil War, he was, like most observers, baffled by the complexities of our newly developing industrial order, by economic issues like free trade and imperialism. Yet he always retained a genuine liberal spirit, and espoused social democracy and a respect for the people, as against the oligarchies of entrenched wealth and power.

We must finally rank Wentworth Higginson as a writer and critic of the second order. But as an individual, as a man of his time, he was remarkable. A man of high moral principle, a gentleman, a man without meanness or rancor, high-minded, devoted to literature and culture in the Arnoldian sense of the best that had been thought and said, a defender of human dignity and of the respect due the individual—whatever his or her race, creed, sex, politics, or national origin—committed to action in behalf of social democracy, preeminently a man of character and personal integrity, of deep compassion and wide sympathies—Wentworth Higginson is a memorable example of what an American man of letters in the nineteenth century could be.

For the reader who is drawn to him, there is no more revealing introduction to the man and writer than his attractive autobiography *Cheerful Yesterdays* (1898). Composed in his seventies, this retrospective of his whole life from the early Cambridge days forward is admirably free of the egotism common in autobiographies. For although Higginson was a man of great prominence in his time, he had the humility to acknowledge "his own extreme unimportance." He was moved to record his times and his own life, but only for whatever benefit they might have to posterity: "When I think of the vast changes which every man of my time has seen, and of the men and women whom I have known,—those who created American literature and who freed millions of slaves,—men and women whom, as the worldly-wise Lord Houghton once wrote me, 'Europe has learned to honour, and would do well to imitate,' then I feel, that whether I will or no, something worth chronicling may be included in the proposed chapters."

Cheerful Yesterdays preserves a fine balance between Higginson's private life and the public history of his time from the 1840s through the 1890s. His account of the Transcendental period, the abolitionist movement, the Civil War, and the literary life of the 1870s cannot of course be taken in isolation from other accounts of these events, for a necessary element of impressionism pervades the work. Nevertheless, in terms of what he observed, his responses are generally faithful to the actualities of his time. Moreover, as a record of his private life, *Cheerful Yesterdays* is informed with that sweetness of temper and undefinable charisma that made him always at-

tractive to his contemporaries. And it is a rich treasury of interpretive personal history, reminiscence, and anecdote. Howard Mumford Jones has even called it a "masterpiece," remarking that "such is the conventional-mindedness of literary historians, they do not recognize the autobiography as an art form. Nevertheless, American letters have produced a great number of these admirable memoirs, and the long golden afternoon of New England gave us a whole library of them, of which Higginson's is one of the most charming" [see excerpt dated 1960].

As he ended the work, Higginson felt that many of the "most important" spiritual events of his life had gone unrecorded. Nevertheless, though his career belonged to his own time, he rightly believed that the record of it would be "chiefly valuable for the light it throws on the period and the place." As a reformer, he lived long enough to see many of his ideals realized in the social transformation of the nation. Nevertheless, he felt that much yet remained to be done, and he expressed the wish, toward the close of his life, that he would "live to see international arbitration secured, civil service reform completed, free trade established; to find the legal and educational rights of the two sexes equalized; to know that all cities are as honestly governed as that in which I dwell; to see natural monopolies owned by the public, not in private hands; to see drunkenness extirpated; to live under absolute as well as nominal religious freedom; to perceive American literature to be thoroughly emancipated from the habit of colonial deference which still hampers it." He hoped, and indeed believed it possible, that "after the progress already made on the whole in these several directions, some future generation may see the fulfillment of what remains." His final words—they constitute the motto of his life—were those of the French iconoclast Proudhon: "Let my memory perish, if only humanity may be free." (pp. 148-52)

James W. Tuttleton, in his Thomas Wentworth Higginson, *Twayne Publishers, 1978, 172 p.*

FURTHER READING

Barbot, Mary Elizabeth. "Emily Dickinson Parallels." *New England Quarterly Review* 14, No. 4 (December 1941): 689-96.
> Examines Higginson's literary influence on Emily Dickinson, comparing passages from *Malbone* and *Outdoor Papers* with some of her poems.

Brooks, Van Wyck. "The Twilight of New England." In his *Sketches in Criticism,* pp. 211-17. New York: E. P. Dutton & Co., 1932.
> Describes "New England decadence" of the late nineteenth century, maintaining that the "*Letters and Journals* of Colonel Thomas Wentworth Higginson do not explain the decline of New England, but they certainly reflect it."

Duclos, Gloria Shaw. "Thomas Wentworth Higginson's Sappho." *New England Quarterly Review* 57, No. 3 (September 1984): 403-11.
> Explores ways in which Higginson's views regarding women influenced his interpretation of Sappho's life and works.

Edelstein, Tilden G. "Emily Dickinson and Her Mentor in Feminist Perspective." In *Nineteenth-Century Women Writers of the English-Speaking World,* edited by Rhoda B. Nathan, pp. 37-43. New York: Greenwood Press, 1986.

Surveys scholarship of the Higginson-Dickinson relationship and attempts to understand why Dickinson initiated it. Defending Higginson, Edelstein notes that "all those twentieth-century Dickinson literary critics and scholars who have decried her choice of Higginson have been unable to suggest a nineteenth-century person who would have been a realistic substitute."

McCormick, Edgar L. "Thoreau and Higginson." *Emerson Society Quarterly,* No. 3 (Second Quarter 1963): 75-8.
Discusses Higginson's criticism of Thoreau, asserting that "no one was more prompt in recognizing Thoreau's genius."

————. "Thomas Wentworth Higginson, Poetry Critic for the *Nation,* 1877-1903." *Serif* 2, No. 3 (September 1965): 15-20.
Analyzes Higginson's strengths and weaknesses as a poetry critic.

Meyer, Howard N. "Thomas Wentworth Higginson." In *The Transcendentalists: A Review of Research and Criticism,* edited by Joel Myerson, pp. 195-203. New York: The Modern Language Association of America, 1984.
Bibliographic essay surveying biographical and critical studies of Higginson. Meyer also provides a summary of Higginson's publication history and information on the locations of his manuscripts.

Morse, Jonathan. "Emily Dickinson and the Spasmodic School: A Note on Thomas Wentworth Higginson's Aesthetics." *New England Quarterly Review* 50, No. 3 (September 1977): 505-09.
Suggests that an examination of the origin and meaning of the term "spasmodic" as related to literature and the reasons Higginson applied it to Dickinson's verse would contribute to a better understanding of the Higginson-Dickinson relationship.

Perry, Bliss. "The Colonel's Quality." In his *The Praise of Folly and Other Papers,* pp. 73-80. 1923. Reprint. Port Washington, N.Y.: Kennikat Press, 1964.
Overview of Higginson's accomplishments as a writer and reformer.

Ward, Theodora V. W. "Emily Dickinson and Thomas Wentworth Higginson." *Boston Public Library Quarterly* 5, No. 1 (January 1953): 3-18.
Describes the development of the personal and literary relationship between Higginson and Dickinson.

Wells, Anna Mary. "The Soul's Society: Emily Dickinson and Colonel Higginson." In *Nineteenth-Century Women Writers of the English-Speaking World,* edited by Rhoda B. Nathan, pp. 221-29. New York: Greenwood Press, 1986.
Traces the development of the Higginson-Dickinson relationship through a detailed examination of the extant correspondence, asserting that "the role of [Higginson] in his relations with Emily Dickinson has been consistently misrepresented and he himself maligned."

Peter Kropotkin

1842-1921

(Born Prince Pyotr Alekseyevich Kropotkin) Russian social philosopher, critic, historian, and geographer.

Kropotkin was the leading exponent of anarchist communism in the late nineteenth and early twentieth centuries. Although his ideas did not differ significantly from those of Pierre-Joseph Proudhon (1809-1865) and Mikhail Bakunin (1814-1876), the founding figures of modern anarchist ideology, Kropotkin is credited with offering a more clear and logical exposition of his predecessors' theories of social organization and political reform. In his best known book, *Mutual Aid: A Factor of Evolution,* he attempted to provide scientific support for the theory that individuals and societies can function in an orderly manner without the control of a government by demonstrating that cooperation is natural within more complex species.

Kropotkin was born in Moscow into an aristocratic family whose lineage, like that of the czar, could be traced to Rurik, a ninth-century warrior credited with founding the Russian empire. Kropotkin's father, a landowner and general in the Russian army, governed his serfs with severity and was an overbearing husband and parent. Kropotkin's mother died when he was three, leaving him in the care of nurses and tutors. At fifteen he entered the Corps of Pages, a school connected with the imperial household, and in 1861 was nominated Sergeant of the Corps, a position which included duties as personal attendant to the czar. The following year, Kropotkin left what could have been a successful court career to serve as an administrator and geologist with the Amur Cossacks in Siberia. In the course of his explorations of the area, he made significant discoveries concerning the structure of mountains in Asia and also developed his theory of mutual aid from observations of animal life in the region. His interest in anarchism began during the 1866 revolt of Polish prisoners in Siberia, after which he left the military, disillusioned with the state's unrealized promises of reform. After studying the natural sciences at the university in St. Petersburg for several years, he investigated glacial deposits in Sweden and Finland for the Russian Geographical Society. On a visit to Switzerland in 1872, he formed a lasting association with the Jura Federation, an organization with anarchist leanings, and returned to Russia to participate in the Chaikovsky Circle, an underground populist movement.

In 1874, Kropotkin was arrested for political agitation and imprisoned in the Peter and Paul fortress, escaping two years later with the help of friends. He settled in Switzerland and founded the revolutionary paper *Le révolté.* After leaving Switzerland in 1881, Kropotkin continued his political activities in France, where he was arrested in Lyons and imprisoned in Clairvaux for his participation in a workers' strike. He served three years of a five-year sentence before efforts on his behalf by geographers and political activists led to his release. Settling in England, Kropotkin began *Freedom,* an anarchist monthly in which he published many of his articles on social and political reform. His reputation as a scientist and social philosopher firmly established by his numerous works and lectures, Kropotkin was looked to as a leader by

anarchist groups throughout Europe. Returning to Russia in 1917 after the revolution, he would not accept a post in the communist government and soon became outspoken in his disapproval of V. I. Lenin's political tactics, which included centralization of authority and the taking of hostages. Under pressure from the government he retired to the small town of Dmitrov, where he worked on his final book, *Etika (Ethics: Origin and Development),* and continued to protest Lenin's dictatorship. Kropotkin died in 1921.

Kropotkin followed closely the anarchist theories of Proudhon and Bakunin, who advocated a social organization of communes that would function through custom and consensus of their individual members without any government. Like Karl Marx, he believed that the workers and peasants would revolt and instinctively establish a socialist system. However, Kropotkin disagreed with Marx's plan for centralized authority, believing that a network of voluntary federations of people with similar skills or interests would avoid the injustices and corruption of power which inevitably accompany hierarchy. He included democracy in this criticism, contending that majority rule was a rule of mediocrity.

Cooperation rather than individualism plays a central role in Kropotkin's anarchist philosophy, providing the framework for social and economic interaction. He believed that workers would naturally band together in order to achieve their common goals, whether these were the manufacture of furniture or the discovery of scientific principles. This faith in humanity's ability to cooperate contradicted the prevailing belief in social Darwinism, which contends that competition within a species eliminates the weaker individuals, naturally selecting those most suited to survive and propagate the species. Thus, competition rather than cooperation would be a normal and desirable process. Kropotkin presented evidence which refuted this theory, demonstrating that in many of the more complex species mutual aid was the norm, making it possible, for instance, for smaller animals to band together to hunt or protect themselves from larger animals. Kropotkin did not dispute Charles Darwin's theory of natural selection; he only emphasized that species compete mainly against other species and natural forces rather than within their own group, an assertion Darwin himself had made. Kropotkin connected his observations of animals with evidence of mutual aid in human history, such as the lack of government in hunting and gathering societies and the cooperative organization of medieval guilds.

Kropotkin devoted much of his writing to such social problems as poverty and crime, which he believed were associated with government. In *Fields, Factories and Workshops,* he criticized England's dependence on other countries for food and raw materials, claiming that importing these products allowed increased manufacturing, a situation that benefited only a fraction of the population. He outlined a plan for self-sufficiency, providing evidence that England could itself produce enough food for its population, accurately predicting the high-yield agriculture that has been developed in the twentieth century. His strategy for integrating farming and manufacture would restructure jobs to allow everyone a more satisfying and productive mixture of manual and intellectual labor. He also wrote on the counter-productivity of prisons, which, he maintained, break the will of prisoners and more firmly entrench them in crime. He believed that social pressure and a natural desire to be part of a community would keep most people from committing crimes and ostracization would suffice to either rehabilitate or eliminate criminals from society.

Critics have praised Kropotkin for his lucid prose and logical explanations of anarchism. While he has been accused of ignoring facts that contradicted his beliefs, his use of scientific data to support his philosophical theories was a notable innovation in the history of the social sciences and his leadership in anarchist movements in the twentieth century has established him as a major figure in modern social and political philosophy.

(See also *Contemporary Authors,* Vol. 119.)

PRINCIPAL WORKS

Paroles d'un révolté (essays) 1885
In Russian and French Prisons (essays) 1887
La conquête du pain (treatise) 1892
    [*The Conquest of Bread,* 1906]
Fields, Factories and Workshops (treatise) 1899
Memoirs of a Revolutionist (memoirs) 1899
Sovremennaya nauka i anarkhizm (treatise) 1901
    [*Modern Science and Anarchism,* 1903]
Mutual Aid: A Factor of Evolution (treatise) 1902

Russian Literature (criticism) 1905; also published as
    Ideals and Realities in Russian Literature, 1915
Grande Révolution (history) 1909
    [*The Great French Revolution: 1789-1793,* 1909]
The Terror in Russia (nonfiction) 1909
Etika (philosophy) 1922
    [*Ethics: Origin and Development,* 1924]

EUGENE LIMEDORFER (essay date 1900)

[*In the following excerpt, Limedorfer praises Kropotkin's* Memoirs of a Revolutionist *for its depiction of Russian life and European social movements and its reflection of Kropotkin's character.*]

Any mention of the name of Kropotkin will bring forth the expression of various and diverse opinions about the man who gave up rank, wealth, position, luxury, and an extremely promising scientific career, renounced his title of Prince, and went forth as plain P. Kropotkin to cast in his lot with the poor, down-trodden, and oppressed. To the Russian Government his name is synonymous with Tsar-murderer; the English shopkeeper sees visions of the red flag, streams of blood, and a carnival of loot following in the trail of the foremost Anarchist in Europe. Some of those who know him well say that he spends his life with no thought for aught else except the verification of his scientific theories; others maintain that Kropotkin is a poet who weaves for himself the most fantastic and beautiful dreams, and mistakes his fancies for realities; there are some who depict him as a sort of wild beast bent solely upon the destruction of all that is held sacred by the vast majority of mankind. Georg Brandes tells us that Kropotkin is more peaceful than Tolstoy himself, and those who know him best love to speak of him as the personification of altruism.

Memoirs of a Revolutionist, the autobiography of Prince Peter Alexeivitch Kropotkin, does not enable us to decide absolutely which of these contradictory opinions is the correct one. We learn very little about the personality of the author from himself. He keeps himself completely in the background, and his presence is rather felt than seen. He seems to be anxious not to say anything about himself, lest the reader should become influenced by his words; he prefers to let actions speak for him, and allows the reader to put his own interpretation upon them, and to construct the author's character according to his own predilection. Once only does Kropotkin give us a real glimpse into his own self. This occurs when he relates the circumstances under which he decided to devote his life to the spreading of knowledge among the masses.

This happened when Kropotkin was thirty years of age, and this decision marks the most important point of his life. His early childhood, interesting as it was; his life in the cadet corps, at the court, as an explorer and geographer, had a marked influence upon his career; but it was not until he had become a teacher of the masses that Kropotkin's life became important. The horrors of serfdom, the rigor of military life, the corruption of official Russia, the hollowness of high society life,—they all make their impressions upon his mind, but he became a revolutionist, a real force in the social movement after he had made his acquaintance with a new world—the life of the working-classes—and after he had found that "he learns from those whom he intends to teach." And so it comes that those parts of the book where he describes the struggle for liberty, where he depicts the enthusiasm of those remarkable men and women who abandoned everything and went out among the artisans and the peasants to educate them, are the most valuable contributions to the study of intellectual progress in Russia. He brings before our mental vision a grand panorama of the great struggle for the principles of human liberty, and in his masterful exposition of the psychology of the Russian reformer we find the explanation of that remarkable devotion to principles, the exalted courage, and utter self-abnegation which is so remarkable a characteristic of the Russian revolutionist.

Kropotkin has condensed, in a truly wonderful way, in a limited space perfect portraits of all the actors in the social movements of Russia, France, England, and Switzerland, beginning in the early sixties and coming down practically to the present day. He gives us an excellent sketch of all those who opposed the spreading of the new thought, and he has drawn such a clear and concise picture of the conditions and circumstances which produced this movement, that we can fully comprehend why and how all the various phases of this struggle originated. The beginnings and development of Russian nihilism, the birth of socialism and anarchism, their propagation and growth, are given in such a masterly way that if the book should contain nothing else but the chapters dealing with them, it would deserve to be ranked with the best textbooks on sociology.

Seldom has there been issued a book which is so full of human interest and which contains so many elements that go to make up an eventful life as is the case with Kropotkin's *Memoirs.* What can be more idyllic than the description of his childhood in Moscow, the picture of his mother, sister, teachers, the old servants, his love for his brother, and the wonderful portraitures of patriarchal life? No one can be callous enough not to perceive the delightful atmosphere that greets him in those pages; a step further and we are touched by the pathetic tales of sufferings on the part of the serfs, we find the harshness and the rigor, often amounting to cruelty, of his father, who tyrannizes his wife, his children, and his serfs. Then we see young Kropotkin recognize the fact that his idols have feet of clay, he notices the vacillations of those in power, he watches their machinations propped up by lies, he sees the Tsar becoming a mere tool in the hands of unscrupulous schemers, and we see compassion and loathing, love and hatred, successively take hold of him. From the brilliant court we follow the author into his prison, we see him a favorite with the emperor and grand dukes; we behold him moving in the highest society circles, then he discards his fine linen and costly dress, dons a sheepskin cloak, and rushes off to mix with the artisans in St. Petersburg. We find the contrast between evenings spent in the luxurious Winter Palace and the weeks and months of life in poverty that were his share in Switzerland; we behold him preaching revolution to the workingmen in France, we follow him to London where he lives an underpaid writer, we are amused at the clumsiness and lack of imagination of the spies that follow him constantly, and we recognize that more than once he was in danger of being killed or kidnapped by men in the pay of the Russian Government. And as for romance—his escape from the fortress of St. Peter and St. Paul will satisfy the wildest imagination, the preparations for his escape and the boldness of the execution of the plan keep one in breathless suspense.

Whether Kropotkin's philosophy of life is correct or not, and be his economic and social theories sound or false, one thing must be admitted by all. Georg Brandes sums it up very happily by saying: "In character he stands comparison with any of the fighters for freedom of any country. None have been more disinterested than he, none have loved mankind more than he does." (pp. 446-48)

Eugene Limedorfer, "Prince and Socialist," in The Critic, *New York, Vol. XXXVI, No. 5, May, 1900, pp. 446-48.*

THE TIMES LITERARY SUPPLEMENT (essay date 1907)

[*In a review of* The Conquest of Bread, *the critic expresses skepticism about the possibility of a successful anarchist revolution as described by Kropotkin.*]

The Conquest of Bread, by Prince Kropotkin, is not very happily named. No one would guess from this enigmatic title that the book is an extremely interesting exposition of the gospel of anarchy. To many, probably to most, people anarchy is a word of fear or disgust; they associate it with murderous and generally cowardly desperadoes, who are the sworn and stealthy enemies of the rest of mankind. To the police, who have a good deal to do with anarchists, it is a word of contempt; they associate it with a peculiarly mean and base type of criminal, whom they do not fear in the least. But there is another view of anarchy, which is much less generally understood. The anarchists of the newspaper and the novel, who occasionally murder a Sovereign or a President, but more often kill a number of innocent bystanders, are either weak-minded fanatics or common criminals who have picked up a theory spun by more ingenious brains than their own and use it as a justification of their criminal acts. The real anarchists never do anything of the kind, or, indeed, anything at all, except talk and write; they theorize and lead blameless or harmless lives, at least in act. Anarchy, in this sense, is a political or economic theory or creed, often confused with Socialism. The mistake is natural enough, because both aim at the regeneration of mankind by destroying what their advocates call the existing "system," by which they mean most of the social customs and arrangements adopted by civilized peoples. But in regard to the customs and arrangements they would substitute they are fundamentally opposed. Anarchy rests all its hopes on individual freedom; it would abolish all government, and rely on free agreement. Collective Socialism, on the other hand, is the very negation of freedom; it would suppress the individual, and rely upon absolute control by "the State."

Now these doctrines, speciously but confusedly advocated, vaguely and confusedly comprehended, are being widely disseminated and accepted in a sort of way. It is desirable that they should be better understood, and anything which contributes to that end is welcome. Prince Kropotkin's plea for Anarchy is, therefore, very opportune. It is not an attack on Socialism, but by emphasizing the principle of freedom it necessarily comes into conflict with the socialistic principle and shows how irreconcilable the two are. As soon as any attempt is made to realize constructively the working out of anarchist and socialist theories they become mutually destructive; and that is brought out clearly in this book. The author believes that the "social revolution" is immediately at hand and will very soon be upon us; and he traces its working out on anarchical lines. The present organizations will dissolve into communistic societies, in which every one will take his place freely and voluntarily. There will be no need of government or coercion; the capitalist will disappear and along with him the State, which is the out-of-the-frying-pan-into-the-fire substitute worshipped by collectivists.

How all this will be accomplished Prince Kropotkin tells us in very clear language and with a transparent simplicity, gentleness, and sweet belief in human nature which disarm criticism and silence argument. The process is mainly one of "springing up" and "shaking down." "Groups of volunteers" will "spring up" to do this, that, and the other; homes will spring up, large public kitchens will spring up, self-devotion will spring up, thousands of societies will spring up "to gratify every taste and every possible fancy." There would be some confusion at first, but "people would shake down amicably." It is a charming picture. The ultimate goal is "wealth and ease for all," which is of course the goal of every kind of Socialism, and (we may observe incidentally) the most dumbfoundering feature of the whole comedy of unreason, since the evil conduct of those who possess wealth and ease and the heroism of those who do not are precisely the grounds on which the entire agitation is based. But Prince Kropotkin is quite right in maintaining that his is the only way in which the millennium can be ushered in. When everybody is ready to behave as he believes everybody will, then we shall have no need of government and shall enter forthwith upon the millennium. It cannot be worked by any boards or committees, and least of all by any elected body; such devices would merely perpetuate the old order under a slightly different name and produce the same results. Unless the great revolution is accompanied by complete communization the people will help themselves, and then order must be restored in the usual way to give collectivism a chance. Then, as Prince Kropotkin shrewdly observes, "if 'order is restored,' the Social Democrats will hang the Anarchists; the Fabians will hang the Social Democrats, and will in their turn be hanged by the reactionaries, and the revolution will come to an end." In short, being men and women, we shall behave as such; and since the existing "system" is the creation of men and women and of nobody else, we shall promptly recreate it. When we are angels we shall behave differently.

"The Gentle Anarchist," in The Times Literary Supplement, *No. 268, March 1, 1907, p. 71.*

LOUISE H. WILLIAMS   (essay date 1921)

[*In the following excerpt, Williams examines Kropotkin's philosophy of social change and self-government in his* Mutual Aid: A Factor of Evolution *and* The Great French Revolution: 1789-1793.]

Kropotkin is many-sided. He is naturalist, scientist, historian, economist, anarchist (self-styled); but always, and most profoundly, he is philosopher.

Now, philosophy is not, as the average Englishman is too much inclined to think, a kind of intellectual game practised by a remote and leisured few. True, it demands some exercise of thought—an occupation he is averse to. But there are innumerable degrees in the evolution of philosophy, and, though it asks of its high priests widest knowledge, of the acolyte it asks only intelligence and veracity. Philosophy of some type is as necessary to the labourer as to the professor. It is no abstruse thing; it means neither more nor less than assessment of circumstances and the adoption of a deliberate attitude to-

wards them. In *Mutual Aid: A Factor of Evolution,* his most famous work, Kropotkin deals throughout with practical philosophy. There is not an ounce of metaphysics in the book. But one plain theory is announced: that Mutual Aid, as practised during the evolution of species, was *at least* as powerful a factor in efficient survival as Mutual Competition and the survival of the strongest; the bulk of the book is taken up with proofs. Now, the value of Kropotkin's proofs is that they are not taken from his own observations alone, but from facts coming under the notice of men who set out to look for something else and found and recorded these by the way.

We are all of us prejudiced in favour of, or against, particular views of life, but the more we correct our bias by considering the views of other truthful people the better for our ultimate statements. Opposing facts may be true; we must assess the relative proportions of truth.

Froude once said of history: "It often seems to me as if history was like a child's box of letters, with which we can spell any word we please. *We have only to pick out such letters as we want, arrange them as we like, and say nothing about those which do not suit our purpose.*" That, unfortunately, is the standpoint of many gifted writers and of nine-tenths of contemporary journalism. It is not the standpoint of Kropotkin in either *Mutual Aid* or *The Great French Revolution: 1789-1793.* He admits his bias—the salt of every earnest man—but presents also the other side; and indeed, the "other side" has had the world its own way for so long it needs no introduction.

When we are confronted with what appears to us a new idea or theory, we can do no more than submit it to the judgment of our experience;—*our* experience, mark you, not that which is traditional. When the notion of Mutual Aid as a prime factor in evolution dawned on Kropotkin it was set over against the idea of Mutual Competition. Both facts were true in Nature; what mattered tremendously was, which was the most proportionately true. From his varied experience—as traveller and prisoner, aristocrat and outcast; as a student of Nature and of ancient history; from association with men of all ranks and of all countries—Kropotkin drew confirmation of his theory sufficient to warrant him in presenting it to the world as of immense importance to the development of civilization.

The whole tendency of thought in recent centuries was against it. The whole structure, political, social, and economic, of Europe was against it. Men who were indifferent to Darwin subscribed whole-heartedly to the Mutual Competition theory under political pseudonyms such as a limited *laissez-faire.*

With the few who were already in a position of vantage it worked excellently; for in the hands of men Competition became a much more murderous weapon than it was as practised by animals. Accepting it in its original sense, it postulated that animals competed to the death for the means of subsistence *when the need was pressing and within the period of scarcity.* Man went further and mortgaged the future. By means of every dodge that his ingenuity could devise, he secured not only what the individual gained during his lifetime, but all profit that might accrue to it, to his successors of legal or lineal descent. Further, he eliminated the factor of continual individual struggle, as it existed amongst animals, and produced abundance of what exists but slightly in Nature, a "parasite" class. As a natural corollary he was impelled to maintain a reserve of available labour that, in all but name, was in a state of slavery—witness industrial history.

Not all men, of course, dwelt quite comfortably under this *régime;* hence the rise of the various philanthropic ameliorative societies. But, as Kropotkin saw, their existence only emphasises the fact that a competitive industrial order depends for its standing-ground on a basis of hunger-driven humanity.

In periods of general prosperity even the poor prosper comparatively and do not assert their condition in the public eye. But in times of world-scarcity, such as the present, the abomination of the social structure is nakedly revealed—to those who cannot turn away. Competition to the death is to be seen in all its degrees at work between nations, classes, even individuals. We shall never have a better opportunity of studying the principle, from causes to results. Even those who deliberately brought it to a crisis are, in spite of themselves, afraid.

Is it not wise, before worse befall us, to try the alternative, the equally true, principle, Mutual Aid?

Combination is the essence of Mutual Aid. The very men who decry its existence in Nature pay unwitting tribute not only to its existence, but to its efficacy, by striving by every means within their power to prevent combination amongst those whom they desire to hold subject. In all countries where, no matter what the government be nominally, real control is in the hands of financiers and merchants, the "Haves" scheme to prevent combination on the part of the "Have-nots." Why? Because combination begets power.

But one perceives in history that it is not so much the very rich as the little rich who are most anxious to maintain a "mere subsistence" class. They themselves have acquired property recently; they know by experience what it means to be without it, and, believing that there will not be enough to go round, they fight the more jealously to retain intact what they have just grasped. The small trader is by circumstances an intransigent.

Kropotkin, in his *Great French Revolution,* shows this convincingly. The "Third Estate" schemed to stir up and use "the people" to pluck *their* power from the flames; but when they saw that these ragged and starving hordes were actually capable of organising themselves, thereby enforcing *their* demands, they became frightened, and promptly tried to break up and disintegrate their unity.

> For in the Paris insurrection leading to July 14, as all through the Revolution, there were two separate currents of different origin: the political movement of the middle classes and the popular movement of the masses. At certain moments during the great days of the Revolution the two movements joined hands in a temporary alliance, and then they gained their great victories over the old *régime.* But the middle classes always distrusted their temporary ally, the people, and gave clear proof of this in July 1789. The alliance was concluded unwillingly by the middle classes; and on the morrow of the 14th, and even during the insurrection itself, they made haste to organise themselves, in order that they might be able to bridle the revolted people.

And again:—

> While the revolutionaries exulted, believing that the Revolution was almost accomplished, the reactionaries knew that the great struggle, the real one, between the past and the future, was only to begin. . . . The reactionaries understood something more. They saw that the middle classes, who until then had sought the support of the people, in order to obtain constitutional laws and to dominate the higher nobility, were going, now that they had seen and felt the strength of the people, to do all they could to dominate the people, to disarm them and to drive them back into subjection.

Returning to *Mutual Aid,* Kropotkin shows that the periods of greatest happiness amongst the greatest number were always those when certain stable productive conditions were brought about by "popular" as opposed to military or political movements—movements such as those which led to the rise of the Free Cities throughout Europe during the Middle Ages. If we compare these movements with those of the later peasant risings throughout France at the close of the eighteenth century, we shall see that they had many points in common. There was the same determination to resist extortion, to find and apply principles of equity in dealing between man and man, and to obtain unhampered access to the means of production, especially land.

It is impossible to enter in detail into the wording of the early city charters or Guild-statutes, but a type of clause customary in them all was one assuming common responsibility for the maintenance of individuals who had become incapable through age, accident, or disease; "Fraternal assistance in necessity of whatever kind" (Guild-statue of Verona, 1303).

Guilds are the natural form of association of the working, the unpropertied people.

> If the institution of the Guild has taken such an immense extension in Asia, Africa, and Europe, if it has lived thousands of years, reappearing again and again when similar conditions called it into existence, it is because . . . it answered to a deeply inrooted want of human nature; and it embodied all the attributes which the State appropriated later on . . . with this difference from the State, that on all these occasions a humane and brotherly element was introduced instead of the formal element which is the essential characteristic of State interference.
>
> *[Mutual Aid]*

The mediæval cities were built, spiritually and materially, by Guilds: the architecture of the period testifies to their value, to the ideal of the architect as to the faithfulness of the mason.

"Self-jurisdiction was the essential point, and self-jurisdiction meant self-administration." "To guarantee liberty" [from extortion] "self-administration and peace was the chief aim of the mediæval city; and labour . . . was its chief foundation." There was communal buying and baking. "In short, if a scarcity visited the city, all had to suffer from it more or less; but apart from the calamities, so long as the free cities existed, no one could die in their midst from starvation, as is unhappily too often the case in our own times" [*Mutual Aid*].

Self-jurisdiction, self-administration, the honour of labour redeemed and the necessities of life guaranteed—such was the outcome of the people's revolt in the Middle Ages. It was achieved by Mutual Aid, working in limited areas in complete accord with common conditions and needs. Set against it the picture of society to-day, under Mutual Competition:— vast remote provinces controlled by a centralised bureaucracy as far out of touch spiritually with the needs and desires of their inhabitants as it is materially; administration markedly inefficient, delayed by the necessity of lengthy "explanations" to a distant headquarters; Labour manipulated, handicapped, and hoodwinked, consequently unwilling, distrustful, and in revolt; seven-tenths of the world-wealth as well as control of the means of production in the hands of a few, whilst of the majority some starve, some linger miserably on the borderline, and the bulk hire themselves out for the day's needs and are entirely without guarantee for the future.

It is impossible, of course, to go back to the actual conditions of the Middle Ages, but, following out Kropotkin's analysis, it is not impossible to rediscover the principles that made them, for the greatest number, the happiest period known to history as well as that yielding the highest quality output.

The first thing we find is really representative government—though not of the brigand princes! Both jurisdiction and administration were plastic—a natural outgrowth of the moral and material conditions prevailing in a given area—and as such they fitted the circumstances and evolved with the times. Kropotkin is a steadfast opponent of present-day State control. A formal bureaucracy possesses neither heart nor conscience; it deals with humanity as a machine; it can neither give nor take. Government from a distance—by one race over another, by peoples psychologically different, even by townsmen over agriculturalists—presents very obvious elements of failure: first, because administration does not keep pace with events; secondly, because the causes of events are frequently misunderstood and the treatment misapplied; thirdly, because such administration is wasteful, obstructive, and frequently unjust for lack of intimate and practical knowledge of the conditions involved.

Smaller states are the most prosperous so far as the bulk of the inhabitants are concerned—as may easily be verified. But self-government is compatable with extensive federation as well as with an excellent international spirit.

But when we talk of spirit we get to the root of things. It was the spirit of the common people that made the Free Cities possible. It was the spirit of the common people that made the French Revolution possible. But the spirit of the common people in England to-day will not carry them far. They suffer from an overdose of wrongly conceived education. A deification of brain and a contempt for fundamental character. A sharpened brain is a prong to pick up riches; honesty may be a weight on the handle.

What does this education produce?

First of all, irresponsibility. The students look to "the State," an independent, outside abstraction, to provide and administer all necessary services.

Secondly, a perverted outlook. Craftsmanship is despised and clerkdom exalted; the clerk is a "gentleman," the carpenter is not.

Thirdly, greed and egoism. Nowhere is the Darwinian formula more rampant. Competition is the universal text in the schools—competition not in being and doing but in getting and keeping. It is not mental acuteness that is lacking in the youth of to-day, but endurance, honesty, and the capacity for self-sacrifice in pursuit of an ideal.

Consequently to all this, the people do not perceive that the roots of well-living must be developed from *within themselves,* and cannot be grafted upon them by any type of outside government or State.

The workmen of the Middle Ages organised *themselves,* evolved their own laws and accepted their own responsibilities. The ragged people of Paris organised their own "districts," evolved their new laws, and in some cases *administered them before the so-called Representative Assembly had put them to the vote.* The peasants in the provinces did likewise. They took the trouble not only to think out but to carry out new methods of communal buying and selling, and of agriculture; and alike in town and country they endeavoured, with a great measure of success, to sink selfish aims in the fight for the common weal.

Principles of equity are incompatible with a policy of "beggar my neighbour."

Principles of irresponsibility are incompatible with self-government.

From Kropotkin's point of view the great fault of the English Labour Movement is its lack of responsibility. It is not prepared, when the moment arises, to assume its duties and carry its possible failures. It talks of "the State," but is not itself, integrally, that "State." The great Trades Unions concern themselves mainly with wages and with the industrial conditions of their particular body. They are not representative of "the people." In fact, the English Labour Movement is not a People's Movement at all; consequently it will disintegrate and fail.

It may be said that Kropotkin idealises "the people"—the common, inconspicuous, lazy, long-suffering, unlovely people. And again it may be said that "the people" have not originated ideas—not formulated them, at all events, in such terms as the world accepts. But they have ever been the first to take action—even sacrificial action—upon such ideas as gripped their hearts.

All the great religions have been spread upon People's Movements; all the signal struggles for liberty have been effected through People's Movements; peace in the world to-day, if attainable at all, will be attainable only through a united Peoples' Movement, bursting the bonds of caste and creed and submerging national prejudice. (pp. 442-48)

> *Louise H. Williams, "Prince Kropotkin's Philosophy in the Light of To-day," in* The Hibbert Journal, *Vol. XIX, No. 3, April, 1921, pp. 441-48.*

GEORGE BOAS   (essay date 1925)

[*In a review of* Ethics: Origin and Development, *Boas discusses the basis of Kropotkin's theory of ethics in animal behavior, criticizing his ideas as overly simplistic.*]

Kropotkin's *Ethics: Origin and Development* is in a way his valedictory. It was written in the little village of Dmitrov away from his library, where he spent his last years in ill health and relative poverty. That it is a system based on mutual aid, justice, and self-sacrifice is no more ironical than that Condorcet's last book, written in hiding from the French Revolutionists, should have been an exposition of the continual progress of the human spirit. It is, of course, a fragment, but a fragment so beautiful and of such noble intent, that one feels a certain reluctance to judge it at all.

As will be expected by readers familiar with *Mutual Aid: A*

Factor of Evolution, Kropotkin's ethics is inspired by the theory that in the natural order there is to be found not merely a record of what had to be done to keep mankind on earth, but also what ought to be done to keep it from going to the Devil. The development of man from the simpler animals is for him one of nature's moral achievements.

That we can go to "nature" for a criticism of our manners is an idea as old as the Greeks. That the animals are better than we is an indignant remark that was made even in the sacred books of the East. But it is very strange to find a man who believes that there is moral progress in the passage of events looking backward to a better time.

Like most zoölogists and anthropologists, he is more interested in the species than in the individual. Mutual aid, justice, self-sacrifice are, by definition, of value largely to the race. They may even prove the annihilation of the individual. They operate as a help in the struggle for existence; they are the separate articles of a "law of nature," which advises not civil war—though it permits interracial war—but the adaptation of the species to the changing environment. The struggle, then, is not between an animal and other animals or between an animal and the environment, but between species or between species and the environment.

This notion, Kropotkin points out generously, was not original with him. Darwin had formulated it also in *The Descent of Man.* Romanes had agreed and had left unfinished at his death a work on animal morality which would have illustrated the same thesis. He has impressive backing. Darwinian ethics, which seemed so romantically grim and haggard, turns out to be on the whole rather cheerful.

The sense of duty, Kropotkin feels, is rooted in sociality. It is because we have a strong sympathy for other men that we desire their approval or follow their commands. All the social animals seem to have this trait as well as primitive man. It may have greater power over their behavior than even the maternal instinct. Its power can be explained naturalistically—*i.e.,* Darwinistically—by the fact that "the less enduring *individual* instinct yields before the more enduring *social* instinct." It aids in the struggle for existence. Its only effective opponent is the feeling of enmity. This feeling is apparently the basis of immorality.

After pointing out the origin of moral ideas in the habits of the social animals, Kropotkin proceeds to trace their development in European philosophy. But a break comes after the chapter on primitive peoples. Whereas that chapter deals with ethics in application, the succeeding deals with ethical theories. There is an obvious difference between the two. This is really unfortunate, for there are plenty of histories of the kind and Kropotkin himself makes liberal use of Jodl's. One regrets that he did not see fit to train his insight upon the development of morals apart from systems of ethics. Merely an anthropological study of historical European man would have shown how strangely detached from his conduct his ethical speculations are. It is too bad that one can not see just how detached.

For Kropotkin the development of moral teaching moves towards a recognition of the ethics of mutual aid. In other words, as ethicists progress, they grow into recognizing what primitive man and the social animals do without reflection. He feels, however, that there are two definite and irreconcilable schools—the naturalistic and the supernaturalistic.

Either the moral conceptions of man are merely the further development of the moral habits of mutual aid, which are so generally inherent in social animals that they may be called a *law* of Nature—and in that event our moral conceptions, in so far as they are the product of reason, are nothing but conclusion arrived at from man's observation of nature, and in so far as they are the product of habit and instinct, they constitute a further development of instincts and habits inherent in social animals. Or our moral conceptions are revelations from above, and all further investigations of morality become merely interpretation of the divine will.

But what he seems to overlook is the puzzle of why supernaturalists observing nature and developing the moral habits of mutual aid should think that they are interpreting the divine will. Is it simply because they are stupid? What survival value has their stupidity?

Kropotkin certainly gives us a picture of a pleasanter natural order than many zoölogical ethicists. They who believe in the savagery of nature, the selfishness and meanness of animals, have their beliefs rudely shaken here. Yet they, too, seem to have some facts on their side. Kropotkin admits that even his primitive Esquimaux occasionally are not quite so mutually helpful as the law of Nature demands. This is a phenomenon not exhibited by other natural events. Falling bodies, litmus paper, electric charges seem to act with exemplary if monotonous regularity. Perhaps that is why they are not concerned with ethics. No one asks as an ethical problem whether a man should walk on his hands or his feet; but some people wonder whether he sould have one wife or many. Ethical problems seem to arise, in part at least, from the diversity of manners, from the necessity of choice, not from uniformity of manners and the impossibility of choice.

Zoölogical and anthropological ethics always leave one with the feeling that though they may show one the origin of our standards, they do not show one their importance. Moreover, they leave untouched those interests of human life which make it so much more complex than the life of animals. All the problems which arise from literary and artistic interests, all the problems which arise from a man's relation to himself, are untouched. No civilized man to speak of worries about the right and wrong of murder, theft, arson, mayhem, and rape. These are things which are taken for granted by everyone but children and their Sunday-school teachers. The problems of a civilized man are rather such things as the standard of workmanship, priority rights to ideas, faithfulness to the economic order, the breaking of contracts, keeping up with the Joneses, and the like. It is difficult to see what light the origin of these problems in simpler tribal adjustments can throw on their solution.

Kropotkin's book is, of course, a vestige of nineteenth-century thinking. It is not a volume in contemporary ethics. It should be judged strictly as an historical event. The nineteenth-century naturalist seemed not only to believe that man was a lower animal, but that he should live like one also. That is a dubious belief to say the least. Yet if these remarks should discourage people from reading this book, it would be a pity. It is important to read it if only to see how it casts in high relief that pathetic faith in human beings and nature which sweetened the lives of our fathers. It seems unbelievable nowadays that anyone could have held Kropotkin's theory and struggled to commit it to writing. We have grown more sophisticated if less sublime. (pp. 245-48)

George Boas, in a review of "Ethics: Origin and Development," in The Journal of Philosophy, *Vol. XXII, No. 9, April 23, 1925, pp. 245-48.*

ROGER N. BALDWIN (essay date 1927)

[*An American sociologist, educator, and author, Baldwin was one of the founders of the American Civil Liberties Union (ACLU). For his work in this and other public service organizations he received the Medal of Freedom, the nation's highest civilian honor. In the following excerpt, Baldwin explains Kropotkin's philosophy of anarchism and his objections to other revolutionary political philosophies.*]

[It] is neither as a scientist nor as a Russian revolutionist that Kropotkin is most significant to the world at large. It is rather as a revolutionary anarchist, who put into anarchism the methods of science. He was in fact a scientist in two wholly unrelated fields,—geography and revolutionary social ethics,—for his anarchism was essentially applied ethics. He was one of the leading authorities of his time both in geodetic mathematics and Siberian geography. He was the first man to formulate a scientific basis for the principle of anarchism,—in its opposition to authority in all forms and in its advocacy of complete social reorganization on the basis of the free cooperation of independent associations. He brought to social science a wealth of training in the natural sciences. Unlike most scientists he states his observations and conclusions so simply that his works were published in popular book and pamphlet form in almost all languages. Their wide appeal was due also to his passion for the education of the masses in revolutionary ideas, feeling that once they understood their powers and mission, they would unite to destroy the State, monopoly and private property.

Mutual aid, sympathy, solidarity, individual liberty through free cooperation as the basis of all social life—these are the positive ideas at the root of Kropotkin's teachings. Abolition of the State, of authority in all forms, of monopoly and class rule, are their negative forms. Coupled with them was a belief,—shared by many revolutionists of all schools,—in an approaching social revolution, a universal seizure of property by the workers and peasants, which would end exploitation and class rule and usher in free cooperation and individual liberty.

He shared with socialists their criticism of capitalism, and in large part their conception that the forms of the economic life of a people determine their social institutions—law, government, religion, and marriage. But he disagreed with them in the use of political methods as a means of achieving power and in their conception of a workers' State. Anarchist-communism, he described, as the "no-government system of socialism." But anarchism as a principle of freedom carried him outside the economic and political struggle into all social relations,—marriage, education, the treatment of crime, the function of law, the basis of morality.

Kropotkin's social outlook was colored by his early contacts with the Russian peasantry. When he thought of the masses, he unconsciously pictured to himself peasants oppressed by landlords and Czars, quite capable of handling their own affairs when a revolutionary upheaval once gave them freedom. His outlook on the working-class was also colored by his limited contacts. He was not close to the working-class struggle as a whole. His only intimate connections were with the Jura Federation in Switzerland, the Russian Jewish workers in London and to a lesser degree with the anarchist workers in Paris. His bitter hostility to Marxian socialism cut him off from the German workers' movement. He knew little of the practical problems of leadership, or of the psychology of action among the workers. And, like many intellectuals, he idealized their capacities.

Kropotkin, unlike many others who called themselves anarchists, notably the Tolstoians, was not opposed to the use of violence. He did not condemn deeds of violence, particularly the assassination of tyrants, but considered them useful acts in the struggle toward liberation. Civil war he regarded as inevitable in the conflict of classes, though he wished it to be limited to the "smallest number of victims and a minimum of mutual embitterment." Even international wars he regarded as sometimes significant of conflict between advanced and reactionary forces. This attitude explains how he could champion the Allied cause in the World War, for he feared the triumph of German militarism would be fatal to the progress of the revolutionary forces which he believed were far more advanced in the Allied countries. His profound love for France, and a strong sentimental attachment to Russia, probably influenced this attitude.

Of the non-resistant anarchism of Tolstoi he wrote, "I am in sympathy with most of Tolstoi's work, though there are many of his ideas with which I absolutely disagree,—his asceticism, for instance, and his doctrine of non-resistance. It seems to me, too, that he has bound himself, without reason or judgment, to the letter of the New Testament." He was also scornful of Tolstoi's idea that the propertied classes could be persuaded to give up their prerogatives without a violent struggle.

Kropotkin objected to being called a "philosophical anarchist" because he said he learned anarchism not from philosophy but from the people. And like many other anarchists he objected to the implication that it was only a philosophy, not a program of action, not a movement rooted in the struggle of the masses. "Philosophical" sounded aloof, too respectable, too pacific. It smacked of books and the study.

To concepts of anarchism other than "anarchist-communism,"—the school founded by Michael Bakunin,—he was inhospitable. The anarchist schools of thought have only one point in common,—the abolition of the State as an institution of compulsion,—and all sects emphasize their points of difference. He regarded "individualist anarchism" of the school of Benjamin Tucker in America and Max Stirner in Germany, as hopelessly conservative, committed only to winning personal liberty without a revolutionary change in the economic system. He said of individualism in general, so often conceived as the leading principle of anarchism: "Individualism, narrowly egotistic, is incapable of inspiring anybody. There is nothing great or gripping in it. Individuality can attain its supreme development only in the highest common social effort." He called the individualism of Nietzsche "spurious," remarking that it could exist "only under a condition of oppression for the masses" and in fact destroyed individuality "in the oppressor himself as well as in the oppressed masses." Ibsen he regarded as the only writer who had achieved a conception of true individualism, but "had not succeeded in expressing it in a way to make it clearly understood." The French anarchist thinker, Pierre Proudhon, inspirer of the "mutualist school" of revolutionary economic changes through the reorganization of banking and money, he considered an impractical dreamer.

Kropotkin did not carry his differences of opinion into the open, except in his relentless opposition to all forms of authoritarianism, which meant a constant state of warfare with authoritarian socialism as represented by the followers of Marx. Besides his opposition to him on principle he had a strong personal dislike for Marx,—who he never met,—largely due to Marx's treatment of Bakunin. Marx, according to common report, had helped spread false rumor that Bakunin had been in the employ of the Russian secret service. Yet when these two once met at the home of George Sand, Marx greeted Bakunin effusively. Kropotkin could not tolerate what he regarded as unpardonable hypocrisy. This feeling was intensified by the discovery that parts of the *Communist Manifesto* had been lifted almost word for word from a work by Considerant. Kropotkin took almost a boyish delight in scoring anything on Marx, and, furthermore, he had contempt for him as a politician.

But aside from a personal feeling which was doubtless the result of his hostility to authoritarian socialism, his differences with Marx on other fundamental points were great. Although he was a materialist, accepting in large part the socialist economic interpretation of history, he did not regard economic forces so overwhelming a factor in the class struggle. All through his work the power of ideas is stressed,—a factor accepted by the Marxians as important but secondary, and originating in the struggle of classes. That struggle itself seemed to Kropotkin less influential in revolutionary progress than arousing the "people" to revolutionary thought and feeling. Such a concept was doubtless based on his early outlook in Russia, where the masses of the peasants stood opposed to a small ruling class. The socialist conception was a sharper, clearer picture of class lines and interests in the industrial west. Yet in his *Great French Revolution: 1789-1793* Kropotkin embodies an interpretation that is shared by the whole socialist-communist school. Indeed, the Soviet Government offered him large returns for the right to use it as a text-book in Russian schools—an offer which Kropotkin characteristically refused because it came from a government.

In his social thinking Kropotkin tended to develop his facts from his theories. He described his method as "inductive-deductive." In his geographical scientific work he got his facts first and developed his theories. The difference in his approach to the two fields was doubtlessly due to his strong feeling on all social issues. Regarding them he was a propagandist at heart, tending to ignore or brush aside the facts that contradicted his interpretations. He maintained that he was always ready to alter his theories in the light of facts, but like all men of deep convictions he cherished them too profoundly to see opposing facts except to demolish them. While much of his work in the social sciences is really scientific,—especially *Mutual Aid* and *Fields, Factories and Workshops,*—preconceptions color large parts of it,—a fact which, however, does not detract greatly from its value.

In his personal life he held with equal tenacity to the standards he had developed. He scrupulously refused to take a penny in compensation for his work for the movement. He refused loans or gifts even when living in pressing poverty. And even at such times he would share the little he had with all who came to him in distress. His habits were marked by moderation in everything but work, in which he was tireless. He was rigid in his opposition to tactics which he thought out of harmony with the broad principles of anarchist-communism, even when the ends appeared good. He con-demned comrades who jumped bail in political cases both because of the breach of faith with bondsmen and the practical effect on securing bail in other cases. He refused to countenance aid to the Russian revolutionists from the Japanese Government at the time of the Russo-Japanese war, both because of its demoralizing influence and his hostility to governments.

Kropotkin is referred to by scores of people who knew him in all walks of life as "the noblest man" they ever knew. Oscar Wilde called him one of the two really happy men he had ever met. Romain Rolland said Kropotkin lived what Tolstoi only advocated. In the anarchist movement he was held in the deepest affection by thousands,—"notre Pierre" the French workers called him. Never assuming a position of leadership, he nevertheless led by the moral force of his personality and the breadth of his intellect. He combined in extraordinary measure high qualities of character with a fine mind and passionate social feeling. His life made a deep impression on a great range of classes,—the whole scientific world, the Russian revolutionary movement, the radical movements of all schools, and in the literary world which cared little or nothing for science or revolution. (pp. 2-8)

> *Roger N. Baldwin, in an introduction to* Kropotkin's Revolutionary Pamphlets *by Peter Kropotkin, edited by Roger N. Baldwin, 1927. Reprint by Benjamin Blom, 1968, pp. 1-12.*

G. D. H. COLE (essay date 1954)

[*Cole, an English economist and novelist, wrote widely on socialism and Marxism in a manner accessible to the common reader and was a prolific author of detective fiction. In the following excerpt, he discusses Kropotkin's vision of agriculture and industry in an anarchist society.*]

[Kropotkin] received a scientific training, and this deeply influenced his thought. Though he was bitterly opposed to capitalist industrialism and an ardent advocate of the independent small producer, he was by no means hostile to machinery or to the use of science to increase productive power. He professed himself quite unable to agree with William Morris's hostility to mechanised industry, though he agreed with him in so much besides. He wanted to liberate mankind from the burden of overwork and looked to technological advance to provide the means. He always argued, however, that the scientists would never use their skill to diminish the burden of human labour as long as they themselves had no direct experience of manual work. The great discoveries of the past, he contended, had come not from scientists in the laboratory but from actual working people, who could make and operate the machines they devised. The professional technicians and scientists had only taken these discoveries made by practical men and improved upon them; and unless the divorce between science and practice could be ended he prophesied that invention would dry up, or where it continued, would fail to take the human factor into account. He also believed that large-scale production, except in the making of intermediate standardised products, was not really economical, and that its advance had been due largely to the cheapness of unskilled labour. When such labour could no longer be exploited he held that it would be found more economical, as well as much better from the standpoint of human happiness, to produce most finished products in relatively small establishments, or even in small workshops; and he put great hopes on the advent of electric power as a means of distributing the power needed for industry over wide areas, in such a way as to make possible both the decentralisation of industry into the countryside and the successful competition of the small workshop with the mass-producing factory. Where the workshop could not hold its own, he favoured factories using large-scale power equipment; but he wanted to see these transferred to villages, and the workers in them enabled to combine industrial with agricultural pursuits. No worker, he contended, should practise only a single trade. He believed, with Fourier, that happiness depended on variety as well as choice of occupation; and he also shared Fourier's belief in the pleasantness of labour, rightly carried on, and above all in the human satisfaction to be derived from intensive agricultural work in producing food of high quality. He made much study of advances in intensive cultivation, and was convinced that even the most populous countries could feed their populations from the produce of their own land if they adopted the right methods.

Kropotkin's belief in the combination of industry and agriculture led him to oppose strongly the *laissez-faire* policies which had made such countries as Great Britain dependent on imported foodstuffs for the means of life; and he also wanted countries to become much more nearly self-supporting, in respect of manufacturers as well as of food, because he believed the search for wider markets and the competition of the industrial countries as exporters to be both an important cause of wars and a factor making for intensified capitalist exploitation. He asserted, and was much criticised for asserting, that world commerce was destined to shrink as one country after another developed its own manufacturing industries and excluded the products of the exporting countries. He urged Great Britain to realise that its manufacturing domination was bound to end, and to take steps, by increasing its agricultural production and diversifying its manufacturers to meet the needs of the home market, to prevent the disaster that would otherwise overtake it when its exports fell into decline.

Kropotkin also took the view—most unfashionable in his day—that there was no real evidence of mass-production driving the arts of small-scale production out of existence. He emphasised both the tenacity with which the small-scale producers were holding out in France and Germany, and the extent to which new forms of small-scale production were springing up to replace those which were superseded by factory methods—including the tendency of large-scale industries to call for the services of small firms in making auxiliary components and subsidiary products. On these grounds he denied Marx's doctrine of increasing capitalist concentration and of the super-session of skill as leading to the reduction of the "labour army" to an undifferentiated mass of "labour-power." He admitted that these tendencies were at work under capitalism, but asserted that there were equally powerful forces making the opposite way, and that these latter would prevail as soon as the workers took matters into their own hands.

In all this he was deeply influenced by what he had seen both in Siberia and in Switzerland, and in the areas of France— Lyons and the French Jura—that he knew best. No doubt, to a large extent, the wish was father to the belief; for Kropotkin wanted the "small men" to survive and the factories, run as workers' Co-operatives, to be kept as small as the technical conditions of efficient production allowed. It was part of his fundamental philosophy that men lived most happily in smallish groups, and that in such groups they could best develop their innate propensities towards mutual aid and democratic ways of life. He laid great stress on the distinction . . . between "natural" and "unnatural" forms of social structure, and on the idea that the large society could operate on a basis of freedom only if it rested on a foundation of self-organising small communities.

Such small communities, he believed, given common ownership and control of the means of production and a "reintegration"—a favourite word of his—of life through the co-ordination of industry with agriculture, could manage without any sort of coercive authority. They would be held together by the bond of their co-operative effort to supply themselves with the means of good living; and the spirit of co-operation, thus established in the basic social units, would readily extend itself to the management of such common affairs as needed to be organised over larger areas. This view was, of course, much too simple; and Kropotkin came no nearer than other Anarchists to confronting the real difficulties in the way. Like most Anarchists, he put great emphasis on the influence of education in preparing men rightly or wrongly for the arts of life. He was strongly critical of contemporary practices in both general and technical education. In general education he held that an immense amount of time was wasted by trying to teach children out of books, or by rote, instead of letting them learn by actual doing and making; and technical education, he held, was for the most part either perverted into training young people for particular routine employments instead of equipping them with a wider craft sense which they could apply in many different fields, or misdirected to the production of managers and supervisors as slave-drivers of exploited workers in mass-producing establishments. He cited instances in which, despite the bad environment of capitalism, better methods were followed in the teaching of small groups of technicians; and his chief praise was accorded wherever he found two conditions satisfied—a stress on the teaching of mathematics and basic science rather than of particular techniques, and a wide opportunity to make things for actual use.

The reader of Kropotkin's writings is struck again and again by the contrast between the essential reasonableness, and even moderation, of what he says about such matters as these, and the intransigeance of his more purely political writings. Even in these, he has little of the bitterness that is characteristic of much Anarchist literature. Even when he was most indignant or furious, he remained an essentially lovable person, and there was in him not the smallest trace of that streak of insanity that is continually showing itself in Bakunin's work. Bakunin managed to be dictatorial as well as the enemy of dictation: Kropotkin had no wish to dictate to anybody. He did really believe in freedom, and regarded coercion as an unnecessary result of wrong social institutions. (pp. 348-52)

G. D. H. Cole, "Anarchists and Anarchist-Communists: Kropotkin," in his Socialist Thought: Marxism and Anarchism, 1850-1890, *Macmillan & Co. Ltd., 1954, pp. 315-60.*

JAMES W. HULSE (essay date 1970)

[*An American educator and historian, Hulse is the author of* Revolutionists in London: A Study of Five Unorthodox Socialists. *In the following excerpt from that work, he analyzes the principal themes in* The Conquest of Bread; Fields, Factories and Workshops; *and* Mutual Aid: A Factor of Evolution.]

La conquête du pain appeared as a book in 1892. There was no English edition until 1906, but a number of chapters appeared in *Freedom* and elsewhere in the 1890s, so that its propositions were readily available to London readers who were interested.

The writing that Kropotkin had done before his arrival in England might be regarded as a rough draft for this work. Even though *La conquête du pain* was . . . a combination of journalistic articles, it had the benefit of Kropotkin's editing of his more mature thinking. During his years in the French prisons, Kropotkin had done much reading and some experimental gardening that had helped to shape his theories about future revolutionary efforts. He had been especially moved by the ideas of Professor Karl Kessler, a zoologist of St. Petersburg University, about the co-operative instinct in nature. He had, in short, added to the raw material from which his ultimate anarchist theory was fashioned. The articles that went into *La conquête du pain* were the first systematic expression of that theory.

When he wrote these pieces, Kropotkin obviously envisioned a new French revolution and he seems to have assumed that the new social order would begin there. He had studied the great Revolution of the 1790s and also the episode of the Commune, and on this record he made his important calculations and projections. His rhetoric is often emotional and provocative, and there is much repetition; *The Conquest of Bread* is not one of his carefully prepared books, but it is a fundamental document of anarchism.

The basic assumptions were elementary. The great revolution could be expected soon, and to be successful it would have to accomplish a total transformation of society very quickly. Revolutionary leaders of the past had spent too much time fulminating over the forms of office and the types of authority they would establish; they had given too little thought to the immediate elimination of human suffering. What was needed were not merely new institutions and regulations, but a complete abolition of government and a new spirit that would swiftly convince the lower classes that the old order was dead.

The great metamorphosis of the masses depended on a new principle of distribution, according to this line of argument. The populace must be convinced by tangible evidence—primarily consisting of an equitable distribution of food—that the day of liberation was at hand. It was the want of basic foodstuffs that had caused previous revolutionary efforts to founder. If this could be overcome, the idlers would become fighters and workers for the common cause and would be equal to any reactionary challenge.

The solution that Kropotkin proposes, after many diversions and generalizations, is common storehouses of food and other essential supplies in the cities where the revolutionary movement has begun:

> Thus the really practical course of action, in our view, would be that the people should take immediate possession of all the food of the insurgent districts, keeping strict account of it all, that none might be wasted, and that by the aid of these accumulated resources every one might be able to tide over the crisis. During that time an agreement would have to be made with the factory workers, the necessary raw material given them and the means of subsistence assured to them while they worked to supply the needs of the agricultural population.

Kropotkin consistently avoided more specific suggestions than this. He was convinced that there could be enough foodstuffs for all insurgents during a revolutionary situation if it were well handled, and it was almost axiomatic that the people had the talent and the will to make an equitable distribution, once they became convinced that the day of liberation had come. He categorically rejected the argument that a government bureau must manage the division. One looks in vain through the work for a substitute or for more precise information about the procedures to be used. Kropotkin had unlimited faith in the people, expecting all the significant problems to evaporate with the political institutions that have been devised to deal with them.

Once the initial hurdle is passed and the revolutionary movement has survived the first trying weeks, its creative collectivity will rapidly provide an abundance for all. In his mind's eye, Kropotkin visualized Paris as he wrote, and he conceived a new commune that would be strong enough to prevent a recurrence of 1871 because it could not be starved. Such a commune could quickly begin to solve its own supply problems:

> "What about land?" It will not be wanting, for it is round the great towns, and round Paris especially, that the parks and pleasure grounds of the landed gentry are to be found. These thousands of acres only await the skilled labour of the husbandman to surround Paris with fields infinitely more fertile and productive than the steppes of southern Russia, where the soil is dried up by the sun. Nor will labour be lacking. To what should the two million citizens of Paris turn their attention when they would be no longer catering for the luxurious fads and amusements of Russian princes, Roumanian grandees, and wives of Berlin financiers?

Each great city would be thus made self-sufficient, and its own factories and shops could supply local needs. Kropotkin enjoyed the luxury of living and developing his theories before the age of the aeroplane and sophisticated weapons of bombardment, and in the 1880s he was not able to imagine types of warfare more deadly than those employed in his own day and in the previous century. His buoyant optimism carried him easily over brutal and bloody aspects of the revolution to the rich life beyond:

> . . . Imagine a society, comprising a few million inhabitants, engaged in agriculture and a great variety of industries—Paris, for example, with the Department of Seine-et-Oise. Suppose that in this society all children learn to work with their hands as well as with their brains. Admit that all adults, save women, engaged in the education of their children, bind themselves to work *5 hours a day* from the age of twenty or twenty-two to forty-five or fifty, and that they follow occupations they have chosen in any one branch of human work considered *necessary.* Such a society could in return guarantee well-being to all its members; that is to say, a more substantial well-being than that enjoyed to-day by the middle classes. And, moreover, each worker belonging to this society would have at his disposal at least 5 hours a day which he could devote to science, art, and individual needs which do not come under the category of *necessities,* but will probably do so later on, when man's productivity will have

augmented, and those objects will no longer appear luxurious and inaccessible.

The use of labour for projects that serve only the idle rich, the division of labour in factories which forces thousands to do tedious boring work, the placing of artificial restrictions on production to elevate prices—all these practices would be eliminated in Kropotkin's ideal community. He confidently believed that land and other resources were available in abundance in every corner of the world, and he expected science and technology to provide many new vistas.

Having read extensively in agricultural journals and having observed new machinery, new fertilizers, and experimental greenhouses in use, Kropotkin gave free rein to his imagination. More completely than most of his contemporaries, Kropotkin foresaw an era when the productivity of land would multiply several times under intensive cultivation. He patiently assembled elaborate statistics and worked out production estimates to demonstrate the possibilities of some types of agriculture. Fortified with figures on hot-house experimentation on Jersey and Guernsey and in the suburbs of London, on practices employed on the American plains, on the raising of cattle, on shipping costs, on labour-time invested in various food-products, he concluded that the earth's potential had been badly underestimated. Only poor systems of cultivation and distribution caused shortages.

The seizure of "bread" during the revolutionary epoch, then, constituted only the first step in the reordering of man's procedures for obtaining food. Kropotkin even anticipated that men would come to see the wisdom of communal kitchens, where the needs of a whole community could be prepared on a single fire. This was a provisional and qualified suggestion however; he would leave open the option of individual kitchens and restaurants.

In many other areas of human life, similar drastic reorientations would begin immediately. His proposals on housing are suggestive. It would be within the ability of the revolutionaries to distribute available housing fairly by expropriating completely the buildings that received too little use. "Groups of volunteers" would probably arise in every district and street to make housing surveys, prepare lists of those that were overcrowded and those that could accommodate the poorly housed. Within a few days, the self-appointed groups would have complete statistics and would make the new distribution of quarters. Again the patience of the underprivileged and aroused populace was assumed. Even if there were not enough buildings to solve all the housing needs immediately, new quarters will be quickly provided.

> When the masons, and carpenters, and all who are concerned in house building, know that their daily bread is secured to them, they will ask nothing better than to work at their old trades a few hours a day. They will adapt the fine houses which absorbed the time of a whole staff of servants, and in a few months homes will have sprung up, infinitely healthier and more conveniently arranged than those of to-day. And to those who are not yet comfortably housed the anarchist Commune will be able to say: "Patience, comrades! Palaces fairer and finer than any the capitalists built for themselves will spring from the ground of our enfranchised city. They will belong to those who have most need of them. The anarchist Commune does not build with an eye to revenues. These monuments erected to its citizens, products of the collective spirit, will

serve as models to all humanity; they will be yours."

Kropotkin regarded a building—like any of the other creations of society—as the product of collective skills and of material gathered from many places and produced by many hands. Hence it is the possession of the community, not the property of him whom the state regards as its owner. He does not indicate how different claims will be adjudicated or how disputes over possession will be settled when expropriation has put all the dwellings under the Commune; he rested on his expectation that good will would prevail. Again he reminded his readers that no central authority could handle the transformation or make the arrangements. Only spontaneous groups, exercising their native communal instincts, will be capable of meeting the challenge.

Even in the more esoteric fields, the new era will provide unprecedented opportunities and abundance. The arts and the professions of writing and publishing would flourish as never before. The artists, by spending parts of their days in the fields or factories, will achieve magnificent results, drawing inspiration from *"ideals held in common."* A writer who prepared a manuscript will no longer seek someone with capital to publish his works; he will be obliged only to "look for collaborators among those who know the printing trade, and who approve the idea of his new work. Together they will publish the new book or journal."

Thus the argument advances, always stopping short of specific description, always leaving technical and practical questions in the minds of the readers. Wages are to be abolished completely and the division of labour will be drastically reduced. International trade will be greatly diminished as region after region becomes self-sufficient in most goods. Toll bridges will become free, museums and libraries will be open to all without charge, and free water will be available in each home. Even the drudgery of the housewife will soon disappear under the impact of technology; Kropotkin anticipated the development of such devices as the automatic washing machine, dishwasher, vacuum cleaner, and other labour-saving household equipment.

Only a lack of collective imagination could provoke a failure, Kropotkin said at several points; ". . . cowardice of the spirit is the rock on which all revolutions have stranded until now." The final passage of the book summarizes and captures the mood of the later sections:

> Inspired by a new daring—thanks to the sentiment of solidarity—all will march together to the conquest of the high joys of knowledge and artistic creation.
>
> A society thus inspired will fear neither dissensions within nor enemies without. To the coalitions of the past it will oppose a new harmony, the initiative of each and all, the daring which springs from the awakening of a people's genius.
>
> Before such an irresistible force "conspiring kings" will be powerless. Nothing will remain for them but to bow before it, and to harness themselves to the chariot of humanity, rolling towards new horizons opened up by the Social Revolution.

Kropotkin's next book, *Fields, Factories and Workshops* may be regarded as a supplement to *The Conquest of Bread.* The essays that went into this volume were written during the same period—the late 1880s and early 1890s. One notable difference is that they were written primarily for English readers and examples were drawn from the English situation; some of the essays appeared first in *The Nineteenth Century*. At the time Kropotkin issued *Fields, Factories and Workshops* in book form in 1898, he may not have anticipated that *The Conquest of Bread*, then available only in French, would be issued in an English edition a few years later.

One of the initial objectives of the essays and the book was to convince Englishmen that their unique leadership in the industrial field was in jeopardy and that their neglect of agriculture in favour of manufacture and trade was an error. Kropotkin deplored the fact that British farm production had declined during the last third of the century, a trend that ran counter to the balanced economic self-sufficiency that he desired for each region. With the same kinds of statistics and some of the same examples that had served him in the earlier work, Kropotkin argued that Great Britain could more than double her food production. He omitted from this work, however, the revolutionary justification for such a development.

The British reliance on her industrial leadership could only be of short duration, according to Kropotkin's reasoning, because manufacturing skills and facilities were developing in all parts of the world. He accurately anticipated that Britain would be embarrassed by her competitors, but he less accurately anticipated that the solution to this would be more reliance on local and domestic industries.

Kropotkin looked at the data that showed ever-larger industrial firms crowding the small producer and handicraft operator out of business, and he refused to accept the conclusion that the evidence suggested.

> Altogether, it may be taken as one of the fundamental facts of the economical life of Europe that the defeat of a number of small trades, artisan work, and domestic industries came through their being incapable of organising the *sale* of their produce—not from the *production* itself.

In his view, the ultimate trend in industry and agriculture would have to be away from great centralized enterprises and towards small, locally-oriented productive units. On this score he found fault with the Marxian Socialists and asserted that Marx himself, had he lived into the 1890s, probably would have abandoned his theories about the concentration of capitalistic enterprises.

Only under special conditions or in certain situations could large and specialized industries exist—ship-building operations and iron foundries were examples. Kropotkin recorded, with obvious delight, a number of instances in which handicraft work of high quality continued to flourish. He was not advocating destruction of mass-production machinery where labour-saving functions could be performed, but artistic design and special types of work would remain in the realm of the craftsman. At several points, Kropotkin's arguments run parallel to those of William Morris.

Complementary to this theme was the idea that "brain work" and "manual work" would be integrated, with virtually all adults sharing the opportunities and the obligations of each kind of work. The great inventions of the nineteenth century had usually not come from the men of science and from the laboratories, he argued, but from the humble workers who knew how to use their hands and "had breathed the atmosphere of the workshop and the building-yard." Division of

labour generally was deplored in anarchist thought, and Kropotkin especially disliked it when mental work had no relationship with physical production. The new creativity that he sought depended on their interaction.

For Kropotkin, the growing population of the world did not constitute a problem; it offered an opportunity. Although some men of his generation were noticing population increases with concern, Kropotkin characteristically welcomed it and took pains to refute the Malthusian hypothesis. He predicted the land could be made so productive that 1,000 people living on 1,000 acres could produce "luxurious vegetable and animal food, as well as the flax, wool, silk and hides necessary for their clothing" simply by using known methods.

> We know that a crowded population is a necessary condition for permitting man to increase the productive powers of his labour.

Not only was Malthus's theory wrong from a technical point of view, but it was also repugnant for the social use that had been made of it:

> . . . Malthus's theory, by shaping into a pseudo-scientific form the secret desires of the wealth-possessing classes, became the foundation of a whole system of practical philosophy, which permeates the minds of both the educated and uneducated, and reacts (as practical philosophy always does) upon the theoretical philosophy of our century.

The idea that the thinking of European men had gone astray, that they had been tricked by wilful exploiters was an important aspect of Kropotkin's thought. Like the later Bolsheviks, who explained many of their failures in terms of erroneous or treacherous use of ideology, Kropotkin regarded the formulation and publicizing of the correct ideology as a most important assignment. This was one of the main reasons for his devotion to the task of creating an anarchist literature during the 1880s and 1890s. He felt the need for a definitive argument—a fresh ideology—that would remedy the damage done by Hobbes in political philosophy, Malthus in economics, and the Darwinians in science. He felt he had the weapons to fashion the correct and "scientific" social philosophy for the new era.

Kropotkin's third significant literary contribution to the body of revolutionary doctrine was a series of articles that eventually became well known under the title of *Mutual Aid*. The point of departure for this series was the Darwinian philosophy of Thomas H. Huxley. In February 1888, the English naturalist had published an essay entitled "The Struggle for Existence in Human Society," which was primarily an argument for an enlarged programme of technical training in Great Britain as a service to citizens in the industrial society. Kropotkin objected not only to this kind of specialization—he took up this question in *Fields, Factories and Workshops*—but also he took exception to the fundamental assumptions the famous Darwinist made at the beginning of his article.

One of Huxley's offensive points was that primitive men—like animals—tend to multiply until food resources are insufficient to sustain the whole population, leading to a vicious struggle in which the strong will prevail. This was simply a restatement of the ideas of Malthus and Darwin, specifying the absence of any moral code in the natural state. The history of civilization, however, is a record of man's efforts to escape this Hobbesian condition, according to Huxley. Hence the desirability of governmental action to try to mitigate the struggles between men and to prepare them for social roles.

Kropotkin disliked not only the conclusions but also the premise, and he had been pondering similar questions for about half a decade when the Huxley article appeared. Returning to the articles by the Russian biologist Kessler that he had read during the period of his incarceration at Clairvaux, and adding to it a variety of information that he had assembled from scholarly works, Kropotkin took issue with Huxley. He willingly consented to write a rebuttal when offered a chance to do so by James Knowles, editor of *The Nineteenth Century.*

The answer to Huxley emerged as eight essays and appeared over a period of more than six years—from the summer of 1890 to the summer of 1896. In 1902, the essays were combined and published as a book. The work was re-issued in 1914, soon after the beginning of the war. Kropotkin hoped at that time that his arguments on communal instincts would help to counteract impressions arising from the barbarities of the war.

Mutual Aid became more than a response to the Darwinists. An elementary philosophy of history is sketched here, and the theories enunciated in *The Conquest of Bread* and *Fields, Factories and Workshops* receive further development. The arguments of the Darwinians are given relatively little attention, most of it in the earliest essays. *Mutual Aid* argues that the Darwinians have ignored some basic facts about the struggle for life and have overemphasized the occasional competition between members of the same species. Those creatures most likely to survive and prosper are not usually those who have triumphed in adversity, but those who have experienced little natural adversity, and this is often a matter of chance, according to Kropotkin. The elimination of birds' eggs by rats, unfavourable weather, and other natural factors have more influence on survival and development of birds than does any struggle for existence within the species. The horses of Siberia, often starved and stunted by the terrible winters, do not grow more fit by virtue of their struggles for existence. It is the horses of more favourable climates that thrive and contribute finer attributes to their progeny, partly because they and their ancestors have escaped the struggles enforced by Siberian winters. Nature's indiscriminate slaughter of individuals in a species more often determines the survivors than do some special qualities of the individuals.

A more important reservation of Kropotkin related to the question of ethics. Huxley drew a sharp line between "nature" and society, finding in nature (and in primitive man) bitter competition for survival, and in society the establishment of methods to diminish the competition. Kropotkin rejected this distinction summarily. The most common characteristic of birds, animals, or men, he believed, was co-operation of individuals within a species, and in the highest orders of creatures the greatest amount of mutual aid existed:

> The first thing which strikes us as soon as we begin studying the struggle for existence under both its aspects—direct and metaphorical—is the abundance of facts of mutual aid, not only for rearing progeny, as recognized by most evolutionists, but also for the safety of the individual, and for providing it with the necessary food. With many large divisions of the animal kingdom mutual aid is the rule. Mutual aid is met with even amidst the lowest animals, and we must be prepared to learn some day, from the students of microscopical pond-life, facts of unconscious mutual support, even from the life of micro-organisms.

Kropotkin then described a large selection of rodents, mammals, insects, and sea-creatures that associate for self-protection and assistance to their neighbours, and he drew from zoological literature some remarkable examples of intuitive co-operation. His own experiences in Asiatic Russia, he testified, provided evidence contrary to the Darwinian thesis.

As he moved on to his consideration of man in the primitive state, Kropotkin revived the theme of the noble savage. The gentle anarchist reviewed an extensive body of writing by anthropological and archaeological scholars to find support for his argument that the typical savage condition involved collective co-operation. Kropotkin proposed that even those practices of savages that troubled Europeans most—infanticide, parricide, blood-revenge, and cannibalism—were founded on the principle of serving the needs of the community as a whole. The clan arrangement had worked well until it was disturbed by the establishment of separate family groups, a preliminary to the accumulation of wealth and property by hereditary units within the clan.

As man passed from the stage of the savage to that of the barbarian—when he accomplished the Neolithic revolution—his preference for collective activity continued, according to Kropotkin's thesis. The natural approach to agriculture was communal, and the great migrations were accomplished collectively. The remarkable achievements of the phase of man's development—the conquering of the wilderness, the developing of domestic industries, and the development of fundamental codes of justice—were among the fruits of this activity. If we think of barbarians in terms of war and slaughter, this is the fault of the historians and chroniclers. The record-keepers have a "pronounced predeliction for the dramatic aspects of history." In our own time, there are many reports of crimes and offences in society, but relatively few of the more frequent and more typical acts of mutual support. So it was with the barbarians, and the epic poems, the annals and the historical remnants inform us of the exceptions, not of the typical circumstances. He argued that contemporary evidence of peoples who are in a transitional stage, just emerging from barbarism, demonstrates the peacefulness of barbarian men.

Kropotkin risked tedious repetition in his argument that man was essentially peaceful, and he even contended that it was the natural peacefulness of man that made possible the rise of the warriors' caste. Because most barbarian men preferred their non-combatant pursuits to warfare, they allowed specialists to undertake the duties of fighting, and this made possible a group of men devoted to militarism, leading to the "States period" of history.

> . . . the deeper we penetrate into the history of early institutions, the less we find grounds for the military theory of origin of authority. Even that power which later on became such a source of oppression seems, on the contrary, to have found its origin in the peaceful inclinations of the masses.

With the rise of militarism, the village communes, which were the standard form of social organization, fell victim to the military rule of the feudal era, with Europe dominated by thousands of petty rulers who could command armed strength. As a result, Europe lapsed into a dark era. In *Mutual Aid,* Kropotkin does not deal with the development of Greek and Roman cultures chronologically. Only later in his essays does one find any substantial comment on the role of the classic civilizations. As the villages fell under the yoke of the local despots, they maintained their habits of mutual aid, and this eventually created the framework for liberation.

In many parts of Europe, medieval towns evolved into institutions which were able to free themselves from the despots and defend themselves from the ravages and exploitation of feudalism. Beginning in about the tenth and eleventh centuries—Kropotkin is not precise with his time references—the medieval city began to emerge with remarkable uniformity throughout Europe. Here, Kropotkin elaborated a thesis that had been briefly foreshadowed in the early sections of *The Conquest of Bread.* The flowering of the medieval city between about the twelfth and fifteenth centuries was one of the outstanding manifestations of mutual aid. He became ecstatic as he discussed the benefits and accomplishments of those communities; he regarded them as the ideal social form. During the era when free cities operated without the restrictions of centralized authority or military rule, they conceived the "truce of God" to limit warfare, developed the craft guilds, erected magnificent cathedrals, cultivated philosophy, improved navigation, and made many other advances that have benefited subsequent generations. According to Kropotkin's reading of medieval studies, the city labourer was well respected and well compensated and his personal liberties were honoured. He was not subjected to long hours and unpleasant conditions of labour, as his descendants have been. "To guarantee liberty, self-administration, and peace was the chief aim of the mediaeval city. . . . " The "fundamental principle" in each city was to assure adequate food and lodging to all. The reader gets the impression that hunger and privation were unknown in the typical city when the federalism of mutual aid existed. Each section and profession within the city exercised its sovereignty wisely and in the public interest.

Yet many of the cities shared unfortunate flaws, and all of them became victims of external pressures that ruined their idyllic conditions. They were frequently at war with the feudal lords who remained in control of the countryside, and they had to maintain armies for defence. All too often, as they liberated the peasantry and their land from the despots, the cities failed to extend the principles of liberty and mutual aid to the countryside. Exploitation of the rural populations continued, creating a gulf of misunderstanding between the urban areas and the rural hinterlands. Compounding the error, the cities neglected agriculture and over-emphasized commerce and industry. Such practices had become common by the sixteenth century, which Kropotkin saw as the twilight of the golden age. Commercialism led the cities into distant trading enterprises, which involved colonial ventures and new military commitments. Mercenary armies were a necessary corollary. Once again, the co-operative instinct proved inadequate to withstand militarism.

In addition, another evil idea existed to undermine the foundations of the medieval city:

> . . . Self-reliance and federalism, the sovereignty of each group, and the construction of the political body from the simple to the composite, were the leading ideas of the eleventh century. But since that time the conceptions had entirely changed. The students of Roman law and the prelates of the Church,

closely bound together since the time of Innocent the Third, had succeeded in paralyzing the idea— the antique Greek idea—which presided at the foundation of the cities. For two or three hundred years they taught from the pulpit, the University chair, and the judges' bench, that salvation must be sought for in a strongly-centralized State, placed under a semi-divine authority; that *one* man can and must be the saviour of society, and that in the name of public salvation he can commit any violence: burn men and women at the stake, make them perish under indescribable tortures, plunge whole provinces into the most abject misery. Nor did they fail to give object lessons to this effect on a grand scale, and with an unheard-of cruelty, wherever the king's sword and the Church's fire, or both at once, could reach. By these teachings and examples, continually repeated and enforced upon public attention, the very minds of the citizens had been shaped into a new mould. They began to find no authority too extensive, no killing by degrees too cruel, once it was "for public safety." And, with this new direction in mind and this new belief in one man's power, the old federalist principle faded away, and the very creative genius of the masses died out. The Roman idea was victorious, and in such circumstances the centralized State had in the cities a ready prey.

Such cities as Paris, Madrid, and Moscow, strategically located and endowed with cunning and unscrupulous lords, became the centres of the revived authoritarian tendencies, and the free cities could not adapt the principles of mutual aid widely enough—either internally among their own populations or externally by defensive federations—to prevent the rise of the monarchies. Their failure to resist successfully permitted the rise of narrow-minded religious and commercial individualism. The determination to seek one's own happiness at the expense of others became common, and the arts and sciences, so vigorous in the medieval period, declined. For Kropotkin, the period from the fifteenth to the eighteenth century was one of decay and lethargy in science and technology.

In spite of this, the mutual aid instinct had survived. At times it is difficult to reconcile this assertion with some of the earlier categorical remarks about the decline of the co-operative idea; Kropotkin's emphatic statements do sometimes seem to be contradictory. But he remained convinced that mutual co-operation prevailed primarily among the poorer classes, among the labourers and in the countryside, in the slums of the modern cities and in the trade union movement. Such institutions as the *artels* of contemporary Russia and collectively-oriented villages of France and Switzerland have survived the ravages of the authoritarian regimes, and the impulse to form co-operatives becomes manifest whenever centralized authorities allow. Kropotkin found a number of examples in France and England in the nineteenth century to support his thesis.

Kropotkin's effort to support his philosophy with scholarly evidence is not quite as successful as he believed it to be. There are many internal indications of his extensive reading and his patience; his command of several languages and his propensity for research directed him to monographs in a broad range of fields, and *Mutual Aid* is generously footnoted. Yet, like *Das Kapital,* it is essentially a polemic and the documentation is obviously selective. The sub-title informed the reader that Kropotkin was considering only one of the factors of evolution, and he was not reticent about the fact he was under-emphasizing some other factors that had been stressed too heavily by the Darwinians.

At times, the evidence that Kropotkin elicits does not seem adequate to sustain the burden of his argument; his characteristically romantic and optimistic sentiments often carry him beyond the facts, and grandiose generalizations follow upon the heels of mundane, narrow data. He was inclined to regard man's experience as basically uniform, acknowledging few important variations. When men passed from the feudal era to the age of the medieval villages and thence to the medieval cities, for example, the experience was basically the same across the continent and in England. One gets no appreciation of the differences between England, France, and eastern Europe, or the various rates of development of the centralized monarchies.

But the fact that Kropotkin ignored some of the historical evidence in fashioning his argument is not as significant as his criticism of scholars of the past, who had selected for their emphasis "the ways and means by which theocracy, military power, autocracy, and, later on, the richer classes' rule have been promoted, established and maintained." He hoped that future historians would find more occasion to document man's co-operative achievements, rather than concentrating on examples of competition and struggle.

As he worked on his articles of the 1886-96 period, Kropotkin obviously thought of providing an example of the kind of history he had in mind, and his attention returned occasionally to the era of the French Revolution. He wrote short pieces and spoke about it from time to time, and like so many of his colleagues, he spent many hours in the Reading Room of the British Museum. From these studies and reflections he eventually produced his large history of the French Revolution, in which he intended to demonstrate the desirable historical technique. However, in the mid-1890s the end of this project was still more than a decade away.

Another need that Kropotkin recognized as he fashioned the basic documents of Communist Anarchism was in the field of ethical philosophy. The movement would have to be provided with a new morality, he believed, since the old values and standards of Europe were inadequate. As early as 1890, he had sketched his ideas on this subject in *Le Révolté,* and the *Freedom* press issued the articles as a thirty-six page pamphlet entitled **Anarchist Morality.** Intermittently for the next two decades Kropotkin worked on this project, but he was not able to give it sustained attention until near the end of his life, when he had returned to post-revolutionary Russia and found himself in a kind of involuntary seclusion. His **Ethics,** like his history of the French Revolution, although a logical continuation of the first three major books, belongs to a later phase of his career. (pp. 55-71)

James W. Hulse, "Kropotkin: The 'Philosophe' of Anarchism," in his Revolutionists in London: A Study of Five Unorthodox Socialists, *Oxford at the Clarendon Press, 1970, pp. 53-76.*

MARTIN A. MILLER (essay date 1970)

[*An American historian, educator, and author, Miller has written primarily on Russian revolutionaries and émigrés of the late nineteenth and early twentieth centuries. In the following excerpt, he discusses the principles set forth in Kropotkin's 1873 manifesto, "Must We Occupy Ourselves with an Examination of the Ideal of a Future System?"*]

The 1873 manifesto ["**Must We Occupy Ourselves with an Examination of the Ideal of a Future System?"**] is Kropotkin's first major essay on politics. Many of the ideas which Kropotkin developed later can already be seen in an earlier form in this document. Fundamentally, the conceptualization of what he later called anarchist communism was a combination of economic egalitarianism and political liberty. Put in another way, he believed man had to be liberated from capitalism and the state in order to be free. It was on the issue of the state that Kropotkin's anarchism distinguished itself most markedly from other varieties of socialist (and populist) thought. He attempted to prove that the state was unnecessary for the accomplishment of the most vital functions needed for survival and defense. On the other hand, the existence of the state was the cause of most of society's evils. Reforming a basically corrupt institution was futile; it had to be entirely swept away in revolution if true progress was to occur.

This line of reasoning led Kropotkin in this essay to a critical examination of all forms of government. He had to refute the presumed benefits of republican and democratic systems of authority as well as to show why the tsarist autocracy in Russia needed to be overthrown. His picture of Western constitutional government was one of acquisitive and egotistical individuals skilled at maneuvering the political party in power to greater exploitation of the masses. The parties themselves were unrepresentative of the people since the majority of the citizens were disenfranchised or ignorant of the realities of politics. Worse, the constitutional parties acted as a bulwark against radical change: by machinations and clever rationales, the parties convinced the masses that they possessed political rights, which in turn served to diminish their revolutionary initiative. Such governments dominated the press, controlled opinion and froze the unequal social class divisions which were a necessary part of any bourgeois system.

Several other subjects which find fuller elaboration in later writings are discussed in detail in the 1873 essay. Kropotkin was quite concerned about the role of education in society. He felt that education as it was institutionalized in contemporary societies was one of the major factors responsible for preserving political, economic, and social inequalities. Students were predominantly from the upper classes and aspired to the highest ranks of the state to receive the rewards it offered. Education was an intellectual luxury unconcerned with the needs of the people at large. Transformed through revolution, education could be adapted to train everyone in a society to perform a necessary task which would in turn dignify the nature of labor and end the class divisions of educated elites and uneducated masses. The focal point for the newly trained masses would be rural communes (*obshchiny*), each of which could produce various products necessary for the welfare of society in general. These small units would voluntarily unite for purposes of exchange or defense for mutual benefit. All of this was to be established without any government, administration, or legal system.

These conceptions received more sophisticated expression in Kropotkin's later essays. [In **"The State: Its Historic Role"**], a historical dimension was added to indicate the influence of anarchy in the past and to show how the whole of history was moving in the direction of the worldwide destruction of governments. While the 1873 manifesto was one of Kropotkin's most graphic illustrations of the postrevolutionary society under anarchism, he returned to this theme in the later essay **"Expropriation."** Here he described in detail the revolutionary tactic of seizing the means of production and all private property, and the methods of reapportioning this as "common property" on an equitable basis among the people. The necessity of abolishing the wage system and the means of replacing it were also considered. Taken together, the 1873 essay and **"Expropriation"** present the clearest picture of the anarchist society of the future which Kropotkin had in mind.

In the later essays Kropotkin introduced conceptions that can be found in other forms in the 1873 manifesto. His stress on the *obshchiny* as the basic units of the future revolutionary order was later superseded by the concept of the free commune. The major difference was that the *obshchina* was primarily a rural agricultural collective community in Russia whereas the commune for Kropotkin was an institution that could operate in an urban setting as well as in the countryside. In theory, the commune served the same function as the Russian *obshchiny,* that of providing a locus for the organizing centers of activities during the revolution and of acting as the foundation for the postrevolutionary society of decentralized, autonomous, and voluntarily cooperating units. Kropotkin also believed that the commune had been the historical force which had stood against the encroaching effects of the state in the past.

Another conception which underwent such an evolution was the notion of the revolutionary party. In the 1873 essay Kropotkin emphasized the importance of a radical party dedicated to populist ideals which was to aid in bringing about the revolution. In his later writings, he was critical of parties because he became convinced that control of the masses by a party elite would lead to worse problems once the revolution was victorious, namely, the establishment of a revolutionary government by a party or faction. Past revolutions had failed precisely because the masses had been convinced by their leaders to establish a representative body which would organize a new revolutionary government. This for Kropotkin was a contradiction in terms. Such a representative body inevitably assumed political authority and thereby degenerated into an obstacle to the realization of a true revolutionary society. Thus, government and revolution were incompatible; "outside of anarchy there is no such thing as revolution" and revolution could only be accomplished by the initiative of the people themselves. Revolutionary authority was no better than the authority it had overthrown.

Two final concepts should be mentioned in connection with the origins of Kropotkin's ideology and the 1873 essay. First, the kind of revolution Kropotkin called for was a social revolution. The concept was already present in the 1873 manifesto and was subsequently expanded. By his use of this term, Kropotkin meant a complete transformation of society. It was intended to go beyond a mere *coup d'état* or even replacing a reactionary government by a so-called revolutionary government. The social revolution was the violent destruction of all governmental forms of legal authority and the transition to autonomous free federations of communes ruling themselves without the state and without capitalism. To achieve this stage of free or anarchist communism, it was imperative to recognize "that the material guarantee of existence of all members of the community shall be the first act of the social revolution." The justice of and rationale for the social revolution was evident from Kropotkin's belief that it was the means of reconquering that which had originally belonged to the people, that which had been usurped from them by princes, priests, and property owners throughout history.

Second, when discussing the mechanics of radical change, Kropotkin repeatedly referred to the people as the basic motivating force. This aspect of his thinking was intimately associated with his experiences in Russia and specifically with the ideology of populism. . . . Kropotkin had come to identify with the plight of the people from an early age in a specific manner. The antithesis between authority and freedom which he encountered in eastern Siberia was conceptualized as a conflict between man and the state. In addition, during the early 1870s while in the Chaikovskii Circle, he accepted the Bakuninist position on the role of the people in the revolutionary struggle. This meant giving priority to the spontaneity of the masses rather than to the consciousness of the intelligentsia as the primary factor in a revolt. The people already possessed the instinct for revolution; intellectuals had to try to understand how the revolutionary potential of the masses actually functioned and how to encourage its expression, but could not attempt to direct or control the drive of the people to rebellion. Kropotkin never lost this unquestioned faith in the revolutionary instinct of the masses. He assumed that they would know what tactics to employ during the actual revolution and that, aside from occasional exceptions, they would be capable of running the new society with justice and without vindictiveness toward their old masters. Examples of the corollary of this position, an intolerant anti-intellectualism, abound in Kropotkin's writings. (pp. 12-17)

> *Martin A. Miller, in an introduction to* Selected Writings on Anarchism and Revolution *by P. A. Kropotkin, edited by Martin A. Miller, The MIT Press, 1970, pp. 1-44.*

EMILE CAPOUYA AND KEITHA TOMPKINS (essay date 1974)

> [*In their introduction to the collection* The Essential Kropotkin, *Capouya and Tompkins describe the relevance of Kropotkin's philosophy to contemporary life.*]

[In] 1974 a specter haunts—not Europe merely, as in Marx's famous phrase—but the world. The specter of the libertarian creed, exorcized again and again with legal sanctions or rites of blood, has risen once more, evoked by the social pressures within industrialized nations. Groping adumbrations of anarchist ideas appear again and again among persons cut off from all connection with the anarchist tradition, who painfully reinvent in response to the force of circumstance the principles developed over a century and a half of the history of a great social movement. In the age of totalitarianism, anarchist themes are once more on the order of the day—not, in the main, as advanced by living anarchists, but thrown up among human beings of the most diverse circumstances, temperament, and opinion who feel in their soul the intimation of the end of the human experiment—by war, by the despoiling of the whole earth, by the progressive enslavement of mankind to the machine in the name of rationalization of industry and of ever-expanding physical production. It is as if the theories of a Godwin, a Proudhon, a Bakunin, a Kropotkin, were too profound and too far seeing to find the requisite points of leverage in the immature forms of industrial organization that those thinkers had before their eyes. Only in our own time are the human contradictions of the system, under their capitalist and communist forms alike, sufficiently developed to answer fully to the critical analysis proposed by anarchism. It is at this moment that a mere listing of the problems universally acknowledged to be the most fateful, corresponding point by point with the strictures and solutions advanced by anarchism, amounts to a clear political and social agenda.

First, a number of issues directly connected with the size of human populations in relation to the limits of available natural resources: Is the formula of Malthus—that the food supply expands arithmetically while population grows by geometric progression—a general and absolute rule or one of limited applicability? The detailed answer given by Peter Kropotkin amounts to a demonstration that the Malthusian doctrine describes the demographic profile of capitalist society in particular, reflecting, among other factors, the consequences of the international division of labor brought about by economic forces which are more or less peculiar to capitalism, and to which finance capital and industrial capital are peculiarly responsive.

Again, is the minute subdivision of the labor process within the boundaries of each nation, and within industries and trades, and indeed within the soul of the individual workman, an inevitable feature of advanced industrial societies? The response of anarchist theory is that the reduction of the worker to no more than a source of undifferentiated labor power (here Bakunin and Kropotkin followed Marx implicitly, and if they did so without acknowledgment it may have been as much because they regarded his doctrine as being self-evident as that they were moved by political partisanship) is the essential feature of one historically specific mode of production—the capitalist mode. (It seems scarcely necessary to remark that the capitalist mode of production has been adopted by those advanced industrial nations that call themselves communist or socialist.) The ends achieved by the system are an astounding proliferation of certain classes of goods, a concentration of political and economic power in fewer and fewer hands, and a relative impoverishment—despite so-called high standards of living—of the working population. That last effect, quite palpable to the worker but generally beyond the ken of middle-class sociologists, operates in two unexpected ways: first, through the degradation of the processes of work, so that a worker cannot aspire to a minimum of creativity in his daily task; then, through the intensification of the work so degraded, to the point that it degrades the worker's character, stultifies him with the hebetude of endlessly repetitive activity, cutting him off from the possibility of self-cultivation, and from the possibility of self-respect and political initiative in his quality of man and citizen. And that helotization of the worker is an immediate function of his role in the process of production, quite without reference to the formal aspect of his impoverishment—that is, the terms of trade that he is powerless to alter, the terms on which he sells his labor in the market and buys his sustenance in the market.

On this general issue, the starting point for the anarchist thinkers was the paradox resumed by Henry George at the turn of the century in the formula, "Progress and Poverty"; the seeming contradiction that Franklin Delano Roosevelt alluded to several generations later in reminding us that one-third of the nation, in the richest country in the world, was ill-fed, ill-clothed, and ill-housed; the anomaly rediscovered at the very height of the Great American Celebration by Michael Harrington, and set down in his book, *The Other America*—that poverty and the ghetto were keeping pace with the long bull market and the affluent suburb, that the American economic system appeared to deal out with the impartiality of physical laws consistent proportions of want and obloquy on the one hand and of luxury and uneasy privilege on the other.

To the demoralization, stultification, and relative penury that are the lot of the worker in the industrialized nations, Kropotkin opposed what he regarded as a perfectly attainable ideal. He began by tracing the effects of carrying on industrial production and commercial exchange in the manner developed under capitalism, and he demonstrated that, for the great majority, the activity was necessarily self-defeating. For instance, it was generally accepted—and still is—that simply on the material level it "did not pay" for England to produce her own foodstuffs; it did pay for her to export manufactured goods (or even pedigreed cattle, for breeding purposes) and buy foodstuffs abroad. But an odd result of the policy was that the average Englishman was nourished on bread and dripping. That fact sets the concept of profitability in a new light. Some Englishmen, indeed, were lavishly rewarded by the system, and could afford to feed their children so that they grew to be taller by a head than other people's children. But most of their fellows contributed their labor and their lives of deprivation to procure meat, vegetables, and fruit for the favored few; the small stature and poor teeth of *their* children were a measure of how imperfectly adjusted to their needs was the system of international production and exchange that assured Britain's "favorable balance of trade."

Views and arguments related to many aspects of Kropotkin's social thought, expressed in books and pamphlets separated by as much as four decades, coalesce here to suggest a full solution to the problem posed by Malthus, showing again that his premises were not absolute but contingent. If the arable land of England, and those portions once arable but long ago converted to pasture and woodland (the process was well under way, of course, before the passage of the Enclosure Acts which gave it formal sanction), were seized, expropriated by the people of England, one basis of the profitability of exporting manufactured goods and importing food would be destroyed. And if the expropriated lands were cultivated in accordance with modern principles, they could support with their product many times the present population.

Now, by "modern principles" Kropotkin did not mean the kind of intensive agriculture dependent on chemical fertilizer, whose immediate advantage in raising gross productivity had set the pattern for advanced agriculture everywhere—a pattern of progressive destruction of the soil and progressive degradation of the quality of the crop. The economic cost of chemical fertilizer, its bad effects upon soil, even the use of natural deposits like nitrates in the form of guano, which made agriculture dependent on a species of mining that was bound in the foreseeable future to exhaust such resources completely—all these objections Kropotkin advanced against the practice of farming with chemicals some fifty years before there was a body of respectable opinion on his side of the question; indeed, the chemical fertilizer industry is still in our own day endowing chairs in universities and granting funds for experiments whose intended effect is to sustain the demand for their product. But Kropotkin was an early convert to what is now called organic farming and gardening. He had seen that the market gardeners in the suburbs of Paris made their own soil from manure—so that, as Kropotkin observed, they could, if they wished, commence operations upon an asphalt pavement—and raised crops of vegetables and fruits of the first quality in astounding abundance, with no expenditure for artificial fertilizer, in the space of a few square yards, feeding Paris and exporting the surplus to England.

In *Fields, Factories and Workshops,* he gives the statistics of the productivity of the French gardeners and suggests how their techniques could be adapted to grain crops; he also tabulates the yearly decline in the acreage that England had allotted to wheat in the last decades of the nineteenth century, till the point was reached at which the country became a regular importer of wheat on a large scale. And all this time the price of grain was rising in Britain. It is in terms of the Q.E.D. that we are to understand his prescribing the expropriation by the people of the arable land of England, and the development of an agriculture that would be truly modern because it would be richly productive without injury to the capital that is the common patrimony, the soil that supports us.

Kropotkin was acutely aware that the practice of an agriculture that had come more and more to resemble an extractive industry had two kinds of unfortunate consequences. The first, as we have come to know feelingly in our own time, was the desecration of the environment. The second was the rise of extensive monocultures, which by their nature contribute greatly to the impoverishment of the soil, but also breed a rural proletariat whose status and fortunes are particularly depressed, the manpower necessary to run what Carey McWilliams' classic phrase describes as "factories in the fields." The decentralization of agriculture and the development of a mixed agriculture were Kropotkin's ideal solutions to both these problems, the environmental and the social; and those solutions were a feature of his larger conception of a mixed economy, as much agricultural as industrial, whose smaller, decentralized units would be favorable to personal development in that they would substitute individual initiative for regimentation—immediately, in the planning and carrying out of the processes of work, and in the long run on a larger field of human activity because of the influence of the kind of political organization with which they would be most compatible. Battalions of machine operatives and field hands sort well with the modern totalitarian systems—those of a relatively amiable cast and those that are naked tyrannies—which almost without exception derive their authority, in theory, from the consent of the governed. In practice, of course, the regimes in question have substituted for the consent of the governed the principle of "virtual representation" that Parliament invented for the benefit of the American colonies. The irony is that the Americans, who made a revolution in order to do away with the sham of virtual representation, live under just such a system to this day, and it is better luck than management—the result of a blessed historical accident—that gives them a milder government to resent than that which the peoples of the Soviet Union are called upon to endure.

Kropotkin did not care for virtual representation because he did not care for class rule, whether on the part of industrial and commercial oligarchies or of a vanguard revolutionary party. He could not but have been familiar with Bakunin's prophetic objection to the Marxist theory of revolution: that the party would soon substitute itself for the people, the central committee for the party, and a smaller cabal or an individual tyrant for the central committee. Leon Trotsky took up the identical formulation during the period of his differences with Lenin before 1917—and after 1917 contributed with all the power of his military and political genius to the fulfillment of the prophecy, which included his own eventual discomfiture and brought calamitous misfortune to the citizens of the Soviet Union.

Why was Kropotkin, almost alone among the committed revolutionaries in the socialist tradition, so penetrated with the intimate connections among the organization of industry and agriculture, the consequences for the land and for the personal fate of the workers, and the nature of the political administration that would lend formality and sanction to those effects? Or rather, why did the Marxians, with the advantage they enjoyed of following the supernal political and social intelligence of modern times—Marx himself—fail to recognize as Kropotkin did that if men and women were ever to come into their full humanity, it must be by virtue of a different kind of social order than the one envisaged by the majority faction within the International Workingmen's Association?

The reasons are complex, but they can be summarized without undue distortion. To begin with, Marxism itself was imbued with the religion of progress, cast in nineteenth-century terms, and departing from them only in that it meant to extend to every human being the privileged existence made possible by the Industrial Revolution—in essence, freedom from want. This creed, we may remark at once, is at bottom the merest good sense of social hygiene, near kin to the ideal of human dignity that effected the American Revolution, the French Revolution, the Russian Revolution, and the Chinese Revolution. But the fact that Marxism was very much in the spirit of the nineteenth century, to the point of sharing the assumptions of persons and institutions far removed from any inclination toward deliberate social revolution, ensured that it would represent in many respects a kind of postgraduate capitalism, and exalt, in the name of the rationalization of industry, the idea of salvation by the machine. The spirit of quantification, the monetization of all values, the quasi-sacred status of expanded material production—these, in the short run of politics, were for Marx, that genuine humanist and master ironist, as much "the Law and the Prophets" as they were for the capitalist entrepreneurs whose idolatrous devotions he contemned and ridiculed.

In contrast, the anarchist strain of socialism was a form of romantic reaction, the necessary antithesis to the religion of mechanical progress. Marxism was fully in accord with what appeared to the nineteenth century to be the wave of the future, and in the twentieth century it has been in accord with the consequences of the systematic regimentation of human beings in the name of increased production—so much so that a large manufacturing plant in the Soviet Union (save for some edulcorations or exacerbations like organized cultural pursuits or mandatory political activities) is indistinguishable in its operations from one in Western Europe or the United States. Perhaps because of the social origins of the persons most influential in the anarchist movement during its classic period, Russian aristocrats and Western European craftsmen, neither of which orders of men feels much natural sympathy with the mechanization of the economy, the social order, and personal life, anarchism's retrograde impulse very early took on the aspect of a romantic protest against the *deus ex machina* of the age. In so doing it assured its peculiar relevance for the latter half of the twentieth century, which, pinched by its special predicament, has brought persons unacquainted with the anarchist tradition to improvise, piecemeal and helter-skelter, the reforms proposed with magisterial scope by Peter Kropotkin.

For the anarchist theorist, moreover, the mixed economy had a particular role to play in the nurture and culture of human beings. Even as the effects of the present division of labor are represented on the international, the national, the regional, and ultimately the personal scale, it was Kropotkin's ideal to exchange specialization of function for a more liberal and liberating activity, whose consequences would revolutionize the lives of individuals and relations among the countries of the world. On the individual level, he hoped for a system of production in which every citizen might contribute to the work of agriculture and industry alike, uniting in his own person planning and execution, theory and practice. The consequences for organizing formal education are obvious, and Kropotkin drew those consequences. He proposed that the acquisition of manual skill, and developing the ability to do physically demanding work be as much a concern of the school curriculum as the acquisition of theoretical knowledge. He also proposed that the processes by which men secure food, clothing, and shelter should be made familiar to every citizen in their connections with the intellectual systems of mathematics, physics, and chemistry, so that useful work might be illuminated with understanding, be better done, and make better men of the doers.

Contrast that with our current educational practice, in which some favored young persons among the poor attend trade schools where they learn, mostly by rote, the operations required of workers in industries that are expressly organized to minimize the necessity for intelligence or initiative on the part of the workers; in which favored young persons in the middle class learn, mostly by rote, the theoretical knowledge that is supposed to equip them for carrying on one or another profession; in which the rich are exposed to literary classics and to the arts and sciences as a preparation for finance, politics, or mere ownership—and left in salutary ignorance about the social cost of their own maintenance; in which the great majority is fitted—by years of custodial discipline and systematic indoctrination rather than by anything that might properly be called education—for the tasks of clerkship, the service jobs, the thousand and one debasing forms of alienated labor that are required by our industrial and commercial system; in which a substantial number are prepared, formally and informally, for lives of destitution, lives on the margin of the industrial and commercial system, spent in urban and rural slums, the armed forces, and the jails.

The education of the mind, the senses, the muscles, familiarity with science as with physical labor, the cultivation of the sympathies, of the humane imagination—these things Kropotkin expected, not unreasonably, to have their effect first upon the individual personality, then upon the character of communities and regions, ultimately upon a world governed by an ideal of the physical, intellectual, and moral well-being of its inhabitants.

A Utopian vision? Undoubtedly. But scarcely dismissable on that account. Firstly, there is in it no hint of an ignoble or simply unworthy appeal, no suggestion that work can or should be rendered superfluous by the efficient organization of computers and servomechanisms, no sordid arrangements to purchase a meaningless leisure for a race that is to be progressively divorced from an intelligent concern with the sources and processes of its own material sustenance. Again, the clear egalitarian bias that suggests that every person is best employed when his work requires him to use mind and body alike, outdoors and within doors, as planner and executor, does not deal in the secret flattery of doctrines that advance the desirability of hierarchies. Kropotkin's vision is demanding, athletic. In his Utopia, distinction is available to everyone—that is, for everyone it must be and can be earned.

Then, Kropotkin shows a psychological acuity most often lacking in apologists for the way we live now, and in reformers, too. He understands that the patterns of human nature that most thinkers accept as given, once and for all, are as much social artifacts as they are the result of physical structure and instinct. The defeated, the incurious, the bellicose, the spiteful character appear to him to be examples of social pathology. He had experienced at firsthand some of the conditions and institutions that are the nurseries of such pathology—prisons, slums, armies, invidious class distinction, want, demeaning toil. He is not so foolish as to imagine that such things have no effect upon the hearts and minds of the human beings who are exposed to them, nor that those exposed to them have by statistical coincidence and inherited talent a special predisposition toward degradation that is denied to persons more fortunately situated in the social order. He assumes that a man or woman not already spiritually crippled by a lifetime of abuse is likely to respond positively to a pattern of living that demands the exercise and expansion of the most manlike faculties—will hunger for just such exercise and seek it fervently. Those who are in the happy position of being able to entertain argument on this subject (most are too overwhelmed by the effects of their social disabilities to do so) are sure to make that very assumption about themselves, that is that they themselves respond to stimulating occupation, to the possibility of using their imagination and initiative. But they are not so sure to extend the principle to their fellow human beings. What is suspect about every form of argument for the genetic inferiority of this or that class or race of mankind is that it is always put forward about other people, never about ourselves. In this instance, too, Kropotkin's plain style is the expression of a most sophisticated spirit: he understands that the favorable view that each of us takes of his own character and actions is not the end of the matter but, in ethics at least, the beginning, requiring to be extended to a reasonably benevolent view of the rest of the species. And he appears not to have struck any compelling reason for supposing that bad morals may be good science.

In his *Memoirs of a Revolutionist,* and again in the essays collected under the title *In Russian and French Prisons,* Kropotkin gave an account of an experience which had been shared by generations of political radicals, including a great many adherents of socialism—the experience of arrest, conviction, and incarceration. Here again he is very nearly alone in having understood the social import of imprisonment in terms that are consistent with the humane passion which is the emotional driving force of socialism. His observations and conclusions, arrived at by the turn of the century, are far in advance of what now goes by the name of modern penology. Having noticed that the great majority of prisoners comes from one social class, and that their number can be accurately predicted from year to year, it was clear to him that the existence of that class was the true ground of antisocial actions—not the bad bloodlines dear to the sociology of the day, carrying the psychic deformations categorized by Max Nordau and Lombroso, and appealed to as a matter of course by Zola. What scientific prejudice looked upon as natural and inevitable, the concentration of bad bloodlines in the poorest class, Kropotkin saw as a comforting illusion. The conditions of life to which that class was subjected would amply explain the incidence of crime within it; there was no reason to appeal to the role of heredity, which in any case had been reduced in Nordau's popular system to a single effect, "degeneration."

Given want, ignorance, and spiritual deprivation, only exceptional individuals among the poor could hope to secure themselves against the fate of their class, whose natural condition was sporadic employment as the "reserve army of industry." The means of life were in the hands of banks, landowners, and industrialists—and their deputies, shopkeepers and the owners of rented dwellings. In a money economy that rationed out grossly inadequate sums to a large portion of the working class, the demands for cash that shopkeepers and landlords made of all would-be purchasers and tenants left a substantial number with insufficient food, poor clothing, and miserable shelter. The consequences for that large group were general desperation, a high disease and mortality rate, prostitution on a scale scarcely conceivable in these more affluent times (mainly because industry has now found profitable uses for female labor), a large number of crimes against property, as with unconscious wit we are accustomed to call them, and a much smaller but still appalling number of crimes against persons—in those days as in ours almost uniformly crimes of the poor against the poor.

By a kind of shorthand, Kropotkin represented as a single quality the psychological traits that might possibly help a poor man or woman to escape the statistical catastrophe connected with membership in the lowest class. That is, singular intelligence, application, ruthlessness, and so forth he resumed under the term "will"—the exercise of a steady determination to perdure in the midst of misery while avoiding its almost unavoidable consequences. The discipline of the prison—of all prisons everywhere—Kropotkin rightly understood as designed specifically to crush the will of the prisoner. Insofar as the process was effective, and over the long run it is very generally effective, its final result is a prisoner trained to abandon forethought, initiative, self-reliance, and all the other qualities implicit in the concept of will. Accordingly, the sure fruits of the prison system are recidivism—a statistically predictable number of continual offenders and offenses—and the existence of a special criminal culture. That culture is indeed socially heritable, whereas the supposedly heritable "criminal tendency" is biological nonsense. (The Y chromosome, that triumph of contemporary scientific sociology, had not been invented in Kropotkin's time, which saved him the labor of exploding it as a significant factor in promoting criminality. *Plus ça change. . . .*)

Kropotkin's conception of crime and its origins identified two contributing causes. The first was the social order, which depended absolutely on the maldistribution of socially created wealth; that is, the property system, which concentrated the ownership of the means of life within a small group and gave its members power over their social inferiors. The laws that reflected this state of affairs were designed to protect and perpetuate it, and Kropotkin regarded the transgressing of those laws as an inevitable consequence of the instincts for self-defense, self-enlargement, and self-realization. His formulation of this aspect of the question argues that the law is literally the origin of crime; it defines all crimes, inventing new categories from time to time and dropping others—for the most part in the interest of the ruling class—and is the point of contact and conflict between the people and the state. The complexity of the law, and, humanly speaking, its arbitrary character, make crime a by-product of the normal function-

ing of society. The cure for the kind of crime that is a perennial feature of the social order and the legal system that defends it is simply the abolition of that social order and that legal system. If there is no invidious affluence, if there is no implacable economic pressure, most of the actions classified as crimes will not occur.

Clearly, Kropotkin did not believe in the Fall of Man—perhaps because in practice only the poor seemed to have inherited Adam's curse. And if the solution proposed by Kropotkin strikes the reader as too sweeping and simpleminded, a panacea rather than a specific, let him call to mind the part of our experience that nevertheless confirms it. The law itself, as we all know perfectly well, makes one large class of crime happen simply by defining it as crime: when the production and sale of alcohol were declared unlawful in the United States, two crimes were created *ipso facto* and on a grand scale, moonshining and bootlegging. And we know very well that social inequities are the absolutely essential conditions for other varieties of offenses: rich women do not become prostitutes, poor women do; rich men do not engage in mugging or burglary, poor men do. And on the other hand, stock fraud, defalcation, or price-fixing are not offenses that are within the reach of most of us. These practices are restricted to persons who have an appreciable share of economic power already and are in a position to take advantage of their fellows in good fortune. These facts, of course, are so plain and so universally understood as to be omitted from most discussions of the subject, so that it is worth remarking on them in the most naïve way. Kropotkin's naïveté is a good part of his genius.

The second cause of crime in Kropotkin's view is an indirect result of social arrangements adopted for the benefit of the ruling class. That is the moral degradation entailed upon the working class not by hard conditions merely but by hard conditions that are mostly man-made and which their victims are nevertheless powerless to change. The habit and the expectation of failure are the most negative aspect of what it is now fashionable to call the culture of poverty. That culture no doubt compares favorably at some points with the culture of invidious affluence—it is hard for the disadvantaged to be as selfishly obtuse about the living conditions of the majority of their fellows because they experience those conditions themselves—but on the whole the moral and esthetic advantage lies with the comfortable classes, just as one would expect. What did we imagine was being mass-produced in the slums, sweetness and light? We knew better than that, but were accustomed to look on such things as being inevitable and therefore not our business. Kropotkin regards the demoralization of the poor as perhaps the worst social evil, the more so in that it is enforced by the common modes of social discipline. Among that class, crimes of violence occur in a much higher proportion than in any other, even when entirely divorced from the prospect of material gain, as in robbery or extortion. Murder (as a matter of statistics the victim is most often a relative or friend of the murderer), assault, rape—these are crimes that testify in Kropotkin's terms to mental and moral sickness, the greater part of which he attributes to the living conditions of the working class. It is a matter for wonder that social theorists should prefer to this reasonable supposition one or another variety of the theory that the poor—meaning most people—are a vast pool of unfavorable genes, a theory, incidentally, that libels the grandparents of most of the theorists in question.

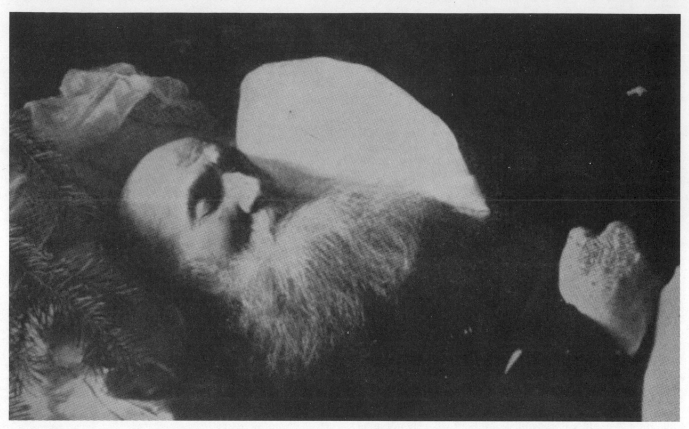

Kropotkin on his deathbed.

It is striking that Kropotkin's method of social analysis was also, and designedly, a method of social therapy. His inveterate habit was to deal with social problems as if they were necessarily susceptible of solution. That would in any case seem to be the part of wisdom, since social phenomena do not generally appear to us to constitute problems until we reach a stage in our evolution that suggests the possibility of making improvements. But, especially in this era of problem-solving, when for two centuries authors have busied themselves with the uniquely modern preoccupation of offering solutions in every department of human affairs, it is easy to overlook a peculiar virtue of Kropotkin's social therapy, and that is its radical, its transcendental character.

Let us consider a familiar case of problem-solving, the concern of that useful class of books whose titles start with the words, "How to." *How to Win Friends and Influence People, How to Get and Keep the Job You Want, How to Make Money in Commodities,* or even *How to Avoid Probate.* One thing is understood about any book that honorably lives up to a title of this kind: it takes the world and mankind as given, and suggests how the reader can profit by what is given, turning to his personal advantage the unchanging structure of the social universe. The instinct exhibited here is prudential. At its best it can be a form of wisdom—not simply laudable but indispensable to the progress of the human race. Indeed, it is probably the impulse to which we owe the fact that at some point our species came down from the trees and began to devise a more ample culture. The instinct in question takes one step at a time, and over periods measurable on the scale contemplated by geology, accomplishes, in terms of civilization, a

work as striking as the raising of a mountain range or the carving of the Grand Canyon. But when mankind has achieved a measure of civilization—some power over natural forces and a degree of self-awareness—the indispensable prudential instinct working through long centuries is no longer adequate. With self-awareness, men's dissatisfactions have grown acute. Intimations of moral possibility not vouchsafed to societies in the savage state exacerbate our present discontents, making them next thing to unbearable.

In the case of our own civilization specifically, another force, and a sinister one, is also at work to intensify the urgency we feel. That is the spiritual underemployment which ravages human beings in industrialized countries, the disease of the will that affects men and women for whom there is no fulfilling occupation, no fulfilling leisure, but only mechanical work and mechanical distractions. Societies so afflicted are more than a little mad, more than a little drawn to self-destruction, as the history of this century must suggest. At such a time the prudential instinct devises atomic weapons and gas chambers, or, with equal innocence and insouciance, data banks and microwave ovens.

In this regard, the prudential instinct seems to pose the question of life in some such terms as these: How to do more cheaply, more efficiently, more effectively, what we are already doing. If we trust blindly to that impulse, two inconveniences are likely to arise in any world that is, like ours, a conditional one. First, the prudential instinct is at war with the ideal of the examined life, whose central question is, how are we to live? That is, not simply, what means shall we adopt, but what means to what end? If our innovations and adaptations are not made in that spirit, then it is a mere accident if to persevere in what we are already doing is not simply to compound a social, political, ethical mistake. Then, it is a matter of experience, especially in an exploitive system directed by the desire for profit, that in innumerable cases practices and products are altered for the worse in the attempt to procure their benefits more cheaply and efficiently in terms of a narrow calculus of money costs. As cheap and efficient methods replace forever the methods and materials adapted to more desirable ends, our standards of what is in fact desirable sink. We forget what is desirable and make do with what is procurable—even developing a refined connoisseurship of the inferior. If we seek a monument, let us bethink ourselves what kind of food affluent Americans have accustomed themselves to find acceptable during the last twenty-five years. Or, if that example appear too trivial, what about the history of the socialist movement during this century of its practical triumph and moral decline? What horrors have socialists not learned to accept, little by little, in the name of socialism?

Peter Kropotkin's attitude appears to be naturally a philosophic one, concentrated upon this central issue. His habit of framing all practical measures in terms of ultimate goals— the habit of a moralist, asking, what is the aim we seek? Is it consistent with our other aims, with our best insights?—is the habit that underlies his method of social criticism and his program of social construction. Not only does that characteristic bent liberate his thought from the hopeless karma entailed upon mere prudential instinct, but it also frees him in an unexpected way for the work of self-analysis that is the beginning of any useful analysis of society.

C. Wright Mills suggested that the task of political sociology was to find the connections between private troubles and public issues; in doing so, the great political theorists always start, like the great poets, from the same point, their sense of the meaning of their own experience. It is that kind of insight that often permits Kropotkin to transcend, like a genuine poet, philosopher, prophet, the habits and interests of his social class, the limitations of his own experience. Kropotkin remarked about the socialist movement in general—of which movement he was, as an anarchist, a conscious, ardent adherent—that its imaginative scope was limited by the social experience of its leaders and doctrinaires, middle class and upper class almost to a man, and imbued with an uncritical faith in theories and social modalities already developed under capitalism.

An argument of the nineteenth century, almost unintelligible today, so far have we lost the genuine impetus toward the reconstruction of society, is that the revolution must not be political only, but social. *La sociale,* the radical Left in France called that needful revolution, omitting the substantive, too well understood as the ground of a thousand debates. *La sociale* implied, among other things, the abolition of the wage system, for unless the working class were in possession of the means of life, and not simply accorded rations at the discretion of leaders, no fundamental change in the condition of that class could be achieved by whatever revolution. And the wage system is an integral feature of capitalist organization, but no more so than representative institutions, which are historically dependent upon so-called free labor—that is, the existence of a proletariat, defined as a class that has nothing but its labor to sell, and must sell its labor in order to live. In his essay, **"Anarchist Communism,"** Kropotkin draws the moral, one completely at odds with Marxian socialism:

Representative government has accomplished its historical mission; it has given a mortal blow to court-rule; and by its debates it has awakened public interest in public questions. But to see in it the government of the future socialist society is to commit a gross error. Each economic phase of life implies its own political phase; and it is impossible to touch the very basis of the present economic life— private property—without a corresponding change in the very basis of the political organization. Life already shows in which direction the change will be made. Not in increasing the powers of the State, but in resorting to free organization and free federation in all those branches which are now considered as attributes of the State.

And in *Modern Science and Anarchism,* he repeats the argument:

Socialism, we have said—whatever form it may take in its evolution towards communism—must find *its own form* of political organization. Serfdom and absolute monarchy have always marched hand in hand. The one rendered the other a necessity. The same is true of capitalist rule, whose political form is representative government, either in a republic or in a monarchy. This is why socialism *cannot* utilize representative government as a weapon for liberating labor, just as it cannot utilize the church and its theory of divine right, or imperialism and Caesarism, with its theory of hierarchy of functionaries, for the same purpose.

A new form of political organization has to be worked out the moment that socialist principles shall enter into our life. And it is self-evident that this new form will have to be *more popular, more decentralized, and nearer to the folk-mote self-government* than representative government can ever be.

Because history, in the capitalist and socialist world alike, has taken a very different path than that suggested by Kropotkin, the power of the ruling classes everywhere has grown in our own day in proportion with the increase in material wealth. That power is now most dramatically represented by the ability of three governments—swollen and turgid with the wealth produced by their enormous populations—to destroy the prospects for civilization and perhaps render the planet uninhabitable in a quarter of an hour. We are sleepwalkers approaching a precipice, and our judgment of the outcome is clouded both by fear and by the habit of living with the possibility of universal destruction. But so far as it is given to us to see the future, the end of the human experiment may well be at hand. The time accorded us before we are extinguished by the folly of the governments of the world may simply prove too short to allow the social inventiveness of mankind to devise the means of salvation.

But if the sentence is not carried out swiftly, there are strong forces at work that may revoke it. To put the matter plainly, those forces will revoke the sentence by destroying the state, whose ultimate expression is atomic bombs. For modern governments are not only more powerful than governments have ever been, with a more absolute grip on the life of every human being, but they are also more unstable and more vulnerable to revolution. That vulnerability is not confined to the advanced industrial countries of the West; the advances in communications have spread a common consciousness around the world in the last half century—that is the meaning of the most striking political phenomenon of our time, the entry upon the stage of history of brown, black, and yellow men armed with automatic weapons. In our time the government of China is as vulnerable as that of France, or Russia, or the United States. Inflation, industrial depression, pollution of the environment, war, depletion and destruction of natural resources—not only are governments helpless to prevent the social catastrophes that take those varied and closely related forms, but it has become quite clear that the coercive state is itself the origin and instrument of those plagues. Society is indeed the human condition, but the state as an expression of society is no longer viable in the proper sense of the word; it will die. Its death flurries are more and more alarming, and may overwhelm the peoples of the world. Or the peoples of the world may dispatch the moribund state before the atomic arsenals are breached.

History presses upon the modern age as it could not do in any former time, when the state had not yet amassed the totalitarian power that is supported by industrialization. If we are not now in a supreme crisis, mankind has never known any. And it is precisely in this era of forced and sharpened choices that the wisdom and humanity of Kropotkin's vision of man commends itself to us. If we do not look upon ourselves as creatures worth saving—and our sense of worth as individuals and as nations has suffered enormously from the unfulfilled promises of the democratic revolutions—then Kropotkin will appeal to us as no more than a figure of a happier time, when hope was permissible, when men knew no better than to hope. But if we have any remnant of virtue as men and women, then Kropotkin will not serve our nostalgia for a golden time. Instead, his social vision will encourage our self-respect, and his social expedients suggest how we may set about making a society that actively encourages the exercise of generosity, dignity, and honor. (pp. vii-xxiii)

> *Emile Capouya and Keitha Tompkins, in an introduction to* The Essential Kropotkin, *edited by Emile Capouya and Keitha Tompkins, Liveright, 1975, pp. vii-xxiii.*

VINCENT C. PUNZO (essay date 1976)

[*In the following excerpt, Punzo assesses the likelihood of Kropotkin's system of federated communities achieving a humane society, particularly as compared to the possibility for success in a centralized state.*]

The following characterization made by Reinhold Niebuhr in 1937 is a good example of the way in which anarchism has been viewed by the majority of political philosophers and theorists. "Anarchism is, in short, a disease. It is the psychosis of infantile idealists who do not know what kind of a world it is in which we are living, what human nature is really like, and what the necessities of government are." Fortunately, there is some indication that a more open outlook on anarchism has begun to develop in the Anglo-American world during the past few years. Whatever one's ultimate judgment on the acceptability of anarchism may be, such a development can be seen to be fortunate for political philosophy in that it represents a step in the deepening and broadening of the dialogue conducted in this area. The critical work of political philosophy has suffered in the past to the extent that anarchism has often been set up as a strawman to be quickly brushed aside so that the political philosopher could move to the task of evaluating and criticizing different forms of state

existence. This essay will offer a challenge to this sort of procedure by drawing together what seems to me to be the essential strands of the case against the ideal of state existence as developed by the Russian anarchist Peter Kropotkin (1842-1921). My exposition will stress the philosophical rather than the tactical side of Kropotkin's anarchism. It will be restricted to that level of reflection which Alfred North Whitehead has described as encompassing the task of philosophy.

Proceeding from the view that humanity has been motivated through history by general ideas that could not be fully encapsulated in the language of a given period, Whitehead sees philosophy as contributing to the development of an organized and systematic comprehension of these ideas:

> But the growth of generality of apprehension is the slowest of all evolutionary changes. It is the task of philosophy to promote this growth in mentality. In so far as there is success, the specialized applications of great ideas are purified from their gross associations with savage fancies. The Carthaginians were a great civilized trading nation. They belonged racially to one of the great progressive sections of mankind. . . . Yet, when Plato was speculating, this great people could so conceive the supreme powers of the Universe that they sacrificed their children to Moloch as an act of religious propitiation. The growth in generality of understanding makes such savagery impossible in corresponding civilizations today.

This paper will treat Kropotkin's critique of state existence on the level of the philosopher's concern with advancing the generality of apprehension. It is hoped that this approach will provide a foundation for purifying the application of our great political ideals from their associations with savage fancies. It is always easier to spot the savagery inherent in the general ideals or principles of another people or of another age than it is to spot analogous savagery in our own culture or in our own time. The evils and inhumanity that are a part of our experience are perceived as being necessary and unavoidable because of the very nature of man, but not as in any way grounded in the ideals according to which our society is organized. The ideals of other peoples are infected with savagery and stand in need of purification, but our ideals are totally pure. Kropotkin's work is useful in offering a challenge to such smugness about our political ideals. Specifically, he challenges the view that the ideal of state existence, especially that of a parliamentary or representative type which is often advanced as the highest expression of this ideal, constitutes the most humane ideal possible for the organization of human society. The thrust of Kropotkin's challenge is to criticize the state as the ideal instrument for the realization of such political values as liberty and justice and to call for the replacement of the state by a system of federated communities as an instrument for such values. This challenge calls for a shift in the underlying general perspective of our political thinking from a concern with finding the appropriate state mechanisms for the realization of human values to a concern with the establishment of a free communal order as the appropriate instrument of such realization. (pp. 3-5)

• • • • •

This section will undertake to present the argument which Kropotkin used to sustain his contention that the modern state has played an essential role in breaking down the communal relations among human beings. That this argument is at the heart of his anarchist communism will be more fully appreciated after we have seen the importance which Kropotkin attaches to community in the achievement of the great ideals of the French Revolution, liberty, equality, fraternity. Although . . . he rejected the dog-eat-dog interpretation of Darwin's work, he saw himself as employing Darwin's evolutionary method in his own criticism of the state. He distinguished this method from a metaphysical approach which he characterized as appealing to natural rights and as developing its view of the state by appeals to such concepts as "Universal Spirit," "Aim of Life," or the "Unknowable." This rejection of a metaphysical method involves a rejection not only of an Hegelian approach to the state, but also of the use of a state of nature involving a war of all against all which was used by seventeenth and eighteenth century political theorists as a means of justifying state existence. Beginning with an imaginary state of nature in which human beings were in constant conflict with one another, these political theorists found it easy to depict the state, born of an equally imaginary social contract, as the source of human progress and salvation.

Kropotkin's critique of the modern state is based on a study of its historical development. Such an approach reveals that human beings lived under such different forms of communal existence as the clan, the village community, and the medieval city for centuries before the birth of the modern state. Kropotkin saw the historical growth of the state as a long process involving a number of false starts and setbacks through the centuries. Working out of the context of such a perspective, the modern state is seen as going through its birth pains from approximately the sixteenth century and as beginning to move out of its adolescence with the defeat of anarchist communitarian tendencies of the French Revolution. However, it was not until the nineteenth century that the modern state achieved its maturity. By this time the mechanisms were in place which made it possible for a whole nation to be mobilized for war at the word of a capital. The bureaucratic network was established, transforming human beings into "officials" who mechanically followed the commands of whoever happened to be in authority. Citizens were fully caught up in the routine of giving mindless obedience to law and of accepting the superiority of their legislators and judges. The school system was by then able to function as an instrument to train youngsters to obey the state and to revere its leaders and officials. By then the industrial system had settled into its comfortable marriage with state power, enabling it to exploit both the riches of nature and the abilities of workers for its own advantage. Finally, science was also by that time comfortably settled in its niche of being a tool for the well-being of this marriage. The state which is the object of Kropotkin's critique is understood by him to be a centralized power which controls the life of a society within certain territorial limits by placing certain vital functions of this society in the hands of a few people. This centralized power uses legislative and policing mechanisms to subject certain classes in society to the domination of others. This conception of the state is clearly not value free. It is rather a conception which Kropotkin sees as corresponding to the nature of the state as that nature has been revealed in history.

Kropotkin is well aware of the ideals on behalf of which political philosophers of the seventeenth and eighteenth centuries defended the rise of the modern state. He shares their trust in the sovereignty of reason, their opposition to the rights claimed by some people to dominate the lives of others, their commitment to equality, and their contribution to the spirit of revolt against aristocracy and privilege. He acknowledges that there were enduring humanitarian ideals, such as equality before the law, and religious and political freedom, involved in the movement toward the modern state and that representative government has rendered service to humanity's struggle against autocracy. Granted all this, Kropotkin insists that the state understood as a hierarchical, centralized structure directing the lives of its citizens is by its very nature inimical to the humanitarian ideals which it claims to serve. Underlying this position is the principle, "that a social institution cannot lend itself to all the desired goals, since, like every organ, it developed according to the function it performed, in a definite direction and not in all possible directions." It is important to understand how Kropotkin interpreted and used this principle because it provides a key methodological point of difference between Kropotkin's anarchism and a statist position.

A statist may readily admit that the history of the modern state is marred by brutal and inhumane episodes, but would insist that such episodes are to be accounted for by certain leaders, or by the defeat of a certain party or individual. In short, the statist does not see such brutality or inhumanity as an indictment of the very character of state existence. If Kropotkin's critique were limited to a mere listing of state evils, the statist could make short work of it by pointing out that these evils have nothing to do with the very nature of state existence. However, as Kropotkin actually employs the principle that a social institution is to be understood by the direction in which it has developed, it is clear that he does not interpret it to mean that we can understand an institution by merely listing the evils and the good points that have been associated with it through history. The thrust of the principle is to move our reflection from the ideals of human equality and liberation which the state claims to serve to a consideration of the hierarchical and pyramidal structure of state existence.

Such a consideration reveals an "insolvable problem" in the state's attempt to function as a servant of society while at the same time claiming the right to force individuals to obey its decisions. At the heart of this insolvable problem lies the fact that the hierarchical structure that is an essential characteristic of the modern state is destructive of the very communal life which it claims to serve and which is necessary to humanity's realization of the ideals of freedom and equality. The modern parliamentary state played a major role in advancing the cause of those who came to control newly developed industrial and technological powers by providing the needed structural mechanisms to open up foreign trade markets and to develop large scale manufacturing processes. Such achievements required the breakdown of the communal order of village life. It was necessary to separate the peasant from his village and, in general, to abolish the local, communal powers that constituted challenges to the state's control over its citizens. Thus, far from being the original principle of community introduced into the lives of a primitive humanity that existed as a "disorderly agglomeration of individuals," the state played a central role in dissolving previously existent communal bonds among human beings so as to organize them along individualistic life styles that were more congenial to the interests of the industrial and commercial classes.

These classes were able to use the state in this manner because intrinsic to the structural dynamics of state existence is the thrust to break down communal life among its members. The state deprives its citizens of the type of environment which human beings need to develop a sense of shared interests and responsibilities insofar as it arrogates to certain "officials" the power to determine the public character of a society by passing laws which control such areas as education, welfare, and the economic and property relations among citizens. Kropotkin describes the outcome of such a state of affairs as follows:

> Today we live side by side without knowing one another. We come together at meetings on an election day: we listen to the lying or fanciful professions of faith of a candidate, and we return home. The State has the care of all questions of public interest; the State alone has the function of seeing that we do not harm the interests of our neighbor, and, if it fails in this, of punishing us in order to repair the evil. . . . You hardly know one another, nothing unites you, everything tends to alienate you from one another, and finding no better way, you ask the Almighty (formerly it was a God, now it is the State) to do all that lies within his power to stop antisocial passions from reaching their highest climax.

The pyramidal structure of state existence is such that effective and significant decisions concerning the direction which society is to take are reserved for those at the top of the pyramid, thereby depriving the great bulk of citizens of the kind of participation in public policy that is essential to the forging of communal ties.

Although she does not refer to Kropotkin's writings, Hannah Arendt has advanced a similar criticism of the modern state in the closing chapter of her book *On Revolution* in which she argues that modern-day state structures have been unable to preserve and develop the treasure that was imbedded in the revolutionary tradition founded in the French and American Revolutions. This treasure entailed the promise of a society in which there was to be sufficient "public space" to enable citizens to engage fully in significant discussions, debates, and decisions concerning issues of public policy. She maintains that representative government under a two-party system has, at best, given the ruled a certain measure of control over their rulers, but it "has by no means enabled the citizen to become a 'participator' in public affairs." There is an oligarchic character to representative government in that the public happiness and public freedom that are involved in a meaningful participation in the dialogue shaping public policy are not widely and generally enjoyed, but are reserved as privileges of a few.

Arendt and Kropotkin also share a similar view on revolutionary councils or communes as the best historical exemplifications of the ideal of a proper public space for the people's involvement in public business. Both see these communes as representing the underlying spirit of revolutionary movements. Writing about the French Revolution, Kropotkin maintains that the communes established during that period differed from the so-called representative bodies of the modern state to which citizens hand over the public business, after having briefly enjoyed the excitement of election fever. The various " 'districts,' 'sections,' 'tribes' " were so organized that the people were able to function as participators rather than as spectators in the ongoing process of public business. Arendt finds this sort of communal spirit running through the American, French, and Russian Revolutions. Unlike Kropotkin, she maintains that it was the American Revolu-

tion which most properly captured the communal character of the revolutionary spirit. However, she does not see the American Revolution as succeeding in the preservation and development of this communal spirit.

There is a further area of agreement between Arendt and Kropotkin concerning the pernicious effect the lack of public space has on the very possibility of the formation of public opinion. Arendt holds that insofar as the Constitution of the United States established a public space available only to the representatives of the people and not the people themselves, it provided no mechanism for combatting lethargy and inattention to public business on the part of the people. Because present state structures fail to provide the public space required for open discussion and public debate that are essential to the formation of public opinion, it is inappropriate to speak of the formation of public opinion within these structures. Public moods are formed under these conditions, not public opinion. Kropotkin conveys a similar message in his description of the way in which citizens existing under state institutions react to issues of public significance.

> In our busy life, preoccupied as we are with the numberless petty affairs of everyday existence, we are all too inclined to pass by many great evils which affect Society without giving them the attention they really deserve. If sensational "revelations" about some dark side of our life occasionally find their way into the daily Press; if they succeed in shaking our indifference and awaken public attention, we may have in the papers, for a month or two, excellent articles and letters on the subject. Many well-meant things may then be said, the most humane feelings expressed. But the agitation soon subsides; and, after having asked for some new regulations or laws, in addition to the hundreds of thousands of regulations and laws already in force; after having made some microscopic attempts at combating by a few individual efforts a deep-rooted evil which ought to be combated by the combined efforts of Society at large, we soon return to our daily occupations without caring much about what has been done. It is good enough if, after all the noise, things have not gone from bad to worse.

Taken out of context of Kropotkin's critique of state structures, this statement may be seen as a repetition of the tired old complaint that people are not willing to get involved in public issues. However, seen within this context, it is clear that the point of the description is to call attention to how hopeless it is to expect people caught up in the life style of state existence to put in the time and effort necessary to the formation of a reflective public opinion on matters of public importance. The structure of state existence contributes to the development of a mind-set and life style among most of its citizens that places matters of public business beyond the scope of their responsibilities. Issues of penal reform, of the underlying justice of an economic system, and of the fairness of judicial processes are not seen as the ongoing business of all the people. That this should be the case is not surprising in view of the fact that the life of a citizen in the modern state is not founded on such values as shared interests and responsibilities, mutual aid and dependence. Under the influence of state structures and capitalism, the individual is led to seek his fulfillment and security in money and at the expense of his fellow man.

The mention of capitalism brings up the issue separating Kropotkin from state socialists. The latter would argue that it is the capitalist system and not state structures that is at the root of the break-down of community. Hence, state socialism is seen as the remedy for this breakdown. Although sharing the socialist criticism of capitalism, Kropotkin holds that socialism cannot escape the requirement that a new form of economic existence demands a new form of political organization. Humanity's political and economic liberation will not be realized by attempts to graft a new form of economic existence on old political forms. Absolute monarchy provided the political life for serfdom. Parliamentarianism provides the political expression for capitalist exploitation. State socialists are involved in a self-defeating enterprise insofar as they are committed to using the hierarchical structures of state existence to develop communal control of the means of production. Those very structures frustrate the development of communal involvement and responsibility that must underlie any meaningful communal control. Unless the political mechanisms relating to the over-all ordering of society are also socialized so as to give people a more meaningful say in this ordering than is possible within the structures of state existence, a so-called socialized economy will be in reality an economy controlled by the few occupying strategic spots in the governmental bureaucracy.

If the socialist ideal is to be properly realized, we must move beyond the structures of the modern "representative" state. "A free society, regaining possession of the common inheritance, must seek, in free groups and free federations of groups, a new organization, in harmony with the new economic phase of history." Kropotkin envisions such a free society as being composed of

> . . . a multitude of associations, federated for all the purposes which require federation: trade federations for production of all sorts,—agricultural, industrial, artistic; communes for consumption, making provision for dwellings, gas works, supplies of food, sanitary arrangements, etc.

These communes may form federations among themselves and also with trade federations. Such federations are seen to be analogous in their unity to the railway companies and postal services of various nations which have been able to cooperate with no reliance on a centralizing power above them which claims to be their principle of union. We can point to the cooperation among multinational corporations in our own day as exemplifying the type of free federations Kropotkin had in mind. The problem with this example is that such unions are established for exploitative purposes and are established by those at the top of the economic pyramid without meaningful communal participation from below. Granted this shortcoming, the fact remains that this example, together with examples of other voluntary international organizations such as international philosophical or scientific associations, is useful as providing living hints of the type of social order which Kropotkin sees as an alternative to state existence.

This brief exposition of Kropotkin's alternative to state forms of existence was offered not as a fully detailed blue-print for the future, but as a sketch of a type of societal order that holds promise of being able to overcome the difficulties in state structures. Kropotkin took the right tack in one of his earliest anarchist writings when he pointed to the futility of trying to present a detailed blueprint of the character of future societies. Recognizing that the humanity of the future will be in a position to learn from our successes and failures and to be aware of problems and possibilities that are present-

ly beyond our comprehension, Kropotkin restricted himself to the task of providing a generalized sketch of a non-statist society that would be useful as a working model for those who accepted his anarchist principles. This paper is not directed to defending Kropotkin's outline of a future society. It is concerned rather with the more basic issue centering in his critique of state existence as being destructive of those social forces of human existence which are essential to the realization of such values as liberty and justice. If this critique can be rationally sustained, it establishes a *prima facie* reason for trying to develop forms of social existence different from the modern state. (pp. 5-12)

• • • • •

If we are to understand the type of social order which is congenial to a communitarian individualism, we must move to a consideration of Kropotkin's ethics of community. His views on the nature of community and on its central importance to the realization of such values as justice and freedom are the key ingredients of this ethics. Kropotkin maintains that humanity's moral existence revolves around three principles, viz., sociality, justice, and magnanimity. There is an interdependence among these principles in that the first provides a basis for the realization of the second, but the first could not sustain itself for long in human existence apart from the development of the second. The same type of relation exists between the second and third principles. . . . Kropotkin attempted to show that sociality understood as an instinct developed in the lives of animals and humans over a long evolutionary movement constitutes the biological foundation of moral existence. Through the development of this instinct, both humans and animals experienced the power of mutual aid, and the joy of social living.

Although grounded in biological instinct, human morality cannot exist simply or exclusively as a matter of instinct or feeling. As human life becomes more complex and as the difficulties of this life increase, the sense of sociability or mutual aid is in danger of losing its hold, with a consequent strengthening of narrowly individualistic habits and passions. The evolutionary development of reason as a factor of human existence has helped prevent this, and has contributed to the strengthening of the sense of sociability. Reason enables human beings to deal with the complexities of their lives by introducing the concept of justice. The development of this concept brings them to see that the right of every individual is as unassailable as the right of every other. If this conception were absent from the human scene, the inevitable collisions among human beings would ultimately mean the disintegration of society.

Intrinsic to this notion of justice is the recognition of equality among all the members of a society. Present societies may talk a great deal about equality, but their failure to realize such equality in the very life styles of their members constitutes a major obstacle to the attainment of a more humane moral level of existence. There can be no real justice in a society in which an equal respect of the rights of all individuals is contradicted at every turn by "existing inequalities of rights and possibilities of development." The equality Kropotkin seeks is political and economic equality. On an economic level, such equality requires that there be an end to the division of labor which separates human beings into those who work with their hands and those who work with their brains. On a political level, it requires an end to hierarchical structures in which human beings are said to hold certain offices which give them a right to rule over other human beings. So long as human beings are pressed into certain moulds or roles by virtue of their economic status or by virtue of the political office they may hold, the very structures of social existence will represent a living contradiction to the achievement of true justice among human beings.

Even if the equality essential to justice were achieved in a society, that society could not long maintain itself unless it moved beyond justice to magnanimity. If every person lived only according to the morality of the trader, taking care in all things that he never gave more than he received, society would eventually come to an end, along with the very principle of equality itself. At this point there is a merging of Kropotkin's conception of magnanimity as the completion of morality and his notion of a humane communal existence. Magnanimity which is the highest development of human morality is also the archimedian point of human community.

> Human society would not exist for more than two consecutive generations if everyone did not give infinitely more than that for which he is paid in coin, in "cheques," or in civic rewards. . . . If middle-class society is decaying, if we have got into a blind alley from which we cannot emerge without attacking past institutions with torch and hatchet, it is precisely because we have given too much to counting. It is because we have let ourselves be influenced into *giving* only to *receive*. It is because we have aimed at turning society into a commercial company based on *debit* and *credit*.

There is a difference between an association of human beings who come together for the purpose of mutual exploitation and a community of human beings whose members are committed to shared goals. Each individual in an association of mutual exploitation is looking out only for his own good, a good not shared by other members each of whom also seeks his own good. It is this difference that underlies Kropotkin's contention that unless magnanimity functions within a social order, that order cannot be just for long. Justice is needed to resolve conflicts among individuals. If every individual in society is concerned exclusively with his own good, thus cutting off the possibility of an appeal being made to certain shared goals in the resolution of conflicts concerning individual goods, there will come a time when the just and non-coercive resolution of conflicts will become impossible. In short, if there is to be justice and community in human life, the goals of individuals must be expanded to include goods that reach beyond their own exclusive well-being.

Kropotkin gives a number of examples of the type of commitment that he sees as central to community. One example is that of the person whose commitment to truth is such that he is willing to give up personal pleasures and comforts in this search and who is not deterred by scoffing ignoramuses. Another example is the revolutionist willing to sacrifice the pleasures of family life in order to work more effectively against social injustices. The soldier willing to face death for his country also exemplifies this commitment. It is not only these striking cases of magnanimity that Kropotkin sees as essential to communal existence.

> Finally it [the "fertility of good will" or magnanimity] is in all those numberless acts of devotion, less striking and therefore unknown and almost always misprized, which may be continually observed especially among women, if we will take the trouble to open our eyes and notice what lies at the very

foundation of human life, and enables it to unfold itself one way or another in spite of the exploitation and oppression it undergoes.

That magnanimity is indispensable to the continued existence of human society is also seen by the fact that statist societies which are so constituted as to encourage bourgeois and aesthete types of individualism find that they must soften the debit-credit morality that characterizes them.

> This stepmother of a society against whom we are in revolt, too, distributes halfpenny dinners to prevent the pillaging of her shops; builds hospitals—often very bad ones, but sometimes splendid ones—to prevent the ravages of contagious diseases. She, too, after having paid the hours of labour, shelters the children of those she has wrecked. She takes their needs into consideration and doles out charity.

In addition to living parasitically off the types of magnanimous behavior mentioned above, statist societies find that they must practice at least a minimal type of magnanimity as an antibiotic against the disease of their own debit-credit morality that threatens their very existence.

Whatever ethological evidence Kropotkin may have to support his notion of the essential sociability of human life, it would appear that he has gone beyond the evidence in expecting to make magnanimity the rule rather than the exception of human life. One need only look around to see that most human beings are interested only in their own well-being. In response to such criticism, Kropotkin takes the approach of ethologists who question the validity of conclusions concerning the nature of animal behavior that have been based on evidence drawn from studies of animals in captivity or in restricted laboratory situations. Similarly, when we attempt to draw conclusions concerning what sort of behavior is "natural" to human beings, we ought to consider the context or habitat within which we find them as we conduct our studies. Although there may be many sermons preached calling for sympathy and mutual aid among human beings and extolling the goodness of helping those in need, the fact of the matter is that anyone who tries to put these values into practice in our present societies is quickly informed that such values may all be appropriate in poetry and Sunday pulpits, but that they certainly are not meant to be put into practice. An individual currently finds himself in a social order in which he may be reduced to the disdained category of a "welfare recipient," if he does not look out for his own narrow self-interest. Granted that human beings find themselves in such a situation, it is not surprising that most will act out of considerations of such self-interest. It is surprising that there are still human beings who persist in behaving magnanimously under such conditions. The aim of anarchist communism is to transform the social context so that magnanimous behavior need not be self-destructive behavior. Finally, Kropotkin maintains that his critics have failed to see that human life shares in the general tendency of life itself to maintain itself through expansion and that an underlying drive in the lives of human beings is to share their abilities, whether intellectual or emotional, with others.

We are now in a position to appreciate what is at the ultimate basis of Kropotkin's indictment of the modern state and of his call for a new social form of existence. Although statists have talked a great deal about liberty and equality, states have been unable to deliver their promises of liberty and equality for all because they are destructive of the very communal life style which is necessary to the proper flowering and maturation of these values. Kropotkin's emphasis on magnanimity and community is meant to show that the search for liberty and equality in their properly human form is doomed to failure unless the search also includes a search for a value analogous to that third ideal of the French Revolution, fraternity. Apart from a communal environment, liberty is perverted and tends to become the liberty to exploit or to be exploited, and equality becomes a mere formality having no place in the real lives of human beings.

• • • • •

The purpose of this section is to present Kropotkin's account of the instruments available to a non-statist community for dealing with anti-social or criminal behavior. This issue has been chosen because Kropotkin has dealt with it at some length in his writings and because his reflections on it will serve to clarify the rational foundations of his ideal of an anarchist communal existence. Central to his handling of the issue is the view that because a free community will deny itself the luxury of prisons, it will not be content with treating crime as a brute, given fact that must be punished. If we would take the time, we would come to see that "crime," or "laziness" do not refer to simple facts of nature, but are words which involve a series of different factors leading to a certain result. In short, we ought to take the same sort of approach toward criminal behavior as we do when we discover that a child cannot hear. Deafness is not accepted as a simple natural fact, but is seen as a problem whose underlying causes must be discovered so that we may find a way of overcoming that problem. Before moving to Kropotkin's attempt to pinpoint the underlying general causes of anti-social behavior, we shall consider his evaluation of the possible means societies may use to combat crime.

He lists three such means: (1) repression as exemplified by current prison systems, (2) moral teaching and exhortation, and (3) the development and perfection of practices of mutual aid. History and practice have shown the impotency of the first option as an instrument to put an end to criminal behavior. More specifically, he argues that prisons are by their very nature self-defeating as means to combat anti-social behavior, or, more positively, as instruments for reform. Although he quotes statistics, he rests his case primarily on a descriptive analysis of the structure of prison life. The analysis involves six points. First, most prisoners see themselves as being essentially no different from many of their fellow citizens not in prison, with the latter being simply more fortunate and successful in their attempts to exploit others than the prisoners themselves have been. This point will be more fully developed when we come to consider the role of modern society in contributing to criminal behavior. Secondly, the character of prison work is inconsistent with a reforming role in that it is done not because of its attractiveness to the prisoner, but out of fear of worse punishment. Moreover, it is so poorly paid that the prisoner sees himself as a paid slave. Thirdly, inmates are isolated from the types of social interactions that would help them develop a sense of community or of involvement in working toward a common good with other members of society. Instead of thus broadening and enriching this conscious life, the narrow world of prison tends to stunt and narrow a prisoner's emotional development.

Fourthly, the regimentation of prison life hinders the growth of a prisoner's ability to make his own choices and makes it difficult for him to develop the strength of character that he may need to overcome temptations to return to a criminal way of life upon his release. This debilitating outcome is grounded in an essential principle of prison organization, viz., that of using the smallest number of guards to guard the largest number of prisoners. "The ideal of prison officials would be thousands of automatons, arising, working, eating and going to sleep by means of electric currents switched on by one of the guards." Fifthly, the tendency of prison clothing and of prison discipline to deprive a prisoner of his sense of self-respect is detrimental to the exercise of a reforming influence on the prisoners. A prisoner is treated not as a human being, but as a numbered thing who must submit to the humiliation of constant searches and who must conceal his disgust at the pettiness of certain guards or of prison life itself. Finally, the character of the relationship between guards and inmates makes it well-nigh impossible for guards to function as sources of reform.

> Forced to live in an enemy's camp, the guards cannot become models of kindness. To the league of prisoners there is opposed the league of jailers. It is the institution which makes them [the guards] what they are—petty, mean persecutors.

To make matters worse, such a situation also engenders among prisoners an outlook on life in which they see themselves on one side and organized society as personified by the guards on the other side as enemies.

Kropotkin is more sympathetic toward moral teaching as a crime-fighting tool than he is toward the repression of prisons. The effectiveness of such teaching is significantly limited, if it is contradicted by the institutional dynamics of a society or by the prevailing life style resulting from such dynamics. Thus, religious teachings may help human beings form proper ideals, but they are not adequate in and of themselves to bring about meaningful changes in the behavior of large numbers of human beings. It is "the daily habits of social life" that play the principal role in the effective determination of social morality. The failure of Christianity to take hold in society is used to illustrate this point. Despite the powerful appeal of the message of a crucified God who died to save all people and who forgave his executioners, Christianity itself eventually lost sight of its own communal message and became an ally of the state in its destruction of communal ties, once it resigned itself to accept the customs, laws, and life style of imperial Rome. Within the context of modern society dominated by the life style of bourgeois individualism, it is easy for persons to treat the Christian message as perhaps a fine theoretical ideal, but to reject it practically as an ideal for saints and not ordinary people.

Kropotkin's defense of mutual aid as the most effective tool against anti-social behavior is intimately bound up with his contention that society must shift from a primarily punitive to a primarily preventive approach to such behavior, an approach that seeks to remedy the underlying causes contributing to criminal behavior. He points to three areas in which such causes may be found, viz., physical, physiological, and social. The reference to physical causes is based on the view that relatively accurate statistical projections can be made concerning the incidence of crime in the future. For example, acts of violence tend to be more numerous in hot than in cold weather. Within agricultural societies, the richness of the harvest seems to play a role in the number of crimes that will be committed during a certain period. Kropotkin seems to cite such facts as a means of weakening the tendency on the part of many to view crime as a happening with no relations to any other factors.

He has more to say about possible physiological factors, such as brain structure, the digestive system, and the nervous system. Although he gave to Lombroso's work on criminal types more credit than it deserved, his handling of the implications of this work retains its validity in our own day. Granted that we may find certain common traits among murderers, the fact that these same traits may be found in those who are not murderers indicates that we must look to environmental conditions as being significant in determining whether these very same tendencies will issue in murderous actions or not. Kropotkin does not deny that an individual may have inherited certain tendencies which may be conducive to criminal behavior, but he emphasizes that these tendencies as they come from the hand of nature are of a rather general type. There is no tendency specifically to murder, although a person may inherit a tendency to seek risk or excitement, or may have a disposition to vanity. Such a disposition may lead to "a maniac like Napoleon the first," or it may lead to the accomplishment of great engineering feats, depending on the circumstances of an individual's life. This outlook on inherited tendencies leads Kropotkin to take a different route from those who argue that the discovery of certain tendencies in individuals at birth should give society the right to exterminate them. He maintains that the discovery of such tendencies places the responsibility on society to provide an environment in which these tendencies can be exercised in a humane manner for humane ends.

In the last analysis, Kropotkin places the greatest emphasis on the role of social structures in contributing to, preventing, or curing criminal behavior. He points out that societies have long taken credit for the achievements of their members. We see this in our own day with countries such as the United States and the Soviet Union hailing the achievements of their respective citizens as indications of the vitality of their social order. Kropotkin has no quarrel with this, provided that we recognize that the achievements of present societies are built on the achievements of the past and of countless unknown men and women. If a society is to take credit for the success of its members, it ought to be willing to share responsibility for their misdeeds. The contributory role of industrialized states to anti-social behavior is described by Kropotkin in the following statement.

> When everything round about us—the shops and the people we see in the streets, the literature we read, the money-worship we meet with every day— tends to develop an unsatiable thirst for unlimited wealth, a love for sparkish luxury, a tendency towards spending money foolishly for every avowable and unavowable purpose; . . . when the watchword of our civilized world is: "Enrich yourself! Crush down everything you meet in your way, by all means short of those which might bring you before a court!" . . . what need is there to talk about inherited criminality when so many factors of our life work in one direction—that of manufacturing beings unsuited for honest existence, permeated with anti-social feelings!

Granted a social structure in which luxury is found side-by-side with degrading poverty and in which one's economic survival requires the exploitation of others, jailers and executioners are necessary. However, unless such a structure is changed, there will be no significant inroads against criminal behavior, no matter how many jailers or executioners are employed.

If criminal behavior is to be prevented or cured, the social order that provides the breeding ground for such behavior must be changed. Specifically, Kropotkin maintains that such prevention and cure depends on the development of a sense of unity and solidarity within a society. Public morality is maintained through the unity of the people, not through policemen and judges. The key to the fight against crime is the development of truly communal relations among human beings that will involve knowing one another and providing moral support and mutual aid for one another. Instead of relying on prisons which simply add to the brutalities and inhumanity of a statist social order, we must learn to depend on "fraternal treatment and moral support," as instruments to prevent and cure criminal behavior. It seems to me that this position represents an alternative to a view that ultimately involves a modern-day equivalent to Aristotle's theory of the natural slave. This theory is implicit in the view that there are "certain people" who can be restrained from rape, muggings, murder, or robbery only through fear of imprisonment or, in some cases, death at the hands of the state. I wonder if there is anyone taking this sort of position who would be willing to include himself among these "certain people." Be that as it may, the position seems to say that certain human beings are by their very nature not susceptible to such humane influences as reason, patience, kindness, good example, or fraternal treatment, but are by nature suited only to be prisoners.

Kropotkin does not claim that fraternal treatment and communal involvement will be completely successful in overcoming criminal behavior. He admits that after doing all that it can to help a delinquent individual, a society may refuse to deal further with him, leaving him free to form another association that is more congenial to him. Moreover, he acknowledges that a society which depends as heavily on free mutual trust as does the communal order he envisions is open to being abused through an exaggeration of its own principles. It is not the fact that there will be no problems that distinguishes an anarchist society from a statist society, but that an anarchist society sees freedom and mutual aid rather than coercion as the best cure for freedom's temporary inconveniences. This acknowledgment that there will be defects and problems in the actual working out of communitarian anarchism is noteworthy because it awakens us to the necessity of comparing ideal with ideal and reality with reality when we embark on a comparative evaluation of the strengths and weaknesses of anarchism and statism. There is an unconscious tendency on the part of defenders of either of these points of view to compare the ideal of the position he defends with existential realities of the position which he opposes. With regard to the specific point at issue in this section, this means that the statist cannot validly claim that Kropotkin's admission of problems in an anarchist society establishes the case for the statist position. For the reality of state existence over the last few hundred years is certainly not a record of unqualified success in dealing with criminal behavior, whether the record is judged from the narrow point of view of stamping out crime by any and all means or from the broader point of view of how morally and humanely states have gone about this task.

· · · · ·

Kropotkin's critique of state existence has been seen to be directed to a defense of the proposition that the proper realization of such values as justice and liberty will always elude statist societies insofar as the essential structures of these societies contribute to the development of an anti-communitarian life style. So long as the great mass of people are excluded from meaningful participation in the decisions affecting the whole of society, so long as the mass of human beings find themselves in an order that encourages individuals to care only for themselves at the expense of others, so long as imprisonment functions as a central weapon against anti-social behavior, there can be no effective realization of humanity's most cherished ideals. The reason for this is that such values as justice, liberty, and security are of a communitarian nature in the sense that they need the communal environment engendered by magnanimity for their proper maturation.

The approach taken in this exposition has been restricted to that most general level of principle which influences or shapes concrete political discussions and decisions. It is inevitable and indeed appropriate that questions will arise as to concrete instruments and application of Kropotkin's communitarian perspective to the present situation. Granted the acceptability of his attempt to replace reliance on the state with a reliance on the workings of the communal powers of human existence, how is such a reliance to be implemented? To undertake anything approaching a direct and thorough answer to this question at the conclusion of what is already an overly long essay would be the height of folly. Instead of such an undertaking, this concluding section will be devoted to a critical reflection on two types of "realism" that would appear to justify a rejection of Kropotkin's communitarian outlook on the grounds that there is absolutely no way of making it effective in the world. I shall try to show that this outlook can retain a viable and positive role on the level of general political principles in face of the criticisms offered by these two types of realism.

Kropotkin's conception of the depth and range of changes that are entailed in the change from a statist to an anarchist, communist society would appear to make him an easy mark for one brand of realism.

> To give full scope to socialism entails rebuilding from top to bottom a society dominated by the narrow individualism of the shopkeeper. It is not as has sometimes been said by those indulging in metaphysical woolliness just a question of giving the worker "the total product of his labor"; it is a question of completely reshaping all relationships, from those which exist today between every individual and his churchwarden or his stationmaster to those which exist between neighborhoods, hamlets, cities, and regions. In every street, in every hamlet, in every group of men gathered around a factory or along a section of the railway line, the creative, constructive, and organizational spirit must be awakened in order to rebuild life—in the factory, in the village, in the store, in production, and in distribution of supplies. All relations between individuals and great centers of population have to be made all over again, from the very moment one alters the existing commercial or administrative organization.

Such an outlook is not likely to find favor with a "managerial or bureaucratic" realist whose approach to political change is restricted to actions such as the rescinding or passing of certain laws, the election or defeat of certain politicians or po-

litical parties, the initiating or terminating of a certain bureau, or the transference of money from one item of the budget to another. The bureaucratic realist is convinced that whatever ails society can be successfully treated by tinkering with certain facets of the given institutional order.

Before Kropotkin's position can be validly rejected because it fails to conform to the demands of this brand of realism, one must show that his diagnosis of the evils of state existence is in error. His position argues that such central social and political evils as crime, poverty, and economic injustice and exploitation are not accidental aberrations of, or superficially related to, state structures; they are rooted in the very nature of these structures. If Kropotkin's contention that an adequate and satisfactory resolution of these evils requires changes reaching down to the very foundations of our political and economic institutions is to be rejected as unrealistic, it must be shown that his assessment of the extent and depth of these evils is mistaken. This point needs to be emphasized because contemporary political thinking has become so enamored of the remedies of bureaucratic realism that instead of trying to find a remedy that suits the full depth and seriousness of certain problems, we find ourselves acknowledging as problems only those areas that can be treated by these remedies. The attractiveness of this approach is understandable. For example, it would certainly be much easier for most of us if criminal behavior could be substantially reduced by such tried and true methods as the hiring of more law enforcement officers and the use of stiffer and longer prison sentences, backed up by a more frequent use of the death penalty. Insofar as these methods are based on the presupposition that criminal behavior is something of a self-enclosed phenomenon, having no connection with the institutional dynamics and prevailing life style of our society, they require no significant change in the lives of most of us. However, if Kropotkin's analysis is right, anyone expecting this sort of approach to make a significant impact on the reduction of criminal behavior is living in a fantasy world. In short, the issue of whether it is Kropotkin or those offering essentially bureaucratic remedies who is the realist requires that one first make a judgment on the validity of Kropotkin's critique of state existence and of his view of the communal character of human existence.

The second type of realism offers a more significant challenge to the acceptability of Kropotkin's general outlook. It is a "structural" realism which argues that the conditions under which human beings presently exist render the possibilities for a free communal existence empty abstractions. The position taken by Heilbroner in his book *An Inquiry into the Human Prospect* exemplifies this type of realism. There are a number of areas in which this position coincides with that taken by Kropotkin. Heilbroner also holds that the political and economic problems confronting us today are beyond the capacities of bureaucratic tinkering within either capitalistic or socialistic systems as presently constituted. Furthermore, he sees extensive decentralization and workers' control as offering attractive humane approaches to our present problems. Finally, he sees intimations in the present for the possibility of the "redirection of history in a diminution of scale, a reduction of immense nation-states toward the 'polis' that defined the appropriate reach of political power for the ancient Greeks." Although attracted to this possibility, Heilbroner sees it as being unrealistic within the present historical context. Thus, he finds himself compelled to conclude that a realistic view of the future must include "the prospect of a far more coercive exercise of national power." This conclusion raises the ironic possibility that Kropotkin's anarchist communism must be rejected as a perspective from which humanity should try to work out its political future because the modern state has been much more effective in destroying the communal resources of human existence than he himself realized. It may be the case that the modern state has been so successful in crushing forms of social existence which would compete with it that humanity now finds itself left only with the power of the centralized state for dealing with its problems, even though it has come belatedly to realize that reliance on this power means that a comparatively small group of human beings control and dominate the lives of the majority.

In assessing the accuracy of Heilbroner's prediction we should not lose sight of the fact that possibilities for the future are not grounded exclusively in the present institutional arrangements, but are a function of the interaction of human consciousness with its world which includes these arrangements. The ideals found in human consciousness, the perspectives which human beings take on their own lives, and the hierarchy which they are willing to establish among competing values have a role to play in the constitution of those possibilities available to humanity for the building of a human future. It is this role which gives significance to philosophy's task of contributing to the growth of generality and of purifying great ideas from their savage fancies. Philosophy must try to prevent human consciousness from being so totally imprisoned by the structures of the present that it has nothing to offer beyond these structures in determining the possibilities for the future. Its reflective criticism of the general principles which play a determining role in the way in which a given society evaluates its strengths, weaknesses, and concrete possibilities must be directed to helping human consciousness distinguish between those evils and shortcomings which are intrinsic to the institutional arrangements and life style of a given society at a given historical period and those evils that are inextricably bound up with the very nature of human existence.

The question of whether or not humanity can in fact develop structures other than those of the centralized state to deal successfully and humanely with the problems that confront humanity today as it faces the future is to be answered not simply by looking at present-day institutions, but also by trying to develop the resources of human consciousness so that it does not merely mirror these institutions but plays an active role in the constitution of humane possibilities for the future. Admittedly, Heilbroner's prediction appears to be highly probable, but probability is not certainty. If human beings are not challenged to acknowledge evils that are intrinsic to state structures and to consider forms of social existence other than the modern state, if the belief that there are no resources available to humanity other than state structures to combat crime and poverty or to secure health, education, and economic well-being is not subjected to critical reflection and questioning, then this probability may indeed become a certainty. Thus, so long as there is the slightest reason to doubt Heilbroner's prediction, we would do well to probe as thoroughly as possible for a type of social order in which all members can play a direct and significant part in the determination of public policy, in which the economic resources of the community are equitably shared with no group so controlling these resources that it is able to accumulate a superabundance of goods while others must struggle for the bare neces-

sities of life, and in which compassionate aid and understanding replace prisons and death penalties as instruments for dealing with anti-social behavior. Kropotkin's critique of state existence and defense of the possibility of a communitarian existence provides a useful generalized perspective within which such a probing into our present situation can be conducted. (pp. 19-32)

Vincent C. Punzo, "The Modern State and the Search for Community: The Anarchist Critique of Peter Kropotkin," in International Philosophical Quarterly, *Vol. XVI, No. 1, March, 1976, pp. 3-32.*

AILEEN KELLY   (essay date 1976)

[*In the following excerpt, Kelly discusses renewed interest in Kropotkin's ideas and analyzes the contradictory components of messianism and nihilism in his philosophy.*]

To observers in the West, the barbarism of Russia's autocracy in the last century was on the whole less bizarre than the moralism of its intelligentsia—its dedication to a vision of a kingdom of God on earth, the reign of universal brotherhood, when man's lost wholeness would be restored. This faith was expressed in very diverse ideologies—conservative and radical, religious and atheistic—but most of its prophets were united on two central beliefs: that the advanced cultures of Western Europe were on the verge of collapse from inner moral decay, and that the main hope for regeneration lay in the uncorrupted instincts of the simple people—in particular the Russian peasant.

The rest of Europe, acquainted with this messianism only in its more sensational manifestations, such as the eccentricity of a world-famous novelist who dressed as a peasant and reviled belles-lettres, attributed it to no more than a curious national tendency toward extremes.

Now the thirst for prophets has spread to the West. The intelligentsia of Europe and America, isolated in a cultural vacuum, morally compromised by association with the new mandarins, and insecure in its values, is increasingly seeking a sense of direction and a positive faith. Solzhenitsyn, a Russian prophet denouncing the moral bankruptcy of the West, is greeted not as an eccentric but as a sage, with a vatic insight into a profound spiritual malaise.

But Solzhenitsyn's message may have less impact than that of another offshoot of the Russian messianic tradition—the anarchism of Bakunin and Kropotkin. Bakunin's belief that the regeneration of the West could be achieved only through total destruction of the existing order inspired many of the revolutionaries of 1968; but it is Kropotkin's influence which is the more significant. The most serene of Russian prophets, Kropotkin was described by Oscar Wilde as "a man with a soul of that beautiful white Christ which keeps coming out of Russia." His gospel of regeneration is attracting a following not only among revolutionary youth but also among writers, teachers, and sociologists. This is a dramatic reversal in the fate of a thinker who, after his death in 1921, was consigned to almost total oblivion for half a century: George Woodcock in his biography of him [see Further Reading] . . . admitted that he was "half-forgotten." Now a new biography has appeared, and all his major writings have been resurrected in a flurry of editions. . . . All his editors, and his biographer, emphasize the relevance of his ideas to our most pressing problems. What has transformed this forgotten prophet into a cult figure, the "essential Kropotkin"? (p. 40)

Kropotkin took the basic theses of his anarchism from Bakunin. These were that the source of all injustice is the state. All revolutions (in particular the Marxist) which seek to replace one form of state by another will merely perpetuate tyranny. Freedom is found by following the instincts of the masses, which lead them to organize themselves in communal associations linked not by authority but by common interests. When the state is destroyed and the people are free to organize themselves as they wish, they will again form such associations.

Kropotkin's specific contribution to anarchism was his attempt to provide a scientific foundation for these theses, to prove that anarchism was not a utopia but on the contrary a form of organization less artificial and better adapted to man's needs than the existing state forms. In numerous articles, in four longer works, *Paroles d'un revolté, The Conquest of Bread, Mutual Aid: A Factor of Evolution,* and *Fields, Factories and Workshops,* and in his unfinished *Ethics: Origin and Development,* he attempted to formulate "a scientific concept of the universe embracing the whole of nature and including man." The basis of this ambitious construction is his theory of ethics, according to which mutual aid, not Darwinian struggle, is the fundamental law of evolution. True morality issues from an instinctive sense of solidarity, prompting men, like animals, to treat others as they themselves wish to be treated. This ethic inspired the earliest form of social organization, the tribe, and later communes and free villages, whose customs were enforced through free cooperation. The opposing state principle of social organization and traditional morality, religion, and law, which enforced obedience by exploiting superstition, is the result of the efforts of minorities to monopolize the common patrimony. All history is a battle between anarchists and jacobins which will soon end with the triumph of the popular ideal; the state will be destroyed, and property, the source of exploitation, will be replaced by "anarchist communism."

Kropotkin's central goal is ethical—the restoration of the harmony of man's powers which the division of labor has destroyed by forcing men to specialize in one monotonous task, reducing them to fragments of human beings. In *Fields, Factories and Workshops* he outlines a system of "integrated labor": each person will engage in agricultural, factory, and intellectual work. Through rational planning and modern technology, industry and agriculture will be completely integrated. The resulting decentralization, whereby regional aggregates of individuals produce and consume most of their agricultural and manufactured produce, will eliminate starvation and the exhaustion of resources. Productivity will be dramatically increased and the working day halved, providing increased leisure for the free development of creativity. Men will be prepared for integrated labor through a system of "integrated education," which will cultivate their mental and physical attributes at the same time.

If the distinction between intellectuals and manual workers were erased, social conflict would be succeeded by community of interest: the individual will "feel his heart at unison with the rest of humanity." No coercion would be needed. Traditional ethics, which posit a conflict between duty and inclination, are a product of the state—anarchism will return to instinctive morality which does not recognize this conflict: "new individuality will attain its highest development in practicing communist sociality in relations with others." Man will attain "full individualization," completeness as an individual and social being.

There is little need to spell out the current appeal of this vision: as the editors of *The Essential Kropotkin,* [Emile Capouya and Keitha Tompkins; see excerpt above] point out eloquently in their introduction, the experience of life in capitalist and communist societies alike is leading many people unacquainted with the anarchist tradition to improvise the reforms embodied in Kropotkin's system. The perfecting of industrialized economies has resulted in an increasing mechanization and quantification of life and a consequent narrowing of spiritual horizons, so that the leisure produced by material progress has become for many a vacuum to be filled by mindless violence. Marxism has proved no solution: the product, like capitalism, of rationalist faith in the supreme importance of material progress, it shares the same values—rationalization, mechanization, quantification.

Pursuit of these values has led communist and capitalist societies alike to increasing incursion of bureaucracy into the few remaining areas open to individual initiative and to a destruction of natural resources on a scale which menaces the existence of future generations. All these problems have directed attention away from the pursuit of quantity to a preoccupation with the quality of existence. Writers like Paul Goodman and Lewis Mumford, who long since pointed to the relevance for our society of Kropotkin's ideas of personal wholeness and cooperative work, are being echoed by sociologists, criminologists, and educationalists; while a strong current of economic theory maintains that a mixed economy is more workable and individual initiative more productive than centralization and regimentation.

There are few therefore who would not subscribe to at least some of Kropotkin's reforms; but to many anarchists any piecemeal approach to reform is totally self-defeating. Anarchism is incompatible with any vestige of traditional attitudes and institutions; it is all or nothing, a total blueprint for the regeneration of man. It is this total faith, not empirical reformism, which is the driving force behind much of the present anarchist revival. Its logic is expressed by Mr. Capouya and Ms. Tompkins as follows: the far-seeing theories of Godwin, Proudhon, and Kropotkin having predicted the human contradictions of our societies, "a mere listing of the problems universally acknowledged to be the most fateful, corresponding point by point with the . . . solutions advanced by anarchism, amounts to a clear political and social agenda." In other words, the profundity of anarchism's critique being self-evident, logic demands that we subscribe to its total blueprint for a new society.

The argument is familiar; all totalitarian ideologies issuing from Enlightenment rationalism have based their claim to hegemony on the assertion that they are "scientific" deductions from an analysis of existing conditions. But their dismal history has amply illustrated that deep insights into the nature of social evils do not of themselves produce effective solutions to them, a point which Bakunin and the anarchist movement were among the first to make with regard to the most impressive of "scientific" social blueprints—that of Marx. Much of the momentum of the anarchist revival derives from the belief that Kropotkin has succeeded where Marx failed in providing a scientific formula for the realization of the kingdom of God on earth. But the theory of mutual aid on which his "scientific" system stands can be seen as a new version of an ancient myth.

Kropotkin's distinction between the drive to solidarity, as the "law" of man's nature, and the drive to domination (also inherent in primitive societies), as a corruption of nature, is a distinction of the order of theology which posits a "higher nature" existing prior to its corrupt manifestation in human societies. Empirical data, based on observation of social man, have so far failed to refute the view that aggression is, to some extent at least, characteristic of our species. Kropotkin claims that anarchism is the direct expression of popular instinct; but popular instinct is often superstitious and attached to tradition, and "anarchist morality," with its rejection of the hold of myth over consciousness, is a pure product of the Enlightenment.

The instinct before which the anarchist intellectual abases himself is a metaphysical abstraction, based on the most ancient of myths, that of a golden age of primal innocence, when man was whole and unified, a myth later incarnated in the Idealist vision of the end of alienation, the resolution of the split between essence and existence. Kropotkin's ideal, like Marx's, is a secular version of this eschatology, supported by the rationalist optimism of the Enlightenment; social evils are seen as the results of extraneous circumstances, for Marx class conflict, for Kropotkin the state, removal of which will suffice to restore man to his true nature.

Even if "barbarian freedom," as Kropotkin calls it, were not entirely the product of romantic nostalgia, it is a crude anachronism to see it as proof of man's ability to harmonize his individual aspirations with the social good. For primitive harmony, such as it was, was the harmony of stagnation, where individuality was little differentiated from the mass; the rational self-directing person who Kropotkin hopes will assent to anarchist morality emerged historically as an antithesis to this primitive harmony through the growing complexity of society, which generated tension between the private individual and abstract social man.

Similarly, the economic effectiveness of Kropotkin's anarchism depends on the technical expertise which began to develop with the division of labor and its hierarchy of roles. No empirical method can demonstrate that human individuality, which, throughout history, has been experienced only in relations of dependence on society and tension and conflict with it, is destined to perfect itself through perfect identification with the social whole, or that a technologically sophisticated economy will reach ultimate perfection by reverting to the primitive democracy and the total integration of functions characterizing early communal existence. Only in the triads of Idealism are such opposites reconciled in harmony; but the Idealist synthesis is the end of history as we know it, the identity of existence and essence, the restoration of man's angelic nature.

Kropotkin's anarchism suffers from the internal contradiction of all millenarian ideologies. Arising as negation, as a rebellion of the personality against the bonds of dogma and entrenched authority, it seeks to impose its own conservatism, its arbitrary end to negation and movement, in the form of one particular system for which it demands total hegemony as the goal of all progress. It is true that Kropotkin emphasizes that anarchist society will develop "in accordance with the ever-growing demands of a free life, stimulated by the progress of science." But in rejecting the concept of tension between the individual and his social environment which has historically been the source of creativity and progress, he rejects progress in the only way we can conceive of it: his utopia is static.

But the tension between negation and faith is more acute in Kropotkin's ideology than in earlier incarnations of this pattern of thought, for the dynamics of his negation led him to a more fundamental questioning of established values than that undertaken by most of the revolutionaries of his time. The same paradox is exhibited by the current cult of Kropotkin in its least critical forms—a questioning of fundamental values brought about by the failure of old faiths is resulting in a determined search for new absolutes to replace them. This suggests that the pattern is closed—that we should be resigned to the fact that only blind faith in absolutes can provide negation with a revolutionary impetus, even at the risk of catastrophe, and that a consistently critical appraisal of existing institutions would lead only to paralyzing skepticism. The relevance for us of Kropotkin's thought may lie less in his solutions than in his contradictions and the light they shed on this problem: on the mechanisms of ideological negation and their relation to faith. (pp. 40-2)

[Kropotkin's] rebellion was deeply conditioned by an established revolutionary tradition. This he acknowledges in his pamphlet *Anarchist Morality* by describing the basis of his anarchism as "nihilist philosophy." If we are to understand the relation between dynamic negation and static utopia in his system, it is with the phenomenon known as nihilism that we must begin.

Nihilism was born with the birth of Russia's intelligentsia, during the period of reaction which followed the failure of the aristocratic elite to force a constitution on the tsar in 1825. Isolated both from the backward masses and the government by their Western culture and moral values, the cultured elite was driven in on the world of ideas, and to the philosophy of the alienated, German Idealism, from which they drew the millenarian ideal of the wholly free and harmonious personality.

Dedication to this ideal led to an intransigent opposition to all existing social and political reality. For the most acutely estranged there was, as Alexander Herzen wrote, "one important consolation: the nakedness of negation, logical ruthlessness," and they channeled their frustrations into left-wing Hegelianism, with its revolutionary assertion of the primacy of the individual over all traditional authorities, all absolutes. The primitive anarchism of the Russian peasant commune seemed to them the social incarnation of this principle, and for the most radical members of their generation, Herzen and Bakunin, anarchism in politics was a logical extension of anarchism in philosophy.

When, as Kropotkin writes in *Anarchist Morality,* the young populists of the 1860s "unfurled the banner of nihilist or rather of anarchist philosophy: to bend the knee to no authority, however respected, to accept no principle . . . unestablished by reason," they were giving a new name to a tradition established by their predecessors. The revolutionary circles of the Sixties sought through a militant materialist philosophy to make their negation more "scientific," and extended their consistency to the strict embodiment in their conduct of the ideal of the just and harmonious society. It was to the most famous of these circles, called after its founder the Chaikovsky circle, that Kropotkin belonged. Though he was in a minority in believing that nihilism demanded total rejection of the state, he frequently referred in later life to the deep impression made on him by the moral nobility of the members of the circle, expressed in the total conformity of their conduct to their principles.

This passion for consistency in negation had a revolutionary dynamism which, far more than the bomb-throwing popularly associated with nihilism, was the movement's distinctive contribution to the Western radical tradition. Enforced isolation in the world of ideas led Russian revolutionaries to give central emphasis to a concept which even the Marxist descendants of Hegel frequently ignored in their preoccupation with economic facts: namely, that the strength of the old order lay perhaps less in its material force than in inner voluntary submission to it, in the eternal readiness of men to surrender responsibility for their self-fulfillment to the abstract constructs of their own reason.

Kropotkin's insight (in *Law and Authority*) into the phenomenon of the fear of freedom, the fact that " 'The Year I of Liberty' has never lasted more than a day, for after proclaiming it men put themselves the very next morning under the yoke of . . . authority," seems a very modern one, but it was also the leitmotif of the writings of Herzen, the founder of Russian populism. Kropotkin often echoed Herzen's observations that the most extreme of revolutionaries in the West were conservatives, liberating men from subjection to the principle of divine right only to enslave them to that of *salus populi*. Though Herzen once called Proudhon "the only free man in Europe," he nevertheless criticized his conservative attitude to the role of women, and Bakunin undertook to instruct him in Paris in 1848 on the liberating implications of Hegelian negation.

Of course, the nihilists were far from being totally consistent; in particular, the materialist philosophies whereby the populists of the Sixties sought to free themselves from superstition encouraged, through their simplistic conception of man's dependence on his environment, a naïve faith in the ease of total social transformation. In this Kropotkin was typical of his time; and this belief in the imminence of utopia sometimes led to the use of authoritarian methods which were in contradiction with the populist goal. But these methods were always strongly criticized within the movement, and until Marxism in the Nineties declared ethics to be irrelevant to revolution, it was only in Russia that debates among revolutionaries centered less on the efficiency of tactics than on their conformity with the moral ideal.

Those who knew Kropotkin only in the West tended to attribute his "impeccable" moral harmony, as Henri Barbusse called it, to a feat of personal saintliness; and the present revival of his ideas, by paying little if any attention to the Russian tradition behind them, perpetuates this view. (pp. 42-3)

It was in his nihilist consistency that Kropotkin contributed most significantly to the European Left. At a time when the first priority was destruction of the enemy, he was almost alone in his uncompromising aversion to the principle that the end justifies the means, emphasizing that this would corrupt the revolution and lead to a new tyranny. When the obtaining of money by theft became popular in Russia as a source of revolutionary funds, he vehemently opposed it, true to the nihilist belief that the revolutionary must be the living embodiment of the future ideal. In his writings the materialist optimism of the Sixties contrasts oddly with the more fundamentally nihilist view that true liberation is an inner process which cannot be brought about by force. While reluctantly conceding that violence was inherent in all revolutions, he emphasized that it could achieve only limited goals:

> in order to conquer, something more than guillotines is required . . . the revolutionary idea . . . which reduces its enemies to impotence by paralysing all the instruments whereby they have governed hitherto. Very sad would be the revolution if it could triumph only by terror.

In the factional squabbles of his time he saw the triumph of the revolution becoming an end in itself, and the original goal of liberty becoming a dispensable extra. In a speech in 1893 he asserted:

> I now see only one party, the anarchist—which respects human life and loudly insists on the abolition of capital punishment, prison torture and punishment of man by man altogether. All the other parties teach every day their utter disrespect of human life. Killing the foe, torturing him in prison, is their principle.

This total consistency in putting the fate of individuals above the purity of dogma, in defending victims of oppression, however insignificant, gave Kropotkin a moral authority extending far beyond anarchist groups. Rudolph Rocker in his memoirs describes him speaking at a demonstration held in London in 1903 in protest against the pogroms against Jews in Russia:

> I still remember him as I saw him that day, his face pale with emotion, his grey beard caught by the wind. His first words were hesitant, as though choked by his deep feeling. Then they came rushing out fiercely, each word like the blow of a hammer. There was a quiver in his voice when he spoke of the suffering of the victims. He looked like some ancient prophet. All the thousands who listened to him were moved to their depths.

There is the same incontestable moral authority in his famous indictment, in a letter to Lenin in 1920, of the Bolsheviks' decision to take hostages in order to protect themselves against possible violence from their opponents:

> How can you, Vladimir Ilich, you who want to be the apostle of new truths and the builder of a new state, give your consent to the use of such . . . unacceptable methods? Such a measure is tantamount to declaring publicly that you adhere to the ideas of yesterday. . . . What future lies in store for communism when one of its most important defenders tramples in this way on every honest feeling?

This is much more than a personal moral stand: it expresses the essence of Russian anarchism as a movement which radically subverted the millenarian tradition from which it sprang.

If the extreme alienation of many of the Russian intelligentsia made them particularly susceptible to the yearning for ultimate "wholeness," the negation which they undertook as a means to that end gained an unexpected momentum as an instrument of self-criticism whose destructive logic constantly counteracted the pull of the millennium, by undermining the absolute pretensions of all utopias, including their own. When Bakunin, carried away by his vision of eternal harmony, resorted to authoritarian methods to hasten its coming, Herzen ruthlessly exposed his inconsistency in his *Letters to an Old Comrade,* which are among the great revolutionary writings on the nature of liberty. Kropotkin, while never relinquishing his visionary ideal, consistently undermined anarchism's hopes of practical success as a revolutionary movement through his intransigent rejection of the coercion of the majority by a minority. In the present wave of enthusiasm for Kropotkin's utopia, Russian anarchism's more radical—and self-critical—contribution to revolutionary thought has been overlooked; if it were emphasized, it could encourage a much more radical line of questioning in current ideological debates.

An answer to whether nihilist consistency, if taken further than Kropotkin took it, would have lost its revolutionary impetus and culminated in an arid skepticism, can be found in the writings of Herzen, the first Russian socialist, and one of the first nihilists. In his famous work *From the Other Shore,* written in 1849, he points out that if progress is seen as the result of the negation by individuals of absolutes and outworn systems, one's own chosen absolutes cannot consistently be excepted from this process. It is much more consistent to assume that the conflict between conservatism and utopia, between a longing for the absolute and negation of it, is not a means to an end, but the end itself, the essence of life and creativity; that general solutions and universal formulae which seek to put an end to this conflict will lead not to universal harmony but to inertia and stagnation, the submergence of the individual in the herd. In a distillation of the insights of the nihilist tradition, Herzen predicts:

> Socialism will develop through all its phases, to its extremes, to absurdities; then a cry of negation will again be torn from the titanic breast of the revolutionary minority, and a battle to the death will begin again in which socialism will take the place now being occupied by conservatism and will be conquered by a new revolution which we cannot yet imagine . . . this is the eternal play of life. . . .

This acceptance that to be consistent with one's ideal of freedom is to recognize that it can only be partially realized in history and never absolutely incarnated in one particular system, one historical type of existence, is, in its delicate balance between faith and skepticism, the most difficult of political attitudes to maintain: but, contrary to a more popular view, it is this true nihilist consistency, rather than utopian faith, which is the most radical heritage of the Russian messianic tradition. (pp. 43-4)

> Aileen Kelly, *"Lessons of Kropotkin,"* in The New York Review of Books, *Vol. XXIII, No. 17, October 28, 1976, pp. 40-4.*

STEPHEN OSOFSKY (essay date 1979)

[*Osofsky is an American political scientist and author. In the following excerpt from his critical study* Peter Kropotkin, *he summarizes Kropotkin's contributions to science and philosophy.*]

Kropotkin's ideas were a living force in his time and remain so today. Many of his insights have stood the test of time remarkably well despite the failure of his views to cohere in a systematic construct. What is lacking in theoretical consistency and logical coherence as he freely analogizes from biology to history to economics is compensated by startling penetration into the implications of capitalist technological and industrial organization for the future of Western society and its physical environment.

As one of the first proponents of a humanly scaled technology and of coupling decentralization of industry with its dispersal to the countryside in search of balanced, wholesome communities, Kropotkin anticipated today's ecological, population-planning, and new-towns movements. In his endeavor to make agriculture on the urban fringe the basis of a realistic regional self-sufficiency, which would simultaneously thin out urban congestion and restore the economic viability of the rural hinterlands, he was a prophetic figure rather than a reactionary rural romantic. And his emphasis on organically intensive rather than technologically intensive agriculture joins a policy debate of the 1970s. In his attack upon Adam Smith's doctrine of the international and regional division of labor and the relative-benefit theory, he made points which radical critics of developmental economics have made only recently. Kropotkin's arguments for a thoroughgoing egalitarianism, economically and socially, and his strong view of the crucial role of education are well worth reading in light of the present IQ controversy. It is possible to argue the relevance of his agro-industrial combines, with their dual economic and political personality, to the Chinese commune; Kropotkin's insight that the "productive forces" of society must be restructured in order to democratize control of the productive process must have relevance to some Chinese and Yugoslav experiments; regional self-sufficiency has long been Maoist policy as has the coordination of artisanal technique with machinism ("walking on two legs"). Kropotkin's high regard for skilled labor and handicrafts, his emphasis upon the organic community, have resonance among a broad, even bewildering, array of social movements and groups today.

Kropotkin's respect for the peasantry and its vocation are in marked contrast to the patronization or theoretical and practical neglect of which many Western Marxists have been guilty. He very early incorporated the peasantry and the agricultural question into the center of the revolutionary agenda. In fact his revolutionary scenario in which the role of the peasant looms large better describes the successful revolutions of this century than Marxist "orthodoxy."

Kropotkin's attempt to prove the scientific imperative of altruism among animals and man remains unconvincing. But as a substantial critique of the "inherently evil" school of human nature and as a refutation of social Darwinism it has proved to be in harmony with the present consensus in the social and natural sciences. Kropotkin's attempt to base human ethics in biology may seem a misguided venture; but his concern with ethics, especially the relationship of revolutionary means to revolutionary ends and the measure of cultural attainment in terms of human satisfaction rather than output, are relevant to our social dialogue today. Many Marxists and neo-Marxists who have grappled with the ugly ramifications of a mass production system and a relentlessly industrialized landscape can turn to Kropotkin for guidance and inspiration. Equally important, Kropotkin has much to say on the question of the practicality of democracy. He hypothesized the relationship between community size and/or workshop size, on the one hand, and the degree of democratization of social relations and the productive process on the other. The question and theory of workers' control was central to Kropotkin's thinking, and this is a question that will not easily be erased from the social agenda.

For Kropotkin the whole man and the authentic life merged in work, but he insisted on the necessity—indeed "blessedness"—of leisure. Kropotkin's views on the significance of art represented his refusal to insulate the aesthetic from the practical. If, as the Greeks and Elizabethans would have it, art and artisan are makers, so can all men consciously make their environment, their community, their history beautiful.

Kropotkin's approach to nature is to include man in it, not to set him apart or see nature as something to be used or overcome. Free from technicist mediation, man's relation to nature is spiritual and aesthetic; it originates in respect for his sole life-support system and for a source of endless intricacies and wonders. Man's living rhythms are akin to and informed by nature's. Essentially this is what Kropotkin means by the irrepressible spontaneity of life. This is not anthropomorphism but a vision of human life in its total context. Kropotkin's views of the sources and motives of human behavior could have benefited from development and revision by passage through the crucible of intellectual exchange. He had his blind spots: his animosity toward Marx, his incongruous Francophilia. As historian and sociologist, he is hardly immune from the teleology and messianism of his era. His historical writings are especially superficial with the exception of his masterpiece on the French Revolution. Indeed much of his work bears the imprint of a flawed first draft. He is almost always sketchy, especially in regard to his writings on revolution, on the transition to and problems confronting the future society.

Many of his predictions about the social and economic trends of his day proved wrong and seem, at least with twenty-twenty hindsight, monuments to wishful thinking. The obvious examples are his belief in a tendency toward decentralization of industrial production and in the growing role of democratic private associations in assuming functions traditionally performed by various levels of government. Yet Kropotkin's powerful indictment of capitalism remains: neither his refusal of an incrementalist approach in order to examine the premises of his society nor his rejection of its value system can be dismissed as utopian. It is true that Kropotkin failed to make anarchism into a formidable revolutionary movement, surely the most grave of his political sins of omission. But despite his organizational failures, which substantially crippled the movement, Kropotkin was quite capable of "practical" politics and was always insistent on concrete proposals. He supported the Allies in World War I in order to keep alive what he believed to be the more progressive historical forces in France and England. The point is not that he was perhaps wrong in his analysis, but that he did feel a stake for his cause in the war's outcome. Kropotkin was frequently drawn into dialogue over incremental changes in society. He entered the lists for penal reform and in condemnation of the Tsarist system of justice; urged bourgeois governments to adopt educational and agricultural reforms. And he was able to revise his views in order to incorporate the lessons of the syndicalist movement, which he had originally accused of trade-unionism.

None of this diluted revolutionary commitment. Kropotkin never played at armchair revolution or at spare-time philosopher-king. He conveyed to friends and foes alike a monumental sense of moral outrage that would not be stilled or suspended for tactical or personal advantages. He was incorruptible and steadfast—yet humanitarian rather than fanatical.

Kropotkin's unflagging service in the cause of man's humanity to man is no small part of his legacy to a particularly brutal century. It became a leitmotif from the early days of challenging social Darwinism to the very end when, enfeebled and politically isolated, he interceded with Lenin on behalf of Bolshevik hostages.

Kropotkin must be adjudged a multi-faceted genius and a moral force. He was a justly famous scientist with distinction in both geography and geology, a pioneer in the field of sociobiology, the author of what remains a classic history of the French Revolution, and a major contributor to the literature on penology. His *Memoirs,* written with distinction and grace and in a characteristically self-effacing manner, are indisputably a classic source on the spirit and life of the privileged in nineteenth-century Russia. His correspondence with his brother constitutes a unique glimpse of the intellectual adolescence of the major anarchist thinker of all time. His arguments in favor of a radical egalitarianism and against the Malthusian-Social-Darwinian axis are among the most trenchant ever made.

As a moral philosopher Kropotkin continues to present us with an invaluable critique of Western society and an indictment of Western man's rapacious attitude toward nature, his self-serving morals, his glib rationalization of the cruel as "practical" in the name of what is sanctimoniously proclaimed the most civilized of societies and social systems. There is validity in faulting Kropotkin for oversimplifying the complexities of moral problems, but he could never be legitimately accused of hypocrisy. This too is no small matter in an age when public officials have scaled new heights of venality and self-righteousness. And for all those implicated in the industrial megathon of the twentieth century, the challenge of Kropotkin's alternative—penultimate dispersal of economic and political power—remains unanswered. (pp. 165-69)

Stephen Osofsky, in his Peter Kropotkin, *Twayne Publishers, 1979, 202 p.*

FURTHER READING

Bartlett, Robert M. " 'Power to Act Is Duty to Act': Peter Kropotkin." In his *They Dared to Live,* pp. 67-70. New York: Association Press, 1948.
    Biographical sketch which focuses on Kropotkin's early life and his dramatic escape from prison.

Bennett, Charles A. "The Ethics of Naturalism." *Nation* 121, No. 3132 (15 July 1925): 97-8.
    Finds that although Kropotkin's *Ethics: Origin and Development* purports to be a history of the development of ethics, the book is biased toward his own system of ethics based on mutual aid.

Berneri, C. *Peter Kropotkin: His Federalist Ideas.* Freedom Press, 1942, 16 p.
    Details the causes of Kropotkin's disillusionment with centralized government and the development of his belief in free communes.

Bernstein, Herman. "Prince Peter Kropotkin." In his *Celebrities of Our Time: Interviews,* pp. 197-204. New York: Joseph Lawren, 1924.

Interview conducted in 1918, in which Kropotkin discussed political and economic conditions in Russia.

Bogardus, Emory S. "Kropotkin and Co-operative Social Thought." In his *The Development of Social Thought,* pp. 381-91. New York: Longmans, Green and Co., 1940.
Includes a brief description of Kropotkin's theory of mutual aid.

Breitbart, Myrna Margulies. "Peter Kropotkin, the Anarchist Geographer." In *Geography, Ideology and Social Concern,* edited by D. R. Stoddart, pp. 134-53. Totowa, N.J.: Barnes and Noble Books, 1981.
Demonstrates the influence of Kropotkin's geographical discoveries on his social and political theories.

Catlin, George. "Individualists and Anarchists." In his *The Story of the Political Philosophers,* pp. 405-34. New York: McGraw-Hill Book Co., 1939.
Contains a brief account of Kropotkin's life and political theories.

Cloete, Stuart. "Kropotkin (A Digest)." In his *The Third Way,* pp. 303-37. Boston: Houghton Mifflin Co., 1947.
Excerpt from Kropotkin's *Mutual Aid: A Factor of Evolution* with a brief introduction by Cloete.

"A Russian Revolutionist." *The Dial* 28, No. 325 (1 January 1900): 9-11.
Examines Kropotkin's *Memoirs of a Revolutionist* for insight into his belief in anarchy.

Eltzbacher, Paul. "Kropotkin's Teaching." In his *Anarchism,* pp. 139-81. New York: Benjamin R. Tucker, 1908.
Explains Kropotkin's philosophy of anarchy through quotations from his works.

Fuchs, J. "A Critical Review of the Revolutionary Legend." *Forum* 43, No. 3 (March 1910): 323-28.
Review of *The Great French Revolution: 1789-1793* which praises Kropotkin for "removing the débris and . . . clearing the ground for a future myth-free history of revolutionary France."

Galois, Bob. "Ideology and the Idea of Nature: The Case of Peter Kropotkin." *Antipode* 8, No. 3 (September 1976): 1-16.
Uses "the framework of the 'idea of nature' to illustrate the link between Kropotkin's thought and the ideological content of geography."

Hare, Richard. "Peter Kropotkin." In his *Portraits of Russian Personalities between Reform and Revolution,* pp. 342-55. London: Oxford University Press, 1959.
Biographical sketch.

Harris, Frank. "Prince Peter Kropotkin." In his *Latest Contemporary Portraits,* pp. 126-38. New York: Macaulay Co., 1927.
Reminiscences.

Joll, James. *The Anarchists.* Boston: Little, Brown and Co., 1964, 303 p.
Includes scattered references to Kropotkin's life and political beliefs.

Lancaster, Lane W. "Peter Kropotkin." In his *Hegel to Dewey,* pp. 244-64. Masters of Political Thought, edited by Edward McChesney Sait, vol. 3. Boston: Houghton Mifflin Co., 1960.
Criticizes the naïveté of Kropotkin's political thought.

Masaryk, Thomas Garrigue. "Modern Anarchism: Kropotkin, Anarchism and Socialism." In his *The Spirit of Russia: Studies in History, Literature and Philosophy,* vol. 2, pp. 378-412. London: George Allen and Unwin, 1919.
Describes Kropotkin's system of thought and compares it to other political philosophies, particularly to that of Bakunin.

Maxey, Chester C. "The Challenge of Proletarianism." In his *Political Philosophies,* pp. 564-94. New York: Macmillan Co., 1938.
Includes a biographical sketch of Kropotkin and an outline of his political theories.

Miller, Martin A. Review of *The Essential Kropotkin,* edited by Emile Capouya and Keitha Tompkins. *Russian Review* 35, No. 2 (April 1976): 203-04.
Criticizes the editors for omissions and distortions of Kropotkin's thought and place in anarchist tradition. Miller also finds their choice of reprinted essays redundant and poorly excerpted.

Montagu, Ashley. Foreword to *Mutual Aid: A Factor of Evolution,* by Peter Kropotkin. Boston: Extending Horizons Books, 1955.
Discusses the circumstances surrounding the composition and publication of *Mutual Aid* and briefly summarizes the book's content.

"Peter Kropotkin." *Nation* 28, No. 19 (5 February 1921): 628-29.
Description of Kropotkin's life and character by a friend who helped him organize *The Terror in Russia.*

"Kropotkin's History of the Development of Ethics: From Primitive Man to Marx, Proudhon and Guyan in a Study of Philosophic Thought." *The New York Times Book Review* (4 January 1925): 11.
Review of Kropotkin's *Ethics: Origin and Development* which finds the book less valuable than if Kropotkin had been able to complete his companion volume on the philosophical justifications of revolution. However, the critic judges that "for the general reader, the book, by reason of its easy manner of discussion, as well as its comprehensiveness, should be a welcome acquisition."

"The French Revolution." *New York Times Saturday Review of Books* (26 February 1910): 101-02, 106.
Finds that Kropotkin wrote *The Great French Revolution: 1789-1793* "in a vigorous manner, but his mental bias in imagining that all social and economic benefits come from the depths, his consistent contempt for the bourgeoisie are destructive to the candid trustworthiness of his hypothesis."

Read, Herbert. "The Death of Kropotkin." *Poetry* 77, No. 1 (October 1950): 21-3.
Obituary tribute to Kropotkin.

Reszler, André. "Peter Kropotkin and His Vision of Anarchist Aesthetics." *Diogenes,* No. 78 (Summer 1972): 52-63.
Investigates Kropotkin's opinions on art in an anarchist society, comparing his views to those of Proudhon and Tolstoy.

Shub, David. "Kropotkin and Lenin." *Russian Review* 12, No. 4 (October 1953): 227-34.
Discusses Kropotkin's opposition to Bolshevism and his correspondence with Lenin in the first few years after the revolution.

"The Anarchist Prince." *Times Literary Supplement,* No. 3606 (9 April 1971): 427.
Review of Kropotkin's *Selected Writings on Anarchism and Revolution,* which recommends the book for its historical interest rather than for what the critic considers its meager inspiration for anarchists.

"Period Pieces of Anarchy." *Times Literary Supplement,* No. 3677 (18 August 1972): 974.
Review of Kropotkin's *The Conquest of Bread* and *Mutual Aid: A Factor of Evolution,* which predicts that "if Kropotkin's works survive, they will survive as historical curiosities of the period in which they were written rather than for the originality and weight of the ideas which they profess."

Van Duyn, Roel. "Kropotkin: A Universal Specialist." In his *Message of a Wise Kabouter,* pp. 13-28. London: Duckworth, 1972.
Description of Kropotkin's life and philosophy which criticizes

his views of authority and aggression as simplistic, while praising his idea of a need-based wage system.

Woodcock, George. "The Explorer." In his *Anarchism: A History of Libertarian Ideas and Movements,* pp. 184-221. Cleveland: Meridian Books, 1962.
    Biographical and critical study which summarizes Kropotkin's major contributions to anarchist theory.

————, and Avakumović, Ivan. *The Anarchist Prince: A Biographical Study of Peter Kropotkin.* New York: Schocken Books, 1971, 465 p.
    Study of Kropotkin's life and works with an annotated bibliography of primary and secondary sources.

Yakobson, Sergius. "Kropotkin's *Russian Literature.*" In *A Garland of Essays Offered to Professor Elizabeth Mary Hill,* edited by R. Auty, L. R. Lewitter, and A. P. Vlasto, pp. 312-21. Cambridge: Modern Humanities Research Association, 1970.
    Discusses the circumstances under which Kropotkin composed and published *Russian Literature* and prints a letter he wrote on the subject to William Morris Colles, a literary agent.

Selma (Ottiliana Lovisa) Lagerlöf

1858-1940

Swedish novelist, short story writer, and autobiographer.

For further discussion of Lagerlöf's career, see *TCLC,* Volume 4.

Lagerlöf was a Swedish novelist and short story writer who combined folklore and history in narratives that are regarded as masterpieces of the storyteller's art. Her works have been widely translated, making her one of Sweden's best-known authors abroad, and she was the first woman to be awarded the Nobel Prize in literature.

Lagerlöf was born at Mårbacka, her family's estate in the province of Värmland in southwestern Sweden. From 1881 until 1885 she attended Stockholm Higher Teacher's College for Women, later recounting that while at the college, studying Swedish and other national literatures, she realized that the rich folklore of her native region could supply her with material for fiction. The death of Lagerlöf's father in 1885, followed by the sale of Mårbacka in 1888 to pay his debts, made it necessary for her to support herself, and she began teaching in the nearby coastal city of Landskrona. During this period she wrote her first novel, *Gösta Berlings saga (Gösta Berling's Saga)*, which was published in 1891. After the success of her short story collection *Osynliga länkar (Invisible Links)* in 1894, Lagerlöf abandoned teaching to pursue a literary career, and her growing financial success enabled her to purchase her childhood home in 1907. Awarded the Nobel Prize in literature in 1909, Lagerlöf used the prize money to buy back the entire Mårbacka estate, where she lived thereafter. Commentators credit Lagerlöf's return to Värmland with inspiring fiction based on her family's history as well as further works based on regional folklore. She also wrote three volumes of memoirs: *Mårbacka, Ett barns memoarer (Memories of My Childhood)*, and *Dagbok för Selma Lagerlöf (The Diary of Selma Lagerlöf)*. She died in 1940 at the age of eighty-one.

Considered Lagerlöf's best novel, *Gösta Berling's Saga* is a vast epic incorporating Värmland folklore and myth into a naturalistic chronicle of Swedish life during the 1820s. Lagerlöf provided detailed accounts of the customs of the period and portrayed figures from legend and myth as having an objective existence, interacting with the townspeople and affecting the action of the story. When *Gösta Berling's Saga* first appeared, critics were confused by the mingling of fantastic and naturalistic elements in the narrative. The novel was reevaluated following a favorable assessment in 1893 by noted Danish critic Georg Brandes. Commentators subsequently commended Lagerlöf's combination of literary Naturalism, sociological commentary, and national folklore in the work, which has come to be considered one of the most important novels in Swedish literature.

The synthesis of folk traditions, history, and compelling narration in *Gösta Berling's Saga* is characteristic of Lagerlöf's fiction. The novel *Antikrists mirakler (The Miracles of Antichrist)*, for example, relates the history and mythology of Italy to contemporary social problems there. The novels *Jerusalem 1: I Dalarne (Jerusalem)* and *Jerusalem 2: I det heli-*

ga landet (In the Holy Land), which are set in the Dalecarlian region of west central Sweden, depict the clash of ancient rural traditions with a modern religious revival. Lagerlöf's strongest influences came from her native province: the novel *Liljecronas hem (Liliecrona's Home)*, for example, based in part on the life of her grandmother, is set on an estate modeled on Mårbacka; and the novels of the Löwensköld trilogy—*Löwensköldska ringen (The General's Ring)*, *Charlotte Löwensköld*, and *Anna Svärd*—draw extensively from Värmland legends, ghost stories, and folk superstitions. Some commentators have speculated that it was in response to criticism about her lack of engagement with contemporary issues that Lagerlöf addressed the issue of war in *Bannlyst (The Outcast)*, written during World War I. This novel is considered one of her weakest, however, and critics evaluating Lagerlöf subsequently have not questioned her judgment in devoting herself to the folkloric themes at which she excelled.

Perhaps Lagerlöf's best-known book outside of Sweden is *Nils Holgerssons underbara resa genom Sverige* (translated in two parts as *The Wonderful Adventures of Nils* and *The Further Adventures of Nils*). Commissioned by the Swedish National Teachers' Society as an introductory geography for schoolchildren, the novel follows a classic fairy-tale plot: a badly behaved boy is punished by being magically transformed to tiny size. Carried aloft by a goose, Nils flies the length and breadth of Sweden before he is returned to his home and proper size. Sweden's geography is described from the air, and as the goose lands to eat and rest, Nils meets people from all parts of the country and learns about their lives. Entertaining and educational, the work is regarded as a masterpiece of children's literature.

Most commentators note that Lagerlöf did not demonstrate a process of development as an author, but rather produced novels and short stories of a uniformly high quality and explored a few recurring themes throughout her works. Hermann Hesse expressed a typical view of her career when he observed that her "first work was already perfect, containing all the essentials of the Lagerlöf's gift; with it the author made her appearance as a finished, mature personality." Her imaginative, folkloric fiction is considered to have been instrumental in the development of a uniquely Swedish national literature.

(See also *Children's Literature Review,* Vol. 7; *Contemporary Authors,* Vol. 108; and *Something about the Author,* Vol. 15.)

PRINCIPAL WORKS

Gösta Berlings saga (novel) 1891
  [*Gösta Berling's Saga,* 1898; also published as *The Story of Gösta Berling,* 1898]
Osynliga länkar (short stories) 1894
  [*Invisible Links,* 1899]
Antikrists mirakler (novel) 1898
  [*The Miracles of Antichrist,* 1899]
Jerusalem 1: I Dalarne (novel) 1901
  [*Jerusalem,* 1903]
Jerusalem 2: I det heliga landet (novel) 1902
  [*In the Holy Land,* 1903; also published as *The Holy City,* 1918]
Herr Arnes penningar (novel) 1903
  [*Herr Arne's Hoard,* 1923; also published as *The Treasure,* 1925]
Kristuslegender (short stories) 1904
  [*Christ Legends,* 1908]
Nils Holgerssons underbara resa genom Sverige (novel) 1906-07
  [Published in two volumes: *The Wonderful Adventures of Nils,* 1907, and *The Further Adventures of Nils,* 1911]
Liljecronas hem (novel) 1911
  [*Liliecrona's Home,* 1914]
Kejsarn av Portugallien (novel) 1914
  [*The Emperor of Portugallia,* 1916]
Troll och människor (short stories) 1915
Bannlyst (novel) 1918
  [*The Outcast,* 1920]
Mårbacka (autobiography) 1922
  [*Mårbacka,* 1924]
Löwensköldska ringen (novel) 1925
  [*The General's Ring,* 1928]
Charlotte Löwensköld (novel) 1925
  [*Charlotte Löwensköld,* 1927]
Anna Svärd (novel) 1928
  [*Anna Svärd* published in *The Ring of the Lowenskölds,* 1931]
Ett barns memoarer (autobiography) 1930
  [*Memories of My Childhood,* 1934]

Dagbok för Selma Lagerlöf (autobiography) 1932
  [*The Diary of Selma Lagerlöf,* 1936]
Skrifter. 12 vols. (novels, short stories, and autobiographies) 1947-49

HERMANN HESSE (essay date 1908)

[*Recipient of the Nobel Prize in literature for 1946, Hesse is considered one of the most important German novelists of the twentieth century. Lyrical in style, his novels are concerned with a search on the part of their protagonists for self-knowledge and for insight into the relationship between physical and spiritual realms. In the following essay, Hesse summarizes Lagerlöf's achievements and offers a favorable assessment of her career.*]

The Swedish author Selma Lagerlöf was born in 1858 and has been prominent in the literary world since the beginning of the nineties. With her first work, **Gösta Berling,** she became famous in Sweden and very soon in the rest of the world. That first work was already perfect, containing all the essentials of the Lagerlöf gift; with it the author made her appearance as a finished, mature personality and since that time she has not changed in any characteristic.

It is this very fact that the person who feels compelled to criticize even what is beautiful may consider a lack in her. In Selma Lagerlöf one does not find the drama of development; her works stand like brothers and sisters, apparently of a like age, side by side, not separated by any profound difference. Perhaps this too is the womanly aspect of her talent: an almost unmoved repose in herself, deep-rooted and firm, a being and growing without division or abrupt transition. Whoever wants to may draw the conclusion from this (apparent or real) lack of conflict, struggle, and development that Selma Lagerlöf is after all not a genius. On the other hand, however, she possesses what is perhaps the most essential characteristic of the person of genius, an inner relationship with all being, a wealth of connections to all the things and creatures of the world, combined with an uncommon, lively, strong memory without which no genius and no art are possible.

In modern Swedish literature this author stands out lonely and remarkable, like some marvelous anachronism. Only the fine, far too little known Verner von Heidenstam shows at times in his best work, *Charles XII,* similar traits. The more recent Swedish writers from Strindberg to Geijerstam have nothing whatever epic about them, they are artists who work entirely subjectively, sensitively analyzing acutely differentiated perceptions, and even the farthest-sighted and most many-sided of them stick close in material and language to their own time and problems, they engage in psychology and support theses. In short, they are modern, they have the typical modern high regard for science, and they attempt to impart a certain scientific air to their books. It is precisely this that Selma Lagerlöf is entirely free from.

How much toil, experiment, and practice preceded **Gösta Berling** we do not know and I trust will never find out. Whether it appeared as the fruit of years of training and effort or as a marvelously easy, inspired achievement, **Gösta Berling,** despite all the warm personal quality of its approach and tone, has over and above this something impersonal, timeless, mythical, something that has grown out of the eternal depths of a nation's being. Its characters, its landscape, its events have been composed, they are works of art, they have the quality of conscious observation about them, but in addition they have a reality, a life of their own that permits us to regard the author not as a maker but as one inspired. It is the spirit of the earth and of the people that wanted to express itself and chose this author as its instrument. Just the way in fairy tales a poor boy runs away and on his travels meets a wise dwarf and overnight becomes rich and powerful and a king and magician, just so Selma Lagerlöf, a Swedish schoolteacher, at some hour encountered the spirit of her native land and became at its touch a great and gifted author.

She writes a style that belongs to no time, whose nuances are very womanly, at times almost homely. She constantly strolls as though in a dream on the breakneck ridge between the genial and the sentimental, between gossip and saga. In the noblest stories she turns aside from the path to pick a few flowers, and to exhibit an almost womanly sentimental love for small things. But she no more than grazes this danger, which she herself hardly suspects. While a timorous devotee shudders with fear that now she must cast off her magic robe and stand there suddenly as a miserable small-town girl, she already has the breezes of eternity playing about her forehead and is uttering words that are as precise, sustaining, and magical as the words of folksong and of the Bible.

Just so with her inventions. The characters without exception have a vivid, lifelike quality that cannot be matched; but this same magician who created them rules them with a fantastic sense of justice, rewards and punishes them according to a commonplace didactic morality, and sometimes makes an ambitious effort to sacrifice her poetry to her somewhat narrow conception of an ethical world order. These are propensities and artistic errors that would cost our greatest poets their necks, whereas in this strange woman they seem barely more than minor flaws.

In this connection I must warn against confusing this writer's morality with her piety. Her morality is that of a schoolmarm; her piety, however, is pure gold, it is inner simplicity and childlikeness, courageous trust and unstinting devotion.

So too is Gösta Berling. He is no hero, rather he is a poor devil, but for many people he has come to mean a hero, has captivated many hearts, has kindled many dazzling lights, bewitched maidens and influenced men. He is a provincial heroic figure become a myth, half still-historical person with individual characteristics, half already poetically transformed into a symbol. Everything that a tiny nation had amassed through many generations of adventure, heroism, great convulsions and great jokes, events and the storyteller's art, had hoarded and only allowed to circulate as small coin, all this becomes in this book a many-colored, rich, magnificent creation.

In a short time *Gösta Berling* captivated the whole world. Naïve people read it naïvely and happily as a splendid story, more sophisticated readers enjoyed it as a work of art, old people warmed themselves at its histories, and youths read it with absorption and excitement. Now if Selma Lagerlöf had been no more than the accidental vessel of a revelation, if she had simply picked up, casual and unaware, the treasures of her native tradition, if all the beauty and effectiveness were due simply to the marvelous material, then with this one great work her art would have been exhausted, or at most a sequel would have followed.

What followed, however, was quite the opposite, a great new book full of passion and splendor, *The Miracles of Antichrist.* Here her qualities and defects can be much more easily distinguished than in *Gösta Berling.* Invention, costuming, and composition of the whole are insignificant, almost dilettantish. And yet the book is marvelous. The action takes place in Sicily in a hill town on Etna and is filled with the southern sun in a way that is rare in northern books. The village life of this town is the real substance of this work, divided up into an ample series of individual pictures painted with marvelous love and even more marvelous vividness. Adroitly and effortlessly these splendid stories, each a gem, are strung together and combined with one another on the loose thread of a hardly perceptible design.

In between times many short tales and legends appeared, among them masterly things, and then followed Selma Lagerlöf's mightiest book, the first volume of *Jerusalem.* This is surely the most beautiful and greatest production of recent Swedish literature, a book about the soul of Sweden, multitudinous and yet unified, tender and powerful, realistic and visionary. The life of the Swedish peasants is portrayed in it, and I know of no other modern book in which the soul of a people has been thus expressed. Nor do I know of any work of fiction in which the religious life and experience of a community has been presented so graphically, so factually, and so sensitively.

The second part of the great work, which takes place in Jerusalem (whither the Dalekarlian community has followed a fanatic), no longer possesses this absolute native perfection. It is, to be sure, still beautiful and impressive enough to surpass many famous novels. But the way these poor mountain dwellers, strayed here from Sweden, feel themselves alien sufferers in the blazing heat of the stony Palestinian city, promised city though it is—here the author sacrifices some of her impeccable strength and assurance. The analysis of world history, the necessity for historical reflection are mostly to blame, more than the foreign soil, for the landscape as well as the oriental street life are pictured beautifully and characteristically, at times with genius.

If the first part did not exist, it would never occur to anyone to criticize the second so severely. But the first volume happens to be such a marvelous work that one reads the second with enormously heightened anticipation and judges it accordingly. For this very reason all the beautiful and absorbing things in it should not be overlooked.

In many scenes in this second part of *Jerusalem,* beautifully and unexpectedly the author's relation to Christ is indicated, a relation that in a later work, *Christ Legends,* finally finds complete expression. This relation is a thing very precious, lovely, and restorative. Selma Lagerlöf's Christ is neither historical nor dogmatic but the popular beloved Germanic Savior whom one must love as one loves the sun, whose features retain from his suffering only the radiant aspect. She talks about him simply and inexhaustibly, the way a pious mother tells her children the stories of the Savior, and in order to be able to tell a great deal and tell it accurately she has read all that was to be found of the old legends. Now she narrates them again, the well-known ones and the obscure ones, Oriental and Italian or Latin, and from her storyteller's lips they flow fresh and ardent, calming every confusion and doubt in the hearer, awakening in his soul everything that has remained pure and true and golden from the days of his childhood.

Whenever people have talked to me with harsh criticism of Selma Lagerlöf and however often I myself have felt doubts about small particulars, here I have always been a devout believer. And where in the whole world of today is there an author who would dare talk to us about Jesus like this—not symbolically, with sociological references, not historically, with critical details, nor in a proselytizing fashion like the Salvation Army, but artlessly as though the theme had no hooks and abysses? That is what Selma Lagerlöf could do.

Of Lagerlöf's remaining books—they are all beautiful and dear to me—**Arne's Treasure** seems to me to deserve special consideration. It is a novella, entirely in the grand, strict ballad style, powerful and exciting as a treasured age-old saga. Arne of Solberga, together with wife, child, and household servants, is murdered by wandering mercenaries for his treasure of gold. The murder occurred at night and the only one to escape was an adopted daughter of the house who thereafter found refuge with a poor fishmonger. She is hardly in any condition to identify the malefactors, nor does she feel called upon or able to help to clear up and avenge the evil deed. Also it appeared that the murderers, along with the treasure they had stolen, had sunk into the fjord in their attempt to flee across the ice. But the innocent victims of the murder are not at peace; visibly and invisibly, they are at work, they cause dreams and win confederates, they arouse horror here and sympathy there, they weave about the escaped murderers an invisible net. Elsalill, the surviving orphan, meanwhile has become innocently involved in an as yet tentative love-game with one of the murderers and is forced half willingly, half under duress, constantly to find and help to find clues until the robbers are discovered, an event that brings about her own death. The fleeing criminals succeed in finding refuge on a ship, which at the moment is locked tight in the ice, yet from hour to hour they expect the breaking-up of the ice and the longed-for chance for departure. But destiny is inescapable: all the bays along the shore become ice-free and navigable, barks and ships everywhere move seawards, only that one fjord and that one ship are locked tight by a wall of pack ice and the wily criminals, who have escaped so often, in the last hour succumb to their punishment. This is enormously effective, pure and inexorable as only great tragedy is, full of the influence of unseen saga-like powers and yet logical and illuminating.

Much by way of gratitude and praise could be said about the splendid "Manor House" saga the enchanting Nils Holgersson, but to what purpose? Whoever has once immersed himself in Lagerlöf's work and come to love it must and will long to read more of her. (pp. 317-23)

> *Hermann Hesse, "Selma Lagerlöf," translated by Denver Lindley, in his* My Belief: Essays on Life and Art, *edited by Theodore Ziolkowski, translated by Denver Lindley and Ralph Manheim, Farrar, Straus and Giroux, 1974, pp. 317-23.*

RANDOLPH BOURNE　(essay date 1918)

[*An American essayist, Bourne is recognized as one of the most astute critics of American life and letters of the early twentieth century. He was a champion of progressive education and pacifism, as well as a fierce opponent of sentimentality in literature.*

In the following excerpt, Bourne favorably reviews The Holy City.]

Miss Lagerlöf's artistic skill never flags. Is there any living novelist who has an imagination at once so luxuriant and so disciplined? Around her simple Swedish people in their simple relations she weaves a magic of all their legendary hopes and fears, that Christianity and their tidy civilization have not been able to destroy. Yet each character of hers emerges beautifully molded and clear, like some delicate head that a gifted peasant has carved out of wood. That form she has become so fond of is most perfectly suited to her quality. She builds up her story in a series of incidents, each of which is a complete story, with its own tension and color, but which weave together into a gorgeous fabric, with each strand infallibly in its place.

She is able in this way to present the life of an entire community, the various characters stealing almost imperceptibly into the narrative and yet indelibly imprinted upon it. She handles this complex interplay of souls with such undeviating skill that her completed story, for all its poignancy of feeling and intricacy of motive, is as clear as a classic tale. She is never wholly immersed in it. She is a master of the tone of sympathetic detachment. She seems to love her characters all the more because she understands them so deeply. They do not need to be sentimentalized over in order to produce the full effect of their pathos, or the fervor of their rugged lives.

Her latest book to be translated into English shows no shadow of turning. **The Holy City** carries on the story told in **Jerusalem** of the Dalecarlian rural people who were tempted from their Northern home by the religious call to spend the rest of their days among the holy shrines in the city of Christ's death. There the personal dramas begun in the Swedish community play themselves out to an end against the background of fanatic zeal. Bo Ingomar Mansson, who has come out to Jerusalem to forget his love for Gertrude, the schoolmaster's daughter, sees her arrive just as he is saved from the temptation to desert the colony and rush home to her. How perfectly that picture sets the tone of the book—the Swedish pilgrims disembarking at Jaffa, solemn and serious with stern rugged faces, rowing towards him over the smooth silvery-blue summer sea! And Ingmar Ingmarsson, who has married Barbro in pique, comes after Gertrude, fleeing unhappy Barbro in his wistful pursuit. But Gertrude has become the most ardent of the pilgrims, going every day at dawn to watch for the coming of the Son of Man, and following through the streets a dervish who thrillingly resembles the Christ. It is not long before she returns to herself, and goes back to Sweden with Bo and the prodigal Ingmar, to whom Barbro has borne an heir and for whom she has suffered.

But with what richness of imagination does the author see this religion-fevered, plague-haunted Jerusalem in which she works out her moving drama! She searches out every nook and cranny and makes the city live almost as a person in all its vivid unhealthiness. The life of this Gordon colony, to which the Swedish pilgrims come, lies dreamily on the borderline of fervent desire and reality. The Americans themselves are characteristic—kindly, prosaic, combining a practical efficiency of working and teaching with a fanatical unreason in the ends they are there for. The poor Swedes suffer from the rumors that are set afloat about the colony by rival sectarians. They live in a stream of ardent wish-fulfilments. The heated air of the arid city shimmers with fantasies for their tired minds. Yet their faithful spirits glow with the glory of legend and religious hope. . . . Miss Lagerlöf has a grave warmth that covers in its comprehending sympathy the passions of many interlocking lives. . . . (p. 167)

Randolph Bourne, "Two Scandanavian Novelists," in The Dial, Chicago, Vol. 65, September 5, 1918, pp. 167-68.

W. GORE ALLEN (essay date 1946)

[*In the following excerpt, Allen discusses the Lutheran background of Lagerlöf's fiction.*]

Selma Lagerlöf was not predestined to her craft: she became what circumstances made her. The first circumstance was poverty: loss of family income and sale of a family estate. She was obliged to train quickly for a suitable profession; and for all the vocation she had received for teaching, she might have become equally well a typist or a nurse. In this alone she was out of sympathy with most contemporary young women; for while they looked eagerly for latch-keys, her one desire was to remain, under parental authority, at home. There, in the seclusion of Mårbacka, a Värmland demesne, she would have led nothing resembling the middle-class English version of a secluded life. Värmland was self-contained as Northumberland or Cornwall, not dead and alive as are the counties which depend on London for their education and amusement. For a girl of Selma's class (her people were "lesser gentry," on good terms with nobility and yeomen, treated with familiar deference by the peasants) there would have been ski-ing, skating, balls, and occasional lectures in the winter, picnics and bathing in the summer, the whole year enriched by happy friendships. It was a well-ordered life, but not by any means a dull one, a place in which you were a foreigner until half a century had passed by since your arrival; a religious culture of which the worst to be said is that it was not cosmic but provincial, and that it neglected modern problems.

The second circumstance which urged Selma Lagerlöf to become a writer was bound up closely with the first. If writing itself was a safety-valve, an escape from the hatefulness of outward things, the material which she used had been given her in Värmland, to guard and cherish wherever life should bring her. Not many years ago (and it must be remembered that Selma Lagerlöf produced her greatest work before the First World War) a girl from Northumberland or Cornwall, driven against her will to London, would have found it natural to re-create on paper the stories which she had heard by word of mouth in childhood. These might have been tales of the Border and the Pilgrimage of Grace, or tales of the smugglers and wreckers; and she would have written them quite literally to pass the time, since the ground had been covered by expert pens already. With the exception of [Gustav] Fröding, whose range was limited to poetic themes, Värmland had not been represented, as the Border was represented by Sir Walter Scott and Cornwall by the Rector of Morwenstowe and Sir Arthur Quiller-Couch. Prior to the Liberal Epoch there were romantics enough in Scandinavia, but their world of romance was artificial as the Hollow Mountain or the Celtic Twilight; not real as a province which is only a few hours away from the capital by train. They made this world, with its trolls and witches, its magic castles, fairy princesses and hobgoblins, because they felt that literature should be more beautiful than life. The contempt which Ibsen and Brandes voiced against them was well merited and overdue. Unless Scandinavian literature went back to reality at once, it would degenerate for all time into pose and polish.

Selma Lagerlöf took this lesson very much to heart. Her first difficulty was to write of a province without being obscurantist; she had therefore to describe people as they were, or as they had been at some time in the course of human history. What may be called her "Lutheran feeling," her essentially Protestant reaction to social and moral problems, helped powerfully in the choice of time: *Gösta Berling's Saga* was set at the end of the eighteenth century, or in the early nineteenth—in days when men were propelled by horses, when squire and parson reigned supreme in their several districts, and when the State did not attempt to fit square pegs into uniform round holes.

All her pegs were square ones. Gösta himself, an unfrocked preacher; the Major's wife, a mannish, domineering woman, who by sheer will-power drew the last inch of wealth from her estate; Ulrika Dillner, an old housekeeper who ran away from her master because she thought him possessed of the Evil Eye. What could a different society have done with a single one of this wayward, improbable collection? A Fascist, or a Socialist régime, would begin with the praiseworthy idea of putting them to work: Gösta, after a period of probation in a home for inebriates, would be sent to lecture upon the Fallacies of Faith; the Major's wife would be placed in charge of slum mothers or unmarried wives; Ulrika Dillner would be psycho-analysed by a doctor whose specialities were terror and frustration. In a Catholic country they might fare better, but the likelihood is that they would not exist at all; if they did, each would be tolerated, but each would be encouraged, somewhat grimly, to behave: after a few years in monastery and convent, Gösta and the Major's wife (the Church would never waste such a natural prioress on a husband) would return to us, spiritually groomed, thoroughly useful members of society, and not in the very least amusing.

Figures of fun are let loose occasionally upon a Protestant society, both because Protestants lack spheres of utility in which to place them, and also because Lutheran Protestants do not take sin with any degree of seriousness at all. If we turn our minds back to the eighteenth century in England, this will not seem too steep a proposition. There Parson Forde, who luckily left us copious diaries, thought it no sin, but rather a mark of elegance, for a cleric to over-indulge himself at table; at that time the one-bottle man was a milksop and a scandal, while the two-bottle man was a pillar of his class and a gift to his profession. When some squire, reading the lessons with obvious relish on the Sabbath, seduced a village maiden, or drove a carriage up the staircase of his mansion, society might cough in his direction if he abandoned the girl or lamed the horses: the actions in themselves were neither disreputable nor sinful.

Selma Lagerlöf has the typically Lutheran attitude to sin: Lutheran as opposed to Calvinistic, for Calvinist societies, as of Switzerland and Scotland, will not condone breaches of the moral law, and they will not allow greater latitude to the wellborn than they vouchsafe to the very poorest. They are egalitarian; Lutheran societies are always oligarchic. Lutherans find it as difficult to believe in sin as they find it easy to make excuses for the sinner. They do not say, as we might expect the Calvinists to do: "This man cannot estrange himself from God, since God has predestined his salvation"; but rather: "This man's actions cannot be too bad, for they are the actions of a believing Christian, and all believing Christians will be saved."

The way of life to which Lutheranism is a contributory factor can be extremely pleasant: the cast of mind which it helps to form is limited, badly equipped, and unresilient. For this faith presupposes, not only a benevolent oligarchy, but a benevolent oligarchy living in the country; not only an acceptance of decent moral standards, but economic circumstances which allow that standard to be kept. When Prussia became a competitive industrial power, Luther's God had to make way for the "Old German God" of Kaiser Wilhelm; when the Industrial Revolution came about in Britain, the Church of England drew strength from Rome and from Geneva. She may have been as fearful of Newman as she was of Whitfield—the fact remains that they pulled her back to Catholic and Calvinist roots; her Lutheran influences could not cope with the realities of a brutal situation. In Sweden there was the same movement from the country to the towns, although it was more gradual and affected smaller numbers; but there was no alternative religion. Societies which were to become Calvinist had become so finally within a hundred years from the Reformation; they were stern and egalitarian then as they are stern and egalitarian now—Sweden was not destined to be either. Within the Catholic Church, the Counter-Reformation won its victories; but the Jesuits are still precluded from Sweden, where in 1911 a further penal law was passed against all Catholics. To the Swedes religion was and is of the Lutheran variety; its answer to social questions remains government by rank, and to moral questions a quiet life in the country.

There are some questions, particularly moral questions, which it will not face at all. It was this weakness, in the work of Selma Lagerlöf, on which the critics pounced when they wrote: "He who is stupid must be pitied, but pitied the more if he lives in Värmland." The critics recognized that a great city cannot become the focal point for any nation unless that nation is prepared to re-examine each one of its thoughts and feelings and ideas. While they brought up their problems for discussion, only to declare themselves unknowing, religious people, of the Lutheran stamp, would not admit that there were problems to discuss. They tried living in the towns as they had always lived upon the land; when that proved impossible they became nostalgic for old days, well proven ways, and simple people. Selma Lagerlöf voiced their sentiments exactly.

> "Oh, children of a later day!" she cried, "I have nothing new to tell you; nothing but what is old and almost forgotten. Tales from the nursery, where the children sit on low stools round the white-haired story-teller, tales from the workmen's kitchen, where the farm labourers and crofters gather about the pine-wood fire . . . talk of the days that are past and gone."

If she shared their sentiments, she shared their reticences also. In her books, amongst the rollicking misfits, male and female, the lovable villains, and the splendidly bad hats, there is enough of human passion, but it is never the passion of desire between the sexes. These people, who are robust in greed and fabulous in pride, become, where love is in question, pale with Lutheran virtue. And the pity is that we cannot believe it. She tries our credulity too hard. The Devil, or his personal agent, we are told, makes an agreement with these decayed gentlemen, these "Cavaliers," whereby they will live safe and provided in a manor house on the one condition that they do no work other than the Devil's. Up to a point they keep their side of the bargain. The Major's wife, former mistress of the manor, is driven out of doors to beg her bread; the house falls to pieces and the estate is ruined; in the neighborhood, children are alienated from their parents, and husbands from their wives. Everyone is suitably terrified, but everyone manages to appreciate the joke.

It would be folly to emulate the critics, who analysed *Gösta Berling's Saga* in the twin obscurities of historical ignorance and personal distaste. They said first that there never were such goings on in ancient Värmland, and secondly—even if evidence in support could be produced, that they preferred to doubt it. Mary Webb, writing of a similar place during the same period, introduces us to sin-eaters, local wizards, and young men haunted by the Devil. We take her word for it, not only because memories of the English country live on in the most urban English, but because the sin-eater swallows seduction with the rest, the wizard exposes his daughter naked for reward, and the young man is tempted to abuse the spiritual adoration of his wife. Mary Webb escaped sufficiently from Lutheranism to paint a living picture: Selma Lagerlöf leaves everything from the calling of banns until the baptism of infants to our imagination.

Reading *Gösta Berling's Saga,* one does not doubt the reality of a devil to the Cavaliers, nor their belief that they had made a compact with him: what one is forced to doubt is that he would have fought left-handed, or with a blunted weapon. The suspicion grows that there is some deception; Satan is only half Satanic; and thus the men who war with him, or against him, are rather less than mortal. As he has been exorcized and fumigated to make him fit for Lutheran society, so the Cavaliers have been emasculated. They are quite harmless, they are even lovable; and we are told towards the end that their motives were always of the highest.

Selma Lagerlöf is no more at home with extremes of goodness than she is with extremes of evil. Amongst various legends which have been bound with her book, *The Queens of Kungahälla,* there is one concerning Catherine Benincasa, the girl saint of Siena. This story demonstrates the Lutheran approach to goodness when that approach is both sympathetic and obtuse. Here is a writer going south, away from the environment she knows, it must be feared in search of local colour. And the colour blinds her; blinds her to such an extent that she is unable to distinguish the wood of faith from the trees of cultus, reverence, and affection. It is on this note that the legend opens:

> It is in St. Catherine's old house in Siena, a day at the end of April, during the week in which her festival is celebrated. The house with the beautiful balcony and many small rooms, which are now turned into chapels and oratories, in the street of the dyers. Thither people are bringing bouquets of white lilies, and the scent of incense and violets hangs about the house. While they do so, they say to themselves, "It seems just as though the little Catherine were quite recently dead and as though those who are going in and out of her house had seen and known her." But, as a matter of fact, no one can believe that she is dead, for in that case there would have been more grief and lamentation, not merely a quiet sense of regret. It seems rather as though a beloved daughter had been just married and taken away from her father's house. . . .

And it is almost on this other note that the legend ends. St. Catherine has been striving for the conversion of Nicola Tunga, a young nobleman condemned to death.

> "Before you came," she said, "I placed my neck on the block in order to see if I could bear it, and I felt that I still have a dread of death and that I do not love Jesus well enough to be willing to die this hour. Nor do I wish you to die, and my prayers have no power." As she said this, he thought, "If I had lived I should yet have won her." And he was glad that he would die before he had dragged down the bright bride of Heaven to the earth. But when he laid his head in her hands, there came to them both a great comfort. "Nicola Tunga," she said, "I see Heaven opening. Angels are hovering about in order to receive your soul." . . .

It is a rare phenomenon for Lutherans to sense the attractiveness of Catholic ceremonial and devotion. In *Gösta Berling's Saga* there is a chapter describing a Värmland church, whose whitewash, as well as the disappearance of plaster saints, Selma Lagerlöf is ready to deplore. One feels that she yearns for the trappings of a drama, but that the drama itself must contain no tragic scenes; and for the Christian Faith, provided that its central fact, a cross, has been removed. Under her hand St. Catherine becomes, not so much a saint, as an extraordinary young woman; a girl whose character was always quite unusual, requiring no preparation for its final renunciation of the world. In the first place, Selma Lagerlöf doubted the efficacy of the Catholic training to sainthood—confession, Holy Communion, constant prayer, and continual self-humiliation; and in the second, she would not admit that the world was a foe to be renounced. As the Cavaliers meant well, so also did the world; as their motives were always of the highest, equally high were the motives of worldly people. Because a Lutheran public could not bear hard facts, they were shown a saint who might have been a daughter of the local manse: she had a sweet disposition, she was given to good works, and, if she had taken a vow of chastity, that was at worst a personal foible.

The vow of chastity was the one thing which made St. Catherine a remarkable person, and which made her memory enduring. Had she refrained from this sacrifice, which the least of them could understand at once, the burghers of Siena, always frugal and suspicious, would not have wasted their money on candles in her honour nor their time on visiting her house. Selma Lagerlöf, and still more her Swedish readers, might understand the sacrifice of sex, but they could not tolerate the renunciation of romance. Therefore the story of a great love, the love of a soul for its Creator, becomes a love story with an unhappy ending. Had Nicola's life been spared, he would have won her. This is so improbable that we are forced from the world of fact into a world of fiction, and from the contemplation of a character to the mere witnessing of puppets. As the Cavaliers fail because they are too good, St. Catherine fails because she is not nearly good enough. Both are shown to us through Lutheran eyes: eyes which are restless but rather vague, kind but extremely sentimental.

Selma Lagerlöf is sometimes attracted to the South, yet only in the North, and only there in times since the Reformation, is she happy as a writer. Her full-length portrait of St. Olav is no more true to life and history than is her thumbnail sketch of the Italian virgin. Here again austerity must yield pride of place to high romance; for we are shown Queen Astrid winning the tough warrior with a feminine guile which barely escapes from being coquettish. Of Catholics in modern Scandinavia she makes no single mention, leaving Sigrid Undset to answer questions of the day on their behalf, through the voice, and through the personality still more, of Father Harold Tangen. She remains within her chosen limits; Lutheran limits which exclude democracy, Socialism, divorce, the urban poor, and which should exclude both the South of Europe and any time—to take two England landmarks—before the abdication of James Stuart or after the accession of Victoria.

It is almost as difficult for us to sum up her literary achievement as it was for Brandes, and the other Scandinavian critics, when they first read *Gösta Berling's Saga.* Because we do not share their view of progress, granting an evolutionary character to history—primitive, medieval, modern; uphill all the way, with a mechanical El Dorado at the top—we shall not regard her as one who wilfully fell back. She was no more reactionary than are whole cultures, and the individual nations which compose them, when they react against a wrong ascent, feeling that it can take them nowhere, and return to a point at which the ways divided. Perhaps she did not return quite far enough; perhaps the Lutheran atmosphere was not an air in which great art could flourish. Certainly it possessed small consolation for those who had entered El Dorado, only to find it an accursed city of the plains.

Yet, if we pronounce these heavy judgments, we shall be taking her too seriously; far more seriously than she herself intended. She was romantic, but we cannot call her a Romantic; she taught school to earn a living, but to think of her as naïve, or over-innocent, or 'missish' would be to study a shadow without once glancing at the figure from whom it was reflected. She was not a born writer in the sense that writing was her obvious vocation: she was a medium to whom the stories whispered: "We must be told: please tell us!" And to have it in this way is to have the better part. (pp. 76-85)

> *W. Gore Allen, "The Protestants," in his* Renaissance in the North, *Sheed & Ward, 1946, pp. 60-86.*

F. S. DE VRIEZE (essay date 1958)

[*In the following excerpt, de Vrieze assesses some characteristics of Lagerlöf's three autobiographical works:* Mårbacka, Memories of My Childhood, *and* The Diary of Selma Lagerlöf.]

According to Selma Lagerlöf, in her memoirs her primary object was to describe the atmosphere and conditions prevailing at the old Mårbacka estate, so that they might be preserved for posterity. This is undoubtedly true: it is plain to see in **Mårbacka.** Unlike Goethe and Hans Christian Andersen whose autobiographical works begin with their birth and are written in the first person, Selma Lagerlöf writes in the third person and begins with her illness and recovery. She was then four years old! Then come the old house keeper's stories, covering the period from Mårbacka's origins up to the early married life of the writer's grandmother. The name of Selma Lagerlöf's grandmother was Lisa Maja Lagerlöf née Wennervik. But this cycle of stories did not nearly exhaust the store of tales about the old Mårbacka. In the following one, "Gamla byggnader och gamla människor," the writer once more starts telling stories about the earliest period in Mårbacka's history, taking the old farm buildings as her starting-point. Selma Lagerlöf does not figure in either of these cycles of stories, nor in the next one "Det nya

Mårbacka." Here once more it is Mårbacka on which interest centres, although notice is taken of Lieutenant Lagerlöf, his wife and his sister Lovisa as well. In the last cycle of stories, "Vardag och fest," it is life at Mårbacka during the writer's childhood on which the stress is laid, although she herself does not figure at all prominently in them. Yet again, excursions into the past are made by means of stories about Lieutenant Lagerlöf's youth!

In the first volume of memoirs Selma Lagerlöf principally describes Mårbacka and the life her ancestors led at this farmstead, as well as the circles in which they moved and on which they left their mark. It is not until the second volume that the writer herself becomes more conspicuous and writes in the first person; although here again her surroundings (the family, the friends and acquaintances and the staff) claim the major part of the reader's attention.

The chief difference with **Mårbacka** is that in **Ett barns memoarer,** a certain development in the character of the young girl is noticeable and this becomes more and more pronounced in the third volume [**Dagbok för Selma Lagerlöf**]. She makes full use of the difficulties encountered during adolescence, which moreover was spent in a new milieu, and this environment likewise figures largely in the book. Unlike the first volume, the second and third recount events in strict (though sometimes invented) chronological order.

In this way a broad panorama of 19th-century life in the Värmland countryside is unfolded before us—social relations; relations within the family itself; the fairly monotonous way of life, especially in winter; the work which went on on the big farm; the dreary life of the day-labourers; the merrymaking, especially amongst the higher ranks of society; belief in the supernatural; the life of the clergymen; the country doctors' visiting; the country customs and, last but not least, the appearance on the scene of numbers of original characters. Ultimately, every writer of memoirs falls back on the atmosphere and conditions of his or her childhood. In order to demonstrate that every writer works these up in his or her individual way, the conscious and unconscious trends perceptible in Selma Lagerlöf's work will be compared with those to be found in the memoirs of certain other well-known writers.

Whereas Selma Lagerlöf has given a broad delineation of the old Värmland history, in particular from a cultural viewpoint, Goethe in his *Dichtung und Wahrheit* has portrayed the history of his own times. Marcel Proust never wrote an autobiography as such, but gives us [in *A la recherche du temps perdu*] a subjective description based on his own memories of French society life, especially in Paris, round about the turn of the century; while Hans Andersen writes about many walks of life in various countries, but only to the extent that they are relevant to his own biography. Selma Lagerlöf and Goethe often so accentuate their surroundings that they themselves are quite inconspicuous, whereas Proust and Andersen are much more openhearted and their work is concentrated on and around their own selves.

Selma Lagerlöf was very much aware of her marked epic talents. She confessed even that she found it terribly difficult to write anything other than stories. Verner von Heidenstam was the one amongst her own generation of writers who meant the most to her, because even in his lyrical writing he had a story to tell. She had such a pronounced aptitude for the epic, that she could not even appreciate lyrical confessions. With her memoirs particularly in mind, Selma Lagerlöf

declared to Esther Ståhlberg (née Elfving) in 1934 that everything she wrote always turned into a story, albeit a perfectly true one.

Closer examination of the conscious and unconscious trends distinguishable in the autobiographical works of Selma Lagerlöf reveals that the writer was quite conscious of a tendency within herself to make the subject-matter interesting. This is apparent from a letter to Valborg Olander, dated May 8th 1930, about Axel Munthe and his book on San Michele. Selma Lagerlöf is of the opinion that Munthe is such a great artist that he would naturally have to lie or fabricate when telling things about himself. (pp. 281-83)

Selma Lagerlöf adopts several methods to make some particular subject interesting.

She may do so by inventing new incidents; by changing the time, the place, or the circumstances of an incident or by letting somebody else experience it. . . .

Then again, the writer may alter people's motives for doing certain things (e.g. reading the Bible). She succeeds in making changes of an often extremely surprising quality, by giving a totally unexpected turn to events. This is not unnaturally less conspicuous in the memoirs than in her other works. (p. 284)

[There is in the autobiographical works] the presence of the so-called "transcendent reality" in many of the chapters, where the changes were made with the object of accentuating the essence of the facts, situations etc. A good biography—and the same can be said of an autobiography—is not a dry summary of exact facts, but a work of art, which makes the past come to life. That Selma Lagerlöf was aware that a series of recorded facts does not represent reality is plain from her comments on an American commission of enquiry into teaching problems. This commission had stenographers take everything down verbatim but realized immediately that their material would have to be adapted in order to reproduce the true state of affairs more faithfully and so to reach the objective: and this required an orderly and imaginative mind.

To take the memoirs in their entirety—the transcendent reality of the first volume consists of a portrayal of Värmland rural life in the 19th century. This originates with and centres on the lives of the ancestors of the writer herself, who accords the typical Värmland milieu a large place. The same goes for the second volume, although Selma Lagerlöf herself is at the centre of things, looking out at the life at Mårbacka (from her individual point of view).

In the third volume, written in the first person singular, like **Ett barns memoarer,** it is the adolescence of Selma Lagerlöf and the powerful development of her imagination during this period spent in another environment, which constitutes transcendent reality. (pp. 284-85)

Transcendent reality is also prominent in Marcel Proust. For him it is the reality of a mystic—beyond the range of material reality and more important and more "real" than this. One can only aspire to transcendent reality by contemplation ("contemplation") or better, involuntary recollection ("mémoire involontaire") brought about by some chance sensation which evokes things of the past with an enhanced clarity and intensity: the intellect, now eliminated, at the time prevented the elements illogically connected with this bit of the past from reaching the level of the conscious mind. . . . However essential recollections are in *La recherche du temps perdu,* this work may certainly not be regarded as autobiographical. Like Selma Lagerlöf, Proust takes a real event or a real person as his starting-point, but in his case it is no more than that. Not only are a number of events in Proust's greatest work purely fictitious, but his personages (with a few exceptions) have traits of character and demeanour borrowed from many people; there is not one gesture, not one inflexion of the voice which he has not really observed, albeit in many different persons. But Selma Lagerlöf has also drawn on various sources for the character and demeanour of her personae, to a far greater extent than is generally appreciated. There is proof of Proust's work not being pure autobiography, in the fact that, unlike Selma Lagerlöf, Goethe and Hans Andersen, he gave places and people fictional names. Even the places which one can locate have been provided with details taken from other towns or villages—a thing that never occurs in Selma Lagerlöf.

Proust is, then, convinced that only involuntary recollection can resuscitate the past in all its glory. Allowances must be made for the neurasthenic Proust's not only having inherited an exceptional sensitiveness and receptiveness from his Jewish mother, but also being confined to bed with chronic asthma for long periods on end. Consequently, he was far more preoccupied with his sensations and recollections than a person leading a more normal life would have been. In the second and third volumes of her memoirs, Selma Lagerlöf has proved that the past can be revived by other means; that is, calling oneself to life again just as one was sixty years ago, with the ideas and experiences of that period alone, and not profiting from life's lesson of the meantime. The author admits [in a letter to Elisabeth Grundtvig of November 5th 1930] that she can never quite achieve reality, but it had helped her greatly to write in this way.

The second distinct tendency in Selma Lagerlöf's autobiographical works was her endeavour not to commit herself or members of her family.

As far as she herself is concerned, the final version of "Efterskrift" is very instructive on this point: she does not mind showing the seamy side of a successful writer's life, but refrains from analysing her father's character and her own, and comparing the two. This trait is brought to light in a letter addressed to Anna Ohlson née Hagman, dated November 22nd 1931. Mrs Ohlson had been going through a very difficult time, but had been very brave about it, so that the writer concludes that neither does she wear her heart upon her sleeve. That Selma Lagerlöf did not flippantly show up the members of her family is proved principally in the case of her father, whose tyranny, egoism and lack of self-control are very much toned down, though not entirely blotted out.

For that matter, the conscious will to spare the family can be to some extent accounted for by the third tendency encountered in the memoirs, namely, her endeavour to create harmony (we find this also, in a lesser degree, in her other works, where discords are often deliberately struck in order to resolve them later).

The writer sets great store by giving a harmonious, and at times even idyllic, picture of her youth, in which the members of her family participate. The chapter "Anna Lagerlöf," which is almost entirely devoted to a short period during which her sister was gentle, lovable and helpful, is clear proof of this. Selma Lagerlöf's pursuit of harmony is certainly the reason for the earlier manuscripts giving a better picture of

the young adolescent girl than the book version. If, in the final text of the book, the writer so firmly represses the young girl's lack of poise and irritability, which are two of the principal traits of puberty, it shows how close to her heart the desire for harmony lies! But it is not only Selma Lagerlöf who cherishes this desire!

The same conscious trend is to be seen in Goethe. He also scrapped hard criticism from his manuscript on more than one occasion (as, for instance, in the case of his sister Cornelie) and preferred besides not to incorporate dramatic scenes into *Dichtung und Wahrheit.*

Hans Andersen, too, who was a man quick to take offence and often in a depressed frame of mind, cut out several violent outbursts, though at times for fear of the consequences. He likewise represented his earliest youth as being more idyllic than it was.

In both Selma Lagerlöf and Hans Andersen a propensity for the dramatic is noticeable. In her novels and shorter stories, the former frequently gives way to this urge, but not without attempting to create a harmonious ending (a few exceptions apart). A different method is, however, used in the memoirs: the dramatic scenes are either omitted or replaced by more sober and harmonious ones. An example of omission is the episode where Miss K.'s jealousy is described, in the chapter "Sjunde och åttonde veckorna"; and of replacement, the story of Selma, Aline Laurell and the practically extinguished candle in "Pastor Unger." The writer, therefore, wanted her memoirs to be more harmonious and more subdued in tone. Dr. J. Ravn has pointed out [in "Selma Lagerlöfs psykiske konstitution," *Bonniers litterära magasin* (1955)], that Selma Lagerlöf, happily for her work as an artist, was not always so harmonious as her contemporaries often supposed. Selma Lagerlöf did not suffer from pessimism as Hans Andersen did: she was convinced that good would triumph in the end, for otherwise mankind would by now have vanished from the face of the earth. However, the happy ending which one finds in most of Selma Lagerlöf's stories, is not principally due to her purposed tendency to make her subject-matter harmonious. She knows quite well that in real life it is not always virtue which is rewarded and that the moral does not always play such an important role as it does in her works. But doing right and good means beauty to her, and that is why her work bears the stamp of aestheticism and is not a question of moral for the sake of a moral! Good and just actions (which are often accompanied by great sacrifices) consequently give her aesthetic, and certainly also moral, satisfaction, so that it is understandable that she wants to see them rewarded.

Besides this propensity for the dramatic, which is often suppressed in favour of harmony—in which Selma Lagerlöf is not alone—we find a propensity for the supernatural in the memoirs. This is expressed not only in the many ghost-stories and descriptions of individuals who are supposed to possess supernatural powers (e.g. the witch of Högbergssäter, Tita Grå, the water sprite etc.), but also in her representation of some particular world of feeling and thought, where magic or the irrational connection between two separate incidents is accepted (e.g. between the drowning of the cats in the brook Ämtan and Lieutenant Lagerlöf's unsuccessful attempts to put an end to the damage caused by this brook).

Selma Lagerlöf herself speaks of always having been drawn to mysticism ("dragning till det mystiska") and to the old folklore of ghosts and supernatural powers, and of its being easier for her to write about things supernatural than about everyday facts and experiences. It is characteristic of Selma Lagerlöf's artistry that things natural and supernatural are completely intermingled. The close connection between her authorship and the world of the supernatural is more pointedly put into words in a letter written to Henriette Coyet in the year 1931. If she had not been able to write about wonders and supernatural powers, she would not have been of much value as a writer. And this inward urge makes her believe that another world must certainly exist. Nor must one lose sight of the fact that it is precisely the world of wonders which is so eminently suitable for depicting suggestively human goodness and its struggle against evil, as well as the goodness of Providence (consider the "conversions" and other sudden psychological changes repeatedly undergone by people in Selma Lagerlöf) both of which themes are extremely important to her work. Furthermore, the wonders usually have a symbolic significance. The writer's symbolism is revealed in the memoirs, in the guise of Marit from Sotbråten and of the "rag-hag", who are concrete representations of adolescent irritability and of jealousy. In the case of the monster within herself, it is not certain if this is merely a symbol of evil, for she may actually have noticed it. As a young woman, especially in her student days in Stockholm, Selma Lagerlöf had lost her religious faith and in the letter to Henriette Coyet in the year 1931, cited above, she mentions that she knows no religion to which she could attach herself (but at the end of her life she showed a preference for the Christian religion). She goes on to say that a belief in God and in her own immortality gives her vitality, whereas unbelief makes her powerless and kills the intuitive life within her. She had already declared on March 4th 1909 in a letter to Professor Valfrid Vasenius, that the poetic strain in her, which aspired to the realms of mysticism, always compelled her to return to the ranks of believers. That a belief in wonders was not alien to her is proved by part of a letter dated November 28th 1913, written to Valborg Olander. The passage is about the holy statue of Lucca which is frightfully ugly and terrifying; still, you can see it is a powerful statue which can perform wonders even at the present day!

A letter written in the summer of 1909 to Valborg Olander shows that Selma Lagerlöf believed in irrational power which can influence the life of human beings. Her brother-in-law does not expect any results from the digging operations at Mårbacka, to find water for an aquaduct. She also presumes nothing can come of it, as her brother-in-law always brings bad luck and believes in failure.

The abundance of abnormal characters in Selma Lagerlöf's works is closely bound up with her propensity for the supernatural: with such people irrational reactions and wonders can certainly be more frequently expected than with matter-of-fact, sensible beings. According to Dr. J. Ravn, the psychically abnormal people in her work are correctly portrayed from both the psychiatric and the psychological angles. (pp. 285-90)

Selma Lagerlöf's modifications resulting from the conscious and unconscious trends just discussed by no means signify that contact with reality had been broken. There appears to be a nucleus of truth present in all the biographical material: in this connection one cannot help thinking of the following statement made in a letter to Esselde dated April 14th 1891: "I allmänhet intresserar det mig ej att skrifva rena lögner. Kan jag få tag i en bit verklighet och förvandla den till poesi

är jag nöjd" ["In general I have no interest in the writing of mere lies. If I can get hold of a bit of reality and can transform it into poetry, I am content"].

What does this nucleus encountered in every part of the memoirs consist of? In other words, what material does the writer take directly from actual facts, without drawing on her imagination?

First, we may enumerate the places where Selma Lagerlöf spent her youth, above all Mårbacka and thereabouts, but also the house of the Afzelius family and the city of Stockholm. Even with place descriptions in her novels and non-autobiographical stories, she gladly uses the surroundings so familiar to her, as a model. (For instance, her Uncle Tullius Hammargren's vicarage at Karlskoga served as a model for the vicarage at Korskyrka in *Charlotte Löwensköld.)*

Secondly, the time when the various incidents took place proves, generally speaking, to be in accordance with the actual facts.

On certain occasions the writer has permitted herself inconsistencies, for the following reasons: for the sake of the composition (in "Den sjuttonde augusti," where performances held over a number of years are compressed into a few birthdays); for the sake of transcendent reality (for instance in "Paradisfågeln," where Selma's leg healed on board the Jakob); and because of her purposed tendency to make the story more interesting (e.g. in "Stolpboden," where the interval between the housekeeper's marriage and her return to Mårbacka is made shorter).

Thirdly, Selma Lagerlöf has in general given a true picture of the appearance, character and life-story of the people in her memoirs. Where this is not so, as for example in the case of Raklitz, Daniel Lagerlöf and his brother, it is to be attributed on the one hand to a more absorbing story thus being possible and on the other, to the writer's not wanting to diverge too much from the description of these people in *Liljecronas hem.* Her attempt to produce harmony appears to be responsible for differences in character sketches (as in the instances of Lieutenant Lagerlöf and Anna Lagerlöf).

Place therefore proves to tally completely with the actual facts, and time tallies for the most part; appearance, character and life-story of the personae to a lesser degree. The writer evidently felt it essential to represent these three aspects—i.e. time, place and personal particulars—with a certain regard for accuracy. This appears from a letter of October 15th 1922 to Valborg Olander. It refers to *Mårbacka*: "Det är sanning alltsammans, men för mig är det nastan svårare att få litet fason på det, som är sannt [!] än på det diktade" ["Everything is truth, but for me it is almost more difficult to give shape to truth than to fiction"]. Selma Lagerlöf acknowledges the share imagination has had in her memoirs, as well as her view that everything in them is true—as can be deduced from her comment on Axel Munthe's artistry, given above, and from her gratification at Karl Otto Bonnier's opinion [expressed in a letter to Selma Lagerlöf of October 3rd 1922], which was that *Mårbacka* compared favourably, as regards powers of imagination and humour, with the best that she had ever written.

The writer of the present thesis may perhaps be permitted, in conclusion, to characterize the Selma Lagerlöf revealed in her memoirs, as a great story-teller, whose endeavour to make her subject-matter more interesting is aided by her propensity for the supernatural, and whose desire to present as harmonious a picture of her youth as possible tempers her inclination to be dramatic and induces her to represent herself and her relatives as being more harmonious than they in fact were. And finally, Selma Lagerlöf may be described as a great artist who is constrained to sacrifice sensible reality in order to depict transcendent reality. (pp. 290-92)

F. S. de Vrieze, in her Fact and Fiction in the Auto-biographical Works of Selma Lagerlöf, Royal Van Gorcum Ltd., 1958, 380 p.

MARGUERITE YOURCENAR   (essay date 1975)

[*A novelist, essayist, poet, and dramatist, Yourcenar was one of the leading figures in modern French literature and the first woman elected to the French Academy. She was a classical scholar and historical novelist who presented psychological analysis of historical figures in her fiction and nonfiction. In the following excerpt, she discusses the epic scope of Lagerlöf's fiction.*]

Various kinds of fiction have been described as a *roman-fleuve* ["river-like novel"]; but Selma Lagerlöf's epic current wells up from the very sources of myth. Its source is among the streams and waterfalls which impetuously feed the forges of Ekeby, in *The Story of Gösta Berling,* with their eddies of melted snow, their foaming superstitions, their dead leaves and debris of the past century mingled with the wild joy of youth. This first work is perhaps the great writer's most spontaneous, a vast hymn to life and at the same time a song of innocent rebellion. The stream then passes through sterner straits: in the first part of *Jerusalem* it reflects the somber green mountains, the storm-raked forests, the fields immemorially hallowed by human labor which Ingmar Ingmarsson and old Matts refuse to leave, even for the Holy Land. Its floodwaters bear the tree trunk which strikes down huge old Ingmar, struggling to save a little band of children swept away by the waters. In the second part of *Jerusalem* the river runs underground, beneath the aridity of the desert. In *The Wonderful Adventures of Nils* it floods all of Sweden, from Lapland to the Sund, reflecting the triangular flights of wild geese accompanied by the rascal Nils, who, by dint of traveling all over the land, participating in man's struggles and sufferings, sharing in the hunted existence of wild creatures, acquires the heart and wisdom he needs to help his old parents on their poor farm. Broadening to an estuary, mingling with the ocean's waters, it surrounds that huge archipelago of sometimes smiling, sometimes somber islands and islets which constitute the tales and novels of Selma Lagerlöf—*Invisible Links, From a Swedish Homestead, The Girl from the Marsh Croft,* many others. In a tale evoking the harsh Sweden of the sixteenth century, *Herr Arne's Hoard,* its icy waves embrace the island where the old priest's murderers are hiding. In *The Outcast* and in *Charlotte Löwensköld,* heavy, tormented, debatable works written later in her career, it is contaminated by the detritus of wickedness and mad selfishness; it sweeps in its eddies the corpses of the Battle of Jutland. Finally, its subsiding wavelets lap the landscapes in which an old lady tenderly reconsiders her childhood.

The characters, too, are of epic scope. Drinker, gambler, debauchee, the renegade minister Gösta burns like a flame, spreading around himself the joy and passion of life. Yet he is also the vagabond who trades for brandy the sacks of grain entrusted to him by a pauper child; the superstitious ungrateful rider of Ekeby who allows his protectress to be driven

from her home because she is accused of witchcraft, though he later reinstates her and keeps vigil at her deathbed; the romantic desperado who dreams of dying in the peace of the Finnish forests, seducer of every beauty and lover of none till the day he weds an abandoned woman who needs his aid, and thereby makes a Faustian end as a useful man. At his side, the Dowager of Ekeby, pipe and oath in her mouth, sometimes decked out in satins and pearls, receiving her Christmas guests, sometimes helping her ore barges navigate the treacherous lake, is one of the most robust female figures the nineteenth-century novel has produced. We hardly know which to prefer among so many unforgettable scenes: the one where she confesses to the young renegade who wants to die that her own life has been as fierce and hard as any vagabond's, and that she would have as many reasons to take her own life as he, if she allowed herself to heed them; the scene where she gives a dinner for her mother, who has come to reproach her for her sins, and the two women insult each other while placidly continuing to eat, the petrified guests not daring to speak or touch the food; or the scene, finally, where, fallen in her turn, she walks to the estate of this virtually centenarian mother and finds her in the dairy, busily ordering the servants about; without a word, the old mistress hands her prodigal daughter the creaming ladle she has hitherto entrusted to no one, thereby restoring her to her rank in her home.

In the two volumes of her novel *Jerusalem,* the current's rhythm matches the slow gait of the peasants. Here the char-

Lagerlöf at Mårbacka.

acters move with caution so as to disturb nothing in established custom or in the mysterious harmony between the spirits of nature and of man, until a crisis of fanaticism hurls some of them on the roads to Palestine. The book begins with the famous pages where Ingmar Ingmarsson, walking behind his plow, imagines he is consulting his father and his forebears gathered on some celestial farm: should he or should he not resolve to seek out, when she has been released from prison, his fiancée condemned to three years' detention for infanticide? Ingmar realizes that Brita would have been ashamed to celebrate her child's baptism before her own wedding, yet the old people are not unaware that the custom of anticipating the nuptial ceremony inveterately prevails in the countryside. "It is hard for a man to understand a bad woman," the imagined father muses. "No, Father, Brita was not bad, she was proud." "That comes to the same thing." How could he marry, as a matter of fact, when the old man's burial in the spring occasioned such heavy expenditures, when there is not enough money to paint and plaster the farm and also give a wedding banquet? But Ingmar, seeing a housepainter passing by on the road with his pails of paint and his brushes, believes he has received the advice his ancestors had promised him: in a long, slow trajectory, each stage of which is a station of the Cross for his pride, he will fetch his fiancée from prison, though she hesitates, fearing the scorn which will be poured on her in her own village. It is Sunday: Ingmar musters the courage to enter the church with her, for she is seized with a sudden desire to attend the service; the other women leave the bench near the door where she sits down. But soon scorn turns to respect; the peasants will recognize in this man capable of enduring his own hard ordeal the worthy successor of the old folk of Ingmarsgard.

When we seek out the source from which Selma Lagerlöf's men and women draw their strength, we think first of the powerful reserves of Protestant austerity in which the author herself was brought up. Accurate in part, this answer is nonetheless too simple. These characters so close to the natural world seem chiefly motivated by a strict adherence to the order of things; their good resolutions grow like trees or well up like springs. We must also take into account a long human heritage which includes not only the warmhearted pre-Reformation folk piety (Swedish Lutheranism never completely broke with the rites and legends of medieval Christianity) but also the legacy of rich and obscure "pagan times." Beneath the Protestant rigidity, her characters' virtue, in the ancient meaning of the word, derives less from the observance of this or that precept or from faith in this or that dogma than from man's deepest powers, those of the race itself. It is not only metaphorically and in the course of a waking dream that Ingmar Ingmarsson is counseled by his ancestors. On one hand, we are so accustomed to despise the conventional morality, considered factitious by so many of us, and on the other to regard greatness of soul as no more than a theatrical convention, that it is difficult, at first, to find such virtues as intimately contained in a human existence as the grain of its wood is present in the oak.

The Danish critic George Brandes, who "launched" Selma Lagerlöf, immediately noted in *Gösta Berling* the "cold purity" of the love scenes. Perhaps he was mistaken: this coldness scorches. His point of view at least suggests that the naturalism of the 1880s could be as mistaken as the paneroticism of our own times about what constitutes a work's passional and sensual depths. The characters of *Gösta Berling,* it is true, do not copulate, or at least do not do so before our eyes, and the adulterous passions of the old mistress of Ekeby manor occurred long before the first chapter. But, as in all high art, it is symbolically and not by physiological details that carnal love is expressed. Even more than the kisses Gösta gives to the little Countess Donna, fierce songs and the speed of the sledge, the cold and the night's flaring torches evoke the lover's orgasm. In the tale from *Invisible Links* in which a peasant ravishes a Troll girl sleeping in the forest, the orgy of butterflies plundering flowers prefigures the young man's emotions in the presence of the lovely naked girl: one is reminded of Baudelaire's "young giantess," but here there is a primeval innocence as well. Selma Lagerlöf inherits her art from the great epic tradition in which sexual relations are either implied or chastely described, whatever the raw realities might have been in the society of the time. Beautiful Helen is presented by Homer as the worthy spouse of Paris; the enormous conjugal delights of Zeus and Hera are signified by the blossoming of flowers on the ground which serves as their couch. In Selma Lagerlöf, marriage, with its joys and its torments, is situated at the very center of life, its sensuous rites remain secret, but under the full skirts and peasant bodices of Brita, of Barbro, or of Anna Svärd, under the well-padded toilettes of that provincial lady Charlotte Löwensköld, we do not doubt the presence of warm flesh.

Symbol again intervenes in the representation of Gabriel and Gertrude's young love in the two parts of *Jerusalem:* it becomes the pure water of the underground spring which Gertrude craves in the delirium of her fever and which Gabriel risks his life to find. On other occasions, the deferred joys of betrothal are allegorized by the building of the house that the bridegroom works at so joyously, and by the sheets and tablecloths woven by the bride. Shameful though it is, as in all traditional societies, adultery is ennobled by a certain aristocratic unconcern in the old mistress of the manor of Ekeby, by a poignant courage in the farmer's wife Ebba, at first driven to despair by the fear of scandal but finally determined to erect, for all to see, a wooden cross engraved with her own name over the grave of her child, to whom her husband has denied the right to sleep in the family plot [in **"The Epitaph"**]. Finally, in this rustic society a wronged girl does not fall quite so low as she would have done in the bourgeois world of the period. Brita, as we have seen, recovers her status despite her infanticide; the girl from the Marsh Croft who forgoes charges against her seducer, rather than causing him to perjure himself before the judge, regains her status in public opinion by this very feat and marries a prosperous peasant.

For us the pagan-Christian opposition is seen at a quasi-primal level, the term "pagan" being supposed to signify the largely imaginary sexual freedom of Antiquity, and the term "Christian," often evoking a religiosity of pure routine, narrowly allied to proprieties and social forms, but from which the great and specifically Christian virtues of charity, humility, poverty, and love of God are absent. In this Scandinavia still so close to its pagan era, the contrast is very differently seen. Pagan elements are perceived as cosmic, *elementary,* in the literal sense of the word, benign or terrible presences irreducible to the human order and surrounding us on all sides; contacts with them remain possible as long as our mind is capable of seeing the invisible within the visible. Thus the enchanting Maja Lisa encounters "The Neck," the fine white magic horse, immemorial genius of the waters, which regards her with the eyes of a human lover [in *Mårbacka*]. The "tomte" watches over the proper upkeep of the house and eliminates its bad masters; it is, as much as the old servants themselves, the conscience of the house [in **"The Tomte of Toreby"**]. Forest spirits warn the charcoal-burner Stark when his rick catches fire, but disappear forever when fanatics cut down the rosebushes in which the "little people" take shelter on his threshold [in *Jerusalem*]. The fisherman helped in his work by mermaids drowns himself when his priest, in order to exorcise him, makes him drink out of the communion chalice a few drops of the lake water which a magical ban forbids him to touch [in **"The Water of the Lake Bay"**]. In the powerful tale **"Banished,"** one of two criminals reduced to living in the woods is a rich Christian peasant outlawed for having killed a monk, while the other, a pagan and the son of a pirate shipwrecker on an isolated island, has never known the relatively settled customs of village life. The peasant whom the half-wild youth reveres as a god gradually teaches him the precepts of the faith he still believes in, though he has broken its commandments. This moral progress paradoxically leads to betrayal: the youth betrays and murders the friend whose soul he believes he is saving by forcing him to undergo punishment. Christian faith and the heroic modes of primitive life destroy each other.

It appears, from certain parts of her early work, that the Selma Lagerlöf of these years saw Christianity as a religion too narrow and too demanding to embrace the whole of reality, and the Cross as the symbol of a salvation which did not necessarily save all mankind. Later in her life, she still said she did not believe in the Redemption; on the other hand, we find an invocation to Jesus in the margin of a book she was reading at the time. These states of her personal belief signify less than the profoundly Christian accent of certain great tales imbued with what we might call the existential fervor of medieval piety. The child who was outraged that an intolerant priest should cast the brightly daubed village saints into the pond reacts to this obtuse puritanism as intensely as to the pietists cutting down the fairies' rosebushes: she, for one, is willing to drink at every spring. [**"Sigurd the Proud,"** the] story of King Olaf Trygvasson, killed by a fierce Viking queen whose advances he has rejected, contains one of the purest Marian visions in literature: Olaf, in a premonitory dream, sees himself defeated during a naval battle, his bloody body lying on the sea's floor; the merciful Mother of God advances into the murky depths which form a cathedral's pillars and vaults around her, raises him up, presses him to her bosom, and slowly bears him out of the sea's blue into the blue of the sky. Even more poignant is the story of King Olaf Haraldson, flouted by a monarch who has sent him for his bride not his legitimate daughter but a slave's bastard. Strongly tempted to kill her, Olaf nonetheless spares the accomplice of this imposture, feeling strong enough to raise this woman to his own level rather than being degraded by her. "Your face shines, King Olaf!" But we must make no mistake here: Olaf is motivated less by Christian humility than by an inner certainty which wells up from deep within his being. On a very high level, this difference vanishes altogether: nonetheless, it is true that Olaf Haraldson, like Ingmar Ingmarsson or Anna Svärd, derives most of his strength from his own inner depths.

In certain tales whose simplicity, even whose good humor, might mislead us, we hear a discordant note, not of irony, as at the same period in the work of Anatole France, but of clear-sighted bitterness, tempering what we took for naïve Christian folklore. Upon St. Peter's supplications, Jesus sends an angel to seek the apostle's mother in the depths of hell and to bring her to heaven [in **"Our Lord and St. Peter"**].

Some of the damned have clung to the angel's wings and the hem of his garments, but the implacable old woman manages to make them let go. When the last of these wretches has fallen back into the abyss, the angel, as though exhausted, lets the woman fall back in her turn and wings his way up out of the infinite abyss. We bear our hell with us: God Himself has not the power to change us sufficiently to enter into heaven.

In many of the tales, pagan and Christian currents run together. Old Agneta, in her cabin on the edge of a glacier, too far from the road to be able to offer a drink to passing travelers, suffers from her useless life. A monk counsels her to aid the dead souls prowling on the mountain, and henceforth, each night, she burns her faggots and candles in order to bestow a feast of light and warmth upon the damned enduring the torments of cold of the ancient Scandinavian hell; she will never again be useless and alone. Old Beda of the Shadows [in **"Our Lord and St. Peter"**] offers food to the neighborhood crones to celebrate the sun which, that day, recovers from an eclipse indicated on the kitchen calendar. In her cold hamlet overhung by the mountain wall, the sun is her best friend: she honors it as an ancestor in the Edda might have done. But a mention of the Lord to whom one owes the sun leads us back from the action of pagan grace to St. Francis's Canticle of the Sun.

The climax of this instinctive syncretism occurs in the **"Legend of the Christmas Rose,"** an exquisite tale one might be tempted to overlook, so many stupid Christmas stories in illustrated magazines having disgusted us with that form of literature. It is the tale of the Goinge Forest, inundated by a flood of light and warmth which melt the snow just before midnight, when all the valley bells begin to ring in the Nativity. The quasi-polar night triumphs anew, but a second, stronger flood makes the grass green again and the leaves sprout; a third brings the migratory birds, which make their nests, lay their eggs, and teach their young to fly, while the creatures of the earth give birth, feed their young, and fearlessly mingle with the lives of men . . . One more pulsation of light and the songs of angels will mingle with that of the birds—but this prodigy, in which even the outlaws hiding in the forest are entitled to participate, ceases when a suspicious monk who regards this phantasmagoria as the work of the Devil strikes down a dove which had perched on his shoulder. The splendor of Christmas will never again return to Goinge. Beyond the profoundly satisfying notion of a biblical Eden, we here approach the sacred world of India: time explodes; plants, animals, and seasons flourish and pass in an instant which we might say was measured by the breath of the Eternal.

Animals, as we have seen, have their share in this reappearance of Eden. It is in the order of things: the Beasts ever fierce or cunning precede the Fall; it retains that primal innocence we human beings have sacrificed. In Selma Lagerlöf's work, it is often a crime committed against an animal which is responsible for the series of human maledictions. During the Christmas season, old Ingmar, surprised by a storm, has boldly taken refuge in a bear's den; he then breaks God's truce by hunting down the powerful creature, who strikes him dead, and the peasant's family buries without honor this man who has violated the terms of a pact [**"God's Truce"**].

In the first part of *Jerusalem,* Barbro's ancestor has whipped to death a blind horse sold him by a dishonest horse trader: his male descendants are born blind and idiot, until the day Ingmar Ingmarsson redeems this sin by a heroic good deed.

In other tales, animal innocence consoles us in our despair over the way of the world. The hermit Hatto [in the story of that name], arms raised motionless like an Indian fakir's, implores God to annihilate this world in which Evil rules. But his knotty arms resemble the branches of a tree, and the wagtails build a nest in the hollow of one of his palms. As though in spite of himself, the holy man takes an interest in the birds' intelligent labor and in their frail masterpiece of twigs and moss. When the nestlings have grown, he protects them against a sparrow hawk, though he knows that all life necessarily proceeds to death. Finally, he stops praying for total annihilation, unable to endure the thought that these innocents should be destroyed. A nest has won out over the iniquity of mankind: "Men, of course, were not worthy of the birds, but perhaps God regarded the universe as Hatto regarded that nest."

In that *Bildungsroman* of 1906, **The Wonderful Adventures of Nils,** birds teach a boy prudence, tenacity, courage. He learns pity by restoring its young to a caged squirrel, and comes to comprehend something about resignation from the old dog that expects nothing but a bullet from its master, and from the old milk cow good for nothing but the knacker since the death of the farmwoman who used to whisper so many secrets over her milking as she leaned against the creature's side. The animals in La Fontaine's fables are human beings deliciously disguised as barnyard or forest creatures; here, sympathy and the feeling of a shared insecurity surmounts the wall between species. When the old lead-goose Akka of Kebnaikaise asks the boy if he doesn't think wild geese deserve to have some patches of land where they will be safe from the hunters, there are some of us on whom the lesson has not been lost.

Two masterpieces immersing the human child in primitive life—Lagerlöf's **Adventures of Nils** and Kipling's *Jungle Books*—were created at about the same time, the turn of that century which has most fiercely sacked and desecrated nature, and thereby man. Selma Lagerlöf acknowledged having been influenced by Kipling, but these two books, produced by such different temperaments, resemble each other as little as the Hindu jungle and the Lapp steppe. The adolescent Mowgli is a kind of young god who possesses "master words," and is aided by the animals to destroy the village against which he seeks revenge, restored to the human world (and for how long?) only by the amorous summons of the spring festival. Nils merely returns to his little farm—we recognize the humble utilitarian ethic which allows the Dalecarlians to survive in the "Jerusalem that kills." *The Jungle Book* and **The Wonderful Adventures of Nils** have suffered the same fate: to be considered as children's books, whereas their wisdom and their poetry are addressed to us all. Selma Lagerlöf, it is true, had consciously written for Swedish schoolchildren, but it is to us that she speaks, over their heads.

In this work so dominated by the notion of a divine or cosmic good, evil seems to be perceived as an accident or a human crime. Lagerlöf's darkest fantastic tales rarely provoke in us the quasi-visceral horror sought by so many lovers of the supernatural. The Devil in **Gösta Berling** is merely a man in costume, and his diabolism is rudimentary. Selma Lagerlöf always refused to say whether the hurricane which precipitates the peasants' conversion in the first part of **Jerusalem** was actually a spiritual tempest, the passage of the Evil One signified by the ancient Wild Hunt of Northern mythologies, or merely a big storm. But it suffices to compare the two parts

of **Jerusalem** to that other murkier masterpiece, Maurice Barrès's *La Colline Inspirée,* to realize that the visionary Dalecarlians retain a kind of heroic integrity to the last; Barrès's dreamers, on the other hand, are mired in a more or less demonic zone where ghosts seethe and riot. This happens, surely, because Barrès, a Catholic by inheritance and by determination, recoils in a terror not untouched by desire before whatever represents for him the temptations of carnal disorder; whereas the Dalecarlians, despised or persecuted as they are, remain in the great tradition of Protestant dissidence.

Evil nonetheless lurks in these books of goodness, in its habitual forms of violence, debauchery, or hypocrisy: these are not merely blackberry-syrup idylls. As early as **The Miracles of Antichrist,** we encounter the story of a feast given by an old Englishwoman to some Sicilian villagers in the ruins of their ancient theater: after singing a few politely applauded ballads of her own country, the foolhardy woman risks an aria from *Norma;* jeers and laughter result, and the delighted crowd compels the wretched woman to repeat her aria over and over again, a grotesque victim flung to wild beasts. The murder of an entire family, in **Herr Arne's Hoard,** is as violent as the reportage by Truman Capote. In **The Outcast,** the scene in which human riffraff, half-sailors, half-malefactors, compel a wretch even viler than themselves to devour a serpent's flesh is virtually unbearable. The Selma Lagerlöf of **Gösta Berling** sympathetically describes the punch flames illuminating the faces of the "riders of Ekeby"; the drunkard mistreated by life in "the Fallen King" from **Invisible Links** is still a kind of sublime wreck, a Rembrandt in a Salvation Army setting. But in **"The Balloon"** the alcoholic is nothing but a sick man, odious as only the weak can be; the story would read as a temperance tract except for the subtle relations between the father and his sons, gentle dreamers who, if they were not lucky enough to die young, would probably end like him. The same refined art in simple forms is orchestrated, at the beginning of **The Ring of the Löwenskölds,** in the conversation of a peasant couple egging each other on to commit a sacrilegious theft without ever uttering the slightest compromising word.

Hypocrisy, vice of self-righteous societies, is everywhere courageously assigned to the lowest circle of all. **Charlotte Löwensköld,** published in 1925, is dominated by the disagreeable personality of Pastor Karl Arthur Ekenstedt, a monster of self-deception who sows misery around him without once ceasing to claim that he is approved and guided by God. With the poisonous Thea, the organist's wife, a wheedling female who has managed to take him for her own, he forms the only repugnant couple in the Swedish novelist's writing; their loathsome figures wandering from fair to fair seem to have emerged from some canvas by Bosch. We are amazed that Selma Lagerlöf should have granted to the two daughters of her old age, the aristocratic Charlotte and the rustic Anna Svärd, such treasures of indulgence in behalf of this crapulous clergyman. Are we to suppose in one of the two women a vestige of tenderness for the man she once loved, and in the other a certain respect for this husband socially so far above herself? Or are we rather in those zones of sensuous penumbra where Selma Lagerlöf sheds no light? One thinks of the charming little Elsalill of **Herr Arne's Hoard,** first loving without recognizing, then loving quite knowingly the murderer who has exterminated her entire family and who, had he been able to, would not have spared her either. "I have loved a wolf," she tells herself. But she continues to love him.

Despite certain touches of almost inevitable moralism, given the time and the place, Selma Lagerlöf does not judge her characters; their actions suffice. The great novelist rarely judges; he is too sensitive to the diversity and specificity of human beings not to see in them the threads of a tapestry whose entirety we do not grasp. Like the French peasant, these Swedish ones obscurely believe it takes a little of everything to make a world. In the tale entitled **"A Story of Halland,"** one of those where Selma Lagerlöf makes us most clearly aware of the inexplicable attraction of one person for another, the young farmer who has abandoned his wretched lands to follow the vagrant Jan, his mother's servant and husband, is not indignant at having been ruined by him or at having been involved in a shady deal which sends him to prison: "He was of another race and had to act according to the laws of his kind." It is not only between the two men but between two modes of life that the author does not choose: that of the sedentary peasant who has never known anything but his heavy habitual burdens, and that of the dissipating vagabond, sometimes faithless and treacherous, but sometimes sweeping others with him into a dance of ecstatic joy.

I have written enough to show that Selma Lagerlöf, where she excels, is the equal of the greatest writers. She does not always excel. Even in her best years, certain works give the impression of troughs between the crests. *The House of Liliencrona* or *From a Swedish Homestead,* among others, though they have the charm of old tales or ballads, would be pale narratives indeed if they were not illuminated by reflections cast upon them by their author's great works. The *Miracles of Antichrist,* published soon after *Gösta Berling,* was received with a mixture of praise and objections; the latter are mainly what prevail today. Lagerlöf's Italian folklore, too hastily absorbed, remains superficially picturesque, and the obviously prefabricated story of a baby Jesus replaced on the altar by a counterfeit who is the Antichrist, i.e., socialism (forty years later, one would have said Communism), is almost irritating in its simplicity. The author has the merit of having seen beneath the tourist's Sicily to an underlying peasant poverty, and it was something to have dared to say in 1894 that the exclusive cult of progress is an atheist form of idolatry, but perhaps it should not have been said in this fashion. A short novel, *Death's Carter,* written in 1912 at the request of a society for the prevention of tuberculosis, deals with problems of the after-life, but despite the experiences to which the author had been exposed, it teaches us little about these marginal regions which has not already been said better elsewhere. The *Emperor of Portugallia,* which dates from 1914, was received admiringly, but it now seems all too easily framed, this tale of a gentle megalomaniac who imagines he is raising his daughter, actually a prostitute in Lund, to the rank of empress.

"My soul has become poor and dark; it has reverted to the wild state," Selma Lagerlöf noted in 1915. Two or three years later, in a poem which remained unpublished during her lifetime, she sits down at her desk, exhausted by her writer's task, which seems to consist in a "desperate gathering up of twigs, straws, and useless bits of bark," then suddenly feels her soul, "that deserter," return to her—and here soul seems to signify genius: "I soared alone above the battlefields," the soul sadly reports. "I advanced with the tormented men in the trenches, I accompanied the refugees on their roads into misery and exile; I was wrecked with the torpedoed ships and lurked in the murderous submarines, waiting for my prey . . . I have suffered the fate of starving peoples; I have kept vigil in cities on which unexpected bombs rained

down . . . I have lived with dethroned princes and among the persecuted who have seized power." Such experiences of identification with the world's pain and suffering should have inspired Selma Lagerlöf to further great achievements as she grew to be an old woman. But exhaustion had come, and the doubt that literature could still serve any real purpose; there was not enough time to let these new experiences ripen as they must in order to be expressed. *The Outcast,* which ends in wartime landscapes, had not been, she knew, a successful work. The twenty years which remained to her were to see the slow gestation of *The Ring of the Löwenskölds,* in which several poignant scenes alternate with delicate portrayals of provincial life of the last century, but in which lengthy digressions and repetitions also abound, and occasionally the melodramatic sequences of a gothic novel. The author, evidently, no longer dominates her work. She struggles to invent an epilogue in which Karl Arthur Ekenstedt dies in the odor of sanctity: this she failed to achieve. Every authentic novelist knows that one does not do as one likes with one's characters.

"I remain perplexed as to the meaning of life," Selma had imprudently confessed to a journalist in 1926. This sage admission provoked the indignation of her public; philosophic doubt was not what her readers expected of their idol. As invariably happens when a writer achieves great fame, her enthusiasts had created a summary notion of her, partly drawn from her great books admired on trust or read only in the hope of finding in them exciting stories, partly from the inevitable publicity organized around her person and her writings. Two years earlier, *Mårbacka,* more accessible than the early masterpieces, had offered her readers a sentimental and playful image of the writer's family past, from which filial piety eliminated all pettiness and conflict. The child Selma was painted with charm but according to conventions adults use in speaking of childhood. There is no harm in an old lady's tenderly evoking her early years, and it would indeed be a hardhearted reader who could resist *Mårbacka's* half-smiling, half-tearful grace. But the great epic storyteller was dead. (pp. 133-51)

> *Marguerite Yourcenar, "Selma Lagerlöf: Epic Storyteller," in her* The Dark Brain of Piranesi and Other Essays, *translated by Richard Howard in collaboration with the author, Farrar, Straus and Giroux, 1984, pp. 129-53.*

VIVI EDSTRÖM   (essay date 1984)

[Edström is a Swedish educator and critic who specializes in children's literature. In the following excerpt from her Selma Lagerlöf, *a study of Lagerlöf's life and works, she discusses* The Wonderful Adventures of Nils. *Edström concludes with an analysis of some chief characteristics of Lagerlöf's fiction.]*

None of Selma Lagerlöf's books has become as well known, both throughout the world and by generations of Swedes, as *Nils Holgerssons underbara resa genom Sverige* (*The Wonderful Adventures of Nils*). The story of a lilliputian who flies through the air over Sweden on the back of a goose has held a special fascination, particularly, it seems, for readers in countries far distant from Sweden, such as Japan and China (a Chinese translation of the book appeared as late as 1980). Very soon after it was published in Sweden, *The Wonderful Adventures of Nils* was translated into both English and German. It has also been filmed. .

The book was originally commissioned for Swedish schools

by the Swedish National Teachers' Society. At the turn of the century, the aim was to enable children to read works of Sweden's foremost writers. The teachers suggested to Lagerlöf that she write a book about the geography of Sweden. Feeling this to be a great responsibility, she approached the task with highest ambitions. "I want this to be one of my best books," she wrote on 22 November 1901 to Alfred Dalin, who handled negotiations between her and the Society.

Lagerlöf was already acquainted with some parts of Sweden, and in her books she had brought vividly to life various Swedish milieus. For the new project, she was forced to extend her knowledge to include the entire country. She began with the same documentary method she had used in *Jerusalem.* Much material was collected for her from different parts of the country: facts about the natural environment, cultural and historical notes, tales and legends, and, as she expressed it in the letter to Dalin, "stories of people who had performed grand or noteworthy or characteristic deeds." Finally, she undertook a special journey to Norrland, the northernmost of the three main regions of Sweden, in order to get an impression of the environment. The task at hand was to describe the country, devoting a reasonably fair amount of discussion to each of its districts. Lagerlöf, as it later turned out, would not be able to escape criticism from certain displeased provinces.

Those who commissioned the book expected a collection of separate tales from different parts of Sweden. But for Lagerlöf, a writer with a love for continuity, the book had to have a unifying idea that could give schoolchildren a feeling of completeness, purpose, and excitement. To provide this, she invented the story of the boy Nils Holgersson, who travels with a flock of wild geese on a journey through Sweden. As Nils discovers the world around him, the readers, following him, become acquainted with their native country. But *The Wonderful Adventures of Nils* is much more than a geography textbook. Besides being a *Bildungsroman* in terms of its hero, it is a book that fosters the general education of its young readers. It can also be called a didactic book, though it lacks, happily, the finger-wagging moral teachings associated with that type of literature.

The book is based on a pattern—typical for Lagerlöf—of guilt, repentence, and reconciliation. At the beginning, Nils, though otherwise an ordinary boy, is extraordinarily indolent and mean. He is punished for this by being banished from the human community, changed into a lilliputian, and exiled to life among the animals in the wilderness.

At first it is only a question of survival for Nils, but soon his possibilities for action increase, and he becomes involved in matters that promote the betterment of both his traveling companions and his environment. Finally, he takes on the function of a hero. At this point, it is time for the author to break the spell. Nils becomes human again—a sign that the process of moral transformation has been completed.

Because its action is based on the dual foundation of myth and realism, its narrative pattern is similar to that of *Gösta Berling's Saga.* The transformation motif affords the possibility of an episodic presentation of events in the present. Anything at all can happen while Nils is on his journey with the wild geese. Concurrently, the time perspective is deepened by the narrator's dealing with what happened before the period of Nils's journey. This is accomplished by including magical encounters between Nils and figures from Sweden's historical and legendary past.

The action begins with the story of the transformation itself. Nils is presented as a nasty, insufferable boy, a problem for his hard-working parents. At the onset, the book was supposed to be aimed at nine-year-old readers, but Lagerlöf, with an unerring sense of a child's curiosity about slightly older children, made her main character a fourteen-year-old. In a way, *The Wonderful Adventures of Nils* is about a puberty crisis, about the dream of escaping from all that is dull and boring and embracing adventure, danger, and excitement. It is also, of course, about the feeling, experienced by many during puberty, of alienation from accepted social norms.

The first chapter is one of the most concentrated and exciting that Lagerlöf has ever written. She begins according to the formula of the fairy tale—"Once upon a time there was a boy"—thereby signaling that anything could happen. But at the beginning everything conforms to down-to-earth reality. The reader is introduced to a small farm in the south of Sweden on a Sunday in early spring. Only three people live there—father, mother, and son. The parents would be quite satisfied with their lot, were it not for their worries about the boy, whom they scarcely can rely on to tend the geese. On this particular Sunday, the boy has refused to accompany his parents to church. They have given him the assignment of reading the day's Biblical text and commentary while he is home alone, and they intend to question him about it when they return. After poring over Luther's *Commentary,* he succumbs to drowsiness and falls asleep. It is now that the fantastic action begins.

When he awakens, he sees, to his surprise, a little elf in the room. At this point, the reader is given a demonstration of the boy's nastiness. Nils teases the imp unmercifully, taking him captive and ignoring his pleas to be freed. But suddenly he feels a burning slap in the face and is transformed into a *Thumbietot (tummetott)*—that is, an imp about the size of Tom Thumb, a "little monster," a "changeling," as Nils later calls himself on different occasions.

He is afraid to appear before people in this guise; he has, however, acquired the ability to communicate with animals. When a young gander on the farm heeds the enticing calls of a flock of wild geese and flies into the air to follow them, Nils tries unsuccessfully to prevent him. Instead, he finds himself going along on their flight, becoming an unusual participant in the journey of a flock of wild geese through Sweden up to Lapland and back again toward the South.

The Wonderful Adventures of Nils continues in the solid tradition established by classic travel and adventure tales, many of which were originally written for children. The motif of the flight afforded considerable narrative advantages. The geography of the country could be presented from above in easily accessible, sweeping panoramas. Fields, for example, appear as patchwork quilts or as borders on mother's apron—domestic images, as it were, that connect the story with the children's experience. For a person who never experienced air travel, Lagerlöf exhibits a manner of observation that corresponds surprisingly well with the optical perspective of air travelers of a later time.

The regions of Sweden are presented in broad outline, as the wild geese fly over them. But since the flock must stop frequently to eat and sleep, numerous occasions arise for showing detailed pictures of the vegetation, the industry, and the culture of various places. In this way, Lagerlöf achieves a double perspective. It is precisely this double perspective that Czeslaw Milosz praises her for in his 1980 Nobel Lecture; specifically, he cites it as a work that "influenced, to a large extent . . . [his] notions of poetry," and speaks of its hero "who flies above the earth and looks at it *from above* but at the same time sees it in every detail." "This double vision," Milosz believes, "may be a metaphor of the poet's vocation": a combination of "avidity of the eye" for the large picture and the endeavor to describe in detail what is seen.

As is customary in the fictional world of Lagerlöf, the story of Nils Holgersson acquaints the reader with many characters. The wild geese form a core group of figures, similar to the cavaliers in *Gösta Berling's Saga.* Interacting with the geese is a series of secondary figures, each of them a significant personality: the eagle Gorgo, the raven Bataki, the stork Herr Ermenrich, and the moose Grayfell. Smirre the fox, the villain of the drama (somewhat reminiscent of Sintram in *Gösta Berling's Saga*) creates a suspenseful atmosphere throughout much of the story by threatening and pursuing the wild geese, who, of course, always succeed in tricking him.

While Lagerlöf took the idea of having a child grow up among animals with human qualities from Kipling's *The Jungle Books* (1894 and 1895), the similarities between the works scarcely extend beyond this main idea. The atmosphere in the two works differs considerably. In *The Wonderful Adventures of Nils,* the reader enters into a typical Lagerlöf world, where the lead goose Akka resembles the imperious Major's Wife of *Gösta Berling's Saga* or the authoritative Ingmar Ingmarsson of *Jerusalem.*

Both on land and in the air, social and psychological dramas are played—the battles, disputes, and decisions of animals, as well as the beautiful love story of Nils's friend the gander and a young female goose, Dunfin. In this interplay of feelings and conflicts, Nils gradually assumes an increasingly important role. His contribution to the flock is reminiscent of what Ingmar Ingmarsson does for the colony in *Jerusalem.* Nils becomes indispensable for the geese, especially for his help in protecting his friends against Smirre the fox.

As counterpart and complement to Nils and his journey through the air, the story includes two other wayfaring children, Osa goose-girl and her little brother Mats. They travel in the same direction as Nils flies, and now and then their paths cross with those of the imp, who helps and protects them.

It is important for the readers to meet a few "real" children with both feet on the ground, who arouse sympathy and admiration. Osa goose-girl and little Mats are abandoned children, plagued by misfortune. Their mother had died of tuberculosis, and their father had simply disappeared. They travel around in search of their father—a motif with a long tradition in literature, going back as far as the search of Telemachus for Odysseus in *The Odyssey.* At the same time, these children serve a concrete, didactic purpose: they educate the readers about tuberculosis, the disease that destroyed their family, and inform people about hygiene and other practical measures for avoiding contagion.

It is noteworthy that Lagerlöf does not include in her book any rosy-cheeked, model children for readers to identify with. An interest in children who do not fare well in the adult world is often predominant in her works. In *Gösta Berling's*

Saga, the daughter of the clergyman from Broby never gets enough to eat because her father is so stingy. In *The Miracles of Antichrist,* Lagerlöf describes child laborers in the mines of Italy. *The Tale of a Manor,* "The Balloon," *Thy Soul Shall Bear Witness,* and *Anna Svärd*—all are examples of stories in which children are ill-treated.

In *The Wonderful Adventures of Nils,* the main purpose of which was to give children "an amicable, beautiful picture of their country" (letter to Dalin, 22 November 1901), Osa goose-girl and Mats manage to get along rather well in spite of everything by making themselves useful to adults, carrying out their orders and running their errands. Their lot is certainly a hard one, but they illustrate one of the main points of the story—that people can cope with even the most difficult circumstances. In one instance, this idea is expressed with almost American optimism: "Even today, cleverness and competence can change a beggar into a prince."

From the standpoint of sexual roles, it is not insignificant that the smartest and most courageous character in the story is a girl. Osa goose-girl is a young counterpart of Akka, the leader of the flock. When the wayfaring children reach Lapland and little Mats dies suddenly as the result of an accident, his sister develops into a genuine heroine. She has to convince the most powerful man in the locality, the director of mines, that Mats is worthy of a respectable funeral. The director is moved by her words of praise in memory of her brother, and he gives her his support. Lagerlöf often depicted burials and funeral processions, scenes that had considerably greater significance in the agrarian Sweden of her day than they do now. She even regarded the story of little Mat's funeral as the high point in the second part of the book. The motif shows her deep respect for the child.

Osa's wanderings end when she finally finds her father, an adult upon whom she can depend; now she can once again be the child she has a right to be. Lagerlöf's view of the adult-child relationship is clear: children are capable of much, but the responsibility must be borne by adults.

The Wonderful Adventures of Nils provides the reader with a wealth of knowledge about the natural and social environment of Sweden. The book also gives a sampling of the problems that people had to struggle with at the time: emigration to American, poverty, and tuberculosis. Special questions are taken up, such as draining of lakes, forestry, and prevention of cruelty to animals. Surprisingly, much is still current; in fact, some of the ecological questions that Lagerlöf was concerned about have become even more acute.

Without minimizing the difficulties and anxieties of existence, the book conveys an optimistic message. In contrast to Strindberg, for example, Lagerlöf is convinced of the importance of industrialization for the country's prosperity. Her story is deeply rooted in "places where contemporary life is flourishing richly and powerfully" (letter to Dalin, 22 November 1901), and it shows the possibilities for advancement through hard work, good will, and solidarity. She embraces the concept that, in Swedish politics, later came to be known as the *folkhemsidé,* or the idea of the People's Home—the notion that the state ought to function as a good home in which everyone contributes to its growth and development.

On the other hand, it would be anachronistic to expect of Lagerlöf a modern view of equality. As in her other books, people are assigned different roles at work and in society. King Oscar II reigns over all—he even intervenes as a deus ex machina in one of the episodes of the book. His elevated position is brought out by the fact that he alone speaks in the plural, whereas the other figures in the book use singular forms in their dialogues. The director of mines in Lapland—a character based on a person Lagerlöf met on her trip to Norrland—also plays an important and decisive role. His patriarchal influence balances Akka's female leadership of the world of the birds. Lagerlöf had originally planned to have a male lead goose, but came later to think better of it.

It is decisive for Lagerlöf's view of humanity that every person in his or her calling has merit and responsibility. Herein lies the book's greatest social significance. An important example of this idea is the description of a woman from Dalecarlia, her hard life and many jobs. It is designed as a tribute to the anonymous workers in an impoverished Sweden. The ideal representative of the country is the Swedish farmer. He is shown as the very model of industriousness, symbolizing honor and diligence, the same qualities possessed by the sons of Ingmar in *Jerusalem.*

The Wonderful Adventures of Nils is a book that not only provides information; it also imparts certain social and moral values to its readers. One social phenomenon stands out as absolutely negative—the emigration to America. While working on the book, Lagerlöf wrote, "Through my reader, I want the young people to get an accurate picture of their country and to learn to love and understand it; I want them also to learn something about its many resources and the possibilities for development that it offers, so that they won't dash off to America at the first temptation" (letter to Josepha Ahnfeldt, 18 November 1904). One episode in the book becomes especially stamped in the readers' consciousness—the story of a sick old farm woman whose cow, unfed and unmilked, lows in the barn. The woman is dying, and she has no one to console her on her deathbed or to continue her work on the farm, for her children have deserted her. They have all emigrated to America. This scene is an admonishment to the schoolchildren of Sweden not to forsake their native land. It also contains the message, typical for the times, that children should remember that they are responsible for their aging parents. In 1910, every fifth Swede lived in America, and children's literature was especially packed with propaganda against emigration. When Lagerlöf was not writing for children, however, her attitude toward emigration was sympathetic; for example, in her speech for women's suffrage in 1911, **"Home and State,"** she equates the emancipation of women with the wave of emigration, precisely in order to show how necessary women's emancipation is.

The story of Nils Holgersson also sets up positive models for the good life. In the chapter "A Little Farm," Lagerlöf introduces her own childhood home as a model for ideal existence. The people there lived simply and unpretentiously, but their life was good because it consisted of a harmonious union of work and pleasure. A well-ordered home life represents one pole in Lagerlöf's concept of what life ought to be. The other is the desire for adventure and new experiences. Nils's flight with the geese and the experience of ever-new landscapes are stimulating features of the story, as well as the description of the radiance of the sun and the beauty of nature in contrast to the darkness of the forest and the fear brought on by nightfall. From the beginning of her career as a writer, motion was fundamental to Lagerlöf. She always regarded traveling most favorably. As she expresses it in *The Wonderful Adventures of Nils,* "The world is wonderful to live in, both for small and big people. It is also a good thing to be free and without cares and to have the whole world open before you."

Lagerlöf's novel about Nils Holgersson is a *Bildungsroman,* in which the protagonist is changed by his experiences. Its pedagogical pattern is a direct outgrowth of the adventures the boy experiences. Although there is nothing pedantic about the novel, certain virtues do stand out as absolute: under no circumstances can one break a promise or resort to violence to achieve a goal. Gratitude, loyalty, and mercy are brought home as moral imperatives, and primary importance is placed upon generosity in communal and personal relationships. Love and concern for his fellow beings are what enable Nils to overcome his egoism and become helpful to others. At first his consideration does not extend beyond the white gander, his only close acquaintance in the strange animal world, but it soon reaches out to the wild geese and to the animals not connected with the flock. Even Smirre the fox, the enemy of the wild geese, is finally conceded a tolerable existence through the efforts of Nils. As an imp, Nils gradually dares to take on the most difficult feats. He is especially good at filing the bars of cages in order to free captive birds. The acknowledgement of his good deeds comes in the form of the favor of Mother Akka, his moral authority.

Thus on his long journey, Nils learns the art of communal living. At the same time, he realizes his own identity. The change that takes place in him is expressed even in the body language of the old and the new Nils. In the penultimate chapter of the book, when Nils has just been changed into a human being and reunited with his parents, we read, "The Nils Holgersson who went away last spring had a heavy and slow gait and slow speech and sleepy eyes, but this one who returned was light and nimble and spoke quickly, and he had eyes that shone and sparkled."

Much has been written about *The Wonderful Adventures of Nils,* but little about the book as a story for children. Quantitatively, the story covers enough pages to fill perhaps ten ordinary children's books; it is the most monumental story ever written for young people. In what way has Lagerlöf striven to appeal to her child audience? Properly speaking, there is no special attempt to cater to children in the book. It is being crafted on an adult level. The children are introduced to adult life in a manner that many today hold up as desirable. Since the young readers are called upon to take responsibility for the future, they must participate in the experiences of adults and submit to their values. In this respect, the story is not childish. An important symbolism lies in the fact that Nils remains diminutive up to the point at which he acquires the norms of the adult world. Only then does he become the size of a normal human being again.

But Lagerlöf did indeed take pains to appeal to children. The lilliputian perspective itself is typical of children's stories, probably because it affords the opportunity to characterize the alienation of children in the world of adults. The well-known fondness of children for animal characters was surely a major reason for the story being rooted in a world other than one inhabited exclusively by humans. Animals who talk and act like human beings belong essentially to the ancient genres of the saga and the fable, which, however, were not primarily intended for children.

In her narrative technique, Lagerlöf aims above all at clarity and lively depiction. Surprises and sudden changes occur incessantly in the story, but they are balanced by meticulous preparation for, and development of, all that takes place. This preparatory technique is an important trait in the narration. The arrival in a new region is preceded by a detailed introduction or by tales, dreams, or other types of allegories. Another method the author employs is to describe first places and types of vegetation and then have Nils speculate about what the landscape under him really is like—a piece of cloth, for example, or a leaf. In his fantasy, Nils projects himself beyond the realm of reality, as a child in the schoolroom can be tempted to fantasize beyond the subject at hand or to seek after further knowledge. Another important feature of the story is repetition, which often lends the work a formulaic character. Repeated phrases, pauses, moments in which the message is brought home—all these structure the story for the reader.

Lagerlöf also devoted considerable care to the level of language in *The Wonderful Adventures of Nils;* in fact, she enlisted the help of experts in determining the language of the book. In no way does one get the impression that the language is that of children. Nils, Osa goose-girl, and little Mats all speak like adults. Paradoxically, the work appears in some instances to be more difficult than certain of Lagerlöf's books for adults. This stems from the fact that the author often assumes a naive tone in her other works; for example, she has a child determine the perspective in *Gösta Berling's Saga,* as she does in the beginning of *Jerusalem* and *The Miracles of Antichrist,* in *Liliecrona's Home,* and in the Mårbacka books. The small tenant farmer's perspective in *The Emperor of Portugallia* is also highly naive. In *The Wonderful Adventures of Nils,* Lagerlöf clearly avoids having Nils's own language or perspective narrow the horizon. At the same time, however, she simplifies Swedish prose by eliminating the plural forms in the colloquial language and by modernizing the spelling. The syntax is plain and clear, with main clauses dominating.

When Lagerlöf began work on her geography of Sweden, she was concerned primarily with the didactic aspects of the project. She knew that children are critical readers, and she was careful not to make any factual errors. Yet a good many so-called experts came down on her when the book was published. She herself conceded confidentially (in a letter to Dalin) that some criticism of zoological points was valid, but that much of it was mere nit-picking.

On the whole, the book was received with exuberant praise and regarded as a valuable gift for children. But there was criticism not only of the factual materials but also of the ideology and the language. Some thought that Nils enjoyed himself too much on his journey and that that could entice children to daydream in school. While Lagerlöf previously had used fantasy as a means of approaching geographical and psychological reality without being faulted for it (she had done this, for example, in *Gösta Berling's Saga*), she drew criticism for blending a "fairy tale" with the depiction of reality in a book for children. This negative evaluation stemmed from the notion that the fantastical features could confuse the facts and lead the children on the wrong path. At the turn of the century, however, pedagogues were beginning to believe that feelings and fantasy were the most important channels through which morals and knowledge could be acquired.

In *The Wonderful Adventures of Nils,* as in Swift's *Gulliver's Travels,* fantasy is a springboard for realism. Milieus, dimensions, explanations, cause-and-effect relationships—all have a precise realistic quality. As Gunnar Ahlström wrote in

[*Den underbara resen. En bok om Selma Lagerlöfs Nils Holgersson*], "With her paradoxical work of art, Selma Lagerlöf succeeded in writing an incredible fairy tale in such a way that it appeals to the readers' sense of familiarity and sense of reality."

Lagerlöf did not write any more books for children, apparently because she feared being classified as an author of children's books. When she refused requests to continue her successful career as a children's author, she stressed that she had to write books in which she did not need to concern herself with anything other than literary qualities. (pp. 58-69)

Lagerlöf was, in the true sense of the word, a storyteller and a creator of living characters. In letters and interviews, she often stressed that she was a listener and observer, but "not one of those who themselves play a significant role on life's stage." According to Lagerlöf, she was happy to remain on the "spectator's bench and then later tell about what others were good enough to experience," but she herself did not play a particularly interesting role in life.

Elin Wägner objects to this self-description by suggesting that Lagerlöf was, without a doubt, much more "knowledgeable about the turbulent game of life than a mere spectator watching from the grandstand could possibly be." While this is true, it is nevertheless interesting that Lagerlöf uses the traditional metaphor of life as a stage upon which all carry out their roles. . . . [This] role playing is an underlying idea in her work. She depicts people in an ever-shifting interplay of roles and relationships, with an understanding of the many possibilities for self-realization that life offers.

The most fruitful sources of information about Lagerlöf's thoughts on various questions are her interviews and letters. This also holds true in the question of how she regards her role and her task as a writer. Letters from the Gösta Berling years, primarily the correspondence with Sophie Adlersparre, are of special interest. What is striking in these letters is Lagerlöf's basic aesthetic view, which she was to hold for the rest of her life. In her literary work, she seeks beauty above all. The idea of the poetic and of poeticizing is characteristic of her purpose as an author. "My task is to bring out the poetically beautiful from even the most shabby situation," she explained to Sophie Adlersparre (21 February 1891). (p. 118)

The fact that Lagerlöf strives for an aesthetic ideal does not mean that she takes an exclusive stance distant from everyday life. On the contrary, she is more of a realist than many writers who are called realists. She had a distinct visual gift, had, as someone expressed it, a strong camera. "For her, imagination was, in a peculiar way, substantiated by the experience of reality," writes the Lagerlöf scholar Gunnar Ahlström [in *Kring Gösta Berlings saga*], who adds, "Realism and truth were no abstract concepts for this imaginative artist, but the basic premises for her narrative art." (p. 120)

Lagerlöf's stories rarely developed out of pure imagination; they had, rather, a clear basis in a story she read or heard, a newspaper article, or some other report. Almost everything she wrote can be traced to such a source, which her imagination helped her reshape. Imagination is also the means by which she interpreted existence. This she explained herself in the following clear and simple manner: "If I can grasp a little bit of reality and change it into poetry, I am satisfied." In this case, poetry means fiction.

Lagerlöf's aesthetic program also included a social attitude and purpose that impart to it an almost didactic function: "I want to teach people the art of bringing a glimmer of beauty into the most simple life." She explained that she wanted, with *Gösta Berling's Saga,* to do something for the tired and work-worn people in her home village. "I wanted the people up there to accept the book as my gift to them in return for the richness of expression and enjoyment that their memory has given me." But it is clear that her aim went far beyond the desire to be a village writer. She wanted to make a contribution to the national literature of Sweden. In a confident moment, she declared that *Gösta Berling's Saga* was something that "the country and the people" needed.

Even when she was working on *Gösta Berling's Saga,* Lagerlöf expressed an ardent wish that she might become a writer for broad audiences. She hoped, she said, that the book would be a genuine *folkbok*—or work of popular literature—a notion that she later came to apply to several of her works. As she wrote to her friend in Landskrona, Elise Malmros, she wanted to approach "the large public, which does not judge, but seizes that which takes its fancy, no matter what the artistic value may be." She herself suggested that she was unusual in her strong interest in the reactions of ordinary people: "Have you ever before heard of a writer who places more value on the judgement of children and servants than on that of professional critics?" But, she confessed, "if I, with all my peculiarities, could be a writer of the people, I would be very glad—no, not glad, but most seriously happy" (letter of 22 February 1891). One should, however, take with a grain of salt the following out-pourings: "I have always felt that it would be all right if the scholars and critics attacked me, as long as I had the people on my side. I want my public to consist of young people and country folk."

Gradually, she did indeed achieve her purpose—her books became popular works. With *Jerusalem,* she received great acclaim from critics as well as from the general reading public. But when the reviews for the second part of the novel were less than enthusiastic, she pointed out with satisfaction on several occasions that she still enjoyed the favor of her readers.

The huge success of her books among the general public rested also on the fact that they came out in inexpensive editions soon after they were published; even the working class could afford to buy them. (pp. 121-22)

There were, of course, other reasons—and deeper ones—for Lagerlöf's popularity than merely the extensive distribution of her works. Ultimately, it rested on her choice of subjects, themes, and styles. Her interest in original narratives, in myths, folktales, fairy tales, and legends led her to delve into the depths of the folk culture. Yet, even though anonymous folk literature was one of her main sources, she often received inspiration from contemporary materials. She was an avid newspaper reader, and the daily newspapers provided her with material for many a story. During her visit to Italy, for example, she absorbed more than the legends of the regions she visited; her reading of newspapers also left its traces in the short stories, as well as in the novel *The Miracles of Antichrist.* (It should perhaps be mentioned that she had a good reading knowledge of Italian.)

In her choice of subjects, Lagerlöf preferred to seek the unknown, that which disclosed a certain primordiality, something primitive or puzzling. As one Lagerlöf scholar ex-

pressed it, she had an "unusual eye for unexploited and artistically fruitful themes" [Nils Afzelius, *Selma Lagerlöf—den förargelseväckande*]. She understood what possibilities a theme might offer, though it be concealed in an anecdote, a ghost story, a letter, a newspaper, or a half-forgotten old book. In this lies the basis for her development as a popular writer.

The question whether her writing style marks her as a popular writer is more complicated. From oral narrative, she doubtless learned to treat a story in a way that maintained its interest. The tension in her stories builds uninterruptedly to a climax, which often brings about a reversal of the situation. The conclusion is always carefully anticipated, but it nevertheless appears unexpected. An important aspect of her narrative technique is that she conceived her stories as being read aloud.

Fairy tales and folktales helped her develop her naive narrative stance—the simple, direct manner of presentation that makes her literary works accessible to all. The chapter on her short stories points out how she employed both of these basic models—the optimistic fairy tale, in which the hero is victorious over the dragons of existence, and the pessimistic folktale, in which man succumbs to the powers. Also, with regard to composition, language, and style, folk literature was a source of inspiration for her writing. Personification and animism are prominent characteristics in her world of narrative, as they are in a fairy tale. Moreover, everything is living and animated.

The Bible, which constituted a common frame of reference for people of Lagerlöf's day, was also an important source of inspiration for her. Its influence can be seen in connection with myths, special motifs and symbols, and, to the greatest degree, in the language. Lagerlöf's general view of existence as a journey in an atmosphere of suffering, and often penitence, has its primary source in the images and ideas of the New Testament. The importance of the Christ figure for her writing has often been pointed out, perhaps even exaggerated, for Lagerlöf's own view was not essentially Christocentric.

Contrasting with Biblical elements, the influence of old Icelandic literature, another important model for her creative work, occasionally breaks through in a most effective manner. The strict fatalism of old Norse literature—found also, incidentally, in folk literature—is confronted with New Testament ideas of mercy and reconciliation, the notions of human good will and the capacity for love—powers that can alter an evil, destructive situation. Lagerlöf's stories are, on the whole, based on the strong contrasting forces of opposing values—for example, revenge and love or sin and justice. *The Treasure* is a typical example of a story charged by all these conflicting elements. At the same time, the Icelandic saga also contributes structurally to the linearity and clarity, not only of that story, but of several others as well—*Jerusalem,* for example.

Lagerlöf, however, is not a popular writer in the sense that she adapts her fiction to the needs and desires of the masses. Current research has emphasized more and more that although her stories are rooted in folk tradition, her narrative technique demonstrates clearly that she is by no means a simple and primitive writer, but a highly conscious artist. This can be seen especially in the composition of her individual novels, in which the structural design—the arrangement of individual chapters, each complete in itself, into a richly diversified causal relationship—demands a high degree of control over the material and ability to structure a narrative. In *Gösta Berling's Saga,* Lagerlöf does not quite achieve complete structural unity, but *Jerusalem* offers an example of a novelistic structure in which each individual episode is a complete story in itself and at the same time an integral part of an ingenious collective plan.

The role of the narrator and the narrative perspective varies in Lagerlöf's works. In some, the narrator plays a major role, introducing and commenting on the story. The first-person narrator in *Gösta Berling's Saga,* for example, creates a special mood, with his passionate outcries and lyrically accented commentary. In other works, the narrator tells the story in a more intimate style, playing the role of cultural intermediary, as, for example, in *The Ring of the Löwenskölds.* Occasionally, there is no explicit narrator. Certain stories are told simply and directly; others are based primarily on insight into the thoughts of the characters.

Lagerlöf's stories often involve a sophisticated alternation between the narrated moment and the depiction of the scenic background. On the whole, the dramatic element in her fiction is very clear. Her inclusion of tragic irony and extreme reversals in the lives of her characters is more reminiscent of the drama of classical antiquity and the Ibsenesque drama than of the folktale. Still, Lagerlöf was no dramatist; the many attempts made, by herself and others, to adapt her novels for the stage were seldom successful.

In certain stories, Lagerlöf adds an observer, a sort of *raisonneur,* who comments on the action. Torarin, the fishmonger in *The Treasure,* is such a figure, as is Lilljänta in *Liliecrona's Home,* the little girl who tries to interpret the tragic events at Lövdala. These characters play a similar role to that of the reader, but since their interpretation of what happens is naive and incomplete, the reader himself is also challenged to work intensively with problems in the text. Although the role of the reader in Lagerlöf's fiction is definitely very important, no attention has, as yet, been paid to it.

Characteristic of Lagerlöf's narrative method is her manner of allowing for various perspectives and ways of interpreting a story and then leaving it up to her readers to take a position regarding the questions presented. Her characters represent not only different standpoints. Frequently they also come from different social classes and speak different kinds of language. In *The Emperor of Portugallia,* for example, the tenant farmers speak a language colored by dialect, and the people of the manor speak cultivated Swedish. One scholar, Erland Lagerroth, has described Lagerlöf's books as dialogue-novels [see *TCLC,* Vol. 4, p. 242]. He also applies the term *polyphonic novel* to some of her works. Lagerlöf's is the voice that "gives voice to the voices" ["Att låta många stämmor tala," *Lagerlöf-studier* (1979)]. The polyphonic elements may be the basis for all narrative literature, especially in its original Homeric meaning of creating an objective picture of reality.

Another feature of Lagerlöf's art that is beginning to attract attention is the often strong discrepancy between what is on the surface and what lies beneath it in her works. On the surface, the stories can appear artless and simple, but upon closer scrutiny they reveal a complicated structure. The question is whether the similarities with the popular narrative extend deeper than the superficial level of the action. The correspondence between the qualities of popular naive literature and the literature of high culture gives Lagerlöf's work its distinctive stamp. Her method is to turn a simple folk motif into a narrative with many different psychological dimensions. One can also assert, however, that psychological developments are shaped into concrete stories patterned after the dramatic structure of folk literature.

To the complex and artistic qualities of Lagerlöf's works belongs also her symbolic language. In an allegorical way, she uses nature myths and other popular tales as images of the powers of existence. As it has been pointed out, in *Gösta Berling's Saga* there is a wealth of personification of various feelings and attitudes, from "the spirit with the icy eyes" to the Dovre witch. The symbolic figure who etches herself most strongly in the reader's memory is, however, Lady Sorrow in *The Tale of a Manor,* the woman with wings made of leather patches, a dream figure, created in a moment of strong inspiration.

On the whole, the ability to mythify existence pervades Lagerlöf's narrative practice. While her characters have distinct social roots, they are, nevertheless, ultimately representatives of various attitudes toward life. Since people have, as a rule, applied the demands of naturalism to Lagerlöf's art, they often have been blind to her method of using a complex interplay of roles, related to each other, to cultivate and analyze humanity in all its forms—from the most wild and uncivilized to the ethereally pure and saintlike. Perhaps the secret of her distinction as a popular writer lies in this exploration of "the soul, that vast country" to which we all belong. As Elin Wägner expresses it, she possessed the ability to "touch with her words something common to human beings all over the world." (pp. 122-26)

Lagerlöf possesses the art of making the reader feel that he has touched upon the very mystery of life. She seeks the most intense moments of human life, in which sloth and inactivity are overcome, and unsuspected powers come rushing forth. Fundamentally, she is one of the great worshipers of life, in which love is both star and center. But she is at the same time a strict moralist, with a strong inner sense of duty. It is precisely the confrontation between Lagerlöf the worshiper of life and Lagerlöf the moralist that causes the sparks to fly in her stories—a confrontation most fascinating in *Gösta Berling's Saga* and more tempered in the rest of her works.

With her unique mythical imagination and narrative talent, Lagerlöf cannot easily be placed into any literary-historical category. She is both a realist and a romantic. Perhaps she should be regarded primarily as a symbolist, for her work is—far more than people usually recognize—permeated with symbols. Often entire stories are illustrations of myths. Life is even "transformed into myth." Nature and landscape, which in themselves are presented concretely, become the bearers of human problems and function as a parallel to them. Nature becomes identical with man, and man becomes identical with nature. This creates an interesting complexity in Lagerlöf's literary works, which, on the whole, also contain a good deal of direct conflict.

Lagerlöf's role as a storyteller has widely overshadowed her importance as a writer with humor, psychological insight, and sharp-sightedness in delineating her characters. She has created a gallery of living characters—well-rounded, believable figures. Here, too, an acute sense of human confusion and vulnerability informs her vision. Lagerlöf, who often felt herself to be cold, empty, and introverted, had the ability to hold her public spellbound with her art. (pp. 133-34)

Vivi Edström, in her Selma Lagerlöf, *translated by Barbara Lide, Twayne Publishers, 1984, 151 p.*

FURTHER READING

Aas, L. "Selma Lagerlöf." *The Bookman,* London LXXIII, No. 433 (October 1927): 7-12.
  Biographical and critical sketch.

Bach, Giovanni, et al. "Swedish Literature." In *The History of Scandinavian Literatures,* by Giovanni Bach, et al., translated by Frederika Blankner, pp. 87-143. 1938. Reprint. Port Washington, N. Y.: Kennikat Press, 1966.
  Brief assessment of Lagerlöf in a chronological overview of Swedish literature through the 1920s.

Cooper, Anice Page. "Selma Lagerlöf: The First Woman of Sweden." In her *Authors and Others,* pp. 81-97. 1927. Reprint. Freeport, N. Y.: Books for Libraries Press, 1970.
  Biographical sketch and favorable assessment of Lagerlöf's works, noting some chief characteristics of her fiction.

Fehrman, Carl. "*Gösta Berlings saga* and Its Transformations." In his *Poetic Creation: Inspiration or Craft,* translated by Karin Petherick, pp. 119-36. Minneapolis: University of Minnesota Press, 1980.
  Examines the process by which Lagerlöf revised *Gösta Berlings*

saga, which she wrote first as a short story and then as a play before casting it into the form of a novel.

Lagerroth, Ulla-Britta. "The Troll in Man—A Lagerlöf Motif." *Scandinavian Studies* 40, No. 1 (February 1968): 51-60.
  Explores Lagerlöf's use of trolls in her fiction as symbols of primitive and destructive aspects of human nature.

Maule, Harry E. *Selma Lagerlöf: The Woman, Her Work, Her Message.* New York: Doubleday, Page & Co., 1926, 89 p.
  Account of Lagerlöf's life and career that includes excerpts from her autobiographical writings and from reviews of her books.

Olson-Buckner, Elsa. *The Epic Tradition in Gösta Berlings Saga.* Brooklyn: Theodore Gaus, 1978, 144 p.
  Examines *Gösta Berlings saga* in relation to the conventions of the literary epic.

Popp, Daniel, and Barksdale, E. C. "Selma Lagerlöf: The Tale-Teller's Fugues." *Scandinavian Studies* 53, No. 4 (Autumn 1981): 405-12.
  Studies Lagerlöf's mixture of folkloric and formal literary traditions in "what might be called 'folkloric-literary' fugues."

Raphael, Robert. "*Gösta Berling* of the Lyric Stage." *Scandinavian Studies* 42, No. 1 (February 1970): 31-8.
  Examines the opera *I cavalieri di Ekebù,* based on *Gösta Berlings saga,* with libretto by Arturo Rossato and score by Riccardo Zandonai.

Setterwall, Monica. "Two Sides of an Ending in *Herr Arnes Penningar.*" *Scandinavian Studies* 55, No. 2 (Spring 1983): 123-33.
  Explores the circumstances surrounding the writing of different conclusions for Swedish and German editions of *Herr Arnes penningar.*

(Sir Charles Otto) Desmond MacCarthy

1877-1952

(Also wrote under the pseudonym Affable Hawk) English critic and essayist.

MacCarthy was one of the most influential literary critics in England during the first half of the twentieth century. Considered a master prose stylist, he was also highly esteemed for the broad learning and tolerant personal philosophy displayed in his reviews and essays.

The only son of a bank official and his wife, MacCarthy was educated at Eton and Trinity College, Cambridge. A precocious and popular undergraduate, he was invited to join the Apostles, Cambridge's most elite intellectual society. Through his acquaintance with members of this group, which included the art critic Roger Fry, philosophers G. E. Moore and Bertrand Russell, and Thoby Stephen, the brother of Virginia Woolf and Vanessa Bell, MacCarthy also became associated with the Bloomsbury Group, the most influential intellectual circle in prewar England. Unable to attend his final examinations due to illness, he left Cambridge with an aegrotat degree in history in 1897 and subsequently began working as a journalist. He married in 1906 and wrote for various periodicals before joining the staff of the *New Statesman* in 1913. MacCarthy remained a full-time contributor to the *New Statesman* for more than fifteen years, signing his column "Affable Hawk," a pseudonym reportedly well suited to both his character and his physical appearance. During the First World War MacCarthy served in a Red Cross unit assigned to the French Army, and he chronicled his wartime experiences in sketches later included in *Memories*. After the war, he became literary editor of the *New Statesman* and wrote theater reviews before serving as co-editor of *Life and Letters* in the late 1920s. In 1928 he also succeeded Sir Edmund Gosse in writing a weekly literary column for the London *Sunday Times*. In later life MacCarthy's gifts as a conversationalist were utilized in a series of BBC Radio broadcasts on literary topics. He was knighted in 1951 for his contributions to literature and the theater, and shortly before his death in 1952 received an honorary doctor of literature degree from Cambridge University.

Beginning with his highly regarded volume of biographical sketches, *Portraits I,* MacCarthy's journalistic works have been collected and republished in book form, including such volumes as *Criticism, Experience, Humanities,* and *Memories.* Among his biographical portraits, those of Herbert Henry Asquith and Henry James are considered notable examples of MacCarthy's ability to identify and express the essential character of his subject through a personal anecdote or characteristic quote. MacCarthy's strengths as a reviewer are rooted in his objective critical outlook and broad-minded personal philosophy, which are characterized by sensitivity, urbanity, and erudition. He wrote on a variety of literary subjects and is especially remembered for his critiques of the works of Henrik Ibsen, Bernard Shaw, and Anton Chekhov. Because of his association with the Bloomsbury Group and other prominent intellectuals of the first decades of the twentieth century, MacCarthy is remembered both as a literary

personality and as a highly esteemed commentator on life and literature during that era.

PRINCIPAL WORKS

The Court Theatre, 1904-1907: A Commentary and Criticism (criticism) 1907
Portraits I (sketches) 1931
Criticism (criticism) 1932
Experience (essays) 1935
Leslie Stephen (lecture) 1937
Drama (criticism) 1940
Shaw (criticism) 1951
Humanities (essays, criticism, and short story) 1953
Memories (essays) 1953
Theatre (criticism) 1954
Desmond MacCarthy: The Man and His Writings (sketches, criticism, and memoirs) 1984

JOSEPH WOOD KRUTCH   (essay date 1932)

[*Krutch is one of America's most respected literary and drama critics. A conservative and idealistic thinker, he was a consistent proponent of human dignity and the importance of literature, and his literary criticism is characterized by such concerns. In the following excerpt, Krutch praises MacCarthy's critical style as presented in* Portraits I.]

In an excellent review recently contributed to *The Nation* Lionel Trilling remarked that no critic could possibly be very effective unless he wrote from some definite point of view. Even narrowness or wrong-headedness was, he maintained, preferable on the whole to mere detachment, because even the narrow and the wrong-headed stand for something, and because it is only by standing for something that one can exert an influence.

Undoubtedly there is much to be said for the contention, and undoubtedly the fact that Desmond MacCarthy does not, in this sense, "stand for anything" has something to do with the further fact that after many years of admirable critical writing he is mentioned far less often than other men who are certainly his superiors in nothing unless it be a more definite assertiveness. And yet, firmly as I believe what Mr. Trilling said, I cannot bring myself to regret Mr. MacCarthy's detachment as much as perhaps I should, or really bring myself to wish that he adhered less consistently to the famous formula: "Je n'impose rien, je ne propose rien; j'expose" ["I impose nothing; I propose nothing: I expose"]. There are, after all, so many activities in which one must be "effective" or fail, so few in which ineffectiveness is compatible with a kind of success. Not only lawyers and statesmen but even novelists and essayists must get somewhere; and I confess that I find something infinitely refreshing in the work of a critic who is content to be merely sensitive, receptive, and intelligent. Some kinds of criticism seem, in other words, the last refuge of that spirit which resists the world's insistence that we do something, go somewhere, or at least say something aggressive and "effective." Is it, I wonder, pure lackadaisical perversity occasionally to feel that one would rather be merely not wrong than either President or, shall we say, a "challenging" critic? Is it not, rather, one of the charms of literature that it does permit just that attitude?

In any event, I must confess that I like Mr. MacCarthy's [*Portraits I*] none the less for the fact that the thirty-four essays which it contains are so plainly in the tradition of Sainte-Beuve and Anatole France. Apparently written at different times and dealing with the most diverse men, they aim chiefly to "expose" their subjects, and they achieve both clarity and a graceful ease of that particular sort which could hardly co-exist with the passionate advocacy of any set of dogmas either literary or moral. If they defend anything, it is just the right of Mr. MacCarthy's kind of intelligence to stand somewhat aside from even the intellectual battles, and it is interesting to speculate whether or not he was aware of a certain pertinence to his own case when he wrote of Arthur Hugh Clough the following acute passage:

> The main point is, I think, that Clough belonged to a type rare among imaginative minds, and was therefore particularly interesting. He was a man who could believe the reason to be divine, but not the will. The will was a useful means of clearing life of muddles, avoiding ignoble things, getting other things done, but it had a horrible way of also dictating to a man what he ought to think, putting its case in the most insidiously persuasive form, saying, "If

you don't batter yourself into a passion over this, if you don't conclude before you have sufficient evidence, you will end by being a burden to yourself and useless to everybody else."

Surely that is a very excellent way of stating the argument by means of which the public is always trying to force the skeptic into action; surely it is only by allowing the will to mix itself up in the affairs of the mind that one ever does come to any general conclusion at all. But surely, also, the coy statement of the argument in that form is enough to persuade the true skeptic that he would rather, after all, stick to his skepticism even if that does mean making him "a burden to himself and useless to everybody else."

Perhaps, however, Mr. MacCarthy's general temper of mind is most clearly revealed in that essay which is concerned with Anatole France and his late conversion to Communist dogmas. Here again the point is not one which has to do with either the usefulness or the dangers of dogmas in themselves, but with the fact that they half destroyed France for the simple reason that they were inappropriate. The man who had rejected all systems of thought had no right suddenly to embrace one, and he could not, as a matter of fact, really embrace opinions to which, "privately and as an artist, he continued to be disloyal. . . . Henceforth he carried on his shoulders, with, it is true, many a shrug, a pack of opinions which, as a skeptic, he had no right to possess."

> All this has been bad for his fame. What is more serious, it goes some way to support the contention of his intellectual opponents that there was nothing helpful, nothing human beings could live by, in his earlier attitude of detachment. If this were true I should be sorry, having still myself some faith in doubt, and in the sense of proportion which doubt engenders. . . . But a skepticism which is not evenly applied all around becomes malicious, and a tolerance which does not tolerate what may be odious to one's self is a sham. After rejecting every religion and every system of thought as impostures held together by sophistry, it was inexcusable in Anatole France to swallow Karl Marx.

The penultimate sentence of that paragraph contains, I think, the most telling warning to those skeptics whom the importunities of the will tempt to renounce their natural doubts. It does not necessarily imply that some men or even most men ought not to believe. But it does show why those who are not really capable of faith are less dangerously and more truly what they are when they do not try to delude either themselves or others. Even a critic who is trying against the grain to be "effective" merely because he thinks he ought is a very sad spectacle. (pp. 603-04)

Joseph Wood Krutch, "On 'Effective' Criticism," in The Nation, *New York, Vol. CXXXIV, No. 3490, May 25, 1932, pp. 603-04.*

E. M. FORSTER   (essay date 1932)

[*Forster was a prominent English novelist, critic, and essayist whose works reflect his liberal humanism. His most celebrated novel,* A Passage to India *(1924), is a complex examination of personal relationships amid the conflicts of the modern world. Although some of Forster's critical essays are considered unsophisticated in their literary assessments, his* Aspects of the Novel *(1927), a discussion of the techniques of novel writing, is regarded as a minor classic in literary criticism. In the following review, Forster favorably appraises* Criticism.]

Mr. MacCarthy is known to his friends, who now number several millions, as a conversationalist. His voice was at first heard over limited areas, such as college courts and drawing rooms; then, by the happy invention of the wireless, it flew into any locality which had the sense to turn it on, and can be heard to-day in highly non-academic circles. It floats across hotel lounges, Air Force barracks, watchmen's shelters, persuasive, civilized, apologetic. "I have been reading . . ." it says, or "I have been thinking of . . ." and inattention becomes impossible. The watchman may grunt, the airmen may shout out "binder," the lounge ladies say "Oh not that Justin what's his name again about books," yet they cannot but listen to Mr. MacCarthy's voice. Whatever he says is fascinating. And whatever he prints becomes fascinating when we supply (as we must occasionally) the vocal accompaniment. He is a talker rather than a writer, and that is one of the reasons why it is difficult to write about him.

He modestly describes [*Criticism*] as "literary journalism." It is scarcely that. It has none of the journalistic demerits—no shallowness or pertness, none of the deficiencies in temper or education that are inseparable from punch. Nor has it the journalistic merit of formal neatness. These little articles do not lie quite right in their little plates. They loll to one side or end abruptly, as if the writer had lost interest in his theme and left its development to the reader. Even the longer articles—like the one on Proust—have this defect (for in written stuff it is a defect) and in the shorter ones (*e.g.* in **"Literary Booms"**) the abruptness is almost painful. One turns the page, agog for more mischief and wisdom, and, alas, all is over already.

This is one's only complaint against the book, and if one has read it with sympathy and understanding, one realizes how unimportant such complaints are. Mr. MacCarthy himself never makes the mistake of scolding people for not being what they are not. Speaking of Samuel Butler he says "The favourite virtue of the humorist is always toleration," and it is his own virtue. He tries to see the best in every writer, even in Miss Gertrude Stein, but (and this is an important point) his standpoint is not so much Christian charity as pagan common sense. Why not look for the best in people? It is foolish to look for anything else. But don't do it in order to display your own kind-heartedness. He mistrusts "niceness," both in himself and others, it is dangerously easy, and one of the accusations he brings against popular critics of to-day is that they exploit their own charms. Butter your authors, and a bit will be left over for you! No! No butter for Mr. MacCarthy. He is tolerant but not at all easy going; he never yields, as Arnold Bennett did, to the temptation of making things jolly all around and of giving young writers a leg up even if they don't deserve it. His integrity is unassailable. It is one of the pillars on which his critical edifice is reared—good temper of the Samuel Butler sort being the other.

Though his approach is philosophic it would be a mistake to burden him with any particular doctrine. He does not belong to the class of critics represented by Matthew Arnold and Tolstoy who try to discover the tests by which good literature can be recognized. Nor does he belong to the far more valuable class which Coleridge adorns: the critics who send us back in excitement to the original. He is neither a teacher nor an inspirer. What he does give us (besides much incidental pleasure) is an improved equipment: "to help the reader to watch himself is part of the function of criticism as I understand it" he writes, and after reading him we are better fitted to cope with literature generally, and also with non-literature, sometimes called life. He educates us by the only efficient method—the indirect—and to be in his company is to acquire civilization. As has been suggested, the full quality of his personality does not come out in the written word; his voice is an integral part of it, and his employment by the B.B.C. is greatly to the credit of that many-sided institution.

Combining as he does the candour that was Cambridge with knowledge of the world, Mr. MacCarthy offers a fascinating problem to the analyst. There is an undergraduate freshness about him, a disinterested ardour for the truth, and yet he is quite an old bird. "Affable Hawk" he styled himself, and the title is apt; he has seen from his perch many reputations rise and fall; he has noted the contradiction that underlies the simplest statements and can say of truth itself that "you can no more sit down and tell it than you can write a poem"; he has learnt about the structure of society; he has visited in country houses and dallied with nobs and snobs. Why, in spite of so much wariness and sophistication, has he cared to follow the gleam? The answer is that though he knows the world he is not knowing about it , and it is knowingness, not knowledge, that rots a critic and is indeed the spiritual death of anyone. He often writes as if he were tired, but he is never slick; that dreadful enamel which many men daub around as they get on in life—that fatal pot of enamel—or is it colour wash?—has been placed by a benign fairy just beyond his reach.

There are twenty-nine reprinted articles in this volume—which is the second of a series. They deal with contemporary writers such as Santayana, Yeats, David Garnett and Joyce or with writers of the past who have affinities with contemporary literature such as Richardson, Defoe, Donne, Browning and Beckford. There are also some articles of a general nature: **"Notes on the Novel"** is particularly bright, and Mr. MacCarthy's own novel in the style of Mr. Hugh Walpole, beginning "The Rev. William Neggit sat at his kneehole table," is so alluring that one wishes he would continue it for ever.

E. M. Forster, "Affable Hawk," in The Spectator, *Vol. 149, No. 5430, July 23, 1932, p. 125.*

GEORGE DANGERFIELD (essay date 1932)

[*Dangerfield is an Anglo-American historian and critic best known for his studies* The Strange Death of Liberal England *(1935) and* The Era of Good Feelings *(1952), a history of the United States during the administrations of presidents James Monroe and John Quincy Adams. In the following excerpt from a review of* Portraits I *and James Milne's* A Window in Fleet Street, *Dangerfield negatively characterizes* Portraits I.]

It may be that in putting these two books [MacCarthy's ***Portraits I*** and James Milne's *A Window in Fleet Street*] together I am doing one or the other of them an injustice. They are both the product of literary journalism—though with MacCarthy, to be sure, one stresses the *literary* and with James Milne the *journalism.*

If Milne is frankly reminiscent, McCarthy starts off wherever he can with such sentences as "I only saw Conrad once"; and neither gentleman is above gossip. Milne's gossip is the more journalistic ("During what proved to be his last visit to London, George Havens Putnam took me with him to lunch at the dignified Athenaeum Club. . . . One of his amusing anecdotes had to do with Mrs. Florence Barclay. . . ."), but MacCarthy's is the more dangerous.

A glance at the table of contents in *Portraits* will make this clear. It is arranged in alphabetical order, which is both convenient for the reader and inconvenient for the author, who must surely blush for such strange groupings as Strindberg, Tetrazzini, and Trollope or Sir William Harcourt, Horace, and Father Ignatius. Nothing but genius—which MacCarthy does not possess—could make such diversity into a book, though a respectable second-rate talent could turn very pleasant little weekly talks out of it. That is why one must call MacCarthy a gossiper. If only he were more apt and if only he were a little malicious at times, he would be something like a *concierge* at a literary hotel. But he merely commits himself to the expected and the kindly. That is why his gossip is mildly "dangerous." Gossip like Miss Rebecca West's, which is sometimes malicious and generally inspired, can shock the comfortable mind with truth; MacCarthy's gossip merely pushes the comfortable mind further back into its sloth.

No review can do justice to thirty-four separate essays. Some things in MacCarthy's work are good—his summing up of Henry James, his short piece on Professor Walter Raleigh. But first impressions are generally right and I shall not forget the effect of turning over the pages of *Portraits:* the inevitable "conversation" with George Moore (is it a comment on Moore that people can seldom write about him except in bad parody?); a dream-dialogue with Bunyan, which contains a deal of intolerable whimsy; a sentence like this from **"Tetrazzini"**—"What, after all, were Queen Victoria's messages to her people but 'a few simple chords touched upon the piano'? I am sure when Jubilee Day was over, she too longed to burst into song."

Is the critic important who can write "Trollope's style never reflects sensitiveness to beauty; it never thrills and seldom amuses"? This is to generalize with a vengeance; or has MacCarthy not read the story of the Bishop's chaplain in *Barchester Towers? Never* is a big word in criticism, though in gossip it is scarcely considered.

Or is the stylist good who can write of Asquith's diction, "The senses have contributed nothing to its vigour, which is intellectual; nor is it at all indebted to random meditations for richness—the laden camels of such dreaming moments have never brought to it their far-fetched consignments of spices and dyes." There is a fatal charm about this, and—as MacCarthy confesses in **"Renan"**—"Charm in literature is rather like a kiss in life; potent, even wonderful at times, at others a trifle or even a nuisance." I fear that those laden camels belong with the trifles and the nuisances.

"Clough" offers some further indication of MacCarthy's limitations. Arthur Clough had cut a poor figure in *Eminent Victorians,* so MacCarthy sets out to justify him, with the result that whatever dubious life Strachey had given the poet is inexorably quenched. Comparisons are not in order here, but it is dangerous to glean where Strachey has reaped. Indeed, it is only on rare occasions that MacCarthy compels our admiration. When he says of George Moore that "his difficulty has perhaps been to find sufficiently strong feelings to remember" he is wobbling across some pretty thin ice; but it takes courage to do that, and one likes him for it. Otherwise his criticism conforms to his own "I slipped into it" which con-

jures up the vision of somebody gently subsiding into the mud. It is not bad criticism, because it is founded upon good taste, but is somewhat soft and complacent, and is neither fresh nor exciting.

In the end, one might say that MacCarthy has facility, an uncertain charm, a surface audition, a decent mind; and that one's real criticism of these essays is that they should never have become a book. Occasional pieces such as these *Portraits* have a purely occasional purpose: read in the weekly periodicals their urbanity may please, and their complacency will harm only those who are in any case not worth helping. (pp. 393-95)

George Dangerfield, in a review of "Portraits I," in
The Bookman, *New York, Vol. LXXV, No. 4, August, 1932, pp. 393-95.*

EDWARD SACKVILLE WEST   (essay date 1935)

[*In the following excerpt from a review of* Experience, *Sackville West praises wisdom, liberalism, and humor in MacCarthy's works.*]

Wisdom is the aroma that disengages itself from [*Experience,* the latest volume] of Mr. MacCarthy's collected journalism. Having written that word "journalism," I am sensible of surprise at the look of it: there is nothing in this book that even remotely recalls the *Daily Express* and its strange system of values. For Mr. MacCarthy, both by his style and by his habit of mind, reminds us more of Montaigne and Hazlitt than of anything much nearer our own day. He is fond of posing as a "man of the 'nineties"; but if we must describe him in a phrase, that phrase would be: "an eighteenth-century Irish gentleman of culture." This is the inheritance which leads him to describe the rhinoceros as "an animal difficult to please"—and what other living writer would describe the rhinoceros with such humorous felicity? The humour—economical and sly—is indeed one of the things that delights us most in this book. When, *à propos* of a remark of George Moore's, he adds, "We are grateful to Mr. Moore for pointing out the delightful quality of that bit of dialogue, but when he goes on to declare that *Wuthering Heights* is poor compared to the novels of Anne Brontë, gratitude is not what we feel"; when, speaking of cookery books, he says, "I do not want to read one by Mr. Bernard Shaw, nor I think by Mr. Hardy, nor one by Mrs. Meynell . . . and it would only be from intellectual curiosity that I would buy one by Ibsen"; when, in describing intoxication, he admits that "I have had to jump into my bed as it passed my corner of the room"—on these occasions, while we laugh, we think at once of the great essayists of a century ago—of Hazlitt and of Lamb. For Mr. MacCarthy, like them, is a famous talker, and the eager amusement and level, generous precision of his conversation find more than an echo in his written style.

How good a novelist Mr. MacCarthy might be if he cared to try his hand at a full-length novel, this volume, far more than its predecessors, serves to show. His account of the trial of Sir Roger Casement, his imaginative study of the old Emperor of Austria, and his description—very moving and vivid—of Red Cross work at the front, possess all the qualities of a highly gifted novelist.

It will be a difficult reader who cannot find in this volume something to amuse, instruct, or stimulate him. Of the three sections into which it is divided, the first two—*Of Human*

Nature and *During the War*—are the most satisfying; the last section is rather scrappy and, although it contains admirable things by the way, the short paragraphs that compose it might have been expanded with advantage. The range, too, is extraordinarily wide, as becomes the descendant of Hazlitt. From **"Cats"** and **"Chess"** to **"The Two Minutes' Silence"** Mr. MacCarthy takes a leisurely way, noticing always those significant details which the more hasty have disregarded as too obvious for mention, and shows them to us illuminated by the pleasing glow of a profound belief in the goodness and worth of human life.

I will quote one passage, as a sample both of the delightful quality of his writing and of the actuality of his preoccupations:

> The cures for day-dreaming may be many; I know of three. One is Dr. Johnson's—constant occupation and company. The second is to secure a little real satisfaction of desire. It may be a petty achievement, far too small to figure in the carnival of a daydream, but the glow it throws dims glories imagined, as the dullest of dawns a festal illumination. The third is to go on piling up fictitious triumphs to such a fantastic height that they crash from the weight of their own absurdity, or, in other words, to make yourself rapidly sick by eating the sweets of imagination by the handful. Afterwards the tone of your stomach revives, and your appetite for solid but meagre realities recovers.

There, it seems to me, speaks the authentic voice of the born essayist—of the writer who collects our scattered and amorphous experiences from us with neat, expert hand, and gives it back before we have time to become impatient—but rearranged, compared, and clarified so that we exclaim: "Good heavens! why did I never think of that?"

> *Edward Sackville West, "The Wisdom of a Liberal," in* The Spectator, *Vol. 154, No. 5565, February 22, 1935, p. 306.*

V. S. PRITCHETT (essay date 1953)

[Considered one of the modern masters of short story writing in English, Pritchett is also one of the world's most respected and well-read literary critics. He writes in the conversational tone of the familiar essay, approaching literature from the viewpoint of a lettered but not overly scholarly reader. In his criticism, Pritchett stresses his own experience, judgment, and sense of literary art, rather than following a codified critical doctrine derived from a school of psychological or philosophical speculation. In the following excerpt from a review of Memories, *Pritchett offers an appreciative overview of MacCarthy's criticism.]*

When I was young I used to turn first of all to the essay of Affable Hawk when the old *New Statesman* came. In that austere and sometimes virginal period of the paper before its brilliant marriage to *The Nation,* these articles were the most luminous and had the finest edge. Affable the hawk was; he would begin his articles with some simple personal sentence which, in the bright sense of journalism, was not a beginning at all, but he soon rose to hover and he always pounced at the moment of precision. His writing was like conversation, but we must add that it came from one of the finest conversationalists of a stern coterie who excelled in the art. It was not vague talk: he knew his thought and I doubt if he would have been easily persuaded from it. All good writing depends on

surprise. In MacCarthy's the surprise lay in the simplicity underlying the civility of the writer, in the clarity and the *natural* choice of image. Also in his wisdom. Most writers value their brains so much that they fear pausing to be wise. There was as well a courtesy towards life and literature that was aristocratic, and an endless curiosity about their interrelation. He wrote an article more or less every week for all his professional life—a huge effort for a man of idle, or at any rate, divided temperament—and his seduction was that, whether he was at his best or not, he used literature not entirely for its own sake, but for the interpretation of human experience. It existed for him as the highest human amenity.

Urbane is a word that has often been used to describe MacCarthy's criticism, but it suggests too much indolent charm, polish and catholicity practised for their own pleasure. It suggests the *belle lettriste* listening to the sound of his own golden voice. MacCarthy's urbanity certainly rested on some assurances that were not lasting: he belonged to the leisured and independent educated class and by 1918 it was dissolving, society was becoming de-civilised and revolutionary, writers were becoming violent. He did not much care for the inelegance of the Twenties or the faiths of the Thirties. But his urbanity was not entirely a mould formed by a bettermannered period than our own. It was not a mould at all; it was an action, not a marmoreal condition. It was nourished by a private conflict. In his memoir to [*Memories*], Mr. Cyril Connolly has one or two good things to say about this:

> Like Sainte-Beuve, he strove to reconcile the wild romantic in him with the studious epicurean and eventually allowed the one to forgive the other.

Or again—

> As a young man he wished both to live fully and write fluently like Byron. His ancestors were men of action (one was a Regency rake) and he was very happy when acting as a special correspondent or getting more movement into his life than the critic's armchair warranted. But we live in an age when we cannot both be Byron and write like him. Genius can only be extracted from talent when it is subjected to a pressure that the possessor will do everything to avoid.

And Mr. Raymond Mortimer in his foreword to the same volume, reinforces the point of the conflict with living:

> I should say . . . that his gusto for life kept him from the ascetic regularity and solitude that authorship usually demands. . . . What delighted him more than art or ideas or landscape was human nature. . . . Goodness knows, he loved words for their own sake. But he loved them first as clues to character.

(p. 315)

[*Memories*] perfectly illustrates the fruits of this division of mind, not only in its literary essays but in its biographical fragments which include a brilliant account of his first day at Eton. The opening essay which compares the work of Trollope, Wells and Bennett, begins with a quotation from Bennett's *Journals.* They are surely not one of the great diaries of their kind in English literature, but MacCarthy looks at them a second time from the point of view of the living man and extracts an epigram:

> Anyhow, he thinks, the mere habit of recording ex-

perience increases the chance of not having lived in vain.

He goes on to the writer, but defines also the man:

> You know those little electric motors which can be fitted to sailing boats and drive them along when the wind drops. They have spoiled sailing, though they are exceedingly convenient. Arnold Bennett was an artist who was born (unfortunately for us, yes and for him too) with such an attachment. He could move rapidly in any direction he wished without waiting for the breath of inspiration; he could make progress without tacking. He was cursed with an irrelevant and impartial efficiency.

Of Wells:

> His method of constructing a book was often just to take the back out of the cart of his mind, tilt up the shafts and let the contents fall with an exhilarating rumble.

MacCarthy's images are there to make his point, not to lead us a dance round it, indeed he uses the image discreetly and times it most carefully. He preferred a few essential ideas to a crowd of brilliant ones. His criticism is not guessed as his gift carries him along. When he says, for example, that in *The Old Wives Tale* Arnold Bennett surpassed his ordinary powers because he rose above the point of view of the people themselves; when he writes of Galsworthy that his dramatic aim seemed to be not to make us live in his characters, but to make us fair-minded towards them, and adds:

> It is all to the good that a play or novel . . . should have a bearing on life as we have observed it, and that an author's mind should be full of the general woe or joy of the world. But only on condition that when once he sits down to write his interest in his people exceeds everything else—

he is making clear fundamental statements about imaginative literature which are frequently bungled by other less clearheaded critics. And he is no less fertile in equally fundamental things about the relation of literature and life. I find this judgment in the excellent conversation on Maupassant, a statement which ought to be framed and put up in every Public Library in England:

> Men are so constituted that they can support with singular composure and courage the misfortunes of others. And though this is not an amiable trait, thanks to it much has been written which is of great benefit even to those who suffer. They have been helped by the strong and indifferent to laugh at many things which might have overwhelmed them.

There is the criticism that incites the creative writer and there is the criticism which irradiates our reading and creates an atmosphere in which literature can live and please. MacCarthy's belonged to the second category. He was not an impressionist, for he did not deal in half-truths and generalities. He was quietly certain. His facts were sound, his detail was chosen carefully to point the definitions he excelled in making. One does, indeed, regret that he did not write at far greater length on some of his subjects, for confined to the two thousand words of the chronic periodical critic, he had to be decisive, where he might have asked more questions. If, for example, Bennett was above his characters in *The Old Wives Tale,* did he not condescend to them? And why? When MacCarthy wrote about novelists he often tended to treat their

novels as memoirs and to regard a story as something found literally in life, rather than as something dramatically invented and imagined. The view of character, the view of life— matters which hardly separate the novelist from the biographer—solely interested him, and he smoothed away the violent differences of genius between the novelists. They were, I fancy, biographers to him. The epicurean, here, certainly swallowed the imaginative man. But this is natural enough: there was a good deal of the 18th-century moralist in MacCarthy, who was diverted by the variety of human beings and who excelled in defining it as it came along; it is a contemplative activity which does not feel the violence of the forces which make people what they are. Or even the necessities. Yet his sociable contemplations were clarifying, calming and succinct. What Mr. Connolly says of MacCarthy in aristocratic society is true of him in criticism:

> He knew not only how everybody pictured themselves, how they expected to be treated, but he saw right through to the inner aspirations of their personality, as if he had known them as children.

When one turns, after this remark, to MacCarthy's sharp and lurid portrait of Lord Alfred Douglas, to the touching and farcical account of his first days at Eton, to the anecdotes about General Gordon or Wilfrid Scawen Blunt, one sees that it is dead right. Clearly MacCarthy could not have been a novelist, for he had to be given his material and he once wrote a few pages to show how easy, and below the serious interest of an equipped and educated man, the writing of novels was. Where could his checked creative instinct have led him? In biography, perhaps, where—on oath, as he said a biographer ought to be—he would have created in unanswerable detail the most amusing fictions. He would have imported them into the social scene where alone, I think, people really lived for him. I doubt if the repressed romantic in him could have borne to think of their solitude. I think he gratified society by being deeply romantic about it. The remark of Mr. Connolly's which I have quoted reveals the imaginative but also worldly perceptiveness of a man who was only half joking when he said that, "on the whole, yes on the whole," he thought he preferred common sense to genius. That was the overt sign of the active man who could never be quite subdued by the unworldly trance, the lonely and insidious dream of literature; and perhaps his surpassing gift as a dramatic critic owed a lot to the excited sense that *here* was the releasing transposition; here was literature in person, walking, talking, feeling, behaving before his ears and eyes. (pp. 315-16)

> *V. S. Pritchett, in a review of "Memories," in* The New Statesman & Nation, *Vol. XLV, No. 1149, March 14, 1953, pp. 315-16.*

LORD DAVID CECIL   (essay date 1953)

[*Cecil was an English educator, critic, and biographer who contributed distinguished studies of the lives and works of Jane Austen, Max Beerbohm, William Cowper, Thomas Hardy, and Charles Lamb, among others. He married MacCarthy's daughter, Rachel, in 1932. In the following essay, which originally appeared as the preface to* Humanities, *Cecil highlights significant aspects of MacCarthy's approach to life and literature.*]

Desmond MacCarthy did not think much of his own work. In his later years, he would with smiling, rueful sadness compare the novels, biographies, dramas he had once dreamed of writing with what he had in fact achieved; a handful of short stories and reminiscences, a heap of reviews. The thought of this contrast did not sour him: he was too sensible and too unegotistic to allow it to do so. But remembering it cast a shadow over his spirit.

It need not have done so. Desmond MacCarthy's achievement was one to be proud of. Moreover, the form it took was in fact the form most suitable to his talent. The long single book was not the right unit for this to display itself, any more than it was for Addison or Hazlitt. Perhaps he had not the faculty for design on a big scale that was needed for it; and certainly it would not have given him the chance to exhibit the variety of his interests and sympathies. This was extraordinary. He is usually described as a literary critic. Indeed, he was one of the best that England ever produced. But the phrase does not portray him completely; for it implies one primarily interested in the art of literature, whereas Desmond MacCarthy, like Dr. Johnson, was first of all a student of human nature. Because he loved and appreciated good writing, he particularly enjoyed studying men as they revealed themselves through the medium of books. But he was just as ready to study them directly in actual persons and events and just as equipped to record his observations in the form of a memoir or a short story. This collection of tales and reviews and reminiscences by him is no heterogeneous hotch-potch, but a unity. For in it he employs different forms to achieve the same end, which was to express his own profound, acute, individual vision of human nature.

It was individual because it was the product of a very individual blend of elements: detachment and sympathy, moral sense and a sense of pleasure. The detachment showed itself in his realism. By birth half Irish, half German-French, he had none of the Englishman's instinctive flinching from painful fact. No doubt much in life was ugly and baffling and disillusioning, but that only made it more interesting to him, only intensified his curiosity to explore it further. To shroud the disagreeable in deceptive and idealising dreams was feeble and futile. For Desmond MacCarthy a grain of fact, however harsh, was worth a ton of daydream, however beguiling.

This sense of the value of fact had been increased by the mental atmosphere in which he grew to maturity. His years at Cambridge had affected him deeply, and Cambridge in the early part of this century was the home of a liberal rationalism which made it a man's first obligation to search for truth by the light of reason, however chilly might be the conclusions to which it led him. Integrity, rationality, truthfulness—these were the watchwords of the circle in which Desmond MacCarthy moved. They are rather depressing watchwords, and on many of his companions they had a depressing effect; imbuing them with a conscientious joyless pedantic agnosticism, more respectworthy than inspiring. Not so Desmond MacCarthy! He accepted the Cambridge principles of thought; intellectually and morally he remained all his life a liberal. But temperamentally he was very unlike the typical English liberal. Here again, his foreign blood may have affected him. Not only was he inexhaustibly inquisitive about life in its every manifestation, but he delighted in it. Seldom can so unworldly a man have taken so much pleasure in the world. Let it be as irresponsible and flamboyant as it pleased; he only responded to it the more. Liberals for the most part are more tolerant politically than personally. They believe that everyone should be permitted to do as he pleases, but

they seldom take pleasure in watching him do it. Desmond MacCarthy did. He enjoyed his fellows all the more because they were diverse.

Further, he liked them. He was not at all put off by the spectacle of human imperfection. The worried, undignified animal called man, bustling about with his unwieldy bundle of inconsistent hopes and fears, virtues and weaknesses, stirred in him the amused sympathetic affection of one who feels himself akin to him and, therefore, has no reason to look on him with dislike or contempt. Or even disrespect: there was nothing of the sentimental cynic about Desmond MacCarthy. His firm grip on fact made him recognise the existence of human virtue, and he had a sharp eye to discern it. Instinctively he was always seeking to do so. Life interested him because it exhibited human character; and for him the centre of every character was its moral centre. After he has noted keenly and with enjoyment a man's idiosyncrasies of aspect or temperament, Desmond MacCarthy always goes on deeper to discover the moral nature behind them. Then, justly but ruthlessly he makes his judgment. The canons he judges by were appropriate to his own mixed nature. On the one hand he believed in honesty, good sense and the courage to face facts; on the other in a readiness to respond to life and to feel deeply and delicately. No amount of brilliance could reconcile him to silliness or false sentiment or hardheartedness. Least of all, hard-heartedness: for all that he appreciated Proust's sensibility so subtly, he could not bring himself to like him for he perceived in him a fundamental coldness. He found Carlyle more lovable, because he discerned, glimmering through all the acrid clouds of bigotry and bias which billowed smokily forth from his personality, the fitful flame of a passionate heart.

It is necessary to stress this moral strain in Desmond MacCarthy because it was this which turned his intelligence into wisdom, which gave depth and significance to his charming, humorous, acute observation of men and things. **"The Mark on the Shutter,"** is, for me, the best short story ever written about a school. Never was there a truer or more entertaining description of boys and masters. But the story is more than a picture of school. For Desmond MacCarthy has the penetration to see this particular school drama as an illustration of laws governing the human drama in general. "Freddy learnt at the time, or thought he had learnt, nothing from all he had been through"; so runs the final paragraph, "but in later life when, either for fun or from curiosity, he would sometimes travel back into the past, he found his experience had taught him three things: that a good conscience is a very private source of happiness in which others can never be much interested; that people have short memories, even for what they once thought important; and that the outraged moral sense of a community is in proportion to the inconvenience suffered at the moment from the delinquent."

A similar wisdom reveals itself in his account of a Labour Party meeting, or his comments on Anglo-Irish relations. But, of course, it is in his criticism that he displays his talents and his view of life most fully. Though he could write shrewdly and sensitively on any play or book, inevitably he liked some sorts better than others: and it is about these that his criticism is most memorable. His preferences were typical. He says somewhere that literature can be divided into the kind that adds the force of reality to imagination, and that which lends the charm of imagination to reality, and that the second is the kind he himself enjoys most. This is true. The books he valued most were those that extended and illuminated his knowledge of human beings. He preferred realism to fantasy; he is more concerned with a writer's matter than his manner, though anything he says about his manner is always acute. For this reason he is more characteristically successful on prose than on poetry. His mode of criticism exhibits first his imaginative sympathy and then his power of judgment. He starts by "placing" his author, defining his point of view and the range of his talent. He then goes on to examine how far the picture of life revealed in his work squares with the facts of experience as he has himself observed them. Finally, he makes a judgment on the quality of the author's moral reaction to life as shown in his picture of it. Tested by such a process, some authors pass, others, though gifted, fail. D'Annunzio fails. The spell he casts by his mastery of language and imaginative exuberance were in Desmond MacCarthy's eyes insufficient compensations for a basic silliness of soul. Swinburne, on the other hand, though apparently a spell-binder of a similar kind, comes off better: "If one has kept one's intelligence alert in spite of the overpowering swing of his verse, one is often surprised at the subtlety and coherence of the poet's thought."

Desmond MacCarthy is most at home, however, with the writers who do not go in for spell-binding; with Tolstoy and Trollope, Ibsen and Chekhov. These last two particularly; for, when Desmond MacCarthy wrote about them, they were still relatively uncharted ground for the critic to work on, and he therefore got a chance to display his greatest gift, which was the capacity to understand and expound some new, fresh vision of reality. Desmond MacCarthy is often counted as a conservative critic. And it is true that he was repelled by the deliberate obscurity and oddness of some modern authors: he thought it cut literature off from the central stream of life. But to the end of his days he welcomed any author who ventured out to explore new territories of human experience: and he had an extraordinary power of discovering what they were after. Of Chekhov and Ibsen he has written more penetratingly than any other Englishman. Read the passage in his review of *The Cherry Orchard* in which he examines in detail a piece of dialogue between Madame Ranevsky and the student Trofimov; see how delicately he interprets each casual, fleeting phrase of their conversation thus teaching us to discern the modulation of mood which directs it. He explains to us Chekhov's mode of expression, and makes us see how it is the perfect vehicle to convey his unique vision of life. Chekhov was the ideal author for Desmond MacCarthy to criticise; for, like his critic, Chekhov combined an unillusioned realism with an unfailing affectionate amusement at the spectacle of the human comedy. No one could better appreciate Chekhov's ruthless charity than Desmond MacCarthy.

Moreover, he approached him from a point of view acquired by a lifelong acquaintance with the great literature of the past; and was thus able to relate him to it. Because he knows his "classics," he can judge in what sense Chekhov is the writer of classic quality. There has been a lot of talk about classical criticism of late years. Mr. T. S. Eliot, to mention no lesser name, has eloquently preached the importance of maintaining a classical standard of criticism. It comes a little oddly from Mr. Eliot, for his own criticism, subtle, idiosyncratic and perverse, is both in its strength and its weakness, highly romantic. But Desmond MacCarthy really was a classical critic. He examined literature always in relation to important and permanent aspects of man's experience, and estimated it by rational and timeless standards deeply grounded in the European tradition of culture and not biased by the prejudice of any school or period. Cocteau is not too modern for him or Ruskin too old-fashioned: nonsense is equally deplorable whether he observes it in an Elizabethan playwright or in Gertrude Stein. If would-be critics to-day genuinely want to acquire a classical point of view, they should study Desmond MacCarthy.

They would learn how to express it too. For Desmond MacCarthy was himself an artist. His writing is a model of what critical prose should be. For he was without the conceit that inspires some critics to expect to find readers, when they have taken no trouble to make their books readable. Desmond MacCarthy was a famous talker, and his style is a talker's style; easy, casual, parenthetical, its unit the sentence rather than the paragraph. But it is conversation glorified and transfigured and purged of its characteristic vagueness and diffuseness. Every sentence is firm and lucid; it gleams at every turn with some picked felicitous phrase—"Swinburne's strong, monotonous melodies," "Hawthorne's pensive, delicate, collected prose," "the passion which smoulders in the dark impersonal eyes" of Rembrandt's Jewish portraits. How delightful too it is when the steady, substantial good sense of Desmond MacCarthy's discourse is lit up by the flicker of his playfulness. "I myself enjoy Swinburne's prose very much, but this is so exceptional a taste that I have been tempted to insert an Agony Column advertisement 'Lonely literary man of moderate means wishes to meet friend; must appreciate Swinburne's prose'."

It is unlikely that any critic of a future generation will want to insert a similar advertisement about Desmond MacCarthy's prose. There will surely be far too many people still enjoying it for such an appeal to be necessary. (pp. vi-xii)

> *Lord David Cecil, in a preface to* Humanities *by Desmond MacCarthy, MacGibbon & Kee, 1953, pp. vi-xii.*

HERMIONE LEE   (essay date 1984)

[*Lee is an English educator and critic who specializes in the works of twentieth-century women writers. In the following excerpt from a review of* Desmond MacCarthy: The Man and His Writings, *Lee re-evaluates MacCarthy's reputation and underscores the strengths of his critical perspective.*]

"He was a supremely good talker. . . . In a charming, expressive voice, male and unmannered but beautifully modulated to convey his ever-changing shades of feeling, his discourse flowed forth, relaxed, leisurely, enthralling" (David Cecil). "He moved through the great houses bestowing the blessings of his wit and the grace of his conversation" (Leon Edel). "He spoke to everyone as if they were all his lifelong guests at some delicious party" (Cyril Connolly). "No one in London was more widely and more wholeheartedly liked. He was adored by persons who detested one another" (Raymond Mortimer).

There is something about the tone of these unanimous tributes which makes the hackles rise. It's partly their blithe assumption that good dinner-party chat must universally be regarded as the acme of civilization—the superficial branch, as it were, of the Cambridge/Bloomsbury/G. E. Moore nexus of beliefs ("Personal affections and aesthetic enjoyments include . . . *by far* the greatest goods we can imagine"); and partly that when someone is praised as a brilliant talker one instantly suspects them of being an insufferable phoney.

MacCarthy's much-indulged insufferableness was, in fact, very well documented: his fecklessness, his laziness, his inability to get out of bed in the morning or get into it at night when his hosts wanted to go to sleep, his chronic eleventh-hourism over dates, deadlines, trains, lunches, appointments, his constant self-reproaches on all these counts, his growing gloom at not having written his great novel or fulfilled his early promise—the Desmond stories are legion. Did you hear the one Morgan tells about Desmond reading a brilliant essay to the Bloomsbury Memoir Club from what turned out to be a blank sheet of paper? Did Virginia ever tell you about the dinner party they gave (Roger was there too) with Leonard's secretary hidden behind a screen to write down Desmond's conversational pearls, and how she came out with nothing much written down at all? Have you heard about Lady Colefax's scheme to raise £300 for Desmond and Molly's debts? So the "table talk" echoes on, and a sense of character remains, most brilliantly (and repeatedly) set down in Virginia Woolf's diaries, where she is sketching him for Bernard in *The Waves.*

> May 1, 1918. His mind had a factitious spryness about it . . . but this wore off, & he yawned, & couldn't stir himself up. . . . Late at night he took to reading Joyce's ms. aloud, & in particular to imitating his modern imitation of a cat's miau, but L. went to bed, & though capable of spending a night in this manner, I had compunction, & decoyed Desmond upstairs, collecting books as he went. Next morning, having observed that breakfast at 8.30 would possibly be early enough, he stayed talking about books till 10 & rambled off quite out of tune for his office.
>
> June 5 1925. He is like a wave that never breaks, but lollops one this way & that way & the sail hangs on ones mast & the sun beats down.
>
> March 22 1928. Desmond comes in, round as a billiard ball; & this is true of his dear bubbling lazy mind; which has such a glitter & lustre now from mere being at ease in the world that it puts me into a good temper to be with him. He describes, analyses, narrates; does not actually talk.

But for all his bubbling inconclusiveness, and his disappointment in his own career (touchingly displayed [in **"To Desmond MacCarthy: Act 22"**] a rueful letter written at fifty-four, in 1931, to his younger self), the literary journalism that came out of his years as literary editor (the "Affable Hawk") of the *New Statesman,* editor of *Life and Letters* and literary critic of the *Sunday Times* is rich and impressive. One's suspicion that he might be bland and superficial, a Bloomsberrian Andrew Lang, . . . is only occasionally borne out. There is a stuffy, uncomprehending put-down of Gertrude Stein, comparing her "jabbering nonsense" to the "intricate pitch-dark rigmaroles" of Mr. Joyce or the incomprehensibility of Mr. Eliot. MacCarthy was no Edmund Wilson, and his sympathies with modernism—as with feminism—are limited (as Virginia Woolf found them when he "sneered" at *Mrs. Dalloway* or derided women for their "intellectual inferiority"). And there are patches of vapid writing, as here on Hardy: "There are green isles of peace and happiness in his stories, but a greyness beats upon them and the ominous murmur of it is heard in their most sheltered recesses." But none

of this matters very much when set against MacCarthy's best work.

He was a first-rate drama critic, and writes perceptively about Ibsen, Shaw, Strindberg and Chekhov (a piece which pleasurably illustrates the English 1920s passion for all things Russian). He has a very acute sense of why certain writers matter to certain generations of readers (it is a pity, for this reason, that the pieces in this collection aren't dated.) Meredith appealed at the turn of the century because he was the first truly post-Darwinian Victorian poet "to assimilate into his poetic conception of the world the idea that death and battle is the law under which all living things exist and come to their proper perfection." Samuel Butler's ironic, sceptical, hedonistic recognition of the necessity for compromise make him a crucial influence on MacCarthy's generation. Kipling was loved in the 1890s not just for being "*the bard* of the British Empire" but because "he idealized for an enormous variety of men their relation to their work." MacCarthy is witty about changing fads in taste (like the use of the words "amusing" and "generous" in art criticism, relics of an unconscious Ruskinianism) and is himself a shrewd barometer.

One of the attractions of the volume is that MacCarthy's moral sympathies and emotional predilections are candidly displayed. There is an interesting essay on Leslie Stephen, not included here, which quotes him as saying: "I have been too much a Jack-of-all-trades." Though MacCarthy makes heroes out of men who work to their utmost and stick to their beliefs (Conrad, James, Goethe) his natural bias is always towards idiosyncratic, self-doubting figures like himself. His way of bringing a character to life is always to dwell on his (and it is usually *his*) moments of doubt. Playing little Bilham to Henry James's Lambert Strether, he recalls him bursting out after lunch: "Yes . . . [writing] is solitude. It is absolute solitude." He notes Asquith, in "a rare gleam of self disclosure" referring to his 1916 defeat as "his wound." He writes with impassioned interest about the paradoxes in Goethe's character (especially on "the limited liability system" in relationships "at which he became early adept"), or about Boswell's self-conscious contradictory impulses, or Disraeli's outrageous sleights-of-hand, or Strindberg's violent quarrels with himself. With his talent for intimate anecdotes, he catches his subjects when they reveal themselves most accurately. Here is Henry James, for example, at his social rounds:

> I was amazed . . . by his standard of decent comfort; and his remark on our leaving what appeared to me a thoroughly well-appointed, prosperous house, "Poor S., poor S.—the stamp of unmistakable poverty upon everything!" has remained in my memory. . . . "I can stand," he once said to me, while we were waiting for our hostess in an exceptionally gilt and splendid drawing-room, "a great deal of gold."

This shows a nice talent for affectionate mockery. I liked, too, Beerbohm's letter to a would-be biographer ("My gifts are small. I've used them very well, and discreetly, never straining them; and the result is that I've made a charming little reputation. But that reputation is a frail plant. Don't over attend to it, Gardener Lynch!") and Herbert Spencer making a joke on the Isle of Wight ("He was on holiday there with G. H. Lewes . . . and at lunch he remarked that the chops were very big for so small an island.") The jokes are part of MacCarthy's great talent, which is for the sympathetic, informed, sensitive penetration of literary character. Why do people find fame after their deaths, he asks himself in the essay on Disraeli? "The idea occurred to me that . . . it was not *in proportion* to the importance either of a man's deeds or his books that he became the object of it, but rather according to the degree in which he appealed himself to the imaginations of those who live after him." It's a humane thought, and might serve as his own epitaph.

Hermione Lee, "Dear Bubbling Desmond," in The Times Literary Supplement, No. 4236, June 8, 1984, p. 628.

RENE WELLEK (essay date 1986)

[*Wellek is an American scholar and the author of* A History of Modern Criticism, *a comprehensive study of the literary critics of the last three centuries. Wellek's critical method, as demonstrated in* A History *and outlined in his* Theory of Literature, *is one of describing, analyzing, and evaluating a work solely in terms of the problems it poses for itself and how the writer solves them. For Wellek, biographical, historical, and psychological information is incidental. Although many of Wellek's critical methods are reflected in the work of the New Critics, he was not a member of that group, and rejected their more formalistic tendencies. In the following excerpt, Wellek discusses MacCarthy's critical principles.*]

Desmond MacCarthy can be described as the most conservative critic of [Bloomsbury Group]. His concept of criticism is practically Arnoldian: it "must be largely a 'criticism of life'. . . a discourse upon human nature and upon good and evil," as the writer (presumably the novelist or playwright) will "create or suggest a rational coherent ideal" of life. MacCarthy remarks, justly I think, that we will be surprised how much of the criticism of Goethe, Coleridge, Sainte-Beuve, Baudelaire, Arnold, is concerned with this question. It is the standard of criticism of George Santayana, whom MacCarthy admires as "the greatest of living critics." When in the preface to his most ambitious collection, *Criticism* (1932), MacCarthy formulates his ideal, he rather rehearses Sainte-Beuve's view of the critic as a "creature without a spiritual home" whose "point of honour is never to seek one," whose "first obligation is to permit himself to be absorbed in the vision of a writer." What matters most is sympathy and the power of the "critic, when he is expounding the literatures of the past, to put the reader at the point of view from which its contemporaries saw that literature, at the same time, of course, judging it from its own; and, confronted by contemporary literature, to show its relations to the world to-day." MacCarthy, in accord with Hennequin, anticipating a strong modern concern, thinks that "the psychology of the reader of a book is almost as much a part of the [critic's] subject as the book itself," though in practice he says little about it. Sometimes, the function of the critic is defined modestly as "not limited to comparison, analysis, and judgment; he may simply make us feel what he has felt." At such moments, MacCarthy admires Leigh Hunt and Swinburne, "the most magnificent sounding board for rapturous admiration," as critics. He seems to advocate "appreciation" and "impressionism" when he criticizes Leslie Stephen as the "least aesthetic" of critics and complains that he is "deficient in the power of transmitting emotions he had derived himself from literature; he seldom, if ever, attempted to record a thrill" (***Leslie Stephen*** [1937]). But in most of his writings MacCarthy is himself a moralist who judges from an ideal of a sane but somewhat gloomy and disillusioned view of life.

MacCarthy belonged to the early admirers of Proust in En-gland. Proust's appeal, he argues, is due to the hope he raises that "aesthetic experience may, after all, fill the place of religious experience—probably a vain hope," he admits. While praising the books he concludes by suspecting the man. "How I should have missed in him, as a man, contact with the common massive satisfactions of life, and the steadiness of fundamental good-nature." This commonsense standard makes MacCarthy reject "obscurity as a literary defect," mysticism as "nearly always pretentious and insincere," Catholicism as "capitulation." MacCarthy is out of sympathy with most modernist experimentation and irrationalist philosophies. He admires D. H. Lawrence as "a religious prophet who was mistaken for a pornographer" but his mysticism is "nonsense to those" (and MacCarthy must consider himself one of them) "to whom belief in civilization seems a first condition of sanity." MacCarthy acknowledges that Lawrence's criticism of modern civilization has some truth in it, and he was deeply impressed by the imagination and vitality of his collection of poems, *Pansies*. MacCarthy has, however, no use for Freudian psychoanalysis: it "has had a bad effect on fiction because it offers easy short-cuts to psychological profundity." A novel by May Sinclair, *The Life and Death of Harriett Frean,* is used as a horrifying example. The whole turn to subjectivity and to the technique of stream of consciousness does not appeal to him. Even Virginia Woolf, whom he admired personally, is criticized. "She gave us, as it were, not the train itself, but the draught a train makes as it flies by." Joyce, though MacCarthy recognizes his "prodigious talents" and linguistic inventiveness, seems to him "a frightened enslaved mind. Much of *Ulysses* is cold, nasty, small and over-serious." The book is "far too much of a self-administered purge." The stream of consciousness is a new artificial convention as artificial as any other. Gertrude Stein is a target of his ridicule. MacCarthy produces a page from *Pitman's Commercial Type-writing Manual* ("she likes a side-saddle; he is laid aside; he has skill," etc.) to dismiss her writing as "piffle." MacCarthy has no use for the "idea that the stuff of literature is a mass of words which can be arranged like coloured pebbles to make a pattern." It "undercuts almost the whole conception of what makes literature valuable to man."

Not surprisingly MacCarthy has little to say about lyrical poetry and its techniques. He apologizes for the "uncertainty of judgements on poetry" as due to "our shifting moods." When in 1921 he reviewed T. S. Eliot he defined his general attitude as "subtle, tender, disillusioned, complicated and cool" and spoke of his "self-productive pride, reserve and sensibility of the dandy-like Laforgue." Eliot is labeled an "ironic sentimentalist." Nowhere does MacCarthy look at the technique of poetry, even when he writes about Donne, Browning, and the highly admired Patmore.

MacCarthy achieves many of his effects by a technique of comparison. Eliot's modern curio shop with a few choice objects in it contrasts with Browning's curiosity shop, "a huge, rambling place, cobwebby, crammed, Rembrandtesque"; Joyce's "superstitious horror of the body and sex" contrasts with the "gay stoicism" of Rabelais; the "sceptical, aesthetic, amoral" Proust with the "emotionally lachrymose, and sentimentally moral" Richardson.

MacCarthy's preoccupation was with theater criticism, much of which is necessarily ephemeral. But he also wrote on his favorite dramatists. His heart went out to Ibsen and Chekhov. Ibsen's theater was for him a "theatre of the soul."

Ibsen's role of social reformer is less important. "Society changes quickly; the soul hardly at all; it is that which makes his work permanent." It is that which "enables him to mingle with a realism which has even a perverse kind of commonness, fantastic symbols—rat wives, wild ducks, houses with lofty towers." Ibsen remains "the dramatist of the future," "our poet," as MacCarthy hopes for a "violent revulsion towards a philosophy which respects the individual and his happiness." Chekhov further defined a philosophy "never formulated," a "feeling rather than a thought," that though "precarious and empty, just because that *is* all, there is a kind of sacredness about it."

Reviewing Eliot's *The Use of Poetry and Criticism,* MacCarthy can endorse his view that art and poetry cannot be a substitute for religion. "But poetry can help us to do one thing which religion helps us to do, to love life spiritually, that is to say, intelligently and disinterestedly." Intelligent and disinterested are good adjectives to qualify MacCarthy's criticism. They do not suffice to make him, as Lord David Cecil would want us to believe, "one of the best [literary critics] that England ever produced" [see excerpt dated 1953]. He remains a minor, appealing figure. (pp. 89-91)

> *René Wellek, "The Bloomsbury Group," in his* A History of Modern Criticism, 1750-1950: English Criticism, 1900-1950, Vol. 5, *Yale University Press, 1986, pp. 55-91.*

FURTHER READING

Beerbohm, Sir Max, et al. "Tributes to Sir Desmond MacCarthy." *The Listener* 47, No. 1217 (26 June 1952): 1031-32.
    Transcription of obituary tributes originally broadcast on BBC Radio by Beerbohm, E. M. Forster, V. S. Pritchett, Philip Hope-Wallace, and C. V. Wedgwood.

Cecil, David. Introduction to *Desmond MacCarthy: The Man and His Writings,* edited by David Cecil, pp. 13-34. London: Constable, 1984.
    Appreciative biographical and critical sketch, the critical section of which appeared for the most part in Cecil's preface to *Humanities* (see excerpt dated 1953).

De Villose, Henry. Review of *Portraits,* by Desmond MacCarthy. *The Adelphi* 26, No. 4 (July-September 1950): 370-71.
    Favorable assessment of the volume occasioned by its reprinting. De Villose praises MacCarthy's sketches as "the harvest of an urbane, mature, modest and receptive intellect, the work of a man whose critical faculties are ever tempered by tolerance, humility, understanding and courtesy."

Review of *Drama,* by Desmond MacCarthy. *The Dublin Magazine* n.s. 16, No. 3 (July-September 1941): 61-2.
    Compares the value of MacCarthy's drama criticism, written at leisure after a play had succeeded, with the more immediate reactions of traditional first-night reviewers.

Gross, John. "Modern Times." In his *The Rise and Fall of the Man of Letters: A Study of the Idiosyncratic and the Humane in Modern Literature,* pp. 233-56. New York: Collier Books, 1970.
    Includes an introductory biographical and critical sketch in a survey of literary figures of the 1920s. According to Gross, "MacCarthy was not a strikingly original critic, nor even, in himself, a particularly important one. His importance was simply that of someone who helped to keep alive a tradition of breadth, enlightenment, rational sociability, civilized forbearance."

Hughes, Richard. "The 'Prestige' of Desmond MacCarthy." *The Spectator* 191, No. 6536 (2 October 1953): 364-67.
    Review of *Humanities* in which Hughes defends MacCarthy's prominence in twentieth-century English letters.

Leavis, Q. D. "Leslie Stephen: Cambridge Critic." *Scrutiny* 7, No. 4 (March 1939): 404-15.
    Disputes aspects of MacCarthy's assessment of the late-Victorian biographer and critic presented in MacCarthy's lecture *Leslie Stephen.*

Marsh, Edward. "Undergraduates." In his *A Number of People: A Book of Reminiscences,* pp. 45-64. New York: Harper & Brothers, 1939.
    Character sketch recalling Marsh's acquaintance with MacCarthy which began at Trinity College, Cambridge, in the mid 1890s.

Mortimer, Raymond. Review of *Experience,* by Desmond MacCarthy. *The New Statesman and Nation* n.s. 9, No. 207 (9 February 1935): 176.
    Favorably appraises *Experience,* commending MacCarthy's philosophy of life and "felicity of phrase."

Pritchett, V. S. "An Urbane Critic." *The Christian Science Monitor* 24, No. 208 (30 July 1932): 8.
    Favorable assessment of *Criticism* asserting that "MacCarthy's opinions are well worth digesting by writers and readers alike."

Richman, Robert. "A Late Edwardian." *New Republic* 130, No. 13, Issue 2053 (29 March 1954): 20-1.
    Discusses MacCarthy's criticism in the context of twentieth-century literary journalism.

Roberts, R. Ellis. "He Writes to Please." *The New Statesman and Nation* n.s. 2, No. 41 (5 December 1931): 718, 720.
    Review of *Portraits,* concluding that "one's chief impression of this book is that Mr. MacCarthy rarely fails to make a man clearer, more intelligible. He has a genuine gift for interpretation, and employs it with great fairness, and no tendency to over-accentuate his own dislikes."

Stein, Jacob A. "Talk Show." *The American Scholar* 54, No. 1 (Winter 1984-85): 135-38.
    Appreciative appraisal of MacCarthy's literary criticism and talent for conversation, occasioned by the publication of *Desmond MacCarthy: The Man and His Writings.*

"Mr. MacCarthy's Portraits." *The Times Literary Supplement,* No. 1568 (18 February 1932): 108.
    Favorable review calling MacCarthy "a brilliant reporter, a born portrait painter" in whose essays the reader may expect "what he amply gives—an individual, immediate and yet often subtle reaction to many uncommon and fascinating human beings."

Woolf, Leonard. "The Years 1913 and 1914." In his *Beginning Again: An Autobiography of the Years 1911-1918,* pp. 84-144. New York: Harcourt, Brace & World, 1963.
    Reminiscence focusing on what Woolf considered the detrimental effects of MacCarthy's journalistic assignments on his ability and ambition to write more serious works.

S(ilas) Weir Mitchell

1829-1914

(Also wrote under the pseudonym Edward Kearsley) American physician, medical writer, novelist, short story writer, and poet.

Noted for his work as a physician specializing in neurology and toxicology, Mitchell was also the author of popular historical novels that were among the best-selling books of his time. He is important in the history of medicine, particularly for his controversial "rest cure," and his experience as a doctor often underlies the themes and subjects of his novels.

Mitchell was born in Philadelphia, the third child of a doctor with a successful practice in that city. He attended the University of Pennsylvania and Jefferson Medical College, earning his M.D. in 1850. After a year of medical study in Paris, he returned to Philadelphia and began assisting his father, assuming the practice shortly thereafter. Mitchell became one of the city's leading physicians; his marriage in 1874 to a member of a prominent Philadelphia family secured his place in the elite society of the city. Mitchell treated many patients who had been wounded in the Civil War, and his earliest publications, such as *Gunshot Wounds and Other Injuries of Nerves,* which he wrote with George R. Morehouse and William W. Keen, included medical studies based on his observations and treatment of war wounded. Mitchell also contributed to the study of venomous poisons and disorders of the nervous system. In the 1870s he began devising the principles of his rest cure, later explicated in such works as *Wear and Tear; or, Hints for the Overworked; Fat and Blood: An Essay on the Treatment of Certain Forms of Neurasthenia and Hysteria;* and *The Evolution of the Rest Treatment.* Combining bed rest, mental inactivity, bland diet, and massage, the "Weir Mitchell Rest Cure" was recommended primarily to women when general malaise, hysteria, neurosis, or neuralgia was diagnosed. Although the rest cure was excoriated by some who underwent it—novelist Charlotte Perkins Gilman, for example, maintained that the restrictions on her physical and intellectual activity imposed by Mitchell's treatment drove her "so near the borderline of utter mental ruin that I could see over"—it was eventually undertaken by thousands of patients in the United States and Europe and recommended by numerous specialists, including Jean Charcot and Sigmund Freud.

Mitchell began publishing short fiction in magazines in the 1860s. These early short stories and novellas appeared anonymously or under a pseudonym because of Mitchell's concern that patients would lose confidence in a physician who dabbled in literature. However, the generally favorable reception accorded his early fiction, and the encouragement of such prominent authors as William Dean Howells and James Russell Lowell, led him to begin publishing under his own name when his works appeared in book form. From the mid-1880s until his death Mitchell produced over a dozen well-received and widely read novels. He died in 1914 at the age of eighty-four.

Mitchell's fiction is characterized by vividly rendered historical settings and an analytic approach to characterization. The

novels *In War Time* and *Roland Blake,* for example, have been commended for realistically depicting the Civil War period, and *Hugh Wynne, Free Quaker* is considered one of the most historically accurate novels about the American Revolution. Critics note that Mitchell's characterizations are presented with the meticulous attention to detail of a case history. His medical training lent authenticity to his depiction of physically, mentally, or emotionally ill individuals who, though rarely central characters, often dominate the novels in which they appear: the bed-ridden and manipulative invalid Octopia Darnell, for example, has received more critical attention than the eponymous protagonist of *Roland Blake,* the novel in which she appears. In one novel, *Constance Trescot,* Mitchell placed an emotionally disturbed character at the center of the action. This story of an unstable woman's revenge for the death of her husband is considered one of his best works. Mitchell's narrative technique is generally considered the weakest element of his fiction, which predominantly reflects the conventional romantic storylines of the genteel tradition in American letters, making his work seem quaint to some critics even at the time that it appeared.

Modern commentary on Mitchell focuses on his rest cure, which has been assessed both as a misogynistic method of controlling women's behavior and, conversely, as a benefit to overburdened people who urgently needed the period of recuperation that the cure provided. Mitchell's novels retain interest primarily for their historical backgrounds and for the insights that he brought to bear on human personality.

PRINCIPAL WORKS

Gunshot Wounds and Other Injuries of Nerves [with George R. Morehouse and William W. Keen] (medical treatise) 1864

THE NATION (essay date 1885)

[*The following is a review of Mitchell's first novel,* In War Time.]

The author of **In War Time** has sketched a group of very life-like personages. He has, moreover, surrounded them with an atmosphere which has a tint of its own. Nor is this effect produced by means so obvious as names of streets or the use of local customs. There is no attempt at disguise of them, but it is not through them that the stranger who may not know Philadelphia is made to recognize a society and its surroundings that are clearly neither of New York nor of Boston. One cannot cite paragraph or page, but, taken as a whole, the nameless something is in the book by which one social circle is distinguished from another. What makes this little world seem more easy and less self-conscious than Boston, more steady than New York, is not to be hit off in a single phrase about Quaker traditions, nor have we room to analyze the subtle differences. Suffice it to say that it is there to give charm to Dr. Mitchell's story.

The idea which underlies the whole can be put in more than one way, even if we forbear any special application to the medical profession: for the soul ignoble by nature there is no hope. A man capable of one cowardly act will surely fail again, under strain. Dr. Wendell could desert his helpless patients in the field-hospital when it was reached by the advancing fire of the enemy, so he can shield his own fatal mistake at the expense of others. This theme is clearly presupposed and carried on throughout the book. The people who surrounded Dr. Wendell are, as we have said, life-like. They are interesting. Some are beautiful and some are brilliant. Given, then, a well-considered theme, and characters in themselves of much more than ordinary promise, why does the book fail of great success? Simply because the third indispensable element is wanting. The story, the incidents, the action—the three terms mean the same thing—lack point and coherence. The power of combination is wanting. The moment the people who are so delightfully described are set to do anything, they become futile or illogical. More than one path is opened in which the reader's conjecture loses itself for nothing. More than one thread is started only to break off abruptly. The war furnishes only a background (and a remote one at that), not motives. A chance meeting at a hospital provides the heroine of the *ingénue* type, but the other incidents taken from the war, except the affair at the field-hospital, are not essential. Dr. Mitchell expects too much credulity from his readers. That a man endowed with every keen and fine sense becoming a gentleman should go to tell the lady who has refused him, that the man he fears she may marry is an arrant coward, is too unlikely. The same keenness of sense which is supposed to prompt him to such a duty would have told him that either the lady herself would have discovered the defect of nature, or that in the other alternative his mission would be hopeless and humiliating. The final catastrophe is too shocking. True, life itself is more dreadful than any fiction; but life proves itself always inevitable. Here the reader saves his sympathy by more than one too obvious chance of escape, and insists it might have been otherwise—so, or so.

It never can be wise to neglect the old rule, discovered long before the evolution of the modern novel, that the principal figure must, so to speak, command the reader. It will not do to make him either a villain or a coward. Be the end never so tragic, the feeling excited must be only terror or pity. If the pity passes into contempt of the man, it is all over with admiration. The sorrowful fate may be heroic, the craven heart never. To have made a man like Dr. Wendell the centre of the action involves the double difficulty, that the reader cannot care for him, and that no other character seems to be natural in any relation to him, for a high-minded, sensitive nature must have felt the fatal want in him. Let the reader drop the last quarter of the book, when it is clear that the young lovers are to be happy, and there is yet hope that Mrs. Westerley may rouse some latent good in Wendell's nature, and he will remember the pleasant pictures, the delicate characterization, the bright sayings in it, rather than the inadequate construction which the reviewer is forced to point out.

A review of "In War Time," in The Nation, *New York, Vol. XL, No. 1030, March 26, 1885, p. 265.*

THE CRITIC, NEW YORK (essay date 1897)

[*In the following review, the critic commends* Hugh Wynne, Free Quaker *for its consistently sustained interest.*]

To say that **Hugh Wynne: Free Quaker** is an ideal story from the reader's standpoint might seem a questionable compliment, yet it would come pretty near the truth. It is interesting from first to last. To one who cares for something more in fiction than the feeling of suspense which the mere maker of plots regards as the chief end of his art—to one who does not seek in literature the same sensations he would experience in watching a game of roulette—to the lover of literature to whom the best writers address themselves, it is certain to appeal effectively. By adopting the form of autobiography Dr. Mitchell enables the reader to look at the life of the last century as if he were a part of it; he finds himself surrounded by the scenes, the manners, and the men and women of a bygone age without experiencing the slightest sensation of surprise. On the contrary, it is with something of a shock that he looks up from an hour's reading of the story, and finds himself among the confusing conditions of a day that seems removed by centuries from the simplicity of '76—especially the simplicity that marked the lives of the Quaker society of Philadelphia.

Hugh Wynne is one of the good, old-fashioned autobiographies that begin with the hero's childhood and end with his marriage; whether in this case he wins in the end the maiden he has pursued from the start, we must leave the reader to discover for himself. Suffice it to say that there is a love story in the book, and that it is a good one, the heroine being anything but a lay figure. What will give the book the vogue it is certain to enjoy is not so much the unfolding of the plot, which is of the simplest, as it is the convincing accuracy of its portrayal of the men and manners of the formative period in the nation's history. Hugh Wynne himself, his stern, old, orthodox father, his simple minded, sweet French mother, his sagacious, courageous and humorous aunt Gainor, the lively and lovable Darthea, and the steadfast friend John Warder, are all real characters, clearly and firmly drawn; but Washington, André, Benedict Arnold and Dr. Rush come and go in the course of the narrative as they might have come and gone in the lives of an actual "lieutenant-colonel on the staff of his excellency General Washington" and his relatives and friends. We have seen no memoirs of the revolutionary time in which these famous personalities seemed truer to the life than they appear in the pages of this romance. Hugh Wynne's interview with the condemned spy André is a most admirable bit of historical novel-writing; and it is only one of many. It will be long before we see a better novel of the last century in America; and perhaps as long a while before we see so good a story of any period in our history. It is easily the author's best work in fiction. His rivals must exert themselves to equal it. (p. 215)

> *A review of "Hugh Wynne: Free Quaker," in* The Critic, *New York, Vol. XXVIII, No. 817, October 16, 1897, pp. 214-15.*

W. D. HOWELLS   (essay date 1901)

[*Howells was the chief progenitor of American Realism and the most influential American literary critic during the late nineteenth century. In the following excerpt, he discusses Mitchell's psychological portraits of characters in the novel* Circumstance.]

It is consoling as often as dismaying to find in what seems a cataclysmal tide of a certain direction a strong drift to the opposite quarter. It is so divinable, if not so perceptible, that its presence may usually be recognized as a beginning of the turn in every tide which is sure, sooner or later, to come. In reform, it is the menace of reaction; in reaction, it is the promise of reform; we may take heart as we must lose heart from it. A few years ago, when a movement which carried fiction to the highest place in literature was apparently of such onward and upward sweep that there could be no return or descent, there was a counter-current in it which stayed it at last, and pulled it back to that lamentable level where fiction is now

sunk, and the word "novel" is again the synonym of all that is morally false and mentally despicable. Yet that this, too, is partly apparent, I think can be shown from some phases of actual fiction which happen to be its very latest phases, and which are of a significance as hopeful as it is interesting. Quite as surely as romanticism lurked at the heart of realism, something that we may call "psychologism" has been present in the romanticism of the last four or five years, and has now begun to evolve itself in examples which it is the pleasure as well as the duty of criticism to deal with. (pp. 872-73)

If the human beings in Dr. Weir Mitchell's very interesting novel of *Circumstance* do not seem so human as those Russians of Gorky [in *Foma Gordyéeff*] and those Kansans of Mr. White [in *Spoils and Stratagems*], it is because people in society are always human with difficulty, and his Philadelphians are mostly in society. They are almost reproachfully exemplary, in some instances; and it is when they give way to the natural man, and especially the natural woman, that they are consoling and edifying. When Mary Fairthorne begins to scold her cousin, Kitty Morrow, at the party where she finds Kitty wearing her dead mother's pearls, and even takes hold of her in a way that makes the reader hope she is going to shake her, she is delightful; and when Kitty complains that Mary has "pinched" her, she is adorable. One is really in love with her for the moment; and in that moment of nature the thick air of good society seems to blow away and let one breathe freely. The bad people in the book are better than the good people, and the good people are best in their worst tempers. They are so exclusively well born and well bred that the fitness of the medical student, Blount, for their society can be ascertained only by his reference to a New England ancestry of the high antiquity that can excuse even dubious cuffs and finger-nails in a descendant of good principles and generous instincts.

The psychological problem studied in the book with such artistic fineness and scientific thoroughness is personally a certain Mrs. Hunter, who manages through the weak-minded and selfish Kitty Morrow to work her way to authority in the household of Kitty's uncle, where she displaces Mary Fairthorne, and makes the place odious to all the kith and kin of Kitty. Intellectually, she is a clever woman, or rather, she is a woman of great cunning that rises at times to sagacity; but she is limited by a bad heart and an absence of conscience. She is bold up to a point, and then she is timid; she will go to lengths, but not to all lengths; and when it comes to poisoning Fairthorne to keep him from changing his mind about the bequest he has made her, she has not quite the courage of her convictions. She hesitates and does not do it, and it is in this point she becomes so æsthetically successful. The guilt of the uncommitted crimes is more important than the guilt of those which have been committed; and the author does a good thing morally as well as artistically in leaving Mrs. Hunter still something of a problem to his reader. In most things she is almost too plain a case; she is sly, and vulgar, and depraved and cruel; she is all that a murderess should be; but, in hesitating at murder, she becomes and remains a mystery, and the reader does not get rid of her as he would if she had really done the deed. In the inferior exigencies she strikes fearlessly; and when the man who has divorced her looms up in her horizon with doom in his presence, she goes and makes love to him. She is not the less successful because she disgusts him; he agrees to let her alone so long as she does no mischief; she has, at least, made him unwilling to feel himself her persecutor, and that is enough for her.

Mrs. Hunter is a study of extreme interest in degeneracy, but I am not sure that Kitty Morrow is not a rarer contribution to knowledge. Of course, that sort of selfish girl has always been known, but she has not met the open recognition which constitutes knowledge, and so she has the preciousness of a find. She is at once tiresome and vivacious; she is cold-hearted but not cold-blooded, and when she lets herself go in an outburst of passion for the celibate young ritualist, Knellwood, she becomes fascinating. She does not let herself go without having assured herself that he loves her, and somehow one is not shocked at her making love to him; one even wishes that she had won him. I am not sure but the case would have been a little truer if she had won him, but as it is I am richly content with it. Perhaps I am the more content because in the case of Kitty Morrow I find a concession to reality more entire than the case of Mrs. Hunter. She is of the heredity from which you would expect her depravity; but Kitty Morrow, who lets herself go so recklessly, is, for all one knows, as well born and as well bred as those other Philadelphians. In my admiration of her, as a work of art, however, I must not fail of justice to the higher beauty of Mary Fairthorne's character. She is really a good girl, and saved from the unreality which always threatens goodness in fiction by those limitations of temper which I have already hinted. (pp. 878-80)

W. D. Howells, "A Psychological Counter-Current in Recent Fiction," in The North American Review, *Vol. 173, No. 6, December, 1901, pp. 872-88.*

ERNEST EARNEST (essay date 1950)

[*Earnest is an American educator and critic. In the following excerpt, he surveys Mitchell's fiction and notes some shortcomings that keep Mitchell's works from the first rank of American fiction.*]

Before 1880 Mitchell had published four stories in the *Atlantic,* one of them, **"The Autobiography of a Quack,"** long enough to require two issues. Only one of the stories carried his name. Another, **"Thee and You,"** published by Lippincott, was signed Edward Kearsley. His reason for anonymity was probably the advice of his conservative elders in the profession who warned that patients might distrust a physician who wrote. . . . Years later . . . when he had achieved literary success, Mitchell was still a little defensive in telling of his decision to continue writing. "Feeling that I could not be injured by literary success, and trusting the good sense of the American people to know whether I was any the less a good doctor because I could write a novel, I continued to thus amuse myself."

In 1880 he published a volume of fiction called *Hephzibah Guinness.* In addition to the novelette of that name it reprinted **"Thee and You"** and added **"A Draft on the Bank of Spain."** With *Hephzibah Guinness* Mitchell entered two areas of fiction he was to develop throughout his life: historical romance and the study of neurotic personality. The story is laid in Philadelphia at the end of the eighteenth century. There is careful representation of costume, furniture, local scenery. Miss Howard's parlor is described as having a half-dozen portraits by Copley and Stuart. There are nests of Chinese teapoys, carved chairs and India cabinets. "The walls were covered with small crimson squares of wall-paper, then just introduced, and the Quaker's foot fell noiselessly on the rich brown and yellow and red of a Turkey carpet." When Arthur Guinness takes a walk, he goes along the willowy

margin of the river, then across the floating bridge at Gray's Ferry, and so up to the high ground back of Woodlands. Though the floating bridge had been replaced, a Philadelphian would instantly recognize the scene.

Not only is the background carefully represented, but also the speech and customs of the time. Two overseers from the Society of Friends visit a home to make sure that discipline was being observed in the matter of dress and furniture. It was a period of "great searchings of the searchings of the heart." Mirrors were taken down and brass clock faces painted over. The story is filled with such details obviously based on research.

In the character of Hephzibah, Mitchell has drawn the portrait of a religious fanatic, so convinced of her own righteousness that she lies and hides important letters to hold her young ward to the Quaker discipline. Hephzibah has all the Freudian implications of a character in one of O'Neill's plays. They are, however, implications only; Mitchell gives no analysis of the springs of her neurotic personality. That sort of thing came later in his work.

The plot is pure nineteenth-century romance: mysterious noble origins, dramatic rescues, a family cursed with inherited insanity, noble rejections and romantic love. Mitchell was seldom good at plots.

There are several recognizable elements from Mitchell's own experience. Elizabeth Howard has resemblances to his sister Elizabeth Mitchell. Both are essentially tragic figures and both are witty, laughing persons. "I should laugh at a jest if I were dying," Miss Howard tells Hephzibah, "—ay, and fear not that God would frown." (pp. 92-4)

With *Hephzibah Guinness* Mitchell had learned to blend his own experiences, his knowledge of Philadelphia history, and his study of neurotic personality. (pp. 94-5)

In writing [*In War Time*] Mitchell drew heavily upon his own war experiences. The scene opens with the arrival at the Filbert Street Hospital in Philadelphia of the ambulances from Gettysburg. Certainly this was an unusual beginning for a novel in that period of saccharine love stories and cloak-and-sword romances.

Much else in the book is unusual. Perhaps the most interesting character is that of the young physician, Dr. Ezra Wendell. Here is a man of unusual sensitivity and imagination, but with a fatal strain of weakness. Thus after Wendell has lost a patient he might possibly have saved, Mitchell comments: "A less imaginative man would have suffered less; a man with more conscience would have suffered longer, and been the better for it." As Wendell is walking home brooding over his carelessness, he stumbles over a piece of bad sidewalk characteristic of Germantown. His meerschaum pipe falls and breaks ". . . a shock which, as he reflected with amazement a moment later, seemed to him—nay, which was—quite as great as that caused by the death of his patient, an hour before."

Obviously Dr. Wendell is no stereotype. (pp. 96-7)

The book is filled with other well-drawn people besides Wendell. There is his righteous, unimaginative sister, who runs his household efficiently, yet torments him with her ritualistic tidyings-up. She carries the same qualities into her personal relationships with disastrous results. There is Mrs. Grace, the busybody, who is a fearful nuisance to the other ladies working for the Sanitary Commission; and Mr. Grace, "who believed in the Pennsylvania Railroad." In Mrs. Grace, Mitchell has drawn that bugbear of every physician: the woman who has determined opinions on medicine and runs from doctor to doctor in search of one who shares her prejudices.

The Morton family is another interesting group. Mrs. Morton is the able, determined woman, frustrated by her marriage to a less able person. Colonel Morton, who had "the amiability so common among selfish people," has found in mistresses a refuge from his strong-minded wife. Thus when the war came he entered the army with enthusiasm and became an able soldier. Mrs. Morton in turn lavished her affection on her semi-invalid son, Edward. Edward, too, is an interesting study of the effects of invalidism. Originally a boy interested only in physical activity, he was injured by a fall from a horse. Gradually he changes into a person who loves books and who lives vicariously in the person of his dashing brother Arthur.

Arthur is a much more typical character, the romantic young soldier. His elder counterpart is Colonel Fox, a Quaker who has abandoned his pacifistic heritage to become the very gentle, perfect knight. Twelve years later Mitchell drew him again as Hugh Wynne. Much more vivid is Alice Westerley, the charming and witty widow, very feminine in her perceptiveness, her loyalties, and her provocativeness. She too is a prototype. Anne Vincent in *Characteristics* and *Dr. North* is much like her. Mitchell obviously admired her greatly, except for her feminine inability to care properly for her fine Madeiras. She is very much the chief woman character in the novel, quite overshadowing the charming young girl, Hester Gray, who provides the necessary romantic counterpart for Arthur Morton. In all his major characters Mitchell is conscious of the complex nature of human motives. It is one of his favorite themes.

In addition to penetrating character studies, *In War Time* is filled with interesting and often provocative ideas. There is the discussion of the effect of the Civil War on medicine and on American life in general. Most important is that war is not glamorized. Eleven years before Crane's *Red Badge of Courage,* Mitchell caused Colonel Fox, a thoroughly brave man, to tell Mrs. Westerley that he has been terribly afraid in battle. And the daredevil young Arthur Morton tells his brother:

> But don't think I like it at all. Anyone who says they like it is stupid or lies. I don't. I never realized until now how dreadful is war; but I think I know that I ought to be here, and why.

Then there are such incidental comments as ". . . manners have a good deal to do with business success in medicine," and again, "a doctor's life has in it . . . a good deal to harm his moral growth and needs watching. It is difficult not to become despotic from mere habit of control, and still harder to be tender and yet decided . . ." A school for girls was condemned because it "applied alike a common system, which admitted of no recognition of individualities," a point of view the "progressive" educators have since claimed as their own invention.

Thus in his first full-length novel Mitchell combined certain elements that became characteristic of him: realistic background, complex and often neurotic personalities, skilfully drawn minor characters, historical material, intellectual discussion, and stereotyped romance. The style is rarely colloquial, never fast moving, but with occasional clever turns of phrase and epigram. Certainly *In War Time* is a novel of more intellectual vigor than most of its contemporaries. It is interesting and alive. (pp. 97-9)

[Mitchell] sent a copy of the novel to George Meredith [see Further Reading], who responded enthusiastically:

> . . . I find it a piece of psychology wrought into a production of art. The story is excellent; and you have done what I constantly protest should be done to give a fruitful report to cultivated readers. You have evolved the story from characters. I look about me in my country vainly for an author who is up to that highwater mark of fiction. The characters are so clearly drawn as they are forcibly conceived, and for that reason the crux of the position between the young medicus and Mrs. Westerley, (to whom my heart is vowed) has the stamp of highest nobility. . . . My wife, my girl, my friends, the fair and masculine alike, are of my mind that the book is both noble and interesting.
>
> Speaking of it to a lady beside me at a dinner-table, I was met by the exclamation, "Why that must be the Dr. Weir Mitchell of Massage!" I praise it on all hands. I shall consider it a privilege to read more of your work and to meet you again.

With such praise from such a source, Mitchell had no further need to hesitate about a literary career. Two years later he published *Roland Blake.* Again Meredith was enthusiastic; he read it twice (Mitchell later said three times) and came to regard it as Mitchell's best novel. The title was a combination of the names of the chivalric hero Roland and the mystic poet and artist William Blake. As might be expected, the book shows therefore some confusion of purpose. And its most interesting character is not Roland Blake at all; it is Octopia Darnell, a superb study of a neurotic woman.

What Mitchell has done is to dramatize the situation described in *Fat and Blood* in which a neurotic woman becomes a chronic invalid and, through her selfish demands, turns her nurse into a neurotic. Thus the twenty-year-old Olivia finds that because of her care for her distant cousin Octopia,

> Her life was absorbed by Octopia, who directed her studies after a fashion, and who was supremely affectionate so long as there was no resistance; when that came Octopia was hurt or nervous, or both, or else, when defeat was near, gave way to such distressing symptoms as commonly routed Olivia and made Mrs. Wynne too uncomfortable for continuous opposition.

This has its inevitable effect upon Olivia:

> Her head ached, and with the consciousness of constant fatigue, the outcome of a life of strain and repression, began to come its certain result, irritability.

The elder woman has "an importunate craving for expressions of love and pity," and her "fondness for physical petting" repels Olivia. The homosexual implication in Octopia's feeling for her cousin is of course carefully veiled, but it is there: Mitchell speaks of the unhealthiness of the relationship, and vividly portrays Olivia's physical repulsion. Not many writers in 1886 could or would have handled such material.

Like its predecessor, *Roland Blake* gives an unglamorous picture of war. There are vivid scenes from the Wilderness Campaign. Mitchell's intimate friend Billings had gone through this campaign as his letters to his wife testify. One wonders if Mitchell overcame his friend's reluctance to discuss the war, for certain scenes have a first-hand realism. There is the dull thud of bullets hitting trees and "the duller sound on limb or trunk of man." Waiting for an attack, one man incessantly wipes his gun-barrel; another buttons and unbuttons his coat. We see men shot, stabbed, beaten down with clubbed muskets, and there are ghastly pictures of the battlefield after a charge. The whole attitude toward war is much more like that of novels after 1920 than of the Charge-of-the-Light-Brigade era. Blake says of war, "It was for me merely a sad duty. I hated it."

Throughout the novel there are provocative ideas such as, "Character is more subject in women than in men to changes physiologically produced. . . ." Or, "The engineer speaks of the breaking-strain in material: the breaking strain in morals was near for Octopia." Or, "The surgeon's idea of 'shock' as a result of sudden physical injury should be imported into the domain of criminal psychology." This last is essentially an anticipation of the trauma theory of psychosis.

There are excellent studies of minor characters: the aged Mrs. Wynne, using her age as a screen against the demands of Octopia and allowing Olivia to assume the burdens, yet at times becoming the great lady who had danced with Lafayette; the ex-slave Judith, malevolent, cautious, unable to shake off her servility to Octopia, yet using a furtive cunning against her.

Despite all these merits, however, the novel is in many ways less good than *In War Time.* The hero is too much the very gentle, perfect knight; the plot thoroughly Victorian. Roland Blake as an intelligence officer in the Union army has received information from the Southern traitor, Richard Darnell, who then attempts to murder him. Yet because of a pledge of secrecy, Blake will not expose Darnell to Olivia, whom they are both wooing. Old Mrs. Wynne allows Octopia to blackmail both her and Olivia in order to prevent the revelation that Olivia's father committed suicide. At almost any point the plot would evaporate if some character did a little sensible plain speaking. Too often coincidence brings important characters together. The elements in the novel which led Meredith to call it noble are the same which a modern reader would call Victorian. Thus *Roland Blake* is a somewhat ill-assorted mixture of realism, psychological brilliance, and Victorian sentimentality. (pp. 99-102)

Out of [his active] social life grew Mitchell's books *Characteristics* and *Dr. North and His Friends.* Really two parts of the same story, they are difficult to classify. He told the editors of the *Critic* that *Characteristics* was not a novel—yet there is no other name for it. To Sarah Butler Wister he wrote that it developed from her suggestion that he write a book of characters. "Of course," he added, "it is not at all the book of your hint." (p. 129)

In these two conversation novels the people spend endless hours over good food and wine, in drawing rooms or at summer resorts—just talking. There are the clever, interesting anecdotes of traveled, important people; the puns and charades of nineteenth-century fashion. But what gives the books substance, in addition to the characterization, is their wealth of interesting discussion. All sorts of things are talked about: medical theory, extra-sensory perception, women's education, philosophy, literature, abnormal psychology—in short these people live in a world of ideas.

Characteristics, the first of the two, is much less well done than *Dr. North;* Mitchell was a better writer at seventy than at sixty. For one thing, the first has less interplay of character, less tension, less drama. For another, it is more provincial, more Philadelphian. In it are such local jokes as that about the conservatism of Philadelphia being due to the fact that its chief cemetery drains into its drinking water. Here too is Mitchell's theory that although a woman has a right to enter any profession, she loses her essential femininity by going into medicine.

In *Dr. North,* on the other hand, one finds such things as a thoughtful discussion of the evidence for extra-sensory perception. Mitchell has Vincent report an instance in which a man seemed to be able to read cards he could not see. This was based upon an experience of his own. At a party a Mr. Van Gaertner had been able to guess the denominations and suits of cards he could not see. To his astonishment Mitchell found that he too could often guess the denomination and color, although he sometimes confused hearts with diamonds. And in his own person as Owen North he says:

> All our abilities, all sensual perceptivity, must have gone through endless ranges of acuteness, and always, in their evolution, certain persons sense in a larger degree than the less developed mass of their fellows.

Mitchell discusses such things as the compulsion to confess or to continually wash the hands. And characteristically, after a penetrating psychological insight, he has Alice North say, "You are a dangerous man, Owen." One of his beliefs is that there should be a psychological consultant for schools.

There is also a good bit of autobiographical material: childhood memories; the account of his experience with the doormat which led to the discovery of the nature of snake venom; incidents from his medical practice. He quotes appreciatively from his own verse and illustrates remarks with quotations from El Din Attar, a reputed contemporary of Omar's. This is of course Mitchell himself, but it caused people to try to buy the works of the mysterious poet. The book department of Wanamaker's, unable to find him listed, asked Mitchell where to obtain the work of El Din Attar.

The two conversation novels, especially *Dr. North,* are by no means an unsuccessful experiment. Like Holmes' *Autocrat of the Breakfast Table,* they are the product of a man with wide-ranging curiosity and breadth of knowledge, a man who is rather vain of his ability as a talker. (pp. 131-32)

[Mitchell] was right in believing *Constance Trescot* his best novel. In fact it can stand comparison with any of its American contemporaries, including those by Henry James. It is a memorable portrait of a possessive woman who becomes a monomaniac, and of a social order—the postbellum South. Constance would be a remarkable portrait in any era; she is especially so in an American novel of 1905. She is described as

> . . . one of those rare women who, for good or ill, attract because of some inexplicable quality of sex. Incapable of analysis, it accounts for divorces and ruined households, even for suicides or murders. It may be faithful to a great passion, and be modified by character and education, and even by religion but it is felt, whether the woman wishes it or not, and she who has it instinctively knows its power.

To the rather restrained George Trescot, who becomes engaged to her on a two weeks' acquaintance, she is rather startling. On his return from a week's absence she flings her arms joyously around him. "Conscious that the embrace was as much hers as his, he cast an uneasy glance about him, fearful of profane eyes, of which she was, to appearance, heedless." After their marriage she is completely possessive. When her sister Susan presents George with an encyclopedia, Constance is annoyed; she wanted to give it herself. Trescot "knew little of women, and nothing of the woman who desires to absorb, so to speak, all the thoughts and feelings of one man, and who as time goes on, becomes jealous of his friends, and even of his work, and, at last, of every hour not given to her."

It is she who arranges for their marriage a year before George had planned it. She did it by persuading her fuddy-duddy uncle and guardian to appoint Trescot as his agent in St. Ann, a southern town in which the uncle owned valuable, contested property.

This uncle, Rufus Hood, is also a well-drawn character. Wealthy by inheritance, he is convinced of his own firmness of purpose and business acumen. In reality he is easily dominated by his strong-minded nieces and is a pompous fool in business.

In St. Ann, Trescot finds sectional feeling strong against the northern millionaire, Hood, who is insistent on dispossessing some ex-Confederate squatters at the same time that he is involved in a suit over a valuable river-front property. Through sympathetic and honorable dealing, Trescot, though a former Union soldier, wins the respect of the community.

Pitted against him in the lawsuit is John Greyhurst, an able but unstable lawyer. Greyhurst, whose evil temper has caused him trouble in the Confederate army and has cost him a divorce, tries to inflame the community and later the jury against Trescot. During the trial Trescot demolishes Greyhurst's case. The latter calls Constance Trescot as a witness, to his own discomfiture. Angered and in danger of financial ruin, he taunts Trescot into what amounts to a challenge for a duel. Trescot, although opposed to dueling and suffering from a war-damaged arm, has no choice under the Southern code. Then Greyhurst, pretending to believe Trescot was drawing a weapon, shoots him down on the street. A local jury acquits him.

The tragedy was an inevitable product of the forces involved: community feeling and southern mores, Greyhurst's ungovernable temper and Rufus Hood's meddling in a dangerous situation. But this is only half of the book. Constance, in her agonized grief over her husband's death, loses her unborn child. On her recovery she dedicates her life to the destruction of Greyhurst. With a devilish ingenuity she haunts the man, ruining him financially and breaking up a love affair. What had been a passionate love becomes an equally passionate and unscrupulous hate. The tragedy is essentially modern rather than Greek; it is not the product of an outside fate, but of psychological forces. It is in the tradition of *Macbeth* and *King Lear*, but its setting is thoroughly American. Compared to James' *The American* it is a much more penetrating study of our national types.

In its psychological insight it does resemble James, but it lacks his ignorance of passionate emotion and his involuted style. Therefore it has been less appealing to a certain type of intellectual.

Like other novels of Mitchell's, it has penetrating comments on human nature. Thus ". . . when Uncle Rufus pinches you [figuratively of course] or me, it is because some one whom he cannot pinch has been pinching him." Or of the doctor:

> He had, however, a fund of pitiful charity, kept full by sad personal experiences and by the physician's vast explanatory knowledge of the lives of men and women, which accepts heredity, education, and environment as matters not to be left out of the consideration of disease or of the motives of men's actions.

Among all of Mitchell's books, *Constance Trescot* has the greatest unity and vigor. (pp. 185-87)

As a . . . novelist Mitchell is less secure in his reputation than as a physician. . . . But as has been suggested in the discussion of individual novels, there are several of considerable merit. *In War Time,* parts of *Roland Blake, Dr. North, Circumstance, Westways,* and above all *Constance Trescot* are still worth reading. In a period when American novels were chiefly designed for hammock reading, Mitchell's have an intellectual quality which is rare among his contemporary writers. The comparisons which most often come to mind are Oliver Wendell Holmes and Henry James. All three were interested in abnormal psychology. Unlike Melville, they made no attempt to solve the riddles of the universe, the problem of evil. They were psychologists, not metaphysicians. Their characters move in an accepted universe. Such problems as they have are the problems of adapting themselves to that universe. Of the three, James is of course the greatest. But Mitchell, using a similar social milieu, has a health which James lacks. Mitchell's characters enjoy good food and drink; they fall in love and marry; they beget children. So often the world of Henry James is an old man's world. Strether in *The Ambassadors* is a thoroughly typical character. James' people are the literary ancestors of Eliot's Prufrocks and Gerontions. Mitchell, on the other hand, tends to write of men and women between twenty-five and forty-five—people at the height of their powers and with a zest for life. Even the maladjusted characters are alive: Octopia Darnell tries to dominate those around her; Mr. Norman, the paranoid, attempts to murder his wife and her fancied lover; Roger Grace, the self-made millionaire, goes on extended binges; Constance Trescot hounds her husband's murderer to his destruction. There is none of the old-maidish resignation of Caroline Spencer in James' *Four Meetings* or the frustration of a Daisy Miller. James wrote of the ineffectuals, the people in the backwaters of life; Mitchell chose men and women battered by war, financial trouble, or imbued with plain cussedness. It is perhaps a commentary on our times that the anemic neuroses of James' men and women are regarded as more significant than the forceful neurotics of Mitchell's books. Certainly it is a commentary on this age that Mitchell's studies in abnormal psychology should seem more important than his more normal characters such as the intelligent men and women of *Dr. North* or the charming Alice Westerley of *In War Time.*

What then keeps Mitchell from being first-rate? Certainly he is more adult than Winston Churchill, Owen Wister, Marion Crawford, or F. Hopkinson Smith. He has more grace than William Dean Howells, a deeper understanding of psychology. There is more history, especially historical detail, in his *Hugh Wynne* than in most of the thirty-two historical romances written during the six years from 1896 to 1902. George Washington swears at Monmouth and gets merry over his wine. In the probing into the bypaths of psychology, the only contemporary who did as much was Henry James.

Part of the answer is Philadelphia. Mitchell never threw off its reticences, its social mores, its emphasis on class and family. He could help to support Walt Whitman, but he could never forget that Walt was not a gentleman. He was a friend of Carnegie's and he put Xerxes Crofter, the malefactor of great wealth, into his books, yet he has no conception of the America of *The Pit* and *The Octopus*. His people are the absentee owners of coal lands, the Philadelphia aristocracy of bankers and lawyers for inherited estates. In their unchallenged position they could afford generous charities, fine distinctions of business honor, and a discriminating taste in Madeira. They had not become the timid George Appleys and H. M. Pulhams of a later day. Mitchell was almost as unconscious of the proletariat as was Henry James.

A more serious fault is his adherence to the love-story convention of his time. With few exceptions there is always the pure, clever, strong-minded girl who refuses to acknowledge to herself that she is in love until the last page. If she is a widow she puts up an even longer battle before she "surrenders." She appears in the stories of Stanley Weyman, of Owen Wister, of Winston Churchill—yes, even in Henry James and Frank Norris. One is forced to believe she must have existed—if only in imitation of a literary fashion. Between 1885 and 1915 she was as ubiquitous as the modern clever career woman who in contemporary novels sleeps with a series of wrong partners before finding love. In Mitchell's day the heroine merely flirted with the wrong man throughout the book, only to marry the hero at last.

As Mitchell demonstrated in *Roland Blake* and *Constance Trescot,* he could draw other types. In fact the adventuress, Mrs. Hunter, in *Circumstances* is an American Becky Sharp. But for the most part he is content to follow convention. At a number of places he hints at the baleful effects of sexual repression, but none of his "good" characters ever violates the strictest propriety or questions the Elsie Dinsmore code. This, combined with the need for happy endings, produces a rather high mortality among rascally or psychotic husbands. In Mitchell's novels unpleasant husbands were not a good insurance risk.

In medicine Mitchell was often in advance of his age; on most social and economic questions he was behind it. . . . His social order is paternalistic; it revolves around the dinner tables of the wealthy. Even the American Revolution becomes an affair of Philadelphia drawing rooms.

As a physician and neurologist Mitchell was able to put much into novels that his contemporaries could not. His fiction has an intellectual quality unusual in his day. Certainly he deserves to be restored to the canon of American literature. Despite the faults of his novels (and they were faults of the time) his work has the flavor of an unusual man. But except in *Constance Trescot* he never let himself go. He never wrote anything which might offend a Philadelphian. (pp. 232-35)

It was this same tendency to conform to the mores of a highly conservative community which perhaps kept him from entertaining more daring theories of psychiatry. There is some point to Emerson's aphorism: "Whoso would be a man must be a nonconformist." Certainly the original thinker or artist must on occasion be something of a nonconformist: he must see beyond the prejudices and limitations of his contemporaries. This habit of conformity is perhaps the chief reason why Mitchell is not regarded as one of the very great. (p. 235)

Ernest Earnest, in his S. Weir Mitchell: Novelist and Physician, *University of Pennsylvania Press, 1950, 279 p.*

JOSEPH P. LOVERING   (essay date 1971)

[*Lovering is an American educator and critic. In the following excerpt, he discusses* Constance Trescot *as Mitchell's most effective novel.*]

In 1905 Silas Weir Mitchell, seventy-six years old, produced his most effective novel, *Constance Trescot,* a story about a vengeful woman who had been grievously wronged when her young husband was treacherously shot to death in a small Southern town. Mrs. Trescot, relentlessly tormented by the memory of her husband's death, brings slow destruction to her husband's slayer and rival lawyer, John Greyhurst, despite the efforts of many people to deflect her from her revenge.

Mitchell constructs his story with increased skill in plotting and in narrative pacing. His setting is a change from the familiar Philadelphia environs: the time is 1870, and the locale is St. Ann, Missouri. The village has been decimated by the war; and Constance and George Trescot, Northerners and newlyweds, have come there from Massachusetts to represent the land holdings of Constance's uncle, Rufus Hood, a stubborn and irreligious Northern Yankee. Most of the St. Ann townsmen are incapable of paying their rentals and sometimes refuse to do so, hiding behing a legal confusion over land titles.

Constance, who has been reared by her uncle, shares his irreligious tendencies. A self-willed young woman, she has urged her husband to accept the difficult post—even though she knows the agent's job is not to her lawyer husband's taste—because it provides the young couple an opportunity for an earlier marriage. The growing resentment against Rufus Hood is led and fostered by John Greyhurst, who is the masculine counterpart of Constance in temperament. He is cast as a passionate Southerner of "unchecked boyhood" with a "drop of Indian or Creole blood in him." He is intelligent, impulsive, and sensitive; he has a definite sexual attraction for Mrs. Trescot from his first meeting with her. Greyhurst, who has built up his own interests in real estate, stands to lose much personally if Hood's interests are capably managed by Trescot.

Trescot, a religious and even-tempered man, seeks a compromise solution to the land settlement in which his wife concurs. When Hood, at the last moment, refuses to accept this proposal, Trescot is ready to resign as the agent; but he does proceed with one final litigation against Greyhurst. In the course of Trescot's success with the trial, his wife's testimony leads to acrimonious statements and finally to open insults from Greyhurst. As the trial ends, word is received that Uncle Rufus has died and has willed that his estate be equally divided between Constance and her sister, Susan, thus resolving the financial problems of the Trescots. As George Trescot crosses the courthouse square to extend a forgiving hand and an assurance of aid to his defeated rival, Greyhurst, angered, mistakes Trescot's hand movement towards his waistcoat as an attempt on his life and impulsively murders the unarmed

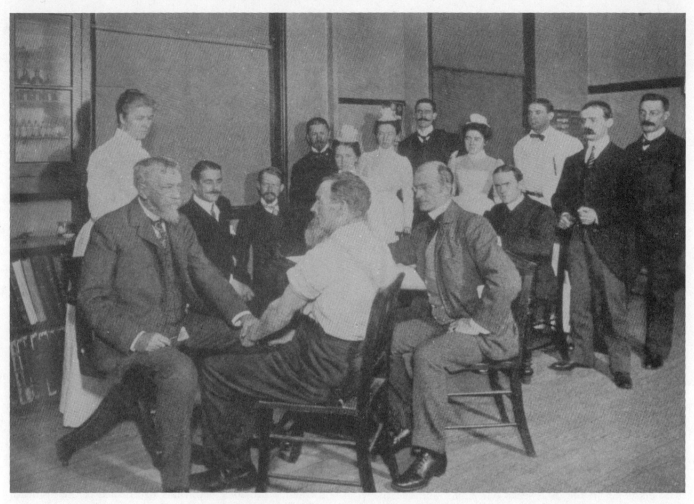

Mitchell at the Orthopedic Hospital, Philadelphia.

Northerner in front of his wife, who, we learn later, was with child.

The last third of the novel is devoted to the revenge of Mrs. Trescot. For a year she slowly recovers from the shock of her husband's death and the loss of the child. She remains away from St. Ann, but she maintains her property there. Greyhurst, freed of any legal guilt in the slaying, has, however, been chastened by the event. Yet he slowly begins to reassume his political leadership in the fast-growing town; and he plans to marry Jeanette Wilson, a San Francisco girl. After a year Constance returns and begins a nightmarish campaign to punish Greyhurst. She begins by recording on her husband's gravestone the facts of the murder. She maneuvers whenever possible to be where Greyhurst can see her in her black dress. She mails him a telegram that is covered with her husband's blood (the telegram he was extracting from his vest at the moment of his death)—the one that indicated his desire for a generous settlement of the court case in spite of his legal victory. She seeks out a charitable organization to which Greyhurst is prominently connected and gives substantial amounts to it with the provision that Greyhurst will not have anything to do with the expenditure of the funds. She buys up, at an overly generous figure, properties that Greyhurst was dependent upon for fulfilling his hopes of a marriage with Jeanette Wilson. Finally, she interferes with his engagement to Jeanette by writing to the girl and revealing the incident of her husband's death. These efforts of Constance Trescot, despite the direct plea of her sister, her minister, Mr. Kent, and her doctor, Dr. Eskridge, culminate in Greyhurst's bursting into her apartment with a pistol. Constance, who coolly spurns his threat, says she is glad to die; thereupon, Greyhurst turns the pistol to his temple and kills himself.

In the character of Constance Trescot, Weir Mitchell for the first time gave concentrated attention to a feminine character of a passionate nature, one who must be considered neurotic in her revenge. Mitchell's lifelong interest in women's nervous ailments and in psychopathology combine to make this novel one of the most absorbing of his narratives. The author never makes the mistake of obtruding his neurological or clinical knowledge upon his main purpose of storytelling.

When the novel opens, Constance Trescot is dark, well-built, about twenty-three years old; she lives with her sister, Susan, at her uncle's house in Massachusetts. The two girls, who are of the "old New England Breed," have been orphaned and brought up separately—Constance, by Rufus; Susan, by an aunt. Specifically, the difference in their rearing has been that of a religious (Episcopal) upbringing for Susan and an irreligious, loosely disciplined childhood for Constance because of Uncle Rufus's ideas.

Moreover, Constance was "one of the rare women who, for good or ill, attract because of some inexplicable quality of sex. Incapable of analysis, it accounts for divorces and ruined households, even for suicides or murders. It may be faithful to a great passion, and be modified by character and education, and even by religion; but it is felt, whether the woman wishes it or not, and she who has it instinctively knows its power." This statement is Mitchell's most explicit one about sexual passion, but similar ones are generally absent from his novels.

Constance had become engaged to George Trescot, a wounded veteran, within two weeks after she first bumped against him at a dance and caused him some discomfort in his wounded arm. There is a possessiveness about her love for George at the outset, and this quality also shows in her demands to her uncle because she plans for an early marriage. She also rather selfishly urges her fiancé into taking the fairly lucrative position as land agent for Uncle Rufus in the South, a dangerous position during the Reconstruction era. Thus the pattern of Constance's girlhood and young womanhood is one of impetuosity and of determination.

The early days of the marriage of George and Constance progress well. Trescot finds the only cloud on his horizon is the wife's lack of a religious faith, for he wants her to share his own spiritual happiness. Mitchell, as we have learned to expect, conveys no scenes of intimacy; but he does emphasize in this novel to some extent the note of Constance's predominantly sexually orientated love. We see her entreaty for George's kisses; on the other hand, she makes a conscious effort to share her husband's religious life by going to church with him. But, as she puts it: "He is my religion."

Her "religion" meets its first test when her husband is shot at by one of the squatters, Tom Griffin, who has been encouraged to shoot him by Greyhurst. Constance's fighting female instincts come to life. She seeks out Coffin and effectively brings him over to her side by retaining him as her handyman. This scheme works, but it increasingly antagonizes Greyhurst and the other litigants. As a result, she really does not serve her husband's interests since he strongly desires a peaceful settlement of the whole controversy.

The trial scene, to which almost three long chapters of the book are devoted, is capably narrated with good balance between courtroom atmosphere, procedures, and suspense. The outcome of the case hinges on the testimony of Tom Coffin and his recognition of old boundary markers in the form of blazed trees, but Greyhurst uses his cross-questioning of Constance Trescot to pointedly insult his opponent, hoping to draw him into an open battle with the townsmen.

After her husband's murder, Constance lives in a state of intermittent awareness and stupor, rigidity and forgetfulness. However, after about nine weeks Constance does regain her health, insists on making a fair adjustment with the squatters over the land issue, and slowly begins her campaign of torture for her husband's killer. Although she goes to Europe for a year, she returns to St. Ann fully aware not only of her purpose to revenge the death of her husband but that his wishes would have been for her to forgive and forget. Her sister, Susan, fruitlessly tries to turn her mind from thoughts of vengeance. So do Dr. Eskridge and Reginald Kent, the Episcopal minister.

Mitchell's own attitude towards his heroine is also interesting to consider, and so is the role of the doctor in the novel. He shifts from his usual pattern of superman-doctor of the Sydney Archer type in *Circumstance,* and Eskridge is not really identifiable as Mitchell's surrogate—although he does come closest to an understanding of the inner turmoil of the main character. She, in turn, confides to Eskridge the nature of her letters to Greyhurst. But Eskridge is definitely not a major character. In other words, it appears that Mitchell was more successful when he remained detached from the central action than when he identified himself with the doctor-hero of his plots.

As for Eskridge's view of Constance, we cite his conclusions after he has made his most urgent plea that she give up her pursuit of Greyhurst: "He began to consider, as he drove into the country, whether he had ever seen any one like Constance Trescot. He at last smiled with the satisfied nod of a man who has found what he was looking for. There was something feline in her delicate ways, her grace of movement, her neatness, the preservation of primitive passions and instincts, her satisfaction in the chase and in torturing. 'Let us add,' said the old doctor, 'the human intelligence, and we have her. . . . It is as near as we shall ever get'."

But Mitchell actually elucidates her character more clearly in his authorial comment and through the events of the story itself. It is abundantly but not obtrusively clear that the irreligious nature of Constance's upbringing, coupled with her passionate nature, has made her a willful, unprincipled, undisciplined woman. She is glimpsed at the end of the novel, a year after the death of Greyhurst, as receiving the news of Reverend Kent's marriage to Susan with a cold sullenness. She has sought in vain to attach herself to Susan, but Susan offers only to help her to help herself. Constance finally leaves the town with a traveling companion, one with whom she has no real friendship.

Constance Trescot's victim has also turned before his death to Dr. Eskridge for help. Greyhurst suffers from vertigo, loss of weight, and a hallucinatory image of the dead Trescot. By accident, Greyhurst had come across a picture of Trescot; and it had so enervated him that he began to have mental visions of the dead man. In the course of this scene, Greyhurst's earlier life is revealed. He sees himself as an "unchecked youth" from which he developed into a passionate, unrestrained adult. This character served to wreck his first marriage and had led to the excesses in his "Western" life before the war. Money had been his chief motive in urging the squatters into the court action against Trescot, but the fatal shooting had tempered his life and he now sought to reestablish himself through a second marriage. Thus the theme of the passionate, undisciplined person as the chief cause of his or her own downfall is reenforced in the characterization of Greyhurst.

Mitchell makes fairly prominent use of nature images—flowers and weather, to orchestrate his theme of psychological revenge. In a passage early in the novel which helps to establish the tone of the whole work, Trescot has been reading to his wife the story of Joseph and his brethren. The forgiveness motif of the Bible story contrasts ironically with the relentless pursuit of revenge of Constance. An earlier quotation has already shown Mitchell's authorial comment on the power of Constance Trescot's sexual appeal, but the following passage is a good example of the author's attempt to symbolize and to dramatize her sexual nature in its destructive possessiveness:

"I am glad I was not Joseph. You will go to bed early, George, and get a good rest."

"Yes; good night."

She kissed him as he sat. As he picked up a book he saw that she had come back.

"Well, dear?"

She seemed to him, as she stood bending over him, like some queenly lily—gracious, sweet, and stately. He said as much, looking up.

"I wanted to kiss you again. That was only ceremonial; this is love."

She threw her arms around him, kissing him passionately. "Now, early; don't read long."

As she turned away, the great red rose she had set on his table of a sudden fell to pieces, the red petals dropping on the table and on the open book he was holding. She raised her hand in a quick gesture, and cried out: "Oh, the rose I gave you!"

Trescot reacts calmly to this meaningful moment; but later, as he sweeps the petals off his open book, he remembers an earlier night in his rooms at Cambridge when a rose had also fallen suddenly to pieces. The incident now gives him a faint sense of unpleasantness, and it seems as "if an unseen hand had crushed it."

Dr. Mitchell, in *Doctor and Patient,* had the following to say about the writing of popular medical treatises on women: "The man who desires to write in a popular way of nervous women and of her who is to be taught how not to become that sorrowful thing, a nervous woman, must acknowledge, like the Anglo-Saxon novelist, certain reputable limitations. The best readers are, however, in a measure cooperative authors, and may be left to interpolate the unsaid. A true book is the author, the book and the reader. And this is not so only as to what is left for the reader to fill in, but also has larger implications." Mitchell used these same guidelines in "reputable limitations" for his fiction.

In contrast to the bare stem and fallen petals of Constance's rose, Susan Hood's growing attachment to Reginald Kent is symbolized as a budding rose; theirs is a love described as fostered by their religious convictions. John Greyhurst, furthermore, ceases to wear a rose in his lapel after the slaying of Trescot.

Mitchell also enriches his narrative by the use of other symbols from nature, and they usually come at crucial moments in the story. The first such significant one occurs when Constance is writing to her husband from the New England coast near Beverly, Massachusetts. As she writes, a dense fog rolls in from the sea. When she goes to the shore and lies on the rocks just above the waves, the fog becomes a great gray wall which shuts out almost all her surroundings. This moment, which comes not too long before her return to St. Ann and her husband's death, symbolizes the complexity of her emotional life and her inability to see into her own life and her passionate involvements.

Earlier in the novel she rejoiced in a great thunder storm as she did in any display of power in nature. At the end of the story, just before Greyhurst's approach to her house for his confrontation with her, a strikingly red sunset occurred. Mr. Kent, also, on his way to see Constance, observes the "splen-

dor of scarlet above the setting sun, and the strange colors cast on the yellow waters of the mighty river below. It was unusual, and, becoming more and more intense, was changing from moment to moment." For Kent, the scene brings a feeling of mysterious awe and glory that he wishes to share with Susan; but he first meets Constance who admits her dislike for red "even when a child." It signifies for her the coming of the night, and she prefers "to live in endless daylight." Thus Mitchell draws his story to a close, with symbolic support from the skyscape; for red is the symbolic color of passion and instinct, as Jung notes in his "On the Nature of the Psyche."

[Mitchell had a] penchant for favoring New England backgrounds for his important characters. . . . They are often people who have come from a powerful colonial ancestry that has included governors and ministers but who also derive from a generation whose fortunes have dwindled and whose offspring are now struggling for a place of importance in life. Ezra Wendell [in *Doctor North and His Friends*] and Roland Blake [in *Roland Blake*] are examples of protagonists whom Mitchell used to illustrate the darker and the brighter sides of human existence. Constance Trescot, who is descended from prominent but ruthless and materialistic New England forebears, boldly contrasts with her own sister, Susan, who has had a different upbringing by her Episcopalian aunt. Thus Mitchell builds a familiar dichotomy between the good and the bad of New England's cultural mores within one narrative.

Constance Trescot represents that side of New England character which has been severed from its spiritual-religious heritage completely. Therefore, Mitchell could find only complete doom for her. When she was trying to please her husband by attending a dying neighbor, the man asked her to read a passage from Scripture. She did so out of a sense of obligation and had come upon the words ". . . the Holy Ghost, the Comforter." She had also read the message, "Peace I leave with you, my peace I give unto you." But neither the dying man nor Constance gained any sustenance from the words. Later, when he asked her to pray with him, she found an excuse to leave him. When she talked over the situation later with her husband, Constance sought some information about the "Comforter"; and George replies in words that have the authority of Mitchell as surrogate: "It is also called the Spirit of Truth, Constance. That which is as old as the world, as old as He who made it, the Spirit before which science bends in worship, that on which the world of morals rests. Isn't that simple enough?" As is customary, the cultureless character in Mitchell's works is especially lacking in literary capability or in receptiveness. It is fair to say that Constance is represented as having come under the wayward, rootless, wildly theoretical and non-dogmatic free-thinking habits of her Uncle Rufus. And it is not difficult to associate Rufus with the mid-nineteenth-century New England of Emerson's time and after, as one for whom formal religion had become a vacuum.

George Trescot, Susan, and Reginald Kent are Mitchell's proof that the Anglican religious tradition is still alive. Moreover, these characters indicate that Mitchell had no bias against the New England type, as did Cooper in several works; but Mitchell is not a propagandist for religion. In this novel the tragic story of Constance Trescot is played out on its own terms. When Mitchell introduces the references to religious and cultural factors in the lives of the characters, it is done to fill out their portraitures; but their actions also indicate and substantiate their cultures as well. George Trescot lives by his ardent faith, but he is no prude. His death results from his efforts to see that more than legal justice prevails in St. Ann.

Greyhurst, probably, comes close to reflecting Mitchell's view of the outlander, culturally speaking, or in other words the man of the South and the West. He attracts because of his showiness and showmanship, but he is a rootless land speculator (tainted with some Creole or Indian blood) whose end is attributed to his unprincipled, passionate, impetuous nature—the masculine counterpart of Constance. Mitchell obviously sees the greatest moral good in following the middle way in moral behavior, as exemplified in the Southern family of General Averill and his wife who have suffered the loss of their sons in the war and who find solace in the Church of England and in sharing in the rebuilding of St. Ann. (pp. 82-91)

I would argue that **Constance Trescot** fails to achieve real tragic import simply because the author lacked enough emotional and dramatic power to sustain his theme, not that he did not know enough about the life of the characters he was representing. It is true that Mitchell wrote the story from the "outside" and that it does have a forceful series of scenes; but the pace of the story, especially in the last stages of Constance's revenge, does not compel the reader's interest. It may be that the very reason for the shortcomings of an otherwise good novel is not that Mitchell failed to give full detail of Constance's change but that he did not portray her with sufficient depth or sympathy. She might have lost some of her human quality if Mitchell had chosen to render her mental disturbance more fully, but the narrative might then also have had to be tightened and strengthened by "inside" rendering of some of the scenes in the manner of James. (p. 92)

Joseph P. Lovering, in his S. Weir Mitchell, Twayne Publishers, Inc., 1971, 176 p.

KELLEY GRIFFITH, JR.   (essay date 1972)

[*In the following excerpt, Griffith considers Mitchell's novels representative of the "genteel romance" that was a popular fictional form from approximately 1890 until 1910.*]

Critics today view S. Weir Mitchell's psychological realism as his main contribution to the development of American fiction. Mitchell's world-wide preeminence as a neurologist and analyst of psychological disorders emphasizes this contribution. He drew upon his medical experience to create such characters as Constance Trescot, a widow neurotically obsessed with revenge; George Dedlow, a quadruple amputee who loses his sense of identity; and Octopia Darnell, whose schizophrenia results from her latent lesbianism.

Yet chroniclers of popular literature place Mitchell within the tradition known as the "genteel romance," which blossomed ephemerally from about 1890 until 1910. This mode of fiction included such writers as Anthony Hope, Richard Harding Davis, George Barr McCutcheon, James Lane Allen, Charles Major, F. Marion Crawford, Mary Johnston, Maurice Thompson, Emerson Hough, Owen Wister, and Winston Churchill. Mitchell himself, although very much aware of the "realism" in his work, said that he hated realism per se. He would take his realism only so far as his sense of

decorum would let him. Beyond that point, he was a writer of "romance."

Few critics have tried systematically and thoroughly to define his romance or, for that matter, the genteel romance. Most critics who place the genteel romance in literary history concentrate on its form. And admittedly form is a blatant characteristic of it. The average genteel romance was set in the past, usually during the American Revolution or Civil War, or during the chivalrous European Renaissance. The hero usually began the romance dispossessed of his estate by a villain who also wanted to dispossess him of the heroine. But after many courageous acts in battle, the hero would defeat the villain and win the heroine for himself. Ethical choices in these romances were simple. The setting was idyllic. Far from being realistic, the hero and the heroine were idealized into almost fairytale form. Emphasis was upon plot and dramatic physical action rather than upon characterization. The lack of relevance and plausibility of these popular romances led critics like Howells and James to mock them and call for greater fidelity to the facts of everyday life.

But of greater historical importance than a formal definition, I think, would be one that includes something about the values underlying the genteel romance. My contention, in fact, is that the value system of the genteel romance is its chief identifying characteristic. Form for the genteel romancer was merely a means to an end—to idealize his values. And the group of writers in the United States who made up the genteel romance "school" all had essentially the same values.

Weir Mitchell's fiction provides a good test for this thesis. His work is typical of the romances popular at the time both in form and content. And his fiction sold well above average over his long career. His most popular romances, **Hugh Wynne, Free Quaker,** and **The Adventures of François,** were best sellers in 1898. He also took greater pains than the other American romancers of the nineties to show a relationship between form and values—a relationship that, in my opinion, they all took for granted. (pp. 247-48)

Mitchell's system of values closely relates to his personal life. His mother, a Presbyterian, made sure that he had a rigid religious training, and his father, a Virginian, made sure that he learned a Virginia "code of honor." As a grown man, he was a fixture of the Philadelphia aristocracy, a social position that gave him numerous prejudices. He believed the upper classes to be innately superior to other people. Though charitable, he was always paternalistic. He believed that women should be subordinate to men. He believed in an extreme sense of propriety, which he associated with being a "gentleman." His sense of "honor" was the essence of his way of life. "The society of that day in Philadelphia [a friend wrote] was the best that the country could provide, and Dr. Mitchell's studies, as well as his native instincts, made him an aristocrat. . . . In his home, correct manners were known and practised. The good social traditions of Philadelphia which are a by-word survived here, for he was their defender and embodiment; his home set the conservative standards of the city" [Ellis P. Oberholtzer, "Personal Memories of Weir Mitchell," *Bookman*, XXXIX (April, 1914)].

Not surprisingly, therefore, the one value under which all others in his romance are subsumed is his belief in the superiority of the aristocracy over the common people. Sometimes his novels seem devoted solely to the didactic purpose of illustrating this belief. **Far in the Forest,** for example, begins with an almost naturalistic statement of how the forest destroys caste: "Caste was unknown. Physical strength and skill with axe or rifle were valued as they must needs be in such a life." But by the absence of "caste," Mitchell means the absence of aristocrats. When some show up, the caste system restores itself. (pp. 248-49)

Mitchell's expression in his fiction of the innate superiority of the aristocracy touches all areas of life, from personal conduct to governmental and social structure. In personal conduct, he lays heavy stress on being courageous, having good manners, and obeying a code of ethics or "honor." But he makes it quite clear that only with good breeding and good "blood" can one have all these attributes to perfection.

A question that Mitchell keeps posing, for example, is, Can one be ethical in a compromising world? Mitchell shows that in his ideal fictional world a "gentleman" can. He creates many situations in which characters have financial crises and as "gentlemen" act ethically. James Penhallow in **Westways** must lay off half his men during a slack business period, but privately he aids them. When he rejoins the army, he sells his share in the iron mill to avoid a conflict of interest. Roger Grace, the wealthy financier in **Circumstance,** is willing to buy stock in a trust company at a loss because he knows that if the stock is suddenly taken off the market, the company will be ruined. Xerxes Crofter in **Characteristics** and **Dr. North** is an unethical Western vulgarian who has won a fortune through immoral business practices. He serves mainly as a foil to North's aristocratic friends, who have no "price."

As for governmental structure, Mitchell believes that the aristocracy should rule, even in democratic America, so he maintains a staunch Hamiltonian Federalism throughout his fiction as the ideal form of government. (pp. 250-51)

Like Mitchell's Federalism, society is a paternalistic structure, with the aristocracy condescendingly "taking care" of the lower classes. In **Westways** Mitchell presents paternalism as an ideal way of life for an entire community. Although Westways is an American town, its social and financial set-up is much like the communities in *Tom Jones* and *Pamela.* The major landowner of Westways (called "Squire" in the novel) owns the principal industry in town, an iron mill, and the townspeople are all economically and socially subservient to him. In fact, only his wife questions his rulings: "Outside of Ann Penhallow's range of authority the Squire's discipline was undisputed and his decrees obeyed." And yet, James Penhallow, the "Squire," is a benevolent man who dispenses his attentions and finances to all the townspeople. They are "his" people and he takes care of them. When the Episcopal church burns down, he builds another one. When the Baptist church needs a new roof, Mrs. Penhallow furnishes the money. When Josiah, a runaway slave, comes destitute from the South, Penhallow gives him money to establish a barber shop. When the poorer people need clothes, the Penhallows have a rummage sale of their old things. When the butcher's business is bad, Mrs. Penhallow buys more meat than she needs. The Penhallows, in other words, hold the town together, and to "hold the town together" is always, in Mitchell's view, a responsibility of the aristocracy.

Finally, Mitchell's patriotism leads him to uphold American aristocracy as superior to European. Democracy and the frontier, he believes, have reduced American aristocracy to its basic elements. European aristocracy, on the other hand, is decadent—it makes manners ends in themselves and thus is inhumane and nonfunctional. Mitchell has George Washington in [*The Youth of Washington*] report that in Europe "men's manners are finished, but so, too, are their virtues."

A striking characteristic of Mitchell's romance is that it supports this aristocratic bias with a rationalism that seems paradoxically to controvert the word "romance." In the late eighteenth and early nineteenth centuries writers like Charles Brockden Brown and Hawthorne associated "romance" with an emotionalism and mysticism that was far from "rational." This difference in philosophical point of view makes the genteel romance quite different from earlier American "romances."

Mitchell more overtly than his contemporary romancers underpins his romance with these rationalistic metaphysics. He believes, for example, in a well-ordered and rational universe, which he equates to a clock: "It is only a great clock, after all," he has one of his characters say in describing the universe. The best way to put ourselves in order with this clock-like universe is to make ourselves like clocks: "We must be like clocks to our great Maker."

Correspondingly Mitchell emphasizes the rationality of man. Man in order to "be like a clock" must be rational. Throughout his fiction Mitchell wages war on emotion. He believes that immorality results from letting the emotions get out of control. . . . (pp. 252-53)

"Self-control," needless to say, is the by-word by which a "gentleman" must live, and it even extends into the realm of love. The love that Mitchell extols is not passionate (ultimately sexual) love but love controlled by reason. Passionate, sexual love, even within the confines of marriage, leads to tragedy or moral disintegration unless checked. James Penhallow in **Westways** "never suspected that to have been less the lover and more the clearsighted outspoken friend would have been better for her [his wife] and for him." The result of Penhallow's surrender to emotion is Ann Penhallow's hysteria and unreasonableness. Constance Trescot loves her husband passionately: "Her love was more passionate than his—of another, perhaps not of so fine a fiber." The result is her moral degeneration after his death. Her monomaniacal hatred of her husband's murderer drives out her compassion and sense of values.

Mitchell's anti-emotionalism also opposes Emersonian mysticism and "mysteriousness" in nature or religion. His love of nature is never mystical. Nature has its "mysteries," but they are scientific mysteries that can be probed and analyzed, and hopefully someday solved by rational processes. One can have a sense of "wonder" at nature. But Mitchell opposes the mystical belief that physical reality is a "correspondence" for a spiritual order and that all reality is "absorbed into a One."

Most important of Mitchell's metaphysical ideas is his belief in evolution. Through it, he applies the Social Darwinian dogma of the survival of the fittest to "explain" the superiority of aristocrats over other classes and to show that such superiority is consonant with the orderliness of a rationally constructed universe.

Evolution, he believes, affects all things and results from the "common sense" of the Creator. The most important effect of evolution on nature is social stratification. Within the human race, some are more dominant than others. These stronger people have "imagination," a quality that Mitchell lets stand for the higher mental abilities of the "fittest." To those who don't have "imagination," Mitchell ascribes animalistic qualities. His villains are always animalistic. Lionel Craig in *Circumstance* is "the unintelligent slave of impulse, and had too little imagination to serve him by predicting unpleasant results. . . . The dog who steals a chop gives no more thought to it than Lionel Craig gave to his theft when he buttoned his waistcoat over the precious autograph of Beethoven's Ninth Symphony." . . . Coffin in *Constance Trescot* has the trust "of a faithful dog" and would just as soon kill a man as not.

Mitchell also places Negroes among the lower orders of human life. John Sherwood's Negro servant has a ferocity "inherited from some faraway African barbarian. I understood it and my man. My own barbaric instincts were merely some thousand years further away" (*John Sherwood*). (pp. 253-55)

The triumph of evolution in the human race is the upper class. For the upper class represents people—families—that have survived and have become the wielders of authority over all other peoples. They are the "fittest." (p. 255)

Ironically, in spite of his professed belief in evolution, Mitchell portrays the social scale as "fixed" instead of evolving. His normal stance is that people in each social position should be happy with what they are and what they have. One of his lower class characters illustrates this philosophy with a parable. A pig wanted out of his field. But after several unsuccessful attempts to get out, it gave up and "after that he was the contentedest pig you ever saw. . . . I guess I'm a good deal like that pig. I've quit trying to get out of my field, and so I just stay here and grin, and take what comes" (*When All the Woods Are Green*). Mitchell believes that people will be much happier if they will remain in their own "fields."

Hugh Wynne, Free Quaker, Mitchell's most celebrated and popular romance, is perhaps the best example of what was appealing to Americans about Mitchell's fiction. It also serves as an excellent illustration of how Mitchell and other genteel romancers manipulated their fiction to glorify their aristocratic, conservative values. Mitchell successfully used a number of techniques to do so. Plot is one of them.

The plot of *Hugh Wynne* is briefly as follows: Hugh Wynne, the scion of an aristocratic Welsh family, grows up a Quaker in Philadelphia. When the American Revolution begins, Hugh joins the new sect of "fighting" Quakers called "Free Quakers." Under the tutelage of his friend, George Washington, Hugh quickly rises through the ranks to become an officer on Washington's staff. After much derring-do, he wins the hand of the aristocratic and coy belle, Darthea Peniston, and fends off the attempts of Arthur Wynne, a cousin and corrupt British officer, to steal Hugh's estate and Darthea. The war over, Hugh and Darthea people his ancestral American home with children and create an idyllic retreat from the foregoing chaos.

The plot of *Hugh Wynne,* in short, perfectly fits the form of the average genteel romance as outlined at the beginning of this essay. But the importance of plot in Mitchell's romances lies less in its form than in how he uses plot conflicts to emphasize the validity of his values. Mitchell's novels are really didactic novels of ideas in which the real conflict is between opposing moral and philosophical forces. Of primary importance to him is the establishment of a conflict between the "good" forces who represent his values and the "bad" who oppose them. Consequently he creates a hero and heroine

who stand almost allegorically for the perfection of his values and villains who are villains because they oppose them. The hero's perfect conquest over the villain and his subsequent happiness with the heroine illustrate the success and efficacy of the author's system of values.

Mitchell's first step in *Hugh Wynne,* therefore, is to give the hero the most important mark of distinction—aristocratic breeding. Hugh, of course, eventually grows up to be strong and courageous and preternaturally wise, but we learn immediately that Hugh is an aristocrat. Mitchell spends the entire first chapter delineating Hugh's lineage. Hugh's stern Quaker father supposedly has put away all class distinctions, but even he tells Hugh that "it is something, in this nest of disloyal traders, to have come of gentle blood." Hugh learns and we learn that his ancestors have consorted with kings and have inhabited for centuries an ancestral Welsh home that looks like a "king's palace." Through this first part of the novel, Mitchell portrays the Quakers unfavorably because of their repression of aristocratic distinctions. The aristocrats like Hugh's mother and his aunt who are proud of being aristocrats are portrayed as mentally sound and wise.

As Hugh moves from his restricted surroundings in Quaker Philadelphia into the broader sphere of the American Revolution the reader becomes more aware of another technique of idealization—Mitchell's use of setting.

Mitchell treats his setting "realistically." In *Hugh Wynne* he lavishes antiquarian attention on particular places in and around Philadelphia. He introduces the reader to the mannerisms and speech of the Philadelphia Quakers and produces exact descriptions of the aristocracy and their homes. In this and other novels, he portrays George Washington with historical accuracy. The key to Mitchell's use of setting, however, is what he excludes from it. He limits his picture of society to the aristocracy. The reader rarely sees members of the lower classes except as servants. Instead, he meets the aristocratic leaders of the American or British forces, whom Mitchell portrays as metaphorically equivalent to Malory's knights of the round table. (pp. 256-58)

Nearly everyone else whom the reader sees fighting the American cause belongs to the old Philadelphia families whose names Mitchell verbally fondles—the Galloways, Cadwaladers, Willings, Shippens, Rawles, Morrises, Pembertons, Whartons, Logans, and Chews. Mitchell even relegates the motivation for fighting the war to aristocratic needs. He says nothing about the ideals contained in the Declaration of Independence or *Common Sense,* nothing about the common man's desire to be free of tyranny. Instead, British malfeasance against America consists entirely of her interference with American trade, by which the aristocrats have made themselves rich.

This restriction of setting not only creates a tone favorable to the aristocratic values Mitchell favors but also establishes an atmosphere of order. Philadelphia's neat street pattern, balanced Georgian architecture, and precise red-brick houses correspond with the social order in the city, the "tranquil sense of unquestioned position." Violent eruptions in society always take place outside the houses of the aristocracy. Inside, life is simple, mannered, and exact. Moral choices are unambiguous. From Mitchell's (and the hero's) point of view, causes like the American Revolution and the Civil War are just without question. Hugh condemns those Americans who remain neutral during the Revolution: "It must be Yes or No, in a war like this." His friend Jack Warder agrees: "It is fortunate when choice is so easy. . . ."

Always, however, there are those who totally reject the "right" choice obvious to the hero and who in so doing reject all of Mitchell's values. These are the villains. They make the genteel romance "work" by giving the plot dramatic physical conflict and by incarnating the forces of evil—i.e., the values that Mitchell dislikes. The most important villain in *Hugh Wynne* is Benedict Arnold, whose villainy stems from his "bad blood" and his prideful attempt to rise above his social place. The foreshadowing of Arnold's dishonor is his courtship of the aristocratic Peggy Shippen. Mitchell says that Arnold is "beneath her" and is "not a gentleman." But Peggy's parents fail to break off the affair, for, as Hugh says, "when a delicate-minded, sensitive, well-bred woman falls in love with a strong, coarse, passionate man, there is no more to be said except, 'take her'." Arnold, recognizing his social inferiority, becomes extravagant and loses control over his "passions." The result is that he abandons the aristocratic values of honesty and patriotism in order to gain wealth and to sate his ego.

The novel's other villain, Arthur Wynne, is an aristocrat—he comes from the European part of Hugh's family—but he is a flawed aristocrat. Mitchell indicates that the best part of the Wynne family came to America, leaving an inferior strain in Wales. Hugh's father is by rights the heir to the Welsh mansion. Arthur is further flawed because he is European. His love of the European vices of gaming and women and ease has taken away his "honor," and he joins Arnold in his willingness to lie, steal, and cheat.

The victory of Mitchell's value system over the forces that oppose it comes at the end of the novel when the Americans conquer the British. Although Arnold's treachery has regretfully brought about the death of the noble André, Providence punishes Arnold. Hugh recalls seeing Arnold after the war with "gloom and disappointment" in his face: "Cain could have borne no plainer marks of vain remorse." Arnold was "poor, broken, shunned, insulted" and "fast going to his grave." Hugh's personal victory comes when he exposes the decadent Arthur and wins Darthea away from him. She in effect is Hugh's prize for being a gentleman of honor. Significantly, Hugh declines the opportunity to win back the Welsh estate. He prefers to remain in America.

The values that Mitchell espouses in his fiction and the methods that he uses to idealize them are characteristic of many, perhaps all, of the genteel romancers of this period. Examples of romances embodying parallel values and techniques abound: Anthony Hope's *Prisoner of Zenda* (1894); George Barr McCutcheon's *Graustark* (1901); Winston Churchill's *Richard Carvel* (1899), *The Crisis* (1901) and *The Crossing* (1904); Richard Harding Davis's *Soldiers of Fortune* (1897); Maurice Thompson's *Alice of Old Vincennes* (1900); F. Marion Crawford's *Saracinesca* (1887), *To Leeward* (1884), *Pietro Ghisleri* (1893), *Katherine Lauderdale* (1894), and *Via Crucis* (1898), and many, many more.

All of these romancers maintain an extreme reverence for strands of European aristocracy, and most of them paradoxically combine this reverence with a super American patriotism. Their love of aristocratic peoples includes an aggressive racism, in which they see nonwhites as subhuman. And their patriotism often condones a white-man's-burden imperialism in which it is right and necessary for the United States to overrun and exploit countries inhabited by nonwhites. In their view Americans are better than other people, and in the United States the lower classes—meaning most of the people—make up an inferior group that should be ruled by those with money and good "blood." The romancers uphold a rationally ordered world in which Providence rewards those aristocrats who keep their "honor" intact. They are very suspicious of emotionalism, sensuality, and the end product of both, a strong sexual relationship.

But most important, they use the romance format to allegorize these values. The hero's journey toward success is like Christian's journey to the Celestial City. The hero and heroine are paragons of the romancer's values. They are aristocrats to perfection and their love is asexual (the romance usually ends with the hero's betrothal to the heroine). The conflict between villain and hero in a setting of pseudo epic scope is really a conflict between two value systems. In the end the hero and the right "side" win and establish forever the goodness of the romancer's values. This marriage of fictional form with the specific values expressed by Mitchell and other romancers is the chief defining characteristic of Mitchell's romance and of the "genteel romance" in general. (pp. 258-61)

> *Kelley Griffith, Jr., "Weir Mitchell and the Genteel Romance," in* American Literature, *Vol. XLIV, No. 2, May, 1972, pp. 247-61.*

SUZANNE POIRIER   (essay date 1983)

[*In the following excerpt, Poirier discusses ways in which physicians represented in Mitchell's fiction reflect his own social values and medical ethics.*]

The power of the physician in the physician-patient relationship has long been apparent to observers and practitioners of medicine. Robert Burton acknowledged it in *The Anatomy of Melancholy* (1621) when he commented that since "the form of health is contained in the physician's mind," patients should exercise "confidence . . . perseverance, obedience, and constancy" toward their physician. Today, as such issues as self-care and patients' rights receive increasing attention, many physicians, such as Howard Brody in *Placebos and the Practice of Medicine* (1980), assume in their patients a "capacity for autonomous, responsible behavior" that enables them to take an active part in the healing process. Yet Brody senses something intangible, "a culturally designated healing context [that itself] can cause changes in symptoms," which still offers physicians a great potential for power over their patients. Over the centuries many physicians, deliberately or not, have abused this power, but many others have labored toward an understanding of their role. Fiction by physicians often reflects this concern. Some of the issues, frustrations, and rewards surrounding the physician's authority can be traced in the writings of [S. Weir Mitchell]. . . . (p. 21)

The topic of the physician-patient relationship seems to have fallen just beyond the boundaries of the variety of critics studying [this writer]. S. Weir Mitchell's non-physician biographers (short, primarily literary studies of Mitchell's work are practically non-existent) write of his medical career but largely record the events of his life and trace the historical and personal themes of his novels; his one physician-biographer gives Freudian case studies of several of Mitchell's more dramatic characters [Richard D. Walter, *S. Weir Mitchell, M.D., Neurologist: A Medical Biography* (1970)]. While all of these writers record the almost magical effect of

Mitchell's personality on his patients, the nature and implications of this relationship are never fully explored. (pp. 21-2)

In 1916 and 1917, shortly after S. Weir Mitchell's death, most medical writing about the physician's conduct dealt with maintaining roles of moral and public leadership. "He must have back of his intelligence character and integrity and high purpose," wrote one physician. Other writers stressed the superior knowledge of physicians but went on to stress the necessity of using such knowledge charitably and honorably: "No doubt he is often powerless to give relief, but a doctor alone is competent to judge of this—not the patient." One doctor described the physician as "a beneficent despot—beloved and feared." Private politics and personal health often became inseparable. The ideal physician "stands for the home and the family," wrote a doctor who went on to argue clearly, though never explicitly, against contraception and abortion. Furthermore, there could be no room for visible doubt. Being too honest with patients usually destroyed their confidence in the physician, thus making it, in one doctor's opinion, "necessary in medical practice to be an actor everywhere and at every step." The overall picture is one of physicians, albeit well-meaning and generally competent, carefully protecting and dictating the physical and moral health of their patients—health by the physicians' own physical and moral definitions.

Finally, one physician from this period complained that only three novelists in the history of literature "have [ever] realized the dignity of medicine" [M. L. Graves, *"Cui Bono—The Doctor and His Ideals," Southern Medical Journal* 10 (1917)]. One of these was S. Weir Mitchell, . . . more famous as a physician than as a writer. Silas Weir Mitchell was one of the founders of neurology in the United States, he was largely responsible for bringing William Osler to Philadelphia in 1884, and he developed therapeutic methods that Freud admitted to incorporating into his own models of psychotherapy. But he was most widely known during his lifetime as the "inventor" of the Weir Mitchell Rest Cure, a treatment which depended to a great extent on the authority and strength of personality of the physician.

The Rest Cure was a regimen of forced rest and feeding to restore sufferers of "neurasthenia," a catchall term for a number of poorly understood nervous conditions. Mitchell believed that nervous exhaustion was linked to anemia: restore the patient's red blood level and the patient's spirits likewise rose. He went to great lengths to ensure such restoration, keeping patients in bed from six to eight weeks, permitting them only to brush their teeth unassisted. Rest was coupled in the treatment with isolation. Mitchell believed that too often family and friends, intrudingly over-concerned or easily manipulated by the patient, were a hindrance rather than a help to cure.

Although Mitchell treated both men and women for neurasthenia, it was primarily women who were prescribed the most extreme isolation—and subsequent dependence on the physician. Thus cut off from contact with everyone except her physician and nurse (who was forbidden to speak about the case with the patient), and unable to do anything to care for or amuse herself, the patient's world came to center entirely around the physician. Such a relationship placed great demands on both physician and patient. Of the physician, Mitchell wrote: "The man who is to deal with such cases must carry with him that earnestness which wins confi-

dence." Of the patient: "Wise women choose their doctors and trust them. The wisest ask the fewest questions."

Such power over his patients did not bother Mitchell because, like so many of his contemporaries, he believed in the virtuousness and good intentions of most physicians. "As a profession," he averred, "it is my sincere conviction that in our adherence to a high code of moral law . . . no like group of men affords as few illustrations of grave moral weaknesses." Mitchell went on to ascribe these noble attributes to the "good" physicians in his novels.

Mitchell's thirteen novels, seven volumes of poetry, and numerous short stories are hardly remembered today although one historical romance, **Hugh Wynne,** was a best seller. At its best, his writing is clever and entertaining; at its worst, it is melodramatic and predictable. Mitchell's most unique novels, ***Dr. North*** and ***Characteristics,*** are "conversational" novels, long reproductions of the intercourse between a group of friends, with only loose plots holding together the evenings and outings of the convivial company. The conversation often lapses into the pedantic, however, in a tone that lacks the easy wit and gentle self-mockery of the garrulous autocrat created by Dr. Oliver Wendell Holmes, of whom Mitchell was a fan and friend.

In these two novels, Mitchell was clearly fictionalizing his own life and friends. The novels' central character, Dr. Owen North, an obvious mouthpiece for his creator, describes himself this way:

> A man of some thirty-six years of age, I was master of three languages, well read in a general way, and, as may have been seen, a practised and interested observer of my fellow men. . . . Mere science had in it for me little that I liked, and it was clear to me that only in my own profession was there what I desired—a combination of ever-changing science, and its constant applications to medicine as an art.

Disease presents to North "an ever-changing science" challenging his imagination and creativity. But the challenge is a uniquely personal one in which he alone seems to confront the enemy. Disease becomes for North a malevolent foe of the *physician* rather than of the patient. Today, North's conviction may sound to us uncomfortably egotistical, as he announces: "What I personally hate is defeat, by death, by incurable ailments. . . . It is, I suspect, the intellectual defeat I so dislike." His words, however, carry the same implications as "the liver in Rm. 256," the quip most frequently used to symbolize depersonalized medicine in the 1980s.

The practice of medicine for North becomes, as he puts it, an "intellectual" battle, a conscious risk-taking, for which a calculated balance between moral and scientific motives is necessary. "Indecision is an awful fool," insists North, but the patient is not totally ignored. An objective understanding of one's own powers and goals should be coupled with an equally objective awareness of the needs of the patient. North criticizes not only the physician who is "too absorbed in the *physical me* to think about that *other me*" of his patients, but also the "soft-mannered and mellifluous doctor" who is so "aggressively gentle" that he will exercise no firmness over his patients. North's concern is for the physician's ability to earn and exercise authority over the patient. That physician is best, he says, who "has the dramatic quality of instinctive sympathy, and, above all, knows how to control it. If he has directness of character too, although he makes mistakes (as who does not?), he will be, on the whole, the best adviser for the sick." Firmness and decisiveness are important to North—not surprising, given the firmness and conviction of North's creator in his own treatment of neurasthenic patients.

The role of adviser in all matters was common to North, as it was to Mitchell and most physicians of his day. When asked by an anxious mother to speak to her daughter, who was intent on attending medical school, North strongly advises that he does "not believe it was best either for the sick or for society for women to be doctors; that, personally, women lose something of the natural charm of their sex in giving themselves either to this or to the other avocations until now in sole possession of man." Although North discusses the value of rest and vacation for overworked businessmen, only once does he advise some form of Mitchell's Rest Cure. He sends an emotional, slightly hunchbacked girl to a German spa to effect a "prolonged separation" from the friends who over-excite her and to whom she is forbidden to write. Sibyl, North concludes, will never be free of her nervousness because her physical condition has weakened her emotional balance, but she does have a hopeful future because she eventually marries a man who will carefully calm her at the first sign of excitement.

It becomes clear while reading any of Mitchell's fiction or nonfiction that he held the general Victorian beliefs about woman's frailty and "place." Such a bias was bound to color his medical advice to women although Mitchell was more sympathetic than most men to women's emotional lives. To women prostrated by the demands of a too-large family or a self-centered husband, Mitchell was often a balm and an inspiration, but to women depressed or anxious because of the roles they were limited to, Mitchell's influence could have disastrous results. Mitchell is one of the few physicians specifically attacked in fiction by other writers, and it is worthwhile to look briefly at these pictures because the main aspect of Mitchell's work presented by these writers is his authoritarianism.

Charlotte Perkins Gilman, social activist at the turn of the twentieth century, divorced her husband when both realized that she could not sanely live solely as a wife and mother. The two of them reached this conclusion only after her treatment by Mitchell, who ordered that she lead "as domestic a life as possible. . . . And never touch pen, brush, or pencil as long as [she] live." This treatment resulted in a "grinding pressure of profound distress" [Charlotte Perkins Gilman, *The Living of Charlotte Perkins Gilman: An Autobiography* (1935)] that eventually found expression in "The Yellow Wallpaper." In the story the main character, who is warned that if she doesn't "pick up faster" she will be sent "to Weir Mitchell in the fall," moves from depression to complete madness. Although she knows that what she needs is "congenial work, with excitement and change," she is forbidden these things. Furthermore, she is not allowed to question her physician. She feels stymied because, as she puts it, "If a physician of high standing . . . assures friends and relatives that there is really nothing the matter with one but temporary nervous depression—a slight hysterical tendency—what is one to do?" She is helpless to pierce the armor of authority. Insanity is her only means of escape or revenge.

The second attack on Mitchell's Rest Cure, if not on Mitchell himself, comes from Virginia Woolf, a twentieth-century British novelist, whose husband, like Sibyl's in Mitchell's novel, spent the whole of their married life safeguarding the equanimity of his wife's emotions. Institutionalized three times by the age of thirty-two for what is now fairly certain to have been manic-depressiveness, Woolf underwent a regimen of total isolation, milk diets, and constant sleep or rest, which continued in varying degrees throughout her life. The treatment clearly echoes Mitchell's therapy, brought in 1888 to England, where it met with wide acceptance. In one of her most famous novels, *Mrs. Dalloway,* Woolf levels an unmitigated attack on the professors of such methods. Again, it is the absolute authority of the physician she criticizes. She creates nerve specialist Sir William Bradshaw, whose own life, and consequently the lives of his patients, is shaped by Proportion: "Worshipping proportion, Sir William not only prospered himself but made England prosper, secluded her lunatics, forbade childbirth, penalised despair, made it impossible for the unfit to propagate their views until they, too, shared his sense of proportion—his, if they were men, Lady Bradshaw's if they were women. . . ."

The necessity or efficacy of the treatments of Gilman and Woolf cannot be judged here. Both women, however, suffered greatly from the administration of the Rest Cure, which was founded on the belief that the doctor always knew—or must act as if he knew—what was best. Any disagreement with the physician on the part of the patient was only proof of the stubbornness of the patient's illness—or of the patient. (pp. 23-7)

> *Suzanne Poirier, "The Physician and Authority: Portraits by Four Physician-Writers," in Literature and Medicine, Vol. 2, edited by Anne Hudson Jones, State University of New York Press, 1983, pp. 21-40.*

FURTHER READING

Brooks, Van Wyck. "Philadelphia." In his *The Confident Years: 1885-1915,* pp. 21-39. New York: E. P. Dutton & Co., 1952.
    Mentions Mitchell's place in the cultural and social life of late nineteenth- and early twentieth-century Philadelphia.

Burr, Anna Robeson. *Weir Mitchell: His Life and Letters.* New York: Duffield & Co., 1929, 424 p.
    Noncritical biography that includes extended quotations from Mitchell's unpublished autobiographical writings.

Burr, Charles W., M. D. *S. Weir Mitchell, Physician, Man of Science, Man of Letters, Man of Affairs.* Philadelphia: College of Physicians, 1920, 31 p.
    Tribute to Mitchell's life and works.

Carman, Bliss. Review of *The Collected Poems of S. Weir Mitchell,* by S. Weir Mitchell. *The Bookman,* New York 4, No. 1 (September 1896): 59-60.
    Favorably reviews Mitchell's collected poetry.

Farrand, Max. "*Hugh Wynne,* a Historical Novel." *The Washington Historical Quarterly* 1, No. 3 (April 1907): 101-08.
    Discusses Mitchell's research techniques and reprints correspondence between Mitchell and history students regarding sources for the novel *Hugh Wynne, Free Quaker.*

Gilman, Charlotte Perkins. "The Breakdown." *The Living of Charlotte Perkins Gilman: An Autobiography,* pp. 90-106. New York: D. Appleton-Century Co., 1935.

Includes Gilman's description of the Weir Mitchell Rest Cure's adverse effect upon her mental and physical well-being.

Howells, W. D. "Recollections of an *Atlantic* Editorship." *The Atlantic Monthly* 100, No. 5 (November 1907): 594-606.
Mentions his preference for Mitchell's early magazine fiction with a medical background.

Leisy, Ernest E. *The American Historical Novel.* Norman: University of Oklahoma Press, 1950, 280 p.
Contains scattered references to Mitchell's historical novels, commending in particular *Hugh Wynne, Free Quaker* for the verisimilitude that resulted from Mitchell's careful research into the historical period in which the novel is set.

Meredith, George. Letter to S. Weir Mitchell. In his *The Letters of George Meredith,* Vol. 2, edited by C. L. Cline, pp. 765-66. Oxford: Clarendon Press, 1970.
Letter of 2 April 1885, largely quoted in the Earnest excerpt in the entry above, thanking Mitchell for a copy of *In War Time* and commending the novel's characterizations.

Quinn, Arthur Hobson. "Weir Mitchell, Pioneer and Patrician." In his *American Fiction: An Historical and Critical Survey,* pp. 305-22. New York: D. Appleton-Century Co., 1936.
Surveys Mitchell's career, noting some characteristics of his major works.

Rein, David M. *S. Weir Mitchell as a Psychiatric Novelist.* New York: International Universities Press, 1952, 207 p.
Discusses Mitchell's application of his scientific and medical background to his fiction.

Richardson, Lyon N. "S. Weir Mitchell at Work." *American Literature* 11, No. 1 (March 1939): 58-65.
Examines Mitchell's process of revision by comparing progressive drafts of the novel *Roland Blake.*

Wagenknecht, Edward. "S. Weir Mitchell: Medicine and Romance." In his *Cavalcade of the American Novel: From the Birth of the Nation to the Middle of the Twentieth Century,* pp. 177-79. New York: Henry Holt and Co., 1952.
Discusses characteristics of Mitchell's fiction, noting in particular the medical and historical nature of the novels. Wagenknecht concludes that "technically, Mitchell contributed little or nothing to the development of the novel."

Walter, Richard D. *S. Weir Mitchell, M.D., Neurologist: A Medical Biography.* Springfield: Thomas, 1970, 232 p.
Biography that includes discussion of Mitchell's fiction.

Williams, Talcott. "Dr. Mitchell as a Writer of Fiction." *The Book News Monthly* 26, No. 2 (October 1907): 89-92.
Positive evaluation of Mitchell's novels, commending particularly *Hugh Wynne, Free Quaker.*

Stanisław Przybyszewski

1868-1927

Polish dramatist, novelist, essayist, editor, and poet.

One of the most influential writers in Polish literature at the turn of the century, Przybyszewski wrote novels and dramas that reflect European artistic and intellectual trends of the era, including the French Decadent movement and the philosophy of Friedrich Nietzsche. Przybyszewski's writings are credited with initiating Young Poland, a cultural movement that rebelled against Naturalism in literature and materialism in philosophical thought, both of which prevailed in Polish letters until the late 1890s. Employing subjective and symbolic forms of literary expression, Przybyszewski's work emphasized a Satanic mysticism and viewed sexual instinct as the primary force in human life.

The son of a village schoolteacher, Przybyszewski was born in Kujawy, a region ruled by Prussia until Poland's independence in 1918. He attended German schools and developed early interests in music, religious studies, and folklore. In 1889 Przybyszewski moved to Berlin to study architecture, changing his curriculum a year later to medicine and psychology. While still a medical student, he began writing *Zur Psychologie des Individuums,* a two-volume psychological treatise in which he developed the view that modern society represses freedom and fulfillment and presented Nietzsche and Frédéric Chopin as examples of artists who sought liberation from social strictures through their works. Przybyszewski subsequently withdrew from his university studies to devote himself to his writing and his interest in the occult. The publication of *Zur Psychologie des Individuums* in 1892 brought Przybyszewski to the attention of Berlin literary society, and he quickly became a central figure among the group of international avant-garde writers and artists who frequented the tavern Zum Schwarzen Ferkel. Among the circle were German poet Richard Dehmel, Norwegian painter Edvard Munch, and Swedish dramatist August Strindberg, who became Przybyszewski's close friend and a strong artistic influence. It was also through this group that Przybyszewski met Dagny Juel, whom he married in 1893. During the 1890s, Przybyszewski published a series of novels typified by *Homo Sapiens,* a work depicting demonic passions and destructive eroticism. The notoriety that Przybyszewski earned for the controversial content of his works was heightened by his flamboyant life-style, particularly by his numerous affairs and several illegitimate children.

Przybyszewski returned to Poland in 1898 to become the editor of *Życie,* an arts and sciences magazine in Kraków. He changed the editorial focus of the journal to reflect his preoccupation with art and published a manifesto titled "Confiteor," which articulated a program of art for art's sake. Soon afterward, Przybyszewski's precepts were adopted as the official creed for the Young Poland movement, and *Życie* provided a forum for the works of Young Poland writers. In 1903 he became widely known as a dramatist through a popular production of his play *Śnieg (Snow)*; thereafter he undertook a series of speaking engagements in Central Europe and Russia. Remaining abroad through World War I, Przybyszewski wrote novels and dramas that were not well received by critics. He returned to Poland in 1918, where he lived in poverty and obscurity until his death in 1927.

Przybyszewski's novels and dramas are notable primarily as illustrations of his studies of psychology and the occult. In these works he portrayed characters possessed by dark psychological forces. Because Przybyszewski's writings posit a libidinal unconscious, critics have compared him to Sigmund Freud. Modern society, according to Przybyszewski, constrains the instincts, and great individuals are forced to convert basic drives into a self-destructive sensuality. In doing so, they approach the state Przybyszewski referred to as the "naked soul," an absolute "primeval source" existing before restrictions were imposed by language and society. The artist best communicates this state through subjective expressions of unconscious forces, rather than through naturalistic portrayals of life. In his best-known novel, *Homo Sapiens,* Przybyszewski used ornate language to trace the dissolution of an artist through alcohol and destructive eroticism. The hedonistic protagonist, Przybyszewski's adaptation of Nietzsche's Superman, provides alternately ecstatic and tormented self-analyses. Przybyszewski's dramas also stress introspection and typically reveal their characters' internal conflicts through monologues. Drawing on conventions of Symbolist theater, his most significant dramas concentrate less on overt action than on evoking an atmosphere of prolonged yearning or anxiety. Such works underscore his synthesis of antinaturalist trends current in European literature at the turn of the century, an achievement for which Przybyszewski is considered one of the most significant modernizing influences in twentieth-century Polish literature.

(See also *Dictionary of Literary Biography,* Vol 66.)

*PRINCIPAL WORKS

Zur Psychologie des Individuums. 2 vols. (essays) 1892
Totenmesse (novel) 1893
Das Werk des Edvard Munch: Vier Beiträge (essays) 1894
De Profundis (novel) 1895
Satans Kinder (novel) 1897
Homo Sapiens. 3 vols. (novel) 1898
   [*Homo Sapiens,* 1915]
"Confiteor" (essay) 1899; published in journal *Życie*
   ["Confiteor" published in journal *The Polish Review,*
   1984]
Dła szczęścia (drama) 1899
   [*For Happiness* published in journal *Poet Lore,* 1912]
"O nová sztukę" (essay) 1899; published in journal *Życie*
Na drogach duszy (essays) 1900
Nad morzem (prose) 1900
†*Goście* (drama) 1901
   [*Visitors* published in *The New York Literary Forum,*
   1980; also published in *Doubles, Demons, and Dream-*
   ers: An International Collection of Symbolist Drama,
   1985]
†*Złote runo* (drama) 1901
Matka (drama) 1902
Poezye proza (poetry) 1902
Śnieg (drama) 1903
   [*Snow,* 1920]
Synowie ziemi. 3 vols. (novel) 1904
Odwieczna baśń (drama) 1906
Śluby (drama) 1906
Gody życia (drama) 1909
Topiel (drama) 1912
Mocny czlowiek. 3 vols. (novel) 1912-13
Krzyk (novel) 1917
Miasto (drama) 1920
Moi współcześni. 2 vols. (memoirs) 1926-30
Mściciel (drama) 1927
Listy. 3 vols. (letters) 1937-54

*All titles are listed as originally written in Polish or German.

†These works are collectively referred to as *Taniec miłości i szczęścia.*

ALEXANDER S. KAUN   (essay date 1915)

[*In the following excerpt, Kaun offers general observations on Przybyszewski's work, focusing on his characterization of Erick Falk, the protagonist of* Homo Sapiens. *For a response to Kaun's comments, see the* Little Review *excerpt below.*]

Homo Sapiens is but a nuance of [Przybyszewski's] multiplex creative spirit, though perhaps a most characteristic nuance. Przybyszewski, like Nietzsche, like Wilde, is a unique mo-

saique, in which the personality, the artist, his life and his works, are inseparable, indivisible units of the wonderful whole. Who can fathom this hellish cosmos, this mare tenebrarum ["sea of darkness"] of the modern man's soul, which the mad Pole has traversed and penetrated to the bottom, and has cast out shrieking monsters and gargoyles illuminated with blinding, dazzling, infernal flames?

I cannot. Perhaps only pale glimpses of reflections.

• • • • •

Those who have heard Przybyszewski play Chopin tell us that no virtuoso can compare with his creative interpretation of his melancholy compatriot. In his profound essay on *Chopin and Nietzsche* I have been impressed not so much with the morbid theory as with the characteristic feature present in all his work—the reflection of his own personality. In his favorite artists, in his heroes, in his women, he has painfully sought an expression of his restless, boundless self. Thus Chopin becomes one of the numerous selves of Przybyszewski. Let me picture the Composer in the light of the Poet.

Specifically Slavic features: extreme subtilty of feeling, easy excitability, passionateness and sensuousness, predilection for luxury and extravagance, and, chief of all, a peculiar melancholy lyricism, which is nothing but the expression of the most exalted egoism, whose sole and highest criterion is his own "I." These, and the profound melancholy of his native limitless plains with their desolate sandy expanses, with the lead-skies over them, have been influences keenly contradicting his flexible, light vivaciousness of the Gallic, his coquettish effeminacy, his love for life and light.

Subtracting the last two strokes, who is it: Chopin or Przybyszewski?

The trait most obviously common to both Poles is the unquenchable yearning, the eternal Sehnsucht ["longing"], which filters through all their productions. In neither of them was it the yearning of healthy natures, in whom, as in a mother's womb, it bears the embryo of fruitful life; it is not the yearning of Zarathustra "in a sunny rapture of ecstacy greeting new, unknown gods with an exalted 'Evoi'!" Chopin's longing, as reflected in Przybyszewski, is tinted with the pale color of anemia peculiar to a representative of a degenerate aristocracy (the Poet's progenitor died of delirium tremens), with his transparent skin projecting the tiniest veins, with his slender figure and prolonged limbs that breathe with each movement incomparable gracefulness, with his overdeveloped intellect which shines in his eyes, as in the eyes of frail children who are doomed to early death. This longing is the incessant palpitation of a nervous, over-delicate nature, something akin to the constant irritability of open wounds, the continuous change of ebbs and flows of morbid sensitiveness, the eternal dissatisfaction of acute emotions, the fatigableness of a too-susceptible spirit, the weariness of one over-satiated with suffering. Yet this longing has in it also wild passion, "the convulsive agony of deadly horror," self-damnation and thirst for destruction, delirium and madness of one who strains his gaze into the vast—and sees nothing.

Indeed I should like to hear Chopin's *Preludes* recreated under the longing fingers of Stanislaw.

• • • • •

Stanislaw Przybyszewski. Do pronounce it correctly, that you may hear the sound of rain swishing through tall grass.

Przybyszewski has come to know himself so thoroughly and unreservedly, and, in himself, to know the modern man of the widest intellectual and artistic horizons, through a long excruciating internal purgatory. From the study of architecture and general aesthetics his restless, ever-searching spirit hurled him into natural sciences in the hope of finding positive answers to his burning questions. He came out loaded with an enormous baggage of facts and information; yet he had not quenched his everlasting dissatisfaction, but had acquired a sceptical "heh-heh" towards life and knowledge. He plunged into psychology, and found Nietzsche—to him the deepest searcher, possessor of the keen eye of a degenerate, which like a wintersun sheds its light with morbid intensity upon snowfields, clearly illuminating each crystal. With a "heh-heh" he dismissed the Loneliest One. For was not Nietzsche driven to create for himself a superman, as a consolation, as a hope, as "a soft pillow upon which could rest his weary inflamed head"? Did he for one moment believe in that ghost which he erected in the heavy hours of despair? Nonsense. Heh-heh. Had not his Falk, [the protagonist of **Homo Sapiens**], been crushed in his struggle to attain liberation and supermanship? Recall Falk's self-rending meditations: "Conscience! Heh-heh-heh! Conscience! How ridiculously silly is your superman! Herr Professor Nietzsche left out of account tradition and culture which created conscience in the course of hundreds of centuries. . . . Oh, how ridiculous is your superman sans conscience!" Thus, step after step, killing god after god, burning his ships behind him, the all-knowing, the all-denying degenerate-nobleman Slav-cosmopolite has ascended the loftiest summit, or, as he would rather say, has descended into deepest hell—Art. An equipment hardly appropriate for an artist who sees "Life Itself" in color and fragrance and petals and varicolored mornings and varicolored nights and Japanese prints and. . . . but you may find the catalogue in the Editor's rhapsody of last month. Przybyszewski's back-ground served him as an Archimedean lever to gauge and fathom the soul of modernity.

• • • • •

Let me attempt to present the quintessence of Przybyszewski's modern Individuum, as he prefers to call an exceptional personality.

He considers himself a superman, aloof from the market-interests of the crowd. He is conscious of the fetters of his instincts and of the gradual sapping of his strength—hence the history of the Individuum turns into a sad monography of suppressed will and distorted instincts, a history of a mountain torrent which cannot find an outlet, and rushes into depth, dissolving obstructing strata, destroying and washing them away, and ruining the structure of the rocks in their very bowels.

Hence the longing for liberation and the yearning for expanse, a perilous "palpitating Sehnsucht and craving of the heights, of the beyond." But this longing has another distinctive symptom: the consciousness of its hopelessness, the clear conviction that the passionately-desired goal is but an idée fixe. In this longing is expressed a spirit that ruins everything in itself with the corrosive acid of reason, a spirit that had long lost faith in itself, that considers its own activity diffidently and critically, a spirit that spies and searches itself, that has lost the faculty of taking itself seriously, that has become accustomed to mock itself and to play with its own manifestations as with a ball; a spirit not satisfied with the highest and finest human perceptions, that has come at last,

after many searchings, to the gloomy decision that all is in vain, that it is incapable of surpassing itself.

Hence the pursuit of enjoyment. But this morbid seeking of enjoyment lacks that direct, self-sufficient bliss that results from the accumulated surplus of productive strength. The modern Individuum is deprived of that healthy instinct, therefore in place of naive joy experienced from the liberation of surcharged power he plunges into self-forgetfulness. All his life is reduced to pure self-narcotization. In the morbid straining of his abnormally-functioning nerves the Individuum-decadent rises to those mysterious borders where the joy and the pain of human existence pass into one another and intermingle, where the two are brought in their extreme manifestations to a peculiar feeling of destructive rapture, to an ecstatic being outside and above himself. All his thoughts and acts acquire a character of something devastating, maniacal, and over all of them reigns a heavy, depressing, wearying atmosphere, like the one before the outbreak of a storm, something akin to the passionate tremor of delirious impotence, something similar to the consumptive flush of spiritual hysteria.

In such clinical terms Przybyszewski sees the modern homo sapiens. Through this prism I perceive his Falk, doomed to utter failure and futility.

• • • • •

Falk an erotomaniac? Nonsense. His sexual relations are as pathological as the functions of his other faculties, not more. In his incessant search for an outlet, for discharge, for some quantity that might fill up his hollowed heart, Falk grasps woman as a potential complement to his emptiness. He fails, naturally. To the artist, woman is a narcotizer and wing-clipper; more often a Dalila or Xantippe than a Cosima Wagner or a Clara Schumann. Neither the exoticism of Ysa, nor the pillow-serviceability of Yanina, nor the medieval fanaticism of Marit, nor Olga's revolutionary resignedness, have the power of checking the hurricane of his questing spirit for more than a moment, such moments when the tormented man erects for his consolation a phantom, be it a superman or a Christ. Falk's quest for self-forgetfulness is futile. He lacks the healthy capacity of us, normal beings, for finding salvation in befogging our vision. No matter how we may indulge in self-analyzation, we usually stop at the perilous point and brake our searching demon with the same happy instinct that closes our eyes automatically at the approach of danger. Falk's mental motor has no brakes; it hurls him into the precipice.

> "I have never suffered on account of a woman," boasts the old rake, Iltis.
>
> "Because your organism is very tough, a peasant's organism, my dear Iltis. Your sensibilities have not yet reached the stage of dependence upon the brain. You are like a hydromedusa which suddenly parts with its feelers stocked with sexual organs and sends them off to seek the female, and then does not bother about them any more. You are a very happy creature, my dear Iltis. But I don't envy you your happiness. I never envy the ox his enjoyment of grass, not even when I am starving."

Przybyszewski's Individuum seeks in woman the miraculous expression of his most intimate, most precious "I." He speaks in one place about the love of the "anointed artist," which is a painful conception of an awful unknown force that casts two souls together striving to link them into one; an intense torment rending the soul in the impossible endeavor to realize the New Covenant, the union of two beings, a matter of absolute androgynism. For such an artist love is "the consciousness of a terrible abyss, the sense of a bottomless Sheol in his soul, where rages the life of thousands of generations, of thousands of ages, of their torments and pangs of reproduction and of greed for life." Now recall Falk's dream:

> He saw a meadow-clearing in his father's forest. Two elks were fighting. They struck at each other with their large horns, separated, and made another terrific lunge. Their horns interlocked. In great leaps they tried to disentangle themselves, turning round and round. There was a crunching of horns. One elk succeeded in freeing himself and ran his horns into the other's breast. He drove them in deeper and deeper, tore ferociously at his flesh and entrails. The blood spurted. . . . And near the fighting animals a female elk was pasturing unmindful of the savage struggle of the passion-mad males. . . . In the centre stood the victor trembling and gory, yet proud and mighty. On his horns hung the entrails of his rival.

The epitome of the sex-problem, heh-heh.

* * * * *

"I don't envy the ox his enjoyment." Przybyszewski despises happiness as something unworthy of an artist. A happy soul, he believes, is a miracle, the squareness of a circle, a whip made of sand. The soul is sombre, stormy, for it is the aching of passion and the madness of sweeps, living over ecstacies of boiling desire, the stupendous anxiety of depths and the boundless suffering of being. For the artist who creates the world not with his brain, but with his soul, all life is one "sale corvée," a filthy burden, eternal horror, despair, and submission, fruitless struggle and impotent stumbling. For this reason love, the greatest happiness for ordinary males, becomes for the artist the profoundest disastrous suffering.

Take away from Przybyszewski his ecstacy of pain, and you rob him of his very essence, of his raison d'être, of his creative breath. When you read his *Poems in Prose* you face a soul writhing in hopeless despair, in futile longing, in maddening convulsions. But you cannot pity the artist. You are aware of the sublime joy in his sorrow, of the unearthly bliss that is wrapped in the black wings of his melancholy. In his poem **"At the Sea,"** the elemental yearning yearing of his soul reaches cosmic dimensions. Only one other poem approaches it in its surcharged grief—Ben Hecht's "Night-Song," if we overlook the latter's redundancy. Allow me to give you a pale translation of the "Introibo" to **"At the Sea"**: . . .

"Introibo"

Thou, who with ray-clad hands wreathest my dreams with the beauty of fading autumn, with the splendor of off-blooming grandeur, with inflamed hues of the burning paradise,—
Radiant mine!
How many pangs have passed as if in a dream, since I saw Thee for the last time, and yet mine heart doth shine amidst the stars which Thou hast strewn in my life, yet the thirsting hands of my blood yearn for the bliss Thou didst once kindle in my soul.
Thou, who in evening twilight spinnest for me with still hands on enchanted harps heavy meditation on moments of joy that have flown away like a distant whisper of leaves,—on suns that, sinking into the sea, sparkle in

the east with bloody dew,—on nights that press to their warm breast tortured hearts,—
Radiant mine!
How many times has the sun set since those hours when with Thy magic songs Thou pacified the sorrow of my soul,—and yet I see Thine eyes, full of moans and sadness, burning in an unearthly rapture, see the radiant hand stretching towards me and grasping mine with a hot cry.
Thou, who transformest stormy nights into sunny days, in the depths of my dreams quenchest reality, removest into an infinite distance all near,—
Thou, who enkindlest in my heart will-o'-the-wisps and bearest unto life black flowers—
Radiant mine!
A thousand times has the world transfigured since Thy look consumed the tarnishing glitter of my soul, and yet I see Thy little child-like face and the golden crown of hair over Thy brow, see how two tears had spread into a pale smile that glowed on Thy mouth, and hear the dark plaint of Thy voice.
Thou, who breakest before me the seals of all mysteries and readest the runes of hidden powers, and in all the madnesses of my life flingest Thyself in a rainbow of blessing from one heaven to the other,—
Never yet has the storm so strewn the rays of my stars, never yet has the aureole played with such bleeding radiancy around Thy head, as now, when I have lost Thee forever.

In another place I called *Homo Sapiens* "the book of the age." Surely there has not been a more stirring work of literature since *Werther*. Will the public respond? Is it true that the wall of American indifferentism is impregnable? I am still optimistic about the intellectual aristocracy of this country; that small circle of the young in spirit, brave searchers and earnest livers, for whom art and life are not merely diversions between meals and business transactions, but the italicized essence of existence. To those few Przybyszewski's book should appeal; those should react. (pp. 17-22)

> *Alexander S. Kaun, "The Ecstacy of Pain," in* The Little Review, *Vol. II, No. 9, December, 1915, pp. 16-23.*

THE LITTLE REVIEW   (essay date 1915)

[*The following comments on* Homo Sapiens *were written in response to Alexander S. Kaun's "The Ecstacy of Pain" (above).*]

[In *Homo Sapiens*] Przybyszewski transplants his readers from their ordinary mental environment into those astral regions where metaphysical subtleties are clothed with reality. Life is dealt with not on the surface strata of its expressions but at its base where motives and ideas and emotions have their source. And in spite of this fact, or rather because of the uncanny clairvoyance of its author there is no perversion or befogging of one's point of view. These nebulous regions are lit up by the ruthless penetration of an artist who is a scientist as well.

One's first sensations are like seeing for the first time with the naked eye the fan of nerves which spread out from the corona radiata, or touching the single nerve trunks with the dissecting knife. In the same manner the pathological Pole brings you into actual contact with the cargos of these nerves, ideas, emotions, sensations. All the concealing layers of evasions and of equivocations have been dissected away; there lies spread out before you sections of naked consciousness. And so subtle has been the dissecting work that there has been no disarrangement and no death. All is still living, still functioning. And your sensation of strangeness, almost of horror, is born out of revulsion against a self-consciousness so intense as to seem almost morbid. "I feel," said a friend of mine, "as if I had been vivisected." Not so much this as that one has been vivisecting. Przybyszewski compels you to co-operate with him in analysing psychological phenomena. At moments you lift your eyes from the page, panting, almost physically exhausted from the effort of concentrating on those tortuous, subtle reactions which occur in the farthest recesses of consciousness and spread upward in waves to the surface, where they often take on curious irrelevant expression.

But that is sheer morbidity, cries your friend the Philistine. It is introspection carried past the point of decency. But to the investigator there is no point past which it is indecent to press. In him there is no affectation of scruple to erect its artificial barricade. He must have transcended all such petty egotism and have depersonalized himself. He is constrained to this by that curiosity which is his master passion, which generates itself and is dynamic in him as hunger or sex are dynamic in the ordinary individual. This curiosity of the artist brooks no bounds, short of the facts against which it brings up abruptly. And so Przybyszewski for all his uncanny subtlety cannot be accused of morbidity since he uses it not to distort but merely to reveal the truth. If he has no false reverence neither has he irreverence. His scalpel, always flashing and leaping, pauses a moment on a state of emotion and, pointing, calls it by name. "For I am I," says Falk. "I am a criminal diabolic nature." Or again:

> And so a certain man is suffering from love induced by auto-suggestion. Very well. But at the same time he loves his wife unqualifiedly. And he loves her so much that there can be no doubt of the reality of his love. In a word he loves both the one and the other.

But such a condition isn't possible, the Philistine will cry out, wounded at his most vulnerable point, his inflexible principles. "A man can't love two women at the same time." This isolated case would undermine the whole monagamistic theory. He sees one of his cherished institutions tottering. And so he takes fright and refutes the fact. "It can't be, it isn't possible." But Przybyszewski continues to stand with the scalpel wearily pointing. "My dear Sir, this is no question of postulates, it's a question of an individual instance. It *is* possible, because it occurs. Falk *does* love two women at the same moment." And the Philistine will doubtless turn away snorting furiously and unconvinced. "Przybyszewski," he will sneer, "that degenerate Pole, always half drunk with cognac, a Slav to boot. What does he know of life or reality? They were all neurasthenics. Look at Artzibashev and Andreyev and Dostoevsky. Yes, let us look at them, and remembering Dostoevsky's epilepsy, remember also Raskolnikov. A criminal's psychology lifted onto paper out of the limbo regions of consciousness by the mammouth Russian's bloody pen. Something more than neurasthenia, this gift of analysis.

What, finally, is Homo Sapiens? Who is this writer-fellow, Falk, with no conscience, with his "criminal, diabolic nature?" Does he only exist to analyse himself, and his tortuous, painful psychologizings? Why is he, what is he?—He is the self-conscious man, par excellence. This book is the epic of consciousness. "The thing must be thought out," says Falk. And nuance by nuance it is thought out, rapidly but faithful-

ly, under your very eyes. You are invited,—no, compelled,—to take part in the operation. Hence your feeling of fatigue. And again, after a page or two, "He examined his own feelings."

"But why a Falk?" the Philistine demands. "Falk is no average man. He is a genius, and as such his psychology is specialized and distinct. Falk is a neurasthenic, victim of erotomania. Even his lucidity is not to his credit. Since he is a writer it is implicit in him, as muscle is in the circus rider. He is bound to analyse his acts, to trace them back to their motives. Falk presents an isolated case. If one is going to deal with consciousness why not choose a less precocious exponent? Why not the everyday consciousness of the average human being?"

And by the same token, why not a Falk, Mr. Philistine, since we are agreed that this is a drama of consciousness. Of what use is the average man in this extremity? The artist is the Homo Sapiens par excellence, for it is in him that consciousness has reached its most complex differentiation. "I am," says Falk, "what they call a highly differentiated individual. I have, combined in me, everything—design, ambition, sincerity of knowledge and ignorance, falsehood and truth. A thousand heavens, a thousand worlds are in me." And recognizing this fact he wrestles with it through some four hundred odd pages. That Falk loved two women, or ten women, is not only possible, but probably inevitable. What in the average man is a temperate reaching out for a few specific joys becomes in a Falk the impulse of his whole being for self-expression. It bursts out along a thousand channels, requiring as many outward aspects as there are sources in his personality. And it is this devious stream of a human consciousness that we are following outward to its expression in words or acts, and backward to its source, as we dissect with Przybyszewski Falk's mental protoplasm.

"Futile," sneers the Philistine, "utterly futile. If that is a Homo Sapiens, give me a subman. Your Falk knew no happiness and he gave none. He only strewed suffering in his wake both for himself and others. He was without scruples and without conscience. Where did he get to with all his differentiation? He wrote a few books, to be sure, but what were they in the scale of the women he ruined, the men he did to death? Even of his own misery? His gift of introspection was a sharp knife turned against himself, since he cried out in the end: 'to be chemically purified of all thoughts.' Homo Sapiens indeed!"

You can see Przybyszewski wearily twisting the scalpel in his nerveless hands, you can see the smile that twists his lips just before they curve about the waiting cognac glass. "No, he was not happy, it is true he did strew misery in his wake. He was neurasthenic and degenerate and criminal. He was all these things and all the other things which you have forgotten or never perceived. For he was Homo Sapiens. And such as he is I have drawn him. Ha, ha—Vive l'Humanité!" (pp. 25-7)

A review of "Homo Sapiens," in The Little Review, *Vol. II, No. 9, December, 1915, pp. 25-7.*

FRANCIS HACKETT   (essay date 1915)

[*Hackett was a respected Irish-American biographer, novelist, and literary critic whose reviews appeared in the* New Republic, *the* Saturday Review of Literature, *and other prominent*

American periodicals. In the following excerpt, Hackett questions the acclaim given to Homo Sapiens *by publisher Alfred A. Knopf and unfavorably reviews the novel.*]

[Przybyszewski], according to Mr. Knopf, is universally conceded to be Poland's greatest living writer; and he advertises **Homo Sapiens** as "a very modern love story" and its hero as a Don Juan, "not even merely the most modern of men, he is the new, the coming man." No enthusiasm for translations can frank this particular kind of nonsense. It is an attempt to plant **Homo Sapiens** in the Nile valley of best-sellers in a manner typically uncritical and questionable. It argues an eagerness for quick success along dubious lines that is absolutely incompatible with the best kind of publishing.

For it is not "universally conceded" that Przybyszewski is "Poland's greatest living writer." He is no more Poland's greatest living writer than Compton Mackenzie is England's greatest living writer, and **Homo Sapiens** is of itself enough to define him as a paste jeweller. As an erotic production, it has popular possibilities, and if to be erotic is the sign of "extreme modernity," it is extremely modern. But it is erotic in rather a literary way. No one, I suppose, will contend that because the truth is usually suppressed about sex in literature, every outspoken version of sex in literature is therefore to be immune from criticism. A superheated version of sex, a version concocted in the imagination, is certainly no more agreeable to the true libertarian than to the pious parish priest. And **Homo Sapiens** presents, as I see it, just that dilation on the frantic excitements of sex which comes from writing out of the imagination. The mind of this highly consonantal Pole has been fed on literature. His "extensive philosophical and esthetic education" has plumed him with grand notions of what life among the literati and illuminati might be. He thinks up the most prodigious café conversations; and in addition the most swooning dances, the most pregnable virgins, the most heartrending suicides, the most sumptuous mistresses, the most indefatigable appetites; and he parades them all in a crackling, self-conscious, perfect-devil manner, with precipices, whirlpools, storms, oceans and cataclysms being leaped, swum and encountered by an irresistible Nietzsche-quoting youth. If this is the best that his country can do, black is the night from Pole to Pole.

Taking pure love to be the result of conforming his hero A and his heroine B, Przybyszewski conceives that B has damaged her value for A by a former relation with C. C is so miffed by the conjunction of AB on the other hand, that he kills himself. As A sees it, AB—BC is unhappiness. So he tries AD, but D learns of the AB relation and drowns herself. Thereupon he resorts to E. E, however, hears of B, and is heartbroken. And when B in turn learns of AD and AE her love instantly expires. In the end A realizes the folly of all mutable relations and at the last moment picks out a safe and immutable love in the person of a quite vague Revolutionary Cause.

It is unfair to **Homo Sapiens** to imply it is uninteresting. It is flashily interesting, rapid and vivid. It is the youthful experiment of a gifted man. But whatever its stylistic merits in Polish, it appears artificial and jerky in English, and deficient except in introspective and erotic intensity and a cleverness of invention. Berlin is the scene of most of the story, though the long episode detailing the seduction of Narit is at the country home of the hero Falk. The atmosphere is that of literary and artistic student life, a Bohemia in which the social epileptics of Falk have a certain credibility. The humanity in which

Russian novels are steeped is totally lacking in this febrile Polish production. It is similar to Russian fiction only in allowing its characters to ask that question so seldom posed in American fiction, the question of the meaning of life. By the mere fact of posing that question at all, **Homo Sapiens,** imitative as it is, has a place in a great tradition. (pp. 150-51)

Francis Hackett, "A Pole Discovered," in The New Republic, *Vol. V, No. 58, December 11, 1915, pp. 150-51.*

BOGDAN CZAYKOWSKI   (essay date 1966)

[*In the following excerpt from an essay comparing Przybyszewski's poetic theories with those of his contemporary Zenon Miriam-Przesmycki, Czaykowski outlines Przybyszewski's aesthetic theories in the context of the Young Poland movement.*]

Various terms have been used to characterize the period in Polish literature known as the "Young Poland" movement: decadence, neoromanticism, modernism, parnassism, symbolism. Each of these terms describes some aspect of the movement; yet taken together they do not give a complete picture of the esthetic views of the representative writers. Moreover, the usefulness of these terms, and indeed the very existence of a literary movement, were denied by the Young Poland writers themselves, who adhered passionately to the principle of individualism in art and who abhorred "the spirit of regimentation."

Yet the period is not devoid of poetic theories, or programmatic writings, whose impact was similar to that of the poetic manifestoes of the 1920's. Two writers in particular influenced contemporary esthetic attitudes and poetic practice: Zenon Miriam-Przesmycki and Stanislaw Przybyszewski. Both shared certain assumptions and viewpoints, yet their poetic theories differed considerably, so much so, in fact, that their writings illustrate clearly two widely divergent trends within the movement. And although they were not the only spokesmen for the young generation of writers—one could mention, for instance, Artur Górski, whose articles entitled "Młoda Polska" in the Cracow Życie (1898) in fact established the movement's name—their theories were by far the most significant and illuminating among those propounded by the Young Poland writers. (p. 45)

Przybyszewski came to Cracow in 1898, at the invitation of a number of writers (Przesmycki among them) to take over the editorship of Życie—already a famous man, the man whom "the Germans considered a genius." The small, ancient town of Cracow witnessed for a while scenes of wild enthusiasm for this genialer Pole ["brilliant Pole"]. But this popularity rapidly changed into notoriety. He shocked by his drunkenness, his unconventional manner of life as well as by his novels, in which the erotic and pathological went hand in hand with lyricism, bathos and mysticism. His satanism, his obsession with sex, and the tragedies of his married life made of him in the eyes of the public a truly demoniac personality. This popular picture of Przybyszewski was not altogether untrue, and his biography and letters make fascinating reading.

His fame as a writer in the German language, and the role he played in the Young Germany movement, have been grossly exaggerated (not least by himself). Yet he was a European figure, a close associate of many German and Scandinavian writers and artists, was read in Germany and Scandinavia, had a bout of popularity in Bohemia, and exerted some influence in Russia.

His mind was lively and alert, but hardly educated; he was moody, irrational and somewhat unbalanced. He amassed a considerable amount of knowledge of the most diverse kind—from medicine, which he studied for a time in Berlin, to medieval mysticism and occultism; he was widely read in contemporary literature, and he had the ability to make use of his knowledge in an impressive way. He was strongly influenced by Nietzsche (which he denied), Huysmans, and a host of other writers and thinkers, and his views on art were by no means original. He was also a talented pianist, and had a passion for Chopin's music.

Przybyszewski's esthetic theory, first expressed in Poland in his manifesto **"Confiteor,"** and developed in shorter and longer studies, was based on the belief in a transcendental reality as opposed to the illusory reality of the senses and of the brain. This transcendental reality he understood as an absolute consciousness, of which the consciousness of the individual, the soul incarnated, was only a very small part. Beyond the thin crust of the conscious life of the individual soul, he asserted, there is a whole *mare tenebrarum* ["sea of darkness"], whose manifestations only seldom come to the surface, in the form of dreams, vague reminiscences, premonitions. The absolute consciousness has none of the divisions into which the senses and the rational mind have divided reality: time and space, colors and sounds, smell, cause and effect—all is one. There is an absolute continuum, sound is both color and smell. In other words (Baudelaire's): "Les parfums, les couleurs, et les sons se répondent" ["The fragrances, the colors, and the sounds themselves reply"].

On the basis of this doctrine Przybyszewski defined art [in **"Confiteor"**] as "the recreation of that which is eternal, independent of change or contingency, free from the fetters of time, space, in short it is the recreation of the essence, i.e. of the soul . . . as it reveals itself in the universe, in humanity or in the individual." Consequently, art is the Absolute, it has no purpose apart from itself and should not be subordinated to anything, whether it is ethics, morality, society, patriotism or entertainment. To use art for social purposes is to degrade it, it is "to drag it down from the heights of the Absolute to the miserable contingency of life." Art is above life. [In a footnote, Czaykowski adds that "Przybyszewski was even more critical of 'democratic art,' art for the people. It consisted, in his view, in the vulgarization of the artist's means of expression. It is in the nature of art to be difficult, it cannot be therefore made easy. And he added: 'The people do not need art, but bread, and when they get their bread, then they will find their way to art by themselves'."]

The only "criterion" of art is the "power" of "energy" with which the life of the soul manifests itself. And hence everything is the province of art: beauty and ugliness, virtue and crime. The artist, Przybyszewski wrote, should treat all these manifestations of the soul on the same level of importance, as long as they are *powerful* manifestations.

Art thus understood became for Przybyszewski "the highest form of religion, and the artist its priest." "He is personal only through the internal power, with which he recreates the states of the soul, otherwise he is a cosmic force, through which Eternity and the Absolute manifest themselves." Przybyszewski identified the artist with the prophet, the magician and sage, and went still further in calling him "ipse philo-

sophus, daemon, deus et omnia" ["himself the philosopher, demon, god, and all things"]. Hence not only is art a-moral, the artist, too, stands above morality, above society, life and fame.

This extreme form of the principle of individualism in art, a principle in many ways central to the Young Poland esthetics, had little to do with the concept of personality. On the contrary, the artist was unique precisely because in his art he was "impersonal" to the point of being an agent of profound forces, a medium through which the voices of the Absolute spoke. In Przybyszewski's view the artist's uniqueness was the uniqueness of the chosen prophet and the fact of being chosen absolved him from all social and moral obligations. The personality of the artist was a consequence of his being an artist, and not vice versa.

Przybyszewski's theory of poetic language reflected a preoccupation similar to that of Przesmycki, namely, the desire to free poetic language from the supremacy of thought. This preoccupation was the consequence of a much wider trend, the upsurge of anti-rationalism in Europe generally. In Poland the trend found a strong resonance, in which Przybyszewski's voice was one of the loudest. While Przesmycki's anti-rationalism was confined mostly to his view of art,— Przybyszewski's pervaded his whole outlook. The difference should be stressed. Przesmycki was not against the rational mind as such, but was concerned with defending the value of poetic or esthetic perception (through mysticism) and wanted to purge poetry of abstract ideas so as to preserve its autonomy both as art and as a distinct contribution to human knowledge. Defending the rights of the imagination, he found in Maeterlinck's concept of the symbol not only a means of upholding the autonomy of art, but also a perfect solution for reconciling the reality of the senses and of the mind with the transcendental reality, the concrete with the infinite. Przesmycki's anti-rationalism was highly intellectual and his concept of the imagination provided a suitable meeting-place for the emotional and the rational.

Przybyszewski's far more extreme irrationalism was reflected both in his "psychology" and in his notion of the creative process, and his attempt to purify poetic language of all thought was radical. His concept of the "metaword" (*metaslowo*) did not even possess the mediating powers of the symbol. In this respect he was much closer to the Expressionists and the Dadaists, than to Przesmycki, who placed greater emphasis on images than on sounds. Similarly, while Przesmycki was interested in literature as art, Przybyszewski's high praise for Mombert was that he had "surmounted literature."

Theories of poetic language often postulate a certain concept of man, and are based on some kind of pseudo-scientific linguistic mythology. This is equally true of Przybyszewski as of many other esthetic writers.

If the irrational, the purely emotional in man is the most valuable from the point of view of art, then the poet should aim at a language free of all rational, logical rigors and associations. But then such a language belonged already to the primitive man. From this it easily follows, that the artist should therefore try to give back to words their primordial character. But how is one to define this long-forgotten quality? Przybyszewski's answer was contained, characteristically enough, in his rhapsodic study of Chopin's music.

In this study Przybyszewski introduced the concept of "meta-music" and—on analogy—the concept of the metaword. And in doing so he gave an imaginative account of what had happened when man created his first word:

> When the first man was making the first word, he did not imitate the sounds of nature, he did not name with a word this or that external object, but:

> Something made a deep impression on his soul. A primeval emotion, whether of passion or vengeance, was welling up in him, until he heard himself give forth a long cry, of astonishment, fear or desire.

> The primitive man did not speak his emotions, he sang them, for long stretches of time, drawlingly, he sang out the whole duration of his emotion.

> This primitive way of expression, of direct recreation of emotions in the form of sound is what I call the metaword, or the metasound.

Some feelings, however, were either so powerful, or so indefinite and fleeting, that even this "singing" language could not express them. It was then that the miracle happened: man created his first musical instrument and produced music for the first time.

Thus, in a way, Przybyszewski too regarded music as that art to which poetry should aspire: "the specific essence of each emotion is the sound and everything can be reduced to it as to the simplest, atomic unit . . . ."

Recalling what he termed Plato's image of ideas as the singing spheres, Przybyszewski capped his argument with his own account of the Fall of Man, which for him consisted in the incarnation of ideas in words:

> . . . as soon as we felt the need for forms and shapes, we became anxious to see ourselves in flesh, and thus we fell down to earth, and ideas fell down with us: we became flesh, and the incarnation of ideas and their fall was consummated in the word. Only some ideas preserved the memory of their ancient state and sing even now.

The second Fall of Man took place when words became "socialized", when they became "names." The artist, urged Przybyszewski, should try to remedy this and return words to their state of emotional expression. For the poet is a man

> who in the process of creation is able to give to a word, or to a sound an emotional character . . . for whom the word is not a symbol, not a name, but a direct expression of emotion, and the sound is not just one of the conventional forms which this or that emotion fills, but a direct recreation of even the smallest glimmer of emotion—such a man is the creator, since he creates the metaword or poetry.

It is clear that for Przybyszewski the metaword and the symbol were two different things. This is explicit in another passage, where Przybyszewski lamented the loss of the metasound, whose place was taken by the symbol, "a simple mathematical sign"—as he called it.

Przybyszewski's most characteristic feature was his anticonventionalism. He was clearly one of the outsiders, to whom there was nothing sacred. Much of his theory can be explained simply in terms of the antagonism he felt for society, and it is not so much the desire to understand art, as the concept of the artist that is central to his esthetics, in which the principle of art for art's sake acquired the idiosyncratic

meaning of artist for the artist's sake. The consequence of Przybyszewski's theories had to be complete anarchy, whether of form or behavior. Yet his concept of poetic language was symptomatic of an important trend, and his elaboration of it is not devoid of poetic beauty. The myth is an attractive one, and quite fundamental. (pp. 48-53)

Bogdan Czaykowski, "Poetic Theories in Poland: Przesmycki and Przybyszewski," in The Polish Review, *Vol. XI, No. 3, Summer, 1966, pp. 45-55.*

MARIA KUNCEWICZ (essay date 1969)

[In the following excerpt, Kuncewicz examines Przybyszewski's Zur Psychologie des Individuums.]

[Przybyszewski's] *Zur Psychologie des Individuums* materialized in an atmosphere heavy with smoke, alcohol, and poverty. The first part, *Chopin und Nietzsche,* was written in 1891, the other, entitled *Ola Hansson,* a year later, and the style of the whole is a mixture of poetic licence, medical student's phraseology, and the philosophical velleities of the age. Its reasoning focuses on two points:

1) the modern individual, as distinct from a representative of the more open, less systematic ages, is subject to so many social restraints that his will for power has to converge on himself, which then breeds pathology. The sadness of seeing one's deepest instincts wither or degenerate finds its compensation in the feeling of superiority over the masses. Men with strong personalities are consumed by a thirst for liberation, while at the same time lacking faith in the possibility of individual freedom.

2) Chopin and Nietzsche are the most perfect representatives of the organic split in the modern individual's psyche. Przybyszewski begins by establishing an analogy between the progress of mankind, and the medical distinction of the two types of illusion: those resulting from a free flight of imagination, and those from compulsion. He believed that Kant and Schopenhauer made their mistakes, fully convinced that they were drawing exact conclusions from their premises. But did Nietzsche really believe in the vision of the superman he had created in his hours of despair? The same distinction can be applied to individualism in the past and in the modern epoch. Mass psychosis which had resulted in the Crusades, the religious wars, and finally the French Revolution, was due to the hypnotic power of individuals endowed with fanatic faith and a brutal creative urge.

Apart from the will for power, the individualism of the present day has nothing in common with this kind of pure frenzy. As he feels the creative urge, a modern individual automatically becomes a pariah, and he knows it full well. His longing for freedom is coupled with realization of the desire's futility. Hence self-irony, hence the mad pursuit of pleasure as means of producing illusions. The creative individual of today receives no spontaneous stimuli; he replaces "the naïve joy of using the overflow of his powers" by the wish for oblivion. Life turns into a perpetual search for oblivion. The morbidity of such pleasures can be seen in the way in which they are experienced.

> In the painful tension of his ineffective nerves the sick individual rises to that secret point where joy and suffering meet, where they become, in their extreme form, a kind of fatal ecstasy transcending and eclipsing one's self. Then all the thoughts and

acts assume the appearance of a destructive mania, the atmosphere of an imminent storm envelops everything, . . . throbbing with vibrations of a mad importance . . ..

Przybyszewski believed that, physiologically speaking, the sharper the artificial stimuli which make people realize the "vegetative" side of life, the stronger the expression of life's pleasure and pain, and the more chances the individual has to survive and perfect the species. A modernist represents the ferment that forces the indifferent mass to climb to a higher degree of awareness. Thus, by making life tragic through sickness and alienation, Nature sacrifices the Individual for the sake of the crowd. His personality is used as an instrument in the same way as all life is turned, for the good of mankind, into one huge sexual process.

Przybyszewski himself was the best example of this thesis. Kazimierz Wyka in his work [(in Polish), 1959] *The Polish Modernism* assigned to him the role of Winkelried in the Polish letters of the period.

> Marching in the first rank, he received in his breast the most vicious blows, he never matured, never changed, he remained petrified in that one gesture; in a sense he was a sublime figure.

On the strength of Przybyszewski's later contribution to Polish culture, this opinion was formulated after almost half a century had elapsed since his German debut. But already then, in 1892, the poet seemed to understand his own nature and its potentialities.

As he passed to the analysis of the antinomies in the character of his protagonists, he stressed the Franco-Polish origin of Chopin, and, although he never mentioned it in the context, we know from his other writings how receptive he was to the legend about Nietzsche's allegedly Polish forbears.

Tęsknota (the Slavic variety of the German *Sehnsucht,* French *Cafard* and English *Spleen*), a blend of objectless longing, regret and pantheism, appears as the most obsessive motive in Przybyszewski's early work. He consequently projected it onto the masterpieces of his two favorite artists. He emphasized their capacity for sombre dreams, and "the savage passion of a hysterical soul for self-destruction." "This laughing chord amidst the gloom of an autumnal night explains better the obscure side of human sensitivity than the whole wisdom of our psychologists," Przybyszewski explains about a chord springing from the painful monotony of the *sostenuto* part of the *Scherzo* in B-minor.

In Przybyszewski's opinion, while Chopin reveals in sound the secret processes going on in the depth of the individual soul, Nietzsche provides them with a philosophical commentary. But they both operate in the twilight zone where sensations and moods float before developing into conscious acts. They are both—Chopin and Nietzsche—pathologically perceptive, and quite aware of the hermetic quality of their respective dreamlands.

Examining further the psychology of the "twin geniuses" as well as his own reactions to Chopin's music and Nietzsche's thought, Przybyszewski obviously wished to integrate them into the decadent world of the nineties, and thus justify his and his friends' excesses.

In *Thus Spake Zarathustra,* not any less than in the *Scherzo* in B-minor, he was above all impressed by the passionate and symbolic character of the authors' effusions.

> In their macrocosmic vision also the element of sex finds its artistic expression, if only in that problem of unassuaged hunger for carnal pleasure which means joy of creation, the eternal affirmation of one's self . . . the commerce of sexes being the most elementary biological law. . . .
>
> Art is intoxication . . . and it must give intoxication . . . intoxication with sex . . . intoxication with twilight and a sultry night in July, intoxication with youth and spring . . . inspiration and Dionysian fury, longing and pain. . . .
>
> Chopin and Nietzsche—two artists of intoxication—will offer us new art; art will cease to be divided into different branches . . . when our senses become so subtle that every word will possess its particular color and sound value.

How far we are from Büchner and Zola! And how near to Plato's ideal essence of all things, how near to Hegel and his ethical ideal, the same for the individual and society; how near to the "objective idealists" and their belief in a human order which man does not create, only discovers it for himself! How near to heresy!

The essay on Ola Hansson begins with the question: "Where is my I?" We learn from Maxime Herman's work that, at the time when the old religion of God was changing into the worship of I, Przybyszewski read the collection of Ola Hansson's stories entitled *Pariah,* dealing with psycho-physiological matters. Przybyszewski explains that:

> It is a study of a brain whose every center had become independent of the other centers; of an abnormally developed soul, a soul where all kinds of eruptions occur without sufficient cause, and where a luminous point can become a limitless sea.

Of course, his interest in Ola Hansson, enhanced by the latter's high praise of the Chopin-Nietzsche parallel, would never have been so intense without the climate of *Lebensangst* ["life-anxiety"] pervading the city of the Hohenzollerns at the dawn of the mechanical age and the upsurge of new social forces. In the *Götterdämmerung* embracing Germany as the great architect of its unity, Bismarck, was ending in Friedrichsruhe his angry years of retirement, "Kaiser der Reise," William II, made his entry on the world scene; he sailed the seven seas, delivered speeches, offered histrionic gestures, while on the empty Bavarian throne the ghost of lunacy watched. In that climate the Berlin bohème felt excited, but insecure. The government balanced precariously between liberalization and a swelling wave of chauvinism. The anti-Polish trend deepened as the Ostmarkverein was founded with the approval of the Kaiser. Divided into two blocs, the Triple Alliance, and the Franco-Russian entente, Europe represented one huge military camp. The rapid progress of colonialism revealed the misery and the savage splendor of what we now call "the third world," creating new political problems and new poetic values. Exoticism in the arts acquired a sharper taste. The "Family of Man" expanded, long vistas opened on a dramatic future, and Baudelaire said:

> Il est plus difficile d'aimer Dieu que de croire en lui. Au contraire, il est plus difficile pour les gens de ce siècle de croire au Diable que de l'aimer. Tout le monde le sent et personne n'y croit.

["It is more difficult to love God than to believe in Him. Conversely, it is more difficult for people of this century to believe in the Devil than to love him. Everyone senses his presence and no one believes in him."]

The budding "Polish Satanist" not only felt the Devil, he also believed in him. Nietzsche pleased him because of his regard for the outcasts. Berlin at the time counted a million and a half inhabitants, and the echo of their philistine voices, as it penetrated the fumes of drunkenness at the "Black Piglet," sounded to a Polish ear like the bleating of demons. The mists of the Gopło Lake [near Przybyszewski's birthplace in Poland] seemed a veil over a paradise lost, and Przybyszewski's heart went out to another exile, another victim of reactionary gods, Ola Hansson, the Swede. Sweden, then, was indeed fighting bitterly the spirit of democracy and its upstart, free thought. Swedish public opinion at that time remained puritanical and aristocratic. It did not approve of such novels as *Sensitiva Amorosa*. [Przybyszewski explained in his memoirs, **Moi współcześni:**]

> Ola Hansson, one of the most wonderful sons of Sweden, managed to escape from his country on the eve of the action brought against him as author of a novel. I said "one of the most wonderful sons" which might sound an empty phrase . . . yet Hansson really was wonderful not only as an artist, but also as a man. Owing to the terror to which a creative mind is subject in Sweden, the greater the talent, the easier it succumbs to a sickness bordering on moral insanity . . . .
>
> In this respect Ola Hansson presents an exception: childishly naive . . . he goes through that poor life of his like a sleepwalker . . . .

When actually writing the essay on Hansson, Przybyszewski, caught as he was between symbolism and naturalism, defended his friend's deterministic point of view which soon was to serve him so well in his own fiction. He found another affinity in the formative effect of the *genius loci*. Extremely sensitive to it himself, he had already stressed the influence of the Slavic plain on Chopin's music. Now he studied the charm of Scania, the native province of Hansson, to show how, through a kind of mimicry, the Swede in his innermost mind had become very much like his country's poetic aspect.

Using further the subject as a springboard for conclusions which he drew from his scientific pursuits, Przybyszewski proceeded to a rapid survey of mankind's psychological history.

> The primitive man reached for impressions automatically, through reflexes . . . he was nothing but an individual. . . . But gradually he learned to store impressions. . . . Between impression and reaction a considerable lapse of time developed, and the chain of consciousness was formed. Man learned how to calculate and compare; series and cycles emerged; individual became personality.

In time, individuality began to interfere with personality. The pure sexual urge was complicated by the impressions stored in the brain. Country, family, religion and nature, all the sentiments related to procreation and conservation, came into play.

Przybyszewski's contention reads that the brain of a modern man does not record impressions on their objective, only their sentimental value. That is why two totally different impressions, as for instance the brow of a girl and a landscape, can be associated. And this is also, according to Przybyszewski, the artistic secret of Nietzsche's *Zarathustra,* and Ola Hansson's whole work. Poetry must become psycho-physiological, which means that an external fact should be expressed through an inner event. Przybyszewski ventures the following definition of symbol: a symbol is a fragment of Nature transformed into nervous vibrations, an impression that strikes at the central junction of all senses so as to make the brain vibrate in its entirety. The best example of this kind of symbolism is *Sensitiva Amorosa,* while in *Pariah* Ola Hansson had demonstrated what was accidental in the ego, and how life developed in the subconscious. In sexual life—which is the theme of *Amorosa*—everything develops beneath the ego, not in it.

Now comes Przybyszewski's personal confession: Through a woman he loves himself; himself attuned to his highest tensions. Why he loves this woman, and not another, does not however depend solely on his system. It depends on the intensity with which he can enjoy a form without the slightest displeasure. Within the sphere of excitement where he experiences sensations of pleasure, there is another, even narrower sphere, in which everything appears as the most intense sensation. The woman enters this narrower frame with all that makes her; *he loves her as the total image of what gives him the most perfect happiness.*

In the same *Sensitiva* Przybyszewski found a confirmation of his favorite theory that *everything in love happens on the borderline of pleasure and pain.* Behind the author's pain the critic discovers Scania, Ola Hansson's morbid, misty country, (just as on the shores of Gopło his own pain had originated, and in the Mazovian fields the nostalgia of Chopin). "The interior world of Ola Hansson is immense because he does not distinguish between normal and pathological things," and as an afterthought, Przybyszewski adds: "A personality like his, not heeding the practical and moral criteria, cannot be understood by a contemporary European who does not yet distinguish the exterior from the inner world."

An ardent, perhaps unconscious, follower of Fichte in his negation of formal logic, Przybyszewski, in writing his study of Hansson, was motivated by the wish to obtain still another corroboration (as it had been in the case of Nietzsche and Chopin) of his theory of the individual and the personal. He praises the Swedish author for exposing the fact of "interior causality being developed in him to its ultimate limit" as he makes of personality a sort of constitutional monarch who tries in vain to master the murky sentiments of the individual.

In one of those lyrical outbursts with which the medical student loved to punctuate his dissertations, he said: "I, the beginning and the end of existence, I enter nothingness." A few lines further: "all that exists, exists only in our head . . . we exist only in our ideas (representations), we are worlds completely closed, completely isolated."

As one now considers Przybyszewski's contribution to the psychology of the individual, one can hardly help visualizing a bowl full of morsels, some of them leftovers from earlier meals, some freshly cooked, swimming in a highly seasoned poetic sauce redolent of sex and metaphysics, while the fumes reach out into the future.

Przybyszewski's idea of the ego is fragmentary, and the structure of his essays somewhat incoherent. The individuality-personality problem was not his discovery, but he presented it in a new form. Although obviously related to his predecessors, he, like Nietzsche, transposed their values onto a poetic plan. Maxime Herman says about the early efforts of the Polish author that "he was continually attentive to the fluctuations of the individual underworld. This estranged him from the naturalists and brought him nearer to the symbolists and the neoromantics." It also made him—I should add—a typical representative of the European malaise at the end of the last century. (pp. 13-19)

Maria Kuncewicz, "A Polish Satanist: Stanisław Przybyszewski," in The Polish Review, Vol. XIV, No. 2, Spring, 1969, pp. 3-20.

DANIEL GEROULD (essay date 1985)

[*Gerould is an American dramatist, critic, and translator who specializes in modern Polish drama, particularly the works of S. I. Witkiewicz. He is the coauthor of a biography of Przybyszewski's daughter, the dramatist Stanisława Przybyszewska, and has translated Przybyszewski's* Visitors *into English. In the following excerpt from his introduction to* Doubles, Demons, and Dreamers: A Collection of Symbolist Drama, *Gerould discusses* Visitors.]

The dramatic epilogue *Visitors*—the last in a series of four plays collectively titled *Love's Dance of Death*—is the theatrical counterpart of a painting by Przybyszewski's friend Edvard Munch. In works such as *The Dance of Life and Death* and *Ashes,* Munch conveys feelings of anxiety, the menace of sexuality, and the ultimate horror of life. A perceptive critic of the Norwegian artist, Przybyszewski declared that Munch's goal was "to express, in fine, the naked psychological state, not mythologically, that is, by means of sensory metaphors, but directly in its coloristic equivalent." *Visitors* is a comparable rendering of the demonic world of psychic phenomena through a painterly use of stark lines, raw colors, and dark engulfing shadows.

Munch depicted Przybyszewski several times. In *Portrait of Stanislaw Przybyszewski,* the Polish writer stares blankly ahead, eyes deranged, cigarette dangling from his mouth, and in *Jealousy,* the same head appears at one side of the canvas, gazing out fixedly—while perceiving in an inner vision the figures of Adam and Eve who stand behind him to his left. During his "Inferno crisis," Strindberg felt that he was pursued by the Satanic Przybyszewski who remained invisible behind a wall of greenery playing Schumann's *Aufschwung.* The author of *Visitors* was, in fact, a brilliant interpreter of Chopin who would sit at the piano (on which there always stood a glass of rum) and play the nocturnes as if in a trance. Przybyszewski calls for the playing of Saint-Saens's *Danse macabre* throughout *Visitors,* but it could be just as well Schumann or Chopin, interpreted by the playwright himself who almost seems to be present in his own drama—in the lower right hand corner of the stage frame, wild-eyed and demented, a cigarette between his lips. Behind him, Adam, Bela, and Pola are figures in his mind's eye, projections of his psyche. Przybyszewski is the play's dreamer; it is a theatre of "the naked soul."

Visitors takes the form of a dance of death in which all humanity is driven by relentless urges in a desperate masquerade. As in Poe's "Masque of the Red Death" and Ensor's paintings, the dead and the dying are celebrants at a masqued ball in carnival time. Przybyszewski's "Haunted Palace"—inspired by Poe—is the habitation of the soul, image of a mind peopled by phantoms, the architecture of a disordered brain. In his evocation of primal desire and psychic terror, Przybyszewski calls upon Aztec rites of sun worship, tales of vampires with frightful black wings, and the paranoia of the persecuting double. *Visitors* is a descent into the vortex of madness from which the only escape is suicide; the mansion dissolves into darkness, much as the House of Usher sinks into the earth.

Within the divided psyche lurks the other self—hidden and unknown—that punishes with guilt for uncommitted crimes. Using the themes of double and shadow, which were often combined in nineteenth-century fantastic literature, Przybyszewski conceives of Adam's shadow as an astral double that has become detached from his body—only to reappear as the moment of death draws near. At the same time that Freud was formulating his theory of the subconscious in *The Interpretation of Dreams,* the author of *Visitors* maintained that "Sexuality is the primal substance of life" and presented the metaphysics of love as a savage battle between the sexes. The world of eros has been infected by an evil spirit. "Nature is wicked, fiendish, lying, crafty," writes Przybyszewski. Laughter in *Visitors* is spasmodic and hollow, the outcry of an anguished demon. A proponent of heretical gnosticism well versed in satanism and infernal rites, Przybyszewski conceived of a church for those like Adam (both the character in *Visitors* and his great ancestor) who are cursed and in despair; the playwright's disciples in Cracow banded together and called themselves the "Sons of Satan." (pp. 19-21)

Daniel Gerould, "The Art of Symbolist Drama: A Re-Assessment," in Doubles, Demons, and Dreamers: An International Collection of Symbolist Drama, edited by Daniel Gerould, Performing Arts Journal Publication, 1985, pp. 7-33.

GRETA N. SLOBIN (essay date 1988)

[*In the following excerpt, Slobin examines Przybyszewski's influence on modern Russian literature.*]

Through his provocative estheticized writing and taboo-breaking behavior, Przybyszewski more than any other Slavic writer epitomized the decadent stance till the end of his life. Paradoxically his works, now almost forgotten, influenced major Russian writers and those of Młoda Polska ["Young Poland"] who moved beyond the tenets of Decadence by the end of the first decade of this century. Przybyszewski's controversial writings of the 1890s and early 1900s expressed the mood of *fin de siècle,* influencing the changing attitudes to art and the quest for new prose.

Considered as the early stage of Symbolism in Russia, the term "decadence" remained current and the two terms were often interchangeable throughout the first decade of the century, even as the younger Symbolists rejected the exclusively esthetic decadent stance. In Poland, the terms modernism, decadence, and symbolism were not adapted and the period 1890-1914 was designated as Neo-Romanticism or Młoda Polska, chronologically corresponding to the Russian Silver Age. (pp. 381-82)

[In Russian literature] Decadence affected the prose of such major poets as Brjusov, Gippius, Belyj, Kuzmin, and Sologub, as well as the writing of Rozanov and Remizov. Although there was no single term comparable to Symbolism in poetry that would unite the variety of trends in modernist prose, its common concern was a quest for new departures from the realist tradition and Victorian morality. The initial impetus came from Decadence which, with Przybyszewski as one of its most vociferous spokesmen, proclaimed a break from existing constraints in the name of new art.

Stanislaw Przybyszewski's unique status as a bohemian artist in Western Europe was partly responsible for his popularity in Russia and Poland. His scandalous life, no less than his shocking prose, embodied the decadent stance of conscious rebellion against existing authority, literary and social. His success as the East-European decadent superstar on the European stage, his meteoric rise as the best-selling author whose influence swept Russia and Poland, had much of a *succès de scandale,* accompanied by biting criticism. Ten volumes of his **Collected Works** were published in Moscow between 1905-1911. His tales, prose poems, essays, and plays were translated immediately and published by the best journals and publishers, with numerous reprintings. His novel **Homo Sapiens** appeared in fifteen editions between 1902-1918!

The reception of the Polish decadent in his own country was no less controversial than in Russia. His influence was summarized by a contemporary with characteristic wit: "He was like an express train going to a quiet Polish station, with all of Europe packed into the luggage compartment." Fortunately, the train also stopped in Russia. Another skeptical critic suggested that Przybyszewski's popularity could be attributed to the fact that he brought the news from the West, rather than producing it at home where it may have passed unnoticed. (p. 384)

Critics remained consistently puzzled by the impact of Przybyszewski's writing. In his article, "Przybyszewski w literaturze rosyjskiej," which appeared after the writer's death in the 1926 issue *Wiadomości literackie,* Paweł Ettinger suggested that his success was not due to the originality of his talent alone, pointing out that the Russian intelligentsia was conscious of a need for literary renovation and that the prose of the Polish decadent was useful in incarnating the slogans of modernism. . . . Ettinger concluded that Przybyszewski's works were a breath of fresh air and a revelation for Russian readers. This was confirmed by such early publications as the two 1906 issues of the journal *Vestnik Evropy* devoted to Polish literature where, in the large essay titled "Sovremennyj pol'skij roman," L. Polonskij referred to Przybyszewski and Tetmajer as "representatives of the very latest word," and to Przybyszewski as a "fighter for the freedom of art and the individual."

In a statement of characteristic bravado, Przybyszewski compared his artistic mission with that of John the Baptist, bringing the message to future followers. Throughout his career Przybyszewski impersonated the self-created myth of the artist as a powerful personality with influence over others, for whom life and art were inseparably bound, reflecting each other. He became as famous for his unconventional life as for his tales of anarchic deeds, dark forbidden passions, usually demonic and fatal, irrevocably striking brothers and sisters, young virgins and worldly men. Before Freud's formulation of the dominant conflict of Eros and Thanatos in the human psyche became widely known, Przybyszewski made destructive sensuality and the hedonism of destruction central in his novels, such as **Deti satany** [**Satans Kinder**] and the best-selling **Homo Sapiens.**

The esthetic principles expounded in Przybyszewski's theoretical writings are reminiscent of the Symbolist theories of "correspondences" and "synesthesia" (the associations of sound-color-touch-smell as a key to meaning). He formulated the concept of the "meta-word" and "meta-sound" based on the example of primitive man who did not speak but sang his emotions in their direct expression. . . . In his programmatic statement **"O nową sztukę,"** published in *Życie* in 1899, Przybyszewski considered the discovery of a totality of impressions in their emotional interdependence as the main feature of "new poetry." He condemned the older, "cerebral art" of the "ancients" who analyzed and split impressions. This denial of the rational and analytical through retrospective emotionalism, the rediscovery of the "ur," came to be redefined as "primitivism."

In the work titled **Na drogach duszy,** his gospel, Przybyszewski formulated the theory of art as a revelation of the eternal and essential "naked soul." . . . He stressed repeatedly that tendentious art was not real art. To place art in the service of utilitarianism was a sacrilege, for art must be "pure." In the foreword to his novel **De Profundis,** titled "Pro domo mea," Przybyszewski takes the opportunity to warn the reader that this is not a popular book, nor is it interested in what is generally known as "normal thought," "logical life of reason," or "real life." The work has little action since it depicts the "life of the soul." Here he defines his approach to sexuality as distinct from the vulgar erotic titillations of Guy de Maupassant. For him, sexuality is an expression of the ancient force of passion, of the mad desire that seeks to create new life. . . . In his worldview, "soul" is far superior in essence to the "stupid brain." Finally, his novel is a protest against contemporary bourgeois culture, the most limited, stupid, and "protestant." Indeed Przybyszewski advocated freedom of the sexual instinct as the new gospel in **Totenmesse** . . . , inextricably tied to his new esthetic program.

No doubt by now the Russian readers will recognize numerous echoes and variations of these themes in Russian modernism. The breaking of sexual and esthetic taboos, the phenomenon of "estheticization of life" (*"žiznetvorčestvo"*) in this period are a part of the literary biographies of Brjusov, Gippius, Belyj, Blok, and Remizov. (pp. 385-86)

The path to renewal in Russian modernism was accomplished by going to extremes first, and Przybyszewski's impact was symptomatic in the first radical gesture of an age that would see many manifestos and new departures within a period of intense artistic activity, compressed into barely more than a decade. (p. 389)

> *Greta N. Slobin, "Polish Decadence and Modernist Russian Prose," in* American Contributions to the Tenth International Congress of Slavists, *edited by Jane Gary Harris, Slavica Publishers, Inc., 1988, pp. 381-91.*

FURTHER READING

Henderson, Robert L. "Chopin and the Expressionists." *Music and Letters* 41, No. 1 (January 1960): 38-45.

Discusses Przybyszewski's writings on Frédéric Chopin.

Klim, George. "Stanisław Przybyszewski: Between Philosophy and Mysticism." *AULLA: Proceedings and Papers of the Twelfth Congress* (5-12 February 1969): 353-54.
    Synopsis of a paper treating Przybyszewski's philosophical thought and its precedents. Klim argues that Przybyszewski's ideas "do not follow Nietzsche, as is often contended, but develop out of several philosophical and mystical trends."

Kosicka, Jadwiga, and Gerould, Daniel. *A Life of Solitude: Stanisława Przybyszewska—A Biographical Study with Selected Letters.* London: Quartet Books, 1986, 239 p.
    Offers substantial biographical information on Przybyszewski in a volume focusing on the life of his daughter, dramatist Stanisława Przybyszewska.

"Polemics and Plain Plays." *The Nation,* New York 110, No. 2857 (3 April 1920): 434-35.
    Encapsulates Przybyszewski's literary career and its significance in brief commentary occasioned by the English-language publication of *Śnieg (Snow).*

"Russian Story of Love and Pathology: Remarkable Analysis of 'Cramps of the Heart and Colic of the Soul' in *Homo Sapiens*." *The New York Times Book Review* (19 December 1915): 516.

Unfavorable review of *Homo Sapiens* in which the critic negatively assesses the protagonist, Erick Falk, and briefly compares the novel to works by contemporary Russian and Slavic authors.

Rose, William John. "The Poets of Young Poland, 1890-1903." *The Slavonic Year-Book* 20 (December 1941): 185-99.
    Summarizes Przybyszewski's life and art in the context of the Young Poland movement.

Sokoloski, Richard. "Stanisław Przybyszewski's 'Confiteor'." *The Polish Review* 29, Nos. 1-2 (1984): 39-45.
    Briefly discusses the significance of Przybyszewski's "Confiteor" in the introduction to an English translation of the manifesto.

Review of *Snow,* by Stanisław Przybyszewski. *Theatre Arts Magazine* 4, No. 3 (July 1920): 259.
    Criticizes the lack of action in the play while praising its psychological insight.

Wilczek, Janus Maria. "Stanisław Przybyszewski's View of Strindberg." *Scandinavian Studies* 57, No. 2 (Spring 1985): 130-46.
    Traces Przybyszewski's relationship with Swedish dramatist August Strindberg using passages of Przybyszewski's letters to illustrate his insight into Strindberg's personality.

Algernon (Charles) Swinburne

1837-1909

(Also wrote under the pseudonym Mrs. Horace Manners)
English poet, dramatist, critic, essayist, and novelist.

For further discussion of Swinburne's life and career, see
TCLC, Volume 8.

Swinburne is renowned as one of the most accomplished lyric
poets of the Victorian era and as a preeminent symbol of rebellion against the conservative values of his time. The explicit and often pathological sexual themes of his most important
collection of poetry, *Poems and Ballads,* delighted some,
shocked many, and became the dominant feature of Swinburne's image as both an artist and an individual. Nevertheless, critics have found that to focus exclusively on the sensational aspects of Swinburne's work is to miss the assertion,
implicit in his poetry and explicit in his critical writings, that
his primary preoccupation was the nature and creation of poetic beauty.

Born into a wealthy Northumbrian family, Swinburne was
educated at Eton and at Balliol College, Oxford, but did not
complete a degree. While at Oxford, he met the brothers William Michael and Dante Gabriel Rossetti, as well as other
members of the Pre-Raphaelite circle, a group of artists and
writers whose work emphasized medieval subjects, elaborate
religious symbolism, and a sensual pictorialism, and who cultivated an aura of mystery and melancholy in their lives as
well as in their works. In 1860 Swinburne published two verse
dramas in the volume *The Queen-Mother and Rosamond,*
which was largely ignored. He achieved his first literary success in 1865 with *Atalanta in Calydon,* which was written in
the form of classical Greek tragedy. The following year the
appearance of *Poems and Ballads* brought Swinburne instant
notoriety. He became identified with the "indecent" themes
and the precept of art for art's sake that characterized many
of the poems of the volume. He subsequently wrote poetry of
many different kinds, including the militantly republican
Song of Italy and *Songs Before Sunrise* in support of the *Risorgimento,* the movement for Italian political unity, as well
as nature poetry. Although individual volumes of Swinburne's poetry were occasionally well received, in general his
popularity and critical reputation declined following the initial sensation of *Poems and Ballads.*

Swinburne's physical appearance, his personality, and the
facts of his life have received much attention from biographers and from commentators exploring biographical bases
of his works. He was small, frail, and possessed of numerous
peculiarities of physique and temperament, including an
overlarge head, nervous gestures, and seizures that may have
been manifestations of a form of epilepsy. Throughout the
1860s and 1870s he drank excessively and was prone to accidents that often left him bruised, bloody, or unconscious.
Until his forties he suffered intermittent physical collapses
that necessitated removal to his parents' home while he recovered. In 1879, Swinburne's friend and literary agent, Theodore Watts-Dunton, intervened during a time when Swinburne was dangerously ill. Watts-Dunton isolated Swinburne
at a suburban home in Putney and gradually weaned him

from alcohol—and from many former companions and habits as well. Swinburne lived another thirty years with Watts-
Dunton, whose role remains controversial. He denied Swinburne's friends access to him, controlled the poet's money,
and restricted his activities. However, commentators agree
that Swinburne's erratic conduct could have resulted in his
death, and Watts-Dunton is generally credited with saving
his life and encouraging him to continue writing into his old
age. Swinburne died in 1909 at the age of seventy-two.

The most important and conspicuous quality of Swinburne's
work is an intense lyricism. Even early critics, who often took
exception to his subject matter, commended his intricately
extended and evocative imagery, metrical virtuosity, rich use
of assonance and alliteration, and bold, complex rhythms. At
the same time, the strong rhythms of his poems and his characteristic use of alliteration were sometimes carried to extremes and rendered his work highly susceptible to parody.
Critics note that his usually effective imagery is at times
vague and imprecise, and his rhymes are sometimes facile and
uninspired. After establishing residence in Putney, Swinburne largely abandoned the themes of pathological sexuality
that had characterized much of his earlier poetry. Nature and
landscape poetry began to predominate, as well as poems
about children. Many commentators maintain that the poet-

ry written during the years at Putney is inferior to Swinburne's earlier work, but others have identified individual poems of exceptional merit among his later works, citing in particular "By the North Sea," "Evening on the Broads," "A Nympholept," "The Lake of Gaube," and "Neap-Tide."

Throughout his career Swinburne also published literary criticism of great acuity. His familiarity with a wide range of world literatures contributed to a critical style rich in quotation, allusion, and comparison. He is particularly noted for discerning studies of Elizabethan dramatists and of many English and French poets and novelists. In response to criticism of his own works, Swinburne wrote essays, including *Notes on Poems and Reviews* and *Under the Microscope,* that are celebrated for their wit and insight. Swinburne also published one novel, *Love's Cross-Currents,* serially under a pseudonym, and left another, *Lesbia Brandon,* unfinished at his death. The first attracted little notice other than some speculation about its authorship. Some critics have theorized that *Lesbia Brandon* was intended as thinly disguised autobiography; however, its fragmentary form resists conclusive interpretation.

During Swinburne's lifetime, critics considered *Poems and Ballads* his finest as well as his most characteristic poetic achievement; subsequent poetry and work in other genres was often disregarded. Since the mid-twentieth century, however, commentators have been offering new assessments of Swinburne's entire career. Forgoing earlier dismissals of Swinburne's voluminous later writings and reexamining individual poems strictly on their own merit, critics have identified works of great power and beauty from all periods of his career.

(See also *Contemporary Authors,* Vol. 105, and *Dictionary of Literary Biography,* Vols. 35 and 57.)

PRINCIPAL WORKS

The Queen-Mother and Rosamond (dramas) 1860
Atalanta in Calydon (drama) [first publication] 1865
Chastelard (drama) [first publication] 1865
Poems and Ballads (poetry) 1866; also published as *Laus Veneris, and Other Poems and Ballads,* 1866
Notes on Poems and Reviews (criticism) 1866
A Song of Italy (poetry) 1867
William Blake (criticism) 1868
Songs before Sunrise (poetry) 1871
Under the Microscope (criticism) 1872
Bothwell (drama) [first publication] 1874
Essays and Studies (criticism) 1875
George Chapman (criticism) 1875
Songs of Two Nations (poetry) 1875
Erechtheus (drama) [first publication] 1876
Poems and Ballads: Second Series (poetry) 1878
A Study of Shakespeare (criticism) 1880
Mary Stuart (drama) [first publication] 1881
Tristram of Lyonesse, and Other Poems (poetry) 1882
A Study of Victor Hugo (criticism) 1886
Locrine (drama) [first publication] 1887
Poems and Ballads: Third Series (poetry) 1889
A Study of Ben Jonson (criticism) 1889
Studies in Prose and Poetry (criticism) 1894
The Tale of Balen (poetry) 1896
Rosamund, Queen of the Lombards (drama) [first publication] 1899

*Love's Cross-Currents (novel) 1901; also published as *A Year's Letters,* 1974
A Channel Passage, and Other Poems (poetry) 1904
Shakespeare (criticism) 1909
Contemporaries of Shakespeare (criticism) 1919
The Complete Works of Algernon Charles Swinburne. 20 vols. (poetry, dramas, novel, essays, criticism, and letters) 1925-27
Lesbia Brandon (unfinished novel) 1952
The Swinburne Letters. 6 vols. (letters) 1959-62

*This work was originally published as *A Year's Letters* in the journal *Tatler* in 1877.

THE SATURDAY REVIEW   (essay date 1866)

[*In the following anonymous review of* Poems and Ballads, *the critic expresses regret that Swinburne draws inspiration from indecent subject matter and commends some technical aspects of Swinburne's poetry.*]

It is mere waste of time, and shows a curiously mistaken conception of human character, to blame an artist of any kind for working at a certain set of subjects rather than at some other set which the critic may happen to prefer. An artist, at all events an artist of such power and individuality as Mr. Swinburne, works as his character compels him. If the character of his genius drives him pretty exclusively in the direction of libidinous song, we may be very sorry, but it is of no use to advise him and to preach to him. What comes of discoursing to a fiery tropical flower of the pleasant fragrance of the rose or the fruitfulness of the fig-tree? Mr. Swinburne is much too stoutly bent on taking his own course to pay any attention to critical monitions as to the duty of the poet, or any warnings of the worse than barrenness of the field in which he has chosen to labour. He is so firmly and avowedly fixed in an attitude of revolt against the current notions of decency and dignity and social duty that to beg of him to become a little more decent, to fly a little less persistently and gleefully to the animal side of human nature, is simply to beg him to be something different from Mr. Swinburne. It is a kind of protest which his whole position makes it impossible for him to receive with anything but laughter and contempt. A rebel of his calibre is not to be brought to a better mind by solemn little sermons on the loyalty which a man owes to virtue. His warmest prayer to the gods is that they should

> Come down and redeem us from virtue.

His warmest hope for men is that they should change

> The lilies and languors of virtue
> For the raptures and roses of vice.

It is of no use, therefore, to scold Mr. Swinburne for grovelling down among the nameless shameless abominations which inspire him with such frensied delight. They excite his imagination to its most vigorous efforts, they seem to him the themes most proper for poetic treatment, and they suggest ideas which, in his opinion, it is highly to be wished that English men and women should brood upon and make their own. He finds that these fleshly things are his strong part, so he sticks to them. Is it wonderful that he should? And at all events he deserves credit for the audacious courage with which he has revealed to the world a mind all aflame with the feverish carnality of a schoolboy over the dirtiest passages in Lemprière. It is not every poet who would ask us all to go hear him tuning his lyre in a stye. It is not everybody who would care to let the world know that he found the most delicious food for poetic reflection in the practices of the great island of the Ægean, in the habits of Messalina, of Faustina, of Pasiphäe. Yet these make up Mr. Swinburne's version of the dreams of fair women, and he would scorn to throw any veil over pictures which kindle, as these do, all the fires of his imagination in their intensest heat and glow. It is not merely "the noble, the nude, the antique" which he strives to reproduce. If he were a rebel against the fat-headed Philistines and poor-blooded Puritans who insist that all poetry should be such as may be wisely placed in the hands of girls of eighteen, and is fit for the use of Sunday schools, he would have all wise and enlarged readers on his side. But there is an enormous difference between an attempt to revivify among us the grand old pagan conceptions of Joy, and an attempt to glorify all the bestial delights that the subtleness of Greek depravity was able to contrive. It is a good thing to vindicate passion, and the strong and large and rightful pleasures of sense, against the narrow and inhuman tyranny of shrivelled anchorites. It is a very bad and silly thing to try to set up the pleasures of sense in the seat of the reason they have dethroned. And no language is too strong to condemn the mixed vileness and childishness of depicting the spurious passion of a putrescent imagination, the unnamed lusts of sated wantons, as if they were the crown of character and their enjoyment the great glory of human life. The only comfort about [**Poems and Ballads**] is that such a piece as **"Anactoria"** will be unintelligible to a great many people, and so will the fevered folly of **"Hermaphroditus,"** as well as much else that is nameless and abominable. Perhaps if Mr. Swinburne can a second and a third time find a respectable publisher willing to issue a volume of the same stamp, crammed with pieces which many a professional vendor of filthy prints might blush to sell if he only knew what they meant, English readers will gradually acquire a truly delightful familiarity with these unspeakable foulnesses; and a lover will be able to present to his mistress a copy of Mr. Swinburne's latest verses with a happy confidence that she will have no difficulty in seeing the point of every allusion to Sappho or the pleasing Hermaphroditus, or the embodiment of anything else that is loathsome and horrible. It will be very charming to hear a drawing-room discussion on such verses as these, for example:—

> Stray breaths of Sapphic song that blew
>   Through Mitylene
> Shook the fierce quivering blood in you
>   By night, Faustine.
>
> The shameless nameless love that makes
>   Hell's iron gin
> Shut on you like a trap that breaks
>   The soul, Faustine.
>
> And when your veins were void and dead,
>   What ghosts unclean
> Swarmed round the straitened barren bed
>   That hid Faustine?
>
> What sterile growths of sexless root
>   Or epicene?
> What flower of kisses without fruit
>   Of love, Faustine?

We should be sorry to be guilty of anything so offensive to

Mr. Swinburne as we are quite sure an appeal to the morality of all the wisest and best men would be. The passionate votary of the goddess whom he hails as "Daughter of Death and Priapus" has got too high for this. But it may be presumed that common sense is not too insulting a standard by which to measure the worth and place of his new volume. Starting from this sufficiently modest point, we may ask him whether there is really nothing in women worth singing about except "quivering flanks" and "splendid supple thighs," "hot sweet throats" and "hotter hands than fire," and their blood as "hot wan wine of love"? Is purity to be expunged from the catalogue of desirable qualities? Does a poet show respect to his own genius by gloating, as Mr. Swinburne does, page after page and poem after poem, upon a single subject, and that subject kept steadily in a single light? Are we to believe that having exhausted hot lustfulness, and wearied the reader with a luscious and nauseating iteration of the same fervid scenes and fervid ideas, he has got to the end of his tether? Has he nothing more to say, no further poetic task but to go on again and again about

> The white wealth of thy body made whiter
>   By the blushes of amorous blows,
> And seamed with sharp lips and fierce fingers,
>   And branded by kisses that bruise.

And to invite new Félises to

> Kiss me once hard, as though a flame
>   Lay on my lips and made them fire.

Mr. Swinburne's most fanatical admirers must long for something newer than a thousand times repeated talk of

> Stinging lips wherein the hot sweet brine
> That Love was born of burns and foams like wine.

And

> Hands that sting like fire,

And of all those women,

>   Swift and white,
>   And subtly warm and half perverse,
> And sweet like sharp soft fruit to bite,
>   And like a snake's love lithe and fierce.

This stinging and biting, all these "lithe lascivious regrets," all this talk of snakes and fire, of blood and wine and brine, of perfumes and poisons and ashes, grows sickly and oppressive on the senses. Every picture is hot and garish with this excess of flaming violent colour. Consider the following two stanzas:—

> From boy's pierced throat and girl's pierced bosom
> Drips reddening round the blood-red blossom.
>   The slow delicious bright soft blood;
> Bathing the spices and the pyre,
> Bathing the flowers and fallen tire,
>   Bathing the blossom by the bud.
>
> Roses whose lips the flame has deadened
> Drink till the lapping leaves are reddened
>   And warm wet inner petals weep;
> The flower whereof sick sleep gets leisure
> Barren of balm and purple pleasure
>   Fumes with no native steam of sleep.

Or these, from the verses to Dolores, so admirable for their sustained power and their music, if hateful on other grounds:—

Cold eyelids that hide like a jewel
   Hard eyes that grow soft for an hour;
The heavy white limbs and the cruel
   Red mouth like a venomous flower;
When these are gone by with their glories
   What shall rest of thee then, what remain,
O mystic and sombre Dolores,
   Our Lady of Pain?

• • • • •

By the ravenous teeth that have smitten
   Through the kisses that blossom and bud,
By the lips intertwisted and bitten
   Till the foam has a savour of blood;
By the pulse as it rises and falters,
   By the hands as they slacken and strain,
I adjure thee respond from thine altars,
   Our Lady of Pain.

• • • • •

Thy skin changes country and colour,
   And shrivels or swells to a snake's.
Let it brighten and bloat and grow duller,
   We know it, the flames and the flakes,
Red brands on it smitten and bitten,
   Round skies where a star is a stain,
And the leaves with thy litanies written,
   Our Lady of Pain.

• • • • •

Where are they, Cotytto or Venus,
   Astarte or Ashtaroth, where?
Do their hands as we touch come between us?
   Is the breath of them hot in thy hair?
From their lips have thy lips taken fever,
   With the blood of their bodies grown red?

It was too rashly said, when *Atalanta in Calydon* appeared, that Mr. Swinburne had drunk deep at the springs of Greek poetry, and had profoundly conceived and assimilated the divine spirit of Greek art. *Chastelard* was enough to show that this had been very premature. But the new volume shows with still greater plainness how far removed Mr. Swinburne's tone of mind is from that of the Greek poets. Their most remarkable distinction is their scrupulous moderation and sobriety in colour. Mr. Swinburne riots in the profusion of colour of the most garish and heated kind. He is like a composer who should fill his orchestra with trumpets, or a painter who should exclude every colour but a blaring red, and a green as of sour fruit. There are not twenty stanzas in the whole book which have the faintest tincture of soberness. We are in the midst of fire and serpents, wine and ashes, blood and foam, and a hundred lurid horrors. Unsparing use of the most violent colours and the most intoxicated ideas and images is Mr. Swinburne's prime characteristic. Fascinated as everybody must be by the music of his verse, it is doubtful whether part of the effect may not be traced to something like a trick of words and letters, to which he resorts in season and out of season with a persistency that any sense of artistic moderation must have stayed. The Greek poets in their most impetuous moods never allowed themselves to be carried on by the swing of words, instead of by the steady, though buoyant, flow of thoughts. Mr. Swinburne's hunting of letters, his hunting of the same word, to death is ceaseless. We shall have occasion by and by to quote a long passage in which several lines will be found to illustrate this. Then, again, there is something of a trick in such turns as these:—

Came flushed from the full-flushed wave.
Grows dim in thine ears and deep as the deep dim soul of
   a star.
White rose of the rose-white water, a silver splendour and
   flame.

There are few pages in the volume where we do not find conceits of this stamp doing duty for thoughts. The Greeks did not wholly disdain them, but they never allowed them to count for more than they were worth. Let anybody who compares Mr. Swinburne to the Greeks read his ode to "Our Lady of Pain," and then read . . . *Antigone* . . . , or any of the famous choruses in the *Agamemnon,* or an ode of Pindar. In the height of all their passion there is an infinite soberness of which Mr. Swinburne has not a conception.

Yet, in spite of its atrocities, the present volume gives new examples of Mr. Swinburne's forcible and vigorous imagination. The **"Hymn to Proserpine"** on the proclamation of the Christian faith in Rome, full as it is of much that many persons may dislike, contains passages of rare vigour:—

All delicate days and pleasant, all spirits and sorrows are
   cast
Far out with foam of the present that sweeps to the surf
   of the past;
When beyond the extreme sea-wall and between the remote sea-gates
Waste water washes and tall ships founder and deep death
   waits,
Where mighty with deepening sides, clad about with the
   seas as with wings,
And impelled of invisible tides and fulfilled of unspeakable
   things,
White-eyed and poisonous-finned, shark-toothed and serpentine-curled,
Rolls under the whitening wind of the future the wave of
   the world.
The depths stand naked in sunder behind it, the storms
   flee away;
In the hollow before it the thunder is taken and snared as
   a prey;
In its sides is the north-wind bound; and its salt is of all
   men's tears;
With light of ruin, and sound of changes and pulse of
   years;
With travail of day after day, and with trouble of hour
   upon hour;
And bitter as blood is the spray; and the crests are as fangs
   that devour;
And its vapour and storm of its steam as the sighing of
   spirits to be;
And its noise as the noise in a dream; and its depth as the
   roots of the sea;
And the height of its heads as the utmost stars of the air;
And the ends of the earth at the might thereof tremble,
   and time is made bare.

The variety and rapidity and sustention, the revelling in power, are not more remarkable here than in many other passages, though even here it is not variety and rapidity of thought. The anapæst to which Mr. Swinburne so habitually resorts is the only foot that suffices for his never-staying impetuosity. In the **"Song in Time of Revolution"** he employs it appropriately, and with a sweeping force as of the elements:—

The heart of the rulers is sick, and the high priest covers
   his head;
For this is the song of the quick that is heard in the ears
   of the dead.

The poor and the halt and the blind are keen and mighty
    and fleet;
Like the noise of the blowing of wind is the sound of the
    noise of their feet.

There are, too, sweet and picturesque lines scattered in the midst of this red fire which the poet tosses to and fro about his verses. Most of the poems, in his wearisomely iterated phrase, are meant "to sting the senses like wine," but to some stray pictures one may apply his own exquisite phrases on certain of Victor Hugo's songs, which, he says,

    Fell more soft than dew or snow by night,
Or wailed as in some flooded cave
Sobs the strong broken spirit of a wave.

For instance, there is a perfect delicacy and beauty in four lines of the hendecasyllabics—a metre that is familiar in the Latin line often found on clocks and sundials, *Horæ nam pereunt et imputantur:*—

When low light was upon the windy reaches,
When the flower of foam was blown, a lily
Dropt among the sonorous fruitless furrows
And green fields of the sea that make no pasture.

Nothing can be more simple and exquisite than

For the glass of the years is brittle wherein we gaze for a
    span.

Or than this:—

In deep wet ways by grey old gardens
Fed with sharp spring the sweet fruit hardens;
  They know not what fruits wane or grow:
Red summer burns to the utmost ember;
They know not, neither can remember,
  The old years and flowers they used to know.

Or again:—

With stars and sea-winds for her raiment

      Night sinks on the sea.

Up to a certain point, one of the deepest and most really poetical pieces is that called the **"Sundew."** A couple of verses may be quoted to illustrate the graver side of the poet's mind:—

The deep scent of the heather burns
About it; breathless though it be,
Bow down and worship; more than we
Is the least flower whose life returns,
Least weed renascent in the sea.

    • • • • •

You call it sundew: how it grows,
If with its colour it have truth,
If life taste sweet to it, if death
Pain its soft petal, no man knows:
Man has no right or sense that saith.

There is no finer effect of poetry than to recall to the minds of men the bounds that have been set to the scope of their sight and sense, to inspire their imaginations with a vivid consciousness of the size and the wonders and the strange remote companionship of the world of force and growth and form outside of man. "Qui se considérera de la sorte," said Pascal, "s'effraiera, sans doute, de se voir comme suspendu dans la masse que la nature lui a donnée entre ces deux abîmes de l'infini et du néant" ["He who considers himself in this man-ner will be frightened, no doubt, to see himself as though suspended in the body nature has given him between those two abysses of infinity and nothingness"]. And there are two ways in which a man can treat this affright that seizes his fellows as they catch interrupted glimpses of their position. He can transfigure their baseness of fear into true poetic awe, which shall underlie their lives as a lasting record of solemn rapture. Or else he can jeer and mock at them, like an unclean fiery imp from the pit. Mr. Swinburne does not at all events treat the lot of mankind in the former spirit. In his best mood, he can only brood over "the exceeding weight of God's intolerable scorn, not to be borne"; he can only ask of us, "O fools and blind, what seek ye there high up in the air," or "Will ye beat always at the Gate, Ye fools of fate." If he is not in his best mood he is in his worst—a mood of schoolboy lustfulness. The bottomless pit encompasses us on one side, and stews and bagnios on the other. He is either the vindictive and scornful apostle of a crushing iron-shod despair, or else he is the libidinous laureate of a pack of satyrs. Not all the fervour of his imagination, the beauty of his melody, the splendour of many phrases and pictures, can blind us to the absence of judgment and reason, the reckless contempt for anything like a balance, and the audacious counterfeiting of strong and noble passion by mad intoxicated sensuality. The lurid clouds of lust or of fiery despair and defiance never lift to let us see the pure and peaceful and bounteous kindly aspects of the great landscape of human life. Of enlarged *meditation,* the note of the highest poetry, there is not a trace, and there are too many signs that Mr. Swinburne is without any faculty in that direction. Never have such bountifulness of imagination, such mastery of the music of verse, been yoked with such thinness of contemplation and such poverty of genuinely impassioned thought. (pp. 145-47)

"Mr. Swinburne's New Poems," in The Saturday Review, *London, Vol. XXII, No. 562, August 4, 1866, pp. 145-47.*

WILLIAM MICHAEL ROSSETTI   (essay date 1866)

[*Rossetti was the older brother of painter and poet Dante Gabriel Rossetti and poet Christina Rossetti. An art and literature critic, he became an important chronicler of his more renowned siblings and of the Pre-Raphaelite circle. In the following excerpt, he discusses the chief characteristics of the poetry in* Poems and Ballads.]

An attentive perusal of [*Poems and Ballads*] will, we think, disclose in it four main currents of influence and feeling—which we set down in descending ratio according to their importance in the work of art; and let us here say once for all that it is as a work of art, mainly if not engrossingly, that we regard these and any other poems which rise above a very restricted æsthetic scope. The currents in question are—

1, the Passionately Sensuous;
2, the Classic, or Antique;
3, the Heterodox, or Religiously Mutinous; and
4, the Assimilative or Reproductive in point of Literary
    Form.

As just stated, we have ranged these influences "in descending ratio according to their importance in the work of art," the particular poems before us. We do not, however, consider that the same ratio would hold good if we were analysing the intrinsic, organic importance of these several influences upon the very mind and personality of the poet. For such an analysis, we might be disposed to place our second and fourth influences, the Classic and Assimilative in Literary Form, ahead of all, and to refer them to another influence, larger and more fundamental still—the intensely, the overpoweringly artistic direction of Mr. Swinburne's mind, and the consequent startling predominance of the literary over other modes of thought or writing, and absorption of all other excellences into the literary or verbally plastic excellence, the excellence of poetic result. In like manner, we should place our third influence, the Heterodox or Religiously Mutinous, including (as in our purview it does) the morally mutinous, above our first-ranked influence, the Passionately Sensuous, which it fairly overlaps in the poet's brain, or in essential relation to his mind and his conception of things. In fact, Mr. Swinburne's mind appears to be very like a *tabula rasa* on moral and religious subjects, so occupied is it with instincts, feelings, perceptions, and a sense of natural or artistic fitness and harmony. These are to him the poetic pounds: be they but taken care of, and those other pence may, with the proverb's leave, take care of themselves. On these moral and religious subjects he seems to have no "innate ideas," no preconceptions, no prejudices. He has no sense of what moral philosophers call a "sanction." Dogmas and doctrines come warranted to him from outside; and there is nothing in him which leaps out to meet the warrant half-way. Thus nude of the qualities of mind which send a man forth to seek for some moral or religious foundation, and which dispose him to accept such as he finds ready to his hand, Mr. Swinburne might have remained neutral enough on such matters, but that others will insist upon knowing all about them, upon proselytizing and evangelizing; and Mr. Swinburne, when he finds he cannot be left alone and unconcerned, flies from neutrality to antagonism, resents what he would naturally leave out of count, and vollies forth "winged words" of the most audacious aim and the least stinted virus. It is in connexion partly with this attitude of mind, and partly with his literary or expressional intensity just previously noted, that we see reason for contemplating the "passionately sensuous" aspect of his work in the *Poems and Ballads.* We conceive it to be very closely related to his moral negativeness (by which term we have no intention, as no right, to assume that Mr. Swinburne is a bad man, but only that the facts of the world and of man naturally and primarily appeal to him on other than their moral showing); related also to the antagonistic excitement consequent upon the coercive administration of those moral and religious "alteratives" of which the British pharmacopœia is so prodigal—and to the fervour of perception and of words which seizes him when fervid subject-matter presents itself to his mental vision, and this because he is so much of an artist, and so little of either a moralist or an immoralist. Thus, strange as it may seem to say so of a book withdrawn from circulation on account of its outrages to decency, and in which "passionate sensuousness" really is a very leading influence, we believe that that influence is, in fact, one of the *less* genuine constituents of the author's mind: there is even something about it too determinate and prepense, too uneasily iterative—not exceptionally genuine, but near to being actually factitious. It would even ring almost hollow to the ear and the apprehension of the reader, were not the sound transmitted through so intense a medium of artistic perception and harmonic expression. We are certainly far from justifying Mr. Swinburne's course in publishing to a world which was pretty well known not to want them such performances as **"Dolores," "Fragoletta,"** and some others—to have done so was both a miscalculation and an *inconvenance,* for which he

has had to pay the penalty which might have been foreseen; but we are equally far from thinking that any positive stigma attaches to his name or his genius on this account, or that there is any true sense of right or justice in those critics who, stopping their ears at his unseemlinesses, refuse to hear, distinct and predominant above them, the flood of noble and divine music which these only mar with casual and separable though perverse discords. To sum up this part of our subject, Mr. Swinburne is "passionately sensuous" in his poems chiefly because the passionate and the sensuous are two ultimate and indestructible elements of poetry; and he over-enforces them in expression chiefly because a mighty intoxication of poetic diction mounts to his head, and pours in an unruly torrent through his lips, and he forgets the often still nobler office of self-mastery and reticence.

The "Classic or Antique" influence is an entirely genuine one with Mr. Swinburne, and cannot be called other than genuine in the part which it plays in his present volume. His mind and his sympathies receive nurture from the antique past. He is a manifest pagan; neither believing in a Christian revelation, nor entering kindly, though he can enter with truth of artistic perception, into a Christian dispensation, and modes of thought and life. This classic influence subserves to some extent his passionate sensuousness; for he can think without intolerance, and write with amazing candour and beauty, about **"Hermaphroditus"** or **"Anactoria."** The poem bearing the latter name is, indeed, one of the most glorious exhibitions of fervent imagination and poetic execution in his volume. The reader is not bound to like it: if he does not admire it, he has but a purblind perception of what poetic workmanship means. The statue in the Louvre, and the Lesbian loves of Sappho, are not germane to the modern mind: let them by all means remain un-germane! Yet let not the artificer or the student of poetry be a mark for the mere mud of nineteenth-century highroads if some "elective affinity" prompts him to penetrate somewhat further than parson or pedagogue into moods of mind and aberrations of passion which were vital enough to some of the great of old, however dead and putrescent they may now most legitimately have become. To these subjects a healthy and open mind stands in the relation expressed by the matron to whom naked men were as so many statues. One might almost say, and not be misunderstood by those whose understanding is worth courting, that everything Greek has become to us as a compound of beauty and of thought, a vestige and an evidence of human soul infused as into Parian marble, marble-like in its purity of appeal to us, and which time has privileged us to love with no gross or abject thought, whatever may be the express image and superscription of the monument. Be it confessed at the same time that Mr. Swinburne receives and transmits the impression without availing himself of this privilege so fully as he might, or, with his exquisite sensibility to beauty of subject-matter and perfection of poetic keeping, ought to, have done. **"Anactoria,"** impure as is its theme, might conceivably be treated with some nearer approach to comparative purity, and certainly without the feline or tigerish dallyings in which "the lust of the flesh" passes into a positive lust of blood, equally unknown (if we are not mistaken) to Greek passion, and unknowable, unless as a nightmare of the imagination, to normal sensualists. Why lay hands doubly lawless upon what can be claimed as rightful property only by such a son of Belial and cretinism as the producer, predestined to a madhouse and a hardly utterable name, of some

> scrofulous French novel
> On grey paper with blunt type,

and embellished with a "woful sixteenth print"? In his other classical poems which touch upon somewhat similarly dangerous ground, **"Phædra"** and **"Hermaphroditus,"** we see no cause for censuring Mr. Swinburne: he imagines and speaks as a poet has a right to do—the only further requirement being the "fit audience."

On the "Heterodox or Religiously Mutinous" influence we have already commented to some extent: it is closely connected with the Classic influence, and is equally genuine, though hardly so deep-seated. Mr. Swinburne, as we have said, is, in intellectual sympathy and culture, a pagan. This gives a positive direction to his thought on religious subjects, which otherwise seems to amount to little beyond negation,—materialism, and the absence of faith in a beneficent Providence. The negative and the positive currents, encountering and joining, roll a considerable volume of turbidity, tumult, and spray. In saying this we desire to guard ourselves carefully against any suspicion of levitical or pharisaic intolerance: we make no complaint of Mr. Swinburne's speculative opinions, but, on the contrary, recognise his right to entertain and express them, whatever they may be. They have done us no harm; and we recommend other readers to persuade themselves of the fact that to them also these opinions of a great poetic genius will do no harm. We say "opinions," feeling that, although Mr. Swinburne very seldom writes otherwise than dramatically, and could not therefore be legally fixed with entertaining as his own the opinions which he puts into the mouths of others, it would nevertheless be affectation to profess serious uncertainty on this point: he, in fact, dramatizes certain opinions, and not their contraries, so continually, because he sympathises with them, and rejoices in giving them words. We would make him welcome to do so. This world, which scandalized readers believe to be regulated by a beneficent Providence, and which Mr. Swinburne (we infer) believes to be regulated by some power of some sort or other which is absolutely inscrutable, unfathomable, and in its operations unamenable to the human reason or sense of right, is big and surprising enough for both opinions: and in the infinite there are possibly infinite disclosures to be made which may prove as astonishing to such readers as to Mr. Swinburne. If readers, only still further scandalized by our summary of the Swinburnian theory, declare that such theory is flat atheism, we shall not concern ourselves to contest the phrase: indeed, our own opinion about the theory is nearly enough the same. There is, as far as we know, only one act of faith, properly so called, possible to be made—namely, the belief in the perfect goodness and justice of the Creative and Disposing Power: all other so-called acts of faith appear, in ultimate analysis, resolvable into persuasion by evidence, which, in the largest sense, includes even that form of belief which consists in the simple acceptance of authority or tradition. Not so this one the supreme act of faith: the whole body of evidence to be brought forward on that most fundamental and vastest of questions, the mysteries and seeming contradictions of it, are so enormous, and so utterly above being cognizable by human intellect or investigation, that no man, it would seem, could ever possibly be convinced of the perfect goodness of the Ruling Power by discovering either the invariableness or the preponderance of its symptoms in the world of nature or of mind. He must take a step from the evidence to the conviction, and that step is faith. The man who has taken that step can alone be rightly said to believe in a God: for to believe in a God who is not all that we can conceive of good and just is to believe not properly in a God, but in a Fate,—or even in a Dæmon, if the sense of shadow, of horror, and of wrong, overpowers that of light, love, and right. Mr. Swinburne, as far as his book shows, never has taken the step in question, never has enacted the act of faith; and, though he seems to believe more or less tentatively and darkly in a supreme Intellect, in a Rule and a Ruler, in something beyond a "fortuitous concourse of atoms," the idea appears to supply to his mind more fuel for fire of resentment and flashes of protest than for anything like a humble, loving, and filial reliance. In fact, what might have been and was shrewdly surmised from *Atalanta in Calydon,* that the sentiments of the famous and overpoweringly eloquent chorus,

> "Yea, with thy hate, O God, thou hast covered us"

(minus the submissive close thereof), were the sentiments of Mr. Swinburne himself, is fully confirmed by various passages in the *Poems and Ballads;* passages which either reinforce the same sentiments dramatically, but with a gusto and insistence not to be mistaken, or, as especially in **"Félise,"** rend the thinnest of dramatic veils, and are manifestly spoken in the author's person. The same is still more clearly the case in the ode **"To Victor Hugo."** Our poet has a singularly acute and terrible conception of the puppet-like condition of man, as acted upon by the forces of Nature and the fiats of her Ruler; and he draws some appalling outlines of it with an equal sense of power and of powerlessness, an equal entireness of despair and of desperation. He jeers and groans in the same act at his and our misery, for the facts appear to him to warrant both moods: "there are passages in his poem" (as was remarked by one of the best English reviews of the *Atalanta*) "which seem to wring from the very roots of human experience the sharpest extract of our griefs." Intellect pitted against a material and moral *pieuvre* appears to be his conception of the state of man; and no wonder that the fight looks to him a most ghastly one, unconvinced as he is (to use the mildest term) of the justice of the Umpire, and convinced, or all but convinced, of the mortality of the soul. His only outlet of comfort is his delight in material beauty, in the fragmentary conquests of intellect, and in the feeling that the fight, once over in this world for each individual, is over altogether; and in these sources of comfort his exquisite artistic organization enables him to revel while the fit is on him, and to ring out such peals of poetry as deserve, we do not fear to say it, to endure while the language lasts. (pp. 16-27)

Of the four main currents of influence and feeling which we noted in the *Poems and Ballads,* we have now discussed all except the one which we termed "the Assimilative or Reproductive in point of literary form." This is one of the most curious specialties of Mr. Swinburne's writings, and may be best commented by a reference to individual poems in his volume. We take them pretty nearly in the order which they hold in the index of contents. The first brace of poems, **"A Ballad of Life"** and **"A Ballad of Death,"** are Italian canzoni of the exactest type, such as Dante, Cavalcanti, Petrarca, and the other mediæval, with many modern, poets of Italy have written; and more especially taking the tinge which works of this class have assumed in Mr. Dante G. Rossetti's volume of translations, *The Early Italian Poets.* The **"Laus Veneris,"** itself sufficiently independent of models, is prefaced by a paragraph in old French purporting to be extracted from a "Livre des Grandes Merveilles d'Amour, escript en Latin et en Françoys par Maistre Antoine Gaget, 1530," but which we confidently father upon Mr. Swinburne himself, along with the extract from the "Grandes Chroniques de France, 1505," appended to **"The Leper,"** and the Greek lines from **"Anth. Sac."** that serve as motto to **"A Litany,"** which poem is a cross between the antiphonal hymnal form and the ideas and phraseology of the Old Testament. These latter are hardly less prominent in the **"Song in Time of Revolution."** **"Phædra"** is in the form of a scene from a Greek tragedy, with the interpolated remarks of the Chorus. **"A Ballad of Burdens"** is moulded upon some of the old French poems, with an "envoy." **"Hendecasyllabics"** and **"Sapphics"** speak for themselves as regards literary relationship. **"At Eleusis"** is an exceptionally long speech spoken by Demeter, as from a Greek tragedy—recalling also such modern work as some of Landor's "Hellenics," or Browning's so-called "Artemis Prologizes." **"A Christmas Carol"** presents quaint, cunning analogies to mediæval writings of the same order. **"The Masque of Queen Bersabe"** is professedly "a miracle play," and treated accordingly. **"St. Dorothy"** is Chaucerian work, even to the extent of intentional anachronisms in the designations of the personages and otherwise. **"The Two Dreams,"** from Boccaccio, is almost in equal measure Keatsian. **"Aholibah"** brings us back again to the Old Testament. Lastly, we have a quintet of ballads, carefully varied in shade, but mainly conforming to the type of the old ballads of North Britain,—**"The King's Daughter," "After Death," "May Janet," "The Bloody Son,"** and **"The Sea-Swallows."**

Now, there is nothing uncommon or surprising in imitative poetry. It is generally bad in itself, and inefficient in imitation; sometimes clever, without imitative success; sometimes imitative to the point of intentional, and very rarely of realized, illusion. The singular thing about Mr. Swinburne's reproductive poems is that they are exceedingly fine pieces of work, exceedingly like their adopted models, startlingly so from time to time, and yet that they belong strictly and personally to Mr. Swinburne, and stand distinctly on the level of original work, with the privileges, difficulties, and responsibilities thereto belonging. It seems quite clear that this poet could do, if he chose, an imitation, a "take-off," of almost any style, so close that only the most knowing critics could detect it: but he always stops short of that extreme point, preserving his own poetic individualism and liberty, exhibiting . . . "the independence and remoulding force of an original work." This state of the case can only, as far as we know, be referred to one cause—the fact that Mr. Swinburne, being truly a poet, a man of imagination, penetrates, by the force of imagination as well as of studentship, into the imaginative identity of poetic models of past time, and thence into their embodying forms. He can create for himself, as he has amply proved; but the determined set of his intellect towards art, and consequently towards literary art, possesses him with so sharp a sympathy for the literary or poetic models of highest style that, as the mood varies, he can pitch his mind into true harmonic concert with Chaucer now, and now with Dante, Sophocles, Keats, or Hugo, and sing, as it were, new vocal music to the accompaniment of these most definite, dominant, and unperishing melodies. In all the roll of poets, we certainly know none who has given such signal proof of his power to enter with re-creative, not imitative, sympathy into so many poetic models of style and form, so diverse and so high; to search their recesses, and extract their essential aroma. A true critic can discern with equal clearness that Mr. Swinburne is a very different sort of writer from a Greek tragedian or a Chaucer, writing things which have a very different ring, and also that his voluntary assimilation to these and other poets is both a genuine and a most singular effort of po-

etry. Such a critic would find it alike impossible to suppose that he was reading in the **"St. Dorothy"** a work really produced by Chaucer, or to miss wondering at the intimate and indwelling Chaucerism of the product.

The foregoing observations, singly and collectively, lead up to the central fact already curtly indicated, that the largest and most fundamental of all the influences acting upon Swinburne is the artistic, or (as one terms it in reference to this particular form of art) the literary, and that his poetry is literary poetry of the intensest kind. It is not only metric eloquence, still less versified rhetoric—something far higher than either: but one hesitates to say whether the primary conception in the poet's mind, the poetic nucleus, or the accretion of images and expressional form which grows and clings to this, the poetic investment, is the more important constituent in the general result. In several instances, however, we would say that the poetic investment is beyond a doubt the more important. Both the great beauties and the faults of Mr. Swinburne's writings are closely connected with this specially artistic or literary turn of his genius, as we shall have occasion to show in the sequel. Shelley has been termed "the poet for poets:" Swinburne might not unaptly be termed "the poet for poetic students." His writings exercise a great fascination over qualified readers, and excite a very real enthusiasm in them: but these readers are not of that wide, popular, indiscriminate class who come to a poet to be moved by the subject-matter, the affectingly told story, the sympathetic interpreting words which, in giving voice to the poet's own emotion or perception, find utterance also for those of the universal and inarticulate heart. Mr. Swinburne's readers are of another and a more restricted order. They are persons who, taking delight in the art of poetry, rejoicing when they find a poet master of his materials and the employment of them, kindle to watch so signal a manifestation of poetic gifts and poetic workmanship, and tender him an admiration which, if less than that of an adept, is more than that of a dilettante. It should be added that, while the beauty of execution is the more special attraction to the more special Swinburnian readers, it is by no means the only one: the poet's conceptions are in fact as vivid as his expressions, and he writes with a fire, and even vehemence, which keep his work, elaborate as it often is in verbal or rhythmical subtlety, lifted clear above any such level as that of euphuism or "word-painting." (pp. 30-6)

> *William Michael Rossetti, in his* Swinburne's Poems and Ballads: A Criticism, *John Camden Hotten, 1866, 80 p.*

A. E. HOUSMAN   (essay date 1910)

[*Housman was an English poet and critic. His* Shropshire Lad *(1896) contains some of the most widely read poems in the English language. The following excerpt is taken from the text of a paper, never delivered, that was originally intended to be part of a series of lectures on English poets. Internal evidence in an unexcerpted portion of the essay indicates that it was written in 1910. In the excerpt below, Housman assesses Swinburne's poetic achievement.*]

When Mr. Swinburne died, April 1909, at the age of 72, he might as well have been dead for a quarter of a century. For a quarter of a century and more he had written nothing that mattered. There were not many to buy his books, and fewer still to read them; the poetasters, except the very poorest, had ceased to try to imitate him; the literary world was much interested in many other things, good, bad and indifferent, but little interested in the poetry of Mr. Swinburne. He still commanded the lip-service of the journalists, who would describe him from time to time as our only great living poet; but this they said, not because they knew anything about such matters or even believed it to be true, but because they hoped, by so saying, to inflict mental anguish on Mr. William Watson or Mr. Stephen Phillips.

Swinburne in fact was one of those not very numerous poets whom their contemporaries have treated with justice. The different attention which he received at different periods very fairly corresponded to differences, at those periods, in the quality of his writing. He was neither steadily overrated, like Byron, nor steadily underrated, like Shelley, nor, like Wordsworth, derided while he wrote well and celebrated when he wrote well no longer: he received the day's wage for the day's work. His first book fell dead, as it deserved; his first good book, *Atalanta in Calydon,* earned him celebrity; his best book, *Poems and Ballads,* was his most famous and influential book; and the decline of his powers, slow in *Songs before Sunrise* and *Bothwell* and *Erectheus,* accelerated in his later writings, was followed, not immediately, but after an interval sufficient to give him the chance of recovery, by a corresponding decline, first slow and then rapid, in public interest and esteem.

There can be no doubt that the enthusiasm provoked by the *Poems and Ballads,* like the loud and transient outcry which frightened its first publisher into withdrawing it from circulation, was due in great measure to adventitious circumstances and to a feature of the book which is now seen to be merely accidental. The poems were largely and even chiefly concerned with a thing which one set of people call love, and another set of people call immorality, each set declaring that the other name is quite wrong, so that people who belong to neither set do not exactly know what to call it; but perhaps one may avoid extremes by calling it Aphrodite. Now in the general life of mankind Aphrodite is quite able to take care of herself; but in literature, at any rate in the literature of that Anglo-Saxon race to which we have the high privilege and heavy responsibility of belonging, she wages an unequal contest with another great divinity, who is called purity by her friends and hypocrisy by her enemies, and whom, again to avoid extremes, one may perhaps call Mrs. Grundy. In the year 1866 the vicissitudes of their secular conflict had brought Mrs. Grundy to the top: she appeared to be sitting on Aphrodite as firmly as the Babylonian woman on her seven mountains in the Book of Revelations; and Swinburne's *Poems and Ballads* were a powerful and timely demonstration in favour of the under dog—if indeed I may apply such a term to either of the fair antagonists. Here was a subject which most poets had ceased to talk about at all, and here was a poet talking about it at the very top of a very sonorous voice: the stone which the builders rejected was become the head of the corner. And although the enthusiasm which this intervention evoked in one camp, like the scandal which it occasioned in the other, was excessive—for Aphrodite has the knack of causing both her friends and her enemies to lose their heads and to make more fuss about her than she is worth—still the stroke was both effective and salutary, and entitles Swinburne to a secure though modest place among the liberators of mankind. The reasonable licence which English literature enjoys today, and which it so seldom abuses, is the result of a gradual emancipation which began with Swinburne's *Poems and Ballads.*

Those to whom this work appealed by its subject and contents, as distinct from its form, were of two classes: there were the simple adherents of Aphrodite, and there were many of those grave men, correct in behaviour and earnest in thought, who regard the relations of the sexes as the most serious and important element in human life. It was the irony of the situation that Swinburne himself belonged to neither class. He was not a libertine, and he was not an earnest thinker about life: he was merely a writer in search of a subject, and a tinder-box that any spark would set on fire. When he had written his book upon this subject, he had done with it, and it hardly appears again in the twenty volumes of his later verse: he was ready for a new subject. In *Songs before Sunrise,* his next volume, his attitude towards Aphrodite was austere, and the finest poem in the book is the Prelude in which he takes his leave of her. *Poems and Ballads* were the effervescence with which a quick and shallow nature responded to a certain influence issuing partly from the Greek and Latin classics, partly from medieval legend, partly from the French literature of the nineteenth century. That effervescence subsided, and around a new subject, Liberty, a new influence, chiefly Mazzini's, provoked a fresh effervescence, not nearly so sparkling. The fact is that, whatever may be the comparative merits of the two deities, Liberty is by no means so interesting as Aphrodite, and by no means so good a subject for poetry. There is a lack of detail about Liberty, and she has indeed no positive quality at all. Liberty consists in the absence of obstructions; it is merely a preliminary to activities whose character it does not determine; and to write poems about Liberty is very much as if one should write an Ode to Elbowroom or a panegyric on space of three dimensions. And in truth poets never do write poems about Liberty, they only pretend to do so: they substitute images.

> Thy face is as a sword smiting in sunder
>   Shadows and chains and dreams and iron things;
> The sea is dumb before thy face, the thunder
>   Silent, the skies are narrower than thy wings.

Then, when they feel that the reader is starving for something more tangible, they generally begin to talk of Athens, which, as it happens, was a slave-state; and in the last resort they fall back on denunciation of tyranny, an abominable institution, no doubt, but at any rate less featureless than Liberty, and a godsend to people who have to pretend to write about her.

But even tyranny is an exhaustible subject, and seven thousand verses exhaust it; and Swinburne, since he could not be still, was forced to be eloquent about other things. He appointed himself to the laureateship of the sea; he cultivated a devotion to babies and young children; finally, under stress of famine and in desperation at the death of themes, he fled to what Johnson calls the last refuge of a scoundrel: he conceived a tardy enthusiasm for his native land, and wrote patriotic poems in imitation of Campbell. And, in addition to all this, he composed a great number of verses about the verses of other poets.

Not one of these subjects was well chosen. The sea is a natural object; and Swinburne had no eye for nature and no talent for describing it. Children and babies are not appropriately celebrated in verse so ornate and so verbose as Swinburne's. As for his patriotic poetry, it may be unfair to call it insincere, but certainly it has no air of sincerity: it is the sort of patriotic poetry one would expect from a man who had written volumes in honour of other nations before he wrote a line in honour of his own.

In truth there was only one theme which Swinburne thoroughly loved and understood; and that was literature. Here was the true centre of his interests, and the source of his genuine and spontaneous emotions. But literature, unfortunately, is neither a fruitful nor even an appropriate subject for poetry. Swinburne himself was uneasily aware of this; and consequently, when he heard it said that his work was grounded not upon life but upon books, it made him angry, and he began to splutter as follows: "The half-brained creature to whom books are other than living things may see with the eyes of a bat and draw with the fingers of a mole his dullard's distinction between books and life: those who live the fuller life of a higher animal than he, know that books are to poets as much part of that life as pictures are to painters or as music is to musicians, dead matter though they may be to the spiritually still-born child of dirt and dullness who find it possible and natural to live while dead in heart and brain." Well, of course it is a sad thing to be a spiritually still-born child of dirt and dullness, and it is peculiarly depressing to be dead in heart and brain when one has only half a brain to be dead in; but it is no use bemoaning one's condition, and we must pass on to consider the parallel which Swinburne draws. Books, he says, are to poets as much part of life as pictures are to painters. Just so: they are to poets that part of life which is not fitted to become the subject of their art. Painters do not paint pictures of pictures, and similarly poets had better not write poems on poems. And Swinburne did worse than take books for his subject: he dragged this subject into the midst of all other subjects, and covered earth and sky and man with the dust of the library. He cannot watch a sunset at sea without beginning to think of Beaumont and Fletcher. He walks along a country road at Midsummer, and it sets him talking about Chaucer, because Chaucer may possibly have done the same thing. He writes an ode for the four hundred and fiftieth anniversary of the foundation of his own school, Eton, in which he contrives to drag in Shakespeare (who was educated at Harrow) but mentions only one Etonian. And who do you think that one Etonian is? Shelley, whom Eton did not quite succeed in tormenting out of his mind: Shelley, who except for his father's influence and intervention, would twice have been expelled: Shelley, whose atheism was traced, by an Eton headmaster, to the difficulty which he found in reconciling the existence of God with the existence of Eton. In short, Swinburne was perpetually talking shop: the bookish spirit in which he looked on nature and mankind, with his head full of his own trade, is essentially the same as the spirit in which *The Tailor and Cutter* annually criticises the portraits in the Royal Academy, interested, not in the artist, not in the subject, but in the cut of the subject's clothes.

I have been speaking of the themes of his *lyrical* poetry, because it is only as a lyrist that Swinburne is important. The themes of his dramatic and narrative works were not ill chosen, and the unsatisfactoriness of those poems was not due to their subject but to Swinburne's lack of talent for narrative and the drama. His plays have a certain empty dignity, but he was not a dramatist nor even, like Browning, a psychologist: his characters are talking masks. In his only considerable narrative poem, **Tristram of Lyonesse,** the prologue, which in essence is lyric, is worth all the rest of the book put together; just as **Atalanta in Calydon** is raised far above his other dramas by the brilliant beauty of its very undramatic lyrics. It is of his lyrical poetry that I am speaking when I say that after the first series of **Poems and Ballads** he was chiefly occupied with bad subjects or with subjects not suited to his genius.

But it has long been a commonplace that the strong side of Swinburne's poetry was not its matter but its manner; and though the matter of **Poems and Ballads** had much to do with the celebrity of the book, it is to its diction and versification that it will mainly owe its place in literature. Of these it is very difficult to speak adequately and justly; to keep the balance between admiration for their extraordinary merit and originality, and due recognition of the fact that they belong essentially to the second order, not to the first.

If a man does not hear the melody of Swinburne's verse, he must be deaf; he would not hear the melody of any verse. But if, as many do, he thinks its melody the best, he must have a gross ear. The man who now calls Swinburne the most musical of poets would, if he had been born one hundred and fifty years earlier, have said the same of Pope. To the ears of his contemporaries Pope's verse was perfection: the inferiority of Milton's and Shakespeare's was not a thing to be disputed about but to be explained and excused. The melody of Pope and of Swinburne have this in common, and owed their acceptation to this, that they address themselves frankly and almost exclusively to what may be called the external ear. This, in different ways and by different methods, they fill and delight: it is a pleasure to hear them, and a pleasure to read them aloud. But there, in that very fact, you can tell that their music is only of the second order. To read aloud poets whose music is of the first, poets so much unlike one another as Blake and Milton, is not a pleasure but an embarrassment, because no reader can hope to do them justice. Their melody is addressed to the inner chambers of the sense of hearing, to the junction between the ear and the brain; and you should either hire an angel from heaven to read them to you, or let them read themselves in silence. None better understood their superiority than Swinburne himself, the finest of whose critical qualities was his capacity to admire excellence unlike his own. His devotees might call him the most melodious of English poets, but he thought that the most melodious lines in English were the first five lines of *Lycidas;* he acknowledged in the Border Ballads a strain of music which no later poetry could reproduce; and he recognised that the best versification of modern times is to be found in the irregular and simple-seeming measures of the *Ancient Mariner.*

Among Swinburne's technical achievements the most conspicuous, if not the greatest, was his development of anapaestic verse. It was he who first made the anapaest fit for serious poetry. Before his time it had been used with some success for the lightest purposes, but when used for purposes other than the lightest it had seldom been managed with skill. At its best it had a simple and rather shallow music:

> The blackbird has fled to another retreat
> Where the hazels afford him a screen from the heat,
> And the scene where his melody charmed me before
> Resounds with his sweet-flowing ditty no more.

But it was notably unsure of foot, and seldom went without stumbling for more than four lines at a time: it was for ever collapsing into such meanness as this:

> There is mercy in every place,
>   And mercy, encouraging thought!
> Gives every affliction a grace
>   And reconciles man to his lot.

Yet this is almost the very stanza which Swinburne dignified and strengthened till it yielded a combination of speed and magnificence which nothing in English had possessed before.

Out of Dindymus heavily laden
   Her lions draw bound and unfed
A mother, a mortal, a maiden,
   A queen over death and the dead.
She is cold, and her habit is lowly,
   Her temple of branches and sods;
Most fruitful and virginal, holy,
     A mother of gods.

She hath wasted with fire thine high places,
   She hath hidden and marred and made sad
The fair limbs of the Loves, the fair faces
   Of gods that were goodly and glad.
She slays, and her hands are not bloody,
   She moves as a moon in the wane,
White-robed, and thy raiment is ruddy,
     Our Lady of Pain.

Other stanzas he invented for it, to display its capacities.

In the darkening and whitening
   Abysses adored,
With dayspring and lightning
   For lamp and for sword,
God thunders in heaven, and his angels are red with the
   wrath of the Lord.

There lived a singer in France of old
   By the tideless dolorous midland sea.
In a land of sand and ruin and gold
   There shone one woman, and none but she.
And finding life for her love's sake fail,
Being fain to see her, he bade set sail,
Touched land, and saw her as life grew cold,
   And praised God, seeing; and so died he.

True, the anapaestic rhythm, even when invested by a master with these alluring splendours, is not, in English, the best vehicle for poetry. Better poetry has been written in iambics and trochaics than will ever be written in anapaests; but still it is an unparalleled achievement, at so late a period of the literature, to have added this new and resonant string to the lyre.

In the second place, not only did he create new metres but he re-created old; and in particular he resuscitated the heroic couplet. It might have been thought, after all the practitioners through whose hands this measure had passed, that nothing remained for it but decent burial. The valley was full of bones; and behold, there were very many in the open valley; and lo, they were very dry. The form which the couplet had taken in the seventeenth century it retained to the nineteenth; and the innovations or reactions of Leigh Hunt and Keats were not improvements. Upon these dry bones Swinburne brought up new flesh and breathed into them a new spirit. In the hands of the last considerable poet who had used it, the metre still went to the tune of Pope and Dryden:

Night wanes—the vapours round the mountains curled
Melt into morn, and Light awakes the world.
Man has another day to swell the past,
And lead him near to little, but his last;
But mighty Nature bounds as from her birth,
The sun is in the heaven, and life on earth;
Flowers in the valley, splendour in the beam,
Health on the gale, and freshness in the stream.
Immortal man! behold her glories shine,
And cry, exulting inly, they are thine.
Gaze on, while yet thy gladdened eye may see;
A morrow comes when they are not for thee:
And grieve what may above thy senseless bier,
Nor earth nor sky will yield a single tear;
Nor cloud shall gather more, nor leaf shall fall,

Nor gale breathe forth one sigh for thee, for all;
But creeping things shall revel in their spoil,
And fit thy clay to fertilise the soil.

These lines are much above Byron's average; they say something worth saying, and they say it capably and with emotion; but their structure is still formal, and their vocabulary a trifle poor. Now take Swinburne:

Thee too the years shall cover; thou shalt be
As the rose born of one same blood with thee,
As a song sung, as a word said, and fall
Flower-wise, and be not any more at all,
Nor any memory of thee anywhere;
For never Muse has bound above thine hair
The high Pierian flower whose graft outgrows
All summer kinship of the mortal rose
And colour of deciduous days, nor shed
Reflex and flush of heaven about thine head,
Nor reddened brows made pale by floral grief
With splendid shadow from that lordlier leaf.

It is hardly recognisable as the same metre. You are free to like it less: it is less brisk and forthright, but its fulness and richness and variety are qualities of which one would never have supposed the couplet to be capable.

In the third place he possessed an altogether unexampled command of rhyme, the chief enrichment of modern verse. The English language is comparatively poor in rhymes, and most English poets, when they have to rhyme more than two or three words together, betray their embarrassment. . . . To Swinburne a sonnet was child's play: the task of providing four rhymes was not hard enough, and he wrote long poems in which each stanza demanded eight or ten rhymes, and wrote them so that he never seemed to be saying anything for the rhyme's sake. His preeminence was most remarkable in the mastery of feminine rhymes, as we call them, rhymes of two syllables. Before Swinburne, few English poets had used them much, and few without doing themselves an injury. They would start swimmingly enough:

How delicious is the winning
Of a kiss at love's beginning,
When two mutual hearts are sighing
For the knot there's no untying.

But unless they made up their mind to desert the scheme it would generally entice them to use words which they would rather not have used:

Yet remember, midst your wooing,
Love has bliss, but love has ruing,
Other smiles may make you fickle,
Tears for other charms may trickle.

The word *trickle,* in that verse, is not preferred to the word *flow* because of its intrinsic merit, but for quite another reason. Swinburne's language, no doubt, is often wanting in clearness and aptness, but that defect is never caused by any difficulty in finding feminine rhymes: they come at call as readily as the others. I will mention one significant detail. The ordinary versifier, if he employs feminine rhymes, makes great use of words ending with *ing:* they are the largest class of these rhymes, and they form his mainstay. Swinburne, so plentiful and ready to hand were his stores, almost disdains this expedient: in all the four hundred and forty lines of **"Dolores,"** for example, he only twice resorts to it.

The ornament of verse especially associated with the name of Swinburne is alliteration. (pp. 60-71)

Swinburne, in much of his writing, employed the artifice so profusely, so wastefully, and indeed so ignorantly, that in the end he brought it into disrepute and sent it out of fashion. The proper function of alliteration is to add speed and force to the motion of verse. How it should be applied, if it is to compass these ends, is a matter on which I might say a good deal; but that belongs rather to a paper on the artifice of versification than to a paper on Swinburne. From Swinburne I will take one example, and I might take hundreds, of how it should not be applied.

> Many a long blithe wave
> Buoyed their blithe bark between the bare bald rocks,
> Deep, steep, and still, save for the swift free flocks . . .

but that is enough. Those verses make on the ear and mind two immediate impressions: they are cumbrous and they are artificial; and if they are analysed it will be found that their unskilful artifice is the chief cause of their cumbrousness. They are the work of a craftsman who has forgotten his trade; who has lost sight of the end proposed, and who actually defeats the end by mechanically hammering away at the means. This is mere bungling; but in the celebrated stanza about the lilies and languors of virtue and the raptures and roses of vice, though the artifice is rather crude and obvious, the effect is nevertheless attained: the verse, though it pays a price for them, does gain force and rapidity. In his best time he used alliteration, never indeed with perfect art, but still with some rectitude of instinct: this he lost in his later years, as he lost almost everything else. He had deafened himself with his own noise, till his verse became downright unpleasant to ears which were still open. His growing obtuseness of perception showed itself most clearly in his employment of trochaic rhythms. This metre he had never written so skilfully as iambics or anapaests, and in the end he may be said to have written it worse than anyone had ever written it before. (pp. 71-2)

If you turn from his versification to his diction, the case is much the same, though it cannot be examined in the same detail. The first impression produced by his style, as it was in 1866, is one of great and even overpowering richness. He seemed to have ransacked all the treasuries of the language and melted the whole plunder into a new and gorgeous amalgam. In the poems of his later life his style was threadbare. It had not become austere: it was as voluble and diffuse as ever, but it had ceased to be rich and various. The torrent streamed on, but it streamed from an impoverished vocabulary, and consisted of a dwindled stock of words repeated again and again. A few favorite epithets were conferred on all manner of different things, instead of different and truly descriptive epithets. If he admired something very much he would not wait to find a word indicative of its quality, but he would call it "god-like"; upon which one of his critics observed that, in view of Mr. Swinburne's theological opinions, to call a thing god-like must be very much the same as calling it devilish good. If an epithet struck him as pretty in itself he would work it to death by associating it with objects to which it had no special appropriateness; and it would be interesting to draw up a list of the various unlike things which he has called "sun-bright" or "flower-soft," or "deep as the sea." This is a fashion of speaking which attains its legitimate culmination in the conversational style of the British workman, who thinks that no noun should be without an adjective, and that one adjective is suitable to every noun.

But even in the days of its early freshness and abundance his diction had the fault that amidst all its magnificence it did not

ring quite true: it would not sustain comparison even with the best contemporary poetry, the best of Tennyson's and Matthew Arnold's, no, nor the best of Coventry Patmore's and Christina Rossetti's. Speaking broadly, it was a diction of the same cast as Pope's. The differences between the two are evident and striking; but their differences are less essential than their resemblance in this point—that they both run in a groove. They impose upon all thought and feeling a set mode of speech: they are mannerisms, and consequently they are imitable. Pope's diction was long imitated successfully; Swinburne's was imitated successfully, but not long, because those who were clever enough to imitate it were also clever enough to see that it was not well worth imitating.

In fact, what Swinburne wrote, and what Pope and Dryden wrote, was not, in the very strictest sense of the word, poetry. It was often capital stuff, and to the taste of many of their contemporaries it was better than the best poetry. But time went on, and the power of its spell was found to wane; its appeal was not to the core of the human mind and the unalterable element in its constitution. I suppose that most people, while admitting that Swinburne's poetry is less poetical than Milton's or even than Tennyson's, would maintain that on the other hand it is much more poetical than Pope's or even Dryden's. Well, I think so too; but I cannot feel sure that I am right in thinking so. The atmosphere of taste in which Swinburne's poetry grew up is not yet altogether dispersed: we ourselves grew up in it, and we have not all grown out of it. But if permanency is any test of merit, then we must remark that the poetry inaugurated by Dryden was supreme for a century and a half, while the influence of Swinburne spent itself within five and twenty years. It began in 1865, it reached its height before 1880, by 1890 there was not much left of it. Here of course it must be borne in mind that Pope and Dryden had two strings to their bow and Swinburne had only one. If Pope's and Dryden's verse were not poetry at all, they still would be very great men of letters and representatives of their age. Their sense, their wit, their knowledge of life and men, and their eminence in those merits which poetry shares with prose, would still preserve for their verse a high place in literature. But if Swinburne's verse had not poetical merit, it would have no merit at all.

Poetry, which in itself is simply a tone of the voice, a particular way of saying things, is mainly concerned with three great provinces. First, with human affection, and those emotions which we assign to the heart: no one could say that Swinburne succeeded or excelled in this province. The next province is the world of thought; the contemplation of life and the universe: in this province Swinburne's ideas and reflections are not indeed identical with those of Mrs. Hemans, but they belong to the same intellectual order as hers: unwound from their cocoon of words they are either superficial or secondhand. Last, there is the province of external nature as perceived by our senses; and on this I must dwell for a little, because there is one department of external nature which Swinburne is supposed to have made his own: the sea.

The sea, to be sure, is a large department; and that is how it succeeded in attracting Swinburne's attention; for he seldom noticed any object of external nature unless it was very large, very brilliant, or very violently coloured. But the sea as a subject of poetry is somewhat barren. Those poets who have a true eye for nature and a sure pen for describing it, spend few words on describing the sea; and their few words describe it better than Swinburne's thousands. It is historically certain

Swinburne at age 31.

that he had seen the sea, but if it were not, it could not with certainty have been inferred from his descriptions: they might have been written by a man who had never been outside Warwickshire. Descriptions of nature equally accurate, though not equally eloquent, have actually been composed by persons blind from their birth, merely by combining anew the words and phrases which they have had read to them from books. When Swinburne writes thus—

> And the night was alive and anhungered of life as a tiger
>   from toils cast free:
> And a rapture of rage made joyous the spirit and strength
>   of the soul of the sea.
> All the weight of the wind bore down on it, freighted with
>   death for fraught:
> And the keen waves kindled and quickened as things
>   transfigured or things distraught.
> And madness fell on them laughing and leaping; and mad-
>   ness came on the wind:
> And the might and the light and the darkness of storm
>   were as storm in the heart of Ind.
> Such glory, such terror, such passion, as lighten and har-
>   row the far fierce East,
> Rang, shone, spake, shuddered around us: the night was
>   an altar with death for priest—

it would be cruel to set against such a passage a single line of Tennyson's or a single epithet of Shakespeare's: I take instead a snatch of verse whose author few of you know and most of you never heard of:

> Hurry me, Nymphs, O, hurry me
> Far above the grovelling sea,
> Which, with blind weakness and bass roar

Casting his white age on the shore,
Wallows along that slimy floor;
With his wide-spread webbed hands
Seeking to climb the level sands,
But rejected still to rave
Alive in his uncovered grave.

Admirers of the sea may call that a lampoon or a caricature, but they cannot deny that it is life-like: the man who wrote it had seen the sea, and the man who reads it sees the sea again.

If even so bare and simple an object as the sea was too elusive and delicate for Swinburne's observation and description, you would not expect him to have much success with anything so various and manifold as the face of the earth. And I am downright aghast at the dullness of perception and the lack of self-knowledge and self-criticism which permitted him to deposit his prodigious quantity of descriptive writing in the field of English literature. That field is rich beyond example in descriptions of nature from the hands of unequalled masters, for in the rendering of nature English poetry has outdone all poetry: and here, after five centuries, comes Swinburne covering the grass with his cartload of words and filling the air with the noise of the shooting of rubbish. It is a clear morning towards the end of winter: snow has fallen in the night, and still lies on the branches of the trees under brilliant sunshine. Tennyson could have surveyed the scene with his trained eye, made search among his treasury of choice words, sorted and sifted and condensed them, till he had framed three lines of verse, to be introduced some day in a narrative or a simile, and there to flash upon the reader's eye the very picture of a snowy and sunshiny morning. Keats or Shakespeare would have walked between the trees thinking of whatever came uppermost and letting their senses commune with their souls; and there the morning would have transmuted itself into half a line or so which, occurring in some chance passage of their poetry, would have set the reader walking between the same trees again. Swinburne picks up the sausage-machine into which he crammed anything and everything; round goes the handle, and out at the other end comes this noise:

> Ere frost-flower and snow-blossom faded and fell, and the
>   splendour of winter had passed out of sight,
> The ways of the woodlands were fairer and stranger than
>   dreams that fulfil us in sleep with delight;
> The breaths of the mouths of the winds had hardened on
>   tree-tops and branches that glittered and swayed
> Such wonders and glories of blossom-like snow or of frost
>   that outlightens all flowers till it fade
> That the sea was not lovelier than here was the land, nor
>   the night than the day, nor the day than the night,
> Nor the winter sublimer with storm than the spring: such
>   mirth had the madness and might in thee made,
> March, master of winds, bright minstrel and marshal of
>   storms that enkindle the season they smite.

That is not all, it clatters on for fifty lines or so; but that is enough and too much. It shows what nature was to Swinburne: just something to write verse about, a material for making a particular kind of sausage.

This inattention or insensibility betrays itself very plainly in his imagery, which is at once profuse and meagre. It is profuse, for he constantly uses metaphors and similes where they are not wanted and do not help the thought; and yet it is meagre, for the same metaphors and similes are perpetually repeated. They are derived from the few natural objects which he had noticed: the sea, the stars, sunset, fire, and flowers, generally of a red colour, such as the rose and the poppy. However, the worst that can be said of them is that they are monotonous, perfunctory, and ineffective. But much worse can be said of another kind of simile, which grows common in his later writings. When a poet says that hatred is hot as fire or chastity white as snow, we can only object that we have often heard this before and that, considered as ornament, it is rather trite and cheap. But when he inverts his comparisons and says that fire is hot as hatred and snow white as chastity, he is a fool for his pains. The heat of fire and the whiteness of snow are so much more sharply perceived than those qualities of hatred and chastity which have heat and whiteness for courtesy titles, that these similes actually blur the image and dilute the force of what is said. But with such similes Swinburne's later works abound: similes to him were part of the convention of poetry, and he mechanically used them when they no longer served, and even when they frustrated, the only purpose which can justify their introduction. In fact he came to write like an automaton, without so much as knowing the meaning of what he said. (pp. 72-7)

It is not . . . for mastery nor even for competent handling of any of the three great provinces of poetry that Swinburne will be known to posterity. And not only so, but he was deficient in some of the qualities which go to constitute excellence on the formal side of poetry: he had little power of construction and little power of condensation. His nearest approach to a good short poem is the **"Garden of Proserpine,"** and that contains 96 lines, though it is true that they are short ones: **"Ilicet"** has about 150, **"The Triumph of Time"** nearly 400, **"Dolores"** more than 400. Of course in this defect Swinburne does not stand alone among eminent poets: he stands with Chaucer and Spenser, whose shorter pieces give hardly a hint of their true powers and excellences. But the defect was a worse misfortune to him than to them, because they in the main were narrative poets, and he was a lyrist. Gray writing to Mason on January 13, 1758, has these words: "Extreme conciseness of expression, yet pure, perspicuous and musical, is one of the grand beauties of lyric poetry. This I have always aimed at, and never could attain." Much less did Swinburne ever attain, what he never even recognised as a mark to aim at, this grand beauty of lyric poetry. Again, the virtue of construction and orderly evolution is almost absent from his lyrics. To take three of his most impressive and characteristic poems, the three which I mentioned last, **"Dolores,"** and **"Ilicet"** and **"The Triumph of Time"**: there is no reason why they should begin where they do or end where they do; there is no reason why the middle should be in the middle; there is hardly a reason why, having once begun, they should ever end at all; and it would be possible to rearrange the stanzas which compose them in several different orders without lessening their coherency or impairing their effect. Almost the only piece which satisfies in this respect is the last good poem he ever wrote, the elegy on the death of Baudelaire, which indeed, if it has not all the fresh and luxuriant beauty of his earlier writing, may yet perhaps be reckoned his very best poem, in virtue of its dignity, and its unusual and uncharacteristic merit of structure and design.

It is therefore by two things mainly, his verse and his language, in the vigour and magnificence which at his best period they possessed, that Swinburne must stand or fall; and by those two things he will not fall but stand. I have said that neither is of the first order; but there is no need that they should be: to things so novel and original it suffices that they

should be good; you cannot demand that they should be the best. Henry the Seventh's chapel is not the most beautiful part of Westminster Abbey; but it is beautiful, and the fabric is more enriched by the addition of that new and different beauty than if the chapel had been built in the purer style of the choir and transepts. Who is the greatest English poet of the nineteenth century it is difficult, gloriously difficult, to say; assuredly not Swinburne; but its two most original poets are Wordsworth, who began the age, and Swinburne, who ended it. (pp. 78-9)

> A. E. Housman, "Swinburne," in The American Scholar, *Vol. 39, No. 1, Winter, 1969-70, pp. 59-79.*

THOMAS E. CONNOLLY   (essay date 1964)

[*Connolly is an American educator and critic. In the following excerpt, he examines influences on Swinburne as a poet and critic and analyzes Swinburne's poetic theory and critical principles.*]

An analysis of Swinburne's poetic theory must be based upon the concept of the end or object of poetry, since it is only in the light of this most general principle that the more particular aspects of his theory can be understood. The accepted belief among critics and literary historians is that Swinburne was initially a wholehearted follower of the art-for-art's-sake school, that he believed the end or purpose of poetry to be solely the expression of the Beautiful, and that he turned to philanthropic or political ideals only when the springs of purely lyric inspiration began to run dry. This notion is essentially false. Swinburne's critical philosophy began and ended with admiration of political poetry. The art-for-art's-sake period was only a temporary departure from his fundamental theory. Because most critics of Swinburne's theory of poetry have depended almost entirely on a chronological analysis of his poetry only, they have fallen into this pit, for his earliest poetry was published during this art-for-art's-sake period. If one examines his critical prose and his letters, he discovers that the art-for-art's-sake period was merely a temporary wandering from the path of his basic and lifelong poetic theory.

Swinburne's belligerent and prolonged veneration of Victor Hugo is a commonplace of literary history. From the time he was a schoolboy at Eton until his death, Swinburne was most vociferously enthusiastic about his *cher et vénéré maître* ["dear and venerated master"]. But when we examine closely the studies of Hugo's influence on him, we find that historians have limited themselves primarily to Hugo's influence on Swinburne's poetic practice. Lafourcade alone has made a study of the influences that molded Swinburne's aesthetic theory, but, in his *La Jeunesse,* he devoted his greatest attention to the influence of Baudelaire and Gautier and, in his more condensed English biography, has swept Hugo aside in favor of Mazzini in the shaping of that theory. What has generally been ignored is the fact that it was from Hugo that Swinburne derived his basic theory of poetry, and that it was Hugo who finally gave him the terms to use in his abandonment of *l'art pour l'art.*

It is, perhaps, difficult for us to appreciate completely the extent to which Swinburne carried his fanaticism for Hugo. In the writings of a man excessively addicted to epithets of the most extreme, we are tempted to discount much of his praise and to take, first with a smile of toleration but eventually with a sigh of boredom, the astounding accumulation of damnatory scorn that he inevitably heaped upon his opponents. But in the case of Hugo, the hundreds of times he repeated such phrases as "supreme poet," "Chief poet of an age," "one of the very greatest among poets and among men," "the greatest dramatist and poet . . . since the death of Shakespeare" must convince even the most sceptical reader that Victor Hugo was one to whom Swinburne sincerely gave lavish and unvarying devotion. He was, together with Shakespeare, Shelley, and the Elizabethan dramatists, a lifelong obsession. (pp. 3-4)

I stress the strong early admiration of Hugo to emphasize two remarks made by Gosse: "It is particularly important to notice that almost all Swinburne's literary convictions were formed while he was at school" [*The Life of Algernon Charles Swinburne*]; and "Before his fortieth year there had set in a curious ossification of Swinburne's intellect. He ceased to form new impressions, while reverting with all his former exuberance to the old" [*Portraits and Sketches*]. In addition, the poet's early literary interests other than Hugo are important. Dickens, Juvenal, Dante, and Shelley, whom he admired, were artists who devoted a good portion of their talents to contemporary political, social, or religious problems. [In his *Life* of Swinburne] Gosse testifies to the influence of others:

> As every development of character in Swinburne was justified and fostered by literature, we may look with confidence to his early reading of such vehement writers as Milton, Landor, and Carlyle for the sources of his rebellious attitude to society.
>
> (pp. 5-6)

Toward the end of his Oxford years, another set of influences came to bear on Swinburne. It was at Birkbeck Hill's rooms that he was introduced to William Morris on November 1, 1857, and almost immediately afterwards to Dante Gabriel Rossetti and Edward Burne-Jones. The real influence of the Pre-Raphaelite Brotherhood, however, did not take place until late in 1860 or early in 1861, after he had left Oxford. Gosse summarizes the result: "Swinburne was drawn aside from the obsession of republicanism by his interest in the new and wonderful world of art his Pre-Raphaelite friends opened out before him."

The influence of Morris was immediate. Lafourcade reports that Morris induced Swinburne to "give up his former models, Aeschylus, Landor, Shelley, Arnold and to study the medieval romances (French and English), Chaucer, the *Morte d'Arthur.*" These were the friends who encouraged Swinburne in the development of his theory of art for art's sake by listening to and praising the poems that later were to cause such a scandal, ***Poems and Ballads.*** The Pre-Raphaelite Brotherhood never actually went so far as Swinburne in adopting the theories of Gautier and Baudelaire, although they introduced him to those theories and encouraged him in his expression of them.

Rossetti had introduced Swinburne, probably during his second year at Oxford (ca. 1857-1858), to *Mademoiselle de Maupin,* in the Preface to which Gautier, "fondateur véritable" ["true founder"] of *l'art pour l'art* in France, set forth his theory. Lafourcade has traced Gautier's influence on Swinburne's ***Notes on Poems and Reviews*** and ***Notes on Some Pictures of 1868,*** in which works he reflects three of Gautier's principles: (1) he refused to accept as the critical standard of art the belief that "all that cannot be lisped in the nursery or fingered in the schoolroom is therefore to be cast out of the library"; (2) he rejected didactic art; and (3) he insisted on form as the only valid critical standard of art.

How or when Swinburne first discovered Baudelaire has never been established, but it is certain that it was during the Pre-Raphaelite association. Whistler was a friend of Baudelaire and may have introduced Swinburne to his works. In addition to tracing the parallels to Gautier, Lafourcade has also shown how Swinburne's theories expressed in ***William Blake*** are derived from Baudelaire's *Notes nouvelles sur Edgar Poe* and *l'Art romantique.* From Baudelaire, he took two important modifications of his theory: (1) he recognized that, although art does not directly seek a moral effect, it is indirectly productive of one; and (2) he accepted without change Baudelaire's classification of the realms of art, science, and moral philosophy: "To art, that is best which is most beautiful; to science, that is best which is most accurate; to morality, that is best which is most virtuous."

Swinburne's earliest criticism was published during this period, in which he was swept away in the current of *l'art pour l'art,* and it has unfortunately been assumed by some that this was the first rather than the second phase of his theory of art. Early in 1862, Swinburne became anxious to have some of his work published. Dante Gabriel Rossetti vainly tried to interest Theodore Martin in producing some of his poetry. When this attempt failed, Monckton Milnes introduced Swinburne to Richard Holt Hutton, who invited him to contribute to the *Spectator.* Accordingly, the first of three articles in which Swinburne reviewed *Les Misérables* appeared on June 21, 1862.

Before the appearance of this article on *Les Misérables,* however, Swinburne had issued a challenging blast that anticipated the style of the later, notorious Swinburnean tirades. In a letter to the editor of the *Spectator* (June 7, 1862), he defended George Meredith's *Modern Love* against the anonymous critic who charged that the author had dealt with a "deep and painful subject on which he had no conviction to express."

Swinburne thundered:

> There are pulpits enough for all preachers in prose; the business of verse writing is hardly to express convictions; and if some poetry, not without merit of its kind, has at times dealt in dogmatic morality, it is all the worse and all the weaker for that. As to subject, it is too much to expect that all schools of poetry are to be for ever subordinate to the one . . . whose scope of sight is bounded by the nursery walls. . . . We have not too many writers capable of duly handling a subject worth the serious interest of man.

Two weeks later, when he started his review of *Les Misérables,* Swinburne could not force himself to apply his new artistic theories with equal vigor to Hugo. His basic admiration for the French poet was producing, this early in his critical career, the principle of the double effect of art that reached its full growth in 1872. He already recognized in the work of Victor Hugo values that were beyond those of a purely artistic nature:

> We may let the social side of the question stand over for the present. Any book above a certain pitch of writing must be taken first of all to be a work of pure art. For we can bring no man's work to a higher standard. All the excellence of moral purpose in the world will never serve for salt to a thing born rotten. Especially in handling any work of the greatest master we have alive we must keep to the real test. No philanthropics or philosophies

that may get between an artist and his work can be permitted to shove by the main question.

And again, a few pages later:

> . . . in all that concerns Enjolras and his company, some sense of personal sentiment and political meaning will slip in at every loophole. All this no doubt improves the book in one sense; gives it heat, directness, sharp clear life, and actual breath; but it is always on the edge of interference with the proper business of so great a book.

We can get some insight into the powerful forces that must have been working against each other in Swinburne when we recall that while he was writing and publishing these reviews of Victor Hugo's book he was also reading Baudelaire for the review of *Les Fleurs du mal* that appeared in the *Spectator* less than a month after the last of the reviews of *Les Misérables.* Swinburne faced the choice of repudiating Hugo on the basis of his newly adopted theory of art or of reconciling that theory with the practice of his idol. As early as 1862, he was well advanced toward the eventual reconciliation.

In the second article on *Les Misérables* (July 26, 1862), he wrote:

> [We] regard a good work of art as the first of all good deeds for an artist, and would consider a fresh Hamlet or a new Ruy Blas cheaply purchased by the hanging without trial of a dozen innocent men. . . . And yet, however we may grudge the best man of us to philanthropy and social schemes, no one has a right to undervalue for an instant the beauty and worth of such work.

His final judgment of the book shows Hugo triumphant over the pure theory of art for art's sake:

> . . . the loftiest form of life and the noblest kind of excellence a book can attain to is to recall . . . the place and likeness of a man in this ascending scale of life. Such a place . . . we must assign to this book. . . . Some books may be sharper-sighted, some may be more complete and faultless, some may have some attraction of colour and savour. This one has in it the breath of human life and the form of human work; it is of a high and rare kind, not to be had for the asking.
>
> (pp. 7-11)

On September 6, 1862, almost a month after the appearance of the last piece on *Les Misérables* that can definitely be assigned to him, Swinburne reviewed *Les Fleurs du mal.* To the casual reader, it would appear that he had reverted to a complete acceptance of the principles of *l'art pour l'art.*

> A French poet is expected to believe in philanthropy, and . . . lend a shove forward to some theory of progress. . . . A poet's business is presumably to write good verses, and by no means to redeem the age and remould society. . . . The mass of readers seem actually to think that a poem is the better for containing a moral lesson or assisting in a tangible and material good work. The courage and sense of a man who at such a time ventures to profess . . . that the art of poetry has absolutely nothing to do with didactic matter at all, are proof enough of the wise and serious manner in which he is likely to handle the materials of his art.

But a few pages later, Swinburne revealed the indirect moral effect of *Les Fleurs du mal.* It is important to remember,

when *William Blake* is discussed, that this attempt to read a moral background into poetry was made as early as 1862.

> Certain critics . . . have discovered what they call a paganism on the spiritual side. . . . There is not one poem of the *Fleurs du mal* which has not a distinct and vivid background of morality to it. Only, this moral side of the book is not thrust forward in the foolish and repulsive manner of a half-taught artist; the background, as we called it, is not out of drawing.
>
> If any reader could extract from any poem a positive spiritual medicine—if he could swallow a sonnet like a moral prescription—then clearly the poet supplying these intellectual drugs would be a bad artist; indeed, no real artist, but a huckster and vendor of miscellaneous wares. But those who will look for them may find moralities in plenty behind every poem of M. Baudelaire's. . . . It is not his or any artist's business to warn against evil; but certainly he does not exhort to it, knowing well enough that the one fault is as great as the other.
>
> (pp. 12-14)

Late in 1866, Swinburne wrote **Notes on Poems and Reviews.** In this, the last affirmation of his full support of *l'art pour l'art,* he followed Gautier in refusing to be dominated by moralistic critics, and he rejected an end outside of art itself:

> . . . if literature indeed is not to deal with the full life of man and the whole nature of things, let it be cast aside with the rods and rattles of childhood. Whether it affect to teach or to amuse, it is equally trivial and contemptible to us. . . .

That Swinburne was motivated to such a violent and late support of the theory of *l'art pour l'art* by the adverse reviews of his own **Poems and Ballads** cannot be doubted. However, even before the publication of this "Laus Diabolo," as he called it, he had recanted in a letter to William Michael Rossetti, who was then seeing the pamphlet through the press. On October 9, 1866, he wrote:

> . . . I am writing a little song of gratulation for Venice with the due reserves and anticipations; and hope to wind up the scheme of the poem by some not quite inadequate expression of reverence towards Mazzini. I have already touched on most other of the later patriots and martyrs—I am half afraid and half desirous to touch on him—i.e. to lay my lips on his feet. . . . After all, in spite of jokes and perversities—malgré ce cher Marquis [de Sade] et ces foutus journaux—it is nice to have something to love and to believe in as I do in Italy. It was only Gabriel and his followers in art (*l'art pour l'art*) who for a time frightened me from speaking out; for ever since I was fifteen I have been equally and unalterably mad—tête montée, as my Mother says—about this article of faith; you may ask any tutor or schoolfellow. I know the result will be a poem more declamatory than imaginative; but I'd rather be an Italian stump-orator than an English prophet; and I meant to make it acceptable to you and a few others of our sort. . . .

A month later, Swinburne completed **William Blake,** that massive work on which he had been laboring for some time. Publication, however, was to be delayed for almost two years, until December 1867. This work reflects the struggle that was going on in him during this period. In **Blake,** both art for art's sake and his revived republicanism are evident. The following excerpt reveals the conflict:

> The contingent result of having good art about you . . . may no doubt be this: that . . . men then living will receive . . . a certain exaltation and insight . . . will become . . . incapable of tolerating bad work, and capable therefore of reasonably relishing the best; which of course implies and draws with it many advantages of a sort you may call moral or spiritual. But if the artist does his work with an eye to such results or for the sake of bringing about such improvements, he will too probably fail even of them. Art for art's sake first of all, and afterwards we may suppose all the rest shall be added to her (or if not she need hardly be overmuch concerned); but from the man who falls to artistic work with a moral purpose shall be taken away even that which he has—whatever of capacity for doing well in either way he may have at starting.

In his own poetic practice Swinburne no longer hesitated: he turned immediately to write political poetry. His first poem of 1867 was the **"Ode on the Insurrection in Candia,"** a weak piece about a subject in which he was not very much interested. Gosse comments on the poem: "He was conscious, I think, of a slight insincerity in the enthusiasm it expressed, for though he was very deeply concerned for Mentana and Custozza, he did not really care whether the Candians rose in insurrection or not." It is important, however, because it shows with what desperation he seized upon a subject to express his republicanism. There can be no doubt that Swinburne was never happy about this ode; in fact, years later he repudiated the poem. Gosse suggested that he include this work in his projected edition of *English Odes,* but [in a letter] Swinburne was quite firm in discouraging him:

> I had already heard with great pleasure of your projected book of select odes. I congratulate you on the prospect of so noble and delightful a task. But I should not like—indeed I should rather object—to be represented by so merely occasional a piece as the Candiote Ode—literally, almost, an impromptu, having been thrown off on the occasion *au courant de la plume* ["off the top of my head"], I think in two sittings: and being in my opinion—except perhaps the *Epode,* which is a little better than the rest—altogether a palpably hasty and comparatively inferior piece of work.

The thick-skinned Gosse must have pressed the inclusion of this poem, for a few days later the poet emphatically insisted on its omission: " . . . I must reiterate that I would rather 'shine by my absence' than be represented by the Candiote impromptu."

I dwell on this later repudiation only to emphasize that Swinburne turned almost in desperation to the only political subject at hand when he decided in his own poetic practice to abandon the principles of art for art's sake.

Shortly after the publication of this poem, Swinburne was introduced to Mazzini and placed himself under his political tutelage. . . . It was not until 1872, when the Pre-Raphaelite ties were essentially broken and the stimulation toward art for art's sake was removed, that Swinburne returned to philanthropic ideals completely. His reluctance to commit himself definitely to these ideals can be seen in this letter (May 7, 1867) to his mother:

> . . . if you are really anxious about [Mazzini's] influence upon me, you may be quite at rest. . . . nothing but good can come from the great honour and delight of being admitted to see and talk with him. . . . all he wants is that I should dedicate and consecrate my writing power to do good and serve others exclusively; which I can't. If I tried I should lose my faculty of verse even. When I can, I do. . . .

When he met Mazzini on March 30, 1867, Swinburne "went down on [his] knees and kissed his hand." Even before this meeting, however, Mazzini had begun to exert an influence upon Swinburne. The poet had sent him a copy of *Atalanta in Calydon,* and then he sent him the "Candiote Ode." On March 10, 1867, Mazzini wrote to Swinburne, and, in forceful language, ordered him to abandon the poetic principles displayed in *Poems and Ballads:*

> I have still to thank you for the gift of your beautiful *Atalanta. . . .* arising . . . from the reading of your masterly Ode on Greece, I cannot help writing a few words to tell you how grateful I felt at the time and how hopeful I feel now; hopeful that the power wich [*sic*] is in you has found out its true direction and that, instead of compelling us merely to admire *you,* you will endeavour to transform *us,* to rouse the sleeping, to compel thought to embody itself into Action. That is the mission of Art; and yours.
>
> . . . the poet ought to be the apostle of a crusade, his word the watchword of the fighting nations and the dirge of the oppressors. Don't lull us to sleep with songs of egotistical love and idolatry of physical beauty: shake us, reproach, encourage, insult, brand the cowards, hail the martyrs, tell us all that we have a great Duty to fulfill, and that, before it is fulfilled, Love is an undeserved blessing, Happiness a blasphemy, belief in God a Lie. Give us a series of "Lyrics for the Crusade." Have not our praise, but our blessing. You *can* if you choose.

The last few sentences very cleverly braid Swinburne's own thoughts—almost his very words—into a whip to lash the poet into action. . . . Before the end of the year, the restraint about writing political poetry, expressed in the letter to his mother, had diminished. To William Michael Rossetti, he wrote on October 6, 1867:

> I think I may some time accomplish a book of political and national poems as complete and coherent in its way as the Châtiments or Drum Taps. This, as you know, Mazzini asked me to attempt—"for us," as he said.

Early in 1869, Swinburne sent Mazzini the dedication to *Songs before Sunrise.* When he accepted it, Mazzini extended the highest compliment possible: " . . . the last beautiful lines," he wrote in March 1869, "will strengthen, if there be need, the firmness of my actual purpose: they *must* be prophetic or a branding reproach." The effect was all that the patriot could have desired. In a letter to William Michael Rossetti, in which he quoted these words of Mazzini, Swinburne announced: " . . . my poetry is 'art and part' in the immediate action of the Republic, having given this feeling at so practical a minute to the leader."

By 1869, therefore, Mazzini had brought Swinburne back to the fold in his poetic practice. From 1869 to 1870, the poet was busy writing the poems for *Songs before Sunrise.* Publication of that volume was delayed, however, until early in

1871 by the transfer of Swinburne's works from Hotten to his new publisher, Ellis. It was not until 1872 that he publicly announced his abandonment of art for art's sake in his critical prose.

Meanwhile, between 1867 and 1872, Hugo expressed a growing cordiality in his letters to Swinburne, and frequently he encouraged the reviving republicanism in the English poet. When he began his correspondence with Swinburne, Hugo had addressed him as "Monsieur." After 1867, however, he began to address him variously as "Mon honorable et cher confrère," "Cher et cordial poète," and "Mon honorable et eminent confrère" ["My honorable and dear colleague," "Dear and cordial poet," "My honorable and eminent colleague"]. (pp. 14-21)

In September 1872, exactly ten years after he had completed his first series of reviews of Hugo's work, Swinburne published his review of *L'Année terrible*. Compare the letter of 1862 in defense of Meredith with the following remark from his latest review: "But there must be somebody on the side of the stars! somebody to stand up for brotherhood, for mercy, for honour, for right, for freedom, and for the solemn splendour of absolute truth."

The following quotation represents the most crucial point in the crystallization of Swinburne's theory of poetry, the reconciliation of political enthusiasm with admiration of form. It was through this reconciliation that he was to justify the rest of his critical judgments and all his subsequent poetry. After the rather startling statement of the need for a humanistic and an ethical voice in poetry, he went on:

> [*L'Année terrible*] at once suggests two points of frequent and fruitless debate between critics of the higher kind. The first, whether poetry and politics are irreconcilable or not; the second, whether art should prefer to deal with things immediate or with things remote. Upon both sides of either question it seems to me that even wise men [including Swinburne?] have ere now been led from errors of theory to errors of decision. The well-known formula of art for art's sake, *opposed as it has ever been to the practice of the poet who was so long credited with its authorship* [italics mine], has like other doctrines a true side to it and an untrue. Taken as an affirmative, it is a precious and everlasting truth. No work of art has any worth or life in it that is not done on the absolute terms of art. . . . Thus far we are at one with the preachers of "art for art!" . . . We admit then that the worth of a poem has properly nothing to do with its moral meaning or design . . . but on the other hand we refuse to admit that art of the highest may not ally itself with moral or religious passion, with the ethics or the politics of a nation or an age. It does not detract from the poetic supremacy of Aeschylus and of Dante, of Milton and of Shelley, that they should have been pleased to put their art to such use: nor does it detract from the sovereign greatness of other poets that they should have no note of song for any such theme. In a word, the doctrine of art for art is true in the positive sense, false in the negative; sound as an affirmation, unsound as a prohibition.

The theory expressed in this excerpt is the direct result of the influence of Hugo. I should like to recall the section that I placed in italics and explore its significance. Who was it that "so long credited" Hugo with the authorship of the expression, *l'art pour l'art?* It was Hugo himself! In 1864, Hugo published *William Shakespeare,* and it was in this work that Swinburne found him openly condemning the principle of art for art's sake. (pp. 21-3)

It is evident that the truant had been brought back to the Master. Hugo's dictum, "aucune perte de beauté ne résulte de la bonté" ["no loss of beauty results from goodness"], permitted Swinburne gracefully to reconcile art for art's sake with such art as was produced in *L'Année terrible.* In his review of that work, Swinburne pontificated:

> We do not therefore rate this present book higher or lower because it deals with actual politics and matter of the immediate day. . . . It is not on this ground that we would base its claim to the reverent study and thankful admiration of men. The first and last thing to be noted in it is the fact of its artistic price and poetic greatness.

At no time from 1872 until the end of his long life did Swinburne ever again disagree with the Master. When he was won back to Hugo's way of thinking, he stayed there. (p. 24)

Swinburne's advocacy of the principles of *l'art pour l'art,* though only a temporary departure from his original belief that the highest and noblest art is that which is devoted to humanitarian ends, did contribute some permanent elements to his theory of poetry. What he retained from the art-for-art's-sake period was the great admiration for technical and formal perfection which he then viewed as an enrichment of the humanitarian end of the work. Unless a work be perfect technically, it cannot exist as a work of art. One of the critical essays written toward the end of his life stated this same principle of the double effect of a work of art. In December 1902, *Harper's Monthly* carried Swinburne's article **"King Lear,"** in which he expressed essentially the same theory that had reached its perfection in his review of *L'Année terrible* exactly thirty years earlier. "Among all its other great qualities," he said of *King Lear,* " . . . it is the first great utterance of a cry . . . on behalf of the outcasts of the world—on behalf of the social sufferer, clean or unclean, innocent or criminal, thrall or free." Here, obviously, he was concerned with the humanitarian effect of the play. The other aspect of his theory came on the next page of the essay: "Not, of course, that it was not his first and last aim to follow the impulse which urged him to do good work for its own sake and for the love of his own art: but this he could not do without delivery of the word that was in him—the word of witness against wrong done by oversight as well as by cruelty, by negligence as surely as by crime."

From a consideration of the end or purpose of poetry it is a reasonable and short step to a consideration of the nature of the poet who creates that poetry. Swinburne seized upon a few classifications and used them over and over again to pigeonhole the poets he discussed. The establishment of such a system of hierarchical orders, though not original, supplied Swinburne with a convenient critical measuring and labeling device. Arnold and Shelley, among others, also used such systems. An examination of Swinburne's hierarchy not only uncovers the basis for his system of classification but also reveals some of his thoughts about the peculiarities of the poetic nature.

Early in his critical career Swinburne made a basic distinction in kind between poets. In 1869, he edited a selection of Coleridge's poems, and, in the **"Introductory Essay on Coleridge,"** he first voiced his theory of the two kinds of poet:

" . . . the ranks of great men are properly divisible, not into thinkers and workers, but into Titans and Olympians. Sometimes a supreme poet is both at once: such above all men is Aeschylus; so also Dante, Michel Angelo, Shakespeare, Milton, Goethe, Hugo, are gods and giants at once. . . ." Having made the basic classification—gods and giants—Swinburne did nothing further to clarify his meaning or to explain the basis of the classification in this essay. He allowed, however, no room in his system for minor poets. To be a poet at all, one must at least be a giant; later he was to admit that one could become a giant under certain circumstances.

Six years later, in his critical essay *George Chapman* (1875), Swinburne revealed the bases for his classifications:

> In [Chapman] we shall find that intellectual energy has taken what it can of the place and done what it can of the work proper to ideal passion. This substitution of an intellectual for an ideal end, of energetic mental action for passionate spiritual emotion as the means toward that end, is as good a test as may be taken of the difference in kind rather than in degree between the first and the second order of imaginative artists. . . . The hard effort of a strong will, the conscious purpose of an earnest ambition, the laborious obedience to a resolute design is as perceptible in Jonson and Chapman as in Shakespeare and in Marlowe is the instinct of spiritual harmony, the loyalty and the liberty of impulse and of work. The lesser poets are poets prepense; the greater are at once the poets of their own making and of nature's, equidistant in their line of life from the mere singing-bird and the mere student.

This quotation contains almost all the elements of Swinburne's division of poets into gods and giants. First, he considered the work of art produced by a giant inferior to that produced by a god. It is inferior because its end is inferior: it is an intellectual, not an ideal end. The distinction that Swinburne makes between gods and giants is simply the distinction between spiritual idealists and rational realists. The second part of this quotation appears on the surface to have more to say than the first. The giants are "poets prepense." These poets, by the very deliberateness of their adoption of a vocation and their rational approach to the objects of their art, have placed the limits of human reason on their work. The gods do not deliberately choose a poetic career; they are co-creators with nature of their own poetic beings or essences. This part of the quotation is simply Swinburnese for the old question, Is the poet made or born?

Swinburne continued to use this system of classification in his article in the *Nineteenth Century* (April 1888), the first part of his study of Ben Jonson. "If poets may be divided into two exhaustive but not exclusive classes—the gods of harmony and creation, the giants of energy and invention—the supremacy of Shakespeare among the gods of English verse is not more unquestionable than the supremacy of Jonson among its giants. . . . No giant ever came so near the ranks of the gods: were it possible for one not born a god to become divine by dint of ambition and devotion, this glory would have crowned the Titanic labours of Ben Jonson."

The concept of a poet being at once a god and a giant is here clarified—the greater may include the lesser talent, but it is impossible for a giant to become a god. Consequently, for the god-poets, *poeta nascitur, non fit* ["a poet is born, not made"];

but if a poet is not born a giant, he can by taking thought add cubits to his height and become one. (pp. 28-31)

Early and late in his critical writings, Swinburne insisted on an unlimited scope for the poet in selecting the material for his poetry. The thought of having someone place a ban on certain subjects was abhorrent to him. He admitted limitations on the poet only with respect to the *quality* and *treatment* of the subject matter; never would he tolerate a limitation of its scope.

The basis for Swinburne's attitude toward poetic subject matter is clear from a passage in *Notes on Poems and Reviews* (1866): "If literature indeed is not to deal with the full life of man and the whole nature of things, let it be cast aside with the rods and rattles of childhood." This essay was Swinburne's attack on those who had charged him with immorality in his own *Poems and Ballads,* and it was essentially an expression of the ideas of *l'art pour l'art* that he had derived from Gautier and others. It is important as the most unrestrained expression of Swinburne's belief that any subject that relates to man is fit for poetic treatment. The basis for such an extension of the material of poetry can be discovered in the same essay. It is the essential goodness of all things in the sight of art: ". . . all things are good in its sight, out of which good work may be produced." (pp. 38-9)

The suitability of a subject for poetic treatment does not depend . . . upon its goodness or evil when measured by any extra-poetic moral standards. Swinburne substituted artistic standards for social, moral, or religious standards in judging the poetic potentiality of any subject. The judgment was made in terms of dignity—human or diabolic—but the nature of the dignity was not defined. There are two possibilities: either the dignity can be intrinsically in the subject or the dignity can result from the representation of the subject by the poet. Swinburne, in his essays, treated both possibilities. (pp. 39-40)

Baudelaire was Swinburne's outstanding example of a poet who so rendered his material as to raise it to a level of poetic dignity: ". . . the pervading note of spiritual tragedy in the brooding verse of Baudelaire dignifies and justifies at all points his treatment of his darkest and strangest subjects." On the other hand, a poor poet is capable of degrading an otherwise perfectly suitable subject. Tennyson is . . . the whipping boy:

> It seems to me that the moral tone of the Arthurian story has been on the whole lowered and degraded by Mr. Tennyson's mode of treatment. . . . [He] has removed not merely the excuse but the explanation of the fatal and tragic loves of Launcelot and Guinevere. . . . Mr. Tennyson has lowered the note and deformed the outline of the Arthurian story, by reducing Arthur to the level of a wittol, Guinevere to the level of a woman of intrigue, and Launcelot to the level of a "correspondent." Treated as he has treated it, the story is rather a case for the divorce-court than for poetry.

Walt Whitman furnished Swinburne with the opportunity for an energetic expression of this same principle. The following quotation is from his "recantation" of Whitman published in 1887 under the title **"Whitmania."** "If anything can justify," said Swinburne, "the serious and deliberate display of merely physical emotion in literature or in art, it must be one of two things: intense depth of feeling, expressed with inspired perfection of simplicity, with divine sublimity of fascination, as by Sappho; or transcendent supremacy of actual and irresistible beauty in such relation of naked nature as was possible to Titian." What Swinburne then went on to condemn in Whitman's poetry was what he considered the brutalization of his subject matter. Had the subject been given the ennobling treatment of a Baudelaire, it might have been converted to noble poetry. Stated more directly in his review **"The Poems of Dante Gabriel Rossetti"** (1870), Swinburne's belief is simply that "a poet of the first order raises all subjects to the first rank, and puts the lifeblood of an equal interest into Hebrew forms or Greek, mediaeval or modern, yesterday or yesterage."

Swinburne pushed this aspect of his theory to such an extreme that he believed a very close relationship existed between the subject matter and the style of a work of art. When the subject matter—either because of some innate quality or the manner in which the poet has treated it—has achieved the spiritual perfection of nobility or dignity, the external, technical quality of the work cannot fail to be similarly perfect:

> But indeed, as with all poets of his rank, so with Mr. Arnold, the technical beauty of his work is one with the spiritual; art, a poet's art above all others, cannot succeed in this and fail in that. Success or achievement of an exalted kind on the spiritual side ensures and enforces a like executive achievement or success; if the handiwork be flawed, there must also have been some distortion or defect of spirit, a shortcoming or misdirection of spiritual supply.

These remarks occur in Swinburne's review of Arnold's poems of 1867. It is appropriate that Swinburne should have expressed this aspect of his theory in a criticism of Arnold's poetry, for these words anticipated by approximately thirteen years the more famous but almost identical pronouncement of Matthew Arnold himself. One cannot read these words without recalling that portion of "The Study of Poetry" in which Arnold said: "The superior character of truth and seriousness, in the matter and substance of the best poetry, is inseparable from the superiority of diction and movement marking its style and manner. The two superiorities are closely related, and are in steadfast proportion one to the other."

On these two aspects of poetic theory—the nature of the poet and the subject of poetry—Swinburne was remarkably thorough and consistent. His own sensational personality has led casual readers to expect him to be chaotic, impulsive, and entirely impressionistic in his critical writings. If one digs down through the welter of words, however, he finds that Swinburne had a hard core of carefully worked-out literary theory. (pp. 45-7)

> *Thomas E. Connolly, in his* Swinburne's Theory of Poetry, *State University of New York, 1964, 144 p.*

ROBERT E. LOUGY   (essay date 1968)

[Lougy is an American educator and critic. In the following excerpt, he relates Swinburne's diminished reputation to the critical reception of disfavor toward Romantic poetry in the twentieth century.]

Osbert Sitwell in *Noble Essences,* a personal chronicle of the Edwardian and Georgian society in which he moved as a young man, recalls sitting next to an old man who was telling him how much he had enjoyed his long life. Speaking of his youth, the old man said:

> If a man—or a schoolboy for that matter—does not get on well, it's his own fault. I well remember, when I first went to Eton, the head boy called us together, and pointing to a little fellow with a mass of curly red hair, said, "If ever you see that boy, kick him—and if you are too far off to kick him, throw a stone. . . ." "He was a fellow named Swinburne," he added. "He used to write poetry for a time, I believe, but I don't know what became of him."

Of course, Swinburne finally left Eton and moved clear of the range of both kicks and stones. But the kicks and stones that he received there metamorphosed into literary judgments, and the schoolboys grew up to become literary critics. One can not be sure which Swinburne found to be more painful, the physical or the verbal attacks, but for his literary reputation the words have been far more detrimental. While it is true that many good poets have had to withstand the same barrage, usually the kicks and stones have been diminished by the passage of time and the distance of the critics from the poet. But for Swinburne, all that the passage of time has effected has been a redirecting of the kicks and the choosing of new and sometimes heavier rocks to throw.

One critic has described Swinburne as breaking "in on that rather agreeably tedious Victorian tea party with the effect of some pagan creature, at once impish and divine, leaping onto the sleek lawn, to deride with its screech of laughter the admirable decorum of the conversation" [T. E. Welby, *A Study of Swinburne*]. And when we realize that this tea party often was less than decorous, as Steven Marcus' book *The Other Victorians* has observed, the impact that Swinburne made becomes less simple to understand. We will probably never be able to understand the impact he made on the undergraduates at Oxford who used to walk around chanting with religious intonations passages from **"Faustine"** or *Atalanta in Calydon,* or on young Thomas Hardy, his eyes glued on Swinburne's volume of poetry, walking, as he later wrote, "along the crowded London streets at my imminent risk of being knocked down." But it was not only the young who realized that an important figure had appeared on the Victorian scene and that his brilliance and temperament made it certain that things would never quite be the same.

Perhaps the most famous account of Swinburne's power to amaze and bewilder more mature men appears in *The Education of Henry Adams,* in which Adams describes his first encounter with Swinburne. Monckton Milnes, Adams, Swinburne, and two other men sat down to dinner at Adams's house, and conversation, we are told, followed the usual channels until Milnes thought "it time to bring Swinburne out." Here is Adams's description of Swinburne's debut:

> Then, at last, if never before, Adams acquired education. . . . For the rest of the evening Swinburne figured alone; the end of the dinner only made the monologue freer. . . . That Swinburne was altogether new to the three types of men-of-the-world before him; that he seemed to them quite original, wildly eccentric, astonishingly gifted, and convulsingly droll, Adams could see; but what more he was, even Milnes hardly dared say. They could not believe his incredible memory and knowledge of literature, classic, medieval, and modern; his faculty of reciting a play of Sophocles or a play of Shakespeare, forward or backward, from end to beginning; or Dante, or Villon, or Victor Hugo.

Cecil Y. Lang in the introduction to his edition of Swinburne's letters comments that Swinburne "in fact leaves the impression that he had read all of English and French literature and most of Greek, Latin, and Italian." In 1863, Swinburne wrote a courageous and perceptive review of Baudelaire's poem at a time when Baudelaire's name was as forbidden on English tongues as Swinburne's was to become. In 1868 he published a full-length study of William Blake, the first serious study of Blake's prophetic books. He mastered most of the major styles in English poetry until he was able to write with ease in each; and as a parodist and satirist he has no equal in the Victorian period, and few in the others. His gift of parody is, of course, most readily seen in **Heptalogia,** a group of seven poems in which he parodies the style and mannerisms of Tennyson, Browning, Patmore, Owen Meredith, Whitman, Rossetti, and his own early verse. His parody of himself is so viciously true that one critic has referred to it as seeming almost "auto-erotic".

A poet's reputation, however, must ultimately rest with his poetry, and not with his criticism, his translations, or his parodies. As Professor Lang has observed about Swinburne: "The central fact about Swinburne criticism is that he has never been judged solely by his best poems." To judge Swinburne only by his early poems is comparable to judging Tennyson solely on the basis of his early imitations of Keats; or to judging Wordsworth by *The Excursion.* The fact that most twentieth-century criticism of his poetry has been merely a reworking of comments made by two of his contemporaries would have appealed to Swinburne's wry sense of humor and to his fascination with those dim-eyed gods who control man's fate. George Meredith in 1861 said of Swinburne: "I don't see any internal centre from which springs anything that he does." Critics referring to the astuteness of this comment too often ignore the fact that in 1861 Swinburne still had four years to go before he published *Atalanta in Calydon* and five years before he published his first major book of poetry, **Poems and Ballads.** Meredith later described Swinburne as "the greatest lyrist England has had . . .". The other comment that has had the tenacity of an oracular judgment is William Morris's statement that "Swinburne's work . . . always seemed to me founded upon literature, not on nature." It has been observed that this is a rather odd comment coming from the author of *The Earthly Paradise;* but it is as incorrect as it is odd. Swinburne's best poetry is definitely concerned with nature—with man's attempt to find an identity within a world from which he is alienated.

Twentieth-century criticism of Swinburne has been generally unfavourable, for the most part, no doubt, because of its dislike and misunderstanding of Romantic poetry. Irving Babbitt, for example, once said that "writing that is romantic . . . is best enjoyed while we are young. A person who is as much taken by Shelley at forty as he was at twenty has, one may surmise, failed to grow up" [*Rousseau and Romanticism*]. T. S. Eliot, to borrow Northrop Frye's metaphor, dumped Swinburne stock on the market in the 1920s, and until recently buyers have been rather reluctant to pick it up. Eliot, in his essays on both Byron and Swinburne [in *The Sacred Wood*] echoes Babbitt's notion that one does (or should) outgrow Romantic poetry. In his essay on Swinburne, Eliot observes of **"The Triumph of Time":** "That so little material as appears to be employed . . . should release such an amazing number of words requires what there is no reason to call anything but genius." This same left-handed praise can be extended to Eliot's essay. Full of these ambiguous pronounce-

ments that it is a sage's privilege to make, his essay is somewhat like God's reply to Job—impressive, but not wholly convincing.

Eliot and the more influential shapers of earlier twentieth-century criticism—men such as Allen Tate, Cleanth Brooks, and John Crowe Ransom—were less than attracted to Romantic poetry. . . . The poetry that met with with their strongest approval was urbane, social, and usually possessed what Eliot defined as "wit" or "a recognition, implicit in the expression of every experience, of other kinds of experience which are possible . . .". They expected of poetry what Eliot expected when he announced [in *On Poetry and Poets*] that "we have come to expect poetry to be something very concentrated, something distilled . . .". (pp. 358-61)

These "new critics," however, are no longer so new, and there has come about a realization that poetry may not fit the criteria established by them and still possibly be good poetry. Looking back upon the criticism and the critical methods prevailing in the 1920s and 1930s, we see a tendency on the part of these critics to rate highest that poetry most amenable to their critical methods; and in this respect, they resemble a physicist who would find it necessary to define all phenomena he did not understand as "unnatural."

Recent critical approaches such as those employed by Northrop Frye and Harold Bloom have opened new accesses to Romantic poetry. Just as irony is one mode of poetry, but is definitely not the only mode, so a study of verbal ambiguity and close *explication de texte* are ways of approaching a poem, but not the only ways. Romantic poetry does in fact withstand a close line-by-line reading, although it does not always yield the most understanding by this approach. For example, Swinburne's poetry if studied in terms of its recurrent imagery and symbols reveals patterns of imagery which are very carefully structured and wholly consistent. These patterns provide a strong argument against those critics who have talked about poetry only in terms of its diffuseness. For not only do those details that were seen as the source of the diffuseness gain added significance as their relationship to the overall pattern becomes clearer, but—as in all good poetry—meaning is finally seen as the total functioning of all the parts becoming a unified whole. Thematic imagery in Swinburne's poetry is often dualistic; images of sun and moon, darkness and light, water and desert, lushness and barrenness. A certain tension or conflict is represented by these opposing images and, in his dramatic lyrics, this tension often provides a symbolic representation of the speaker's mind. Much of Swinburne's best poetry is dramatic in nature; in fact, Swinburne himself described his poems as "dramatic, many-faced, and multifarious . . .". Although his poems were so heavily attacked for their "erotic" nature by the Victorian press and public that his first publisher refused to continue publishing them, one sees that those poems which deal most thoroughly with eroticism, such as the Sappho poems of **"Laus Veneris,"** are not defences of eroticism, but rather exposures, through the techniques of dramatic monologue, of eroticism's ultimate failure. Swinburne preceded Steven Marcus's recent study of *My Secret Life* by about a hundred years in showing that eroticism must produce frustrations which can be gratified only by destruction of others or by destruction of self. Eroticism for Swinburne is never the perpetual panacea that it is in pornography; on the contrary, it leads to physical suffering, to spiritual emptiness, and ultimately to either a literal or a metaphysical death.

The conflict in Swinburne's poetry, however, is by no means always caused by erotic frustration. Swinburne, like most of the later nineteenth-century poets, had lost faith in that transcendental vision the Romantics strove so hard to retain; and in such poems as **"The Triumph of Time"** and **"Laus Veneris,"** we see the speaker trying to define those phenomena which surround him and attempting to reduce the conflict between nature and himself by creating a universe which is both explicable and desirable. The speaker moves towards what look like solutions, only to discover that they are ultimately illusions that must be destroyed by the same consciousness that created them. Swinburne often depicts man as living in a world governed by the oppressiveness of a time that has been stripped of religious significance. Such a recognition of time and its consequences explains both the Victorians' looking back towards the past, whether it be medieval or Greek, for an era when time was less oppressive (or so they believed), and their looking for ways to transcend this time, one of these ways being a sense of mission or destiny. Swinburne, however, although he intensely loved and admired the Greek civilization, never believed that it could be resurrected in the nineteenth century. A poem such as the **"Hymn to Proserpine,"** for example, shows the agonies of an individual caught between a world he loves but cannot have, and a world he lives in but cannot accept.

The attempt to rid oneself of time's oppressiveness makes up the quest of much nineteenth-century poetry; and Swinburne's poetry could be studied just in terms of how he variously confronts the problem of time. In his earlier poetry of 1865-1870, the most thorough treatment of time's relationship to a man who finds himself living in a wholly secular cosmos is the long poem, **"The Triumph of Time."** Each of the solutions towards which the Victorian poets reached, such as the redemptive quality of faith, of art, or the ability of love to allow one to transcend the agony of the moment, is confronted by the speaker and ultimately discarded. In the process of the poem, the speaker reaches for these solutions, but discovers that each is unsatisfactory. As the poem concludes, the only possible answer that he sees is one of a stoic endurance: "I shall go my ways, tread out my measures, / Fill the days of my daily breath." In the two longer poetic dramas, *Atalanta in Calydon* and *Erectheus,* Swinburne works with mythic material which allows him to envision artistically a world in which time is the vanquished rather than the victor because events occur within a teleological rather than a fortuitous universe. Man, of course, is still vulnerable to time, but the agonies of the modern consciousness are lessened because the possibility of "experienced continuity," in George Poulet's term, is assured by man's ability to effect meaningful action.

Swinburne wrote all his poetry after Darwin's *Origin of the Species* appeared in 1859, and he not only accepted the implications of the theory of evolution but also incorporated it in his poetry. He found the theory to be not the frightening spectre that it is in the poetry of Tennyson, but rather saw in it a freedom from the old myths that had enslaved man. Thus, closer in thought to Blake and Shelley than to Tennyson and Browning, Swinburne both repudiated the dualism implicit in Tennyson and Browning and condemned man's imprisoning of his senses and potentialities by creating the fiction of a supernatural being and the institutions that perpetuated this fiction. Many of his later poems focus upon the theme of freedom from political and religious tyranny. And in his poetry of freedom as well as in his poetry of humanity, we see

an effort still to transcend or escape the oppressiveness of existence removed from duration. For if man is seen not only as an isolated being whose identity can be assured solely by a consciousness of those intense moments of experience which are always fleeing (the type of consciousness that created both the agony and the ecstasy of such men as Walter Pater), but also as a man who contains within himself that God who is the culmination rather than the origin of man's spiritual growth, then the sense of duration can be experienced because man is then united to all men, past, present, and future.

But this vision of hope is only a part, a later part, of Swinburne's poetry. Until he reached it, and even after he reached it, he confronts in his poems those powers of darkness and chaos which he can only describe, not alleviate. This latter aspect, this darker vision of his poetry, is one of the reasons for the stylized structure and form of his poems. Beneath the deceivingly smooth surface of many of his poems is a vision as dark as Baudelaire's or Dostoevsky's. The aesthetes, or the "stylists" as Morse Peckham more accurately calls them, found it necessary to impose a stylistic barrier between their vision and the communication of this vision. This barrier existed both in their poetry and in their lives, and was not restricted only to the later poets; for as Lionel Trilling reminds us in his study of Matthew Arnold, "when dandyism was at work, Arnold produced poetry but when dandyism failed, poetry failed too." This stylistic barrier also made possible a more thorough communication of experience. At the same time that Swinburne was attacking virtually every sacred cow of the Victorian age, Thomas Hardy was being required by his publishers to delete a scene in which he had depicted Alec d'Urberville carrying Tess in his arms. Swinburne's poetry, then, is a method of communicating experience while attempting to protect oneself from the full effects of that experience. And at the same time, it is an attempt to impose upon a world without meaning or intrinsic value the order and control that art can provide. (pp. 361-64)

Robert E. Lougy, "Swinburne's Poetry and Twentieth-Century Criticism," in The Dalhousie Review, *Vol. 48, No. 3, Autumn, 1968, pp. 358-65.*

JOHN D. ROSENBERG (essay date 1968)

[*Rosenberg is an American educator and critic who has written critical studies of John Ruskin and Alfred Tennyson and edited editions of Tennyson and Swinburne. In the following essay, he assesses various characteristics of Swinburne's poetry, commending in particular his skillful use of poetic language.*]

Swinburne is a poet not of natural objects but of natural energies—of winds and surging waters. His scale is macrocosmic, his focus less upon the small celandine than upon the spines of mountains, less upon things seen than forces felt. At times he is nearly a blind poet, all tongue and ear and touch. His poetry moves away from the art of painting and toward the art of music; after reading Swinburne one retains not an image but a tonality and a rhythm.

Traditionally, the English poet has prided himself on particularity, which English criticism has exalted as the clearest sign of genius. Donne's "bracelet of bright haire about the bone" has dazzled the critics for half a century. The modern reader's very conception of poetry has been shaped by the practices of the Metaphysical poets and by Keats's dictum that the poet must have "distinctness for his luxury." We are at a loss in reading a poet who, like Swinburne, is diffuse not by default but by design.

From the perspective of Keats's principles, Gerard Manley Hopkins is in the main stream of nineteenth-century verse and Swinburne is the eccentric. For Hopkins' attempt to etch in words the dappled individuality of things was as much a cultural as a personal concern. Hopkins was simply an extreme exponent of the impulse to render with absolute accuracy the distinct profusion of nature itself. One recognizes the same impulse in the splendid exactitude of Tennyson's verse and Ruskin's prose, in the bright, crowded, microscopically accurate foliage of the Pre-Raphaelites, in Browning's eft, queer, creeping things, or, for that matter, in the solid clutter of any Victorian mantelpiece.

Memory betrays us into believing Swinburne to be far more ornate than he is. Dismissed as overlush and decadent, he is in point of diction the most *austere* of the greatly gifted poets of his century. Early in his career he evokes the heady, Pre-Raphaelite scent of oversweet violets, but in his greatest poetry Swinburne is more starkly monosyllabic than Wordsworth. The knight doomed to a sexually joyless service in **"Laus Veneris"** craves death in a stanza containing thirty-seven sparse words, all but four of them monosyllables:

> Ah yet would God this flesh of mine might be
> Where air might wash and long leaves cover me,
>   Where tides of grass break into foam of flowers,
> Or where the wind's feet shine along the sea.

[In his introduction to *The Novels of Swinburne*] Edmund Wilson condemns Swinburne for his "generalizing visageless monosyllables"; I would praise him as the supreme master in English of the bleak beauty of little words.

Wilson has argued that Swinburne the poet is a nullity and that his true gifts lay with the novel, in which he escapes the monotonous vocabulary of his verse: "He can never surprise or delight by a colloquial turn of phrase, a sharply observed detail, a magical touch of color." This might be helpful if it were true, which it is not, or if it were reasonable to condemn Swinburne for not succeeding in what he did not attempt to do. If there are few sudden glories in his verse, they are suppressed in the interests of a more sustained harmony. Great art, he believed, does not vex or fret the beholder with "mere brilliance of point and sharpness of stroke, and such intemperate excellence as gives astonishment the precedence of admiration: such beauties as strike you and startle and go out" [Swinburne, **"Matthew Arnold's New Poems"**]. Hopkins pushes language as far as it can go toward pointedness and sharpness of stroke; Swinburne moves it with equal daring in the opposite direction, diffusing where Hopkins concentrates, generalizing where Hopkins specifies. Together, they are the linguistic bravos of Victorian verse.

By diffuseness, however, I mean something very different from vagueness. The vague poet cannot see or speak clearly—in short, is not a poet. Swinburne is often called vague, but no one who has read his best poetry closely could ever accuse him of imprecision or carelessness with words. T. S. Eliot did not look closely enough at a famous chorus of Swinburne and charged him with laxity:

> Before the beginning of years
>   There came to the making of man
> Time, with a gift of tears;
>   Grief, with a glass that ran. . . .

The verses appear to make a "tremendous statement, like statements made in our dreams," Eliot writes of this chorus from *Atalanta in Calydon*; "when we wake up we find that the 'glass that ran' would do better for time than for grief, and that the gift of tears would be as appropriately bestowed by grief as by time" ["Swinburne as Poet" in his *Selected Essays*].

The reversed verses that Eliot prefers—time with an hourglass, grief with tears—are trite, and Swinburne wisely avoided them. But he had more positive reasons for overturning our expectation, as immediately becomes clear if we complete Eliot's truncated quotation:

> . . . Grief, with a glass that ran;
> Pleasure, with pain for leaven;
>   Summer, with flowers that fell;
> Remembrance fallen from heaven,
>   And madness risen from hell;
> Strength without hands to smite;
>   Love that endures for a breath:
> Night, the shadow of light,
>   And life, the shadow of death.

The chorus, like the play it mirrors, is about the terrible ambiguity of the god's gifts to men. We are given the bittersweet gift of time, but it passes even as it is given, and hence our tears; yet the pangs of grief also fade with the hours, like the summer blossom. As we read the lines, we are half aware of the conventional imagery underlying them, our mind reacting as does our ear to a departure from regular rhythm, half hearing the normal beat and half hearing the eccentric.

Swinburne constantly breaks down our habitual word associations, but the rupture is so slight that we scarcely notice it. The kind of gentle dislocation that Eliot condemned in the chorus from *Atalanta* gives to Swinburne's poetry the quality of a prolonged, mildly mixed metaphor, a quality which Eliot himself brilliantly exploited in his own poetry. This sense of disorientation, together with Swinburne's insistent, mesmeric meters, induces a surrealist heightening of consciousness that we associate with dreaming and that Swinburne realized with beautiful daring in **"The Leper,"** a ballad about a necrophiliac monk who makes love to the remnants of his lady. Grotesquely explicit, the poem is also inexplicably lovely, like the disintegrating lady, "sweeter than all sweet." The word *sweet* floats like a perfume throughout **"The Leper."** It recurs most often at those moments when the sense of the poem is most repugnant, sweet sound and fetid sense miraculously counterpoised through thirty-five stanzas.

Swinburne's adjectives, as with *sweet* in **"The Leper,"** have a way of detaching themselves from the nouns they adjoin and modifying instead whole lines or stanzas. He deliberately suppresses the specifying, limiting function of the adjective in order to discharge its meaning through the total poem. The search for *le mot juste* ["the exact word"] is, in the young Swinburne at least, the search for *le ton juste* ["the exact tone"], for the word which will not stick like a burr in the consciousness but serve unnoticed as a supporting note in a chord of color. Hence the intentional blandness of his diction, and his overfondness for generalizing modifiers like *bright, sad, light, glad,* and *sweet.* Swinburne's earlier, Pre-Raphaelite imitations are especially rich in such diction and should be read as *études* in verbal coloration. The opening lines of **"A Ballad of Life,"** the first of the *Poems and Ballads* of 1866, offer the reader a conditioning exercise in those lightly limiting adjectives and bland plural nouns that enable

Caricature of Swinburne as Pan.

Swinburne to arrange words as if they were pigments, or notes in a scale. Pairs of *glads, sweets,* and *sads* resolve themselves into a single neutral chord, as muted as a flame rained upon:

> I found in dreams a place of wind and flowers,
>   Full of *sweet* trees and colour of *glad* grass,
>   In midst whereof there was
> A lady clothed like summer with *sweet* hours.
> Her beauty, fervent as a fiery moon,
>   Made my blood burn and swoon
>   Like a flame rained upon.
> Sorrow had filled her shaken eyelids' blue,
> And her mouth's *sad* red heavy rose all through
>   Seemed *sad* with *glad* things gone.

In these flawless minor lyrics—**"A Ballad of Life," "Hermaphroditus," "A Match," "Before the Mirror," "The Roundel"**—language takes on a life independent of any ostensible subject. Words, severed from the soil of things, send out aerial roots of their own.

One seems to be overhearing an exquisitely beautiful voice singing at a distance; the melody carries, but the words come muffled, as if in a foreign tongue:

> If love were what the rose is,
>   And I were like the leaf,
> Our lives would grow together
> In sad or singing weather,
> Blown fields or flowerful closes,
>   Green pleasure or grey grief;

> If love were what the rose is,
>   And I were like the leaf.

• • • • •

> If you were queen of pleasure,
>   And I were king of pain,
> We'd hunt down love together,
> Pluck out his flying-feather,
> And teach his feet a measure,
>   And find his mouth a rein;
> If you were queen of pleasure,
>   And I were king of pain.

(**"A Match"**)

Self-engendered, self-contained, the poem is inspired not by the emotion of love but by the emotion of poetry itself.

All that Swinburne learned in composing these exercises in verbal color he put to use in the much later and more ambitious *Tristram of Lyonesse.* The "Prelude" to *Tristram* usually makes its way into the anthologies, but the rest of the poem is virtually unread, although it is one of the great erotic poems in English. *Tristram* is undervalued largely because the wrong demands have been made upon it. As narrative or as a drama of action the poem inevitably disappoints, in precisely the ways that Wagner's *Tristan and Isolde* disappoints. In both of these essentially *lyrical* re-creations of the legend, action and characterization are wholly subordinate to the all-absorbing theme of love. Just as there are no independent arias in *Tristan,* so there are no striking images in Swinburne's *Tristram* that are not repeated as leitmotifs and thus reabsorbed into the enveloping texture of the verse. The Londoner who read Swinburne's poem upon its publication in 1882 and then, just one month later, heard the English première of Wagner's music drama might well have felt a certain *déjà entendu* [sense of something "already known"].

From its opening lines to its close, **Tristram of Lyonesse** is about four lips that "become one burning mouth." As so often in Swinburne, the "image" is more tactile than visual. It first appears when Tristram and Iseult drink the potion; it recurs in a series of variants, most notably in Tristram's praise of "the mute clear music of her amorous mouth," a line whose enunciation moves the mouth into the position of a kiss. The image closes the poem as Iseult bows her head over the dead Tristram, "And their four lips became one silent mouth."

Although love is doomed, bleak, sick and sterile in almost all of Swinburne's poetry, in **Tristram** one senses his unique exultation in portraying sex that is fulfilled, however fated. Perhaps it is *because* the lovers are so clearly foredoomed that he could write so richly of their fulfillment. In this central legend symbolizing the love-sickness of the Western world, Swinburne creates by far his healthiest love poetry:

> Only with stress of soft fierce hands she prest
> Between the throbbing blossoms of her breast
> His ardent face, and through his hair her breath
> Went quivering as when life is hard on death;
> And with strong trembling fingers she strained fast
> His head into her bosom; till at last,
> Satiate with sweetness of that burning bed,
> His eyes afire with tears, he raised his head
> And laughed into her lips; and all his heart
> Filled hers; then face from face fell, and apart
> Each hung on each with panting lips, and felt
> Sense into sense and spirit in spirit melt.

These lines occur in Canto II, "The Queen's Pleasance," the poem's great *Liebesnacht* in which rest at last gains mastery "in the lovely fight of love and sleep." All of nature is absorbed into the passion of love, until the perfumed air seems an extension of the lovers' breath, the soft grass an extension of their bodies. The erotic interpenetration of nature and man is one of the poem's pervasive motifs, most remarkably realized in lines from Canto I describing a spring sunrise and the parallel dawning of womanhood in Iseult. Images of light, heat, florescence and flame all fuse into a single Turnerian chord of color, as Iseult herself comes to full flower under the "august great blossom" of the sun:

>   . . . she felt
> Through her own soul the sovereign morning melt,
> And all the sacred passion of the sun;
> And as the young clouds flamed and were undone
> About him coming, touched and burnt away
> In rosy ruin and yellow spoil of day,
> The sweet veil of her body and corporal sense
> Felt the dawn also cleave it, and incense
> With light from inward and with effluent heat
> The kindling soul through fleshly hands and feet.
> And as the august great blossom of the dawn
> Burst, and the full sun scarce from sea withdrawn
> Seemed on the fiery water a flower afloat,
> So as a fire the mighty morning smote
> Throughout her, and incensed with the influent hour
> Her whole soul's one great mystical red flower
> Burst, and the bud of her sweet spirit broke
> Rose-fashion, and the strong spring at a stroke
> Thrilled, and was cloven, and from the full sheath came

> The whole rose of the woman red as flame:
> And all her Mayday blood as from a swoon
> Flushed, and May rose up in her and was June.

Swinburne concluded **Tristram of Lyonesse** with a final verse paragraph that, to my knowledge, has no precedent in any version of the legend. King Mark builds the lovers a stone chapel at the sea's edge, and in their death the lovers undergo a second doom. For the waves shatter the chapel and the sea closes over their uncoffined bones. Fulfilled love in Swinburne pays the penalty of double death.

The association of love with death is the underlying theme of almost all of Swinburne's major poetry. He is of course best known for a variant on that theme—the pain implicit in all pleasure. Virtually incapable of using the word *pleasure* without its alliterative opposite, Swinburne is undeniably sadomasochistic, but this lurid aspect of his lyricism has obscured his true achievement. His greatest love poetry is addressed not to those literary ladies with sharp teeth—Dolores, Faustine, and the rest—but to his bitter, salt mother the sea, and to those bleakly beautiful, ravaged margins of earth that yield their substance to her.

Swinburne is the laureate of barrenness in all its forms. I find myself further from the essential matter of his poetry when I learn, as his critics stress of late, that he was fond of being whipped, than when I read his nobly sad letter congratulating Edmund Gosse on his marriage:

> I suppose it must be the best thing that can befall
> a man to win and keep the woman that he loves
> while yet young; at any rate I can congratulate my
> friend on his good hap without any too jealous af-
> terthought of the reverse experience which left my
> own young manhood "a barren stock." . . .

The signs of that "reverse experience" are everywhere in Swinburne's poetry. In the autobiographical **"Thalassius,"** for example, Swinburne tells of his painful encounter with the young god of Love. Terrifyingly transformed, Love "waxes immeasurable" and from his erected height says to the poet:

> O fool, my name is sorrow;
> Thou fool, my name is death.

Of course, Swinburne's trauma in love would not have so scarred him were it not for an antecedent disposition toward being bruised. His peculiar vulnerability and ambivalence to pain express themselves in the figure of the *femme fatale* who dominates all of his early writing. Although she is a familiar type in nineteenth-century literature, this "fair fearful Venus made of deadly foam" objectifies Swinburne's personal sense of the deathliness of desire and the desirability of death. The hero of **Chastelard,** for example, commits the curiously passive indiscretion of watching Mary Stuart disrobe, in order to compel her to behead him. In an ecstasy of self-prostration, Chastelard says to his Queen:

> Stretch your throat that I may kiss all round
> Where mine shall be cut through; suppose my mouth
> The axe-edge to bite so sweet a throat in twain
> With bitter iron, should not it turn soft
> As lip is soft to lip?

Chastelard is too specialized in theme and derivative in style to engage the general reader, although as an exercise in unrelenting eroticism, this mid-Victorian *Salomé* retains the power to shock. In **Atalanta** Swinburne steps outside the torrid circle of his obsessions and creates a world as bright, virginal and swift as *Chastelard* is sick with too many roses. Yet he still manages to use the myth of the virgin huntress as a vehicle for his private sensibility. Atalanta is a *frigid* Venus who destroys her lover Meleager as mercilessly as Aphrodite destroys Hippolytus.

No tact is fine enough to discriminate among all the various shades in Swinburne's portrait of love. At times he takes a schoolboy's hot delight simply in handling the theme. At times he writes like a patrician revolutionary attacking sexual prudery as John Stuart Mill attacked intellectual conformity. Occasionally love serves him as an excuse for embroidering rhymes in which birds or flowers would do as well. But the theme can get out of hand, as in **"Anactoria,"** in which he writes with morbid power of the pleasures of inflicting pain:

> I would find grievous ways to have thee slain,
> Intense device, and superflux of pain;
> Vex thee with amorous agonies, and shake
> Life at thy lips, and leave it there to ache;
> Strain out thy soul with pangs too soft to kill,
> Intolerable interludes, and infinite ill;
> Relapse and reluctation of the breath,
> Dumb tunes and shuddering semitones of death.

• • • • •

> Ah that my lips were tuneless lips, but pressed
> To the bruised blossom of thy scourged white breast!
> Ah that my mouth for Muses' milk were fed
> On the sweet blood thy sweet small wounds had bled!
> That with my tongue I felt them, and could taste
> The faint flakes from thy bosom to thy waist!
> That I could drink thy veins as wine, and eat
> Thy breasts like honey! that from face to feet
> Thy body were abolished and consumed,
> And in my flesh thy very flesh entombed!

• • • • •

> Would I not plague thee dying overmuch?
> Would I not hurt thee perfectly? not touch
> Thy pores of sense with torture, and make bright
> Thine eyes with bloodlike tears and grievous light?
> Strike pang from pang as note is struck from note,
> Catch the sob's middle music in thy throat,
> Take thy limbs living, and new-mould with these
> A lyre of many faultless agonies?

The horror of the last couplet is heightened by its exquisite verbal wit, as faultless as Marvell's green thought in a green shade.

The passion in **"Anactoria"** goes well beyond Swinburne's desire throughout *Poems and Ballads* to *épater le bourgeois* ["shock the middle classes"]. Only in two or three prose passages of *Lesbia Brandon* does one sense the same overwhelming pressure toward personal release, the same breathing closeness of the author to his text. Elsewhere in *Poems and Ballads* Swinburne handles similar themes in cooler tones. Poems whose sadism and anti-theism aroused or shocked generations of readers seem today to veer away from blasphemy toward burlesque. Yet Swinburne's death occasioned a sermon by the Vice Dean of Canterbury Cathedral on the need of Christ's blood itself to wash away "the pollution which Swinburne's poetry introduced into English literature."

Instead of pollution, I find a certain innocence in Swinburne's perversity. As in his letters, with their Etonian slang and naughty allusions to the Divine Marquis, his eroticism is

often more infantile than immoral. Perhaps critical judgment is so unsettled over Swinburne because he is at once a great poet of the solitude of loving and a precocious schoolboy making off-color rhymes. Nor does it simplify matters that he is possibly the most gifted parodist and mimic in English. Swinburne in jest often appears most in earnest, and his apparent earnestness is often a jest, as in his hymn to Notre Dame des Sept Douleurs:

> Could you hurt me, sweet lips, though I hurt you?
>   Men touch them, and change in a trice
> The lilies and languors of virtue
>   For the raptures and roses of vice;
> Those lie where thy foot on the floor is,
>   These crown and caress thee and chain,
> O splendid and sterile Dolores,
>   Our Lady of Pain.

• • • • •

> Thou wert fair in the fearless old fashion,
>   And thy limbs are as melodies yet,
> And move to the music of passion
>   With lithe and lascivious regret.
> What ailed us, O gods, to desert you
>   For creeds that refuse and restrain?
> Come down and redeem us from virtue,
>   Our Lady of Pain.

In this litany of a sadomasochist's lust, Dolores presides over the marriage of Pleasure and Pain in a ceremony that suggests a black mass. Beneath the deftly controlled surface, one recognizes several of the major themes of *Poems and Ballads*: the intricate connection of pleasure and pain; the dual desire to experience and inflict suffering; a will to fall prey to the destructive sexual force of woman, and the fear of so falling; a need for total self-abasement and a counterimpulse to rebel; a deeply religious reverence before a mystery, and as profound a desire to blaspheme.

God is the supreme sadist in *Poems and Ballads.* Swinburne defies Him eloquently and delightedly: "Him would I reach, him smite, him desecrate," he writes in **"Anactoria"** of the God who grinds men in order to feed the mute, melancholy lust of heaven. At times Swinburne's poetry of pure defiance achieves a Job-like integrity; at times it suggests a schoolboy's provoking his headmaster to lay on the rod. This anti-theist verse never succeeds as great poetry, although it is often great rhetoric, as in the **"Hymn to Proserpine,"** with its lament for the conquest of the pagan world by the pale Galilean.

Swinburne's rebellion against the tyrant God finds its complement in his worship of man. One recalls that this blasphemer of the pieties of his age once arrived at a dinner party bearing a footstool, so that he could pay proper homage to Robert Browning. In his verse, as in his life, Swinburne was both rigidly defiant and pliantly responsive, self-exultant and self-abasing, a rebel and a mimic. His long sequence of poems of praise begins with tributes to Walter Savage Landor and Victor Hugo in *Poems and Ballads* and ends, some fifty years later, with his humble effusions to the babies of Wimbledon Common.

Swinburne's second volume of poems, *Songs before Sunrise,* is in all apparent respects the opposite of *Poems and Ballads.* Erotic verses give way to marching songs in praise of Italian liberation. We leave the sultry atmosphere of the boudoir and breathe instead the bracing air of the *Risorgimento*; our Lady of Liberty displaces our Lady of Pain. Yet the two ladies inspire in Swinburne similar emotions of self-prostration and worship. In **"The Oblation,"** for example, he addresses Liberty as if she were a stern lover under whose feet he craves to be trampled:

> All things were nothing to give
>   Once to have sense of you more,
>   Touch you and taste of you sweet,
> Think you and breathe you and live,
>   Swept of your wings as they soar,
>   Trodden by chance of your feet.

The sincerity of Swinburne's attachment to the goddess of Liberty is unassailable, although he composed many of his odes to her while walking to a brothel where he paid to be flogged.

The fault with *Songs before Sunrise* and its companion volume, *Songs of Two Nations,* is not their covert pathology but their dullness. Dolores and Faustine at least could bite, but Lady Liberty merely bores. Perhaps the themes of sexual humiliation and theological defiance in *Poems and Ballads* are intrinsically richer than the parallel themes of hero-worship and political rebellion in *Songs before Sunrise.* At any rate, the abstract diction, the manic, trumpet-blast tone, the rhetorical straining—"O soul, O God, O glory of liberty"—soon exhaust the reader's capacity to respond.

With startling self-knowledge, Swinburne anticipated the cause of his relative failure in *Songs before Sunrise.* [The critic adds in a footnote that " 'Failure' is too harsh a term. There are at least a dozen distinguished poems in the volume, among them 'Super Flumina Babylonis,' 'Hertha,' 'Before a Crucifix,' 'Hymn of Man,' 'Genesis,' 'Christmas Antiphones,' 'Siena,' 'Cor Cordium,' 'Tiresias,' 'On the Downs,' 'Messidor,' and 'Non dolet'." But none of these reaches the standard set in *Poems and Ballads,* 1866, by 'Laus Veneris' and 'The Triumph of Time' and attained again in *Poems and Ballads,* 1878, by 'A Forsaken Garden' and 'A Vision of Spring in Winter.' I should add that other critics disagree with my tepid estimate of *Songs before Sunrise,* among them T. Earle Welby and Swinburne himself."] "There is I think room for a book of songs of the European revolution," he wrote to William Michael Rossetti on beginning the volume, "and if sung as thoroughly as Hugo or as Whitman would sing them, they ought to ring for some time to some distance of echo. The only fear is that one may be disabled by one's desire—made impotent by excess of strain." The love of liberty was one of the most abiding and intense emotions that Swinburne knew. His rhetorical excess in *Songs before Sunrise* marks his ineffectual effort to translate great conviction into great art.

All that is forced or febrile in *Songs before Sunrise* achieves quiet fulfillment in the *Poems and Ballads* of 1878. In the first series of *Poems and Ballads,* one felt the exuberance of genius discovering itself; in the second series the voice has achieved self-mastery and sings in chaste magnificence. The volume appeared during the grimmest period of Swinburne's life, when he lived alone in London in suicidal dissipation. One senses the solitude, but none of the squalor. In the splendid elegies to dead poets interspersed through *Poems and Ballads,* Swinburne seems to lay his own youth to rest and prepare to retire from the exercise of his highest powers. One year after the volume was published, he was removed from his rooms in Great James Street by his friend Theodore Watts-Dunton and taken to live at Putney. For thirty years their home at "No. 2, The Pines," served Swinburne as a kind

of suburban sanitorium. "The Pines" became the tomb of a great poet and the birthplace of a distinguished man of letters who wrote on Shakespeare and Victor Hugo, Marlowe and Mary, Queen of Scots. One of the finest lyrics in *Poems and Ballads* is entitled **"A Vision of Spring in Winter"**; the volume itself is a pervision of Swinburne's long winter, seen from the last moment of his spring.

The leitmotif of *Poems and Ballads* is the triumph of time over love, over life, and over the generative powers of earth and man. These are Swinburne's essential themes, and *Poems and Ballads,* 1878, is remarkable only in that it plays upon them more persistently and with his subtlest music. The sado-masochistic verses of *Poems and Ballads,* First Series, are less the heart of Swinburne's poetic matter than a variation on this larger theme of the forces in nature that divide and destroy us. **"Laus Veneris," "The Leper,"** and **"Anactoria"** are extreme cases of the classic Swinburne situation in which lovers are, so to speak, disjointed. Once in the First Series—in **"The Triumph of Time"**—and once in the Second Series—in **"A Forsaken Garden"**—all of these elements meet in perfect balance. They are Swinburne's archetypical lyrics, adjacent stanzas of a single, larger poem.

In both poems one feels the full force of loss, and the counter-force of its acceptance. This stoicism of the heart, which falls short of bitterness on the one hand, and the sentimentality of unresisted regret on the other, is the defining note of Swinburne's love poetry. It is struck in the opening stanza of **"The Triumph of Time,"** in which the propulsive rush of the meter paces time's triumph over the lovers, changing all things except the fact of their separation:

> Before our lives divide for ever,
>   While time is with us and hands are free,
> (Time, swift to fasten and swift to sever
>   Hand from hand, as we stand by the sea)
> I will say no word that a man might say
> Whose whole life's love goes down in a day;
> For this could never have been; and never
>   Though the gods and the years relent, shall be.

I mentioned the lovers in **"The Triumph of Time,"** but, remarkably, there are scarcely any lovers in Swinburne's poetry. There is much passion but little conjunction; emotion is felt but not communicated and not returned. Swinburne has mistakenly acquired the reputation of an erotic poet; he is rather the poet of love's impossibility. Perhaps that is why, even in his most sensual verses, one feels a peculiar innocence, just as in his most moving love poetry one feels a profound barrenness:

> It will grow not again, this fruit of my heart,
>   Smitten with sunbeams, ruined with rain.
> The singing seasons divide and depart,
>   Winter and summer depart in twain.
> It will grow not again, it is ruined at root,
> The bloodlike blossom, the dull red fruit;
> Though the heart yet sickens, the lips yet smart,
>   With sullen savour of poisonous pain.

All of Swinburne's finer love poetry is set by the sea—the cold, clean "mother-maid" who is more palpable than the evershadowy girl who refuses, or is unaware of, the poet's love. The return to the sea in **"The Triumph of Time"** occurs near the poem's end, in three stanzas more strange than Swinburne's critics have yet acknowledged:

> I will go back to the great sweet mother,

Mother and lover of men, the sea.
I will go down to her, I and none other,
  Close with her, kiss her and mix her with me;
Cling to her, strive with her, hold her fast;
O fair white mother, in days long past
Born without sister, born without brother,
  Set free my soul as thy soul is free.

O fair green-girdled mother of mine,
  Sea, that art clothed with the sun and the rain,
Thy sweet hard kisses are strong like wine,
  Thy large embraces are keen like pain.
Save me and hide me with all thy waves,
Find me one grave of thy thousand graves,
Those pure cold populous graves of thine
  Wrought without hand in a world without stain.

I shall sleep, and move with the moving ships,
  Change as the winds change, veer in the tide;
My lips will feast on the foam of thy lips,
  I shall rise with thy rising, with thee subside;
Sleep, and now know if she be, if she were,
Filled full with life to the eyes and hair,
As a rose is fulfilled to the roseleaf tips
  With splendid summer and perfume and pride.

The lines are at once infantile—"save me and hide me"—and overwhelming. One recalls that Swinburne's earliest memory was of shrieking with delight as his father tossed him head-first into the waves. Fifty years later he wrote to his sister of the ecstasy he felt in swimming off the Sussex Downs:

> I ran like a boy, tore off my clothes, and hurled myself into the water. And it was but for a few minutes—but I was in Heaven! The whole sea was literally golden as well as green—it was liquid and living sunlight in which one lived and moved and had one's being. And to feel that in deep water is to feel—as long as one is swimming out, if only a minute or two—as if one was in another world of life, and one far more glorious than even Dante ever dreamed of in his Paradise.

That paradise held many pleasures, among them the pleasure of death—that primordial return to "the great sweet mother," whose rocking rhythms Swinburne captures in lines that, like some fluid lullaby, mix the image of love-making with the image of drowning: "My lips will feast on the foam of thy lips, / I shall rise with thy rising, with thee subside." The passage is animistic in its primitiveness of emotion. The decadent, verbally sophisticated Swinburne was in another part of his being pre-civilized, a wind-worshiper and a sea-worshiper whose poetry springs from sources more antique than words.

In **"A Forsaken Garden,"** as in **"The Triumph of Time,"** this fusion of the artificial with the aboriginal achieves a fragile power. The setting is an eighteenth-century garden gone to seed and thorn. A faint, salt-sprayed scent of faded flowers and ghostly lovers hovers over the opening stanzas. It is springtime, but neither leaves nor loves will bloom again in this rocky wasteland poised over the sea. The actual garden that inspired the imagined garden of the poem was on the Isle of Wight, where Swinburne spent the springs of his childhood in a setting of near-tropical luxuriance. In late summer the Swinburnes drove north to the family seat at Capheaton, Northumberland, where the bare moors, gray seas, and autumnal summits must have seemed, to the young Swinburne, like winter suddenly overlaid upon spring. The two seasons became forever fixed in his mind in their sudden proximity and sharpness of contrast, so that he could scarcely feel the

one without its opposite. The sea that rolls through the great closing stanzas of **"A Forsaken Garden"** is a chill, northern sea, a blast of death bringing a second ruin, as in *Tristram of Lyonesse,* to a rich but ravaged landscape:

> All are at one now, roses and lovers,
>   Not known of the cliffs and the fields and the sea.
> Not a breath of the time that has been hovers
>   In the air now soft with a summer to be.
> Not a breath shall there sweeten the seasons hereafter
>   Of the flowers or the lovers that laugh now or weep,
> When as they that are free now of weeping and laughter
>   We shall sleep.
>
> Here death may deal not again for ever;
>   Here change may come not till all change end.
> From the graves they have made they shall rise up never,
>   Who have left nought living to ravage and rend.
> Earth, stones, and thorns of the wild ground growing,
>   While the sun and the rain live, these shall be;
> Till a last wind's breath upon all these blowing
>   Roll the sea.
>
> Till the slow sea rise and the sheer cliff crumble,
>   Till terrace and meadow the deep gulfs drink,
> Till the strength of the waves of the high tides humble
>   The fields that lessen, the rocks that shrink,
> Here now in his triumph where all things falter,
>   Stretched out on the spoils that his own hand spread,
> As a god self-slain on his own strange altar,
>   Death lies dead.

As in all of his most powerful verse, Swinburne writes here not of time present, but of a time immemorially before time, or of the eternity that follows time. The steady pulse of the monosyllables, the starkness of the diction, the open generalized barrenness of the setting—"earth, stones, and thorns"—evoke some primordial drama of the elements, as though nature suddenly shed the coloration of millennia and resolved back into earth, water, fire, and wind. The lifeless landscape is charged with hidden life, only to make its final ravagement the more complete: the wind breathes, the rocks shrink, the sea rises, the gulfs drink, the fields are humbled. The wreck is so total that Death itself, with nothing mutable left to prey upon, lies dead. The personification ought to ring hollow—a poetical flourish in an elemental landscape. But this touch of artifice makes more awesome the larger, cosmic death that Swinburne heard blowing through nature like a low bone-shaking rumble and that he here evokes in the form of the wind's last breath rolling sea over earth in the final Deluge.

One hears the same elemental music in **"At a Month's End,"** another lyric of doomed love in *Poems and Ballads,* Second Series. The lovers, no longer in love, stand by night at the sea's edge and watch the serried spears of the waves storm toward the shore:

> Hardly we saw the high moon hanging,
>   Heard hardly through the windy night
> Far waters ringing, low reefs clanging,
>   Under wan skies and waste white light.
>
> With chafe and change of surges chiming,
>   The clashing channels rocked and rang
> Large music, wave to wild wave timing,
>   And all the choral water sang.

The lapsed love plays itself out against a background of alliterative choiring of the elements. Drifting clouds, waves, gulls, wind, the earth's margins, these are the phenomena on which

Swinburne's senses instinctually fix, the background of earth against which his people stand, dwarfed and apart:

> Across, aslant, a scudding sea-mew
>   Swam, dipped, and dropped, and grazed the sea:
> And one with me I could not dream you;
>   And one with you I could not be.
>
> As the white wing the white wave's fringes
>   Touched and slid over and flashed past—
> As a pale cloud a pale flame tinges
>   From the moon's lowest light and last—
>
> As a star feels the sun and falters,
>   Touched to death by diviner eyes—
> As on the old gods' untended altars
>   The old fire of withered worship dies—
>
> • • • • •
>
> So once with fiery breath and flying
>   Your winged heart touched mine and went,
> And the swift spirits kissed, and sighing,
>   Sundered and smiled and were content.

The lovers in **"At a Month's End"** seem not only lost to each other but eclipsed by the larger motions of nature around them. Always in Swinburne the pure, fluid power of wind and sea sweeps everything before it, just as the cataclysmic rush of avalanche and inundation obliterates the paltry human figures in J. M. W. Turner's *Val d'Aosta*. Like Turner, too, Swinburne finds in the vast undifferentiated sea the visible emblem of his genius, with its exaltation of energy over form, infinite nuance over discrete detail. One stanza from **"At a Month's End"** might have come from Turner's own catalogue descriptions of his seascapes:

> Faint lights fell this way, that way floated,
>   Quick sparks of sea-fire keen like eyes
> From the rolled surf that flashed, and noted
>   Shores and faint cliffs and bays and skies.

One recognizes in both artists the same sophisticated virtuosity, alongside an enormous responsiveness to the aboriginal forces of nature. Swinburne's landscapes, like Turner's, abstract all the sharp, divisible aspects of nature into an elemental luminosity and motion, such as God might have beheld on completing the Creation:

> . . . one clear hueless haze of glimmering hues
> The sea's line and the land's line and the sky's.
>
>   **("Thalassius")**

"Indistinctness is my forte," Turner retorted to a patron who chided him for vagueness, a fault which modern critics still impute to Turner's early admirer, Swinburne. Both men practice a highly structured art that has nonetheless freed itself from the canons of conventional representation. No single word in a Swinburne poem quite corresponds to a given thing, just as no single dab of paint on a Turner canvas corresponds to a natural object; the correspondence is always between the total configuration of the poem or painting and the total configuration of nature. The adjective floating freely away from its substantive in a Swinburne poem is equivalent to the blob of pigment that is neither sea nor foam nor sky, but all of these, in a Turner painting. Such an art prizes color over outline, light over form, music over meaning. Its concern, as Swinburne wrote of poetry [in **"Notes on the Text of Shelley"**], but might as well have written of Impressionism in general, "is rather to render the effect of a thing than the thing itself." I had read the following lines from *Atalanta in*

Calydon many times before they actually sprang into focus as a splendid rendering not of the thing itself, but of its effect upon the sun-dazed beholder. Althaea describes the bright blur of approaching hunters, as they ride between her and the slanted morning light:

> . . . for sharp mixed shadow and wind
> Blown up between the morning and the mist,
> With steam of steeds and flash of bridle or wheel,
> And fire, and parcels of the broken dawn,
> And dust divided by hard light, and spears
> That shine and shift as the edge of wild beasts' eyes,
> Smite upon mine; so fiery their blind edge
> Burns, and bright points break up and baffle day.

Swinburne's love of mixed effects gives to his descriptive verse much of its Turnerian quality. His poetry is charged with the tension of delicately poised opposites: shadows thinned by light, lights broken by shade, sunset passing into moonrise, sea merging with sky. He is obsessed by the moment when one thing shades off into its opposite, or when contraries fuse, as in **"Hermaphroditus,"** one of his earliest and finest poems. Yet apart from his profound esthetic affinity with Turner, there is the unique idiosyncrasy of Swinburne himself, who was equipped with superb senses, each of which must have transmitted a peculiar counterpoint. This basic, polarizing rhythm runs through his being and manifests itself in his compulsive use of alliterating antitheses in prose and verse. Much in Swinburne that has been criticized as mere mannerism—paradox, alliteration, elaborate antithesis—strikes me as deriving from his deepest impulses, although the question of "sincerity" is always vexing in his verse. In a sense, Swinburne *perceived* in paradoxes, and his recurrent synesthetic images express perfectly that passing of pain into pleasure, bitter into sweet, loathing into desire, which lay at the root of his profoundest experiences. He loves nature best in her moments of transition, as if drawn to dusk and dawn as the day's hermaphrodisms:

> Over two shadowless waters, adrift as a pinnace in peril,
>   Hangs as in heavy suspense, charged with irresolute light,
> Softly the soul of the sunset upholden awhile on the sterile
>   Waves and wastes of the land, half repossessed by the night.
>
>   **("Evening on the Broads")**

His imagery of these times of change is most mixed and rich, as when, in **"Evening on the Broads,"** he fuses touch, sound, and sight to describe twilight at sea as "a molten music of colour"; and in a line from **"Laus Veneris"** that is wisest not to gloss at all, the knight is maddened by erotic fumes rising from "the sea's panting mouth of *dry* desire."

At times Swinburne will elaborate a single antithesis into an entire poem. **"A Vision of Spring in Winter"** is a beautifully poised evocation of life arising from dormancy as the poet himself declines from spring toward winter; the countermovements of rebirth and loss are as delicately juxtaposed as the snowdrop set in the vanishing snow at the poems' opening. Muted antithesis is also at the heart of **"Ave atque Vale,"** an elegy to Baudelaire in which Swinburne uncannily evokes the mixed, sweetly-acrid scent of *Les Fleurs du Mal*. The elegiac convention of strewing flowers takes on sudden, sensuous reality as one *smells* the very leaves of Baudelaire's book, the paradoxical

> Half-*faded fiery* blossoms, *pale* with *heat*
> And full of *bitter* summer, but more *sweet*

To thee than on the gleanings of a northern shore . . .

The poem pays its subject the high tribute of perfect imitation. At its close we move away from the bitter-sweet scent of *Les Fleurs du Mal* to the chill smell of the earth that is to receive the poet's body. There is no "far-off divine event" to lighten grief, no advance to pastures new; only death, and this grim tribute of one great poet to another:

> For thee, O now a silent soul, my brother,
>   Take at my hands this garland, and farewell.
>   Thin is the leaf, and chill the wintry smell,
> And chill the solemn earth, a fatal mother,
>   With sadder than the Niobean womb,
>   And in the hollow of her breasts a tomb,
> Content thee, howsoe'er, whose days are done;
>   There lies not any troublous thing before,
>   Nor sight nor sound to war against thee more,
> For whom all winds are quiet as the sun,
>   All waters as the shore.

Only once again, in **Tristram of Lyonesse,** did Swinburne achieve the sustained excellence of **Poems and Ballads,** Second Series. He continued to publish volumes of verse into our own century, but for the most part the later poetry is a peculiarly vacant sort of versage that exists still-born in a world of its own. One thinks of Swinburne's increasing deafness at Putney, and somehow the poetry suggests a muted soliloquy. The saddest lines in all of Swinburne appear in **"A Midsummer Holiday"** (1884), dedicated to Watts-Dunton. The setting is indistinguishable from those great, bleak earlier lyrics of the sea's encroachments on the land; here, however, the sea has shrunk to a suburban pond reflecting the ghost of a dead poet:

> Friend, the lonely land is bright for you and me
> All its wild ways through: but this methinks is best,
> Here to watch how kindly time and change agree
> Where the small town smiles, a warm still sea-side nest.

Yet there are moments of astonishing strength in late Swinburne. Much of **"By the North Sea,"** more of the unknown **"Evening on the Broads,"** all of **"A Nympholept"** defeat one's impulse to impose a curve of growth, flowering, and decline upon the actual pattern of his creativity. Swinburne always wrote a good deal of dead and silly verse, rather more of both toward the end of his career. That his most lifeless poetry is in all formal respects—meter, diction, and subject—virtually indistinguishable from his greatest poetry is one of the mysteries of his art. His genius is extraordinary above all for its *intermittency*; the verse-making engine spins constantly for half a century, but the surges of engaged power are sudden and unpredictable. Tennyson called him "a reed through which all things blow into music." Sometimes the melody carries; often it does not. Swinburne had a curious passion for monotony, which was undoubtedly linked to his love of bleak, monochromatic effects. Out of this love came his most powerful poetry; out of it also came whole poems too like his own description of the Dunwich coast:

> Miles, and miles, and miles of desolation!
> Leagues on leagues on leagues without a change!
>   **("By the North Sea")**

One's final reservation toward Swinburne has to do with a certain arrested development. Wordsworth's genius flowers, then endlessly wanes: *Tintern Abbey* unfolds an organic evolution of growths, losses, and gains. Neither Swinburne nor his verse seems to undergo much change; a single note is struck early and held obsessively long. The reader wants a richer range of subject, more nuance of idea. Swinburne composes by compounding, not synthesizing. Too often, his method is merely quantitative: "I have added yet four more jets of boiling and gushing infamy to the perennial and poisonous fountain of Dolores." One wishes that his eccentric genius could have retained all its power while ridding itself of rigidity and repetitiveness. It did not, and the death of development in Swinburne may have been as large a loss to English poetry as the physical death of Keats. (pp. vii-xxxiv)

> *John D. Rosenberg, in an introduction to* Swinburne: Selected Poetry and Prose *by Algernon Swinburne, edited by John D. Rosenberg, The Modern Library, 1968, pp. vii-xxxiv.*

ANTONY H. HARRISON   (essay date 1977)

[*In the following excerpt, Harrison examines Swinburne's poetic use of language, in particular his ability to reflect in his poetry the limitations and impermanence of life.*]

Swinburne's poetry has repeatedly been attacked for vagueness, diffuseness, and emotional as well as prosodic extravagance. Although the imagery of his verse is generally concrete and graphic, readers are frequently baffled or dismayed by the apparent dissolution of meaning that seems inevitably to occur in the Swinburnean lyric. And although his techniques of composition clearly constitute an intentional "style," critics often insist that Swinburne's "rhapsodic vagaries" can be properly understood only in psychological or biographical terms. They suggest that because of its idiosyncrasies, his poetry is not susceptible to the usual kinds of critical analysis at all. Such reactions, though precipitate, are understandable, for it was often characteristic of Swinburne, as it was of the French symbolists, to use the versatility of grammar to undercut the possibilities in language for precise meaning. In fact, the diffuse effect of Swinburne's verse is a result of both its subject matter and Swinburne's craftsmanship.

John D. Rosenberg describes Swinburne's poetry as deliberately diffuse: "No single word in a Swinburne poem quite corresponds to a given thing. . . . The adjective floating freely away from its substantive in a Swinburne poem is equivalent to the blob of pigment that is neither sea nor foam nor sky, but all of these, in a Turner painting. Such an art prizes color over outline . . . music over meaning" [see excerpt dated 1968]. This seems an accurate general characterization of Swinburne's verse, but it does not begin to deal in adequate detail with the technique and final effect of the poems that are so often dismissed as vague. As Rosenberg implies, the charge of vagueness results from the correct initial response to Swinburne's deliberately expansive rather than reductive use of language. But to appreciate the complexity of Swinburne's achievement as a poet, we must extend and supersede first responses by means of patient inquiry. Such inquiry is best begun by determining Swinburne's attitude toward his medium of expression and is completed only when we have become sensitive to the extraordinary effects of his characteristic exploitation of the evanescent properties of language.

In the fourth major chorus of **Atalanta in Calydon,** Swinburne deals by implication with the ponderous and precarious subject of the relations between language, life, and death. The chorus concludes with the assertion that "words divide and rend; / But silence is most noble till the end." And it opens with a passage that powerfully suggests the complexity of Swinburne's attitude toward language:

> Who hath given man speech? or who hath set therein
> A thorn for peril and a snare for sin?
> For in the word his life is and his breath,
>   And in the word his death,
> That madness and the infatuate heart may breed
>   From the word's womb the deed
> And life bring one thing forth ere all pass by,
> Even one thing which is ours yet cannot die—
>   Death.

Language here is represented as symbolic action ("From the word's womb the deed"). Moreover, in Swinburne's early monism the end of all action is represented as implicit in its beginning ("in the word his life is . . . / and his death"). Indeed, life cannot be conceived without man's mad and "infatuate heart" at once conceiving of death, because no action can be conceived as perpetual. Speech is symbolic of both life (desire) and its necessary counterpart, death (relief), as well as of man's passion to be simultaneously possessed of both. Of course, language is, at the same time, the primary vehicle for the expression of all our contradictory passions, of our desire for consummations to every action we initiate. Whereas George Eliot conceived of a "roar on the other side of silence," Swinburne perceives it on this side; it consists in man's inevitable attempts to express passion in language, including the passion for immortality, as well as the passionate and contradictory desire for an end to passions. The possibility of redemption from our cravings and yearnings exists only when those attempts are silenced. As Swinburne insists in **"Il-icet"** and throughout his early poems, the ultimate, imperturbable silence is found solely in "The poppied sleep, the end of all," where "the heart of wrath is broken, / Where long love ends as a thing spoken."

Of all things transient, Swinburne repeatedly suggests, speech is the most fleeting. Even poets, the supreme masters of speech, are bound to perish. Sappho in **"Anactoria"** sustains a suspiciously long assertion that she will be made immortal through the affinities of her "song" with man's inescapable passions and the objects of nature. She claims that,

> . . . in the light and laughter, in the moan
>
> And music, and in grasp of lip and hand
> And shudder of water that makes felt on land
> The immeasurable tremor of all the sea,
> Memories shall mix and metaphors of me.

But the memory of her passions and her song will necessarily diminish as the generations pass. At the crescendo of her increasingly desperate monologue, Sappho envisions her posthumous union with all natural things and "all high things forever"—a result of "my songs once heard in a strange place" which shall "cleave to men's lives." She insists that she shall not die,

> For [men] shall give me of their souls, shall give
> Life, and the days and loves wherewith I live,
> Shall quicken me with loving, fill with breath,
> Save me and serve me, strive for me with death.

[In] spite of Sappho's yearning for immortality, she cannot conceive of eternal existence in her perennial state of unfulfilled sexual desire for Anactoria. And her song, through which she hopes to remain immortal, is merely the expression of passions which, she is aware, can be finally quelled only in death:

> Alas, that neither moon nor snow nor dew
> Nor all cold things can purge me wholly through,
> Assuage me nor allay me nor appease,
> Till supreme sleep shall bring me bloodless ease.

Like **"Anactoria,"** nearly all of the poems in *Poems and Ballads,* First Series, simultaneously illustrate the power of men's passions and the impossibility of adequately and permanently gratifying them. At the same time, these lyrics embody young Swinburne's preoccupation with the fact of mortality, and, as a reflection of it, the evanescence of man's self-expression in language. As a result, much of Swinburne's early verse, while straining language in the attempt to describe states of intense passion, forces upon the reader an awareness of the impermanence of things spoken, the weightless qualities of language that can be worked poetically to leave no definable impress on even the most receptive mind. In most of these poems, expression imitates idea. Often, our perception of syntactical structure dissolves into preoccupation with rhythm and sound. Indeed, perhaps unique in Victorian poetry is Swinburne's ostensibly unlimited resourcefulness in making a poetic virtue out of an acknowledged deficiency of the medium in which he is working. (pp. 16-18)

"Anactoria" can be seen as both a thematic and technical model for the pieces in *Poems and Ballads* that deal with human yearning for a complete passionate consummation described as impossible to attain in life. In **"The Triumph of Time," "Phaedra,"** and **"Hymn to Proserpine,"** for example, death is described as the ultimate anodyne and an alternate, if not ultimate, consummation to passion. For Sappho all pleasure is mixed with pain, and perfect pleasure is death:

>   O that I
> Durst crush thee out of life with love, and die,
> Die of thy pain and my delight, and be
> Mixed with thy blood and molten into thee!

In spite of the concrete manner in which desire is portrayed here, the craving for relief from human passions, as expressed by Swinburne's poetic personae, is always uncontainable and its infinite, immedicable nature is always reinforced by the language in which yearning is expressed. In spite of the graphic imagery of the above passage, we feel compelled to suspend belief and assume that its meaning is metaphorical rather than literal. Yet the problems of interpretation with which it forcefully confronts us are not dissolved by describing the statement as merely a hyperbolic expression of consummate sado-masochism. Sappho is yearning (desperately, bitterly) for real pain, real delight, and real death simultaneously—not for merely metaphorical or vicarious oblivion. The words *literally* characterize the intensity and nature of Sappho's complex passion in the vivid description of an impossible act. We are forced here to accept the impossible to the extent that it *is* realized in language. As in this passage, Swinburne's verse is frequently nonmimetic, but purely expressive. We are, after all, incapable of visualizing the act Sappho describes. Yet, the powerful physicalness of Sappho's yearning to be "Mixed with thy blood and molten into thee" prevents either a metaphorical or a mimetic reading and forces us to receive her words as we would the ravings of a mad woman, as pure expression and exclusively symbolic action.

From almost every piece in *Poems and Ballads* we can cull illustrations of other techniques Swinburne employs to break down the reader's apprehension of explicit meaning in the process of heightening emotional force. The most impressive examples occur in poems where death is hailed as an anodyne and the possibilities for dissolution in death are explored through the dissolution of meaning in language (a representation of the dissolution of consciousness). In these poems Swinburne's language is, finally, always grammatical; literal meanings are decipherable, but resonances can be pursued until they dissolve just beyond intelligibility, as they do in the poem **"Hermaphroditus."** For Swinburne the statue of Hermaphroditus in the Louvre constitutes a mythical but palpable representation of that insatiable state of desire expressed by Sappho in **"Anactoria."** Because of his sexual duality, the mythical Hermaphroditus is not merely sexually impotent, but impotent as well for action in the world, a still birth, suspended between sleep and life in a perpetual state of yearning, possessed of the *combined* desires of man and woman. The statue is the physical representation of insupportably intense, insatiable human passions.

With delicate empathy, in the first sonnet of the **"Hermaphroditus"** sequence, Swinburne is able to induce in the reader a state of being and yearning—a state of suspended action—approaching that which the statue projects; but, in order to do so, he must temporarily dissolve the possibility for meaning to be derived from the language he uses:

> Lift up thy lips, turn round, look back for love,
>   Blind love that comes by night and casts our rest;

• • • • •

> Two loves at either blossom of thy breast
> Strive until one be under and one above.
> Their breath is fire upon the amorous air,
>   Fire in thine eyes and where thy lips suspire:
> And whosoever hath seen thee, being so fair,
>   Two things turn all his life and blood to fire;
> A strong desire begot on great despair,
> A great despair cast out by strong desire.

The last two lines define the relationship of the viewer (and the reader) to the statue as one of helpless identification. The rhetorical structure and the effect here is that of a paradox: the second line inverts the order of the subject and object of the first. "Cast out," of course, meaningfully replaces "begot on," as we become aware on closer scrutiny, and although the initial effect is the same as that of a paradox, i.e., intellectual immobility, the final effect is to heighten our sense of the statue's desire. Literally, the despair concomitant with Hermaphroditus' dual sexuality *generates* a desire (for unisexuality and the possibility of sexual gratification) powerful enough to overthrow and effectually abolish despair. But in order to explain the process verbally, "despair" must remain in visible equipoise with "desire," its child. Here syntax imitates the passion represented, while seeming at first to undermine meaning because of our expectations of such a rhetorical structure. These last lines leave us in a momentary state of intellectual suspension parallel to Hermaphroditus' suspension in a purgatory of sexual yearnings which "shall not be assuaged till death be dead." Here, as in **"Anactoria,"** Swinburne uses accepted mechanical properties of language to undermine its potential for precise meaning, and to approach the pure and perfect expression of an ostensibly ineffable emotional state.

Swinburne employs similarly simple but subtle grammatical structures expansively to define the impermanence and contradictions inherent in conceptual states as well. **"Ilicet,"** for example, is a lyric in which an anonymous persona attempts conceptually and negatively to describe the nature of death. The subject is the same as in Swinburne's poems of atheistic iconoclasm: the relationship of death to life and to the passions and pretensions of the living. Yet it is written not in the context of reproach to the "Pale Galilean" or any other god, nor as an apostrophe to an ultimate god, but rather as a credo of consummate fatalism. The poem is sometimes ironically patronizing, sometimes elaborately critical of human yearnings for an afterlife and the wretchedness endured by those who believe in gods that allow "this dust" to "gather flesh hereafter":

> They find no fruit of things they cherish;
> The goodness of a man shall perish,
>   It shall be one thing with his sin.

• • • • •

> Nay, where the heart of wrath is broken,
> Where long love ends as a thing spoken,
>   How shall thy crying enter there?

Death is hailed not as an anodyne or recompense, but rather as both the locus of nonbeing and a supreme fact:

> There is an end of joy and sorrow;
> Peace all day long, all night, all morrow.

• • • • •

> Outside of all the worlds and ages,
> There where the fool is as the sage is,
>   There where the slayer is clean of blood,
> No end, no passage, no beginning.

The only "god" the persona of this poem acknowledges is relentless Fate, which he characterizes by means of deft but gentle inversions of New Testament figures:

> Shall these grave-clothes be rent in sunder;
>   He that hath taken, shall he give?
> He hath rent them: shall he bind together?
> He hath bound them: shall he break the tether?
>   He hath slain them: shall he bid them live?
> A little sorrow, a little pleasure,
> Fate metes us from the dusty measure
>   That holds the date of all of us.

Ironically, in the process of articulating his alternative credo, the speaker manages to apotheosize death. While he admonishes the world for its futile yearning for salvation and afterlife, for its unjustified faith in "high gods," Swinburne dextrously subverts the speaker's stance and suggests that, in spite of himself, the persona yearns for something beyond death:

> Not for [the high gods'] love shall Fate retire,
> Nor they relent for our desire,
>   Nor the graves open for their call.
> The end is more than joy and anguish,
> Than lives that laugh and lives that languish,
>   The poppied sleep, the end of all.

The syntactical ambiguity of the last three lines allows them to be read in two ways. Both phrases of the last line can be perceived in apposition to "the end" of the fourth quoted line. However, alternatively, the comparative "more" can be read as applying not only to "joy," "anguish," and both instances of "lives," but also to "the poppied sleep, the end of all." So that "the end" becomes "more than" the "end of all," and the very notion of absolute death is undercut, as is the finality of the poem's ending, whose grammatical ambiguity forces us back into the labyrinth of language used to accomplish it. Moreover, characteristically, the music of the verse—particularly the internal rhymes of "anguish," "laugh," and "languish"—serve to break down the distinctions between very different emotional states. Swinburne's use of assonance here strives to imitate the speaker's skeptical *ennui* by subverting any attempt simply to reduce language to definable meaning. We do feel the power of the speaker's fatalism and his sense of life's, as death's, monolithic character. At the same time, however, we are made aware that the speaker's admonitions are merely "things spoken," transient and artificial. By the poem's conclusion our faith in the possibility that there in fact exists an "end" which is "more than joy and anguish" is undermined, as is our conviction that there exists any end at all to our equivocal and passionate yearning for ends.

Swinburne's use of complex and purely expressive grammatical constructions in this poem and the others cited from *Poems and Ballads,* First Series, constitutes a kind of preludium to his later practice. In major (and egregiously neglected) works, such as *Erechtheus,* "Thalassius," "On the Cliffs," *Tristram of Lyonesse,* and "The Lake of Gaube," Swinburne employs intentionally diffuse and involved grammar with significantly greater frequency than in the lyrics of *Poems and Ballads.* The standard explanation is that his dithyrambic and vacant later poems were written in his premature dotage, when in the protective custody of Theodore Watts-Dunton. Yet, if the effect of Swinburne's prosody in the later poems is examined with the care we have applied to the lyrics treated here, his practice at Putney is logically seen as an extension of expressive techniques developed in his early works. For instance, in the second stanza of **"The Lake of Gaube"** (1899) Swinburne describes the salamanders that densely inhabit the mountains around the lake. Having stressed, in the first stanza, how all elemental creation beneath the sun-god lies "prone in passion, blind with bliss unseen," Swinburne proceeds to depict the exuberant life of the beautiful salamanders:

> And living things of light like flames in flower
> That glance and flash as though no hand might tame
> Lightnings whose life outshone their stormlit hour
> And played and laughed on earth, with all their power
> Gone, and with all their joy of life made long
> And harmless as the lightning life of song,
> Shine sweet like stars when darkness feels them strong.

This passage employs some prosodic techniques similar to those already discussed. The most conspicuous are separation and accretion. The simple grammar of this single sentence is that "living things . . . Shine sweet like stars." As in much of Swinburne's later poetry, however, our perception of grammar dissolves as we attempt to absorb the accretion of highly expressive, descriptive detail between the subject and predicate. Here Swinburne's intent is to demonstrate the "Glad glory, thrilled with sense of unison" that, in the first stanza, he perceives as characteristic of every object in the passively receptive world of nature. Therefore, as the description of the salamanders is extended, these "living things" undergo a series of metaphoric transformations that demonstrate their intricate and organic relationship to a constellation of natural phenomena. In brief, the salamanders are like "flames in flower," a metaphoric reduction of multi-forked "lightnings" whose "joy of life" is like the "lightning life of song." Moreover, the salamanders shine "sweet like stars," as the flowers of the stanza's first line do. Because we lose track of grammar in the course of these transformations, the

series affects us as a group of appositions, so that, in effect, flames, flowers, lightnings, song, and stars become identified. The stanza as a whole creates a powerful sense of the essential interrelations among all objects and all experience, which is Swinburne's central philosophical preoccupation. Appropriately, this description precedes the poet's own "rapturous plunge" into the lake where he undergoes a kind of self-dissolution and integration with both organic nature and the spiritual world beneath it. For the poet the lake of Gaube becomes "a symbol revealed" of "infinite heaven."

The prosodic techniques discussed here, along with those treated earlier, mark Swinburne as a central transitional figure between the Romantic and Symbolist movements in poetry. On the one hand, Swinburne's purely expressive use of language stresses the total involvement of the self with human passions, with nature, and with some ultimate reality beyond both. On the other hand, it allows him to enforce on the reader the essential unity and interchangeability of all phenomena. Throughout his career Swinburne was interested in poetry as a vehicle for the expression of both passion and ideas, as the political lyrics of *Songs Before Sunrise* and *Songs of Two Nations* adequately demonstrate. Yet he perceived clearly that ideas embodied in language are, in effect, reductive distillations of feeling; and poetry, he believed, is properly the vehicle for expressing passions, whether sexual, political, or aesthetic. Swinburne adhered to one basic precept in his best poetry: that all areas of human thought and feeling are ultimately indivisible and irreducible, that language—and verse, as the supreme form of language—is, at its best, purely expressive of the "multitudinous unity" of man's vibrant and ineluctably synthetic life. In Swinburne's characteristic philosophical monism, passion, politics, and aesthetics inevitably merge into metaphysics. (pp. 18-20)

> *Antony H. Harrison, "Swinburne's Craft of Pure Expression," in* The Victorian Newsletter, *No. 51, Spring, 1977, pp. 16-20.*

WILLIAM E. BUCKLER   (essay date 1980)

[Buckler is an American educator and critic. In the following excerpt, he offers a reappraisal of Swinburne and a defense of him as a poet who derived inspiration more from literature than from life.]

It has taken a century for Swinburne's reputation as an indispensable man of letters to pass beyond the polemical stage: he has finally become a part of the warp and woof of modern thinking about modern letters. Critics have become shy of denying that Swinburne was one of the imperious shapers of the language, structures, consciousness, and aesthetics with which the twentieth century began its career in poetry and criticism. His conspicuous faults are still intact as are his extraordinary strengths, and the debate over the "essential" character and value of his poetry will continue as long as it is read. But our freedom from the critical monism that laced our sensibilities at mid-century and our new willingness to admit that an exciting literary realization is what makes a day of literary study worthwhile have moved us off-center and made us critically available to new literary recognitions and experiences. It has not been an extreme alteration: most people's methodologies, like Swinburne's conspicuous faults, are still intact; and *pluralism* and *impressionism,* while obviously relevant terms, are too vague or too heavily weighted to be precisely usable. Nor was an extreme alteration needed: the polemical century in Swinburne criticism (say, 1866-1966) could not have been sustained had there not been good poetry-readers on both sides of the issue. Moreover, we should not overgeneralize our critical availability to Swinburne: the group of critics and students of modern aesthetic continuities who do not feel threatened by Swinburne's sexual sensibility, ideological consciousness, linguistic explosiveness, and subject matter derring-do is still relatively small, and it is most unlikely that the undergraduates of the 1980s will march around the quadrangles chanting **"Dolores."** What *is* likely is that the process of literary placement, now in visible flow, will continue uninterrupted and that Swinburne's part in moving literary matters forward when they threatened to stagnate in the acknowledged successes of Tennyson and Browning will gain firmer and crisper, if not universal, recognition and acknowledgment.

Swinburne's part in moving literary matters forward was itself very literary, resulting in that superb bookishness so ably and ardently defended in the "Dedicatory Epistle" to the collected *Poems* (1904). For Swinburne, great books were major spiritual events in human history, quintessentially alive and usable; great artists were the tutors, the singing-masters of men. With Shelley, Swinburne believed that "A poet is the combined product of such internal powers as modify the nature of others; and of such external influences as excite and sustain those powers; he is not one, but both. Every man's mind is, in this respect, modified by all the objects of nature and art; by every word and every suggestion which he ever admitted to act upon his consciousness; it is the mirror upon which all forms are reflected, and in which they compose one form." Swinburne had a deep, liturgical reverence for the writers, texts, myths which formed his literary inheritance, and he celebrated, in both poetry and prose, his keen sense of gratitude for what writers had given him (along with his penetrating awarenesses of the distinctive qualities of their imaginative labors) more broadly, more graciously, and more profoundly than any other English poet has ever done. The "external influences" that excited and sustained his "internal powers" were primarily literary: he had, from schoolboy days, a truly remarkable availability to the literary imagination, and he yielded without trepidation to its transforming influences, so that by the time he went up to Oxford, he was estranged from his own generation by the specialized character of his imaginative experience.

Thus, it is no petulant challenge to the ultimate stature of Tennyson, Browning, and Arnold to say that Swinburne's first volume of dramatic lyrics, **Poems and Ballads** (1866), is more accomplished than *Poems, Chiefly Lyrical* (1830), *Pauline* (1833), and *The Strayed Reveller, and Other Poems* (1849) on the basis, not of a single criterion, but of a whole cluster of criteria: the firmness of its language, the precision of its imagery, the boldness of its experiential probings, the dramatic redirection it attempts to give to poetic purpose (creative awareness rather than moral judgment, perception *is* meaning), the far-reaching character of its experiments with form, the breadth and originality of its literary frame of reference. Swinburne might possibly top out early, but he came on initially with extraordinary imaginative zest and technical finish.

Special note should be taken of Swinburne's conscientious craftsmanship, one of the most experimental and varied of the nineteenth century. He was fascinated with all species of genre, with poetic forms as means of rendering perception,

and the formal constructs to which he turned his hand were very numerous indeed: sonnets and sonnet sequences, odes, choriambics, sestinas and double sestinas, elegies, sapphics, ballads and double ballads, triads, nocturnes, epitaphs, poetic drama in the Greek mode, poetic drama in the Elizabethan mode, masques, dramatic narratives, threnodies, dirges, epicedes, rondels, roundels, rondeaux, dialogues, monologues, soliloquies, litanies, monotones, epilogues, verse translations, verse adaptations, and so forth. The implications of such a catalogue, however incomplete, thoroughly contradict easy statements about the "lawlessness" of Swinburne's poetry. He was deeply devoted to the rubrics of poetry in a large variety of manifestations; and although he was impatient of imitation gone sterile and wooden in its effects—imitation that had lost its soul, as he said of Arnold's Greek imitation *Merope,* Swinburne's desire to give "fuller scope and freer play of wing to the musical expression" should not be interpreted as licentiousness. "Law, not lawlessness, is the natural condition of the poetic life," he wrote in the "Dedicatory Epistle"; "but the law must be itself poetic and not pedantic, natural and not conventional."

Besides being a brilliant amateur in Greek and Roman literature, Swinburne had so full and firm a grasp of the new poetry of the nineteenth century in Europe that some of the most distinctive poets and characteristic movements seem to converge upon him and his work. He was a close student of Blake, Byron, and Shelley, feeling the full force and unstability of their varied Romanticism; he was dedicated in a special way to Hugo, Baudelaire, and Mallarmé, earning a high reputation among the French for an exceptional understanding of their literature; he wrote incisively on such contemporary English authors as Rossetti, Morris, Arnold, Meredith, Charlotte Brontë, Tennyson, and Dickens, maintaining currency with the literary nuances through which the spiritual ambience of his own time could be intuited. His interest in the literature and art of the Middle Ages was reenforced by his close association with the Pre-Raphaelites, as was his modified aestheticism; and he was a shaping practitioner in the Symbolist and Impressionist movements. Finally, Swinburne was perhaps the period's most accomplished critical student of Elizabethan and Jacobean drama. Thus, he brought balance and brilliance to almost every important aspect of the nineteenth-century literary enterprise. He was as austerely literary as Sappho and Aeschylus, as psychically free as Blake, as urgently engaged as Shelley, and as "modern" as Whitman, Hopkins, and Hardy.

Shelley had spoken of powers that "modify the nature of others": thus, to the poet as the *creation* of his age, as Swinburne in many ways was, Shelley added the poet as *creator* of his age, as Swinburne in many ways tried to be. Like his great predecessors in the poetic art, Swinburne tried to induce illumination through beauty, to lend his talent out, to show others how soul-serviceable letters could be; like his contemporaries, he employed as his most characteristic method a dramatic conception energized by an importunate lyricism. As is true also of Tennyson and Browning, both qualities must be yielded to Swinburne if one would give his poetry a chance to work. By denying him the former, by refusing to acknowledge that Swinburne's poetry is "dramatic, many-faced, multifarious," one essentially denies him his birthrights as a modern poet—such rights as poetic access to the historical imagination; the ability to gain entry into the self-enclosures of strange but representative imaginary *personae* (metaphor, myth); the indispensable recognition that modern poetry, the creation of an age of collapsed structures, is increasingly a poetry of the missed mediate word in which the author's primary concern is with the truth (fidelity, affectiveness) of his representation rather than with ideological conveyance. Such far-reaching denials would threaten the viability of any modern poet—of Tennyson, for example, and Browning and Arnold; and they threaten the viability of Swinburne by reducing his poetry to the verbal diffuseness that T. S. Eliot [in "Swinburne as Poet"] called "one of his glories," but that ultimately strips Swinburne of the peculiar creative center—the generative apprehension peculiarly Swinburne's own—from which his special language strategies organically emerge. Swinburne claimed that his poetry was "dramatic, many-faced, multifarious," and the critic who chooses to deny the claim accomplishes nothing but the impoverishment, in a significant degree, of modern English poetry.

Just how Swinburne sought to "modify the nature of others" is the chief concern of the serious critic of his poetry: it enables one to see better the dramatic principle by which his poems are structured, and it redefines what is meant by the content of his poetry. Poetry itself became the subject of much nineteenth-century literary endeavor when writers began to realize that the imagination was itself in the profoundest difficulty as secular man floundered about in an infinity of secular details. This is one of the central awarenesses that Tennyson and his contemporaries had inherited from the earlier Romantics: science and fable were at war with each other over the consciousness of man; and Matthew Arnold, who repeatedly drew attention to the hazards of multitudinousness, reiterated the faith that poetry would survive religion in recognition that the counterproposition was arguable too. Swinburne and his generation inherited an acute version of this anxiety: it was perhaps the chief motive behind both the go-for-broke, no-compromises extravagance of the art-for-art's-sake movement and the stabilizing effect of that movement on the literary endeavors of that same generation. Like Wellington in his use of squares at the Battle of Waterloo, they needed a technique for closing ranks against the onslaughts of a positivistic, materialistic mentality (natural science, sociology, political economy, religious literalness and dogmatism), and the technique they adopted was aesthetic and attitudinal: they declared that the integrity of art depended upon the autonomy of art. As a guide to the proper motive in the actual writing act, such an aesthetic attitude is beyond criticism: it is a practical technique for keeping the pen from pandering to both the pulpit and the proletariat; but as guide to the appropriate subject matter of art, it is simply inadequate. Swinburne pointed to this distinction in his review of Victor Hugo's *L'Année terrible*: "In a word, the doctrine of art for art is true in the positive sense, false in the negative; sound as an affirmation, unsound as a prohibition . . . while we refuse to any artist on any plea the license to infringe in the least article the letter of the law [of autonomy], to overlook or overpass it in the pursuit of any foreign purpose, we do not refuse to him the liberty of bringing within the range of it any subject that under these conditions [the integrity of the work of art] may be so brought and included within his proper scope of work." Thus, even after he had freed himself from the more simplistic and dogmatic forms of art for art's sake, Swinburne still maintained, in the broader tradition of aesthetic poetry, that for an artist in the act of composition to prefer any object over artistic beauty would inevitably by false in art. This is, perhaps, the closest one can serviceably draw the aesthetic toga around Swinburne: he was certainly devoted throughout his career to high imaginative principle and to imaginative purity of literary execution; the question of how much of a purist he was in art-for-art's-sake doctrines at a given moment in his career, though legitimate as a subject of aesthetic discourse, is surely impedimental (and may even be false) to a discussion of his special poetic achievement.

We begin, then, with a useful cluster of critical inclinations toward Swinburne's poetic canon: that he was especially responsive to the literary (particularly the poetic) experience of the whole Western tradition, being unusually attentive to the literary structures that his predecessors and contemporaries had found imaginatively useful; that he was explicitly devoted to the dramatic (or impersonative) principle, even in lyric poetry and even when the *structure* used was not specifically dramatic; that the energy of his poetry has a lyric source, not just an importunate lyricism of technique, but also what one of his earliest critics called a "terrible earnestness" fueling that technique; that he functioned in the highly developed nineteenth-century tradition of aesthetic poetry, with its customary emphasis on imaginative principle and careful workmanship; and that his primary object as a poet, the object to which he devoted all of his resources as a poet, was to "modify the nature of others." (pp. 227-33)

Swinburne's poetry lay too long in an inadequately marked grave. He suffered the sentence of a magnificently gifted poet who refused to massage the sentiments, to add grace to the melancholy, of self-harrowing modern man. Instead, he removed, relentlessly and one by one, the sacrosanct vestments by which man dressed up and disguised reality and allowed his priests and kings to suborn the testimony of consciousness. The most thoroughly homocentric of English poets, Swinburne saw man, not by the measure of thought or creed or moral habit, not as derivatively social or political: philosophy and religion, ethics and socio-political institutions either diminished man or positively enslaved him. Swinburne was the poet of consciousness and of the instrument of consciousness, language; and his poetry is an exultant, freely but severely structured revel of language, not for its own sake, but as a jubilant celebration of consciousness. This, in turn, leads to two defining characteristics of his work: its almost exclusive dependence upon literature itself—the quintessential language—for its referents; and its almost exclusive emphasis on the apprehending awareness rather than the apprehended object. Swinburne thus found his validating models, not in the conceptualizing proclivities of an enlightened neoclassicism nor in the sensuous precision and concreteness of touch, taste, and smell of Wordsworthian-Keatsian Romanticism. Schooled in Blake and Shelley and Baudelaire, he turned more and more to the literature of tragic apprehension—to the Elizabethan and Jacobean dramatists and to the Greek tragedians—as he more deeply perceived that the consciousness of man finds its most ennobling stature in the complexities of tragic awareness. (pp. 255-56)

William E. Buckler, "The Poetry of Swinburne: An Essay in Critical Reenforcement," in his The Victorian Imagination: Essays in Aesthetic Exploration, *New York University Press, 1980, pp. 227-59.*

KERRY McSWEENEY   (essay date 1981)

[*In the following excerpt, McSweeney contrasts the sensational reputation of* Poems and Ballads *with a close examination of the classical and philosophical themes of four poems from the collection:* "Itylus," "Hymn to Proserpine," "Anactoria," *and* "Laus Veneris."]

It would be idle to attempt to play down the sensational aspects of ***Poems and Ballads***: the self-conscious, flaunted decadence; the celebration of strange sexual passions; the attempt to *épater le bourgeois.* These are the qualities which accounted for the volume's notoriety a hundred years ago, and which are still synonymous with it today. But it may be said that these are not the only, and not the most intrinsically important, aspects of ***Poems and Ballads,*** and that the meaning and distinction of several of the volume's strongest poems have been obscured by its reputation. It is mainly in these poems, not in the conventional exercises or lurid shockers, that the pervasive concerns of Swinburne's most deeply felt and authentic poetry are foreshadowed.

"Itylus" is an example. Through the nightingale's recollection the poem retells the ghastly story of Tereus, Procne, Philomela, and the slaying of Itylus. It is a fine exercise in delayed meaning, for only gradually do the full circumstances of the nightingale's appeal to her sister, the swallow, became clear. What the poem basically does is dramatize two different kinds of existence. The sisters have both lived through the same hideous experiences, but they are very different singers, who make mutually exclusive kinds of poetry. All of the ad-

Caricature of Swinburne and Watts-Dunton by Max Beerbohm.

jectives describing the swallow suggest her swiftness and lightness. Her heart is "full of the spring," and she annually follows the sun into the south. The nightingale, on the other hand, is a creature belonging to the night. Her heart is an unquenchable "molten ember" and she is "fulfilled" not by seasonal renewal but by feeding "the heart of the night" with the fire of her song. She can neither forget the past nor forgive the "changing swallow" her forgetfulness: "Thou hast forgotten, O summer swallow, / But the world shall end when I forget." The "heart's division" that separates the sisters is two different responses to a world of gross tragedy and personal violation. Swinburne does not arrange his poem to suggest which of these responses he favours, nor is there any reason why he should do so. One might associate the swallow with the husband in Robert Frost's "Home Burial," who is able to assuage his grief over the death of his young child by living in the present, yielding to the rhythms of the natural cycle, and turning to fresh tasks—unlike his wife who, like the nightingale, thinks "the world's evil" and refuses to be consoled. But one might also reflect that the swallow seems an Edgar Linton type, lacking the passion and stature of Heathcliff, who cannot be reconciled to his loss. In any event, it is not hard to understand what **"Itylus"** is doing in the first ***Poems and Ballads.*** What the sisters have experienced suggests an analogy to the world of these early poems. It is what may be called a *fleurs du mal* world, where vice is stronger than virtue and weakness dominates will. To sing like the nightingale is to make personal trauma the subject matter of poetry, to live locked in the harshness of the past and keep always present "the grief of the old time." To sing like the swallow is to be able to naturalize grief, to find something glad "in thine heart to sing," and to become renewed through identification with natural process.

"Hymn to Proserpine," one of Swinburne's most negative statements on the human condition, is another example. The poem's concerns—mutability, mortality, and the ambiguous nature of the poet's privileged insight—Swinburne will repeatedly return to throughout his poetic career, but his treatment of them will seldom be so despairing. The poem is a dramatic soliloquy; its speaker a Roman of the fourth century A.D., a pagan poet who, like Julian the Apostate (whose supposed last words are the poem's epigraph), thinks that Christianity does not represent an advance over the pagan gods. But Swinburne's poem is not really about the reaction of a classical pagan to the new religion of Christ in the way that Browning's "Cleon" or Pater's *Marius the Epicurean* is. The speaker has no real faith in the pagan gods; for him they are simply metaphors, and he feels that Christianity and the Christian pantheon (the "New Gods" crowned in the city) are simply another set of metaphors which will also pass away.

The poem's basic tension is between the speaker's desires and his overpowering awareness of mutability, which he calls "Time" or "Fate." The overthrow of the pagan by the Christian gods is simply one instance of mutability's work. For the speaker, the only reality is change, which terrifies him. His only release from this pained awareness comes from sensation, his sensuous pleasure in both natural and human beauty. But since this beauty all too quickly fades, his release is short-lived. The sharper his pleasure, the keener his realization of its transience: "Laurel is green for a season, and love is sweet for a day; / But love grows bitter with treason, and laurel outlives not May." This is the situation that Pater would describe a decade later in the famous "Conclusion" to

The Renaissance. But the speaker of the **"Hymn to Proserpine"** cannot maintain the ecstasy of burning always with a "hard, gemlike flame"; he is too overwhelmed by his awareness of what Pater called the "awful brevity" of human life.

His languorous mood and world-weary manner also recall the early Yeats. For him, as for Yeats' Happy Shepherd: "The woods of Arcady are dead / And over is their antique joy." But while Yeats' singer is at least able to assert that "Words alone are certain good," Swinburne's poet is unable to find certainty or joy in his vocation as a poet: "I am sick of singing: the bays burn deep and chafe." Apollo, symbol of poetry and poetic life, is the god who slays his own worshippers: though "a beautiful god to behold," he is "a bitter god to follow." The speaker's sole utterance has become a chant of oblivion, and it is a measure of his estangement from natural process that he views death more as an escape from the meaningless flux of life than as a necessary part of it, more as life's extinction than its completion. Only at one moment does he seem to remember what Swinburne in his later poetry will seldom forget, that death is an integral part of the natural world and its cyclic change, and that an individual's life is rooted in this process: "O daughter of earth, of my mother, her crown and blossom of birth, / I am also, I also, thy brother; I go as I came unto earth." One may say that the speaker has not yet learned fully to accept death as a condition of life, and to accept the circumstances of his life as tolerable. At least implicitly, there is a connection between this and his inability to fulfil himself as a poet. In later poems of Swinburne, an acceptance of death as the completion of life, beyond which there is nothing else, is closely linked to an affirmation of the value of poetry and the poetic vocation, and to a recognition of the bonds of love and compassion that bind poets (and, by extension, all men) together in their common mortality. But the speaker of the **"Hymn to Proserpine"** has not yet learned that although death destroys a man, the idea of death saves him.

"Anactoria" is another dramatic monologue about an unhappy poet. It is not the sadistic effusion it is sometimes taken to be, but a poem about the fate of poets and the nature of poetic vocation. The speaker of **"Anactoria"** is Sappho, the lyric poetess of antiquity, for Swinburne "simply nothing less . . . than the greatest poet who ever was at all." She also appears in **"Sapphics,"** another of the first *Poems and Ballads*. There, as the representative of poetry and the poetic life, she is opposed to Aphrodite, the Venus of **"Hymn to Proserpine,"** who represents an exclusive devotion to physical love. Sappho's song can make the gods "wax pale: such a song was that song," and almost move the "implacable Aphrodite." Her song gives her "a crown forever," but because she sings to her own devotees, and not to Venus, the goddess of love withdraws her amorous retinue from Lesbos, leaving the island barren. The point of this dream-poem is obscure, but its main theme is clear: the opposition between the erotic life and the influential but isolating gift of poetry. The theme of **"Anactoria"** is the same.

"Sapphics" describes the poetess' song as

> her visible song, a marvel,
> Made of perfect sound and exceeding passion,
> Sweetly shapen, terrible, full of thunders,
>   Clothed with the wind's wings.

This is a not unfair description of **"Anactoria,"** a poem of great technical virtuosity. A mosaic of elaborations of various Sapphic fragments, the poem is flawed by a certain looseness of organization, but one can nevertheless discern a basic conflict and its resolution. The opening line—"My life is bitter with thy love"—introduces one pole of the poem's tension: Sappho's perverted and sadistic emotions towards her beloved, best epitomized in the chilling line: "Yea, all thy beauty sickens me with love." Opposed to this is her awareness of her vocation as a poet and, consequently, of her closeness to the natural world. What happens in the poem is that her initial, almost total, submersion in her compulsive love gradually gives way before an increasingly exultant realization of her poetic powers, so that by the poem's conclusion she is able to chant an extraordinary hymn to the powers of poetry.

Only after she has been speaking for some time does Sappho first mention her poetic gifts, and then in passing—"Though my voice die not till the whole world die." Soon after this comes the poem's most unnerving moment—when Sappho desires to exchange her poetic gifts for the fulfilment of her sadistic lust:

> Ah that my lips were tuneless lips, but pressed
> To the bruised blossom of thy scourged white breast!
> Ah that my mouth for Muses' milk were fed
> On the sweet blood thy sweet small wounds had bled!

Her most despairing cry comes soon after: "Yea, though their alien kisses do me wrong, / Sweeter thy lips than mine with all their song." Swinburne next allows Sappho an extended vituperation against "God," a section which is something of an intrusion into the poem. With the end of this tirade, **"Anactoria"** abruptly modulates into the sustained brilliance of its closing section, beginning "Thee too the years shall cover"—lines which Hardy described in a letter to Swinburne as presenting "the finest *drama* of Death and Oblivion . . . in our tongue." This section grows out of the few lines of a Sapphic fragment: "When you are dead you will lie unremembered for evermore; for you will have no part in the roses that come from Pieria; nay, obscure here, you will move obscure in the house of Death, and flit to and fro among such of the dead as have no fame." To have "the high Pierian flower" is to have the gift of poetry; not to have it is to "be not anymore at all, / Nor any memory of thee anywhere." Sappho asserts that, unlike her beloved, she will not wholly perish because her poems will survive, and that with men's perceptions of the natural world memories and metaphors of her "shall mix." She goes on to claim for the poetic life an additional consolation, another way in which poets may be said to be immortal. Sappho foresees that, like the apotheosized Keats at the climax of Shelley's "Adonais," she will be "made one with Nature" and become "a portion of the loveliness" which once she made more lovely through her singing:

> Of me the high God [of death] hath not all his will.
> Blossom of branches, and on each high hill
> Clear air and wind, and under in clamorous vales
> Fierce noises of the fiery nightingales,
> Buds burning in the sudden spring like fire,
> The wan washed sand and the waves' vain desire,
> Sails seen like blown white flowers at sea, and words
> That being tears swiftest, and long notes of birds
> Violently singing till the whole world sings—
> I Sappho shall be one with all these things,
> With all high things forever.

Sappho's assertions of a mixture of natural and creative immortality are so triumphant and unqualified, and so uncharacteristic of Swinburne's vision, as to make one reflect that, however closely the young Swinburne's vision, may have identified with its speaker, **"Anactoria"** is after all a dramatic poem. For Swinburne seldom if ever makes such claims in his own voice; and in **"Ave atque Vale,"** which one might call his definitive statement on the fate of poets, Swinburne will offer a quite different account of poetic immortality, including that of Sappho. And in another dramatic poem from the 1866 *Poems and Ballads,* the triumphant conclusion is of a quite different kind from that of **"Anactoria."**

The speaker of **"Laus Veneris"** is Tannhäuser, the knight of medieval legend. Like **"Anactoria,"** his poem is rather longer and more rambling than one would wish it to be. But it is wrong to say "the poem has no logical development; nor . . . any emotional development. One simply joins the knight in spirit as he moves through the conflicting emotions which obsess him. There is no escape from them and no hope of bringing them into unity" [Barbara Charlesworth, *Dark Passages*]. On the contrary, there is in the poem a real development and a final emotional unity.

A poem which resembles **"Laus Veneris"** in interesting ways is Tennyson's "Tithonus." Each has at its centre an immortal goddess and an exhausted human lover who is condemned to live forever. Like Tithonus, Tannhäuser longs for naturalistic fulfilment, to return to the world of "happy men that have the power to die." There is a crucial difference between the two poems, however, which underlines a basic aspect of Swinburne's vision. **"Tithonus"** ends with an enormously poignant lament for the tears of things, with the speaker's haunting wish one day to be dead. Tannhäuser, on the other hand, comes to resolve his dilemma in a much more affirmative manner.

Unlike most of Swinburne's poems, **"Laus Veneris"** relies for its basic situation on a Christian framework—that of sin, repentance, and redemption. In **"Notes on Poems and Reviews"**—his apologia for the first *Poems and Ballads*—Swinburne put forward an interpretation of the poem in keeping with its Christian framework, chastely saying: "Once accept or admit the least admixture of pagan worship, or of modern thought, and the whole story collapses into froth and smoke." But there is good reason to think that much of the **"Notes"** was written with tongue in cheek, and in any event it is clear that Swinburne was being disingenuous in his remarks on **"Laus Veneris,"** for Christian belief is hardly what the poem advocates, and it is not against a Christian background that the poem must be viewed if it is to be understood.

Tannhäuser speaks the poem from inside the Horsel with Venus, where he is condemned (so he thinks) to remain until the end of the world. He is exhausted and enervated, his psychological condition mirrored in the oppressive heat and desiccation of the Horsel, in contrast is the freshness and movement of the natural world outside, to which Tannhäuser longs to be united:

> Ah yet would God this flesh of mine might be
> Where air might wash and long leaves cover me,
>   Where tides of grass break into foam of flowers,
> Or where the wind's feet shine along the sea.
>
> Ah yet would God that stems and roots were bred
> Out of my weary body and my head,
>   That sleep were sealed upon me with a seal,
> And I were as the least of all his dead.

It is in the world of nature and natural process that death, the release from the bonds of Venus, is to be found:

> Alas, but surely where the hills grow deep,
> Or where the wild ways of the sea are steep,
>   Or in strange places somewhere there is death.

Simultaneously repelled by and attracted to Venus, Tannhäuser goes on to recount the strength of her bittersweet charms, and to tell the story of his life. Finally comes the poem's astonishing conclusion: it does not end with Christian resignation to the will of God, with Tannhäuser's despair, with a Tithonus-like death wish, or with a hint of eventual redemption (the blossoming of the Pope's staff is not mentioned in the poem). At the end of **"Laus Veneris,"** Tannhäuser, with a ringing rhetorical insistence, comes fully to accept his fate:

> Ah love, there is no better life that this;
> To have known love, how bitter a thing it is,
>   And afterwards be cast out of God's sight;.
> Yea, these that know not, shall they have such bliss
>
> High up in barren heaven before his face
> As we twain in the heavy-hearted place,
>   Remembering love and all the dead delight,
> And all that time was sweet with for a space?
>
> For till the thunder in the trumpet be,
> Soul may divide from body, but not we
>   One from another; I hold thee with my hand,
> I let mine eyes have all their will of thee,
>
> I seal myself upon thee with my might,
> Abiding alway out of all men's sight
>   Until God loosen over sea and land
> The thunder of the trumpets of the night.

Tannhäuser has come to accept what is as good. He realizes that what he possesses inside the Horsel is enough to sustain him and preferable to a "barren heaven" beyond. This distillation of peace and resignation out of apparent defeat and damnation is sudden and unexpected, and one should not fail to notice just how striking a resolution it is. It is as if the lotos eaters had ended their chant with a fuller self-consciousness than Tennyson grants them, and had decided to remain in contentment in the lotos land simply because there was no longer any other place for them to go. Doubtless, this kind of resolution is morally intolerable to some; and it is certainly in contrast to the ethical vigour and idealizing propensities of much Victorian literature. But as this theme is handled in Swinburne's poetry it does have an impressive dignity which it would be quite unreasonable to despise. (pp. 126-32)

In his later poetry, Swinburne came to develop more fully and more positively the themes of **"Itylus,"** **"Hymn to Proserpine,"** **"Anactoria,"** **"Laus Veneris,"** and some other of the first *Poems and Ballads.* These early poems tend to present the poet's deepest concerns in an oblique, even a semi-disguised manner, but they can be nevertheless recognized: a concern with natural process and its relation to man; a preoccupation with death and change; a questioning of poetry's value in a world of mutability and mortality. A fairly consistent contrast runs through these poems: on the one hand, an unhealthy sensuality, a world-weariness, and a sense that the only possible poems are cries of perverted delight or chants of despair; on the other hand, a sense of the healing qualities of the natural world, a realization of the value of poetic vocation, and a determination to accept the circumstances of one's life as tolerable, whatever they happen to be. The former qualities have given *Poems and Ballads* its notoriety; the latter give it much of its distinction. (pp. 133)

Kerry McSweeney, "Swinburne's Internal Centre,"

in his Tennyson and Swinburne as Romantic Naturalists, *University of Toronto Press, 1981, pp. 123-52.*

ROBERT PETERS (essay date 1982)

[*Peters is an American educator, critic, and poet. In the following excerpt, he offers an examination of Swinburne's poetic theory and technique, maintaining that Swinburne has been too often underappreciated because of inadequate critical assessments.*]

[In] the late forties, I was something of an esthete, wrote my dissertation (under the supportive eye of Jerome Buckley) on the poets of the 1890s and the several arts. I cultivated Bohemian types. I was increasingly fascinated by late Victorian aesthetics, and particularly with the writers and artists of the so-called Decadence—Wilde, Beardsley, Symons, Symonds, Pater, Solomon, Dowson, Gray, and Johnson. Once I had received the PhD. and was settled into teaching, I began to see Swinburne as an almost archetypal figure looming just ahead of, and inspiring, the late Victorian art for art's sake movement. Since I enjoyed his poetry greatly, on its own terms, I wanted somehow to convey my enthusiasm to students as exactly as I could. Obviously, to appear before a class and chant selections from **Poems and Ballads; First Series** for fifty minutes, no matter how adept one is, is a bore—and the students who would respond to that treatment would respond at a skin-deep level. I sought to be more analytical about Swinburne. Behind his much noted plethora of words, his impressive, largely ignored verse techniques anticipated later movements in English poetry, including the much admired sprung-rhythms of Gerard Manley Hopkins. His ideas on religion and society, though derivative of Aeschylus, Shelley, Hugo, and Blake, were nonetheless sufficiently his own in their iconoclasm. He was much more than a pale imitation of other writers, or the facile singer of mindless anapestic feet.

I desired (and still desire) that my students perceive Swinburne as a magnificently vital writer, relevant to our times, stirring for both his music and his humanitarianism. If they are to look closely they will find an amazing verse craftsmanship based on the best traditional poets from the ancient Greeks forward. He demands so much more of the attentive reader than a sensuous passivity. Even his abstractions, skillfully employed, possess vitality and magic. One problem is, of course, that Swinburne is a poet who shows little development throughout a long career. This in itself makes writing about him difficult for interpreters and critics, and is responsible for the usual complaint that since there was no growth, and since he wrote for so many years, he succeeded mainly in producing a dulling monotony of ideas and effects. I know of no other poet so proficient in his art in the early stages of his career as he was during later ones. To assume that such a poet is inferior and mediocre because of this is a mistake. What Swinburne requires is something other than the usual critical treatment, where a critic proceeds from volume one and works through volume ten charting all the changes of thought and technique. Swinburne's methods and ideas can be examined in representative poems from any point in his long career. A sequential study, volume by volume, would be repetitious. (pp. 138-39)

As a young professor at Wayne State University, I began gathering notes towards a lengthy study of Swinburne's poetry. Before long I realized that if I were to understand this vast body of work, knowing something about his theories of poet-

ry would be essential. I turned to his criticism, finding there an incredible array of pieces on a vast assembling of writers, ranging throughout English and Continental literature. Reading him was a joy—even at his most crabbed and tortured there seemed a design; he often parodied the pompous critics of the age (he mocked Arnold in particular). He struck me as a civilized and urbane Carlylean figure, but one devoting his iconoclastic energies to literature and art rather than to overtly metaphysical and social themes, as Carlyle had done. And although he later turned vituperative towards Carlyle, calling him *Thomas Cloacinus,* one doesn't read far in Swinburne's criticism before one senses his vast debts to Carlyle—the rambunctious humor, the devastating ironies, the imitation of voices for purposes of parody, the complex Germanic sentence structures, the ruthless independence of mind and feeling, the name-calling and energetic blastings of assorted human pretensions.

Swinburne's criticism constitutes a body of work unique in its range and style. It is a sheer pleasure to read; and it made fearless pronouncements unpopular in their time: Swinburne extolled Charlotte Brontë over George Eliot, Byron over the other Romantic poets, Chapman over other Elizabethan poets, Browning over Matthew Arnold. His work on the Elizabethans, incidentally, and on William Blake, stimulated fresh assessments of these hitherto neglected writers. His contributions to Elizabethan studies remain seminal.

The result of my interest in Swinburne's criticism was *The Crowns of Apollo: Swinburne's Principles of Literature and Art.* Realizing that Impressionist criticism was greatly out of fashion and generally ridiculed by New Critics and others in the early sixties, I decided to systematize Swinburne's thinking about other poets, dramatists, novelists, and about art and aesthetics in general. I discovered in those vast pages of the monumental Bonchurch edition of the **Works** that there was indeed something of a single whole arranged around the most strenuous principles. Swinburne's vivid sense of tradition going back to the ancients impressed me. I had no idea I would find so much substance and so much connecting tissue.

A few comments, then, by way of pointing directions: Swinburne pioneered in realizing the enormous power of synesthesia as a device both for poetry and for criticism. He managed to incorporate in a single telling image or metaphor, nervous in its evocations, a remarkable blending of sense impressions, anticipating what the French symbolists were later to do. These are exactly the qualities John D. Rosenberg, in his excellent essay on Swinburne's poetry [see essay dated 1968], describes as "Swinburne's love of mixed effects," giving to the work a "Turnerian quality." The poetry, Rosenberg says, "is charged with the tension of delicately poised opposites: shadows thinned by light, lights broken by shade, sunset passing into moonrise, sea merging with sky. He is obsessed by the moment when one thing shades off into its opposite, or when contraries fuse. . . ." Rosenberg continues by noting Swinburne's "superb senses, each of which must have transmitted a peculiar counterpoint. This basic, polarizing rhythm," Rosenberg continues, "runs through his being and manifests itself in his compulsive use of alliterating antitheses in prose and verse." His recurring synthetic images are the result of Swinburne's perceptions experienced as "paradoxes."

Swinburne provided a seminal corrective to the Victorian writer's obsession with exuberant detail. While he himself early shared some of the Pre-Raphaelite enthusiasm for such exuberance, he insisted that such detail must be subordinated to a principle he derived from his thinking about William Blake, that each detail, well-employed, must contribute to an idea of "gathering form." Swinburne was an organicist in his theories, believing in something like a Platonic ladder of cognition—aesthetic effects ring higher and higher until finally they are spun into that exalted, transcendent realm of Beauty so prized by Shelley and the Romantics. *Passion* was Swinburne's word for the excitement we feel experiencing art. And there are varieties of *passion,* he insisted, on a scale moving from lower to higher. His theories were always dynamic—as his principle of "gathering form" shows. A fine work of art exudes *energy,* and, like one of Swinburne's ubiquitous ocean waves, accumulates force and "form" as it drives towards the shore. As it nears land, its energies gather into a stunning visual impressionist whole. As a critic, and by example as a poet, Swinburne was a major countervoice to the didacticism and moralizing so prevalent in Victorian writing. He proclaimed that the first business of the poet is to write fine verses and not to "redeem the age and remould society." Didacticism in art he lambasted as "the frantic and flatulent assumptions of quasi-secular clericalism." Inspired by Blake's example again, he insisted that art can never be the "handmaid of religion, exponent of duty, servant of fact, pioneer of morality" [*William Blake*]. And he supplied this warning for the trimmers: Those "who try to clip or melt themselves down to the standard of current feeling, to sauce and spice their natural fruits of mind with such condiments as may take the palate of common opinion, deserve to disgust themselves and others alike." In the mid 1860s when these pronouncements (and a host of others like them) appeared, Swinburne's was indeed a minority voice, one to be echoed shortly by James McNeill Whistler and Oscar Wilde.

Another of Swinburne's virtues as a critic was his amazing ability to enter chameleon-like into a piece of literature. He is, I think, the finest of Impressionist critics. At his best he renders in generally stunning prose an equivalent for what he has read and perceived. He explained his method in one of his pieces on Victor Hugo:

> This style of Victor Hugo's is not easy to catch and reproduce effectively. To find fault with it, lay a finger on the flaws and knots of it, set a mark against this or that phrase—even to seize on some salient point and hold it up in the way of parody—these are the easy things to do. It has singular alternations of fluent power and sharp condensed angular thought; moves now softly and freely, now with a sort of abrupt military step, a tight-laced, short-breathed kind of march, as it were; a style broken and split up into bright, hard fragments of spar, that have a painful sparkle in them, and rough, jagged notches and angles; then, again, it shifts into quite another likeness, becomes flexible, soft, sinuous, as the over-growth of trees or grass; with a passionate eager beauty in it that dilates every word and sentence to the full; a feverish excess of blood, a tremulous intensity of life. It is hard at times to keep up with the pace of it; the very written words seem to have a conscience and a vitality in them, to heave and beat with the fever of excited thought, to quiver with actual sensuous passion. Moreover, the style expands and opens up into vast paragraphs, coherent, indeed, but only as water coheres; "tumbling, weltering spaces of sea with no good anchorage for miles," that drift the reader breathless out of reach of rope or spar. Evidently, however, this matter, too, is best as it is; these are the forms

into which the great thought and purpose of the writer naturally cast themselves, they fall and lap of their own accord into those folds and creases, and so the meaning of the book gets clothed and set out as suits it best.

The critical approaches we have valued in our own time have been more analytical, more attentive to poems and plays as "verbal constructs," more self-consciously scientific and, I think, boring to read. A poem is not an intricately jewelled watch in which every part functions as moving cogs and wheels; there must be space in art for the flawed work, for passages of decreasing intensity, pauses for the reader to catch his breath before he is spun on towards the heights. Here, obviously, Swinburne shares with Ruskin and Carlyle, and most of the Victorian poets, the idea of the flawed work, characteristic of most long poems with their passages of quiet alternating with passages of intensity. The Victorians seemed to feel that such imperfections or modified orchestrations in works of art remind us mortals that we too fall short of perfection. The achievement is in the striving; or, as Browning wrote, "A man's reach should exceed his grasp, or what's a Heaven for?"

Swinburne seemed to have twentieth-century critics in mind when he warned: "If we insist on having hard ground under foot all the way we shall not get far." Freedom rather than rigidity, flexibility rather than a stereotyped approach, he felt, best provide critics with opportunities for success.

Obviously Swinburne's poetry no less than his criticism requires some detailing of its unique qualities. He has been badly read and too easily dismissed. And Swinburne is a difficult poet to be specific about. He is intellectually complex and fond of paradox. He is as complex a technician and craftsman as any other poet of his age. Today's students, by reading and sensing him carefully, can touch the well-springs of earlier poetry better than they can by reading most other Victorian poets—Swinburne was indeed conscious of a classical tradition of art preceding him. It is a truism to say that his *Atalanta in Calydon* is the finest Greek verse drama written in the nineteenth century. And young poets, drenched today in free verse techniques and projective verse journalese, anxious to learn their craft, would profit, I think, by immersing themselves in Swinburne's poetry.

Another much-heard truism about Swinburne is that once he has bitten you (he might have preferred *fanged* or *whipped*), you become a passionate aficionado. So my apologies for being an enthusiast. I sincerely hope, however, that what I have to say about his poetry will stimulate a few readers to read him with more care than they might otherwise have done.

First, I shall briefly examine Swinburne's facility for subordinating to an informing artistic effect observations made from nature. Second, I shall examine some instances of his use of synesthesia. Third, I shall comment on his impressionism and shall hope, however briefly, to describe his Impressionist verse style. I realize, of course, that I am excluding other valuable topics from my discussion: Swinburne's sexuality, his passion for liberty, his humor present in his self-parodies and in his parodies of other poets, his virtues as a novelist, his verse dramas. To a degree, I suppose, his sexuality and his humanitarianism are implied throughout my discussion, as is his detachment from his chaotic times, so enamored of evolutionary theories, science, and commerce. His insistence on the fixed, all-encompassing attributes of art can still enrich our own troubled spirits in an ill-centered, threatening age. For he asserts the profoundest of human values—those of the human spirit free from constricting religious, social, and political ties. He breathes a kind of anarchism of enlightened souls, inspirited by the transcendent, aesthetic feelings generated by art.

Swinburne had his say about the verbal decoration proliferating in much Victorian poetry—an important phenomenon since tortuous lines and sentence patterns and complicated sceneries—gingerbread—constitute a major Victorian verse style. There are Browning's elaborate catalogues of Renaissance lumber rooms, of natural settings with their eft-things, *pompion-plants, Oak-worts,* gourd-fruits, honeycombs, and finches; Tennyson's landscape and medieval sceneries, his massive, highly complicated verse paragraphs twisting and turning in folds innumerable (see the description of Arthur's throne in "Lancelot and Elaine"); William Morris' luxuriously described towers and turret-roofs, Philip J. Bailey's and Sydney Dobell's verbal foliage; George Meredith's complex nature description and genre-bits; Rossetti's Willowwood settings; and Francis Thompson's involved gingerbread verse— "Corymbus for Autumn," for example, which is nearly swamped by excessive metaphors and a diction *fleshed out* from various verbal storehouses, past and present.

In these matters, as in nearly all others, Swinburne was his own man. Apart from his brief dalliance with the Pre-Raphaelites, reflected best in sections of **"Laus Veneris," "The Sundew,"** the slaughter of the boar passage in **Atalanta in Calydon,** and the battle scenes of **Erectheus,** Swinburne's work reflects little of this gingerbread style. He himself complained of the "fretted" traceries he found in Tennyson's verse, and in the work of Tennyson's followers. He preferred poets—like Arnold of *New Poems* and much of Walter Savage Landor—who didn't assault us with visual exactitudes. In these poets "nothing is thrust or pressed upon our eyes." These poets have a "Greek spirit." Readers "breathe and move" through their landscapes, and are not "tripped up and caught at in passing by intrusive and singular and exceptional beauties which break up and distract the simple charm of general and single beauty, the large and musical unity of things."

Swinburne's own transformations of poetic materials are as much intellectual and abstract as they are feverish and passionate. At their purest, his symbols attach themselves to objects at few points—sometimes at none, as in the following couplet from **Songs Before Sunrise** where Love as a vaguely rendered sky bends over a lover without touching her:

> Love, like a clear sky spread
> Bends over thy loved head.

Or, from **Bothwell:**

> Her soul is as a flame insatiable
> And subtle as thin water.

The success of such imagery depends upon our willingness to suspend disbelief in the heightened and transformed qualities of such lucent metaphors. Swinburne's imagination seemed to work best in a Watteau-like haze shimmering somewhere in a special zone between the physical and the transcendent, developing penumbras of meaning. He preferred to dissolve the solid and the visible; at his most characteristic engaging the reader in a play of light and shadow of an almost purely aesthetic-intellectual kind. Even when he is most erotic, the

trappings of his poems are apt to be generalized rather than specific. A passage from **"Hesperia"** describing a femme fatale in her bower, contains thorns, leaves, snakes, gleaming eyes, hissing tongues, foam, desert dew, and lips. All of these are curiously inexact. While there are gleams, there is little or no color. When Dolores' lip-foam blends with the "cold foul foam of the snakes" winding round her, we are still dealing with abstractions. The action itself, repellent to most non-snake lovers, remains conceptual—we construct a scene of particular intensity, of a woman's incredible lust projected via her manipulation of the snakes; she is a creature vastly larger than life—a symbol, if you will.

Another poem, **"In the Bay,"** a panegyric to Marlowe and Shelley, envisions the souls of these earlier poets projected against a sunset. Although Swinburne gives the illusion of a real locale—"here, where light and darkness reconciled / hold earth between them as a weanling child"—the setting is merely an illusion. Nature makes way for some artificial personifications: light and darkness are parents and earth the "weanling child" who in Marlow's times held a promise lost in Swinburne's.

Swinburne preferred poems then in which natural details are kept subordinate to some developing figure. He introduced thematic motifs and then improvised in a somewhat circular fashion rather than in a swift but logical flow from image to image and sound to sound. He resembled a composer developing materials for a sonata. His ideal paralleled one he discerned in Shelley—Shelley, Swinburne said, sought "to render the effect of a thing rather than the thing itself; the soul and spirit of life rather than the living form, the growth rather than the thing grown." Swinburne's figures and his visual details acquire a conceptual acuteness, what Paul de Reul, [in *L'oeuvre de Swinburne*], called "the coloring of an idea" in Swinburne. What de Reul saw was that Swinburne's best symbols, based in reality, strive to escape the limitations of the actual. Nature seemed inadequate for Swinburne, and, again according to de Reul, it is this disdain for the concrete, the known, and the familiar that most estranges Swinburne from readers.

Swinburne's treatment of the landscape of **"At Eleusis"** is revealing. The countryside is a human body in distress, sterilized by Demeter. Images of doors, iron locks, and plows imposed on sexually charged references to *womb, seed,* and *mate,* deprive the poem of the realism in details we might find in Tennyson, Robert Browning, or Rossetti. Even the lines in which raping men "widen the sealed lips" of the land, with their Miltonic overtones, are intellectualized and artful. The ploughed fields ache as a body aches, the wind personified is frustrated, the burnt fields lie helpless.

Swinburne would have found Tennyson's defense of the following passage from *Maud* thoroughly uncongenial:

> I know the way she went
> Home with her maiden posy.
> For her feet have touch'd the meadows
> And left the daisies rosey.

When a critic complained of the facility of this verse, Tennyson defended himself by explaining that when one's feet disturb a patch of white daisies one does indeed expose their rosy undersides—a botanical fact!

Swinburne's method of simplifying natural details for an allegorical or symbolic effect is particularly clear in a passage from **"At Eleusis"** describing Persephone's rape by Hades. The passage is a kind of play of Whistlerian whiteness—the flowers are not named—except that we are told after the event transpires that they are white or purple "waifs . . . of the pasturage." Hardly very specific. The event itself is mythical and is, therefore, at a remove from the passions of real human beings. Hades' passion is stylized and conceptualized.

As Persephone reclines in her bed of wild flowers, chill water slides over her reddening feet, killing "the throbs in their soft blood." Birds—we are told neither genus nor number—perch by her elbow, peck at her hair, and stretch their necks "more to see her than even to sing." The actual abduction is presented in an elaborately constructed verse sentence, distanced by the intrusion of the speaker proclaiming her own reverence for Persephone's body. The reporting is curiously decorative, abstract, and bloodless. Here is the passage:

> For Hades holding both *white* wrists of hers
> UNLOOSED the girdle and with *knot* by *knot*
> *Bound* her between his wheels upon the *seat,*
> BOUND her pure body, holiest yet and dear
> To me and God as always, clothed *about*
> With BLOSSOMS LOOSENED as her knees *went* DOWN
> *Let* fall as she let go of this and this
> By tens and twenties, tumbled to her *feet,*
> *White* waifs or purple of the PASTURAGE.

The sentence is a model of balanced stylistic effects: alliteration and repetitions of key words, confined mainly to the left side of the passage, and masculine rhymes and half-rhymes, arranged for the most part on the right side, developing around *seat* and *feet.* Obviously, as my italics show, Swinburne's longitudinal division of his verse sentence is only approximate; his effects are intertwined and cross over. The crisp qualities of the monosyllabic *bound* echo similar properties in a majority of the masculine end-words on the opposite right-hand side of the sentence. Moreover, *bound* pairs with *down,* connecting both sides and underscoring the tying-up motif—*knot, unloosened, loosened, bound.* Also, *let,* appearing twice in line 7, helps to interweave the halves. The stylistic effect produced, nicely complements the transpiring action, as reported by Demeter. The illusion of reportage is maintained, if somewhat artificially, through curiously flattened prepositional phrases: in line 1 an ordinary possessive is expanded in a Rossettian fashion—"white wrists of hers"; in line 3, the pair of linked adverbial phrases, "between his wheels upon the seat" are splayed out foreshadowing some of the colloquial woodenness of "holiest yet and dear / To me and God as always" and the flat vagueness of "of this and this."

By allowing bare natural metaphors to stand for themselves without much adornment, and by rendering these metaphors as abstractions rather than as palpable, definable, classifiable objects in the physical universe, Swinburne achieves a classical tone. Art, he insisted, is not life: realms of the spirit are distinct from the insane, confusing varieties of forms in actual life—to abstract these forms is a technical means of creating art: the flowers, animals, birds, and trees of such poems need never pass as definitions for the botanist or the geologist.

Intimately related to Swinburne's transformations of natural detail is his pioneering use of synesthesia. His model was certainly in part Baudelaire and his famous theory of *correspondences,* where the universe becomes a forest of symbols, and where a conjoining *or* blending of metaphors of the senses clusters around a single image. Also, quite apart from Baude-

laire's influence, Swinburne's own intensities of mind and feeling led him to such images—to cluster sense responses was to artificialize, to naturalize, image behind that metaphor.

Several examples appear in his early masterpiece **"Laus Veneris,"** his treatment of the Venus and Tannhäuser story written in fiery quatrains inspired by Fitzgerald's *Rubaiyat of Omar Khayyam.* One of the most elaborate of his synesthetic passages occurs early in the poem. Tannhäuser who has sapped Venus sexually—she is asleep beside him—hallucinates and imagines Love (Amor/Cupid) standing near Venus's head. The knight confuses Cupid with Christ—the love god wears a crown of thorns. His lusting flesh is on fire. Initially, then, Swinburne's image is complex—is the image Christian or is it pagan? Obviously, in the Christian Knight's psyche it is both. Suddenly, however, there are other fascinating accretions. Love, "wan," suddenly becomes sea spume "blown up the salt burnt sands":

> Hot as the brackish waifs of yellow spume
> That shift and steam—loose clots of acrid fume
> From the sea's panting mouth of dry desire. . . .

Sight, touch, taste, sound commingle in a rich texture of effects. We *see* "wan" Love, we *see* foam blowing onto the hot sands, we *see* yellow spume, we *see* clots of fume. We *touch,* in a sense, the burned sands, and *feel* the hot spume. We *taste* the brackish spume. We hear the sea's panting mouth. The sea becomes an enormous leviathan of lust. What an evocation of fires! The passage resembles the traditional epic simile, in that the forward motion of the poem seems to delay itself in order to allow the poet to embroider his theme. Swinburne's passage, however, goes far beyond the generally simple contributions of the ordinary epic simile; his blending of sense effects is an artful attempt to induce us to *sense* lust as it overwhelms Tannhäuser's mind. Yes, Swinburne here is partially literal, or true to nature; we do see, almost as if we are observing a stylized etching of the beach, the foam reaching the heated sands. But Swinburne's genius refuses to allow us to linger long over such an easily fabricated picture; for he suddenly personifies the sea, in an incredible image of a huge sea-monster, a leviathan of lust. We have moved a considerable distance from the rather straightforward image of the Cupid/Christ wearing his gilt thorns—a blend of Christian and pagan myths. Swinburne wins us over by his skillful blending of sense impressions. His art here triumphs over what another poet, say a William Morris, would have handled in a straightforwardly literal, decorative fashion. It seems to me that the incredible image of the panting sea anticipates what Symbolist poets were to do a generation or so after Swinburne.

One more image, among several equally useful, from **"Laus Veneris,"** will demonstrate that Swinburne's use of synesthesia was a consciously developed technique, and not simply a rare, chance occurrence. Tannhäuser's account of a battle fought to wrest the Holy Land away from the pagans is realized in a tissue of sensory images. The Knight's recall of the battle involves his senses of smell, sound (shriek of spears and bows snapping, the breathing of the battle itself), and sight. The whole recalling becomes a stunning visual object, rendered finally almost as a Beardsleyesque graphic design of serpentine line—as the opposing ranks of "beautiful mailed men" move into combat, the pure lines of those ranks slip into a snake's sinuous movement. Swinburne renders a visual pattern in cool, almost detached terms, as it transpires in the

Knight's psyche. For a moment the recollection frees Tann-häuser from his lustful obsession with Venus—but not for long. In an instant, and with a stroke of genius, Tannhäuser moves the metaphor of the snake as it images the battle lines over into his obsession with Venus as his femme fatale. The transition is entirely credible in terms of Swinburne's central theme of lust Venusian. This is, I feel, an exceptional moment in Victorian poetry. Swinburne's reference in developing his stunning visual motifs here, as nearly always, is art and not verifiable reality. To see that charged moment just before the hosts of mailed men engage in battle as a sinuous line of light (and sound) means that one must in a sense time-stop vision. The warriors remain inactive until the perceiver has *seen* the image of light, has made an engraving or a painting in his mind, and, guided by Swinburne, lets go and senses the motion as a gradual slipping of lines into a vision of chaotic battle. Even here, however, the reader is suddenly returned to the Venus theme; it is Venus now that he sees, Venus as serpent. Art, for Swinburne, seemed to provide the distance he required between raw events and their presence in his imagination. In his fashioning of such splendid images he is in the company of painters.

Impressionism is a term that literary critics have borrowed from painting. To simplify, in painting, impressionism refers to the juxtaposition of minute strokes of color, to be combined by the perceiver's eye and blent into tones the painter desired. For example, in a canvas by Monet (or by Renoir, Degas, or Pissarro) we perceive green by visually fusing juxtaposed small strokes of yellow and blue. The effect produced is of an atmospheric shimmer of greens produced without our losing the properties of the tints constituting the greens. The impressionist painter captures the play of sunlight over surfaces, fragmenting objects into tints and hues, infusing the atmosphere with colors absorbed from those objects. In Monet's *Sunflowers,* the air around the vase is as alive with color as the vase itself and the scrap of Persian carpet on which it rests.

In applying *impressionism* to poetry, it is easy to sidestep the issue of verse technique and record instead some quivering, hesitant emotion, or describe passages flickering with sunlight. But such recordings will not suffice. We must look, as Pater said, to "the literary architecture" of the poems in question, to see whether that architecture "involves not only foresight of the end in the beginning, but also development or growth of design in the process of execution," leading to some "unity of the whole." We have already seen something of the nervousness behind Swinburne's particular creation of symbols and moods. Nervousness, obviously, implies flickering and evanescence. Speed and motion are among Swinburne's chief characteristics—the Apollonian dance, derived from Apollo, god of poetry, himself, spins, whirls, and moves through Swinburne's poetry. The swift anapestic line generates much of the kineticism we associate with Swinburne. At its best, the poetry has an impressive architecture, in Pater's sense. Towards understanding how his verse impressionism works, as words play against words, and lines against lines, I shall examine two passages from his late masterpiece **"By the North Sea."** The whole poem is an elaborate metaphor for the act of Apollonian creation and the dominance of art over all transiency.

The first stanza of **"By the North Sea,"** part of the dedication, presents a trio of characteristic Swinburnian images—*sea, wind,* and *sun* (or, *sound, breath,* and *light*) symbolizing

the free creative spirit of man. Death, a shadow cast by life upon fate, symbolizes life's ironic triumph over fate. The passage sustains two predominant sounds: *th* and *t*. There is a remarkable absence of sharp imagery and detail. The first stanza is an *abba abba* pattern: the rhymes or near-rhymes are *breath, create, passionate, faith, safe, great, fate,* and *death:*

> Sea, wind, and sun, with light and sound and breath
>   The spirit of man fulfilling—these create
>   That joy wherewith man's life grown passionate
> Gains heart to hear and sense to read and faith
> To know the secret word our Mother saith
>   In silence, and to see, though doubt wax great,
>   Death as the shadow cast by life on fate,
> Passing, whose shade we call the shadow of death.

If one divides this stanza more or less medially (possible because of the disposition of the caesurae and the natural pauses), one sees that end rhymes indigenously allow the right portion to carry richer sounds than the left. The images, pallid and bare, call little attention to themselves and evoke quietly penetrating relationships. In the total music of the passage, separate words are subordinated to an overriding effect of blent senses in combination. In general, masculine rhymes (*create, great, fate*) occur at the ends of lines where the reader pauses to absorb the metaphysical content. Swinburne involves us in complex, intellectual abstractions. Faster soft-rhyme echoes (*breath, faith, death*) carry us swiftly into the succeeding lines where they halt, usually at a caesura placed skillfully midway through.

This oscillation between soft and harsh effects, between *th* sounds and explosives, produces a verbal shimmer, ubiquitous in **"By the North Sea."** This effect can be compared to the Impressionist painter's practice of juxtaposing small nervous strokes of color. To alternate *breath* and *create* as key sounds attracting individual echoes is not of course unusual. What is unusual is the exclusive dependence on such controls within this tightly knit stanza. Note, for example, the several internal effects echoing *breath* and *create* in one form or another: *spirit, heart, secret, doubt; wherewith, however, though,* and *death* are the more obvious examples.

In grasping Swinburne's nuances, we enjoy a complex Impressionist art. His sound patterns, so full of shadings, are an exercise in impressionism by association. Nervous on-going designs assemble around key words . . . *death* is an example. In this instance feminine words dominate: *boundless, endless, blossoms, fruitless, powerless.* Flickering white swallows and fluttering grass, though seemingly precise are, in fact, vague; yet they serve as nervous images flashing through the dusky, cloudlit skies. The landscape itself is desolate—a more expanded version of the sterile site he celebrates in **"A Forsaken Garden."** The vast landscape is shot through with swiftly moving negative energies. In an impressionist, restless, flickering way, we juggle his positives and negatives, motifs of pleasure and pain. The birds' songs "fall," the image borrowing impact from the visual detail of frightened wings seen as "lightnings that flee." Swinburne manages to create a complex tissue of mental and auditory effects implying their opposites, a quality unique in his poetry and particularly successful in **"By the North Sea."**

Delicate impressionist rhymes based on certain key polysyllabic feminine words (*hunger, passion, hunger, winter*) culminate (stanza 6) in a potent image of storm and floundering ships, symbolizing the rage of the sea. Destructive and ravenous, the sea is no longer the life-giver. This oscillation between roles requires a certain alertness from the reader, a shift of mind, a counterpart to the quick fluctuations of sight and sound everywhere in the poem. As Swinburne presents his swiftly rendered symbols, transitions are minimal. Verse sentences pile upon one another, their solidity arising from an assemblage of various impressionist effects and not from any solid rational progression of thought and feeling. As lines race forward, clustered with paradoxical meanings and actions, images assume symbolic force. The attention they require of us is not dissimilar to some of the effects found in the work of Baudelaire, Verlaine, Rimbaud, Laforgue, and Mallarmé; in this sense, developing his own style, Swinburne anticipates these writers.

Midway in **"By the North Sea,"** our view moves leisurely from land out to the sea's yellow edge which devours the land and beyond, to flickering clouds and more birds. Here, all human problems dissolve into the earth, where they "sink under / Deep as deep in water sinks a stone." Impressionist seeing creates a special joy in freedom:

> Tall the plumage of the rush-flower tosses,
>   Sharp and soft in many a curve and line
> Gleam and glow the sea-coloured marsh-mosses
>   Salt and splendid from the circling brine.
> Streak on streak of glimmering seashine crosses
> All the land sea-saturate as with wine.

The passage is fresh and buoyant, glimmering as it does with streaks of sea-shine. Curves and lines suggested by broad expanses of marsh vegetation abound, always generally rather than specifically seen. Tossing rush-flowers produce ample, rounding curves; there is a massed single impression of beauty. All hues are carefully controlled, in the manner of Whistlerian merged tones. Only the generalized billowing contours of the flowers divide these massed forms from the sea—which sheds a metallic light and assumes various tints of blue. Earlier in the poem the sea was wan, grey, and sunless. Sensations of touch and taste weave through visual and kinetic ones. Lines describing natural forms are both sharp and soft. The marsh mosses are salty. Combined, these motifs produce a single effect, a beautiful climax for the stanza—the land is "sea-saturate as with wine." The whole landscape is stained with color, without distinctive configurations. Accompanying the various plays of sunlight, a surface impressionism, are verbal and thematic motions playing throughout, enhancing the visual effects. The whole landscape is stained with color, without distinctive configurations. The allusion to *wine* carries, of course, connotations of color and taste and, in addition, possesses ceremonial or ritualistic overtones and evokes an epic past. In summary, while these lines produce a surface impressionism of sunlight as it transforms a landscape and breaks up the precise contours of individual objects, they do a good deal more. A verbal and thematic motion plays throughout, enhancing the visual effects.

The interplay of contrasting, swiftly moving sets of rhymes characterizes Swinburne's verse impressionism at its best. *Tosses, mosses,* and *crosses* relaxed, on-going, and soft, are checked and drawn in by clipped, long-vowelled monosyllables (*line, brine, wine*). In addition to managing such skillful interweavings of sense images and alternating end rhymes with their positive auditory effects, Swinburne characteristically treats the stanza as a unit more or less divided medially, a sort of form with a vertebra. The compound subjects of lines 3-5, and the streaks of line 6, show this. Contributing also is

the weight provided by the rhymes *tall, salt,* and *all* of lines 1, 4, and 6. These tight rhymes comprise part of the frame for the section (aided also by the assonance of *gleam* and *streak* of lines 3 and 5) and are in tensile balance with those softer feminine end rhymes which seem to dissolve in the distance.

We move next to a muted view featuring a "low grey sky" cloven by "clear grey steeples," a Whistlerian motif of grey on grey with the heavier grey pricked out by spires. The latter symbolize human fearlessness before the "blast of days and nights that die" and prepare for the final irony, the crumbling of graveyard and church into the sea. Unfortunately the stanza is loose and uninspired. Grey is the hue of a man's troubled face and of clouds troubling the land. The transferences happen too easily. The "towers and tombs" watching "stern and sweet" over the lonely dunes lack symbolic power. Interwoven *in* sounds constitute the best technical feature here. Stanzas 6-8 blend these sounds: *thinned, sinned,* and *wind* as end rhymes in stanza 6; *wander, squander,* and *yonder* in 7; *olden, golden,* and *beholden* in 8.

The vision of Odysseus materializes slowly, as the poet laments that only in pre-Homeric times did the present landscape bear signs of life and death. In the present, this sterile waste is more a symbol of death than a real locale: "Here is Hades, manifest, beholden, / Surely, surely here, if aught be sure." The place is "the border-line" between life and death. Life's wild motions, its "lightning joys and woes," occur here only to expire. This is the same Hades, the speaker says, where Hercules met Anticleia's spirit and found proof that souls after death love even more intensely than in life. In this symbolic underworld love "lives and stands up re-created."

But Hercules suffers since he, the only mortal allowed to cross death's threshold and live, is unable to grasp his mother's shade. The brief meeting is painfully but delicately described, concluding the vision and returning the speaker to the present "all dispeopled here of visions" and "forlorn of shadows": "Ghostless, all its gulfs and creeks and reaches / Sky, and shore, and cloud, and waste, and sea."

These final symbols, elemental and abstract, recall Shelley's and Whitman's similar handling of broad motifs: procreant large forces of nature and the universe stilled and colored by the poet's mood. For Swinburne they are consciously pallid. There is perhaps more of a hunger for the past in Swinburne than in the other poets; nor does Swinburne embrace the disparate natural and social forces of a vivid present, as one finds them in "Song of Myself"; nor does he absorb much of Shelley's remarkable power to transform classical material into a symbolic equivalent for a vital, apocalyptic social and ethical vision transpiring in a graspable future (see *Prometheus Unbound,* particularly the final act). Swinburne here joins the ranks, if he is not, indeed, the leader, of those writers (Arnold, Pater, John Addington Symonds, Oscar Wilde, and Arthur Symons among them) who contrasted their hunger for a romanticized past with a desperate Philistine present. Swinburne's label for the latter was "the new Gaza where we live." It is in such passages as these that Swinburne is most purely the early Victorian aesthete. (pp. 140-56)

Robert Peters, "Swinburne: A Personal Essay and a Polemic," in The Victorian Experience: The Poets, *edited by Richard A. Levine, Ohio University Press, 1982, pp. 138-57.*

PAULINE FLETCHER (essay date 1983)

[*In the following excerpt, Fletcher maintains that Swinburne's poetry of bleak, solitary landscapes and seascapes emphasizes natural cycles of birth, growth, death, and decay.*]

Swinburne is a great romantic mythmaker, and nowhere is his mythmaking more apparent than in his treatment of landscape. His love of wild and solitary settings springs not merely from his rejection of society, but from the most profound and passionate depths of his nature. His feeling for the more sublime aspects of nature, and particularly for the sea, has an intensity that is probably unsurpassed in English poetry. He should be remembered not only for the shocking crime of introducing Dolores to the Young Person, but for throwing open the Victorian drawing room and exposing its inmates to the elemental clash of wind and waves, and to the stark beauties of a landscape untouched by man.

It was perhaps necessary to break some windows before people would take notice of what lay outside the drawing room, and Swinburne performed this task with relish. For one thing, he subverted the traditional associations of the garden, transforming it from a symbol of paradisal innocence into something disturbingly different. Even when he exploits the conventional associations, as in **"The Two Dreams,"** which is based on Boccaccio and contains an enclosed rose garden, he introduces a subversive note. Much of the poem is disarmingly traditional, being written in pseudo-Chaucerian English. The heroine is straight out of a medieval romance:

> Her face was white, and thereto she was tall;
> In no wise lacked there any praise at all
> To her most perfect and pure maidenhood.

And when the hero dies he sounds remarkably like Chaucer's Troilus; "O help me, sweet, I am but dead." The rose garden is introduced in similarly conventional terms: "There grew a rose-garden in Florence land / More fair than many." However, in the detailed description of the garden, Chaucer and Boccaccio give way to pure Swinburne:

> Even this green place the summer caught them in
> Seemed half deflowered and sick with beaten leaves
> In their strayed eyes; these gold flower-fumèd eves
> Burnt out to make the sun's love-offering,
> The midnoon's prayer, the rose's thanksgiving,
> The trees' weight burdening the strengthless air,
> The shape of her stilled eyes, her coloured hair,
> Her body's balance from the moving feet—
> All this, found fair, lacked yet one grain of sweet
> It had some warm weeks back: so perisheth
> On May's new lip the tender April breath;
> So those same walks the wind sowed lilies in
> All April through, and all their latter kin
> Of languid leaves whereon Autumn blows—
> The dead red raiment of the last year's rose—
> The last year's laurel, and the last year's love,
> Fade, and grow things that death grows weary of.

The idyllic spring freshness of the medieval garden has been replaced by a garden in the full and oppressive heat of summer, presaging the further change of winter in its "half deflowered" blooms and "beaten leaves." Like Browning, Swinburne sees the garden not as a static paradise, but as embodying the change and decay that its rich growth implies. Moreover, the seasonal change mirrors the decaying passion of the lovers, now in the summertime of their satiety. It is the intense quality of their passion and of life in the garden that forces both toward extinction. The flowers do not merely perfume the air; they burn themselves out in an extravagant love-offering to the sun. The trees produce such an abundance of foliage that they burden "the strengthless air." The lovers have lived at the same intensity, but they are condemned to watch their passion fade slowly. At least last year's rose dies and is the sweeter for producing new blossoms. Human lovers cannot hope for such a renewal. She, sensing the decay of passion in him, revives their love with an embrace so violent that he dies. Like the speaker in Browning's "Porphyria's Lover," she prefers the eternal possession of death to the hazards of a life that is subject to the flux of time.

The garden of **"The Two Dreams"** is not only subject to time; its idyllic quality is also subverted by the evil nature of the dreams recounted by the lovers. She tells how she saw "a live thing flaked with black / Specks of brute slime and leper-coloured scale," crawling from his mouth and then devouring him. He, after enjoying the "tender little thornprick of her pain," describes his own dream, in which he received a kiss that wounded him. Cruelty has entered the garden, and it operates at a more disturbing level than that of the cruel mistress of the courtly love tradition. The woman of **"The Two Dreams,"** whose kiss is death, is first cousin to a long line of fatal women that includes Keats's "La Belle Dame Sans Merci," and Rossetti's somber ladies. They reach their most extreme development in Swinburne's Dolores, Our Lady of Pain.

"Dolores" also represents a more extreme subversion of the garden. The Lady of Pain is herself a "garden where all men may dwell," which is "lit with live torches," and drenched with blood and tears. Such a garden is not merely antisocial; it is a deliberate affront to society. Tennyson's early gardens had been antisocial places of solitary withdrawal, but they had always represented an attempt to recover the innocence of Eden. Swinburne's gardens, far from being Edenic, are often not even Gardens of Earthly Delights; they are more likely to be Gardens of Infernal Pleasures, presided over by sinister women or implacable goddesses.

Lucrezia Borgia is one such fatal woman, addressed by the poet in **"A Ballad of Life,"** but her sinister qualities are played down in the poem, and she emerges as something of a "stunner" in a Pre-Raphaelite setting:

> I found in dreams a place of wind and flowers,
>   Full of sweet trees and colour of glad grass,
>   In midst whereof there was
> A lady clothed like summer with sweet hours.
> Her beauty, fervent as a fiery moon,
>   Made my blood burn and swoon
>   Like a flame rained upon.
> Sorrow had filled her shaken eyelids' blue,
> And her mouth's sad red heavy rose all through
>   Seemed sad with glad things gone.

This could have been written for one of Rossetti's paintings; it has a static, pictorial, brooding quality unusual in Swinburne, and the flowers, trees, and grass suggest the kind of woodland bower beloved of Rossetti. One word, however, marks it as belonging to Swinburne, and that is "wind." It has already been noted that Rossetti almost always finds the wind a hostile element, whereas Swinburne delighted in it, and even imports it, somewhat incongruously, into this otherwise hushed, Pre-Raphaelite landscape.

In fact, it may not be too much of an exaggeration to say that Rossetti's heaven, the enclosed, protected space, was Swinburne's hell. In **"Laus Veneris"** the horror of the knight's fate is conveyed most powerfully through the feeling of claustrophobia within the Venusberg:

> Inside the Horsel here the air is hot;
> Right little peace one hath for it, God wot;
>   The scented dusty daylight burns the air,
> And my heart chokes me till I hear it not.

The prisoner of Venus longs for death, so that he might merge with the free, elemental forces outside the gloomy cavern:

> Ah yet would God this flesh of mine might be
> Where air might wash and long leaves cover me,
>   Where tides of grass break into foam of flowers,
> Or where the wind's feet shine along the sea.

This yearning for freedom from lust through union with the great cosmic forces is one of the most enduring themes in Swinburne's poetry, but there is a part of him that also saw subjection to a beautiful, ruthless woman as a kind of paradise. He has to explore that paradise of lust in order to discover what a hell it really represents, and the knight of Venus who is "damned to joyless pleasure," is nevertheless damned because he has gained his pleasure too well. It is significant that Morris, in his version of the legend, imagines the pleasures that tempt the knight very differently. His Venus inhabits a kind of utopian pastoral landscape, a natural paradise, which palls through its unchanging perfection. In Swinburne's **"Laus Veneris"** there is practically no landscape within the mountain. The landscape is all outside, and represents the freedom the knight has lost. The natural world is now the yearned-for paradise, just as Venus was the once yearned-for love. The two represent the basic dualism of Swinburne's nature: the desire for freedom set against the desire for subjugation, or, as Harold Nicolson expresses it [in his *Swinburne*], "the impulse towards revolt and the impulse towards submission." In **"Laus Veneris"** the subjugation to lust is shown as destructive and sterile, while the elemental world represented by the "wind's wet wings" outside the prison of love remains, as elsewhere in Swinburne, the true object of desire.

The fascination with corruption and the fatal woman persists, however, and finds expression in Swinburne's fine elegy, **"Ave atque Vale."** He imagines Baudelaire "at the great knees and feet / Of some pale Titan-woman," an image derived directly from Baudelaire's "La Géante." In "La Géante" the sleeping woman is compared to a mountain. Swinburne seems to have developed this image, associating the Titan woman more specifically with the earth and with great natural forces: her "awful tresses . . . still keep / The savour and shade of old-world pine-forests / Where the wet hill-winds weep." She thus moves away from the Dolores type of cruel lover, closer to an earth goddess. She should perhaps be identified with Proserpine, Queen of the Underworld and daughter of the earth-goddess, Demeter. According to Walter Pater, Proserpine was not, in the earliest myths, clearly separated from her mother: "Demeter—Demeter and Persephone, at first, in a sort of confused union—is the earth, in the fixed order of its annual changes, but also in all the accident and detail of the growth and decay of its children." The emphasis in Swinburne is, of course, on "decay," and he imagines that in the underworld Baudelaire will find strange, poisonous flowers similar to those he created in life:

> Where all day through thine hands in barren braid
> Wove the sick flowers of secrecy and shade,

> Green buds of sorrow and sin, and remnants grey,
> Sweet-smelling, pale with poison, sanguine-hearted.

Such "fleurs du mal" are a ghastly parody of the floral tributes traditionally offered in the classical pastoral elegy, and they celebrate qualities that are the reverse of those usually associated with the garden. In place of innocence, purity, and fruitfulness, this anti-garden produces sin, secrecy, and barrenness; instead of being associated with the control of violent passion, it is a place for the cultivation of extreme license. It is associated with death rather than with life, and links with what Swinburne sees as Baudelaire's desire for "sleep and no more life." Oblivion is the chief consolation offered in this stark elegy, and the only real immortality is to be found in the "shut scroll" of poems, which ensures a continuing communion of souls between the dead and the living. Dim intimations of some afterlife in a classical Hades are recognized as nothing more than the products of the poet's imagination, "Yet with some fancy, yet with some desire, / Dreams pursue death as winds a flying fire."

In an earlier poem, **"The Garden of Proserpine,"** Swinburne had allowed his dreams to pursue death as an end to be desired for its own sake. Rejecting the pastoral world of "men that sow to reap," he celebrates "fruitless fields of corn" and the barren gardens of death:

> No growth of moor or coppice,
>   No heather-flower or vine,
> But bloomless buds of poppies,
>   Green grapes of Proserpine,
> Pale beds of blowing rushes
> Where no leaf blooms or blushes
> Save this whereout she crushes
>   For dead men deadly wine.

Proserpine offers death, but she also offers a life beyond the turmoil of passion. To enter her garden is to enter a still, closed world, cut off from the freshness and freedom of wind and waves. In this respect it resembles the world of the Venusberg, but in this poem Swinburne's protagonist is strongly attracted to the place "where all trouble seems / Dead winds' and spent waves' riot." The death wish expressed in this poem is basically negative and escapist; the speaker is "tired of tears and laughter" and "weary of days and hours." Swinburne was later to deal with the death wish differently and more positively, but at this point the desire seems to be for deliverance from "too much love of living."

It is significant that Swinburne's Proserpine seems to have no desire to return from the realm of death. She "Forgets the earth her mother, / The life of fruits and corn." This fleeting reference to Demeter is the only mention the poet makes of that side of Proserpine which is traditionally associated with the seasonal renewal of life in the world. (pp. 191-98)

In both [**"Hymn to Proserpine"** and **"The Garden of Proserpine"**] the underworld is the realm of death or sleep, and neither goddess nor poet visits it in order to return, regenerated, to the world of light. In **"Ave atque Vale"** there is a suggestion that Baudelaire's knowledge of "Secrets and sorrows unbeheld of us: / Fierce loves, and lovely leaf-buds poisonous" was akin to the infernal knowledge of Proserpine. In her strange garden he, the "gardener of strange flowers," may find blossoms similar to those of his poetic vision, but there will be no return from the underworld for him either. Swinburne is, in this poem, absolute for death. (pp. 201-02)

In his poem **"A Forsaken Garden,"** Swinburne describes a

more realistic and earthly version of the garden of death, one that is poised at the center of indifference, in the void after the process of dissolution has been completed, but before the new life can begin. This is expressed in the ambiguous, one might say amphibious nature of the garden:

> In a coign of the cliff between lowland and highland
>   At the sea-down's edge between windward and lee,
> Walled round with rocks as an inland island,
>   The ghost of a garden fronts the sea.
> A girdle of brushwood and thorn encloses
>   The steep square slope of the blossomless bed
> Where the weeds that grew green from the graves of its
>   roses
>   Now lie dead.

It is "between lowland and highland," between "windward and lee," and, belonging to neither land nor sea, it is an "inland island." Its wall of rocks is neither quite natural, nor is it the traditional ivy-covered, man-made wall of the *hortus conclusus.* What Rosenberg calls "this fusion of the artificial with the aboriginal" [see essay dated 1968] is also suggested in the "square" of the abandoned bed, which has a wild girdle of "brushwood and thorn." These details are not merely decorative. In giving the garden such ambiguity, Swinburne places it in limbo between land, order, and civilization on the one hand, and sea, chaos, and wilderness on the other. It is also caught between life and eternity. Life belongs to the land and to the "meadows that blossom and wither"; its chief characteristic is that it is subject to time, change, and mortality. Eternity belongs to the sea. This point is made by the ghostly lover: "look forth from the flowers to the sea; / For the foam flowers endure when the rose-blossoms wither."

But the rose has long since withered in this forsaken garden,

Drawing of Swinburne by Sir William Rothenstein.

and now there remains "naught living to ravage and rend." What does remain will not decay:

> Earth, stones and thorns of the wild ground growing,
>   While the sun and the rain live, these shall be:
> Till a last wind's breath upon all these blowing
>   Roll the sea.

It is in this stasis, this imitation of eternity, that Swinburne recovers for his anti-garden one of the most important qualities of the traditional garden, since for most poets the ideal garden is either a static world of repose and meditation, or a place where lovers may meet for a precious moment caught and held out of the flux of time, the moment made eternal. For Swinburne, this repose is only possible in the garden of death. His forsaken garden has achieved such a perfection of barrenness that it has, paradoxically, defeated death, at least until the apocalypse:

> Till the slow sea rise and the sheer cliff crumble,
>   Till terrace and meadow the deep gulfs drink,
> Till the strength of the waves of the high tides humble
>   The fields that lessen, the rocks that shrink,
> Here now in his triumph where all things falter,
>   Stretched out on the spoils that his own hand spread,
> As a god self-slain on his own strange altar,
>   Death lies dead.

Man can achieve a similar triumph over death, but only by surrendering to death, as this garden has done. Such a surrender is envisaged in **"The Triumph of Time,"** in which the speaker turns from an earthly lover, who has failed him, to the bleak margins of the sea, where he gazes on a landscape of endurance:

> But clear are these things; the grass and the sand,
>   Where, sure as the eyes reach, ever at hand,
> With lips wide open and face burnt blind,
>   The strong sea-daisies feast on the sun.

There is stoic resignation in this barren scene with its "strong sea-daisies," and one is reminded of the landscape in Arnold's "Resignation," in which "solemn wastes of heathy hill / Sleep in the July sunshine still." However, Arnold's landscape is one that seems "to bear rather than rejoice"; Swinburne's goes beyond passive resignation. The wide open lips of the daisies imply an appetite for life, or perhaps for death. Moreover, although the faces of the daisies are "burnt blind" by the heat, they also feast on the sun, so that they both take and give life; the roles of victim and predator are reciprocal. Since Swinburne usually associates the sun with Apollo, god of song and poetry, the daisies may also be seen as symbols of the poet himself, and of his peculiar relationship to the source of his inspiration.

The passion of the daisies for the sun is paralleled by the apparent desire of the landscape to merge with the sea:

> The low downs lean to the sea; the stream,
>   One loose thin pulseless tremulous vein,
> Rapid and vivid and dumb as a dream,
>   Works downward, sick of the sun and the rain.

The description of the falling stream would seem to owe something to Tennyson's streams in "The Lotos-Eaters," which, "like a downward smoke, / Slow-dropping veils of thinnest lawn, did go," but in fact Swinburne's purposes are quite different. Tennyson is primarily concerned with a beautiful visual effect, and secondly with an emotional effect: the great delicacy and slow movement of the dropping veils enhance the languorous calm of the island paradise. Swinburne has moved further from the school of picturesque landscape description than Tennyson. In describing the stream as "One loose thin pulseless tremulous vein," he is not drawing attention to its pictorial qualities. He is making a statement about its relationship to the sea. The stream is part of the body of the sea, a "vein," but "pulseless" because it has become detached or "loose." In tremulous longing it hastens downward, "sick of the sun and the rain" because they are the agents of the cycle in which the stream is caught up, separated from, and then returned to its mother, the sea, through evaporation and precipitation. This passage of seemingly vague, diffuse Swinburnian description yields the most precise meanings. Even "The low downs lean to the sea" is a scientifically accurate account of the gradual erosion of the land by physical forces, rather than an example of the pathetic fallacy.

The scientific accuracy of the passage is, however, given emotional coloring by identification of the speaker with the stream. He too is "born of the sea":

> I will go back to the great sweet mother,
>   Mother and lover of men, the sea.
> I will go down to her, I and none other,
>   Close with her, kiss her and mix her with me;
> Cling to her, strive with her, hold her fast.

In the sea he is able to achieve that perfect union with the beloved that he had desired of the woman he loved:

>   were you once sealed mine,
> Mine in the blood's beat, mine in the breath,
> Mixed into me as honey in wine,
>   Not time, that sayeth and gainsayeth,
> Nor all strong things had severed us then.

Denied this immortality, he chooses to mingle with the sea, becoming, like the stream, "A pulse of the life of thy straits and bays, / A vein in the heart of the streams of the sea."

The immortality offered by the sea is, however, that of eternal change. To surrender to its bitter embrace is to surrender to the principle of mutability:

> I shall sleep, and move with the moving ships,
>   Change as the winds change, veer in the tide;
> My lips will feast on the foam of thy lips,
>   I shall rise with thy rising, with thee subside.

Such a surrender implies the complete extinction of personality, but this loss is seen as a guarantee of freedom. He asks the sea to "Set free my soul as thy soul is free," and claims that, once freed from the body, "Naked and glad would I walk in thy ways, / Alive and aware of thy ways and thee."

Although the sea in **"The Triumph of Time"** promises freedom, it still has many of the characteristics of the cruel mistress, whose "large embraces are keen like pain." In **"Hesperia"** the sea is associated with Our Lady of Sleep rather than with Our Lady of Pain, and the poet imagines a more peaceful and gentle surrender, resulting, however, in an even more complete loss of personality and its burdens. In **"The Triumph of Time"** he is still pitting his strength against the sea: he will "cling to her, strive with her, hold her fast." In **"Hesperia"** there is no struggle:

> And my heart yearns baffled and blind, moved vainly toward thee, and moving
> As the refluent seaweed moves in the languid exuberant stream,

Fair as a rose is on earth, as a rose under water in prison,
That stretches and swings to the slow passionate pulse of the sea,
Closed up from the air and the sun, but alive, as a ghost rearisen,
Pale as the love that revives as a ghost rearisen in me.

The loss of will and separate identity implied by this passage represents a further stage in the death process, and is therefore, paradoxically, closer to the possibility of new life. Trapped in their underwater prison without sun or air, the roses of the sea are in the realm of death, and yet, as they sway in the saline bath of the Great Mother, they are also in the womb of life, "alive as a ghost rearisen."

In terms of Swinburne's personal myth, as outlined in **"Thalassius,"** this return to the sea and consequent resurrection can be seen as the commitment of the poet to his art. In **"Thalassius"** the poet is born of the sea and the sun. Leaving the sea, he encounters Love, who is also Sorrow and Death; then he rides for a while in the fierce, wild train of Lust. Finally sickened, he returns to the sea, falls into a deep sleep, and awakens "Pure as one purged of pain that passion bore." The process of regeneration begins, and "the earth's great comfort and the sweet sea's breath / Breathed and blew life in where was heartless death." His poetic awakening, which follows, is described in terms that suggest the submergence of the individual soul in the great cosmic rhythms of the sea:

> Now too the soul of all his senses felt
> The passionate pride of deep sea-pulses dealt
> Through nerve and jubilant vein
> As from the love and largess of old time,
> And with his heart again
> The tidal throb of all the tides keep rhyme
> And charm him from his own soul's separate sense
> With infinite and invasive influence
> That made strength sweet in him and sweetness strong,
> Being now no more a singer, but a song.

(pp. 202-08)

In **"On the Cliffs"** . . . the animating source seems to come from man rather than from nature. The poem opens with a powerful description of the bleak landscape bordering the North Sea, with its "gaunt woods," "wan wild sparse flowers," and "steep green sterile fields." This barren landscape must be brought to life by the song of the lyric poet, Sappho, here embodied in the nightingale, whose "ruling song has thrilled / The deep dark air and subtle tender sea." Before her voice was heard, "Dumb was the field, the woodland mute, the lawn / Silent; the hill was tongueless as the vale." Nature is so much dead matter without the life given to it by the perceiving poet. "For Wordsworth," writes David Riede [in *Swinburne: A study of Romantic Myth-making*], "the informing force in nature is a mysterious pantheistic deity; for Swinburne, it is poetry." This, at least, emerges quite clearly from **"On the Cliffs."** But Swinburne was not a didactic poet. Less theoretical than Wordsworth, he is often caught in the flux of changing moods and feelings, and his various seas, like Tennyson's, speak with many voices.

In **"The Garden of Cymodoce,"** for example, he sings a song of rapturous praise of the sea, and of that "favourite corner of all on earth known to me, the island of Sark." There he states that he has loved the sea with a love "more strong / In me than very song," which certainly implies that the sea has a reality that equals, or even surpasses, his poetry. In other poems he sings not of a beautiful and beneficent sea, but of a sea that is

Wild, and woful, and pale, and grey,
A shadow of sleepless fear,
A corpse with the night for bier.

("Neap-Tide")

Often the sea is associated with death and destruction, as in the very fine poem **"By the North Sea,"** where the "waters are haggard and yellow / And crass with the scurf of the beach." This sea is a devourer of corpses, the mate of Death, and it borders a land that is bleak and desolate:

A land that is lonelier than ruin;
A sea that is stranger than death:
Far fields that a rose never blew in,
Wan waste where the winds lack breath;
Waste endless and boundless and flowerless
But of marsh-blossoms fruitless as free:
Where earth lies exhausted, as powerless
To strive with the sea.

The poet, however, finds consolation in this bleak wasteland. Its barren emptiness confers the peace of oblivion:

Slowly, gladly, full of peace and wonder
Grows his heart who journeys here alone.
Earth and all its thoughts of earth sink under
Deep as deep in water sinks a stone.

Emerging from this Center of Indifference, he perceives a new beauty in the landscape, which has undergone a "sea-change":

Tall the plumage of the rush-flower tosses,
Sharp and soft in many a curve and line
Gleam and glow the sea-coloured marsh-mosses
Salt and splendid from the circling brine.
Streak on streak of glimmering seashine crosses
All the land sea-saturate as with wine.

The sea has claimed this land for its own, saturating it with brine and rendering it useless to man; the "pastures are herdless and sheepless." But in so doing, the sea has transformed it into a landscape of strange, gleaming beauty, like a Turner painting. The process traced in these stanzas encapsulates the movement of the poem as a whole from Death, through the Void, to a renewal of life and beauty. This renewal only comes after a total acceptance of death. Nothing, not even the graves of the dead, can stand against time and the destructive power of the sea.

Nothing, that is, save the wind, whom the sea recognizes as "her lord and her lover." The wind is powerful and free because he gives no hostages to time; he has no possessions or material body to lose. He therefore achieves immortality, but is doomed to seek, never to find, "but seeking rejoices / That possession can work him no wrong." The poet identifies with the wind, and can achieve a similar immortality through his song, but he must accept both "the boon and the burden / Of the sleepless unsatisfied breeze." Part of that burden entails the sacrifice of ordinary life, its goals and rewards:

For the wind's is their doom and their blessing;
To desire, and have always above
A possession beyond their possessing,
A love beyond reach of their love.
Green earth has her sons and her daughters,
And these have their guerdons; but we
Are the wind's and the sun's and the water's,
Elect of the sea.

Swinburne's choice of bleak landscapes and seascapes is therefore a necessary part of his vocation as a poet. Ordinary men and women may receive the reward of the rich pastoral life implied in "green earth," but they will decay with that earth. The poet will pay for his immortality by inhabiting landscapes that are "herdless and sheepless."

Sometimes the poet finds it impossible to make the sacrifice demanded of him in order to become one of the "elect of the sea." This happens in **"Evening on the Broads,"** in which no joyful union between poet and sea or wind takes place. In this poem the sea is presented as a less than perfect lover: she rejects light and love because she has "None to reflect from the bitter and shallow response of her heart." But the poet is equally ungenerous, giving nothing of himself to the sea. He remains a detached and critical observer, "here by the sand-bank watching, with eyes on the sea-line." However, the mood of the poet fluctuates, and there is a slow rise and fall of hopefulness and despair, perhaps corresponding to the rhythm of the sea itself. (pp. 209-12)

["The Lake of Gaube" is] one of Swinburne's few poems inspired by mountain scenery. The lake celebrated in this remarkable poem is in the central Pyrenees, near Cauteretz. It is the same region that was visited by Tennyson and Hallam in 1830, and that inspired the beautiful scenic description in "Oenone." . . . Tennyson was to modify the early version of this poem by softening and humanizing the picturesque landscape in the 1842 version. Swinburne does not humanize the landscape in **"The Lake of Gaube"**; he emphasizes its sublime and terrible qualities.

He has little interest, however, in the picturesque qualities of the scene. Even in the opening stanza, which comes closest to being pictorial, the emphasis is on the unifying power of the sun:

The lawns, the gorges, and the peaks, are one
Glad glory, thrilled with sense of unison
In strong compulsive silence of the sun.

The speaker desires to become part of this "glad glory," but in order to achieve this, he must submit to the extinction of his own separate personality by plunging into the dark, icy waters of the lake. . . . **"The Lake of Gaube"** is a death poem, but through this "death" the "spirit may experience utter freedom and self-obliviousness or a moment of annihilation preceding renewal."

In **"A Nympholept"** the speaker bathed himself in the fiery light of noon and was granted knowledge of the God who is both darkness and light. Now he must dive into the darkness in order to arrive at unity with the sun, and he must submit to the dark not simply without fear, but with ecstasy:

As the bright salamander in fire of the noonshine
exults and is glad of his day,
The spirit that quickens my body rejoices to pass
from the sunlight away,
To pass from the glow of the mountainous flowerage,
the high multitudinous bloom,
Far down through the fathomless night of the water,
the gladness of silence and gloom.
Death-dark and delicious as death in the dream
of a lover and dreamer may be,
It clasps and encompasses body and soul with
delight to be living and free.

Such a rhapsodic invocation of the realm of death looks forward to D. H. Lawrence's "Bavarian Gentians," in which oblivion is seen as a consummation, the embrace of the dark god amidst "the splendour of torches of darkness, shedding darkness on the lost bride and her groom." But Swinburne's swimmer breaks out of the darkness after his moment of oblivion, and "Shoots up as a shaft from the dark depth shot, sped straight into sight of the sun." He has earned his right to join earth, air, and mountains in their "sense of unison" beneath the sovereign power of the sun, and since the sun is associated with Apollo, it becomes possible . . . to see the plunge into the lake as "a superb image for the freedom and joy of poetic creation and of man's union with nature."

A useful comparison might also be drawn between this dive into the dark lake and Empedocles' leap into the volcano in Arnold's poem. For Empedocles, the leap is an act of despair leading to extinction, although he does, as has been pointed out, recover the sense of the sublime for a brief moment before death. For Swinburne, extinction is the necessary prelude to a renewed sense of life and, in particular, to the accession of poetic power. Swinburne recovers the sense of the sublime for the Victorians by exploring and accepting its terrible aspects. He is attracted to those landscapes which "excite the ideas of pain and danger," and which are, therefore, "productive of the strongest emotion which the mind is capable of feeling" [Edmund Burke, *The Sublime and the Beautiful*].

The eighteenth-century sublime had degenerated into the picturesque, in which the observer is separated from the landscape, and the terrors of the scenery are turned into a checklist of set emotions for the tourist. Swinburne completely rejects the picturesque, desiring to become a part of the landscape. Arnold's Empedocles had seen that only by the leap into the volcano could a sense of primal terror be regained that would purge life of its triviality. But Arnold was too much of a pessimist, caught in the web of Victorian doubt, to believe that there could be anything after that leap. Swinburne, although rejecting Christianity and the Christian afterlife more completely than Arnold, nevertheless accepts death as part of the process whereby the soul achieves true life and freedom.

Swinburne is the great poet of paradoxes, which are basic to his philosophy that true freedom can only be achieved by the unity of such opposites as flesh and spirit, life and death, light and darkness, pain and pleasure. It is therefore fitting that his landscapes should be at once completely antisocial, and yet in a certain respect completely humanized, since in most of them the division between man and the landscape has disappeared. In a truly reciprocal relationship, man becomes part of the cosmic song, but he is also the singer of that song. (pp. 220-23)

> Pauline Fletcher, "Swinburne: The Sublime Recovered," in her Gardens and Grim Ravines: The Language of Landscape in Victorian Poetry, *Princeton University Press, 1983, pp. 191-223.*

RIKKY ROOKSBY (essay date 1988)

[*In the following excerpt, Rooksby counters claims that Swinburne's later poetry was of a uniformly low quality, assessing examples drawn from the later works as among Swinburne's finest verse.*]

F. L. Lucas wrote of Swinburne [in *Ten Victorian Poets*] that "the heart of him is in **Atalanta** and **Poems and Ballads;** after thirty, his bloom begins to fade" and that at Putney "the nightingale in him died of too much midnight oil." But the more one reads the later poetry the more one sees that the

nightingale did not die, he simply changed his tune, and because that tune does not appear to be as rich or as obvious it is often missed altogether. Most modern Swinburnians would agree with his most recent editor, Leonard Findlay [in *Swinburne: Selected Poems*], that Swinburne "was still capable of fine work in old age, a capacity rare enough among lyric poets." Although critics have given special praise to five of the late poems—**"By the North Sea," "On the Cliffs," "Thalassius," "A Nympholept,"** and **"The Lake of Gaube"**—by analyzing some of the problems of the later poetry and discussing its characteristic techniques and themes, we can add to these five.

The first problem facing the reader of Swinburne's later poetry is that there is so much of it, and, more significantly, that the best poems so closely resemble the worst, and, furthermore, that the successes are utterly unpredictable in their occurrence. As John Drinkwater wrote [in *Swinburne: An Estimate*], "Whilst with other poets a glance is sufficient to tell us which pages to pass over and which to absorb, each page of Swinburne has to be examined carefully before any determination can be made." Prolonged random exploration in these ten Putney volumes can be exasperating in the extreme. Swinburne wrote too many poems, and too many of what Robert Graves once called "unnecessary" poems. Graves had in mind those uninspired poems written out of boredom, obligation, or the craftsman's desire to "keep the hand in": "Every poet knows in his heart which are the necessary and which the unnecessary poems. But too often he tries to fool himself that all are necessary. Necessary poems are rare" [*The Crowning Privilege*]. There are a large number of aesthetic failures in the later poetry, poems that, though they often employ the same metrics, diction, and subjects as the successes, nevertheless read as uninspired. Swinburne's overrestricted lifestyle, and the vagaries of circumstance, or fate, meant he had little opportunity for inspirational experiences. For this reason his holidays in Wiltshire, Sussex, Norfolk, and the Channel Islands were important for the poetry, for they at least provided some stimulus.

Without the inner compulsion experienced by the majority of poets in the composition of their best work, the repetitious elements in Swinburne's later work—especially with regard to diction—doom his unnecessary poems from the outset. But in his finest later lyrics this limited vocabulary becomes irrelevant because our attention is pulled through the surface of the poetry into the depths of Swinburne's imaginative vision. One aspect of his repetitious diction, his use of imagery drawn from the elemental life of nature, is habitual because it is a formal expression of the essential cast or bias of his perception; for [as editor Lawrence Binyon noted in *Selected Poems by A. C. Swinburne*], "the elements, water, fire, wind . . . are his constant inspiration," not to mention the foundation of his reality. When the creative fire is there we do not notice stock phrases like "clothed round" because they disappear in the overall effect, whereas in the failures those favored words stand out like bricks in an unplastered wall. The opening of **"The Centenary of Alexandre Dumas"** affords a good example of this:

> Sound of trumpets blowing down the merriest winds of
> morn,
> Flash of hurtless lightnings, laugh of thunders loud and
> glad,
> Here should hail the summer day whereon a light was
> born

> Whence the sun grew brighter, seeing the world less dark
>   and sad.
> Man of men by right divine of boyhood everlasting,
>   France incarnate, France immortal in her deathless boy,
> Brighter birthday never shone than thine on earth, fore-
>   casting
>   More of strenuous mirth in manhood, more of manful
>   joy.

This has all the effect of being blindfold at a badly organized fireworks display on a wet night: one hears the striking of matches, the sizzle of blue touchpaper, the muted woosh of a rocket, and the faint sigh from the spectators—but one actually sees nothing. Swinburne was sixty-seven when this poem was published, and it is above all the tired verse of an old man. The diction is hyperbolic, the phrasing verges on Victorian greeting-card verse, and the meter is lifeless, devoid of the mercurial energy of Swinburne at his best. Compare the second line with the immeasurably livelier "shed like rain and shaken / Far as foam that laughs and leaps along the sea." Even the alliteration sounds jaded, and Swinburne actually manages to make the eighth line mumble.

This poem is typical of a group of eulogies that tend more to failure than success. There are exceptions, including the elegy for Richard Burton and several of the roundels, but generally this kind of poem is ruined by language erupting into apotheosis: theological metaphors lead to a literary idolatry that overwhelms the humanity of the subject. The result is sometimes comic, as in **"Burns: An Ode"**:

> A fire of fierce and laughing light
> That clove the shuddering heart of night
> Leapt earthward, and the thunder's might
>   That pants and yearns
> Made fitful music round its flight:
>   And earth saw Burns.

If the subject had been Blake's Orc this would have read differently; as it is, the style has outstripped the subject and the reader is irritated by the discrepancy between them. The stanza, however, provokes other intriguing questions. Swinburne is usually neatly labelled as an atheist and a materialist. So what is this pre-birth "fire"? "Leapt earthward"—from where? Either Swinburne is producing here the kind of mythopoeic poetry he is not widely credited with or we need to re-think our view of his thought.

Elsewhere, Swinburne's impulse to eulogize great works of human devising can also lead to careless writing, as with his reference to an old church's "Arch and vault without stain or fault." How could a church have a "stain" in the moral sense? Does he mean rising damp? We cannot get around this by reading "stain" as an aesthetic term because it then becomes redundant; "fault" fulfills that task much better.

We can put aside other groups of poems, at least for the time being: the lyrics in praise of babies and infants (though some, including **"A Dark Month,"** will be of value to the careful biographer), the nationalistic pieces, and poems like those on the Jacobean playwrights that are highly condensed forms of impressionistic literary criticism only a specialist could really appreciate. By selective quotation Swinburne can effortlessly be made to seem the least rewarding poet in the language. But a poet deserves to be judged by his better work and by a careful examination of his technical characteristics when they are being used to best effect.

Critics often accuse Swinburne of being imprecise, yet we can counter this by referring to his diction and similes and to the techniques that govern them. As John D. Rosenberg pointed out in a seminal essay, Swinburne often creates his most moving and beautiful effects with an austere diction that relies heavily on monosyllables [see essay dated 1968]. An elegiac lyric entitled **"Threnody"** begins:

> Watching here alone by the fire whereat last year
> Sat with me the friend that a week since yet was near,
>   That a week has borne so far and hid so deep.

The lines proceed without a syntactical pause and capture the rambling sentences of someone dazed with grief, and the bleak diction is entirely fitting. The vagueness of "hid so deep" is absolutely right for the context while communicating a subtle suggestion of "deep as the sea," a favorite image of Swinburne's. So-called imprecision is working here for a purpose. The same type of tight-lipped, short, almost conversational statement occurs in the triplet of roundels, **"Past Days,"** where Swinburne recalls holidays spent with a now deceased friend:

> Where we went, we twain, in time foregone,
> Forth by land and sea, and cared not whether,
>   If I go again, I go alone.

We meet with this kind of writing in much of **"To a Seamew."** These are all poems of loss, but Swinburne can also use such plain diction to the opposite emotional effect, as with the classic last line of **"A Nympholept"**—"And nought is all, as am I, but a dream of thee"—where the speaker experiences a state of ecstatic union. The grammar suggests the loss of self by subjugating "I" to the "thee" at the end of the sentence. At the close of a poem of 273 lines, the line has a remarkable intensity despite being constructed from apparently unpromising material; the effect evokes the use of blank spaces in Japanese ink-sketches to express the Absolute.

This austerity of diction suits very well the descriptive poems that deal with the more desolate aspects of nature, as in **"By the North Sea"**:

> A land that is lonelier than ruin;
>   A sea that is stranger than death:
> Far fields that a rose never blew in,
>   Wan waste where the winds lack breath;
> Waste endless and boundless and flowerless
>   But of marsh-blossoms fruitless as free:
> Where earth lies exhausted, as powerless
>   To strive with the sea.

The landscape is rendered in a gray wash, there are no color words and visual detail is kept to a minimum, as befits a poem whose subject is a dismal stretch of water and a submerged town; instead of beauty and fecundity, the locale is sterile and alienating. The meter and the feminine rhymes contribute to this impression of a desolate shore by way of their regular emphasis, felt in an almost subliminal way while the reader concentrates on the denotative meaning of the stanza.

In other poems, when Swinburne chooses to celebrate more picturesque scenes, he can use color and lighting in a manner all the more striking for the contrast. Examples of this would include much of **"On the South Coast,"** with its descriptions of plots of land gleaming in the sunset as "Rosy-grey, or as fiery spray full-plumed, or greener than emerald," the sky in **"Le Casquettes"** with "red rose-leaflets of countless cloud," and the fertile beauty of **"A Ballad of Sark"**:

> High beyond the granite portal arched across

Like the gateway of some godlike giant's hold
Sweep and swell the billowy breasts of moor and moss
East and westward, and the dell their slopes enfold
Basks in purple, glows in green, exults in gold.
Glens that know the dove and fells that hear the lark
Fill with joy the rapturous island, as an ark
Full of spicery wrought from herb and flower and tree.

This is clearly very different both in method and final effect from **"By the North Sea."** Where the latter evokes only waste, grayness, and mist, these lines suggest life, vivid color, and tangible landmarks. The same intensity is in the fifth stanza of **"The Palace of Pan,"** where the sun is likened unto a bird "caught" in the "toils" of the branches, "toils" being a splendidly weighty verb for the motion of branches in a wind. The simile is developed further:

As the shreds of a plumage of gold on the ground
    The sun-flakes by multitudes lie,
Shed loose as the petals of roses discrowned
On the floors of the forest engilt and embrowned
    And reddened afar and anigh.

With regard to the subject of this simile, there is a controlled and resonant use of ambiguity. At first, the "plumage of gold" refers to the scattering of light on the forest floor via the foliage of the trees; this appeals to the imagination because it turns intangible light into a concrete object. By the end of the stanza, the "plumage" also refers to the leaves and their autumnal colors. The transition is made by a secondary simile of the "sun-flakes" being like the petals of roses that fall at the same time. Each image blends into the next, but the device is precisely the sort of thing that draws the charge of vagueness. In fact, it expresses Swinburne's holistic view of nature, in which all parts of the whole are related and interdependent, and register the seasonal changes as one: sun, rose, leaf, and wood all show the signs of autumn. As we have already seen with his syntax, specific formal features of the poetry very often enact a deeper perception. When the perceptions are either not understood or unfamiliar, the techniques are liable to be misunderstood also. Some of Swinburne's perceptions are as strange to us as the style of the poetry, and the former embrace much more than simply the sado-masochism of *Poems and Ballads.*

Swinburne's writing has a precision of its own; that is, in accord with his aesthetic aims and his themes. His best similes will repay close examination, as does this one from **"The Ballad of Melicertes"**:

As the sea-shell utters, like a stricken chord,
Music uttering all the sea's within it stored,
    Poet well-beloved, whose praise our sorrow saith,
So thy songs retain thy soul.

The conceit is, of course, traditional: the singer lives on in the immortal form of his art; but it is well expressed, and given that in the later poetry the sound and energy of the sea are often associated with song, the seashell image takes on a greater richness. There is an additional irony in the formal beauty of Swinburne's own lines creating a place in which the dead poet's songs also echo. The Swinburnian simile will "work out" as well as a metaphysical conceit. The difference is that Swinburne was not interested in unusual or inventive analogies since, as he writes in **"A Singing Lesson,"** a poem cannot be good if it is "Far-fetched and dear-bought" in technique. The poetry aspires to uniformity of finish and a constant lyrical intensity by invariably placing the emphasis on the rhythm of a line and on the overall shape of the whole

poem, throughout which the emotion moves without hindrance and without distraction. It deliberately discourages the reader from pausing over specific details. For "As the turn of wave should it sound, and the thought / Ring smooth," as he put it in the same poem, showing that even when expounding a point connected with something as abstract as the craft of poetry, Swinburne is compelled to turn to the elements for an image.

These similes sometimes demonstrate considerable compression of thought and feeling. Swinburne's reputation is for creating on a symphonic scale over hundreds of lines, but he can also move us with a few words. In the "Dedication" to his play *The Sisters* we find the lines:

But where of old from strong and sleepless wells
The exulting fountains fed their shapely shells,
Where light once dwelt in water, dust now dwells.

Like the seashell simile this has an almost classical turn, like white marble, and one notes the tactile "shapely." Line three is an image whose implications lead straight to the core of Swinburne's abiding concerns: the mystery of time and change, and the suffering this inevitably involves for humanity. Elsewhere, his choice of simile will provoke a startling shift of perspective, as when he describes a tempest that confronts

        The might of marshalled fleets
And sheds it into shipwreck, like a rose
        Blown from a child's light grasp in sign
That earth's high lords are lords not over breeze and brine.

The abrupt switch that turns the ships to petals in a child's hand is perfect for the idea of vulnerability involved. A final example of the precision of Swinburne's best similes is to be found in **"Elegy,"** which begins "Auvergne, Auvergne, O wild and woful land"; the poem describes Le Puy:

The huddled churches clinging on the cliffs
    As birds alighting might for storm's sake cling,
Moored to the rocks as tempest-harried skiffs
    To perilous refuge from the loud wind's wing.

Both similes have important ramifications. Firstly, as birds the churches will eventually fly away when Christianity passes into history like the pagan cults it eclipsed centuries ago, since Swinburne takes this kind of long-term view. Secondly, there is the macabre suggestion that the churches will "fly" when they topple into the void through the natural processes of decay. Swinburne was fascinated by the frailty of human creations—be they faiths, ships, or building—in the face of the forces of nature and time. The second simile is ironic, wrought from a deep skepticism, for the churches seen here as taking "perilous refuge" claim to be refuges of an eternal kind for the human soul.

From these examples we can see that the landscape poems tend to be more successful than perhaps any other class of poem in Swinburne's later poetry.

Two effects which characterize Swinburne's landscape pieces are their panoramic quality and their tendency to produce a very powerful reduction of any specific objects that happen to be included in them. He has few rivals when it comes to creating a vast landscape bereft of anything that might suggest the planet is occupied by homo sapiens; his habitats are places only of gulls, sea mews, grass, moor, sand, cliffs, wind, rain, and sun. They are distinguished by an elemental purity and a quality of being very old, far older than the mind of man. The time, in our definition of time, to which the opening lines of **"Evening on the Broads"** refer, is quite irrelevant; the poem was published in 1880 but it could just as well be set in 1880 B.C. or 188,000 B.C.:

> Over two shadowless waters, adrift as a pinnace in peril,
>   Hangs as in heavy suspense, charged with irresolute light,
> Softly the soul of the sunset upholden awhile on the sterile
>   Waves and wastes of the land, half repossessed by the night.
> Inland glimmer the shallows asleep and afar in the breathless
>   Twilight: yonder the depths darken afar and asleep.

Both the length of the lines (dactylic hexameters) and the poem itself (140 lines) contribute to producing the panorama. The lines move slowly, owing to the syntax that halts the flow of the sixth line after one stress, and all the important nouns are plural. The subject of the first sentence, the soul of the sunset, is delayed until the third line, thereby producing the sort of diffusion which Rosenberg has compared to the painting of Turner. Sky, sea, and broads merge into one another, and the whole tableau seems to be full of changing light; the shallows "glimmer," the sea "darkens," and the sunset is "charged" with "irresolute" light. The result is a mobile, not static, picture.

"Evening on the Broads" is, in its early stages, a swirl of luminescent color, but for bleaker daylight conditions yet the same impression of space one need look no further than **"By the North Sea"**:

> Firm and fast where all is cloud that changes
>   Cloud-clogged sunlight, cloud by sunlight thinned,
> Stern and sweet, above the sand-hill ranges
>   Watch the towers and tombs of men that sinned
> Once, now calm as earth whose only change is
>   Wind, and light, and wind, and cloud, and wind.

Again, against our natural bias, the grammar insists that what we would consider the central reference point in the scene, the "towers and tombs," are only a part, by delaying mention of them to the fourth line. The poetry refuses to reflect faithfully our anthropocentric perspectives; for this reason they come in the middle and not at the opening where they could be seized upon and everything else made subordinate to them. The last line shows Swinburne's calculated use of repetition to depict an essentially featureless landscape.

We can only feel the full scope of this panoramic writing when we read poems like **"By the North Sea"** or **"Evening on the Broads"** in their entirety. The same is true of the second effect of the landscape pieces, complementary to the impression of space. Where a panorama is evoked, there is an alteration of perspective for the onlookers, for they must expand their attention in order to begin to take in the immensity of what they are looking at. Adjusting to the macrocosmic scale, the mind sees beyond what is close at hand. For the first one hundred lines **"Evening on the Broads"** makes very little reference to the world of humanity; all is elemental energy and the fading western light. When the reference does finally appear, slipped in as a subordinate clause in a sentence of eight lines in which the reader gropes forward for a main noun that does not come until the eighth line, the change in perspective is very powerful: "Here, far off in the farther extreme of the shore as it lengthens / Northward, lonely for miles, ere ever a village begin." The shock of seeing the village as so isolated, small, and vulnerable, and described and

introduced in such a casual manner, is considerable. The poem does not didactically state that in the context of the might of nature's forces and geological time, human societies are both unprotected and ephemeral, it manipulates us into being abruptly confronted with the fact with the jolt of a fall through a trap door. This pancentricism, with its characteristic reducing of the human world to insignificance, occurs in a number of late poems, with various subtle variations. In the Auvergne **"Elegy"** is a passing allusion to "Thy steep small Siena," and **"Les Casquettes"** has the poignant sketch of "the league-long length of its wild green border, / And the small bright streets of serene St. Anne." In **"The Cliffside Path,"** Swinburne looks back from the cliff top to where "Low behind us lies the bright steep murmuring town," and in the second stanza of **"Neap-tide"** is the same delaying effect previously discussed when the towns are placed in a broader context:

> The fair wild fields and the circling downs,
>   The bright sweet marshes and meads
>   All glorious with flowerlike weeds,
> The great grey churches, the sea-washed towns,
>   Recede as a dream recedes.

"On the South Coast" provides a nocturnal variation when he writes "East and west on the brave earth's breast glow girdle-jewels of gleaming towns." The same kind of perception is in Swinburne's letters, as in this one of November 1887:

> The downs sweep away inland, melting into each other and rising and falling and swelling and sinking like waves of a greater sea, caught and fixed in the act of motion—nothing but the infinite range of softly-rounded heights to be seen to left or right when you look northward; but turning east you see Shoreham with its broad estuary lying (as it seems) quite near at hand, but looking a tiny village.

In **"A Haven"** Swinburne incorporates this effect into the refrain of the poem, "Where the small town smiles, a warm still sea-side nest." Rosenberg finds this refrain and the lines that immediately precede it in the final stanza "the saddest lines in all of Swinburne": "The setting is indistinguishable from those great, bleak, earlier lyrics of the sea's encroachments on the land; here, however, the sea has shrunk to a suburban pond reflecting the ghost of a dead poet." He clearly feels (quite rightly) that something is being diminished in the poem. But I would argue that it is the town, not the sea, that has shrunk, and though the town is described in what seems like an invincibly cozy manner, in context the refrain is less confident than it seems:

> Many a lone long mile, by many a headland's crest,
> Down by many a garden dear to bird and bee,
> Up by many a sea-down's bare and breezy breast,
> Winds the sandy strait of road where flowers run free.
> Here along the deep steep lanes by field and lea
> Knights have carolled, pilgrims chanted, on their quest,
> Haply, ere a roof rose toward the bleak strand's lee,
> Where the small town smiles, a warm still sea-side nest.

The wilder aspects of the countryside, the phrase "ere a roof rose," and the sudden sense of past centuries all subtly warn the reader that the town is not necessarily the "nest" it appears to be.

The diminishing effect is most moving in the elegies. The speaker in the third roundel of **"Past Days"** surveys a landscape only to exclaim:

> These we loved of old: but now for me the blasting
> Breath of death makes dull the bright small seaward
>   towns,
> Clothes with human change these all but everlasting
>   Cliffs and downs.

In this instance the towns are reduced not only by nature but also by death. These lines illustrate Swinburne's simple diction and his panoramic mode. Critics have often said that he is fascinated by opposites and antitheses, and some of these contrasts, such as the pleasure-pain contrast, are well known. We can regard the images of town and wide open space as another example. And the contrast becomes even more striking when Swinburne substitutes a human figure for the town, as in this magical couplet from *Tristram of Lyonesse* where Iseult "Cast the furs from her and subtle embroideries / That wrapped her from the storming rain and spray"; where the vulnerability of human life, embodied in the beauty of the woman, is vividly contrasted with the force of the elements. Furthermore, Swinburne's ability to create a panorama also involves a corresponding change in our view of time.

The landscape poems often express an awareness of stretches of time that dwarf the individual human life. In **"Barking Hall: A Year After"** he writes of the oak-trees that "storms and centuries rock . . . still to rest," and more impressively in **"Past Days"** of

> Cliffs and downs and headlands which the forward-
>   hasting
> Flight of dawn and eve empurples and embrowns,
> Wings of wild sea-winds and stormy seasons wasting
>   Cliffs and downs,
>
> These, or ever man was, were

With a rapidity strongly reminiscent of high-speed photography, the land colors before our eyes as the seasons bloom and fade in mere seconds, dawn and eve chasing each other as they did for H. G. Wells's time traveller. The stanza stresses both the antiquity and the comparatively unchanging aspect of the scene, and both make human life seem but a fleeting moment.

A variation upon this effect occurs when Swinburne recollects a distant moment of human history while describing a locality of beauty. **"On a Country Road"** is a good example of this. It succeeds as a eulogy of Chaucer because unlike **"The Centenary of Alexandre Dumas"** and **"Burns: An Ode"** the praise seems unforced and we have a vividly realized portrait of the English poet in a precise location:

> Along these low pleached lanes, on such a day,
> So soft a day as this, through shade and sun,
> With glad grave eyes that scanned the glad wild way,
> And heart still hovering o'er a song begun,
> And smile that warmed the world with benison,
> Our father, lord long since of lordly rhyme,
> Long since hath haply ridden, when the lime
> Bloomed broad above him, flowering where he came.
> Because thy passage once made warm this clime,
> Our father Chaucer, here we praise thy name.

It is a symbolic portrait of man as a singer, a creator, at one with the environment. Chaucer's creativity is linked with that of the sun, the sun as Apollo being for Swinburne the source of poetic inspiration. The third line suggests the unity of man and world as the "glad" eyes of the poet reflect the "glad wild way." An adroit choice of words like "pleached" and "Bloomed broad" supply naturalistic detail, and the verb

"hovering" evokes delicately the initial stages of composition. The occasional instance of the Swinburnian triple stress—"glad wild way," "lord long since"—amid the iambic pentameter hints at a bubbling joy just kept in check.

Swinburne's handling of the contrast between the nineteenth-century present and the fourteenth-century past is evident in the way he plays off the imaginative reality with the sense of time past. The important phrases in this connection are "on such a day" and the repetition of "long since." The nearest analogy for the final effect is photographic double exposure: Chaucer is there, and yet not there. Eventually, at the close of the poem, the sense of how distant Chaucer is overcomes the act of memory: the feeling expressed earlier that each turn "might bring us face to face" is dismissed by the final metaphor "even as bees about the flowering thyme, / Years crowd on years."

Elsewhere, Swinburne presents the reader with a scene in the present which is really a memory, but only reveals this fact at the very end of the poem in a highly dramatic manner. The laughter and feet of children echo throughout the haunting lyric **"In a Rosary,"** which describes a sheltered place of beauty and peace (like the mill-garden in the poem of that title) apparently quite the opposite of the ruined places of poems such as **"A Forsaken Garden."** But in the final stanza, Swinburne pulls the rug out from under our feet in no uncertain terms:

> Swept away, made nothing now for ever, dead,
> Still the rosary lives and shines on memory, free
> Now from fear of death or change as childhood, fled
> Years on years before its last live leaves were shed:
> None may mar it now, as none may stain the sea.

The rosary is hurled into the past, and we realize with a shock that the rest of the poem was an elaborate deceit since the present tense is used until the end. The last stanza enacts the line "Ere delight may dream it lives, its life is done." The implications touch more than just the rosary, for the children also are "made nothing now for ever," and the last line is yet another example of Swinburne's ability to phrase powerful lines from simple words. The sea is infinitely suggestive as an image of the All, into which roses, children, and—one might add with a nod to the earlier poetry—poets and lovers, are gathered. The abrupt framing of the rosary as the past impresses the reader with a sense of the fleeting quality of human existence.

A central theme of the landscape poems is impermanence, in particular as caused by the processes of physical erosion. In **"The Cliffside Path"** Swinburne writes of the wind being "lord and change is sovereign of the strand"; the wind also features at the end of **"Evening on the Broads."** The opening of the former poem affords a typical anatomy of geological decay:

> Breach by ghastlier breach, the cliffs collapsing yield:
> Half the path is broken, half the banks divide;
> Flawed and crumbled, riven and rent, they cleave and
>   slide
> Toward the ridged and wrinkled waste of girdling sand
> Deep beneath.

The rhythmic stress produced by the grouping of phrases, the pronounced caesura, and the trochaic meter all emphasise the decay and the fascinated horror of the speaker. Implicit in the fascination is the knowledge spelt out in the third stanza, "Soon, where late we stood, shall no man ever stand." This focus on the irrevocability of change is characteristic of Swinburne.

Descriptions like this, of ruined coastlines, are given extended treatment in the longer poems but can also be condensed into a sonnet, as with **"A Solitude."** The poems linger over images of human artifacts overwhelmed by the seas of time, and where other poets would call a halt, Swinburne keeps going. They might have been content to end the Tristram legend with the lovers lying in the tomb, but he cannot resist telling how the tomb eventually crumbles with the cliff into the sea. Shipwrecks were another favorite image of his for the same reason. Small wonder he should write, with evident emotion, in a letter of January 1876,

> Fancy a cathedral city, which had its Bishop and members and six great Churches, one a minister, and an immense monastery and hospital for lepers—and now the sea has slowly swallowed all but two shells of ruined masonry, and just twenty cottages, inn and school included. This is Dunwich—literally built on the sand—on and behind a high crumbling sea-bank, looking out to a sea where the nearest land is Denmark.

and go on to add, "I did a good deal of verse there." He refers to **"By the North Sea,"** his greatest hymn to earthly mutability, using Dunwich as the exemplum for an anti-Theist homily upon human vanity:

> Here is all the end of all his glory—
>   Dust, and grass, and barren silent stones.
> Dead, like him, one hollow tower and hoary
>   Naked in the sea-wind stands and moans,
> Filled and thrilled with its perpetual story:
>   Here, where earth is dense with dead men's bones.

Not for Swinburne the selection of one ghost, one stone, one "mute inglorious Milton"; his attention is on the sheer ghastly multiplicity of the dead, described with ruthless concentration:

> Tombs, with bare white piteous bones protruded,
>   Shroudless, down the loose collapsing banks,
> Crumble, from their constant place detruded,
>   That the sea devours and gives not thanks.
> Graves where hope and prayer and sorrow brooded
>   Gape and slide and perish, ranks on ranks.

The observable processes of entropy are shown directly mocking the doctrines of orthodox religion. The phrase "gives not thanks" parodies liturgical sentiment, and "constant" is quietly ironic. The brutal realism of "gape" and "slide" violate the dignity of "brooded." The poem is tilting also at the idea of bodily resurrection, a theme handled by Hardy in a number of Swinburnian pieces including "The Levelled Churchyard." Hardy indulges in a little droll graveyard humor, writing of how each dead maiden fears "the final Trumpet / Lest half of her should rise herself, / And half some sturdy strumpet!" This graphically shows a difference in temper between the poets. Hardy gains on wit but loses on magnitude; the latter holds Swinburne's interest.

Seemingly from the foregoing discussion the later poetry is unremittingly bleak, and Swinburne sees humanity confronted with a world that is fundamentally hostile. But this is only half the picture, because the later poetry includes a number of moments where we discover a meaningful communion between the human spirit and the environment.

A. E. Housman alleged that Swinburne had "no eye for nature and no talent for describing it" and that he "seldom noticed any object of external nature unless it was very large, very brilliant, or very violently coloured [see excerpt dated 1910]. This is untrue, of both his letters and poetry. As [Cecil Y. Lang, the editor of an edition of Swinburne's letters] remarked, "Even in unlikely places there are many bits of almost Pre-Raphaelite detail and evidences of close observation." Take, for example, the lines "Up to the sea, not upon it or over it, upward from under / Seems he to gaze, whose eyes yearn after it here from the shore," an accurate record of the illusion, which one sometimes has when standing on a beach looking at the horizon, that the ocean is higher than one's head. And from the same poem, the phrase "Moving inland alway again" captures the impression a rough incoming tide gives of being about to overwhelm the beach within a few moments. In the letters there are passages like this comment of January 1892: "The shadows of the frozen sprays or sprigs of heather against the sun at noon on the hard bright ground were so lovely that one had to stop and stare at them."

When they appear in the poems, specific details are important in a general sense because the beauty of the natural world at least partially compensates for the fact of impermanence, and Swinburne glories in it. In **"Off Shore,"** there are stanzas which could only have been written by a swimmer who had looked down through the water to see

> Bright bank over bank
>   Making glorious the gloom,
> Soft rank upon rank,
>   Strange bloom after bloom,
> They kindle the liquid low twilight, the dusk of the dim
>   sea's womb.

Words that normally relate to the sense of touch are used here in a visual capacity to give the impression of looking through the water—for example, "soft." And just prior to this stanza is the evocative line that refers to the "wild-weed forests of crimson and russet and olive and gold" of the sea. And when, in **"The Lake of Gaube,"** Swinburne remembers the salamanders seen forty years back in 1862 and gives them a symbolic value, he nevertheless keeps sight of their physical reality:

> The deep mild purple flaked with moonbright gold
>   That make the scales seem flowers of hardened light,
> The flamelike tongue, the feet that noon leaves cold,
>   The kindly trust in man, when once the sight
>   Grew less than strange.

Quite apart from the effectiveness of the description of their skin, with the daring "moonbright gold" and the scales like "hardened light," Swinburne also gives us the startlingly accurate "feet that noon leaves cold." The way in which the creatures are introduced in the poem says much about his view of nature: "Flowers dense and keen as midnight stars aflame / And living things of light like flames in flower." The perception is deliberately blurred by the reversal of the simile that likens the flowers to flame and the salamanders to flowers of light; each appears as what it essentially is, a part of a single greater whole, manifestations of the one Life of nature. Swinburne's technique turns description of the lizards half-hidden amid the undergrowth into the formal expression of an abstract truth.

One of the most important phrases in the poem is "Fear held the bright thing hateful." As a precondition of the experience of communion with nature, the later poetry insists humanity must accept change, banish fear, and open into empathy. A number of poems demonstrate this empathy. One thinks of the desolate **"To a Seamew,"** where the speaker gazes longingly after the freedom of the bird whose "cry from windward clanging / Makes all the cliffs rejoice," and of this stanza from **"Lines on the Death of Edward John Trelawny"**:

> Wings that warred with the winds of morning,
>   Storm-winds rocking the red great dawn,
>   Close at last, and a film is drawn
> Over the eyes of the storm-bird, scorning
> Now no longer the loud wind's warning,
>   Waves that threaten or waves that fawn.

Without sentimentality, the verse captures the muscular effort of the bird that "warred" against the wind whose power is evoked by the transference of "rocking" to the very dawn itself, a technique oddly reminiscent of Ted Hughes; the phrase, "a film is drawn / Over the eyes," performs the difficult task of rendering the moment of death. It has the authenticity of a detail Swinburne had noted for himself. As a whole, the stanza is full of compassion for the bird, spreading wider in the knowledge that the human subject of the elegy has also died and so shall the speaker. A similar empathy, illustrated by close observation, can be felt in **"To a Cat,"** which blends gentle mockery of the cat's condescension, self-deprecation, and very real questions such as "What within you wakes with day / Who can say?" before concluding with an invocation of the "love-lit law" of St. Francis of Assisi.

A careful reading of the late poetry and the letters, putting aside the exotic dementia of the Swinburne of biographical legend, suggests a poet who drew a deep satisfaction from woods, downs, lakes, seas, and their varied inhabitants, and who liked nothing better than to be in wild weather. Here he is, at sixty-six, in a letter of June 1903, standing on a lakeshore with it "pouring . . . rain in sheets":

> But what was my enjoyment to that of the happy and lovely birds I stood still in the drenching rain to watch? The whole length of the lake was covered with flocks of swallows flying along and across, dipping and rising, hovering and loitering in air so as to lose nothing of the delicious pleasure of the shower-bath. I never knew they were so fond of being bathed in water pouring straight down from heaven. . . . Nor did I ever see a tenth part, I think, of so many swallows together. One flew close up to me and looked into my eyes with a bright friendly glance (I ventured to think) as who should say "Isn't it lovely weather?"

The passage shows clearly the empathy which informs a poem like **"The Lake of Gaube"** or **"To a Cat,"** and that the image of an essentially deaf and blind Swinburne who could respond only to the sea (because it is big) and the smell of old books does him a grave injustice. From this intense feeling for nature and landscape he drew the inspiration for many fine late poems. Some of these encounters with the natural world haunted him, sometimes across many years, as in the case of **"The Lake of Gaube"**; others make an evident impression all the more surprising because they are not conventionally romantic or picturesque. In a letter of December 1887, Swinburne describes a nocturnal walk in Sussex, which he dreams of "night and day," along a road that "runs from nowhere to nowhere, and is so lonely, with a vast stretch of fen or pastureland on either side, that to be alone there in the dark without even starlight and with a wild wind blowing was

like a dream—and simply delicious." That he never wrote a poem about this experience is a great pity, because it might have given us an antithetical partner to **"A Nympholept."** As Lang pointed out, the letters often record seed-incidents that spark off poems, as with **"A New Year's Eve,"** an elegy for Christina Rossetti. Swinburne commented, "I looked out of [the] window just before beginning to write, and have never seen a more magnificent heavenful of stars"; the first line is "The stars are strong in the deeps of the lustrous night." So intimate is the relationship between the poems and the locale of their genesis, that Swinburne will sometimes make remarks like this on **"The Interpreters"**: that since it "was born out of doors on a hot day" it "ought to be read by midsummer sunlight if the mood it was made in is to be appreciated."

The intensity of the best of Swinburne's later poems of nature indicates that not only are they concerned with the experience of unity with the energies of the whole ecosystem of the planet, but also that the rejection of the concept of something akin to pantheism in the poetry is mistaken. This issue emerges in a close reading of **"Loch Torridon,"** a poem relatively unknown, but one which provides examples of almost every technique and theme cited in the course of this discussion. A careless reading will dismiss the structure and varied rhythms of the poem as mere showmanship. In fact, the different stanzas and rhythms—the latter ranging from anapestic trimeter, iambic and trochaic tetrameters and pentameters, to characteristic anapestic hexameters—are crucial for expressing the different experiences and moods of the travelers in the course of the three sections of the poem. **"Loch Torridon"** charts their journey from moor to house to sea, from dusk to night to dawn, from exertion to sleep to joy, and from trial to rest to communion; the list could go on. The dusk sequence, where the sun "forsook us at our need" and there is a descent into the "dark sharp sudden gorge," uses two quite irregular stanzas made up of lines of varying length and stress, as well as inversion of the iambic foot and much enjambment, as in the emphatic "Where we thought to have rested, rest / Was none" and "ere the day / Sank." These, coupled with a convoluted syntax and a grammar that, again, seems to lose the humans in other features of the scene—as with "We followed" in stanza two, relegated to a subordinate position in a sentence seventeen lines long—all work to enact the troubled plight of the travelers. Whereas in stanzas three and six, dealing with the sea and sleep respectively, couplet rhyming and more regular rhythms suggest the certitudes and assurance of the speaker:

> All night long, in the world of sleep,
> Skies and waters were soft and deep:
> Shadow clothed them, and silence made
> Soundless music of dream and shade.

These lines from stanza six are quite rightly incantatory; the stanza as a whole is a tour-de-force of circling, echoing repetitions of words like "shadow," "soft," "silence," and the parallelism that generates "All night long," "All above us," "All around us," "All unseen," and "All unheard" in a mere sixteen lines. There is nothing more Lethean in the whole of Swinburne. This is immediately followed by a dramatic surge of energy:

> And the dawn leapt in at my casement: and there, as I
>   rose, at my feet
> No waves of the landlocked waters, no lake submissive
>   and sweet.

The shift into anapests is not gratuitous; it exactly expresses the joy of the speaker waking to see the goal of the journey, the sea itself.

Other typical Swinburne features in **"Loch Torridon"** include panoramic description ("From mountain to mountain the water was kindled"), crafted paradox ("passionless rapture," "noiseless noise," "soundless music"), geological time ("stern hill-ranges / That hardly may change their gloom"), the impermanence of humanity ("The tribes . . . / . . . erased and effaced") and the diminishing effect ("the kindliest of shelters / That ever awoke into light"). The opening line—"The dawn of night more fair than morning rose"—is a fine piece of defamiliarization: dusk is not normally thought of as night-rise instead of sunset. But the most compelling aspect is the way the journey is seen as a quest in the pilgrim's sense, almost an allegory of a descent, with the fading of the light, into darkness and fear, only to discover that "limitless" night is "adorable," and that the light returns and brings to the swimmers in "The kingdom of westward waters" the experience of unity. The act of swimming in the later poetry is a potent symbol for Swinburne's elemental communion. Several earlier phrases support the possibility of this reading, most notably the comparison of the path into the gorge to "the dim still pass whence none turns back"—by which Swinburne surely means death—the reference to the sea "sweet and strange as heaven may be" shortly followed by "The sea, that harbours in her heart" where "harbours" is being used in a paradoxical sense. A harbor usually keeps the sea out, but here the sea, or whatever it represents, is itself a harbor. In short, **"Loch Torridon"** may be Swinburne's equivalent to D. H. Lawrence's "Ship of Death." For just as the frequent references to the presences of the night, the winds and the waters make it quite possible to read the poem as at least in some sense pantheistic, so the intensity of the final passages, the boat passing between the cliffs into open sea, the swimmers directing their attention away from land and out to the boundlessness of the ocean, the feeling of transcendence, the very language and structure of the whole poem, lead us to the thought that **"Loch Torridon"** may embody Swinburne's deepest intuitions about the nature of death. (pp. 413-29)

> *Rikky Rooksby, "Swinburne without Tears: A Guide to the Later Poetry," in* Victorian Poetry, *Vol. 26, No. 4, Winter, 1988, pp. 413-30.*

FURTHER READING

Arvin, Newton. "Swinburne as a Critic." *The Sewanee Review* 32, No. 4 (October 1925): 405-12.
    Assesses Swinburne as "an important and memorable critic" but "not a great critic," citing his tendency to overpraise or summarily dismiss a work under consideration based on personal preference.

Beach, Joseph Warren. "Swinburne." In his *The Concept of Nature in Nineteenth-Century English Poetry,* pp. 455-69. New York: Pageant Book Co., 1956.
    Examines political, spiritual, and humanistic convictions underlying Swinburne's nature poetry.

Beerbohm, Max. "No. 2 The Pines." In his *And Even Now,* pp. 55-88. New York: E. P. Dutton & Co., 1921.
    Anecdotal reminiscence about visits to Swinburne and Watts-Dunton at Putney.

Beetz, Kirk H. *Algernon Charles Swinburne: A Bibliography of Secondary Works, 1861-1980.* Metuchen, N. J.: Scarecrow Press, 1982, 227 p.
    Chronologically arranged annotated bibliography of criticism.

Brown, E. K. "Swinburne: A Centenary Estimate." *The University of Toronto Quarterly* 6 (January 1937): 215-35.
    Approbatory assessment of Swinburne as a lyric poet.

Chew, Samuel C. *Swinburne.* Boston: Little, Brown, and Co., 1929, 335 p.
    Critical study of Swinburne's prose and poetry.

Drinkwater, John. *Swinburne: An Estimate.* London: J. M. Dent & Sons, 1913, 215 p.
    Study of Swinburne's lyric poetry, dramas, and criticism.

Greenberg, Robert A. "Swinburne and the Redefinition of Classical Myth." *Victorian Poetry* 14, No. 3 (Autumn 1976): 175-95.
    Examines ways that Swinburne, in his second poetry collection *Songs before Sunrise,* utilized classical myths and legends to address contemporary concerns.

Hargreaves, H. A. "Swinburne's Greek Plays and God, 'The Supreme Evil'." *Modern Language Notes* 76, No. 7 (November 1961): 607-16.
    Examines Swinburne's indictment of divine treatment of humankind in *Atalanta in Calydon* and *Erechtheus.*

———. *Swinburne's Medievalism: A Study in Victorian Love Poetry.* Baton Rouge: Louisiana State University Press, 1988, 205 p.
    Examines the influence of medieval literature of courtly love on Swinburne's poetry.

Henderson, Philip. *Swinburne: Portrait of a Poet.* New York: Macmillan Publishing Co., 1974, 305 p.
    Critical biography.

Hepburn, James. "Swinburne Corrupted." In his *Critic into Anti-Critic,* pp. 33-59. Columbia, S.C.: Camden House, 1984.
    Explores the possibility that several of Swinburne's poems about unrequited love are autobiographical.

Hughes, Randolph. "Algernon Charles Swinburne: A Centenary Survey." *The Nineteenth Century* 121, No. 724 (June 1937): 721-63.
    Counters negative assessments of Swinburne with a favorable evaluation of him as a critic and poet.

Hyder, Clyde Kenneth. Introduction to *Swinburne Replies: Notes on Poems and Reviews, Under the Microscope, Dedicatory Epistle,* by Algernon Charles Swinburne, edited by Clyde Kenneth Hyder, pp. 1-14. Syracuse: Syracuse University Press, 1966.
    Examines several critical essays in which Swinburne discusses his own poetry and addresses his critics.

———. Introduction to *Swinburne as Critic,* by Algernon Charles Swinburne, edited by Clyde K. Hyder, pp. 1-22. London: Routledge & Kegan Paul, 1972.
    Assesses Swinburne's critical theories, methods, and "the range of his knowledge and the quality of his taste."

———, ed. *Swinburne: The Critical Heritage.* London: Routledge & Kegan Paul, 1970, 255 p.
    Reprints important reviews of Swinburne's major works through *Poems and Ballads: Second Series.*

Lafourcade, Georges. "Swinburne and Keats: An Essay." In *Swinburne's "Hyperion" and Other Poems,* by Algernon Charles Swinburne, edited by Georges Lafourcade, pp. 25-114. London: Faber & Gwyer, 1927.

Critical discussion of both poets, including some comparison of their treatment of similar themes.

———. *La jeunesse de Swinburne (1837-1867)*. 2 vols. Paris: Société d'édition les belles lettres, 1928.
Important French-language study of Swinburne's life and works through the publication of *Poems and Ballads*.

———. *Swinburne: A Literary Biography*. London: G. Bell and Sons, 1932, 314 p.
Biography concentrating on the circumstances surrounding the writing and publication of Swinburne's principal works.

Lang, Cecil Yelverton. "Swinburne's Lost Love." *PMLA* 74, No. 1 (March 1959): 123-30.
Considers different theories regarding the identity of the woman to whom biographers believe Swinburne proposed marriage.

Mackail, J. W. *Swinburne*. 1909. Reprint. Folcroft, Pa.: Folcroft Press, 1969, 27 p.
Tribute presented as a lecture on the occasion of Swinburne's death, pronouncing him the last great Victorian poet.

McGann, Jerome J. *Swinburne: An Experiment in Criticism*. Chicago: University of Chicago Press, 1972, 321 p.
Critical commentary cast in the form of dialogue between several contemporaries and acquaintances of Swinburne.

McSweeney, Kerry. "Swinburne's 'Thalassius'." *The Humanities Association Bulletin* 22, No. 1 (Winter 1971): 50-5.
Examines biographical elements in the poem "Thalassius."

Murdoch, W. G. Blaikie. "Memories of Swinburne," in his *Memories of Swinburne: With Other Essays*, pp. 17-35. 1910. Reprint. Folcroft, Pa.: Folcroft Library Editions, 1975.
Tribute to Swinburne by a friend.

Murfin, Ross C. "Athens Unbound: A Study of Swinburne's *Erechtheus*." *Victorian Poetry* 12, No. 3 (Autumn 1974): 205-17.
Considers the lyrical drama *Erechtheus* to be representative of the "controlled poetry of ideas which Swinburne developed in his middle period."

Nicolson, Harold. *Swinburne and Baudelaire*. Oxford: Oxford at the Clarendon Press, 1930, 21 p.
Assessment of both poets with some comparison of their work.

Ober, William B. "Swinburne's Masochism: Neuropathology and Psychopathology." In his *Boswell's Clap and Other Essays: Medical Analyses of Literary Men's Afflictions*, pp. 43-88. Carbondale: Southern Illinois University Press, 1979.
Theorizes that Swinburne's psychopathology was due to neuropathologic brain damage at birth.

Panter-Downes, Mollie. *At the Pines: Swinburne and Watts-Dunton in Putney*. Boston: Gambit, 1971, 196 p.
Account of the household maintained by Swinburne and Theodore Watts-Dunton.

Peters, Robert L. *The Crowns of Apollo: A Study in Victorian Criticism and Aesthetics*. Detroit: Wayne State University Press, 1965, 209 p.
Study of Swinburne's aesthetic and critical principles.

Richardson, James. "Swinburne: Purity and Pain." In his *Vanishing Lives: Style and Self in Tennyson, D. G. Rossetti, Swinburne, and Yeats*, pp. 116-36. Charlottesville: University Press of Virginia, 1988.
Examines often contradictory imagery of "cruelty, tenderness, coldness, shame, purity, pain, passion" in Swinburne's poetry.

Riede, David G. *Swinburne: A Study of Romantic Mythmaking*. Charlottesville: University Press of Virginia, 1978, 227 p.
Maintains that "Swinburne's major works show a continuous grappling with the works of the earlier romantics, and his career shows a steady progression to a more and more truly imaginative mythopoeic mode, eventually culminating in a unique, personal, fully articulated myth."

Rutland, William R. *Swinburne: A Nineteenth Century Hellene*. Oxford: Basil Blackwell, 1931, 410 p.
Examines the influence of ancient Greek literature on Swinburne.

Saintsbury, George. "Mr. Swinburne." In his *The Collected Essays and Papers of George Saintsbury, 1875-1920*, pp. 220-30. London: J. M. Dent & Sons, 1923.
Positive reassessment of *Poems and Ballads*.

———. "A Reconsideration of Swinburne." In his *Last Vintage: Essays and Papers*, pp. 72-6. London: Methuen & Co., 1950.
Commends Swinburne's poetic achievement.

Shmiefsky, Marvel. "Swinburne's Anti-Establishment Poetics." *Victorian Poetry* 9, No. 3 (Autumn 1971): 261-76.
Maintains that Swinburne's aestheticism placed him in reaction to moralistic tendencies in late Victorian literature.

Victorian Poetry 9, No. 1-2 (Spring-Summer 1971): 1-260.
Special issue devoted to studies of Swinburne, including critical and biographical essays by Cecil Y. Lang, Robert E. Lougy, David A. Cook, Donald C. Stuart, and Kerry McSweeney.

Walder, Anne. *Swinburne's Flowers of Evil: Baudelaire's Influence on "Poems and Ballads, First Series."* Stockholm: Uppsala, 1976, 157 p.
Considers thematic and topical links between the poetry of Charles Baudelaire and Swinburne.

Zeiger, Melissa. " 'A Muse Funereal': The Critique of Elegy in Swinburne's 'Ave atque Vale'." *Victorian Poetry* 24, No. 2 (Summer 1986): 173-88.
Maintains that Swinburne's elegiac "Ave atque Vale" represents a rejection of the consolations of faith offered by the traditional elegy.

Mark Twain

1835-1910

(Pseudonym of Samuel Langhorne Clemens; also wrote under the pseudonyms Thomas Jefferson Snodgrass, Josh, Muggins, Soleather, Grumbler, and Sieur Louis de Conte) American novelist, short story writer, journalist, essayist, memoirist, and dramatist.

The following entry presents criticism of Twain's novel *A Connecticut Yankee in King Arthur's Court* (1889). For a discussion of Twain's complete career, see *TCLC*, Volumes 6 and 12; for a discussion of the novel *The Adventures of Huckleberry Finn,* see *TCLC,* Volume 19.

Hailed as a masterpiece of social satire, *A Connecticut Yankee in King Arthur's Court* is also viewed as one of Twain's most complex and problematic works of fiction. Although Twain stated that his primary intention in writing the novel was to expose the absurdity of those institutions and cultural dogmas he believed had impeded positive social change in Europe for centuries, critics generally interpret Twain's narrative as a much more ambiguous and multifaceted response to the subject of human progress. The stature of *A Connecticut Yankee* as Twain's most important work after *The Adventures of Huckleberry Finn* is therefore based not only on its enormous popularity but also on its interest for critics and scholars.

Commentators believe that Twain began work on *A Connecticut Yankee* shortly before the publication of *The Adventures of Huckleberry Finn* in December 1884. Twain later noted that he had been given a copy of *Le morte d'Arthur,* Sir Thomas Malory's Arthurian cycle, by George Washington Cable during their joint speaking tour in the fall of 1884, and that he had immediately begun to make notes for a satire of the book. His first reference to the story that eventually became *A Connecticut Yankee* appears in his notebook covering the period from October 1884 to April 1885, where he wrote: "Dream of being a knight errant in armor, in the Middle Ages. Have the notions & habits of thought of the present day mixed with the necessities of that. No pocket in the armor. Can't scratch. Cold in the head—can't blow. . . . Iron gets redhot in the sun—leaks in the rain. . . . and freezes me solid in the winter. . . . Always getting struck by lightning. Fall down and can't get up." Further evidence shows that work on the novel progressed slowly at first: in November 1886, when Twain gave a reading from the unfinished manuscript, only the first three chapters had been completed. At that point, he set the project aside.

By the end of the following summer Twain had resumed work on *A Connecticut Yankee,* but with a slightly different plan for the novel. Originally conceived as a light satire, as is revealed in the aforementioned notebook entry, the novel had now taken on what Twain described in a letter as a "funereal seriousness." Critics note that a number of factors contributed to this shift in tone, the most crucial being Twain's increasing contempt for European monarchies and his outrage at English critic Matthew Arnold's attacks on American society. After the publication of Arnold's most derogatory comments in 1887 and 1888, Twain began to unleash his

anger in lengthy diatribes, some of which were included in *A Connecticut Yankee.* Later, when Twain's English publishers, Chatto and Windus, proposed deletions to make the novel more palatable to their readers, Twain refused, saying that the novel had been written specifically to enlighten English people about the shortcomings of their way of life. Twain's bitterness is clear in the ironic concluding sentence of his letter to Chatto and Windus: "So many Englishmen have done their sincerest best to teach us something for our betterment that it seems to me high time that some of us should substantially recognize the good intent by trying to pry up the English nation to a little higher level of manhood in turn."

A Connecticut Yankee was published simultaneously in the United States and England, with no deletions, in December 1889. While American reviews were predominantly favorable, English critics were incensed by what they considered Twain's blasphemous treatment of one of their most cherished national legends. Conservative journals did not review the novel, and Andrew Lang, one of Twain's most steadfast English admirers, refused to read it, remarking that Twain did not possess the knowledge "which would enable him to be a sound critic of the Middle Ages." However, the furor over *A Connecticut Yankee* was relatively short-lived, curtailed in part by Twain's more sympathetic portrait of the English in his next novel, *The American Claimant.*

One of the most notable experiments with the subject of time travel in world literature, *A Connecticut Yankee* recounts the adventures of Hank Morgan, a foreman at a Hartford arms factory who, after being hit on the head by a disgruntled employee, awakens in the kingdom of Camelot in the year 528. Intensely pragmatic, Morgan quickly reconciles himself to his situation and decides that if fate has thrust him into the past, he will take full advantage of the situation and "boss the whole country inside of three months" by using his superior learning. After defeating Merlin in a contest in which the magician's powers are pitted against the Yankee's scientific knowledge, Morgan is granted official power and given the title "The Boss." He then sets about transforming Arthurian society by introducing nineteenth-century technical innovations and by attempting to instill in the people his own ideals of freedom and democracy. However, when his activities evoke the censure of the church, the people turn against him. In the ensuing battle, Morgan uses all his knowledge of nineteenth-century weaponry but is nevertheless defeated. Merlin appears and, angered at having been displaced by Morgan, puts him into a deep sleep which will last for centuries. The novel ends with Morgan awakening back in his own century to find that he no longer belongs there and wishes to return to the society that rejected him.

Twain hoped to demonstrate in *A Connecticut Yankee* how monarchy, aristocracy, and organized religion had enslaved the minds and bodies of humanity throughout history, thus contradicting the romanticized depiction of the Middle Ages in such popular works as Sir Walter Scott's *Ivanhoe* (1819) and Alfred Lord Tennyson's *Idylls of the King* (1842-85). Morgan, often described as Twain's most autobiographical character, repeatedly denounces the loutishness of King Arthur, who has no political acumen and in fact no qualifications whatever for the position he holds; the wickedness and brutality of the aristocracy, whose privileges are unearned and abused; and the credulity of the people, who have been literally beaten into submission. He also emphasizes the sheer discomfort of rural existence, particularly its lack of cleanliness and labor-saving machinery. Morgan's many denunciations of the Catholic church as an archaic institution that encourages submissive behavior are augmented by the plot of the novel, which casts the church as the sworn enemy of progress. Generally couched in humor, Morgan's comments sometimes reflect Twain's "funereal seriousness" in their bitter tone, as when Morgan expresses his outrage after a young mother is burned at the stake for stealing food for her children. Early detractors of the book pointed out that Twain's criticisms were unfounded since, in order to serve his rhetorical purpose, he had attributed to Arthurian England many features drawn from other periods and places. However, Twain acknowledged such amalgamations and explained in his preface to the novel: "The ungentle laws and customs touched upon in this tale are historical, and the episodes which are used to illustrate them are also historical. It is not pretended that these laws and customs existed in England in the sixth century; no, it is only pretended that inasmuch as they existed in the English and other civilizations of far later times, it is safe to consider that it is no libel upon the sixth century to suppose them to have been in practice in that day also. One is quite justified in inferring that whatever one of these laws or customs was lacking in that remote time, its place was competently filled by a worse one."

Although *A Connecticut Yankee* is ostensibly a celebration of the great strides made by civilization between the medieval period and the late nineteenth century, many view the work as an unintentional statement of Twain's cynicism about what he called "the damned human race" and the possibility of meaningful progress in human society. Critics have noted that, when confronted with a choice between freedom, with its inherent risks, and the oppressive but familiar domination of the Church, the citizens of Camelot choose the latter. Although Morgan maintains in the novel that "training is all there is *to* a person" and attempts to retrain the citizens of Camelot, the failure of his endeavor is sometimes viewed as a profound statement concerning the tendency toward superstition and cowardice that dominates human nature. However, a number of critics have pointed out that Morgan's defeat is no more than a technical necessity imposed by the time-travel element of Twain's narrative and, in the words of Everett Emerson, "without broad implication."

A more vigorous critical controversy has arisen over the question of whether or not Hank Morgan represents a sympathetic figure and the related issue of the actual focus of the satire in *A Connecticut Yankee.* Although Twain stated that his intent was to criticize archaic institutions such as monarchy and aristocracy, many commentators, beginning with Gladys Bellamy in her 1950 study *Mark Twain as a Literary Artist,* have detected what they consider to be profoundly negative elements in Twain's portrait of Morgan and the technological progress he symbolizes. Expanding upon Bellamy's observations, subsequent commentators have suggested that while Twain approved of technology on one level, his profound longing for his own pastoral youth, clearly demonstrated in *The Adventures of Huckleberry Finn,* and his increasing disillusionment with industrial civilization led him to create a narrative that ultimately condemns modern technology rather than medieval institutions. Such critics note in particular the sympathetic aspects of Twain's portrait of Camelot as well as the primarily destructive nature of Morgan's innovations, which include dynamite and Gatling guns. However, this widespread interpretation of *A Connecticut Yankee* has been opposed by critics who, while acknowledging ambiguities in the novel, nevertheless accept Twain's own estimation of its essential meaning. Representing this point of view, Louis J. Budd has concluded: "To say that *A Connecticut Yankee* falls into nostalgia for a pre-industrial Eden is to play up a minor thread instead of the bold, obvious pattern."

Recognition of the tonal ambiguities of *A Connecticut Yankee* has led some to concur with Bernard DeVoto's description of the novel as "chaos," an assessment based on the conclusion that Twain's ambiguous attitude toward his subject matter caused him to lose control of his narrative. Such commentators often judge the work a failure. Most critics, however, view the ambiguities in the novel as not at all detrimental to its overall effectiveness. As a result, *A Connecticut Yankee* remains among the most popular of Twain's writings, valued for its humor, its pragmatic sensibility, and its profound insights into the essential nature of humankind.

(See also *Contemporary Authors,* Vol. 104; *Dictionary of Literary Biography,* Vols. 11, 12, 23, 64, and 74; *Concise Dictionary of American Literary Biography, 1865-1917;* and *Yesterday's Authors of Books for Children,* Vol. 2.)

SYLVESTER BAXTER   (essay date 1889)

[The following excerpt is taken from Baxter's positive review of A Connecticut Yankee in King Arthur's Court.*]*

Of all the extraordinary conceits that have germinated in his fruitful imagination, nothing more delicious has ever occurred to Mark Twain than that of running riot among the legendary times of our ancestral race by placing *A Connecticut Yankee in King Arthur's Court. . . .* Here is a rare field for the unbridled play of fancy, and right bravely has the author used his opportunity. There is a most audacious rollicking around among the dusty bric-a-brac of chivalry—which is not handled at all gently—and a merry tossing about of poetic finery in a way that ruthlessly exposes in their literal ugliness the illusively mantled facts. Of course there is most abundant fun, and Mark Twain's rich humor never coursed more freely than here, where just provocation is never absent. But there is much more than this; the sources of the claims of aristocratic privileges and royal prerogatives that yet linger in the world are so exposed to the full glare of the sun of 19th century common sense, are shown in so ridiculous an aspect, that the work can hardly fail to do yeoman service in destroying the still existing remnants of respect for such pretensions. Through the book there is a steady flowing undercurrent of earnest purpose, and the pages are eloquent with a true American love of freedom, a sympathy with the rights of the common people, and an indignant hatred of oppression of the poor, the lowly and the weak, by the rich, the powerful and the proud. While much false glamour is dispelled by resolving it into absurdity under the touchstone of truth, the book is marked by real beauty, by a poetry of style worthy of its rich material, with much sympathetic tenderness, as well as frankness of speech. The quaint early English speech is handled with the same artistic skill that characterized the author's facile handling of the stately Elizabethan in that lovely idyll of childhood, *The Prince and the Pauper,* and the constant admixture of a concisely expressive American vernacular thereto makes a contrast of lingual coloring that is unspeakably delightful.

We may fancy that the same matter-of-fact Englishman who seriously reasoned that certain statements in *Innocents Abroad* were preposterously absurd, and could not be based upon fact, might again step forward to break a lance against this book by showing, from historical and philological data, that such a language could not possibly have been spoken in the sixth century, since the English tongue did not exist, and that the use of Norman French names before the conquest is anachronistic in the highest degree! But this is an excursion back into the England of the chronicles, and not of strict chronology, and that eminent ethnologist, Tylor, would undoubtedly perceive with delight the accuracy of scientific perception in the treatment of human nature which marks the book. For, in order to characterize with truth a past period we must make ourselves familiar with some existing state of society that is analogous therewith. Only under such conditions can a faithful historical romance be written, for otherwise the writer cannot fail to modernize his work, and falsify its life with 19th century sentiments that could not have been known in a previous age. By resorting to the principle that "distribution in time" is paralleled by "distribution in space," we may solve many a problem. So there is a certain aspect of sober truth in this most fanciful tale, and, just as the Con-

necticut Yankee went back into the days of King Arthur's court, so might he go out into the world today, into Central Asia or Africa, or even into certain spots in this United States of ours, find himself amidst social conditions very similar to those of 1300 years ago, and even work his astonishing 19th century miracles with like result. For it is a fact that, when Frank Hamilton Cushing astounded the Zuni Indians with an acoustic telephone constructed of two tomato cans and a string, they deemed him a magician, and tried him for witchcraft. And, for parallels of the inhumanities which, as we here read of them, seem to have been left far behind us in the track of the centuries, we have but to look with George Kennan into the dungeons of Siberia; and, in our own country, read the records of the investigations into the horrors of the almshouses, jails and lunatic hospitals here in this enlightened commonwealth of Massachusetts so late as the time of Horace Mann, or look to the record of the nameless barbarities of negro slavery alive in the memories of men still young. How the conscience and the sympathies of the world have quickened with the advent of the railway, the steamship and the telegraph! We have, after all, but just passed out across the threshold of the dark ages, and, in view of the few steps we have taken, we can hardly doubt that we are yet to make an infinitely mightier progress into the light of a genuine civilization, putting far behind us the veneered barbarism of the present, that still retains the old standards of conduct and intercourse for our guidance in all "practical" affairs. (pp. 148-50)

Sylvester Baxter, in an extract in Mark Twain: The Critical Heritage, *edited by Frederick Anderson with Kenneth M. Sanderson, Barnes & Noble, Inc., 1971, pp. 148-52.*

WILLIAM DEAN HOWELLS   (essay date 1890)

[Howells was the chief progenitor of literary Realism in the United States and the most influential American critic of the late nineteenth century. In espousing Realism, Howells sought to disperse "the conventional acceptations by which men live on easy terms with themselves" in order that they might "examine the grounds of their social and moral opinions." The author of nearly three dozen novels, he also wrote perceptive criticism of the works of numerous prominent nineteenth-century authors, including Henry James and Mark Twain. In the following excerpt, Howells applauds the humor and mordant social satire of A Connecticut Yankee in King Arthur's Court.*]*

[In *A Connecticut Yankee in King Arthur's Court*] our arch-humorist imparts more of his personal quality than in anything else he has done. Here he is to the full the humorist, as we know him; but he is very much more, and his strong, indignant, often infuriate hate of injustice, and his love of equality, burn hot through the manifold adventures and experiences of the tale. What he thought about prescriptive right and wrong, we had partly learned in *The Prince and the Pauper,* and in *Huckleberry Finn,* but it is this last book which gives his whole mind. The elastic scheme of the romance allows it to play freely back and forward between the sixth century and the nineteenth century; and often while it is working the reader up to a blasting contempt of monarchy and aristocracy in King Arthur's time, the dates are magically shifted under him, and he is confronted with exactly the same principles in Queen Victoria's time. The delicious satire, the marvellous wit, the wild, free, fantastic humor are the colors of the tapestry, while the texture is a humanity that lives in every fibre. At every moment the scene amuses, but it is all the time an object-lesson in democracy. It makes us glad of our republic and our epoch; but it does not flatter us into a fond content with them; there are passages in which we see that the noble of Arthur's day, who battened on the blood and sweat of his bondmen, is one in essence with the capitalist of Mr. Harrison's day who grows rich on the labor of his underpaid wagemen. Our incomparable humorist, whose sarcasm is so pitiless to the greedy and superstitious clerics of Britain, is in fact of the same spirit and intention as those bishops who, true to their office, wrote the other day from New York to all their churches in the land:

> It is a fallacy in social economics, as well as in Christian thinking, to look upon the labor of men and women and children as a commercial commodity, to be bought and sold as an inanimate and irresponsible thing. . . . The heart and soul of a man cannot be bought or hired in any market, and to act as if they were not needed in the doing of the world's vast work is as unchristian as it is unwise.

Mr. Clemens's glimpses of monastic life in Arthur's realm are true enough; and if they are not the whole truth of the matter, one may easily get it in some such book as Mr. Brace's *Gesta Christi,* where the full light of history is thrown upon the transformation of the world, if not the church, under the influence of Christianity. In the mean time, if any one feels that the justice done the churchmen of King Arthur's time is too much of one kind, let him turn to that heart-breaking scene where the brave monk stands with the mother and her babe on the scaffold, and execrates the hideous law which puts her to death for stealing enough to keep her from starving. It is one of many passages in the story where our civilization of to-day sees itself mirrored in the cruel barbarism of the past, the same in principle, and only softened in custom. With shocks of consciousness, one recognizes in such episodes that the laws are still made for the few against the many, and that the preservation of things, not men, is still the ideal of legislation. But we do not wish to leave the reader with the notion that Mr. Clemens's work is otherwise than obliquely serious. Upon the face of it you have a story no more openly didactic than *Don Quixote,* which we found ourselves more than once thinking of, as we read, though always with the sense of the kindlier and truer heart of our time. Never once, we believe, has Mark Twain been funny at the cost of the weak, the unfriended, the helpless; and this is rather more than you can say of Cid Hamet ben Engeli. But the two writers are of the same humorous largeness; and when the Connecticut man rides out at dawn, in a suit of Arthurian armor, and gradually heats up under the mounting sun in what he calls that stove; and a fly gets between the bars of his visor; and he cannot reach his handkerchief in his helmet to wipe the sweat from his streaming face; and at last when he cannot bear it any longer, and dismounts at the side of a brook, and makes the distressed damsel who has been riding behind him take off his helmet, and fill it with water, and pour gallon after gallon down the collar of his wrought-iron cutaway, you have a situation of as huge a grotesqueness as any that Cervantes conceived.

The distressed damsel is the Lady Corisande; he calls her Sandy, and he is troubled in mind at riding about the country with her in that way; for he is not only very doubtful that there is nothing in the castle where she says there are certain princesses imprisoned and persecuted by certain giants, but he feels that it is not quite nice: he is engaged to a young lady in East Hartford, and he finds Sandy a fearful bore at first,

though in the end he loves and marries her, finding that he hopelessly antedates the East Hartford young lady by thirteen centuries. How he gets into King Arthur's realm, the author concerns himself as little as any of us do with the mechanism of our dreams. In fact the whole story has the lawless operation of a dream; none of its prodigies are accounted for: they take themselves for granted, and neither explain nor justify themselves. Here he is, that Connecticut man, foreman of one of the shops in Colt's pistol factory, and full to the throat of the invention and the self-satisfaction of the nineteenth century, at the court of the mythic Arthur. He is promptly recognized as a being of extraordinary powers, and becomes the king's right-hand man, with the title of The Boss; but as he has apparently no lineage or blazon, he has no social standing, and the meanest noble has precedence of him, just as would happen in England to-day. The reader may faintly fancy the consequences flowing from this situation, which he will find so vividly fancied for him in the book; but they are simply irreportable. The scheme confesses allegiance to nothing; the incidents, the facts follow as they will. The Boss cannot rest from introducing the apparatus of our time, and he tries to impart its spirit, with a thousand most astonishing effects. He starts a daily paper in Camelot; he torpedoes a holy well; he blows up a party of insolent knights with a dynamite bomb; when he and the king disguise themselves as peasants, in order to learn the real life of the people, and are taken and sold for slaves, and then sent to the gallows for the murder of their master, Launcelot arrives to their rescue with five hundred knights on bicycles. It all ends with the Boss's proclamation of the Republic after Arthur's death, and his destruction of the whole chivalry of England by electricity.

We can give no proper notion of the measureless play of an imagination which has a gigantic jollity in its feats, together with the tenderest sympathy. There are incidents in this wonder-book which wring the heart for what has been of cruelty and wrong in the past, and leave it burning with shame and hate for the conditions which are of like effect in the present. It is one of its magical properties that the fantastic fable of Arthur's far-off time is also too often the sad truth of ours; and the magician who makes us feel in it that we have just begun to know his power, teaches equality and fraternity in every phase of his phantasmagory.

He leaves, to be sure, little of the romance of the olden time, but no one is more alive to the simple, mostly tragic poetry of it; and we do not remember any book which imparts so clear a sense of what was truly heroic in it. With all his scorn of kingcraft, and all his ireful contempt of caste, no one yet has been fairer to the nobility of character which they cost so much too much to develop. The mainly ridiculous Arthur of Mr. Clemens has his moments of being as fine and high as the Arthur of Lord Tennyson; and the keener light which shows his knights and ladies in their childlike simplicity and their innocent coarseness throws all their best qualities into relief. This book is in its last effect the most matter-of-fact narrative, for it is always true to human nature, the only truth possible, the only truth essential, to fiction. The humor of the conception and of the performance is simply immense; but more than ever Mr. Clemens's humor seems the sunny break of his intense conviction. We must all recognize him here as first of those who laugh, not merely because his fun is unrivalled, but because there is a force of right feeling and clear thinking in it that never got into fun before, except in *The Bigelow Papers.* Throughout, the text in all its circumstance and meaning is supplemented by the illustrations of an artist whc has entered into the wrath and the pathos as well as the fun of the thing, and made them his own.

This kind of humor, the American kind, the kind employed in the service of democracy, of humanity, began with us a long time ago; in fact Franklin may be said to have torn it with the lightning from the skies. Some time, some such critic as Mr. T. S. Perry (if we ever have another such) will study its evolution in the century of our literature and civilization; but no one need deny himself meanwhile the pleasure we feel in Mr. Clemens's book as its highest development. (pp. 153-56)

William Dean Howells, in an extract in Mark Twain: The Critical Heritage, *edited by Frederick Anderson with Kenneth M. Sanderson, Barnes & Noble, Inc., 1971, pp. 152-56.*

JAMES ASHCROFT NOBLE   (essay date 1890)

[*In the following English review of* A Connecticut Yankee in King Arthur's Court, *Noble objects to Twain's satirical treatment of the Arthurian legends.*]

It cannot be said that Mr. Clemens has never done better work than is to be found in *A Yankee at the Court of King Arthur;* and, indeed, if the plain truth must be told, his new book is utterly unworthy of him. Though burlesque is the cheapest kind of humour which can be produced by men whose humorous faculty is of the slenderest sort, it has a field in which it may legitimately exploit itself; but the Arthurian legends, which, to us of the age of Tennyson, have become saturated with spiritual beauty and suggestiveness, lie a long way outside the boundary of this "scanty plot." If Mark Twain can now find no better raw material for the manufacture of small jokes than the story of the Quest of the Sangraal, he had better retire from a business which up to this time, he has conducted with distinguished success. We laugh at *Tom Sawyer* and *Huck Finn,* and enjoy the laugh because we feel we have a right to it. If we laugh at the new book we are ashamed of ourselves, for we know that the laugh has been obtained on false pretences, and that it bears an unpleasant resemblance to that cacchination which has been described as "the crackling of thorns under a pot."

James Ashcroft Noble, in a review of "A Yankee at the Court of King Arthur," in The Academy, *Vol. XXXVII, No. 929, February 22, 1890, p. 130.*

THE SPECTATOR   (essay date 1890)

[*In the following negative review of* A Connecticut Yankee in King Arthur's Court, *an English critic objects to Twain's irreverent use of the Arthurian legends and judges the novel a "sorry performance."*]

Nothing in its way could well be more deplorable than the latest and certainly not the least ambitious example of Transatlantic humour,—*A Yankee at the Court of King Arthur.* Mark Twain has surpassed himself as a low comedian in literature by the manner in which he has vaulted at a bound into the charmed circle of Arthurian romance. The gallant deeds of the Knights of the Round Table have enlisted many pens, since the far off years in which Sir Thomas Malory gave them a setting in the exquisite prose of *Morte d'Arthur,* to the present century in which the genius of the Laureate has conjured back the days of chivalry and interpreted the moral significance of the old allegory, in poetry that is already classic,— the *Idylls of the King.* Let it be granted at once that Lord Tennyson has idealised, as only a supreme poet can, the life and aspirations which, according to tradition, prevailed at the Court which King Arthur kept in that mystic border-land where legend and history meet and blend in indissoluble union. Possibly the Knights were far other than Tennyson has portrayed them; yet Geraint and Lancelot, Pelleas and Bedivere, Galahad and Percevale, as we now know them, are men of like passions with ourselves, and as we witness their "bursts of great heart and slips in sensual mire," it seems as if we beheld as in a glass the glory and the shame of human life.

Camelot may be a beautiful dream; but Connecticut is a hard reality about which no illusions are possible. Hitherto, Dagonet has held undisputed sway as the only fool at the Court of King Arthur, but he, it seems, is scarcely up to modern requirements; so Mark Twain has come to the rescue with a brand-new specimen of the breed, in the shape of this Yankee "Boss." He swaggers upon the scene with jaunty assurance and proceeds to disport himself after the manner of his kind. Once at Camelot, this 'cute, enterprising, conceited product of the nineteenth century duly "plays the fool exceedingly," airing his choice slang and cutting his insufferable capers in a way which was certainly calculated to astonish the natives. How the "Boss" started a newspaper, arrived at the conclusion that King Arthur's Knights were a "childlike and innocent lot," denounced Merlin as a "cheap old humbug," and discovered that in the Quest of the Holy Grail there were "worlds of reputation, but no money,"—is it not written in this coarse and clumsy burlesque, of which America in general, and Mark Twain in particular, ought already to be heartily ashamed? Mr. Howells [see excerpt above] is, however, in raptures over this sorry performance, and goes out of his way to describe, on behalf of the American public, Mark Twain as "our arch-humorist," in whose latest work "delicious satire," "marvellous wit," "unrivalled fun," and we know not what beside, are to be found by those who appreciate this kind of vulgar and boisterous horse-play. We are even assured, on the same unimpeachable authority, that *A Yankee at the Court of King Arthur* is an "object-lesson in democracy;" but the humour of such a conception scarcely justifies Mr. Howells's expression, "simply immense," until we place it side by side with that critic's oracular declaration that the grotesque medley itself is a revelation of Mark Twain's "intense conviction," and that this screaming farce, which ends in the destruction of the chivalry of England by means of electricity, is "obliquely serious."

Mark Twain is quite right about the Quest of the Holy Grail, for it—in common with other enterprises the memory of which mankind will not willingly let die—had "worlds of reputation in it, but no money." Possibly, however, he may find a tangible consolation in the fact—since reverence fails to keep pace with knowledge in the present generation—that these broad grins at the expense of his betters are likely to bring him "worlds" of money, if no reputation.

"Mark Twain's Camelot," in The Spectator, *Vol. 64, No. 3223, April 5, 1890, p. 484.*

STEPHEN LEACOCK   (essay date 1932)

[*Leacock was a prominent Canadian humorist and the author*

of numerous collections of satirical sketches. In the following excerpt, he praises both the style and content of A Connecticut Yankee in King Arthur's Court.]

To many of us who are old enough to remember most of Mark Twain's works from the time of their appearance, there is a certain list which seemed then and seem now the real Mark Twain. The rest don't matter. The list includes **Roughing It, Life on the Mississippi, The Innocents Abroad, Tom Sawyer** (a little grudgingly), **The Adventures of Huckleberry Finn,** and, most certainly and beyond controversy, the **Connecticut Yankee.** We don't need to care what the critics say; we can recall the sheer unadulterated joy of that first perusal.

The story is based thus:

A Connecticut Yankee, a factory boss, skilled in all mechanical arts, is "put to sleep" by a crack on the head with a crowbar from an employee. He wakes up to find himself—not forward in time as most Utopians are, but backward. He is lying on a grassy bank in the woodland country of King Arthur's England. To him approaches a knight in "old time iron armour from head to heel." "Fair sir, will ye joust?" asks the knight. "Will I which?" says the Yankee.

And with that the tale is on. The Yankee, about to be put to death, recalls the fact that an eclipse happened that very year and day, and "puts out" the sun. This beats out Merlin and makes the Yankee a magician. He rules King Arthur's England; introduces machinery, fights the superstitions of the church, the cruelty of the law, the brutality of the strong— only to meet disaster at the end.

It is a strange and wonderful tale, and carries with it not only a story but a meaning. By and through his Yankee Mark Twain is denouncing all the things that he hated—hereditary power, the church, aristocracy, privilege, superstition. He is able, under the guise of humour, to give vent to the fierce elemental ideas of justice and right and equality, hatred of oppression and religious persecution, by which he was inspired. In other books this could only be incidental—a word, a phrase, a quoted speech. Here it was the whole book.

It was no wonder that such a book called forth plenty of criticism, even of denunciation; no wonder that many of Mark Twain's English admirers turned their backs on him. The book seemed to challenge this. In the first place, from the point of view of the historian, if taken seriously, it is contemptible. The date of the story is fixed by a solar eclipse which is part of its machinery as the year 528 A.D. The time is that of King Arthur. But the author has lumped into it in an indistinguishable mass the manners and customs of ten centuries, all the tyrannies of all the countries he ever heard of (except America)—the Dark Ages, the Middle Ages, the Old Régime in France; all the aristocracies of Europe, with especial reference to the English, past and present; with this, and running all through it, is a denunciation, by name, of the Roman Catholic Church.

Witness, for example, the following typical quotations:

> It was pitiful for a person born in a wholesome free atmosphere to listen to their humble and hearty outpourings of loyalty towards their king and church and nobility; as if they had any more occasion to love and honour king and church and noble than a slave has to love and honour the lash. . . .

> Before the day of the Church's supremacy in the world, men were men and held their heads up.

> Any established church is an established crime, an established slave pen.

> A privileged class, an aristocracy, is but a band of slave-holders under another name.

Now of course it is not really the fictitious Yankee speaking here, but the author himself. The voice is Yankee but the hand is from Missouri.

Such criticism of England, past and present, from a citizen of the American Republic, was a little too much like a child of light reproving the children of darkness. Against the tyranny of aristocracy could be set the rising tyranny of the trust; the criminals and bandits of King Arthur's time (whenever it was) were soon to be overmatched by the gangsters of the United States; against the power of the church stood the social tyranny of Puritanical America; denunciations of slavery came ill from a writer brought up in a slave-holding family in the greatest slave state the world ever saw, and the rack and stake of the Middle Ages could be paralleled in the hellfires of the Southern lynchers.

At best it was Satan rebuking sin, the pot calling the kettle black. Underneath was the insult that Mark Twain really thought America a far superior place to England, a fact of which the next generation were not so assured. But the delusion of American freedom died hard.

Yet real lovers of Mark Twain's work, those who understand it, will "wipe all that out." When the **Yankee** book appeared, it was read by thousands with sheer unadulterated joy from cover to cover; by thousands who didn't care a rush for historical accuracy, and were as willing to fuse all the centuries together as the author was. To such readers the burlesque of chivalry was a delight; it was glorious to think of King Arthur's knights set to play baseball and to ride round with advertising boards instead of hunting the Holy Grail. The reader threw off the dead weight of literary reverence and roared at the fun of it. And the denunciation of cruelty and tyranny, and the triumph of machine-power, the revolver against the knight on horseback—all that was equally thrilling. It didn't matter where the tyranny was or when it was; the reader had a notion that the institutions of dark ages were dark indeed, and exulted in their overthrow.

These readers were right. The **Yankee** is the most "artistic" of all Mark Twain's works; the burlesque the most unbroken, the theme the most continuous and consistent. The book **Huckleberry Finn** is imperfect as art when it breaks or nearly breaks into burlesque; in other books the burlesque is imperfect when it breaks into sentiment. The **Yankee** is a complete artistic conception, carried unbroken to a finish. Such faults as it has, in the technique of humour, lie elsewhere. Mark Twain never could convey the idea of prolixity except by getting prolix; to convey the idea of an interminable speech, he makes one; as witness the talk of Alisande in the tale and many of his characters elsewhere. Art should do better than that. (pp. 104-09)

Stephen Leacock, in his Mark Twain, *Peter Davies Limited, 1932, 167 p.*

WALTER BLAIR (essay date 1942)

[*An American critic, Blair was the author of several major studies of American humorists. In the following excerpt, he identifies some objects of criticism in* A Connecticut Yankee in King Arthur's Court.]

When Clemens got the idea of writing *A Connecticut Yankee in King Arthur's Court,* he had been having a fine time reading an old book to which he had been introduced by a companion on a lecture trip—the quaint story of King Arthur and his court as it had been told by Thomas Malory in the fifteenth century. He might also have seen—but apparently did not—a book which was the runaway best seller of the day—Edward Bellamy's *Looking Backward.* This popular book was a novel telling how a young Bostonian who fell into a hypnotic sleep in 1887 awoke to find himself in the world of the year 2000. His fascinating story was largely about what he had found in the society of that distant future. Internal evidence suggests that the two books together gave Twain the idea that it would be fun to write about a character who had had a similar experience, but external evidence proves that he did not read Bellamy's novel until after he had finished his own. By sheer coincidence Clemens, too, made a New Englander fall sleep and awaken to find himself in another era. Twain's Yankee, however, instead of shifting his life into the future, was transported to the past—back to the time of King Arthur in the year 528.

The humorist wrote the story of how Hank, the Yankee superintendent in the Colt factory in Connecticut, after being knocked out by a worker with a crowbar, awoke in a field near Camelot. The slangy talk of a nineteenth-century Yankee alongside the stately language of the Middle Ages was amusing, and his exposition of what a man of the industrial age thought of a feudal society was also comical. And when the Yankee, thanks to his predicting an eclipse, became a dictator and put into practice all sorts of new-fangled plans, incongruities leaped up everywhere—knights in armor and plug hats, knights playing baseball, the news of chivalry written up in a country newspaper, Simon Stylites, attached to a sewing-machine, turning around on his pillar. The book was full of such broad fun.

But, like Bellamy's book, Clemens' story was more than a contrast between civilizations. Because, in the world of 2000, he had found a utopia with many advantages over the society of 1887, Bellamy had made his book a social criticism. Urged on by the fact that he, like his contemporary, had many strongly held notions of his own, Mark Twain also used his book to set forth his ideas about things in general and in particular. Ideas came out through the talk and through the adventures of Hank—so many ideas that many pages of the novel were cluttered up with them.

Hank was a common American, "an ignoramus"—as Mark said he was—in many ways. Looking at the fine tapestries on medieval walls, he kept remembering the hideous pictures on his wall at home in nineteenth-century America and longing for a sight of them.

> Not a chromo [he moaned]. I had been used to chromos for years, and I saw now that without my suspecting it a passion for art had got into the fabric of my being, and was become a part of me. It made me homesick to look around over this proud and gaudy but heartless barrenness and remember that in our home in East Hartford, all unpretending as it was, you couldn't go into a room but you would find an insurance-chromo, or at least a three-color God-Bless-Our-Home over the door; and in the parlor we had nine.

Or the Yankee noticed the way the aristocracy observed the forms of religion and was not keen-eyed enough to notice how little these forms meant:

> I will say this much for the nobility: that, tyrannical, murderous, rapacious, and morally rotten as they were, they were deeply and enthusiastically religious. Nothing could divert them from the regular and faithful performance of the pieties enjoined by the Church. More than once I have seen a noble who had gotten his enemy at a disadvantage, stop to pray before cutting his throat; more than once I had seen a noble, after ambushing and despatching his enemy, retire to the nearest wayside shrine and humbly give thanks, without even waiting to rob the body . . . . All the nobles of Britain, with their families, attended divine service morning and night daily, in their private chapels, and even the worst of them had family worship five or six times a day besides.

The naïve visitor seemed bowled over by such piety. Many of the other notions which Hank cherished and made known were just as stupid as this—the half-baked judgments of an uneducated man.

But, though Hank shared the stupidities of ordinary Americans, he was a good man, he had been brought up in a country where people in general had the right view of things, and usually, when he pondered important matters, he made good use of his horse sense. It was as easy as pie, for example, for him to see what a horrible thing the aristocratic form of government was for the people in the land where it was in operation:

> And the people! They were the quaintest and simplest and trustingest race; why, they were nothing but rabbits. It was pitiful for a person born in a wholesome free atmosphere to listen to their humble and hearty outpourings of loyalty toward their king and Church and nobility; as if they had any more occasion to love and honor the king and church and noble than a slave has to love and honor the lash. . . . ! Why, dear me, *any* kind of royalty, howsoever modified, *any* kind of aristocracy, however pruned, is rightly an insult; but if you are born and brought up under that sort of arrangement you probably never find it out for yourself, and don't believe it when somebody else tells you.

That was doctrine which could be preached in America without much danger. It—and much of the other preaching in the book—seemed to apply entirely to other countries. But Clemens was not satisfied with social criticism which hit countries across the sea but did not hit America. In the tradition of Jack Downing, Hosea Biglow, and other humorous commentators in homespun, the Yankee tore into the United States as well as other lands.

The book was written and published at a time when Americans in increasing numbers were beginning to see that their system could do with a good deal of tinkering. In the years since the Civil War, the tie-up between big business and government had reached such impudent heights that many had begun to voice their disgust. Bellamy's book had been only one in a great flood of similar books calling attention to a need for changes of a vital sort. In 1884, after many years of Republican rule, the dissatisfied faction had managed at last to cast enough votes to defeat Blaine and to put Grover Cleveland into office. Cleveland was a stuffy fellow and a poor hand at politics, but he had a better notion than any successful American political leader between Abraham Lincoln and Theodore Roosevelt of what was wrong with the country, and he had enough courage to try to do things. He tried to reform the civil service, tried to cut down graft, tried to get the tariff whittled down to a reasonable size. But one after another of his sensible reforms bumped up against a stone wall of resistance.

Clemens, who had been a vigorous supporter of Cleveland's candidacy, made his book speak in favor of the President. Along with the low comedy and the snaps at England in the *Yankee* were passages which one way and another backed up Cleveland's most important policies—the policies repudiated by the electorate in 1888 when Cleveland, running for a second term, was defeated.

A fable about military examinations in Arthur's kingdom had to do with spoils-system appointments. The Yankee told how he had introduced, among other innovations in the country, a West Point, where army officers were carefully taught all the complexities of warfare. When, however, an examination was held, though the West Pointers knew answers to all questions asked, the commissions were all given to chuckleheads who knew nothing about military matters. The reason was that the West Point students were commoners, while the numskulls were nobles. For readers engaged in the red-hot arguments of the day, this passage attacked not only unqualified men who got offices because of their birth but also those who got offices because of their party politics.

Another passage about the King's evil appropriation hit at another bad practice against which Cleveland fought—the huge profits of contractors and commercial centers made possible by pork-barrel laws. This Arthurian law, whereby money was handed out to all the citizens, said Hank, "was just the River and Harbor bill of that government for the grip it took on the treasury and the chance it offered for skimming the surplus."

Then, too, there was a whole chapter on the hottest issue of the day—the tariff question. Civil War tariffs, which had come in as emergency measures, had continued to apply in peacetime. All through the 1880's the government had collected an annual surplus of a hundred million dollars—a great temptation to grafters; prices had soared, and protected trusts had flourished. In 1887, Cleveland had sent a message to Congress flaying the tariff evils. In the election of 1888, protection was the most-discussed issue.

To treat this matter Mark Twain put into his fantastic yarn Hank's account of a discussion he had with a blacksmith he met during the course of a trip through the country—a long talk about wages in a free-trade district as compared with wages in a district where a tariff was in force. The smith, an utter ass, started things by smugly pointing out how high wages were in his parts compared with those in Hank's district. Hank countered by showing that, proportionately, the people in his section could buy more with what they earned. Then the Yankee pointed out that he had "knocked the stuffing out of the high wages" the smith had been so excited about. But the smith, being a fool, could not see the point— could not see it even after poor Hank had made it time after time, using all the illustrations that came to his mind:

> "What I say is this. With us *half* a dollar buys more than a *dollar* buys with you—and *therefore* it stands to reason and the commonest kind of com-

mon sense, that our wages are *higher* than yours. . . . "

It was a crusher.

But alas, it didn't crush. No, I had to give it up. What those people valued was *high wages;* it didn't seem to be a matter of any consequence to them whether the high wages would buy anything or not. They stood for "protection," and swore by it, which was reasonable enough, because interested parties had gulled them into the notion that it was protection that had created their high wages.

It was an effective kind of propaganda Mark was using here. Laughter was turned against the opponent of free trade, and the fool attitude was tied up with protectionism while the wise Yankee stood for free trade. A book that sold by the hundred thousands amused people with buffoonery and clowning while at the same time it slipped in little sermons like this on the most disputed issues of the day. (pp. 203-09)

> *Walter Blair, "Mark Twain, Hank, and Huck," in his* Horse Sense in American Humor from Benjamin Franklin to Ogden Nash, *The University of Chicago Press, 1942, pp. 195-217.*

CARL VAN DOREN (essay date 1948)

[*Van Doren is considered one of the most perceptive American critics of the first half of the twentieth century. In the following excerpt, he discusses the ambivalent perspective of* A Connecticut Yankee in King Arthur's Court.]

It is difficult, reading *A Connecticut Yankee in King Arthur's Court,* not to feel sometimes that the book must have been written by two different persons: one of them with a lingering old affection for the days of the Round Table and the other full of dry contempt for all such faded nonsense. Take, for example, the episode of the smallpox hut, when King Arthur without the slightest hesitation picks up the young girl dying of the disease and carries her to her stricken mother. "Here," the narrative runs,

> was heroism at its last and loftiest possibility, its utmost summit; this was challenging death in the open field unarmed, with all the odds against the challenger, no reward set upon the contest, and no admiring world in silks and cloth-of-gold to gaze and applaud; and yet the king's bearing was as serenely brave as it had always been in those cheaper contests where knight meets knight in equal fight and clothed in protecting steel. He was great now; sublimely great. The rude statues of his ancestors in his palace should have an addition—I would see to that; and it would not be a mailed king killing a giant or a dragon, like the rest, it would be a king in commoner's garb bearing death in his arms that a peasant mother might look her last upon her child and be comforted.

And yet in a page or two the king is again the same royal blockhead he is through most of the story.

Or take the first impression the Yankee get of Arthur's Court.

> There was a fine manliness observable in almost every face; and in some a certain loftiness and sweetness that rebuked your belittling criticisms and stilled them. A most noble benignity and purity reposed in the countenance of him they called Sir

Galahad, and likewise in the king's also; and there was majesty and greatness in the giant frame and high bearing of Sir Launcelot of the Lake.

But then, almost at once, when Launcelot's captives are presented to Queen Guenever, "it was touching to see the queen blush and smile, and look embarrassed, and happy, and fling furtive glances at Sir Launcelot that would have got him shot in Arkansas, to a dead certainty."

The two persons who seem to have collaborated in the *Yankee* were of course both in Mark Twain's nature, which included a genuine sense of what he found great in history and at the same time a keen sense of what was foolish or vicious in ancient customs that some modern readers thought beguiling. His interest in the Arthurian legends began early in 1885 when, in a bookstore in Rochester, he came upon Sir Thomas Malory's *Le Morte d'Arthur,* was at once fascinated by it, and learned that George Washington Cable regarded it as one of the most beautiful books in the world. Mark Twain read and re-read Malory in the copy Cable bought and gave to him that day, in alternating moods of delight and burlesque. At a time when Tennyson and Swinburne and William Morris were glorifying medieval England in romantic lay poems, Mark Twain conceived the idea of a kind of counter-romance which would show how uncomfortable it might be, in fact, for a man of the nineteenth century to try living in sixth-century conditions. One night, according to Mark Twain's note-book, he dreamed he was a knight-errant in armor. The armor had no pockets. The knight had a cold in the head and no handkerchief. The iron was blazing in summer, freezing in winter. It was struck by lightning. The knight fell down and could not get up alone. It seems never to have occurred to Mark Twain in his dream, if he knew it when he was awake, that knights did not travel in their armor, only fought in it, and that he was imagining discomforts out of misinformation. Still, his prevailing aim was to burlesque the old tales of knighthood, and his rough naturalism was no further from the truth than the soft romance of his poetic contemporaries.

Just as, in *Innocents Abroad,* Mark Twain had taken Americans of his own day to Rome and Greece and Egypt and the Holy Land and shown them to be as ready to laugh as to be awed, so now he would take a Connecticut Yankee, brisk and brash, back into the Arthurian age and show him unawed and triumphant. There the Yankee would match his radical wits with the conservative traditions of Court and Church, his inventions with their superstitions. To make the contrast emphatic, and convincing, Mark Twain had to create a character who was a mechanic, an all-round handyman. Since Mark Twain then lived in Hartford, to make his hero a Connecticut Yankee was a compliment to the adopted state, but it was also in an American tradition to think of Connecticut as notable for the varied ingenuities of its native sons. Moreover, Mark Twain liked to tell stories in the first person. Samuel L. Clemens, taking the pseudonym Mark Twain, had in a sense created a character who was not quite Clemens, but instead was only the part of Clemens that appeared in public. This had made him freer to recount, in his special idiom, the adventures of *Innocents Abroad* and *Roughing It. The Gilded Age* and *Tom Sawyer,* told in the third person, had not been so good as *Huckleberry Finn,* told in the first by an imaginary narrator. Now in the *Yankee* the story would appear to be told by the actual man who had gone to Camelot in the flesh and taken Connecticut with him for contrast.

"I am an American," the Yankee says in introducing himself.

I was born and reared in Hartford, in the state of Connecticut—anyway, just over the river, in the country. So I am a Yankee of the Yankees—and practical; yes, and nearly barren of sentiment, I suppose—or poetry, in other words. My father was a blacksmith, my uncle was a horse-doctor, and I was both, along at first. Then I went over to the great arms factory and learned my real trade; learned all there was to it; learned to make everything: guns, revolvers, cannon, boilers, engines, all sorts of labor-saving machinery. Why, I could make anything a body wanted—anything in the world, it didn't make any difference what; and if there wasn't any quick new-fangled way to make a thing, I could invent one—and do it as easy as rolling off a log. I became head superintendent; had a couple of thousand men under me.

His character thus established, the Yankee can go on to his adventures, which Mark Twain intended to make true for the Yankee, not necessarily true for other men. In a more balanced, more considered story the Yankee would have seemed superior to the wizards and warriors of Camelot by virtue of his mechanical skills; but also he would now and then have been inferior because of his intellectual and spiritual limitations. *A Connecticut Yankee* is not balanced or considered. From time to time the hero exhibits a strain of poetry and more than a strain of sentiment. Again and again his story betrays Mark Twain's own assumption that mechanical inventions are the true index of human progress and success. The Yankee's opinion about monarchy and hierarchy are unmistakably Mark Twain's. The Yankee, if he had been rigorously presented, would have known nothing about the England of centuries after the sixth. But Mark Twain does not hesitate to say in his Preface:

> It is not pretended that these laws and customs existed in England in the sixth century; no, it is only pretended that inasmuch as they existed in the English and other civilizations of far later times, it is safe to consider that it is no libel upon the sixth century to suppose them to have been in practice in that day also. One is quite justified in inferring that whatever one of these laws and customs was lacking in that remote time, its place was competently filled by a worse one.

Mark Twain was neither an antiquarian, determined to get his history always accurate in the story, nor a strict dramatist, determined to keep his hero always in character. *A Connecticut Yankee* was conceived in burlesque, but executed through many of its pages in anger. For Mark Twain profoundly hated tyranny and cruelty and superstition, and he could not ridicule them in cold blood. It is he, rather than the Yankee in character, who rises to diatribes against kinghood and aristocracy and ecclesiastical oppression. It is he, rather than the Yankee, who tells the teasing and yet oddly tender love story of the Yankee and the Demoiselle Alisande Carteloise whom he calls Sandy. These distinctions, however, are only critical niceties. For Mark Twain, once in the current of his narrative, bothered little about the character of his hero and instead went on in a rush of broad comedy, hitting any heads he liked to hit, going to any length of burlesque that amused him. If there was much revolutionary ardor in his story, so was there much of the rowdy humor of the American frontier in which he had grown up and from which he had learned his vigorous art. He sounds, as an earlier critic has observed, sometimes like a barbarian of genius who has burst into the court of some narrow kingdom. He shatters a thousand delicately poised decorums—many of them harmless enough—and exposes a thousand obnoxious shams.

A Connecticut Yankee, published in 1889, has lost some of the force it had for readers of its own year. There are no longer so many languishing admirers of the Middle Ages as there were then. There are no longer so many persons irritated by the languishers and delighted to see their extravagant adorations ridiculed. Some of the Yankee's irreverences now seem vulgarisms. It is not now quite so funny as then to see a knight unhorsed in a tournament with the help of a lasso; not quite so climactic to see all the chivalry of England electrocuted by charged wires. Those same knights, when they arrive on bicycles barely in time to save King Arthur, in disguise, from being hanged are magnificent:

> The grandest sight that ever was seen. Lord, how the plumes streamed, how the sun flamed and flashed from the endless procession of webby wheels!. . . Well, it was noble to see Launcelot and the boys swarm up onto that scaffold and heave sheriffs and such overboard. And it was fine to see that astonished multitude go down on their knees and beg their lives of the king they had just been deriding and insulting. And as he stood apart there, receiving this homage in rags, I thought to myself, well, really there *is* something peculiarly grand about the gait and bearing of a king, after all.

The difference is merely that these knights are on the Yankee's side, the electrocuted knights on the other.

Yet the inconsistencies of the book, the variations in tone from matter-of-fact to idyl to tragedy to hilarious clowning, do not deprive the *Yankee* of its share of Mark Twain's natural fun and charm. Most burlesque is written with a kind of arid, niggling ill humor. Mark Twain even in his most burlesquing mood, here as elsewhere, is never far from his other inescapable moods of romance and poetry and rich laughter. If there is anger in his burlesque, so is there good humor: the burlesque, anger, and good humor that are Mark Twain. (pp. v-viii)

> *Carl Van Doren, in a foreword to* A Connecticut Yankee in King Arthur's Court *by Samuel L. Clemens, The Heritage Press, 1948, pp. v-viii.*

JOHN DeWITT McKEE   (essay date 1960)

[*In the following excerpt, McKee examines the revolutionary social ideas presented in* A Connecticut Yankee in King Arthur's Court.]

Much has been said about Mark Twain's final ability to achieve perspective in *The Adventures of Huckleberry Finn.* The same thing might be said—and with the same amount of truth—about *A Connecticut Yankee in King Arthur's Court.* And the qualification must be made, because Mark Twain was never able to achieve true objectivity. In a sense Huckleberry Finn on the Mississippi and Hank Morgan in Camelot are both Mark Twain. As Bernard DeVoto believes, this strange man could not objectify his fiction, and, paradoxically, he could not make the direct revelation of autobiography.

But if Mark Twain is a personal and private writer in that his viewpoint character is almost always, in essence, himself, he is also universal in that he is hardly ever speaking only of America in the nineteenth century or, as in *Joan,* of France

of the fifteenth century, or of England of the sixth century; he is speaking of and to mankind. For that reason a study of *A Connecticut Yankee* as a revolutionary document should be a rewarding one.

Bernard DeVoto has interpreted *Huckleberry Finn* as a social criticism, or at least as having social implications concerning America, and others have followed him in that interpretation. If this interpretation is valid, and I think it is, then the evaluation of *A Connecticut Yankee* as a social document is at least equally so. John R. Hoben [see Further Reading] makes a good case for Twain's feud with Matthew Arnold and his increasing Anglophobia as the catalyst which turned *A Connecticut Yankee* into a scathingly anti-British harangue, and, more than incidentally, into a much better book than it might otherwise have been. But, granting the Anglophobia, and granting the need of some such catalyst as Arnold's superior attitude toward America, granting even the prevailing American penchant for twisting the lion's tail, *A Connecticut Yankee in King Arthur's Court* is far more than a blast at England, far more than a blast at the twin anachronisms of Church and State. This book, written at the peak of Twain's power, at the edge of the long descent, is a revolutionary novel. (p. 18)

[In his *Mark Twain's America*] Mr. DeVoto quotes a letter from Edmund Clarence Stedman to Mark Twain:

> Some blasted fool will surely jump up and say that Cervantes polished off chivalry long ago, etc. After a time he'll discover, perhaps, that you are going at the *still existing* radical principles or fallacies which made "chivalry" possible once and servility and flunkeyism and tyranny possible now.

And Mark Twain himself says, in his preface to *A Connecticut Yankee:*

> The ungentle laws and customs touched upon in this tale are historical, and the episodes which are used to illustrate them are also historical. It is not pretended that these laws and customs existed in England in the sixth century; no, it is only pretended that inasmuch as they existed in English and other civilizations of far later times, it is safe to consider that it is no libel upon the sixth century to suppose them to have been in practice in that day also. One is quite justified in inferring that whatever one of these laws and customs was lacking in that remote time, its place was competently filled by a worse one.

Twain's attacks on the Catholic Church "as the begetter of slavery, the enfranchisement of privilege and corruption and injustice, the source of cruelty and superstition and intolerance . . . " have long been noted; and his bitter laughter at the traditions of kingship and the chivalric tradition—which has come down today to empty titles and guided tours through the feudal castles—is part of the explicit satire of the book.

But it is the institution itself which is evil; the individual may be good or evil himself, regardless of the institution. Hence before Merlin puts Hank Morgan into his thirteen-century sleep, the Yankee machinist has grown to like King Arthur, and to respect him. Hence there is a kindly priest to take the child of the condemned young mother. "Law is intended to mete out justice," the priest says. "Sometimes it fails. This cannot be helped. We can only grieve, and be resigned, and pray for the soul of him who falls unfairly by the arm of the law, and that his fellows may be few. The law sends this poor young thing to death—and it is right. But another law had placed her where she must commit her crime or starve with her child—and before God that law is responsible for both her crime and her ignominious death!"

Thus it is not the king nor the priest who is at fault; it is the institution, the State, which moves stupidly and often with unknowing and uncaring cruelty, and the Church, which abets the state by perpetuating and encouraging superstition.

We see King Arthur as a man when he goes on his tour in disguise, and he is a good man. The only priest we see is a good man, caught in the toils of the institution he serves. The same comparison is made between individual common men and humanity in the mass. Marco is a simple, good man. Dowley, the smith, overpays his help at the risk of the law. The king himself, at the risk of the Church's displeasure and of his own life, helps Hank in the smallpox hut. But humanity in the mass is as evil as the institutions it erects. Mobs make picnics out of hangings and run along beside the tumbril shouting obscenities and singing ribald songs. Pilgrims on a holy quest watch the whipping of a slave girl and comment on "the expert way in which the whip was handled."

Hank Morgan's attitude toward mankind fluctuates continually between man's innate goodness, a romantic faith in education, and a conviction that the human race is damned. When Marco offers to go to the gallows rather than report his relatives for killing the lord and burning the castle, Hank says:

> There it was, you see. A man *is* a man, at bottom. Whole ages of abuse and oppression cannot crush the manhood clear out of him . . . . Yes, there is plenty good enough material for a republic in the most degraded people that ever lived—even the Russians; plenty of manhood in them—even in the Germans—if one could but force it out of its timid and suspicious privacy, to overthrow and trample in the mud any throne that ever was set up, and any nobility that ever supported it. . . .

When he first discovered that he was in the sixth century, Hank reconciled himself to it this way:

> If . . . it was really the sixth century, all right, I didn't want any softer thing: I would boss the whole country inside of three months; for I judged I would have the start of the best-educated man in the kingdom by a matter of thirteen hundred years and upward. . . .

In another place, he says, "Training—training is everything; training is all there is *to* a person. We speak of nature; it is folly; there is no such thing as nature; what we call by that misleading name is merely heredity and training. . . ." Yet only a few lines further on, he says, "And as for me, all that I think of in this plodding and pilgrimage, this pathetic *drift between the eternities,* is to lock out and humbly live a pure and high and blameless life, and save that one microscopic item in me that is truly *me:* the rest may land in Sheol for all I care."

The only banner around which the novel finds a kind of unity is the banner of revolution. The human race may be damned; nothing ultimately may be done for this sorry creature, man; but at the very least a revolution might ameliorate some of his suffering while he drifts pathetically between eternities. Stedman focused the importance of this aspect of the book

when he spoke of "tyranny . . . now." Twain was beating no dead horse when he railed against the monarchy of the sixth century. Witness the references to Russia and to Germany in the passages already quoted, and Twain's insistence on a broad application of the story in the passage quoted from the preface.

The revolutionary aspect of the novel begins with Hank Morgan's analysis of the power of the Catholic Church, an analysis which continues throughout the book, but is at its clearest when Hank compares the power of the king, who is a slave to the Church, with his own intellectual and political powers as The Boss—The Boss who is outside the power of the Church. It is clearer, too, in his comparison of the hereditary power of the nobility and of his own power, drawn from the people. "Unlimited power *is* the ideal thing when it's in safe hands," Hank says. The trouble is, the only safe hands are perfect hands, and the only perfect hands are the hands of God. Among necessarily imperfect men, Hank concludes, "an earthly despotism is not only a bad form of government, it is the worst form of government."

Although in the end he sees them as slaves of their own apathy, everywhere Hank Morgan is on the side of the people. Of the French Revolution, he says:

> There were two "Reigns of Terror," if we would but remember it and consider it; the one wrought murder in hot passion, the other in heartless cold blood; the one lasted mere months, the other lasted a thousand years; the one inflicted death on ten thousand persons, the other upon a hundred millions . . . What is the horror of swift death by the ax compared with lifelong death from hunger, cold, insult, cruelty, and heartache?

Did Mark Twain take up the clothes symbol from Carlyle's *Sartor Resartus* and cut it to fit the pattern of his own democratic doctrine? From the internal evidence, it would seem so.

> You see, my kind of loyalty was loyalty to one's country, not to its institutions, or its office-holders. . . . Institutions are extraneous, they are [the country's] mere clothing, and clothing can wear out, become ragged, cease to be comfortable, cease to protect the body from winter, disease and death. To be loyal to rags, to shout for rags, to die for rags—that is the loyalty of unreason, it is pure animal; it belongs to monarchy, was invented by monarchy, let monarchy keep it. . . . The citizen who thinks he sees that the commonwealth's political clothes are worn out, and yet holds his peace and does not agitate for a new suit is disloyal; he is a traitor. . . .

As always in *A Connecticut Yankee,* Mark Twain's attack here is a double-barrelled one, and he soon lets go the other barrel at the Church in the matter of political liberty:

> Concentration of political power is bad; and an Established Church is only a political machine; it was invented for that; it is nursed, cradled, preserved for that; it is an enemy to human liberty, and it does no good which it could not do better in a split-up and scattered condition. . . .

Hank Morgan could work nineteenth-century magic for sixth-century England. He could build it factories and shot-towers and schools, but he could not give it liberty; for that there had to be a revolution. The monarchy and the Church and their evils had grown too deeply into the soil of England to be rooted out in any other way; and the people, the soil upon which this corruption had fed itself for so many centuries, were inured to the corruption. The damned, as Mr. DeVoto says, had accepted their damnation.

". . . all gentle cant and philosophizing to the contrary notwithstanding," Hank Morgan says, "no people in the world ever did achieve their freedom by goody-goody talk and moral suasion: it being immutable law that all revolutions that succeed must *begin* in blood, whatever may answer afterward."

It seems to me that we have in *A Connecticut Yankee in King Arthur's Court* what could have been one of the greatest and most passionate expressions of democratic faith in the nineteenth century. That it failed to live up to its potential can be laid, I think, to several causes. In the first place, Mark Twain functioned almost exclusively as a critic of his time. He could diagnose, but he could not prescribe. In the second place, he seemingly could not sustain the savage satire which makes up most of the democratic testament; he must forever, by his very nature and literary training, slip from wit into humor and from humor into sheer burlesque. Finally, he gave a slender idea—the idea of what would happen if a nineteenth century Connecticut gun-maker were suddenly dumped into sixth century England—too great a load to carry. This willing little pony has been made to carry a Clydesdale's portion of slavery, injustice, tyranny, the chivalric tradition, the despotism of the Church, the pitiable apathy of men, their superstition and their child-like ignorance. No wonder Mark Twain occasionally found himself riding off in all directions. He is like Hank Morgan at the tournament: there are too many enemies against whom to break a lance.

But for all its faults, it may be that *A Connecticut Yankee* has more things to say to more people than even *Huckleberry Finn,* Twain's one generally admitted masterpiece. Insofar as its main purpose is concerned, one could no more call *A Connecticut Yankee* mere frontier humor than one could call "A Modest Proposal" a whimsical essay.

Hank Morgan's revolution failed, and we can see in that failure, if we will, what Mr. DeVoto calls futility; but I prefer to think that, given enough young men who have been freed from the tyrannies and superstitions of their fathers, and enough time and patience to educate those young men—perhaps only a few at first, but with each generation, more—mankind may finally find its way out of Merlin's cave. (pp. 18-20, 24)

> *John DeWitt McKee, "A Connecticut Yankee as a Revolutionary Document," in* Mark Twain Journal, *Vol. XI, No. 2, Summer, 1960, pp. 18-20, 24.*

CHARLES S. HOLMES   (essay date 1962)

[*In the following excerpt, Holmes discusses the fundamental ambiguity of Twain's attitude toward technical progress in* A Connecticut Yankee in King Arthur's Court.]

Most readers have taken *A Connecticut Yankee in King Arthur's Court* as though it were one of Twain's early books—a fantasy-version of *The Innocents Abroad* perhaps, in which the values of democratic, enlightened America triumph over the caste system and superstition of medieval England. But this it surely is not. The fable of the Yankee mechanic's effort to transform the bad old world of King Arthur ends in break-

down and failure, not in triumph. The book is ultimately destructive of all value, and its real affinities are with such later works as *Pudd'nhead Wilson* and *The Mysterious Stranger.* It expresses not Mark Twain's certainties, but the deep contradictions in his feelings about his own career, about American culture, and finally, about life itself.

Something of the fundamental ambiguity of the book can be seen in the character of Hank Morgan, the rowdy Hartford mechanic who introduces "soap and civilization" to medieval England. Conceived in part as an answer to Matthew Arnold's strictures upon the American character, he is first of all a national archetype. In his brag and cocky assurance, his hustle and inventiveness, and his indifference to fine art and culture, he is the epitome of the nineteenth-century American common man. His father is a blacksmith and his uncle a horse-doctor. He is "nearly barren of sentiment . . . or poetry," he tells us, but he can "make anything." The dark and mysterious world of the Middle Ages is for him simply a situation full of "opportunities for a man of pluck and enterprise." He is the New-World Robinson Crusoe: thrown into a world without soap, matches, gas, books, coffee, tea, or tobacco, his response is to lay the following imperatives upon himself—"Invent, contrive, create, reorganize."

He is also a reformer and idealist. In his effort to redeem the benighted world of the Middle Ages he is more than anything else a missionary, embodying in this role as well as in his role as pioneer and mechanic not only a national trait but a central fact of Twain's own nature. When Howard Taylor tried to dramatize the novel, Twain was outraged at his failure to represent this aspect of the Yankee: "He has captured but one side of the Yankee's character—his rude animal side, his circus side; the good heart and the high intent are left out of him."

Yet there are a good many contradictions in the Yankee's character, suggesting that Twain was not altogether sure what he really thought of him. If in some respects he is intended to be a national culture-symbol, in others, as James Cox has pointed out, he is more like a caricature or parody. His crude and clownish behavior is in part dictated by his function as mocker of Old World culture, but the extravagance of his buffoonery suggests that Twain, like Swift, viewed his protagonist with some irony. The Yankee is full of missionary zeal, yet he has only contempt for the people he intends to salvage. "Rabbits," he calls them. His imagination is fired with the "dream of a republic," yet he confidently predicts that he "will boss the whole country inside of three months," and establishes a total dictatorship based on the power of his modern inventions. He congratulates himself on the superior qualities of his mind in contrast to the superstitious ignorance of Merlin and the fantasy-ridden illusions of Sandy, yet at the end of the book, it is the self-confident, practical-minded Yankee who is the dupe, the victim of his own naïve expectations.

In short, the character of the Yankee is somewhat ambiguously conceived. Democratic culture-hero, Carlylean strong man, clown, gull, and auctorial projection, he reveals some of the irresolutions in Twain's mind and the problematical intention of the novel itself.

The Utopian program with which the Yankee hopes to transform the conditions of life in the Middle Ages is a grab-bag of the popular optimisms of the nineteenth century in America: faith in education, in political and social democracy, in the promise of the machine, and in the inevitable superiority of the present to the past. The connection between technological and moral progress was a central theme in Lecky's *History of European Morals,* a book which was much on Twain's mind when he wrote *A Connecticut Yankee,* and in such popularized accounts of the American achievement as Andrew Carnegie's *Triumphant Democracy.* "The first thing you want in a new country is a patent office; then work up your school system; and after that, out with your paper," says the Yankee. Under his benevolent dictatorship England becomes "a happy and prosperous country." The factory system is well established, schools and colleges are everywhere, a "complete variety of Protestant congregations" is to replace the Established Church, and universal suffrage and a republican form of government are projected. Steamboats ply the Thames, a railroad is already in operation, and telephones, typewriters, and sewing machines are "working their way into favor."

It is tempting to see this clutter of popular ideology as deliberately ironic, particularly in the light of the conclusion of the book, but this would be to overlook the fact that almost all the elements of the Yankee's program represent values to which Twain himself subscribed, with varying degrees of enthusiasm, throughout his early and middle life. He was particularly excited by the achievements of modern technology, which he saw as clear guarantees of the superiority of modern times to all of the past. In the famous letter on Whitman's seventieth birthday, instead of congratulating the old poet on his trail-blazing career in the world of letters, Twain elected to speak of what to him were the real wonders of the age: "The steam press . . . the telegraph . . . the electrotype . . . the sewing machine and the amazing, infinitely varied and innumerable products of coal tar, those latest and strangest marvels of a marvellous age."

Thus, the technological emphasis of the brave new world in *A Connecticut Yankee* is something more than the reflection of the popular American belief in progress through applied science. For Twain it was the expression of a deeply felt personal involvement. Invention was to him the spirit of the age, and throughout his life he pursued a bizarre variety of machines and gadgets with the intensity of the true believer. Hank Morgan speaks for Twain when he refers to the great inventors—Gutenberg, Watt, Whitney, Morse, and others—as "after God, the creators of this world." The Paige typesetting machine, into which he so recklessly poured his financial and emotional resources in the decade of the eighties, became not only the focus of his commitment to the ideal of "machine culture," but the embodiment of his dream of success as businessman, inventor, and author. It was the machine to end all machines. "All the other wonderful inventions of the human brain sink . . . into commonplace contrasted with this awful mechanical miracle," he wrote his brother Orion on the occasion of its first successful performance, January 5, 1889. And when he adds that after two or three weeks' tinkering "we shall speak out the big secret and let the world come and gaze," he sounds like Hank Morgan, about to expose his "vast system of clandestine factories and workshops to an astonished world." Moreover, it was a machine closely connected with writing, and hence with creation and with art. It is significant that Twain, a great literary inventor (in the Poundian sense), so often makes the connection between mechanical invention and other forms of creation. He called Paige "a poet . . . whose sublime creations are written in steel," and he often spoke of the machine as though it possessed a character and intelligence of its own. "It is a cunning

devil, knowing more than any man that ever lived," he wrote to Orion, betraying some of his latent uneasiness about its reliability, and he urged Howells to "come and see this sublime magician of iron and steel work his enchantments." The typesetter touched Twain's imagination on many levels, but the secret source of its power may well have been his sense that it represented a possible reconciliation of forces at war within himself and within American society at large. In the typesetter, the worlds of art, technics, and business might be made one. That they never were may in part explain the doubts and frustrations which gradually darkened his horizons in the late '80's and the '90's.

In any case, the typesetter venture was at the center of Twain's experience at the time he was writing *A Connecticut Yankee.* (He wrote Theodore Crane that he wanted to complete the novel on the day the machine was finished.) The story of the wonder-working mechanic and the beneficent revolution brought about through his special skills is clearly a projection of Twain's vast hopes for the typesetter, just as the disintegration and failure of the Yankee's whole experiment embodies the intimations of disaster (never openly acknowledged) which made the whole venture an agony of uncertainty for Twain.

For no sooner has Hank Morgan's Utopia been fairly launched than it begins to founder. A six-weeks' absence is all it takes. He returns from France to find that the bustling modern culture he had so hopefully established has completely disappeared. The Church has taken over, and is determined to "snuff out" the Yankee's "beautiful civilization." It is all as though the Yankee and his enlightened ideals had never existed. The basic pattern of the book—early success and ultimate failure—represents Twain's ambiguous feelings about his own career and about the age. One of Pudd'nhead Wilson's calendar epigrams reads, "Every one is a moon and has a dark side which he never shows to anybody." In the last section of *A Connecticut Yankee* Twain showed his. For all his public commitment to progress, social legislation, and the common man, he really distrusted the whole fabric of American life, and beneath the outward appearance of success with which his life was attended in the 1880's, he was insecure, uncertain, and disturbed.

There were strong personal reasons why the subject of failure should force its way into his work at this time. The business ventures into which he had plunged with such confidence and bravado, certain that the role of business man would suit him better than that of author, were in a precarious state. The publishing business was slipping downhill; indeed, one of the reasons he wrote *A Connecticut Yankee* was that the firm needed a successful book if it was to stay in business. The typesetter, for all the promise it held out, struck terror deep into his soul. He had started out in 1880 with a modest investment of $3,000. By 1887 it was costing him more than $3,000 a month.

In addition, he was suffering from doubt and anxiety about his artistic career. For all his prolific energy and phenomenal success, Twain never overcame his neurotic fear of failure. He required constant encouragement, advice, and applause to bolster up his security. The need for popular success and the fear of losing it may have been the underlying motives for the conception of the Yankee as a magician who destroys all rivals to the awe, amazement, and enthusiasm of huge crowds (as at Merlin's Tower and the Holy Fountain), and whose career is one personal triumph after another—until the end, when he is deserted by all save his band of faithful boys. The aftermath of the Holy Fountain episode, in which a false magician steals the Yankee's audience with some fraudulent mumbo jumbo, is especially interesting in this connection. The Yankee eventually exposes the false magician, but he adds this anxious remark: "A man can keep his trademark current in such a country, but he can't sit around and do it; he has got to be on deck and attending to business right along." *A Connecticut Yankee* was Twain's first book since 1885, and he was characteristically uncertain about it. He wrote Howells shortly before the book was published, "I don't think I'll send out any other press copy—except perhaps to Stedman. I'm not writing for those parties who miscall themselves critics, and I don't care to have them paw the book at all. It's my swan-song, my retirement from literature permanently. . . ."

But one must look beyond autobiography to temperament and philosophy for an explanation of the theme of failure in *A Connecticut Yankee.* The essential melancholy and pessimism which were the underside of Twain's energy and appetite for experience made the collapse of the Yankee's whole experiment inevitable. (So, of course, did history. Everyone knows that the Dark Ages were not, in fact, suddenly transformed into the nineteenth century.) The curious determinism from which he derived so much comfort and upon which he came to rely more and more as life proved more and more delusive runs like an iron chain throughout the book, imprisoning men in the patterns of their upbringing. Mired in their ancient superstitions and prejudices, what hope is there that the benighted people of King Arthur's time could ever throw off the institutions that had shaped them, and become free, enlightened, independent? "Did you think you had educated the superstition out of these people?" asks Clarence, as he tells the Boss of the collapse of their social experiment. "I certainly did think it," answers the Boss. "Well then, you may unthink it," says Clarence. Only a handful of boys has been truly saved. Too young to remember the old ways, and plastic enough to receive the stamp of the Boss's democratic ideals, they are the only true products of the Boss's experiment. The older people reverted at the first pressure. "It revealed them to themselves, and it revealed them to me, too," says Clarence.

The picture of man as a helpless product of his background had always appealed to Mark Twain as a prime subject for fiction. One thinks of Huck's struggle with his socially-created conscience, and of the pathetic half-brothers, Tom Driscoll and Valet de Chambre, in *Pudd'nhead Wilson.* As early as 1883 he was making elaborate preparations for a story (characteristically unfinished) about the Sandwich Islands, which, in its intended treatment of the theme of a man's bondage to his early upbringing and the inevitable failure of any effort to convert people to a new dispensation, is very obviously an early trying-out of some of the leading ideas of the Connecticut Yankee. In a letter to Howells he said that "the hidden motive" of the story would "illustrate a but-little considered fact in human nature: that the religious folly you are born in you will *die* in, no matter what apparently reasonabler religious folly may seem to have taken its place. . . ."

But underlying the determinism of *A Connecticut Yankee* is a far more fundamental reason for the breakdown of the Yankee's experiment, and that is the profound distrust of life and contempt for human nature which after about 1890 became the dominant note in Twain's work. "It is the strangest thing," he wrote in his notebook in 1895, "that the world is not full of books that scoff at the pitiful world, and the useless universe and violent, contemptible human race—books that laugh at the whole petty scheme and deride it." He saw man as "a poor joke—the poorest that was ever contrived," and history as nothing but a series of crimes. The Yankee's view of the people of Arthur's England is shaped by this basic misanthropy. In their timid submissiveness to their oppressors they are nothing but sheep. "They swung their caps and shouted for the republic for about one day, and there an end!" They really prefer slavery. With the first pressure from the Church and the nobility they fall back into their old attitudes. "Imagine such human muck as this," remarks the Yankee bitterly.

The basic paradox of the Yankee's position is obvious: if man is so limited and so unworthy, why bother with Utopian social reorganizations? Why care if man only proves to be what you have said he was all along? The answer is, of course, that Mark Twain held two opposed views of human nature, and was never able to bring them into any kind of relationship. On the one hand, he was wholeheartedly committed to the democratic-humanitarian-optimistic ideals of the eighteenth and nineteenth centuries: he stood for liberty, justice, enlightenment, reform. On the other hand, his sensitive and melancholy temperament inclined him to see human nature as "the most consummate sham and lie ever invented." The warfare between these incompatible positions is largely responsible for the rages and diatribes of Twain's private life and a good many of the contradictions and irresolutions in his art.

In the work of his early and middle years, where the balance was tipped in the direction of life and hope (*Huckleberry Finn,* for example), the problem was not acute, particularly since he was able to siphon off much of his distress at humanity's transgressions in the form of humor; but in such later pieces as *A Connecticut Yankee* and *The Mysterious Stranger,* where the certainty of human depravity competes on even terms with the old belief and the desire to reform, fundamental contradictions in meaning emerge. That Twain was aware that these contradictions could not be logically resolved is suggested by the fact that both stories end in a progressive retreat from reality—the gradual revelation that life is simply an illusion in *The Mysterious Stranger,* and the retreat to the cave and the final dissolve into dream in *A Connecticut Yankee.*

The Yankee's withdrawal to the cave, facing a hostile world with a small band of boys, expresses Twain's deepest feelings about himself and his whole relationship to life. His inmost self never left Hannibal and the world of boyhood, and his instinct was more and more to face life from that imaginative vantage point. The image of the Yankee and his boys in the cave is one of those wonderful symbolic tableaux in Twain—like Huck and Jim on the raft—which catch up a richness of meaning extending far beyond the confines of any particular story. Readers may see in it not only Twain's estrangement from the age and his instinctive retreat to the simpler, safer position of boyhood; it can also be seen as a culture image of a less reassuring sort than that which dominates *Huckleberry Finn:* the Boss, crouching in his cave and surrounded by his electric fence, is modern technological man. When he is through exercising his weapons, there will be even less left of civilization than there was before he began his wonder-working transformation.

The gesture of cosmic destruction which climaxes the Yankee's effort to modernize medieval England looks forward to **The Mysterious Stranger** in motivation and final effect. There is nothing like it in the earlier work. In both stories, the baffled idealist, unable to reconcile himself to the gap between what he hopes of human nature and what he sees, simply unmakes the world which has such painful contradictions in it. The destruction of the knights in **A Connecticut Yankee** is tantamount to elimination of the whole adult world: the Boss and his boys are alone in the silence after the electric fence has done its work.

The dream setting of **A Connecticut Yankee** completes the movement away from reality which characterizes the final sequence. The permissiveness of the form doubtless appealed to Twain, who would find its invitation to a certain degree of looseness, ambiguity, and contradiction congenial; but, more important, it served for him a genuinely expressive purpose. He was always acutely conscious of the world of fantasy and dream which lay beyond the borders of pragmatic reality. His letters, notebooks, and autobiographical fragments are full of wonder-filled accounts of his own vivid dreams and of notations on the similarities and differences between the kind of reality to be found in dream and that in the everyday world. The possibility of confusing dream and reality was a subject which particularly interested him. In his earlier, more self-confident years he tended to view this as a comic human failing, but as his troubles mounted and his inability to understand life grew more and more frustrating, he was drawn more and more to consider life under the aspects of fantasy, dream, and illusion.

The effect of the dream framework in **A Connecticut Yankee** is thus to heighten the already considerable ambiguity of the tale. In the story told to Mark Twain by the Yankee, the values are, in general, clear enough: the Yankee's experiences in King Arthur's England are a hallucination, the wild fantasy of a man hit on the head by a crowbar; reality is the nineteenth century, with its Colt arms factories and its practical point of view. But within the dream-world of King Arthur, the Yankee is the reality-principle. He stands for common sense, efficiency, the empirical approach to problems. Merlin and Sandy represent the principle of fantasy, superstition, and magic. The criticism of fantasy and illusion by common sense and reality is clearly part of the central design of the book; yet this design becomes a good deal less clear when we take into account the narrative frame provided by the introductory "A Word of Explanation" and the concluding "Final P. S. by M. T." At the very outset the Yankee is presented to us not as the self-confident factory superintendent from Hartford, but as "a curious stranger," who seemed, as he talked, "to drift away imperceptibly out of this world and time," into a world of "spectres and shadows." He is, in short, a representative of the world of dream, not of common-sense reality. The point is easily missed at first, because Twain brushes it only lightly as he moves into his tale, but the "P. S." returns to it in a way that cannot be ignored. The old Yankee, now dying, confuses dream and reality: as he speaks, it is clear that his Arthurian dream is now reality to him, and that his return to the nineteenth century, "with an abyss of thirteen centuries yawning . . . between me and all that is dear to me," is simply a bad dream.

The dream framework thus reverses the dominant values of the story itself. After his sojourn in the land of King Arthur, the Yankee no longer believes in the superiority or the reality of the nineteenth century. He has rejected the world of science and common sense, and has chosen instead the dream world of the Middle Ages. In this connection, his marriage to Sandy, which at first seems merely a burlesque or a sentimental gesture, takes on some importance. Sandy is the incarnation of the medieval past, of fantasy and illusion, and in marrying her, the Yankee signifies his commitment to her world, and prepares us for his reversal of form in the frame chapters. So while the body of the narrative purports to show the triumph of Yankee common sense and nineteenth-century reality over fantasy and the past, the dream framework calls all this into question.

Whether or not Twain was fully aware of the countercurrents of meaning in his final sequence and in the dream framework, it must be recognized that they are genuinely expressive. The Yankee's surprising commitment to fantasy and the past, for example, is clearly a protest on the part of the romantic and daydreaming side of Twain's nature against the "science and common sense" values asserted by the side committed to pragmatism and progress, just as the suggestion that the nineteenth century and all that we have taken to be real may be only dream-stuff is an expression of his basic uncertainty about the values of the age he lived in. The central scheme of the novel is thus not a static contrast between two sets of value (democracy, technology, common sense—the present—versus the caste system, superstition, fantasy—the past), but a reversible interplay, in which each set of terms acts progressively upon the other, so that by the time the conclusion is reached both schemes of value have been thoroughly undercut. The total effect of the contradictions, inconsistencies, and ambiguities of **A Connecticut Yankee** is to give the whole tale a quality of dubiety much more representative of Twain's real response to life (particularly in the late 1880's and 1890's, when his position seemed more and more precarious) than of the rather simple-minded confidence in nineteenth-century democratic culture which has commonly been taken as the message of the book. (pp. 462-72)

> Charles S. Holmes, " 'A Connecticut Yankee in King Arthur's Court:' Mark Twain's Fable of Uncertainty," in South Atlantic Quarterly, Vol. 61, No. 4, Autumn, 1962, pp. 462-72.

HAROLD ASPIZ   (essay date 1962)

[*In the following essay, Aspiz emphasizes the influence of William E. H. Lecky's interpretation of European history in Twain's depiction of medieval England.*]

The relationship between **A Connecticut Yankee in King Arthur's Court** and William E. H. Lecky's *History of European Morals from Augustus to Charlemagne* (1869) provides valuable insights into Mark Twain's fictional method and ideological development. Twain "digested every word and line" of the *History,* and profusely annotated his own copy. In Lecky's work he found the kind of commentary on humanity which reinforced his own conclusions. An astute reader, he recognized an ambivalence in Lecky's thought akin to the ambivalence readers may recognize in Mark Twain's own thought. Lecky's pioneer study provided more than a statement of the superiority of the nineteenth century over all other centuries and a qualified affirmation of inevitable progress. It also documented his misgivings about the upgrading of human nature as a concomitant of technical or social advancement. Thus Lecky's *History,* like Twain's novel, came to grips with the central dilemma in nineteenth-century thought: the faith in the perfectibility of humanity through democratic social organization and scientific progress, on the one horn, and the dogma that human nature is static, obtuse, damned, or molded by uncontrollable forces, on the other horn.

The *History* was a treasury of ideas into which Mark Twain dipped liberally to compose *A Connecticut Yankee.* His borrowings were of three sorts. First, he used Lecky as a source, conscious or otherwise, of characters, incidents, and bits of "local color," particularly in the middle section of the novel. This relationship between the two works not only accounts for the genesis and development of much of the novel but also illuminates Mark Twain's frequent practice of priming his ebbing "tank" of inspiration with other men's writings. Twain's borrowing of incidents from Lecky is very complex. Although his footnote to Chapter XXII ("The Holy Fountain") declares that "All the details concerning the hermits, in this chapter, are from Lecky, but greatly modified," he actually derives major portions of some half dozen chapters from Lecky's *History.* The excesses of the desert saints are telescoped from five pages in the *History* into 200 words. . . . Lecky's details about St. Simeon Stylites are modified to make the old hermit more ludicrous; even his profitable harnessing to a sewing machine combines Lecky's picture of the old man bowing in prayer atop a pillar and his final description of the aged saint "with long white beard and gentle aspect, weaving his mats beneath the palm trees, while daemons vainly tried to disturb him by their stratagems." Sandy's story in Chapter XXI ("The Pilgrims") about the monastery well, which materialized after the Abbot Theodosius had prayed for it but which dried up after some monks constructed a bath nearby, is found in a short passage of the *History* immediately preceding the description of St. Simeon Stylites. Lecky's declaration that sixth-century monasticism had reached "the secluded valleys of Wales and Ireland" helped make it possible to people the Valley of Holiness with desert characters and to identify the abbot's well with a purely British well in Malory's *Morte D'Arthur.* At this well we encounter not only Sir Dinadan, the purveyor of "rotten" and "petrified" jokes in *A Connecticut Yankee,* but also Sir Ozana le Cure Hardy. Transformed by the Yankee to a peddler of plug hats in the novel, the latter dignitary quits his Arthurian well to bring the bad news of the failure of the desert well to the Yankee.

After the well's restoration, an event accompanied by brilliant pyrotechnics, the Yankee confutes Merlin and an Eastern magician who claims to be able to see what is happening in far-away places. This action, which fills the second half of Chapter XXIV ("The Rival Magician") is related to a strange passage . . . which mingles accounts of magic which backfires, "illuminations," and long-distance extrasensory perception. The second half of Chapter XXVI ("The First Newspaper"), describing the cure for the king's evil, is a reworking of two consecutive, and derivative, footnotes in the *History* and supplies a valuable insight into Mark Twain's technique of adapting borrowed materials. Finally, Mark Twain's marginalia show that his touching picture of slavery was strongly colored by his deep absorption with Lecky's contrast between the relatively mild form of slavery under pagan Roman law and its more debasing counterpart under Christianity. He drew numerous comparisons between slavery under early Christianity and slavery in the American South, and he probably felt justified (the whole novel is a gay abjuration of histo-

ricity anyway) in endowing Arthurian slavery with the characteristics and pathos of American slavery as he remembered it.

Second, Mark Twain took from Lecky the unifying theme of the novel—the theme of training and of the conflict between those dedicated souls who attempt to raise the level of humanity and the mass of men unwilling to think for themselves. Finally, Mark Twain translated the thematic concepts developed with Lecky's help into the fictional framework of the novel. Using the *History* as our vade mecum, we can see that Twain constructed a novel with a well-defined theme and a large measure of artistic unity.

Essentially, *A Connecticut Yankee in King Arthur's Court* is a "laboratory" novel, whose theme of "training" is best understood in the light of Lecky's *History.* The novel proposes to examine whether the mass of men can be trained to make proper use of modern technology and democratic self-government. The problem is presented in terms of the two complementary sub-themes (both of major importance in the *History*) whose interaction supplies most of the novel's dramatic tension. The first of these concepts is that (whose conduct is the product of his hereditary and environmental influences) can be trained to abandon his trust in the dark past and to raise himself to higher social, intellectual, and moral levels. The second concept (tinged with a melancholy mechanistic determinism) is that man is so deeply rooted in his dark past that he will inevitably revert to irrational, superstitious behavior.

The more optimistic of the sub-themes evolves in terms of the Yankee's program to achieve nineteenth-century capitalism in the sixth century. Like Lecky, Mark Twain finds the moral climate of his own day balmier than that of the past. Like Lecky, he sees a nation's *mores* as part of its social superstructure, shaped by prevailing economic and political relationships. Lecky argued that "The morals of men are more governed by their pursuits than by their opinions." "Industrial progress," he claimed, "ultimately brings a moral improvement," and "the virtues that spring from equality increase." He attributed the world's first social and intellectual progress to the rise of capitalism and the emergence of modern science. These new phenomena produced the habits of rational thought, wholesale skepticism, and self-reliance which dispelled the "superstitious torpor" and "blind credulity" thrust upon the "dark ages" as "the first of duties."

Lecky's thesis makes it possible to interpret the Yankee's program to alleviate the social and economic backwardness of the "more or less tamed animals" among whom he is "cast away" in King Arthur's sixth-century England. "Like another Robinson Crusoe," he sets out "to make life bearable . . . invent, create, reorganize things": he gives the Britons soap, telegraphs, telephones, sewing machines, steamboats, insurance, taxation, and a legal code. He attempts, in other words, to *create* a nineteenth-century milieu—to institute, at breakneck speed, an "industrial revolution" by concentrating on political, economic, and technological change. His stress on material progress rather than on the illumination of the spiritual darkness of Arthur's subjects is, in effect, an endorsement of Lecky's thesis that the moral stupor which supposedly characterized the "dark ages" disappeared—more or less automatically—with the advent of capitalism. Most of the Yankee's efforts are directed toward achieving capitalism, toward altering the basic fabric of sixth-century society. Like Lecky, the Yankee seems to feel that favorable attendant changes in the social superstructure are inevitable and that the end product of his efforts will be a nation of practical, moral, free-thinking republicans.

The pessimistic sub-theme concerns the ingrained superstitions which reassert themselves at unexpected moments to overwhelm the most reasonable minds. Both Lecky and Twain accused the Church of making belief a virtue, skepticism a sin, and man a fallen being whose mortality allegedly resulted from his sinful pride—that is, his daring to question authority.

> Above all [writes Lecky in a passage which could serve as an epitomization of this sub-theme] the conditions of true enquiry had been cursed by the Church. A blind unquestioning credulity was inculcated as the first of duties, and the habit of doubt, of the impartiality of a suspended judgment, of the desire to hear both sides of a disputed question and to emancipate the judgment from unreasoning prejudice, were in all consequence condemned. . . .

And Mark Twain assailed these medieval practices, by way of a bitter marginal comment, for having "exercised an influence of the most rotten character upon the moral history of the world."

> In moments when the controlling judgment has relaxed its grasp [Lecky wrote in another key passage] old intellectual habits resume their sway, and images painted on the imagination will live, when the intellectual propositions on which they rested have been wholly abandoned. In hours of weakness, in the feverish and anxious moments that are known to all, when the mind floats passively upon the stream, the phantoms which reason had exorcised must have often reappeared and the bitterness of an ancient tyranny must have entered upon the soul.

The tendency to revert to old and discredited thought patterns—a theme wholly in harmony with Lecky's *History*—receives both explicit statement and dramatic development in the novel. How frequently the Yankee seems on the verge of success when Arthur or his subjects revert to the old modes of thought! The novel's very ending—the ruin of the Yankee's reform program and the British nation's abandonment of reason within a Pisgah-sight of the promised land of the nineteenth-century—is a dramatic statement of Lecky's concept of reversion.

The theme of training, with its positive and negative sub-themes, combines with the personality of the Yankee to unify the dramatic structure of the novel and to lend it a large measure of artistic coherence. The theme makes it possible for us to follow the novel's development in the five segments into which it can be divided.

In the first segment (through Chapter X), the Yankee, a clever mechanic and shrewd administrator, is introduced to the "childlike and innocent" sixth-century Britons. Their conduct represents "mere animal training; they are white Indians . . . without brains enough to bait a fishhook with" and their crudity makes the Yankee observe (echoing Lecky's bias) that no gentlemanly or ladylike conduct was seen in the world until the start of the nineteenth century. The Yankee, "like another Robinson Crusoe," decides to master his environment, becomes prime minister ("The Boss"), and after four uneventful years (seven pages later) during which he has

viewed life in Camelot as "a curious thing," he appears to have accomplished only three things. He has concluded that the Church is at the root of feudal abuse; he has established a Department of Agriculture and Morals; and he has set up his surreptitious Man-Factory to train a handful of independent-minded men for an as yet unspecified purpose.

In the second segment (through Chapter XXI), we are afforded an insight into the nature of the feudal mind and are presented with the Yankee's program to change matters. Here Mark Twain dispatches the Yankee and Sandy on a mock-chivalric "quest." But although the Yankee is obviously an "innocent" in armor, Twain's ridicule of knightly customs and of Malory's never-never stories is the kind of biting buffoonery evident in his attacks (in *Life on the Mississippi* and *The Adventures of Huckleberry Finn*) on feudal vestiges in the ante bellum South. Quotations of Malory's diction and Sandy's garrulous imitations of it represent more than delightful jousting with "the terrible German language," for such speech exhibits the mental deficiencies of King Arthur and his subjects. The benighted Clarence, for instance, sounds like Malory at first, but after he has become the Yankee's right-hand man he speaks a marvelously colloquial English.

This segment also elaborates upon a deterministic observation Mark Twain had made in his marginalia: "All moral perceptions," he had said, "are acquired by the influences around us; these influences begin in our infancy; we never get a chance to find out whether they are innate or not." Similarly, the Yankee remarks, upon witnessing the equanimity of that enchanting murderess Queen Morgan le Fay and her defense of a merciless law:

> We speak of nature; it is folly; there is no such thing as nature; what we call by that misleading name is merely heredity and training. We have no thoughts of our own; they are merely transmitted to us, trained into us. All that is original in us, and therefore creditable or discreditable in us, can be covered up and hidden by the point of a cambric needle. . . .

Faulty training also explains the obtuseness of the suffering masses and the irrational behavior of Sandy, who charmingly insists that her porkers are bewitched noblewomen.

To counteract the pitiful results of feudal training, the Yankee designs a revolutionary retraining program whose success, he feels, requires only the development of a *cadre* of leaders who can think independently and feel no loyalties to the old order. He announces his long-range objectives and the sequence in which he hopes to achieve them. First, he will ridicule knight errantry out of existence. Second, he will undermine Church and State with a program of cleanliness. (Seemingly a flippant notion, this goal—as can be seen in the next segment—clearly symbolizes his struggle to uproot superstition.) Third, he will campaign for education. Finally, he will establish political freedom. The ensuing collapse of the old order will rob the Church of its power and "abolish [feudal] oppression from this land and restore to all people their stolen rights without disobliging anybody."

The third segment (through Chapter XXVI) develops all of the novel's principal ideas: that error sanctified by tradition is the cause of the "dark ages"; that reversion to baseless superstition is an ingrained habit; and that modern science is the real miracle which must replace specious miracles if progress is to be made. Following Lecky closely, Mark Twain probes the superstitious depths to which humanity can sink. Here we see the self-torture of the hermits; the magician who claimed to know what was happening in far-away places; the miracle of the king's touch; and the well which dried up, supposedly through divine displeasure, because the monks had bathed in its waters; the superstition-ridden populace.

Learning that the monks had endowed the failure of the well with a mystic interpretation, the Yankee observes:

> Old habit of mind is one of the toughest things in the world. It transmits itself like physical form and feature; and for a man, in those days, to have had an idea that his ancestors hadn't had, would have brought him under suspicion of being illegitimate.

"Old habit of mind" underlies the excesses of the desert saints, the credulity of the masses, the belief in the spurious miracles of Merlin, and the near ruin of the Boss's reputation as the magician who had performed "the showiest [and most practical] bit of magic in history" at the hands of a charlatan whose unsupported assertions convince the Boss's fans that he can tell what is happening in distant places. Baseless faith, like that of the people in the king's touch, says the Yankee, echoing Lecky, once more is akin to the superstitious awe which permits the existence of monarchies and all other frauds and abuses.

The fourth segment (through Chapter XXXVIII) is once again picaresque. The Yankee—a novice no longer—travels with the king—Twain's only case study in the retraining of a benighted individual. Although the most manly specimen feudalism can breed, the king is too obtuse to understand the self-evident propositions of nineteenth-century ethics or politics. Even when he is made to realize that his serfs are debased by the laws which he imposes, he cannot (because of his faulty training) regard them as anything but animals. Again, his humanity is not at fault:

> He was born so, educated so, his veins are full of ancestral blood that was rotten with this sort of unconscious brutality brought down from a long procession of hearts that had each done its share toward poisoning the stream.

The cardinal fact, however, is that the king *is* made to understand the nineteenth-century facts of life. Retraining *does* work. After passing through the baptism of slavery and discovering his own humanity, he who was a royal bigot ends as a man.

The king's unrehabilitated subjects are even less perceptive than he. Although victimized by feudal and ecclesiastical brutality, they are no more free from baseless prejudice than their overlords or the "poor white" of the ante bellum South who, debased by the slavery in whose midst they lived, nevertheless died eagerly for its defense. All exhibit the Lecky syndrome: a combination of bad training, fear, and baseless conformity makes them revert to unreasonable behavior. This is the point of the three chapters (XXXI, XXXII, XXXIII) in which the Yankee tries to teach the elements of crackerbarrel economics to the anachronistic village capitalists. Blind to the simplest logic, intimidated by irrational class loyalties, and terrorized by the prospect of having to think for themselves, they become conformists, informers to the very powers which wrong them. The most wretched members of society, the hapless slaves, betray the Boss and the King into slavery, because the latter appear to be nonconformists. "You

must not take any chances on those poor fellows if you can avoid it," says the Yankee.

The fifth and final segment begins with the Yankee's entering the lists against the flower of Arthurian chivalry. His lariat and six-shooter having prevailed over armor and spear, "Knight-errantry was a doomed institution. The march of civilization was begun." The Yankee's revolutionary program, which he clearly restates at this point, was on the high road to success. He envisioned disestablishing the Church and establishing unlimited manhood suffrage when Arthur should die, perhaps in two-score years. (Moses dwelt forty years in the wilderness, rearing a generation which felt no loyalty to Egypt; the Yankee may have reasoned that he needed a similar period to develop a new generation, rooted in the new order and owing no fealty to feudal institutions.)

Although he ultimately "broke the back of knight-errantry" and "exposed the nineteenth-century to the inspection of the sixth," his program ended in dismal failure. In part, this sad turn of events is a tribute to the melancholy conclusion of Malory's tale. But primarily the denouement represents a valid dramatic climax in terms of the theme of reversion. The entire British nation—terrorized by the Church's interdict against all those who supported the Boss's administration—abandons its manhood, cringingly returns to an animal existence, and leaves the Boss with only Clarence and fifty-two teenage supporters, whose non-feudal minds had been molded during the Yankee's tenure of office. The seeming triumph of his program had made him forget for a moment how deeply rooted were the superstitions of the age and that "Habit," in Pudd'nhead Wilson's words, "is habit and not to be flung out the window by any man but coaxed downstairs a step at a time." The level-headed Clarence had to disabuse him of his belief that he had "educated the superstition out of those people"—a delusion which the masses themselves seem to have shared for a time; "it is in their blood and bones," he protested.

This novel's ending ought not to be interpreted, however, as a denial of the possibility of human progress. In the final analysis, Mark Twain does not reject the concept (to cite Pudd'nhead Wilson once again) that "Training is everything." If the peach was once a bitter almond and the cauliflower an uneducated cabbage, may not man hope for improvement through nurture? "Training toward higher and higher and ever higher ideals," Mark Twain concludes in *What Is Man?*, his putative credo of unalloyed despair, "is worth any man's thought and labor and diligence." But man's reliance on the deadweight of superstition, his fear to think independently, and his willingness to support the very forces which debase him have circumscribed his social and moral progress in the thirteen centuries spanned by *A Connecticut Yankee in King Arthur's Court.* (pp. 15-25)

Harold Aspiz, "Lecky's Influence on Mark Twain," in Science and Society, *Vol. XXXI, No. 1, Winter, 1962, pp. 15-25.*

JAMES D. WILLIAMS (essay date 1964)

[*In the following excerpt, Williams suggests that an examination of early drafts of* A Connecticut Yankee in King Arthur's Court *contradicts the widely held view that Twain altered the plot of the novel as a result of his increasing contempt for English society.*]

"I SAW HE MEANT BUSINESS."

Frontispiece by Dan Beard for A Connecticut Yankee in King Arthur's Court.

In 1889, Mark Twain got free advertising for his forthcoming "keen and powerful satire of English Nobility and Royalty" by free-swinging attacks on England and all things un-American. On December 10, for example, in an interview in the New York *Times,* he derided English publishers who refused to print his "utter contempt for their pitiful Lords and Dukes" and then—with notable inconsistency—went on to deplore the dissemination of foreign literature in America. Americans, he asserted, could afford "to look down and spit upon miserable titled nonentities." He was carried away by indignation as he bemoaned the existence of "perfectly respectable women" in America who were willing "to sell themselves to anything bearing the name of Duke." And finally, if we may trust the interviewer, he stated flatly that his purpose in *A Connecticut Yankee* was to "get at" the Englishman by satirizing "the shams, laws, and customs of today under pretense of dealing with the England of the sixth century."

These remarks were in line with the advertising policy Mark Twain and his publisher Fred Hall had agreed on—"whatever makes fun of royalty and nobility . . . will suit the American public well"—and might have been largely a bid for sales. But Mark Twain's letters and notebook entries prove that his Angolophobia was not merely for public consumption. It is now generally agreed that during the late

1880's he went through a phase of extreme hostility to England—especially to English aristocracy—accompanied by high confidence in the beneficence of American democracy, capitalism, and technology. But the precise effect of these shifting opinions on *A Connecticut Yankee* is less easy to determine, although it is clear that Mark Twain's conception of the novel was anything but stable during composition. The statement of intention quoted above, for example, might be contrasted with his 1886 assertion that he was "only after the life of that day, that is all; to picture it; to try to get into it; to see how it feels and seems." Authorial comments such as these have given rise to the current belief that the *Yankee* began as a simple "contrast" but for various reasons—primarily Mark Twain's resentment of English criticisms of America—became a satire after the third chapter had been completed. This view is both critically misleading and unsupported by what we know of the actual planning and revising of *A Connecticut Yankee.*

To begin with, we can establish no point in time, or in the text, as marking a clear change in general intention. Even with the novel nearly half finished, Mark Twain insisted that "fun" was its primary purpose and planned to accompany it with a free copy of Malory. And yet he had long believed that the society of the "Middle Ages" was not simply quaint but radically evil and falsely glamorized. History provided him with intense moral issues as well as opportunities for comic irreverence, and as an artist who delighted in broad strokes he was deeply involved with the past. He had once considered giving a contemporary setting to *The Prince and the Pauper,* but found that it did not seem "real." His favorite "answer" to English critics of America was to refer them to their national past. Even his unwritten but cherished appendix to *A Connecticut Yankee* was simply an attack on the manners and morals of the eighteenth century. It could not have supported his contention that the novel satirized by indirection the "shams, laws and customs of today." Moreover, he made this claim only briefly and at a time when his animosity towards England was being freely vented in notebook entries, letters, and interviews, which apparently afforded him the same sort of relief as did his "unmailed letters."

In *A Connecticut Yankee,* Mark Twain presented a series of pathetic and outrageous scenes of brutal oppression in forms largely non-existent in the England and America of the 1880's. Even his ridicule of such perennial follies as credulity, snobbery, and superstition was cast in terms generally flattering to his readers. He assumed that British criticism of the *Yankee* proceeded from wounded sensibilities, but for most English readers the satire was surely a slap on the wrist rather than a body blow. It was specifically the unavoidable contemporary English parallels to Mark Twain's Arthurdom that inspired English critics to describe the satire in the *Yankee* as "stale," "second-hand," and "very trite."

It is difficult, therefore, to accept [Gladys Bellamy's assertion in her *Mark Twain as a Literary Artist*] that "most critics now agree that *A Connecticut Yankee* was written to point up the injustices both of Victoria's England and of Mark Twain's America." If such agreement exists, it is based on the understanding that what is apparently peripheral in the novel reflects the author's central intention. To classify the *Yankee* as an "inverted satire" is both to misread it and to damn it. In the context of Mark Twain's inveterate antimedievalism, we cannot infer a single initial intention from the series of burlesque "contrasts" which he rarely used but continued to plan almost until the *Yankee* was completed. Ambiguities in tone were present from the beginning, when he outlined a heavily nostalgic love story similar to the Dillsberg legend in *A Tramp Abroad* or planned the destruction of a medieval army by a few men with modern weapons—an "effect" adumbrating the cruelly adolescent "dream of glory" element in the *Yankee.* Perhaps the most significant departure from initial intentions was the decision to submit King Arthur to his own cruel laws, a procedure borrowed from *The Prince and the Pauper.* It should be noted that with the novel half finished, and at a time when he was stuffing his notebooks with scathing attacks on contemporary England, Mark Twain deliberately turned to the sort of historical cruelties which could only blunt and muffle satiric concern with the present.

The current theory that Mark Twain's attitude toward King Arthur and his knights became more severely critical beginning with the fourth chapter mistakes tangential remarks for a major shift in tone. Hank Morgan sees Arthurdom from the beginning in terms of the ante bellum South of *Life on the Mississippi.* The picturesque and legendary Camelot becomes on closer inspection a wretched Arkansas village plus a castle. Hogs wallow in the mud amid hordes of unwashed children. Freemen humbly salute Sir Kay, who contemptuously ignores them. Chained slaves are in evidence. The knights are presented as credulous liars, insensitive to suffering, brainless, verbose, and dirty. Like the village loafers in *Huckleberry Finn,* they delight in dog fights. Hank Morgan's conclusion that he is in an asylum recalls **"The Tournament in A.D. 1870,"** in which Mark Twain labeled the knight "a braggart, a ruffian, a fantastic vagabond and an ignoramus." The fact that the knights are described as unconsciously indelicate in the fourth chapter of the *Yankee* is no sign that Mark Twain's attitude toward them had changed. He had already dubbed them "White Indians," and verbal and sexual indecency had long been part of his catalogue of the evils of an aristocratic past. The first important intrusion of a satiric tone inappropriate to the narrator did not occur until Chapter VIII, a tirade on reverence, nobility, and the Catholic Church. Thereafter, the narrative mask was frequently discarded, and humor often entirely subordinated to moral indignation and pathos. The chapters on Morgan le Fay's dungeons, for example, were written under the influence of a rereading of Carlyle, and Mark Twain himself was troubled by their "funeral seriousness." But his zaniest burlesque continued to crop up in the midst of his angriest, most pathetic, and melodramatic scenes.

Mark Twain claimed he had carefully eliminated passages in the *Yankee* that were potentially offensive to the English, thus suggesting that the original text had a sharper satiric thrust. But the available evidence does not support his assertion that he and Stedman had dug out many "darlings" so that the publisher Chatto would accept the novel. On the contrary, several passages added to the manuscript during revision were among the novel's most direct attacks on royalty and the Church; and one of the latest additions—a passage on the Royal Grant—was a clear sally against a still existing abuse. The manuscript leads one to believe that most cuts in the text were made more with general propriety than national sensibilities in mind. The *Yankee* was advertised as "thoroughly clean, wholesome, humorous, instructive, and patriotic," but Mark Twain's notebook suggestions for direct satire of contemporary England often had decidedly vulgar or sexual overtones. Particularly if one considers discarded plans for the novel as well as eliminated passages, it appears that Mark Twain's chief aims in revision were to tone down some of the wildest burlesque, to eliminate the "vulgar," and to modify attacks on the Church that might also have offended Protestants.

Some discarded burlesque inspirations for the *Yankee* were not unlike incidents in the published novel. Among them was the plan to have the Boss place bets on a hermit during a competition in austerities. Another involved a contest among bards, which the Boss would win by reciting Tennyson and Shakespeare. But a number of the jokes that occurred to Mark Twain during composition undermined whatever unity of character and tone he had managed to establish. For example, the story that the Boss repeats fifteen times at the monastery—until his English audience "disintegrates"—was initially about a "celebrated jumping frog of Calaveras County." And Sandy's version of the same tale originally broke all hearts in the adjacent nunnery. The nuns' tears washed away a wing of the asylum, drowned sixty orphans, and gave Merlin the chance to claim he had started up the fountain. Another briefly considered burlesque impulse was in direct conflict with the romantic nostalgia of the love story. The Boss would sadly forego marriage with the talkative Sandy because of an "obstacle" which would not be overcome until a bout of scarlet fever had left her hilariously deaf and dumb.

Most of the discarded ideas for the *Yankee* stemmed from a fairly mechanical proliferation of burlesque "contrasts" which Mark Twain continued to jot down as late as 1888. At various times he planned to include knights charging a locomotive, getting their picture taken, insuring their armor, "dating" the Lady of Shallott by phone, and engaging in a number of other activities of the "grailing by rail" variety. With fourteen chapters completed, he planned the Boss's introduction of steam engines, fire companies, aluminum, vaccination, and lightning rods, but the whole business of technological innovation failed to catch his deeper interest, and it was probably not until the novel was near completion that he added some summarizing passages on this subject.

The "germ" of the *Yankee* developed into a good example of unrestrained burlesque calmed down in revision. In the earlier version, Sandy threw rocks at Hank's helmet while he called balls and strikes, and only after braining the horse did she manage to jar the helmet loose with the shaft of a lance. An equally unrestrained but funnier account of the Boss's wildly successful farming and real estate speculation in "hermit dirt" was omitted—perhaps as vulgar. Other major elisions were the "Letter from the Recording Angel"—a satire of American business worked into the novel with obvious strain—and the Boss's lengthy and absurd calculations of casualties during the battle of the Sand Belt, which Stedman objected to as "technical humor" and which made a shambles of any significance the final catastrophe was intended to have.

A number of "vulgar" passages were cut from *A Connecticut Yankee,* including some *double entendres* inspired by the tails of Sandy's "princesses," a comparison of hermits and sewers, and several references to nakedness. (Chief among the latter was a passage on the effect of putting undershirts on nude statues, an idea Mark Twain had already presented—using fig leaves—in *A Tramp Abroad.*) Two comments on the sexual immorality of medieval clergy were toned down. All that remains of them are the merry songs of Morgan le Fay's chaplain and the mere presence of a foundling home in the Valley of Holiness. Finally, he eliminated two long passages on the Boss's plan to erect monuments to royal mistresses as the true "divine right" rulers of England. These passages, on which the second paragraph of the *Yankee* preface seems to comment, might have been regarded as particularly offensive to the English, even though Swift, for example, had less humorously made the same point in the previous century; but mistresses, royal or otherwise, were not really appropriate in a thoroughly clean and wholesome book from which such words as "bastard," "prostitute," "rump," "buttocks," "damn," "nipple," "stark naked," "disemboweled," and "devil" had been carefully stricken.

Charles Webster, as the publisher of the Pope's biography, could assure Mark Twain that Catholics did not buy books anyway; but there were a number of passages in the *Yankee* that even Protestants might have found offensive, and while Mark Twain wished to instruct, he had no desire to offend. Nevertheless, he may have agreed with Webster on Catholic reading habits, since on the one hand he inserted in the manuscript the direct and extreme attack on the Catholic Church in Chapter VIII, but on the other omitted the lengthy comparison of Sandy's veneration of pigs with the (Presbyterian) doctrine of infant damnation. The desire to avoid offense may not have been the only reason for cutting the latter passage, in which the Boss suddenly and untypically despises his own feeling of superiority to Sandy. He recalls an American trick of placing a tall mirror at one end of a dimly lit room, so that a stranger assumes it is a door which someone is approaching from the other side. After vainly trying to dodge by his own reflection, the stranger calls it a fool, idiot, and ass before realizing that he is addressing himself. Similarly, the Boss concludes, Sandy slobbering over hogs is simply the mirror image of his recent American Presbyterian self. The lesson that we should at least pretend to honor each other's superstitions is perfectly apt and typical of Mark Twain, but it tends to undercut both the theme of moral progress and the character of the narrator, who was originally conceived as an "innocent" mask for satire of religiosity.

Some other eliminated comments on religion also involved inconsistencies in characterization. Thus it was clearly inappropriate for Sandy to deride burnt offerings and votive candles to the Virgin. The Boss himself was at first envisioned as a "Brother Jonathan," complete with pious ejaculations *à la* George Cable, but either his foolish piety or his increasingly direct comments on religion had to be sacrificed. (At one point, for example, Mark Twain planned to have the Boss convert the hermit Marinel to Presbyterianism as a punishment for his dreadful cures. Marinel would be delighted, since a Presbyterian hermit is a sort of ultimate in the revolting.) Finally, almost all indirect satire of religiosity was cut, and the Boss's Presbyterianism ceased to be a subject of ridicule. The fading of Hank Morgan as an "innocent" point of view for religious satire was paralleled by his increasing historical and literary sophistication. Mark Twain continued to use him as an "ignoramus" for indirect satire on such subjects as chromos, but verbal revisions show that he often gave his narrator a deliberately literate or even literary style, and late additions like the passage on the joys of intellectual work suggest how little concern he finally had for his original conception of a shrewd and pious buffoon.

Many of the undeveloped or discarded ideas for satire of England in the *Yankee* did not occur to Mark Twain until 1888 or later and were frequently of dubious propriety. The subject of Anglo-American marriages, for example, provoked his unrestrained contempt. He thought of having market reports on rich girls from a republic and a bench show of mongrel children, in his notebook he went so far as to suggest that the English dukes "bought" by American heiresses were for the most part syphilitic. A less virulent idea from 1887—the Boss's still undetected substitution of chimpanzees for the royal family—appeared in the novel in the moderated form of Clarence's proposal for a family of royal cats.

Discarded but unobjectionable ideas for satire of contemporary England involved such relatively minor "abuses" as the use of lithographed sermons, the sale of advowsons, and the privateness of English public parks. But such topics must have struck him as rather tame, and as late as the summer of 1889 he was hoping to add to the *Yankee* a chapter in which women would be stripped and whipped, though the only possible contemporary reference was to Russia. Clearly, Mark Twain's appetite for scenes of extreme brutality and pathos contributed to the frustration of his belated attempts to satirize "the shams, laws, and customs" of contemporary England.

The notebook entries, the manuscript, and the published novel do not support the thesis that *A Connecticut Yankee* began simply as a humorous contrast and then—because of a conscious change in intention—became at a specific point an "inverted satire." Throughout the period of composition,

Mark Twain's ability to resist the "damned human race" theme was uncertain, but specific outbursts against contemporary England were for the most part too late, or too tame, or too indelicate for inclusion in the novel. The *Yankee* works out in action ideas on chivalry, slavery, and progress which had been dominant in Mark Twain's thinking for twenty years. His Anglophobia, on the other hand, had shallow roots and was poor in associations. (Even in 1883, after all, he had seen England as the greatest of all nations.) Consequently, and despite his claims to the contrary, he seems to have had more trouble *including* satire of England in his novel than in toning it down or eliminating it. His 1889 references to the *Yankee* as an attack on England were certainly not detached estimates of his intentions during composition nor of his actual accomplishment. And however great may be our interest in the conflicting historical and social philosophies underlying the *Yankee,* the novel survives neither as a theory of history nor as an "inverted satire," but rather as a giddy, shrewd, and violent realization of that ordinary fantasy in which a hostile world is reduced to impotence before the unchanged yet conquering dreamer. (pp. 288-97)

> James D. Williams, "Revision and Intention in Mark Twain's 'A Connecticut Yankee'," in American Literature, *Vol. XXXVI, No. 3, November, 1964, pp. 288-97.*

HENRY NASH SMITH   (essay date 1964)

[*Smith is an American critic and educator who has written extensively on the works of major American novelists. In the following excerpt, he examines the narrative weaknesses created by Twain's ambivalent attitude toward the subjects of his satire in* A Connecticut Yankee in King Arthur's Court.]

Mark Twain's *A Connecticut Yankee in King Arthur's Court* is one of the most characteristic productions of the decade when Americans generally first realized they were entering the modern world. The Civil War had given a decided impetus to the mechanization of industry in this country, and the process had gained speed in the post-Civil War decades. By the 1880's a revolutionary change began to be apparent to most people in the United States—not only factory workers and dwellers in the industrial cities, but also farmers, especially in the West, who were using machines to expand agricultural production and found themselves dependent on the new railway systems to send their crops to markets in the East and in Europe.

The pace and scope of industrialization placed unprecedented strains on American society and American culture. The traditional system of values, the beliefs about men, institutions, and the universe that had guided the lives of earlier generations, were coming to seem irrelevant. New conceptions of value, a new ethics, a new philosophy had to be created. As always, imaginative writers had the task of synthesizing fact and theory into images that could be understood by the public at large. Mark Twain's *A Connecticut Yankee* is an effort to perform this task. Although it is basically comic in conception and contains some of his most irresistible humor, it is of all Mark Twain's books the most urgently focused on the state of the nation and of the world at the moment of writing. The burlesque tale expresses a philosophy of history and a theory of the capitalist system created by the industrial revolution—and the story breaks under the pres-

sure of the thought and emotion that the writer poured into it. (pp. 6-7)

The diverse strains of thought and feeling that converge in the character of Mark Twain's Yankee are all aspects of American self-consciousness in the later nineteenth century, but we can distinguish two clusters of images embodied in this protagonist that derive from radically different sources and are never fully synthesized. In some of his roles the Yankee is a figure out of the past. He is an avatar of the American Adam dwelling in the Garden of the World, whose vague but resplendent features can be discerned in Cooper's Natty Bumppo, the yeoman farmer dear to agrarian tradition, Frederick Jackson Turner's frontiersman, and the idealized "self " of Whitman's *Leaves of Grass*. Because the Yankee is a transatlantic innocent confronting an ancient and corrupt Europe, he also resembles the narrator of *The Innocents Abroad.* In fact, he belongs to the long line of vernacular protagonists in Mark Twain's books which includes the tenderfoot in *Roughing It,* the cub pilot in *Life on the Mississippi* and, of course, Huck Finn. The Yankee's colloquial language, his lowly rural origins, his uncultivated practical common sense, and his magnificent indifference toward the pretensions of titled aristocrats all attest to this side of his ancestry. Yet he also embodies significant traits that are foreign to Mark Twain's earlier vernacular characters. One of these novelties is his command of industrial technology. Another is his highly developed political awareness. He is a constitutional and legal theorist and is well versed in the outstanding events of modern history. He knows what he is trying to do in a way that sets him apart from his predecessors.

Although the Yankee is a philistine with reference to the arts, his consciousness of his historical mission makes him an intellectual. Unlike Huck Finn, who is not at ease with concepts, the Yankee is passionately devoted to general ideas such as progress, civilization, justice, equality before the law, universal suffrage, representative government, free trade, and separation of church and state. His principles are American in the sense that they were cherished by virtually all Americans in the nineteenth century, but they are too abstract for folklore and too serious to be useful in comedy, oral or otherwise. In characterizing Hank Morgan, Mark Twain attempted to engraft upon an almost entirely nonintellectual tradition of folk humor an ideology of enlightenment and republicanism.

In the broadest sense, we may say that Mark Twain was trying to depict a protagonist who represented the American common man functioning within an exemplary industrial and political order which he himself created. To put the matter in yet more general terms, Mark Twain was asking himself whether the American Adam, who began as representative of a preindustrial order, could make the transition to urban industrialism and enter upon a new phase of his existence by becoming a capitalist hero. Many of the confusions in the character and actions of Hank Morgan—particularly the extent to which he both is and is not an entrepreneur and businessman—take on clarity and meaning if we examine them in the light of this over-all intention. I shall therefore examine first the vernacular elements in Mark Twain's Yankee and then the functions dictated by his ideology.

The vernacular humor of Hank Morgan is his most obvious trait. The device of burlesquing Malory creates almost endless comic opportunities in the handling of romantic conventions of chivalry as if they governed everyday life in Arthurian Britain. To the newcomer from the nineteenth century the inhabitants naturally seem at first simply lunatics. Later he thinks of them as "big boobies" or "white Indians" or tame animals. He analogizes their yarns about forests and enchantments drear with tall tales of the American West, ridicules Malory's endless paratactic sentences as a medium of conversation, takes a common-sense reductionist view of the Grail quest, and notes the impropriety of having high-born damsels accompany knights-errant on long overland journeys without a chaperon. At its best, the burlesque is so brilliant that it disarms criticism, as in the excursion to the enchanted pigsty.

As the story develops, however, the burlesque leads into a bitter vein of satire growing out of the fact that the narrator is an American in conflict with Englishmen. Mark Twain becomes preoccupied with American resentments against nineteenth-century Britain. (pp. 67-70)

Hank Morgan as quintessential American philistine and democratic has behind him the weight of all Mark Twain's animus against genteel attitudes. The Yankee invader of Arthur's kingdom is "low" in tone. (Dan Beard, the illustrator of the book, appropriately shows him dressed in a loud checked suit and plug hat, swaggering with his hands in his pockets, putting his feet on the furniture, and in one of the most memorable drawings tickling the nose of a gigantic British lion with a straw.) Like the narrator of *The Innocents Abroad,* the Yankee is irreverent because he mocks at the shadowy grandeurs and romantic associations of the age of chivalry in a period when Tennyson's *Idyls of the King* and "Galahad," Lowell's *The Vision of Sir Launfal,* and the paintings of Burne-Jones had canonized feudal knighthood as one of the major symbols of genteel values.

It is significant that on both sides of the Atlantic, the figure of the knight was accepted as the antithesis of the sordid businessman. A reviewer of *A Connecticut Yankee* for the Edinburgh *Scots Observer* called the book "a 'lecture' in dispraise of monarchical institutions and religious establishments as the roots of all evil, and in praise of Yankee 'cuteness and Wall Street chicanery as compared to the simple fidelity . . . of the knightly ideal." The London *Daily Telegraph* stated the question posed by the book as follows: "Which, then, is to be most admired—the supremacy of a knight or the success of a financier? Under which king will the Americans serve—the ideal or the real? Will they owe allegiance to King Arthur or Jay Gould?" In this country, Sidney Lanier's long poem "The Symphony" opposed chivalry to all-blighting trade in a fashion that merges chivalry with Christianity and makes trade the root of all evil.

It will thus be evident that the burlesque of Malory engaged cultural issues of great intensity. As adversary of the Knights of the Round Table the Yankee expresses . . . irreverence. . . . His aggressive philistinism tends to identify him with the anti-poetic, anti-sentimental businessman. And all these traits cohere about a tendentious image of the democratic American patriot conceived as the antithesis of the typical British aristocrat. Beard was amply justified in making Hank Morgan explicitly into Uncle Sam. In the final sequence the Yankee is suddenly supplied with a suggestive goatee and striped trousers, and he becomes at last fully allegorical with the addition of a top hat bearing a plume labeled "Macaroni." In this drawing the Yankee bestrides a book labeled "Common Sense" and levels a quill pen like a lance at the midriff of a bloated aristocrat suggesting Henry VIII.

But Mark Twain was not prepared at the outset to accept the full implications of the Anglophobia he had invoked in the creation of his protagonist. It will be recalled that in the early chapters he pays rather incongruous tribute to the dignity and grandeur of Launcelot and Galahad; and even after the Yankee has begun his attack on feudalism we are given occasional glimpses of noble behavior such as King Arthur's unhesitating exposure of himself to smallpox when he bears in his arms a dying child. By and large, however, the vestiges of reverence for the chivalric ideal are obliterated by the Yankee's increasingly violent polemic against the feudal order. In comic terms this takes the form of a campaign to make chivalry ridiculous. The Yankee employs knights as traveling salesmen for stove polish and mouth wash, or as conductors on railway trains. They are mounted on bicycles; they play baseball in armor; they are frightened by the pipe smoke issuing from the visor of his helmet, as if he were a fire-breathing dragon. The comic contrast between medieval and modern manners rests on the assumption that American common sense and commercial realism are axiomatically superior to the other-worldly ineptitude of the knights. The businessman is the moral norm invoked by the satire: his unromantic usefulness throws into relief the impractical absurdity of feudalism. This is the general mood of Mark Twain's readings before the Military Service Institute in 1886, and the newspaper accounts make clear that not only the audience of officers, businessmen, and politicians but also the reporters were enchanted by the implied endorsement of American Gilded Age culture and the businessman ideal.

The mockery of feudalism could of course readily move beyond vernacular comedy to overt hostility. We recall that, especially toward the end of the book, the knights become simply the enemy, to be blown up by dynamite bombs or shot with revolvers or, at the very last, destroyed in a mass slaughter. These expressions of aggressive feeling in the plot are supported by frequent denunciations of the harsh laws and the caste system of Arthur's kingdom. The book amply justifies Mark Twain's description of it to his English publisher as "a Yankee mechanic's say against monarchy and its several natural props." But the values embodied in the character of the Yankee are too largely taken for granted, and the "say against monarchy" replaces the imaginative mode of comedy with mere rhetoric. (pp. 72-6)

Simply as a literary idea, the notion of viewing the European past through the eyes of an adult spokesman for the American vernacular tradition was as promising as any Mark Twain had ever hit upon. It was a misfortune that he allowed himself to be diverted from his original plan into the well-worn ruts of Anglophobia and sentimental melodrama. Both the attack on nineteenth-century England and the doctrinaire polemic against feudalism were essentially irrelevant to the imaginative core of the story. The crude hostility to which Mark Twain committed himself in this fashion ruled out any approach to the ironic complexity of vision that he had achieved in *Huckleberry Finn.*

The transition from a comic to a melodramatic mode . . . indicates that Mark Twain had begun to draw upon a store of ideas and attitudes quite different from the motives he had taken over from native backwoods humor. He had implied as much when he told [a correspondent] he was writing a contrast of civilizations. The contrast, of course, was between poverty-stricken, ignorant, tyrannical feudalism and the enlightened industrial capitalism of the nineteenth century.

Mark Twain, in common with virtually all his contemporaries, held to a theory of history that placed these two civilizations along a dimension stretching from a backward abyss of barbarism toward a Utopian future of happiness and justice for all mankind. The code name for the historical process thus displayed was progress, and in nineteenth-century America it had the status of a secular theology.

The current notion of progress had a considerable basis in Mark Twain's own experience. For he had himself passed from the tranquil preindustrial world of Hannibal in the 1840's to Hartford in the highly industrialized Connecticut Valley, where during most of the 1880's he had been preoccupied with what he considered the most amazing of modern inventions, the Paige typesetter. The sixth-century Britain of Hank Morgan's adventures shows many points of similarity to the slaveholding Missouri of Mark Twain's childhood. The prewar South, for example, is described in *Life on the Mississippi* as having been debilitated by a chivalry-disease contracted from reading Walter Scott's medieval romances, and in *Pudd'nhead Wilson* Mark Twain would implant a hollow but fanatically cherished ideal of chivalry in Dawson's Landing, one of his many versions of Hannibal. The institution of slavery introduced unhistorically into Arthurian Britain is documented with incidents drawn from the supposedly authentic *Autobiography* of Charles Ball, an American Negro slave. Hank Morgan explicitly compares the peasants of Abblasoure Manor with the misguided poor whites who served in the ranks of the Confederate Army to defend an aristocratic order that kept them degraded and impoverished. Most significant of all, perhaps, the landscape of Britain is described by means of words and images identical with those Mark Twain would apply in his *Autobiography* to the Quarles Farm near Hannibal that he had known as a boy.

Thus Mark Twain's own observation had deeply impressed upon him the pattern of rapid transition from a backward agrarian society with corrupt institutions and ideals to an industrial society enjoying all the benefits of machine technology and enlightened republican government. The contrast between medieval and modern civilizations was, accordingly, the obvious conceptual framework for the Yankee's adventures in Arthurian Britain.

The most obvious exemplification of progress in the story is the Yankee's technological achievements—his creation of a complex of factories, railways, and telegraph and telephone lines. This aspect of the contrast between civilizations is an allegory of the industrial revolution; its emphasis is primarily economic. But the contrast also has a political aspect in the depiction of outrageous laws by means of which the nobles of Arthur's realm oppress the people. In this respect the story is an allegory of the French Revolution, which the Yankee mentions with enthusiasm.

Hank Morgan was meant to be a representative American both in his practical knowledge of machines and in his devotion to republican institutions. But at different times Mark Twain emphasized first one aspect and then the other. His introductory remarks for readings from the unfinished manuscript before a Baltimore audience in January 1888 stressed the Yankee's technology:

> Conceive of the blank & sterile ignorance of that day, & contrast it with the vast & many-sided knowledge of this. Consider the trivial miracles & wonders wrought by the humbug magicians & enchanters of that old day, & contrast them with the mighty miracles wrought by science in our day of steam & electricity. Take a practical man, thoroughly equipped with the scientific [magic] enchantments of our day & set him down alongside of Merlin the head magician of Arthur's time, & what sort of a show would Merlin stand?

Here, evidently, "civilization" is equated with knowledge, and knowledge with technology. Chapter X of the novel, describing the creation of the Yankee's hidden industrial system, is entitled "Beginnings of Civilization." To mention only one other passage, when Clarence reports his preparations for a last stand in Merlin's cave, he explicitly refers to "all our vast factories, mills, workshops, magazines, etc." as "our civilization."

After the book was published Mark Twain continued on various occasions to interpret "civilization" in similar fashion. Thus in an unpublished reply to Paul Bourget's criticism of the United States (probably written in 1894) he sets out to list the components of modern civilization, most of which he claims as American contributions. The first five items are political and legal: "Political Liberty," "Religious Liberty," "Reduction of Capital Penalties," "Man's Equality before the Law," and "Woman's rights." But No. 6 is "Application of Anaesthesia in Surgery." And with No. 7 ("The First Approximately Rational Patent Law") and No. 8 ("Development of Patents") he begins a list of mechanical inventions that reaches almost one hundred items before the writer begins to tire of the game.

Despite Mark Twain's stated beliefs, however, the theme of technological advance is only meagerly dealt with in *A Connecticut Yankee.* Man-factories are mentioned, but the only products of the Yankee's system of technical education that appear on stage are the fifty-two shadowy boy technicians in the cave at the end, none of them given an identity or even a name, and none represented as performing any concrete action. Despite Mark Twain's occasional efforts to give fictional substance to the Yankee's mechanical prowess, he actually performs no constructive feat except the restoration of the holy well; and it will be recalled that the technology in this episode does not go into repairing the well, but into the fraudulent display of fireworks with which he awes the populace. (pp. 81-6)

The inadequate development of the theme of technology seriously impairs the contrast of civilizations in the story. Mark Twain devotes much more attention to material that is in a broad sense political—the various procedures for demonstrating the evils of feudalism and the merits of republican government. Yet here also he runs into difficulties. The polemic against feudalism implies an unqualified endorsement of the American system of government, which the Yankee makes explicit by comments such as his quotation of the Constitution of Connecticut to the effect that "all political power is inherent in the people." In the abstract, his program rests on the assumption that under free political institutions, industrialization will achieve Utopian results without interference by the state: the classical doctrine of laissez-faire liberalism. [In *Mark Twain: Social Philosopher* (1962)] Mr. Louis J. Budd has demonstrated that, generally speaking, Mark Twain shared the belief in this doctrine held in his day by all but the most extreme left-wing thinkers.

Yet there are a number of indications in *A Connecticut Yankee* that he was troubled by growing doubts concerning the liberal creed. Like Warner and Howells, he had misgivings about the unrestrained operation of the profit motive. His uneasiness appears in his ambiguous handling of the Yankee's commercial ambitions. The early chapters present the protagonist as a cunning operator bent on making money. When Hank Morgan says that if an eclipse of the moon had been imminent he could have sold it short, or that "Merlin's stock was flat," the most obvious effect is of comic incongruity between this jargon of the stock market and the tone of Malory's fictive world. Nevertheless, the cumulative effect of the Yankee's commercial imagery is to suggest detachment on Mark Twain's part. The Yankee's exploitation of the eclipse is of course justifiable as a means of saving his life, but the manner in which he takes advantage of the situation to make himself economic master of the country seems somewhat cynical. The very title "The Boss" in which he takes so much pleasure has unpleasant overtones ("Boss" Tweed of Tammany had been a household word in the United States since the 1860's). Only later, when the Yankee becomes preoccupied with his attack on feudalism and loses interest in economic activity, does Mark Twain identify himself with the narrator. And even then his distaste for merely commercial motives continues to reappear occasionally—as for example, in the Yankee's gleeful and self-satisfied account of his debasement of the currency or, more strongly, in the complacency of his remark that when he noticed signs of a breakdown in the hermit harnessed to a sewing machine, "I stocked the business and unloaded, taking Sir Bors de Ganis into camp financially along with certain of his friends: for the works stopped within a year, and the good saint got him to his rest."

On the other hand, in the final sequence, when Launcelot buys up wildcat railway stock and bankrupts Sir Agravaine and Sir Mordred, Clarence comments with the writer's apparent approval: "He skinned them alive, and they deserved it—anyway, the whole kingdom rejoiced." Many of the references to speculation here and elsewhere have a certain innocence, as if Mark Twain were simply amusing himself by applying to the Knights of the Round Table terms borrowed from the stock market. This vein of humor harks back to the irresponsible gaiety of his journalism in the 1860's. The connection with earlier comic devices is particularly close in the Yankee's casual comparison of his own plans with Joseph's "splendid financial ingenuities." Such verbal horseplay may well have had no connection in the writer's mind with the realities of Gilded Age financial piracies. Yet Mark Twain undoubtedly felt some of the distaste for large-scale speculation that was so deep-seated in Warner and Howells. More than one reviewer of *A Connecticut Yankee* noticed that Beard had given the instantly recognizable features of Jay Gould to a slave driver represented in a full-page drawing as standing with a whip in his hand and one foot planted on the breast of a prostrate female slave. Sylvester Baxter referred to the picture and characterized Gould as a notorious billionaire and stock gambler. The satirical allusion had no basis in the text, but when Mark Twain was interviewed by a reporter for the New York *Times,* he said he was "delighted at the way the artist has entered into the spirit of the book in executing the illustrations, and pointed specially to a fine portrait of Jay Gould in the capacity of 'the slave driver'."

In later years Mark Twain became convinced that financial tycoons had had an evil influence on American civilization. During the last decade of his life he jotted down a revealing page of notes for an essay on recent American history:

THE START. Benton—Pac. RR—only 3 rich men

then, of very humble origin: Astor, skins, Girard (college—stolen) Vand. boating—in Cin (Longworth) . . . not another in Amer. Vand. first to consolidate a trust. Gould followed CIVIL WAR & California sudden-riches disease with a *worse* one, s.r. [secured riches?] by swindling & buying courts. Cal. & Gould were the beginners of the moral rot, they were the worst things that ever befel Amer; they created the hunger for wealth when the Gr. Civ. had just completed its youth & its ennobling WAR—strong, pure, clean, ambitious, impressionable—ready to make choice of a life-course & move with a rush; *they & circumstances* determined the choice. . . . Circumst. after Vand. wrought railways into systems; then Standard Oil; Steel Trust; & Carnegie. CALIF—causes Pac. R. R. UNCLE TOM WAR TELEGRAPH. to *restrict* slavery—circum. *abolished* it. GOULD, R. by theft.—R. R. wrecker & buyer of courts. CABLE. CONSOLIDATION invented by Vander. Other RRs follow. STAND. O. begins CON of *Manufac.* FILIPINE & S. A.—CHINA. MORGAN consolidates steel, copper, cables, ships, the WORLD's commerce—Europe began to decline.

At this point the projected essay looks toward a future in which Morgan takes over all power in the United States, "meditates a monarchy," and in short consummates the liquidation of the American republican experiment. For our purposes it is enough to notice that Gould is bracketed with the California gold rush as one of the two "worst things that ever befel America."

Although Mark Twain may not have reached this degree of hostility toward financiers at the time he wrote *A Connecticut Yankee,* the transformation of the Round Table into a stock exchange and the outbreak of civil war in the kingdom as a result of financial rivalries cannot be wholly devoid of meaning. Just as the Yankee's technological revolution tends to dwindle into a rather childish contest with Merlin, so his creation of an industrial system leads to economic anarchy rather than an orderly and prosperous society. Mark Twain's difficulties in plot construction were paralleled by difficulties in developing the themes of his story. Hank Morgan's vernacular common sense and freedom from pretense veered off into Anglophobia. His plan for proclaiming a republic was frustrated by the operations of speculators. These perversions of the thematic pattern bespeak a crisis in Mark Twain's thought and feeling about progress, a crisis so severe that it led to an almost complete loss of control over his materials. The world of the novel falls into a chaos which is reflected in the diction, the tone, the very rhythms of the prose. The contrast of civilizations drops from sight, and the Yankee's Promethean mission ends in absolute failure. (pp. 90-5)

Mark Twain could not work out adequately his contrast of medieval and modern civilizations because the protagonist who represented the modern world in the story was an inadequate vehicle for depicting industrial capitalism. In more metaphorical terms, the American Adam representing an older agrarian or pre-agrarian order could not be made into a Prometheus creating and administering an economic system comparable in complexity to the actual economic system of post-Civil War America.

Adam and Prometheus—American Adam and American Prometheus—are cultural symbols, and to state Mark Twain's dilemma in these terms is to imply that the failure of his undertaking in *A Connecticut Yankee* was due to forces affecting all perceptive men of his generation—including for example Henry Adams, who found that the modern world resisted his effort to interpret it by means of scientific concepts, and Frederick Jackson Turner, whose archetypal frontiersman was even less able than Hank Morgan to function in an urban industrial society because he knew nothing about machine technology. (pp. 104-05)

Yet if Hank Morgan's story can be read as a parable dealing with the same historical subject as *The Education of Henry Adams,* his defeat is also due to a conflict within Mark Twain's mind between a conscious endorsement of progress and a latent revulsion against the non-human imperatives of the machine and all it stood for in the way of discipline and organization. Again, Mark Twain was not alone in experiencing such emotions; much evidence has been gathered to demonstrate the existence of a "covert culture" in this country from the early nineteenth century onwards which associated machines with images of destruction and menace. But his latent hostility to machines and technological progress was unusually strong. Even though he disclaimed exact fidelity to history, his choice of medieval Britain as the setting for his fable meant that he could not hope to represent the Yankee's undertaking as permanently successful. Mark Twain may not have realized fully at the outset what the implications of this decision were, but they must have been present in his mind in some fashion. Let me mention . . . the evidences in the story itself that he felt a nostalgia for a half-remembered, half-imagined preindustrial world: the images associated with his uncle's farm near Hannibal that crop up so vividly in his descriptions of landscapes in Arthurian Britain; the hints that the Yankee's industrial system is a potential menace; the consistently destructive effects of technology in the story; and above all the strange ending of the framework narrative, in which the dying Yankee proclaims himself to be "a stranger and forlorn" in the modern world, "with an abyss of thirteen centuries yawning . . . between me and all that is dear to me, all that could make life worth the living!"

These words are addressed in delirium to his beloved Sandy; his yearning for his Lost World is expressed in conventional terms, but it is nevertheless erotic. Since the Lost World is also identified with memories of childhood, one might conjecture that Mark Twain's latent hostility to industrialism is related to the psychological conflict between Eros and civilization that Herbert Marcuse has explored. But the prelogical fantasies of this sort are buried too deeply to be more than glimpsed. The overt narrative presents a conflict expressed in terms more congruous with Hank Morgan's announced effort to bring enlightenment and progress to medieval Britain. He identifies the force that has defeated him as "superstition," the structure of habit imposed on all men by the conditions of their lives in society. Another name for this ineradicable evil is "training," the conditioning that implants reverence for established authority in every man's mind from childhood. The brute fact is that men love their chains and turn against the saviors who would force freedom on them. In the final sequence of the novel, the human fear of rationality seems categorical and primal: it is a secularized version of Original Sin, and no means of redemption is in sight.

Mark Twain's proclamation of this doctrine through a protagonist with whom he is now fully identified reveals an absolute despair. It is true that his comments on the book after it was finished show he was not fully conscious of its meaning. Nevertheless, at some point in the composition of this fable

he had passed the great divide in his career as a writer. What had happened to him was too complex to be made out at this distance in time, but one aspect of it is clear. When he found it impossible to show how the values represented by his vernacular protagonist could survive in an industrial society, he lost his faith in the value system of that society. Henceforth he worked as a writer in a kind of spiritual vacuum. His imagination was virtually paralyzed. He was never again able to reach the level of his achievement in *Adventures of Huckleberry Finn.* Frustrated in his attempt to come to terms with the industrial revolution, he gave up the modern world for lost, and during the rest of his career devoted most of his energy to composing variations on the theme expressed in his slogan of "the damned human race." That indomitable writer's imagination of his spent itself for two decades in a series of demonstrations that, as the dying Yankee believed, the world is too absurd to be anything but a dream. (pp. 105-08)

> *Henry Nash Smith, in his* Mark Twain's Fable of Progress: Political and Economic Ideas in "A Connecticut Yankee," *Rutgers University Press, 1964, 116 p.*

GERALD ALLEN (essay date 1966)

[*In the following excerpt, Allen discusses what he views as Twain's failure to formulate a consistent attitude toward either the sixth or the nineteenth century in* A Connecticut Yankee in King Arthur's Court.]

In recent years there has been no dearth of commentary on Mark Twain's *A Connecticut Yankee in King Arthur's Court,* yet there is a surprising divergence of method and opinion in what has been said. Critics have examined this increasingly puzzling book in terms of Twain's view of history, his attitudes during the composition, and the curiously ironic turns of the story, but satisfactory evaluations of the work as a whole have proved difficult. There is ample reason to believe that when Mark Twain set out to write *A Connecticut Yankee* he planned to expose those "ungentle laws and customs" of predemocratic society by contrast to nineteenth-century America. He began by transporting his Yankee, Hank Morgan, backwards in time to a world which was a mixture of Arthurian and medieval England. As his work progressed, Twain became fully aware of the satiric possibilities at his disposal. Hank Morgan's jibes at the society in which he found himself became more pointed, and the book as a whole seemed to orient itself towards a direct attack on the feudal past. But if readers were expecting only anti-English invective from *A Connecticut Yankee* they soon realized their mistake when the book was published in 1889. Twain's satire had a double edge. American reformers at once hailed the book as a new *Looking Backward,* and reviewers delighted in making Twain's criticisms of contemporary American life explicit. Twain himself was pleased by the illustrations, which were made by the socialist Dan Beard. Beard's illustrations constituted a rather more direct anti-American satire than anything in Twain's story, for one drawing of a slave-driver was soon recognized as a caricature of Jay Gould. Thus in its final form *A Connecticut Yankee* is an ambivalent work. It proclaims itself as an attack on outmoded (un-American) social customs and then, almost in spite of itself, turns into a commentary on the very society which it had meant to extol—an irony of which Twain may or may not have been aware. Mark Twain's Yankee arrives in sixth-century England, he rails against feudal and ecclesiastical injustices, and he vows to replace them with the American Utopia of the nineteenth century. But almost as soon as Hank Morgan's "new deal" goes into effect its inadequacies begin to manifest themselves. After an encouraging start, the situation grows steadily worse, and at last the Church marshals its forces against the Yankee. He is finally brought down to defeat in a costly battle. In spite of his confident boasting, Hank Morgan is able to bring little more than confusion to England. His project is an utter failure.

Because of the ambiguous direction of the satire in *A Connecticut Yankee,* readers have often not known just what to make of the book. Is it complimenting or condemning America, or is Twain himself confused? The ambiguity is genuine, as several studies have shown by an examination of the book within the context of Mark Twain's thought and development as a writer. From this point of view, the uncertainties of intent in *A Connecticut Yankee* appear to reflect the author's own doubts as he wavered between a boisterous assertion of the values of American culture and a fundamentally pessimistic attitude towards human nature. Since it embodies both alternatives, the book is found to be as inconsistent as its author and hence, in spite of its attractiveness, a failure. But in this and other views the salient feature of *A Connecticut Yankee* is either passed over lightly or neglected altogether. Why should Twain and his book be inconsistent in this way, and what does such an inconsistency suggest about the cultural ambience in which it was written? Within a cultural context the inconsistencies of *A Connecticut Yankee* are not so much faults as they are features of considerable importance. I do not suggest that the book should be read as a cultural expression simply to demonstrate that yet another reading is possible. This would be pointless, since, in spite of its fine comedy and intriguing implications, it is (at best) no masterpiece. *A Connecticut Yankee* deserves the first attention of anyone interested in late nineteenth-century American literature because of what it says about that literature. In its ragged but surprisingly complete way, the book expresses more consistently and engagingly than any other work the seminal attitude of American writers between 1870 and 1910. In a time when the old ideals of progress were being subjected to the experiences of the Civil War, political corruption, and massive industrialization, Twain is completely in tune.

The voice of the Yankee is, throughout the book, that of the American Man epitomized. At the outset, Hank Morgan proclaims himself as such, and in the process he reveals both his strengths and his weaknesses: "I am a Yankee of the Yankees—and practical; yes, and nearly barren of sentiment, I suppose—or poetry, in other words. . . . Why, I could make anything a body wanted—anything in the world, it didn't make any difference what." In his first utterance Hank Morgan embodies the ambiguous equation of material and total progress which lurked in the nineteenth century's, and Twain's, world view. In the flush of his success with machines, he believes that he can provide for any of man's wants. This generalization of the Yankee's statement may seem crude, and yet it is likely that in the nineteenth century the fallacy of such reasoning would have seemed less apparent, or, perhaps, less significant. Machines had indeed provided for many of man's wants for the first time. The Yankee's belief that he could "make anything a body wanted" turns out to be mistaken, though it encourages him to undertake his ambitious project. His failure is really a failure of knowledge, or, more disastrously, it is the failure which comes from acting on a false assumption of knowledge. The Yankee, not

unlike his intellectual ancestors of the Enlightenment, confidently believes that he knows all of the laws which regulate human conduct. His confidence is so great that he is unable to suspect that his system may not be comprehensive. It is, in fact, those aspects of human nature beyond the limitations of his knowledge which reduce his plans to nothing.

The inadequacies of the Yankee's approach become apparent almost as soon as he begins his work in the sixth century. They are doubly harmful because they cause him to misinterpret both himself and the people around him. There are a number of incidents which suggest that his motives are not fully explained by what ought to be a reasonable, benevolent concern for humanity. "If," he concludes after finding himself in England, "it was really the sixth century, all right, I didn't want any softer thing: I would boss the whole country inside of three months." Such a statement casts some doubt on his benevolence. Though Twain's thesis would demand a typical nineteenth-century man to rise above any man of the sixth century, there is something unfair or sinister about the way the Yankee seizes power. He does it not so much by absolute ability as by the mere fact of his cultural superiority. In effect, he has no competition other than what at first appears to be the negligible amount offered by Merlin, the court magician. Worse still, he jealously guards his monopoly on technological knowledge. With a keen sense for the theatrical, he disguises his scientific ability as magic, and he maintains his position in the kingdom only by keeping the people ignorant of the rational basis for his extraordinary powers. Even to the elect, the students of his Man-factory, he tries to maintain a certain aura of supernatural power. He rises to a position of authority by perpetrating a brilliant hoax on the bewildered society of the sixth century, and, in effect, he becomes the kind of absolute ruler he claims to despise most.

Mark Twain's humor in *A Connecticut Yankee* has always accounted for a large part of the enormous popularity of the book. Yet the ambivalence which is apparent in the Yankee's motives is also found in his comic actions. Beneath the theatrical effect, what he calls the "circus" side of his nature, there often lie curiously incongruous implications of cruelty and inhumanity. In a last minute show of ingenuity, for example, the Yankee blows up a group of knights, who are charging towards him and King Arthur, with a dynamite bomb. Similarly, he agrees with Morgan Le Fay, "Mrs. Le Fay," as he calls her, that the musicians in her castle should be hanged for their hideous rendition of "In the Sweet Bye and Bye." Finally, he decides once and for all to "break the back of knight-errantry," and he does it by shooting Sir Sagramor and nine other challengers in a tournament with a revolver. Twain's unfailingly comic presentation of these situations glosses over the element of potent evil in the Yankee's actions. To anyone who cares to look beyond the comedy, these scenes suggest the familiar lesson of power misused. This lesson, moreover, is not altogether lost on the Arthurians themselves. The king insists that Hank Morgan accept a title, but Hank consistently refuses, saying that the only valid title is one which comes from the people. The title which the people choose rings forth with full irony. It is "the Boss," the classic form of address which slaves used to their masters and the term which the American population at large used to refer to corrupt politicians. Their choice of title is a telling indication of their attitude towards the mechanical wizard from the nineteenth century.

The confines of the Yankee's ideological knowledge limit his interpretation of the people around him just as they limit his understanding of himself. He is constantly frustrated by the inability of the Arthurians to think in a logical way, and their failure almost always sends him into a rage. The Yankee's conversations with Sandy mark the fruitless confrontation of the rational and the primitive mind. When Sandy notes that Morgan Le Fay's castle is "many" leagues away, the Yankee doggedly demands, "*How* many?" to which Sandy can only reply:

> Ah, fair sir, it were woundily hard to tell, they are so many, and do so lap the one upon the other, and being made all in the same image and tincted with the same color, one may not know the one league from its fellow, nor how to count them except they be taken apart, and ye wit well it were God's work to do that.

The Yankee in turn expects that she can tell him the direction of Morgan's castle, but Sandy is no help on this matter either: "Ah, please you, sir, it hath no direction from here; by reason that the road lieth not straight, but turneth evermore; wherefore the direction of its place abideth not."

This insistence that all experience be subject to measure and reason explains in part the Yankee's attitudes towards the society of the sixth century. It is an attitude which fails to do that society full justice. The recurrent metaphor for describing the people he finds is the metaphor of childhood. To Hank Morgan's way of thinking, the inhabitants of sixth-century England may be dismissed as children since they have not yet grown into an awareness of the rational laws which help to explain the world around them. This outlook causes him to objectify the faults of Arthurian England into institutional forms, and the dominant institutions of slavery, aristocracy, and the Church come under heavy attack in the book. The famous diatribe against monarchies, in which Twain compares the intelligence of kings to that of tomcats, represents the extreme of the Yankee's ideological nature. One cannot help feeling that Twain is seeking an explanation of evil which is altogether too simple. To cast the eccentricities of human action into an objective, institutional form is to be able to eliminate them more easily. Hank Morgan, however, seems to have little idea of the relationship between the individual failings of men and the composite failings of society. Individual characters he often sees sympathetically. The king is presented as a silly, doting, even likeable old man who is never quite conscious of, or responsible for, any misdoings to which he is a part. The aristocracy, when it is presented as an abstract group, comes out somewhat worse than the monarchy, although individual characters, like Morgan Le Fay, are at least seen with a mixture of humor and rage. But the Church, which has no single representative, is the real culprit. Its religious character is almost irrelevant; only its vast temporal and psychological powers are to be feared.

The Church is presented as a formidable antirational force which the Yankee recognizes from the beginning as his chief enemy. Its offense is to inculcate feudal doctrines, mysticism, and superstition in order to keep the people in poverty and to maintain its own worldly interests. Worst of all, it officially encourages the belief in a joyful afterlife in order to keep the masses resigned to exploitation. The Yankee approaches the whole problem of the Church from a materialistic viewpoint. The outcome of the Church's irrational hold on the people is economic degradation. The Church's reward, conversely, is great wealth. The Church thus becomes a convenient ex-

planation for the irrationalities of human conduct which puzzle the Yankee. In the end, its power over the people is instrumental in the Yankee's defeat. The Yankee at first has great success with his technological program, and he believes that in his schools he is educating the more capable men into the principles of modern society. Near the end of the book, however, the Church imposes an interdict, and almost all of the Yankee's men desert him because of their fear of eternal damnation. "We imagined we had educated it out of them," Clarence, one of the few faithful students, reports; "they thought so, too; the Interdict woke them up like a thunderclap!" The Church's hold turns out to be deeply rooted. Thus the Yankee discovers, in spite of his earlier confidence, that education is not all, and that he has in a very crucial way misjudged the powers which motivate men.

The extraordinary conclusion of *A Connecticut Yankee* comes about from a coalition of institutions which Hank Morgan finds most onerous, with the ironic complicity of at least one of the modern institutions which he himself has introduced, the stock market. Foremost among these is, of course, the Church, which conspires to keep the Yankee out of the country until the technological and financial machinery which he has set up runs awry. While he is in France, trouble does arise. Sir Lancelot has become involved in a massive railroad transaction on the stock market in which he has fleeced several other prominent knights. In retaliation, they go to King Arthur to reveal Queen Guenever's adultery, something of which the king had been naïvely unaware. A civil war ensues, and the Church takes advantage of the public commotion to move in unnoticed against the Yankee with the interdict. Though Twain follows the traditional legend in having the kingdom fall because of Lancelot and Guenever, he casts the real burden of responsibility on the inevitable confrontation of the forces of reaction represented by the Church and the forces of progress which the Yankee represents. "Well, if there hadn't been any Queen Guenever, it wouldn't have come so early," Clarence explains to the Yankee when he returns to find the country in chaos, "but it would have come anyway. It would have come on your account by and by." Only a short while before, the Yankee had felt that he had nearly achieved his dream of a nineteenth-century Utopia in Arthurian England. His projects seemed to be curing the maladies of sixth-century life, and perfection appeared to be near:

> Slavery was dead and gone; all men were equal before the law; taxation had been equalized. The telegraph, the telephone, the phonograph, the typewriter, the sewing-machine, and all the thousand willing and handy servants of steam and electricity were working their way into favor.

But "Ah, what a donkey I was!" is his final disillusioned comment.

Disgusted by the irrationality of human behavior, the Yankee desperately turns to technology in order to save himself and his vision of society. The end result of the war which follows is that he, even with his superior knowledge, has only invented a more efficient way of killing people. His technology is powerless to combat the real enemies of his Utopian vision, just as technology was powerless to establish it in the first place. His smashing military victory accomplishes precisely nothing towards re-establishing the Yankee's beautiful civilization:

> Within ten short minutes after we had opened fire,

armed resistence was totally annihilated, the campaign was ended, we fifty-four were masters of England! Twenty-five thousand men lay dead around us.

But how treacherous is fortune! In a little while—say an hour—happened a thing, by my own fault, which—but I have no heart to write that. Let the record end here.

Clarence tells what happened in a postscript, and the incident which he describes is Twain's most damning indictment of the Yankee's failings. Clarence, the Yankee, and fifty-two of the Yankee's students are trapped in the cave from which they had mounted their attack by a mountain of dead bodies. Suddenly, a mysterious old woman appears in the cave, and she addresses them with malicious satisfaction: "Ye were conquerors; ye are conquered! These others are perishing—you also. Ye shall all die in this place—every one—except *him* [the Yankee]. He sleepeth now—and shall sleep for thirteen centuries." At this point, the old woman reveals her identity. Her revelation is completely astonishing: "I am Merlin!" She is Merlin the court magician whom the Yankee had easily dismissed as a preposterous charlatan. Here Merlin reveals himself as something else. He is a *good* magician, and a symbol of the forces of evil which the Yankee has misjudged. The Yankee, in his self-confidence, grossly underrates Merlin and the powers for which he stands, and it is Merlin who strikes the final blow.

Seen in terms of Hank Morgan's ambitious proposals at the beginning and his failure at the end, *A Connecticut Yankee* is a parable about the idea of material progress. By virtue of what Hank says, he is the exponent of the idea of progress in its crudest form, but by virtue of what happens to him he embodies its limitations. His criticisms of the old order are often just, but by example he calls into question his own ideals and the very culture which shared them. *A Connecticut Yankee* is therefore a valuable key to the intellectual ambience of late nineteenth-century America. During this period, America and specifically American culture became a dominant concern of prose writers. To evaluate the social, political, and economic inequities of contemporary life, these writers turned, either directly or by implication, to a reexamination of the ideology upon which their culture was nominally based. *A Connecticut Yankee* is a microcosmic manifestation of their concern. Within Twain's own work, it foreshadows a despair which is a logical extension of the futile attempt to explain the fullness of human experience in a neatly schematic way. Twain was to be repelled by his failure to the opposite extreme—into, that is, an implicit solipsism which denied all values outside the individual mind. *The Mysterious Stranger* voices such a view: "Nothing exists save empty space. . . . You are but a thought!" Also akin in spirit to *A Connecticut Yankee* are William Dean Howells' scrupulous examinations of American moral life and Henry James' novels of international contrast. Howells' almost journalistic method reflects his conviction that solutions are to be found in the simple organization—or reorganization—of things. James, on the other hand, with his complex attitude towards aesthetic perception as a basis for active morality, tries to avoid categorical name-calling of the kind which plagued Twain's thought; and, I believe, he succeeds. In its impulse, at least, *A Connecticut Yankee* is of a company with Henry Adams' individualistic pair of books, *The Education of Henry Adams* and *Mont St. Michel and Chartres;* and, to range slightly further afield, it shares both impulse and structure

with the enormously popular Utopian novels of the late 1880's, for it is, in effect, a Utopian novel in reverse.

A Connecticut Yankee is not only akin to these works, it is central to them and to this period of American literature—if we choose to emphasize the former rather than latter word. This is so for three reasons. The first of these is that Twain, in *A Connecticut Yankee,* is on a collision course with the most perplexing dilemma of late nineteenth-century American thought, a dilemma which finds place, either directly or indirectly, in almost all fiction of the time. How, Americans were asking, can one understand a burgeoning industrial society through the old rubrics of the American myth; how—a much more crucial question—can one control such a society by traditional modes of social thought? Twain suggests an answer in the character of Hank Morgan, the swaggering proponent of material progress, the Yankee of the Yankees. The rubrics which Hank Morgan trusts are those of the Enlightenment in a particularly American, and materialistic, form. Thus armed, he sets out to fashion a society and to create among the Arthurians the Utopia which the American myth promised. His abilities, of course, do not match the task; his knowledge is severely limited, and his society comes to grief. Hank Morgan would not have understood Condorcet's remark, made some hundred years before: "the labours of recent ages have done much for the progress of the human mind, but little for the perfection of the human race; that they have done much for the honour of man, something for his liberty, but so far almost nothing for his happiness." Twain suggests that America may be headed the same way as Hank Morgan's England; and though Twain himself may not have admitted this, there were many of his contemporaries—like Henry Adams and Ignatius Donnelly, to cite two men otherwise unrelated by talent or sensibility—who would.

A second reason for valuing *A Connecticut Yankee* is that the book *is,* on artistic grounds, a failure. Hank Morgan is by no means an unequivocally ironic figure. It is often very difficult to see whether Twain is agreeing with him or making light of him. The resulting ambivalence suggests, and this is the case, that Twain is confused and unsure of his thesis. But successes put forth answers, while failures define the questions more precisely. *A Connecticut Yankee* hovers in a most engaging way above the gap between question and answer, and, as a failure, it suggests so much about other works of the time. If it were not, however, for Twain's unfailing sense of the comic (a third valuable feature of the book) all this would be too burdensome. Indeed, the book has most often been read merely for its comedy, and, as a result, has been misunderstood. But, for anyone who cares to look at *A Connecticut Yankee* in the ways I have suggested, the comedy provides a catalyst for the book's chaotic substance. The effect produced is at once slapstick and sinister, uproariously funny and profoundly relevant. (pp. 435-46)

Gerald Allen, "Mark Twain's Yankee," in The New England Quarterly, *Vol. XXXIX, No. 4, December, 1966, pp. 435-46.*

JAMES M. COX (essay date 1966)

[*Cox is an American critic and educator specializing in American literature. In the following analysis of* A Connecticut Yankee in King Arthur's Court, *he discusses the novel in the context of Twain's life and literary career.*]

A Connecticut Yankee in King Arthur's Court holds much

the same position in Mark Twain's career that *Pierre* occupies in Melville's. Before both books stand single masterpieces; after them comes work of genuine merit, work of a higher order than they themselves represent, but work more quietly desperate, as if the creative force behind it had suffered a crippling blow. Moreover each book displays its author's ambitious effort to scale heights hitherto unattempted. Finally, the books share a similarity of substance, reaching resolutions involving self-destruction for the artist-hero. Melville's Pierre is a writer so caught in the involutions of love and creativity that suicide becomes a last refuge. Mark Twain's Hank Morgan, a brash superintendent of a Hartford Machine Shop transported into a sixth-century feudal world, assumes the role of a superman inventor in an effort to revolutionize the Arthurian world by accelerating the course of history. He does revolutionize it, only to destroy his technological marvels and defeat himself. Despite a certain audacity of conception, however, both works disintegrate into extravagant failures. Each involves an excess of energy, as if the energy invested had not been fully assimilated, leaving the author to force his way toward a destructive ending which would perforce break the identification between himself and the artist-hero.

Such a struggle is particularly evident in *A Connecticut Yankee.* The most revealing comment on the unfulfilled effort is Mark Twain's reply to Howells' praise of the novel: "Well, my book is written—let it go. But if it were only to write over again there wouldn't be so many things left out. They burn in me; & they keep multiplying & multiplying; but now they can't ever be said. And besides, they would require a library—& a pen warmed-up in hell." This humorous exaggeration rests on two central assumptions: that the book is an incomplete expression of suppressed attitudes, and that the suppressions are self-generatively threatening the writer's personality. The entire passage points to the final incompleteness of *A Connecticut Yankee,* corroborating the incompleteness of the novel; or—to put it inversely—the novel realizes the sense of incompleteness which the remark suggests. In this respect it is a new kind of failure for Mark Twain. He had failed before, and failed often, but usually in the midst of successes. For example, there is the failure of *The Innocents Abroad*—a failure of concentration and economy. And there is the failure of *Roughing It,* a failure to realize the true structure of the book. And even in *Huckleberry Finn*, there is, after everything one can say about the ending, a failure of proportion. But in all these instances the failure is directly related to and defined by a discovery in form.

In *A Connecticut Yankee,* however, the failure is as central and pervasive as it is in *The Prince and the Pauper.* Moreover, it is of greater magnitude for the simple reason that *A Connecticut Yankee* pretends to be more than *The Prince and the Pauper.* The earlier book had been addressed to a juvenile audience on the one hand and to a respectable audience on the other. It was a book which could be read aloud in the parlor to all the family. If it seemed tame, Mark Twain could rest in the solace of not having claimed it was profound, and also in the knowledge of having subtly conveyed the impression that the book had been written to please the respectable world in which he found himself. *A Connecticut Yankee* was a different thing. It was not peripheral but central; it was not respectable but genuinely irreverent; it offered itself not as an exercise but as an experiment. Like *Huckleberry Finn,* it did not come quickly but slowly, five years elapsing between the time of his first notebook entry in the late fall of 1884 and the

date of publication in December, 1889. That first notebook entry—"Dream of being a knight errant in armor in the Middle Ages"—was supposedly inspired by Mark Twain's reading of Sir Thomas Malory to whose book he had been introduced by George W. Cable on their lecture tour in the fall of 1884.

Not until a year later, in December, 1885, did he actually begin to write; by March, 1886 he had written "A Word of Explanation" and the first three chapters. Then, much as he had done with *Huckleberry Finn,* he simply let the manuscript gather dust for a year and a half before returning to write sixteen chapters at Quarry Farm during the summer of 1887. This summer burst of writing carried him into Chapter 20, where Sandy and the Boss visit the Ogre's Castle. But when he returned to Hartford and the business world, his writing stopped. Not until he returned to Quarry Farm in July, 1888 did he begin the sustained assault which carried through disappointments and frustrating delays to the end of the manuscript in the spring of 1889. This brief history of the composition points up the similarity between the emergence of *Huckleberry Finn* and *A Connecticut Yankee.* In each instance there was a beginning, a long delay, a return, another hesitation, and a final sustained push to, or near to, a conclusion.

But similarities have a way of pointing up essential differences, the difference in this instance being that the creative enterprise of *A Connecticut Yankee,* insofar as it parallels that of *Huckleberry Finn,* is on a slighter scale. The total time of its composition is shorter, the initial burst of writing is much less decisive, and the *literary* waste required to complete the book is almost minimal compared to the failures which marked the way toward the success of *Huckleberry Finn.* Yet—and here is the issue—*A Connecticut Yankee* sounds bigger than *Huckleberry Finn.* It makes more noise; it seems more aspiring; it is much more liberal; it exposes the evil as well as the folly of man and his institutions. It thus becomes the central book for those critics who want to see Mark Twain as a robust frontier spirit at war with tradition, and also for those who wish to measure literature in terms of political liberalism and social conscience. (pp. 198-201)

Yet for all the audacity the *Yankee* seems to have, it is actually a much tamer, safer performance. This fact is immediately evident in the Preface. Whereas the Preface to *Huckleberry Finn* was defiant and nihilistic, humorously warning the reader to look for something at the cost of his life, the *Yankee* Preface begins:

> The ungentle laws and customs touched upon in this tale are historical, and the episodes which are used to illustrate them are also historical. It is not pretended that these laws and customs existed in England in the sixth century; no, it is only pretended that inasmuch as they existed in the English and other civilizations of far later times, it is safe to consider that it is no libel upon the sixth century to suppose them to have been in practice in that day also. One is quite justified in inferring that whatever one of these laws or customs was lacking in that remote time, its place was competently filled by a worse one.

Already there is the fatal appeal of *The Prince and the Pauper:* the appeal to history and at the same time the apology for fiction under the assurance of exposing eternal injustices. In a word, the Preface promises satire rather than humor, seriousness rather than mere laughter. Yet the language of *A Connecticut Yankee* was apparently vernacular, not genteel as it had been in *The Prince and the Pauper.* Promising a revolutionary revision of the past it invaded, it seemed a secure armor against the sentimentality of the earlier work. Yet *A Connecticut Yankee,* for all its hardheaded irreverence, succumbed to sentimentality.

The form of *A Connecticut Yankee* is what may be called an inverted Utopian fantasy. A graphic way to see the inversion is to compare it with Edward Bellamy's *Looking Backward,* which appeared in 1887 and was a best seller by the time the *Yankee* was ready for publication. Mark Twain himself was extremely fond of Bellamy's book, though he apparently did not read it until after the *Yankee* was completed. In Bellamy's dream fantasy Julian West is precipitated into the future, where, faced with the material and ideological evolution evident in the year A.D. 2000, his own nineteenth century appears meager and startlingly inadequate. Through all his experience, West remains the observer, the listener, the interrogator who assimilates the persuasive criticism which the imaginary age affords. Bellamy's central achievement is to realize the terms of the Utopian fantasy, which is to say he conveys the notion of a dream of reason. Thus his hero finds himself being constantly persuaded that truths he had believed, values he had held, and causes he had supported are nothing more than outworn attitudes and trappings of a dead age. Being reasonable in the face of the disparity, he submits to the superior argument and assents to the promise of the strange new world.

Mark Twain, however, instead of sending his hero into an imaginary future territory outside history where the terms of criticism could operate freely to create the dream of reason, plunged him into history as if to invade and reform the past. The Yankee is not the innocent interlocutor but the chief actor of his chronicle. Just as his machine-shop lingo collides with the Malory-ese of the Age of Chivalry, his democratic ideology does battle with the aristocratic and religious dogmas of the king's realm. The superintendent of a Colt Arms machine shop, he emerges into the sixth-century Arthurian world and is able to see this feudal pastoral from the presumable advantage of democratic industrialism. Unable to resist the lure of potential power residing in his technological advantage, he finds himself "inventing" labor-saving devices, instigating reforms, and organizing the people in an effort to proclaim a republic in England. For a brief moment his regime prevails; but the Church, never quite defeated, plays upon the superstition of the populace, declares an interdict, and sends an army against the Yankee; he in turn blows up his technological world, along with the assaulting forces of Church and Chivalry. Surrounded and poisoned by the vast corpse he has made of the past, the Yankee is condemned to a thirteen-century sleep by Merlin, the old-time magician whom he initially ridiculed.

The energy generated by this incongruity between chivalric past and practical present made up—as near as one can tell—the central impulse for beginning the book. Mark Twain's letters and notebook entries say as much, and the early portions of the book itself, even after all revisions were made, are essentially built upon a burlesque contrast between two styles: Morgan's rough-neck, irreverent abruptness set against the exaggerated impersonation of Malory's circumlocutive archaism. There are, particularly in the early chapters and from time to time throughout the book, amusing moments when

Mark Twain is able to exploit the possibilities of the contrast to genuine advantage. His mounting the knights on bicycles, for example, or forcing them to wear placards advertising such items as Persimmons Soap or Peterson's Prophylactic Toothbrushes, have the genuine force of burlesque incongruity and exceed the expectations of the situation. And his utilizing the waste power of a genuflecting ascetic in order to operate a shirt factory has about it the old reckless irreverence which still has power to shock a safe gentility.

But as Morgan gains power in the Arthurian world, the democratic assumptions on which his identity rests assert themselves, causing the burlesque contrast to assume satiric form. Such a change produces a marked transformation of Hank Morgan's character. For insofar as the burlesque contrast is the dominant impulse, Hank Morgan is essentially the showman, his characterizing compulsion being his urge to gain attention. Wherever he appears, the Yankee must shine, and more than food or women or even life itself, he loves the effect. In a rare moment of insight, he observes that the crying defect of his character is his desire to perform picturesquely. His whole style—given to overstatement from the moment he appears until he finally collapses under Merlin's spell—is in large part a manifestation of his desire to show off. Even the sad-faced Mark Twain ruefully observes of the Yankee's dying call to arms, "He was getting up his last 'effect'; but he never finished it."

But as the satiric impulse comes to the fore, the surprise, bewilderment, and amusement with which Morgan had originally beheld the Arthurian world are displaced by the indignation he feels upon discovering the atrocities at the heart of chivalry. Whereas the burlesquing Morgan had been intent upon making fun of chivalry, the satiric Morgan becomes determined to make war upon it. Yet the satiric Morgan can never really be effective, because the narrow range of his burlesque style cannot tolerate enough analytic intelligence or wit to discharge his growing indignation. Instead, his outrage tends to reduce his democratic ideology to clamorous fulmination and noisy prejudice, so that he becomes an object of curiosity rather than an effective satiric agent. Constantly advertising his ideas, his mechanical aptitude, and his stagey jokes, he becomes a grotesque caricature of the nineteenth century he advocates. Prancing through every conceivable burlesque and flaunting himself before the stunned Arthurian world into which he bursts, he begins to be the real buffoon of the show he manages.

Mark Twain recognized the Yankee's limitations, going so far as to confide to his illustrator Dan Beard, ". . . this Yankee of mine . . . is a perfect ignoramus; he is boss of a machine shop; he can build a locomotive or a Colt's revolver, he can put up and run a telegraph line, but he's an ignoramus, nevertheless." Aware of Morgan's career and Twain's own statements, certain critics have maintained that Mark Twain was directing his fire upon the nineteenth century as much as upon the sixth. Thus Parrington insisted [in *Main Currents in American Thought* (1930)] that Twain was "trimming his sails to the chill winds blowing from the outer spaces of a mechanistic cosmos," and Gladys Carmine Bellamy has more recently observed [see Further Reading] that the book is "a fictional working out of the idea that a too-quick civilization breeds disaster."

Plausible though such arguments are in the light of the Yankee's ultimate failure, the logic of the narrative and the tone which sustains it move in precisely the opposite direction.

For although the Yankee finally destroys himself, Mark Twain's major investment is in the Yankee's attitudes. After all, most of those attitudes were the same ones Mark Twain himself swore by at one time or another during his public life; and the usual response to the novel has been—and inevitably will continue to be—that he was lampooning monarchy, religion, and chivalry. There is abundant evidence that Mark Twain himself intended just such criticism. As early as 1866, he was attacking feudalism in the Sandwich Islands, and his belief in the superiority of democracy to monarchy goes back to the very beginning of his career; his hatred of an established church stretches equally far back—and further forward. Ten years after the Yankee's diatribes against organized religion, Mark Twain took special pleasure in mounting a sustained, logical attack upon Mary Baker Eddy, whose Christian Science he feared would become the official religion of the Republic. There is also clear evidence, as John B. Hoben long ago observed [see Further Reading], that some of the Yankee's attitudes have their exact counterparts in Mark Twain's hostile responses to Matthew Arnold's strictures upon American culture. Finally, Howard Baetzhold has shown [see Further Reading] that Mark Twain's picture of feudal England is at times almost a direct transcript of the elder George Kennan's lectures and writings on Russia, both of which Mark Twain particularly approved.

What becomes evident is that during the composition of the ***Yankee,*** the hostility, anger, and indignation which were permanent aspects of his personality came into much fuller play. As he had done while writing ***Huckleberry Finn,*** he *gave himself up to these emotions.* To read his notebooks of either period is to come across long passages in which fury and brooding animus are often indulged, much as if the writer were cultivating those emotions in order to motivate himself to write. But whereas in the vernacular of ***Huckleberry Finn*** he had discovered a vehicle to convert the indignation which stands behind both humor and satire into the ironic observation, apparent indifference, and mock innocence which constitute them, the vernacular of Hank Morgan lacked the inverted point of view which would convert the emotions of rage and hate into humor. Instead of being the instrument which transfers the indignation from writer to reader, as in the case of satire, or converts it to pleasure, as in the case of humor, Morgan—who is conceived as a rowdy agent of burlesque—comes to be invested with the indignation of his creator. He is therefore not fully dramatized and remains part of the author, who seems to struggle more and more desperately to free him into character. It is just this struggle which makes the ending seem like a fantasy in which the author is driving the mechanism of his hero faster and faster until it flies apart. Thus in the closing chapters of the book, what began as a burlesque dream assumes the character of a nightmare in which Morgan is electrocuting knights so rapidly and so thoroughly that the dead, being merely an alloy of brass and buttons, are impossible to identify. Trapped at the center of his destruction, the Yankee is condemned by Merlin to a thirteen-century sleep from which he awakens to find himself a stranger in his once familiar nineteenth century. Unmoored from space, adrift in time, he lies down at last to death.

This relatively "sad" ending to what had begun as a burlesque contrast is what makes the book seem a turning point in Mark Twain's career, embodying as it does the shift from joy to despair, from dream to nightmare. The whole nature of the enterprise, in which Mark Twain finds himself killing the character who had given utterance to so many of his own criticisms and opinions, makes biographical speculation wellnigh inevitable. It is possible, for example, to show that Mark Twain's increasing involvement with the Paige Typesetter during the years the novel took shape had much to do with his growing desperation in the ***Yankee.*** For it was during these years, in the wake of his success with General Grant, that Mark Twain invested all his available capital in the typesetter. There is a sense in which the Yankee's demise is both a foreshadowing and a rehearsal of the fall which Mark Twain must have begun to see awaiting him. There is even a correspondence between the Yankee—whom Mark Twain indulges and almost glorifies, then brings to grief—and James Paige—the inventor of the typesetter who, like the Yankee, worked in the Colt Arms factory and was at first Mark Twain's hero, later his devil. The intricate relationship between book and typesetter is nowhere better revealed than in a letter Mark Twain wrote to his wife's brother-in-law, Theodore Crane, when, racing to finish the **Yankee,** he was also awaiting the advent of the mechanical miracle which Paige kept toying with.

> I am here in Twichell's house at work, with the noise of the children and an army of carpenters to help. Of course they don't help, but neither do they hinder. It's like a boiler-factory for racket . . . but I never am conscious of the racket at all, and I move my feet into position of relief without knowing when I do it. . . . I was so tired last night that I thought I would lie abed and rest, today; but I couldn't resist. . . . I want to finish the day the machine finishes, and a week ago the closest calculations for that indicated Oct. 22—but experience teaches me that their calculations will miss fire, as usual.

The process of composition as Mark Twain describes it—a dumbly driven effort going on almost outside himself—is perfectly explained by his wish to finish the book on the day the machine was to be completed. He was saying, in effect, that he was a machine-driven writer; but more important, he revealed that the novel had come to be identified with the machine. There is, however, the hint of fatal doubt about Paige's invention. To accommodate his writing to its schedule was to be anchored to perpetual uncertainty. The machine was not perfected on October 22; nor was the novel completed on that date. Not until eight months later, after seasons of ecstatic hope punctuated by periods of depression or anxious alarm about the mechanical marvel, did Mark Twain succeed in completing his novel. As for the machine, it was never really completed. Paige, constantly taking it apart in an effort to perfect it to the last dimension of its complexity, was overtaken by the simpler Mergenthaler linotype. As for Mark Twain, he was left in bankruptcy.

That Mark Twain could bring the book to an end and break the identification discloses how much writing was his real business. It was the act he had ultimately to rely upon to recover from the financial involvements of his business ventures. Yet the recovery was as costly as it was desperate, for it required killing the Yankee. And the Yankee in the book is not simply a businessman or a mechanic in the Arthurian world, but an *inventor* as well; his power was indivisibly a part of Mark Twain's creative impulse. Killing the Yankee was symbolically a crippling of the inventive imagination, as if Mark Twain were driven to maim himself in an effort to survive. Understandably he considered this radical redefinition of himself to be the logical end of his writing life and went so far as to say jokingly to Howells that his career was over and he wished "to pass to the cemetery unclodded." Of course, his career was not over. He wrote again and again, not simply because there were financial necessities which required it, but because writing was at last his life.

The priority of writing in Mark Twain's life brings us back to the matter of form in the *Yankee.* For it is finally the form—which is to say the style and character of Hank Morgan—that failed Mark Twain. Though a change in his outlook took place during the process of composition, and though this change is reflected in the book, it is difficult to say—as it was difficult to say about *Huckleberry Finn*—how much the art, fed into the life and how much the life fed the art. Thus, while it can be said that Mark Twain's investment in his publishing house and the Paige Typesetter "caused" him to run into writing difficulty, it is also possible to argue that Mark Twain's increasing tendency to invest in business rather than in art was a result, not a cause, of a lesion in his own creative faculties.

That there was such a lesion is evident in the slender frame he cast round the *Yankee.* In that frame—appropriately entitled "A Word of Explanation"—he employed the author-meets-narrator stratagem as a device for getting into the narrative and also for introducing his narrator. Following a guided tour through Warwick Castle, itself a representative of the storied past of the tourist's imagination, the author encounters a stranger "who wove such a spell about me that I seemed to move among the specters and shadows and dust and mold of a gray antiquity, holding speech with a relic of it!" Here is the familiar impersonation of the clichés of travelogue nostalgia, and throughout the introduction, Mark Twain continues to portray himself as the dreamy-eyed tourist bent on caressing images of the past. In this moment of sentimental retrospection—while the guide is attempting to explain the presence of a bullet hole in an ancient piece of armor—the stranger appears, like the fabulous genie come from a bottle, and into Mark Twain's ear alone proclaims himself the author of the bullet hole. The "electric surprise of the remark" momentarily shatters the tourist's dream, and by the time he recovers, the stranger has disappeared. That evening, however, sitting by the fire at the Warwick Arms, "steeped in a dream of the olden time," Mark Twain is again abruptly confronted by the stranger, who, knocking upon the door to interrupt the dream, takes final charge of the narrative.

The frame makes clear that Morgan, instead of being a companion character, is a projection, or, more accurately, an anti-mask of the tourist Mark Twain's stock nostalgia. In the same way that Morgan has put a bullet hole in the antique armor, he punctures the sentimental dream of the past. Moreover, he comes unbidden to menace the dreamer and his retrospective vision. Speaking with casual and confident authority, he proclaims himself the antithesis of sentimentality. "I am a Yankee of Yankees—and practical; yes, and nearly barren of sentiment, I suppose—or poetry, in other words." His entire narrative, appropriately preserved on a palimpsest, is the record of an attempt to overwrite as well as override the past.

The Yankee's role, as defined in the frame, is thus one of burlesquing "Mark Twain's" tourist version of the past. Taken together in the frame, Morgan and "Mark Twain" could be considered as the essential mechanism of Mark Twain's burlesque. There are the two attitudes—nostalgia and irreverence—in collision; both attitudes are at the heart of Mark

Twain's creative impulse. For in order to make the irreverence work, Mark Twain had to impersonate reverence. Even as he specialized in burlesquing the piety of retrospection, he had to cultivate his longing for the past. Sentimental as that longing could be—he speaks in his *Autobiography* of "the pathetic past, the beautiful past, the dear and lamented past"—it nevertheless inspired, at the same time it drove him back upon, his memory.

Probably his chief protection against this intense longing for the past, which he indulged as necessarily as he had to indulge anger and indignation, was his capacity for burlesque. Burlesque was the means of both mocking and checking the nostalgic impulse. In *The Innocents Abroad* Mark Twain, by discovering a perspective along the borderland between pathos and ridicule, had developed a style which contained both attitudes in a new synthesis. Yet in the frame of *A Connecticut Yankee* he reverted to the simple division of polite tourist and vulgar companion—a division he had used in his *Travels with Mr. Brown,* only to transcend it in *The Innocents Abroad.* In giving over the narrative to Hank Morgan, Mark Twain attempted to transcend the essential division at the heart of the burlesque impulse; but in displacing "Mark Twain" with Morgan rather than Huck Finn, he had no way of producing the mock gravity so essential to his earlier humor. With Morgan as narrator, there was no possibility of impersonating pained seriousness or genteel piety. For Morgan is, as he proudly proclaims, a Yankee of Yankees and barren of sentiment. Instead of embodying the underside of language and experience in the manner of Huck Finn, Hank is the rowdy and irreverent genie of burlesque. Although both Hank and Huck are involved in reconstructing history, the mode of reconstruction is opposite at nearly every point. Huck is the apparently helpless figure drifting upon the current of the mighty Mississippi; Hank is both director and chief actor in his drama. Huck thinks all his heroism is wrong; Hank is sure that his revolution is right. But whereas Huck's successive evasions bring us to the awareness that a real revolution has taken place, Hank's revolutionary indignation involves him in an ever-enlarging fantasy.

All of which brings us to Hank Morgan's style, for Hank's style, like Huck's, will tell everything about the book. It is a loud and boisterous style, given to bluntness and dogmatic attitude. Unlike Huck's Southwestern vernacular, Morgan's Yankee lingo is essentially correct as far as its grammar is concerned. Though it runs toward a jaunty boastfulness and apparently reckless contempt for conventional attitudes, it does not play havoc with the proprieties of grammar. In the final analysis, Hank's vernacular is rather conventional language masquerading as burly, rough talk.

In Huck's vernacular, Mark Twain used the illusion of illiteracy to secure the impression of simplicity while at the same time retaining a complex syntactical structure. Set against the implications of conventional syntax, the illiteracies make possible a style capable of a vast range of expressive utterance. Take, for example, Huck's reflection upon Mary Jane Wilks's offer to pray for him:

> Pray for me! I reckon if she knowed me she'd take a job that was more nearer her size. But I bet she done it, just the same—she was just that kind. She had the grit to pray for Judus if she took the notion—there warn't no back-down to her, I judge. You may say what you want to, but in my opinion she had more sand in her than any girl I ever see;

in my opinion she was just full of sand. It sounds like flattery, but it ain't no flattery. And when it comes to beauty—and goodness, too—she lays over them all.

Here Huck's language defines perfectly the breach between his reality and her convention. Mary Jane can approve of him only sentimentally, only because she refuses to know the extent of his sin; and Huck can approve of her only in metaphors which are unwittingly abrasive. In a very real sense his praise of her "ain't no flattery." Yet neither Mary Jane's banality, Huck's self-depreciation, nor the implicit irony of his metaphors disturb the sentiment of his approval. Compare Huck's art of language to Hank's description of a girl he meets upon entering Camelot:

> Presently a fair slip of a girl, about ten years old, with a cataract of golden hair streaming down over her shoulders, came along. Around her head she wore a hoop of flame-red poppies. It was as sweet an outfit as ever I saw, what there was of it. She walked indolently along, with a mind at rest, its peace reflected in her innocent face. . . . But when she happened to notice me, *then* there was a change! Up went her hands, and she was turned to stone; her mouth dropped open, her eyes stared wide and timorously, she was a picture of astonished curiosity touched with fear. And there she stood gazing, in a sort of stupefied fascination, till we turned a corner of the wood and were lost to her view. That she should be startled at me instead of at the other man, was too many for me.

This passage is as representative as it is revealing. The features which distinguish the passage as vernacular are clear—and few. First of all, there is a certain exaggeration of metaphor and figure, as illustrated by the "cataract of golden hair streaming down over her shoulders," and "hoop of flame-red poppies." This exaggeration is also present in other areas of the style. It is evident when the Yankee speaks of "astonished curiosity" and "stupefied fascination." The method here is to call into service an adjective which overlaps the meaning of the noun in an effort to intensify the description. This doubling effect, while it can produce a certain flamboyance of description, is more likely to result—as in the passage under scrutiny—in a redundancy and loss of nuance.

Aside from the exaggeration, the Yankee's style is pervaded with literary clichés. There is the "fair slip of a girl," the "golden hair," the "flame-red poppies," the "mind at rest." Then there are the elaborately stylized locutions—"Up went her hands," "her eyes stared wide and timorously," "she was a picture of astonished curiosity," and "there she stood gazing." These two tendencies—the one toward exaggeration and loud intensity, the other toward literary cliché—reach their logical end in the last sentence of the passage, where the sentence begins with the stilted noun clause as a subject and ends by veering into colloquialism. The entire passage illustrates the essential rhythm and feature of Morgan's language. Grounded in clichés and conventional syntax, its character emerges by means of exaggeration and calculated vulgarity. The exaggeration is achieved largely by relying on clichés which generalize images and impersonate Arthurian gentility; the slang is the means of dissociating from and exposing the overelaborate impersonation.

These revelations about Hank Morgan's style put us directly in touch with his action and his character, for Morgan's action bears the same relation to his style that Hucks action bore to his. Huck, it is worth remembering, was helplessly involved in doing the thing which his society disapproved—freeing a slave. It was an action which he himself disapproved but could avoid no more than he could avoid his grammatical blunders. Both morally and grammatically he "hadn't had no start." The humor in the book lay in involving Huck in a wrong action which his society might abhor yet the reader would heartily approve. Such a strategy required either setting the action in a primitive society and using space or geography as the point of reference; or setting the book in time and using history as the referent. The game lay in playing upon the reader's—and author's—instinctive belief in progress; and Mark Twain had played it admirably in *Huckleberry Finn.* Not only had he involved his protagonist in a revolution which his reader inexorably approved; the hero could not help himself. He simply found himself helplessly and ironically in revolution against a society which he kept thinking he should admire.

In *A Connecticut Yankee,* Mark Twain tried much the same strategy. His Yankee, finding himself in the Arthurian world, sets about revolting against the monarchy and the Catholic Church—institutions which were fairly safe game for a nineteenth-century Yankee. Certainly Mark Twain could count on a general audience approval of these aims almost as much as he could count on their disapproval of slavery. But the great difference between the Yankee and Huck is that the Yankee is a reformer whereas Huck is a helpless rebel. The Yankee acts upon principle and moral confidence; he is finally a Yankee, an abolitionist, an American, who never doubts that he is right. Huck, the fugitive and helpless outcast, acts out of a sense of being always wrong.

The Yankee's assurance that he is in the right contributes as much as anything else to alienating him from the reader. For a real problem arises the moment the Yankee begins to establish his republic. It is not that the reader disapproves of the Yankee's republicanism, but that he cannot approve the revolutionary zeal which goes along with it. As long as he is simply amused at the contrast between his own century and the quaint absurdities of the Arthurian world, the Yankee at least remains plausible; but when he begins to rail at the injustice of the past, his indignation becomes misplaced. The direction of the book discloses that the *intention* of the narrative can neither sustain nor account for the emotion of the central figure; for the emotion—the indignation—is a manifestation of the failure and inadequacy of the intention. The intention of the narrative is a burlesquing or *making fun* of the past. But what begins as making fun becomes making war. Insofar as the Yankee begins to make war upon the Arthurian kingdom he loses his sense of show and pleasure. His indignation is the index to his capacity, not for the destruction of the past, but for self-destruction.

Even more important, the Yankee's revolution is really as correct as his style. It *sounds* like revolution but is actually thoroughly safe and respectable gentility. Small wonder that Howells, who was himself at the threshold of a great "conversion" to political liberalism, should have congratulated his friend upon the bravery of the novel. And so, of course, did E. C. Stedman. Actually there is no courage about the novel. It marks a great turning back for Mark Twain—a turning back in technique and a betrayal of humor. Worst of all, Mark Twain seems to have been self-deceived since he apparently thought the Yankee was a rebel. Yet the reality of the situation is that there is scarcely anything rebellious about

A photo of Twain with journalist George Alfred Townsend (left) and editor David Gray taken at the Mathew Brady Studio.

the Yankee. His language, as we have seen, is the index of his tameness. Although he sounds and thinks as if he were rebellious, he is quite clearly echoing the sentiments of a society fairly sunk in the complacent and institutionalized "liberalism" which had sponsored the Civil War in 1860-65.

That is why the book, seen in a certain light, amounts to fighting the Civil War again. It is, after all, a tale of the Yankee doing battle with chivalry. Mark Twain himself had made it eminently plain in *Life on the Mississippi* that the South he could not abide was the South which had created itself in the image of Walter Scott and chivalry. Henry Nash Smith, in a fine discussion of Mark Twain's images of Hannibal ["Mark Twain's Images of Hannibal: From St. Petersburg to Eseldorf," *University of Texas Studies in English* (1958)] has shown decisively how the entire Arthurian kingdom is a thinly veiled picture of Southern regional culture which Mark Twain, as he grew older, came more and more to criticize. Smith points out that Arthur's Britain is "a projection of the benighted South," a "negative image of Hannibal, of Hannibal as Bricksville."

Into this "backward" region the Yankee marches to free the people from religion, aristocracy, and slavery. It is here that he seeks to establish his republic. Insofar as the action of the book amounts to a fighting of the Civil War, Mark Twain assumes the role of the Yankee; he puts on—or better, indulges in—the Yankee conscience and commits aggression after aggression upon the South in himself. For Hank Morgan does, almost from the beginning, what Huck is finally driven helplessly to do—he commits himself to the Northern conscience. This commitment Mark Twain evidently believed was rebellious; actually it is nothing less—or more—than the *approved*

action. Huck's rebellion lay not at all in his "All right, then, I'll *go* to hell," but in his rejection of conscience—of hell and heaven—altogether. Having committed himself to the "approved" rebellion, Hank Morgan sounds off louder and louder about it—and the more he commits himself to it, the less real rebellion there can be. This is Hank Morgan's and Mark Twain's self-deception—a self-deception which the style reveals. For Hank's supposed vernacular is not really vernacular at all but indulged colloquialism. It is, in a word, slang, which is to say that it is simply put-on vernacular. Mark Twain, in *A Connecticut Yankee,* succumbed to the lure of mere lingo, which so many writers since his time have done. He wanted to have a hero with an ideology *and* a vernacular. The vernacular was to ground the character in "reality" and give him a "realistic" and recognizable "social" quality. Such a hero really knows what ideas are and showily makes bright philosophical formulations in the rough and salty savor of colloquial speech. But what happens in *A Connecticut Yankee,* and in many another such attempt, is simply a faking and collapse in both directions. The ideas are so crudely simplified in Morgan's vernacular that they actually become pretentious evasions. And the vernacular is nothing but a *show,* an act. It is not necessary to the action, but simply decoration, a contrast. Nothing more than one of Hank Morgan's *effects,* it is in the last analysis an affectation.

To see this failure is to see the crucial difference between vernacular and slang. Slang is a patronizing indulgence of metaphor by someone consciously taking imaginative flights for purposes of mystification, in-group solidarity, or protective, secret communication. Vernacular, however, . . . is the "lower" or illiterate language whose very "incorrectness" at once indulgently implies a correct grammar and at the same time subverts the literary vision. The more a book is committed to a vernacular hero, the more it necessarily must produce a vision which displaces the genteel values it plays upon. *Huckleberry Finn* did carry such a vision—so much so that the vernacular and vision wait upon each other to produce a new reality of form and action. In the world of childhood which Huck's language reconstructed lay the central confrontations and discoveries which Mark Twain's humor could make. There lay the pleasure principle, which somehow gave the lie to the adult reality principle.

But in moving from Southwestern boy to Yankee adult, Mark Twain actually regressed. The Yankee is in many ways Tom Sawyer grown up—but Tom Sawyer grown up is, alas, somehow grown down. Mark Twain had refused to let Tom grow up on the grounds that he would "just be like all the other one-horse men in literature." And Morgan, if we look at him carefully, does do little but be like other one-horse men. That is why he comes to believe in himself, to take himself seriously. In *Tom Sawyer,* Mark Twain had kept Tom's speech contained within a frame—a frame half-indulgently patronizing, half-burlesque, which both indulges and exposes Tom's essential conformity with and imitation of adult ways. The indulgent narration of *Tom Sawyer* had greatly enriched Tom's reality by showing that it was somehow absurd yet pleasurably *real* in a lost nostalgic way.

When he dropped himself—the "Mark Twain" narrator— out of the action in *A Connecticut Yankee,* he could never compensate for the loss of perspective; instead, he was drawn inevitably to invest the fantasy Yankee with "serious" values. But the fate of the slang form inexorably produced a reduction in the intellectual content of Hank's "thought" and an attendant excess of emotion. The result is an increased amount of sound about ideas, yet a reduction of sense in expressing them.

The conclusion to be drawn from an examination of *A Connecticut Yankee* is that Mark Twain was deceived into believing that slang and vernacular were one and the same. But in vernacular humor, the *form* indulgently inverts conventional values, whereas in slang the *character* must attack them. The one inverts relationships and values; the other moves toward overt judgment and criticism. To realize the possibilities of slang form, Mark Twain would have had to reduce Hank Morgan's intelligence, thereby producing a burlesque, or increase his capacities of criticism and move toward satire. Yet he was able to do neither. It was as if the writer, having reached the top of his form in vernacular, was actually deceived by his masterpiece into believing that the sound of language was identical with its form. By failing to realize the necessities of his form, Mark Twain was never able to be fully responsible to the book he was making. (pp. 202-21)

James M. Cox, in his Mark Twain: The Fate of Humor, *Princeton University Press, 1966, 321 p.*

TOM H. TOWERS   (lecture date 1969)

[*In the following essay, Towers discusses inhumanity and lack of community as central concerns in* A Connecticut Yankee in King Arthur's Court.]

In general, criticism of *A Connecticut Yankee* must come down to a consideration of two closely related matters: the true object of Twain's satire, and the proper understanding of Hank Morgan's apparently ambiguous role in the novel. However, whether critics have made Twain the enemy of the middle ages or of the nineteenth century, whether they have understood Hank as the frustrated prophet of a higher civilization or as the egomaniacal destroyer of primitive innocence, most, I think, have concentrated too exclusively on the explicitly social and institutional materials of the book.

Twain, of course, seems to invite exactly that kind of interest. Most of *Yankee*'s most memorable scenes demonstrate the degrading folly of superstition, or the vanity of monarchy and feudalism, or the cynical cruelty of established religion. At the same time though, Hank—and Twain—are concerned with realities more elemental than church and state. I believe that the most basic theme in *A Connecticut Yankee* has to do not with institutionalized life in society so much as with the necessary absence of human love and community. It is this sorry fact of the human condition, and not the interdict or Hank's technology that at last destroys Hank Morgan, and with him Twain's hope for mankind.

When Hank revives after his transforming "misunderstanding conducted with crowbars," he awakens to what seems at first a second Eden. He finds himself in "a soft, reposeful summer landscape, as lovely as a dream, and as lonesome as Sunday." Hank and his captor, Sir Kay, are alone, except for "a fair slip of a girl, about ten years old, with a cataract of yellow hair streaming down over her shoulders." As befits her apparent innocence, the girl is naked except for "a hoop of flame-red poppies" around her head. Hank recognizes in the child "a mind at rest, its peace reflected in her innocent face." But the "peace" of the girl and the blessedness of the landscape itself are more apparent than real. The girl, innocent or not, is naked only because she has the misfortune to be the daughter of a "freeman" too poor to clothe her; and as Hank and Sir Kay continue on their way to Camelot, Hank's sense of the "fair, reposeful summer day" yields to his increasing awareness of human suffering.

The men they encounter "look like animals," and their homes are "wretched cabins" standing in "small fields and garden patches in an indifferent state of cultivation." Camelot itself, Hank discovers, is little more than a "wilderness of thatched cabins," lined by a network of "mere crooked alleys" where "hogs roamed and rooted contentedly about." Arthur's court seems similarly disordered and brutish. It is "a tumultuous chaos," a "storm of howlings and barkings," as the knights and ladies, in the best Arkansas fashion, divert themselves with a dog fight. As Hank stands by, waiting his turn with the other prisoners, he thinks of the courtiers as "childlike and innocent" in their "winning naivety." But as he better understands their "guileless relish" in the common talk of "blood and suffering," he perceives that chivalry, in fact, exists without human feeling or real moral knowledge. The nobles go on with their banquet and their boasting, oblivious to the prisoners who stand among them "caked with black and stiffening drenchings of blood," and Hank realizes that his captors—and his fellow prisoners too—are unreasoning savages, "white Indians," or, as he later explains to Sandy, "a sort of polished-up court of Comanches."

Everything in Hank's later adventures bears out the implication of these opening scenes. Virtually every episode in the novel has its trace of gratuitous cruelty or violence. The festive tournament is followed by a night filled with the screams of the dying losers. During his travels with Sandy, Hank finds the idyllic English countryside populated almost entirely by "freemen," whose only expectation is "life-long death from hunger, cold, insult, cruelty and heartbreak." Every castle has its dungeon, and Morgan le Fay's differs from the rest only in being fuller. The comic scene in which Hank liberates the bewitched "countess" and her sister swine is followed at once by the dismal encounter with the slave caravan. Later, during Hank's tour with Arthur, even more striking evidences of "savagery" are commonplace. There is the pathos of the smallpox hut, the horror of the prisoners burned alive in the chapter called "The Tragedy of the Manor-House," and at last, of course, the enslavement and projected execution of Hank and the king themselves.

Hank repeatedly calls attention to the savage, brutish conditions of medieval life. Englishmen are "animals," "white Indians," "big boobies" continuing into "full age and beyond" the mindless cruelties of children; they are a "nation of worms," "groping and grubbing automata"; they are "barbaric," "juvenile," and perhaps most degrading of all, they are "cow-boys." Appropriately enough, Hank, a civilized castaway in this savage land, thinks of himself as Columbus or Cortez, the "champion of hard unsentimental common-sense and reason." Shortly after he has been installed as "The Boss," he says, " 'I saw that I was just another Robinson Crusoe cast away on an uninhabited island, with no society, but some more or less tame animals, and if I wanted to make life bearable I must do as he did—invent, contrive, create, reorganize things; set brain and hand to work, and keep them busy'." But what Hank, as a later—or earlier—Robinson Crusoe, must at last set his "brain and hand to work" on is not merely superstition, nor ignorance, nor injustice, nor economic and political backwardness, but rather the innate perversity of the "damned human race." Underlying all the suffering and the inhumanity in the novel is a single tragic but simple fact—each man, by his nature, is spiritually alone, imprisoned in a savage self, and cannot be redeemed by love nor ever live in true peace with other men. Thus, there can be no community, no humanity, no real compassion or pity.

When he first reconciles himself to the fact that he is indeed in the sixth century and not the county asylum, Hank exclaims, " 'I shall never see my friends again—never, never again'." The intuition of that cry, of course, is ironically confirmed in the ending of the novel. Hank Morgan eventually dies a stranger, but now a stranger in his own century. And in his final delirium he cries out pathetically to the Sandy of his dream; he has been, he says, " 'set down in that strange England, with an abyss of thirteen centuries yawning between me and you! between me and my home and friends! between me and all that is dear to me, all that could make life worth the living! It was awful—awfuller than you can ever imagine'."

The events of the novel demonstrate that Hank's original fear and the ultimate realization of the dreaded isolation are not agonies special to Hank, but are indeed the common lot of mankind, at least in the savage state of the sixth century. In the dungeons of Arthur's nobles, it is common to separate husbands from wives, allowing each partner to destroy himself in the ordeal of supposing the other dead. Morgan le Fay's most exquisite torture is periodically to allow her most hated prisoner to glimpse from his cell what appear to be the funerals of his family; his greatest pain is his separation from those who survive, the necessity of suffering in solitude the grief that can be assuaged only by being shared. As in **Huck Finn** and **Pudd'nhead Wilson,** the cruelest evil of slavery in **A Connecticut Yankee** is the division of families on the auction block. The keenest anguish of the woman in the smallpox hut is her inability to help or even to see her dying children. And, of course, one of the clearest instances of the inhumanity of the medieval church is the ban which has cast the woman and her family officially outside the range of human sympathy, even in the hour of death itself.

The most fundamental manifestation of the savagery of Arthurian England, then, is not that men must suffer the abuse and injustice of priest and noble, but that in their suffering they must be alone, yearning for the liberation of love, but forever denied it. The separation of families, the casual imprisonments, the universal distrust which makes natural allies betray each other, are all only symbolic of the pervasive spiritual isolation which is the chief characteristic of the savage life.

When the sixth century characters even notice such intolerable conditions, it is to shrug them off as the necessary price that must be paid to preserve the Christian culture. Except for a few nameless slaves and freemen, only Hank recognizes and responds to the human outrage of frustrated love and shattered community. His tour with Sandy, for example, can be seen as a series of confrontations in which he uses his brain and his authority to free prisoners, to restore families, and generally to alleviate the horror of isolation. However, in his more general and programmatic response to this condition, Hank assumes that the agony of isolation, like the discomfort of owning but a single change of clothes, proceeds from faulty institutions and a generally backward idea of society. The trouble, he thinks, is that both noble and freemen accept the established order as divine necessity, and so routinely sacrifice their own humanity and that of others to maintain that

order. Consequently, just as Hank sets out to destroy superstition with science, or to relieve poverty through technology, he undertakes to ameliorate the oppression of spiritual isolation by transforming Britains from "worms" to men. In his "man-factory" Hank educates likely freemen in the ways of moral, social, and economic independence. He teaches his candidates to reject the authority of institutions, especially that of the church and the aristocracy, and to rely on their own reason and their own consciences. In addition, he equips them to become the bearers of nineteenth century technology and political economy. The premise, obviously, is that once men are free from the oppression of an established church and a feudal hierarchy, and free also from the even more degrading oppression of physical want, they will be free from the inhuman isolation that Hank assumes to be the direct consequence of poverty and repression. In the new order Hank strives for, men will cease to be "worms"; they will be no longer the victims of brutalizing savagery, but the masters of liberating civilization, no longer a mass of tormented isolatos, but loving members of a truly human community.

As we all know, the culmination of Hank's endeavors is the battle of the sand-belt, and the great wall of corpses within which Hank and his cadets apparently must die. But the reasons for that disaster, I think, have little to do with the destructiveness of what Hank calls his "labor-saving machinery" or with the inadequacy of nineteenth century industrialism generally. I would argue, indeed, that in every outward regard Hank vastly improves the quality of English life. From the institution of the "go-as-you-please" church to the substitution of baseball for the chivalric tournament, Hank has worked to make the lives of most Englishmen, if not perfect, at least much better than they were. Hank's projects fail, in the end, because he has mislocated the origins of human savagery and mistaken the causes of the suffering he hopes to cure.

This point, perhaps, can be illustrated by a brief look at the efficient causes of the division of the round table and the resultant interdict. The catastrophe comes about because of the greed and the selfish ambition of Sir Launcelot. Early in the novel Hank points out that knightly "adventures" were in fact "simply duels between strangers," more appropriate to amoral children than to men of "full age and beyond." After Hank has transformed the round table into the stock exchange, Launcelot transfers his "childish" appetite for violent combativeness from the lists to the counting house. He corners the market in the stock of the London, Canterbury, and Dover Railroad, and by the time he "compromises" with the knights who have been caught short, he has "skinned them alive." The injured parties retaliate by carrying to Arthur the story of Launcelot's long-standing adultery with Guinivere, and the machinery of civil war is set in motion. The "modern," "democratic" state is as susceptible to antihuman ambition and appetite as the age of chivalry. Launcelot's economic savagery is just a newer version of his sexual savagery. Both in his manipulation of the market and in his seduction of Arthur's queen, we see the kind of primal violation of trust and moral sympathy that must culminate in the dissolution of community and in the savage horror of isolation. In short, the men Hank earlier calls "animals" or "Indians" are such, not because of their institutions, but from their natures.

As I have suggested, Hank is virtually alone in his sensitivity to the terror of human isolation and in his efforts to relieve it. But even Hank betrays the very community he apparently strives to establish. The clearest example of Hank's failure is his conduct after he and the king, betrayed first by the freeman, Marco, and later by their "noble" rescuer, have been sold into slavery. Typically, Hank sees in their situation an opportunity to win Arthur over to his own abolitionist position. When the king at last agrees to abolish slavery—if he can only get free from it himself, Hank sets to work on the great "effect" that will liberate them. Like Tom Sawyer "freeing" Jim, Hank devises an elaborate, ultimately destructive scheme; he plans to overcome the slave-master, change clothes with him, chain him to the slave coffle, and march triumphantly to Camelot. Hank admits, "One could invent quicker ways [of getting free], and fully as sure ones; but none that would be as picturesque; none that could be made so dramatic. . . . It might delay us months, but no matter, I would carry it out or break something." When Hank finally sets his plan in motion he bungles it from the beginning. Instead of assaulting the slave-driver, he sets upon a perfect stranger. (Ironically his fight for freedom becomes exactly the "duel between strangers" he condemns in the knights.) The slave-trader, when he discovers Hank's escape, beats the remaining slaves, who, finally provoked too far, turn on him and kill him. In another blunder, deriving again from his desire for "effect," Hank causes himself to be recaptured and sentenced to death, along with Arthur and the rest of the slaves. Before the rescue party can arrive on bicycles, three of the slaves have been hanged. Thus, in his desire to make a grand entrance into Camelot, Hank has unfeelingly wasted the lives of the very men he hoped to save. Much the same point might be made in regard to the great climactic tournament in which Hank shoots ten knights in order once more to humiliate Merlin, this time in the "final struggle for supremacy between the two master sorcerers of the age." Thus, long before his "death," suffered in pathetic separation from Sandy and Hello Central, Hank yields to his own inveterate savagery, and thereby destines himself to his solitary end.

In **Huck Finn** society is destructive to true selfhood and to human love. We see this most clearly, perhaps, in the final episodes where, once more in society, Huck loses his sense of the free self and becomes a cruder version of Tom Sawyer, while Jim degenerates into the stage darkey. The real and valid community discovered in nature vanishes in civilization. In **Huck Finn,** though, there is always the river, and at the end of the novel, the territory. Huck, in society, may be unable to realize his humanity, but he can "light out for the territory"—he can keep out of the way of society, and hopefully, in the revitalizing benevolence of nature he can attain to what civilization everywhere denies. But in **A Connecticut Yankee** there is no such hope. Nowhere in this novel does Twain suggest any possible life for man outside of society. Hank can turn for spiritual sustenance to Sandy or to Clarence, but not to a primitive, unspoiled nature. For Hank there is no river nor any territory.

In **Yankee,** then, man is condemned to civilization. Filled, as Hank is, with the apprehension of isolation and its agony, man can strive to create a better civilization in the desperate hope that he can thereby attain to genuine community. But in the novel no institution or set of institutions is proof against the innate savagery of men, their essentially inhuman selfishness. Twain's final vision of the human condition in this work shows Hank, who in spite of all his faults, has honestly yearned towards the blessedness, the "mind at rest" of the innocent child, imprisoned by his own benevolent ambition

within the great fortress of rotting corpses, destined not to love and the new life of the spirit, but to ages long loneliness and death. (pp. 190-97)

> *Tom H. Towers, "Mark Twain's 'Connecticut Yankee': The Trouble in Camelot," in* Challenges in American Culture, *Ray B. Browne, Larry N. Landrum, William K. Bottorff, eds., Bowling Green University Popular Press, 1970, pp. 190-98.*

WILLIAM K. SPOFFORD   (essay date 1970)

[*In the following analysis of Twain's portrait of Hank Morgan, Spofford suggests that Morgan's defeat is the result of his intellectual shortcomings.*]

In "A Word of Explanation," Hank Morgan introduces himself to Twain as "a Yankee of the Yankees—and practical; yes, and nearly barren of sentiment, I suppose—or poetry, in other words." This is, however, a rather modest evaluation. The Connecticut Yankee is egotisical and brutal. As one critic states it, "despite his Utopianism, [Hank] has a relentless and unforgiving contempt for the human race." Though he may seem to possess superior intelligence, this is only so in relation to the sixth century. In his own nineteenth century, as Twain expressed it to his illustrator, Dan Beard, "he is a perfect ignoramus; he is boss of a machine shop; he can build a locomotive or a Colt's revolver, he can put up and run a telegraph line, but he's an ignoramus nevertheless." Hank Morgan possesses all of these traits, and herein lies the key to the failure of the revolution. Before examining the Boss's character, however, we should briefly glance at two attitudes which were with Twain from the beginning of the composition of **A Connecticut Yankee in King Arthur's Court.**

On March 22, 1886, Twain presented **"The New Dynasty"** to the Monday Evening Club of Hartford. In this essay he gives his wholehearted support to the American labor movement, attacking the slave-like treatment being handed the "working millions, in all ages," and especially in the nineteenth century United States. Twain's sympathies are for the oppressed masses, and he asks, "Who are the oppressors? The few: the king, the capitalist, and a handful of other overseers and superintendents." According to Howard Baetzhold, chapter one of "The Autobiography of Sir Robert Smith of Camelot" (what we know as "A Word of Explanation" and chapters one through three of **A Connecticut Yankee**) was probably written in January and February, 1886. The proximity of Twain's presentation to the Monday Evening Club and the composition of this portion of the manuscript gives particular significance to the fact that Hank Morgan is a "head superintendent [with] a couple of thousand men under me."

Second, all critics agree that one of the primary influences upon **A Connecticut Yankee** was Lecky's *History of European Morals*. Twain first came in contact with this study in the early 1870's and read it several times thereafter. It is impossible to determine the degree to which this source was informative, to which corroborative of Twain's thinking. But a faith in cultural advancement and a fear of cultural reversion is a syndrome common to both works. The doctrine of progress maintains that it is possible to train man "to abandon his trust in the dark past and to raise himself to higher social, intellectual, and moral levels." Hank Morgan's emphasis on training, on education, and his apparent progress during the first forty chapters exemplifies this faith. But a hesitancy to wholly accept this philosophy resides in "the danger that men, once liberated by modern rational thought, might slip back into their old slavish and superstitious ways." Hence the last section of the novel, in which all of England cowers under the Church's Interdict.

This basic cycle of progression and regression, I believe, was in Twain's mind from the start. He had planned to use the same structure in his novel on the Sandwich Islands on which he worked in January, 1884. The novel, which never materialized, was to treat social revolution inspired by the Christianizing and civilizing influences of missionaries in the early nineteenth century. But at the conclusion of the novel, according to Fred W. Lorch, the main character was to succumb to "the strength and the pull of the old superstitions and the idolatrous practices." Lorch further notes that Twain's primary source, J. J. Jarves' *History of the Hawaiian Islands,* gave Twain "his picture of the oppressive role of pagan chiefs and priests." I am sure that in Twain's mind these would be categorized with kings and superintendents.

Mark Twain was fully aware of the implications in the literary application of the structural cycle he was to employ in *A Connecticut Yankee* two years prior to the start of composition. This suggests that Twain never intended the Republic to be successfully established. And a close examination of the text reveals that in Hank Morgan Twain created a figure who would insure that the revolution would fail.

The Yankee's attitude toward himself remains consistent throughout the novel. He has no doubts that he will be able to "boss the whole country inside of three months," just as he is confident to the end in his ability to establish a Republic. He is a "superior man," with "knowledge, brains, pluck, and enterprise." This egotism determines his attitude toward the masses, in whose behalf he supposedly instigates his revolution. He looks with scorn and disdain upon the commoners. To him they are "white Indians," "animals" who do not reason, "a nation of worms," "modified savages," "innumerable clams," "sheep," and finally "human muck." Hank considers himself "a giant among pygmies, a man among children, a master intelligence among intellectual moles." Dowley, the blacksmith, is certainly not presented in a favorable light, but the Boss appears little better. Both are equally obnoxious. When Hank has no success with his nineteenth century economics, the teaching of which in this sixth century context is an absurd undertaking to begin with, he states, "The first statesman of the age, the capablest man, the best-informed man in the entire world, the loftiest uncrowned head that had moved through the clouds of any political firmament for centuries, sitting here apparently defeated in an argument by an ignorant country blacksmith." . . . (pp. 15-16)

[In *Mr. Clemens and Mark Twain*] Justin Kaplan has further pointed out that "the very names the Yankee gives his institutions—'civilization factories' and, a dehumanizing pun, 'man factories'—suggest not the fervent brotherhood of Whitman's utopian democracy but instead a bleak, industrial collectivism, the nightmare society of a monolithic state ruled by the Boss." This is in keeping with the Yankee's brutally insensitive nature. When applied to the masses, it is in terms of "educating his *materials* up to revolution grade" (my italics) in the "factory where I'm going to turn groping and grubbing automata into *men*." When applied to the nobility, it is even more obtuse. In the aftermath of the tournament of chapter nine, Hank shows his usual unconcern for the knights. In attempting to repair mutilated chivalry, "[the sur-

geons] ruined an uncommon good old cross-cut saw for me, and broke the sawbuck, too, but I let it pass. And for my axe—well, I made up my mind that the next time I lent an axe to a surgeon I would pick my century." When Clarence informs him of the war's casualties in chapter forty-two, Hank worries about his right-fielder and his "peerless shortstop." Similarly, discussion of the Church committee's testing of the dynamite torpedoes gives rise to gruesome punning on the word "report," and the knight's first assault on the Sand Belt results in, as Hank puts it, a "homogeneous protoplasm, with alloys of iron and buttons."

Throughout the novel the undercurrent of the Boss's dehumanizing brutality comes to the surface, casting suspicious shadows on the ideals toward which he is supposedly striving. But the more far-reaching troubles for the Yankee are rooted in Hank's problems with ideology. There are three basic concepts which the superior intellect of the Yankee seems to have difficulty grasping. He measures progress in the most superficial terms, enthusiastically interpreting any material improvement as synonomous with cultural advancement. He advocates the equality of men and a republican government, but both the fundamental precept and the institution are contrary to his nature. And, finally, Morgan speaks throughout the novel of the importance of training, but he does not realize the implications of the doctrine as they relate to his plans for the future of England.

The Boss's first official act is the establishment of a patent office, because "a country without a patent office and good patent laws was just a crab, and couldn't travel any way but sideways or backways." Hank fails to see the worthlessness of such an anachronistic institution. He applies the values and needs of the nineteenth century to the sixth century. The only person who has the knowledge and the facilities with which to invent anything is the Yankee, himself, and he is the Boss. As such, he does not need the protection of laws. But lest we put any stock in the Yankee's "progress," Twain reduces the concept ad absurdum. Sir Ossaise of Surluse sells stove-polish in preparation for the advent of the stove, while Ozana le Cure Hardy sells plughats to eventually extinguish "knighthood by making it grotesque and absurd." The Boss is very pleased to see not only the new money circulating, but also the corresponding jargon coming into fashion. He comments that "we were progressing, that was sure." His enthusiasm is particularly appropriate in the light of his materialistic mentality.

Similarly, the Yankee's view of democracy is singularly warped. After the showman's life-saving performance of magic, that is, his production of an eclipse, he is elevated to the highest position attainable in a feudal society. In his own eyes he is akin to a god, for "I was the substance; the king himself was the shadow. My power was colossal." The first democratic election is instigated by a mumbling blacksmith, who happens to speak of Hank as "The Boss." The populace is quite taken by this appellation, and Hank interprets its rapid spread as the affirmative vote of all England. He thinks to himself, not without satisfaction and a little pride, "THE BOSS. Elected by the nation. That suited me." Ironically, the antecedent of "that" is ambiguous. Hank goes on modestly to equate his new station with that of the king or the queen, and I suspect that he is more concerned about his new title than about the bogus democratic process by which he was raised to the office. Hank makes the same association with royalty at the sight of the Holy Fountain, immediately following its restoration. His description of the scene omits mention of his own aspect, but we can assume that the show-man is playing the effect for all it is worth. "When I started to the chapel, the populace uncovered and fell back reverent-ly to make a wide way for me, as if I had been some kind of superior being—and I was. I was aware of that."

The Yankee plans to institute a modified monarchy until Ar-thur's death; in thirty years he feels that the popular mentali-ty will be equipped for the Republic. This is an essentially sound evaluation. And things seem to progress very smooth-ly. With the defeat of knight-errantry in the lists, with lasso and revolver, "the march of civilization was begun." But in Hank's own words, "How empty is theory in the presence of fact!" At heart the Boss is not a liberal; he is a despot, and not particularly enlightened at that. He is, therefore, quite pleased with the Gestapo tactics of his knights, "the most ef-fective spreaders of civilization we had." If a person cannot be persuaded to purchase the latest technological advance, such as a melodeon or a prohibition journal, the knights "re-moved him and passed on." When the Church's Interdict, supported by knight-hood, prevents the establishment of his Republic, Hank chooses the only truly democratic course of action—the liquidation of all his political opposition. The Boss declaims to his loyal fifty-two, "While one of these [knights] remains alive, our task is not finished, the war is not ended. We will kill them all."

Lastly, the Yankee never fully realizes the implications of the doctrine of training. Though he complains throughout the novel of the inbred and virtually unalterable feudal mentality, he is taken completely by surprise when the country reverts to its old ways under the Interdict. His absolute faith in prog-ress blinds him to the possibility of cultural regression. Hank recognizes at the outset that the philosophical bearing of the people "is not an outcome of mental training, intellectual for-titude, reasoning; it is mere animal training." He knows that the feudal mentality is dominated by "childish, idiotic, chuckle-headed, chicken-livered superstitions." In fact, the showman rises to power by capitalizing upon just this super-stitious ignorance. This is *the* medieval mentality, and it is not confined to the masses alone.

While Sandy dotes on her porcine princes the Boss observes, "The power of training! of influence! of education! It can bring a body up to believe anything." The theory of training even applies to the Yankee himself, for were he to undress in front of Sandy, Hank knows he would be embarrassed. He explains that "the prejudices of one's breeding are not gotten rid of just at a jump." Hank's most concise statement on the doctrine, as it applies to mankind in general, is found in chap-ter eighteen.

> Training—training is everything; training is all there is *to* a person. We speak of nature; it is folly; there is no such thing as nature; what we call by that misleading name is merely heredity and train-ing. We have no thoughts of our own, no opinions of our own; they are transmitted to us, trained into us.

Yet, despite the fact that this concept is repeated over and over again by the Yankee himself, he cannot see the regres-sive, negative aspect of this doctrine. He does not forsee the failure of his insurrection. He does not comprehend before-hand that the principle upon which he bases his capacity to establish the Republic contains within itself the assurance that the revolution will not succeed if prematurely instigated.

The Yankee is practical; he is no theoretician. Ironically, Clarence, his prize pupil, has to explain to him why he has not "educated the superstition out of those people," and why there remain only fifty-two boys, between the ages of fourteen and seventeen, to defend his cause.

> Because all the others were born in an atmosphere of superstition and reared in it. It is in their blood and bones. We imagined we had educated it out of them; they thought so, too; the Interdict woke them up like a thunderclap!

As evidenced in the portrayal of the Connecticut Yankee, Twain never intended the revolution to succeed. Despite Hank Morgan's seemingly superior intelligence and ability, we soon come to understand that it is only relative to the era in which he is placed. Twain impresses this upon us through Hank's "practical" and insensitive character and by endow-ing the Boss with a superficial concept of progress, a warped notion of democracy, and an incomplete comprehension of the significance of training. Throughout the novel Twain thus implicitly and explicitly undermines the Yankee's goal. And despite all the humor and the showmanship of Hank Morgan, we are left, in the final analysis, with "an ignoramus neverthe-less." (pp. 16-18)

> *William K. Spofford, "Mark Twain's Connecticut Yankee: An Ignoramus Nevertheless," in* Mark Twain Journal, *Vol. XV, No. 2, Summer, 1970, pp. 15-18.*

JUDITH FETTERLEY   (essay date 1973)

> [*In the following excerpt, Fetterley regards Hank Morgan as a profoundly negative character who manipulates and humili-ates others to satisfy his ego.*]

There is a recurrent image in *A Connecticut Yankee in King Arthur's Court,* which, when examined, reveals an impulse behind the writing of the story as central to it as the satiric and burlesque motives embedded in the title. Hank repeated-ly pictures himself with his hand hovering over a switch, his finger resting lightly on a button, which, if thrown or pushed, will flood the world with light or blow it to bits. He imagines himself at the center of some great machine, all of whose power can be activated only by him. Surely much of the satis-faction of this image lies in the disproportion between the ef-fort he must expend—the merest impulse of a finger—and the result he can achieve; much of its delight resides in the ease with which he can produce vast changes in the world. This ease is the index of his control and the mark of his superiori-ty. It is a most revealing image. And part of what it reveals is the fact that the conception of the story evoked for Mark Twain the image of a character who would have immense possibilities of power. From the start, *A Connecticut Yankee* offered Mark Twain the opportunity for indulging in a fanta-sy of omnipotence.

Mark Twain's investment in the fantasy of power is, however, continually balanced by his perspective on its implications. From the very beginning the possession of immense power is seen as ambivalent, and Hank as a character is ambiguous. This ambivalence is captured in the opening situation of the novel, describing Hank's first use of power, and, concomi-tantly, his first spectacle—namely, the eclipse. The eclipse is at once destructive and creative, at once a blotting out and a bringing back, both the threat of darkness and the gift of light. Hank announces the eclipse as a threat: "Go back and tell the king that at that hour I will smother the whole world in the dead blackness of midnight; I will blot out the sun, and he shall never shine again; the fruits of the earth shall rot for lack of light and warmth, and the peoples of the earth shall famish and die, to the last man!" His relish for the destructive capacity of his power is already evident. Clarence, while willing to help Hank, voices the fears that such power evokes in others when he begs Hank to "do the blessed sun no hurt." But when Hank himself refers to the eclipse from the vantage point of success, he presents it as an act of creation, regarded as such by the population which honors him "as the man who had by his unaided might saved the globe from destruction."

Hank's love of the theatrical is as obvious as that of his proto-type, Tom Sawyer. He is forever using theatrical metaphors and imagery, and the word "effects" is a constant element in his talk. It is nearly the last word on Hank in the book and it provides an excellent way into his psychology as a show-man. What stands behind this word, as far as Hank is con-cerned, is the desire for power over others and the ability to *affect* them. Hank seeks to control people as he controls a ma-chine, by switches and buttons; perhaps this is the central im-plication behind the contradictions of his plan to send "auto-mata" to a "Man-factory" to turn them into men. The thrill for the showman is in manipulating the emotions of people, working them up and down at will, like turning the hermit into a shirt factory, while all the time remaining himself abso-lutely unmoved and unaffected:

> It was immense—that effect! Lots of people shrieked, women curled up and quit in every direc-tion, foundlings collapsed by platoons. The abbot and the monks crossed themselves nimbly and their lips fluttered with agitated prayers. Merlin held his grip, but he was astonished clear down to his corns; he had never seen anything to begin with that, be-fore. Now was the time to pile in the effects.

The showman succeeds, of course, only to the extent to which people wish to be affected. As Hank contemptuously realizes, people love spectacles. They want to be moved and to feel they have had an intense experience. Thus the showman can do what he wants to as long as the members of his audience are assured that he is not actually going to damage them, ei-ther physically or in their self-esteem. But it is difficult for the showman to avoid threatening his audience, because the pos-session of power over them releases the ambivalence of his na-ture and constantly invites him to express the immense ego-tism of his personality and its concomitant contempt for oth-ers. Tom nearly loses control over the people of St. Peters-burg when he threatens to humiliate them by appearing at his own funeral. Hank, too, finds humiliation a natural extension of his desire to control people and discovers in the process that the power to manipulate is double-edged.

This pattern is played out most clearly in the chapter entitled "Dowley's Humiliation." Hank has carried out his plan of in-viting Dowley, the self-made and self-satisfied blacksmith, and a couple of other men to Marco's for a meal where, un-known to the guests, he has laid in a spread the like of which the century has never seen. Hank is only moderately interest-ed in the pleasure his scheme gives to the Marcos. He is more interested in the opportunities it presents for enhancing his own image. But his main focus, as the title of the chapter and the structure of the plan indicate, is the puncturing of Dowley and what is, for Hank, his false sense of self-importance. The situation is perfectly constructed to make Dowley inflict much of the damage on himself. He is led on, through his ego-tism, to puff himself, and Hank has only to sit back and watch him collapse under the "effect" of the lavish spread. Hank, however, controls the danger inherent in this humiliation and brings Dowley back to a relative sense of ease. But he does this only in order to work the same trick again. He lets the conversation drift into the area of political economy and quickly spots the chance to puncture Dowley and wipe an-other self-satisfied smirk off his face. The subject is "protec-tion" versus "free trade," Dowley holding forth for the for-mer and Hank arguing with what seems to him impeccable logic for the latter. But Dowley refuses to be convinced, and, far from losing his smirk, increases it with every "absurdity" he detects in Hank's reasoning. This is an impossible situa-tion for Hank; he himself is being affected rather than affect-ing, being humiliated rather than humiliating. So he sets out to create an "effect" that will put him back in control.

As Hank sets about his trap, we observe again the psychology of the showman. He goes for Dowley in a completely cool and collected way, knowing exactly where each point will lead and where the plan will ultimately end, but never letting his victim have the slightest inkling, a strategy which increases both his control over the situation and the intensity of the ef-fect he can produce. Nor does he let Dowley know that he is out to get him, for the intent is thoroughly disguised under the playful tone and casual drift of the conversation. When Hank springs his trap by showing that he knows enough about Dowley to get him put in the stocks and probably killed in the process, the victim is taken totally by surprise and the effect is tremendous. Dowley is astonished and petrified. While humiliation punctures the proud man and inflates the humiliator, enlarging his ego in proportion to the other's de-flation, the manipulation of fear leaves the victim rigid, like stone—the effect is inherent in the words "astonished" and "petrified." The manipulator, on the other hand, is left free and flexible, in control of both body and emotions. This situa-tion is repeated later, in the fight between Hank and the knights of England. Sir Sagramor is an image of stone, inflexi-ble, rigid, a "tower of iron." Hank is the image of absolute ease, flexibility, and control. Again emphasis is laid on the contrast between the minimal effort Hank makes and the co-lossal effort Sir Sagramor must expend, only to achieve hu-miliation and defeat: ". . . it was a game of tag, with all the advantage on my side; I whirled out of his path with ease whenever I chose, and once I slapped him on the back as I went to the rear." Again the contrast extends to the emotions. Hank remains perfectly cool while Sir Sagramor becomes more and more enraged. Finally he charges at Hank with all the force he can command. In response, Hank simply con-verts Sir Sagramor's passion into the momentum necessary to drag him off his horse. He uses Sir Sagramor's strength against him just as he used Dowley's egotism against him. This, of course, is the ultimate humiliation, not simply to make a fool of a person but to make that person at root re-sponsible for what has happened to him.

It is obvious that a large component of the showman's per-sonality is egotism. Hank's egotism is reflected in the title he delights in, "The Boss." Like Tom Sawyer's "The Black Avenger," or "The Traveler," or "The Erronort," the defi-nite article states that there is only one and that the person holding the title is unique. Hank's conviction that he is a su-perior being is everywhere apparent. What is not so apparent, however, is the extent to which Hank's egotism is related to the rest of his character. Despite his frequent democratic pronouncements, his occasional "a man is a man, at bottom," or his perception that a king can be a man, Hank has a basic contempt for people. The feeling permeates his character from his first reflection that the prisoners at King Arthur's court are mere "white Indians" to his final verdict, "Imagine such human muck as this." The only figures who are exempt from this judgment are Clarence and the boys, who are simply replicas of Hank, and Sandy, who, after she has served the ends of satirizing romance, falls quietly into the category of idealized womanhood.

Behind much of Hank's contempt lies the conviction that he can do what others do far better than they can. His contempt is an inverse expression of his own egotism. This fact emerges even in the smallest details of the story. For instance, Hank's animus against Sir Dinadan and his wretched joke of tying metal mugs to dogs' tails derives essentially from his resentment at the fact that such an unimaginative and simple-minded trick can gain attention for its perpetrator. His resentment is at root a form of jealousy of a rival showman. The same emotions arise in his confrontation with the rival magician in the Valley of Holiness, and his contempt for the court in the one case and the people of the Valley in the other is a product of his disgust at their being attracted by so paltry a talent. Behind this emotion, of course, is Hank's belief that he could provide a far better joke and a far better spectacle. What Hank cannot tolerate is another's self-satisfaction, as when Sir Dinadan laughs at his own joke, being immensely pleased with himself and his effect and expecting Hank to respond. But the showman cannot bear being audience. He has no desire to build up another's ego through his laughter. Thus Sir Dinadan's joke seems almost an insult to Hank. The fact that the joke is about the humiliation of "a humorous lecturer who flooded an ignorant audience with the killingest jokes for an hour and never got a laugh" is equally suggestive of Hank's sensitivity to his own humiliation.

It is clear that Hank feels he is not sufficiently appreciated. Much of his contempt for others must be seen in this light. Thus Hank fulminates against the people who, because he has no title, no inherited name, admire and fear him "as an animal is admired and feared" but give him neither reverence nor respect. His outrage against injustice takes on new significance from this perspective; the injustice lies in the self-importance of others—"the possessor's old and inbred custom of regarding himself as a superior being"—and their failure to see that Hank himself is the "superior being." Hank's sense of not being sufficiently appreciated is further manifest in the pattern of betrayal which emerges from the book. Part of the texture of the scene with the rival magician, it is even more pronounced in the sequence of events that begins with Hank and the king's visit to the smallpox hut and the subsequent stay with the Marcos. Hank becomes a hero in Marco's eyes when he denounces him for setting off to betray his cousins who have set fire to the manor of Abblasoure and murdered the Baron. But Marco betrays Hank in spite of all that Hank has given him, and arouses the village and its dogs to track him down. The climax of this sequence occurs when the "gentleman," who arrives in the nick of time to save Hank and the king from the wrath of the village, suddenly drops chains on them and has them sold as slaves.

This pattern of treachery and betrayal recurs significantly at the end of the book. The doctors, apparently solicitous for the health of Hank's child, prove to be merely the paid spies of the church. And so does "every officer of [the] ship" and "every man of the crew." During the final battle, Hank is moved by compassion for the suffering of the wounded and goes out to see if he can relieve them. As he bends over a knight who has asked for help, the man stabs him. And finally comes Merlin, appearing in the guise of a healer at a time when help is most needed and disguised as one of the people for whom Hank is presumably fighting. But Hank's personal betrayal grows out of the larger betrayals that initiate the ending of the story. As Arthur has been betrayed for many years by Launcelot and Guenevere, so they in turn are finally betrayed by Mordred and Agravaine. Mordred, left in command at Arthur's departure for France, turns traitor, not simply to Arthur but to the entire kingdom, for he calls down the wrath of the church upon it. Thus, when Hank returns to England, he enters a situation built on multiple treacheries and the stage is prepared for his own final betrayal. The people, intimidated by the church, gather not to his side but to that of the enemy. "*All England*—ALL ENGLAND!—*is marching against you!*" It is the ultimate betrayal. And Hank's reaction to it is the ultimate expression of the egotism that underlies this sense of betrayal, the conviction that he is too good for the world in which he finds himself. It is pearls before swine, Hank Morgan and the "human muck."

Hank's betrayal, however, is ultimately a self-betrayal. That is the meaning played out in the record of Clarence's postscript and caught in this image of one dead knight electrocuting a second knight, a friend, as he lays a hand on his shoulder. The source of Hank's self-betrayal lies essentially in the characteristic which now claims our attention, his aggression. It is no accident that Hank enters the world of King Arthur through a brawl; he is a violent man. Throughout the book Hank is filled with indignation, anger, outrage. He is himself much of the time a seething volcano just barely under control, always on the verge of exploding. This may explain why the imagery of explosion dominates the novel and why Hank is fascinated at once with the idea of a volcano and the thought of controlling it. Certainly much of what makes the experience of the book uncomfortable is the fact that we, as readers, are forced at many points to participate in these emotions. William Dean Howells commented in his review of *A Connecticut Yankee,* "There are incidents in this wonder-book which wring the heart for what has been of cruelty and wrong in the past, and leave it burning with shame and hate for the conditions which are of like effect in the present." In many scenes, especially those which take place when Hank and the king travel as slaves, the book ceases to be a self-contained aesthetic experience; instead, the reader is made so angry that he wants to get up out of his chair and smash something, preferably the perpetrator of the cruelty he has just witnessed. This reaction in effect makes him over in the image of Hank and directs him toward an understanding of both Hank's character and his tale.

Like Huck, Hank feels the suffering of others acutely; like Huck, he has a conscience that forever holds before him pictures of cruelty that he can not forget; like Huck's, his adventures present a telling record of man's inhumanity to his fellows. But Huck's perceptions are only rarely formulated into statements about human nature, and they issue at once in a desperate desire to avoid aggression and a guilty sense of being somehow responsible for it all. Hank's perceptions are continually formulated into general condemnations of the human race and his capacity to feel turns into indignation, a hatred of hating, a desire to aggress against the aggressors and kill the killers. This reaction constitutes the dynamics of Chapter XVII, "In The Queen's Dungeons," which opens with the remark, "I had a great desire to rack the executioner." Later in the chapter Hank attempts to praise Morgan Le Fay for paying for the page she has killed, and comments, " 'Madame, your people will adore you for this.' Quite true, but I meant to hang her for it someday, if I lived." The extreme statement of this reaction, however, occurs in Hank's remarks on the French Revolution, "it being immutable law that all revolutions that will succeed must *begin* in blood, whatever may answer afterward. If history teaches anything, it teaches that."

Like Tom Sawyer's and in contrast to Huck Finn's, all of Hank's aggression is deflected outward in one form or another. The contempt noted above is certainly one of these forms, for it is a mode of attack on another person. Even Hank's perceptions of cruelty frequently turn into contempt, both for the victim and the victimizer. Equally, his perceptions of his own discomfort turn to contempt. When Huck is bothered by clothes, he describes the feeling and takes off the clothes. When Hank is bothered by his armor, he fulminates against the human beings who have been so stupid as to invent and wear the stuff. Hank is without self-criticism. The only fault of his own which he notes is his excessive ingenuity, but the criticism is presented in such a way that it becomes a covert form of praise. Hank does not really believe his cleverness is at fault; he believes it has been sabotaged by the stupidity of the people around him who climb the wrong tree or accept his tip-off about the escaped slave. He is singularly free from guilt. His few scattered references to the conscience are so out of character and context as to be meaningless. They make sense only as Hank at these points ceases to be a fictional persona and becomes a mouthpiece for the feelings of Mark Twain, or, better, Samuel L. Clemens.

Hank is so free from self-criticism and self-perspective that he can criticize in others what are patently his own characteristics. Henry Nash Smith in *Mark Twain: The Development of a Writer* perceptively suggests the contradictions and hypocrisies in Hank Morgan's character. He notes, for instance, that despite the Yankee's claims to be a harbinger of truth, despite his contempt for Merlin as a fraud, a liar, and a fake, "all his effects . . . are achieved by fraudulent methods." The element of contradiction is equally apparent in Hank's reaction to the knights of the Round Table. He criticizes them for their love of fighting, but a fight has placed Hank himself into his situation. One would be hard put to distinguish between the miscellaneous brawls at the Colt Arms Factory and the battles of the Round Table, except that, if anything, we find the fights in King Arthur's world less reprehensible for the very features which disgust Hank: "As a general thing—as far as I could make out—these murderous adventures were not forays undertaken to avenge injuries, nor to settle old disputes or sudden fallings out; no, as a rule they were simply duels between strangers—duels between people who had never even been introduced to each other, and between whom existed no cause of offense whatever." In *Adventures of Huckleberry Finn,* Mark Twain implied that this pure animal activity without the complications of consciousness to corrupt it was better than the "honorable" feuding of the Grangerfords and Shepherdsons; in *The Mysterious Stranger* he would overtly praise it. This difference between forms of aggression is fully dramatized in the person of Arthur, who delights in fighting almost as a sport. Unlike Hank, who fights bitterly for the Right, the king fights without rancor or

hatred or contempt, simply for the love of it: "What joy flamed up in the king's eye! . . . He had been fasting long, he was hungry for a fight."

Clearly, aggression is part of the personality of the showman. It is present in his use of his power to humiliate; it is caught in the very metaphors used: wilt, shrivel, puncture, deflate. Behind the desire to make someone look ridiculous is the desire to destroy that person, if not literally, then in terms of his power over the minds of others, his image in their eyes. Thus Hank encourages the knights of the Round Table to ride around the country with sandwich boards on their backs advertising soap, toothbrushes, stove polish: " . . . it was a furtive, underhand blow at this nonsense of knight errantry, though nobody suspected that but me." The aggression behind the showman's desire to affect is equally apparent. One of the effects Hank most delights in is that of terror; he enjoys watching people dissolve in fear and trembling before him. It is equally part of the showman's character in his role of raconteur: "At last I ventured a story myself; and vast was the success of it. . . . the fifth time I told it, they began to crack in places; the eighth time I told it, they began to crumble; at the twelfth repetition they fell apart in chunks; and at the fifteenth they disintegrated, and I got a broom and swept them up." The delightful effect of the funny story is imagined as the annihilation of the audience.

Aggression seems to be always a part of Hank's playfulness. It emerges in the small detail of the toy gun which he invents for use as a purse, and it is a pervasive element in his jokes:

> The noise at night would have been annoying to me ordinarily, but I didn't mind it in the present circumstances, because it kept me from hearing the quacks detaching legs and arms from the day's cripples. They ruined an uncommon good old crosscut saw for me, and broke the saw-buck, too, but I let it pass. And as for my ax—well, I made up my mind that the next time I lent an ax to a surgeon I would pick my century.

> The poor queen was so scared and humbled that she was even afraid to hang the composer without first consulting me. I was very sorry for her—indeed, any one would have been, for she was really suffering; so I was willing to do anything that was reasonable, and had no desire to carry things to wanton extremities. I therefore considered the matter thoughtfully, and ended by having the musicians ordered into our presence to play that Sweet Bye and Bye again, which they did. Then I saw that she was right, and gave her permission to hang the whole band.

> But the thing which clean broke my heart was something which happened in front of our old barrack in a square, while we were enduring the spectacle of a man being boiled to death in oil for counterfeiting pennies. It was the sight of a newsboy—and I couldn't get at him!

Perhaps a more accurate way of looking at these passages is to see them as attempts on Hank's part to control his aggression. The last two passages in particular follow hard on scenes of intense indignation, Hank's rage at the queen's wanton killing of a page and his horror at the vision of a young mother hanged for stealing a piece of cloth. This burlesque is an elaborate mockery of his indignation and as such is a form of control over it. By treating as a joke situations which have previously made him burn with anger, Hank manages, at least momentarily, to see the absurdity of his indignation and to divert its damaging and dangerous emotion into a kind of laughter.

There are other ways in which Hank attempts to control his aggressions. He is, for instance, always thinking, reflecting, philosophizing. What he achieves on occasion is a sublimation of emotion in thought, a dissipation of the intensity of particular feelings through large generalizations about human nature. And some of these generalizations serve particularly well. Certainly this is one way of looking at the constant references Hank makes to the deterministic philosophy of "training." Bernard DeVoto in "The Symbols of Despair" has suggestively discussed the relationship between Mark Twain's evolution of a deterministic philosophy and his need to absolve himself from blame for the tragedies of his later years. In *A Connecticut Yankee in King Arthur's Court* the philosophy is equally functional, though in a different way. If men are not responsible for what they do, if they have no choice, if everything is simply a matter of their training, then they cannot be blamed or hated, but must rather be retrained—sent to a "Man-factory." This way of perceiving humanity, which Hank succeeds in holding from time to time, does, at those moments, serve to control his aggression.

Ultimately, of course, Hank's aggression is uncontrollable and his attempts to divert it through jokes and philosophy fail. As Allen Guttmann has observed in his brief study of the Yankee's negative aspects, "The Boss's wake is strewn with terror and with corpses." And, of course, the ending of the book is an excessive statement of uncontrolled aggression. But if Hank fails to control his aggression, he does not fail in the age-old gambit, central to the experience of *Huckleberry Finn,* of legitimizing his aggression by presenting it as right and just. In this connection Hank is Tom Sawyer and the Grangerfords seen from the inside. We watch not simply the action produced but the mind at work producing it. Hank has a whole panoply of modes for legitimizing his aggression, but the main one is provided by the simplifications of his melodramatic imagination, his capacity to see things as Good and Bad, with himself, of course, representing the Good. This is particularly clear in the creation of Morgan Le Fay, who although grotesque and ridiculous, is still presented as the epitome of evil. The same approach is taken with numerous minor characters, such as the slave driver. Certainly anything done against such people is legitimate. This process of simplification can also be observed in Hank's treatment of the Catholic Church. As pure evil, with its symbol, appropriately, the blackness of the Interdict, it conveniently serves as the scapegoat for all the ills of the world Hank inhabits. He has no qualms about attacking it in any fashion: "It being my conviction that any Established Church is an established crime, an established slave-pen, I had no scruples, but was willing to assail it in any way or with any weapon that promised to hurt it." And as he here justifies all means because of the end in view, so does he justify the slaughter which takes place at the end of the book, for the knights, by virtue of their association with the church, deserve to be killed.

A striking example of the utility of simplification is provided at the beginning of Chapter XVII:

> The priests told me about this, and were generously hot to have him punished. Something of this disagreeable sort was turning up every now and then. I mean, episodes that showed that not all priests were frauds and self-seekers, but that many, even

the great majority, of these that were down on the ground among the common people, were sincere and right-hearted, and devoted to the alleviation of human troubles and sufferings. Well, it was a thing which could not be helped, so I seldom fretted about it, and never many minutes at a time; it has never been my way to bother much about things which you can't cure. But I did not like it, for it was just the sort of thing to keep people reconciled to an Established Church.

Of course, the scene is treated humorously; it is one of Hank's few stabs at laughing at himself, but it is more revealing than qualifying, for it demonstrates that even when Hank perceives complications he does not allow them to affect his way of thinking. His perception about the priests becomes merely a tactical problem in his attempt to melodramatize the nation.

Another mode available to Hank for justifying his aggression is the imagination of betrayal basic to his character. If people betray one, then they become legitimate objects of attack; retaliation becomes a matter of self-defense and, indeed, justice. Thus all Hank's feelings of betrayal lead to a massive justification for his final battle in which Good is pitched against Evil, the Betrayed against the Betrayers. This process of justification is dramatized near the end. Hank is moved by his "conscience" to take pity on the knights of England and spare them from annihilation. He writes a message offering them amnesty if they will surrender and shows it to Clarence. But Clarence neatly releases his conscience by describing to him how the knights would receive his message and messenger: "Dismember me this animal, and return him in a basket to the base-born knave who sent him; other answer have I none!" The knights would betray Hank's trust; therefore it is right, just, finally necessary to annihilate them.

While Hank is thoroughly successful in directing his aggression outward, by the end of the book his success is equally his defeat; his destruction of others is also self-destruction. The ending of the book carries out the implications present from the start that power is double-edged, and at the end, as at the beginning, Hank is in a trap of his own making. But the ending of the book is not simply an expression of the ambivalence inherent in the possession of power; it is equally an exorcism of the fantasy of power which lies at the heart of *A Connecticut Yankee in King Arthur's Court.* The absurdity of the ending, its grotesquely comic exaggerations, the constant intrusion into it of the element of burlesque, beginning with Clarence's references to photographs taken of the queen at the stake and with Hank's response to Clarence's casualty list, and continuing through the final scenes when Hank describes the reception of his proclamation to his army, all express Mark Twain's vision of the absurdity which his character and story had become. Originally conceived as a successor to Huck Finn, a character who would adopt the latter's role of traveling through a corrupt world and exposing its corruption, Hank turned out to be another Tom Sawyer. Armed with the gospels of democracy, Hank sets out to do battle with the evils of monarchy, aristocracy, and church, with all the tyranny of privilege that lives on egotism, self-righteousness, hypocrisy, and aggression. But in the process of hating privilege and attacking its various forms, Hank takes on each of the qualities that it embodies. What Mark Twain discovered in writing *A Connecticut Yankee* was the underside of the personality of the reformer and satirist. The character who set out to reform the world turned out to be one of its greatest evils, and the comic exaggerations of the ending are an elaborate joke on the fantasies of power, aggression, and egotism which are at the root of the reforming impulse.

The final index of Mark Twain's awareness of the nature of his character and of the meaning of his story lies in the tone of the frame that concludes the novel. Far from indignantly turning on Hank and destroying him in a burst of righteous anger, an approach which would simply have made the author into another version of his character, Mark Twain renders his character pathetic and thus finally severs whatever bonds of identification may have existed between them:

> Presently his fingers began to pick busily at the coverlet, and by that sign I knew that his end was at hand. With the first suggestion of the death-rattle in his throat he started up slightly, and seemed to listen: then he said: "A bugle? . . . It is the king! The drawbridge, there! Man the battlements!—turn out the—"
>
> He was getting up his last "effect", but he never finished it.

If Hank Morgan is a study of the reformer, he is equally a study of the entertainer, a study which presents the reverse side of the vision embodied in *The Adventures of Tom Sawyer.* If *A Connecticut Yankee in King Arthur's Court* presents the underside of the reformer's character, it equally presents the underside of the entertainer's character, exposing, as it does, his insatiable egotism, which precludes any self-perspective and makes him incapable of bearing the jokes of others, and the aggressive passion to manipulate and humiliate which lies at the root of his performance. (pp. 667-79)

> *Judith Fetterley, "Yankee Showman and Reformer: The Character of Mark Twain's Hank Morgan," in* Texas Studies in Literature and Language, *Vol. XIV, No. 4, Winter, 1973, pp. 667-79.*

DAVID KETTERER (essay date 1974)

[*In the following excerpt, Ketterer examines the implications of the recurring image of the eclipse in* A Connecticut Yankee in King Arthur's Court.]

Hank Morgan's use of a solar eclipse in order to impress upon King Arthur and his court that a mighty magician—superior to Merlin—stands before them is undoubtedly the most impressive episode in *A Connecticut Yankee in King Arthur's Court,* Mark Twain's time-travel version of the international novel. Arthur is at least as affected as the reader, and as a consequence, Hank is transformed from being a prisoner into being the Boss. But the reader is perhaps not likely to fully appreciate, and Arthur not at all, that on a thematic and symbolic level, this blotting out and temporary displacement of one heavenly body by another parallels the "transposition of epochs—and bodies [human and stellar]," which is the donnée of the novel—the displacement of nineteenth-century America by sixth-century Britain, and subsequently the displacement, tentative, then total, of sixth-century Britain by nineteenth-century America. By equating this "epoch-eclipse" with the apparent extinction of the sun, Twain is implying that the posited world transformation is conceivably an event of apocalyptic proportions.

Because this revelation is a continuing process, the book is repeatedly given to fiery reminders of the epoch-eclipse that has taken place. Indeed the work is remarkable for the number of explosions that occur and for images that draw on the sun's various qualities: its fieriness, its circularity, its color, and its role as a source of light. As I hope to demonstrate, all these instances depend upon "The Eclipse" chapter for their essential meaning.

If all the rather intricate connections I shall argue for are not immediately obvious to the reader, they are even less apparent to Hank, although, as the narrator, he is the source of all the information. Hank, being a narrowly pragmatic exhibitionist and something of a boor, is incredibly obtuse, unaware, and quite incapable of questioning his own attitudes. These limitations manifest themselves in a hackneyed and exaggerated speech which admirably serves the purposes of comedy and burlesque at the expense both of Arthur's England and of himself as a representative nineteenth-century "Yankee." But what Hank's style does not allow for, as James M. Cox has made very clear [see excerpt dated 1966], is enough "analytic intelligence or wit to discharge his growing indignation" when the novel moves from an essentially burlesque to an essentially satiric stance. In other words, because Hank cannot function satisfactorily as a satiric norm, and because, outside of the frame, there is no "Mark Twain" narrator, the novel lacks an acceptable perspective on reality. All the reader has is the very limited perspective implied by Hank's style, a perspective that would certainly not generate and would seemingly deny the possibility of any subtle imagistic design. My analysis of imagistic patterning, which follows, must, then, infer a sophisticated consciousness that is otherwise explicitly absent from the novel. An explanation as to why Twain excluded from his satire a normative and intelligent consciousness which might have provided a convincing source for imagistic significance, in favor of a philistine who is a most unconvincing source, must await the further development of my argument.

Lest the reader miss the sun's function as an apocalyptic image, Twain is careful to associate the eclipse with that biblical prefiguration of the Apocalypse, the Flood: " . . . when the silver rim of the sun pushed itself out, a moment or two later, the assemblage broke loose with a vast shout and came pouring down like a deluge to smother me with blessings and gratitude." It is assumed that Hank's incantation, timed with the astronomical process, is the causal factor. So it is that Hank escapes death at the stake by fire or, in symbolic terms, survives the apocalypse and successfully enters the new world. Previously, after being hit on the head in the nineteenth century, the old "world went out in darkness"—like a light. Now we learn that "the eclipse had scared the British world almost to death: that while it lasted . . . the churches, hermitages, and monkeries overflowed with praying and weeping poor creatures who thought the end of the world had come." As Hank notices "my eclipse beginning," he exclaims, "I was a new man." During the eclipse he literally puts on the new man by donning the sixth-century clothes that befit his new status.

As a further exhibition of his power and in order to consolidate his position, Hank arranges the first of many explosions. His "magic" causes Merlin's tower, conceivably an apocalyptic symbol in its own right, to blow up:

> I made about three passes in the air, and then there was an awful crash and that old tower leaped into the sky in chunks, along with a vast volcanic fountain of fire that turned night to noonday [previous-

ly, noonday had been turned into night, since the eclipse occurred at approximately twelve noon], and showed a thousand acres of human beings groveling on the ground in a general collapse of consternation."

I contend that the symbolic relationship between the eclipse and this explosion, pointed up here by the specific time reversal, is intended as applying to the remaining explosive fires in the book.

No sooner has Hank adjusted to the displacement of the nineteenth century by the sixth than he attempts to reverse the process. It is his particular aim to replace the monarchy and the aristocracy with a democracy, and it is toward this end that the only title he is willing to accept is that granted by the entire nation: "THE BOSS." Just as, during the eclipse, the moon threw the sun into shadow, so democracy will eclipse monarchy. "I was no shadow of a king; I was the substance; the king himself was the shadow," affirms Hank. And in a voice very reminiscent of Huckleberry Finn, Hank continues, "It is enough to make a body ashamed of his race to think of the sort of froth that has always occupied its thrones without shadow of right or reason. . . . " Is it a mistake to deduce from the shadow image the light necessary to produce shadow and from there to recall the sun once more? However this may be, Dan Beard's illustrations, which accompanied the original text, frequently make overt what Twain only implies. In this case, a drawing of the solar eclipse has the sun symbolic of the "Divine Rights of Kings VI ceny," while the moon, which bears the legend "The Earth belongs to the People XIX ceny," casts the "shadow of right and reason."

Concurrently, Hank manages surreptitiously to install most nineteenth-century technical improvements, notably electric light, and thereby the emergent nineteenth century is associated with explosive fire: "There it was, as sure a fact, and as substantial a fact as any serene volcano, standing innocent with its smokeless summit in the blue sky [the sun is shining!] and giving no sign of the rising hell in its bowels." Meanwhile, in his despair at turning Sandy, his traveling companion, into a pragmatic nineteenth-century American woman, Hank can conceive the transformation only by blowing her up: "It may be that this girl had a fact in her somewhere, but I don't believe you could have . . . got it with the earlier forms of blasting, even; it was a case for dynamite." The attention paid to Hank's pipe, which causes Sandy to faint, is not accidental. Its forceful effect may be more accurately attributable to its function as a symbol of the apocalyptic change associated with Hank. Surely the episode in which Hank, mistaken for "one of those fire-belching dragons," routs "half a dozen armed men and their squires" is a little too fantastic in anything other than symbolic terms. Hank should be seen as a Prometheus bringing to the Middle Ages the fire of the nineteenth century. Just as Prometheus is assisted by Hercules, so Hank's displacement depends upon being hit on the head by "a fellow we used to call Hercules." It should also be noted that Hank's father, like Vulcan, was a blacksmith.

Announcing, in his Tom Sawyer voice, "You can't throw too much style into a miracle," Hank takes pains that the restoration of the dry fountain in the Valley of Holiness doesn't lack the apocalyptic element: "Then I touched off the hogshead of rockets, and a vast fountain of dazzling lances of fire [here fire and flood are identified] vomited itself towards the zenith [the position of the sun at greatest strength and, in traditional

symbology, a point of exit from the world of space and time—the eclipse, it will be recalled, occurred at midday on June 21, the time at which the sun is at its zenith in the Western Hemisphere] with a hissing rush, and burst in mid-sky into a storm of flashing jewels!" The cry of exultation that follows might be an appropriate response to a sight of the jeweled New Jerusalem descending from the sky's zenith, although mention of "flashing jewels" may not itself warrant such an extension. This event is written up in the newspaper that Hank has founded, the *Weekly Hosannah and Literary Volcano,* with the phrase "INFERNAL FIRE AND SMOKE AND THUNDER!" in large print. The column "Local Smoke and Cinders" is presented as being representative of the rest of the paper. If Marshall McLuhan is right about the impact of the Gutenberg revolution, and, at a later point, Gutenberg, along with Watt, Arkwright, Whitney, Morse, Stephenson, and Bell are credited, "after God," as "the creators of this world," Hank could find no surer means than a newspaper of displacing a sixth-century reality by a nineteenth-century reality. It is then meaningful that the newspaper by its titles and headline is associated with apocalyptic heat. No wonder that Hank, upon reading this first edition, feels, "Yes, this was heaven."

The journey Hank and Arthur make through the kingdom is undertaken with the intention of opening Arthur's eyes to that reality of sixth-century England of which Hank has become aware in the earlier part of the book. There are two disconnected worlds or realms of experience in sixth-century England, since the romantic experience of Arthur, his knights, and the aristocracy is quite distinct from the actual living conditions of the majority of the population. The nineteenth-century experience is similarly dual: there is the technological utopia in which Hank believes, his own form of romanticism, and the dehumanized Armageddon that is much closer to a possible future reality. There are, then, essentially four worlds in *A Connecticut Yankee:* two negative visions—of the sixth century and of the nineteenth century—and two corresponding positive visions. Twain's purpose is to have Arthur undergo an apocalypse of mind in recognizing the negative reality of his time, and subsequently to have Hank experience a similar apocalyptic revelation concerning the negative reality of his epoch. The effect of this movement is of course to imply an essential lack of differentiation between the sixth century and the nineteenth century.

While traveling with the king incognito, Hank engineers another miracle, which consists of another explosion, in order to dispose of some troublesome knights. Thus we are provided with an objective correlative for Arthur's dawning realization about the sham of chivalry. By noting that the conflagration "resembled a steamboat explosion on the Mississippi," Hank associates it with a new and different world and consequently with the notion of apocalyptic transformation. A fifth instance of fire, the manor-house fire and the death of the lord of the manor, is intended as symbolic of the end of an old, feudal world. For accompaniment "there was an ear-splitting explosion of thunder, and the bottom of heaven fell out; the rain poured down in a deluge"—the mixture of fire and flood as before.

Hank's efforts to update the sixth-century economy allow Twain to draw symbolically on a further characteristic of the sun—its circularity. Dan Beard diagrams the revolution as a coinlike sun emerging over the horizon. Around its edges are the words "free trade." The new "currency" Hank introduces, plus the notion of "a trade union, to *coin* [italics mine] a new phrase," must be seen for the puns contained if these measures are to impart their total meaning; likewise the description of the "gun-purse," which uses different-sized shot for money and which Hank offers as an explanation for the phrase "Paying the shot." In other words, the new money and the new world of mind it signifies entail destruction. Revolutionary ideas must be circulated to be effective—hence the rather weird information, regarding the gun-purse, that "you could carry it in your mouth," wherefrom, of course, might issue that "Paying the shot" line, which "would still be passing men's lips, away down in the nineteenth century."

It is Arthur's experience as a slave—as a part of that slave band which Hank had witnessed earlier—that, more than anything else, encourages the emergence of his new awareness and heroic stature. Once again the revelation and reversal of fortune is accompanied by fire. The slave-holders smoke Arthur and Hank out of the tree in which they were hiding: "They raised their pile of dry brush and damp weeds higher and higher, and when they saw the thick cloud begin to roll up and smother the tree, they broke out in a storm of joy-clamors." One might here recall Hank's earlier experience, when "the fagots were carefully and tediously piled about my ankles, my knees, my thighs, my body," just prior to the eclipse. I would incidentally not insist upon the addition of the symbolic dimension to all the incidents and images involving fire were it not for two factors: first, the apparently deliberate referral back to the eclipse that most of these fiery verbal details encourage, and second, the coincidence of these combustible elements with moments of major transformation and revelation.

In a following episode Hank and Arthur, still slaves, witness the actual burning of a witch: "They fastened her to a post; they brought wood and piled it about her; they applied the torch, while she shrieked and pleaded and strained her two younger daughters to her breast; and our brute, with a heart solely for business, lashed us into position about the stake and warmed us into life and commercial value by the same fire that took away the innocent life of that poor harmless mother." Again we recall Hank's possibly similar fate at the stake, but the incident is particularly important to the process of revelation that Arthur is undergoing. In addition, this incident illustrates particularly well the dual nature of an apocalypse: it is both destructive and creative. Shortly afterward, Hank and Arthur witness a similar atrocity: the hanging of a young girl after a priest has pulled her baby from her arms. The priest pledges to look after the child: "You should have seen her face then! Gratitude? Lord, what do you want with words to express that? *Words are only painted fire; a look is the fire itself* (my italics). She gave that look, and carried it away to the treasury of heaven, where all things that are divine belong." Here fire is specifically equated with divine will and thereby with apocalyptic revelation. Fire figures yet again in the next episode, which features "a man being boiled to death in oil for counterfeiting pennies"—for inability to adapt to Hank's new currency?

Hank and Arthur are finally rescued, Arthur with his neck in a noose, when, in response to Hank's telephone call, five hundred knights come cycling to his aid, seemingly having harnessed the power and aggression of the sun itself: "Lord, how the plumes streamed, how the sun flamed and flashed from the endless procession of webby wheels!" It might be noted in passing, that the idea of the sun as a fiery wheel goes back to antiquity. Hank describes this spectacle as "the grandest sight that ever was seen." Yet at a later point, when an army, similarly sun-coated since "the sun struck the sea of armor and set it all aflash," aligns itself *against* Hank, the impression is even more formidable: "I hadn't ever seen anything to beat it." In between these two moments Hank suffers a major reversal. The remaining action consists of an escalated series of violent encounters between Hank, or the nineteenth century, and Arthur's knights, or the sixth century. As I hope to demonstrate, the association of the knights with the sun is not accidental. This climactic Armageddon is a kind of literal equivalent to the solar eclipse, the symbolic import of which I trust I have made sufficiently clear. But whereas the solar eclipse seemingly signaled the displacement of the sixth century by the nineteenth for the people of Arthur's England and the displacement of the nineteenth century by the sixth for Hank, the concluding Armageddon signifies, for the world of King Arthur, a final if costly victory of the sixth-century reality over that of the nineteenth century and, for Hank personally, a displacement of the sixth century by the nineteenth century. In a sense, then, both sides win and both sides lose.

The tournament between Hank and Sir Sagramour, motivated at the beginning of the book, is in reality "a duel not of muscle but of mind," a "mysterious and awful battle of the gods," because the real conflict is that between two magicians, Hank and Merlin. It is described in terms of a conflict of the elements of fire and air. To the repeated blasts of apocalyptic bugles, Sir Sagramour, and after him other knights, engage Hank in combat. All fall prey to the "snaky spirals" of Hank's lasso, which is linked with a whirlwind. Thus Hank "whirled" out of Sir Sagramour's path, which occasions a "whirlwind of applause," while, afterward, Lancelot falls "with the rush of a whirlwind." Sir Lancelot is described as "the very sun of their shining system," while one of his predecessors charges "like a house afire." Sir Lancelot's fall is greeted with a "thunder-crash of applause." After Merlin steals his lasso, Hank is compelled to use his revolver to halt the five hundred knights who then bear down upon him. Hank's subsequent challenge to take on with fifty assistants *"the massed chivalry of the whole earth and destroy it"* is not taken up initially. However, the double syntactic ambiguity of the italicized section of the challenge (the words "massed chivalry" may be a description of the "whole earth," the "it" may refer back to the "whole earth") allows for the implication that he will destroy the whole world, and makes the cosmic and apocalyptic nature of the upcoming conflict readily apparent.

Following the civil war between the king's party and Sir Lancelot's over Guinevere, which began when Lancelot thwarted the king's intention to "purify her with fire" (we might well recall once more Hank's own experience at the stake), and the civil war between Arthur's group and Sir Mordred's for possession of the kingdom, during which Arthur is killed, both Hank and Mordred find themselves bereft of power by force of the Church Interdict. However, Clarence, Hank's chief helper, has prepared Merlin's cave for a siege, whereupon Hank declares his republic. (Actually the cave is as much Plato's as Merlin's, given Twain's concern with the nature of reality. . . .) At the battle of the sand-belt, Hank, Clarence, and fifty-two boys, one for each week of the solar year, prepare to take on the Church army. The detailed description of Hank's fortification is, I believe, meaningful. Twelve electrified wire fences circle the cave concentrically, while, around the outer fence, lies the mined sand-belt. The planetary, somewhat Copernican setup of this design, confused possibly with the twelve signs of the zodiac *"belt,"* to create a mix of sixth-century and nineteenth-century cosmologies suggests to me that the sand-belt, which is presumably yellow in color, should be symbolically identified as the path of the sun. If this is the case, Hank's choice of analogy in the congratulatory proclamation to his army is deliberate: "So long as the planets shall continue to move in their orbits, the BATTLE OF THE SAND-BELT will not perish out of the memories of men." It would seem that Twain intends some equation between the battle and cosmological phenomena, an eclipse of the sun for example.

The ensuing holocaust has all the requisite apocalyptic features. The knights first advance to "the blare of trumpets," only to be "shot into the sky with a thunder-crash, and become a whirling tempest of rags and fragments." The "smell of burning flesh" is noticeable first, and then the carnage itself becomes visible when Hank "touched a button and set fifty electric suns aflame on the top of our precipice." The solar eclipse turned day into night; now Hank turns night into day. (To our ears, incidentally, the reference to "fifty electric suns" gains in intensity with its ominous implication of megatonnage.) When the eclipse was total, the multitude "groaned with horror." Now, as a host of knights are electrocuted, "There was a groan you could *hear!*" The "deluge" of congratulations that Hank received for returning the sun, now becomes a "withering deluge of fire" directed at the remaining knights. The deluge here is both literal and metaphorical, composed of both fire and water, since Hank opens the sluice gates in order to fill the now-surrounding ditch caused by the explosion of the torpedoes and thus drown many of the knights like Pharaoh's army. But my point here is that these ordered repetitions are purposeful.

Hank's victory is pyrrhic only. Merlin, disguised as a woman, works his most effective enchantment—more truly impressive than any of Hank's magical accomplishments—and puts the wounded Boss to sleep for thirteen centuries. (It may be recalled that Merlin's first accomplishment in the novel is to send all of Arthur's court to sleep during his droning rehearsal of Arthur's adventures with the Lady of the Lake.) However, Merlin's victory, too, is short-lived. A moment later, in the midst of a delirious cackle, he electrocutes himself. Subsequently, the remainder of Hank's followers gradually die off for reasons Clarence explains: "We were in a trap, you see—a trap of our own making. If we stayed where we were, our dead would kill us; if we moved out of our defences, we should no longer be invisible. We had conquered; in turn we were conquered." Following the end of Hank's manuscript, we obtain the truly apocalyptic revelation, a revelation indirectly hinted at throughout, namely that the sixth century does not displace the nineteenth century in any real sense, nor does the nineteenth century displace the sixth century, because there is no essential difference between them.

The eclipse of the sun is a false apocalyptic image, *at least in the sense that I have so far implied.* And the same goes for the related fiery, circular, luminous yellow elements I have been cataloging. They are all "effects" in so far as they relate to the usurpation of one historical world by another. Nevertheless, these elements, outside of Hank's usage of them, do have a "factual" and symbolic reality as apocalyptic imagery in so far as they herald the revelation that any apocalyptic transformation, from an Eden in the past to a utopia in the future, is all myth. Gradually we are made aware that the most startling fact about the sixth century in relation to the nineteenth is the lack of significant differentiation. It is no accident that Hank's story is inscribed on a palimpsest and that underlying his writing are "Latin words and sentences: fragments from old monkish legends." The common parchment is more important than the apparent differences imbedded in successive historical records. And it is this essential lack of differentiation that prepares the reader for the genuine apocalyptic revelation with which the book concludes.

Careful attention to the imagery associated with the sun is in itself revealing. Shortly after his spectacular demonstration, Hank draws attention to the current belief that "he could have blown out the sun like a candle." There is some irony to this statement, as the sun-candle world of mind comes, during the course of the book, to be associated with nineteenth-century America and not sixth-century Britain. This process gets under way with Hank's decision to wait for an opportune moment before *flooding* sixth-century England with nineteenth-century electric light: "I was turning on my light one-candle-power at a time, and meant to continue to do so." He was, nevertheless, ready, like God to "flood the midnight world with light any moment." Somewhat weirdly, except as a part of this process, Hank, in full armor, speaks of himself as being "snug as a candle in a candle-mould." And, at the end of the novel, when Hank appears to be losing ground to the Church, Dan Beard provides an illustration of a monk snuffing the candle of the nineteenth century, an illustration presumably based on this description of Camelot: "From being the best electric-lighted town in the kingdom and the most like a recumbent sun of anything you ever saw, it was becoming simply a blot—a blot upon darkness—that is to say, it was darker and solider than the rest of the darkness, and so you could see it a little better; it made me feel as if maybe it was symbolical—a sort of sign that the Church was going to *keep* the upper hand, now, and *snuff out* [italics mine] all my beautiful civilization just like that." Once again, snuffing out the candle and the eclipse of the sun are clearly related, although the import is completely reversed. But this confusion seems to imply that if the two transformations can be imaged in the same terms, perhaps the similarities between the two epochs are more important than the differences.

Similarities between sixth-century Britain and nineteenth-century America quickly assert themselves. The major common denominator is slavery. In large measure, Twain's source for the Old World of the sixth century is the pre-Civil War South. Furthermore economic thinking is as muddled in King Arthur's time as in Hank's day, due to the failure to realize that the important thing is not how much you earn but how much you can purchase with it. Twain was fond of blaming Sir Walter Scott for causing the Civil War by romanticizing aristocratic behavior. It becomes apparent, in *A Connecticut Yankee,* that Scott has a predecessor in this activity in Malory, who presented a similarly romantic version of chivalry, which Twain derides by parody—witness Merlin's opening story, the style of which is later taken up by Sandy's rambling narrative.

From this comparison between Malory and Scott it is but a short step to the recognition that men are all the same under the skin. Hank refers with approval to a prisoner's critical assertion, "If you were to strip the nation naked and send a stranger through the crowd, he couldn't tell the king from a quack doctor, nor a duke from a hotel clerk." The later portion of the narrative, with the king and the Boss traveling incognito, effectively bears this point out. Nor is there any fundamental distinction between good and evil. The essential similarity between the sinister Morgan Le Fay and our hero, Hank Morgan, pointed to by their common name, becomes increasingly obvious as the book goes on. As Edmund Reiss suggests, Hank's surprise at Morgan Le Fay's beauty is a means of indicating the ambiguity of good and evil, but "what appalls the Yankee in the character of Morgan Le Fay are the same insensitivities Twain objects to in the Yankee's character." A further distinction is eroded when we learn of Hank's factory, where he plans "to turn groping and grubbing automata into *men*," which raises, in the modern reader's mind, the equal likelihood of turning men into automata. What superficial distinctions do exist are all a consequence of training and inherited ideas. Since man is essentially without free will, he might fittingly be considered allegorically as a slave, which is how Dan Beard presents him, chained to two iron balls of debt.

Clearly, since our recognition of material reality depends upon our ability to make meaningful distinctions, the discovery that meaningful distinctions do not exist would tend to throw that state of reality into question. It is, then, a relatively small distance from demonstrating an essential homogeneity to asserting that there is no reality or that reality is a dream—the truly apocalyptic revelation of the postscript. There is, however, one further logical intermediary step: the business of eradicating any distinction between reality and appearance or reality and unreality. It is all shown to be a matter of phenomenology. Toward the end of the book, Hank's entire conception of reality comes to depend upon the health of his child. Thus this description of her recovery:

> Then our reward came: the center of the universe turned the corner and began to mend. Grateful? It isn't the term. There *isn't* any term for it. You know that, yourself, if you've watched your child through the Valley of the Shadow and seen it come back to life and sweep night out of the earth [like the sun?] with one all illuminating smile that you could cover with your hand.

In the circumstances, this image of the creation is most appropriate and in no way inflated.

Now is the appropriate time to recall Hank's status in the novel as narrator, because the perceptual idiopathic bias that his child's recovery highlights is endemic. To the degree that all events are filtered through the hardheaded, burlesque, "Yankee" consciousness of Hank, the entire account is "unreal." Hank's idiosyncrasies translate themselves into a style that is ultimately as "unreal" as the Malory romance he ridicules. For example, although one might speak descriptively of Hank's "ordeal" at the stake, the use of quotation marks should be taken as ironic, because Hank is simply insufficiently serious and insufficiently aware to experience the incident as more than a spectacular show, albeit somewhat uncomfortable. Similarly, Hank's practical and rather callous application of the energy expended by the bowing hermit on his pillar to run a sewing machine reflects on his total incomprehension of the realities of religious ardor.

The image of this hermit standing against the "background of sky," producing energy at the rate of "1244 revolutions in 24 minutes and 46 seconds" to make shirts which "sold like smoke" shares certain qualities with the sun, and now I can perhaps seek to further justify my imagistic use of that body

as a viable approach to the novel. My point is that Twain's narrative strategy blurs the distinction between an event or incident considered externally and the subjective image whereby events and images are understood. Given that Twain's aim is an impression of the unreality of reality, it makes sense that a reader might find his bearings, or clue to the novel's "reality principle," in the imagery, by definition unreal, particularly since the entire narrative, which is a statement of Hank's consciousness, might be conceived as having the same ontological status as imagery. There is, then, good reason for the disjunction raised earlier. Twain chooses to dissociate his intricate imagistic patterns from a poetic consciousness capable of comprehending them and instead locates them in the mundane, "effective" rhetoric of a practical man, because such a stance turns out to be an extreme but representative form of unreality. Ultimately the form of Hank's narrative *is* the primary reality of the novel, and it is there that the ambiguous imagistic import of the eclipse is appropriately if paradoxically "grounded." Indeed the "truth" of the novel has much to do with what appears to exist but is independent of factual justification.

Twain's point about the idiopathic nature of perception is more strongly made by dramatizing the weird conceptions of sixth-century humanity—of Sandy in particular. Where Hank sees pigs in a sty, she sees enchanted princesses in an enchanted castle. Sandy ponders:

> And how strange is this marvel, and how awful—that to the one perception it is enchanted and dight in a base and shameful aspect; yet to the perception of the other it is not enchanted, hath suffered no change, but stands firm and stately still, girt with its moat and waving its banners in the blue air from its towers.

Although men differ only in their training, such differences as do exist are sufficiently powerful to mold external reality! It is indeed tempting, incidentally, to extend the connotations of the sand-belt to the name Sandy!

To confuse swine with members of the aristocracy, and then a few pages on to refer to the band of slaves that perambulate through the novel as "bundled together like swine," is not just a matter of being uncomplimentary to the nobility, nor is it just a means of pointing to an essential lack of distinction between animals, nobles, and slaves. It is, more especially, a further and final confusion of reality and unreality. The slave chain, as I have argued, is an image of humanity. Hank and the king do not suddenly become slaves toward the end of the novel to be "sold at auction, like swine"; this is but a concrete manifestation of their continual situation. But this conception of human reality, by being linked to Sandy's unique perception of swine, is, then, equally a picture of human unreality. The swine image comes to stand for both the aristocracy and the slaves, but primarily for the Circe-like force of illusion.

The apocalyptic discovery with which the book is concerned is the understanding that no apocalyptic transformation has occurred. The true apocalyptic revelation is not that the sixth-century world is so different but that it is identical and identically unreal. In this context, the concluding doubt in Hank's mind as to which is the dream, the sixth century or the nineteenth century, makes perfect sense. Apparently back in the nineteenth century, Hank, delirious, believes he is speaking to Sandy in the sixth century: "I seemed to be a creature out of a remote unborn age, centuries hence, and even *that* was as real as the rest! Yes, I seemed to have flown back out of that age into this of ours, and then forward to it again, and was set down, a stranger and forlorn in that strange England, with an abyss of thirteen centuries yawning [pun intended?] between me and you. . . ." He begs Sandy to shield him from "these hideous dreams."

This revelation is in alignment with, but does not depend for justification upon, those other moments in the book when the reality of a dream world is particularly pressing. Can we be sure that everything is not merely the narrator's dream—after all, Hank's second entrance occurs after midnight and after the narrator has read a stretch of Malory with the intention that it put him to sleep? In fact, as Twain's notebook entry tells us, his original idea for the story derived from a dream following his reading Mallory, "a dream of being a knight errant in armor in the middle ages." Certainly Camelot is "as lovely as a dream." and Hank "moved along as one in a dream." Toward the end of the book, Hank's dreams are of the nineteenth century: "In my dreams, along at first, I still wandered thirteen centuries away, and my unsatisfied spirit went calling and harking all up and down the unreplying vacancies of a vanished world."

The apocalyptic solution implied in *A Connecticut Yankee* and subsequently stated directly in *The Mysterious Stranger* and in Twain's late symbolic writings is that all reality is a dream. Apparently the inhabitants of sixth-century Britain were absolutely correct in their intuition that the eclipse of the sun betokens the end of the world. As an image, the eclipse and the related details chronicled earlier connote not the transformation of realities but the end of reality, the final apocalypse. The images of apocalypse that figure in Hank's final pronouncements suggest the impact of such an extreme philosophical position: "A bugle. . . . It is the king! . . . turn out the—" Are we not justified in hypothesizing the adjective "apocalyptic" before bugle, in identifying "the king" as God rather than Arthur, and, in completing the phrase as "turn out the light," recall, a final time, the episode detailing the extinction of the sun, which now darkens both the sixth century and the nineteenth century? The frame narrator interprets this as Hank "getting up his last 'effect'," but the quotation marks around "effect" are fortunate. In a reality that turns out to be a dream, a special effect must be granted its measure of actuality. (pp. 213-32)

David Ketterer, "Epoch-Eclipse and Apocalypse: Special 'Effects' in 'A Connecticut Yankee', " in his New Worlds for Old: The Apocalyptic Imagination, Science Fiction, and American Literature, *Indiana University Press, 1974, pp. 213-32.*

CLARK GRIFFITH (essay date 1975)

[*In the following analysis of* A Connecticut Yankee in King Arthur's Court, *Griffith views the character of Hank Morgan as an unsuccessful synthesis of two central tendencies in Twain's fiction, comic exaggeration and moral criticism.*]

Few would deny that *A Connecticut Yankee in King Arthur's Court* eventually becomes a book that is almost savagely divided against itself. Why, for example, should Mark Twain so relentlessly expose the ugliness and horror of the Arthurian old order, only to reserve for Merlin, the least attractive spokesman for the old order, a last, grim triumph? Or why did he seem to conceive of Hank Morgan as the clever, increasingly creative nineteenth-century man, yet turn Hank at last into a raging tyrant, whose cataclysmic tantrums destroy himself and everything else in sight? One might reply, of course, that ending this story in any satisfactory manner had to pose unusual problems for Twain. It could have been no easy task for him to find the logical stopping place for Hank's adventures in Camelot, and then devise the means of transporting Hank back again across the distance of 1,300 years. Conceding the awkwardness, however, does not minimize the question of how Twain chose to resolve it. Among the various possibilities available to him (at least two are implied by earlier developments in the narrative) why did he select the one particular conclusion that most subverted the tone, the spirit, the wit, and (above all) the characters and character-relationships of the work he had already written?

The answer is discoverable in the way Twain now sees and presents two basic situations out of his earlier fiction. In the past, the situations could attract and repulse him, sometimes simultaneously. But he had managed to control his feelings, largely by seeing to it that the situations themselves remained separate and discontinuous. Each had to be the defining condition of only one character at a time. Now, by contrast, both are merged into the single career of the man from Hartford—and Twain's ambivalences suddenly become certainties. The will to play games for the sake of gamesmanship, as opposed to a capacity for entertaining moral issues and executing moral choices: these are the ways of life between which the Connecticut Yankee, as book and man, are made to move. Before Twain is finished, he has had to see through each way to its essential worthlessness. Moreover, he has had to deflate both ways in terms of the strangely paradoxical relationship they bear to one another. And in the process, finally, he has had to destroy Hank Morgan twice over, and consign him and his future to the mirthful, mocking grin of a Black Magician.

The first situation is one that Twain builds out of the conventions of the distinctively American tall tale. Obviously his story *is* a "stretcher"; and by its very organization we are reminded that, more than any other of Twain's longer works, *A Connecticut Yankee* can be read as tall tale in an extended form. There is the frame structure, reminiscent of Southwestern humor, with the voice of Mark Twain at the beginning and end, while within the frames Mark Twain listens to (or subsequently reads from) the voice of the raconteur. And the raconteur himself has clearly been patterned upon the storyteller of an earlier comic tradition. Arriving inexplicably at Camelot, Hank Morgan comes as a stranger into a world which both resists and threatens him. Very soon, however, he has drawn upon two favorite tactics of the comic hero, and used them in order to feel perfectly at home in a new locale.

First of all, he debunks. As G. W. Harris' Sut Luvingood or the hunter in Thorpe's "Big Bear of Arkansas" overcame the pomposities of their listeners by making the audience appear small and absurd, so Hank undercuts the pretensions of Camelot through a process of laying bare all its shabbiness. He scales his surroundings down in size, and thereby lays claim to a kind of mastery over those surroundings, by pointing to the grease beneath the Round Table, the rat on the head of the drowsing King, the tedium of Merlin's narratives, the follies of grail-chasing, the inconveniences of wearing armor—in short, to the childishness and idiocies that stand just behind the chivalric ideal.

His second tactic is that of outwitting his new environment, and outwitting it, strictly on its own terms. As Thorpe's hero routed other bear hunters by emerging as the bear-hunter-supreme, or as Sut could thwart lesser mischief-makers by inventing still more devilment, so Hank takes advantage of certain natural affinities between the Arthurians and himself, and he consistently beats his hosts by playing their game more efficiently than they can. In a world which sets great store by fantasy and gaudy display, the Yankee steps forth center-stage as the gaudiest of the fantasizers.

Hence the quality of his early adventures. We must accept as a sort of poetic fiction the premise that, with the information and memory of a Greenwich astronomer, Hank can recall how an eclipse of the sun was scheduled for the summer solstice of 528 A.D. And we have to take for granted as other, similar unlikelihoods the exact timing of the eclipse (so that it commences in just the moment when a torch is being applied to the victim's stake) and Hank's prophecy of the thunder storm which will presently set Merlin's tower ablaze. The point is, however, that all these fictions are completely appropriate to the type of narrative that Twain is writing. He has located Hank not in a real-life situation and, for that matter, not even in a pseudo-historical context, but has set him down in the larger-than-life atmosphere of the tall tale. This is an atmosphere which thrives on improbabilities, since it defines a world where ordinary limitations are always kept secondary to the power of the fantasizer, and where even natural law is never allowed to interfere with the triumphs of the fantasizing hero.

Or, in a more general way, consider the first of the changes that Hank imposes upon the Arthurian countryside. Examining them from the standpoint of strict plausibility, we would need to ask: where, in the world, does Hank get the raw materials for his tools and inventions; how does he manage to round up the workmen necessary for the mines and factories he opens; how does he keep hidden from most of the Arthurians such notoriously public utilities as the telegraph, telephone, newspaper, and electric light? And here again our questions would be meaningless. During his first days at Camelot, Hank is not simply the technologically superior Yankee in a land of intellectual pygmies; rather, we are asked to assume what he himself has grown to believe: that his feats are the truly magical achievements of a true shaman. Thus he is as little bounded by actualities as was Thorpe's hero in his pursuit of the supernatural big bear. Cast to be the protagonist of a "stretcher," he is as privileged to manipulate his environment, to sport with reality and reshape it for his own playful ends, as was the fictional Davy Crockett of a famous folktale, who awoke one morning to find the earth "friz" to its axis, but set it to rotating again with a ton or two of hot bear oil.

But if Hank invites comparison with Sut, the hunter and the fictional Crockett, another "borrowing" proves even more illuminating. The truth is that he resembles no one so much as that other tall-tale hero, whom Twain himself had created a dozen years earlier. He is cut to the exact dimensions of a Tom Sawyer, grown to manhood now, yet still blessed with the privileges and prerogatives which Tom had once enjoyed.

The Paige typesetting machine, on which Twain lost nearly $300,000.

Like Tom, Hank dominates a world where, despite very occasional setbacks, he is generally free to do whatever he wishes. He therefore shares with Tom that miraculous talent for turning fancy to fact, as he indulges in the most outlandish daydreams or perceives the most farfetched connections, and then settles back to watch their fulfillment in actual experience. And if at far-off St. Petersburg, Tom could vex and grieve his neighbors and yet, in a society of "show-offs," still be acclaimed hero of the hour, it is even so for Hank. From having been feared and distrusted initially, the Yankee is soon a popular favorite of the Arthurians, who correctly recognize him as one of theirs and are, in fact, often fondest of him during those moments when his disdain for them seems most boorish.

In the light of his affiliations with Tom Sawyer, one can imagine a radically different ending for the Yankee's adventures. Having vanquished the flower of British knighthood, Hank would marry Sandy and father Hello Central; he would find the means of silencing Merlin forever, and so settle down finally as the unchallenged and invincible Boss, an absolute ruler of all he surveyed. This is where the tall tale, as told classically, should have ended. No doubt it would have been the ending in the unlikely event that either Sut Luvingood or the mythical Crockett might have invaded Arthurian England, and it certainly would have been the ending in the event that Tom Sawyer had gone calling on Camelot. As a matter of fact, it comes close to being the conclusion which Twain suggests when he is approximately four-fifths of the way through the narrative. With Hank's corralling the knights in Chapter XXXIX, we seem to have reached that abundance of good spirits, that restoration of the hero's dominance, that slackening of tension and air of "happily ever afterward," which are traditionally the wrap-ups of the comic tale. The baseball game, described at the close of Chapter XL, might have appeared as a somewhat abrupt last episode. All the same, it would not have been inconsistent with the mood of the opening chapters. Hank Morgan, master showman, elevated to be Supervisor of Sports and Revelries at the Court of King Arthur. Toward some such final view of Hank, the tall tale seems destined to push us.

The book cannot end on this note, however, because even as Twain refurbishes the tall tale to fit *A Connecticut Yankee,* he has all along been put in the position of having to question the moral adequacies of both the tall-tale hero and the kind of world which this figure must occupy. In themselves, his doubts represent nothing new. As early as 1865, in a newspaper sketch called **"Story of the Bad Little Boy,"** he had shown how the fantasizer's "charmed life" makes Jim a cute little scamp for a while, but within a few years (and only three pages of text) converts him into an adult monster who "brained his family with an axe one night . . . and is universally respected and belongs to the legislature." And if the **"Bad Little Boy"** seems a piece too slight for many inferences, then a decade later, in *The Adventures of Tom Sawyer,* Twain's latent mistrust of fantasizing has become unmistakable. All is merry as a circus insofar as Tom, the Fantasizer Compleat, projects and attends his own funeral or has turned daydreams about buried treasure into the discovery of an actual fortune. Let more serious and morally demanding matters be interjected, though, and suddenly it is as if Twain can no longer be imaginatively attuned to his protagonist. Either he glosses over Tom's rôle in the proceedings (as is surely the case in the exoneration of Muff Potter, where the courtroom scene constitutes a failure of the imagination); or (as in the

rescue of the Widow Douglas) he must find a new and totally different type of character to resolve the crisis.

In Twain's terms, then, fantasizing is an enviable yet not entirely harmless pastime. To be effective, it requires good luck, gregariousness, the will to win in a world willing to be treated as spectacle—and also complete moral insouciance. There is, in fact, more than a little of the Faustian in the make-up of a successful fantasizer. For though he conjures no pacts with Satan (and hence is spared even the thought of final retribution), the extraordinary ability he has to command life is dependent upon his being forgiven all the ordinary responsibilities of living. The fantasizer had better be portrayed as a child therefore, and viewed strictly from the outside so that his essential callousness will seem less evident. What is more, he had better be shown as the occupant of a childishly unreal world, where brutalities are rewarded with public honors, and into which, at the very least, nothing profound, or morally taxing, or affecting to the heart, or threatening to the ego must ever penetrate.

And much as this total immunity to experience could fascinate Mark Twain, the nature of his material in *A Connecticut Yankee* kept him from granting it indefinitely to Hank Morgan. Introducing Hank into novel surroundings, Twain might *at first* project Camelot as the never-never land of fantasy. But, as his preface has already warned, Camelot will likewise reveal matters of a considerably deeper import: it is to show us the "ungentle laws and customs" of history. Conceiving of Hank as only a voice, furthermore, Twain could *for a time* indulge him to sound like the freewheeling and all-triumphant comic hero. But, by virtue of his first-person presentation, it also became necessary for Twain to construct a personality behind the voice. After a while, he had to look inside this character who speaks, and make something more of him than a mere verbal presence, amidst wholly physical episodes.

The drift of the book is thus increasingly to juxtapose the externally real with an inner capacity for pondering reality, for worrying about its shortcomings, and for wishing to change its moral structure. And as this happens, the issue is complicated by Twain's creating within the Yankee the one faculty which no fantasizer can safely possess, or with the acquisition of which the Faustian self can never hope to survive. Hank is endowed with a conscience. Whereupon, so my thesis goes, Twain gradually shifts him out of the first situation of his earlier fiction and conducts him into the second.

True to his rôle in the tall tale, Hank enters the sixth century not as a weary traveler, but as one who simply awakens to find himself already arrived. And for the first eleven chapters of his story, he continues to be a basically static magician, working his wonders from atop the "breezy height" and behind the "great . . . closed gates" of the castle. But thereafter Twain makes him mobile (and his field of vision more spacious and panoramic) by sending the Yankee on a series of three long journeys.

The effect of his expedition with Sandy is that, intermittently at least, it does compel Hank to see. He is brought back "down the hill" from Camelot, and into a world which discloses, beneath the grubby and laughable, some less enchanting aspects of Arthurian life: a corrupt and indifferent church, the oppressiveness of the feudal social structure, the miseries and degradations of the British peasant. Now, his relationship with his hosts deepens somewhat, as Hank makes his famous reflection concerning their need for a "new deal," a fresh distribution of wealth and power, and a bit later, in the presence of the forty-seven prisoners from Morgan le Fay's dungeons, he openly avows the existence of his conscience, speaking of it as a "trouble and bother" to be sure, yet conceding how it can nonetheless stir him to anger in the midst of what he calls scenes of the "grisly" and "terrible."

Of course the norms of the touring aristocrat remain more nearly personal than social. Hank is still The Boss after all, for whom creating knight-vendors seems a racier enterprise than challenges to the priesthood—and still every inch the showman, whose concern for a party of slaves is readily overborne by an obsession with sending "John W. Merlin home on a shingle." Yet through two wry ironies, Twain suggests changes in the Yankee that have already forced him a short, tentative step beyond the tall tale. He cloaks Hank with medieval armor to display his continuing superiority over every kind of physical experience, while, at the same time, chinks begin to appear in his armor of detachment which make him subject to the new experience of compassion. And letting Hank humor Sandy with the pretense that noblewomen can be enchanted into hogs, Twain has simultaneously given him an inkling of what it might mean to turn a greedy, sluggish culture into a nation of free men. Thus, if his first expedition returns The Boss to another flourish of fireworks and putdowns in the Valley of Holiness, it has also served a deeper purpose. By it, Hank is rehearsed for the moment in Chapter XXVII, when he will be joined by the King and sets forth a second time.

There are significant differences between the two journeys. The first had skirted a carefully generalized underworld. Horror was kept at a safe distance by Hank's observing it from the outside (so that the victims tended to be nameless and faceless) and by his habit of confusing atrocities along the way with Arthurian quaintnesses. In the second, on the other hand, the Yankee progressively becomes the victim. Traveling in a disguise that can only render him vulnerable, he is, by turns, the beleaguered peasant, a potential victim of disease, the fugitive on the run, the slave in manacles, an imprisoned felon, and the felon on the gallows. And the closer he draws to the center of life, the greater Twain's willingness is to modify another technique of narration. Incongruity was the key to the first journey, the sudden turn in the road that disclosed modern gadgets in an ancient setting. But the grimness of the second is consistently the result of similarity. Hank now follows a road which often seems to lead straight out of the sixth century and into a series of more recent settings.

The shift is evident among the sufferers from smallpox. At this point Camelot recedes from view, and we find the Yankee enveloped by the atmosphere (and hence the issues and chronology) of *A Modest Proposal* and the *Journal of the Plague Year*. A similar telescoping is achieved through his disquisition on economics (addressed to an audience with the occupations and oddly plebeian surnames of a renaissance comedy) and his ordeals as a slave. First the experiences remind Hank of later centuries; next they actually appear to relocate him in the world of *A Shoemaker's Holiday*, in the last days of Bourbon France, in the antebellum American South, in industrial Europe, or in the America of Grover Cleveland. Seen in this way, finally, the descriptions of London are not a pointless anachronism of Twain's, but rather his quite conscious attempt to end their journey by delivering the King

and The Boss into the modern city—the human cesspool which is at once Twain's own (he had already portrayed it in *The Prince and the Pauper)* and that of Hogarth and Fielding, of Blake and Dickens.

What results is a journey across space that is likewise treated as an expedition forward in time and, ultimately, as a pilgrimage into the self. These are no longer specifically Arthurian evils which confront Hank; he is exposed to something far broader—is adrift on that dreadful continuity of suffering and stupidity which has afflicted societies whenever and wherever human beings have gathered. He has been transported from make-believe into the spectacle of history. And in the face of the spectacle, the Yankee looks inward to find that his quest for utopia can be delayed no further. The vaguely imagined reforms of someday become a positive program, as thinking back to Camelot (but to a Camelot he now envisions as one source of modern history) Hank pledges that soon in Britain there will be

> a modified monarchy . . . then the destruction of the throne, nobility abolished, every member of it bound out to some useful trade, universal suffrage instituted, and the whole government placed in the hands of the men and women of the nation there to remain.

So, the aroused conscience prevents *A Connecticut Yankee* from continuing in the vein of the tall tale. Summoning up bicycle brigades or imposing his will on unruly knights might have served as Hank's proper exit, if Twain had left him to practice magic within the friendly seclusion of Camelot. But for a traveler through history, who has both seen and been the worst that civilization exhibits, these same episodes must be means to a higher end, entering wedges into the moral transformation of humanity. Hank's sense of more serious achievement, at the beginning of Chapter XL, may strike us as overly smug, and no doubt there is a fair share of Crystal Palace gimmickry in certain of the materialistic changes he goes on to enumerate:

> Schools everywhere, and several colleges; a number of good newspapers. . . .

> Slavery was dead and gone; all men were equal before the law; taxation had been equallized. The telegraph and telephone, the typewriter, the sewing machine, and all the willing and handy servants of steam and electricity were working their way into favor.

Let us give him his due, however, as, after three years of remaking the world that Arthur botched, the Yankee stands on the pier, prepared to commence his third long journey. By abolishing slavery, autocracy, and a parasitical knighthood, he *has* eradicated many of the blights on sixth-century society. He *has* struck out at the modified savagery through which he traveled earlier, and sought to replace it with a "happy and prosperous country."

But of course he has done so at the price of renouncing his status as a tall-tale hero. Once committed to social forays, Hank is no longer free. Instead, Twain shows us The Boss become a servant to his moral idealism; and following Chapter XXXIX, we are abruptly conscious of him as a driven and fretful father-figure: the parent who has given life to Hello Central and a new social order and whose freedoms are delimited as he responds to *their* needs with an intense moral earnestness. Nor is he any longer doing sleight-of-hand tricks on a permissive landscape for the delight of an easily en-thralled human audience. Instead, Twain makes it clear that he has declared war on the engrained values of history: is ar-rayed against that most implacable of all foes, which is the force of a conservative, superstitious, rigidly institutionalized human society. And so, above all, he can no longer feel at home in the world he would redeem. Instead, he finds himself increasingly at odds with the community that applauded his showmanship as the embodiment of its own highest aspira-tions, but that has little taste for the comments which he ad-dresses to it for its own moral welfare. Inevitably therefore the Yankee must lose his last tournament. He loses not solely because history dictates the loss (though that obviously is part of it), but because, by entering his irresistible conscience into the lists against intractable custom and tradition, *he* in-vites the interdict and assures his place in the Arthurian Göt-terdämmerung of Malory and Tennyson. Yet even here, one suspects that it is not too late to spare him the manner of his defeat.

For in the end, after the Church and Nobility have had their day, there is still open to Mark Twain the revision of a plan he had jotted down in 1886, just as he was getting into his new book. Hank would stay in Britain (or perhaps sail back from France) to fight beside an enlightened Arthur at Salisbury. He would incur a second blow on the head, and be aroused presently to find that he is restored to the nineteenth century. Then, it might scarcely seem logical to show him mourning his "lost land . . . so fresh and new"; (Twain's notebook entry can only have applied to the opening third of the narra-tive). But it might be possible to portray the homecoming as a time of genuine moral insight.

Suppose from the standpoint of Hartford, Hank awakens to this realization: Left to itself, the dynamo has produced not Paradise, but only modern Connecticut, a place whose under-lying associations have persistently included the factory, the city, munitions-making, the insane asylum, and fifteen-year-old Puss Flanagan, doing child labor at the telephone compa-ny. But if he has judged too narrowly the means of revolution, keep him aware that concerning the need for moral and social rejuvenation he was never mistaken. Addressing it toward the last, the Yankee spoke to the sixth century as a techno-crat—and also as a humanitarian. He could legitimately have echoed Whitman to the élite of the Round Table: "I am the man, I suffer'd, I was there." And now, still the possessor of unique knowledge, let him bring his insights to bear upon the near end of history. Have him close his story with the deter-mination that he will yet help to wrest happiness and prosper-ity out of an atmosphere that has proved fully as light-denying, as inimical to personal freedom and dignity, as was the Arthurian nightmare.

These suggestions are in keeping with Twain's conception of Hank down to the close of Chapter XL. And out of them, or something like them, Twain might have brought to comple-tion the bold reworking of a *rite de passage,* which he implied when he spoke of his protagonist as combining a "rude ani-mal side, [a] circus side" with a "good heart & high intent." From the circus side that darkened life (or claimed to) for its own gratification, to the high intent that undertook to raise the darkness of both ancient Britain and modern America; from encastled Faustus to Prometheus on the highroads: here, through three long journeys, would have been the course of Hank's development. Moreover, not even interdict or Götterdämmerung could finally have stilled his good

heart. For though he lost a battle against corruption, the Yankee would have learned at Salisbury how better to fight the continuing war.

The book cannot end on this note, however, because even as Twain seems about to turn Faustian Munchausen into a Pro-methean Odysseus, he has had to see through to the bitter end of the metamorphosis. In itself his vision is nothing new, of course. He had grasped the essentials as early as 1865, when Jacob Blivens, his "good little boy," may first offend us as a hopeless prig, but is soon rushing to the aid of a blind man (and being thrashed for his pains), and ends his story by blast-ing to smithereens both himself and a group of persecuted dogs he had set out to rescue. And if Jacob remains a figure from burlesque, then his recognition that "it is not healthy to be good," has, by 1876, taken a considerably bleaker turn in a sketch which Twain wrote about another character from Connecticut. *Is there* any *way,* cries the morally tormented speaker of **"A Recent Carnival of Crime in Connecticut,"** "Is there *any* way of satisfying that malignant invention . . . called conscience?" To which his morally exacerbating con-science replies, *none whatsoever:* "My business—and my joy—[are] to make you repent of *every*thing you do."

It is ever the double burden of Mark Twain's Promethean fig-ures. They are distinguishable, on the one hand, by their per-ception of the need to be obligated and their willingness (however reluctantly they arrive at it) to accept obligation. But on the other, they are set apart by the discovery that each new acceptance brings them punishment, rejection, and the rôle of moral outcast in both the eyes of society and their own eyes. Theirs is the rage that comes from existing in a condi-tion of complete moral and social futility. And yielding to the rage in 1888, Twain had to emerge from his chronicle of the sixth century in the only way he now knew how. From having first presented Hank as a skylarking Tom Sawyer grown up, Twain so alters Hank in the middle portions of the book that, on the last pages, the Yankee must reappear in the image of Twain's other first-person narrator who traveled toward an unhappy encounter with his sensitive conscience. At the close of his third journey, in other words, Hank returns to Britain as an adult Huckleberry Finn.

Oh, he is Huck with certain variations. When Huck weighed his personal conviction against the intransigence of social or-thodoxy, there were three consequences. Out of a profound unworthiness, he first supposed that in standing alone he could not possibly be right; so, speaking through clenched teeth, he condemned himself to hell in the very moment of his moral glory. Next, equating the loneliness he then felt with living death, he sought to purchase his way back into the community; he dissipated a part of his anger by becoming once again Tom Sawyer's lackey, the accessory to Tom's fun and games which he knew society expected him to be. But in order to resume playing in the world, Huck had to do yet a third thing, the one we find so difficult to forgive that we are often strangely content to ignore it. Since the fact of Jim could not be reconciled with the wish for social acceptance, Huck was compelled to slay Jim symbolically. Far more than Tom Sawyer (who, after all, will never see him except as a slave), it is Huck Finn who reduces Jim from human being to object; who substitutes for the richly evocative companion on the raft the figure of a fawning, shambling minstrel darky; who, having discovered to his astonishment that Jim can suf-fer, nonetheless permits Jim to be bitten by rats and hounded through the bayous—who, in short, neutralizes Jim as a moral and emotional dilemma through the expedient of acting as if Jim had ceased to exist as a personality. That, unless we choose to sentimentalize and distort what happens, has to be the meaning of the last twenty-one chapters of Huck's adventures. It is the tale of a transformation, in which his erstwhile beneficiary is converted by Huck into an actual victim, the deliberately and self-consciously created scapegoat.

Now Hank by contrast is too old for Huck's humility, just as he has been made too inflexible of purpose to share Huck's capacity for last-minute accommodation. All that remains to him is the sheer rage which caused the speaker in **"Carnival of Crime"** to "murder" his conscience—and which Huck finally expended in the "murder" of Jim. And impelled by the rage, Hank shifts from symbolic homicide to an all too literal act of genocide. Convinced he is right, the Yankee machine-guns out of existence the community which has turned on him and declined to accept his rightness. Yet our horror at what he does must be both underscored and mitigated by our sense that Hank's self-image was a just and earned one. Surely he was right; or surely it was right for Twain to bring him the long way he came from selfishness to altruism. Accordingly, his destructiveness on the Sand Belt is not simply the behavior of a tyrant run wild and not simply a last, grotesque reversion to childhood. It is not nearly so much these as it is a gesture of guilt and a gesture occasioned by frustrated love. Laying waste Arthurian England (and himself), the Yankee acknowledges that precisely because he has been given a conscience, has been made to experience moral and emotional commitments, he can no longer bear to look upon the "grisly" and "terrible" without in some way—ultimately in any way!—trying to banish them from sight.

Which means that from still another perspective the analogy with Huckleberry Finn holds firm. In the bitterness of his old age, Mark Twain was to seize upon oblivion as the moralist's best defense against engagements with life. Thus Huck would become crazy or perhaps a drunkard, his anxieties eased at last (his involvements with the Jims of this world all conveniently forgotten), as he wandered from town to town in a mental haze. And what has Twain made Hank do at the Sand Belt, except take up a reality grown intolerable and thrust it to oblivion? If the Yankee brings ruin during what Twain once thought of calling "the Battle of the Broken Heart," he brings it in sorrow and imposes it upon ruins which others have created before him. The desolation of London, the ravaging of the English countryside, the fall of utopia into disorder and civil war: all were accomplished facts by the time he returned to the kingdom. Unable to charm them away (for Faustian trickery is of no value against historical realities) and equally unprepared to restore their lost innocence (for the Promethean will can bend only the bendable), Hank has but one viable option. Like Huck, he must neutralize the unbearable; as best he can, he must blast from view those circumstances which will cause him anguish and repentance, however he confronts them. It is as if Huck Finn, seeing that there was no countering a world whose moral boundaries were Tom Sawyer-Miss Watson at one end and Bricksville-Duke-and-Dauphin at the other—as though in the straits of such a vision, Huck had performed the understandable, the conscionable, the perhaps even charitable action of blowing Jim and himself to bits before the front door of the Silas Phelps plantation.

The tensions of *A Connecticut Yankee* are rooted more deeply than in the surface contrasts of past vs. present, pastoral vs. technology, church vs. state, or monarchy vs. democracy. These are the issues that Mark Twain uses to keep the book going. Underlying them all, however, we find another, more fundamental, and far more melancholy paradox. It springs from Twain's perception that a character may be elevated up out of the amorality of the mere humorous anecdote—and yet, in the exchange of rôles, be forced to do fully as much damage as the Bad Little Boy. Or it consists of his recognition that the morally committed hero will have to lose his soul in the pursuit of some great and noble enterprise—and so end up no differently from the tall-tale fantasizer, who never had a soul to lose.

The result is that process of double deflation and double destruction referred to at the beginning. Twain deflates the tall tale, by showing how it can exist only at the price of moral blindness. Hank deflates moral insight, by demonstrating how the practice of morality is as futile as it is ruinous. Responsibility erodes freedom, to be itself undermined by the responsible man's failure to make his last, most vital dream come true. When Twain is finished, both the situations of his earlier fiction—the carefree fantasizing of *The Adventures of Tom Sawyer,* the movement toward moral heroism in *The Adventures of Huckleberry Finn*—are brought down in shambles.

The shambles part, moreover, part to disclose Mark Twain's acceptance of two terrible certainties, and his first brush with nothingness. What began in the spirit of fun failed Twain because the further he pursued the new narrative, the more certain he became that fun alone could no longer be a worthy subject for his fiction. What next became a novel of education failed him because, as Twain plotted its course, the book led not just to the image of virtue become a casualty in the sixth century (that could have been rectified, as we have seen); it led to the certainty that frustration and nihilism must *always* be the ends of wisdom. The world assembled in *A Connecticut Yankee* is ultimately as devoid of joy as it is destitute of the grounds for hope. Consequently, it is a world good for nothing—except perhaps as a place to give the last word to Merlin.

For the change in Merlin's rôle stands in exact counterpoint to the part played by the Yankee. The tall tale had made him butt, the addled, ineffectual Bre'r Merlin, whom Hank could spoof with charm and impunity. But as is often observed, Merlin emerges from the conclusion of the story as a true demon, the weaver of black spells and incantations: in a word, the Devil's spokesman. And to him, everything else belongs. His laughter, echoing across an otherwise silent landscape, is not merely the last important sound we are to hear from *A Connecticut Yankee;* it is the logical stopping place for a book which has measured mankind comically and morally, found life to be wanting in both respects, and so has had to give it over to the mirthful and mocking powers of darkness. The frozen features of Merlin thus serve to remind us of the long way that Twain has come (with Hank) from fun to despair, and of the fact that having come this way, he (like Hank) has no retreat in view. It may not be, as Clarence supposes, that the grin of Merlin will endure for thirteen centuries. As readers of Mark Twain, nevertheless, we shall see it again repeatedly, leering out at us from between the lines of virtually every important work Twain would compose from 1890 until the end of his life. (pp. 28-46)

Clark Griffith, "Merlin's Grin: From 'Tom' to 'Huck' in 'A Connecticut Yankee'," *in* The New England Quarterly, *Vol. XLVIII, No. 1, March, 1975, pp. 28-46.*

EVERETT CARTER   (essay date 1978)

[*In the following excerpt, Carter challenges the idea that* A Connecticut Yankee in King Arthur's Court *satirizes nineteenth-century industrialism as well as European institutions and supports the reading of the novel as Twain's argument for the moral and material superiority of nineteenth-century America over feudal Europe.*]

Interpretations of Mark Twain's fiction about knight errantry, *A Connecticut Yankee in King Arthur's Court,* have changed with successive generations of American commentators. Like the Spanish readers of *Don Quixote,* American readers of *A Connecticut Yankee* have divided into "hard" critics who have seen the book as an attack on sentimentalism about the past, and, increasing in number, those "soft" critics who have read it as either ambivalent or as an attack on technology and the American faith in material progress. The terms "hard" and "soft" are those of a scholar commenting upon the division between schools of commentaries on *Don Quixote,* the "hard" critics of Cervantes' masterpiece insisting upon its defense of reality, the "soft" critics interpreting the work as a defense of the dauntless power of the imagination to remake reality nearer to the dream.

The new "soft" reading of *Don Quixote* has been essential to interpretations of Spanish culture; Unamuno, the first of the "soft" critics of our century, suggested that Don Quixote, rejecting the miserable real for the hopeless dream, is the symbol of what is good, holy, and tragic in the Spanish soul. The fact that one modern American commentator has suggested that the Yankee's enemy, Merlin, plays a similar role in Mark Twain's romance is an index of how far criticism has come from the nineteenth-century assumptions that *A Connecticut Yankee* was a satire on English chivalry. Like the controversy over *Don Quixote,* the controversy about the Yankee has been couched in terms that leave no doubt that for twentieth-century readers there is something eponymous about Hank Morgan. Hank is not only a Connecticut Yankee; he is *The Yankee,* and his fate, like the fate of Cervantes' hero and of the book in which he appears, is more than a falling out among scholars; it has something to do with a country's feeling about itself and its role in the Western world. In 1889, most readers, the illustrator Dan Beard among them, thought they were reading a book about a Yankee's praiseworthy attempt to make a better world. In the second half of the twentieth century, some critics, among them our most influential, have seen it as a premonition of what they assume is an American danger to the world: a story that ends in massive destruction of a large number of the inhabitants of an underdeveloped country is obviously suggestive to the modern mind.

My purpose here is to try to find out what is the probable meaning of *A Connecticut Yankee.* In doing so, I accept both the terminology and the method of E. D. Hirsch's *Validity in Interpretation.* Hirsch urges the distinction between "meaning" and "significance," with "meaning" restricted to the meaning that the author meant. I address myself to this meaning alone. About significance I shall not comment. No one is going to convince the modern readers who see the book as a reinforcement of their dread of American technological progress that it is anything other. I shall not try. I shall simply try to answer the question: "What, in all probability, and on the basis of all the internal and external evidence, did Mark Twain mean by the total fiction *A Connecticut Yankee in King Arthur's Court?*"

In evaluating the external evidence which bears upon the novel's meaning, the first problem to resolve is the probable attitude of Mark Twain towards his narrator, Hank Morgan. Did Mark Twain identify with and sympathize with Hank? Or did he create a narrator whom the reader must criticize, whose attitudes the reader is directed to reject? The answer to this question need not suppose constant authorial identification with the narrator: Mark Twain, after all, had been completely one with Huck Finn's "sound heart" and yet he had satirized minor aspects of Huck's attitude. All that need be asked is "did the writer generally identify with and approve of his narrator and the general course of his narrator's behavior?"

The external evidence that Mark Twain disbelieved in Hank's values consists of a statement to Dan Beard that the Yankee is "an ignoramus." The context of this expression is a description of the protagonist in so favorable a light that Beard made his portraits of the Yankee uniformly sympathetic, although obviously Beard's Yankee is far from refined. Mark Twain, himself a philistine, would not have regarded this as a serious shortcoming. However, he made Hank even more philistine than himself, and Hank's blindness to the beauties of medieval painting and tapestry provides one of the relatively rare instances of Twain's satirizing his protagonist.

Against this lone piece of dubious evidence outside the work itself which might indicate the author's adverse attitude towards the narrator, there are arrayed several indications that Mark Twain sympathized deeply with his Connecticut Yankee. The notebook entries that announce the first glimmerings of the idea for the book, and Twain's working notes for the development of the plot identify the author with the protagonist, suggest he is like Mark Twain's hero, Ulysses S. Grant, and use the first person in outlining the story: "I gave a knight a pass to go holy-grailing. . . . I did everything I could to bring knight-errantry into contempt." After saying that "the whole tribe" will be away on the quest, Twain asks: "Is here my chance to push a R R along, while they are out of my way?" After writing the first thirty-two chapters, he paused to think about the conclusion of his book, and he wrote himself a memorandum: "I make a *peaceful* revolution and introduce advanced civilization."

Even more directly, Mark Twain is on record as approving of his protagonist. The circumstances which led to his expression of approval were these: Howard Taylor had asked for and had received permission to rework the novel for the stage. When Twain read the dramatization he was disappointed, and he focused his criticism on Taylor's failure to do justice to the Yankee. "The new play," Twain wrote his wife, ". . . has captured but one side of the Yankee's character—his rude animal side, his circus side; the good heart & the high intent are left out of him. . . . I told Taylor he had degraded a natural gentleman to a low-down blackguard."

The external evidence seems weighted in Hank's favor; the internal evidence which bears upon Mark Twain's attitude towards his narrator concerns the Yankee's philistinism and his seemingly inhuman attitude towards the chivalry he is trying to destroy. His philistinism is announced at the beginning: Hank describes himself as "nearly barren of sentiment . . . or poetry. . . . " He stands amid medieval glories of sculpture, painting, and tapestry and complains that there is no "insurance-chromo, or at least a three-color-God-Bless-Our-Home over the door." But this lack of a refined aesthetic sense is a minor flaw (and probably not a flaw, at all, in the eyes of Mark Twain). More serious are the several instances where Hank sounds close to megalomania in his desire to reform the medieval world. When he declares, near the end, referring to the massed knights, "We will kill them all," he seems like the Hitler to whom one "soft" commentary has come close to comparing him. "There is a time," Hank says, "when one would like to hang the whole human race. . . ." He describes with apparent relish the "steady drizzle of microscopic fragments of knights and hardware and horse-flesh" that result from his use of dynamite. He considers using "a person of no especial value" to place a bomb down a well. He hooks up a repetitively bowing hermit to a machine and, after he wears him out, he unloads him on Sir Bors de Gans. Finally he approves (although he had not himself prepared) the electrified fences that wipe out England's chivalry.

These constitute an almost complete list of the charges against Hank. If we add to them his willingness to cheat in business, to hang some musicians who play off-key, and to murder a boring would-be humorist, we have the complete indictment. But there is evidence to support a contention that the author did not consider these actions as fundamentally immoral or as more than occasionally and humanly foolish. In the instance of Hank's apparently callous actions, Twain either agreed with their necessity or, in less important cases, took it for granted that his audience would understand the comic-epic tone which permits us to laugh unreservedly at the obliteration of Tom in a Tom and Jerry cartoon, without agonizing about the realities of pain. For example, when Hank asks Clarence if some committee members had made their report (they had just walked over a landmine), Clarence answers that it was "Unanimous." Until the final pages, when Twain's rage against aristocratic privilege got out of hand, Twain was working confidently in the comic world of frontier humor where overstatement about death and destruction was a standard mode of evoking laughter. Many of the seemingly inhuman reactions of Hank take this form, a form linked to the author's own perhaps tasteless but nevertheless comic hyperbole.

Others of Hank's actions are meant to be taken seriously, and in these instances there is a weight of evidence to indicate Twain's sympathies with his protagonist. When planning the activities of the narrator, he not only used the "I," but in the writing sometimes forgot that he was using a specious rather than an actual first-person. Hank's enormous pride when the first newspaper comes out, and as he watches the favorable reaction of a reader, is not the feeling of a Connecticut factory foreman, but rather that of a Missouri journalist: "Yes, this was heaven; I was tasting it once, if I might never taste it more." When Hank expresses his views of England and Russia, they are views that Mark Twain held and which were, according to the two most thorough accounts of the genesis of *A Connecticut Yankee* [Howard G. Baetzhold, "The Course of Composition of *A Connecticut Yankee*," *American Literature* (Jan., 1961) and John B. Hoben, "Mark Twain's *A Connecticut Yankee*: A Genetic Study," *American Literature* (Nov. 1946)], the major impulses for the revival of his interest in the narrative in 1887-1888; Hank's words are usually paraphrases of Twain's letters and notebook entries during those years. He could look into the future, says Hank, and see En-

gland "erect statues and monuments to her unspeakable Georges and other royal and noble clothes-horses, and leave unhonored the creators of this world—after God—Gutenberg, Watt, Arkwright, Whitney, Morse, Stephenson, Bell." Said Mark Twain in a speech in Baltimore in January, 1889, "Conceive of the blank and sterile ignorance of that day, and contrast it with the vast and many-sided knowledge of this. Consider the trivial miracles and wonders wrought by the humbug magicians and enchanters of that old day, and contrast them with the mighty miracles wrought by science in our day of steam and electricity."

From the opening of the tale to its end, Mark Twain treated his alter-ego sympathetically, weighting plot and characterization heavily in his favor. When, at the beginning, Clarence unwittingly dooms him to seeming certain death by his well-meaning acceleration of the date of execution, Hank is considerate of the boy's feelings even at the moment that would tempt most men to relieve their own feelings in recrimination: "I had not the heart to tell him," says Hank, "his good-hearted foolishness had ruined me." When Hank comes upon a dying woman in a peasant's hut, he comforts her, and stays with her even when he knows she is dying of small-pox. "Let me come in and help you—you are sick and in trouble," are his words. His aim in urging the king to travel incognito and his motivation for allowing himself to be kept in the chain-gang, is to open the king's eyes to the horrors of slavery. When they are opened, and the king says he will abolish the evil institution, Hank says he is "ready and willing to get free, now," for his mission has been accomplished. A thoroughly middle-class husband and father, Hank is properly concerned for the good name and well-being of his wife and child. He marries Sandy because he is "a New Englander and in my opinion this sort of partnership [their unwedded companionship] would compromise her." Their marriage results in "the dearest and perfectest comradeship that ever was." The illness of their child compels his absence at the crucial moment of his new country's history: the child is sick; the good father unhesitatingly takes her to the sea-shore. Dan Beard, the illustrator of the first edition, underscored the firm position of the Yankee at the heart of middle-class values with his full-page illustration of a benign and solicitous Yankee, standing next to a beautiful and adoring Sandy, both holding the recumbent "Hello Central," while on the wall behind them is the inevitable framed embroidery of "God Bless Our Home."

Most important of all, Twain sympathetically gave Hank a fatal, but entirely praiseworthy weakness: a reluctance to use violence when the opinion of the sansculotte Mark Twain of 1888 was that bloodshed is the only means of accomplishing major social change. It is "the immutable law," says Hank, echoing sentiments Mark Twain had confided to Howells, "that all revolutions that will succeed must *begin* in blood, whatever may answer afterward. . . . What this folk needed, then, was a Reign of Terror and a guillotine, and I was the wrong man for them." In the end, it is Hank's humanitarianism (viewed by Clarence as his "mistimed sentimentalities") that causes his final tragic sleep. Clarence reports that Hank proposed to go out to help the wounded knights; Clarence strenuously opposes the project; Hank insists, and it is on this errand of mercy that he is treacherously stabbed by one of the knights. Clarence, in what are almost the final words of the epilogue, calls Hank "our dear good chief."

Hank, the eponymous Yankee, then, is a good and trustworthy narrator whose weaknesses are occasionally satirized but who usually carries the burden of authorial attitudes. This fact about the narrator is central to the answer of the next and the most important question: the meaning of *A Connecticut Yankee* with regard to the progress of mankind through the application of reason to the physical and social world, an application that has resulted in the technological society. When Hank engages in his duel with Merlin and with knight errantry, the duel is not simply a conflict between two men, but between two ways of life, between two cultures with their attendant deities, "a mysterious and awful battle of the gods": the god of science on the one hand, the god of superstition on the other. "I was a champion . . . ," Hank says, "but not the champion of the frivolous black arts, I was the champion of hard unsentimental common-sense and reason."

There are three pieces of external evidence that might support a proposition that *A Connecticut Yankee* is not a book in praise of commonsense and reason, but is rather an attack on these and a defense of a lost world of the imagination. One is a notebook entry written very early in the gestation of the work when Twain predicted that his Yankee would mourn "his lost land" and would be "found a suicide." A second piece of external evidence is the fact that Twain was outraged, in August or September, 1887, by the Langdon family's sharp business practices, a concern which led him to write a section, unused in the final version, satiric of nineteenth-century commercialism. The third piece of external evidence is the most famous: Twain's letter to Howells, after the dean of American letters had read and praised the book: Twain replied that there were many things left unsaid, that if he were to say them it would take "a pen warmed-up in hell."

All three pieces of evidence are ambiguous, but all three more logically support a view that the meaning of the work is a defense of the American nineteenth century than the reverse. The early notebook reference to Hank's longing for a sixth-century, a "new" and "virgin" England can be read as a reference to the century and the country as Hank had reformed them, a land and a time that held the memories of his wife and child, a time and a land that, in the same entry, he contrasts with the degradation not of nineteenth-century America, but of nineteenth-century England. Concerning his anger at Andrew Langdon's sharp business practices: Twain's awareness of the curse of financial greed had long been a motive of his satire; since *The Gilded Age,* sixteen years before, he had deplored this disease in a system that he otherwise considered far superior to those of other lands and times. To satirize those ancient evils which persisted into the present was consistent with his reformist purposes; it was this meliorist urge that Dan Beard pointed up by using the face of Jay Gould on the body of the medieval slave-driver, and that William Dean Howells and Clarence Stedman noticed in their reviews. What is more significant than the fact that Twain continued to criticize the shortcomings of his contemporary society is the fact that, in the final version of *A Connecticut Yankee,* he decided to omit a specific satire of this example of a contemporary evil.

The third, and more often quoted bit of external evidence consists of that cry to Howells that he would need a "pen warmed-up in hell" to say the unsaid things of *A Connecticut Yankee.* There is little reason to believe that the unsaid things would have been attacks on common-sense, republicanism, and technology. There is every reason to believe that the unsaid things were further scathing attacks on monarchy, for-

eign despotisms, and aristocratic pretensions. Exactly two months after his cry for a hell-warmed pen, he crowed to Howells that "These are immense days. . . . There'll be plenty to sneer & depreciate & disenthuse—on the other hand, who can lift a word of the other sort, in the name of God let him pipe up! I want to print some extracts from the Yankee that have in them the new (sweet) breath of republics." The same week he wrote the hell-warmed pen letter, he wrote to Sylvester Baxter to gloat over the fall of the Brazilian monarchy, and to link the last chapters of *A Connecticut Yankee* with that happy demise. Within three months he wrote to his English publisher: "I wanted to say a Yankee mechanic's say against monarchy and its several natural props." From 1885 to 1889 his notebooks and letters are full of rage against English arrogance, Russian tyranny, commercial speculation and greed, and those prolongations of medieval prejudices into the nineteenth century which made the South and the slavery system the subject of nostalgic sentimentalizing. These had been the evils against which Twain had been fulminating for years; he had never expressed the need for a weapon with which to attack technological progress and liberal democracy, while he had often raged against royalty, aristocracy, and hereditary privilege. To take the angry satirist's cry for a pen warmed in hell as a cry for a tool with which to attack republican progress would be an improbable introduction of a new and unexpected attitude; to take the phrase as a reference to his hatred of those past and foreign institutions about which he had frequently expressed himself would be a more probable inference.

The letter to his English publisher constitutes one of six direct, unambiguous statements of authorial purpose, six declarations of intent which provide a substantial body of support for a reading of *A Connecticut Yankee* as a defense of democracy, technology, and progress. Every time Mark Twain expressed himself about what he meant in writing the book, he tried to say bluntly that he was defending the American nineteenth century and attacking a brutish and inhumane past. The letter to the English publisher not only made the identification between author and narrator: "I wanted to say a Yankee mechanic's say . . . ," but it went on to declare: ". . . the book was not written for America; it was written for England. So many Englishmen have done their sincerest to teach us something for our betterment that it seems to me high time that some of us should substantially recognize the good intent by trying to pry up the English nation to a little higher level of manhood in turn." Twain's changing the name of the Yankee from the neutral "Robert Smith" to a familiar form of the name of the pirate who harried English trade routes is, in this context, no reflection on the character of Hank Morgan, but is rather the humorist's signal of the direction of his satire. Twain's angry response to English criticism of America, and his defense of his country, was one of his preoccupations in the years he was writing *A Connecticut Yankee;* he has left notes for a talk attacking English and defending American society: ". . . If you scrape off our American crust of shabby politicians," the unfinished draft reads, "you will find a nation underneath of as sterling a character, & with as high purposes at heart. . . ." The draft did not complete the terms of the comparison, but the meaning is unambiguous. Equally unequivocal is the introduction to several excerpts from *A Connecticut Yankee* which appeared in the *Century Magazine* in November, 1889. There Twain described the work as "a bitter struggle for supremacy . . . , Merlin using the absurd necromancy of the time and the Yankee beating it easily and brilliantly with the more splendid necromancy of the nineteenth century—that is, the marvels of modern science." After a few chapters, Twain wrote a summary of the plot: "Meantime the Yankee is very busy; for he has privately set himself the task of introducing the great and beneficent civilization of the nineteenth century, and of peacefully replacing the twin despotisms of royalty and aristocratic privilege with a 'Republic on the American plan.' . . . " In 1906, he dictated his memories about the book; they were that he had been ". . . purposing to contrast that English life . . . with the life of modern Christendom and modern civilization—to the advantage of the latter, of course."

In addition to these declarations of purpose in letter, introduction, and memoir, Twain wrote three prefaces that announce the intended meaning of the work. One, published as an appendix in A. B. Paine's biography, accounts for the fact that he chose England, and not Russia (or Belgium) as the object of his satire. "I have drawn," he wrote, "no laws and no illustrations from the twin civilizations of Hell and Russia. To have ventured into that atmosphere would have defeated my purpose: which was to show a great & genuine progress in Christendom in these few later generations, toward mercifulness—a wide and general relaxing of the grip of the law." This was one of his tries at an introduction; another emphasized that his attack was not only upon the false worship of the English past, but upon the sentimentalizing of history in general: "The strange laws," this unpublished preface went, "which one encounters here and there in this book, are not known to have existed in King Arthur's time, of course, but it is fair to presume that they did exist, since they still existed in Christian lands in far later times—times customarily called, with unconscious sarcasm, 'civilized and enlightened.' The episodes by which these laws are illustrated in this book are not invention, but are drawn from history; not always from English history, but mainly from that source. Human liberty—for white people—may fairly be said to be one hundred years old this year; what stood for it in any previous century of the world's history cannot be rationally allowed to count." This seems clear enough, but even more to the point was another unpublished preface that was directed at the reader who might make the mistake of preferring the past to the present: "One purpose of the book," Mark Twain wrote, "is to entertain the reader—if it may have the happy luck to do that. Another is, to remind him that what is called Christian Civilization is so young and new that it had not yet entered the world when our century was born. . . . If any are inclined to rail at our present civilization, why there is no hindering him; but he ought to sometimes contrast it with what went before, & take comfort—and hope, too."

In the face of this evidence of authorial purpose, few commentators have implied that Mark Twain intended to write an attack on progress and technology. Instead, modern revision of the work's meaning has either ignored the question of authorial intent (after all, academic critics had been warned off by the dread of committing "the intentional fallacy") or has argued that authorial intent was subverted by the act of creation: behind the new commentaries has hovered the critical ideology which insists upon the independence of the work of art: "trust the tale, not the teller." The tale, for the "soft" critics, tells us that the Yankee is at least a well-meaning fool or at most an authoritarian villain whose obsession with technology brings about the destruction of civilization. (pp. 418-29)

While occasionally concerned with internal evidence drawn from other portions of the book, these revisions of *A Connecticut Yankee*'s meaning have usually concentrated on the conclusion: the catastrophic scenes of the slaughter of the knights, the destruction of the technological civilization, the triumph of Merlin, the thirteen-century-long sleep of the Yankee, and his sad death while calling out for his lost life in the sixth century. Any interpretation of the meaning of the romance must address itself to the construction of the plot of *A Connecticut Yankee* with particular attention to its development towards this ending: towards the electrocution of the knights, the dynamiting of the factories, and the defeat of the Yankee. What were the causes of the Yankee's failure? Who and what was responsible for the downfall of his civilization?

To support a contention that this ending constitutes a subconscious inversion of the author's conscious intention, several necessary conditions would have to be proven. One is that there was a sudden shift, an undermining of the author's meaning as the work progressed, a reversal of previous mood and tone. The second is that the ending was unusually, even unbearably painful for the author: certainly a subconscious fear that exploded previous convictions and that subverted conscious desires would be something to which he would be loathe to return. A third is that the sadness of the ending, the change from comedy to tragedy, was a statement about human institutions and not about man's cosmic fate, a statement about society and not about metaphysics. An ending that described common-sense, reason, and technology as destructive forces inside of history would be truly a subversion of authorial intent; a plot whose denouement showed an awareness of the immutable human condition, condemned to eventual earthly separation from home and love, would be a shift in mood, but not a change in social commitment: within the larger, inescapable terms of human existence, this ending might say, men can still make choices that will make society better or worse; the crucial point is whether the Yankee offered a better choice than that which was offered in the past.

First the question: was the ending an unforeseen reversal of previous plans for the novel? It seems not to have been. From the beginning, as we have seen, Mark Twain planned an ending in which the Yankee would "mourn his lost land." In Chapter 8, "The Boss," a chapter written in the summer of 1887 a full eighteen months before he wrote the ending, Mark Twain put in Hank's mouth the following prediction about the conclusion of his adventure: "Yes, in power I was equal to the king. At the same time there was another power that was a trifle stronger than both of us put together. That was the Church. I do not wish to disguise that fact. I couldn't if I wanted to. But never mind about that, now; it will show up in its proper place, later on." Then, in September, 1888, still nine months before he wrote the conclusion, Twain made the entry in his notebook where he both identified himself with the protagonist, and then summarized the ending: "I make a *peaceful* revolution and introduce advanced civilization. The Church overthrows it with a 6 year interdict."

The frustration of England's premature progress, the failure of the Yankee to reform the medieval world was the ending Mark Twain had decided upon possibly as early as 1885, probably as early as 1887, and certainly by the autumn of 1888. It was no sudden change, no turning of a creator's subconscious against his conscious wishes. Furthermore the very form of the ending—the carnage of the knights, electrocuted by charged barbed wire and mowed down by machine guns—had been one of the earliest incidents Mark Twain had devised; he had written of precisely this kind of battle in 1886, when no more than three chapters had been completed. Some of these "adventures of Sir Robert Smith of Camelot" were read before the Military Service Institute of Governor's Island on November 11, 1886. According to a reporter's version, Sir Robert Smith "took a contract from King Arthur to kill off, at one of the great tournaments, fifteen kings and many acres of hostile armored knights. When, lance in rest, they charge by squadrons upon him, he, behind the protection of a barbed wire fence charged with electricity, mowed them down with Gatling guns that he had made for the occasion." After finishing the book in 1889, Twain gave another reading of it before a military audience, this time the cadets of West Point. He included the scene of the Battle of the Sand-Belt, and in his reading notes—a paste-up of pages from the first edition—he identified the 52 loyal "boys" with the audience before him, substituting the word "cadet" for "boy" when the latter first appeared, and ended his reading with a description of the military victory: ". . . the campaign was ended, we fifty-four were masters of England! Twenty-five thousand men lay dead around us." Then he crossed out the remaining paragraphs that dealt with Hank's wounding and his defeat.

The carnage at the end, then, is no aberration but a conventional mode of frontier hyperbole in which Mark Twain frequently indulged, which he had planned for three years to be part of his novel, and which he read with obvious relish before audiences properly appreciative of the progress of military weaponry; one may deplore its childish ferocity or its possibly misplaced admiration, but one can scarcely use it to prove a sudden reversal of authorial intent, or a pathological change in customary style. Above all, since Mark Twain conceived the scene early and returned with relish to it late, he was obviously untraumatized by its possible implications for his belief in the blessings of technology.

The ending, then, was both planned by and was untraumatic for its author; it was something Mark Twain had decided upon early, and with unusual care for an author who was self-admittedly a poor constructor of plots. But there is certainly a difference in tone between the ending of *A Connecticut Yankee* and almost everything Mark Twain had written before; all of his previous works had concluded "happily": *The Gilded Age* with Washington Hawkins coming to his senses; *The Prince and the Pauper* with the regaining of the Prince's position and with the improved fortunes of the pauper; *Tom Sawyer* with the finding of Injun Joe and the winning of the reward; *Huckleberry Finn* with the freedom of Jim from slavery and of Huck from his father's tyranny; *Life on the Mississippi* with paeans to Northern progress. The sense of weariness and sadness at the end of *A Connecticut Yankee* is a changed tone. Very early in its writing, Mark Twain knew that the Yankee would have to lose and began to prepare his readers for his hero's downfall. The crucial question is: to what causes did the book assign the Yankee's failure? Were they causes inherent in the Yankee's beliefs or moral structure? Did Hank cause the terrible ending of *A Connecticut Yankee*? Or did Mark Twain take care to assign the reasons for the disaster to other elements of history? And what did this assignation of guilt tell us about forces in history that should be encouraged, and those discouraged, in order to achieve a better society?

Mark Twain made Hank but a minor, and morally guiltless, cause of the final catastrophe: he was too humane in his efforts to reform an evil society. With Hank absent, drawn from his post by the needs of a sick child, forces that the romance identifies as evil and reactionary, and that Hank (still according to the authorial voice) had been too soft-hearted to make impotent, these forces nullify his reforms. In self-defense and in defense of a small besieged band of loyal followers, victims of an unprovoked aggression by armored soldiers who outnumber them 500-1, soldiers who would torture and kill them and then reinstitute serfdom and slavery, Hank uses advanced technology to destroy the enemy. There is no evidence that Twain thought Hank's self-defense reprehensible. The major causes of the disaster, as Twain described them, are, first, the growing corruption of the Round Table, specifically the adultery of Launcelot and Guenever, and second, and most important, the opening that this corruption made for the exercise of the decisive cause: the power of an absolute church.

The corruption of the Round Table was fixed as a moving force in the denouement from the beginning of the conception of *A Connecticut Yankee.* Immediately after he outlined the burlesque of knight-errantry for the Military Institute of Governor's Island in 1886, Twain reassured Mrs. A. W. Fairbanks that he would not besmirch the work she loved, the *Morte Darthur,* and its "beautiful" characters. He did not keep his promise with regard to the whole of Malory's romance; it comes in for pretty rough treatment in Chapter XV; but as a counterpoint to the broad burlesque of knight errantry and of its chronicler, Mark Twain introduced and intermittently sustained the serious traditional subplot concerning the gallant and praiseworthy members of the chivalric orders: Galahad, Launcelot, and, above all, the king himself. The king is more than a king, says Hank, he is "a man." Galahad, the Yankee tells us, has a "noble benignity and purity." Launcelot has "majesty and greatness," and it is he who comes riding to Hank's rescue—on a bicycle. The part of the *Morte Darthur* that Mark Twain seized upon was the tragic and fatal adultery that resulted in the waste of Malory's admirable characters; in *A Connecticut Yankee* it was this crime against nineteenth-century middle-class morality that leads directly to the death of that portion of the chivalry of England that was praiseworthy, leaving only the dregs of aristocracy to be destroyed by Hank and Clarence and their fifty-two loyal cadets.

The adultery is suggested as early as the third chapter, upon Hank's first view of the Knights of the Round Table. He sees the queen fling the kind of "furtive glances at Sir Launcelot that would have got him shot in Arkansas, to a dead certainty." A few moments later, the court explodes in a riot of indecency, using language that "would make a Comanche blush." Hank is stripped, and stands before the knights and ladies "naked as a pair of tongs." Queen Guenever, says Hank, "was as naïvely interested as the rest." Dan Beard obligingly emphasized the meaning of this scene by drawing a small picture of Guenever, looking anything but naïve, as she presumably appraises the object before her. In Chapter XXVI, written during the summer of 1886, Hank describes the mournful look of King Arthur, when Hank suggests that he tell Guenever that he is going away. "Thou forgettest," says the king, "that Launcelot is here; and where Launcelot is, she noteth not the going forth of the king, nor what day he returneth." Hank then observes: "Yes, Guenever was beautiful, it is true, but take her all around she was pretty slack." When

Hank returns from his trip of mercy to find his partially re-formed country in ruins, Clarence tells him of the Civil War that resulted when Arthur found out about Guenever's and Launcelot's adultery; it is a tale of the destruction of all of the worthy knights, of the death of Arthur, and of the queen's retirement to a nunnery. Moral slackness had destroyed what was good in knight errantry.

Sexual immorality, however, was but a contributory cause of the disaster; it had been but the weakening of the body politic, making it susceptible to the final fatal disease. The disease, announced by Mark Twain in both notebook and text, was the power of the absolute church. It was a power exercised when both the adultery of court life and the morally opposite fidelity of Hank to wife and family made it possible for the Church to exercise its latent strength. While Hank is away, caring for his child, the Church, stronger than both Hank and the king, makes its move; the Church, Hank says sadly when he returns from France, was going to "*keep* the upper hand, now, and snuff out all my beautiful civilization. . . ." Again, Dan Beard obliged by visualizing these lines in a full-page illustration of a smirking monk placing a bishop's miter over a bright candle labeled "19th Century," and entitling the drawing: "Snuffing Out the Candle."

The failure of the Yankee, then, is accounted for: minor blame is assigned to Hank for the venial sin of sentimentality, major blame to the mortal sins of Launcelot and Guenever and, most important, of the reactionary church. In only one place in the narrative is there the suggestion that progress through technology itself is the wrong course for humanity. This is the paragraph where Hank, describing his hidden factories, uses the analogy of a volcano, and compares them to the lava's "rising hell": "Unsuspected by this dark land," Hank says, "I had the civilization of the nineteenth century booming under its very nose! . . . There it was . . . as substantial a fact as any serene volcano, standing innocent with its smokeless summit in the blue sky and giving no sign of the rising hell in its bowels."

Comparing technology to a hell, the metaphor seems on the face of it to be loaded with negative feelings about the beneficence of applied science. Perhaps. One might also observe that "hell" did not always have negative connotations for an author who would rather be consigned to the Puritan hell than the Puritan heaven, who asked for his pen to be warmed in the infernal regions, and who might quite typically have described what was going to happen to aristocracy and church as, from their standpoint, a diabolical eruption. Furthermore the possibly negative import of the metaphor is contradicted by the surrounding allusions where technology is associated with light, and backward England with darkness.

The metaphor of the volcano is the one piece of internal evidence that might support the view that the cause of the disaster was technology itself; everywhere else there is the suggestion that Hank's prescription for the cure of social ills—the prescription of the faith in progress through reason, common sense, and applied science—is sound. What is perhaps true, although the internal evidence is far from clear, is that the general metaphysical framework in which this belief was embedded began to show signs of stress by the time Mark Twain was finishing *A Connecticut Yankee.* This framework had been built of a certain view of human nature—that it is essentially good—, and a corresponding view of universal law—that it too is moral and tends to work by assuring the betterment of human institutions over the course of history. Both

optimisms are questioned by the conclusion of Mark Twain's fiction.

The disappointment Hank suffers when he returns to find not only the chivalry of England massed against him, but the people of England as well, revives his (and Mark Twain's) latent ambivalence towards the common man and towards the doctrine of his natural goodness. Where at the beginning of his adventures in medieval England, Hank used the word "muck" literally, to describe the streets of Camelot, Hank uses the term at the end of the novel to describe the people themselves: "Imagine such human muck as this; conceive of this folly!" This constitutes the "massive disillusionment" to which revisionist criticism of *A Connecticut Yankee* refers. It is incontestable that the Yankee is disappointed, and that his faith in humanity has been shaken. However, it had never been a faith without an admixture of both doubt and realism; earlier in the work, Hank had faced the problem posed for his hope of progress by the complex nature of man, and had come out of the experience with a renewed, if chastened, conviction that in the main there is enough good in human nature to justify a hope for society's improvement. The situation was this: travelling incognito, Hank and the king had come upon a frightful example of the operations of the archaic customs of England, laws that had resulted in mass cruelties and executions. Hank found that the peasants support the lords. "The painful thing," he observed, ". . . was the alacrity with which this oppressed community had turned their cruel hands against their own class. . . . It was depressing to a man with a dream of a republic in his head." Then, as it often did, the distance between narrator and author collapsed, and Mark Twain began to talk of his own experiences, experiences in the American South outside the range of a descendant of New England blacksmiths and horsedoctors: "It reminded me of a time thirteen centuries away, when the 'poor whites' of our South . . . were . . . pusillanimously ready to side with slave-lords . . . for the upholding and perpetuating of slavery." There was a redeeming factor, however, a small one, but enough to modify Hank's pessimism: "secretly the 'poor white' did detest the slave-lord and feel his own shame." This was enough "for it showed that a man is at bottom a man. . . ." That this is straightforward and not ironic is made clear a moment later when Hank describes the bravery of one of the peasants and declares: "There it was, you see. A man *is* a man, at bottom. Whole ages of abuse and oppression cannot crush the manhood clear out of him." Yes, he continues, "there is plenty good enough material for a republic in the most degraded people that ever existed. . . ." Then, as mask and author once more abruptly coalesce, he adds: "—even the Russians." At this point, the most extended discussion of the problem of the moral nature of man in *A Connecticut Yankee,* Hank concluded: "there was no occasion to give up my dream yet a while." The abandonment of the dream would be forced not by the nature of man, but by the nature of radically corrupt human institutions.

The second part of the metaphysical structure that supported the American belief in progress was an attitude toward the power behind history, be it God, Nature, or Universal Law: the sense that the movement of events was both purposeful and, in the long run, moral. There is some support for the proposition that Mark Twain's shaky allegiance to this faith was undergoing stress, and that the stress is reflected in the ending of *A Connecticut Yankee.* When the Yankee is described in Twain's notebook as "mourning his lost land," when in the frame of the narrative he smiles "one of those pathetic, obsolete smiles of his," when, in his dreams, he still wanders "thirteen centuries away," his unsatisfied spirit ". . . calling and harking all up and down the unreplying vacancies of a vanished world," we seem to have taken a long step toward the final pessimisms of *The Mysterious Stranger.* If, in his longing for his vanished world, Hank is longing for Camelot as Camelot, and if he feels himself a stranger in the nineteenth century as the nineteenth century, then, indeed, *A Connecticut Yankee,* as fiction, subverted its author's announced intention.

That this is not true can be proven by an examination of the portrait of medieval England as we find it in *A Connecticut Yankee.* The sixth century landscapes are idyllic, but its villages are vile and the life of its people is a hell for all but noble and aristocrat. It is a pastoral land whose dream-like beauty is, for Hank, "as lonesome as Sunday." In the course of his incognito wanderings, Hank comes upon a telegraph station of his underground army of progress. "In this atmosphere of telephones and lightning communication . . . ," Hank says, "I was breathing the breath of life again after long suffocation. I realized then, what a creepy, dull, inanimate horror this land had been to me all these years."

The apparently idyllic land contained a culture that made a horror out of natural goodness. Even the most favored of the aristocrats were prevented from enjoying it. The most eloquent description of pre-technological England, a description full of sentimental cliches like "sylvan solitudes," comes at the beginning of the chapter called "Slow Torture," a chapter devoted to the intolerable life inside a coat of armor. A second flowery passage describing "blessed God's untainted dew-freshened, woodland-scented, air" comes after the description of Morgan le Fay's tortured victims, and is followed by Hank's description of the suffocation of mind and body in "the moral and physical stenches of that intolerable old buzzard-roost."

This pretechnological England, naturally beautiful, humanly terrible, was transformed by Hank without, apparently, harming the landscape. Like "another Robinson Crusoe," he invented, contrived, created, and made a good society. "Consider the three years sped," he said proudly. "Now look around on England. A happy and prosperous country, and strangely altered. Schools everywhere, and several colleges. . . . Slavery was dead and gone; all men were equal before the law; taxation had been equalized. The telegraph, the telephone, the phonograph, the type-writer, the sewing machine, and all the thousand willing and handy servants of steam and electricity were working their way into favor. . . ." The list of accomplishments goes on, and ends with: "I was getting ready to send out an expedition to discover America."

There is reason to believe, then, that Hank's longing is not for a pretechnological Eden, but for an England that the Yankee, like Robinson Crusoe, had made bearable by the exercise of his ingenuity. However, more powerful motives than nostalgia operated at the end of *A Connecticut Yankee* to give the comedy its serious turn. One was Mark Twain's consideration of a cyclical, repetitive theory of the movements of history. While the immediate cause of the downfall of Hank's society was the immorality of the Queen, Clarence suggests, without contradiction, that the end would have come "by and by," and would be caused by Hank himself. Merlin's taunt: "Ye were conquerors, ye are conquered," has the ring of the mockery of the goddess of Fortune, the deity of an inevitable turning back upon itself of all human enterprise.

The second tragic motive, and a more important one, was Mark Twain's growing awareness, at the age of fifty, of the inevitable private failures of men, whatever the fate of their societies. Men must die; men must be separated from their earthly loves. Except for those fortunate, or self-deluding, enough to have a traditional religious faith, men must face the fact that time is man's enemy, cutting him away from his worldly affections. Hank's final delirium is entirely about these private sadnesses; he raves about Sandy and about their child, not about politics or technology. The bathetic ending of *A Connecticut Yankee* has nothing to do with the relative merits of republics or monarchies, progress or tradition. This is the human condition, says the novel's ending; but given the unalterable limits of this condition, man can still ask the question: what should man then do? And the answer *A Connecticut Yankee* gives, just as Mark Twain's tract *What Is Man?,* written years later, would give, is that within the severe restrictions and limitations of man's condition, he can try to act for human, for worldly improvement.

The available evidence, then, external and internal, suggests that the meaning of *A Connecticut Yankee* is, as the author repeatedly said it was, that the American nineteenth century, devoted to political and religious liberalism and to technology, was better than the traditional past. The efforts of modern men to continue a progress towards a fulfillment of material goals is shown to be a worthy mission of man. Mark Twain's fictional excursion into history was, as he insisted it was, for the purpose of saying to the reader: you've been poor following European models; you've become rich following American models; rich is better. Twentieth-century interpreters who find an opposed significance in the work must ask themselves whether that significance is an "appropriate" extension of authorial meaning. (pp. 430-40)

Everett Carter, "The Meaning of 'A Connecticut Yankee'," in American Literature, *Vol. 50, No. 3, November, 1978, pp. 418-40.*

WILLIAM J. COLLINS   (essay date 1986)

[*In the following excerpt, Collins discusses the originality and narrative implications of Twain's framing device in* A Connecticut Yankee in King Arthur's Court.]

Commentary on Mark Twain's *A Connecticut Yankee in King Arthur's Court* has concentrated overwhelmingly on the social criticism contained in the book-within-a-book, the palimpsest account of Hank Morgan's adventures in sixth-century England. One is safe in stating that, outside of science fiction criticism, few if any critics deal seriously with the framing device, the account of the tourist Mark Twain's encounter with Morgan in Warwick Castle and the methods that propel the Yankee into the past and back again to his native nineteenth century. Yet that frame constitutes one of Twain's most important contributions to what would become known as science fiction.

Philip Klass [see Further Reading] has noted the novel's success in treating, for almost the first time in Anglo-American fiction, one of the most prevalent devices of imaginative literature: "All backward-in-time stories come from . . . *A Connecticut Yankee.* . . . [There] was no such story before. And every such story since uses themes he discovered in that book." David Ketterer [see excerpt dated 1974] is equally emphatic:

Time travel into the past raises all kinds of paradoxical and science-fictional possibilities centering on the problem of historical anachronism. That Twain realistically faces the anachronism issue constitutes a major point in any argument for considering *A Connecticut Yankee* an example of classic science fiction.

Indeed, the three basic "themes," perhaps better stated as "challenges," of time-travel fiction are present in Twain's novel: the mechanics of traveling backward to the historical event; the paradoxes involved in visiting the presumably fixed past, from which no report of a time traveler has reached the present; and the method of returning the time traveler to his own present day. Lacking any analogues upon which he might improve, Twain's development of these challenges is embryonic. But read in the wake of later, more sophisticated approaches to time travel, *A Connecticut Yankee* demonstrates how successfully Twain identified the genre's inherent problems.

For the forward-in-time segment, Morgan's return to the nineteenth century, there were already precedents, though in many of them the fantastic element was vitiated by the ubiquitous "It was all a dream." Suspended animation as a device to move a human far beyond his normal lifespan appears to have exploded onto the literary scene during the writing of *A Connecticut Yankee;* W. H. Hudson's *The Crystal Age,* whose protagonist is caught in a landslide and preserved miraculously for several thousand years, had appeared in 1887, and Edward Bellamy was putting the insomniac protagonist of his *Looking Backward* into a hundred-and-thirteen-year sleep via hypnosis while Twain was putting the finishing touches to his own novel. And of course all three Americans had before them the exemplar of Washington Irving's Rip van Winkle.

The trip backward through time, which receives its first major fictional treatment in the Twain novel, is a much more difficult challenge because, as Fritz Leiber has pointed out, "Time travel is quite impossible . . . because it would change the past, disordering history and unfixing the framework of reality." Leiber goes on to quote Thomas Aquinas that such a feat would be beyond even the power of God. And, of course, our own perceptions, if we can trust them, confirm that no one from the future has visited us. And yet, the great question "what if . . . "—common to all speculative fiction—nowhere unfolds more temptation than in the contemplation of a visit to some enigmatic historical period or some grand turning point of human destiny.

In order to fulfill at least fictionally the longing for intimate contact with the past, some writers, such as H. G. Wells, invented machines that, in spite of all known laws of physics, worked. Others, like John Taine, have cloaked their time travel in extradimensional mathematics of which present-day science is ignorant. Still others, and Mark Twain was only the first, simply provide an unexplained and unexplainable natural accident that, somehow, momentarily tears the fabric of time (whatever that is!), allowing a random temporal displacement of the protagonist. The blow on the head that precipitates Hank Morgan back to Arthurian England is only slightly more awkward a device than the lightning strike that propels Martin Padway from twentieth- to sixth-century Rome in L. Sprague de Camp's *Lest Darkness Fall,* written a half century after the Twain novel on which it is obviously modeled.

Twain's realization of the paradoxes involved in a visit to the past must involve the reader in something of an act of faith. Paradox abounds, but to what degree Twain was aware of just how sophisticated were the problems he posed probably can never be determined with total accuracy. However, a close examination of the use of paradox in *A Connecticut Yankee* not only illuminates the ambiguous nature of the novel's framing device but also reveals a hitherto unrecognized contribution by Twain as innovator of science fiction themes.

The reader's awareness of Twain's use of paradox begins with the Warwick Castle guide's explanation of the bullet hole in the suit of armor:

> Ancient hauberk, date of the sixth century, time of King Arthur and the Round Table; said to have belonged to the knight Sir Sagramor le Desirous; observe the round hole through the chain-mail in the left breast; can't be accounted for; supposed to have been done with a bullet since invention of firearms—perhaps maliciously by Cromwell's soldiers.

This is followed by Morgan's statement that he had done it himself. If Cromwell's soldiers are indeed responsible for the bullet hole, then Morgan is a madman or a liar despite his palimpsest and his deathbed delirium, which seems to confirm his veracity or at least his belief in his own tale. The bullet hole is the only tangible evidence that Morgan has journeyed through time, unless we consider that the practical Yankee lacks the creative imagination to fabricate his palimpsest testament. If the reader steps outside the novel, however, Morgan's story becomes less and less credible. In his years as The Boss, Morgan has given, according to his story, foundries, mining, new coinage, telephones, bicycles, and printing to sixth-century England. Yet in our world there is no trace of any of his works, though artifacts less substantial and more ancient have survived. Nor could the most thorough purge of his contributions by a vengeful Catholic Church so completely obliterate not only their physical presence but also their memory, however blurred by time. One might make a case for his massacre of massed knighthood as a source, corrupted by time, for the cataclysmic battle between Arthur and Mordred; but no electric wires have yet been unearthed at Salisbury. The only proof, if such it is, of Morgan's presence in the sixth century remains the ambiguous bullet hole.

Thus far, the few critical writings on *A Connecticut Yankee* as science fiction have centered on Twain's invention of the idea of contemporary man in conflict with the mores of a past age. In doing so, they have overlooked the central paradox of the novel. Morgan, somehow translated from nineteenth-century America to sixth-century Britain, encounters—King Arthur's court, as Malory describes it! By the late nineteenth century, scholarship concerning the Matter of Britain was sufficiently developed that, at the very least, readers of Malory, Chrétien de Troyes, and Wolfram von Eschenbach were aware that Camelot was a Never-Never Land, a clothing by the romance writers of the last Roman Britons and their leader Artus in the armor of the twelfth century, in order to produce a nostalgic utopia as a mirror of their own corrupt society. Thus, Morgan must be a liar and the bullet hole a Cromwellian desecration.

If, that is, there is only one past. But for many years science fiction writers, notably Philip K. Dick in *The Man in the High Castle* and Keith Roberts in *Pavane,* have dealt with alternative presents produced by historical events that turned out differently from what we know to be our history. As Jorge Luis Borges has described it in his short story "The Garden of Forking Paths,"

> [Ts'ui Pen] did not believe in a uniform, absolute time. He believed in an infinite series of times, in a growing, dizzying net of divergent, convergent and parallel times. This network of times which approached one another, forked, broke off, or were unaware of one another for centuries, embraces *all* possibilities of time.

Consciously or not, then, by placing Hank Morgan in a sixth-century England that in our collective history is a fabulation concocted by a series of romance writers six centuries after the fact, Mark Twain has invented not only, for all practical purposes, the time travel tale but also the alternative history. The blow on Hank Morgan's head has sent him not only back through time but across it, across a rift in the seams of possibility, to one of the infinity of worlds in which Malory is not a fabulator but a historian.

Twain's primacy as inventor of the alternative history, at least for the English language, is less open to question than is his primacy as inventory of the fully developed time-travel story. Both the anonymous "An Anachronism, or Missing One's Coach," published by the *Dublin University Magazine* in 1838 (in which the protagonist briefly finds himself talking to the Venerable Bede in the eighth century), and Edward Page Mitchell's "The Clock That Went Backward," from the *New York Sun* in 1881, qualify as genuine predecessors of Twain's in the realm of time travel (even if both totally lack literary influence). Robert Silverberg, however, has advanced the claim that Edward Everett Hale's "Hands Off," published in *Harper's New Monthly* the same year as Mitchell's short story, thus eight years prior to *A Connecticut Yankee*, is "the first known example of the world-of-maybe story." Jan Pinkerton has also examined the Hale story, providing evidence that although "Hands Off " can be legitimately considered a precursor of the alternative history, it does not qualify because the narrator is a supernatural being (thus rendering it fantasy by definition) and because the world with which he might have interfered exists only on a conditional, not an actual, basis.

Whereas Hale's cross-time traveler is a spirit, Twain's is most definitely fleshly. But Morgan's return to and presence in a shared nineteenth century with Twain-as-narrator pose another paradox. If Morgan had indeed been thrown both back through and across time by the blow on the head, if he has left as his monument to Arthur's England printing, literacy, sophisticated mining and metallurgical techniques, as well as the massacre of every last living male member of the nation's nobility, how then has his cave/tomb returned to the Twain-Morgan nineteenth century? Of course Twain lacks the answer (L. Sprague de Camp, faced with a similar problem in *Lest Darkness Fall,* leaves his protagonist in the sixth century). But based on later refinements of the alternative history theme, readers can supply their own speculations: perhaps Merlin's cave is itself an extratemporal entity; perhaps the cave has, over the centuries, crossed the parallel worlds, drawn to the "real" world because of the attraction of Morgan's sleeping body to its own rivulet of the time stream; perhaps Ts'ui Pen's remark that the strands of the garden of forking paths "bifurcate, intersect" justifies the cave's moving from its Malory-as-historian line to one of the Malory-as-fabulator lines.

But there is a further question inherent in the paradox: is Twain and Morgan's reality the reader's reality? Remember the "drowning voice of the salaried cicerone" who guides Twain and Morgan around Warwick Castle: "Ancient hauberk, date of the sixth century, time of King Arthur and the Round Table"? "Sixth century"? "Time of King Arthur"? We know that, whoever Arthur or Artus really was, he and his companions did not wear twelfth-century armor. Even in "our" nineteenth century such armor on exhibit would have been correctly labeled. One might accuse a creative museum guide of playing on the popular confusion of history and literature to slip in a reference to King Arthur's court, but Twain's "salaried cicerone" quite obviously has no such poetry in his soul. Just as obviously, Twain and Morgan are neither in "our" nineteenth century nor in one proceeding lineally from the sixth century that Morgan briefly reformed but rather in one of the infinity of nineteenth centuries that spans the distance between the two, perhaps closer to Morgan's than to ours in that there also Malory is a historian.

In "our" universe, Twain's novel is essentially one of social criticism, conceived in a brilliant framing device that doubly identifies the author as a pioneer of science fictional themes. In the castle guide's universe, Twain's novel is really Morgan's scarcely believable manuscript with a Foreword and a "Final P. S." by tourist and author Mark Twain. In at least one of the infinity of parallel universes, *A Connecticut Yankee in King Arthur's Court* must be a historical novel with speculative overtones, a novel that celebrates the age that produced England's liberation from the oppression of church and nobility by the martyred Sir Boss and its era of prosperity inaugurated by Clarence, the gallant fifty-two, and Hank's heir, Hello-Central Morgan. (pp. 109-14)

> *William J. Collins, "Hank Morgan in the Garden of Forking Paths: 'A Connecticut Yankee in King Arthur's Court' as Alternative History," in* Modern Fiction Studies, *Vol. 32, No. 1, Spring, 1986, pp. 109-14.*

JANE GARDINER (essay date 1987)

[*In the following excerpt, Gardiner argues that the essential conflict in* A Connecticut Yankee in King Arthur's Court *is not between modern science and medieval superstition, as has been widely asserted, but between clearly beneficial mechanical innovations and more sophisticated and potentially dangerous forms of technical progress.*]

An enormous amount of criticism of Mark Twain's *A Connecticut Yankee in King Arthur's Court* has, and quite rightly, concerned itself with the ambivalences of the author or (and probably the same thing) those of his protagonist, Hank Morgan, toward progress. Kenneth Roemer, for example, sees Twain as floundering between worship and fear of "progress," and this is only a subtle shift from Jay Martin's statement that "Twain simultaneously entertains the opposite views of history as decline and history as progress." Most critics, and again quite reasonably, make an association between "progress and technology"—as when Vernon Parrington says that Twain, in writing *Connecticut Yankee,* "was already trimming his sails to the chill winds blowing in from the mechanistic cosmos," or when Henry Nash Smith sees Twain as "oscillat[ing] between the brave new world of science and technology, and nostalgia for the simple agrarian world that the industrial revolution was destroying before his eyes." What is interesting about most of these discussions is that they tend to accept as given the ground of the argument and align themselves on one or the other side of it. The ground is that, in **Connecticut Yankee** (and in the mind of the author), backwardness is opposed to progress, pastoral England to industrial America, romance to realism, and magic, superstition, and faith to science, technology, and reason. The argument thus polemically constructed demands that the critic attempt to determine whether the author (sometimes via his protagonist) had, ultimately, greater sympathy for one of these given "sides" or for the other. Was Twain a closet pastoralist or was he, as Everett Carter has attempted to re-assert [see excerpt dated 1978] in the wake of an army of "revisionists," a strict nineteenth-century technological progressive?

While this is a perfectly valid approach—and an approach which is difficult for even a casual reader of the novel to avoid—one cannot but observe that argument along these lines has caused much scholarly ink to be spilled to no apparent resolution of the dispute. I would like to suggest that a certain shift in the dialectical focus might be productive; might, in fact, throw up the possibility of an explanation of those ambivalences and ambiguities which run through the novel and so concern its readers. The shift in ground that I have in mind requires a re-examination of what has, inevitably, become the core of many scholars' interpretations of the novel: the series of duels fought between Hank Morgan and Merlin (and, once, with another "surrogate Merlin" rival magician) in which, ostensibly, nineteenth-century science is pitted against sixth-century magic.

The first skirmish in this war is Hank's battle for survival at the stake when, with the aid of a timely eclipse (and, presumably, a habit of memorizing *Whitaker's Almanac*), Hank "proves" that he can put out the sun—and then bring it back—when Merlin's incantations could not prevent the darkness. The second duel occurs when Hank blows up Merlin's tower with lightning and dynamite, and shows himself to be a greater magician than Merlin who, again, could not prevent the destruction by incantations. The third battle is also won by Hank when he restores the flow of the miraculous waters at "The Valley of Holiness"—a feat which Merlin could not accomplish with spells, and which Hank performs with scientific "know-how." The fourth duel takes place between Hank and a stranger magician, a Merlin-surrogate (Merlin having been rendered *hors de combat* after his latest humiliation), who is defeated by Hank's use of a secret telephone. The fifth episode occurs near the end of the novel, when Hank uses a revolver to defeat Sir Sagramor in the lists, despite the latter's "magic veil" supplied for his "protection" by Merlin. In point of fact, however, Hank, who purports to despise "magic" and "superstition," always defeats Merlin on Merlin's own ground: that of magic. Although Hank uses science to perform his "miracles," he unfailingly disguises the scientific basis of his achievements from the people and, one begins to suspect, from himself, and pretends, instead, that his powers are magical.

In this pretense of supernatural powers, Hank's very first "miracle" sets the pattern. Despite having none of the accompanying flares and bangs of later wonders, the eclipse is passed off as necromancy when Hank says, "let the enchantment dissolve and pass harmless away!" By the time we reach Hank's second duel with Merlin (the destruction of Merlin's tower), we read "wonderful necromancer as I was pretending to be" and, when we arrive at "The Valley of Holiness" with

its blocked well, we find Hank saying to a monk, "I can do this miracle; I shall do this miracle; yet I do not try to conceal from you that it is a miracle to tax the occult powers to the last strain." Soon after that, and even more significantly, in speaking of a telephone installed in a hermit's abandoned cave—the telephone that is secretly used and passed off as magic in the defeat of the visiting magician—Hank muses to himself, "the home of the bogus miracle become the home of a *real one*, the den of a medieval hermit turned into a telephone office!" (emphasis added). At this point, all reference to, perhaps all notion of, pretense in respect of Hank's perception as well as promotion of *his* magic has been lost from his reflections and, finally, after the duel with Sir Sagramor, Hank comments that "every time the magic of fol-de-rol tried conclusions with the magic of science, the magic of fol-de-rol got left." The accumulated significance of these battles is, in short, that Hank comes to see science as the real magic and himself as the better magician; and, having thus accepted the reality of "magic," and its difference from "science" being, if anything, merely one of degree, the final encounter between the two antagonists is particularly appropriate. Merlin casts an effective spell (his first) on Hank, which puts Hank to sleep for thirteen centuries. Having thus ended Hank's power by the use of magic, Merlin falls on Hank's electrified fence and is killed instantly, a victim of Hank's superior magic. The honors are so nearly equally divided between "science" and "fol-de-rol" that one is tempted to wonder whether there is really any difference between the two.

While Hank's first encounter with Merlin establishes a close association between "science" and "magic," in another respect there is an important divergence between the first duel and subsequent ones. In the first encounter Hank is fighting for survival whereas, in subsequent meetings, the duel with Merlin is a fight for power. This is important because the battle of the eclipse, unlike all the other battles of "magic," is not won by Hank's control of science-based technology, but by something over which he has, in reality, no control whatsoever. Moreover, although he is thought by the population to have the supreme power of creation and destruction when he blots out—and then relights—the sun, this is the one occasion in a battle with Merlin when that power is not, in fact, his. In other words, Hank's real power of creation and destruction, as well as his real power of technology, manifests itself in those duels after the first one; those in which the prize also is power: political power. However, in all but one of the duels fought with Merlin for possession of political power in Arthur's kingdom, the tool Hank uses to defeat his rival is also power: electric power. Thus, in blowing up Merlin's tower, Hank uses an electrical charge to detonate dynamite; at The Valley of Holiness a "pocket electrical battery" creates the spectacle by igniting fireworks (although the actual water flow is achieved by pumps); a telephone causes the humiliation of the surrogate Merlin; and electrified fences finally defeat Merlin and the massed chivalry of England. Only the defeat of Sir Sagramor, with a bullet from a revolver, is secured by some means unconnected with electrical power. In all the other duels Hank holds the power of creation or destruction by having the power of electricity. Not for nothing does he begin and end his account of his attempts to "modernize" sixth-century England with the twin images of his hand on the switch; the first when he says "I stood with my hand on the cock, so to speak, ready to turn it on and flood the midnight world with light at any moment"; the second when, at the end, he "touched a button. . . . All our noble civilization-factories went up in the air and disappeared from the earth." Power. Magic.

Lest we miss the point, Twain, writing in the November 1889 issue of *Century Magazine,* restates the paradox as "Merlin using the absurd necromancy of the time and the Yankee beating it easily and brilliantly with the more splendid necromancy of the nineteenth century—the marvels of modern science." Picking up on this unquestioningly and apparently without recognizing the paradox, Stephen Leacock in his "Appreciation" in the "Stormfield" edition of *A Connecticut Yankee* says that "there is a contrast between the childish 'magic' of Merlin and the practical knowledge of the Yankee, who can make telephones and telegraphs and introduce in the place of Merlin's spells the 'magic' of electricity." Subsequent critics repeat the same paradox with, it seems, no more consciousness than Leacock.

The strange thing about this unthinking acceptance of what is, after all, a paradox set up by Twain in a work of fantasy, is that such a paradox could not have gone unquestioned at any previous time in the nineteenth century. One has only to look back at the ante-Bellum social reformers (the real-life fathers of Hank Morgan) to see that an allegation of "magic" made in respect of science would have been quickly decried. The true nineteenth-century attitude toward science was expressed not by Twain but by Josiah Warren, social reformer and organizer of "utopian" communes: "Science is simple and definite, and easy to comprehend and uniform in its results." This was an assertion which any nineteenth-century social reformer, prior to the years during which Twain was writing *A Connecticut Yankee,* would have accepted. Such was the popular view of "science" as distinctly different from, and opposed to, magic (or miracles) that even social philosophers as absurdly metaphysical as Fourier and the Fourierists had to cloak their fantasies in a pretense of science in order to attain credibility in nineteenth-century America: "the application of science to the pursuits of life shall, through daily use, become as familiar as the mother tongue."

How, then, could Twain create, and his contemporaries and subsequent readers so blithely accept, an assertion so contrary to the nineteenth-century understanding of the relationship between science and the supernatural as Twain's comment on "the more splendid necromancy of the nineteenth century—that is, the marvels of modern science"? A clue can be found, I believe, in the words of another prominent social reformer of the nineteenth century. At about the same time as Josiah Warren was pronouncing "science" to be "simple and definite, and easy to comprehend and uniform in its results," Robert Owen was maintaining that "mechanism . . . may be made the greatest of blessings to humanity," a sentiment that Hank Morgan, with his "people factories," could surely have agreed with. "Science" as it was understood in the mid-nineteenth century was rational precisely because it was mechanical. It ceased to be rational, and became miraculous, in the decade before Twain published *A Connecticut Yankee* because it was no longer the same science. When Twain wrote of "modern science" as "the splendid necromancy of the nineteenth century," he was referring to that supremely modern science that is what Leacock calls "the magic of electricity." This is a totally different science from the "mechanism" that Robert Owen (and Hank Morgan in his role of social reformer) had in mind when they contemplated a technological basis of social progress.

Thus the true ambivalence which Twain creates in his novel

is the paradox of a "magical science," an ambivalence to which such contradictions as those usually debated by critics are secondary. The tension is not, primarily, between pastoral and industrial, primitive and progressive, faith and reason or magic and science, but between two different kinds of nineteenth-century science. The first kind represents "reason," "progress," "civilization," and the second kind of science represents—and in *A Connecticut Yankee* is represented *as*—magic. The former kind exists in the novel in the bicycle, the sewing-machine, the railroad and sundry other contraptions donated by Hank to improve the lives of Arthur's subjects and the prosperity of His Majesty's entrepreneurial Chief Minister. The latter kind of science exists not as machines, but as power. This power cannot—unlike the poor saint who drives Hank's sewing-machine—be seen or understood; nevertheless its *effects* can be seen, and those effects can be hugely creative or apocalyptically destructive. This power, which does indeed seem magical, and which Hank uses to enormous effect throughout the novel, is electricity.

The suddenness of the onset of this new science can scarcely be overstated. Before 1878 (the dating of the new epoch can be conveniently—and fairly honestly—fixed with the invention of Edison's incandescent lamp), science was all that Josiah Warren and Robert Owen held it to be. After that it bore no relationship to the world of "science" as Warren, Owen—or Twain, or anyone, for that matter—understood it. In the first place, electricity was a *power*—not a machine—and a power that was totally unlike any previous power. It was invisible, incomprehensible (seriously, how many people *really* understand electricity?) and deadly. Secondly, this power, and the technology that utilized it, was invading people's lives and homes in a way that the old water or steam power had never done. Finally, this electrically-based technology was breaking in upon people's lives, including those of the Clemenses of Hartford, Connecticut, with an unheard-of speed in the very decade in which Twain was writing *A Connecticut Yankee.*

The bare statistics of the period are frightening enough, even to a twentieth-century reader; consider the impact of the reality upon the people of the time. In 1878 Bell's first telephone system, complete with switchboard, was operating in New Haven, Connecticut. It had twenty-one telephones connected to it—and this merely two years after Bell had shown the prototype telephone at the Philadelphia Centennial Exhibition. In 1880 the nation had 138 telephone *exchanges,* and a year later there were 408. The invention of the multiple switchboard in 1883 simplified transmission of calls by allowing each operator access to every line in her exchange. In 1885 the first long-distance line (from New York to Philadelphia) was begun, and by 1892 New York, Boston, and Chicago were all connected by telephone lines. Meanwhile, Thomas Edison, four years after inventing a workable incandescent light for home use (arc-lights had been in use as street lighting in the late 1870s but could not be used in confined spaces because of the huge surge of electricity required and because of the high-powered glare of the lights), opened the Edison Electric Light Company's central generating plant at Pearl Street in New York. It initially supplied power to 2,323 lamps. Two years later (1884), the power from this plant fed 11,272 lamps in 500 homes. A sister company also supplied individual home generators which served 10,424 lamps in 1882, and 59,173 in 1885.

Similarly rapid was the application of electricity to machinery. In 1879 the first experimental electric railway-line was shown at the Berlin Industrial Exhibition, and in 1882 the Crystal Palace Electrical Exhibition in London included a display of electrical machinery. In 1884, in the U.S.A., Frank J. Sprague's Electric Railway and Motor Company was incorporated and in 1887 the company received a contract to build an electric street-railway in Richmond, Virginia. This railway was successfully operating in 1888. Thus, the year before Twain published *A Connecticut Yankee,* the era of the horse came to an end—although the age of the electrical motor really had its origins in the invention of the transformer (1885) and then the inductor motor (1889). Until the invention of the transformer, all electric motors ran on direct current. Although direct current had the advantage over alternating current in transportation, where an easily adjustable speed was important, it had limited range of transmission and was far less economical than alternating current. The transformer and the alternator made alternating current safer and easier to use than before, and thus opened the way to the large-scale application of electrical power to machines of many kinds—including household appliances.

Should there be any doubt about the enormous changes brought about by this new power, one should consider the forms of energy which had, hitherto, run the industrial revolution. Gas, transmitted through pipes, burned to produce heat and light; that was no miracle. Steam power and water power could be seen and their workings understood by everyone. Likewise, the machines which ran on steam or water power were relatively simple gadgets; mere hand tools with an external source of power applied to them. It may have taken millennia to invent a weaving machine, but the principle was an ancient one known to everybody. Once they had seen it, most people could put together a clumsy replica; could certainly repair a faulty one. A paddle steamer was little more than an Indian canoe with another source of power attached to it. In the 1880s, however, electrically-based technology was producing machines of a more complex nature; machines whose principles were based upon a scientific theory that could not be readily understood; machines that did much more than reproduce the action of an ancient hand-tool with greater speed and accuracy; machines like the induction motor and the dynamo.

Furthermore, as science was passing out of the realm of common understanding, its applications were passing more and more into direct confrontation with the lives of people; the more incomprehensible electrically-based technology became, the more it impinged upon people's lives. Before the 1880s people saw machines at their places of work; they saw railroad trains and steam-boats, and may even have ridden on them. The 1880s saw electrified street transportation, and homes run with the aid of (it may have seemed *by*) this strange new power that could strike a man dead instantly. The Clemens' household of Hartford, Connecticut, was in the middle of this domestic revolution, as Twain's *Notebooks* show. In 1885 he noted, "the telephone must be driven out, for it is useless—at any rate at night when the electric lights are burning," and in 1889 or 1890 he notes (the context is not supplied): "Maid below, no extra charge, electric bell right below. Or in our room." Ordinary people were being assaulted in their streets and in their homes by a technology that was not, in Josiah Warren's phrase, "easy to comprehend," and the impact was all the greater because more and more people were concentrated in the cities where they could not escape this new scientific age. By 1889 civilization had become virtu-

ally equated with technology—as Hank's foray into Arthurian England suggests—but a new and awful kind of technology it seemed to be. An omnipotent and supreme power had arrived.

The accelerating importance as well as the awfulness of this new power may be grasped by the modern reader from a perusal of the contemporary journals. A newspaper, by its very nature, indicates the immediate impact upon the general public of current events in a way that a history, for example, cannot. In the year 1885, the "Index" to the *New York Times,* for the first time, has "Electricity" printed in bold type as a sub-heading and lists under it various reports and editorials pertaining to the topic. This form is continued throughout the decade. Previously, entries about electricity had been too few to warrant such a sub-section. After 1885 the *New York Times'* reports upon electricity are almost equally divided between the beneficial aspects of the power—the electrification of street-cars (the approaching demise of the stinking horse was nowhere regretted), subways, elevated railways, lights—and the more frightening uses of electricity. An electric "torpedo" receives notice on February 18, 1886; in 1887 a bill is introduced in the New York State Legislature to provide for electrocution of criminals convicted of a capital crime. This bill is signed in 1888 and in 1889 a murderer is the first person sentenced to die by the means allotted to Merlin in *A Connecticut Yankee.*

Both intentional and unintentional death by electrocution are the subjects of articles appearing in the *North American Review* in 1889—the year of publication of *A Connecticut Yan-*

Twain in 1872.

kee. One Eldridge T. Gerry notes that "over ninety cases of accidental death by such [electrical] contacts during the past two years are recorded, and in every case the action of the current was so instantaneous as to leave not the shadow of a doubt that death was literally quicker than thought," and thus advocates, in an undoubtedly unconscious parody of Josiah Warren, capital punishment by electrocution as "painless, instantaneous, and uniform in its results." In the same volume, Thomas Edison admits that "a number of accidents, many of them attended with fatal results, have occurred to pedestrians on the streets of New York and other cities through the medium of fallen wires," and, after mentioning a particularly gruesome accident "witnessed a few days ago in New York by several thousand people," announces that the present rate of fatal accidents is nothing to what it will be in the future, but that the adoption of underground wiring (as advocated, and eventually enforced, by the municipality of New York) or a move to alternating current would actually increase the death rate. This latter point appears to be supported in an accompanying article by Harold P. Brown, "New York State Expert on Electrical Execution," who blames alternating current for "the terrible, needless slaughter of unoffending men." How far in his cheek is Mark Twain's tongue when he comments in his *Notebooks* that "the Electric Light Co's [are] permitted to murder men and horses unrebuked"?

If the author of *A Connecticut Yankee* seems ambivalent in his attitude toward "science" and "progress," surely the ambivalence lies here. Hank Morgan, as social reformer, brings "civilization" to Arthurian England with the mechanics of the industrial revolution. But Hank Morgan, in destroying that civilization, does it with the new power of electricity; and Hank Morgan, in destroying the power of Merlin, uses the power of electricity and presents it as "magic." When Hank pushes the buttons to destroy the knights ("men and horses") of England and to destroy his new machine-based civilization, he is doing what the inhabitants of American cities knew—and may, themselves, have seen—could be done with electricity. It is surely reasonable to assume that Twain did not escape the general confusion and disorientation that the "new science" was inflicting on his contemporaries. That it *was* inflicting confusion and disorientation is not mere supposition. One only needs look at *The Education of Henry Adams,* a book which Leo Marx has said is dominated by "a sense of the transformation of life by technology." This is particularly true of the last part of the book. After having considered his education terminated in 1871, Adams finds himself in the position of being forcibly re-educated in 1892. Beginning with Chapter 21, "Twenty Years After (1892)," *The Education* is a chronicle of a man confronted by a new power of science and technology for which he is unprepared and for which nothing in his previous life and education have fitted him to understand. In Paris, in 1892, Adams writes: "As [Adams] saw the world it was no longer simple and could not express itself simply. . . . Under the first blast of this furnace-heat, the lights seemed fairly to go out. He felt nothing in common with the world as it promised to be." The metaphor used by Adams, here, echoes the last major act of Hank Morgan. In a surge of power, darkness descends upon the old, "simple" world of the industrial revolution and both Henry Adams and Hank Morgan (the latter wandering, delirious, in a later Britain) are left confused by the new world they have come to.

Eight years later, Henry Adams is in Paris again, at the Great

Exposition. The focus of his attempt to understand the events of recent years is, not for the first time, the dynamo. As he looks at the dynamo, he writes:

> [T]he dynamo became a symbol of infinity. As he grew accustomed to the great gallery of machines, he began to feel the forty-foot dynamos as a moral force, much as the early Christians felt the Cross. . . . Before the end, one began to pray to it; inherited instinct taught the natural expression of man before silent and infinite force. Among the thousand symbols of ultimate energy, the dynamo was not so human as some, but it was the most expressive. . . .
>
> For Adams's objects its value lay chiefly in its occult mechanism. Between the dynamo in the gallery of machines and the engine-house outside, the break of continuity amounted to abysmal fracture. . . . No more relation could he discover between the steam and the electric current than between the Cross and the cathedral. The forces were interchangeable if not reversible, but he could see only an absolute *fiat* in electricity as in faith.

Nowhere in literature is the nature of the mystical ("occult") power that is electricity more eloquently described. Unlike the Cross, however, the theology of the dynamo introduced a Manicheism into the "theology" of science that, in Twain's novel, is reflected in the twin images of Hank, finger on the switch, waiting to "flood the midnight world with light" or to blow "all our noble civilization-factories in[to] the air." This was not the science Twain—or Adams, or Warren—knew of old.

Perhaps we might allow Henry Adams the last word. In "The Grammar of Science" (1903), he notes that, previously, almost all scientific thought had stressed unity and order:

> One God, one Law, one Element,
> And one far-off, divine event,
> To which the whole creation moves.

But, adds Adams, "suddenly, in 1900, science raised its head and denied." I would suggest that Adams' date owes something to a millennialistic desire for symmetry, and something, also, to the chance date of his personal epiphany. The denial had, in fact, been made in the decade of the 1880s, and the ambivalences of *A Connecticut Yankee* are a reflection of that denial. (pp. 448-57)

> Jane Gardiner, " 'A More Splendid Necromancy': Mark Twain's 'Connecticut Yankee' and the Electrical Revolution," in Studies in the Novel, *Vol. XIX, No. 4, Winter, 1987, pp. 448-58.*

FURTHER READING

Baetzhold, Howard G. " 'The Autobiography of Sir Robert Smith of Camelot': Mark Twain's Original Plan for *A Connecticut Yankee.*" *American Literature* 32, No. 4 (January 1961): 456-61.
    Examines published accounts of Twain's reading from an early draft of *A Connecticut Yankee* on 11 November 1886.

———. "The Course of Composition of *A Connecticut Yankee:* A Reinterpretation." *American Literature* 33 (May 1961): 195-214.

Discusses the composition of *A Connecticut Yankee,* suggesting emendations to John B. Hoben's widely accepted account (cited below) and noting the influence of George Kennan's articles concerning the Russian monarchy, which appeared in *Century* magazine in 1888.

Bellamy, Gladys. "Moralism versus Determinism." In her *Mark Twain as a Literary Artist,* pp. 305-25. Norman: University of Oklahoma Press, 1950.
Includes a brief discussion of *A Connecticut Yankee in King Arthur's Court* in which Bellamy notes the underlying pessimism of the novel.

Blues, Thomas. "A Connecticut Yankee: 'Ah, What a Donkey I Was'." In his *Mark Twain and the Community,* pp. 27-54. Lexington: University Press of Kentucky, 1970.
Analysis of the relation between Hank Morgan and the Arthurian community in *A Connecticut Yankee.* Blues argues that the novel fails because "Mark Twain could no longer effect the stratagem central to the structural coherence of each of his previous novels, his protagonist's commitment to the community whose values and stability he paradoxically repudiates."

Brodwin, Stanley. "Wandering between Two Gods: Theological Realism in Mark Twain's *A Connecticut Yankee.*" *Studies in the Literary Imagination* 16, No. 2 (Fall 1983): 57-82.
Examines the role of Twain's Protestant, utopian ideals in shaping the narrative of *A Connecticut Yankee.*

Budd, Louis J. "Uncle Sam." In his *Mark Twain: Social Philosopher,* pp. 111-44. Bloomington: Indiana University Press, 1962.
Analyzes the social and political attitudes reflected in *A Connecticut Yankee,* focusing on Twain's liberalism, his contempt for European monarchies, and his endorsement of modern technology.

Butcher, Philip. " 'The Godfathership' of *A Connecticut Yankee.*" *CLA Journal* 12, No. 3 (March 1969): 189-98.
Suggests that, despite Twain's unwillingness to acknowledge the fact, George Washington Cable contributed to the writing of *A Connecticut Yankee* by introducing Twain to Malory's *Morte d'Arthur,* by engaging him in conversations that parodied the style of Malory's book, and by serving as a model of humanitarianism.

Dinan, John S. "Hank Morgan: Artist Run Amuck." *Massachusetts Studies in English* 3, No. 3 (Spring 1972): 72-7.
Analysis of Hank Morgan as the antithesis of the artist-hero figure in American literature. Dinan notes: "One of the most intriguing indictments against Hank is that which accuses him of being both a dangerous, irresponsible artist and a poor critic of his artistic creations. He is an artist controlled by his artifacts, an artist deficient in human sensibility—an artist run amuck."

Emerson, Everett. *The Authentic Mark Twain: A Literary Biography of Samuel L. Clemens.* Philadelphia: University of Pennsylvania Press, 1984, 330 p.
Supplies background information concerning the composition of *A Connecticut Yankee.*

Fienberg, Lorne. "Twain's Connecticut Yankee: The Entrepreneur as a Daimonic Hero." *Modern Fiction Studies* 28, No. 2 (Summer 1982): 155-67.
Suggests that the problematic ending of *A Connecticut Yankee* can best be understood by viewing Morgan as a character whose very success produces the conditions that inevitably lead to his downfall.

Fluck, Winfried. "The Restructuring of History and the Intrusion of Fantasy in Mark Twain's *A Connecticut Yankee in King Arthur's Court.*" In *Forms and Functions of History in American Literature: Essays in Honor of Ursula Brumm,* edited by Winfried Fluck, Jürgen Peper, and Willi Paul Adams, pp. 134-48. Berlin: Erich Schmidt Verlag, 1981.

Views *A Connecticut Yankee* as an unintentionally negative depiction of nineteenth-century technological progress. Fluck explains: "Because Twain was an artist who did not force his own experiences into a strict preconceived aesthetic pattern, but composed in a rather spontaneous fashion, he gave expression to cultural fantasies and emotions which were no official part of his doctrine of progress."

Foner, Philip S. "Politics and Government." In his *Mark Twain Social Critic,* pp. 65-124. New York: International Publishers, 1958.
Discusses Twain's attacks on the church, aristocracy, and monarchy in *A Connecticut Yankee.*

Geismar, Maxwell. "Failure and Triumph." In his *Mark Twain: American Prophet,* pp. 110-41. New York: McGraw-Hill, 1970.
Discussion of *A Connecticut Yankee* in which Geismar emphasizes the ambivalent tone of the novel.

Giddings, Robert, ed. *Mark Twain: A Sumptuous Variety.* London: Vision, 1985, 255 p.
Includes two essays concerning *A Connecticut Yankee.* In a discussion of picaresque elements in Twain's work entitled "Mark Twain and the Future of Picaresque," Lyall Powers argues that Twain's portrait of Hank Morgan is more consistent than is generally acknowledged. In "Towards the Absurd: Mark Twain's *A Connecticut Yankee, Pudd'nhead Wilson,* and *The Great Dark,*" Peter Messent discusses Twain's use of the figure of the stranger in his later works, suggesting that such figures indicate both Twain's move toward "a fiction of displacement, of isolation, of restlessness," and his disillusionment with realism as a literary method.

Girgus, Sam B. "Conscience in Connecticut: *Civilization and Its Discontents* in Twain's Camelot." *New England Quarterly* 51, No. 4 (December 1978): 547-60.
Applies elements of Freudian psychological theory to *A Connecticut Yankee,* focusing on Twain's interest in conscience and his own feelings of guilt.

Goldstien, Neal L. "Mark Twain's Money Problem." *Bucknell Review* 19, No. 1 (Spring 1971): 37-54.
Views Hank Morgan's fascination with commerce as a manifestation of Twain's obsession with money at the time he wrote *A Connecticut Yankee.*

Green, Martin. "Twain and Whitman: The Problem of 'American' Literature." In his *Re-appraisals: Some Commonsense Readings in American Literature,* pp. 113-43. London: Hugh Evelyn, 1963.
Reassesses Twain's literary achievements. Green considers *A Connecticut Yankee* a more appropriate and more successful vehicle for Twain's humor than *The Adventures of Huckleberry Finn,* noting: "The important part of [*A Connecticut Yankee*] is the friendly, uncritical, but lively irony it directs at the Yankee himself and what he stands for."

Guttmann, Allen. "Mark Twain's *Connecticut Yankee:* Affirmation of the Vernacular Tradition?" *New England Quarterly* 33, No. 2 (June 1960): 232-37.
Brief analysis of plot and characterization in *A Connecticut Yankee.* Guttmann concludes: "The Boss represents a turning-point in the hard road from ill-founded optimism to starkest nihilism. Mark Twain, when he finished the *Connecticut Yankee,* was a man who had lost his belief in the Idea of Progress."

Hansen, Chadwick. "The Once and Future Boss: Mark Twain's Yankee." *Nineteenth-Century Fiction* 28, No. 1 (June 1973): 62-73.
Considers Hank Morgan a prototype of the modern totalitarian dictator.

Harris, Susan K. "*A Connecticut Yankee in King Arthur's Court:* Hank Morgan." In her *Mark Twain's Escape from Time: A Study of Patterns and Images,* pp. 44-59. Columbia and London: University of Missouri Press, 1982.

Discusses the importance and significance of alienation in Twain's characterization of Hank Morgan.

Henderson, Harry B., III. "Twain: The Varieties of History and *A Connecticut Yankee*." In his *Versions of the Past: The Historical Imagination in American Fiction,* pp. 175-97. New York: Oxford University Press, 1974.

Views *A Connecticut Yankee* as Twain's attempt to "revolutionize the nineteenth-century historical novel and adapt it to the progressive social imagination."

Hoben, John B. "Mark Twain's *A Connecticut Yankee:* A Genetic Study." *American Literature* 18, No. 3 (November 1946): 197-218.

Discusses the composition of *A Connecticut Yankee.* From his examination of pertinent documents, Hoben concludes that Twain originally conceived of the novel as a light satire of the Arthurian romances but that his celebrated disagreements with Matthew Arnold, which peaked during the composition of *A Connecticut Yankee,* affected his view of the English people and altered the tone of the novel.

Johnson, James L. "A Connecticut Yankee." In his *Mark Twain and the Limits of Power: Emerson's God in Ruins,* pp. 120-54. Knoxville: University of Tennessee Press, 1982.

Analyzes *A Connecticut Yankee* as the turning-point in Twain's view of the relation between the individual and material circumstances. Johnson contends that in previous novels, Twain had demonstrated an Emersonian belief in the power of the individual to shape or transcend material existence, while in *A Connecticut Yankee,* he was forced to acknowledge the destructive potential of such power.

Jones, Joseph. "Utopia as Dirge." *American Quarterly* 2, No. 3 (Fall 1950): 214-26.

Compares dystopian aspects of *A Connecticut Yankee* with those of Aldous Huxley's *Brave New World* and George Orwell's *Nineteen Eighty-Four.*

Kegel, Paul. "Henry Adams and Mark Twain: Two Views of Medievalism." *Mark Twain Journal* 15, No. 3 (Winter 1970-71): 11-21.

Compares the portraits of medieval society presented in *A Connecticut Yankee* and Henry Adams's *Mont-Saint-Michel and Chartres.*

Klass, Philip. "An Innocent in Time: Mark Twain in King Arthur's Court." *Extrapolation* 16, No. 1 (December 1974): 17-32.

Examines the narrative problems Twain encountered in his experimentation with the subject of time displacement.

Knight, Stephen. " 'A New Deal': Mark Twain's *A Connecticut Yankee at King Arthur's Court* and the Modern Arthurian Legend." In his *Arthurian Literature and Society,* pp. 187-216. New York: St. Martin's Press, 1983.

Discusses Twain's satirization of medieval society, nineteenth-century England, and modern technology in *A Connecticut Yankee.*

Lorch, Fred W. "Hawaiian Feudalism and Mark Twain's *A Connecticut Yankee in King Arthur's Court.*" *American Literature* 30, No. 1 (March 1958): 50-66.

Argues that "many of the basic concepts of feudal society and its practices which come under attack in the *Yankee* had their inception in Mark Twain's early observations of life in the Sandwich Islands." Lorch suggests that Twain's intention to write a satire of medieval society predated his reading of Malory's *Morte d'Arthur.*

Maynard, Reid. "Mark Twain's Ambivalent Yankee." *Mark Twain Journal* 14, No. 3 (Winter 1968-69): 1-5.

Summarizes critical approaches to *A Connecticut Yankee* and disagrees with critics who view the primary focus of Twain's satire as nineteenth-century technology.

Miller, Robert Keith. "Invincible Stupidity: *A Connecticut Yankee*

in King Arthur's Court." In his *Mark Twain,* pp. 113-35. New York: Frederick Ungar, 1983.

Argues that the key to resolving the questions of interpretation surrounding *A Connecticut Yankee* lies in Twain's description of the novel as simply a "contrast" of the two civilizations depicted.

Pressman, Richard S. "A Connecticut Yankee in Merlin's Cave: The Role of Contradiction in Mark Twain's Novel." *American Literary Realism, 1870-1910* 16, No. 1 (Spring 1983): 58-72.

Suggests that, although Twain did not intend to criticize the failures of modern technology and democratic institutions in *A Connecticut Yankee,* such criticisms are nevertheless implicit in the narrative.

Reed, Walter. "*The Confidence-Man* and *A Connecticut Yankee in King Arthur's Court:* The Novel, the Original, and the New." In his *An Exemplary History of the Novel: The Quixotic versus the Picaresque,* pp. 197-231. Chicago and London: University of Chicago Press, 1981.

Discusses *A Connecticut Yankee* as an inversion of the quixotic theme, with the anti-Romantic Hank Morgan attempting to reshape a Romantic reality to fit his pragmatic desires.

Rust, Richard Dilworth. "Americanisms in *A Connecticut Yankee.*" *South Atlantic Bulletin* 33, No. 3 (May 1968): 11-13.

Examines Twain's use of American colloquial speech in *A Connecticut Yankee.*

Salomon, Roger B. "The Fall of Prometheus: *A Connecticut Yankee.*" In his *Twain and the Image of History,* pp. 95-132. New Haven, Conn.: Yale University Press, 1961.

Discusses the tonal ambiguity of *A Connecticut Yankee.* Salomon concludes: "If the official theme of the book is the progress that Western Society has made since the Middle Ages, the theme of the Yankee's own story, on the contrary, is the absurdity of optimism and the impermanence of progress (or the illusory nature of progress) because of the aggressiveness and rapacity of modern industrial man, the false promise of technology and—ultimately—because of the deep-rootedness of human evil."

Sloane, David E. E. "*A Connecticut Yankee:* A Culmination of American Literary Comedy." In his *Mark Twain as a Literary Comedian,* pp. 146-67. Baton Rouge and London: Louisiana State University Press, 1979.

Reading of *A Connecticut Yankee* in which Sloane views the novel as an exemplification of Twain's skepticism about human progress.

Spengemann, William C. "The Yankee Pirate: *A Connecticut Yankee in King Arthur's Court.*" In his *Mark Twain and the Backwoods Angel: The Matter of Innocence in the Works of Samuel L. Clemens,* pp. 84-104. Kent, Ohio: Kent State University Press, 1966.

Interprets *A Connecticut Yankee* as an essentially Romantic narrative in which Twain expresses nostalgia for the pastoral setting of his youth. Spengemann notes: "Clemens purports to show the great progress mankind has made since the sixth century—a progress in which he officially believed. However, his gnawing distrust of commercialism and social institutions, and his continued interest in the innocent past, with its agrarian economy and its stable traditions, subverted these aims."

Stead, William T. "Mark Twain's New Book: A Satirical Attack on English Institutions." *Review of Reviews* 1, No. 2 (February 1890): 144-56.

Positive review of *A Connecticut Yankee.* Stead asserts: "To those who endeavor to understand what the mass of men who speak English are thinking . . . this book of Mark Twain's is one of the most significant of our time."

Trainor, Juliette. "Symbolism in *A Connecticut Yankee in King Arthur's Court.*" *Modern Language Notes* 66, No. 6 (June 1951): 382-85.

Suggests that Twain's use of the story of Lancelot and the Giants in *A Connecticut Yankee* symbolizes his own quest to topple the twin giants of church and monarchy.

Williams, James D. "The Use of History in Mark Twain's *A Connecticut Yankee*." *PMLA* 80, No. 1 (March 1965): 102-10.
    Examines the historical sources upon which Twain drew in creating his portrait of medieval society.

Wilson, Robert H. "Malory in the *Connecticut Yankee*." *Studies in English* 27, No. 1 (June 1948): 185-206.
    Discusses Twain's use of specific elements drawn from Malory's *Morte d'Arthur* in order to clarify the extent of Malory's influence in the creation of *A Connecticut Yankee*.

Twentieth-Century
Literary Criticism

Cumulative Indexes
Volumes 1-36

This Index Includes References to Entries in These Gale Series

Contemporary Literary Criticism

Presents excerpts of criticism on the works of novelists, poets, dramatists, short story writers, scriptwriters, and other creative writers who are now living or who have died since 1960. Cumulative indexes to authors and nationalities are included, as well as an index to titles discussed in the individual volume. Volumes 1-56 are in print.

Twentieth-Century Literary Criticism

Contains critical excerpts by the most significant commentators on poets, novelists, short story writers, dramatists, and philosophers who died between 1900 and 1960. Cumulative indexes to authors, nationalities, and titles discussed are included in each new volume. Volumes 1-34 are in print.

Nineteenth-Century Literature Criticism

Offers significant passages from criticism on authors who died between 1800 and 1899. Cumulative indexes to authors, nationalities, and titles discussed are included in each new volume. Volumes 1-24 are in print.

Literature Criticism from 1400 to 1800

Compiles significant passages from the most noteworthy criticism on authors of the fifteenth through eighteenth centuries. Cumulative indexes to authors, nationalities, and titles discussed are included in each new volume. Volumes 1-11 are in print.

Classical and Medieval Literature Criticism

Offers excerpts of criticism on the works of world authors from classical antiquity through the fourteenth century. Cumulative indexes to authors, titles, and critics are included in each volume. Volumes 1-3 are in print.

Short Story Criticism

Compiles excerpts of criticism on short fiction by writers of all eras and nationalities. Cumulative indexes to authors, nationalities, and titles discussed are included in each new volume. Volumes 1-4 are in print.

Children's Literature Review

Includes excerpts from reviews, criticism, and commentary on works of authors and illustrators who create books for children. Cumulative indexes to authors, nationalities, and titles discussed are included in each new volume. Volumes 1-19 are in print.

Contemporary Authors Series

Encompasses five related series. *Contemporary Authors* provides biographical and bibliographical information on more than 92,000 writers of fiction, nonfiction, poetry, journalism, drama, motion pictures, and other fields. Each new volume contains sketches on authors not previously covered in the series. Volumes 1-127 are in print. *Contemporary Authors New Revision Series* provides completely updated information on active authors covered in previously published volumes of *CA*. Only entries requiring significant change are revised for *CA New Revision Series*. Volumes 1-27 are in print. *Contemporary Authors Permanent Series* consists of updated listings for deceased and inactive authors removed from the original volumes 9-36 when these volumes were revised. Volumes 1-2 are in print. *Contemporary Authors Autobiography Series* presents specially commissioned autobiographies by leading contemporary writers. Volumes 1-9 are in print. *Contemporary Authors Bibliographical Series* contains primary and secondary bibliographies as well as analytical bibliographical essays by authorities on major modern authors. Volumes 1-2 are in print.

Dictionary of Literary Biography

Encompasses three related series. *Dictionary of Literary Biography* furnishes illustrated overviews of authors' lives and works and places them in the larger perspective of literary history. Volumes 1-87 are in print. *Dictionary of Literary Biography Documentary Series* illuminates the careers of major figures through a selection of literary documents, including letters, notebook and diary entries, interviews, book reviews, and photographs. Volumes 1-6 are in print. *Dictionary of Literary Biography Yearbook* summarizes the past year's literary activity with articles on genres, major prizes, conferences, and other timely subjects and includes updated and new entries on individual authors. Yearbooks for 1980-1988 are in print. A cumulative index to authors and articles is included in each new volume.

Concise Dictionary of American Literary Biography

A six-volume series that collects revised and updated sketches on major American authors that were originally presented in *Dictionary of Literary Biography*. Volumes 1-3 are in print.

Something about the Author Series

Encompasses two related series. *Something about the Author* contains heavily illustrated biographical sketches on juvenile and young adult authors and illustrators from all eras. Volumes 1-57 are in print. *Something about the Author Autobiography Series* presents specially commissioned autobiographies by prominent authors and illustrators of books for children and young adults. Volumes 1-8 are in print.

Yesterday's Authors of Books for Children

Contains heavily illustrated entries on children's writers who died before 1961. Complete in two volumes. Volumes 1-2 are in print.

Literary Criticism Series
Cumulative Author Index

This index lists all author entries in the Gale Literary Criticism Series and includes cross-references to other Gale sources. References in the index are identified as follows:

AAYA: *Authors & Artists for Young Adults,* Volumes 1-2
CAAS: *Contemporary Authors Autobiography Series,* Volumes 1-10
CA: *Contemporary Authors* (original series), Volumes 1-129
CABS: *Contemporary Authors Bibliographical Series,* Volumes 1-3
CANR: *Contemporary Authors New Revision Series,* Volumes 1-28
CAP: *Contemporary Authors Permanent Series,* Volumes 1-2
CA-R: *Contemporary Authors* (revised editions), Volumes 1-44
CDALB: *Concise Dictionary of American Literary Biography,* Volumes 1-6
CLC: *Contemporary Literary Criticism,* Volumes 1-58
CLR: *Children's Literature Review,* Volumes 1-20
CMLC: *Classical and Medieval Literature Criticism,* Volumes 1-4
DLB: *Dictionary of Literary Biography,* Volumes 1-90
DLB-DS: *Dictionary of Literary Biography Documentary Series,* Volumes 1-7
DLB-Y: *Dictionary of Literary Biography Yearbook,* Volumes 1980-1988
LC: *Literature Criticism from 1400 to 1800,* Volumes 1-12
NCLC: *Nineteenth-Century Literature Criticism,* Volumes 1-26
SAAS: *Something about the Author Autobiography Series,* Volumes 1-9
SATA: *Something about the Author,* Volumes 1-57
SSC: *Short Story Criticism,* Volumes 1-5
TCLC: *Twentieth-Century Literary Criticism,* Volumes 1-36
YABC: *Yesterday's Authors of Books for Children,* Volumes 1-2

Ainsworth, William Harrison
1805-1882 .... **NCLC 13**
See also SATA 24; DLB 21

Ajar, Emile 1914-1980
See Gary, Romain

Akhmadulina, Bella (Akhatovna)
1937- .... **CLC 53**
See also CA 65-68

Akhmatova, Anna 1888-1966.... **CLC 11, 25**
See also CAP 1; CA 19-20;
obituary CA 25-28R

Aksakov, Sergei Timofeyvich
1791-1859 .... **NCLC 2**

Aksenov, Vassily (Pavlovich) 1932-
See Aksyonov, Vasily (Pavlovich)

Aksyonov, Vasily (Pavlovich)
1932- .... **CLC 22, 37**
See also CANR 12; CA 53-56

Akutagawa Ryunosuke
1892-1927 .... **TCLC 16**
See also CA 117

Alain-Fournier 1886-1914 .... **TCLC 6**
See also Fournier, Henri Alban
See also DLB 65

Alarcon, Pedro Antonio de
1833-1891 .... **NCLC 1**

Alas (y Urena), Leopoldo (Enrique Garcia)
1852-1901 .... **TCLC 29**
See also CA 113

Albee, Edward (Franklin III)
1928- ... **CLC 1, 2, 3, 5, 9, 11, 13, 25, 53**
See also CANR 8; CA 5-8R; DLB 7;
CDALB 1941-1968

Alberti, Rafael 1902- .... **CLC 7**
See also CA 85-88

Alcott, Amos Bronson 1799-1888 .. **NCLC 1**
See also DLB 1

Alcott, Louisa May 1832-1888 .... **NCLC 6**
See also CLR 1; YABC 1; DLB 1, 42;
CDALB 1865-1917

Aldanov, Mark 1887-1957 .... **TCLC 23**
See also CA 118

Aldington, Richard 1892-1962...... **CLC 49**
See also CA 85-88; DLB 20, 36

Aldiss, Brian W(ilson)
1925- .... **CLC 5, 14, 40**
See also CAAS 2; CANR 5; CA 5-8R;
SATA 34; DLB 14

Alegria, Fernando 1918-........... **CLC 57**
See also CANR 5; CA 11-12R

Aleixandre, Vicente 1898-1984 ... **CLC 9, 36**
See also CANR 26; CA 85-88;
obituary CA 114

Alepoudelis, Odysseus 1911-
See Elytis, Odysseus

Aleshkovsky, Yuz 1929-........... **CLC 44**
See also CA 121

Alexander, Lloyd (Chudley) 1924- .. **CLC 35**
See also CLR 1, 5; CANR 1; CA 1-4R;
SATA 3, 49; DLB 52

Alger, Horatio, Jr. 1832-1899..... **NCLC 8**
See also SATA 16; DLB 42

Algren, Nelson 1909-1981 .... **CLC 4, 10, 33**
See also CANR 20; CA 13-16R;
obituary CA 103; DLB 9; DLB-Y 81, 82;
CDALB 1941-1968

Alighieri, Dante 1265-1321 .... **CMLC 3**

Allen, Roland 1939-
See Ayckbourn, Alan

Allen, Woody 1935- .... **CLC 16, 52**
See also CANR 27; CA 33-36R; DLB 44

Allende, Isabel 1942- .... **CLC 39, 57**
See also CA 125

Allingham, Margery (Louise)
1904-1966 .... **CLC 19**
See also CANR 4; CA 5-8R;
obituary CA 25-28R

Allingham, William 1824-1889 ... **NCLC 25**
See also DLB 35

Allston, Washington 1779-1843.... **NCLC 2**
See also DLB 1

Almedingen, E. M. 1898-1971...... **CLC 12**
See also Almedingen, Martha Edith von
See also SATA 3

Almedingen, Martha Edith von 1898-1971
See Almedingen, E. M.
See also CANR 1; CA 1-4R

Alonso, Damaso 1898- .... **CLC 14**
See also CA 110

Alta 1942-..................... **CLC 19**
See also CA 57-60

Alter, Robert B(ernard) 1935-..... **CLC 34**
See also CANR 1; CA 49-52

Alther, Lisa 1944-.............. **CLC 7, 41**
See also CANR 12; CA 65-68

Altman, Robert 1925-.............. **CLC 16**
See also CA 73-76

Alvarez, A(lfred) 1929-........... **CLC 5, 13**
See also CANR 3; CA 1-4R; DLB 14, 40

Alvarez, Alejandro Rodriguez 1903-1965
See Casona, Alejandro
See also obituary CA 93-96

Amado, Jorge 1912-............ **CLC 13, 40**
See also CA 77-80

Ambler, Eric 1909-............. **CLC 4, 6, 9**
See also CANR 7; CA 9-12R

Amichai, Yehuda 1924- ...... **CLC 9, 22, 57**
See also CA 85-88

Amiel, Henri Frederic 1821-1881 .. **NCLC 4**

Amis, Kingsley (William)
1922- ...... **CLC 1, 2, 3, 5, 8, 13, 40, 44**
See also CANR 8; CA 9-12R; DLB 15, 27

Amis, Martin 1949- .... **CLC 4, 9, 38**
See also CANR 8; CA 65-68; DLB 14

Ammons, A(rchie) R(andolph)
1926- .... **CLC 2, 3, 5, 8, 9, 25, 57**
See also CANR 6; CA 9-12R; DLB 5

Anand, Mulk Raj 1905-........... **CLC 23**
See also CA 65-68

Anaya, Rudolfo A(lfonso) 1937- .... **CLC 23**
See also CAAS 4; CANR 1; CA 45-48

Andersen, Hans Christian
1805-1875 .... **NCLC 7**
See also CLR 6; YABC 1

Anderson, Jessica (Margaret Queale)
19??-........................ **CLC 37**
See also CANR 4; CA 9-12R

Anderson, Jon (Victor) 1940- .... **CLC 9**
See also CANR 20; CA 25-28R

Anderson, Lindsay 1923- .... **CLC 20**

Anderson, Maxwell 1888-1959 ..... **TCLC 2**
See also CA 105; DLB 7

Anderson, Poul (William) 1926- .... **CLC 15**
See also CAAS 2; CANR 2, 15; CA 1-4R;
SATA 39; DLB 8

Anderson, Robert (Woodruff)
1917-....................... **CLC 23**
See also CA 21-24R; DLB 7

Anderson, Roberta Joan 1943-
See Mitchell, Joni

Anderson, Sherwood
1876-1941 ...... **TCLC 1, 10, 24; SSC 1**
See also CAAS 3; CA 104, 121; DLB 4, 9;
DLB-DS 1

Andrade, Carlos Drummond de
1902-1987 .... **CLC 18**
See also CA 123

Andrewes, Lancelot 1555-1626 .... **LC 5**

Andrews, Cicily Fairfield 1892-1983
See West, Rebecca

Andreyev, Leonid (Nikolaevich)
1871-1919 .... **TCLC 3**
See also CA 104

Andrezel, Pierre 1885-1962
See Dinesen, Isak; Blixen, Karen
(Christentze Dinesen)

Andric, Ivo 1892-1975 .... **CLC 8**
See also CA 81-84; obituary CA 57-60

Angelique, Pierre 1897-1962
See Bataille, Georges

Angell, Roger 1920-.............. **CLC 26**
See also CANR 13; CA 57-60

Angelou, Maya 1928-.......... **CLC 12, 35**
See also CANR 19; CA 65-68; SATA 49;
DLB 38

Annensky, Innokenty 1856-1909... **TCLC 14**
See also CA 110

Anouilh, Jean (Marie Lucien Pierre)
1910-1987 ...... **CLC 1, 3, 8, 13, 40, 50**
See also CA 17-20R; obituary CA 123

Anthony, Florence 1947-
See Ai

Anthony (Jacob), Piers 1934- ...... **CLC 35**
See also Jacob, Piers A(nthony)
D(illingham)
See also DLB 8

Antoninus, Brother 1912-
See Everson, William (Oliver)

Antonioni, Michelangelo 1912-..... **CLC 20**
See also CA 73-76

Antschel, Paul 1920-1970
See Celan, Paul
See also CA 85-88

Anwar, Chairil 1922-1949 .... **TCLC 22**
See also CA 121

Apollinaire, Guillaume
   1880-1918 . . . . **TCLC 3, 8**
   See also Kostrowitzki, Wilhelm Apollinaris
   de

Appelfeld, Aharon 1932- . . . . **CLC 23, 47**
   See also CA 112

Apple, Max (Isaac) 1941- . . . . **CLC 9, 33**
   See also CANR 19; CA 81-84

Appleman, Philip (Dean) 1926- . . . . . **CLC 51**
   See also CANR 6; CA 13-16R

Apuleius, (Lucius) (Madaurensis)
   125?-175? . . . . **CMLC 1**

Aquin, Hubert 1929-1977 . . . . **CLC 15**
   See also CA 105; DLB 53

Aragon, Louis 1897-1982 . . . . **CLC 3, 22**
   See also CA 69-72; obituary CA 108;
   DLB 72

Arbuthnot, John 1667-1735 . . . . **LC 1**

Archer, Jeffrey (Howard) 1940- . . . . **CLC 28**
   See also CANR 22; CA 77-80

Archer, Jules 1915- . . . . **CLC 12**
   See also CANR 6; CA 9-12R; SAAS 5;
   SATA 4

Arden, John 1930- . . . . **CLC 6, 13, 15**
   See also CAAS 4; CA 13-16R; DLB 13

Arenas, Reinaldo 1943- . . . . **CLC 41**

Aretino, Pietro 1492-1556 . . . . **LC 12**

Arguedas, Jose Maria
   1911-1969 . . . . **CLC 10, 18**
   See also CA 89-92

Argueta, Manlio 1936- . . . . **CLC 31**

Ariosto, Ludovico 1474-1533 . . . . **LC 6**

Aristophanes
   c. 450 B. C.-c. 385 B. C. . . . . . . **CMLC 4**

Arlt, Roberto 1900-1942 . . . . **TCLC 29**
   See also CA 123

Armah, Ayi Kwei 1939- . . . . **CLC 5, 33**
   See also CANR 21; CA 61-64

Armatrading, Joan 1950- . . . . **CLC 17**
   See also CA 114

Arnim, Achim von (Ludwig Joachim von
   Arnim) 1781-1831 . . . . **NCLC 5**

Arnold, Matthew 1822-1888 . . . . . . **NCLC 6**
   See also DLB 32, 57

Arnold, Thomas 1795-1842 . . . . . . **NCLC 18**
   See also DLB 55

Arnow, Harriette (Louisa Simpson)
   1908-1986 . . . . **CLC 2, 7, 18**
   See also CANR 14; CA 9-12R;
   obituary CA 118; SATA 42, 47; DLB 6

Arp, Jean 1887-1966 . . . . **CLC 5**
   See also CA 81-84; obituary CA 25-28R

Arquette, Lois S(teinmetz) 1934-
   See Duncan (Steinmetz Arquette), Lois
   See also SATA 1

Arrabal, Fernando 1932- . . . **CLC 2, 9, 18, 58**
   See also CANR 15; CA 9-12R

Arrick, Fran 19??- . . . . **CLC 30**

Artaud, Antonin 1896-1948 . . . . . **TCLC 3, 36**
   See also CA 104

Arthur, Ruth M(abel) 1905-1979 . . . . **CLC 12**
   See also CANR 4; CA 9-12R;
   obituary CA 85-88; SATA 7;
   obituary SATA 26

Artsybashev, Mikhail Petrarch
   1878-1927 . . . . **TCLC 31**

Arundel, Honor (Morfydd)
   1919-1973 . . . . **CLC 17**
   See also CAP 2; CA 21-22;
   obituary CA 41-44R; SATA 4;
   obituary SATA 24

Asch, Sholem 1880-1957 . . . . **TCLC 3**
   See also CA 105

Ashbery, John (Lawrence)
   1927- . . . **CLC 2, 3, 4, 6, 9, 13, 15, 25, 41**
   See also CANR 9; CA 5-8R; DLB 5;
   DLB-Y 81

Ashton-Warner, Sylvia (Constance)
   1908-1984 . . . . **CLC 19**
   See also CA 69-72; obituary CA 112

Asimov, Isaac 1920- . . . . **CLC 1, 3, 9, 19, 26**
   See also CLR 12; CANR 2, 19; CA 1-4R;
   SATA 1, 26; DLB 8

Astley, Thea (Beatrice May)
   1925- . . . . **CLC 41**
   See also CANR 11; CA 65-68

Aston, James 1906-1964
   See White, T(erence) H(anbury)

Asturias, Miguel Angel
   1899-1974 . . . . **CLC 3, 8, 13**
   See also CAP 2; CA 25-28;
   obituary CA 49-52

Atheling, William, Jr. 1921-1975
   See Blish, James (Benjamin)

Atherton, Gertrude (Franklin Horn)
   1857-1948 . . . . **TCLC 2**
   See also CA 104; DLB 9

Atwood, Margaret (Eleanor)
   1939- . . . . **CLC 2, 3, 4, 8, 13, 15, 25, 44;**
                                         SSC 2
   See also CANR 3, 24; CA 49-52; SATA 50;
   DLB 53

Aubin, Penelope 1685-1731? . . . . **LC 9**
   See also DLB 39

Auchincloss, Louis (Stanton)
   1917- . . . . **CLC 4, 6, 9, 18, 45**
   See also CANR 6; CA 1-4R; DLB 2;
   DLB-Y 80

Auden, W(ystan) H(ugh)
   1907-1973 . . . . . **CLC 1, 2, 3, 4, 6, 9, 11,**
                                         14, 43
   See also CANR 5; CA 9-12R;
   obituary CA 45-48; DLB 10, 20

Audiberti, Jacques 1899-1965 . . . . . . **CLC 38**
   See also obituary CA 25-28R

Auel, Jean M(arie) 1936- . . . . **CLC 31**
   See also CANR 21; CA 103

Austen, Jane 1775-1817 . . . . **NCLC 1, 13, 19**

Auster, Paul 1947- . . . . **CLC 47**
   See also CANR 23; CA 69-72

Austin, Mary (Hunter)
   1868-1934 . . . . **TCLC 25**
   See also CA 109; DLB 9

Avison, Margaret 1918- . . . . **CLC 2, 4**
   See also CA 17-20R; DLB 53

Ayckbourn, Alan 1939- . . . . **CLC 5, 8, 18, 33**
   See also CA 21-24R; DLB 13

Aydy, Catherine 1937-
   See Tennant, Emma

Ayme, Marcel (Andre) 1902-1967 . . . **CLC 11**
   See also CA 89-92; DLB 72

Ayrton, Michael 1921-1975 . . . . **CLC 7**
   See also CANR 9, 21; CA 5-8R;
   obituary CA 61-64

Azorin 1874-1967 . . . . **CLC 11**
   See also Martinez Ruiz, Jose

Azuela, Mariano 1873-1952 . . . . **TCLC 3**
   See also CA 104

"Bab" 1836-1911
   See Gilbert, (Sir) W(illiam) S(chwenck)

Babel, Isaak (Emmanuilovich)
   1894-1941 . . . . **TCLC 2, 13**
   See also CA 104

Babits, Mihaly 1883-1941 . . . . **TCLC 14**
   See also CA 114

Bacchelli, Riccardo 1891-1985 . . . . . **CLC 19**
   See also CA 29-32R; obituary CA 117

Bach, Richard (David) 1936- . . . . **CLC 14**
   See also CANR 18; CA 9-12R; SATA 13

Bachman, Richard 1947-
   See King, Stephen (Edwin)

Bacovia, George 1881-1957 . . . . **TCLC 24**

Bagehot, Walter 1826-1877 . . . . . . **NCLC 10**
   See also DLB 55

Bagnold, Enid 1889-1981 . . . . **CLC 25**
   See also CANR 5; CA 5-8R;
   obituary CA 103; SATA 1, 25; DLB 13

Bagryana, Elisaveta 1893- . . . . **CLC 10**

Bailey, Paul 1937- . . . . **CLC 45**
   See also CANR 16; CA 21-24R; DLB 14

Baillie, Joanna 1762-1851 . . . . **NCLC 2**

Bainbridge, Beryl
   1933- . . . . **CLC 4, 5, 8, 10, 14, 18, 22**
   See also CA 21-24R; DLB 14

Baker, Elliott 1922- . . . . **CLC 8**
   See also CANR 2; CA 45-48

Baker, Russell (Wayne) 1925- . . . . . . **CLC 31**
   See also CANR 11; CA 57-60

Bakshi, Ralph 1938- . . . . **CLC 26**
   See also CA 112

Bakunin, Mikhail (Alexandrovich)
   1814-1876 . . . . **NCLC 25**

Baldwin, James (Arthur)
   1924-1987 . . . . . **CLC 1, 2, 3, 4, 5, 8, 13,**
                                         15, 17, 42, 50
   See also CANR 3; CA 1-4R;
   obituary CA 124; CABS 1; SATA 9;
   DLB 2, 7, 33; DLB-Y 87;
   CDALB 1941-1968

Ballard, J(ames) G(raham)
   1930- . . . . **CLC 3, 6, 14, 36; SSC 1**
   See also CANR 15; CA 5-8R; DLB 14

Balmont, Konstantin Dmitriyevich
   1867-1943 . . . . **TCLC 11**
   See also CA 109

Balzac, Honore de
   1799-1850 . . . . **NCLC 5; SSC 5**

Bellow, Saul
1915- ..... **CLC 1, 2, 3, 6, 8, 10, 13, 15, 25, 33, 34**
See also CA 5-8R; CABS 1; DLB 2, 28; DLB-Y 82; DLB-DS 3; CDALB 1941-1968

Belser, Reimond Karel Maria de 1929-
See Ruyslinck, Ward

Bely, Andrey 1880-1934........... **TCLC 7**
See also CA 104

Benary-Isbert, Margot 1889-1979... **CLC 12**
See also CLR 12; CANR 4; CA 5-8R; obituary CA 89-92; SATA 2; obituary SATA 21

Benavente (y Martinez), Jacinto
1866-1954 .... **TCLC 3**
See also CA 106

Benchley, Peter (Bradford)
1940- .... **CLC 4, 8**
See also CANR 12; CA 17-20R; SATA 3

Benchley, Robert 1889-1945 .... **TCLC 1**
See also CA 105; DLB 11

Benedikt, Michael 1935- .... **CLC 4, 14**
See also CANR 7; CA 13-16R; DLB 5

Benet, Juan 1927-................. **CLC 28**

Benet, Stephen Vincent
1898-1943 .... **TCLC 7**
See also YABC 1; CA 104; DLB 4, 48

Benet, William Rose 1886-1950 ... **TCLC 28**
See also CA 118; DLB 45

Benford, Gregory (Albert) 1941-.... **CLC 52**
See also CANR 12, 24; CA 69-72; DLB-Y 82

Benn, Gottfried 1886-1956........ **TCLC 3**
See also CA 106; DLB 56

Bennett, Alan 1934- .... **CLC 45**
See also CA 103

Bennett, (Enoch) Arnold
1867-1931 .... **TCLC 5, 20**
See also CA 106; DLB 10, 34

Bennett, George Harold 1930-
See Bennett, Hal
See also CA 97-100

Bennett, Hal 1930-................ **CLC 5**
See also Bennett, George Harold
See also DLB 33

Bennett, Jay 1912-................ **CLC 35**
See also CANR 11; CA 69-72; SAAS 4; SATA 27, 41

Bennett, Louise (Simone) 1919-..... **CLC 28**
See also Bennett-Coverly, Louise Simone

Bennett-Coverly, Louise Simone 1919-
See Bennett, Louise (Simone)
See also CA 97-100

Benson, E(dward) F(rederic)
1867-1940 .... **TCLC 27**
See also CA 114

Benson, Jackson J. 1930-.......... **CLC 34**
See also CA 25-28R

Benson, Sally 1900-1972 .... **CLC 17**
See also CAP 1; CA 19-20; obituary CA 37-40R; SATA 1, 35; obituary SATA 27

Benson, Stella 1892-1933........ **TCLC 17**
See also CA 117; DLB 36

Bentley, E(dmund) C(lerihew)
1875-1956 .... **TCLC 12**
See also CA 108; DLB 70

Bentley, Eric (Russell) 1916-....... **CLC 24**
See also CANR 6; CA 5-8R

Berger, John (Peter) 1926- ...... **CLC 2, 19**
See also CA 81-84; DLB 14

Berger, Melvin (H.) 1927-......... **CLC 12**
See also CANR 4; CA 5-8R; SAAS 2; SATA 5

Berger, Thomas (Louis)
1924- .... **CLC 3, 5, 8, 11, 18, 38**
See also CANR 5; CA 1-4R; DLB 2; DLB-Y 80

Bergman, (Ernst) Ingmar 1918-..... **CLC 16**
See also CA 81-84

Bergson, Henri 1859-1941........ **TCLC 32**

Bergstein, Eleanor 1938-........... **CLC 4**
See also CANR 5; CA 53-56

Berkoff, Steven 1937-............. **CLC 56**
See also CA 104

Bermant, Chaim 1929-............. **CLC 40**
See also CANR 6; CA 57-60

Bernanos, (Paul Louis) Georges
1888-1948 .... **TCLC 3**
See also CA 104; DLB 72

Bernhard, Thomas 1931-1989 .... **CLC 3, 32**
See also CA 85-88

Berriault, Gina 1926-............. **CLC 54**
See also CA 116

Berrigan, Daniel J. 1921-........... **CLC 4**
See also CAAS 1; CANR 11; CA 33-36R; DLB 5

Berrigan, Edmund Joseph Michael, Jr.
1934-1983
See Berrigan, Ted
See also CANR 14; CA 61-64; obituary CA 110

Berrigan, Ted 1934-1983 .... **CLC 37**
See also Berrigan, Edmund Joseph Michael, Jr.
See also DLB 5

Berry, Chuck 1926- .... **CLC 17**

Berry, Wendell (Erdman)
1934- .... **CLC 4, 6, 8, 27, 46**
See also CA 73-76; DLB 5, 6

Berryman, John
1914-1972 ..... **CLC 1, 2, 3, 4, 6, 8, 10, 13, 25**
See also CAP 1; CA 15-16; obituary CA 33-36R; CABS 2; DLB 48; CDALB 1941-1968

Bertolucci, Bernardo 1940- .... **CLC 16**
See also CA 106

Besant, Annie (Wood) 1847-1933 ... **TCLC 9**
See also CA 105

Bessie, Alvah 1904-1985........... **CLC 23**
See also CANR 2; CA 5-8R; obituary CA 116; DLB 26

Beti, Mongo 1932- .... **CLC 27**
See also Beyidi, Alexandre

Betjeman, (Sir) John
1906-1984 .... **CLC 2, 6, 10, 34, 43**
See also CA 9-12R; obituary CA 112; DLB 20; DLB-Y 84

Betti, Ugo 1892-1953 .... **TCLC 5**
See also CA 104

Betts, Doris (Waugh) 1932-.... **CLC 3, 6, 28**
See also CANR 9; CA 13-16R; DLB-Y 82

Bialik, Chaim Nachman
1873-1934 .... **TCLC 25**

Bidart, Frank 19??-............... **CLC 33**

Bienek, Horst 1930-............ **CLC 7, 11**
See also CA 73-76; DLB 75

Bierce, Ambrose (Gwinett)
1842-1914?...............**TCLC 1, 7**
See also CA 104; DLB 11, 12, 23, 71, 74; CDALB 1865-1917

Billington, Rachel 1942-........... **CLC 43**
See also CA 33-36R

Binyon, T(imothy) J(ohn) 1936- .... **CLC 34**
See also CA 111

Bioy Casares, Adolfo 1914-.... **CLC 4, 8, 13**
See also CANR 19; CA 29-32R

Bird, Robert Montgomery
1806-1854 .... **NCLC 1**

Birdwell, Cleo 1936-
See DeLillo, Don

Birney (Alfred) Earle
1904- .... **CLC 1, 4, 6, 11**
See also CANR 5, 20; CA 1-4R

Bishop, Elizabeth
1911-1979 ...... **CLC 1, 4, 9, 13, 15, 32**
See also CANR 26; CA 5-8R; obituary CA 89-92; CABS 2; obituary SATA 24; DLB 5

Bishop, John 1935-............... **CLC 10**
See also CA 105

Bissett, Bill 1939-................. **CLC 18**
See also CANR 15; CA 69-72; DLB 53

Bitov, Andrei (Georgievich) 1937-... **CLC 57**

Biyidi, Alexandre 1932-
See Beti, Mongo
See also CA 114, 124

Bjornson, Bjornstjerne (Martinius)
1832-1910 .... **TCLC 7**
See also CA 104

Blackburn, Paul 1926-1971 ...... **CLC 9, 43**
See also CA 81-84; obituary CA 33-36R; DLB 16; DLB-Y 81

Black Elk 1863-1950 .... **TCLC 33**

Blackmore, R(ichard) D(oddridge)
1825-1900 .... **TCLC 27**
See also CA 120; DLB 18

Blackmur, R(ichard) P(almer)
1904-1965 .... **CLC 2, 24**
See also CAP 1; CA 11-12; obituary CA 25-28R; DLB 63

Blackwood, Algernon (Henry)
1869-1951 .... **TCLC 5**
See also CA 105

Blackwood, Caroline 1931- .... **CLC 6, 9**
See also CA 85-88; DLB 14

Blair, Eric Arthur 1903-1950
See Orwell, George
See also CA 104; SATA 29

Blais, Marie-Claire
1939- .... **CLC 2, 4, 6, 13, 22**
See also CAAS 4; CA 21-24R; DLB 53

Blaise, Clark 1940-............... CLC 29
See also CAAS 3; CANR 5; CA 53-56R;
DLB 53

Blake, Nicholas 1904-1972
See Day Lewis, C(ecil)

Blake, William 1757-1827 .... NCLC 13
See also SATA 30

Blasco Ibanez, Vicente
1867-1928 .... TCLC 12
See also CA 110

Blatty, William Peter 1928-........ CLC 2
See also CANR 9; CA 5-8R

Blessing, Lee 1949-............... CLC 54

Blish, James (Benjamin)
1921-1975 .... CLC 14
See also CANR 3; CA 1-4R;
obituary CA 57-60; DLB 8

Blixen, Karen (Christentze Dinesen)
1885-1962
See Dinesen, Isak
See also CAP 2; CA 25-28; SATA 44

Bloch, Robert (Albert) 1917-....... CLC 33
See also CANR 5; CA 5-8R; SATA 12;
DLB 44

Blok, Aleksandr (Aleksandrovich)
1880-1921 .... TCLC 5
See also CA 104

Bloom, Harold 1930- .... CLC 24
See also CA 13-16R; DLB 67

Blount, Roy (Alton), Jr. 1941- ..... CLC 38
See also CANR 10; CA 53-56

Bloy, Leon 1846-1917........... TCLC 22
See also CA 121

Blume, Judy (Sussman Kitchens)
1938- .... CLC 12, 30
See also CLR 2, 15; CANR 13; CA 29-32R;
SATA 2, 31; DLB 52

Blunden, Edmund (Charles)
1896-1974 .... CLC 2, 56
See also CAP 2; CA 17-18;
obituary CA 45-48; DLB 20

Bly, Robert (Elwood)
1926- .... CLC 1, 2, 5, 10, 15, 38
See also CA 5-8R; DLB 5

Bochco, Steven 1944?-............ CLC 35

Bodker, Cecil 1927- .... CLC 21
See also CANR 13; CA 73-76; SATA 14

Boell, Heinrich (Theodor) 1917-1985
See Boll, Heinrich
See also CANR 24; CA 21-24R;
obituary CA 116

Bogan, Louise 1897-1970..... CLC 4, 39, 46
See also CA 73-76; obituary CA 25-28R;
DLB 45

Bogarde, Dirk 1921-.............. CLC 19
See also Van Den Bogarde, Derek (Jules
Gaspard Ulric) Niven
See also DLB 14

Bogosian, Eric 1953- .... CLC 45

Bograd, Larry 1953-.............. CLC 35
See also CA 93-96; SATA 33

Bohl de Faber, Cecilia 1796-1877
See Caballero, Fernan

Boiardo, Matteo Maria 1441-1494 .... LC 6

Boileau-Despreaux, Nicolas
1636-1711 .... LC 3

Boland, Eavan (Aisling) 1944-...... CLC 40
See also DLB 40

Boll, Heinrich (Theodor)
1917-1985 ... CLC 2, 3, 6, 9, 11, 15, 27,
39
See also Boell, Heinrich (Theodor)
See also DLB 69; DLB-Y 85

Bolt, Robert (Oxton) 1924-........ CLC 14
See also CA 17-20R; DLB 13

Bond, Edward 1934-....... CLC 4, 6, 13, 23
See also CA 25-28R; DLB 13

Bonham, Frank 1914-............. CLC 12
See also CANR 4; CA 9-12R; SAAS 3;
SATA 1, 49

Bonnefoy, Yves 1923-........ CLC 9, 15, 58
See also CA 85-88

Bontemps, Arna (Wendell)
1902-1973 .... CLC 1, 18
See also CLR 6; CANR 4; CA 1-4R;
obituary CA 41-44R; SATA 2, 44;
obituary SATA 24; DLB 48, 51

Booth, Martin 1944-.............. CLC 13
See also CAAS 2; CA 93-96

Booth, Philip 1925-.............. CLC 23
See also CANR 5; CA 5-8R; DLB-Y 82

Booth, Wayne C(layson) 1921- ..... CLC 24
See also CAAS 5; CANR 3; CA 1-4R;
DLB 67

Borchert, Wolfgang 1921-1947 ..... TCLC 5
See also CA 104; DLB 69

Borges, Jorge Luis
1899-1986 ... CLC 1, 2, 3, 4, 6, 8, 9, 10,
13, 19, 44, 48; SSC 4
See also CANR 19; CA 21-24R; DLB-Y 86

Borowski, Tadeusz 1922-1951...... TCLC 9
See also CA 106

Borrow, George (Henry)
1803-1881 .... NCLC 9
See also DLB 21, 55

Bosschere, Jean de 1878-1953..... TCLC 19
See also CA 115

Boswell, James 1740-1795.......... LC 4

Bottoms, David 1949-............. CLC 53
See also CANR 22; CA 105; DLB-Y 83

Boucolon, Maryse 1937-
See Conde, Maryse
See also CA 110

Bourget, Paul (Charles Joseph)
1852-1935 .... TCLC 12
See also CA 107

Bourjaily, Vance (Nye) 1922-....... CLC 8
See also CAAS 1; CANR 2; CA 1-4R;
DLB 2

Bourne, Randolph S(illiman)
1886-1918 .... TCLC 16
See also CA 117; DLB 63

Bova, Ben(jamin William) 1932-.... CLC 45
See also CLR 3; CANR 11; CA 5-8R;
SATA 6; DLB-Y 81

Bowen, Elizabeth (Dorothea Cole)
1899-1973 ..... CLC 1, 3, 6, 11, 15, 22;
SSC 3
See also CAP 2; CA 17-18;
obituary CA 41-44R; DLB 15

Bowering, George 1935-........ CLC 15, 47
See also CANR 10; CA 21-24R; DLB 53

Bowering, Marilyn R(uthe) 1949-... CLC 32
See also CA 101

Bowers, Edgar 1924- .... CLC 9
See also CANR 24; CA 5-8R; DLB 5

Bowie, David 1947- .... CLC 17
See also Jones, David Robert

Bowles, Jane (Sydney) 1917-1973.... CLC 3
See also CAP 2; CA 19-20;
obituary CA 41-44R

Bowles, Paul (Frederick)
1910- .... CLC 1, 2, 19, 53; SSC 3
See also CAAS 1; CANR 1, 19; CA 1-4R;
DLB 5, 6

Box, Edgar 1925-
See Vidal, Gore

Boyd, William 1952-........... CLC 28, 53
See also CA 114, 120

Boyle, Kay 1903- .. CLC 1, 5, 19, 58; SSC 5
See also CAAS 1; CA 13-16R; DLB 4, 9, 48

Boyle, Patrick 19??-.............. CLC 19

Boyle, Thomas Coraghessan
1948- .... CLC 36, 55
See also CA 120; DLB-Y 86

Brackenridge, Hugh Henry
1748-1816 .... NCLC 7
See also DLB 11, 37

Bradbury, Edward P. 1939-
See Moorcock, Michael

Bradbury, Malcolm (Stanley)
1932- .... CLC 32
See also CANR 1; CA 1-4R; DLB 14

Bradbury, Ray(mond Douglas)
1920- .... CLC 1, 3, 10, 15, 42
See also CANR 2; CA 1-4R; SATA 11;
DLB 2, 8

Bradford, Gamaliel 1863-1932..... TCLC 36
See also DLB 17

Bradley, David (Henry), Jr. 1950- .. CLC 23
See also CANR 26; CA 104; DLB 33

Bradley, John Ed 1959-........... CLC 55

Bradley, Marion Zimmer 1930-..... CLC 30
See also CANR 7; CA 57-60; DLB 8

Bradstreet, Anne 1612-1672.......... LC 4
See also DLB 24; CDALB 1640-1865

Bragg, Melvyn 1939- .... CLC 10
See also CANR 10; CA 57-60; DLB 14

Braine, John (Gerard)
1922-1986 .... CLC 1, 3, 41
See also CANR 1; CA 1-4R;
obituary CA 120; DLB 15; DLB-Y 86

Brammer, Billy Lee 1930?-1978
See Brammer, William

Brammer, William 1930?-1978 ..... CLC 31
See also obituary CA 77-80

Brancati, Vitaliano 1907-1954..... TCLC 12
See also CA 109

Carr, John Dickson   1906-1977 ...... **CLC 3**
  See also CANR 3; CA 49-52;
  obituary CA 69-72

Carr, Virginia Spencer   1929-....... **CLC 34**
  See also CA 61-64

Carrier, Roch   1937- .... **CLC 13**
  See also DLB 53

Carroll, James (P.)   1943-.......... **CLC 38**
  See also CA 81-84

Carroll, Jim   1951- .... **CLC 35**
  See also CA 45-48

Carroll, Lewis   1832-1898......... **NCLC 2**
  See also Dodgson, Charles Lutwidge
  See also CLR 2; DLB 18

Carroll, Paul Vincent   1900-1968.... **CLC 10**
  See also CA 9-12R; obituary CA 25-28R;
  DLB 10

Carruth, Hayden   1921- .... **CLC 4, 7, 10, 18**
  See also CANR 4; CA 9-12R; SATA 47;
  DLB 5

Carter, Angela (Olive)   1940-..... **CLC 5, 41**
  See also CANR 12; CA 53-56; DLB 14

Carver, Raymond
  1938-1988 .... **CLC 22, 36, 53, 55**
  See also CANR 17; CA 33-36R;
  obituary CA 126; DLB-Y 84, 88

Cary, (Arthur) Joyce (Lunel)
  1888-1957 .... **TCLC 1, 29**
  See also CA 104; DLB 15

Casares, Adolfo Bioy   1914-
  See Bioy Casares, Adolfo

Casely-Hayford, J(oseph) E(phraim)
  1866-1930 .... **TCLC 24**
  See also CA 123

Casey, John   1880-1964
  See O'Casey, Sean

Casey, Michael   1947-.............. **CLC 2**
  See also CA 65-68; DLB 5

Casey, Warren   1935- .... **CLC 12**
  See also Jacobs, Jim and Casey, Warren
  See also CA 101

Casona, Alejandro   1903-1965 ...... **CLC 49**
  See also Alvarez, Alejandro Rodriguez

Cassavetes, John   1929-........... **CLC 20**
  See also CA 85-88

Cassill, R(onald) V(erlin)   1919-... **CLC 4, 23**
  See also CAAS 1; CANR 7; CA 9-12R;
  DLB 6

Cassity, (Allen) Turner   1929- .... **CLC 6, 42**
  See also CANR 11; CA 17-20R

Castaneda, Carlos   1935?-.......... **CLC 12**
  See also CA 25-28R

Castelvetro, Lodovico   1505-1571..... **LC 12**

Castiglione, Baldassare   1478-1529 ... **LC 12**

Castro, Rosalia de   1837-1885 ..... **NCLC 3**

Cather, Willa (Sibert)
  1873-1947 ...... **TCLC 1, 11, 31; SSC 2**
  See also CA 104; SATA 30; DLB 9, 54;
  DLB-DS 1; CDALB 1865-1917

Catton, (Charles) Bruce
  1899-1978 .... **CLC 35**
  See also CANR 7; CA 5-8R;
  obituary CA 81-84; SATA 2;
  obituary SATA 24; DLB 17

Cauldwell, Frank   1923-
  See King, Francis (Henry)

Caunitz, William   1935- .... **CLC 34**

Causley, Charles (Stanley)   1917-..... **CLC 7**
  See also CANR 5; CA 9-12R; SATA 3;
  DLB 27

Caute, (John) David   1936-........ **CLC 29**
  See also CAAS 4; CANR 1; CA 1-4R;
  DLB 14

Cavafy, C(onstantine) P(eter)
  1863-1933 .... **TCLC 2, 7**
  See also CA 104

Cavanna, Betty   1909-............. **CLC 12**
  See also CANR 6; CA 9-12R; SATA 1, 30

Cayrol, Jean   1911-................ **CLC 11**
  See also CA 89-92

Cela, Camilo Jose   1916-......... **CLC 4, 13**
  See also CANR 21; CA 21-24R

Celan, Paul   1920-1970 ...... **CLC 10, 19, 53**
  See also Antschel, Paul
  See also DLB 69

Celine, Louis-Ferdinand
  1894-1961 ..... **CLC 1, 3, 4, 7, 9, 15, 47**
  See also Destouches,
  Louis-Ferdinand-Auguste
  See also DLB 72

Cellini, Benvenuto   1500-1571 .... **LC 7**

Cendrars, Blaise   1887-1961........ **CLC 18**
  See also Sauser-Hall, Frederic

Cernuda, Luis (y Bidon)
  1902-1963 .... **CLC 54**
  See also CA 89-92

Cervantes (Saavedra), Miguel de
  1547-1616 .... **LC 6**

Cesaire, Aime (Fernand)   1913- .. **CLC 19, 32**
  See also CANR 24; CA 65-68

Chabon, Michael   1965?-........... **CLC 55**

Chabrol, Claude   1930- .... **CLC 16**
  See also CA 110

Challans, Mary   1905-1983
  See Renault, Mary
  See also CA 81-84; obituary CA 111;
  SATA 23; obituary SATA 36

Chambers, Aidan   1934- .... **CLC 35**
  See also CANR 12; CA 25-28R; SATA 1

Chambers, James   1948-
  See Cliff, Jimmy

Chandler, Raymond   1888-1959 ... **TCLC 1, 7**
  See also CA 104

Channing, William Ellery
  1780-1842 .... **NCLC 17**
  See also DLB 1, 59

Chaplin, Charles (Spencer)
  1889-1977 .... **CLC 16**
  See also CA 81-84; obituary CA 73-76;
  DLB 44

Chapman, Graham   1941?- .... **CLC 21**
  See also Monty Python
  See also CA 116

Chapman, John Jay   1862-1933 ..... **TCLC 7**
  See also CA 104

Chappell, Fred   1936- .... **CLC 40**
  See also CAAS 4; CANR 8; CA 5-8R;
  DLB 6

Char, Rene (Emile)
  1907-1988 .... **CLC 9, 11, 14, 55**
  See also CA 13-16R; obituary CA 124

Charyn, Jerome   1937- .... **CLC 5, 8, 18**
  See also CAAS 1; CANR 7; CA 5-8R;
  DLB-Y 83

Chase, Mary Ellen   1887-1973....... **CLC 2**
  See also CAP 1; CA 15-16;
  obituary CA 41-44R; SATA 10

Chateaubriand, Francois Rene de
  1768-1848 .... **NCLC 3**

Chatterji, Bankim Chandra
  1838-1894 .... **NCLC 19**

Chatterji, Saratchandra
  1876-1938 .... **TCLC 13**
  See also CA 109

Chatterton, Thomas   1752-1770 .... **LC 3**

Chatwin, (Charles) Bruce
  1940-1989 .... **CLC 28, 57**
  See also CA 85-88, 127

Chayefsky, Paddy   1923-1981....... **CLC 23**
  See also CA 9-12R; obituary CA 104;
  DLB 7, 44; DLB-Y 81

Chayefsky, Sidney   1923-1981
  See Chayefsky, Paddy
  See also CANR 18

Chedid, Andree   1920-............. **CLC 47**

Cheever, John
  1912-1982 ..... **CLC 3, 7, 8, 11, 15, 25;**
                                          SSC 1
  See also CANR 5; CA 5-8R;
  obituary CA 106; CABS 1; DLB 2;
  DLB-Y 80, 82; CDALB 1941-1968

Cheever, Susan   1943-.......... **CLC 18, 48**
  See also CA 103; DLB-Y 82

Chekhov, Anton (Pavlovich)
  1860-1904 ...... **TCLC 3, 10, 31; SSC 2**
  See also CA 104, 124

Chernyshevsky, Nikolay Gavrilovich
  1828-1889 .... **NCLC 1**

Cherry, Caroline Janice   1942-
  See Cherryh, C. J.

Cherryh, C. J.   1942-.............. **CLC 35**
  See also CANR 10; CA 65-68; DLB-Y 80

Chesnutt, Charles Waddell
  1858-1932 .... **TCLC 5**
  See also CA 106, 125; DLB 12, 50

Chester, Alfred   1929?-1971 .... **CLC 49**
  See also obituary CA 33-36R

Chesterton, G(ilbert) K(eith)
  1874-1936 .... **TCLC 1, 6; SSC 1**
  See also CA 104; SATA 27; DLB 10, 19,
  34, 70

Ch'ien Chung-shu   1910-........... **CLC 22**

Child, Lydia Maria   1802-1880 .... **NCLC 6**
  See also DLB 1, 74

Child, Philip   1898-1978 .... **CLC 19**
  See also CAP 1; CA 13-14; SATA 47

Childress, Alice   1920-............ **CLC 12, 15**
  See also CLR 14; CANR 3; CA 45-48;
  SATA 7, 48; DLB 7, 38

Chislett, (Margaret) Anne   1943?- ... **CLC 34**

Cooper, J. California 19??- .... **CLC 56**
See also CA 125, 127

Cooper, James Fenimore
1789-1851 .... **NCLC 1**
See also SATA 19; DLB 3;
CDALB 1640-1865

Coover, Robert (Lowell)
1932- .... **CLC 3, 7, 15, 32, 46**
See also CANR 3; CA 45-48; DLB 2;
DLB-Y 81

Copeland, Stewart (Armstrong)
1952- .... **CLC 26**
See also The Police

Coppard, A(lfred) E(dgar)
1878-1957 .... **TCLC 5**
See also YABC 1; CA 114

Coppee, Francois 1842-1908 ...... **TCLC 25**

Coppola, Francis Ford 1939- .... **CLC 16**
See also CA 77-80; DLB 44

Corcoran, Barbara 1911- .... **CLC 17**
See also CAAS 2; CANR 11; CA 21-24R;
SATA 3; DLB 52

Corman, Cid 1924- .... **CLC 9**
See also Corman, Sidney
See also CAAS 2; DLB 5

Corman, Sidney 1924-
See Corman, Cid
See also CA 85-88

Cormier, Robert (Edmund)
1925- .... **CLC 12, 30**
See also CLR 12; CANR 5, 23; CA 1-4R;
SATA 10, 45; DLB 52

Corn, Alfred (Dewitt III) 1943-..... **CLC 33**
See also CA 104; DLB-Y 80

Cornwell, David (John Moore)
1931- .... **CLC 9, 15**
See also le Carre, John
See also CANR 13; CA 5-8R

Corso, (Nunzio) Gregory 1930-... **CLC 1, 11**
See also CA 5-8R; DLB 5, 16

Cortazar, Julio
1914-1984 ..... **CLC 2, 3, 5, 10, 13, 15,
33, 34**
See also CANR 12; CA 21-24R

Corvo, Baron 1860-1913
See Rolfe, Frederick (William Serafino
Austin Lewis Mary)

Cosic, Dobrica 1921- .... **CLC 14**
See also CA 122

Costain, Thomas B(ertram)
1885-1965 .... **CLC 30**
See also CA 5-8R; obituary CA 25-28R;
DLB 9

Costantini, Humberto 1924?-1987... **CLC 49**
See also obituary CA 122

Costello, Elvis 1955-.............. **CLC 21**

Cotter, Joseph Seamon, Sr.
1861-1949 .... **TCLC 28**
See also DLB 50

Couperus, Louis (Marie Anne)
1863-1923 .... **TCLC 15**
See also CA 115

Cousteau, Jacques-Yves 1910-...... **CLC 30**
See also CANR 15; CA 65-68; SATA 38

Coward, (Sir) Noel (Pierce)
1899-1973 .... **CLC 1, 9, 29, 51**
See also CAP 2; CA 17-18;
obituary CA 41-44R; DLB 10

Cowley, Malcolm 1898-1989 .... **CLC 39**
See also CANR 3; CA 5-6R; DLB 4, 48;
DLB-Y 81

Cowper, William 1731-1800 ...... **NCLC 8**

Cox, William Trevor 1928- ...... **CLC 9, 14**
See also Trevor, William
See also CANR 4; CA 9-12R

Cozzens, James Gould
1903-1978 .... **CLC 1, 4, 11**
See also CANR 19; CA 9-12R;
obituary CA 81-84; DLB 9; DLB-Y 84;
DLB-DS 2; CDALB 1941-1968

Crabbe, George 1754-1832 .... **NCLC 26**

Crace, Douglas 1944-............. **CLC 58**

Crane, (Harold) Hart
1899-1932 .... **TCLC 2, 5**
See also CA 104; DLB 4, 48

Crane, R(onald) S(almon)
1886-1967 .... **CLC 27**
See also CA 85-88; DLB 63

Crane, Stephen
1871-1900 .... **TCLC 11, 17, 32**
See also YABC 2; CA 109; DLB 12, 54, 78;
CDALB 1865-1917

Craven, Margaret 1901-1980 .... **CLC 17**
See also CA 103

Crawford, F(rancis) Marion
1854-1909 .... **TCLC 10**
See also CA 107; DLB 71

Crawford, Isabella Valancy
1850-1887 .... **NCLC 12**

Crayencour, Marguerite de 1903-1987
See Yourcenar, Marguerite

Creasey, John 1908-1973.......... **CLC 11**
See also CANR 8; CA 5-8R;
obituary CA 41-44R

Crebillon, Claude Prosper Jolyot de (fils)
1707-1777 .... **LC 1**

Creeley, Robert (White)
1926- .... **CLC 1, 2, 4, 8, 11, 15, 36**
See also CANR 23; CA 1-4R; DLB 5, 16

Crews, Harry (Eugene)
1935- .... **CLC 6, 23, 49**
See also CANR 20; CA 25-28R; DLB 6

Crichton, (John) Michael
1942- .... **CLC 2, 6, 54**
See also CANR 13; CA 25-28R; SATA 9;
DLB-Y 81

Crispin, Edmund 1921-1978........ **CLC 22**
See also Montgomery, Robert Bruce

Cristofer, Michael 1946- .... **CLC 28**
See also CA 110; DLB 7

Crockett, David (Davy)
1786-1836 .... **NCLC 8**
See also DLB 3, 11

Croker, John Wilson 1780-1857 .. **NCLC 10**

Cronin, A(rchibald) J(oseph)
1896-1981 .... **CLC 32**
See also CANR 5; CA 1-4R;
obituary CA 102; obituary SATA 25, 47

Cross, Amanda 1926-
See Heilbrun, Carolyn G(old)

Crothers, Rachel 1878-1953...... **TCLC 19**
See also CA 113; DLB 7

Crowley, Aleister 1875-1947 ...... **TCLC 7**
See also CA 104

Crowley, John 1942-
See also CA 61-64; DLB-Y 82

Crumb, Robert 1943-............. **CLC 17**
See also CA 106

Cryer, Gretchen 1936?- .... **CLC 21**
See also CA 114, 123

Csath, Geza 1887-1919.......... **TCLC 13**
See also CA 111

Cudlip, David 1933-.............. **CLC 34**

Cullen, Countee 1903-1946 .... **TCLC 4**
See also CA 108, 124; SATA 18; DLB 4,
48, 51

Cummings, E(dward) E(stlin)
1894-1962 .... **CLC 1, 3, 8, 12, 15**
See also CA 73-76; DLB 4, 48

Cunha, Euclides (Rodrigues) da
1866-1909 .... **TCLC 24**
See also CA 123

Cunningham, J(ames) V(incent)
1911-1985 .... **CLC 3, 31**
See also CANR 1; CA 1-4R;
obituary CA 115; DLB 5

Cunningham, Julia (Woolfolk)
1916- .... **CLC 12**
See also CANR 4, 19; CA 9-12R; SAAS 2;
SATA 1, 26

Cunningham, Michael 1952- .... **CLC 34**

Currie, Ellen 19??- .... **CLC 44**

Dabrowska, Maria (Szumska)
1889-1965 .... **CLC 15**
See also CA 106

Dabydeen, David 1956?-........... **CLC 34**
See also CA 106

Dacey, Philip 1939- .... **CLC 51**
See also CANR 14; CA 37-40R

Dagerman, Stig (Halvard)
1923-1954 .... **TCLC 17**
See also CA 117

Dahl, Roald 1916-............ **CLC 1, 6, 18**
See also CLR 1, 7; CANR 6; CA 1-4R;
SATA 1, 26

Dahlberg, Edward 1900-1977... **CLC 1, 7, 14**
See also CA 9-12R; obituary CA 69-72;
DLB 48

Daly, Elizabeth 1878-1967........ **CLC 52**
See also CAP 2; CA 23-24;
obituary CA 25-28R

Daly, Maureen 1921-............. **CLC 17**
See also McGivern, Maureen Daly
See also SAAS 1; SATA 2

Daniken, Erich von 1935-
See Von Daniken, Erich

Dannay, Frederic 1905-1982
See Queen, Ellery
See also CANR 1; CA 1-4R;
obituary CA 107

D'Annunzio, Gabriele 1863-1938.... **TCLC 6**
See also CA 104

Author Index

Follett, Ken(neth Martin) 1949- .... **CLC 18**
See also CANR 13; CA 81-84; DLB-Y 81

Fontane, Theodor 1819-1898 ..... **NCLC 26**

Foote, Horton 1916- .... **CLC 51**
See also CA 73-76; DLB 26

Forbes, Esther 1891-1967 .... **CLC 12**
See also CAP 1; CA 13-14;
obituary CA 25-28R; SATA 2; DLB 22

Forche, Carolyn 1950- .... **CLC 25**
See also CA 109, 117; DLB 5

Ford, Ford Madox 1873-1939 ... **TCLC 1, 15**
See also CA 104; DLB 34

Ford, John 1895-1973 .... **CLC 16**
See also obituary CA 45-48

Ford, Richard 1944- .... **CLC 46**
See also CANR 11; CA 69-72

Foreman, Richard 1937- .... **CLC 50**
See also CA 65-68

Forester, C(ecil) S(cott)
1899-1966 .... **CLC 35**
See also CA 73-76; obituary CA 25-28R;
SATA 13

Forman, James D(ouglas) 1932- .... **CLC 21**
See also CANR 4, 19; CA 9-12R; SATA 8,
21

Fornes, Maria Irene 1930- .... **CLC 39**
See also CA 25-28R; DLB 7

Forrest, Leon 1937- .... **CLC 4**
See also CAAS 7; CA 89-92; DLB 33

Forster, E(dward) M(organ)
1879-1970 .... **CLC 1, 2, 3, 4, 9, 10, 13,
15, 22, 45**
See also CAP 1; CA 13-14;
obituary CA 25-28R; DLB 34

Forster, John 1812-1876 .... **NCLC 11**

Forsyth, Frederick 1938- ...... **CLC 2, 5, 36**
See also CA 85-88

Forten (Grimke), Charlotte L(ottie)
1837-1914 .... **TCLC 16**
See also Grimke, Charlotte L(ottie) Forten
See also DLB 50

Foscolo, Ugo 1778-1827 .... **NCLC 8**

Fosse, Bob 1925-1987 .... **CLC 20**
See also Fosse, Robert Louis

Fosse, Robert Louis 1925-1987
See Bob Fosse
See also CA 110, 123

Foster, Stephen Collins
1826-1864 .... **NCLC 26**

Foucault, Michel 1926-1984 .... **CLC 31, 34**
See also CANR 23; CA 105;
obituary CA 113

**Fouque, Friedrich (Heinrich Karl) de La
Motte** 1777-1843 .... **NCLC 2**

Fournier, Henri Alban 1886-1914
See Alain-Fournier
See also CA 104

Fournier, Pierre 1916- .... **CLC 11**
See also Gascar, Pierre
See also CANR 16; CA 89-92

Fowles, John (Robert)
1926- .... **CLC 1, 2, 3, 4, 6, 9, 10, 15, 33**
See also CANR 25; CA 5-8R; SATA 22;
DLB 14

Fox, Paula 1923- .... **CLC 2, 8**
See also CLR 1; CANR 20; CA 73-76;
SATA 17; DLB 52

Fox, William Price (Jr.) 1926- ..... **CLC 22**
See also CANR 11; CA 17-20R; DLB 2;
DLB-Y 81

Frame (Clutha), Janet (Paterson)
1924- .... **CLC 2, 3, 6, 22**
See also Clutha, Janet Paterson Frame

France, Anatole 1844-1924 .... **TCLC 9**
See also Thibault, Jacques Anatole Francois

Francis, Claude 19??- .... **CLC 50**

Francis, Dick 1920- .... **CLC 2, 22, 42**
See also CANR 9; CA 5-8R

Francis, Robert (Churchill)
1901-1987 .... **CLC 15**
See also CANR 1; CA 1-4R;
obituary CA 123

Frank, Anne 1929-1945 .... **TCLC 17**
See also CA 113; SATA 42

Frank, Elizabeth 1945- .... **CLC 39**
See also CA 121, 126

Franklin, (Stella Maria Sarah) Miles
1879-1954 .... **TCLC 7**
See also CA 104

Fraser, Antonia (Pakenham)
1932- .... **CLC 32**
See also CA 85-88; SATA 32

Fraser, George MacDonald 1925- .... **CLC 7**
See also CANR 2; CA 45-48

Frayn, Michael 1933- ...... **CLC 3, 7, 31, 47**
See also CA 5-8R; DLB 13, 14

Fraze, Candida 19??- .... **CLC 50**
See also CA 125

Frazer, Sir James George
1854-1941 .... **TCLC 32**
See also CA 118

Frazier, Ian 1951- .... **CLC 46**

Frederic, Harold 1856-1898 ...... **NCLC 10**
See also DLB 12, 23

Fredman, Russell (Bruce) 1929-
See also CLR 20

Fredro, Aleksander 1793-1876 ..... **NCLC 8**

Freeling, Nicolas 1927- .... **CLC 38**
See also CANR 1, 17; CA 49-52

Freeman, Douglas Southall
1886-1953 .... **TCLC 11**
See also CA 109; DLB 17

Freeman, Judith 1946- .... **CLC 55**

Freeman, Mary (Eleanor) Wilkins
1852-1930 .... **TCLC 9; SSC 1**
See also CA 106; DLB 12

Freeman, R(ichard) Austin
1862-1943 .... **TCLC 21**
See also CA 113; DLB 70

French, Marilyn 1929- .... **CLC 10, 18**
See also CANR 3; CA 69-72

Freneau, Philip Morin 1752-1832 .. **NCLC 1**
See also DLB 37, 43

Friedman, B(ernard) H(arper)
1926- .... **CLC 7**
See also CANR 3; CA 1-4R

Friedman, Bruce Jay 1930- .... **CLC 3, 5, 56**
See also CANR 25; CA 9-12R; DLB 2, 28

Friel, Brian 1929- .... **CLC 5, 42**
See also CA 21-24R; DLB 13

Friis-Baastad, Babbis (Ellinor)
1921-1970 .... **CLC 12**
See also CA 17-20R; SATA 7

Frisch, Max (Rudolf)
1911- ...... **CLC 3, 9, 14, 18, 32, 44**
See also CA 85-88; DLB 69

Fromentin, Eugene (Samuel Auguste)
1820-1876 .... **NCLC 10**

Frost, Robert (Lee)
1874-1963 ... **CLC 1, 3, 4, 9, 10, 13, 15,
26, 34, 44**
See also CA 89-92; SATA 14; DLB 54

Fry, Christopher 1907- .... **CLC 2, 10, 14**
See also CANR 9; CA 17-20R; DLB 13

Frye, (Herman) Northrop 1912- .... **CLC 24**
See also CANR 8; CA 5-8R

Fuchs, Daniel 1909- .... **CLC 8, 22**
See also CAAS 5; CA 81-84; DLB 9, 26, 28

Fuchs, Daniel 1934- .... **CLC 34**
See also CANR 14; CA 37-40R

Fuentes, Carlos
1928- .... **CLC 3, 8, 10, 13, 22, 41**
See also CANR 10; CA 69-72

Fugard, Athol 1932- ... **CLC 5, 9, 14, 25, 40**
See also CA 85-88

Fugard, Sheila 1932- .... **CLC 48**
See also CA 125

Fuller, Charles (H., Jr.) 1939- ...... **CLC 25**
See also CA 108, 112; DLB 38

Fuller, (Sarah) Margaret
1810-1850 .... **NCLC 5**
See also Ossoli, Sarah Margaret (Fuller
marchesa d')
See also DLB 1, 59, 73; CDALB 1640-1865

Fuller, Roy (Broadbent) 1912- .... **CLC 4, 28**
See also CA 5-8R; DLB 15, 20

Fulton, Alice 1952- .... **CLC 52**
See also CA 116

Furphy, Joseph 1843-1912 .... **TCLC 25**

Futrelle, Jacques 1875-1912 ...... **TCLC 19**
See also CA 113

Gaboriau, Emile 1835-1873 ...... **NCLC 14**

Gadda, Carlo Emilio 1893-1973 .... **CLC 11**
See also CA 89-92

Gaddis, William
1922- .... **CLC 1, 3, 6, 8, 10, 19, 43**
See also CAAS 4; CANR 21; CA 17-20R;
DLB 2

Gaines, Ernest J. 1933- ...... **CLC 3, 11, 18**
See also CANR 6, 24; CA 9-12R; DLB 2,
33; DLB-Y 80

Gale, Zona 1874-1938 .... **TCLC 7**
See also CA 105; DLB 9

Gallagher, Tess 1943- .... **CLC 18**
See also CA 106

Gallant, Mavis
1922- .... **CLC 7, 18, 38; SSC 5**
See also CA 69-72; DLB 53

Gallant, Roy A(rthur) 1924- .... **CLC 17**
See also CANR 4; CA 5-8R; SATA 4

Gallico, Paul (William) 1897-1976 ... **CLC 2**
See also CA 5-8R; obituary CA 69-72;
SATA 13; DLB 9

Galsworthy, John 1867-1933 ...... **TCLC 1**
See also CA 104; DLB 10, 34

Galt, John 1779-1839 .... **NCLC 1**

Galvin, James 1951- .... **CLC 38**
See also CANR 26; CA 108

Gamboa, Frederico 1864-1939 ..... **TCLC 36**

Gann, Ernest K(ellogg) 1910- ...... **CLC 23**
See also CANR 1; CA 1-4R

Garcia Lorca, Federico
1899-1936 .... **TCLC 1, 7**
See also CA 104

Garcia Marquez, Gabriel (Jose)
1928- .... **CLC 2, 3, 8, 10, 15, 27, 47, 55**
See also CANR 10; CA 33-36R

Gardam, Jane 1928- .... **CLC 43**
See also CLR 12; CANR 2, 18; CA 49-52;
SATA 28, 39; DLB 14

Gardner, Herb 1934- .... **CLC 44**

Gardner, John (Champlin, Jr.)
1933-1982 .... **CLC 2, 3, 5, 7, 8, 10, 18,
28, 34**
See also CA 65-68; obituary CA 107;
obituary SATA 31, 40; DLB 2; DLB-Y 82

Gardner, John (Edmund) 1926- ..... **CLC 30**
See also CANR 15; CA 103

Garfield, Leon 1921- .... **CLC 12**
See also CA 17-20R; SATA 1, 32

Garland, (Hannibal) Hamlin
1860-1940 .... **TCLC 3**
See also CA 104; DLB 12, 71

Garneau, Hector (de) Saint Denys
1912-1943 .... **TCLC 13**
See also CA 111

Garner, Alan 1935- .... **CLC 17**
See also CLR 20; CANR 15; CA 73-76;
SATA 18

Garner, Hugh 1913-1979 .... **CLC 13**
See also CA 69-72; DLB 68

Garnett, David 1892-1981 .... **CLC 3**
See also CANR 17; CA 5-8R;
obituary CA 103; DLB 34

Garrett, George (Palmer, Jr.)
1929- .... **CLC 3, 11, 51**
See also CAAS 5; CANR 1; CA 1-4R;
DLB 2, 5; DLB-Y 83

Garrigue, Jean 1914-1972 .... **CLC 2, 8**
See also CANR 20; CA 5-8R;
obituary CA 37-40R

Gary, Romain 1914-1980 .... **CLC 25**
See also Kacew, Romain

Gascar, Pierre 1916- .... **CLC 11**
See also Fournier, Pierre

Gascoyne, David (Emery) 1916- .... **CLC 45**
See also CANR 10; CA 65-68; DLB 20

Gaskell, Elizabeth Cleghorn
1810-1865 .... **NCLC 5**
See also DLB 21

Gass, William H(oward)
1924- .... **CLC 1, 2, 8, 11, 15, 39**
See also CA 17-20R; DLB 2

Gautier, Theophile 1811-1872 ..... **NCLC 1**

Gaye, Marvin (Pentz) 1939-1984 ... **CLC 26**
See also obituary CA 112

Gebler, Carlo (Ernest) 1954- ...... **CLC 39**
See also CA 119

Gee, Maggie 19??- .... **CLC 57**

Gee, Maurice (Gough) 1931- ...... **CLC 29**
See also CA 97-100; SATA 46

Gelbart, Larry (Simon) 1923- ...... **CLC 21**
See also CA 73-76

Gelber, Jack 1932- .... **CLC 1, 6, 14**
See also CANR 2; CA 1-4R; DLB 7

Gellhorn, Martha (Ellis) 1908- ..... **CLC 14**
See also CA 77-80; DLB-Y 82

Genet, Jean
1910-1986 ... **CLC 1, 2, 5, 10, 14, 44, 46**
See also CANR 18; CA 13-16R; DLB 72;
DLB-Y 86

Gent, Peter 1942- .... **CLC 29**
See also CA 89-92; DLB 72; DLB-Y 82

George, Jean Craighead 1919- ..... **CLC 35**
See also CLR 1; CA 5-8R; SATA 2;
DLB 52

George, Stefan (Anton)
1868-1933 .... **TCLC 2, 14**
See also CA 104

Gerhardi, William (Alexander) 1895-1977
See Gerhardie, William (Alexander)

Gerhardie, William (Alexander)
1895-1977 .... **CLC 5**
See also CANR 18; CA 25-28R;
obituary CA 73-76; DLB 36

Gertler, T(rudy) 1946?- .... **CLC 34**
See also CA 116

Gessner, Friedrike Victoria 1910-1980
See Adamson, Joy(-Friederike Victoria)

Ghelderode, Michel de
1898-1962 .... **CLC 6, 11**
See also CA 85-88

Ghiselin, Brewster 1903- .... **CLC 23**
See also CANR 13; CA 13-16R

Ghose, Zulfikar 1935- .... **CLC 42**
See also CA 65-68

Ghosh, Amitav 1943- .... **CLC 44**

Giacosa, Giuseppe 1847-1906 ...... **TCLC 7**
See also CA 104

Gibbon, Lewis Grassic 1901-1935 ... **TCLC 4**
See also Mitchell, James Leslie

Gibbons, Kaye 1960- .... **CLC 50**

Gibran, (Gibran) Kahlil
1883-1931 .... **TCLC 1, 9**
See also CA 104

Gibson, William 1914- .... **CLC 23**
See also CANR 9; CA 9-12R; DLB 7

Gibson, William 1948- .... **CLC 39**
See also CA 126

Gide, Andre (Paul Guillaume)
1869-1951 .... **TCLC 5, 12, 36**
See also CA 104, 124; DLB 65

Gifford, Barry (Colby) 1946- .... **CLC 34**
See also CANR 9; CA 65-68

Gilbert, (Sir) W(illiam) S(chwenck)
1836-1911 .... **TCLC 3**
See also CA 104; SATA 36

Gilbreth, Ernestine 1908-
See Carey, Ernestine Gilbreth

Gilbreth, Frank B(unker), Jr.
1911- .... **CLC 17**
See also CA 9-12R; SATA 2

Gilchrist, Ellen 1935- .... **CLC 34, 48**
See also CA 113, 116

Giles, Molly 1942- .... **CLC 39**
See also CA 126

Gilliam, Terry (Vance) 1940-
See Monty Python
See also CA 108, 113

Gilliatt, Penelope (Ann Douglass)
1932- .... **CLC 2, 10, 13, 53**
See also CA 13-16R; DLB 14

Gilman, Charlotte (Anna) Perkins (Stetson)
1860-1935 .... **TCLC 9**
See also CA 106

Gilmour, David 1944-
See Pink Floyd

Gilroy, Frank D(aniel) 1925- .... **CLC 2**
See also CA 81-84; DLB 7

Ginsberg, Allen
1926- .... **CLC 1, 2, 3, 4, 6, 13, 36**
See also CANR 2; CA 1-4R; DLB 5, 16;
CDALB 1941-1968

Ginzburg, Natalia 1916- ...... **CLC 5, 11, 54**
See also CA 85-88

Giono, Jean 1895-1970 .... **CLC 4, 11**
See also CANR 2; CA 45-48;
obituary CA 29-32R; DLB 72

Giovanni, Nikki 1943- .... **CLC 2, 4, 19**
See also CLR 6; CAAS 6; CANR 18;
CA 29-32R; SATA 24; DLB 5, 41

Giovene, Andrea 1904- .... **CLC 7**
See also CA 85-88

Gippius, Zinaida (Nikolayevna) 1869-1945
See Hippius, Zinaida
See also CA 106

Giraudoux, (Hippolyte) Jean
1882-1944 .... **TCLC 2, 7**
See also CA 104; DLB 65

Gironella, Jose Maria 1917- .... **CLC 11**
See also CA 101

Gissing, George (Robert)
1857-1903 .... **TCLC 3, 24**
See also CA 105; DLB 18

Gladkov, Fyodor (Vasilyevich)
1883-1958 .... **TCLC 27**

Glanville, Brian (Lester) 1931- ...... **CLC 6**
See also CANR 3; CA 5-8R; SATA 42;
DLB 15

Glasgow, Ellen (Anderson Gholson)
1873?-1945 .... **TCLC 2, 7**
See also CA 104; DLB 9, 12

Glassco, John 1909-1981 .... **CLC 9**
See also CANR 15; CA 13-16R;
obituary CA 102; DLB 68

Glasser, Ronald J. 1940?- .... **CLC 37**

Glendinning, Victoria 1937- .... **CLC 50**
See also CA 120

Glissant, Edouard 1928- .... **CLC 10**

Gloag, Julian 1930- .... **CLC 40**
See also CANR 10; CA 65-68

Gluck, Louise (Elisabeth)
  1943- .... CLC 7, 22, 44
  See also CA 33-36R; DLB 5

Gobineau, Joseph Arthur (Comte) de
  1816-1882 .... NCLC 17

Godard, Jean-Luc 1930- .... CLC 20
  See also CA 93-96

Godden, (Margaret) Rumer 1907- ... CLC 53
  See also CLR 20; CANR 4, 27; CA 7-8R;
  SATA 3, 36

Godwin, Gail 1937- .... CLC 5, 8, 22, 31
  See also CANR 15; CA 29-32R; DLB 6

Godwin, William 1756-1836 ...... NCLC 14
  See also DLB 39

Goethe, Johann Wolfgang von
  1749-1832 .... NCLC 4, 22

Gogarty, Oliver St. John
  1878-1957 .... TCLC 15
  See also CA 109; DLB 15, 19

Gogol, Nikolai (Vasilyevich)
  1809-1852 .... NCLC 5, 15; SSC 4
  See also CAAS 1, 4

Gokceli, Yasar Kemal 1923-
  See Kemal, Yashar

Gold, Herbert 1924- .... CLC 4, 7, 14, 42
  See also CANR 17; CA 9-12R; DLB 2;
  DLB-Y 81

Goldbarth, Albert 1948- .... CLC 5, 38
  See also CANR 6; CA 53-56

Goldberg, Anatol 1910-1982 .... CLC 34
  See also obituary CA 117

Goldemberg, Isaac 1945- .... CLC 52
  See also CANR 11; CA 69-72

Golding, William (Gerald)
  1911- ..... CLC 1, 2, 3, 8, 10, 17, 27, 58
  See also CANR 13; CA 5-8R; DLB 15

Goldman, Emma 1869-1940 ...... TCLC 13
  See also CA 110

Goldman, William (W.) 1931- .... CLC 1, 48
  See also CA 9-12R; DLB 44

Goldmann, Lucien 1913-1970 ...... CLC 24
  See also CAP 2; CA 25-28

Goldoni, Carlo 1707-1793 .... LC 4

Goldsberry, Steven 1949- .... CLC 34

Goldsmith, Oliver 1728?-1774 .... LC 2
  See also SATA 26; DLB 39

Gombrowicz, Witold
  1904-1969 .... CLC 4, 7, 11, 49
  See also CAP 2; CA 19-20;
  obituary CA 25-28R

Gomez de la Serna, Ramon
  1888-1963 .... CLC 9
  See also obituary CA 116

Goncharov, Ivan Alexandrovich
  1812-1891 .... NCLC 1

Goncourt, Edmond (Louis Antoine Huot) de
  1822-1896 .... NCLC 7

Goncourt, Jules (Alfred Huot) de
  1830-1870 .... NCLC 7

Gontier, Fernande 19??- .... CLC 50

Goodman, Paul 1911-1972 .... CLC 1, 2, 4, 7
  See also CAP 2; CA 19-20;
  obituary CA 37-40R

Gordimer, Nadine
  1923- ...... CLC 3, 5, 7, 10, 18, 33, 51
  See also CANR 3; CA 5-8R

Gordon, Adam Lindsay
  1833-1870 .... NCLC 21

Gordon, Caroline
  1895-1981 .... CLC 6, 13, 29
  See also CAP 1; CA 11-12;
  obituary CA 103; DLB 4, 9; DLB-Y 81

Gordon, Charles William 1860-1937
  See Conner, Ralph
  See also CA 109

Gordon, Mary (Catherine)
  1949- .... CLC 13, 22
  See also CA 102; DLB 6; DLB-Y 81

Gordon, Sol 1923- .... CLC 26
  See also CANR 4; CA 53-56; SATA 11

Gordone, Charles 1925- .... CLC 1, 4
  See also CA 93-96; DLB 7

Gorenko, Anna Andreyevna 1889?-1966
  See Akhmatova, Anna

Gorky, Maxim 1868-1936 .... TCLC 8
  See also Peshkov, Alexei Maximovich

Goryan, Sirak 1908-1981
  See Saroyan, William

Gosse, Edmund (William)
  1849-1928 .... TCLC 28
  See also CA 117; DLB 57

Gotlieb, Phyllis (Fay Bloom)
  1926- .... CLC 18
  See also CANR 7; CA 13-16R

Gould, Lois 1938?- .... CLC 4, 10
  See also CA 77-80

Gourmont, Remy de 1858-1915 .... TCLC 17
  See also CA 109

Govier, Katherine 1948- .... CLC 51
  See also CANR 18; CA 101

Goyen, (Charles) William
  1915-1983 .... CLC 5, 8, 14, 40
  See also CANR 6; CA 5-8R;
  obituary CA 110; DLB 2; DLB-Y 83

Goytisolo, Juan 1931- .... CLC 5, 10, 23
  See also CA 85-88

Gozzi, (Conte) Carlo 1720-1806 .. NCLC 23

Grabbe, Christian Dietrich
  1801-1836 .... NCLC 2

Grace, Patricia 1937- .... CLC 56

Gracq, Julien 1910- .... CLC 11, 48
  See also Poirier, Louis

Grade, Chaim 1910-1982 .... CLC 10
  See also CA 93-96; obituary CA 107

Graham, Jorie 1951- .... CLC 48
  See also CA 111

Graham, R(obert) B(ontine) Cunninghame
  1852-1936 .... TCLC 19

Graham, W(illiam) S(ydney)
  1918-1986 .... CLC 29
  See also CA 73-76; obituary CA 118;
  DLB 20

Graham, Winston (Mawdsley)
  1910- .... CLC 23
  See also CANR 2, 22; CA 49-52;
  obituary CA 118

Granville-Barker, Harley
  1877-1946 .... TCLC 2
  See also CA 104

Grass, Gunter (Wilhelm)
  1927- .. CLC 1, 2, 4, 6, 11, 15, 22, 32, 49
  See also CANR 20; CA 13-16R; DLB 75

Grau, Shirley Ann 1929- .... CLC 4, 9
  See also CANR 22; CA 89-92; DLB 2

Graves, Richard Perceval 1945- .... CLC 44
  See also CANR 9, 26; CA 65-68

Graves, Robert (von Ranke)
  1895-1985 ... CLC 1, 2, 6, 11, 39, 44, 45
  See also CANR 5; CA 5-8R;
  obituary CA 117; SATA 45; DLB 20;
  DLB-Y 85

Gray, Alasdair 1934- .... CLC 41
  See also CA 123

Gray, Amlin 1946- .... CLC 29

Gray, Francine du Plessix 1930- .... CLC 22
  See also CAAS 2; CANR 11; CA 61-64

Gray, John (Henry) 1866-1934 .... TCLC 19
  See also CA 119

Gray, Simon (James Holliday)
  1936- .... CLC 9, 14, 36
  See also CAAS 3; CA 21-24R; DLB 13

Gray, Spalding 1941- .... CLC 49

Gray, Thomas 1716-1771 .... LC 4

Grayson, Richard (A.) 1951- .... CLC 38
  See also CANR 14; CA 85-88

Greeley, Andrew M(oran) 1928- .... CLC 28
  See also CAAS 7; CANR 7; CA 5-8R

Green, Hannah 1932- .... CLC 3, 7, 30
  See also Greenberg, Joanne
  See also CA 73-76

Green, Henry 1905-1974 .... CLC 2, 13
  See also Yorke, Henry Vincent
  See also DLB 15

Green, Julien (Hartridge) 1900- .. CLC 3, 11
  See also CA 21-24R; DLB 4, 72

Green, Paul (Eliot) 1894-1981 ...... CLC 25
  See also CANR 3; CA 5-8R;
  obituary CA 103; DLB 7, 9; DLB-Y 81

Greenberg, Ivan 1908-1973
  See Rahv, Philip
  See also CA 85-88

Greenberg, Joanne (Goldenberg)
  1932- .... CLC 3, 7, 30
  See also Green, Hannah
  See also CANR 14; CA 5-8R; SATA 25

Greenberg, Richard 1959?- .... CLC 57

Greene, Bette 1934- .... CLC 30
  See also CLR 2; CANR 4; CA 53-56;
  SATA 8

Greene, Gael 19??- .... CLC 8
  See also CANR 10; CA 13-16R

Greene, Graham (Henry)
  1904- ..... CLC 1, 3, 6, 9, 14, 18, 27, 37
  See also CA 13-16R; SATA 20; DLB 13, 15;
  DLB-Y 85

Gregor, Arthur 1923- .... CLC 9
  See also CANR 11; CA 25-28R; SATA 36

Gregory, Lady (Isabella Augusta Persse)
  1852-1932 .... TCLC 1
  See also CA 104; DLB 10

Harper, Frances Ellen Watkins
  1825-1911 . . . . TCLC 14
  See also CA 111, 125; DLB 50

Harper, Michael S(teven) 1938- . . CLC 7, 22
  See also CANR 24; CA 33-36R; DLB 41

Harris, Christie (Lucy Irwin)
  1907- . . . . CLC 12
  See also CANR 6; CA 5-8R; SATA 6

Harris, Frank 1856-1931 . . . . TCLC 24
  See also CAAS 1; CA 109

Harris, George Washington
  1814-1869 . . . . NCLC 23
  See also DLB 3, 11

Harris, Joel Chandler 1848-1908 . . . TCLC 2
  See also YABC 1; CA 104; DLB 11, 23, 42

Harris, John (Wyndham Parkes Lucas)
  Beynon 1903-1969
  See Wyndham, John
  See also CA 102; obituary CA 89-92

Harris, MacDonald 1921- . . . . CLC 9
  See also Heiney, Donald (William)

Harris, Mark 1922- . . . . CLC 19
  See also CAAS 3; CANR 2; CA 5-8R;
  DLB 2; DLB-Y 80

Harris, (Theodore) Wilson 1921-. . . . CLC 25
  See also CANR 11; CA 65-68

Harrison, Harry (Max) 1925- . . . . . . CLC 42
  See also CANR 5, 21; CA 1-4R; SATA 4;
  DLB 8

Harrison, James (Thomas) 1937-
  See Harrison, Jim
  See also CANR 8; CA 13-16R

Harrison, Jim 1937- . . . . CLC 6, 14, 33
  See also Harrison, James (Thomas)
  See also DLB-Y 82

Harrison, Tony 1937- . . . . CLC 43
  See also CA 65-68; DLB 40

Harriss, Will(ard Irvin) 1922- . . . . . . CLC 34
  See also CA 111

Harte, (Francis) Bret(t)
  1836?-1902. . . . . TCLC 1, 25
  See also CA 104; SATA 26; DLB 12, 64,
  74; CDALB 1865-1917

Hartley, L(eslie) P(oles)
  1895-1972 . . . . CLC 2, 22
  See also CA 45-48; obituary CA 37-40R;
  DLB 15

Hartman, Geoffrey H. 1929- . . . . CLC 27
  See also CA 117, 125; DLB 67

Haruf, Kent 19??- . . . . CLC 34

Harwood, Ronald 1934- . . . . CLC 32
  See also CANR 4; CA 1-4R; DLB 13

Hasek, Jaroslav (Matej Frantisek)
  1883-1923 . . . . TCLC 4
  See also CA 104

Hass, Robert 1941- . . . . CLC 18, 39
  See also CA 111

Hastings, Selina 19??- . . . . CLC 44

Hauptmann, Gerhart (Johann Robert)
  1862-1946 . . . . TCLC 4
  See also CA 104; DLB 66

Havel, Vaclav 1936- . . . . CLC 25, 58
  See also CA 104

Haviaras, Stratis 1935- . . . . CLC 33
  See also CA 105

Hawkes, John (Clendennin Burne, Jr.)
  1925- . . . . . . CLC 1, 2, 3, 4, 7, 9, 14, 15,
                        27, 49
  See also CANR 2; CA 1-4R; DLB 2, 7;
  DLB-Y 80

Hawthorne, Julian 1846-1934 . . . . . TCLC 25

Hawthorne, Nathaniel
  1804-1864 . . . NCLC 2, 10, 17, 23; SSC 3
  See also YABC 2; DLB 1, 74;
  CDALB 1640-1865

Hayashi Fumiko 1904-1951 . . . . . . TCLC 27

Haycraft, Anna 19??-
  See Ellis, Alice Thomas

Hayden, Robert (Earl)
  1913-1980 . . . . CLC 5, 9, 14, 37
  See also CANR 24; CA 69-72;
  obituary CA 97-100; CABS 2; SATA 19;
  obituary SATA 26; DLB 5, 76;
  CDALB 1941-1968

Hayman, Ronald 1932-. . . . . CLC 44
  See also CANR 18; CA 25-28R

Haywood, Eliza (Fowler) 1693?-1756 . . LC 1
  See also DLB 39

Hazzard, Shirley 1931- . . . . CLC 18
  See also CANR 4; CA 9-12R; DLB-Y 82

H(ilda) D(oolittle)
  1886-1961 . . . . CLC 3, 8, 14, 31, 34
  See also Doolittle, Hilda

Head, Bessie 1937-1986. . . . . CLC 25
  See also CANR 25; CA 29-32R;
  obituary CA 109

Headon, (Nicky) Topper 1956?-
  See The Clash

Heaney, Seamus (Justin)
  1939- . . . . CLC 5, 7, 14, 25, 37
  See also CANR 25; CA 85-88; DLB 40

Hearn, (Patricio) Lafcadio (Tessima Carlos)
  1850-1904 . . . . TCLC 9
  See also CA 105; DLB 12

Hearne, Vicki 1946- . . . . CLC 56

Heat Moon, William Least 1939-. . . CLC 29

Hebert, Anne 1916- . . . . CLC 4, 13, 29
  See also CA 85-88; DLB 68

Hecht, Anthony (Evan)
  1923- . . . . CLC 8, 13, 19
  See also CANR 6; CA 9-12R; DLB 5

Hecht, Ben 1894-1964 . . . . CLC 8
  See also CA 85-88; DLB 7, 9, 25, 26, 28

Hedayat, Sadeq 1903-1951. . . . . . . TCLC 21
  See also CA 120

Heidegger, Martin 1889-1976 . . . . . . CLC 24
  See also CA 81-84; obituary CA 65-68

Heidenstam, (Karl Gustaf) Verner von
  1859-1940 . . . . TCLC 5
  See also CA 104

Heifner, Jack 1946- . . . . CLC 11
  See also CA 105

Heijermans, Herman 1864-1924 . . . TCLC 24
  See also CA 123

Heilbrun, Carolyn G(old) 1926-. . . . . CLC 25
  See also CANR 1; CA 45-48

Heine, Harry 1797-1856
  See Heine, Heinrich

Heine, Heinrich 1797-1856 . . . . NCLC 4

Heinemann, Larry C(urtiss) 1944- . . CLC 50
  See also CA 110

Heiney, Donald (William) 1921-
  See Harris, MacDonald
  See also CANR 3; CA 1-4R

Heinlein, Robert A(nson)
  1907-1988 . . . . . . CLC 1, 3, 8, 14, 26, 55
  See also CANR 1, 20; CA 1-4R;
  obituary CA 125; SATA 9; DLB 8

Heller, Joseph
  1923- . . . . CLC 1, 3, 5, 8, 11, 36
  See also CANR 8; CA 5-8R; CABS 1;
  DLB 2, 28; DLB-Y 80

Hellman, Lillian (Florence)
  1905?-1984. . . . . CLC 2, 4, 8, 14, 18, 34,
                          44, 52
  See also CA 13-16R; obituary CA 112;
  DLB 7; DLB-Y 84

Helprin, Mark 1947- . . . . . CLC 7, 10, 22, 32
  See also CA 81-84; DLB-Y 85

Hemingway, Ernest (Miller)
  1899-1961 . . . CLC 1, 3, 6, 8, 10, 13, 19,
           30, 34, 39, 41, 44, 50; SSC 1
  See also CA 77-80; DLB 4, 9; DLB-Y 81;
  DLB-DS 1

Hempel, Amy 1951- . . . . CLC 39
  See also CA 118

Henley, Beth 1952-. . . . . CLC 23
  See also Henley, Elizabeth Becker
  See also DLB-Y 86

Henley, Elizabeth Becker 1952-
  See Henley, Beth
  See also CA 107

Henley, William Ernest
  1849-1903 . . . . TCLC 8
  See also CA 105; DLB 19

Hennissart, Martha
  See Lathen, Emma
  See also CA 85-88

Henry, O. 1862-1910 . . . TCLC 1, 19; SSC 5
  See also Porter, William Sydney
  See also YABC 2; CA 104; DLB 12, 78, 79;
  CDALB 1865-1917

Henry VIII 1491-1547. . . . . LC 10

Hentoff, Nat(han Irving) 1925-. . . . . . CLC 26
  See also CLR 1; CAAS 6; CANR 5;
  CA 1-4R; SATA 27, 42

Heppenstall, (John) Rayner
  1911-1981 . . . . CLC 10
  See also CA 1-4R; obituary CA 103

Herbert, Frank (Patrick)
  1920-1986 . . . . CLC 12, 23, 35, 44
  See also CANR 5; CA 53-56;
  obituary CA 118; SATA 9, 37, 47; DLB 8

Herbert, Zbigniew 1924- . . . . CLC 9, 43
  See also CA 89-92

Herbst, Josephine 1897-1969. . . . . . . CLC 34
  See also CA 5-8R; obituary CA 25-28R;
  DLB 9

Herder, Johann Gottfried von
  1744-1803 . . . . NCLC 8

Horwitz, Julius 1920-1986......... CLC 14
See also CANR 12; CA 9-12R;
    obituary CA 119

Hospital, Janette Turner 1942-..... CLC 42
See also CA 108

Hostos (y Bonilla), Eugenio Maria de
    1893-1903 .... TCLC 24
See also CA 123

Hougan, Carolyn 19??-............ CLC 34

Household, Geoffrey (Edward West)
    1900-1988 .... CLC 11
See also CA 77-80; obituary CA 126;
    SATA 14

Housman, A(lfred) E(dward)
    1859-1936 .... TCLC 1, 10
See also CA 104, 125; DLB 19

Housman, Laurence 1865-1959 ..... TCLC 7
See also CA 106; SATA 25; DLB 10

Howard, Elizabeth Jane 1923- ... CLC 7, 29
See also CANR 8; CA 5-8R

Howard, Maureen 1930- ..... CLC 5, 14, 46
See also CA 53-56; DLB-Y 83

Howard, Richard 1929- ...... CLC 7, 10, 47
See also CANR 25; CA 85-88; DLB 5

Howard, Robert E(rvin)
    1906-1936 .... TCLC 8
See also CA 105

Howe, Fanny 1940- .... CLC 47
See also CA 117; SATA 52

Howe, Julia Ward 1819-1910 ..... TCLC 21
See also CA 117; DLB 1

Howe, Tina 1937-................ CLC 48
See also CA 109

Howells, William Dean
    1837-1920 .... TCLC 7, 17
See also CA 104; DLB 12, 64, 74;
    CDALB 1865-1917

Howes, Barbara 1914- .... CLC 15
See also CAAS 3; CA 9-12R; SATA 5

Hrabal, Bohumil 1914-............ CLC 13
See also CA 106

Hubbard, L(afayette) Ron(ald)
    1911-1986 .... CLC 43
See also CANR 22; CA 77-80;
    obituary CA 118

Huch, Ricarda (Octavia)
    1864-1947 .... TCLC 13
See also CA 111; DLB 66

Huddle, David 1942- .... CLC 49
See also CA 57-60

Hudson, W(illiam) H(enry)
    1841-1922 .... TCLC 29
See also CA 115; SATA 35

Hueffer, Ford Madox 1873-1939
See Ford, Ford Madox

Hughart, Barry 1934-............ CLC 39

Hughes, David (John) 1930- .... CLC 48
See also CA 116; DLB 14

Hughes, Edward James 1930-
See Hughes, Ted

Hughes, (James) Langston
    1902-1967 ..... CLC 1, 5, 10, 15, 35, 44
See also CANR 1; CA 1-4R;
    obituary CA 25-28R; SATA 4, 33;
    DLB 4, 7, 48, 51

Hughes, Richard (Arthur Warren)
    1900-1976 .... CLC 1, 11
See also CANR 4; CA 5-8R;
    obituary CA 65-68; SATA 8;
    obituary SATA 25; DLB 15

Hughes, Ted 1930- ..... CLC 2, 4, 9, 14, 37
See also CLR 3; CANR 1; CA 1-4R;
    SATA 27, 49; DLB 40

Hugo, Richard F(ranklin)
    1923-1982 .... CLC 6, 18, 32
See also CANR 3; CA 49-52;
    obituary CA 108; DLB 5

Hugo, Victor Marie
    1802-1885 .... NCLC 3, 10, 21
See also SATA 47

Huidobro, Vicente 1893-1948 ..... TCLC 31

Hulme, Keri 1947- .... CLC 39
See also CA 123

Hulme, T(homas) E(rnest)
    1883-1917 .... TCLC 21
See also CA 117; DLB 19

Hume, David 1711-1776............. LC 7

Humphrey, William 1924-......... CLC 45
See also CA 77-80; DLB 6

Humphreys, Emyr (Owen) 1919-.... CLC 47
See also CANR 3, 24; CA 5-8R; DLB 15

Humphreys, Josephine 1945-.... CLC 34, 57
See also CA 121, 127

Hunt, E(verette) Howard (Jr.)
    1918- .... CLC 3
See also CANR 2; CA 45-48

Hunt, (James Henry) Leigh
    1784-1859 .... NCLC 1

Hunter, Evan 1926- .... CLC 11, 31
See also CANR 5; CA 5-8R; SATA 25;
    DLB-Y 82

Hunter, Kristin (Eggleston) 1931-... CLC 35
See also CLR 3; CANR 13; CA 13-16R;
    SATA 12; DLB 33

Hunter, Mollie (Maureen McIlwraith)
    1922- .... CLC 21
See also McIlwraith, Maureen Mollie
    Hunter

Hunter, Robert ?-1734............. LC 7

Hurston, Zora Neale
    1891-1960 .... CLC 7, 30; SSC 4
See also CA 85-88; DLB 51

Huston, John (Marcellus)
    1906-1987 .... CLC 20
See also CA 73-76; obituary CA 123;
    DLB 26

Huxley, Aldous (Leonard)
    1894-1963 .. CLC 1, 3, 4, 5, 8, 11, 18, 35
See also CA 85-88; DLB 36

Huysmans, Charles Marie Georges
    1848-1907
See Huysmans, Joris-Karl
See also CA 104

Huysmans, Joris-Karl 1848-1907 .. NCLC 7
See also Huysmans, Charles Marie Georges

Hwang, David Henry 1957-........ CLC 55
See also CA 127

Hyde, Anthony 1946?-............ CLC 42

Hyde, Margaret O(ldroyd) 1917- ... CLC 21
See also CANR 1; CA 1-4R; SATA 1, 42

Ian, Janis 1951- .... CLC 21
See also CA 105

Ibarguengoitia, Jorge 1928-1983.... CLC 37
See also obituary CA 113, 124

Ibsen, Henrik (Johan)
    1828-1906 .... TCLC 2, 8, 16
See also CA 104

Ibuse, Masuji 1898-.............. CLC 22

Ichikawa, Kon 1915-.............. CLC 20
See also CA 121

Idle, Eric 1943-
See Monty Python
See also CA 116

Ignatow, David 1914-...... CLC 4, 7, 14, 40
See also CAAS 3; CA 9-12R; DLB 5

Ihimaera, Witi (Tame) 1944-....... CLC 46
See also CA 77-80

Ilf, Ilya 1897-1937 .... TCLC 21

Immermann, Karl (Lebrecht)
    1796-1840 .... NCLC 4

Ingalls, Rachel 19??-.............. CLC 42
See also CA 123

Ingamells, Rex 1913-1955 .... TCLC 35

Inge, William (Motter)
    1913-1973 .... CLC 1, 8, 19
See also CA 9-12R; DLB 7;
    CDALB 1941-1968

Innaurato, Albert 1948-........... CLC 21
See also CA 115, 122

Innes, Michael 1906-
See Stewart, J(ohn) I(nnes) M(ackintosh)

Ionesco, Eugene
    1912- .... CLC 1, 4, 6, 9, 11, 15, 41
See also CA 9-12R; SATA 7

Iqbal, Muhammad 1877-1938 ..... TCLC 28

Irving, John (Winslow)
    1942- .... CLC 13, 23, 38
See also CA 25-28R; DLB 6; DLB-Y 82

Irving, Washington
    1783-1859 .... NCLC 2, 19; SSC 2
See also YABC 2; DLB 3, 11, 30, 59, 73,
    74; CDALB 1640-1865

Isaacs, Susan 1943- .... CLC 32
See also CANR 20; CA 89-92

Isherwood, Christopher (William Bradshaw)
    1904-1986 .... CLC 1, 9, 11, 14, 44
See also CA 13-16R; obituary CA 117;
    DLB 15; DLB-Y 86

Ishiguro, Kazuo 1954?-........ CLC 27, 56
See also CA 120

Ishikawa Takuboku 1885-1912 .... TCLC 15
See also CA 113

Iskander, Fazil (Abdulovich)
    1929- .... CLC 47
See also CA 102

Ivanov, Vyacheslav (Ivanovich)
    1866-1949 .... TCLC 33
See also CA 122

Lafayette, Rene
See Hubbard, L(afayette) Ron(ald)

Laforgue, Jules 1860-1887....... NCLC 5

Lagerkvist, Par (Fabian)
1891-1974 .... CLC 7, 10, 13, 54
See also CA 85-88; obituary CA 49-52

Lagerlof, Selma (Ottiliana Lovisa)
1858-1940 .... TCLC 4, 36
See also CLR 7; CA 108; SATA 15

La Guma, (Justin) Alex(ander)
1925-1985 .... CLC 19
See also CA 49-52; obituary CA 118

Lamartine, Alphonse (Marie Louis Prat) de
1790-1869 .... NCLC 11

Lamb, Charles 1775-1834....... NCLC 10
See also SATA 17

Lamming, George (William)
1927- .... CLC 2, 4
See also CANR 26; CA 85-88

LaMoore, Louis Dearborn 1908?-
See L'Amour, Louis (Dearborn)

L'Amour, Louis (Dearborn)
1908-1988 .... CLC 25, 55
See also CANR 3; CA 1-4R;
obituary CA 125; DLB-Y 80

Lampedusa, (Prince) Giuseppe (Maria
Fabrizio) Tomasi di
1896-1957 .... TCLC 13
See also CA 111

Lampman, Archibald 1861-1899 .. NCLC 25

Lancaster, Bruce 1896-1963....... CLC 36
See also CAP 1; CA 9-12; SATA 9

Landis, John (David) 1950-........ CLC 26
See also CA 112

Landolfi, Tommaso 1908-1979... CLC 11, 49
See also obituary CA 117

Landon, Letitia Elizabeth
1802-1838 .... NCLC 15

Landor, Walter Savage
1775-1864 .... NCLC 14

Landwirth, Heinz 1927-
See Lind, Jakov
See also CANR 7; CA 11-12R

Lane, Patrick 1939-............. CLC 25
See also CA 97-100; DLB 53

Lang, Andrew 1844-1912........ TCLC 16
See also CA 114; SATA 16

Lang, Fritz 1890-1976 .... CLC 20
See also CA 77-80; obituary CA 69-72

Langer, Elinor 1939- .... CLC 34
See also CA 121

Lanier, Sidney 1842-1881 .... NCLC 6
See also SATA 18; DLB 64

Lanyer, Aemilia 1569-1645 .... LC 10

Lapine, James 1949-............. CLC 39

Larbaud, Valery 1881-1957....... TCLC 9
See also CA 106

Lardner, Ring(gold Wilmer)
1885-1933 .... TCLC 2, 14
See also CA 104; DLB 11, 25

Larkin, Philip (Arthur)
1922-1985 ... CLC 3, 5, 8, 9, 13, 18, 33,
39
See also CA 5-8R; obituary CA 117;
DLB 27

Larra (y Sanchez de Castro), Mariano Jose de
1809-1837 .... NCLC 17

Larsen, Eric 1941- .... CLC 55

Larsen, Nella 1891-1964 .... CLC 37
See also CA 125; DLB 51

Larson, Charles R(aymond) 1938-... CLC 31
See also CANR 4; CA 53-56

Latham, Jean Lee 1902-........... CLC 12
See also CANR 7; CA 5-8R; SATA 2

Lathen, Emma .... CLC 2
See also Hennissart, Martha; Latsis, Mary
J(ane)

Latsis, Mary J(ane)
See Lathen, Emma
See also CA 85-88

Lattimore, Richmond (Alexander)
1906-1984 .... CLC 3
See also CANR 1; CA 1-4R;
obituary CA 112

Laughlin, James 1914-............ CLC 49
See also CANR 9; CA 21-24R; DLB 48

Laurence, (Jean) Margaret (Wemyss)
1926-1987 .... CLC 3, 6, 13, 50
See also CA 5-8R; obituary CA 121;
SATA 50; DLB 53

Laurent, Antoine 1952- .... CLC 50

Lautreamont, Comte de
1846-1870 .... NCLC 12

Lavin, Mary 1912-...... CLC 4, 18; SSC 4
See also CA 9-12R; DLB 15

Lawler, Raymond (Evenor) 1922-... CLC 58
See also CA 103

Lawrence, D(avid) H(erbert)
1885-1930 .... TCLC 2, 9, 16, 33; SSC 4
See also CA 104, 121; DLB 10, 19, 36

Lawrence, T(homas) E(dward)
1888-1935 .... TCLC 18
See also CA 115

Lawson, Henry (Archibald Hertzberg)
1867-1922 .... TCLC 27
See also CA 120

Laxness, Halldor (Kiljan) 1902- .... CLC 25
See also Gudjonsson, Halldor Kiljan

Laye, Camara 1928-1980........ CLC 4, 38
See also CA 85-88; obituary CA 97-100

Layton, Irving (Peter) 1912-..... CLC 2, 15
See also CANR 2; CA 1-4R

Lazarus, Emma 1849-1887....... NCLC 8

Leacock, Stephen (Butler)
1869-1944 .... TCLC 2
See also CA 104

Lear, Edward 1812-1888 .... NCLC 3
See also CLR 1; SATA 18; DLB 32

Lear, Norman (Milton) 1922- ...... CLC 12
See also CA 73-76

Leavis, F(rank) R(aymond)
1895-1978 .... CLC 24
See also CA 21-24R; obituary CA 77-80

Leavitt, David 1961?-............. CLC 34
See also CA 116, 122

Lebowitz, Fran(ces Ann)
1951?- .... CLC 11, 36
See also CANR 14; CA 81-84

Le Carre, John 1931-... CLC 3, 5, 9, 15, 28
See also Cornwell, David (John Moore)

Le Clezio, J(ean) M(arie) G(ustave)
1940- .... CLC 31
See also CA 116

Leduc, Violette 1907-1972......... CLC 22
See also CAP 1; CA 13-14;
obituary CA 33-36R

Ledwidge, Francis 1887-1917...... TCLC 23
See also CA 123; DLB 20

Lee, Andrea 1953- .... CLC 36
See also CA 125

Lee, Andrew 1917-
See Auchincloss, Louis (Stanton)

Lee, Don L. 1942-................. CLC 2
See also Madhubuti, Haki R.
See also CA 73-76

Lee, George Washington
1894-1976 .... CLC 52
See also CA 125; DLB 51

Lee, (Nelle) Harper 1926-......... CLC 12
See also CA 13-16R; SATA 11; DLB 6;
CDALB 1941-1968

Lee, Lawrence 1903- .... CLC 34
See also CA 25-28R

Lee, Manfred B(ennington) 1905-1971
See Queen, Ellery
See also CANR 2; CA 1-4R, 11;
obituary CA 29-32R

Lee, Stan 1922-................... CLC 17
See also CA 108, 111

Lee, Tanith 1947-................ CLC 46
See also CA 37-40R; SATA 8

Lee, Vernon 1856-1935 .... TCLC 5
See also Paget, Violet
See also DLB 57

Lee-Hamilton, Eugene (Jacob)
1845-1907 .... TCLC 22

Leet, Judith 1935- .... CLC 11

Le Fanu, Joseph Sheridan
1814-1873 .... NCLC 9
See also DLB 21, 70

Leffland, Ella 1931- .... CLC 19
See also CA 29-32R; DLB-Y 84

Leger, (Marie-Rene) Alexis Saint-Leger
1887-1975
See Perse, St.-John
See also CA 13-16R; obituary CA 61-64

Le Guin, Ursula K(roeber)
1929-............... CLC 8, 13, 22, 45
See also CLR 3; CANR 9; CA 21-24R;
SATA 4, 52; DLB 8, 52

Lehmann, Rosamond (Nina) 1901- ... CLC 5
See also CANR 8; CA 77-80; DLB 15

Leiber, Fritz (Reuter, Jr.) 1910-.... CLC 25
See also CANR 2; CA 45-48; SATA 45;
DLB 8

Leino, Eino 1878-1926.......... TCLC 24

Morgenstern, Christian (Otto Josef Wolfgang)
1871-1914 .... TCLC 8
See also CA 105

Moricz, Zsigmond 1879-1942 ..... TCLC 33

Morike, Eduard (Friedrich)
1804-1875 .... NCLC 10

Mori Ogai 1862-1922............ TCLC 14
See also Mori Rintaro

Mori Rintaro 1862-1922
See Mori Ogai
See also CA 110

Moritz, Karl Philipp 1756-1793 ...... LC 2

Morris, Julian 1916-
See West, Morris L.

Morris, Steveland Judkins 1950-
See Wonder, Stevie
See also CA 111

Morris, William 1834-1896 .... NCLC 4
See also DLB 18, 35, 57

Morris, Wright (Marion)
1910- .... CLC 1, 3, 7, 18, 37
See also CA 9-12R; DLB 2; DLB-Y 81

Morrison, James Douglas 1943-1971
See Morrison, Jim
See also CA 73-76

Morrison, Jim 1943-1971.......... CLC 17
See also Morrison, James Douglas

Morrison, Toni 1931-..... CLC 4, 10, 22, 55
See also CA 29-32R; DLB 6, 33; DLB-Y 81;
AAYA 1

Morrison, Van 1945- .... CLC 21
See also CA 116

Mortimer, John (Clifford)
1923- .... CLC 28, 43
See also CANR 21; CA 13-16R; DLB 13

Mortimer, Penelope (Ruth) 1918-.... CLC 5
See also CA 57-60

Mosley, Nicholas 1923-........... CLC 43
See also CA 69-72; DLB 14

Moss, Howard
1922-1987 .... CLC 7, 14, 45, 50
See also CANR 1; CA 1-4R; DLB 5

Motion, Andrew (Peter) 1952-...... CLC 47
See also DLB 40

Motley, Willard (Francis)
1912-1965 .... CLC 18
See also CA 117; obituary CA 106

Mott, Michael (Charles Alston)
1930- .... CLC 15, 34
See also CAAS 7; CANR 7; CA 5-8R

Mowat, Farley (McGill) 1921- ..... CLC 26
See also CLR 20; CANR 4; CA 1-4R;
SATA 3; DLB 68

Mphahlele, Es'kia 1919-
See Mphahlele, Ezekiel

Mphahlele, Ezekiel 1919-.......... CLC 25
See also CA 81-84

Mqhayi, S(amuel) E(dward) K(rune Loliwe)
1875-1945 .... TCLC 25

Mrozek, Slawomir 1930-........ CLC 3, 13
See also CA 13-16R

Mtwa, Percy 19??-............... CLC 47

Mueller, Lisel 1924-.......... CLC 13, 51
See also CA 93-96

Muir, Edwin 1887-1959 .... TCLC 2
See also CA 104; DLB 20

Muir, John 1838-1914 .... TCLC 28

Mujica Lainez, Manuel
1910-1984 .... CLC 31
See also CA 81-84; obituary CA 112

Mukherjee, Bharati 1940- .... CLC 53
See also CA 107; DLB 60

Muldoon, Paul 1951-............. CLC 32
See also CA 113; DLB 40

Mulisch, Harry (Kurt Victor)
1927- .... CLC 42
See also CANR 6; CA 9-12R

Mull, Martin 1943-............... CLC 17
See also CA 105

Munford, Robert 1737?-1783......... LC 5
See also DLB 31

Munro, Alice (Laidlaw)
1931- .... CLC 6, 10, 19, 50; SSC 3
See also CA 33-36R; SATA 29; DLB 53

Munro, H(ector) H(ugh) 1870-1916
See Saki
See also CA 104; DLB 34

Murasaki, Lady c. 11th century-... CMLC 1

Murdoch, (Jean) Iris
1919- ...... CLC 1, 2, 3, 4, 6, 8, 11, 15,
22, 31, 51
See also CANR 8; CA 13-16R; DLB 14

Murphy, Richard 1927-........... CLC 41
See also CA 29-32R; DLB 40

Murphy, Sylvia 19??-............. CLC 34

Murphy, Thomas (Bernard) 1935-... CLC 51
See also CA 101

Murray, Les(lie) A(llan) 1938- ..... CLC 40
See also CANR 11; CA 21-24R

Murry, John Middleton
1889-1957 .... TCLC 16
See also CA 118

Musgrave, Susan 1951- .... CLC 13, 54
See also CA 69-72

Musil, Robert (Edler von)
1880-1942 .... TCLC 12
See also CA 109

Musset, (Louis Charles) Alfred de
1810-1857 .... NCLC 7

Myers, Walter Dean 1937- .... CLC 35
See also CLR 4, 16; CANR 20; CA 33-36R;
SAAS 2; SATA 27, 41; DLB 33

Nabokov, Vladimir (Vladimirovich)
1899-1977 .... CLC 1, 2, 3, 6, 8, 11, 15,
23, 44, 46
See also CANR 20; CA 5-8R;
obituary CA 69-72; DLB 2; DLB-Y 80;
DLB-DS 3; CDALB 1941-1968

Nagy, Laszlo 1925-1978........... CLC 7
See also obituary CA 112

Naipaul, Shiva(dhar Srinivasa)
1945-1985 .... CLC 32, 39
See also CA 110, 112; obituary CA 116;
DLB-Y 85

Naipaul, V(idiadhar) S(urajprasad)
1932- .... CLC 4, 7, 9, 13, 18, 37
See also CANR 1; CA 1-4R; DLB-Y 85

Nakos, Ioulia 1899?-
See Nakos, Lilika

Nakos, Lilika 1899?- .... CLC 29

Nakou, Lilika 1899?-
See Nakos, Lilika

Narayan, R(asipuram) K(rishnaswami)
1906- .... CLC 7, 28, 47
See also CA 81-84

Nash, (Frediric) Ogden 1902-1971 .. CLC 23
See also CAP 1; CA 13-14;
obituary CA 29-32R; SATA 2, 46;
DLB 11

Nathan, George Jean 1882-1958... TCLC 18
See also CA 114

Natsume, Kinnosuke 1867-1916
See Natsume, Soseki
See also CA 104

Natsume, Soseki 1867-1916..... TCLC 2, 10
See also Natsume, Kinnosuke

Natti, (Mary) Lee 1919-
See Kingman, (Mary) Lee
See also CANR 2; CA 7-8R

Naylor, Gloria 1950- .... CLC 28, 52
See also CANR 27; CA 107

Neihardt, John G(neisenau)
1881-1973 .... CLC 32
See also CAP 1; CA 13-14; DLB 9, 54

Nekrasov, Nikolai Alekseevich
1821-1878 .... NCLC 11

Nelligan, Emile 1879-1941........ TCLC 14
See also CA 114

Nelson, Willie 1933-............. CLC 17
See also CA 107

Nemerov, Howard 1920- .... CLC 2, 6, 9, 36
See also CANR 1; CA 1-4R; CABS 2;
DLB 5, 6; DLB-Y 83

Neruda, Pablo
1904-1973 .... CLC 1, 2, 5, 7, 9, 28
See also CAP 2; CA 19-20;
obituary CA 45-48

Nerval, Gerard de 1808-1855...... NCLC 1

Nervo, (Jose) Amado (Ruiz de)
1870-1919 .... TCLC 11
See also CA 109

Neufeld, John (Arthur) 1938- ...... CLC 17
See also CANR 11; CA 25-28R; SAAS 3;
SATA 6

Neville, Emily Cheney 1919-...... CLC 12
See also CANR 3; CA 5-8R; SAAS 2;
SATA 1

Newbound, Bernard Slade 1930-
See Slade, Bernard
See also CA 81-84

Newby, P(ercy) H(oward)
1918- .... CLC 2, 13
See also CA 5-8R; DLB 15

Newlove, Donald 1928- .... CLC 6
See also CANR 25; CA 29-32R

Newlove, John (Herbert) 1938-..... CLC 14
See also CANR 9, 25; CA 21-24R

Author Index

Olson, Theodore 1937-
See Olson, Toby

Olson, Toby 1937- .... CLC 28
See also CANR 9; CA 65-68

Ondaatje, (Philip) Michael
1943- .... CLC 14, 29, 51
See also CA 77-80; DLB 60

Oneal, Elizabeth 1934-
See Oneal, Zibby
See also CA 106; SATA 30

Oneal, Zibby 1934-............... CLC 30
See also Oneal, Elizabeth

O'Neill, Eugene (Gladstone)
1888-1953 .... TCLC 1, 6, 27
See also CA 110; DLB 7

Onetti, Juan Carlos 1909-....... CLC 7, 10
See also CA 85-88

O'Nolan, Brian 1911-1966
See O'Brien, Flann

O Nuallain, Brian 1911-1966
See O'Brien, Flann
See also CAP 2; CA 21-22;
obituary CA 25-28R

Oppen, George 1908-1984 .... CLC 7, 13, 34
See also CANR 8; CA 13-16R;
obituary CA 113; DLB 5

Orlovitz, Gil 1918-1973 .... CLC 22
See also CA 77-80; obituary CA 45-48;
DLB 2, 5

Ortega y Gasset, Jose 1883-1955 ... TCLC 9
See also CA 106

Ortiz, Simon J. 1941-............. CLC 45

Orton, Joe 1933?-1967....... CLC 4, 13, 43
See also Orton, John Kingsley
See also DLB 13

Orton, John Kingsley 1933?-1967
See Orton, Joe
See also CA 85-88

Orwell, George
1903-1950 .... TCLC 2, 6, 15, 31
See also Blair, Eric Arthur
See also DLB 15

Osborne, John (James)
1929- .... CLC 1, 2, 5, 11, 45
See also CANR 21; CA 13-16R; DLB 13

Osborne, Lawrence 1958- .... CLC 50

Osceola 1885-1962
See Dinesen, Isak; Blixen, Karen
(Christentze Dinesen)

Oshima, Nagisa 1932- .... CLC 20
See also CA 116

Oskison, John M. 1874-1947..... TCLC 35

Ossoli, Sarah Margaret (Fuller marchesa d')
1810-1850
See Fuller, (Sarah) Margaret
See also SATA 25

Otero, Blas de 1916- .... CLC 11
See also CA 89-92

Owen, Wilfred (Edward Salter)
1893-1918 .... TCLC 5, 27
See also CA 104; DLB 20

Owens, Rochelle 1936-............. CLC 8
See also CAAS 2; CA 17-20R

Owl, Sebastian 1939-
See Thompson, Hunter S(tockton)

Oz, Amos 1939- ... CLC 5, 8, 11, 27, 33, 54
See also CA 53-56

Ozick, Cynthia 1928-.......... CLC 3, 7, 28
See also CANR 23; CA 17-20R; DLB 28;
DLB-Y 82

Ozu, Yasujiro 1903-1963 .... CLC 16
See also CA 112

Pa Chin 1904-................... CLC 18
See also Li Fei-kan

Pack, Robert 1929-.............. CLC 13
See also CANR 3; CA 1-4R; DLB 5

Padgett, Lewis 1915-1958
See Kuttner, Henry

Padilla, Heberto 1932-............ CLC 38
See also CA 123

Page, Jimmy 1944-............... CLC 12

Page, Louise 1955-............... CLC 40

Page, P(atricia) K(athleen)
1916- .... CLC 7, 18
See also CANR 4, 22; CA 53-56; DLB 68

Paget, Violet 1856-1935
See Lee, Vernon
See also CA 104

Palamas, Kostes 1859-1943 .... TCLC 5
See also CA 105

Palazzeschi, Aldo 1885-1974...... CLC 11
See also CA 89-92; obituary CA 53-56

Paley, Grace 1922-.......... CLC 4, 6, 37
See also CANR 13; CA 25-28R; DLB 28

Palin, Michael 1943- .... CLC 21
See also Monty Python
See also CA 107

Palma, Ricardo 1833-1919........ TCLC 29
See also CANR 123

Pancake, Breece Dexter 1952-1979
See Pancake, Breece D'J

Pancake, Breece D'J 1952-1979 .... CLC 29
See also obituary CA 109

Papadiamantis, Alexandros
1851-1911 .... TCLC 29

Papini, Giovanni 1881-1956....... TCLC 22
See also CA 121

Parini, Jay (Lee) 1948- .... CLC 54
See also CA 97-100

Parker, Dorothy (Rothschild)
1893-1967 .... CLC 15; SSC 2
See also CAP 2; CA 19-20;
obituary CA 25-28R; DLB 11, 45

Parker, Robert B(rown) 1932-...... CLC 27
See also CANR 1, 26; CA 49-52

Parkin, Frank 1940-.............. CLC 43

Parkman, Francis 1823-1893..... NCLC 12
See also DLB 1, 30

Parks, Gordon (Alexander Buchanan)
1912- .... CLC 1, 16
See also CANR 26; CA 41-44R; SATA 8;
DLB 33

Parnell, Thomas 1679-1718 .... LC 3

Parra, Nicanor 1914-.............. CLC 2
See also CA 85-88

Pasolini, Pier Paolo
1922-1975 .... CLC 20, 37
See also CA 93-96; obituary CA 61-64

Pastan, Linda (Olenik) 1932- ...... CLC 27
See also CANR 18; CA 61-64; DLB 5

Pasternak, Boris 1890-1960... CLC 7, 10, 18
See also obituary CA 116

Patchen, Kenneth 1911-1972 ... CLC 1, 2, 18
See also CANR 3; CA 1-4R;
obituary CA 33-36R; DLB 16, 48

Pater, Walter (Horatio)
1839-1894 .... NCLC 7
See also DLB 57

Paterson, Andrew Barton
1864-1941 .... TCLC 32

Paterson, Katherine (Womeldorf)
1932- .... CLC 12, 30
See also CLR 7; CA 21-24R; SATA 13, 53;
DLB 52

Patmore, Coventry Kersey Dighton
1823-1896 .... NCLC 9
See also DLB 35

Paton, Alan (Stewart)
1903-1988 .... CLC 4, 10, 25, 55
See also CANR 22; CAP 1; CA 15-16;
obituary CA 125; SATA 11

Paulding, James Kirke 1778-1860.. NCLC 2
See also DLB 3, 59, 74

Paulin, Tom 1949- .... CLC 37
See also CA 123; DLB 40

Paustovsky, Konstantin (Georgievich)
1892-1968 .... CLC 40
See also CA 93-96; obituary CA 25-28R

Paustowsky, Konstantin (Georgievich)
1892-1968
See Paustovsky, Konstantin (Georgievich)

Pavese, Cesare 1908-1950 .... TCLC 3
See also CA 104

Payne, Alan 1932-
See Jakes, John (William)

Paz, Octavio 1914-.. CLC 3, 4, 6, 10, 19, 51
See also CA 73-76

Peacock, Thomas Love
1785-1886 .... NCLC 22

Peake, Mervyn 1911-1968....... CLC 7, 54
See also CANR 3; CA 5-8R;
obituary CA 25-28R; SATA 23; DLB 15

Pearce, (Ann) Philippa 1920-....... CLC 21
See also Christie, (Ann) Philippa
See also CLR 9; CA 5-8R; SATA 1

Pearl, Eric 1934-
See Elman, Richard

Pearson, T(homas) R(eid) 1956- .... CLC 39
See also CA 120

Peck, John 1941- .... CLC 3
See also CANR 3; CA 49-52

Peck, Richard 1934-............... CLC 21
See also CLR 15; CANR 19; CA 85-88;
SAAS 2; SATA 18

Peck, Robert Newton 1928-........ CLC 17
See also CA 81-84; SAAS 1; SATA 21

Peckinpah, (David) Sam(uel)
1925-1984 .... CLC 20
See also CA 109; obituary CA 114

Powell, Padgett 1952-.............. CLC 34
    See also CA 126

Powers, J(ames) F(arl)
    1917- .... CLC 1, 4, 8, 57; SSC 4
    See also CANR 2; CA 1-4R

Pownall, David 1938-............. CLC 10
    See also CA 89-92; DLB 14

Powys, John Cowper
    1872-1963 .... CLC 7, 9, 15, 46
    See also CA 85-88; DLB 15

Powys, T(heodore) F(rancis)
    1875-1953 .... TCLC 9
    See also CA 106; DLB 36

Prager, Emily 1952-.............. CLC 56

Pratt, E(dwin) J(ohn) 1883-1964.... CLC 19
    See also obituary CA 93-96

Premchand 1880-1936 .... TCLC 21

Preussler, Otfried 1923-........... CLC 17
    See also CA 77-80; SATA 24

Prevert, Jacques (Henri Marie)
    1900-1977 .... CLC 15
    See also CA 77-80; obituary CA 69-72;
    obituary SATA 30

Prevost, Abbe (Antoine Francois)
    1697-1763 .... LC 1

Price, (Edward) Reynolds
    1933-............ CLC 3, 6, 13, 43, 50
    See also CANR 1; CA 1-4R; DLB 2

Price, Richard 1949-............. CLC 6, 12
    See also CANR 3; CA 49-52; DLB-Y 81

Prichard, Katharine Susannah
    1883-1969 .... CLC 46
    See also CAP 1; CA 11-12

Priestley, J(ohn) B(oynton)
    1894-1984 .... CLC 2, 5, 9, 34
    See also CA 9-12R; obituary CA 113;
    DLB 10, 34; DLB-Y 84

Prince (Rogers Nelson) 1958?- ..... CLC 35

Prince, F(rank) T(empleton) 1912-.. CLC 22
    See also CA 101; DLB 20

Prior, Matthew 1664-1721.......... LC 4

Pritchard, William H(arrison)
    1932- .... CLC 34
    See also CANR 23; CA 65-68

Pritchett, V(ictor) S(awdon)
    1900-................ CLC 5, 13, 15, 41
    See also CA 61-64; DLB 15

Procaccino, Michael 1946-
    See Cristofer, Michael

Prokosch, Frederic 1908-1989.... CLC 4, 48
    See also CA 73-76; DLB 48

Prose, Francine 1947-............. CLC 45
    See also CA 109, 112

Proust, Marcel 1871-1922 .. TCLC 7, 13, 33
    See also CA 104, 120; DLB 65

Pryor, Richard 1940-............. CLC 26
    See also CA 122

Przybyszewski, Stanislaw
    1868-1927 .... TCLC 36
    See also DLB 66

Puig, Manuel 1932- .... CLC 3, 5, 10, 28
    See also CANR 2; CA 45-48

Purdy, A(lfred) W(ellington)
    1918- .... CLC 3, 6, 14, 50
    See also CA 81-84

Purdy, James (Amos)
    1923-............ CLC 2, 4, 10, 28, 52
    See also CAAS 1; CANR 19; CA 33-36R;
    DLB 2

Pushkin, Alexander (Sergeyevich)
    1799-1837 .... NCLC 3

P'u Sung-ling 1640-1715 .... LC 3

Puzo, Mario 1920-......... CLC 1, 2, 6, 36
    See also CANR 4; CA 65-68; DLB 6

Pym, Barbara (Mary Crampton)
    1913-1980 .... CLC 13, 19, 37
    See also CANR 13; CAP 1; CA 13-14;
    obituary CA 97-100; DLB 14; DLB-Y 87

Pynchon, Thomas (Ruggles, Jr.)
    1937- .... CLC 2, 3, 6, 9, 11, 18, 33
    See also CANR 22; CA 17-20R; DLB 2

Quasimodo, Salvatore 1901-1968 ... CLC 10
    See also CAP 1; CA 15-16;
    obituary CA 25-28R

Queen, Ellery 1905-1982 .... CLC 3, 11
    See also Dannay, Frederic; Lee, Manfred
    B(ennington)

Queneau, Raymond
    1903-1976 .... CLC 2, 5, 10, 42
    See also CA 77-80; obituary CA 69-72;
    DLB 72

Quin, Ann (Marie) 1936-1973 .... CLC 6
    See also CA 9-12R; obituary CA 45-48;
    DLB 14

Quinn, Simon 1942-
    See Smith, Martin Cruz
    See also CANR 6, 23; CA 85-88

Quiroga, Horacio (Sylvestre)
    1878-1937 .... TCLC 20
    See also CA 117

Quoirez, Francoise 1935-
    See Sagan, Francoise
    See also CANR 6; CA 49-52

Rabe, David (William) 1940-... CLC 4, 8, 33
    See also CA 85-88; DLB 7

Rabelais, Francois 1494?-1553........ LC 5

Rabinovitch, Sholem 1859-1916
    See Aleichem, Sholom
    See also CA 104

Rachen, Kurt von 1911-1986
    See Hubbard, L(afayette) Ron(ald)

Radcliffe, Ann (Ward) 1764-1823 .. NCLC 6
    See also DLB 39

Radiguet, Raymond 1903-1923 .... TCLC 29

Radnoti, Miklos 1909-1944 ...... TCLC 16
    See also CA 118

Rado, James 1939-................ CLC 17
    See also CA 105

Radomski, James 1932-
    See Rado, James

Radvanyi, Netty Reiling 1900-1983
    See Seghers, Anna
    See also CA 85-88; obituary CA 110

Rae, Ben 1935-
    See Griffiths, Trevor

Raeburn, John 1941- .... CLC 34
    See also CA 57-60

Ragni, Gerome 1942-............. CLC 17
    See also CA 105

Rahv, Philip 1908-1973 .... CLC 24
    See also Greenberg, Ivan

Raine, Craig 1944-............... CLC 32
    See also CA 108; DLB 40

Raine, Kathleen (Jessie) 1908- ... CLC 7, 45
    See also CA 85-88; DLB 20

Rainis, Janis 1865-1929.......... TCLC 29

Rakosi, Carl 1903-............... CLC 47
    See also Rawley, Callman
    See also CAAS 5

Ramos, Graciliano 1892-1953 ..... TCLC 32

Rampersad, Arnold 19??-.......... CLC 44

Ramuz, Charles-Ferdinand
    1878-1947 .... TCLC 33

Rand, Ayn 1905-1982........ CLC 3, 30, 44
    See also CA 13-16R; obituary CA 105

Randall, Dudley (Felker) 1914-...... CLC 1
    See also CANR 23; CA 25-28R; DLB 41

Ransom, John Crowe
    1888-1974 .... CLC 2, 4, 5, 11, 24
    See also CANR 6; CA 5-8R;
    obituary CA 49-52; DLB 45, 63

Rao, Raja 1909- .... CLC 25, 56
    See also CA 73-76

Raphael, Frederic (Michael)
    1931-..................... CLC 2, 14
    See also CANR 1; CA 1-4R; DLB 14

Rathbone, Julian 1935- .... CLC 41
    See also CA 101

Rattigan, Terence (Mervyn)
    1911-1977 .... CLC 7
    See also CA 85-88; obituary CA 73-76;
    DLB 13

Ratushinskaya, Irina 1954- .... CLC 54

Raven, Simon (Arthur Noel)
    1927-..................... CLC 14
    See also CA 81-84

Rawley, Callman 1903-
    See Rakosi, Carl
    See also CANR 12; CA 21-24R

Rawlings, Marjorie Kinnan
    1896-1953 .... TCLC 4
    See also YABC 1; CA 104; DLB 9, 22

Ray, Satyajit 1921-................ CLC 16
    See also CA 114

Read, Herbert (Edward) 1893-1968 .. CLC 4
    See also CA 85-88; obituary CA 25-28R;
    DLB 20

Read, Piers Paul 1941- ...... CLC 4, 10, 25
    See also CA 21-24R; SATA 21; DLB 14

Reade, Charles 1814-1884 .... NCLC 2
    See also DLB 21

Reade, Hamish 1936-
    See Gray, Simon (James Holliday)

Reading, Peter 1946- .... CLC 47
    See also CA 103; DLB 40

Reaney, James 1926-............. CLC 13
    See also CA 41-44R; SATA 43; DLB 68

Rebreanu, Liviu 1885-1944 .... TCLC 28

Rechy, John (Francisco)
1934- . . . . CLC 1, 7, 14, 18
See also CAAS 4; CANR 6; CA 5-8R;
DLB-Y 82

Redcam, Tom 1870-1933 . . . . TCLC 25

Redgrove, Peter (William)
1932- . . . . CLC 6, 41
See also CANR 3; CA 1-4R; DLB 40

Redmon (Nightingale), Anne
1943- . . . . CLC 22
See also Nightingale, Anne Redmon
See also DLB-Y 86

Reed, Ishmael 1938- . . CLC 2, 3, 5, 6, 13, 32
See also CA 21-24R; DLB 2, 5, 33

Reed, John (Silas) 1887-1920 . . . . . . TCLC 9
See also CA 106

Reed, Lou 1944- . . . . CLC 21

Reeve, Clara 1729-1807 . . . . NCLC 19
See also DLB 39

Reid, Christopher 1949- . . . . CLC 33
See also DLB 40

Reid Banks, Lynne 1929-
See Banks, Lynne Reid
See also CANR 6, 22; CA 1-4R; SATA 22

Reiner, Max 1900-
See Caldwell, (Janet Miriam) Taylor
(Holland)

Reizenstein, Elmer Leopold 1892-1967
See Rice, Elmer

Remark, Erich Paul 1898-1970
See Remarque, Erich Maria

Remarque, Erich Maria
1898-1970 . . . . CLC 21
See also CA 77-80; obituary CA 29-32R;
DLB 56

Remizov, Alexey (Mikhailovich)
1877-1957 . . . . TCLC 27
See also CA 125

Renan, Joseph Ernest
1823-1892 . . . . NCLC 26

Renard, Jules 1864-1910 . . . . TCLC 17
See also CA 117

Renault, Mary 1905-1983 . . . . CLC 3, 11, 17
See also Challans, Mary
See also DLB-Y 83

Rendell, Ruth 1930- . . . . CLC 28, 48
See also Vine, Barbara
See also CA 109

Renoir, Jean 1894-1979 . . . . CLC 20
See also obituary CA 85-88

Resnais, Alain 1922- . . . . CLC 16

Reverdy, Pierre 1899-1960 . . . . CLC 53
See also CA 97-100; obituary CA 89-92

Rexroth, Kenneth
1905-1982 . . . . . . CLC 1, 2, 6, 11, 22, 49
See also CANR 14; CA 5-8R;
obituary CA 107; DLB 16, 48; DLB-Y 82;
CDALB 1941-1968

Reyes, Alfonso 1889-1959 . . . . TCLC 33

Reyes y Basoalto, Ricardo Eliecer Neftali
1904-1973
See Neruda, Pablo

Reymont, Wladyslaw Stanislaw
1867-1925 . . . . TCLC 5
See also CA 104

Reynolds, Jonathan 1942?- . . . . . . CLC 6, 38
See also CA 65-68

Reynolds, Michael (Shane) 1937- . . . CLC 44
See also CANR 9; CA 65-68

Reznikoff, Charles 1894-1976 . . . . CLC 9
See also CAP 2; CA 33-36;
obituary CA 61-64; DLB 28, 45

Rezzori, Gregor von 1914- . . . . CLC 25
See also CA 122

Rhys, Jean
1890-1979 . . . . . . CLC 2, 4, 6, 14, 19, 51
See also CA 25-28R; obituary CA 85-88;
DLB 36

Ribeiro, Darcy 1922- . . . . CLC 34
See also CA 33-36R

Ribeiro, Joao Ubaldo (Osorio Pimentel)
1941- . . . . CLC 10
See also CA 81-84

Ribman, Ronald (Burt) 1932- . . . . CLC 7
See also CA 21-24R

Rice, Anne 1941- . . . . CLC 41
See also CANR 12; CA 65-68

Rice, Elmer 1892-1967. . . . . CLC 7, 49
See also CAP 2; CA 21-22;
obituary CA 25-28R; DLB 4, 7

Rice, Tim 1944- . . . . CLC 21
See also CA 103

Rich, Adrienne (Cecile)
1929- . . . . CLC 3, 6, 7, 11, 18, 36
See also CANR 20; CA 9-12R; DLB 5, 67

Richard, Keith 1943- . . . . CLC 17
See also CA 107

Richards, I(vor) A(rmstrong)
1893-1979 . . . . CLC 14, 24
See also CA 41-44R; obituary CA 89-92;
DLB 27

Richards, Keith 1943-
See Richard, Keith
See also CA 107

Richardson, Dorothy (Miller)
1873-1957 . . . . TCLC 3
See also CA 104; DLB 36

Richardson, Ethel 1870-1946
See Richardson, Henry Handel
See also CA 105

Richardson, Henry Handel
1870-1946 . . . . TCLC 4
See also Richardson, Ethel

Richardson, Samuel 1689-1761 . . . . LC 1
See also DLB 39

Richler, Mordecai
1931- . . . . CLC 3, 5, 9, 13, 18, 46
See also CA 65-68; SATA 27, 44; DLB 53

Richter, Conrad (Michael)
1890-1968 . . . . CLC 30
See also CA 5-8R; obituary CA 25-28R;
SATA 3; DLB 9

Richter, Johann Paul Friedrich 1763-1825
See Jean Paul

Riding, Laura 1901- . . . . CLC 3, 7
See also Jackson, Laura (Riding)

Riefenstahl, Berta Helene Amalia
1902- . . . . CLC 16
See also Riefenstahl, Leni
See also CA 108

Riefenstahl, Leni 1902- . . . . CLC 16
See also Riefenstahl, Berta Helene Amalia
See also CA 108

Rilke, Rainer Maria
1875-1926 . . . . TCLC 1, 6, 19
See also CA 104

Rimbaud, (Jean Nicolas) Arthur
1854-1891 . . . . NCLC 4

Ringwood, Gwen(dolyn Margaret) Pharis
1910-1984 . . . . CLC 48
See also obituary CA 112

Rio, Michel 19??- . . . . CLC 43

Ritsos, Yannis 1909- . . . . . . CLC 6, 13, 31
See also CA 77-80

Ritter, Erika 1948?- . . . . CLC 52

Rivera, Jose Eustasio 1889-1928. . . TCLC 35

Rivers, Conrad Kent 1933-1968. . . . . . CLC 1
See also CA 85-88; DLB 41

Roa Bastos, Augusto 1917- . . . . CLC 45

Robbe-Grillet, Alain
1922- . . . . . . CLC 1, 2, 4, 6, 8, 10, 14, 43
See also CA 9-12R

Robbins, Harold 1916- . . . . CLC 5
See also CANR 26; CA 73-76

Robbins, Thomas Eugene 1936-
See Robbins, Tom
See also CA 81-84

Robbins, Tom 1936- . . . . CLC 9, 32
See also Robbins, Thomas Eugene
See also DLB-Y 80

Robbins, Trina 1938- . . . . CLC 21

Roberts, (Sir) Charles G(eorge) D(ouglas)
1860-1943 . . . . TCLC 8
See also CA 105; SATA 29

Roberts, Kate 1891-1985 . . . . CLC 15
See also CA 107; obituary CA 116

Roberts, Keith (John Kingston)
1935- . . . . CLC 14
See also CA 25-28R

Roberts, Kenneth 1885-1957 . . . . . . TCLC 23
See also CA 109; DLB 9

Roberts, Michele (B.) 1949- . . . . CLC 48
See also CA 115

Robinson, Edwin Arlington
1869-1935 . . . . TCLC 5
See also CA 104; DLB 54;
CDALB 1865-1917

Robinson, Henry Crabb
1775-1867 . . . . NCLC 15

Robinson, Jill 1936- . . . . CLC 10
See also CA 102

Robinson, Kim Stanley 19??- . . . . CLC 34
See also CA 126

Robinson, Marilynne 1944- . . . . CLC 25
See also CA 116

Robinson, Smokey 1940- . . . . CLC 21

Robinson, William 1940-
See Robinson, Smokey
See also CA 116

Sagan, Francoise
    1935- . . . . CLC 3, 6, 9, 17, 36
    See also Quoirez, Francoise
    See also CANR 6

Sahgal, Nayantara (Pandit) 1927- . . . CLC 41
    See also CANR 11; CA 9-12R

Saint, H(arry) F. 1941- . . . . CLC 50

Sainte-Beuve, Charles Augustin
    1804-1869 . . . . NCLC 5

Sainte-Marie, Beverly 1941-
    See Sainte-Marie, Buffy
    See also CA 107

Sainte-Marie, Buffy 1941- . . . . CLC 17
    See also Sainte-Marie, Beverly

Saint-Exupery, Antoine (Jean Baptiste Marie
    Roger) de 1900-1944 . . . . TCLC 2
    See also CLR 10; CA 108; SATA 20;
    DLB 72

Saintsbury, George 1845-1933 . . . . . TCLC 31
    See also DLB 57

Sait Faik (Abasiyanik)
    1906-1954 . . . . TCLC 23

Saki 1870-1916 . . . . TCLC 3
    See also Munro, H(ector) H(ugh)
    See also CA 104

Salama, Hannu 1936- . . . . CLC 18

Salamanca, J(ack) R(ichard)
    1922- . . . . CLC 4, 15
    See also CA 25-28R

Salinas, Pedro 1891-1951 . . . . TCLC 17
    See also CA 117

Salinger, J(erome) D(avid)
    1919- . . . . CLC 1, 3, 8, 12, 56; SSC 2
    See also CA 5-8R; DLB 2;
    CDALB 1941-1968

Salter, James 1925- . . . . CLC 7, 52
    See also CA 73-76

Saltus, Edgar (Evertson)
    1855-1921 . . . . TCLC 8
    See also CA 105

Saltykov, Mikhail Evgrafovich
    1826-1889 . . . . NCLC 16

Samarakis, Antonis 1919- . . . . CLC 5
    See also CA 25-28R

Sanchez, Luis Rafael 1936- . . . . CLC 23

Sanchez, Sonia 1934- . . . . CLC 5
    See also CA 33-36R; SATA 22; DLB 41

Sand, George 1804-1876 . . . . NCLC 2

Sandburg, Carl (August)
    1878-1967 . . . . CLC 1, 4, 10, 15, 35
    See also CA 5-8R; obituary CA 25-28R;
    SATA 8; DLB 17, 54; CDALB 1865-1917

Sandburg, Charles August 1878-1967
    See Sandburg, Carl (August)

Sanders, (James) Ed(ward) 1939- . . . CLC 53
    See also CANR 13; CA 15-16R, 103;
    DLB 16

Sanders, Lawrence 1920- . . . . CLC 41
    See also CA 81-84

Sandoz, Mari (Susette) 1896-1966 . . CLC 28
    See also CANR 17; CA 1-4R;
    obituary CA 25-28R; SATA 5; DLB 9

Saner, Reg(inald Anthony) 1931- . . . . CLC 9
    See also CA 65-68

Sannazaro, Jacopo 1456?-1530 . . . . LC 8

Sansom, William 1912-1976 . . . . . . CLC 2, 6
    See also CA 5-8R; obituary CA 65-68

Santiago, Danny 1911- . . . . CLC 33
    See also CA 125

Santmyer, Helen Hooven
    1895-1986 . . . . CLC 33
    See also CANR 15; CA 1-4R;
    obituary CA 118; DLB-Y 84

Santos, Bienvenido N(uqui) 1911- . . . CLC 22
    See also CANR 19; CA 101

Sappho c. 6th-century B.C.- . . . . CMLC 3

Sarduy, Severo 1937- . . . . CLC 6
    See also CA 89-92

Sargeson, Frank 1903-1982 . . . . CLC 31
    See also CA 106, 25-28R; obituary CA 106

Sarmiento, Felix Ruben Garcia 1867-1916
    See also CA 104

Saroyan, William
    1908-1981 . . . . . CLC 1, 8, 10, 29, 34, 56
    See also CA 5-8R; obituary CA 103;
    SATA 23; obituary SATA 24; DLB 7, 9;
    DLB-Y 81

Sarraute, Nathalie
    1902- . . . . CLC 1, 2, 4, 8, 10, 31
    See also CANR 23; CA 9-12R

Sarton, Eleanore Marie 1912-
    See Sarton, (Eleanor) May

Sarton, (Eleanor) May
    1912- . . . . CLC 4, 14, 49
    See also CANR 1; CA 1-4R; SATA 36;
    DLB 48; DLB-Y 81

Sartre, Jean-Paul (Charles Aymard)
    1905-1980 . . . CLC 1, 4, 7, 9, 13, 18, 24,
                                        44, 50, 52
    See also CANR 21; CA 9-12R;
    obituary CA 97-100; DLB 72

Sassoon, Siegfried (Lorraine)
    1886-1967 . . . . CLC 36
    See also CA 104; obituary CA 25-28R;
    DLB 20

Saul, John (W. III) 1942- . . . . CLC 46
    See also CANR 16; CA 81-84

Saura, Carlos 1932- . . . . CLC 20
    See also CA 114

Sauser-Hall, Frederic-Louis 1887-1961
    See Cendrars, Blaise
    See also CA 102; obituary CA 93-96

Savage, Thomas 1915- . . . . CLC 40

Savan, Glenn 19??- . . . . CLC 50

Sayers, Dorothy L(eigh)
    1893-1957 . . . . TCLC 2, 15
    See also CA 104, 119; DLB 10, 36

Sayers, Valerie 19??- . . . . CLC 50

Sayles, John (Thomas)
    1950- . . . . CLC 7, 10, 14
    See also CA 57-60; DLB 44

Scammell, Michael 19??- . . . . CLC 34

Scannell, Vernon 1922- . . . . CLC 49
    See also CANR 8; CA 5-8R; DLB 27

Schaeffer, Susan Fromberg
    1941- . . . . CLC 6, 11, 22
    See also CANR 18; CA 49-52; SATA 22;
    DLB 28

Schell, Jonathan 1943- . . . . CLC 35
    See also CANR 12; CA 73-76

Scherer, Jean-Marie Maurice 1920-
    See Rohmer, Eric
    See also CA 110

Schevill, James (Erwin) 1920- . . . . . . CLC 7
    See also CA 5-8R

Schisgal, Murray (Joseph) 1926- . . . . . CLC 6
    See also CA 21-24R

Schlee, Ann 1934- . . . . CLC 35
    See also CA 101; SATA 36, 44

Schlegel, August Wilhelm von
    1767-1845 . . . . NCLC 15

Schlegel, Johann Elias (von)
    1719?-1749 . . . . LC 5

Schmidt, Arno 1914-1979 . . . . CLC 56
    See also obituary CA 109; DLB 69

Schmitz, Ettore 1861-1928
    See Svevo, Italo
    See also CA 104, 122

Schnackenberg, Gjertrud 1953- . . . . . CLC 40
    See also CA 116

Schneider, Leonard Alfred 1925-1966
    See Bruce, Lenny
    See also CA 89-92

Schnitzler, Arthur 1862-1931 . . . . . . TCLC 4
    See also CA 104

Schorer, Mark 1908-1977 . . . . CLC 9
    See also CANR 7; CA 5-8R;
    obituary CA 73-76

Schrader, Paul (Joseph) 1946- . . . . . CLC 26
    See also CA 37-40R; DLB 44

Schreiner (Cronwright), Olive (Emilie
    Albertina) 1855-1920 . . . . TCLC 9
    See also CA 105; DLB 18

Schulberg, Budd (Wilson)
    1914- . . . . CLC 7, 48
    See also CANR 19; CA 25-28R; DLB 6, 26,
    28; DLB-Y 81

Schulz, Bruno 1892-1942 . . . . TCLC 5
    See also CA 115, 123

Schulz, Charles M(onroe) 1922- . . . . CLC 12
    See also CANR 6; CA 9-12R; SATA 10

Schuyler, James (Marcus)
    1923- . . . . CLC 5, 23
    See also CA 101; DLB 5

Schwartz, Delmore
    1913-1966 . . . . CLC 2, 4, 10, 45
    See also CAP 2; CA 17-18;
    obituary CA 25-28R; DLB 28, 48

Schwartz, Lynne Sharon 1939- . . . . . CLC 31
    See also CA 103

Schwarz-Bart, Andre 1928- . . . . CLC 2, 4
    See also CA 89-92

Schwarz-Bart, Simone 1938- . . . . CLC 7
    See also CA 97-100

Schwob, (Mayer Andre) Marcel
    1867-1905 . . . . TCLC 20
    See also CA 117

Sciascia, Leonardo
    1921-1989 . . . . CLC 8, 9, 41
    See also CA 85-88

Scoppettone, Sandra 1936- . . . . CLC 26
    See also CA 5-8R; SATA 9

Shuster, Joe 1914- . . . . **CLC 21**

Shute (Norway), Nevil 1899-1960 . . . **CLC 30**
See also Norway, Nevil Shute
See also CA 102; obituary CA 93-96

Shuttle, Penelope (Diane) 1947- . . . . . **CLC 7**
See also CA 93-96; DLB 14, 40

Siegel, Jerome 1914- . . . . **CLC 21**
See also CA 116

Sienkiewicz, Henryk (Adam Aleksander Pius)
1846-1916 . . . . **TCLC 3**
See also CA 104

Sigal, Clancy 1926- . . . . **CLC 7**
See also CA 1-4R

Sigourney, Lydia (Howard Huntley)
1791-1865 . . . . **NCLC 21**
See also DLB 1, 42, 73

Siguenza y Gongora, Carlos de
1645-1700 . . . . **LC 8**

Sigurjonsson, Johann 1880-1919 . . . **TCLC 27**

Silkin, Jon 1930- . . . . **CLC 2, 6, 43**
See also CAAS 5; CA 5-8R; DLB 27

Silko, Leslie Marmon 1948- . . . . **CLC 23**
See also CA 115, 122

Sillanpaa, Franz Eemil 1888-1964 . . . **CLC 19**
See also obituary CA 93-96

Sillitoe, Alan
1928- . . . . **CLC 1, 3, 6, 10, 19, 57**
See also CAAS 2; CANR 8, 26; CA 9-12R;
DLB 14

Silone, Ignazio 1900-1978 . . . . **CLC 4**
See also CAAS 2; CANR 26; CAP 2;
CA 25-28, 11-12R,; obituary CA 81-84

Silver, Joan Micklin 1935- . . . . **CLC 20**
See also CA 114, 121

Silverberg, Robert 1935- . . . . **CLC 7**
See also CAAS 3; CANR 1, 20; CA 1-4R;
SATA 13; DLB 8

Silverstein, Alvin 1933- . . . . **CLC 17**
See also CANR 2; CA 49-52; SATA 8

Silverstein, Virginia B(arbara Opshelor)
1937- . . . . **CLC 17**
See also CANR 2; CA 49-52; SATA 8

Simak, Clifford D(onald)
1904-1988 . . . . **CLC 1, 55**
See also CANR 1; CA 1-4R;
obituary CA 125; DLB 8

Simenon, Georges (Jacques Christian)
1903-1989 . . . . **CLC 1, 2, 3, 8, 18, 47**
See also CA 85-88; DLB 72

Simenon, Paul 1956?-
See The Clash

Simic, Charles 1938- . . . . **CLC 6, 9, 22, 49**
See also CAAS 4; CANR 12; CA 29-32R

Simmons, Charles (Paul) 1924- . . . . . **CLC 57**
See also CA 89-92

Simmons, Dan 1948- . . . . **CLC 44**

Simmons, James (Stewart Alexander)
1933- . . . . **CLC 43**
See also CA 105; DLB 40

Simms, William Gilmore
1806-1870 . . . . **NCLC 3**
See also DLB 3, 30

Simon, Carly 1945- . . . . **CLC 26**
See also CA 105

Simon, Claude (Henri Eugene)
1913- . . . . **CLC 4, 9, 15, 39**
See also CA 89-92

Simon, (Marvin) Neil
1927- . . . . **CLC 6, 11, 31, 39**
See also CA 21-24R; DLB 7

Simon, Paul 1941- . . . . **CLC 17**
See also CA 116

Simonon, Paul 1956?-
See The Clash

Simpson, Louis (Aston Marantz)
1923- . . . . **CLC 4, 7, 9, 32**
See also CAAS 4; CANR 1; CA 1-4R;
DLB 5

Simpson, Mona (Elizabeth) 1957- . . . **CLC 44**
See also CA 122

Simpson, N(orman) F(rederick)
1919- . . . . **CLC 29**
See also CA 11-14R; DLB 13

Sinclair, Andrew (Annandale)
1935- . . . . **CLC 2, 14**
See also CAAS 5; CANR 14; CA 9-12R;
DLB 14

Sinclair, Mary Amelia St. Clair 1865?-1946
See Sinclair, May
See also CA 104

Sinclair, May 1865?-1946 . . . . . . **TCLC 3, 11**
See also Sinclair, Mary Amelia St. Clair
See also DLB 36

Sinclair, Upton (Beall)
1878-1968 . . . . **CLC 1, 11, 15**
See also CANR 7; CA 5-8R;
obituary CA 25-28R; SATA 9; DLB 9

Singer, Isaac Bashevis
1904- . . . . **CLC 1, 3, 6, 9, 11, 15, 23, 38;**
SSC 3
See also CLR 1; CANR 1; CA 1-4R;
SATA 3, 27; DLB 6, 28, 52;
CDALB 1941-1968

Singer, Israel Joshua 1893-1944 . . . **TCLC 33**

Singh, Khushwant 1915- . . . . **CLC 11**
See also CANR 6; CA 9-12R

Sinyavsky, Andrei (Donatevich)
1925- . . . . **CLC 8**
See also CA 85-88

Sirin, V.
See Nabokov, Vladimir (Vladimirovich)

Sissman, L(ouis) E(dward)
1928-1976 . . . . **CLC 9, 18**
See also CANR 13; CA 21-24R;
obituary CA 65-68; DLB 5

Sisson, C(harles) H(ubert) 1914- . . . . . **CLC 8**
See also CAAS 3; CANR 3; CA 1-4R;
DLB 27

Sitwell, (Dame) Edith 1887-1964 . . . **CLC 2, 9**
See also CA 9-12R; DLB 20

Sjoewall, Maj 1935-
See Wahloo, Per
See also CA 61-64, 65-68

Sjowall, Maj 1935-
See Wahloo, Per

Skelton, Robin 1925- . . . . **CLC 13**
See also CAAS 5; CA 5-8R; DLB 27, 53

Skolimowski, Jerzy 1938- . . . . **CLC 20**

Skolimowski, Yurek 1938-
See Skolimowski, Jerzy

Skram, Amalie (Bertha)
1847-1905 . . . . **TCLC 25**

Skrine, Mary Nesta 1904-
See Keane, Molly

Skvorecky, Josef (Vaclav)
1924- . . . . **CLC 15, 39**
See also CAAS 1; CANR 10; CA 61-64

Slade, Bernard 1930- . . . . **CLC 11, 46**
See also Newbound, Bernard Slade
See also DLB 53

Slaughter, Carolyn 1946- . . . . **CLC 56**
See also CA 85-88

Slaughter, Frank G(ill) 1908- . . . . **CLC 29**
See also CANR 5; CA 5-8R

Slavitt, David (R.) 1935- . . . . **CLC 5, 14**
See also CAAS 3; CA 21-24R; DLB 5, 6

Slesinger, Tess 1905-1945 . . . . **TCLC 10**
See also CA 107

Slessor, Kenneth 1901-1971 . . . . **CLC 14**
See also CA 102; obituary CA 89-92

Slowacki, Juliusz 1809-1849 . . . . . **NCLC 15**

Smart, Christopher 1722-1771 . . . . **LC 3**

Smart, Elizabeth 1913-1986 . . . . **CLC 54**
See also CA 81-84; obituary CA 118

Smiley, Jane (Graves) 1949- . . . . **CLC 53**
See also CA 104

Smith, A(rthur) J(ames) M(arshall)
1902-1980 . . . . **CLC 15**
See also CANR 4; CA 1-4R;
obituary CA 102

Smith, Betty (Wehner) 1896-1972 . . . **CLC 19**
See also CA 5-8R; obituary CA 33-36R;
SATA 6; DLB-Y 82

Smith, Cecil Lewis Troughton 1899-1966
See Forester, C(ecil) S(cott)

Smith, Charlotte (Turner)
1749-1806 . . . . **NCLC 23**
See also DLB 39

Smith, Clark Ashton 1893-1961 . . . . **CLC 43**

Smith, Dave 1942- . . . . **CLC 22, 42**
See also Smith, David (Jeddie)
See also CAAS 7; CANR 1; DLB 5

Smith, David (Jeddie) 1942-
See Smith, Dave
See also CANR 1; CA 49-52

Smith, Florence Margaret 1902-1971
See Smith, Stevie
See also CAP 2; CA 17-18;
obituary CA 29-32R

Smith, John 1580?-1631 . . . . **LC 9**
See also DLB 24, 30

Smith, Lee 1944- . . . . **CLC 25**
See also CA 114, 119; DLB-Y 83

Smith, Martin Cruz 1942- . . . . **CLC 25**
See also CANR 6; CA 85-88

Smith, Martin William 1942-
See Smith, Martin Cruz

Smith, Mary-Ann Tirone 1944- . . . . . **CLC 39**
See also CA 118

Smith, Patti 1946- . . . . **CLC 12**
See also CA 93-96

Smith, Pauline (Urmson)
1882-1959 .... TCLC 25
See also CA 29-32R; SATA 27

Smith, Rosamond 1938-
See Oates, Joyce Carol

Smith, Sara Mahala Redway 1900-1972
See Benson, Sally

Smith, Stevie 1902-1971.... CLC 3, 8, 25, 44
See also Smith, Florence Margaret
See also DLB 20

Smith, Wilbur (Addison) 1933- ..... CLC 33
See also CANR 7; CA 13-16R

Smith, William Jay 1918- .... CLC 6
See also CA 5-8R; SATA 2; DLB 5

Smollett, Tobias (George) 1721-1771 .. LC 2
See also DLB 39

Snodgrass, W(illiam) D(e Witt)
1926- .... CLC 2, 6, 10, 18
See also CANR 6; CA 1-4R; DLB 5

Snow, C(harles) P(ercy)
1905-1980 .... CLC 1, 4, 6, 9, 13, 19
See also CA 5-8R; obituary CA 101;
DLB 15

Snyder, Gary (Sherman)
1930- .... CLC 1, 2, 5, 9, 32
See also CA 17-20R; DLB 5, 16

Snyder, Zilpha Keatley 1927- ...... CLC 17
See also CA 9-12R; SAAS 2; SATA 1, 28

Sodergran, Edith 1892-1923....... TCLC 31

Sokolov, Raymond 1941- .... CLC 7
See also CA 85-88

Sologub, Fyodor 1863-1927 .... TCLC 9
See also Teternikov, Fyodor Kuzmich
See also CA 104

Solomos, Dionysios 1798-1857 ... NCLC 15

Solwoska, Mara 1929-
See French, Marilyn
See also CANR 3; CA 69-72

Solzhenitsyn, Aleksandr I(sayevich)
1918- ... CLC 1, 2, 4, 7, 9, 10, 18, 26, 34
See also CA 69-72

Somers, Jane 1919-
See Lessing, Doris (May)

Sommer, Scott 1951- .... CLC 25
See also CA 106

Sondheim, Stephen (Joshua)
1930- .... CLC 30, 39
See also CA 103

Sontag, Susan 1933-... CLC 1, 2, 10, 13, 31
See also CA 17-20R; DLB 2

Sophocles
c. 496? B.C.-c. 406? B.C. ...... CMLC 2

Sorrentino, Gilbert
1929- .... CLC 3, 7, 14, 22, 40
See also CANR 14; CA 77-80; DLB 5;
DLB-Y 80

Soto, Gary 1952-................. CLC 32
See also CA 119

Souster, (Holmes) Raymond
1921- .... CLC 5, 14
See also CANR 13; CA 13-16R

Southern, Terry 1926- .... CLC 7
See also CANR 1; CA 1-4R; DLB 2

Southey, Robert 1774-1843 .... NCLC 8

Southworth, Emma Dorothy Eliza Nevitte
1819-1899 .... NCLC 26

Soyinka, Akinwande Oluwole 1934-
See Soyinka, Wole

Soyinka, Wole 1934- .. CLC 3, 5, 14, 36, 44
See also CA 13-16R; DLB-Y 86

Spackman, W(illiam) M(ode)
1905- .... CLC 46
See also CA 81-84

Spacks, Barry 1931-.............. CLC 14
See also CA 29-32R

Spanidou, Irini 1946-............. CLC 44

Spark, Muriel (Sarah)
1918- .... CLC 2, 3, 5, 8, 13, 18, 40
See also CANR 12; CA 5-8R; DLB 15

Spencer, Elizabeth 1921- .... CLC 22
See also CA 13-16R; SATA 14; DLB 6

Spencer, Scott 1945-.............. CLC 30
See also CA 113; DLB-Y 86

Spender, Stephen (Harold)
1909- .... CLC 1, 2, 5, 10, 41
See also CA 9-12R; DLB 20

Spengler, Oswald 1880-1936 ...... TCLC 25
See also CA 118

Spenser, Edmund 1552?-1599 .... LC 5

Spicer, Jack 1925-1965 .... CLC 8, 18
See also CA 85-88; DLB 5, 16

Spielberg, Peter 1929- .... CLC 6
See also CANR 4; CA 5-8R; DLB-Y 81

Spielberg, Steven 1947- .... CLC 20
See also CA 77-80; SATA 32

Spillane, Frank Morrison 1918-
See Spillane, Mickey
See also CA 25-28R

Spillane, Mickey 1918- .... CLC 3, 13
See also Spillane, Frank Morrison

Spinoza, Benedictus de 1632-1677 .... LC 9

Spinrad, Norman (Richard) 1940-... CLC 46
See also CANR 20; CA 37-40R; DLB 8

Spitteler, Carl (Friedrich Georg)
1845-1924 .... TCLC 12
See also CA 109

Spivack, Kathleen (Romola Drucker)
1938- .... CLC 6
See also CA 49-52

Spoto, Donald 1941-.............. CLC 39
See also CANR 11; CA 65-68

Springsteen, Bruce 1949- .... CLC 17
See also CA 111

Spurling, Hilary 1940-............. CLC 34
See also CANR 25; CA 104

Squires, (James) Radcliffe 1917-.... CLC 51
See also CANR 6, 21; CA 1-4R

**Stael-Holstein, Anne Louise Germaine Necker,
Baronne de** 1766-1817....... NCLC 3

Stafford, Jean 1915-1979...... CLC 4, 7, 19
See also CANR 3; CA 1-4R;
obituary CA 85-88; obituary SATA 22;
DLB 2

Stafford, William (Edgar)
1914- .... CLC 4, 7, 29
See also CAAS 3; CANR 5, 22; CA 5-8R;
DLB 5

Stannard, Martin 1947- .... CLC 44

Stanton, Maura 1946- .... CLC 9
See also CANR 15; CA 89-92

Stapledon, (William) Olaf
1886-1950 .... TCLC 22
See also CA 111; DLB 15

Starbuck, George (Edwin) 1931-.... CLC 53
See also CANR 23; CA 21-22R

Stark, Richard 1933-
See Westlake, Donald E(dwin)

Stead, Christina (Ellen)
1902-1983 .... CLC 2, 5, 8, 32
See also CA 13-16R; obituary CA 109

Steele, Timothy (Reid) 1948-....... CLC 45
See also CANR 16; CA 93-96

Steffens, (Joseph) Lincoln
1866-1936 .... TCLC 20
See also CA 117; SAAS 1

Stegner, Wallace (Earle) 1909-... CLC 9, 49
See also CANR 1, 21; CA 1-4R; DLB 9

Stein, Gertrude 1874-1946... TCLC 1, 6, 28
See also CA 104; DLB 4, 54

Steinbeck, John (Ernst)
1902-1968 ... CLC 1, 5, 9, 13, 21, 34, 45
See also CANR 1; CA 1-4R;
obituary CA 25-28R; SATA 9; DLB 7, 9;
DLB-DS 2

Steiner, George 1929-............. CLC 24
See also CA 73-76

Steiner, Rudolf(us Josephus Laurentius)
1861-1925 .... TCLC 13
See also CA 107

Stendhal 1783-1842............. NCLC 23

Stephen, Leslie 1832-1904........ TCLC 23
See also CANR 9; CA 21-24R, 123;
DLB 57

Stephens, James 1882?-1950 .... TCLC 4
See also CA 104; DLB 19

Stephens, Reed
See Donaldson, Stephen R.

Steptoe, Lydia 1892-1982
See Barnes, Djuna

Sterling, George 1869-1926 .... TCLC 20
See also CA 117; DLB 54

Stern, Gerald 1925- .... CLC 40
See also CA 81-84

Stern, Richard G(ustave) 1928-... CLC 4, 39
See also CANR 1, 25; CA 1-4R

Sternberg, Jonas 1894-1969
See Sternberg, Josef von

Sternberg, Josef von 1894-1969..... CLC 20
See also CA 81-84

Sterne, Laurence 1713-1768.......... LC 2
See also DLB 39

Sternheim, (William Adolf) Carl
1878-1942 .... TCLC 8
See also CA 105

Stevens, Mark 19??-.............. CLC 34

Stevens, Wallace 1879-1955..... TCLC 3, 12
See also CA 104, 124; DLB 54

Tarkington, (Newton) Booth
   1869-1946 . . . . TCLC 9
   See also CA 110; SATA 17; DLB 9

Tasso, Torquato 1544-1595 . . . . LC 5

Tate, (John Orley) Allen
   1899-1979 . . . . CLC 2, 4, 6, 9, 11, 14, 24
   See also CA 5-8R; obituary CA 85-88;
   DLB 4, 45, 63

Tate, James 1943- . . . . CLC 2, 6, 25
   See also CA 21-24R; DLB 5

Tavel, Ronald 1940- . . . . CLC 6
   See also CA 21-24R

Taylor, C(ecil) P(hillip) 1929-1981 . . CLC 27
   See also CA 25-28R; obituary CA 105

Taylor, Edward 1644?-1729 . . . . LC 11
   See also DLB 24

Taylor, Eleanor Ross 1920- . . . . CLC 5
   See also CA 81-84

Taylor, Elizabeth 1912-1975 . . . CLC 2, 4, 29
   See also CANR 9; CA 13-16R; SATA 13

Taylor, Henry (Splawn) 1917- . . : . . . CLC 44
   See also CAAS 7; CA 33-36R; DLB 5

Taylor, Kamala (Purnaiya) 1924-
   See Markandaya, Kamala
   See also CA 77-80

Taylor, Mildred D(elois) 1943- . . . . . CLC 21
   See also CLR 9; CANR 25; CA 85-88;
   SAAS 5; SATA 15; DLB 52

Taylor, Peter (Hillsman)
   1917- . . . . . . CLC 1, 4, 18, 37, 44, 50
   See also CANR 9; CA 13-16R; DLB-Y 81

Taylor, Robert Lewis 1912- . . . . CLC 14
   See also CANR 3; CA 1-4R; SATA 10

Teasdale, Sara 1884-1933 . . . . TCLC 4
   See also CA 104; SATA 32; DLB 45

Tegner, Esaias 1782-1846 . . . . NCLC 2

Teilhard de Chardin, (Marie Joseph) Pierre
   1881-1955 . . . . TCLC 9
   See also CA 105

Tennant, Emma 1937- . . . . CLC 13, 52
   See also CAAS 9; CANR 10; CA 65-68;
   DLB 14

Teran, Lisa St. Aubin de 19??- . . . . . CLC 36

Terkel, Louis 1912-
   See Terkel, Studs
   See also CANR 18; CA 57-60

Terkel, Studs 1912- . . . . CLC 38
   See also Terkel, Louis

Terry, Megan 1932- . . . . CLC 19
   See also CA 77-80; DLB 7

Tertz, Abram 1925-
   See Sinyavsky, Andrei (Donatevich)

Tesich, Steve 1943?- . . . . CLC 40
   See also CA 105; DLB-Y 83

Tesich, Stoyan 1943?-
   See Tesich, Steve

Teternikov, Fyodor Kuzmich 1863-1927
   See Sologub, Fyodor
   See also CA 104

Tevis, Walter 1928-1984 . . . . CLC 42
   See also CA 113

Tey, Josephine 1897-1952 . . . . TCLC 14
   See also Mackintosh, Elizabeth

Thackeray, William Makepeace
   1811-1863 . . . . NCLC 5, 14, 22
   See also SATA 23; DLB 21, 55

Thakura, Ravindranatha 1861-1941
   See Tagore, (Sir) Rabindranath
   See also CA 104

Thelwell, Michael (Miles) 1939- . . . . CLC 22
   See also CA 101

Theroux, Alexander (Louis)
   1939- . . . . CLC 2, 25
   See also CANR 20; CA 85-88

Theroux, Paul
   1941- . . . . CLC 5, 8, 11, 15, 28, 46
   See also CANR 20; CA 33-36R; SATA 44;
   DLB 2

Thesen, Sharon 1946- . . . . CLC 56

Thibault, Jacques Anatole Francois
   1844-1924
   See France, Anatole
   See also CA 106

Thiele, Colin (Milton) 1920- . . . . CLC 17
   See also CANR 12; CA 29-32R; SAAS 2;
   SATA 14

Thomas, Audrey (Grace)
   1935- . . . . CLC 7, 13, 37
   See also CA 21-24R; DLB 60

Thomas, D(onald) M(ichael)
   1935- . . . . CLC 13, 22, 31
   See also CANR 17; CA 61-64; DLB 40

Thomas, Dylan (Marlais)
   1914-1953 . . . . TCLC 1, 8; SSC 3
   See also CA 104, 120; DLB 13, 20

Thomas, Edward (Philip)
   1878-1917 . . . . TCLC 10
   See also CA 106; DLB 19

Thomas, John Peter 1928-
   See Thomas, Piri

Thomas, Joyce Carol 1938- . . . . CLC 35
   See also CA 113, 116; SATA 40; DLB 33

Thomas, Lewis 1913- . . . . CLC 35
   See also CA 85-88

Thomas, Piri 1928- . . . . CLC 17
   See also CA 73-76

Thomas, R(onald) S(tuart)
   1913- . . . . CLC 6, 13, 48
   See also CAAS 4; CA 89-92; DLB 27

Thomas, Ross (Elmore) 1926- . . . . . . CLC 39
   See also CANR 22; CA 33-36R

Thompson, Ernest 1860-1946
   See Seton, Ernest (Evan) Thompson

Thompson, Francis (Joseph)
   1859-1907 . . . . TCLC 4
   See also CA 104; DLB 19

Thompson, Hunter S(tockton)
   1939- . . . . CLC 9, 17, 40
   See also CANR 23; CA 17-20R

Thompson, Judith 1954- . . . . CLC 39

Thomson, James 1834-1882 . . . . . . NCLC 18
   See also DLB 35

Thoreau, Henry David
   1817-1862 . . . . NCLC 7, 21
   See also DLB 1; CDALB 1640-1865

Thurber, James (Grover)
   1894-1961 . . . . . . CLC 5, 11, 25; SSC 1
   See also CANR 17; CA 73-76; SATA 13;
   DLB 4, 11, 22

Thurman, Wallace 1902-1934 . . . . . . TCLC 6
   See also CA 104, 124; DLB 51

Tieck, (Johann) Ludwig
   1773-1853 . . . . NCLC 5

Tillinghast, Richard 1940- . . . . CLC 29
   See also CANR 26; CA 29-32R

Timrod, Henry 1828-1867 . . . . NCLC 25

Tindall, Gillian 1938- . . . . CLC 7
   See also CANR 11; CA 21-24R

Tiptree, James, Jr. 1915-1987 . . . CLC 48, 50
   See also Sheldon, Alice (Hastings) B(radley)
   See also DLB 8

Tocqueville, Alexis (Charles Henri Maurice
   Clerel, Comte) de 1805-1859 . . NCLC 7

Tolkien, J(ohn) R(onald) R(euel)
   1892-1973 . . . . CLC 1, 2, 3, 8, 12, 38
   See also CAP 2; CA 17-18;
   obituary CA 45-48; SATA 2, 32;
   obituary SATA 24; DLB 15

Toller, Ernst 1893-1939 . . . . TCLC 10
   See also CA 107

Tolson, Melvin B(eaunorus)
   1900?-1966 . . . . CLC 36
   See also CA 124; obituary CA 89-92;
   DLB 48, 124

Tolstoy, (Count) Alexey Nikolayevich
   1883-1945 . . . . TCLC 18
   See also CA 107

Tolstoy, (Count) Leo (Lev Nikolaevich)
   1828-1910 . . . . TCLC 4, 11, 17, 28
   See also CA 104, 123; SATA 26

Tomlin, Lily 1939- . . . . CLC 17

Tomlin, Mary Jean 1939-
   See Tomlin, Lily
   See also CA 117

Tomlinson, (Alfred) Charles
   1927- . . . . CLC 2, 4, 6, 13, 45
   See also CA 5-8R; DLB 40

Toole, John Kennedy 1937-1969 . . . . CLC 19
   See also CA 104; DLB-Y 81

Toomer, Jean
   1894-1967 . . . . . CLC 1, 4, 13, 22; SSC 1
   See also CA 85-88; DLB 45, 51

Torrey, E. Fuller 19??- . . . . CLC 34
   See also CA 119

Tournier, Michel 1924- . . . . . . CLC 6, 23, 36
   See also CANR 3; CA 49-52; SATA 23

Townshend, Peter (Dennis Blandford)
   1945- . . . . CLC 17, 42
   See also CA 107

Tozzi, Federigo 1883-1920 . . . . TCLC 31

Trakl, Georg 1887-1914 . . . . TCLC 5
   See also CA 104

Transtromer, Tomas (Gosta)
   1931- . . . . CLC 52
   See also CA 117

Traven, B. 1890-1969 . . . . CLC 8, 11
   See also CAP 2; CA 19-20;
   obituary CA 25-28R; DLB 9, 56

Tremain, Rose   1943-.............. **CLC 42**
  See also CA 97-100; DLB 14

Tremblay, Michel   1942-.......... **CLC 29**
  See also CA 116; DLB 60

Trevanian   1925- .... **CLC 29**
  See also CA 108

Trevor, William   1928- ..... **CLC 7, 9, 14, 25**
  See also Cox, William Trevor
  See also DLB 14

Trifonov, Yuri (Valentinovich)
      1925-1981 .... **CLC 45**
  See also obituary CA 103, 126

Trilling, Lionel   1905-1975 .... **CLC 9, 11, 24**
  See also CANR 10; CA 9-12R;
      obituary CA 61-64; DLB 28, 63

Trogdon, William   1939-
  See Heat Moon, William Least
  See also CA 115, 119

Trollope, Anthony   1815-1882 ..... **NCLC 6**
  See also SATA 22; DLB 21, 57

Trotsky, Leon (Davidovich)
      1879-1940 .... **TCLC 22**
  See also CA 118

Trotter (Cockburn), Catharine
      1679-1749 .... **LC 8**

Trow, George W. S.   1943-......... **CLC 52**
  See also CA 126

Troyat, Henri   1911-............. **CLC 23**
  See also CANR 2; CA 45-48

Trudeau, G(arretson) B(eekman)   1948-
  See Trudeau, Garry
  See also CA 81-84; SATA 35

Trudeau, Garry   1948-............. **CLC 12**
  See also Trudeau, G(arretson) B(eekman)

Truffaut, Francois   1932-1984...... **CLC 20**
  See also CA 81-84; obituary CA 113

Trumbo, Dalton   1905-1976 .... **CLC 19**
  See also CANR 10; CA 21-24R;
      obituary CA 69-72; DLB 26

Tryon, Thomas   1926-........... **CLC 3, 11**
  See also CA 29-32R

Ts'ao Hsueh-ch'in   1715?-1763........ **LC 1**

Tsushima Shuji   1909-1948
  See Dazai Osamu
  See also CA 107

Tsvetaeva (Efron), Marina (Ivanovna)
      1892-1941 .... **TCLC 7, 35**
  See also CA 104, 128

Tunis, John R(oberts)   1889-1975 ... **CLC 12**
  See also CA 61-64; SATA 30, 37; DLB 22

Tuohy, Frank   1925- .... **CLC 37**
  See also DLB 14

Tuohy, John Francis   1925-
  See Tuohy, Frank
  See also CANR 3; CA 5-8R

Turco, Lewis (Putnam)   1934- ...... **CLC 11**
  See also CANR 24; CA 13-16R; DLB-Y 84

Turgenev, Ivan   1818-1883 .... **NCLC 21**

Turner, Frederick   1943-.......... **CLC 48**
  See also CANR 12; CA 73-76; DLB 40

Tutuola, Amos   1920- .... **CLC 5, 14, 29**
  See also CA 9-12R

Twain, Mark
      1835-1910 .... **TCLC 6, 12, 19, 36**
  See also Clemens, Samuel Langhorne
  See also DLB 11, 12, 23, 64, 74

Tyler, Anne   1941-.... **CLC 7, 11, 18, 28, 44**
  See also CANR 11; CA 9-12R; SATA 7;
      DLB 6; DLB-Y 82

Tyler, Royall   1757-1826......... **NCLC 3**
  See also DLB 37

Tynan (Hinkson), Katharine
      1861-1931 .... **TCLC 3**
  See also CA 104

Tytell, John   1939- .... **CLC 50**
  See also CA 29-32R

Tzara, Tristan   1896-1963......... **CLC 47**
  See also Rosenfeld, Samuel

Uhry, Alfred   1947?-.............. **CLC 55**
  See also CA 127

Unamuno (y Jugo), Miguel de
      1864-1936 .... **TCLC 2, 9**
  See also CA 104

Underwood, Miles   1909-1981
  See Glassco, John

Undset, Sigrid   1882-1949......... **TCLC 3**
  See also CA 104

Ungaretti, Giuseppe
      1888-1970 .... **CLC 7, 11, 15**
  See also CAP 2; CA 19-20;
      obituary CA 25-28R

Unger, Douglas   1952-............. **CLC 34**

Unger, Eva   1932-
  See Figes, Eva

Updike, John (Hoyer)
      1932- ...... **CLC 1, 2, 3, 5, 7, 9, 13, 15,
                      23, 34, 43**
  See also CANR 4; CA 1-4R; CABS 2;
      DLB 2, 5; DLB-Y 80, 82; DLB-DS 3

Urdang, Constance (Henriette)
      1922- .... **CLC 47**
  See also CANR 9, 24; CA 21-24R

Uris, Leon (Marcus)   1924-....... **CLC 7, 32**
  See also CANR 1; CA 1-4R; SATA 49

Ustinov, Peter (Alexander)   1921-.... **CLC 1**
  See also CANR 25; CA 13-16R; DLB 13

Vaculik, Ludvik   1926- .... **CLC 7**
  See also CA 53-56

Valenzuela, Luisa   1938-........... **CLC 31**
  See also CA 101

Valera (y Acala-Galiano), Juan
      1824-1905 .... **TCLC 10**
  See also CA 106

Valery, Paul (Ambroise Toussaint Jules)
      1871-1945 .... **TCLC 4, 15**
  See also CA 104, 122

Valle-Inclan (y Montenegro), Ramon (Maria)
      del   1866-1936............... **TCLC 5**
  See also CA 106

Vallejo, Cesar (Abraham)
      1892-1938 .... **TCLC 3**
  See also CA 105

Van Ash, Cay   1918-.............. **CLC 34**

Vance, Jack   1916?-.............. **CLC 35**
  See also DLB 8

Vance, John Holbrook   1916?-
  See Vance, Jack
  See also CANR 17; CA 29-32R

Van Den Bogarde, Derek (Jules Gaspard
      Ulric) Niven   1921-
  See Bogarde, Dirk
  See also CA 77-80

Vanderhaeghe, Guy   1951- .... **CLC 41**
  See also CA 113

Van der Post, Laurens (Jan)   1906-... **CLC 5**
  See also CA 5-8R

Van de Wetering, Janwillem
      1931- .... **CLC 47**
  See also CANR 4; CA 49-52

Van Dine, S. S.   1888-1939....... **TCLC 23**

Van Doren, Carl (Clinton)
      1885-1950 .... **TCLC 18**
  See also CA 111

Van Doren, Mark   1894-1972..... **CLC 6, 10**
  See also CANR 3; CA 1-4R;
      obituary CA 37-40R; DLB 45

Van Druten, John (William)
      1901-1957 .... **TCLC 2**
  See also CA 104; DLB 10

Van Duyn, Mona   1921-.......... **CLC 3, 7**
  See also CANR 7; CA 9-12R; DLB 5

Van Itallie, Jean-Claude   1936- ..... **CLC 3**
  See also CAAS 2; CANR 1; CA 45-48;
      DLB 7

Van Ostaijen, Paul   1896-1928..... **TCLC 33**

Van Peebles, Melvin   1932- ...... **CLC 2, 20**
  See also CA 85-88

Vansittart, Peter   1920-............ **CLC 42**
  See also CANR 3; CA 1-4R

Van Vechten, Carl   1880-1964 ..... **CLC 33**
  See also obituary CA 89-92; DLB 4, 9, 51

Van Vogt, A(lfred) E(lton)   1912-..... **CLC 1**
  See also CA 21-24R; SATA 14; DLB 8

Varda, Agnes   1928- .... **CLC 16**
  See also CA 116, 122

Vargas Llosa, (Jorge) Mario (Pedro)
      1936- .... **CLC 3, 6, 9, 10, 15, 31, 42**
  See also CANR 18; CA 73-76

Vassilikos, Vassilis   1933-......... **CLC 4, 8**
  See also CA 81-84

Vazov, Ivan   1850-1921.......... **TCLC 25**
  See also CA 121

Veblen, Thorstein Bunde
      1857-1929 .... **TCLC 31**
  See also CA 115

Verga, Giovanni   1840-1922 .... **TCLC 3**
  See also CA 104, 123

Verhaeren, Emile (Adolphe Gustave)
      1855-1916 .... **TCLC 12**
  See also CA 109

Verlaine, Paul (Marie)   1844-1896.. **NCLC 2**

Verne, Jules (Gabriel)   1828-1905 ... **TCLC 6**
  See also CA 110; SATA 21

Very, Jones   1813-1880........... **NCLC 9**
  See also DLB 1

Vesaas, Tarjei   1897-1970......... **CLC 48**
  See also obituary CA 29-32R

Vian, Boris 1920-1959 . . . . TCLC 9
See also CA 106; DLB 72

Viaud, (Louis Marie) Julien 1850-1923
See Loti, Pierre
See also CA 107

Vicker, Angus 1916-
See Felsen, Henry Gregor

Vidal, Eugene Luther, Jr. 1925-
See Vidal, Gore

Vidal, Gore
  1925- . . . . CLC 2, 4, 6, 8, 10, 22, 33
See also CANR 13; CA 5-8R; DLB 6

Viereck, Peter (Robert Edwin)
  1916- . . . . CLC 4
See also CANR 1; CA 1-4R; DLB 5

Vigny, Alfred (Victor) de
  1797-1863 . . . . NCLC 7

Villiers de l'Isle Adam, Jean Marie Mathias
    Philippe Auguste, Comte de,
  1838-1889 . . . . NCLC 3

Vinci, Leonardo da 1452-1519 . . . . . . LC 12

Vine, Barbara 1930- . . . . CLC 50
See also Rendell, Ruth

Vinge, Joan (Carol) D(ennison)
  1948- . . . . CLC 30
See also CA 93-96; SATA 36

Visconti, Luchino 1906-1976 . . . . CLC 16
See also CA 81-84; obituary CA 65-68

Vittorini, Elio 1908-1966 . . . . . . CLC 6, 9, 14
See also obituary CA 25-28R

Vizinczey, Stephen 1933- . . . . CLC 40

Vliet, R(ussell) G(ordon)
  1929-1984 . . . . CLC 22
See also CANR 18; CA 37-40R;
  obituary CA 112

Voight, Ellen Bryant 1943- . . . . CLC 54
See also CANR 11; CA 69-72

Voigt, Cynthia 1942- . . . . CLC 30
See also CANR 18; CA 106; SATA 33, 48

Voinovich, Vladimir (Nikolaevich)
  1932- . . . . CLC 10, 49
See also CA 81-84

Von Daeniken, Erich 1935-
See Von Daniken, Erich
See also CANR 17; CA 37-40R

Von Daniken, Erich 1935- . . . . CLC 30
See also Von Daeniken, Erich

Vonnegut, Kurt, Jr.
  1922- . . . . CLC 1, 2, 3, 4, 5, 8, 12, 22, 40
See also CANR 1; CA 1-4R; DLB 2, 8;
  DLB-Y 80; DLB-DS 3

Vorster, Gordon 1924- . . . . CLC 34

Voznesensky, Andrei 1933- . . . CLC 1, 15, 57
See also CA 89-92

Waddington, Miriam 1917- . . . . CLC 28
See also CANR 12; CA 21-24R

Wagman, Fredrica 1937- . . . . CLC 7
See also CA 97-100

Wagner, Richard 1813-1883 . . . . NCLC 9

Wagner-Martin, Linda 1936- . . . . CLC 50

Wagoner, David (Russell)
  1926- . . . . CLC 3, 5, 15
See also CAAS 3; CANR 2; CA 1-4R;
  SATA 14; DLB 5

Wah, Fred(erick James) 1939- . . . . . . CLC 44
See also CA 107; DLB 60

Wahloo, Per 1926-1975 . . . . CLC 7
See also CA 61-64

Wahloo, Peter 1926-1975
See Wahloo, Per

Wain, John (Barrington)
  1925- . . . . CLC 2, 11, 15, 46
See also CAAS 4; CANR 23; CA 5-8R;
  DLB 15, 27

Wajda, Andrzej 1926- . . . . CLC 16
See also CA 102

Wakefield, Dan 1932- . . . . CLC 7
See also CAAS 7; CA 21-24R

Wakoski, Diane
  1937- . . . . CLC 2, 4, 7, 9, 11, 40
See also CAAS 1; CANR 9; CA 13-16R;
  DLB 5

Walcott, Derek (Alton)
  1930- . . . . CLC 2, 4, 9, 14, 25, 42
See also CANR 26; CA 89-92; DLB-Y 81

Waldman, Anne 1945- . . . . CLC 7
See also CA 37-40R; DLB 16

Waldo, Edward Hamilton 1918-
See Sturgeon, Theodore (Hamilton)

Walker, Alice
  1944- . . . . . . CLC 5, 6, 9, 19, 27, 46, 58;
                                                    SSC 5
See also CANR 9, 27; CA 37-40R;
  SATA 31; DLB 6, 33; CDALB 1968-1988

Walker, David Harry 1911- . . . . CLC 14
See also CANR 1; CA 1-4R; SATA 8

Walker, Edward Joseph 1934-
See Walker, Ted
See also CANR 12; CA 21-24R

Walker, George F. 1947- . . . . CLC 44
See also CANR 21; CA 103; DLB 60

Walker, Joseph A. 1935- . . . . CLC 19
See also CANR 26; CA 89-92; DLB 38

Walker, Margaret (Abigail)
  1915- . . . . CLC 1, 6
See also CANR 26; CA 73-76; DLB 76

Walker, Ted 1934- . . . . CLC 13
See also Walker, Edward Joseph
See also DLB 40

Wallace, David Foster 1962- . . . . CLC 50

Wallace, Irving 1916- . . . . CLC 7, 13
See also CAAS 1; CANR 1; CA 1-4R

Wallant, Edward Lewis
  1926-1962 . . . . CLC 5, 10
See also CANR 22; CA 1-4R; DLB 2, 28

Walpole, Horace 1717-1797 . . . . LC 2
See also DLB 39

Walpole, (Sir) Hugh (Seymour)
  1884-1941 . . . . TCLC 5
See also CA 104; DLB 34

Walser, Martin 1927- . . . . CLC 27
See also CANR 8; CA 57-60; DLB 75

Walser, Robert 1878-1956 . . . . TCLC 18
See also CA 118; DLB 66

Walsh, Gillian Paton 1939-
See Walsh, Jill Paton
See also CA 37-40R; SATA 4

Walsh, Jill Paton 1939- . . . . CLC 35
See also CLR 2; SAAS 3

Wambaugh, Joseph (Aloysius, Jr.)
  1937- . . . . CLC 3, 18
See also CA 33-36R; DLB 6; DLB-Y 83

Ward, Arthur Henry Sarsfield 1883-1959
See Rohmer, Sax
See also CA 108

Ward, Douglas Turner 1930- . . . . CLC 19
See also CA 81-84; DLB 7, 38

Warhol, Andy 1928-1987 . . . . CLC 20
See also CA 89-92; obituary CA 121

Warner, Francis (Robert le Plastrier)
  1937- . . . . CLC 14
See also CANR 11; CA 53-56

Warner, Rex (Ernest) 1905-1986 . . . . CLC 45
See also CA 89-92; obituary CA 119;
  DLB 15

Warner, Sylvia Townsend
  1893-1978 . . . . CLC 7, 19
See also CANR 16; CA 61-64;
  obituary CA 77-80; DLB 34

Warren, Mercy Otis 1728-1814 . . . NCLC 13
See also DLB 31

Warren, Robert Penn
  1905-1989 . . . CLC 1, 4, 6, 8, 10, 13, 18,
                                          39, 53; SSC 4
See also CANR 10; CA 13-16R; SATA 46;
  DLB 2, 48; DLB-Y 80

Washington, Booker T(aliaferro)
  1856-1915 . . . . CLC 34
See also CA 114, 125; SATA 28

Wassermann, Jakob 1873-1934 . . . . . TCLC 6
See also CA 104; DLB 66

Wasserstein, Wendy 1950- . . . . CLC 32
See also CA 121

Waterhouse, Keith (Spencer)
  1929- . . . . CLC 47
See also CA 5-8R; DLB 13, 15

Waters, Roger 1944-
See Pink Floyd

Wa Thiong'o, Ngugi
  1938- . . . . CLC 3, 7, 13, 36
See also Ngugi, James (Thiong'o); Ngugi wa
  Thiong'o

Watkins, Paul 1964- . . . . CLC 55

Watkins, Vernon (Phillips)
  1906-1967 . . . . CLC 43
See also CAP 1; CA 9-10;
  obituary CA 25-28R; DLB 20

Waugh, Auberon (Alexander) 1939- . . CLC 7
See also CANR 6, 22; CA 45-48; DLB 14

Waugh, Evelyn (Arthur St. John)
  1903-1966 . . . CLC 1, 3, 8, 13, 19, 27, 44
See also CANR 22; CA 85-88;
  obituary CA 25-28R; DLB 15

Waugh, Harriet 1944- . . . . CLC 6
See also CANR 22; CA 85-88

Webb, Beatrice (Potter)
  1858-1943 . . . . TCLC 22
See also CA 117

Wiggins, Marianne 1948-......... **CLC 57**

Wight, James Alfred 1916-
See Herriot, James
See also CA 77-80; SATA 44

Wilbur, Richard (Purdy)
1921-............. **CLC 3, 6, 9, 14, 53**
See also CANR 2; CA 1-4R; CABS 2;
SATA 9; DLB 5

Wild, Peter 1940-............... **CLC 14**
See also CA 37-40R; DLB 5

Wilde, Oscar (Fingal O'Flahertie Wills)
1854-1900 .... **TCLC 1, 8, 23**
See also CA 104; SATA 24; DLB 10, 19,
34, 57

Wilder, Billy 1906-............... **CLC 20**
See also Wilder, Samuel
See also DLB 26

Wilder, Samuel 1906-
See Wilder, Billy
See also CA 89-92

Wilder, Thornton (Niven)
1897-1975 ...... **CLC 1, 5, 6, 10, 15, 35**
See also CA 13-16R; obituary CA 61-64;
DLB 4, 7, 9

Wiley, Richard 1944-............. **CLC 44**
See also CA 121

Wilhelm, Kate 1928-............... **CLC 7**
See also CAAS 5; CANR 17; CA 37-40R;
DLB 8

Willard, Nancy 1936-........... **CLC 7, 37**
See also CLR 5; CANR 10; CA 89-92;
SATA 30, 37; DLB 5, 52

Williams, C(harles) K(enneth)
1936-.................... **CLC 33, 56**
See also CA 37-40R; DLB 5

Williams, Charles (Walter Stansby)
1886-1945 .... **TCLC 1, 11**
See also CA 104

Williams, Ella Gwendolen Rees 1890-1979
See Rhys, Jean

Williams, (George) Emlyn
1905-1987 .... **CLC 15**
See also CA 104, 123; DLB 10

Williams, Hugo 1942-............. **CLC 42**
See also CA 17-20R; DLB 40

Williams, John A(lfred) 1925-.... **CLC 5, 13**
See also CAAS 3; CANR 6, 26; CA 53-56;
DLB 2, 33

Williams, Jonathan (Chamberlain)
1929-...................... **CLC 13**
See also CANR 8; CA 9-12R; DLB 5

Williams, Joy 1944-............. **CLC 31**
See also CANR 22; CA 41-44R

Williams, Norman 1952-......... **CLC 39**
See also CA 118

Williams, Paulette 1948-
See Shange, Ntozake

Williams, Tennessee
1911-1983 .... **CLC 1, 2, 5, 7, 8, 11, 15,**
19, 30, 39, 45
See also CA 5-8R; obituary CA 108; DLB 7;
DLB-Y 83; DLB-DS 4;
CDALB 1941-1968

Williams, Thomas (Alonzo) 1926-... **CLC 14**
See also CANR 2; CA 1-4R

Williams, Thomas Lanier 1911-1983
See Williams, Tennessee

Williams, William Carlos
1883-1963 .... **CLC 1, 2, 5, 9, 13, 22, 42**
See also CA 89-92; DLB 4, 16, 54

Williamson, David 1932-......... **CLC 56**

Williamson, Jack 1908-........... **CLC 29**
See also Williamson, John Stewart
See also DLB 8

Williamson, John Stewart 1908-
See Williamson, Jack
See also CANR 123; CA 17-20R

Willingham, Calder (Baynard, Jr.)
1922-.................... **CLC 5, 51**
See also CANR 3; CA 5-8R; DLB 2, 44

Wilson, A(ndrew) N(orman) 1950- .. **CLC 33**
See also CA 112; DLB 14

Wilson, Andrew 1948-
See Wilson, Snoo

Wilson, Angus (Frank Johnstone)
1913-............. **CLC 2, 3, 5, 25, 34**
See also CANR 21; CA 5-8R; DLB 15

Wilson, August 1945-.......... **CLC 39, 50**
See also CA 115, 122

Wilson, Brian 1942-............. **CLC 12**

Wilson, Colin 1931-............. **CLC 3, 14**
See also CAAS 5; CANR 1, 122; CA 1-4R;
DLB 14

Wilson, Edmund
1895-1972 .... **CLC 1, 2, 3, 8, 24**
See also CANR 1; CA 1-4R;
obituary CA 37-40R; DLB 63

Wilson, Ethel Davis (Bryant)
1888-1980 .... **CLC 13**
See also CA 102; DLB 68

Wilson, John 1785-1854.......... **NCLC 5**

Wilson, John (Anthony) Burgess 1917-
See Burgess, Anthony
See also CANR 2; CA 1-4R

Wilson, Lanford 1937-....... **CLC 7, 14, 36**
See also CA 17-20R; DLB 7

Wilson, Robert (M.) 1944-....... **CLC 7, 9**
See also CANR 2; CA 49-52

Wilson, Sloan 1920-............. **CLC 32**
See also CANR 1; CA 1-4R

Wilson, Snoo 1948-............... **CLC 33**
See also CA 69-72

Wilson, William S(mith) 1932- ..... **CLC 49**
See also CA 81-84

**Winchilsea, Anne (Kingsmill) Finch, Countess
of** 1661-1720.................. **LC 3**

Winters, Janet Lewis 1899-
See Lewis (Winters), Janet
See also CAP 1; CA 9-10

Winters, (Arthur) Yvor
1900-1968 .... **CLC 4, 8, 32**
See also CAP 1; CA 11-12;
obituary CA 25-28R; DLB 48

Wiseman, Frederick 1930-......... **CLC 20**

Wister, Owen 1860-1938 .... **TCLC 21**
See also CA 108; DLB 9

Witkiewicz, Stanislaw Ignacy
1885-1939 .... **TCLC 8**
See also CA 105

Wittig, Monique 1935?-........... **CLC 22**
See also CA 116

Wittlin, Joseph 1896-1976......... **CLC 25**
See also Wittlin, Jozef

Wittlin, Jozef 1896-1976
See Wittlin, Joseph
See also CANR 3; CA 49-52;
obituary CA 65-68

Wodehouse, (Sir) P(elham) G(renville)
1881-1975 ... **CLC 1, 2, 5, 10, 22; SSC 2**
See also CANR 3; CA 45-48;
obituary CA 57-60; SATA 22; DLB 34

Woiwode, Larry (Alfred) 1941-... **CLC 6, 10**
See also CANR 16; CA 73-76; DLB 6

Wojciechowska, Maia (Teresa)
1927-...................... **CLC 26**
See also CLR 1; CANR 4; CA 9-12R;
SAAS 1; SATA 1, 28

Wolf, Christa 1929-........ **CLC 14, 29, 58**
See also CA 85-88

Wolfe, Gene (Rodman) 1931-....... **CLC 25**
See also CANR 6; CA 57-60; DLB 8

Wolfe, George C. 1954-........... **CLC 49**

Wolfe, Thomas (Clayton)
1900-1938 .... **TCLC 4, 13, 29**
See also CA 104; DLB 9; DLB-Y 85;
DLB-DS 2

Wolfe, Thomas Kennerly, Jr. 1931-
See Wolfe, Tom
See also CANR 9; CA 13-16R

Wolfe, Tom 1931-... **CLC 1, 2, 9, 15, 35, 51**
See also Wolfe, Thomas Kennerly, Jr.

Wolff, Geoffrey (Ansell) 1937- ..... **CLC 41**
See also CA 29-32R

Wolff, Tobias (Jonathan Ansell)
1945-...................... **CLC 39**
See also CA 114, 117

Wolitzer, Hilma 1930-............ **CLC 17**
See also CANR 18; CA 65-68; SATA 31

Wollstonecraft (Godwin), Mary
1759-1797 .... **LC 5**
See also DLB 39

Wonder, Stevie 1950-............. **CLC 12**
See also Morris, Steveland Judkins

Wong, Jade Snow 1922-........... **CLC 17**
See also CA 109

Woodcott, Keith 1934-
See Brunner, John (Kilian Houston)

Woolf, (Adeline) Virginia
1882-1941 .... **TCLC 1, 5, 20**
See also CA 104; DLB 36

Woollcott, Alexander (Humphreys)
1887-1943 .... **TCLC 5**
See also CA 105; DLB 29

Wordsworth, Dorothy
1771-1855 .... **NCLC 25**

Wordsworth, William 1770-1850.. **NCLC 12**

Wouk, Herman 1915-......... **CLC 1, 9, 38**
See also CANR 6; CA 5-8R; DLB-Y 82

Wright, Charles 1935- .... **CLC 6, 13, 28**
See also CAAS 7; CA 29-32R; DLB-Y 82

Wright, Charles (Stevenson) 1932-.. **CLC 49**
See also CA 9-12R; DLB 33

Author Index

Literary Criticism Series
Cumulative Topic Index

This index lists all topic entries in the Gale Literary Criticism Series *Contemporary Literary Criticism,*
Literature Criticism from 1400 to 1800, Nineteenth-Century Literature Criticism, and *Twentieth-Century Literary Criticism.*

TCLC Cumulative Nationality Index

AMERICAN

Adams, Henry **4**
Agee, James **1, 19**
Anderson, Maxwell **2**
Anderson, Sherwood **1, 10, 24**
Atherton, Gertrude **2**
Austin, Mary **25**
Barry, Philip **11**
Baum, L. Frank **7**
Beard, Charles A. **15**
Belasco, David **3**
Benchley, Robert **1**
Benét, Stephen Vincent **7**
Benét, William Rose **28**
Bierce, Ambrose **1, 7**
Black Elk **33**
Bourne, Randolph S. **16**
Bradford, Gamaliel **36**
Bromfield, Louis **11**
Burroughs, Edgar Rice **2, 32**
Cabell, James Branch **6**
Cable, George Washington **4**
Cather, Willa **1, 11, 31**
Chandler, Raymond **1, 7**
Chapman, John Jay **7**
Chesnutt, Charles Waddell **5**
Chopin, Kate **5, 14**
Comstock, Anthony **13**
Cotter, Joseph Seamon, Sr. **28**
Crane, Hart **2, 5**
Crane, Stephen **11, 17, 32**
Crawford, F. Marion **10**
Crothers, Rachel **19**
Cullen, Countee **4**
Davis, Rebecca Harding **6**
Davis, Richard Harding **24**
Day, Clarence **25**
DeVoto, Bernard **29**
Dreiser, Theodore **10, 18, 35**

Dunbar, Paul Laurence **2, 12**
Dunne, Finley Peter **28**
Fisher, Rudolph **11**
Fitzgerald, F. Scott **1, 6, 14, 28**
Fletcher, John Gould **35**
Forten, Charlotte L. **16**
Freeman, Douglas Southall **11**
Freeman, Mary Wilkins **9**
Futrelle, Jacques **19**
Gale, Zona **7**
Garland, Hamlin **3**
Gilman, Charlotte Perkins **9**
Glasgow, Ellen **2, 7**
Goldman, Emma **13**
Grey, Zane **6**
Hall, James Norman **23**
Harper, Frances Ellen Watkins **14**
Harris, Joel Chandler **2**
Harte, Bret **1, 25**
Hawthorne, Julian **25**
Hearn, Lafcadio **9**
Henry, O. **1, 19**
Hergesheimer, Joseph **11**
Higginson, Thomas Wentworth **36**
Hopkins, Pauline Elizabeth **28**
Howard, Robert E. **8**
Howe, Julia Ward **21**
Howells, William Dean **7, 17**
James, Henry **2, 11, 24**
James, William **15, 32**
Jewett, Sarah Orne **1, 22**
Johnson, James Weldon **3, 19**
Kornbluth, C. M. **8**
Kuttner, Henry **10**
Lardner, Ring **2, 14**
Lewis, Sinclair **4, 13, 23**
Lewisohn, Ludwig **19**
Lindsay, Vachel **17**
London, Jack **9, 15**

Lovecraft, H. P. **4, 22**
Lowell, Amy **1, 8**
Marquis, Don **7**
Masters, Edgar Lee **2, 25**
McCoy, Horace **28**
McKay, Claude **7**
Mencken, H. L. **13**
Millay, Edna St. Vincent **4**
Mitchell, Margaret **11**
Mitchell, S. Weir **36**
Monroe, Harriet **12**
Muir, John **28**
Nathan, George Jean **18**
Nordhoff, Charles **23**
Norris, Frank **24**
O'Neill, Eugene **1, 6, 27**
Oskison, John M. **35**
Porter, Gene Stratton **21**
Rawlings, Marjorie Kinnan **4**
Reed, John **9**
Roberts, Kenneth **23**
Robinson, Edwin Arlington **5**
Rogers, Will **8**
Rölvaag, O. E. **17**
Rourke, Constance **12**
Runyon, Damon **10**
Saltus, Edgar **8**
Sherwood, Robert E. **3**
Slesinger, Tess **10**
Steffens, Lincoln **20**
Stein, Gertrude **1, 6, 28**
Sterling, George **20**
Stevens, Wallace **3, 12**
Tarkington, Booth **9**
Teasdale, Sara **4**
Thurman, Wallace **6**
Twain, Mark **6, 12, 19, 36**
Van Dine, S. S. **23**
Van Doren, Carl **18**

Nationality Index

Title Index to Volume 36